Get started with your **Connected Casebook**

Redeem your code below to access the **e-book** with search, highlighting, and note-taking capabilities; **case briefing** and **outlining** tools to support efficient learning; and more.

1. Go to www.casebookconnect.com
2. Enter your access code in the box and click **Register**
3. Follow the steps to complete your registration and verify your email address

If you have already registered at CasebookConnect.com, simply log into your account and redeem additional access codes from your Dashboard.

ACCESS CODE:
Scratch off with care.

STXT99506273716

Is this a used casebook? Access code already redeemed? Purchase a digital version at **CasebookConnect.com/catalog**.

If you purchased a digital bundle with additional components, your additional access codes will appear below.

"I liked being able to search quickly while in class."

"Being able to highlight and easily create case briefs was a fantastic resource and time saver for me!"

"I loved it! I was able to study on the go and create a more effective outline."

For technical support, please visit http://support.wklegaledu.com.

27624

10053081-0002

NATIONAL SECURITY LAW AND THE CONSTITUTION

ASPEN CASEBOOK SERIES

NATIONAL SECURITY LAW AND THE CONSTITUTION

SECOND EDITION

GEOFFREY S. CORN
Professor of Law
South Texas College of Law Houston

JIMMY GURULÉ
Professor of Law
Notre Dame Law School

JEFFREY D. KAHN
Professor of Law
Southern Methodist University Dedman School of Law

GARY CORN
Program Director, Technology, Law & Security Program, and Adjunct Professor of Law
American University Washington College of Law
and
Senior Fellow in National Security and Cybersecurity
R Street Institute

Published by Wolters Kluwer in New York.

Wolters Kluwer Legal & Regulatory U.S. serves customers worldwide with CCH, Aspen Publishers, and Kluwer Law International products. (www.WKLegaledu.com)

To contact Customer Service, e-mail customer.service@wolterskluwer.com, call 1-800-234-1660, fax 1-800-901-9075, or mail correspondence to:

Wolters Kluwer
Attn: Order Department
PO Box 990
Frederick, MD 21705

Printed in the United States of America.

1 2 3 4 5 6 7 8 9 0

ISBN 978-1-5438-1071-4

Library of Congress Cataloging-in-Publication Data

Names: Corn, Geoffrey S., author. | Gurulé, Jimmy, author. | Kahn, Jeffrey, 1971- author. | Corn, Gary, author.
Title: National security law and the constitution / Geoffrey S. Corn, Professor of Law, South Texas College of Law Houston; Jimmy Gurulé, Professor of Law, Notre Dame Law School; Jeffrey D. Kahn, Professor of Law, Southern Methodist University, Dedman School of Law; Gary Corn, Program Director, Technology, Law & Security Program, and Adjunct Professor of Law, American University Washington College of Law and Senior Fellow in National Security and Cybersecurity R Street Institute.
Description: Second edition. | New York : Wolters Kluwer, [2021] | Series: Aspen casebook series | Includes bibliographical references and index. | Summary: "A highly accessible casebook for students studying National Security Law"—Provided by publisher.
Identifiers: LCCN 2020029784 (print) | LCCN 2020029785 (ebook) | ISBN 9781543810714 (hardback) | ISBN 9781543823417 (ebook)
Subjects: LCSH: National security—Law and legislation—United States. | Constitutional law—United States. | LCGFT: Casebooks (Law)
Classification: LCC KF7209 .C67 2021 (print) | LCC KF7209 (ebook) | DDC 343.73/01—dc23
LC record available at https://lccn.loc.gov/2020029784
LC ebook record available at https://lccn.loc.gov/2020029785

About Wolters Kluwer Legal & Regulatory U.S.

Wolters Kluwer Legal & Regulatory U.S. delivers expert content and solutions in the areas of law, corporate compliance, health compliance, reimbursement, and legal education. Its practical solutions help customers successfully navigate the demands of a changing environment to drive their daily activities, enhance decision quality and inspire confident outcomes.

Serving customers worldwide, its legal and regulatory portfolio includes products under the Aspen Publishers, CCH Incorporated, Kluwer Law International, ftwilliam.com and MediRegs names. They are regarded as exceptional and trusted resources for general legal and practice-specific knowledge, compliance and risk management, dynamic workflow solutions, and expert commentary.

Summary of Contents

Contents

PART III
CRIME AND NATIONAL SECURITY

Preface

The basic structure of our casebook has been retained in this new edition. This reflects our commitment to the goal identified in the preface of the first edition, "to offer students insights into the complex process of national security legal practice by focusing on essential legal sources and national security issues touching on the full spectrum of national security powers." The changes we have made, in addition to the necessary task of updating coverage of all subjects to reflect developments since our first publication in August 2016, fall into two broad categories.

The first category is a pedagogical one. This new edition responds to lessons learned from students and teachers who have shared with us their experiences using the first edition. We have expanded the range of different approaches for instructors to explore the topics presented in this book. A principal change has been to exchange our previous commitment to a 14-week/14-chapter casebook for a more flexible approach that allows for a variety of ways to introduce and select topics to cover in a semester of standard length. The chapters that follow those in Part I, which establishes foundations and frameworks on which to build a course on national security law, are independent units that may be selected and organized according to the needs and preferences of the instructor.

The most obvious pedagogical change in Part I is the addition of a new first chapter, "An Introduction to the 'National Security' Constitution." This chapter takes a close look at a slower pace at a single case: *Hamdi v. Rumsfeld*, 542 U.S. 507 (2004). This is an important case in its own right, to which reference is made in subsequent chapters. But this first chapter is intended to allow newcomers to the field to acquaint themselves, in an absorbable way, with some of the themes, techniques, institutions, sources of law, and (it must be said) some of the ubiquitous jargon common to the many facets of national security law.

The second category reflects changes in organization, scope, and coverage. First, we welcome Colonel Gary Corn (U.S. Army, Ret.) as our co-author. Professor Corn, now the program director for the Technology, Law and Security Program at American University Washington College of Law, most recently served as the Staff Judge Advocate to U.S. Cyber Command, the capstone to a distinguished career spanning over twenty-seven years as a military lawyer.

Second, existing topics have been reorganized while retaining our focus on the Constitution as "the foundation for the exercise of all national security powers."

Thus, while Part I remains centered on this constitutional framework, and the friction points built into it, coverage has been reconfigured to add a chapter devoted to frictions especially associated with the foreign affairs powers of the Congress and the President. Similarly, a new chapter has been added to Part V that reflects the increasing importance of computer networks as part of the essential infrastructure of—and, therefore, an expanding battlespace in—our society. At the same time, we have endeavored to keep each chapter a manageable length. We have written a casebook, not a treatise, and our choices reflect our aim to provide students with a serious introduction to a difficult subject, one that enlightens but does not overwhelm.

National security law, like all law, is a field defined not only by recognized precedents and seemingly well-anchored guideposts but also by constant flux, with new challenges and twists on old issues. At the time this preface is being written, the world finds itself in the grip of a pandemic that has upended settled expectations of every sort with blinding speed. In the United States, leaders at the local, state, and federal levels finds themselves rediscovering legal powers, reconsidering their limits, and sometimes relearning old lessons from the friction points that characterize our unique federal approach to governance. We are reminded of the variety of guises in which threats to national security can appear. Now, more than ever, an understanding of the question at the heart of national security law—"how the interests of security and liberty are reconciled"—is crucially important.

Geoffrey S. Corn
Jimmy Gurulé
Jeffrey D. Kahn
Gary P. Corn
August 2020

Acknowledgments

The authors would like to thank the rights holders for their permission to reproduce the following material:

Bolivians train anti-air gun on Paraguayan airplane on May 24, 1934. The Chaco War was fought over the Chaco Boreal wilderness. Photograph. Everett Collection Historical/Alamy.
Pre-Chaco War Borders. Chile. 1906 map. Photograph. Antiqua Print Gallery/ Alamy.

NATIONAL SECURITY LAW AND THE CONSTITUTION

PART I

THE CONSTITUTIONAL FRAMEWORK

CHAPTER 1

An Introduction to the "National Security" Constitution

Inter arma silent leges is a Latin phrase often attributed to the Roman lawyer and statesman Cicero. Loosely translated, the English equivalent is: "In times of war, the law is silent." In slightly different form, Cicero allegedly spoke these words in defense of a friend accused of murdering a political rival. Although these words were spoken to advance an argument of self-defense, the trial itself took place in highly charged political circumstances. The stakes were high: "the Forum and all the temples in its neighbourhood were occupied by troops."[1]

What does *"inter arma silent leges"* mean in the context of national security law in the United States? As suggested by this very book, which is so full of laws and legal opinions issued in times of war and national security crisis, our law does not actually cease to function. Rather, the questions are more nuanced and sometimes more subtle. *Which* law functions and for what reasons? When, and how, does one *body* of law replace another? How are the rights of individuals affected by threats, real or perceived, to the state? Who interprets these laws? If the interpretor is a judge, what deference should be given to the judgments of non-judicial actors?

These are not easy questions to answer. And the answers themselves do not remain unchanged over time. Oliver Wendell Holmes, Jr. famously declared: "The life of the law has not been logic: it has been experience."[2] He then explained what he meant:

> The felt necessities of the time, the prevalent moral and political theories, intuitions of public policy, avowed or unconscious, even the prejudices which judges share with their fellow-men, have had a good deal more to do than the syllogism in determining the rules by which men should be governed. The law embodies the story of a nation's development through many centuries, and it cannot be dealt with as if it contained only the axioms and corollaries of a book of mathematics.

---

1. M.T. CICERONIS, ORATIO PRO TITO ANNIO MILONE vii (Cambridge University Press, 1886) (from the introduction by Q. Asconius Pedianus).
2. OLIVER WENDELL HOLMES, JR., THE COMMON LAW 1 (1881).

Judges, like generals and senators, presidents and attorney generals, soldiers and advisers, and lawyers and citizens, are human beings. They are subject to fear, revulsion, and doubt as much as to courage, compassion, and certainty. And the contexts in which their decisions are made often help us to study the choices they make.

With these thoughts in mind, this introductory chapter focuses on a single case, *Hamdi v. Rumsfeld*, 542 U.S. 507 (2004). The lead petitioner in the caption is Yaser Esam Hamdi, who at the time of the events in this case was a twenty-year-old United States citizen living in Afghanistan. The lead respondent is Donald H. Rumsfeld, who at the time was the U.S. Secretary of Defense under President George W. Bush.

This important Supreme Court case will be referenced in several chapters in this book. Its careful study will be rewarded. But it is also a difficult case in which the Justices wrestle over the meaning of two acts of Congress (the 2001 Authorization for the Use of Military Force and the 1971 Non-Detention Act); an executive decision (to detain indefinitely a United States citizen as an enemy combatant captured in Afghanistan); and the meaning of two Supreme Court cases from very different times and contexts in U.S. history (a Civil War era case, *Ex parte Milligan*, and a case from World War II, *Ex parte Quirin*). The case also raises issues concerning international law (the Geneva Convention relative to the Treatment of Prisoners of War).

Unusually, this chapter will intersperse notes and questions *between* the different opinions offered in the case instead of leaving them all for the end. The components of the case are the judgment of the Court accompanied by a plurality opinion by Justice O'Connor joined by Chief Justice Rehnquist and Justices Kennedy and Breyer, a concurring opinion by Justice Souter joined by Justice Ginsburg, a dissenting opinion by Justice Scalia joined by Justice Stevens, and another dissenting opinion by Justice Thomas.

In closing, consider the view expressed by Justice Scalia at the end of his opinion:

> Many think it not only inevitable but entirely proper that liberty give way to security in times of national crisis — that, at the extremes of military exigency, *inter arma silent leges*. Whatever the general merits of the view that war silences law or modulates its voice, that view has no place in the interpretation and application of a Constitution designed precisely to confront war and, in a manner that accords with democratic principles, to accommodate it.

This book is about exploring the metes and bounds of that thought. Consider the first case:

Hamdi v. Rumsfeld
542 U.S. 507 (2004)

Justice O'Connor announced the judgment of the Court and delivered an opinion, in which The Chief Justice, Justice Kennedy, and Justice Breyer join.

I

On September 11, 2001, the al Qaeda terrorist network used hijacked commercial airliners to attack prominent targets in the United States.

Approximately 3,000 people were killed in those attacks. One week later, in response to these "acts of treacherous violence," Congress passed a resolution authorizing the President to "use all necessary and appropriate force against those nations, organizations, or persons he determines planned, authorized, committed, or aided the terrorist attacks" or "harbored such organizations or persons, in order to prevent any future acts of international terrorism against the United States by such nations, organizations or persons." Authorization for Use of Military Force (AUMF). Soon thereafter, the President ordered United States Armed Forces to Afghanistan, with a mission to subdue al Qaeda and quell the Taliban regime that was known to support it.

This case arises out of the detention of a man whom the Government alleges took up arms with the Taliban during this conflict. His name is Yaser Esam Hamdi. Born in Louisiana in 1980, Hamdi moved with his family to Saudi Arabia as a child. By 2001, the parties agree, he resided in Afghanistan. At some point that year, he was seized by members of the Northern Alliance, a coalition of military groups opposed to the Taliban government, and eventually was turned over to the United States military. The Government asserts that it initially detained and interrogated Hamdi in Afghanistan before transferring him to the United States Naval Base in Guantanamo Bay in January 2002. In April 2002, upon learning that Hamdi is an American citizen, authorities transferred him to a naval brig in Norfolk, Virginia, where he remained until a recent transfer to a brig in Charleston, South Carolina. The Government contends that Hamdi is an "enemy combatant," and that this status justifies holding him in the United States indefinitely—without formal charges or proceedings—unless and until it makes the determination that access to counsel or further process is warranted.

In June 2002, Hamdi's father filed the present petition for a writ of habeas corpus, naming as petitioners his son and himself as next friend. The elder Hamdi alleges in the petition that he has had no contact with his son since the Government took custody of him in 2001, and that the Government has held his son "without access to legal counsel or notice of any charges pending against him." Although his habeas petition provides no details with regard to the factual circumstances surrounding his son's capture and detention, Hamdi's father has asserted in documents found elsewhere in the record that his son went to Afghanistan to do "relief work," and that he had been in that country less than two months before September 11, 2001, and could not have received military training. The 20-year-old was traveling on his own for the first time, his father says, and "[b]ecause of his lack of experience, he was trapped in Afghanistan once the military campaign began."

[The] Government filed a response and a motion to dismiss the petition. It attached to its response a declaration from one Michael Mobbs (hereinafter Mobbs Declaration), who identified himself as Special Advisor to the Under Secretary of Defense for Policy. Mobbs indicated that in this position, he has been "substantially involved with matters related to the detention of enemy combatants in the current war against the al Qaeda terrorists and those who support and harbor them (including the Taliban)." He expressed his "familiar[ity]" with Department of Defense and United States military policies and procedures applicable to the detention, control, and transfer of al Qaeda and Taliban personnel, and declared that "[b]ased upon my review of relevant records and reports, I am also familiar with the facts and circumstances related to the capture of . . . Hamdi and his detention by U.S. military forces."

Mobbs then set forth what remains the sole evidentiary support that the Government has provided to the courts for Hamdi's detention. The declaration states that Hamdi "traveled to Afghanistan" in July or August 2001, and that he thereafter "affiliated with a Taliban military unit and received weapons training." It asserts that Hamdi "remained with his Taliban unit following the attacks of September 11" and that, during the time when Northern Alliance forces were "engaged in battle with the Taliban," "Hamdi's Taliban unit surrendered" to those forces, after which he "surrender[ed] his Kalishnikov assault rifle" to them. Mobbs states that Hamdi was labeled an enemy combatant "[b]ased upon his interviews and in light of his association with the Taliban." According to the declaration, a series of "U.S. military screening team[s]" determined that Hamdi met "the criteria for enemy combatants," and "[a] subsequent interview of Hamdi has confirmed the fact that he surrendered and gave his firearm to Northern Alliance forces, which supports his classification as an enemy combatant."

The District Court found that the Mobbs Declaration fell "far short" of supporting Hamdi's detention. It criticized the generic and hearsay nature of the affidavit, calling it "little more than the government's 'say-so.'" It ordered the Government to turn over numerous materials for *in camera* review[.]

The Government sought to appeal the production order. The Fourth Circuit reversed. It instead stressed that, because it was "undisputed that Hamdi was captured in a zone of active combat in a foreign theater of conflict," no factual inquiry or evidentiary hearing allowing Hamdi to be heard or to rebut the Government's assertions was necessary or proper.

II

The threshold question before us is whether the Executive has the authority to detain citizens who qualify as "enemy combatants." [T]he Government has never provided any court with the full criteria that it uses in classifying individuals as such. It has made clear, however, that, for purposes of this case, the "enemy combatant" that it is seeking to detain is an individual who, it alleges, was "'part of or supporting forces hostile to the United States or coalition partners'" in Afghanistan and who "'engaged in an armed conflict against the United States'" there. We therefore answer only the narrow question before us: whether the detention of citizens falling within that definition is authorized.

The Government maintains that no explicit congressional authorization is required, because the Executive possesses plenary authority to detain pursuant to Article II of the Constitution. We do not reach the question whether Article II provides such authority, however, because we agree with the Government's alternative position, that Congress has in fact authorized Hamdi's detention, through the AUMF.

Our analysis on that point, set forth below, substantially overlaps with our analysis of Hamdi's principal argument for the illegality of his detention. He posits that his detention is forbidden by 18 U.S.C. § 4001(a) [(the Non-Detention Act), which] states that "[n]o citizen shall be imprisoned or otherwise detained by the United States except pursuant to an Act of Congress." The Government again presses two alternative positions. First, it argues that § 4001(a), in light of its legislative history and its location in Title 18, applies only to "the control of civilian prisons and related detentions," not to military detentions. Second, it maintains that § 4001(a) is satisfied, because Hamdi is being detained "pursuant to an Act of Congress" — the AUMF. Again, because we conclude that the Government's second assertion is correct, we do not address the first. In other words, for the reasons that follow, we conclude that the AUMF is explicit congressional authorization for the detention of individuals in the narrow category we describe (assuming, without deciding, that such authorization is required), and that the AUMF satisfied § 4001(a)'s requirement that a detention be "pursuant to an Act of Congress" (assuming, without deciding, that § 4001(a) applies to military detentions).

There can be no doubt that individuals who fought against the United States in Afghanistan as part of the Taliban, an organization known to have supported the al Qaeda terrorist network responsible for [the September 11, 2001] attacks, are individuals Congress sought to target in passing the AUMF. We conclude that detention of individuals falling into the limited category we are considering, for the duration of the particular conflict in which they were captured, is so fundamental and accepted an incident to war as to be an exercise of the "necessary and appropriate force" Congress has authorized the President to use.

There is no bar to this Nation's holding one of its own citizens as an enemy combatant. In *Ex parte Quirin* (1942), one of the detainees, Haupt, alleged that he was a naturalized United States citizen. We held that "[c]itizens who associate themselves with the military arm of the enemy government, and with its aid, guidance and direction enter this country bent on hostile acts, are enemy belligerents within the meaning of . . . the law of war." While Haupt was tried for violations of the law of war, nothing in *Quirin* suggests that his citizenship would have precluded his mere detention for the duration of the relevant hostilities. Nor can we see any reason for drawing such a line here. A citizen, no less than an alien, can be "part of or supporting forces hostile to the United States or coalition partners" and "engaged in an armed conflict against the United States"[;] such a citizen, if released, would pose the same threat of returning to the front during the ongoing conflict.

Hamdi objects, nevertheless, that Congress has not authorized the *indefinite* detention to which he is now subject. As the Government concedes, "given its unconventional nature, the current conflict is unlikely to end with a formal cease-fire agreement." If the Government does not consider this unconventional war won for two generations, and if it maintains during that time that

Hamdi might, if released, rejoin forces fighting against the United States, then the position it has taken throughout the litigation of this case suggests that Hamdi's detention could last for the rest of his life.

It is a clearly established principle of the law of war that detention may last no longer than active hostilities. See Article 118 of the Geneva Convention (III) Relative to the Treatment of Prisoners of War, Aug. 12, 1949.

If the practical circumstances of a given conflict are entirely unlike those of the conflicts that informed the development of the law of war, that understanding may unravel. But that is not the situation we face as of this date. Active combat operations against Taliban fighters apparently are ongoing in Afghanistan. The United States may detain, for the duration of these hostilities, individuals legitimately determined to be Taliban combatants who "engaged in an armed conflict against the United States." If the record establishes that United States troops are still involved in active combat in Afghanistan, those detentions are part of the exercise of "necessary and appropriate force," and therefore are authorized by the AUMF.

Ex parte Milligan (1866) does not undermine our holding about the Government's authority to seize enemy combatants, as we define that term today. In that case, the Court made repeated reference to the fact that its inquiry into whether the military tribunal had jurisdiction to try and punish Milligan turned in large part on the fact that Milligan was not a prisoner of war, but a resident of Indiana arrested while at home there. That fact was central to its conclusion. Had Milligan been captured while he was assisting Confederate soldiers by carrying a rifle against Union troops on a Confederate battlefield, the holding of the Court might well have been different. The Court's repeated explanations that Milligan was not a prisoner of war suggest that had these different circumstances been present he could have been detained under military authority for the duration of the conflict, whether or not he was a citizen.

Moreover, as Justice Scalia acknowledges, the Court in *Quirin* dismissed the language of *Milligan* that the petitioners had suggested prevented them from being subject to military process. *Quirin* was a unanimous opinion. It both postdates and clarifies *Milligan*, providing us with the most apposite precedent that we have on the question of whether citizens may be detained in such circumstances.

To the extent that Justice Scalia accepts the precedential value of *Quirin*, he argues that it cannot guide our inquiry here because "[i]n *Quirin* it was uncontested that the petitioners were members of enemy forces," while Hamdi challenges his classification as an enemy combatant. But it is unclear why, in the paradigm outlined by Justice Scalia, such a concession should have any relevance. Justice Scalia envisions a system in which the only options are congressional suspension of the writ of habeas corpus or prosecution for treason or some other crime. He does not explain how his historical analysis supports the addition of a third option — detention under some other process after concession of enemy-combatant status — or why a concession should carry any different effect than proof of enemy-combatant status in a proceeding that comports with due process.

Further, Justice Scalia largely ignores the context of this case: a United States citizen captured in a *foreign* combat zone. Justice Scalia refers to only one case involving this factual scenario—a case in which a United States citizen-prisoner of war (a member of the Italian army) from World War II was seized on the battlefield in Sicily and then held in the United States. The court in that case held that the military detention of that United States citizen was lawful.

Justice Scalia can point to no case or other authority for the proposition that those captured on a foreign battlefield (whether detained there or in U.S. territory) cannot be detained outside the criminal process.

Moreover, Justice Scalia presumably would come to a different result if Hamdi had been kept in Afghanistan or even Guantanamo Bay. This creates a perverse incentive. Military authorities faced with the stark choice of submitting to the full-blown criminal process or releasing a suspected enemy combatant captured on the battlefield will simply keep citizen-detainees abroad. Indeed, the Government transferred Hamdi from Guantanamo Bay to the United States naval brig only after it learned that he might be an American citizen. It is not at all clear why that should make a determinative constitutional difference.

III

Even in cases in which the detention of enemy combatants is legally authorized, there remains the question of what process is constitutionally due to a citizen who disputes his enemy-combatant status. Hamdi argues that he is owed a meaningful and timely hearing and that "extra-judicial detention [that] begins and ends with the submission of an affidavit based on third-hand hearsay" does not comport with the Fifth and Fourteenth Amendments. The Government counters that any more process than was provided below would be both unworkable and "constitutionally intolerable."

First, the Government urges the adoption of the Fourth Circuit's holding below—that because it is "undisputed" that Hamdi's seizure took place in a combat zone, the habeas determination can be made purely as a matter of law, with no further hearing or factfinding necessary. This argument is easily rejected. As the dissenters from the denial of rehearing en banc noted, the circumstances surrounding Hamdi's seizure cannot in any way be characterized as "undisputed," as "those circumstances are neither conceded in fact, nor susceptible to concession in law, because Hamdi has not been permitted to speak for himself or even through counsel as to those circumstances."

The Government's second argument requires closer consideration. This is the argument that further factual exploration is unwarranted and inappropriate in light of the extraordinary constitutional interests at stake. Under the Government's most extreme rendition of this argument, "[r]espect for separation of powers and the limited institutional capabilities of courts in matters of military decision-making in connection with an ongoing conflict" ought to eliminate entirely any individual process, restricting the courts to investigating only whether legal authorization exists for the broader detention scheme. At most, the Government argues, courts should review its determination that a citizen is an enemy combatant under a very deferential "some evidence" standard. Under this review, a court would assume the accuracy of the Government's articulated basis for Hamdi's detention, as set forth in the Mobbs Declaration, and assess only whether that articulated basis was a legitimate one.

In response, Hamdi emphasizes that this Court consistently has recognized that an individual challenging his detention may not be held at the will of the Executive without recourse to some proceeding before a neutral tribunal to determine whether the Executive's asserted justifications for that detention have basis in fact and warrant in law. See, *e.g., Zadvydas v. Davis* (2001).

The ordinary mechanism that we use for balancing such serious competing interests, and for determining the procedures that are necessary to ensure that a citizen is not "deprived of life, liberty, or property, without due process of law," is the test that we articulated in *Mathews v. Eldridge* (1976). *Mathews* dictates that the process due in any given instance is determined by weighing "the private interest that will be affected by the official action" against the Government's asserted interest, "including the function involved" and the burdens the Government would face in providing greater process. The *Mathews* calculus then contemplates a judicious balancing of these concerns, through an analysis of "the risk of an erroneous deprivation" of the private interest if the process were reduced and the "probable value, if any, of additional or substitute procedural safeguards." We take each of these steps in turn.

It is beyond question that substantial interests lie on both sides of the scale in this case. Hamdi's "private interest . . . affected by the official action," is the most elemental of liberty interests — the interest in being free from physical detention by one's own government. Nor is the weight on this side of the *Mathews* scale offset by the circumstances of war or the accusation of treasonous behavior, for it is clear that commitment for *any* purpose constitutes a significant deprivation of liberty that requires due process protection, and at this stage in the *Mathews* calculus, we consider the interest of the *erroneously* detained individual.

On the other side of the scale are the weighty and sensitive governmental interests in ensuring that those who have in fact fought with the enemy during a war do not return to battle against the United States. [T]he law of war and the realities of combat may render such detentions both necessary and appropriate, and our due process analysis need not blink at those realities.

[W]e believe that neither the process proposed by the Government nor the process apparently envisioned by the District Court below strikes the proper constitutional balance when a United States citizen is detained in the United States as an enemy combatant.

We therefore hold that a citizen-detainee seeking to challenge his classification as an enemy combatant must receive notice of the factual basis for his classification, and a fair opportunity to rebut the Government's factual assertions before a neutral decisionmaker.

At the same time, the exigencies of the circumstances may demand that, aside from these core elements, enemy-combatant proceedings may be tailored to alleviate their uncommon potential to burden the Executive at a time of ongoing military conflict. Hearsay, for example, may need to be accepted as the most reliable available evidence from the Government in such a proceeding. Likewise, the Constitution would not be offended by a presumption in favor of the Government's evidence, so long as that presumption remained a rebuttable one and fair opportunity for rebuttal were provided. Thus, once the Government puts forth credible evidence that the habeas petitioner meets the enemy-combatant criteria, the onus could shift to the petitioner to rebut that evidence with more persuasive evidence that he falls outside the criteria. A burden-shifting scheme of this sort would meet the goal of ensuring that the errant tourist, embedded journalist, or local aid worker has a chance to prove military error while giving due regard to the Executive once it has put forth meaningful support for its conclusion that the detainee is in fact an enemy combatant.

We think it unlikely that this basic process will have the dire impact on the central functions of warmaking that the Government forecasts. The parties agree that initial captures on the battlefield need not receive the process we have discussed here; that process is due only when the determination is made to *continue* to hold those who have been seized. The Government has made clear in its briefing that documentation regarding battlefield detainees already is kept in the ordinary course of military affairs. Any factfinding imposition created by requiring a knowledgeable affiant to summarize these records to an independent tribunal is a minimal one. [I]t does not infringe on the core role of the military for the courts to exercise their own time-honored and constitutionally mandated roles of reviewing and resolving claims like those presented here. Cf. *Korematsu v. United States* (1944) (Murphy, J., dissenting) ("[L]ike other claims conflicting with the asserted constitutional rights of the individual, the military claim must subject itself to the judicial process of having its reasonableness determined and its conflicts with other interests reconciled").

In so holding, we necessarily reject the Government's assertion that separation of powers principles mandate a heavily circumscribed role for the courts in such circumstances. We have long since made clear that a state of war is not a blank check for the President when it comes to the rights of the Nation's citizens. *Youngstown Sheet & Tube* (1952).

Because we conclude that due process demands some system for a citizen-detainee to refute his classification, the proposed "some evidence" standard is inadequate. Any process in which the Executive's factual assertions go wholly unchallenged or are simply presumed correct without any opportunity for the alleged combatant to demonstrate otherwise falls constitutionally short.

Aside from unspecified "screening" processes and military interrogations in which the Government suggests Hamdi could have contested his classification, Hamdi has received no process. An interrogation by one's captor, however effective an intelligence-gathering tool, hardly constitutes a constitutionally adequate factfinding before a neutral decisionmaker.

There remains the possibility that the standards we have articulated could be met by an appropriately authorized and properly constituted military tribunal.

Indeed, it is notable that military regulations already provide for such process in related instances, dictating that tribunals be made available to determine the status of enemy detainees who assert prisoner-of-war status under the Geneva Convention. *See* Headquarters Depts. of Army, Navy, Air Force, and Marine Corps, Enemy Prisoners of War, Retained Personnel, Civilian Internees and Other Detainees, Army Regulation 190-8, ch. 1, § 1-6 (1997). In the absence of such process, however, a court that receives a petition for a writ of habeas corpus from an alleged enemy combatant must itself ensure that the minimum requirements of due process are achieved. We have no reason to doubt that courts faced with these sensitive matters will pay proper heed both to the matters of national security that might arise in an individual case and to the constitutional limitations safeguarding essential liberties that remain vibrant even in times of security concerns.

IV

Hamdi unquestionably has the right to access to counsel in connection with the proceedings on remand. No further consideration of this issue is necessary at this stage of the case.

* * *

The judgment of the United States Court of Appeals for the Fourth Circuit is vacated, and the case is remanded for further proceedings.

It is so ordered.

NOTES AND QUESTIONS

1. One hundred six days after this judgment on October 11, 2004, Yaser Esam Hamdi was released to his family in Saudi Arabia, where he renounced his U.S. citizenship pursuant to an agreement with the Justice Department. According to a Defense Department press release, "considerations of United States national security did not require his continued detention" but "operational and security considerations" prevented further elaboration. Jerry Markon, *Hamdi Returned to Saudi Arabia*, Wash. Post, Oct. 12, 2004. A Department of Justice press release was only slightly more expansive:

   The United States and enemy combatant Yaser Esam Hamdi and his counsel have signed an agreement that allows Hamdi to be released from United States custody and transferred to the Kingdom of Saudi Arabia, where he is a citizen. The agreement requires Hamdi, once he arrives in Saudi Arabia, to renounce any claim he has to U.S. citizenship and to abide by strict travel restrictions.

   Mr. Hamdi was taken into the custody of U.S. armed forces after he surrendered as part of a Taliban military unit. Like many other enemy combatants captured and detained by U.S. armed forces in Afghanistan who have been subsequently released, the United States has determined that Mr. Hamdi could be transferred out of United States custody subject to strict conditions that ensure the interests of the United States and our national security. As we have repeatedly stated, the United States has no interest in detaining enemy combatants beyond the point that they pose a threat to the U.S. and our allies.[3]

Why didn't the government proceed with the process the *Hamdi* Court deemed necessary for his continued detention?

2. How broadly or narrowly applicable to other cases is the plurality opinion? What is the range of factual circumstances that it covers?

3. What legal authorities does the United States identify as sources of its power to detain Hamdi? What are the implications of accepting one source instead of another?

4. Does this opinion include an argument about the separation of powers? What is its role?

5. The powers and authorities that U.S. officials wield must ultimately be traced to their source in the U.S. Constitution. The constitutional rights possessed by a U.S. citizen constrain how such powers may be used. When such officials act outside the United States, the constitutional source of their power does not change. Do the constitutional rights of citizens also remain the same when asserted abroad? To ask the question in shorthand, does (should) the Constitution "follow the flag"? Is this the wrong case to answer this question, since Hamdi's case was decided after he was brought to the United States?

Hamdi v. Rumsfeld
542 U.S. 507 (2004)

Justice SOUTER, with whom Justice GINSBURG joins, concurring in part, dissenting in part, and concurring in the judgment.

[In] this Court [Hamdi] presses the distinct argument that the Government's claim [that he is an "enemy combatant"], even if true, would not implicate any authority for holding him that would satisfy 18 U.S.C. § 4001(a) (Non-Detention Act), which bars imprisonment or detention of a citizen "except pursuant to an Act of Congress."

The threshold issue is how broadly or narrowly to read the Non-Detention Act, the tone of which is severe: "No citizen shall be imprisoned or otherwise detained by the United States except pursuant to an Act of Congress." Should the severity of the Act be relieved when the Government's stated factual justification for incommunicado detention is a war on terrorism, so that the Government may be said to act "pursuant" to congressional terms that fall short of explicit authority to imprison individuals? With one possible though important qualification, the answer has to be no.

[The] circumstances in which the Act was adopted point the way to this interpretation. The provision superseded a cold-war statute, the Emergency

---

3. *Statement of Mark Corallo, Director of Public Affairs, Department of Justice, Regarding Yaser Hamdi,* Sept. 22, 2004.

Detention Act of 1950, which had authorized the Attorney General, in time of emergency, to detain anyone reasonably thought likely to engage in espionage or sabotage. That statute was repealed in 1971 out of fear that it could authorize a repetition of the World War II internment of citizens of Japanese ancestry; Congress meant to preclude another episode like the one described in *Korematsu v. United States* (1944). While Congress might simply have struck the 1950 statute, in considering the repealer the point was made that the existing statute provided some express procedural protection, without which the Executive would seem to be subject to no statutory limits protecting individual liberty. See 117 Cong. Rec. 31544 (1971) (Emergency Detention Act "remains as the only existing barrier against the future exercise of executive power which resulted in" the Japanese internment). It was in these circumstances that a proposed limit on Executive action was expanded to the inclusive scope of § 4001(a) as enacted.

The fact that Congress intended to guard against a repetition of the World War II internments when it repealed the 1950 statute and gave us § 4001(a) provides a powerful reason to think that § 4001(a) was meant to require clear congressional authorization before any citizen can be placed in a cell. It is not merely that the legislative history shows that § 4001(a) was thought necessary in anticipation of times just like the present, in which the safety of the country is threatened. To appreciate what is most significant, one must only recall that the internments of the 1940s were accomplished by Executive action. Although an Act of Congress ratified and confirmed an Executive order authorizing the military to exclude individuals from defined areas and to accommodate those it might remove, the statute said nothing whatever about the detention of those who might be removed; internment camps were creatures of the Executive, and confinement in them rested on assertion of Executive authority. When, therefore, Congress repealed the 1950 Act and adopted § 4001(a) for the purpose of avoiding another *Korematsu*, it intended to preclude reliance on vague congressional authority (for example, providing "accommodations" for those subject to removal) as authority for detention or imprisonment at the discretion of the Executive (maintaining detention camps of American citizens, for example). In requiring that any Executive detention be "pursuant to an Act of Congress," then, Congress necessarily meant to require a congressional enactment that clearly authorized detention or imprisonment.

[T]here is one argument for treating the Force Resolution as sufficiently clear to authorize detention of a citizen consistently with § 4001(a). Assuming the argument to be sound, however, the Government is in no position to claim its advantage.

Because the Force Resolution authorizes the use of military force in acts of war by the United States, the argument goes, it is reasonably clear that the military and its Commander in Chief are authorized to deal with enemy belligerents according to the treaties and customs known collectively as the laws of war. Accordingly, the United States may detain captured enemies, and *Ex parte Quirin* (1942) may perhaps be claimed for the proposition that the American citizenship of such a captive does not as such limit the Government's power to deal with him under the usages of war. Thus, the Government here repeatedly argues that Hamdi's detention amounts to nothing more than customary detention of a captive taken on the field of battle: if the usages of war are fairly authorized by the Force Resolution, Hamdi's detention is authorized for purposes of § 4001(a).

There is no need, however, to address the merits of such an argument in all possible circumstances. For now it is enough to recognize that the Government's stated legal position in its campaign against the Taliban (among whom Hamdi was allegedly captured) is apparently at odds with its claim here to be acting in accordance with customary law of war and hence to be within the terms of the Force Resolution in its detention of Hamdi. In a statement of its legal position cited in its brief, the Government says that "the Geneva Convention applies to the Taliban detainees." Hamdi presumably is such a detainee, since according to the Government's own account, he was taken bearing arms on the Taliban side of a field of battle in Afghanistan. He would therefore seem to qualify for treatment as a prisoner of war under the Third Geneva Convention, to which the United States is a party.

By holding him incommunicado, however, the Government obviously has not been treating him as a prisoner of war, and in fact the Government claims that no Taliban detainee is entitled to prisoner of war status. This treatment appears to be a violation of the Geneva Convention provision that even in cases of doubt, captives are entitled to be treated as prisoners of war "until such time as their status has been determined by a competent tribunal." Art. 5. The Government answers that the President's determination that Taliban detainees do not qualify as prisoners of war is conclusive as to Hamdi's status and removes any doubt that would trigger application of the Convention's tribunal requirement. But reliance on this categorical pronouncement to settle doubt is apparently at odds with the military regulation, Enemy Prisoners of War, Retained Personnel, Civilian Internees and Other Detainees, Army Regulation 190-8, ch. 1, §§ 1-5, 1-6 (1997), adopted to implement the Geneva Convention, and setting out a detailed procedure for a military tribunal to determine an individual's status. One of the types of doubt these tribunals are meant to settle is whether a given individual may be, as Hamdi says he is, an "[i]nnocent civilian who should be immediately returned to his home or released." Thus, there is reason to question whether the United States is acting in accordance with the laws of war it claims as authority.

Whether, or to what degree, the Government is in fact violating the Geneva Convention and is thus acting outside the customary usages of war are not matters I can resolve at this point. What I can say, though, is that the Government has not made out its claim that in detaining Hamdi in the manner described, it is acting in accord with the laws of war authorized to be applied against citizens by the Force Resolution. I conclude accordingly that the Government has failed to support the position that the Force Resolution authorizes the described detention of Hamdi for purposes of § 4001(a).

It is worth adding a further reason for requiring the Government to bear the burden of clearly justifying its claim to be exercising recognized war powers before declaring § 4001(a) satisfied. Thirty-eight days after adopting the Force Resolution, Congress passed the USA PATRIOT ACT; that Act authorized the detention of alien terrorists for no more than seven days in the absence of criminal charges or deportation proceedings. It is very difficult to believe that the same Congress that carefully circumscribed Executive power over alien terrorists on home soil would not have meant to require the Government to justify clearly its detention of an American citizen held on home soil incommunicado.

Because I find Hamdi's detention forbidden by § 4001(a) and unauthorized by the Force Resolution, I would not reach any questions of what process he may be due in litigating disputed issues in a proceeding under the habeas statute or prior to the habeas enquiry itself. I would therefore vacate the judgment of the Court of Appeals and remand for proceedings consistent with this view.

Since this disposition does not command a majority of the Court, however, the need to give practical effect to the conclusions of eight Members of the Court rejecting the Government's position calls for me to join with the plurality in ordering remand on terms closest to those I would impose. Although I think litigation of Hamdi's status as an enemy combatant is unnecessary, the terms of the plurality's remand will allow Hamdi to offer evidence that he is not an enemy combatant, and he should at the least have the benefit of that opportunity.

It should go without saying that in joining with the plurality to produce a judgment, I do not adopt the plurality's resolution of constitutional issues that I would not reach. It is not that I could disagree with the plurality's determinations (given the plurality's view of the Force Resolution) that someone in Hamdi's position is entitled at a minimum to notice of the Government's claimed factual basis for holding him, and to a fair chance to rebut it before a neutral decisionmaker; nor, of course, could I disagree with the plurality's affirmation of Hamdi's right to counsel. On the other hand, I do not mean to imply agreement that the Government could claim an evidentiary presumption casting the burden of rebuttal on Hamdi, or that an opportunity to litigate before a military tribunal might obviate or truncate enquiry by a court on habeas.

NOTES AND QUESTIONS

1. Justice Souter seems to perceive the case as best resolved through statutory interpretation, not constitutional interpretation. Why? If Congress had rescinded the Non-Detention Act before adopting the AUMF, would Justice Souter have joined Justice O'Connor's opinion?
2. Justice Souter writes that the legislative history of the Non-Detention Act recognized its need in "times just like the present, in which the safety of the country is threatened." Is military detention of citizens found abroad and alleged to be "enemy combatants" comparable to the detention of citizens under suspicion

because of their racial ancestry? Does Justice Souter's argument depend on the strength of that comparison or is he making a different point?

3. Justice Souter's opinion makes frequent reference to Hamdi's "incommunicado" detention. Would Justice Souter have reached a different conclusion if Hamdi had been given access to his lawyer but nothing else?

Article 4 of the Third Geneva Convention establishes the qualification for prisoner of war status. In order to fall under the scope of Article 4, an individual must be captured in the context of an international (inter-state) armed conflict. Specifically, Article 4 provides, in part:

A. Prisoners of war, in the sense of the present Convention, are persons belonging to one of the following categories, who have fallen into the power of the enemy:

(1) Members of the armed forces of a Party to the conflict as well as members of militias or volunteer corps forming part of such armed forces.

(2) Members of other militias and members of other volunteer corps, including those of organized resistance movements, belonging to a Party to the conflict and operating in or outside their own territory, even if this territory is occupied, provided that such militias or volunteer corps, including such organized resistance movements, fulfil the following conditions:

(a) that of being commanded by a person responsible for his subordinates;

(b) that of having a fixed distinctive sign recognizable at a distance;

(c) that of carrying arms openly;

(d) that of conducting their operations in accordance with the laws and customs of war.

(3) Members of regular armed forces who profess allegiance to a government or an authority not recognized by the Detaining Power.

. . .

It is common that a detainee's status as a prisoner of war will be obvious, for example, when the detainee is captured in the enemy's uniform with military identification. However, in some situations, it is not clear whether a detainee falls within the scope of Article 4. In response to such uncertainty, Article 5 of the Convention provides:

The present Convention shall apply to the persons referred to in Article 4 from the time they fall into the power of the enemy and until their final release and repatriation.

Should any doubt arise as to whether persons, having committed a belligerent act and having fallen into the hands of the enemy, belong to any of the categories enumerated in Article 4, such persons shall enjoy the protection of the present Convention until such time as their status has been determined by a competent tribunal.

Article 5 does not indicate the requisite composition or structure of a status determination tribunal. For the U.S. military, Army Regulation 190-8 provides this flesh to the Article 5 bones. According to this joint service regulation, an Article 5 tribunal shall consist of three commissioned officers, ideally one military police officer, one military intelligence officer, and one judge advocate (a military lawyer). The hearing is non-adversarial, and there is no right to counsel or representation. The sole function of the tribunal is to determine whether a detainee qualifies as a prisoner of war pursuant to Article 4.

United States armed forces began capturing and detaining Taliban and al Qaeda fighters in October of 2001, after the initiation of ground combat operations in Afghanistan. Initially, the conflict was treated as non-international because Afghanistan was considered a failed state. In response to Secretary of State Colin Powell's strong recommendation to reconsider this position, President Bush reversed course. (Excerpts from some of these memos are reproduced in Chapter 2.)

In a memorandum dated February 7, 2002, titled "Humane Treatment of Taliban and al Qaeda Detainees," President Bush concluded that the armed conflict with the Taliban was international in character, thereby bringing the Third Geneva Convention into force. However, in the same memorandum, he also concluded that neither Taliban nor al Qaeda detainees qualified as prisoners of war. Taliban detainees, although captured during an international armed conflict, failed to satisfy the four criteria implicitly applicable to members of regular armed forces. President Bush therefore concluded that there was "no doubt" as to their non–prisoner of war status. As for al Qaeda detainees, the President determined that they were captured during the course of a distinct non-international armed conflict with the United States, and therefore were not even entitled to consideration of whether they qualified as prisoners of war.

Thus, all captives would be detained pursuant to the law of war because of their status as members of enemy belligerent groups engaged in hostilities against the United States, but none would be designated as prisoners of war nor provided a status review tribunal pursuant to Article 5 and Army Regulation 190-8.

Hamdi v. Rumsfeld
542 U.S. 507 (2004)

Justice SCALIA, with whom Justice STEVENS joins, dissenting.

Where the Government accuses a citizen of waging war against it, our constitutional tradition has been to prosecute him in federal court for treason or some other crime. Where the exigencies of war prevent that, the Constitution's Suspension Clause, Art. I, § 9, cl. 2, allows Congress to relax the usual protections temporarily. Absent suspension, however, the Executive's assertion of military exigency has not been thought sufficient to permit detention without charge. No one contends that the congressional Authorization for Use of Military Force, on which the Government relies to justify its actions here, is an implementation of the Suspension Clause. Accordingly, I would reverse the judgment below.

I

When a citizen was deprived of liberty because of alleged criminal conduct, those procedures [deemed necessary as "due process of law"] typically required committal by a magistrate followed by indictment and trial. To be sure, certain types of permissible *non*-criminal detention—that is, those not dependent upon the contention that the citizen had committed a criminal act—did not require the protections of criminal procedure. However, these fell into a limited number of well-recognized exceptions—civil commitment of the mentally ill, for example, and temporary detention in quarantine of the infectious. It is unthinkable that the Executive could render otherwise criminal grounds for detention non-criminal merely by disclaiming an intent to prosecute, or by asserting that it was incapacitating dangerous offenders rather than punishing wrongdoing.

These due process rights have historically been vindicated by the writ of habeas corpus.

II

The relevant question, then, is whether there is a different, special procedure for imprisonment of a citizen accused of wrongdoing *by aiding the enemy in wartime.*

Justice O'Connor, writing for a plurality of this Court, asserts that captured enemy combatants (other than those suspected of war crimes) have traditionally been detained until the cessation of hostilities and then released. That is probably an accurate description of wartime practice with respect to enemy *aliens.* The tradition with respect to American citizens, however, has been quite different. Citizens aiding the enemy have been treated as traitors subject to the criminal process.

[C]itizens have been charged and tried in Article III courts for acts of war against the United States, even when their noncitizen co-conspirators were not. For example, two American citizens alleged to have participated during World War I in a spying conspiracy on behalf of Germany were tried in federal court. A German member of the same conspiracy was subjected to military process. During World War II, the famous German saboteurs of *Ex parte Quirin* (1942), received military process, but the citizens who associated with them (with the exception of one citizen-saboteur, discussed below) were punished under the criminal process.

The modern treason statute basically tracks the language of the constitutional provision. Other provisions of Title 18 criminalize various acts of warmaking and adherence to the enemy. See, *e.g.*, § 32 (destruction of aircraft or aircraft facilities), § 2332a (use of weapons of mass destruction), § 2332b (acts of terrorism transcending national boundaries), § 2339A (providing material support to terrorists), § 2339B (providing material support to certain terrorist organizations), § 2382 (misprision of treason), § 2383 (rebellion or insurrection), § 2384 (seditious conspiracy), § 2390 (enlistment to serve in armed hostility against the United States). The only citizen other than Hamdi known to be imprisoned in connection with military hostilities in Afghanistan against the United States *was* subjected to criminal process and convicted upon a guilty plea. See *United States v. Lindh*, 212 F. Supp. 2d 541 (E.D. Va. 2002) (denying motions for dismissal).

There are times when military exigency renders resort to the traditional criminal process impracticable. English law accommodated such exigencies by allowing legislative suspension of the writ of habeas corpus for brief periods. Our Federal Constitution contains a provision explicitly permitting suspension, but limiting the situations in which it may be invoked. Although this provision does not state that suspension must be effected by, or authorized by, a legislative act, it has been so understood, consistent with English practice and the Clause's placement in Article I.

III

Of course the extensive historical evidence of criminal convictions and habeas suspensions does not *necessarily* refute the Government's position in this case. When the writ is suspended, the Government is entirely free from judicial oversight. It does not claim such total liberation here, but argues that it need only produce what it calls "some evidence" to satisfy a habeas court that a detained individual is an enemy combatant. Even if suspension of the writ on the one hand, and committal for criminal charges on the other hand, have been the only *traditional* means of dealing with citizens who levied war against their own country, it is theoretically possible that the Constitution does not *require* a choice between these alternatives.

I believe, however, that substantial evidence does refute that possibility. [Justice Scalia here discusses legal writings from 1679 through 1812.]

Further evidence comes from this Court's decision in *Ex parte Milligan*. There, the Court issued the writ to an American citizen who had been tried by military commission for offenses that included conspiring to overthrow the Government, seize munitions, and liberate prisoners of war. The Court rejected in no uncertain terms the Government's assertion that military jurisdiction was proper "under the 'laws and usages of war' ":

> "It can serve no useful purpose to inquire what those laws and usages are, whence they originated, where found, and on whom they operate; they can never be applied to citizens in states which have upheld the authority of the government, and where the courts are open and their process unobstructed."

Milligan is not exactly this case, of course, since the petitioner was threatened with death, not merely imprisonment. But the reasoning and conclusion of *Milligan* logically cover the present case. The Government justifies imprisonment of Hamdi on principles of the law of war and admits that, absent the war, it would have no such authority. But if the law of war cannot be applied to citizens where courts are open, then Hamdi's imprisonment without criminal trial is no less unlawful than Milligan's trial by military tribunal.

Milligan responded to the argument, repeated by the Government in this case, that it is dangerous to leave suspected traitors at large in time of war:

> "If it was dangerous, in the distracted condition of affairs, to leave Milligan unrestrained of his liberty, because he 'conspired against the government, afforded aid and comfort to rebels, and incited the people to insurrection,' the *law* said arrest him, confine him closely, render him powerless to do further mischief; and then present his case to the grand jury of the district, with proofs of his guilt, and, if indicted, try him according to the course of the common law. If this had been done, the Constitution would have been vindicated, the law of 1863 enforced, and the securities for personal liberty preserved and defended."

Thus, criminal process was viewed as the primary means — and the only means absent congressional action suspending the writ — not only to punish traitors, but to incapacitate them.

The proposition that the Executive lacks indefinite wartime detention authority over citizens is consistent with the Founders' general mistrust of military power permanently at the Executive's disposal.

IV

The Government argues that our more recent jurisprudence ratifies its indefinite imprisonment of a citizen within the territorial jurisdiction of federal courts. It places primary reliance upon *Ex parte Quirin*, a World War II case upholding the trial by military commission of eight German saboteurs, one of whom, Herbert Haupt, was a U.S. citizen. The case was not this Court's finest hour. The Court upheld the commission and denied relief in a brief *per curiam* issued the day after oral argument concluded; a week later the Government carried out the commission's death sentence upon six saboteurs, including Haupt. The Court eventually explained its reasoning in a written opinion issued several months later.

Only three paragraphs of the Court's lengthy opinion dealt with the particular circumstances of Haupt's case. The Government argued that Haupt, like the other petitioners, could be tried by military commission under the laws of war. In agreeing with that contention, *Quirin* purported to interpret the language of *Milligan* quoted above (the law of war "can never be applied to citizens in states which have upheld the authority of the government, and where the courts are open and their process unobstructed") in the following manner:

> "Elsewhere in its opinion . . . the Court was at pains to point out that Milligan, a citizen twenty years resident in Indiana, who had never been a resident of any of the states in rebellion, was not an enemy belligerent either entitled to the status of a prisoner of war or subject to the penalties imposed upon unlawful belligerents. We construe the Court's statement as to the inapplicability of the law of war to Milligan's case as having particular reference to the facts before it. From them the Court concluded that Milligan, not being a part of or associated with the armed forces of the enemy, was a non-belligerent, not subject to the law of war. . . ."

In my view this seeks to revise *Milligan* rather than describe it. *Milligan* had involved (among other issues) two separate questions: (1) whether the military trial of Milligan was justified by the laws of war, and if not (2) whether the President's suspension of the writ, pursuant to congressional authorization, prevented the issuance of habeas corpus. The Court's categorical language about the law of war's inapplicability to citizens where the courts are open (with no exception mentioned for citizens who were prisoners of war) was contained in its discussion of the first point. The factors pertaining to whether Milligan could reasonably be considered a belligerent and prisoner of war, while mentioned earlier in the opinion, were made relevant and brought to bear in the Court's later discussion, of whether Milligan came within the statutory provision that effectively made an exception to Congress's authorized suspension of the writ for (as the Court described it) "all parties, not prisoners of war, resident in their respective jurisdictions, . . . who were citizens of states in which the administration of the laws in the Federal tribunals was unimpaired." *Milligan* thus understood was in accord with the traditional law of habeas corpus I have described: Though treason often occurred in wartime, there was, absent provision for special treatment in a congressional suspension of the writ, no exception to the right to trial by jury for citizens who could be called "belligerents" or "prisoners of war."

But even if *Quirin* gave a correct description of *Milligan*, or made an irrevocable revision of it, *Quirin* would still not justify denial of the writ here. In *Quirin* it was uncontested that the petitioners were members of enemy forces. They were "*admitted* enemy invaders," (emphasis added), and it was "undisputed" that they had landed in the United States in service of German forces. The specific holding of the Court was only that, "upon the *conceded* facts," the petitioners were "plainly within [the] boundaries" of military jurisdiction (emphasis added).[3] But where those jurisdictional facts are *not* conceded where the petitioner insists that he is *not* a belligerent—*Quirin* left the pre-existing law in place: Absent suspension of the writ, a citizen held where the courts are open is entitled either to criminal trial or to a judicial decree requiring his release.

V

It follows from what I have said that Hamdi is entitled to a habeas decree requiring his release unless (1) criminal proceedings are promptly brought, or (2) Congress has suspended the writ of habeas corpus. A suspension of the writ could, of course, lay down conditions for continued detention, similar to those

---

3. The plurality complains that . . . I have identified [only one case] in which "a United States citizen [was] captured in a *foreign* combat zone." Indeed it is; such cases must surely be rare. But given the constitutional tradition I have described, the burden is not upon me to find cases in which the writ was *granted* to citizens in this country *who had been captured on foreign battlefields*; it is upon those who would carve out an exception for such citizens (as the plurality's complaint suggests it would) to find a single case (other than one where enemy status was admitted) in which habeas was *denied*.

that today's opinion prescribes under the Due Process Clause. But there is a world of difference between the people's representatives' determining the need for that suspension (and prescribing the conditions for it), and this Court's doing so.

The plurality finds justification for Hamdi's imprisonment in the Authorization for Use of Military Force. This is not remotely a congressional suspension of the writ, and no one claims that it is. I do not think this statute even authorizes detention of a citizen with the clarity necessary. But even if it did, I would not permit it to overcome Hamdi's entitlement to habeas corpus relief. The Suspension Clause of the Constitution, which carefully circumscribes the conditions under which the writ can be withheld, would be a sham if it could be evaded by congressional prescription of requirements *other than the common-law requirement of committal for criminal prosecution* that render the writ, though available, unavailing. If the Suspension Clause does not guarantee the citizen that he will either be tried or released, unless the conditions for suspending the writ exist and the grave action of suspending the writ has been taken; if it merely guarantees the citizen that he will not be detained unless Congress by ordinary legislation says he can be detained; it guarantees him very little indeed.

Having found a congressional authorization for detention of citizens where none clearly exists; and having discarded the categorical procedural protection of the Suspension Clause; the plurality then proceeds, under the guise of the Due Process Clause, to prescribe what procedural protections *it* thinks appropriate. It claims authority to engage in this sort of "judicious balancing" from *Mathews v. Eldridge* (1976), a case involving . . . *the withdrawal of disability benefits!* Whatever the merits of this technique when newly recognized property rights are at issue (and even there they are questionable), it has no place where the Constitution and the common law already supply an answer.

There is a certain harmony of approach in the plurality's making up for Congress's failure to invoke the Suspension Clause and its making up for the Executive's failure to apply what it says are needed procedures—an approach that reflects what might be called a Mr. Fix-it Mentality. The plurality seems to view it as its mission to Make Everything Come Out Right, rather than merely to decree the consequences, as far as individual rights are concerned, of the other two branches' actions and omissions. Has the Legislature failed to suspend the writ in the current dire emergency? Well, we will remedy that failure by prescribing the reasonable conditions that a suspension should have included. And has the Executive failed to live up to those reasonable conditions? Well, we will ourselves make that failure good, so that this dangerous fellow (if he is dangerous) need not be set free. The problem with this approach is not only that it steps out of the courts' modest and limited role in a democratic society; but that by repeatedly doing what it thinks the political branches ought to do it encourages their lassitude and saps the vitality of government by the people.

VI

Several limitations give my views in this matter a relatively narrow compass. They apply only to citizens, accused of being enemy combatants, who are detained within the territorial jurisdiction of a federal court. This is not likely to be a numerous group; currently we know of only two, Hamdi and Jose Padilla. Where the citizen is captured outside and held outside the United States, the constitutional requirements may be different. Moreover, even within the United States, the accused citizen-enemy combatant may lawfully be detained once prosecution is in progress or in contemplation. See, *e.g., United States v. Salerno* (1987). The Government has been notably successful in securing conviction, and hence long-term custody or execution, of those who have waged war against the state.

I frankly do not know whether these tools are sufficient to meet the Government's security needs, including the need to obtain intelligence through interrogation. It is far beyond my competence, or the Court's competence, to determine that. But it is not beyond Congress's. If the situation demands it, the Executive can ask Congress to authorize suspension of the writ—which can be made subject to whatever conditions Congress deems appropriate, including even the procedural novelties invented by the plurality today. To be sure, suspension is limited by the Constitution to cases of rebellion or invasion. But whether the attacks of September 11, 2001, constitute an "invasion," and whether those attacks still justify suspension several years later, are questions for Congress rather than this Court. If civil rights are to be curtailed during wartime, it must be done openly and democratically, as the Constitution requires, rather than by silent erosion through an opinion of this Court.

* * *

Because the Court has proceeded to meet the current emergency in a manner the Constitution does not envision, I respectfully dissent.

NOTES AND QUESTIONS

1. As Justice Scalia observes, *Mathews v. Eldridge* was a case concerning the constitutionality of procedures used to terminate the respondent's social security disability benefits. It is a key case in the analysis of procedural due process issues. Can it be transposed to a case concerning military detention in the context of an armed conflict? If the issue is what process is due, should it matter if what is at stake is the property or the liberty of the individual?

2. Does Justice Scalia's opinion include an argument about the separation of powers? How does it differ from any separation of powers concerns raised in Justice O'Connor's plurality opinion?

3. Justice Scalia writes: "Where the citizen is captured outside and held outside the United States, the constitutional requirements may be different." Why? Compare your answer to the answer you gave to question 5 under Justice O'Connor's plurality opinion.

4. How does the identification of different "key" facts trigger different legal conclusions? What *are* the "key" facts in *Hamdi* for purposes of applying *Ex parte Milligan* and/or *Ex parte Quirin*?

5. Now that you have read both Justice O'Connor's and Justice Scalia's views of *Milligan* and *Quirin*, consider each case more closely. As you do so, try to iden-tify the points on which these two Justices disagree. How would you charac-terize their disagreements? What are their starting assumptions? What are the assumptions from which *you* start in concluding which one is more persuasive?

Ex parte Milligan

Ex parte Milligan, 71 U.S. 2 (1866), is from the Civil War era. Lambdin P. Milligan, in Justice Davis's description, "is a citizen of the United States; has lived for twenty years in Indiana; and, at the time of the grievances complained of, was not, and never had been in the military or naval service of the United States." (He also hap-pened to be a lawyer.) Chief Justice Chase, concurring in the opinion of the Court, implied but did not say that Milligan was part of a "powerful secret association" known generally as "Copperheads" and organized as the "Order of the Sons of Liberty." This group, "composed of citizens and others, existed within the state, under military organization, conspiring against the draft, and plotting insurrec-tion, the liberation of the prisoners of war at various depots, the seizure of the state and national arsenals, armed cooperation with the enemy, and war against the national government." What no one could claim, however, was that Milligan or his fellow citizens were members of the Confederate Army or its spies or affiliates.

What to do with such types? The commander of the military district of Indiana (an administrative district, not in any way a martial government) ordered Milligan's arrest. Milligan was rousted from his home, found guilty of "certain charges and specifications" before a military commission convened at Indianapolis, and sen-tenced to be hanged.

But the courts in Indiana were open at the time and, indeed, a grand jury empaneled in Indianapolis had adjourned without handing down any indictment against Milligan. This was an important legal fact. In 1863, Congress had passed "An Act Relating to Habeas Corpus." The law authorized presidential suspension of the writ of habeas corpus "whenever, in his judgment, the public safety may require it." But the law also required that if the military held persons "otherwise than as prisoners of war" who were "citizens of states" where the courts were open and operating, such persons must be identified to the federal court in that jurisdiction. If a grand jury then adjourned without indicting such a person, the court could order his discharge from military confinement. The statute made no mention of any military authority to do more than detain such persons. Other statutes and practices were at best unclear whether someone like Milligan (e.g., not a "prisoner of war" or a spy or a deserter) fit the category of "triable by" military authority as then understood under the customary laws of war.[4]

4. What these were, exactly, was also not certain. Indeed, it fell to a law professor named Francis Lieber to codify such rules for the first time in 1863 in what became known as the "Lieber Code," or more formally, General Orders No. 100, Instructions for the Government of Armies of the United States in the Field.

Milligan argued that the military commission lacked jurisdiction to try him. The government, on the other hand, argued for the sweeping authority of martial law: "[I]n a time of war the commander of an armed force (if in his opinion the exigencies of the country demand it, and of which he is to judge), has the power, within the lines of his military district, to suspend all civil rights and their remedies, and subject citizens as well as soldiers to the rule of his will; and in the exercise of his lawful authority cannot be restrained, except by his superior officer or the President of the United States."

The Court rejected this argument as going too far: "[T]his is not a question of the power to proclaim martial law, when war exists in a community and the courts and civil authorities are overthrown." Indiana had been threatened by enemy invasion. But that was all: "On her soil there was no hostile foot; if once invaded, that invasion was at an end, and with it all pretext for martial law." Further, the Court found it "difficult to see how the safety for the country required martial law in Indiana. If any of her citizens were plotting treason, the power of arrest could secure them, until the government was prepared for their trial, when the courts were open and ready to try them. It was as easy to protect witnesses before a civil as a military tribunal; and as there could be no wish to convict, except on sufficient legal evidence, surely an ordained and established court was better able to judge of this than a military tribunal composed of gentlemen not trained to the profession of the law."

Therefore, the Court issued its famous holding:

> It follows, from what has been said on this subject, that there are occasions when martial rule can be properly applied. If, in foreign invasion or civil war, the courts are actually closed, and it is impossible to administer criminal justice according to law, then, on the theatre of active military operations, where war really prevails, there is a necessity to furnish a substitute for the civil authority, thus overthrown, to preserve the safety of the army and society; and as no power is left but the military, it is allowed to govern by martial rule until the laws can have their free course. As necessity creates the rule, so it limits its duration; for, if this government is continued after the courts are reinstated, it is a gross usurpation of power. Martial rule can never exist where the courts are open, and in the proper and unobstructed exercise of their jurisdiction. It is also confined to the locality of actual war. Because, during the late Rebellion it could have been enforced in Virginia, where the national authority was overturned and the courts driven out, it does not follow that it should obtain in Indiana, where that authority was never disputed, and justice was always administered.
>
> But it is insisted that Milligan was a prisoner of war, and, therefore, excluded from the privileges of the statute. It is not easy to see how he can be treated as a prisoner of war, when he lived in Indiana for the past twenty years, was arrested there, and had not been, during the late troubles, a resident of any of the states in rebellion. If in Indiana he conspired with bad men to assist the enemy, he is punishable for it in the courts of Indiana; but, when tried for the offence, he cannot plead the rights of war; for he was not engaged in legal acts of hostility against the government, and only such persons, when captured, are prisoners of war. If he cannot enjoy the immunities attaching to the character of a prisoner of war, how can he be subject to their pains and penalties?

Ex parte Quirin

Ex parte Quirin is from World War II. How it came to be decided shows our system of laws in both its best and worst light. On the one hand, the resolution of the case by the Supreme Court seems like rushed justice. The Court issued a brief per curiam judgment with no opinion to explain its reasons two days after it heard the case. *Ex parte Quirin*, 63 S. Ct. 1 (1942). What the Court termed its "extended opinion" was filed three months later, on October 29, long after most of the defendants had already been executed. *Ex parte Quirin*, 63 S. Ct. 2 (1942). On the other hand, the case only reached the Supreme Court in the first place because the appointed defense counsel, Col. Kenneth C. Royall, defied President Roosevelt's wishes in order to seek judicial review outside the military system hastily set up to convict them.

The case came about because of some rather hapless Nazi saboteurs. After undergoing training in sabotage, four were transported by German submarine across the Atlantic and landed on a Long Island beach in mid-June 1942; four others landed on a beach in Florida.[5] All were almost immediately discovered thanks in large part to the decision of one of their number to turn himself in.[6] On July 2, President Roosevelt ordered the appointment of a military commission to try the men for war crimes, prescribing on the same day the regulations for trial and appeal and denying access to any civil court.

Appointed military counsel for the defendants argued that the commission proceedings deprived the petitioners of their Fifth and Sixth Amendment rights and that the President's order was in conflict with rules established by Congress in its Articles of War. The Court dispensed with both arguments rather quickly. The President had authority "incident to the conduct of war . . . not only to repel and defeat the enemy, but to seize and subject to disciplinary measures" enemy combatants who have violated the law of war. Congress added to that authority its own authorization to use military commissions to do so. In its first substantive nod to *Ex parte Milligan*, the Court acknowledged the possible existence of acts

---

5. Hapless though they clearly were, the threat they represented is easy to understand. According to Attorney General Biddle, "[e]ach group possessed a substantial supply of TNT and other high explosives and fuses, timing devices and detonators, which, in the hold of a boat or in a locker of the waiting room of a railroad station, set off at a crowded moment would have caused unimaginable damage and loss of life. . . . They carried the layouts of three plants of the Aluminum Company of America, of the Niagara Falls hydroelectric plant, of the New York water supply system, and of a number of key industries." FRANCIS BIDDLE, IN BRIEF AUTHORITY 325 (1962). Recounting the threat, Biddle invoked the "Black Tom" explosion described in Chapter 2 of this casebook. *Id.* at 326-27.

6. An excellent summary treatment of the strange facts of this case is found in LOUIS FISHER, MILITARY TRIBUNALS AND PRESIDENTIAL POWER 91-129 (2005). According to his account, the government sought to avoid a criminal trial in part to preserve the public's false impression "that uncanny FBI organizational skills had quickly exposed the plot," not, as was actually the case, the cold-feet confession of one of the would-be saboteurs. But what might seem a decision motivated by an attempt to avoid government embarrassment could still have national security implications: "The government did not want to broadcast how easily German U-boats had reached American shores undetected." *Id.* at 95. Attorney General Biddle, it seems, also worried about the probability of conviction on criminal charges carrying adequately severe penalties available in the civil courts. *Id.*

"not triable by military tribunal here, either because they are not recognized by our courts as violations of the law of war or because they are of that class of offenses constitutionally triable only by a jury. It was upon such grounds that the Court denied the right to proceed by military tribunal in *Ex parte Milligan*." *Id.* at 11. But, the Court concluded, such a circumstance was not present.

One of the petitioners, Herbert Haupt, claimed to be a U.S. citizen. (The government argued that he had lost this citizenship either because he "elected to maintain German allegiance and citizenship" or because "by his conduct [he] renounced or abandoned" it. *Id.* at 7.) The Court dismissed the issue in two stages. First, the Court noted:

> Citizenship in the United States of an enemy belligerent does not relieve him from the consequences of a belligerency that is unlawful because in violation of the law of war. Citizens who associate themselves with the military arm of the enemy government and with its aid, guidance and direction enter this country bent on hostile acts are enemy belligerents within the meaning of the Hague Convention and the law of war. It is as an enemy belligerent that petitioner Haupt is charged with entering the United States, and unlawful belligerency is the gravamen of the offense of which he is accused.[7]

Second, the Court distinguished Milligan:

> Petitioners, and especially petitioner Haupt, stress the pronouncement of this Court in the Milligan case, that the law of war "can never be applied to citizens in states which have upheld the authority of the government, and where the courts are open and their process unobstructed." Elsewhere in its opinion, the Court was at pains to point out that Milligan, a citizen twenty years resident in Indiana, who had never been a resident of any of the states in rebellion, was not an enemy belligerent either entitled to the status of a prisoner of war or subject to the penalties imposed upon unlawful belligerents. We construe the Court's statement as to the inapplicability of the law of war to Milligan's case as having particular reference to the facts before it. From them the Court concluded that Milligan, not being a part of or associated with the armed forces of the enemy, was a non-belligerent, not subject to the law of war save as—in circumstances found not there to be present and not involved here—martial law might be constitutionally established.
>
> The Court's opinion is inapplicable to the case presented by the present record. We have no occasion now to define with meticulous care the ultimate boundaries of the jurisdiction of military tribunals to try persons according to the law of war. It is enough that petitioners here, upon the conceded facts, were plainly within those boundaries, and were held in good faith for trial by military commission, charged with being enemies who, with the purpose of destroying war materials and utilities, entered or after entry remained in our territory without uniform—an offense against the law of war. We hold only that those particular acts constitute an offense against the law of war which the Constitution authorizes to be tried by military commission.[8]

The Court denied the habeas petitions.

Between the Court's brief per curiam placeholder on July 31, and the "extended opinion" filed in late October, all eight petitioners were found guilty by the military

---

7. *Ex parte Quirin*, 63 S. Ct. 2, 15-16 (1942) (internal citations omitted).
8. *Id.* at 19-20 (internal citations omitted).

commission. Six petitioners, including Haupt, were executed by electric chair. Haupt's parents, who helped him hide for a brief period in Chicago before his capture, were convicted of treason and eventually stripped of their citizenship and deported. The father's protracted experience of the civilian criminal justice system—his first conviction and death sentence was reversed on appeal, see *United States v. Haupt*, 136 F.2d 661 (7th Cir. 1943), following which he was retried, convicted, and had his life sentence upheld in *United States v. Haupt*, 152 F.2d 771 (7th Cir. 1945), *aff'd Haupt v. United States*, 330 U.S. 631 (1947)—suggests the process that the son's secret military trial had avoided.

Hamdi v. Rumsfeld
542 U.S. 507 (2004)

Justice THOMAS, dissenting.

The Executive Branch, acting pursuant to the powers vested in the President by the Constitution and with explicit congressional approval, has determined that Yaser Hamdi is an enemy combatant and should be detained. This detention falls squarely within the Federal Government's war powers, and we lack the expertise and capacity to second-guess that decision. As such, petitioners' habeas challenge should fail, and there is no reason to remand the case.

I

The Founders intended that the President have primary responsibility—along with the necessary power—to protect the national security and to conduct the Nation's foreign relations. They did so principally because the structural advantages of a unitary Executive are essential in these domains.

I acknowledge that the question whether Hamdi's executive detention is lawful is a question properly resolved by the Judicial Branch, though the question comes to the Court with the strongest presumptions in favor of the Government. The plurality agrees that Hamdi's detention is lawful if he is an enemy combatant. But the question whether Hamdi is actually an enemy combatant is of a kind for which the Judiciary has neither aptitude, facilities nor responsibility and which has long been held to belong in the domain of political power not subject to judicial intrusion or inquiry. That is, although it is appropriate for the Court to determine the judicial question whether the President has the asserted authority, we lack the information and expertise to question whether Hamdi is actually an enemy combatant, a question the resolution of which is committed to other branches.

II

Although the President very well may have inherent authority to detain those arrayed against our troops, I agree with the plurality that we need not decide that question because Congress has authorized the President to do so [in the AUMF].

Accordingly, the President's action here is "supported by the strongest of presumptions and the widest latitude of judicial interpretation." *Dames & Moore* (internal quotation marks omitted). The question becomes whether the Federal Government (rather than the President acting alone) has power to detain Hamdi as an enemy combatant. More precisely, we must determine whether the Government may detain Hamdi given the procedures that were used.

III

I agree with the plurality that the Federal Government has power to detain those that the Executive Branch determines to be enemy combatants. But I do not think that the plurality has adequately explained the breadth of the President's authority to detain enemy combatants, an authority that includes making virtually conclusive factual findings. In my view, the structural considerations discussed above, as recognized in our precedent, demonstrate that we lack the capacity and responsibility to second-guess this determination.

In a case strikingly similar to this one, the Court addressed a Governor's authority to detain for an extended period a person the executive believed to be responsible, in part, for a local insurrection. Justice Holmes wrote for a unanimous Court:

> "When it comes to a decision by the head of the State upon a matter involving its life, the ordinary rights of individuals must yield to what *he deems* the necessities of the moment. Public danger warrants the substitution of executive process for judicial process. This was admitted with regard to killing men in the actual clash of arms, and we think it obvious, although it was disputed, that the same is true of temporary detention to prevent apprehended harm." *Moyer v. Peabody* (1909) (citation omitted; emphasis added).

The Court answered Moyer's claim that he had been denied due process by emphasizing:

> "[I]t is familiar that what is due process of law depends on circumstances. It varies with the subject-matter and the necessities of the situation. Thus summary proceedings suffice for taxes, and executive decisions for exclusion from the country. . . . Such arrests are not necessarily for punishment, but are by way of precaution to prevent the exercise of hostile power."

In this context, due process requires nothing more than a good-faith executive determination.[3] To be clear: The Court has held that an Executive, acting pursuant to statutory and constitutional authority, may, consistent with the Due Process Clause, unilaterally decide to detain an individual if the Executive deems this necessary for the public safety *even if he is mistaken.*

---

3. Indeed, it is not even clear that the Court required good faith. See *Moyer* ("It is not alleged that [the Governor's] judgment was not honest, if that be material, or that [Moyer] was detained after fears of the insurrection were at an end").

Moyer is not an exceptional case. [I]n *U.S. v. Salerno* (1987), the Court explained that the Due Process Clause "lays down [no] categorical imperative." The Court continued:

> "We have repeatedly held that the Government's regulatory interest in community safety can, in appropriate circumstances, outweigh an individual's liberty interest. For example, in times of war or insurrection, when society's interest is at its peak, the Government may detain individuals whom the Government believes to be dangerous."

The Government's asserted authority to detain an individual that the President has determined to be an enemy combatant, at least while hostilities continue, comports with the Due Process Clause. As these cases also show, the Executive's decision that a detention is necessary to protect the public need not and should not be subjected to judicial second-guessing. Indeed, at least in the context of enemy-combatant determinations, this would defeat the unity, secrecy, and dispatch that the Founders believed to be so important to the warmaking function.

I therefore cannot agree with Justice Scalia's conclusion that the Government must choose between using standard criminal processes and suspending the writ. Justice Scalia relies heavily upon *Ex parte Milligan*, and three cases decided by New York state courts in the wake of the War of 1812. I admit that *Milligan* supports his position. But because the Executive Branch there, unlike here, did not follow a specific statutory mechanism provided by Congress, the Court did not need to reach the broader question of Congress' power, and its discussion on this point was arguably dicta, as four Justices believed (Chase, C.J., joined by Wayne, Swayne, and Miller, JJ., concurring in judgment).

Accordingly, I conclude that the Government's detention of Hamdi as an enemy combatant does not violate the Constitution. By detaining Hamdi, the President, in the prosecution of a war and authorized by Congress, has acted well within his authority. Hamdi thereby received all the process to which he was due under the circumstances. I therefore believe that this is no occasion to balance the competing interests, as the plurality unconvincingly attempts to do.

IV

Ultimately, the plurality's dismissive treatment of the Government's asserted interests arises from its apparent belief that enemy-combatant determinations are not part of "the actual prosecution of a war," or one of the "central functions of warmaking." This seems wrong: Taking *and holding* enemy combatants is a quintessential aspect of the prosecution of war. Moreover, this highlights serious difficulties in applying the plurality's balancing approach here. First, in the war context, we know neither the strength of the Government's interests nor the costs of imposing additional process.

Second, it is at least difficult to explain why the result should be different for other military operations that the plurality would ostensibly recognize as "central functions of warmaking." As the plurality recounts:

> "Parties whose rights are to be affected are entitled to be heard; and in order that they may enjoy that right they must first be notified. It is equally fundamental that the right to notice and an opportunity to be heard must be granted at a meaningful time and in a meaningful manner."

Because a decision to bomb a particular target might extinguish *life* interests, the plurality's analysis seems to require notice to potential targets. To take one more example, in November 2002, a Central Intelligence Agency (CIA) Predator drone fired a Hellfire missile at a vehicle in Yemen carrying an al Qaeda leader, a citizen of the United States, and four others. It is not clear whether the CIA knew that an American was in the vehicle. But the plurality's due process would seem to require notice and opportunity to respond here as well. I offer these examples not because I think the plurality would demand additional process in these situations but because it clearly would not. The result here should be the same.

I realize that many military operations are, in some sense, necessary. But many, if not most, are merely expedient, and I see no principled distinction between the military operation the plurality condemns today (the holding of an enemy combatant based on the process given Hamdi) from a variety of other military operations. In truth, I doubt that there is any sensible, bright-line distinction. It could be argued that bombings and missile strikes are an inherent part of war, and as long as our forces do not violate the laws of war, it is of no constitutional moment that civilians might be killed. But this does not serve to distinguish this case because it is also consistent with the laws of war to detain enemy combatants exactly as the Government has detained Hamdi.

Undeniably, Hamdi has been deprived of a serious interest, one actually protected by the Due Process Clause. Against this, however, is the Government's overriding interest in protecting the Nation. If a deprivation of liberty can be justified by the need to protect a town [in *Moyer*], the protection of the Nation, *a fortiori*, justifies it.

For these reasons, I would affirm the judgment of the Court of Appeals.

NOTES AND QUESTIONS

1. How does Justice Thomas's approach to the case differ from that found in the plurality opinion?
2. Compare Justice Thomas's view of the President's powers with those of the other Justices. What types of arguments do the Justices use to advance their different positions?
3. Justice Thomas argues that "the question whether Hamdi is actually an enemy combatant is of a kind for which the Judiciary has neither aptitude, facilities nor responsibility and which has long been held to belong in the domain of political

power not subject to judicial intrusion or inquiry." Is this a legal question or a factual question? Why is the judicial branch poorly placed to answer it? Is the judicial branch equally lacking in "aptitude, facilities [and] responsibility" to decide or is one of these characteristics of greater concern than the others?

4. If you felt that *Mathews v. Eldridge* was not a case readily transposable to a case concerning military detention of an enemy combatant captured in a foreign country, is *Moyer v. Peabody* similarly ill-suited for such use?

5. Justice Thomas quotes Justice Oliver Wendell Holmes, writing for the Court in *Moyer*: "Public danger warrants the substitution of executive process for judicial process." Is that an example of *"Inter armes silent leges"* or a matter of one branch of government appropriately deferring to another?

CHAPTER 2

Lessons of History

The past is a foreign country: they do things differently there.
—*L.P. Hartley*[1]

At 8:46 on the morning of September 11, 2001, American Airlines Flight 11 crashed into the North Tower of the World Trade Center in lower Manhattan.[2] A few minutes after nine o'clock, United Airlines Flight 175 crashed into the South Tower. Roughly thirty minutes later, American Airlines Flight 77 crashed into the Pentagon. Twenty-five minutes later, United Airlines Flight 93 crashed in a field near Shanksville, Pennsylvania. It is widely believed that but for a revolt of the passengers on board, Flight 93 would have crashed into the White House or the Capitol. All four planes had been hijacked by terrorists working together. The principal architect of the plot was Khalid Sheikh Mohammed. He was supported by Osama bin Laden and the organization he led, al Qaeda (Arabic for "the base").

Two hundred forty-six people lost their lives on board these four aircraft (excluding the nineteen hijackers). Almost three thousand people were killed in the destruction in lower Manhattan and at the Pentagon. Such an attack had never occurred in U.S. history. Many Americans felt that their world changed that day.

It is extreme understatement to note that this attack made a profound impact on U.S. law and society. The impact of those domestic changes soon extended worldwide. On September 18, 2001, Congress authorized the President "to use all necessary and appropriate force against those nations, organizations, or persons he determines planned, authorized, committed, or aided the terrorist attacks . . . or harbored such organizations or persons, in order to prevent any future acts of international terrorism against the United States by such nations, organizations, or persons." Pub. L. No.

---

1. L.P. Hartley, The Go-Between 9 (1953).

2. The facts provided in these first two paragraphs come from the Final Report of the National Commission on Terrorist Attacks upon the United States (the 9/11 Commission Report) (2004).

107-40, 115 Stat. 224. Exceptionally, Congress authorized the President to use military force without identifying the enemy by a specific name or country.

> Congress has declared war eleven times in five different conflicts and authorized military force (without "declaring war") on many more occasions. The enemy is not always named. In 1819, Congress authorized President Monroe to employ "public armed vessels" to protect the U.S. merchant fleet from "piratical aggressions and depredations." Act of Mar. 3, 1819, ch. 77, 3 Stat. 510. This remains current law. *See* 33 U.S.C. § 381.

The U.S.-led invasion of Afghanistan began in October 2001. By mid-January 2002, detainees from Afghanistan (who were believed to be fighters for either al Qaeda or the Taliban, but who sometimes turned out to be neither)[3] were arriving at Camp X-Ray, a facility at the U.S. naval station located at Guantánamo Bay, Cuba. Following his capture in 2003, Khalid Sheikh Mohammed was interrogated, tortured, and subjected to trial by military commission at Guantánamo Bay. As of this writing in mid-2020, his trial along with four co-defendants seems unlikely to start before the twentieth anniversary of the 9/11 attacks has passed. See Carol Rosenberg, *The 9/11 Trial: Why Is It Taking So Long?* N.Y. Times, April 17, 2020. (Ironically, the historical justification for a military commission — as opposed to a court-martial — was its speed.)

In the United States, the USA PATRIOT Act, 130 pages of the Statutes at Large, was approved by both houses of Congress within three days of its introduction and then signed into law by President Bush on October 26, 2001. Pub. L. No. 107-56, 115 Stat. 272. The law enhanced domestic and foreign surveillance authorities, defined new crimes (including an expanded definition of material support for terrorism), augmented controls on financial transactions, and removed obstacles to inter-agency cooperation and intelligence sharing. Security at airports, previously the responsibility of private firms hired by commercial airlines, was federalized in a new agency, the Transportation Security Administration (TSA). Aviation and Transportation Security Act, Pub. L. No. 107-71, 115 Stat. 597, Nov. 19, 2001. The TSA became a component of the cabinet-level Department of Homeland Security, which was created a year later. Homeland Security Act of 2002, Pub. L. No. 107-296, 116 Stat. 2135, Nov. 25, 2002.

Were there lessons that those responsible for these decisions could have learned from past responses to earlier threats? Had those lessons been heeded, could the worst errors and excesses of mass surveillance, extrajudicial detention and torture,

---

3. *WikiLeaks: Many at Guantanamo "Not Dangerous,"* BBC News, Apr. 25, 2011, http://www.bbc .com/ news/world-us-canada-13184845 ("At least 150 people were revealed to be innocent Afghans or Pakistanis—including drivers, farmers and chefs—rounded up during intelligence gathering operations in the aftermath of 9/11."); *Most Guantanamo Detainees Are Innocent: Ex-Bush Official,* CBC News, Mar. 19, 2009, http://www.cbc.ca/news/world/most-guantanamo-detainees-are-innocent-ex-bush-official-1.804550 (quoting Lawrence Wilkerson, former Chief of Staff to Secretary of State Colin Powell, saying that many detainees "clearly had no connection to al-Qaeda and the Taliban and were in the wrong place at the wrong time. Pakistanis turned many over for $5,000 a head").

and the quagmire of military commissions, among other issues, been avoided? Or is every national security crisis, in some sense, *sui generis*, i.e., of its own kind and not susceptible to useful comparison? Does our nation's respect for the rule of law ultimately reestablish the traditional balance between security and liberty over time?

If national security threats are comparable, how are comparisons helpfully made to judges, policy-makers, and other officials (and unhelpful comparisons avoided)? Lawyers are sometimes criticized for "law office" history, i.e., reducing a complex historical event with multiple causes to simpler, more linear, mono-causal explanations. "When lawyers, judges, and legal scholars turn to history, they do so because they believe, and want their readers to believe, that a historical pedigree adds authority to their argument. They believe and want their readers to believe, in other words, that their claim is weightier because this or that happened in this or that way in the past." Larry D. Kramer, *When Lawyers Do History*, 72 Geo. Wash. L. Rev. 387, 395 (2003). Is it coincidence that "law office" history tends to favor the client's position?

This chapter explores these questions in three parts. First, we ask, "Is the enemy 'new' and does it matter?" How did lawyers use history to advance their policy preferences and support their legal arguments in the months after September 11, 2001? Second, we explore the counter-argument to a claim of historical uniqueness: There is "nothing new under the sun," which is shorthand for the idea that reactions to conflicts are predictably similar over time. This idea is explored through a case study of the entry of the United States into World War I, including a little remembered terrorist attack that occurred just a few miles but eighty-five years away from the destruction of the Twin Towers in lower Manhattan. Third, we explore the parallels between post-9/11 counterterrorism efforts and the Cold War—the standoff between the United States and the Soviet Union from 1946-1990 that was fought in small proxy conflicts against the background of an omnipresent fear of apocalyptic nuclear war.

NOTES AND QUESTIONS

1. A few minutes before eight o'clock on the morning of December 7, 1941, Imperial Japan launched a surprise attack on the U.S. naval base at Pearl Harbor, in the American Territory of Hawaii. Hundreds of Japanese military aircraft destroyed much of the U.S. Pacific Fleet. Two thousand three hundred thirty-five military personnel and sixty-eight civilians were killed. Compare this event to the 9/11 attack. How are they comparable or not comparable?

2. Most would agree that few participants in the policy-making process could, would, or should undergo the lengthy and rigorous academic training of professional historians. What differences in professional training do you perceive among lawyers and others in that process (e.g., analysts, military officers, diplomats, politicians, etc.) that might make those cohorts prone to using history well or poorly?

3. All major departments of the federal government have official historians. The Office of the Historian of the State Department, for example, is legally tasked with the publication of the official history of U.S. foreign policy, a series called *Foreign Relations of the United States* (FRUS), begun in 1861 and now exceeding 450 volumes. These men and women played no role whatsoever in the policy debates that followed 9/11. Should they have?

I. IS THE ENEMY "NEW" AND DOES IT MATTER?

In the months after September 11, 2001, lawyers for top policy-makers debated whether the Geneva Conventions provided legal constraints on the general treatment of detainees. In particular, could detainees qualify for the special status of POWs, the primary benefit of which would be to grant them certain privileges while in detention under the Geneva Convention Relative to the Treatment of Prisoners of War (GPW)? For now, put to one side the particular details of the legal arguments (grounded in the law of armed conflict discussed in Chapter 8). Evaluate the independent value of arguments from history. Are these arguments persuasive? Consistent? What are their strengths and weaknesses?

> The Geneva Conventions are four international treaties adopted in 1949 and three additional protocols later adopted by many (but not all) previous signatories, called "High Contracting Parties." The Conventions, the only treaties adopted by every nation in the world, are the foundation for humanitarian protection of victims armed conflicts, and a central component of the law of armed conflict (the "law of wars"). These treaties aim to mitigate suffering of victims of war (the wounded and sick, shipwrecked, civilians, and prisoners of war) and thereby advance the humanitarian interests of all participants in hostilities.

The White House Counsel, Alberto Gonzales, drafted a four-page memo to President Bush about the post-9/11 struggle against terrorism that both agreed would be "a new kind of war."[4] Outlining positives and negatives to applying the Geneva Convention, the memo concluded as follows:

DRAFT
1/25/2002 — 3:30 P.M.

January 25, 2002

MEMORANDUM FOR THE PRESIDENT

From: Alberto R. Gonzales
Subject: Decision re Application of the Geneva
           Convention on Prisoners of War to the
           Conflict with Al Qaeda and the Taliban

* * *

---

4. Memorandum for the President from Alberto R. Gonzales, Decision re Application of the Geneva Convention on Prisoners of War to the Conflict with Al Qaeda and the Taliban, January 25, 2002, reprinted in The Torture Papers: The Road to Abu Ghraib 118 (Karen J. Greenberg & Joshua L. Dratel eds., 2005).

As you have said, the war against terrorism is a new kind of war. It is not the traditional clash between nations adhering to the laws of war that formed the backdrop for GPW [Geneva Convention III on the Treatment of Prisoners of War]. The nature of the new war places a high premium on other factors, such as the ability to quickly obtain information from captured terrorists and their sponsors in order to avoid further atrocities against American civilians, and the need to try terrorists for war crimes such as wantonly killing civilians. In my judgment, this new paradigm renders obsolete Geneva's strict limitations on questioning of enemy prisoners and renders quaint some of its provisions requiring that captured enemy be afforded such things as commissary privileges, scrip (i.e., advances of monthly pay), athletic uniforms, and scientific instruments.

Gonzales rejected a number of arguments in favor of applying GPW to the conflict before returning to his primary point: "More importantly, as noted above, this is a new type of warfare — one not contemplated in 1949 when the GPW was framed — and requires a new approach in our actions toward captured terrorists."[5]

Others made similar arguments for an across-the-board determination that, as a legal matter, the Geneva Conventions did not apply to fighters for al Qaeda or the Taliban. Attorney General John Ashcroft, in particular, made arguments from history, relying on two judicial precedents and reference to the Vietnam War. His letter to the President is reproduced on the next two pages. Before you read it, consider the sources on which he based his argument.

The first of the two Supreme Court cases that he cites is *Clark v. Allen*, 331 U.S. 503 (1947), which concerned how certain treaties with Germany affected a dispute between German and U.S. nationals over a will. Was defeated Nazi Germany, then under occupation by Allied forces, the same Germany that signed a Treaty of Friendship in 1923? The Court held that "the question whether a state is in a position to perform its treaty obligations is essentially a political question." *Id.* at 514. In other words, courts should not resolve in (i.e., courts would declare "nonjusticiable") disputes involving such determinations.

The second case, *Perkins v. Elg*, 307 U.S. 325 (1939), concerned an even older treaty, the Naturalization Convention and Protocol of 1869 between the United States and Sweden. Marie Elg, born in the United States, moved to Sweden as a child, where her parents resumed their Swedish citizenship. When Elg reached majority, she returned to the United States only to be told she was a deportable alien. In the face of inconsistent executive branch interpretation of the treaty and implementing statute, the Supreme Court, while admitting "[w]e are reluctant to disagree with the opinion of the Attorney General," interpreted the treaty itself in favor of Marie Elg.

Finally, the Attorney General referenced the abysmal treatment of American soldiers captured by the North Vietnamese.

---

5. *Id.*

Here is the Attorney General's short letter to the President:[6]

Office of the Attorney General
Washington, D. C. 20530

February 1, 2002

The President
The White House
Washington, DC

Dear Mr. President:

With your permission, I would like to comment on the National Security Council's discussion concerning the status of Taliban detainees. It is my understanding that the determination that al Qaeda and Taliban detainees are not prisoners of war remains firm. However, reconsideration is being given to whether the Geneva Convention III on prisoners of war applies to the conflict in Afghanistan.

There are two basic theories supporting the conclusion that Taliban combatants are not legally entitled to Geneva Convention protections as prisoners of war:

1. During relevant times of the combat, Afghanistan was a failed state. As such it was not a party to the treaty, and the treaty's protections do not apply;

2. During relevant times, Afghanistan *was* a party to the treaty, but Taliban combatants are not entitled to Geneva Convention III prisoner of war status because they acted as unlawful combatants.

If a <u>determination</u> is made that Afghanistan was a failed state (Option 1 above) and not a party to the treaty, various legal risks of liability, litigation, and criminal prosecution are minimized. This is a result of the Supreme Court's opinion in *Clark v. Allen* providing that when a President <u>determines</u> that a treaty does not apply, his determination is fully discretionary and will not be reviewed by the federal courts.

Thus, a Presidential determination against treaty applicability would provide the highest assurance that no court would subsequently entertain charges that American military officers, intelligence officials, or law enforcement officials violated Geneva Convention rules relating to field conduct, detention conduct or interrogation of detainees. The War Crimes Act of 1996 makes violation of parts of the Geneva Convention a crime in the United States.

In contrast, if a determination is made under Option 2 that the Geneva Convention applies but the Taliban are <u>interpreted</u> to be unlawful combatants not subject to the treaty's protections, *Clark v. Allen* does not accord American officials the same protection from legal consequences. In cases of Presidential <u>interpretation</u> of treaties which are confessed to apply, courts occasionally refuse to defer to Presidential interpretation. *Perkins v. Elg* is an example of such a case. If a

---

6. Memo from FindLaw: http://news.findlaw.com/wsj/docs/torture/jash20102ltr.html.

The President
Page 2
February 1, 2002

court chose to review for itself the facts underlying a Presidential interpretation that detainees were unlawful combatants, it could involve substantial criminal liability for involved U.S. officials.

We expect substantial and ongoing legal challenges to follow the Presidential resolution of these issues. These challenges will be resolved more quickly and easily if they are foreclosed from judicial review under the *Clark* case by a Presidential determination that the Geneva Convention III on prisoners of war does not apply based on the failed state theory outlined as Option 1 above.

In sum, Option 1, a determination that the Geneva Convention does not apply, will provide the United States with the highest level of legal certainty available under American law.

It may be argued that adopting Option 1 would encourage other states to allege that U.S. forces are ineligible for Geneva Convention III protections in future conflicts. From my perspective, it would be far more difficult for a nation to argue falsely that America was a "failed state" than to argue falsely that American forces had, in some way, forfeited their right to protections by becoming unlawful combatants. In fact, the North Vietnamese did exactly that to justify mistreatment of our troops in Vietnam. Therefore, it is my view that Option 2, a determination that the Geneva Convention III applies to the conflict in Afghanistan and that Taliban combatants are not protected because they were unlawful, could well expose our personnel to a greater risk of being treated improperly in the event of detention by a foreign power.

Option 1 is a legal option. It does not foreclose policy and operational considerations regarding actual treatment of Taliban detainees. Option 2, as described above, is also a legal option, but its legal implications carry higher risk of liability, criminal prosecution, and judicially-imposed conditions of detainment -- including mandated release of a detainee.

Clearly, considerations beyond the legal ones mentioned in this letter will shape and perhaps control ultimate decision making in the best interests of the United States of America.

Sincerely,

John Ashcroft
Attorney General

Others disagreed with the conclusion that the Geneva Conventions did not apply. Secretary of State Colin Powell argued that "while no one anticipated the precise situation that we face, the GPW was intended to cover all types of armed conflict and did not by its terms limit its application."[7] The State Department's Legal Advisor, William H. Taft IV, responded to the Gonzales memo with the following argument:[8]

The Legal Advisor
Department of State
Washington

February 2, 2002

MEMORANDUM

To: Counsel to the President
From: William H. Taft, IV
Subject: Comments on Your Paper on the Geneva Convention

The paper should make clear that the issue for decision by the President is whether the Geneva Conventions apply to the conflict in Afghanistan in which U.S. armed forces are engaged. The President should know that a decision that the Conventions do apply is consistent with the plain language of the Conventions and the unvaried practice of the United States in introducing its forces into conflict over fifty years. It is consistent with the advice of DOS lawyers and, as far as is known, the position of every other party to the Conventions.

... A decision that the Conventions do not apply to the conflict in Afghanistan in which our armed forces are engaged deprives our troops there of any claim to the protection of the Convention in the event they are captured and weakens the protections accorded by the Conventions to our troops in future conflicts.

On February 7, 2002, President Bush made his decision. Neither al Qaeda detainees nor Taliban detainees would qualify for POW status under the Geneva Convention. As a general matter, "none of the provisions of Geneva apply to our

---

7. Memorandum to Counsel to the President and Assistant to the President for National Security Affairs from Colin L. Powell, Draft Decision Memorandum for the President on the Applicability of the Geneva Convention to the Conflict in Afghanistan, January 26, 2002, reprinted in Greenberg & Dratel, *supra* note 4, at 122.

8. Memorandum to Counsel to the President from William H. Taft IV, Comments on Your Paper on the Geneva Convention, reprinted in Greenberg & Dratel, *supra* note 4, at 129.

conflict with al Qaeda in Afghanistan or elsewhere throughout the world because, among other reasons, al Qaeda is not a High Contracting Party to Geneva."[9]

NOTES AND QUESTIONS

1. How much authority should "old" law possess to influence the course of a "new kind of war"? Do old Supreme Court opinions have more or less power than old treaties or statutes? How should policy-makers and their lawyers determine which legal sources may be discarded as obsolete or quaint and which remain vital?

2. How persuasive is the example from the Vietnam War? The Việt Cộng (a.k.a. National Liberation Front) was a guerrilla insurgency in South Vietnam with close ties to the North Vietnamese Army. There is substantial evidence that throughout the war these insurgents and the conventional military forces of North Vietnam did not abide by the Geneva Conventions. The mistreatment and torture of U.S. POWs continued throughout the war regardless of the U.S. position on Geneva. The Việt Cộng were no more entitled to POW status than al Qaeda forces in 2001. Yet, they were treated as POWs. Why? Precedential value for future conflicts as law or policy? Compliance with Geneva Convention obligations is not contingent on compliance by an adversary. Are the Việt Cộng enough like al Qaeda or the Taliban to legitimate the analogy?

3. President Bush declined to apply the Geneva Conventions to al Qaeda because that terrorist organization was not a "High Contracting Party," a status only states could attain. Isn't that rather "old" thinking about the parties to armed conflicts today and the treaties (or customary international law) that attempt to moderate their conduct?

4. What exactly did Mr. Gonzales perceive to be new about the post-9/11 struggle? Suppose a German Luftwaffe captain were captured in England during the Blitz of London in WWII. Would British officials feel the same need that Alberto Gonzales described "to quickly obtain information . . . in order to avoid further atrocities" against Londoners? If "Bomber" Harris (Air Chief Marshal Sir Arthur Travers Harris of the Royal Air Force, whose nighttime bombing raids on German cities killed hundreds of thousands) had fallen into the hands of Nazi officials, should he have been tried "for war crimes such as wantonly killing civilians" in the fire-bombing of Dresden?

II. THERE IS NOTHING NEW UNDER THE SUN

Here is an alternative perspective on these historical questions: American history reveals the cyclical nature of national security assessments, especially by the judicial branch. As an example, consider this argument by a former Assistant Attorney

---

9. Memorandum for the Vice President, the Secretary of State, the Secretary of Defense, the Attorney General, Chief of Staff to the President, Director of Central Intelligence, Assistant to the President for National Security Affairs, Chairman of the Joint Chiefs of Staff from President George Bush, Humane Treatment of al Qaeda and Taliban Detainees, February 7, 2002, reprinted in Greenberg & Dratel, *supra* note 4, at 134.

General in the U.S. Department of Justice. This lawyer, Charles Warren, was instrumental in helping to draft legislation to fill perceived gaps in national security.

> If, however, any question should now be raised as to the power of Congress to punish under Military Law the operations of a spy outside of the "theatre of active military operations," the Court would be confronted with the problem: What is the modern definition of the latter phrase? Has not the modern system of warfare modified, or rather, extended, the meaning of "theatre of military operations"? When an enemy abandons the old system of warring by use of troops and spies, and adopts the plan of introducing into its foe's country corps of civilian enemies employed to aid the external military operations by acts of internal, domestic violence, the whole country thus attacked by these hostile activities has, in fact, become part of the zone of operations of the war.[10]

Warren wanted to subject civilians accused of belligerent acts to trial by military tribunal. When did Charles Warren live and work? What legislation was the fruit of his efforts? This was not an argument for the USA PATRIOT Act of 2001 or for the Military Commissions Act of 2006. Warren made these arguments in 1919. Nothing new under the sun in 2001?

Consider this evaluation of the work of the judiciary during the McCarthy period of the 1950s: "At that time, as it had done so often before, the nation's judiciary condoned the violations of civil liberties that were claimed to be essential for America's defense. It soon recanted, and, again as happened so often in the past, became more protective of individual rights. Because that pattern of repression and repentance occurs during almost every major crisis in our nation's history, it cannot be viewed as a temporary aberration, but rather as a normal part of American political life."[11]

It is not surprising, this argument goes, to find excesses in the government's response when the United States finds itself under threat. And it is equally unexceptional therefore to note that a "return to normalcy" follows: The pendulum swings back.

Should this assumption be questioned? Does the pendulum return to the place it was before the United States entered the war? Or does it return to a new starting point that then affects the *next* cycle of responses? Is American political life really that predictable? Don't changes in technology, or new political ideologies, not to mention the recursive effect of living with *awareness* of past national security situations and the official reactions to them, affect present-day decision making?

NOTES AND QUESTIONS

1. Play a game to test your predisposition to one position or another about the value of a historical perspective. On the next page are four dates and five federal statutes. Match the federal law with the date of its enactment. Notice that there is one more statute than there are dates to match with it. Cross out the law that is fictitious. Was the fake one easy to identify?

---

10. Charles Warren, *Spies, and the Power of Congress to Subject Certain Classes of Civilians to Trial by Military Tribunal*, 53 AM. L. REV. 209-10 (1919).

11. Ellen Schrecker, *"Mere Shadows": The Early Cold War*, in SECURITY V. LIBERTY: CONFLICTS BETWEEN CIVIL LIBERTIES AND NATIONAL SECURITY IN AMERICAN HISTORY 68 (Daniel Farber ed., 2008).

Date of Enactment:

> A. July 6, 1798   B. May 16, 1918   C. June 28, 1940   D. Oct. 26, 2001

Federal Statute:

1. Upon the President's public proclamation "[w]henever there is a declared war between the United States and any foreign nation or government, or any invasion or predatory incursion is perpetrated, attempted, or threatened against the territory of the United States, . . . citizens, denizens, or subjects of the hostile nation or government, being males of the age of fourteen years and upward, who shall be within the United States, and not actually naturalized, shall be liable to be apprehended, restrained, secured, and removed, as alien enemies."

2. Authorizing criminal prosecution of any person who knowingly provides "any property, tangible or intangible, or service, . . . training, expert advice or assistance . . . except medicine or religious materials" to certain foreign organizations that the Secretary of State so designates, resulting upon conviction in up to life imprisonment.

3. Authorizing criminal prosecution of any person found to "organize or help to organize any society, group, or assembly of persons who teach, advocate, or encourage the overthrow or destruction of any government in the United States by force or violence; or to be or become a member of, or affiliate with, any such society, group, or assembly of persons, knowing the purposes thereof," resulting upon conviction in up to ten years imprisonment followed by prohibition for five years following conviction of employment by the United States including by any corporation the stock of which is wholly owned by the United States.

4. Authorizing the President, through the Attorney General, to prohibit the maintenance of dual citizenship between the United States and any state "engaged in armed conflict or open hostility with the United States, or whose citizens constitute a substantial share of the members of a non-state organization" similarly engaged, and granting the President the power to denationalize any such U.S. citizen who does not renounce that dual affiliation within a period established by presidential proclamation.

5. Authorizing criminal prosecution of any person who, "when the United States is at war, shall utter, print, write, or publish any disloyal, profane, scurrilous, or abusive language about the form of government of the United States, or the Constitution of the United States, or the military or naval forces of the United States, or the flag of the United States, . . . or any language intended to bring the [same] into contempt, scorn, contumely, or disrepute, [or] willfully advocate, teach, defend, or suggest the doing of any of the acts or things in this section," resulting upon conviction in up to twenty years imprisonment.

2. Does the arc of history (like Dr. Martin Luther King, Jr.'s arc of the moral universe, bending toward justice) bend gently in the right direction?

A. Case Study: The Road to U.S. Involvement in World War I

On April 2, 1917, President Woodrow Wilson famously declared that the United States must enter World War I because "[t]he world must be made safe for democracy." In the same address to a joint session of Congress, he described the threat as direct, immediate, and global, "civilization itself seeming to be in the balance."

On September 20, 2001, President George W. Bush told a joint session of Congress that he would direct "every necessary weapon of war to the destruction and to the defeat of the global terror network," declaring, "This is civilization's fight. This is the fight of all who believe in progress and pluralism, tolerance and freedom." As noted on page 35, authorization for the use of military force had been approved two days earlier by joint resolution.

Does the experience of the United States in joining WWI, and its aftermath for U.S. domestic law after its conclusion, especially the first "Red Scare" of 1919-1920, offer useful comparisons for today? Is WWI an example of the effects of fighting a "new" kind of war (at the time) or evidence that there is nothing new under the sun?

1. The Road to War

War broke out in Europe in July 1914. The United States did not rush to join the Allied Powers and no single act is easily characterized as an obvious catalyst for U.S. involvement. On May 7, 1915, almost 1,200 lives were lost (including 128 U.S. citizens) when the *Lusitania* was sunk by a German torpedo. Even revelations that the cruise liner was carrying tons of munitions in its hold did not alter U.S. public opinion, which continued to favor isolation.

Hours before dawn on July 30, 1916, German agents set fires at a munitions depot called Black Tom Island in New York Harbor (where U.S.-manufactured explosives, dynamite, and shells were stored before their trans-Atlantic shipment, mostly to the United Kingdom and France, while the United States remained, officially, neutral). The resulting explosions killed seven (including an infant), caused tens of millions of dollars in damage, shattered thousands of windows in Manhattan and Jersey City, and were felt as far away as Philadelphia. Shrapnel from the blasts damaged the Statue of Liberty (closing access to the torch up to the present day). The official commemorative plaque at the site of the explosion informs visitors that "[y]ou are walking on a site which saw one of the worst acts of terrorism in American history." According to one of its chroniclers: "Had the explosions occurred during the daylight hours of a business day, the casualties could easily have reached the thousands, especially in the jammed financial district of Lower Manhattan." JULES WITCOVER, SABOTAGE AT BLACK TOM 21 (1989).

War in Europe, begun in 1914, did not reach the United States until 1917. In February, Germany maintained a policy of unrestricted submarine warfare against military and merchant vessels alike, including those of ostensibly neutral powers such as the United States. As winter 1917 turned to spring, as many as seven U.S. merchant vessels had been sunk by German submarines. British interception of a German communique to Mexico, the famous Zimmermann telegram proposing a German-Mexican alliance if the United States entered the war, further inflamed sentiment against Germany.

President Woodrow Wilson convened a special joint session of Congress on April 2, 1917, beginning his remarks by disclaiming authority to act alone: "I have called the Congress into extraordinary session because there are serious, very serious, choices of policy to be made, and made immediately, which it was neither right nor constitutionally permissible that I should assume the responsibility of making." 55 CONG. REC. 102 (Apr. 2, 1917).

Senate Joint Resolution 1, adopted by the Senate on April 4, and by Congress on April 6, declared war. Its brevity is striking; it is reproduced here in full:

Document Courtesy of the National Archives

2. Wartime Legislation

In his April 2 speech, President Wilson asked for complete national mobilization of a war economy and the addition of 500,000 men into the armed forces.

Legislation quickly followed. An April 6, 1917, adoption implemented the Alien Enemies Act of 1798 (an excerpt is quoted as the first statute in the game you played on page 45 above). The proclamation and an executive order that followed led to the arrest of 6,300 aliens in the United States and the military internment of 2,300.[12] The President's proclamation declared that alien enemies were prohibited from possessing firearms or ammunition, nor could they possess or use any wireless apparatus, nor reside, remain, or enter any locality designated by the President as a prohibited area. Registration, deportation, and internment were also all contemplated in the proclamation. This action might be contrasted to the President's assurance in his remarks to Congress that

> [w]e shall, happily, still have an opportunity to prove that friendship in our daily attitude and actions towards the millions of men and women of German birth and native sympathy who live amongst us and share our life, and we shall be proud to prove it towards all who are in fact loyal to their neighbours and to the Government in the hour of test. They are, most of them, as true and loyal Americans as if they had never known any other fealty or allegiance. . . . If there should be disloyalty, it will be dealt with with a firm hand of stern repression; but, if it lifts its head at all, it will lift it only here and there and without countenance except from a lawless and malignant few.

The Espionage Act was introduced on April 2, "an amalgamation of seventeen bills prepared in the attorney general's office,"[13] and passed into law on June 15, 1917. Pub. L. No. 65-24, 40 Stat. 217. As its name implies, it prohibited and criminally punished espionage of various forms. In addition, § 3 of the Act authorized twenty years' imprisonment to any person who "when the United States is at war, shall willfully cause or attempt to cause insubordination, disloyalty, mutiny, or refusal of duty, in the military or naval forces of the United States, or shall willfully obstruct the recruitment or enlistment service of the United States."

This law was upheld as applied to the conviction of Charles T. Schenck and Elizabeth Baer, leaders of the Socialist Party in the United States. In opposition to the war, they circulated leaflets that Justice Oliver Wendell Holmes described as follows:

> In impassioned language it intimated that conscription was despotism in its worst form and a monstrous wrong against humanity in the interest of Wall Street's chosen few. It said, "Do not submit to intimidation," but in form at least confined itself to peaceful measures such as a petition for the repeal of the act. The other and later printed side of the sheet was headed "Assert Your Rights." It stated reasons for alleging that any one violated the Constitution when he refused to recognize "your

---

12. Paul L. Murphy, World War I and the Origin of Civil Liberties in the United States 74 n.4 (1979) (citing Attorney General's reports for 1917 and 1918).

13. *Id.* at 76.

right to assert your opposition to the draft," and went on, "If you do not assert and support your rights, you are helping to deny or disparage rights which it is the solemn duty of all citizens and residents of the United States to retain." It described the arguments on the other side as coming from cunning politicians and a mercenary capitalist press, and even silent consent to the conscription law as helping to support an infamous conspiracy.[14]

Schenck and Baer argued that their conviction violated their First Amendment rights. In powerful words (although stating a constitutional test subsequently discarded for a stronger one), Justice Holmes upheld their convictions:

> We admit that in many places and in ordinary times the defendants in saying all that was said in the circular would have been within their constitutional rights. But the character of every act depends upon the circumstances in which it is done. The most stringent protection of free speech would not protect a man in falsely shouting fire in a theatre and causing a panic. It does not even protect a man from an injunction against uttering words that may have all the effect of force. The question in every case is whether the words used are used in such circumstances and are of such a nature as to create a clear and present danger that they will bring about the substantive evils that Congress has a right to prevent. It is a question of proximity and degree. When a nation is at war many things that might be said in time of peace are such a hindrance to its effort that their utterance will not be endured so long as men fight and that no Court could regard them as protected by any constitutional right.[15]

What role should this history play in assessing these issues today? In the words of Alberto Gonzales, should even this limited respect for free speech be regarded as an "obsolete" or "quaint" luxury from a bygone era? Or does the later development of a stronger test applied even in wartime suggest that the relevant history in this case is one of increasing protections of liberty in the face of increasingly noxious ideologically motivated violence?

The Sedition Act was passed on May 16, 1918. Pub. L. No. 65-150, 40 Stat. 553. In the words of one scholar, this was "the first time since 1798 that the government had formally outlawed speech, and it eventually produced the largest number of political prisoners in American history to that point."[16] The Sedition Act expanded the bounds of the Espionage Act, adding to the previous offense under § 3 the crime committed by anyone who "shall willfully utter, print, write or publish any disloyal, profane, scurrilous, or abusive language about the form of government of the United States, or the Constitution of the United States, or the military or naval forces of the United States, or the flag of the United States, or the uniform of the Army or Navy of the United States . . . and whoever shall willfully advocate, teach, defend, or suggest the doing of any of the acts or things in this section enumerated, and whoever shall by word or act support or favor the cause of any country with

---

14. *Schenck v. United States*, 249 U.S. 47, 51 (1919).

15. *Id.* at 52 (internal citations omitted).

16. Alan Brinkley, *World War I and the Crisis of Democracy*, in Farber, *supra* note 11, at 31 (citing ALAN DAWLEY, CHANGING THE WORLD: AMERICAN PROGRESSIVES IN WAR AND REVOLUTION 157 (2003)).

which the United States is at war or by word or act oppose the cause of the United States. . . ."

This law was also upheld. *Abrams v. United States*, 250 U.S. 616 (1919). The crime in *Abrams* also included leafleting, by four anarchists and a socialist, including a circular entitled "The Hypocrisy of the United States and her Allies" and decrying American policy toward the newly created "proletarian republic in Russia." The leaflets were distributed in the final months of WWI. Their First Amendment defense was rejected by Justice Clarke, who noted, "This contention is sufficiently discussed and is definitely negatived in *Schenck*" and elsewhere. *Id.* at 619.

This time, Justice Holmes dissented, although not with a ringing endorsement of free speech in wartime:

> I never have seen any reason to doubt that the questions of law that alone were before this Court in the Cases of *Schenck* [and others] were rightly decided. . . . The power undoubtedly is greater in time of war than in time of peace because war opens dangers that do not exist at other times. But as against dangers peculiar to war, as against others, the principle of the right to free speech is always the same. It is only the present danger of immediate evil or an intent to bring it about that warrants Congress in setting a limit to the expression of opinion where private rights are not concerned. Congress certainly cannot forbid all effort to change the mind of the country. Now nobody can suppose that the surreptitious publishing of a silly leaflet by an unknown man, without more, would present any immediate danger that its opinions would hinder the success of the government arms or have any appreciable tendency to do so.[17]

Holmes did object to the lengthy punishment inflicted on "these poor and puny anonymities," whom he felt deserved "the most nominal punishment." Having diminished their beliefs and their power to persuade others to join them, Holmes then penned some of the most famous words ever written about the American conception of free speech:

> Persecution for the expression of opinions seems to me perfectly logical. If you have no doubt of your premises or your power and want a certain result with all your heart you naturally express your wishes in law and sweep away all opposition. To allow opposition by speech seems to indicate that you think the speech impotent, as when a man says that he has squared the circle, or that you do not care whole heartedly for the result, or that you doubt either your power or your premises. But when men have realized that time has upset many fighting faiths, they may come to believe even more than they believe the very foundations of their own conduct that the ultimate good desired is better reached by free trade in ideas — that the best test of truth is the power of the thought to get itself accepted in the competition of the market, and that truth is the only ground upon which their wishes safely can be carried out. That at any rate is the theory of our Constitution. It is an experiment, as all life is an experiment. Every year if not every day we have to wager our salvation upon some prophecy based upon imperfect knowledge. While that experiment is part of our system I think that we should be eternally vigilant against attempts

---

17. *Id.* at 627-28.

to check the expression of opinions that we loathe and believe to be fraught with death, unless they so imminently threaten immediate interference with the lawful and pressing purposes of the law that an immediate check is required to save the country.[18]

Holmes's words are often quoted in debates about the value of the marketplace of ideas, of opposing speech with more speech. Less frequently remembered is the argument from history with which Holmes ended his dissent:

> I wholly disagree with the argument of the Government that the First Amendment left the common law as to seditious libel in force. History seems to me against the notion. I had conceived that the United States through many years had shown its repentance for the Sedition Act of 1798 (Act of July 14, 1798, c. 74, 1 Stat. 596), by repaying fines that it imposed. Only the emergency that makes it immediately dangerous to leave the correction of evil counsels to time warrants making any exception to the sweeping command, "Congress shall make no law abridging the freedom of speech."[19]

The Sedition Act of 1798 was extraordinarily controversial from the start. It was a major political issue in the election of 1800, since the governing Federalist Party of John Adams had used the law as a weapon against political adversaries (the first trial convicted a sitting Member of Congress). It was allowed to expire and Thomas Jefferson used his pardon power to undo numerous convictions that preceded his assumption of office.

NOTES AND QUESTIONS

1. In all likelihood, you probably had never heard of the "9/15" terrorist attack on Black Tom. Will students a century from now be similarly unfamiliar with the "9/11" terrorist attack on the World Trade Center? Why or why not? Should they? Would such knowledge necessarily affect their reactions to similar events in their own day?

2. Compare S. Joint Res. 1, declaring war on Imperial Germany, with the Authorization for Use of Military Force quoted on the first page of this chapter. Imperial Germany had allied with the Austro-Hungarian Empire, but President Wilson told Congress, "I take the liberty, for the present at least, of postponing a discussion of our relations with the authorities at Vienna. We enter this war only where we are clearly forced into it because there are no other means of defending our rights." Why not declare war "against those nations, organizations, or persons he determines planned, authorized, committed, or aided the [submarine] attacks"? Alternatively, why didn't President Bush seek a declaration of war against Afghanistan, where al Qaeda's leadership operated under the protection of the Taliban, the de facto governing authority of that country from 1996 until the U.S.-led invasion in October 2001?

---

18. *Id.* at 630.
19. *Id.* at 630-31.

3. What do you make of Justice Holmes's turn to history at the end of his dissent in *Abrams v. United States*? How much does it add to his primary argument? What would you want to know in order to assess its merits?

B. The Red Scare

A restoration to the *status quo ante* did not immediately follow the November 1918 armistice that ended World War I. Rather, the first "Red Scare" developed out of increasing anxiety over the effects of the Russian Revolution that President Wilson had initially welcomed in his April 2, 1917, speech to a joint session of Congress. The Red Scare led to the Palmer Raids (named after Attorney General A. Mitchell Palmer, who aggressively pursued anarchists after the bombing of his home), the rise of J. Edgar Hoover, and helped catalyze the growth of a then modest component of the Justice Department—the Bureau of Investigation. This would grow to become the federal agency we know today as the FBI. The Red Scare also led to the formation of the National Civil Liberties Bureau. Following the Palmer Raids of 1919-1920, this organization was renamed the American Civil Liberties Union, which is widely known today.

The Bolshevik Revolution in Russia in March and November 1917 (February and October under the Julian calendar used in Russia at the time) led to rising anxiety about worldwide revolution. This fear grew particularly acute after the surrender of Germany ended World War I but ushered in a series of global economic crises that seemed to foment worker unrest and seed ever stronger revolutionary fervor. In such an economic and social climate, anarchist and communist groups were increasingly suspected of posing threats to entrenched economic interests and even to the authority of governments themselves.

Terrorist organizations multiplied even prior to the 1917 Russian revolutions. The strongest were transnational, messianic, and intent on destroying the Russian state. By any measure, they were more successful than al Qaeda at their goals. By mid-1907, terrorists had assassinated Czar Alexander II (on the fifth attempt), his son the Grand Duke, the Chief of the Gendarmes, an Education Minister, two Interior Ministers, a Prime Minister, and over a thousand officials. During 1907, terrorist violence averaged eighteen casualties a day. From January 1908 to May 1910, 732 officials and 3,051 citizens were killed and 4,000 wounded in terror attacks.

Textbox facts drawn from Jeffrey Kahn, *"Protection and Empire": The Martens Clause, State Sovereignty, and Individual Rights*, 56 Va. J. Int'l L. 1 (2016).

These fears seemed to have been realized in a wave of bombings and terrorist attacks in the spring and summer of 1919 that, according to the FBI, offer "a window into an era and lessons that apply to current events."[20] As the FBI's official history

---

20. http://www.fbi.gov/philadelphia/about-us/history/famous-cases/famous-cases-1919-bombings.

describes the night of June 2, 1919: "In seven U.S. cities in June 1919, all within approximately 90 minutes of one another, bombs of extraordinary capacity rocked some of the biggest urban areas in America, including New York; Boston; Pittsburgh; Cleveland; Patterson, New Jersey; Washington, D.C.; and Philadelphia."[21] One such bomb, placed on the doorstep of Attorney General Mitchell Palmer, caused extensive damage to his home and terrified his family.

The Palmer Raids that were called in response to the bombings soon became a *cause célèbre* among progressive and reformist legal circles. A citizens' blue ribbon committee that included legal luminaries Zachariah Chafee, Jr., Felix Frankfurter, Ernst Freund, and Roscoe Pound concluded that, under the direction of the office of the Attorney General, "[w]holesale arrests both of aliens and citizens have been made without warrant or any process of law; men and women have been jailed and held *incommunicado* without access of friends or counsel; homes have been entered without search-warrant and property seized and removed; other property has been wantonly destroyed; workingmen and workingwomen suspected of radical views have been shamefully abused and maltreated." Worst of all, as a result of these illegal acts as well as the development of a network of informants and *agents provocateurs*, American institutions "have been seriously undermined, and revolutionary unrest has been vastly intensified. No organizations of radicals acting through propaganda over the last six months could have created as much revolutionary sentiment in America as has been created by the acts of the Department of Justice itself." TO THE AMERICAN PEOPLE: REPORT UPON THE ILLEGAL PRACTICES OF THE UNITED STATES DEPARTMENT OF JUSTICE 3, 7 (National Popular Government League, May 1920).

Archival records suggest that—Attorney General Palmer's protests to the contrary—the Labor Department's Immigration Bureau was used as the cat's paw of the Department of Justice and its Bureau of Investigation to provide a pretext for the mass arrests. According to one scholar, records at the National Archives also reveal the strong pressure (successfully) brought to bear by a young J. Edgar Hoover, working in the Justice Department, on his counterparts at the Labor Department to change departmental guidelines for the conduct of deportation hearings (which fell under the latter agency's jurisdiction). For example, just days before the January 1920 raids, an alien would be advised of his right to counsel at the "beginning of the hearing." This was changed to "as soon as such hearing has proceeded sufficiently in the development of the facts to protect the Government's interests . . ." with only a preference noted for the previous practice.[22]

One result of the raids was the country's first mass deportation. On December 21, 1919, the *U.S.S. Buford* sailed for Finland carrying 249 deported aliens, including Emma Goldman, under guard by 200 armed soldiers.[23] Two weeks later, immigration raids led by the Justice Department's Bureau of Investigation (but using the authority over immigration placed in the Labor Department) occurred simultaneously in

---

21. *Id.*

22. REGIN SCHMIDT, RED SCARE: FBI AND THE ORIGINS OF ANTICOMMUNISM IN THE UNITED STATES 287-88 (2000).

23. *Id.* at 275.

thirty-one cities, focusing on communist organizations; thousands of people were arrested and sweeping seizures were made of documents netted in the raids.[24]

The FBI notes in its history that "[m]uch like today's Joint Terrorism Task Forces, in June 1919 '[t]he plan . . . worked out by the federal authorities in its efforts to combat anarchy . . . combined activities of all federal, state, and local police authorities in every part of the country.' Then as now, the Bureau's approach to defeating terrorism in 1919 relied heavily on intelligence." The brutality of the Palmer Raids "and the abuse of the rights of those detained in the raids, though, led to a significant backlash against the Attorney General and the Bureau. The public's support for the strong suppression of potentially dangerous aliens clearly had limits."[25]

NOTES AND QUESTIONS

1. Do the excesses of the Red Scare suggest that war does *not* necessarily lead to post-war reduction of civil liberties? After all, the Palmer Raids resulted from a fear of anarchists and revolutionaries, which was not the reason the United States entered WWI.
2. Alternatively, does the Red Scare suggest that power granted to fight an international conflict can be used to tackle domestic problems? Or that the line between international and domestic is not always clear?
3. One scholar offers a provocative institutional explanation for the Red Scare and the rise of J. Edgar Hoover. "The lesson is clear: those who do the dirty work of repression are basically bureaucrats whose primary concerns are advancing their careers and promoting the interests of their agencies. . . . To attempt to end repression by destroying the FBI or the CIA is to approach the problem from the wrong end. The solution lies not in flailing the technicians of political espionage, but in reforming the system which they serve."[26] Other scholars focus on the role of individual leaders in shaping the institutions that execute their personal vision. Evaluate the merits of these arguments. What does history teach of the role of institutions, rather than personalities, in shaping policy choices?

III. COMPARISONS ACROSS HISTORY: THE COLD WAR AND THE POST-9/11 ERA

Notwithstanding President Wilson's rosy prediction, made weeks after the overthrow of Tsar Nicholas II, that "assurance has been added to our hope for the future peace of the world by the wonderful and heartening things that have been happening within the last few weeks in Russia," the Union of Soviet Socialist Republics that emerged from the rubble of four hundred years of Romanov rule did not become a "fit partner for a League of Honour" that was "fighting for freedom in the world,

---

24. *Id.* at 278.
25. See *supra* note 20.
26. Michal R. Belknap, *The Mechanics of Repression: J. Edgar Hoover, the Bureau of Investigation and the Radicals 1917-1925*, Crime and Social Justice, No. 7 (spring-summer 1977), pp. 49-58, at 56.

for justice, and for peace." After joining the Allied Powers to defeat Nazi Germany, the Soviet Union emerged as America's greatest adversary after WWII. Compare President Wilson's words, above, spoken on the eve of American entry into WWI in 1917, to President Eisenhower's view of the Soviet threat roughly four decades later:

> It commands our whole attention, absorbs our very beings. We face a hostile ideology—global in scope, atheistic in character, ruthless in purpose, and insidious in method. Unhappily the danger it poses promises to be of indefinite duration. To meet it successfully, there is called for, not so much the emotional and transitory sacrifices of crisis, but rather those which enable us to carry forward steadily, surely, and without complaint the burdens of a prolonged and complex struggle—with liberty the stake.[27]

Now compare President Eisenhower's description to the one offered by President George W. Bush of an entirely different enemy, still another four decades later:

> Al Qaeda is to terror what the Mafia is to crime. But its goal is not making money, its goal is remaking the world and imposing its radical beliefs on people everywhere. The terrorists practice a fringe form of Islamic extremism that has been rejected by Muslim scholars and the vast majority of Muslim clerics; a fringe movement that perverts the peaceful teachings of Islam. . . . We have seen their kind before. They're the heirs of all the murderous ideologies of the 20th century. By sacrificing human life to serve their radical visions, by abandoning every value except the will to power, they follow in the path of fascism, Nazism and totalitarianism. And they will follow that path all the way to where it ends in history's unmarked grave of discarded lies.[28]

Is it reasonable to compare communist subversives and Soviet spies to terrorists and al Qaeda? The Cold War to the "War on Terror" (an appellation of the Bush Administration) or the war against ISIS? Some have sharply criticized this analogy with the past. During the oral argument in *Holder v. Humanitarian Law Project*, 561 U.S. 1 (2010), Justice Scalia took issue with the comparison:

> *Justice Scalia:* I think it's very unrealistic to compare these terrorist organizations with the Communist Party. Those cases involved philosophy. The Communist Party was—was—was more than a—than an organization that—that had some unlawful ends. It was also a philosophy of—of—of extreme socialism. And—and many people subscribed to that philosophy. I don't think that Hamas or any of these terrorist organizations represent such a philosophical organization.
>
> *David D. Cole:* Your Honor, this—this Court accepted Congress's findings. Congress's findings were not that this was a philosophical debating society, but that it was an international criminal conspiracy directed by our enemy to overthrow us through terrorism.

Critics of the comparison might point out that the nuclear threat from a Soviet superpower is different from the risk of nuclear attack from terrorist groups with "no scruples about employing any weapon or tactic," as one national intelligence

---

27. Farewell Radio and Television Address to the American People, Jan. 17, 1961, Public Papers of the Presidents of the United States, Dwight D. Eisenhower, 1960-1961, p. 1037 (GPO, 1961).

28. George W. Bush, Address to Joint Session of Congress, Sept. 20, 2001.

estimate described one threat. The travel restriction of a few Communist rabble-rousers is nothing compared to the dangers of terrorists who would take advantage of the nation's "virtually unpatrolled borders." Detection, deterrence, and control are essential given the higher stakes of today. Just consider the scenario posed in a recently unclassified FBI memo: "[A] saboteur could easily pose as a Mexican 'wet-back' and get into the country without detection, presumably carrying an atomic weapon in his luggage."[29]

On the other hand, consider a thumbnail sketch drawn from a few years at the height of Cold War anxieties. We might start by noting that the sources of the quotations in the preceding paragraph might surprise you. They are not about post-9/11 terrorism. They were all excerpted from sources written in the early 1950s, during the Cold War. The first quote is from a CIA report in 1951 about Soviet agents. The second is from a *New York Times* article in 1953. The FBI memo was also written in 1953.

In 1950, Congress expressed its conclusion (referenced by David Cole, above) that there existed a Communist movement that "in its origins, its development, and its present practice, is a world-wide revolutionary movement whose purpose it is, by treachery, deceit, infiltration into other groups (governmental and other-wise), espionage, sabotage, terrorism, and any other means deemed necessary, to establish a Communist totalitarian dictatorship in the countries throughout the world through the medium of a world-wide Communist organization." Subversive Activities Control Act, § 2(1), Pub. L. No. 81-831, 64 Stat. 987.

By 1952, the year the Supreme Court decided the famous case of *Youngstown Sheet & Tube v. Sawyer* (which we examine in detail in Chapter 4), the Soviet Union had successfully tested three atomic bombs. The Korean War was entering its third year, with hundreds of thousands of military and civilian casualties. President Truman's proclamation of a national emergency to fight the "world conquest by communist imperialism" led Congress to pass the Emergency Powers Continuation Act, extending the statutory duration of a wide variety of exceptional presidential powers. Pub. L. No. 82-450, 66 Stat. 330, July 3, 1952. Senator Joseph McCarthy had discovered communists infiltrating the U.S. government.[30] Witch hunts followed in state, industrial, and private settings.

These institutional views reflected sentiment in society at large. ". . . [I]t is easy to compile a list of the McCarthy era's silliest moments, the ridiculous lengths to which overcautious officials, nervous employers, or publicity-hungry politicians went to guard the nation from the supposed threat of domestic communism. Nonetheless, to treat such excesses as aberrations resulting from some kind of col-lective hysteria trivializes what was one of the most serious outbreaks of political repression in American history. The congressional inquisitions, political pros-ecutions, and private blacklists that constituted what we now call McCarthyism could not have gained such traction within the nation's political culture had they

---

29. This paragraph is excerpted from Jeffrey Kahn, Mrs. Shipley's Ghost: The Right to Travel and Terrorist Watchlists 236, 326 (2013).

30. This paragraph is excerpted from Kahn, *supra* note 29, at 33.

not contained considerable plausibility and corresponded at least in some ways with what American policy makers and public opinion perceived as a real threat to the nation's security."[31] Evaluate these sentiments as you read the case study that follows.

NOTES AND QUESTIONS

1. Stewart Baker, former General Counsel for the National Security Agency and the first Assistant Secretary for Policy at the Department of Homeland Security, rejected the notion that the Cold War and post-9/11 eras were meaningfully comparable: "The Communist threat is like the Confederate threat. It's historical and easy to see as inherently improbable [and] tends to trivialize the threat. . . . The wars that you've won always look like you were bound to win them." Parse this comment. For what different reasons is the comparison criticized? Which persuade you? Why?

2. Edward Snowden, who leaked government surveillance practices on an unprecedented scale, is considered a whistleblowing hero by some and a traitor to his country by others. He was indicted, *inter alia*, under 18 U.S.C. § 793(d) (concerning the gathering, transmitting, or losing of defense information). This statute has its origins in the Espionage Act of 1917, Pub. L. No. 65-24, 40 Stat. 217. Much of the language of this provision remains the same as it did in the original statute. Is this an example of the "revenge of the past," a national security act from another time returning to haunt the present, or does the past simply have nothing to do with this law remaining on the books? Does it matter to you whether the statute may have been abused in the past but now seems a sensible precaution for the protection of state secrets? Does its existence on the books, however applied in practice, suggest that the balance between liberty and security did not return to the *status quo ante*? Should it have?

A. Case Study: Colonel Rudolf Abel of the KGB

Early in the morning of June 21, 1957, two special agents of the FBI pushed their way into Room 839 at the Hotel Latham in Manhattan.[32] The FBI agents sat a sleepy and half-naked man on his bed and identified themselves as charged with investigating matters of internal security. They questioned the man for twenty minutes, insinuating knowledge of his espionage activities by addressing him as "Colonel." The FBI agents told the man, who later identified himself only as Rudolf Abel, that "if he did not 'cooperate,' he would be arrested before he left the room."

When Abel refused, the FBI agents signaled agents of the Immigration and Naturalization Service (the INS, then under the authority of the Department of

---

31. Schrecker, *supra* note 11, at 69-70.
32. This section is drawn from Jeffrey Kahn, *The Case of Colonel Abel*, 5 J. NAT'L SEC. L. & POL'Y 263-301 (2011).

Justice), who were waiting outside. Under the close observation of the FBI agents, the INS agents arrested Abel, searched him and the contents of his room, and seized several items as evidence of Abel's alienage. Immediately after Abel had "checked out" of the hotel with an INS escort, the FBI agents obtained permission from the hotel manager to search Room 839 themselves. There they found a cipher pad, a hollowed-out pencil, and microfilm, all of which became evidence used to convict him at his criminal trial.

As everyone in Room 839 knew, Abel was a Soviet spy. In fact, it would later be determined that Abel was in charge of all Soviet espionage in North America, and had been for nearly a decade. He was an extraordinary catch and a serious challenge for U.S. national security. His work was aimed at the destruction of the United States. As his prosecutor told the jury at his trial, Abel's work was "directed at our very existence and through us at the free world and civilization itself."

Neither the FBI nor the INS sought a warrant signed by a federal judge or a United States Commissioner (the precursor to a United States magistrate judge) to arrest Abel or to search his room. The immigration agents possessed only an administrative order signed by another Justice Department official, the INS District Director in New York, granting them authority to detain Abel on a suspected immigration violation. The initial decision to bypass the standard warrant procedure was perhaps driven by difficulties of surveillance, although Abel's whereabouts were known long enough before his arrest to have obtained a judicially authorized arrest warrant had one been sought. "We were well aware of what he was when we picked him up," the Commissioner of Immigration, Lt. Gen. Joseph M. Swing, told reporters. "Our idea at the time was to hold him as long as we could. . . . [W]e were holding him in the hope that sufficient evidence could be gathered to indict him." The Commissioner said that his officers would not have arrested Abel had the FBI not requested that they do so. In other words, the immigration law was used as a pretext for the INS to arrest the man instead of the FBI.

But there seems to be more to this story, for it may not have been mere doubt about the *power* to detain Abel that led to this tandem operation. Another explanation for the FBI's warrantless arrest may have been the FBI's desire to keep Abel's detention secret; a warrant would have required an arraignment, the opportunity for legal counsel, and the potential for press coverage. What transpired *after* Abel's detention suggests that avoiding the publicity that a standard arrest and arraignment would generate may well have influenced the FBI's approach.

At the Hotel Latham, the INS gave Abel a written order to appear at INS offices in Manhattan to show cause why he should not be deported. Perhaps because he was "the most professional spy we have yet encountered" (as his prosecutor later informed a rapt press corps), Abel remained there for only a few hours. Instead, later that day, he was secretly bustled onto a special plane waiting for him in Newark and flown thirteen hours to a federal detention center in McAllen, Texas. He was held there for almost seven weeks. During this time the FBI (not the INS) questioned him in lengthy interrogation sessions and without a lawyer. The FBI hoped to turn him into a double agent or at least obtain intelligence about Soviet espionage.

Colonel Abel met threats and blandishments alike with stony silence. The FBI finally gave up, he was processed through deportation proceedings (for which he was permitted a lawyer), found deportable, but still not deported. Instead, after three more weeks of interrogation without the benefit of any counsel, Abel was returned to New York to face charges of espionage. Only with the announcement of his indictment on August 7 did his forced disappearance come to an end.

Abel was charged with atomic espionage. His court-appointed lawyer argued his case twice before the Supreme Court (claiming a Fourth Amendment violation in the pretextual immigration arrest) but lost. *Abel v. United States*, 362 U.S. 217 (1960). Nevertheless, Abel was spared execution—conspiracy to transmit atomic secrets, count one of the indictment, was a capital offense—largely because of his lawyer's foresight and skill in articulating the national interest in preserving Abel's life for an exchange of agents at some future date; instead, he was sentenced to thirty years in prison. Abel would not complete his sentence. On the cold morning of February 10, 1962, Abel was exchanged for captured U-2 pilot Francis Gary Powers on the Glienicke Bridge that connected Potsdam with Soviet-controlled East Berlin. These events have been dramatized by Steven Spielberg in the film *Bridge of Spies* (2015).

Abel's attorney, James Donovan, would be the one to hand Abel over in that exchange but, more importantly, it was he who negotiated the swap in the first place. Thus, the appointment of Donovan was more crucial than anyone could have anticipated. Donovan was following in the honorable tradition of American lawyers who, once appointed, zealously defend the interests of their clients no matter how infamous or unpopular, often for little or no compensation. Three judges of the U.S. Court of Appeals for the Second Circuit ended their opinion affirming Abel's conviction by thanking Donovan and his assistants, who "represented the appellant with rare ability and in the highest tradition of their profession. We are truly grateful to them for the services which they have rendered." *United States v. Abel*, 258 F.2d 485, 502 (1958). Nevertheless, Donovan (who had no doubt of his client's guilt) suffered considerable notoriety and probably sacrificed his prospects for a political career. The calumny he suffered in the press and public opinion found parallel fifty years later. A senior official at the United States Department of Defense, ignorant of or uninterested in the lessons of the past, crudely attacked the lawyers working pro bono to represent detainees at Guantanamo Bay.[33] He was rightly excoriated by the private bar as well as members of the Bush Administration, who ultimately forced his apology and resignation.[34]

---

33. Neil A. Lewis, *Official Attacks Top Law Firms over Detainees*, N.Y. Times, Jan. 13, 2007, at A1 (reporting comments by Charles D. Stimson, the deputy assistant secretary of defense for detainee affairs, "I think, quite honestly, when corporate C.E.O.'s see that those firms are representing the very terrorists who hit their bottom line back in 2001, those C.E.O.'s are going to make those law firms choose between representing terrorists or representing reputable firms, and I think that is going to have major play in the next few weeks. And we want to watch that play out.").

34. *Official Quits After Remark on Lawyers*, N.Y. Times, Feb. 3, 2007.

Abel had been held by federal agents in solitary confinement and total secrecy for forty-eight days, two thousand miles from the place of his initial arrest, without meaningful access to counsel, and without having appeared before any judicial officer for any reason. As Justice Brennan put it in his dissenting opinion, "[a]s far as the world knew, he had vanished." The Justice Department had used the immigration laws as a pretext to accomplish this secret arrest, which was otherwise impossible in our system of criminal justice.

Compare Abel's seizure and extraordinary detention to that of suspected terrorists in the years after September 11, 2001. (These cases are analyzed further in Chapter 8.) For example, American citizen Jose Padilla was detained on a judicially authorized material witness warrant for thirty-three days in 2002. Ostensibly, the arrest was to secure his testimony for the ongoing grand jury investigation into the September 11th attacks, but in reality the arrest was preventive detention on suspicion that he was plotting a major terrorist attack himself. On the eve of a hearing about Padilla's legal status (at which he would have been represented by counsel), the warrant was vacated at the government's request and Padilla was transferred to military custody, where he was held as an enemy combatant for almost four years with no substantial contact with counsel (the first six months of that time without any judicial decision regarding the lawfulness of his detention). *See Padilla ex rel. Newman v. Bush*, 233 F. Supp. 2d 564, 571 (S.D.N.Y. 2002); *Hanft v. Padilla*, 546 U.S. 1084 (2006).

In 2011, the Supreme Court decided the case of Abdullah Al-Kidd, another American who alleged that the federal material witness statute was used as a pretext to arrest, interrogate, and mistreat him on the basis of terrorism suspicions that were insufficient to satisfy the Fourth Amendment's requirements for a lawful arrest. *Ashcroft v. al-Kidd*, 563 U.S. 731 (2011). The Supreme Court declined to resolve the difficult issues presented by the allegations of pretext in the case. In a concurring opinion joined by Justices Ginsburg, Breyer, and Sotomayor, Justice Kennedy noted "the difficulty of these issues," and observed that the Court's holding left "unresolved whether the Government's use of the Material Witness Statute in this case was lawful." *Id.* at 744-45.

But even Padilla and Al-Kidd were not made to disappear in the way that Abel did. The material witness statute used to justify their detention at least required that a neutral magistrate authorize a warrant for their seizure and that they be brought to a court for a public hearing shortly after being seized, a hearing at which they had the right to be represented by counsel.[35] Abel was only provided counsel for the few hours consumed by his deportation hearing; the rest of his summer was spent in lawyerless, secret detention and subject to frequent interrogation. Padilla's detention also differed significantly from Abel's in that it was announced almost immediately by the Attorney General (ironically enough, at a press conference in Moscow).

---

35. 18 U.S.C. § 3144 incorporates by reference 18 U.S.C. § 3142(f): "The hearing shall be held immediately upon the person's first appearance before the judicial officer unless that person, or the attorney for the Government, seeks a continuance. Except for good cause, a continuance on motion of such person may not exceed five days (not including any intermediate Saturday, Sunday, or legal holiday), and a continuance on motion of the attorney for the Government may not exceed three days. . . . At the hearing, such person has the right to be represented by counsel, and, if financially unable to obtain adequate representation, to have counsel appointed."

Post-9/11, transparency has not always been the default. In the immediate aftermath of the terrorist attacks, Attorney General John Ashcroft had authorized the use of material witness warrants and arrest on immigration violations to pursue the investigation of the attacks. (Not a single conviction, or even charge, for terrorism-related crimes resulted from the 762 persons seized, detained, and sometimes unlawfully and brutally treated as a result of these immigration-related arrests.[36]) Chief Immigration Judge Michael Creppy ordered the closure of "special interest" immigration hearings that many subsequently suspected to have involved the same pretextual conduct evidenced in Abel's case. His e-mail to all immigration judges read, in part: "[T]he Attorney General has implemented additional security procedures for certain cases in the Immigration Court. Those procedures require us to hold the hearings individually, to close the hearings to the public, and to avoid discussing the case or otherwise disclosing any information about the case to anyone outside the Immigration Court."[37]

A circuit split resulted that the Supreme Court declined to resolve. The Sixth Circuit held that the Creppy order violated the First Amendment. *Detroit Free Press v. Ashcroft*, 303 F.3d 681 (6th Cir. 2002). The Third Circuit, on the other hand, sustained Judge Creppy's closure order by distinguishing immigration hearings from other judicial hearings with a greater tradition of openness. *North Jersey Media Group v. Ashcroft*, 308 F.3d 198 (3d Cir. 2002), *cert. denied*, 538 U.S. 1056 (2003).

The justification offered by the FBI for closed deportation hearings was very similar to the national security interest advanced in keeping Abel's arrest a secret: "[I]nsight gleaned from open proceedings might alert vigilant terrorists to the United States' investigative tactics and could easily betray what knowledge the government does—or does not—possess." *Id.* at 200.

In the words of Yogi Berra, was this déjà vu all over again?

B. Conclusion

None should gainsay the value of studying history. "To be ignorant of what occurred before you were born," Cicero said, "is to remain always a child." But history is not easy to use and, when misused, can be quite dangerous. How should lawyers assess, and even use themselves, arguments from history? If you now have a greater sense of the advantages and pitfalls of a historical perspective on national security issues, this chapter was worth writing.

---

36. OFFICE OF THE INSPECTOR GENERAL, U.S. DEPARTMENT OF JUSTICE, SUPPLEMENTAL REPORT ON SEPTEMBER 11 DETAINEES' ALLEGATIONS OF ABUSE AT THE METROPOLITAN DETENTION CENTER IN BROOKLYN, NEW YORK (2003); John Mintz, *Nominee Criticized over Post-9/11 Policies*, WASH. POST, Jan. 12, 2005, at A10.

37. Memorandum from Michael Creppy to all immigration judges and court supervisors, September 21, 2001, *available at* https://web.archive.org/web/20040430101711/http:/archive.aclu.org/court/creppy_memo.pdf.

In closing, consider the admission of Niall Ferguson:

[After] researching the life and times of Henry Kissinger, I have come to realize that my approach was unsubtle. In particular, I had missed the crucial importance in American foreign policy of the *history deficit*: the fact that key decision makers know almost nothing not just of other countries' pasts but also of their own. Worse, they often do not see what is wrong with their ignorance. Worst of all, they know just enough history to have confidence but not enough to have understanding. Like the official who assured me in early 2003 that the future of a post-Saddam Iraq would closely resemble that of post-Communist Poland, too many highly accomplished Americans simply do not appreciate the value, but also the danger, of historical analogy.[38]

NOTES AND QUESTIONS

1. Do past experiences of injustice or government excess embolden courts in subsequent conflicts toward opinions more protective of civil liberties, albeit too late to remedy the injuries of those victimized by such past state action? Could the Alien and Sedition Acts be passed today? Are internment camps for citizens or aliens more or less likely? Could Colonel Abel be detained in secret were he seized today?

2. Do changes in technology minimize or neutralize entirely these apparent gains for civil liberty? Are targeted surveillance efforts of any concern when computer power exists to capture, analyze, and indefinitely retain *all* communications in our society?

3. Is the executive branch or the legislative branch more likely to be a danger to civil liberty?

---

38. NIALL FERGUSON, KISSINGER: 1923-1968: THE IDEALIST 31 (2015).

CHAPTER 3

Governing Frictions

The doctrine of the separation of powers was adopted by the convention of 1787 not to promote efficiency but to preclude the exercise of arbitrary power. The purpose was not to avoid friction, but, by means of the inevitable friction incident to the distribution of the governmental powers among three departments, to save the people from autocracy.
— Justice Louis Brandeis[1]

John Locke and the Baron de Montesquieu are largely credited with originating the concept of the separation of governmental powers. LOCKE, TWO TREATISES OF GOVERNMENT (1690); MONTESQUIEU, DE L'ESPRIT DES LOIS (1748). Locke advanced the metaphor of a social contract between rulers and ruled, and defended revolution in response to repressive government. These ideas had particular salience in colonies that originally owed their existence to corporate charters. Montesquieu's conception of structural checks and balances as a means to protect liberty naturally appealed to colonists as well, given their increasingly limited opportunities for self-rule. Indeed, James Madison expressly invoked Montesquieu to argue that the separation of powers, "this essential precaution in favor of liberty," was embedded in the United States Constitution. THE FEDERALIST NO. 47.

And yet, in the same essay, Madison argued that compliance with that maxim is wholly possible when "the legislative, executive and judiciary departments are by no means totally separate and distinct from each other." In fact, Madison went on to argue that "unless these departments be so far connected and blended, as to give to each a constitutional control over the others, the degree of separation which the maxim requires as essential to a free government, can never in practice, be duly maintained." THE FEDERALIST NO. 48. This chapter explores this argument as it

---

1. *Myers v. United States*, 272 U.S. 52, 85 (1926) (Brandeis, J., dissenting).

applies in the particular case of national security. Just how "separate and distinct" does the separation of powers require governing structures to be, not only to protect the citizen's liberty against his or her own government, but in order to protect the nation's security against foreign threats?

Section I introduces some theory and history. Section II examines frictions between the branches of the federal government. Section III explores frictions that may develop within a branch. Section IV studies federal-state friction. Section V offers some comparative views from other countries.

I. THE THEORY OF SEPARATION OF POWERS: FRICTION

It is important to understand that the doctrine of separation of powers, then and now, concerns the value of distinct, formal *institutions* of governance. First among these is an independent, powerful legislature. But that is not to suggest the absence of other power centers outside of, and often influencing, such institutions. Even the archetypal European absolute monarch, Louis XIV of France (who reigned from 1643 to 1715), was forced to reckon with aristocrats, bureaucrats, and clergy, as well as regional and other cross-cutting political currents and forces. The characteristic that makes for an "absolute monarchy" is the absence of a strong parliament, a separate *institutional* repository of government power.

Indeed, it was just such a strong parliament on the other side of the English Channel—a parliament that was only willing to raise an army controlled by the Commons (the lower house of the bicameral legislature, the Parliament of England), not the King—that propelled England into civil war under Charles I. The interregnum commonwealth under Oliver Cromwell (which followed the execution of Charles I and abolition of the upper house of parliament, the House of Lords, in 1649) descended into a tyranny of an absolute *non*-monarchical sort before the Restoration. A legislature, it turned out, could be just as dangerous to individual liberty as a single ruler if there were no independent government institutions with which it was required to share power. Monarchs returned, but they shared power with a parliament that became (compared to French and other continental European legislative bodies) increasingly stronger and more independent. As the historian S.E. Finer observed in comparing eighteenth-century monarchical government on either side of the English Channel: "The [British] executive was (and still is) the Crown. This is not the same as the 'natural person' of the king or queen and herein lies the first difference between the character of the Hanoverians [the eighteenth- and nineteenth-century monarchs of what became the United Kingdom] and the French Bourbons [which included Louis XIV]: the latter ruled in their own persons whereas the kings of Britain could personally do very little without the assent of Parliament."[2]

---

2. For an excellent comparative discussion of this political and legal-institutional historical development, see S.E. FINER, III THE HISTORY OF GOVERNMENT: EMPIRES, MONARCHIES, AND THE MODERN STATE 1350 (1997).

The English legal heritage (e.g., independent courts, juries, the concept of the "common law" itself) was of foundational importance to the development of the United States. But some constitutional structures created by the Framers of the U.S. Constitution were reactions to the English system of parliamentary monarchy that they knew (and despised) under George III.[3] Royal governors of the colonies often clashed with popularly elected local legislatures (although in more peaceful encounters than colonists clashed with the king's soldiers). The governors' dependence on the Crown for the payment of their salaries was seen as an affront to the independence (and power) of colonial assemblies. In fact, the initial privileging of legislative over executive authority in the Articles of Confederation may be traced to the so-called Stamp Act Congress, a collection of representatives from many of the colonial assemblies that met in 1765 to denounce the Act's imposition of "taxation without representation." It was this same approach that was adopted in response to the Intolerable Acts (the American name for a series of laws passed by the British Parliament in response to the Boston Tea Party) to convene the First Continental Congress in 1774.

Prior to the adoption of the Constitution, the government of the rebelling colonies—the "united States of America," as the Declaration of Independence informed George III—lacked a chief executive altogether. The Articles of Confederation adopted in late 1777 authorized collective action only through "the united states in congress assembled." A "Committee of the States" with an annually rotating presidency (whose main function lay in the root *president* shares with the verb *to preside*) was established "to appoint such other committees and civil officers as may be necessary for managing the general affairs of the united states under their direction" when the congress was in recess. *See* Art. IX, cl. 5. This weak collective of state delegates, however, had virtually no power to act, even in an emergency. What powers the committee was granted were limited to the terms of the recess, required the consent of nine states, and excluded virtually all national security authorities. *See* Art. X. Even in regard to foreign relations and foreign trade, the separate states had the upper hand, retaining their sovereign legislative power to impose "imposts and duties on foreigners" and control "the exportation or importation of any species of goods or commodities whatsoever." *See* Art. IX, cl. 1. Retention of such powers showed continued suspicion of centralized government dating back to the trade conflicts that sparked the Revolutionary War.

This weak alliance of separate sovereign states did not last long. It was really just a treaty organization to "secure and perpetuate mutual friendship and intercourse among the people of the different states," as Article IV of the Articles of Confederation candidly expressed. There were simply too many sovereigns in this confederacy, each retaining "its sovereignty, freedom and independence, and every Power, Jurisdiction and right, which is not by this confederation expressly

---

3. Several limitations on legislative power in the U.S. Constitution also originate in colonial controversies, including the severe restriction on direct taxation (a response to the Stamp Act, among other taxes), the Third Amendment (a reaction to the Quartering Act of 1765), and the Fourth Amendment's requirement that warrants "particularly" describe the limits of a search (a reaction to the general writs of assistance deployed to combat smuggling).

delegated" to the national government. *See* Art. II. The national government (to the extent that a central authority was created) had no independent courts and no independent power to tax. The end of the war for independence also ended the need for solidarity, exposing fissures between states that left the national government unable to pay its debts or conduct foreign affairs with any confidence. With so little power transferred from the states to the central government, there was, ironically, no need for separation of powers within the latter.

The Constitutional Convention in Philadelphia during the summer of 1787 produced a much more powerful national government. As Justice Kennedy noted two centuries later, "[t]he Framers split the atom of sovereignty."[4] Ceasing to be true sovereigns with autonomy in foreign trade and other international affairs, the states ceded more than the "expressly" delegated powers to a national government, which was now given sole powers over national defense, international trade, and foreign affairs. An elastic clause following the enumerated powers of Congress authorized any legislation "necessary and proper" to execute both the foregoing listed powers and any other powers granted the government, individual departments, and officers of the United States. The Articles of Confederation had no such "necessary and proper" clause. A solitary president, endowed with power from his own national election, replaced the presiding official of a committee of states and served as a permanent, civilian commander in chief. Federal courts, which Congress was now empowered to establish, would interpret federal laws subject to real federal enforcement no longer subject to the whim and caprice of "the several states."

Compare clauses of the 1777 Articles of Confederation with the 1787 Constitution.

Under the Articles, "the united states in congress assembled shall have the sole and exclusive right and power of determining on peace and war . . . of sending and receiving ambassadors" and "entering into treaties and alliances." To do these things, as well as to "appoint a commander in chief of the army or navy," required the assent of nine states.

The Constitution declares the President sole and permanent "Commander in Chief." The President has power "to make Treaties" that are ratified by a two-thirds vote of the Senate. Senate approval is needed to appoint an ambassador, but the President has sole authority to receive foreign ambassadors. Congress retains the sole power "to declare war."

A truly national government with truly national powers required true constraints. And for that reason, the structural protections of the doctrine of separation of powers returned. The first three articles of the 1787 Constitution assign legislative, executive, and judicial powers to separate institutions. The lines of separation, however, left much for subsequent political resolution. For example, only one court was actually established by the text of Article III of the Constitution,

---

4. *U.S. Term Limits v. Thornton*, 514 U.S. 779 (1995) (Kennedy, J., concurring).

the Supreme Court, which had jurisdictional limits that Congress could change to some degree. Likewise, the President's election depended on state delegations organized in an Electoral College and, quite possibly, final resolution in the House of Representatives. To which institution the Vice President belonged—legislature or executive—was ambiguous.

It would be a mistake to conclude from those assignments that separating the *types* of power allocated wholly separated authority over distinct, substantive *subjects* to the Congress, the President, and the courts. Certainly, it cannot be said that each branch has *exclusive* authority over almost any policy subject. Much more frequently, the subject matter is shared between branches that must cooperate in the use of divided powers.

Consider, for example, the allocations of power over the subject of the country's armed forces. Graphically, these allocations may be represented as in the table below, organized by the location of the power under the Constitution's respective headings:

Article I	Article II	Article III
"The Congress shall have Power . . . To raise and support Armies . . .; To provide and maintain a Navy; To make Rules for the Government and Regulation of the land and naval Forces . . ." (Art. I, § 8, cl. 12-14) "The Congress shall have Power . . . To declare War, grant Letters of Marque and Reprisal, and make Rules concerning Captures on Land and Water . . ." (Art. I, § 8, cl. 11)	"The President shall be Commander in Chief of the Army and Navy of the United States. . . ." (Art. II, § 2, cl. 1) ". . . shall Commission all the Officers of the United States." (Art. II, § 3, cl. 1)	"Treason against the United States, shall consist only in levying War against them, or in adhering to their Enemies, giving them Aid and Comfort. No Person shall be convicted of Treason unless on the Testimony of two Witnesses to the same overt Act, or on Confession in open Court." (Art. III, § 3, cl. 1)

This representation clearly separates what the Constitution says about the topic according to where the Constitution says it. But the table obscures a fact that more careful reading makes clear: All three branches seem to have some authority over the same subject matter. An alternative graphic might centralize the focus of attention on the subject matter, making clearer that all three institutions have overlapping jurisdictions of competing kinds. Indeed, perhaps a fourth entity also has some relation to those already named: the states from which conscripts may be drawn for the federal army and from which militias (national guard) may be formed for both state and federal use.

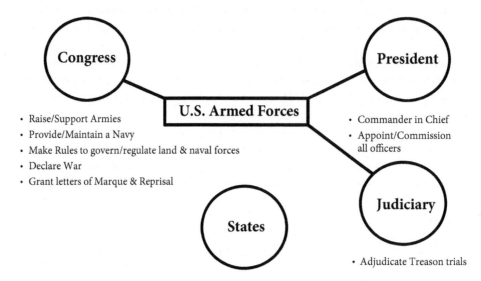

It becomes clear that this separation of powers obscures considerable ambiguity in the interplay—the friction—between the institutions that wield them. How should one determine the boundaries of authority allocated to different branches over the same subjects?

Take the example of a U.S. soldier accused of treason. The Constitution defines this crime but leaves to Congress a limited power to declare the nature of the punishment imposed. "No Person," we read in Article III, "shall be convicted of Treason unless on the Testimony of two Witnesses to the same overt Act, or on Confession in open Court." Must that court be an Article III court? Certainly, the *definition* and *restrictions* on the prosecution of treason are to be found in Article III, in which the civilian court system is established. But the power of Congress "to constitute Tribunals inferior to the supreme Court" is located in Article I. Must these tribunals be civilian institutions (not military ones)? How should the judicial power be construed in light of the legislative power to make rules to govern and regulate the armed forces? Article III, § 2, Cl. 3 appears to require that "[t]he Trial of all Crimes, except in Cases of Impeachment," be "by Jury; and such Trial shall be held in the States where the said Crimes shall have been committed." But that same provision also provides that Congress may direct where the trial shall occur when the crime is not committed within any State.

Or take the example of the establishment of the armed forces themselves. Congress seems unambiguously to have that power. But Article I, § 8, Cl. 12 (which grants the power to "raise and support Armies") restricts Congress from making any appropriation of money for that purpose "for a longer Term than two Years." This requires the repeated interaction of the political branches to fund the army. Could Congress circumvent the President's Commander-in-Chief power by refusing to make any such appropriations, instead granting letters of marque and reprisal to privateers (discussed at page 72, below)? The Constitution provides federal power "for calling forth the Militia"—which appears to be a military force organized under the authority of the separate states of the Union—for limited purposes: "to execute the Laws of the Union, suppress Insurrections and repeal [sic] Invasions." When called to such service, Article II, § 2 makes the President the Commander in Chief of "the Militia of the several States." But the Constitution does not provide the President with a power similar to that concerning the federal armed forces to appoint their officers; this is reserved "to the States respectively." Who appropriates revenue for such uses? The states? Congress? Does the appropriations limitation apply to militias, too?

In *McCulloch v. Maryland*, Chief Justice Marshall seemed to derive the power to "conduct a war" from Congress's enumerated powers to declare one and to raise the armies and navies to fight one. He described these as "among the enumerated powers of government," referring to legislative powers granted in Article I, § 8 of the Constitution. 4 Wheat. (17 U.S.) 316, 407 (1819). But the context of Marshall's opinion, in which these references occur, clearly describes a vision of a national government, i.e., the combined authority of the federal executive and the legislature. Where the power of the legislating institution ends and the executing institution begins (not to mention the interventions of the judicial power itself) has been contested from the very beginning.

NOTES AND QUESTIONS

1. What information beyond the "plain meaning" of the text should inform a lawyer's advice regarding the separation of powers?
2. What exactly does it mean to "split the atom of sovereignty"?
3. The Framers considered a proposal to grant Congress power "to make war." The proposal was rejected in favor of the phrase "to declare war." What's the difference? Would the former phrasing have eased or complicated separation of powers questions?

II. FRICTIONS *BETWEEN* BRANCHES OF THE FEDERAL GOVERNMENT

Friction in the exercise of constitutional authority over foreign affairs and national security is most obvious and immediate in the interaction between Congress and the executive branch. The seminal cases in this area, in particular *United States v. Curtiss-Wright Export Corporation* and *Youngstown Sheet & Tube v. Sawyer*, are examined in detail in Chapter 4. It should be noted, however, that the judicial involvement indicated by the very existence of these cases is unusual. The courts often defer to the political branches in disputes about competing authority over national security. Is this because national security issues present inherently political questions that the courts have deemed not justiciable by them? Are there other reasons to insulate national security policy from judicial intervention? As the subject matter of these cases indicates, judicial deference comes to an abrupt end when the courts detect infringement of the rights of individuals. Detection of a sufficient violation of the separation of powers, apart from the structural protection it can provide for individual rights, has been even less frequent.

This section first considers the array of complementary and competing authorities that Congress and the President exercise. Consideration then follows of the role of the courts to influence (or not) the exercise of those powers.

A. Congressional Powers and Limits

1. Powers

Unlike the British Parliament at Westminster (which is subject, perhaps, to the self-constraint of its longstanding customs and treaty obligations), the United States Congress is not endowed with a complete set of legislative powers. The first article of the Constitution provides only that "[a]ll legislative powers herein granted" shall be vested in a bicameral national legislature. The enumeration of these powers is itself part of what limits them, notwithstanding the elastic nature of the "Necessary and Proper" Clause that concludes the list (which names some, but not all, of Congress's powers) found in Article I, § 8.

What are the primary powers relating to national security? They are not difficult to list, or even broadly describe. Their exercise, however, is another matter.

To regulate Commerce. In his early and influential treatise on the Constitution, Joseph Story described this power as "vital to the prosperity of the union; and without it the government would scarcely deserve the name of a national government; and would soon sink into discredit and imbecility." COMMENTARIES ON THE CONSTITUTION OF THE UNITED STATES § 1057 (2d ed. 1851). The power to regulate *domestic* interstate commerce has been applied to everything from produce to civil rights. Power over *foreign* commerce is similarly potent, being the source of trade embargoes, such as the one still in place against Cuba. Although President Obama instructed his Secretary of State to reestablish diplomatic relations with Cuba in December 2014, only Congress can lift the embargo.

To establish an uniform Rule of Naturalization. . . . It is often said that Congress has plenary power over naturalization, by which is meant complete power vis-à-vis other institutional actors such as the President or states. The power is indeed sweeping—Congress may selectively or collectively grant citizenship—but this characterization is not entirely accurate. Citizenship, for example, may be conferred by treaty or by the admission of new states into the union. In the former case, the Senate's assent would be required, *see* Art. II, § 2, cl. 2, but the treaty power is one shared with the President, the only constitutional actor with authority to "make" treaties. And although Congress has the power to admit new states into the Union, Article IV, § 3 requires the consent of state legislatures in certain instances.

The naturalization power has also been described as the only enumerated power "that is unrestrained by constitutional limitations on its exercise." JOHNNY H. KILLIAN ET AL., THE CONSTITUTION OF THE UNITED STATES OF AMERICA: ANALYSIS AND INTERPRETATION 283-84 (2004). Thus, the First Amendment does not prevent Congress from denying naturalization to anyone advocating, or even holding, a wide range of beliefs or memberships (such as communism or membership in the Communist Party of the United States), just as the Equal Protection Clause works no limitation on any choice of exceptions (e.g., to those deemed to have "made a contribution to the national security or to the national intelligence mission of the United States," viz. foreign spies). *See* 8 U.S.C. §§ 1424(a)(2) & (e)(1)-(4).

To define and punish . . . Offenses against the Law of Nations. Responsibility for enforcing (as well as operating under) what was called the "law of nations," viz. public international law, is an essential attribute of sovereignty. When Congress acts within the limits of that power, the result is a shared responsibility with the other branches. The executive branch is entrusted with the enforcement, through prosecution of such crimes, punishable upon conviction by a constitutionally acceptable tribunal. A good example of the use of this power is the War Crimes Act of 1996, Pub. L. No. 104-192, 110 Stat. 2104, which amended Title 18 to add criminal penalties for war crimes resulting from a grave breach of the Geneva Conventions. This statute, among other things a long overdue implementation of the United States's non-self-executing obligation to provide criminal penalties for grave breaches, is an example of how Congress as a whole can influence the international obligations established by the President working only with the Senate. Just how this clause may limit Congress's power "to define" such offenses remains open to debate. In *Al Bahlul v. United States*, 792 F.3d 1, 15 (D.C. Cir. 2015), the petitioner was convicted by a military commission convened to try violations of the law of war. He challenged his conviction for *conspiring* to commit war crimes as beyond the jurisdiction of the tribunal, arguing that such a conspiracy offense does not exist under the relevant international law. Judge Rogers and Judge Tatel agreed that "Congress cannot, pursuant to the Define and Punish Clause, declare an offense to be an international war crime when the international law of war concededly does not." Judge Henderson dissented: "My colleagues contend — as a matter of constitutional law, not simple comity — that the Congress cannot authorize military-commission trials unless the international community agrees, jot and tittle, that the offense in question violates the law of war. And the content of international law is to be determined by — who else? — the Judiciary, with little or no deference to the political branches. But the definition and applicability of international law is, in large part, a political determination, and the decision to try an alien enemy combatant by military commission is part and parcel of waging war." *Id.* at 28 (internal citations omitted).

Following rehearing *en banc*, four of six judges in the majority (Judges Henderson, Brown, Griffith, and Kavanaugh) concluded that "consistent with Articles I and III of the Constitution, Congress may make conspiracy to commit war crimes an offense triable by military commission." Two judges did not reach the question in affirming the judgment of the U.S. Court of Military Commission Review, while Judges Rogers, Tatel, and Pillard dissented, concluding that "Article III of the Constitution bars Congress from making inchoate conspiracy an offense triable by a law-of-war military commission." *Al Bahlul v. United States*, 840 F.3d 757 (D.C. Cir. 2016) (per curiam) (en banc), *cert. denied*, 138 S. Ct. 313 (2017). This case is covered in greater detail in Chapter 10.

To declare War, grant Letters of Marque and Reprisal, and make Rules concerning Captures on Land and Water.   Letters of marque and reprisal grant private parties (i.e., non-state actors) permission to attack citizens of other countries and seize their property. Similarly, "rules concerning captures" govern legal issues arising out of such seizures. Without such commissioning instruments, these individuals would be pirates. The power has long since fallen into desuetude but was a prominent part of eighteenth- and early nineteenth-century conflicts. During the American Revolutionary War, privateers at sea functioned much like minutemen on land as important supplements to American forces opposing a stronger British opponent. But when it was used, this power, too, could be shared. In the act by which the United States entered the War of 1812, Congress declared war on the United Kingdom and authorized the President "to use the whole land and naval force of the United States to carry the same into effect [i.e., the war "hereby declared to exist"], and to issue to private armed vessels of the United States commissions or letters of marque and general reprisal, in such form as he shall think proper, and under the seal of the United States, against the vessels, goods, and effects of the government of the said United Kingdom of Great Britain and Ireland, and the subjects thereof." Act of June 18, 1812, 2 Stat. 755.

Some scholars read these powers in combination with the power to declare war as evidence that Congress occupies the entire field of war making: Whether a full-scale "declared" war or a simmering "undeclared" conflict or fighting carried out by privateers, Congress alone had the power to authorize such armed actions. Louis Fisher, Presidential War Power 6-7 (2d ed. 2004). Others argue that these clauses simply do not speak to the division of war-making authorities between the political branches. *See* J. Gregory Sidak, *The Quasi War Cases—And Their Relevance to Whether "Letters of Marque and Reprisal" Constrain Presidential War Powers*, 28 Harv. J.L. & Pub. Pol'y 465 (2005); *see also* Ingrid Wuerth, *The Captures Clause*, 76 Chi. L. Rev. 1683 (2009).

What limits the meaning of the Declare War Clause? Recall the drafting decision to change the power "to make war" to the power "to declare war." The verb "declare" has been interpreted as a limitation with varying degrees of intensity in debates going back to the First Congress. Some saw its purpose as a structural mechanism to slow any rush to war by requiring (through bicameralism and presentment) the concurrence of all political actors in the federal government. Others perceived little more than the need to express an exception for the President to act alone, if need be, to repel attacks (but not initiate them, which required a congressional declaration) until such concurrence could be reached. An extreme version of this position argues that "to declare" meant nothing more than "to notify" the enemy to be opposed in the armed conflict; the President was fully endowed with the power to use force—the essence of executive power. Still others argued that a declaration of war *against* the United States required no answer by Congress for the President to act completely unencumbered by such restraints, i.e., the power "to declare" meant the power "to initiate," not "to respond decisively" (which is just what a Commander in Chief should do). The intermediate question—to what extent a president may use force in the pursuit of national interests, but in the absence of an urgent defensive need or congressional approval—remains highly charged and unanswered.

Regardless of the origins of the choice of the verb "to declare," Congress has made that power a trigger for dozens of statutory authorities. To cite one example, consider the power granted by the Alien Enemies Act, Ch. 66, 1 Stat. 577 (1798), authorizing the President, "[w]henever there shall be a declared war," to direct the manner and degree to which "all natives, citizens, denizens, or subjects of the hostile nation or government, being males of the age of fourteen years and upwards, who shall be within the United States, and not actually naturalized shall be liable to be apprehended, restrained, secured and removed, as alien enemies." The law was amended during World War I to its current form, 50 U.S.C. § 21, which expands its scope to include women. Act of April 16, 1918, Pub. L. No. 65-131, 40 Stat. 531. (The Nineteenth Amendment gave women citizens the right to vote in 1920.)

To raise and support Armies, but no Appropriation of Money to that Use shall be for a longer Term than two Years; To provide and maintain a Navy; To make Rules for the Government and Regulation of the land and naval Forces.   These provisions contain the mechanism for meaningful use of a power to declare war: procurement and administration of a fighting force. The drafters of the Constitution were well aware of the problems experienced by the Continental Congress and Confederation in raising troops. Deprived of the power "to raise and support Armies," the national government relied on a system of requisitions made to the separate states, which filled these quotas with variable completeness and timeliness. At the same time, many believed that a standing army — especially one controlled by a distant federal government—would be a threat to liberty.

The solution found in the Constitution to this dilemma is a structural one. The Congress could raise and support armies, but only by appropriations made every two years. Madison believed that this was "the best possible precaution against danger from standing armies." THE FEDERALIST NO. 41. Or, as Joseph Story put it, "unless the necessary supplies are voted by the representatives of the people every two years, the whole establishment must fall." COMMENTARIES ON THE CONSTITUTION OF THE UNITED STATES § 1188 (2d ed. 1851). This requirement may be seen to be a check both on the legislature (imposing more frequent action by a collective political body is a natural brake) and the executive (whose ambitions may be thwarted by a stubborn refusal to fund them).

Justice Story did not specify which of these checks was more needed, satisfied that "there would seem to be every human security against the possible abuse of the power" to raise armies. But the drafters of these provisions may well have recalled the seventeenth-century British Parliament's opposition to a king empowered both to raise his armies and to deploy them. In that light, these clauses are structural protections against excessive power in the executive as Commander in Chief. Professor John Yoo is associated with a robust defense of the executive-checking utility of the clause: "Even with today's modern conflicts, waged by America's large standing militaries, the great expense in conducting war requires the president to seek supplemental appropriations from Congress. In the course of approving these measures, Congress can consider fully the merits of war, and it can easily forestall hostilities by refusing to appropriate a single dollar." JOHN YOO, THE POWERS OF WAR AND PEACE 22 (2005).

Others query just how easy the task may be—was it really true that "the whole establishment must fall"? The Clause has not fared particularly well against the development of precedents that seem to weaken its force. What to do, for example, with money left over? Could appropriated funds remain available until expended? Could contracts be made that extended beyond two years? Consider the following important interpretation of the Appropriations Clause by the Attorney General. The Secretary of War (precursor to the Secretary of Defense) wanted to know whether the Navy could contract with an English munitions company. The problem was that fulfillment of the contract would probably extend over the course of two years, in seeming conflict with the Appropriations Clause of Article I, § 8, Cl. 12.

United States Attorney General
CONSTITUTIONAL PROHIBITION—
APPROPRIATIONS FOR ARMIES
25 U.S. Op. Atty. Gen. 105 (1904)

The words "to that use" refer to the raising and supporting [sic] armies, so that the clause is as if it had read "no appropriation of money to raise and support armies shall be for more than two years." The question is, therefore, whether the appropriations here considered "for mountain guns, with their carriages, packing outfits, accessories and ammunition," are appropriations to raise and support armies. To raise and support an army is one thing. To render it effective, by equipping it with guns, ammunition, and other means for attack and defense, is another; and the word "equip" was, in military parlance, so common and well known as to preclude the idea that the framers of the Constitution intended the words "raise and support" as including, or as the equivalent of, "raise, support, arm or equip," and thus to limit appropriations for forts, fortifications, heavy ordnance, arms, ammunition, and other means for the public defense to such as must be expended within two years.

That the inhibition was not intended to go beyond the ordinary meaning of the term "raise and support," nor to forbid Congress, in time of peace, to prepare for war by erecting and arming forts and fortifications, providing arsenals, heavy artillery, arms, ammunition, and other means for the common defense and public safety, even though this should require appropriations for more than two years, is manifest: First, from the fact that, had a matter of such vast importance been actually intended, it would have been expressed with the clearness and precision which characterizes the whole of the Constitution, and would not have been left to what is, at best, a very doubtful inference from an ambiguous expression; and, second, it is manifest from the broad, unlimited powers conferred upon Congress in other parts of that instrument.

Thus, the power to declare war is also the power to prepare for, maintain, and carry on war, offensive and defensive; of constructing and arming forts and fortifications, providing heavy artillery, arms, ammunition, and all other means of warfare. This may and often does require appropriations for more than two years. The power to do these things was not intended to be taken away or restricted by the inhibition of appropriations to raise and support armies. The two purposes were different. The one was to raise and support armies, and to guard against excess in this the power was limited; the other was to arm, equip, and render effective such armies as we might have within the previous limitation, and to provide for the common defense. And, as to this latter purpose, no restriction is imposed.

Clause 17, section 8, Article I, which gives to the Government exclusive jurisdiction over all places purchased by the consent of a State, "for the erection of forts, magazines, arsenals, dockyards, and other needful buildings," confers upon Congress an unlimited power to procure sites for, erect, arm and supply, at will, these forts, magazines, arsenals, and other needful buildings for military purposes; and the fact that, in order to do these things, appropriations for more than two years would be required, in no wise detracts from or restricts the exercise of this power.

The wide and unlimited power to levy and collect taxes, etc., to "provide for the common defense and general welfare" fully authorizes Congress to provide forts, magazines, arsenals, guns, ammunition, and military stores and supplies, without reference to whether or not the appropriations therefor extend over more than two years; and, in reading this and the other clauses referred to, it is impossible to suppose that the powers thus conferred without condition or restriction were, in fact, intended to be limited and qualified by the clause here considered.

I have no hesitation in reaching the conclusion that the appropriations forbidden by Article I, section 8, clause 12 of the Constitution are those only which are to raise and support armies in the strict sense of the word "support," and that the inhibition of that clause does not extend to appropriations for the various means which an army may use in military operations, or which are deemed necessary for the common defense, or which may be provided as a measure of precaution irrespective of the existence or magnitude of any present army.

The opinion had long legs. Forty-four years later, it supported the opinion that the Clause presented no obstacle to appropriating funds for the "procurement of aircraft and aeronautical equipment to remain available until expended." 40 U.S. Op. Atty. Gen. 555 (1948). In 1956, Congress authorized billions of dollars in appropriations over the course of more than a decade for construction of the interstate highway system, called the National System of Interstate and Defense Highways "[b]ecause of its primary importance to the national defense." Pub. L. No. 84-627,

70 Stat. 374, 378, § 108(a). The sheer enormity of the Pentagon—like that of an aircraft carrier—would not seem to express much anxiety about the biennial appropriations process.

To provide for calling forth the Militia to execute the Laws of the Union, suppress Insurrections and repeal Invasions; To provide for organizing, arming, and disciplining, the Militia, and for governing such Part of them as may be employed in the Service of the United States, reserving to the States respectively, the Appointment of the Officers, and the Authority of training the Militia according to the discipline prescribed by Congress[.] This power bespeaks the peculiarities of a federal relationship: two sovereigns governing one population. When the Constitution was debated and drafted, a standing army was perceived to be a threat to the citizen's liberty. But that was not all. Its control by the national government—replacing the system of requisitions used to fight the Revolutionary War—seemed a potential threat to the sovereignty of the individual states. What was once a militia of dubious fighting strength and questionable training was transformed by a series of statutes into what is now known as a State National Guard, the members of which are simultaneously enlisted in the National Guard of the United States subject to "calling forth" for the reasons stated in the Clause. Within the parameters of this Clause, which reserves the choosing of officers and training (according to Congress's standards) to the states, the Militia/National Guard is available as a supplement to (and, indeed, can be roughly incorporated into) the U.S. Army.

The relationship of the two Militia Clauses, as the relationship of a State National Guard to the National Guard of the United States, can seem complicated. It was concisely summarized by Justice Stevens for a unanimous Court:

> [T]he Militia Clauses do not constrain the powers of Congress "to provide for the common Defence," to "raise and support Armies," to "make Rules for the Government and Regulation of the land and naval Forces," or to enact such laws as "shall be necessary and proper" for executing those powers. [F]ar from being a limitation on those powers, the Militia Clauses are—as the constitutional text plainly indicates—additional grants of power to Congress.
>
> The first empowers Congress to call forth the militia "to execute the Laws of the Union, suppress Insurrections and repel Invasions." [W]hen a National Guard unit retains its status as a state militia, Congress could not "impress" the entire unit for any other purpose. Congress did, however, authorize the President to call forth the entire membership of the Guard into federal service during World War I, even though the soldiers who fought in France were not engaged in any of the three specified purposes. Membership in the Militia did not exempt them from a valid order to perform federal service, whether that service took the form of combat duty or training for such duty. The congressional power to call forth the militia may in appropriate cases supplement its broader power to raise armies and provide for the common defense and general welfare, but it does not limit those powers.
>
> The second Militia Clause enhances federal power in three additional ways. First, it authorizes Congress to provide for "organizing, arming and disciplining the Militia." It is by congressional choice that the available pool of citizens has been formed into organized units. Over the years, Congress has exercised this power in

various ways, but its current choice of a dual enlistment system is just as permissible as the 1792 choice to have the members of the militia arm themselves. Second, the Clause authorizes Congress to provide for governing such part of the militia as may be employed in the service of the United States. Surely this authority encompasses continued training while on active duty. Finally, although the appointment of officers "and the Authority of training the Militia" is reserved to the States respectively, that limitation is, in turn, limited by the words "according to the discipline prescribed by Congress." If the discipline required for effective service in the Armed Forces of a global power requires training in distant lands, or distant skies, Congress has the authority to provide it.[5]

NOTES AND QUESTIONS

1. James Madison, writing in THE FEDERALIST NO. 48, criticized "[t]he founders of our republics" for a narrow vision of the threat to liberty: "[T]hey seem never for a moment to have turned their eyes from the danger to liberty from the overgrown and all-grasping prerogative of an hereditary magistrate [i.e., the king], supported and fortified by an hereditary branch of the legislative authority. They seem never to have recollected the danger from legislative usurpations; which by assembling all power in the same hands, must lead to the same tyranny as is threatened by executive usurpations." Did the Framers give Congress too much power?

2. Madison thought "a principal source" of national security would be naval forces, not armies, since the United States (like the British Isles) was blessed with the natural defenses of deep water borders. This had the added advantage of protecting the citizenry against their own government, since a navy, far less than a standing army, is "happily such as can never be turned by a perfidious government against our liberties." THE FEDERALIST NO. 41. Although a core component of the nation's armed forces, the Navy has not been the principal actor in recent conflicts. Nor has its existence noticeably reduced the size of our land forces. The isolation previously accorded by geography now seems more permeable and less protective. To what extent, if at all, should interpretation of the Constitution's war powers change when the original factual predicates no longer describe our world?

3. In his treatise on constitutional law, Supreme Court Justice Joseph Story called the power to declare war *ultima ratio regum*, "the last resort of sovereigns." Clausewitz, on the other hand, called war "nothing but the continuation of policy with other means." Can the nature of the legal limits on the war power be understood apart from the political reasons for armed conflict in the first place?

4. Those who perceived standing armies to be a threat to liberty did not always differentiate between the political branches. History offers many examples of tyranny from both kings and parliaments, not the least being the armies raised to fight the English Civil War. More recently, Professor John Yoo has relied on

---

5. *Perpich v. Department of Defense*, 496 U.S. 334, 349-51 (1990) (internal citations and footnotes omitted).

the Appropriations Clause, not as a restraint on Congress, but as a means to empower the legislature to restrain an aggressive president: "While Congress never declared war in Korea or Vietnam, among many other places, it had every opportunity to control those conflicts through its funding powers. That it did not was a reflection of a lack of political will rather than a defect in the constitutional design." JOHN YOO, THE POWERS OF WAR AND PEACE 143 (2005). Are there other factors beyond political will and constitutional design that might limit the practical utility of the Appropriations Clause?

5. In October 2002, Senator Robert Byrd (D-WV) gave a fiery speech in the Senate opposing S.J. Res. 46 authorizing the use of force in Iraq. He accused his colleagues of abdicating their constitutional roles because of political pressure (the vote was roughly a month before the general elections). The Framers, he said, "did foresee the frailty of human nature. And they saw the inherent danger of concentrating too much power in one individual. . . . That is why the Framers bestowed on Congress—not the President—the power to declare war." 148 CONG. REC. S9870-02. Do the legal limits on the war power adequately address "the frailty of human nature"? How do you know?

2. Limits

As already noted, the most obvious limit on congressional power is the fact that the powers are enumerated. Only those powers "herein granted" (primarily in Article I, § 8) are given to Congress. Some of the powers granted are subject to internal limits (e.g., the extent of the power may be limited by the choice of words conveying it—what does "declare" mean?) or limitations placed immediately after the power is conveyed (e.g., military appropriations must be biennial).

In addition to these internal limits, Congress is generally restrained by a number of external limits that should be quite familiar to law students. Some of these limits are found in Article I, § 9, where, for example, we find restrictions on the use of Congress's power to lay and collect taxes, and regulate commerce. Other limits, of varying degrees of generality, are found in the Bill of Rights, which provides due process and equal protection restrictions, describes the constitutional floor for the conduct of criminal and civil procedure, and establishes other fundamental enumerated (and unenumerated) rights that neither Congress nor the President may infringe without sufficient, judicially determined, cause.

Some limitations seem particularly directed to constrain Congress in its response to national security concerns. The Third Amendment, for example, prohibits the quartering of troops in private homes in peacetime without express permission and in wartime except "in a manner prescribed by law." This provision, with obvious roots in the hated British practice of quartering troops in private homes during the Revolution, has never been the subject of an opinion of the Supreme Court. Another example: Congress may not alter the elements of the crime of treason, the only crime with a definition that is constitutionally fixed. *See* Art. III, § 3, cl. 1.

Perhaps the most well-known restriction on Congress in this category concerns its ability to interfere with the ancient right to the writ of habeas corpus. The medieval Latin phrase roughly translates as "you shall have the body," as in "you, the jailor, shall have the body of the prisoner delivered to the court for examination by a judicial magistrate." The writ is powerful because it provides access to a source of authority beyond the jailor. Suspending the privilege to the writ leaves no recourse for restoring the prisoner's freedom by declaring his or her seizure unlawful. The "privilege" of the Great Writ (as the Constitution puts it) can be dated to 1215, when the Barons at Runnymede demanded it of King John in the Magna Carta.

The Constitution denies any power to suspend the writ of habeas corpus "unless when in Cases of Rebellion or Invasion the public Safety may require it." Art. I, § 9, cl. 2. Notice, however, that the denial is in the passive voice: "The Privilege of the Writ of Habeas Corpus shall not be suspended. . . ." On whom is the restriction placed? The location of the clause suggests that Congress may not suspend it. But not all of the limitations in Article I, § 9 are directed at Congress. (The emergence of both statutory and constitutional sources of habeas protection has made this area very complex. A more detailed examination of the writ and its limitations is found in Chapter 11.)

Congress is constrained in its legislative power by the prohibition on passing any bills of attainder or ex post facto laws. In some ways, these prohibitions are related, although the Ex Post Facto Clause was subject to an early interpretation limiting its application to penal and criminal statutes. *Calder v. Bull*, 3 Dall. (3 U.S.) 386, 393 (1798). The word attainder comes from the same Latin root that forms the word stain or taint. A bill of attainder legislatively declares a person or group of persons outlaws, or otherwise punishes them, without a judicial trial. In other words, attainder is essentially the verdict of a *legislative* trial (which, if the term has meaning outside of a trial of impeachments, *see* Art. I, § 3, cl. 7, could mean any process or none at all). Bills of attainder may have a long provenance, but their apparent attraction to some legislators—and rejection by some judges—can be found in a modern context. Should the meaning of a "bill of attainder" be fixed by its original understanding in the law of eighteenth-century England and America, or could one be found in the intended effects and purposes of newer circumstances? *See, e.g., United States v. Lovett*, 328 U.S. 303 (1946) (holding that a section of the Urgent Deficiency Appropriation Act of 1943 that prohibited compensation to three civil servants deemed subversives by a House committee was an unlawful bill of attainder).

B. Presidential Powers and Limits

Article II of the Constitution is much shorter than Article I. It provides the President a numerically smaller complement of powers. Many of these powers—to appoint officials, to make treaties, to fill up vacancies—require the concurrence (or, with regard to the latter, the absence) of the Senate.[6]

---

6. Interestingly, the President also has power to mediate in the affairs of the Congress. The annual "State of the Union" address comes from the power/obligation "from time to time give to the Congress Information of the state of the Union, and recommend to their Consideration such Measures as he shall judge necessary and expedient." The President has a power to order either or both Houses of Congress into session "on extraordinary Occasions," and to adjourn them when they cannot negotiate the time of the adjournment themselves. The power "to grant reprieves and pardons for offenses against the United States" excepts from the President's discretion any case of impeachment (brought by the House of Representatives and tried by the Senate).

Appointments and Removals.   As head of the executive branch, the President has the power to control its composition. This manifests itself in the textually explicit power to nominate all of its component officials and (with the agreement of the Senate) sign their commissions.[7] To the extent that the Senate is unavailable for its "advice and consent" function, this power extends to filling up vacancies with term-limited commissions. The President is also understood to have an implied removal power that Congress can only modify if its restrictions do not "impede the President's ability to perform his constitutional duty," *Morrison v. Olson*, 487 U.S. 654 (1988).

Directive Authority.   The power of appointment—textually explicit and directly exercised by the President—may be contrasted with the more limited powers that the Constitution seems to provide the President to compel the actions of executive branch officials. This is a much more indirect authority. Beyond the power of appointment (which the President shares with Congress), the President's *textual* authority extends only to the power "to require the Opinion in writing, of the principal Officer in each of the executive Departments, upon any subject relating to the Duties of their respective Offices." Art. II, § 2, cl. 1. Indeed, the duty to "take Care that the Laws be faithfully executed" is written in the passive voice. Execution of the law may not always fall, strictly speaking, to the President. The existence of so-called independent agencies—those specially insulated against presidential removal and directive authority—further complicate the famous claim that once sat on President Truman's desk: "The Buck Stops Here."

Thus, the high school civics notion of an executive branch pyramid with the President sitting at the apex is far too simplistic. True, many statutes provide direct authority to the President to act, a power that he is often entitled to delegate to lower level officials. But, generally speaking, the statutes that create the various departments delegate authority directly to officials in those agencies, *not* to the President. It is political power, operating alongside institutional power, that often works to maintain the pyramid structure. For it is "only" through the twin powers of appointment and removal—and the political allegiances that those powers create, reflect, and are sometimes bound by—that the President influences an enormous and sprawling federal bureaucracy.

What is more, the authorities these officials execute conform to the policies that *Congress* adopts through legislation. It is hornbook law that Congress—the only body granted legislative power—cannot delegate any of it. *Marshall Field & Co. v. Clark*, 143 U.S. 649, 692 (1892) ("That congress cannot delegate to the president is a principle universally recognized as vital to the integrity and maintenance of the system of government ordained by the constitution."). So long as Congress provides an "intelligible principle" by which agencies may act within the confines of the policy adopted by Congress (and even "fill in the

---

7. Of course, Article II also provides that the President "shall nominate, and by and with the Advice and Consent of the Senate, shall appoint . . . Judges of the Supreme Court."

gaps" within those parameters with binding regulations), no unconstitutional delegation occurs.[8]

Military Authority. Notwithstanding the ambiguities of presidential directive authority, there are some presidential powers for which Truman's sign was entirely accurate. "The President shall be Commander in Chief of the Army and Navy of the United States, and of the Militia of the several States, when called into the actual Service of the United States." Art. II, § 2, cl. 1. This power is shared with no one, although the President is free to delegate some decision making to his military commanders and civilian leaders of the Defense Department and the various departments of the armed forces that partially compose it.[9]

Some, including Alexander Hamilton (no opponent of national power), have taken a rather narrow view of this power, arguing that the President's "authority would be nominally the same with that of the King of Great-Britain, but in substance much inferior to it. It would amount to nothing more than the supreme command and direction of the military and naval forces, as first General and Admiral of the confederacy: while that of the British King extends to the *declaring* of war and to the *raising* and *regulating* of fleets and armies; all which by the Constitution under consideration would appertain to the Legislature." THE FEDERALIST NO. 69.

As the country grew, and its military entanglements and foreign affairs grew more complex, broader interpretations of the "Commander in Chiefship" emerged. In many ways, debates over this Clause of the Constitution mirror those about the degree to which the Declare War Clause empowers or limits Congress. Several cases emerged from the Civil War. Could the President blockade the ports of states in open rebellion, even absent a congressional declaration of war? Yes.[10] Could the

---

8. It is important to distinguish between delegations regarding domestic policy and those implicating foreign affairs. In its relatively short heyday, the nondelegation doctrine was used to strike down several pieces of New Deal legislation. But dicta in *Carter v. Carter Coal Co.*, 298 U.S. 238 (1936) (striking down the Bituminous Coal Conservation Act of 1935 as an unconstitutional assertion of the Commerce Clause power and as an unconstitutional delegation of legislative powers to fix hours and wages in the nation's coal industry) written by the same Justice who shortly thereafter wrote the opinion for the Court in *United States v. Curtiss-Wright Export Corp.*, 299 U.S. 304 (1936), suggested a different application in relation to "external affairs of the Nation and in the field of international law." See the text box "*Curtiss-Wright* in Context" in Chapter 4, on pages 134-135.

9. The Department of Defense is an executive department of the United States. *See* 10 U.S.C. § 111(a). It is composed of the "departments" of the Army, Navy, and Air Force, among other components. *Id.* § 111(b)(6)-(8). But are the Army, Navy, and Air Force themselves executive agencies, or something else? Geoff Corn and Eric Jensen argue that this perspective is constitutionally problematic: "[T]he military is more properly understood as a national agency with controls explicitly divided between the executive and legislative branches." *See* Geoffrey Corn & Eric Talbot Jensen, *The Political Balance of Power over the Military: Rethinking the Relationship Between the Armed Forces, the President, and Congress*, 44 HOUS. L. REV. 553, 560 (2007).

10. *See The Prize Cases*, 2 Bl. (67 U.S.) 635, 670 (1862) ("Whether the President in fulfilling his duties, as Commander-in-chief, in suppressing an insurrection, has met with such armed hostile resistance, and a civil war of such alarming proportions as will compel him to accord to them the character of belligerents, is a question to be decided *by him*, and this Court must be governed by the decisions and acts of the political department of the Government to which this power was entrusted. . . . The proclamation of blockade is itself official and conclusive evidence to the Court that a state of war existed which demanded and authorized a recourse to such a measure, under the circumstances peculiar to the case.") (emphasis in original).

President, solely by virtue of his Commander-in-Chief authority, hire spies and secret agents (and object to litigation of the secret contract)? Yes.[11] But more often than not, the questions are less susceptible to black-and-white answers. May the President subject civilians to military justice? Maybe.[12]

With the rise to global power after World War II and the contestation with a rival superpower during the Cold War, judicial answers to these and other questions about the power of the President as Commander in Chief did not become any easier and, in fact, in some cases issued less frequently. All modern presidents have ordered military action without congressional authorization, let alone a formal declaration of war (as noted in Chapter 2, formal declarations of war have been the exception, not the rule). In 1973, following Cold War proxy wars in Korea and Vietnam, Congress adopted the War Powers Resolution, Pub. L. No. 93-148, 87 Stat. 555 (codified at 50 U.S.C. §§ 1541-1548), purporting to limit the President's power to commit troops abroad and requiring various notification and time limits when such commitments are made. As a general matter, the judiciary has not participated in the resolution of these issues, which it has left to the political branches. (A detailed examination of this topic is the subject of Chapter 7.)

To whom is a military officer responsible? Like civilian officers of the United States, military officers are appointed by the President by and with the advice and consent of the Senate unless Congress chooses another method permitted by the Appointments Clause of the Constitution. But, while the President can fire at will the Secretary of Defense, he has no power to remove even a newly commissioned second lieutenant, even in time of war, except as Congress establishes by statute. *See* 10 U.S.C. § 804(a) & § 1161. On the other hand, Congress cannot remove any particular commissioned military officer, even by impeachment; Article II, § 4 provides only that "all civil Officers of the United States, shall be removed from Office on Impeachment for, and Conviction of, Treason, Bribery, or other high Crimes and Misdemeanors." If it is true that "[o]nce an officer is appointed, it is only the authority that can remove him, and not the authority that appointed him, that he

---

11. *See Totten v. United States*, 92 U.S. 105, 106-07 (1876) ("[The President] was undoubtedly authorized during the war, as commander-in-chief of the armies of the United States, to employ secret agents to enter the rebel lines and obtain information respecting the strength, resources, and movements of the enemy; and contracts to compensate such agents are so far binding upon the government as to render it lawful for the President to direct payment of the amount stipulated out of the contingent fund under his control. . . . [In the event of a contractual dispute,] its agents in those services must look for their compensation to the contingent fund of the department employing them, and to such allowance from it as those who dispense that fund may award. The secrecy which such contracts impose precludes any action for their enforcement.").

12. *See Ex parte Milligan*, 4 Wall. (71 U.S.) 2, 127 (1866) ("If, in foreign invasion or civil war, the courts are actually closed, and it is impossible to administer criminal justice according to law, *then*, on the theatre of active military operations, where war really prevails, there is a necessity to furnish a substitute for the civil authority, thus overthrown, to preserve the safety of the army and society; and as no power is left but the military, it is allowed to govern by martial rule until the laws can have their free course. As necessity creates the rule, so it limits its duration; for, if this government is continued *after* the courts are reinstated, it is a gross usurpation of power. Martial rule can never exist where the courts are open, and in the proper and unobstructed exercise of their jurisdiction. It is also confined to the locality of actual war.") (emphasis in original).

must fear and, in the performance of his functions, obey," *Bowsher v. Synar*, 478 U.S. 714, 726 (1986) (internal quotation omitted), does it then follow that a military officer serves two distinct political masters?

Foreign Affairs. The President has the singular power to receive Ambassadors and other public Ministers. This is a power not shared with the Senate, unlike the President's own ambassadorial nominations, which are subject to Senate confirmation. Chapter 6 will explore in detail the policy-making authority between Congress and the President in foreign affairs, which is not nearly so clear as it would appear to be in relation to domestic affairs. The President also enjoys the exclusive power to negotiate treaties although, if these are signed, they are subject to Senate ratification by two-thirds of those present (i.e., of a quorum present to do business). Whether the President may, without Senate consent, terminate a treaty that has been ratified by the Senate is a more complicated and less resolved question.

Indeed, when President Carter gave notice in December 1978 of his intention to terminate a mutual defense treaty with the Republic of China (Taiwan) *without* Senate consent (the President recognized the People's Republic of China — "Mainland China" — as the sole government of China a few weeks later), Senator Barry Goldwater and others filed suit to stop him. The various judicial opinions this produced, discussed further in Chapter 6 at pages 219-220, are a case study in the Court's wariness to become too closely involved in the resolution of such questions.

More generally, does the President possess only those powers enumerated, in the same way that the enumerated legislative powers found in Article I, § 8 limit Congress? What about powers implied by textually explicit powers? Or "inherent" in the nature of executive power itself? Those who defend the existence of powers beyond those listed in the text often point to differences in the vesting clauses for the political branches. Unlike Congress, the President's powers are not limited to those "herein granted." Instead, the Vesting Clause in Article II endows the President with "the executive Power." For some interpreters, that definite article "the" makes all the difference, granting not just enumerated powers but those implied by them as well as those inherent in the concept of executive action.

Those who take a narrower view do so equally strongly. Perhaps the most concise expression of this position was made by Judge David Pine, whose opinion at the district court level started the case of *Youngstown Sheet & Tube Co. v. Sawyer* toward its destination in the Supreme Court. Judge Pine rejected the Justice Department's argument for inherent executive power to respond to a national security emergency:

> The President therefore must derive this broad "residuum of power" or "inherent" power from the Constitution itself, more particularly Article II thereof, which contains the grant of Executive power. . . . These are the only sections which have any possible relevancy, and their mere enumeration shows the utter fallacy of defendant's claim. Neither singly nor in the aggregate do they grant the President, expressly or impliedly, as that term has hereinabove been defined, the "residuum of power" or "inherent" power which authorizes him, as defendant claims, to take such action as he may deem to be necessary, including seizure of plaintiffs' properties, whenever in his opinion an emergency exists requiring him to do so in the public

interest. Instead, in Congress is lodged, within Constitutional limitations, the power to "provide for the common defense and general welfare," Art. I, Sec. 8.[13]

In the case that follows, Judge Ellis wrote that "[t]he state secrets privilege is an evidentiary privilege derived from the President's constitutional authority over the conduct of this country's diplomatic and military affairs and therefore belongs exclusively to the Executive Branch." In what way is this privilege derived? Is it implied by these constitutional authorities? Inherent in the concept of the chief executive of a sovereign state? Would resolution of this debate, one way or another, lead to a different result in the case below? What other powers may be derived from those found in the text of Article II?

El-Masri v. Tenet

437 F. Supp. 2d 530 (E.D. Va. 2006)

Plaintiff in this civil suit claims to be an innocent victim of the United States' "extraordinary rendition" program[1] and seeks redress from the former Director of the Central Intelligence Agency (CIA), private corporations allegedly involved in the program, and unknown employees of both the CIA and the private corporations. At issue is whether the assertion of the state secrets privilege by the United States is valid, and, if so, whether this privilege prevents this case from proceeding.

Plaintiff Khaled El-Masri is a German citizen of Lebanese descent. His allegations begin on New Year's Eve 2003 when he claims he was seized by Macedonian authorities while attempting to cross the border between Serbia and Macedonian. Following his abduction, El-Masri alleges the Macedonian authorities imprisoned him in a Skopje hotel room for 23 days, refusing to let him contact a lawyer, a German consular officer, a translator or his wife, and interrogating him continuously about his alleged association with Al Qaeda, an association he consistently denied. After thirteen days of this treatment, El-Masri alleges he commenced a hunger strike to protest his detention, and he did not eat again in Macedonia.

On January 23, 2004, El-Masri claims several men in civilian clothes entered his hotel prison room. They forced El-Masri to make a statement that he had not been mistreated by his captors, and would shortly be flown back to Germany. After his captors videotaped this statement, El-Masri states he was blindfolded and driven to what sounded like an airstrip approximately one hour from Skopje. Still blindfolded, he alleges he was led to a building where he was beaten, stripped of his clothing, and sodomized with a foreign object.

---

13. *Youngstown Sheet & Tube v. Sawyer*, 103 F. Supp. 569, 573-74 (D.D.C. 1952) (internal citations and footnotes omitted).

1. The complaint alleges that since the early 1990s the CIA has been operating interrogation centers in countries where the United States believes legal safeguards do not constrain efforts to interrogate suspected terrorists. This practice is commonly known as "extraordinary rendition."

He further alleges he was dragged naked to a corner of the room where his captors removed his blindfold only for him to be blinded again by a camera's flash. When he regained his sight, he claims he saw seven or eight men dressed in black and wearing black ski masks. El-Masri contends that these men were members of a CIA "black renditions" team, operating pursuant to unlawful CIA policies at the direction of defendant Tenet. These men, he alleges, dressed him in a diaper, a tracksuit and earmuffs. He claims he was then blindfolded, shackled and dragged to an airplane where his captors injected him with a sedative that rendered him nearly unconscious. In this drugged state, he states he was secured inside the aircraft and thereafter only dimly remembers the airplane landing once and taking off again before finally depositing him in a place that El-Masri knew from the air temperature was not Germany. Indeed, El-Masri was to discover later that he had been flown to Kabul, Afghanistan.

Upon reaching Kabul, El-Masri claims he was again beaten and then placed in a small, cold cell. He contends this prison was a CIA-run facility known as the "Salt Pit," an abandoned brick factory north of the Kabul business district. El-Masri alleges he was detained in the "Salt Pit" for the next four months, during which time he was repeatedly interrogated about his alleged association with terrorists, including September 11 conspirators Mohammed Atta and Ramzi Binalshibh. He points out that although the prison facility was nominally run by Afghans, two of his interrogators identified themselves as Americans. He claims he repeatedly beseeched his captors to contact the German government on his behalf, but these requests were denied.

In March, El-Masri contends he and several other inmates commenced another hunger strike to protest their continued confinement. After 27 days without food, El-Masri states he was brought before two unmasked persons he believes were CIA agents in charge of the "Salt Pit." These men refused to accede to El-Masri's demands to release him, to charge him with a crime, or to allow him to contact a German official. Although the American official denied these requests, El-Masri contends the official conceded to El-Masri that El-Masri's detention was a mistake, but that he could not agree to El-Masri's release without permission from Washington. At this point, El-Masri states he was returned to his cell where he continued his hunger strike. After ten more days without nourishment, El-Masri asserts his captors fed him forcibly by inserting tubes into his nose and his mouth through which they pumped liquid sustenance. Soon thereafter, El-Masri states he was given canned food and books to read. El-Masri alleges that his hunger strike had a deleterious effect on his health; he lost sixty pounds over the course of his detention.

El-Masri contends that the CIA had determined soon after his arrival in Afghanistan that they were detaining an innocent man. Further, he contends that Tenet knew this fact by April 2004 and that Secretary of State Condoleeza Rice knew by early May that El-Masri was the victim of mistaken identity. Nonetheless, El-Masri says he remained imprisoned in Kabul until May 28, 2004, after which he was flown in a private jet, again blindfolded, from Kabul to Albania, where he was deposited by his captors on the side of an abandoned road. With the assistance of Albanian authorities, El-Masri eventually made his way back to his home in Germany only to find that his wife and four children, believing he had abandoned them, had left Germany to live in Lebanon. El-Masri asserts that he remains deeply traumatized by his abduction and treatment during his detention.

El-Masri asserts three separate causes of action. The first claim is brought against Tenet and the unknown CIA agents pursuant to the cause of action recognized by the Supreme Court in *Bivens v. Six Unknown Named Agents of the Federal Bureau of Narcotics*, 403 U.S. 388 (1971), for violations of El-Masri's Fifth Amendment right to due process. Specifically, El-Masri contends that Tenet and John Does 1-10 violated the Due Process Clause's prohibition against anyone acting under color of U.S. law (1) to subject any person held in U.S. custody to treatment that "shocks the conscience," or (2) to deprive any person of liberty in the absence of legal process. El-Masri's second cause of action is brought against all defendants pursuant to the Alien Tort Statute (ATS) for violations of international legal norms prohibiting prolonged arbitrary detention. Likewise, El-Masri's final cause of action is brought pursuant to the ATS for each defendant's violation of international legal norms prohibiting cruel, inhuman, or degrading treatment.

[T]he United States filed a statement of interest[,] a formal claim of the state secrets privilege[,] submitted both an unclassified and a classified ex parte declaration of the Director of the CIA (DCI) [and] moved to intervene in the suit in order to protect its interests in preserving its state secrets. Concurrent with the motion to intervene, the United States moved for dismissal or for summary judgment on the ground that maintenance of the suit would invariably lead to disclosure of its state secrets.

Determining whether the state secrets privilege has been validly asserted requires an understanding of the nature and purpose of the privilege and of who may assert it. The state secrets privilege is an evidentiary privilege derived from the President's constitutional authority over the conduct of this country's diplomatic and military affairs and therefore belongs exclusively to the Executive Branch. As such, it must be formally asserted by the head of the Executive Branch agency with control over the state secrets at issue, and then only after that person has personally considered the matter. If validly asserted the state secrets privilege permits the government to "block discovery in a lawsuit of any information that, if disclosed, would adversely affect national security." More particularly, "the various harms, against which protection is sought by invocation of the privilege, include impairment of the nation's defense capabilities, disclosure of intelligence-gathering methods or capabilities, and disruption of diplomatic relations with foreign governments." Given the vitally important purposes it serves, it is clear that while the state secrets privilege is commonly referred to as "evidentiary" in nature, it is in fact a privilege of the highest dignity and significance.

How searching the judicial inquiry must be depends on the particular circumstances of the case, for it is well-settled that the depth of a court's inquiry increases relative to the adverse party's need for the information the government seeks to protect. . . . In those cases where the claimed state secrets are at the core of the suit and the operation of the privilege may defeat valid claims, courts must carefully scrutinize the assertion of the privilege lest it be used by the government to shield "material not strictly necessary to prevent injury to national security." But, in undertaking this inquiry, courts must also bear in mind the Executive Branch's preeminent authority over military and diplomatic matters and its greater expertise relative to the judicial branch in predicting the effect of a particular disclosure on national security. Accordingly, the judiciary must accept the executive branch's assertion of the privilege whenever its independent inquiry discloses a "reasonable danger that compulsion of the evidence will expose military matters which, in the interest of national security, should not be divulged." Importantly, once the court is satisfied that any disclosure of the putative secrets "might have a deleterious effect on national security, 'the claim of the privilege will be accepted without requiring further disclosure.'"

Finally, it is important to note that, unlike other privileges, the state secrets privilege is absolute and therefore once a court is satisfied that the claim is validly asserted, the privilege is not subject to a judicial balancing of the various interests at stake. Thus, the adverse party's need for privileged information affects only the depth of the judicial inquiry into the validity of the assertion and not the strength of the privilege itself, for "even the most compelling necessity cannot overcome the claim of privilege if the court is ultimately satisfied that military secrets are at stake."

Given these governing principles, there is no doubt that the state secrets privilege is validly asserted here. To begin with, the privilege has been formally asserted by the appropriate Executive Branch official, the DCI, who has done so by submitting an ex parte classified declaration labeled "JUDGE'S EYES ONLY," and also an unclassified declaration for the public record. The latter document states in general terms that damage to the national security could result if the defendants in this case were required to admit or deny El-Masri's allegations. The former is a detailed explanation of the facts and reasons underlying the assertion of the privilege. It is, of course, inappropriate to reveal here the substance of the DCI's classified ex parte declaration, for to do so would compromise "the very thing the privilege is designed to protect." It is enough to note here that the substance of El-Masri's publicly available complaint alleges a clandestine intelligence program, and the means and methods the foreign intelligence services of this and other countries used to carry out the program. And, as the public declaration makes pellucidly clear, any admission or denial of these allegations by defendants in this case would reveal the means and methods employed pursuant to this clandestine program and such a revelation would present a grave risk of injury to national security. This conclusion finds firm support in the details disclosed in the DCI's classified ex parte declaration.

Plaintiff's argument that government officials' public affirmation of the existence of a rendition program undercuts the claim of privilege misses the critical distinction between a general admission that a rendition program exists, and the admission or denial of the specific facts at issue in this case. A general admission provides no details as to the means and methods employed in these renditions, or the persons, companies or governments involved. Nor is the government's assertion of the privilege here intended to protect from disclosure this general information. Instead, the government seeks to protect from disclosure the operational details of the extraordinary rendition program, and these details are validly claimed as state secrets. Accordingly, El-Masri's argument that generalized public admissions somehow undercut the government's right to protect the specific details of the "extraordinary rendition" program are unavailing.

Nor is the strength of the government's privilege somehow diminished by either El-Masri's complaint or the numerous media, government or other reports discussing renditions, often relying largely on El-Masri's allegations. It is self-evident that a private party's allegations purporting to reveal the conduct of the United States' intelligence services overseas are entirely different from the official admission or denial of those allegations. Furthermore, neither the United States' claim of privilege, nor a judicial acceptance of that claim is tantamount to an admission that El-Masri's factual allegations are true. The applicability of the state secrets privilege is wholly independent of the truth or falsity of the complaint's allegations. While a public admission of the alleged facts would obviously reveal sensitive means and methods of the country's intelligence operations, a denial of the alleged facts would also be damaging, as it may raise an inference of veracity in those cases where the government does not deny similarly sensitive allegations but asserts the state secrets privilege instead. For this reason, the CIA has appropriately adopted the policy of neither admitting nor denying allegations regarding the means, methods, persons, entities or countries used in its foreign intelligence operations. In light of this sensible policy, and on the basis of the DCI's public and classified ex parte declarations, the Court finds the United States' privilege is validly asserted in this case.

If a court finds that the state secrets privilege has been validly asserted, it must then determine whether the case must be dismissed to prevent public disclosure of those secrets, or whether special procedural mechanisms may be adequate to prevent disclosure of the state secrets. Resolution of this issue will depend on the centrality of the privileged material to the claims or defenses asserted by either party. In sum, the question is whether El-Masri's claims could be fairly litigated without disclosure of the state secrets absolutely protected by the United States' privilege.

In the instant case, this question is easily answered in the negative. To succeed on his claims, El-Masri would have to prove that he was abducted, detained, and subjected to cruel and degrading treatment, all as part of the United States' extraordinary rendition program. As noted above, any answer to the complaint by the defendants risks the disclosure of specific details about the rendition argument. These threshold answers alone would reveal considerable detail about the CIA's highly classified overseas programs and operations.

Thus, while dismissal of the complaint deprives El-Masri of an American judicial forum for vindicating his claims, well-established and controlling legal principles require that in the present circumstances, El-Masri's private interests must give way to the national interest in preserving state secrets. The United States' motion to dismiss must therefore be granted.

It is important to emphasize that the result reached here is required by settled, controlling law. It is in no way an adjudication of, or comment on, the merit or lack of merit of El-Masri's complaint. Nor does this ruling comment or rule in any way on the truth or falsity of his factual allegations; they may be true or false, in whole or in part. Further, it is also important that nothing in this ruling should be taken as a sign of judicial approval or disapproval of rendition programs; it is not intended to do either. In times of war, our country, chiefly through the Executive Branch, must often take exceptional steps to thwart the enemy. Of course, reasonable and patriotic Americans are still free to disagree about the propriety and efficacy of those exceptional steps. But what this decision holds is that these steps are not proper grist for the judicial mill where, as here, state secrets are at the center of the suit and the privilege is validly invoked.

Finally, it is worth noting that putting aside all the legal issues, if El-Masri's allegations are true or essentially true, then all fair-minded people, including those who believe that state secrets must be protected, that this lawsuit cannot proceed, and that renditions are a necessary step to take in this war, must also agree that El-Masri has suffered injuries as a result of our country's mistake and deserves a remedy. Yet, it is also clear from the result reached here that the only sources of that remedy must be the Executive Branch or the Legislative Branch, not the Judicial Branch.

"A crisis that challenges the President equally, or perhaps primarily, challenges Congress," Justice Jackson said, concurring in *The Steel Seizure Case* (*Youngstown Sheet & Tube Co. v. Sawyer*, 343 U.S. 579, 654 (1952). Jackson openly worried about the practical power of Congress to limit the President: "I have no illusion that any decision by the Court can keep power in the hands of Congress if it is not wise and timely in meeting its problems. . . . We may say that power to legislate for emergencies belongs in the hands of Congress, but only Congress itself can prevent power from slipping through its fingers."

This was not a new concern, but an echo of the same anxiety expressed by James Madison in THE FEDERALIST NO. 41: "It is in vain to oppose constitutional barriers to the impulse of self-preservation. It is worse than in vain; because it plants in the Constitution itself necessary usurpations of power, every precedent of which is a germ of unnecessary and multiplied repetitions." Madison was defending the maintenance of a standing federal army in times of peace. But do his words also reveal the tension between the need for the separation of powers ("ambition must be made to counteract ambition," Madison himself says later, in THE FEDERALIST NO. 51) and the need to clear obstacles to action in the face of perceived threats to national security?

NOTES AND QUESTIONS

1. James Madison, writing in THE FEDERALIST NO. 48, worried about a legislature that "is every where extending the sphere of its activity, and drawing all power into its impetuous vortex." Has that concern played out?

2. Denying President Truman the authority to order his Secretary of Commerce to seize possession of the nation's steel mills, Justice Hugo Black wrote: "In the framework of our Constitution, the President's power to see that the laws are faithfully executed refutes the idea that he is to be a lawmaker. . . . The President's order does not direct that a congressional policy be executed in a manner prescribed by Congress—it directs that a presidential policy be executed in a manner prescribed by the President. . . . The Constitution did not subject this law-making power of Congress to presidential or military supervision or control." *Youngstown Sheet & Tube Co. v. Sawyer*, 343 U.S. 579, 587-88 (1952). Did Black think Truman had exceeded his constitutional authority by assuming lawmaking powers, by assuming directive authority over Secretary Sawyer, or both?

3. In February 2003, General Eric Shinseki, the 34th Chief of Staff of the Army, told the Senate Armed Services Committee that "several hundred thousand troops" could be required in postwar Iraq. This statement contradicted the public opinions of Secretary of Defense Donald Rumsfeld and Deputy Secretary of Defense Paul Wolfowitz, who later told the House Budget Committee that General Shinseki's estimate was "wildly off the mark." Eric Schmitt, *Pentagon Contradicts General on Iraq Occupation Force's Size*, N.Y. TIMES, Feb. 28, 2003, at A14. Secretary Wolfowitz was criticized for hiding cost estimates from Congress; General Shinseki retired four months later. In his parting remarks, he observed that "when some suggest that we, in the Army, don't understand the importance of civilian control of the military—well, that's just not helpful—and it isn't true." He also warned: "Beware the 12-division strategy for a 10-division Army." Retirement Ceremony remarks (as prepared), June 11, 2003. Were General Shinseki's civilian superiors at the Pentagon right to rebuke him? Or was his candor a good example of how military experts should provide their best professional judgment to both political branches?

4. When Congress asks for the candid opinion of a military officer, can the President (or his delegate) countermand that request? Does it depend on the nature of the opinion? On a state of war or peace?

5. Given that the plaintiff El-Masri is not a U.S. citizen with any substantial connection to the United States (other than the torture he alleges), what institutional mechanisms are likely to produce the remedy that Judge Ellis suggests he "deserves"? Is the political process likely to produce one? Should constitutional rights, such as due process of law, extend to limit the actions of government officials acting abroad? If not, what part of the Constitution provides authority for an official abroad to act as El-Masri alleged?

C. Judicial Powers and Limits

"It is emphatically the province and duty of the judicial department to say what the law is." *Marbury v. Madison*, 1 Cranch (5 U.S.) 137, 177 (1803). Chief Justice Marshall was clear as to the reason why:

> The very essence of civil liberty certainly consists in the right of every individual to claim the protection of the laws, whenever he receives an injury. One of the first duties of government is to afford that protection. In Great Britain the king himself is sued in the respectful form of a petition, and he never fails to comply with the judgment of his court. [The] government of the United States has been emphatically termed a government of laws, and not of men. It will certainly cease to deserve this high appellation, if the laws furnish no remedy for the violation of a vested legal right.[14]

How this might be accomplished in the face of executive and congressional opposition, however, was precisely the dilemma that led the Chief Justice to deny Marbury's claim to his commission (while in the process securing the power of constitutional judicial review for the Court). Recall that Thomas Jefferson's Secretary of State, James Madison, "declined to acknowledge the propriety of the suit even by appearing through counsel." William W. Van Alstyne, *A Critical Guide to Marbury v. Madison*, 1969 DUKE L.J. 1, 5. And President Jefferson's supporters in Congress abolished two terms of the Supreme Court, forcing the Court to delay decision of Marbury's petition for fifteen months. Act of April 29, 1802, ch. 31, 2 Stat. 156-57, §§ 2-3. This was a concrete example of the weakness that one of Madison's co-authors of the Federalist Papers described: The judiciary "has no influence over either the sword or the purse, no direction either of the strength or of the wealth of the society, and can take no active resolution whatever. It may truly be said to have neither Force nor Will, but merely judgement; and must ultimately depend upon the aid of the executive arm even for the efficacy of its judgments." Alexander Hamilton, THE FEDERALIST No. 78.

Notwithstanding this judicial dependence on the executive branch, the reader may still be surprised to realize just how relatively new is the judicial sense that the President could be directly made subject to a judicial order. The historic Supreme Court opinion that broke this barrier, *Youngstown Sheet & Tube v. Sawyer*, is discussed in Chapter 4. For purposes of our discussion of judicial power and its limits, however, it is worth noting some of the legal battles in the lower courts that followed the President's executive order to his Commerce Secretary to seize possession of the nation's steel mills on the eve of labor strikes that (President Truman argued) could affect national security by disrupting the flow of materiel to troops fighting in Korea. The first conflict arose the day after the President's order: Several mill executives moved in federal district court for a temporary restraining order to prevent

---

14. *Id.* at 163.

the government's continuing possession. District Judge Alexander Holtzoff denied the motion. His first and foremost reason was the uncertainty of his own power:

> There are several matters that the court must weigh in this instance. Although, nominally, and technically, an injunction, if granted, would run solely against the defendant Sawyer, actually and in essence it would be an injunction against the President of the United States, because it would have the effect of nullifying and stopping the carrying out of the President's Executive Order for the seizure of the plants. It is very doubtful, to say the least, whether a Federal Court has authority to issue an injunction against the President of the United States, in person. . . . This does not mean that the President is above the law, or that he has unlimited powers, but merely that the coercive remedy of an injunction may not be directed against him, just as it may not be directed against the Congress. The court, it seems to me, should not do by indirection what it could not do directly, irrespective of whether the court has the power so to do. This is a consideration that should affect the exercise of the court's discretion.[15]

Undeterred, the mill executives sought injunctive relief on the merits. The case was transferred to a different judge of the same court, David A. Pine, who scheduled extensive briefing followed by oral argument two weeks later. Assistant Attorney General Holmes Baldridge represented the government. Judge Pine, more boldly than his predecessor in the case, held "that the acts of defendant are illegal and without authority of law." *Youngstown Sheet & Tube v. Sawyer*, 103 F. Supp. 569, 573 (D.D.C. 1952). The opinion obscures a telling exchange that occurred during oral argument. Professor Marcus vividly describes the scene:

> Before the remaining industry attorneys had a chance to criticize the government's theories, Judge Pine suggested that the government speak for itself. Almost immediately, Baldridge got into trouble. He stated that "our position is that there is no power in the Courts to restrain the President and . . . Secretary Sawyer is the alter ego of the President and not subject to injunctive order of the Court." What would happen to you if the President ordered Secretary Sawyer to put you in jail right now and have you executed tomorrow? Judge Pine asked. Would the court be unable to protect you? Baldridge floundered for an answer until Judge Pine observed: "On the question of the deprivation of your rights you have the Fifth Amendment; that is what protects you."[16]

To be more precise, what protects you is only the insistence of a *court*, exercising judicial power to forbid some action on the ground that the action would violate the Fifth Amendment or some other provision of statutory or constitutional law. It is therefore telling that, notwithstanding the bold confrontation with AAG Baldridge, Judge Pine ultimately proved himself as unwilling as Judge Holtzoff to

---

15. *Youngstown Sheet & Tube Co. v. Sawyer*, 103 F. Supp. 978, 980-81 (D.D.C. 1952) (internal citations and footnotes omitted).

16. Maeva Marcus, Truman and the Steel Seizure Case: The Limits of Presidential Power 117 (1994).

issue an injunction directly against the President of the United States. Rather, he preferred to hold that Secretary Sawyer, the defendant (though in name only), "is subject to an injunction, and the President not only is not a party but he is not an indispensable party to this action." 103 F. Supp. at 576.

What explains this caution? Consider the following Civil War-era case, decided by Justice Taney riding circuit. On May 26, 1861, Taney received a petition from John Merryman, sent from his place of confinement in Fort McHenry near Baltimore. Merryman alleged that in the middle of the preceding night, he had been "aroused from his bed by an armed force pretending to act under military orders from some person to your petitioner unknown." Merryman wrote that no due process, no warrant, but only the order of a mistaken army general, was the source of his detention. Nevertheless, the commander of Fort McHenry, George Cadwalader, kept him under close custody, refusing to allow his legal counsel access to the written papers directing Merryman's detention. Justice Taney immediately signed an order issuing a writ of habeas corpus to General Cadwalader, who was ordered to appear in court, with Merryman, at eleven o'clock the next day.

The order and writ were issued by the clerk of the circuit court and a U.S. marshal served it on General Cadwalader. At eleven o'clock, May 27, 1861, a Colonel Lee arrived at the court with General Cadwalader's return to the writ in hand. It described Merryman's arrest at the command of other officers, and informed the court that Merryman had been charged with treason. Cadwalader's return continued:

> He has further to inform you, that he is duly authorized by the president of the United States, in such cases, to suspend the writ of habeas corpus, for the public safety. This is a high and delicate trust, and it has been enjoined upon him that it should be executed with judgment and discretion, but he is nevertheless also instructed that in times of civil strife, errors, if any, should be on the side of the safety of the country. He most respectfully submits for your consideration, that those who should co-operate in the present trying and painful position in which our country is placed, should not, by any unnecessary want of confidence in each other, increase our embarrassments. He, therefore, respectfully requests that you will postpone further action upon this case, until he can receive instructions from the president of the United States, when you shall hear further from him.

Upon confirming that Col. Lee had not brought Merryman with him to the Court, Taney issued an order of contempt of court against General Cadwalader, ordering him to appear in person at noon the next day. The next day, at noon, a marshal informed Taney that upon his arrival at Fort McHenry to serve the writ, "I was not permitted to enter the gate."

After ruling from the bench that Merryman was "entitled to be set at liberty and discharged immediately from imprisonment," Taney indicated that he would issue a written opinion later that week.

Ex parte Merryman
17 F. Cas. 144 (1861)

TANEY, Circuit Justice.

The application in this case for a writ of habeas corpus is made to me under the 14th section of the judiciary act of 1789 [1 Stat. 81], which renders effectual for the citizen the constitutional privilege of the writ of habeas corpus. That act gives to the courts of the United States, as well as to each justice of the supreme court, and to every district judge, power to grant writs of habeas corpus for the purpose of an inquiry into the cause of commitment. The petition was presented to me, at Washington, under the impression that I would order the prisoner to be brought before me there, but as he was confined in Fort McHenry, in the city of Baltimore, which is in my circuit, I resolved to hear it in the latter city, as obedience to the writ, under such circumstances, would not withdraw General Cadwalader, who had him in charge, from the limits of his military command.

The case, then, is simply this: a military officer, residing in Pennsylvania, issues an order to arrest a citizen of Maryland, upon vague and indefinite charges, without any proof, so far as appears; under this order, his house is entered in the night, he is seized as a prisoner, and conveyed to Fort McHenry, and there kept in close confinement; and when a habeas corpus is served on the commanding officer, requiring him to produce the prisoner before a justice of the supreme court, in order that he may examine into the legality of the imprisonment, the answer of the officer, is that he is authorized by the president to suspend the writ of habeas corpus at his discretion, and in the exercise of that discretion, suspends it in this case, and on that ground refuses obedience to the writ.

As the case comes before me, therefore, I understand that the president not only claims the right to suspend the writ of habeas corpus himself, at his discretion, but to delegate that discretionary power to a military officer, and to leave it to him to determine whether he will or will not obey judicial process that may be served upon him. No official notice has been given to the courts of justice, or to the public, by proclamation or otherwise, that the president claimed this power, and had exercised it in the manner stated in the return. And I certainly listened to it with some surprise, for I had supposed it to be one of those points of constitutional law upon which there was no difference of opinion, and that it was admitted on all hands, that the privilege of the writ could not be suspended, except by act of congress.

But being thus officially notified that the privilege of the writ has been suspended, under the orders, and by the authority of the president, and believing, as I do, that the president has exercised a power which he does not possess under the constitution, a proper respect for the high office he fills, requires me to state plainly and fully the grounds of my opinion, in order to show that I have not ventured to question the legality of his act, without a careful and deliberate examination of the whole subject.

The clause of the constitution, which authorizes the suspension of the privilege of the writ of habeas corpus, is in the 9th section of the first article. This article is devoted to the legislative department of the United States, and has not the slightest reference to the executive department.

It is the second article of the constitution that provides for the organization of the executive department, enumerates the powers conferred on it, and prescribes its duties. And if the high power over the liberty of the citizen now claimed, was intended to be conferred on the president, it would undoubtedly be found in plain words in this article; but there is not a word in it that can furnish the slightest ground to justify the exercise of the power.

He is not empowered to arrest anyone charged with an offence against the United States, and whom he may, from the evidence before him, believe to be guilty; nor can he authorize any officer, civil or military, to exercise this power, for the fifth article of the amendments to the constitution expressly provides that no person "shall be deprived of life, liberty or property, without due process of law" — that is, judicial process.

Even if the privilege of the writ of habeas corpus were suspended by act of congress, and a party not subject to the rules and articles of war were afterwards arrested and imprisoned by regular judicial process, he could not be detained in prison, or brought to trial before a military tribunal, for the article in the amendments to the constitution immediately following the one above referred to (that is, the sixth article) provides, that "in all criminal prosecutions, the accused shall enjoy the right to a speedy and public trial by an impartial jury of the state and district wherein the crime shall have been committed, which district shall have been previously ascertained by law; and to be informed of the nature and cause of the accusation; to be confronted with the witnesses against him; to have compulsory process for obtaining witnesses in his favor; and to have the assistance of counsel for his defence."

The only power, therefore, which the president possesses, where the "life, liberty or property" of a private citizen is concerned, is the power and duty prescribed in the third section of the second article, which requires "that he shall take care that the laws shall be faithfully executed." He is not authorized to execute them himself, or through agents or officers, civil or military, appointed by himself, but he is to take care that they be faithfully carried into execution, as they are expounded and adjudged by the co-ordinate branch of the government to which that duty is assigned by the constitution. It is thus made his duty to come in aid of the judicial authority, if it shall be resisted by a force too strong to be overcome without the assistance of the executive arm; but in exercising this power he acts in subordination to judicial authority, assisting it to execute its process and enforce its judgments. With such provisions in the constitution, expressed in language too clear to be misunderstood by any one, I can see no ground whatever for supposing that the president, in any emergency, or in any state of things, can authorize the suspension of the privileges of the writ of habeas corpus, or the arrest of a citizen, except in aid of the judicial power. He certainly does not faithfully execute the laws, if he takes upon himself legislative power, by suspending the writ of habeas corpus, and the judicial power also, by arresting and imprisoning a person without due process of law.

If the president of the United States may suspend the writ, then the constitution of the United States has conferred upon him more regal and absolute power over the liberty of the citizen, than the people of England have thought it safe to entrust to the crown; a power which the queen of England cannot exercise at this day, and which could not have been lawfully exercised by the sovereign even in the reign of Charles the First.

But the documents before me show, that the military authority in this case has gone far beyond the mere suspension of the privilege of the writ of habeas corpus. It has, by force of arms, thrust aside the judicial authorities and officers to whom the constitution has confided the power and duty of interpreting and administering the laws, and substituted a military government in its place, to be administered and executed by military officers. For, at the time these proceedings were had against John Merryman, the district judge of Maryland, the commissioner appointed under the act of congress, the district attorney and the marshal, all resided in the city of Baltimore, a few miles only from the home of the prisoner. Up to that time, there had never been the slightest resistance or obstruction to the process of any court or judicial officer of the United States, in Maryland, except by the military authority. And if a military officer, or any other person, had reason to believe that the prisoner had committed any offence against the laws of the United States, it was his duty to give information of the fact and the evidence to support it, to the district attorney; it would then have become the duty of that officer to bring the matter before the district judge or commissioner, and if there was sufficient legal evidence to justify his arrest, the judge or commissioner would have issued his warrant to the marshal to arrest him; and upon the hearing of the case, would have held him to bail, or committed him for trial, according to the character of the offence, as it appeared in the testimony, or would have discharged him immediately, if there was not sufficient evidence to support the accusation. There was no danger of any obstruction or resistance to the action of the civil authorities, and therefore no reason whatever for the interposition of the military.

Yet, under these circumstances, a military officer, stationed in Pennsylvania, without giving any information to the district attorney, and without any application to the judicial authorities, assumes to himself the judicial power in the district of Maryland; undertakes to decide what constitutes the crime of treason or rebellion; what evidence (if indeed he required any) is sufficient to support the accusation and justify the commitment; and commits the party, without a hearing, even before himself, to close custody, in a strongly garrisoned fort, to be there held, it would seem, during the pleasure of those who committed him.

Such is the case now before me, and I can only say that if the authority which the constitution has confided to the judiciary department and judicial officers, may thus, upon any pretext or under any circumstances, be usurped by the military power, at its discretion, the people of the United States are no longer living under a government of laws, but every citizen holds life, liberty and property at the will and pleasure of the army officer in whose military district he may happen to be found.

In such a case, my duty was too plain to be mistaken. I have exercised all the power which the constitution and laws confer upon me, but that power has been resisted by a force too strong for me to overcome. It is possible that the officer who has incurred this grave responsibility may have misunderstood his instructions, and exceeded the authority intended to be given him; I shall, therefore, order all the proceedings in this case, with my opinion, to be filed and recorded in the circuit court of the United States for the district of Maryland, and direct the clerk to transmit a copy, under seal, to the president of the United States. It will then remain for that high officer, in fulfilment of his constitutional obligation to "take care that the laws be faithfully executed," to determine what measures he will take to cause the civil process of the United States to be respected and enforced.

NOTES AND QUESTIONS

1. It is quite clear from the tenor of the opinion that Justice Taney did not perceive much legal difficulty in the case. Why, then, such a pathetically weak final paragraph?
2. On the other hand, what alternatives did Taney have to avoid his conclusion that his power "has been resisted by a force too strong for me to overcome"?
3. Does this case present dangers to the rule of law that Chief Justice Taney's predecessor, Chief Justice Marshall, did not face in his confrontation with President Jefferson in *Marbury v. Madison*? Marshall had to wonder what would result if he ordered Marbury commissioned as a Justice of the Peace, only to have the President and his Secretary of State refuse to execute the order. Is there a greater threat to the authority of the courts and to the rule of law when a military commander disregards a court order, than the risks presented by refusal by the civilian Commander in Chief?

History has shown that United States courts have not been overly eager to resolve disputes that raise national security questions. When confronted with such litigation, judges have often found the plaintiffs to lack standing,[17] to have raised

---

17. Constitutional standing comprises three elements: "First, the plaintiff must have suffered an injury in fact—an invasion of a legally protected interest which is (a) concrete and particularized, and (b) actual or imminent, not conjectural or hypothetical. Second, there must be a causal connection between the injury and the conduct complained of   the injury has to be fairly . . . traceable to the challenged action of the defendant, and not the result of the independent action of some third party not before the court. Third, it must be likely, as opposed to merely speculative, that the injury will be redressed by a favorable decision." *Lujan v. Defenders of Wildlife*, 504 U.S. 555, 560-61 (1992) (internal citations, footnotes, quotation and editorial marks omitted).

a political question,[18] and/or to have presented claims that are not justiciable for other reasons.[19] Most of the so-called non-justiciability doctrines are asserted to originate in the "case or controversy" requirement for federal jurisdiction established in Article III, § 2, Cl. 1.

Chapter 4, Government Interaction, will further explore these doctrines in the national security context. For now, consider simply how their application both affects the separation of powers and friction that can develop in the practice of national security decision making and exposes what might be called the judiciary's inherent institutional anxiety about its authority, power, and role vis-à-vis the political branches. Or, as Alexander Hamilton expressed it in THE FEDERALIST NO. 78: "[T]he judiciary is beyond comparison the weakest of the three departments of power;[footnote 1] that it can never attack with success either of the other two; and that all possible care is requisite to enable it to defend itself against their attacks." The footnote in this quotation was Hamilton's, and he cited to Montesquieu, whom he quoted as saying: "of the three powers above mentioned, the Judiciary is next to nothing."

Is that—*should* that—be true in "a government of laws, and not of men"?

Dellums v. Bush
752 F. Supp. 1141 (D.D.C. 1990)

HAROLD H. GREENE, District Judge.

This is a lawsuit by a number of members of Congress who request an injunction directed to the President of the United States to prevent him from initiating an offensive attack against Iraq without first securing a declaration of war or other explicit congressional authorization for such action.

On August 2, 1990, Iraq invaded the neighboring country of Kuwait. President George Bush almost immediately sent United States military forces to the Persian Gulf area to deter Iraqi aggression and to preserve the integrity of Saudi Arabia.

---

18. Justice Brennan provided the most cited summary of the Court's various grounds for invoking its political question doctrine, which he described as "essentially a function of the separation of powers. Prominent on the surface of any case held to involve a political question is found a textually demonstrable constitutional commitment of the issue to a coordinate political department; or a lack of judicially discoverable and manageable standards for resolving it; or the impossibility of deciding without an initial policy determination of a kind clearly for nonjudicial discretion; or the impossibility of a court's undertaking independent resolution without expressing lack of the respect due coordinate branches of government; or an unusual need for unquestioning adherence to a political decision already made; or the potentiality of embarrassment from multifarious pronouncements by various departments on one question." *Baker v. Carr*, 369 U.S. 186, 217 (1962).

19. For example, the Court refuses to give advisory opinions, and most famously refused to do so in 1793 when President Washington sought advice on the legal implications of U.S. neutrality in the war between Britain and France. The Court has sometimes declined to decide cases that have been rendered moot for the particular litigants or that it deems not yet to have ripened to a state sufficient for adjudication. Invoking its prudential standing doctrines (which are entirely discretionary bars to judicial access), the Court has sometimes avoided difficult issues of extra-territorial application of the Constitution. *See, e.g.*, Jeffrey Kahn, *Zoya's Standing Problem, or, When Should the Constitution Follow the Flag?*, 108 MICH. L. REV. 673 (2010).

The United States, generally by presidential order and at times with congressional concurrence, also took other steps, including a blockade of Iraq, which were approved by the United Nations Security Council, and participated in by a great many other nations.

On November 8, 1990, President Bush announced a substantial increase in the Persian Gulf military deployment, raising the troop level significantly above the 230,000 then present in the area. At the same time, the President stated that the objective was to provide "an adequate *offensive* military option" should that be necessary to achieve such goals as the withdrawal of Iraqi forces from Kuwait.

The House of Representatives and the Senate have in various ways expressed their support for the President's past and present actions in the Persian Gulf. However, the Congress was not asked for, and it did not take, action pursuant to Article I, § 8, cl. 11 of the Constitution "to declare war" on Iraq. On November 19, 1990, the congressional plaintiffs brought this action, which proceeds on the premise that the initiation of offensive United States military action is imminent, that such action would be unlawful in the absence of a declaration of war by the Congress, and that a war without concurrence by the Congress would deprive the congressional plaintiffs of the voice to which they are entitled under the Constitution. The Department of Justice, acting on behalf of the President, is opposing the motion for preliminary injunction, and it has also moved to dismiss.

The Department raises a number of defenses to the lawsuit—most particularly that the complaint presents a non-justiciable political question, that plaintiffs lack standing to maintain the action, that their claim violates established canons of equity jurisprudence, and that the issue of the proper allocation of the war making powers between the branches is not ripe for decision.

POLITICAL QUESTION

[T]he Constitution grants to the Congress the power "To declare War." To the extent that this unambiguous direction requires construction or explanation,[5] it is provided by the framers' comments that they felt it to be unwise to entrust the momentous power to involve the nation in a war to the President alone; Jefferson explained that he desired "an effectual check to the Dog of war"; James Wilson similarly expressed the expectation that this system would guard against hostilities being initiated by a single man.

The congressional power to declare war does not stand alone, however, but it is accompanied by powers granted to the President. Article II, § 1, cl. 1 and Section 2 provide that "[t]he executive powers shall be vested in a President of

---

5. While the Constitution itself speaks only of the congressional power to declare war, it is silent on the issue of the effect of a congressional vote that war not be initiated. However, if the War Clause is to have its normal meaning, it excludes from the power to declare war all branches other than the Congress. It also follows that if the Congress decides that United States forces should not be employed in foreign hostilities, and if the Executive does not of its own volition abandon participation in such hostilities, action by the courts would appear to be the only available means to break the deadlock in favor of the constitutional provision.

the United States of America," and that "[t]he President shall be Commander in Chief of the Army and Navy. . . ."

It is the position of the Department of Justice on behalf of the President that the simultaneous existence of all these provisions renders it impossible to isolate the war-declaring power. The Department further argues that the design of the Constitution is to have the various war- and military-related provisions construed and acting together, and that their harmonization is a political rather than a legal question. In short, the Department relies on the political question doctrine.

That doctrine is premised both upon the separation of powers and the inherent limits of judicial abilities. In relation to the issues involved in this case, the Department of Justice expands on its basic theme, contending that by their very nature the determination whether certain types of military actions require a declaration of war is not justiciable, but depends instead upon delicate judgments by the political branches. On that view, the question whether an offensive action taken by American armed forces constitutes an act of war (to be initiated by a declaration of war) or an "offensive military attack" (presumably undertaken by the President in his capacity as commander-in-chief) is not one of objective fact but involves an exercise of judgment based upon all the vagaries of foreign affairs and national security. Indeed, the Department contends that there are no judicially discoverable and manageable standards to apply, claiming that only the political branches are able to determine whether or not this country is at war. Such a determination, it is said, is based upon "a political judgment" about the significance of those facts. Under that rationale, a court cannot make an independent determination on this issue because it cannot take adequate account of these political considerations.

This claim on behalf of the Executive is far too sweeping to be accepted by the courts. If the Executive had the sole power to determine that any particular offensive military operation, no matter how vast, does not constitute war-making but only an offensive military attack, the congressional power to declare war will be at the mercy of a semantic decision by the Executive. Such an "interpretation" would evade the plain language of the Constitution, and it cannot stand.

That is not to say that, assuming that the issue is factually close or ambiguous or fraught with intricate technical military and diplomatic baggage, the courts would not defer to the political branches to determine whether or not particular hostilities might qualify as a "war." However, here the forces involved are of such magnitude and significance as to present no serious claim that a war would not ensue if they became engaged in combat, and it is therefore clear that congressional approval is required if Congress desires to become involved.

Notwithstanding these relatively straightforward propositions, the Department goes on to suggest that the issue in this case is still political rather than legal, because in order to resolve the dispute the Court would have to inject itself into foreign affairs, a subject which the Constitution commits to the political branches. That argument, too, must fail.

While the Constitution grants to the political branches, and in particular to the Executive, responsibility for conducting the nation's foreign affairs, it does not follow that the judicial power is excluded from the resolution of cases merely because they may touch upon such affairs. The court must instead look at "the particular question posed" in the case. *Baker v. Carr*, 369 U.S. 186 (1962). In fact, courts are routinely deciding cases that touch upon or even have a substantial impact on foreign and defense policy. *Japan Whaling Assn. v. American Cetacean Soc.*, 478 U.S. 221 (1986); *Dames & Moore v. Regan*, 453 U.S. 654 (1981); *Youngstown Sheet & Tube Co. v. Sawyer*, 343 U.S. 579 (1952); *United States v. Curtiss-Wright Export Corp.*, 299 U.S. 304 (1936).

The Department's argument also ignores the fact that courts have historically made determinations about whether this country was at war for many other purposes—the construction of treaties, statutes, and even insurance contracts. These judicial determinations of a de facto state of war have occurred even in the absence of a congressional declaration.[14]

Plaintiffs allege in their complaint that 230,000 American troops are currently deployed in Saudi Arabia and the Persian Gulf area, and that by the end of this month the number of American troops in the region will reach 380,000. They also allege, in light of the President's obtaining the support of the United Nations Security Council in a resolution allowing for the use of force against Iraq, that he is planning for an offensive military attack on Iraqi forces.

Given these factual allegations and the legal principles outlined above, the Court has no hesitation in concluding that an offensive entry into Iraq by several hundred thousand United States servicemen under the conditions described above could be described as a "war" within the meaning of Article I, § 8, cl. 11 of the Constitution. To put it another way: the Court is not prepared to read out of the Constitution the clause granting to the Congress, and to it alone, the authority "to declare war."

STANDING

The Department of Justice argues next that the plaintiffs lack "standing" to pursue this action.

For the purpose of determining standing on a motion to dismiss, the Court must "accept as true all material allegations of the complaint, and must construe the complaint in favor of the complaining party." Accordingly, plaintiffs' allegations of an imminent danger of hostilities between the United States forces and Iraq must be accepted as true for this purpose.

---

14. In the *Prize Cases*, 67 U.S. 635 (1863), the Court was asked to determine whether the Civil War, which Congress had never officially declared to be a war, constituted a war for the purpose of determining whether the right of prize existed. The owners of the captured ships claimed that the Civil War was not a war because it had not been officially declared. The Court responded that they "cannot ask a court to affect a technical ignorance of the existence of a war, which all the world acknowledges to be the greatest civil war known in the history of the human race."

Plaintiffs further claim that their interest guaranteed by the War Clause of the Constitution is in immediate danger of being harmed by military actions the President may take against Iraq. That claim states a legally-cognizable injury, for as the Court of Appeals for this Circuit stated in a leading case, members of Congress plainly have an interest in protecting their right to vote on matters entrusted to their respective chambers by the Constitution.

The right asserted by the plaintiffs in this case is the right to vote for or against a declaration of war. In view of that subject matter, the right must of necessity be asserted before the President acts; once the President has acted, the asserted right of the members of Congress—to render war action by the President contingent upon a prior congressional declaration of war—is of course lost.

The Department also argues that the threat of injury in this case is not immediate because there is only a "possibility" that the President will initiate war against Iraq, and additionally, that there is no way of knowing before the occurrence of such a possibility whether he would seek a declaration of war from Congress.

That argument, too, must fail, for although it is not entirely fixed what actions the Executive will take towards Iraq and what procedures he will follow with regard to his consultations with Congress,[16] it is clearly more than "unadorned speculation," that the President will go to war by initiating hostilities against Iraq without first obtaining a declaration of war from Congress.

With close to 400,000 United States troops stationed in Saudi Arabia, with all troop rotation and leave provisions suspended, and with the President having acted vigorously on his own as well as through the Secretary of State to obtain from the United Nations Security Council a resolution authorizing the use of all available means to remove Iraqi forces from Kuwait, including the use of force, it is disingenuous for the Department to characterize plaintiffs' allegations as to the imminence of the threat of offensive military action for standing purposes as "remote and conjectural" for standing purposes. For these reasons, the Court concludes that the plaintiffs have adequately alleged a threat of injury in fact necessary to support standing.

RIPENESS

Although the Court rejects several of defendant's objections to the maintenance of this lawsuit, and concludes that, in principle, an injunction may issue at the request of Members of Congress to prevent the conduct of a war which is about to be carried on without congressional authorization, it does not follow that these plaintiffs are entitled to relief at this juncture. For the plaintiffs are met with a significant obstacle to such relief: the doctrine of ripeness.

It has long been held that, as a matter of the deference that is due to the other branches of government, the Judiciary will undertake to render decisions

---

16. These concerns touch also on the determination of ripeness addressed by the Court, *infra.*

that compel action by the President or the Congress only if the dispute before the Court is truly ripe, in that all the factors necessary for a decision are present then and there. The need for ripeness as a prerequisite to judicial action has particular weight in a case such as this. The principle that the courts shall be prudent in the exercise of their authority is never more compelling than when they are called upon to adjudicate on such sensitive issues as those trenching upon military and foreign affairs. Judicial restraint must, of course, be even further enhanced when the issue is one—as here—on which the other two branches may be deeply divided. Hence the necessity for determining at the outset whether the controversy is truly "ripe" for decision or whether, on the other hand, the Judiciary should abstain from rendering a decision on ripeness grounds.

In the context of this case, there are two aspects to ripeness, which the Court will now explore.

A. ACTIONS BY THE CONGRESS

No one knows the position of the Legislative Branch on the issue of war or peace with Iraq; certainly no one, including this Court, is able to ascertain the congressional position on that issue on the basis of this lawsuit brought by fifty-three members of the House of Representatives and one member of the U.S. Senate. It would be both premature and presumptuous for the Court to render a decision on the issue of whether a declaration of war is required at this time or in the near future when the Congress itself has provided no indication whether it deems such a declaration either necessary, on the one hand, or imprudent, on the other.

For these reasons, this Court has elected to follow the course described by Justice Powell in his concurrence in *Goldwater v. Carter*, 444 U.S. 996 (1979). In that opinion, Justice Powell provided a test for ripeness in cases involving a confrontation between the legislative and executive branches that is helpful here.[23] In *Goldwater*, President Carter had informed Taiwan that the United States would terminate the mutual defense treaty between the two countries within one year. The President made this announcement without the ratification of the Congress, and members of Congress brought suit claiming that, just as the Constitution required the Senate's ratification of the President's decision to enter into a treaty, so too, congressional ratification was necessary to terminate a treaty.

Justice Powell proposed that "a dispute between Congress and the President is not ready for judicial review unless and until each branch has taken action asserting its constitutional authority." He further explained that in *Goldwater* there had been no such confrontation because there had as yet been no vote in

---

23. That is so even though Justice Powell spoke only for himself. The Supreme Court, in a brief order, remanded the *Goldwater* case to the lower court with instructions to dismiss. Four different views were expressed by the various justices. However, several other courts have adopted Justice Powell's reasoning.

the Senate as to what to do in the face of the President's action to terminate the treaty with Taiwan, and he went on to say that the

> Judicial Branch should not decide issues affecting the allocation of power between the President and Congress until the political branches reach a constitutional impasse. Otherwise we would encourage small groups or even individual Members of Congress to seek judicial resolution of issues before the normal political process has the opportunity to resolve the conflict. . . . It cannot be said that either the Senate or the House has rejected the President's claim. If the Congress chooses not to confront the President, it is not our task to do so.

Justice Powell's reasoning commends itself to this Court. The consequences of judicial action in the instant case with the facts in their present posture may be drastic, but unnecessarily so. What if the Court issued the injunction requested by the plaintiffs, but it subsequently turned out that a majority of the members of the Legislative Branch were of the view (a) that the President is free as a legal or constitutional matter to proceed with his plans toward Iraq without a congressional declaration of war,[26] or (b) more broadly, that the majority of the members of this Branch, for whatever reason, are content to leave this diplomatically and politically delicate decision to the President?

It would hardly do to have the Court, in effect, force a choice upon the Congress[27] by a blunt injunctive decision, called for by only about ten percent of its membership, to the effect that, unless the rest of the Congress votes in favor of a declaration of war, the President, and the several hundred thousand troops he has dispatched to the Saudi Arabian desert, must be immobilized. Similarly, the President is entitled to be protected from an injunctive order respecting a declaration of war when there is no evidence that this is what the Legislative Branch as such — as distinguished from a fraction thereof — regards as a necessary prerequisite to military moves in the Arabian desert.

All these difficulties are avoided by a requirement that the plaintiffs in an action of this kind be or represent a majority of the Members of the Congress: the majority of the body that under the Constitution is the only one competent to declare war, and therefore also the one with the ability to seek an order from the courts to prevent anyone else, *i.e.*, the Executive, from in effect declaring war. In short, unless the Congress as a whole, or by a majority, is heard from, the controversy here cannot be deemed ripe; it is only if the

---

26. It might be that these legislators are content to follow some of the historical patterns, including those involving the hostilities in Vietnam and Korea where there was no declaration of war, or that they deem the consultations had in recent months and weeks between the Executive and congressional leaders to constitute adequate compliance with Article I, § 8, cl. 11 of the Constitution.

27. The plaintiffs argue that "Congress cannot, and should not, be able to read the War Powers Clause out of the Constitution by failure to act." However, plaintiffs are not entitled to receive relief from action or non-action of their colleagues in Congress through a suit for an injunction against the President.

majority of the Congress seeks relief from an infringement on its constitutional war-declaration power that it may be entitled to receive it.[29]

B. Actions Taken By the Executive

The second half of the ripeness issue involves the question whether the Executive Branch of government is so clearly committed to immediate military operations that may be equated with a "war" within the meaning of Article I, § 8, cl. 11, of the Constitution that a judicial decision may properly be rendered regarding the application of that constitutional provision to the current situation.[30]

Plaintiffs assert that the matter is currently ripe for judicial action because the President himself has stated that the present troop build-up is to provide an adequate offensive military option in the area. His successful effort to secure passage of United Nations Resolution 678, which authorizes the use of "all available means" to oust Iraqi forces remaining in Kuwait after January 15, 1991, is said to be an additional fact pointing toward the Executive's intention to initiate military hostilities against Iraq in the near future.[31]

The Department of Justice, on the other hand, points to statements of the President that the troops already in Saudi Arabia are a peacekeeping force to prove that the President might not initiate more offensive military actions. In addition, and more realistically, it is possible that the meetings set for later this month and next between President Bush and the Foreign Minister of Iraq, Tariq Aziz, in Washington, and Secretary of State James Baker and Saddam Hussein in Baghdad, may result in a diplomatic solution to the present situation, and in any event under the U.N. Security Council resolution there will not be resort to force before January 15, 1991.

Given the facts currently available to this Court, it would seem that as of now the Executive Branch has not shown a commitment to a definitive course of action sufficient to support ripeness.[34] In any event, however, a final decision on that issue is not necessary at this time.

Should the congressional ripeness issue be resolved in favor of a finding of ripeness as a consequence of actions taken by the Congress as a whole, there

---

29. Of course, should Congress pass a resolution authorizing the President's proposed actions in the Persian Gulf area, one byproduct would be that the instant action would be mooted.

30. The Court rejects defendant's contention that the issue can never be ripe until hostilities have actually broken out. That argument would insulate the President from even the grossest violations of the War Clause of the Constitution, for a congressional vote after war has begun would likely to be without practical effect (as would also be the alternative suggestion that the Congress could always cut off funds for our fighting forces while they are engaged in military operations).

31. On December 3, one day before the hearing in the instant case, Secretary of Defense Dick Cheney testified to the Senate Armed Services Committee that "I do not believe the President requires any additional authorization from the Congress before committing U.S. forces to achieve our objectives in the Gulf."

34. Obviously, while plaintiffs cannot be expected to pinpoint precisely the time when the Executive will take action that is equivalent to war, constitutional ripeness demands that their submission be more definite and more immediate than it is now.

will still be time enough to determine whether, in view of the conditions as they are found to exist at that time, the Executive is so clearly committed to early military operations amounting to "war" in the constitutional sense that the Court would be justified in concluding that the remainder of the test of ripeness has been met. And of course an injunction will be issued only if, on both of the aspects of the doctrine discussed above, the Court could find that the controversy is ripe for judicial decision. That situation does not, or at least not yet, prevail, and plaintiffs' request for a preliminary injunction will therefore not be granted.

For the reasons stated, it is this 13th day of December, 1990

ORDERED that plaintiffs' motion for preliminary injunction be and it is hereby denied.

United States v. Richardson
418 U.S. 166 (1974)

Mr. Chief Justice BURGER delivered the opinion of the Court.

Respondent brought this suit in the United States District Court on a complaint in which he recites attempts to obtain from the Government information concerning detailed expenditures of the Central Intelligence Agency. According to the complaint, respondent wrote to the Government Printing Office in 1967 and requested that he be provided with the documents "published by the Government in compliance with Article I, section 9, clause (7) of the United States Constitution." The Fiscal Service of the Bureau of Accounts of the Department of the Treasury replied, explaining that it published the document known as the Combined Statement of Receipts, Expenditures, and Balances of the United States Government. Several copies of the monthly and daily reports of the office were sent with the letter. Respondent then wrote to the same office and, quoting part of the CIA Act, asked whether this statute did not "cast reflection upon the authenticity of the Treasury's Statement." He also inquired as to how he could receive further information on the expenditures of the CIA. The Bureau of Accounts replied stating that it had no other available information.

In another letter, respondent asserted that the CIA Act was repugnant to the Constitution and requested that the Treasury Department seek an opinion of the Attorney General. The Department answered declining to seek such an opinion and this suit followed. Respondent's complaint asked the court to "issue a permanent injunction enjoining the defendants from publishing their 'Combined Statement of Receipts, Expenditures and Balances of the United States Government' and representing it as the fulfillment of the mandates of Article I Section 9 Clause 7 until same fully complies with those mandates." In essence, the respondent asked the federal court to declare unconstitutional that provision of the Central Intelligence Agency Act which permits the Agency to account for its expenditures "solely on the certificate of the Director. . . ." 50 U.S.C. § 403j(b). The only injury alleged by respondent was that he "cannot obtain a document that sets out the expenditures and receipts" of the CIA but on the contrary was "asked to accept a fraudulent document." The District Court granted a motion for dismissal on the ground respondent lacked standing and that the subject matter raised political questions not suited for judicial disposition.

The Court of Appeals sitting en banc, with three judges dissenting, reversed, holding that the respondent had standing to bring this action. The Court of Appeals concluded that the CIA statute challenged by the respondent was integrally related to his ability to challenge the appropriations since he could not question an appropriation about which he had no knowledge.

We conclude that respondent lacks standing to maintain a suit for the relief sought and we reverse.

As far back as *Marbury v. Madison*, this Court held that judicial power may be exercised only in a case properly before it—a "case or controversy" not suffering any of the limitations of the political-question doctrine, not then moot or calling for an advisory opinion. In *Baker v. Carr*, this limitation was described in terms that a federal court cannot "pronounce any statute, either of the state or of the United States, void, because irreconcilable with the constitution, except as it is called upon to adjudge the legal rights of litigants in actual controversies."

The party who invokes the (judicial) power must be able to show not only that the statute is invalid but that he has sustained or is immediately in danger of sustaining some direct injury as the result of its enforcement, and not merely that he suffers in some indefinite way in common with people generally.

We need not and do not reach the merits of the constitutional attack on the statute; our inquiry into the "substantive issues" is for the limited purpose indicated above. The mere recital of the respondent's claims and an examination of the statute under attack demonstrate how far he falls short of the standing criteria. Although the status he rests on is that he is a taxpayer, his challenge is not addressed to the taxing or spending power, but to the statutes regulating the CIA, specifically 50 U.S.C. § 403j(b). That section provides different accounting and reporting requirements and procedures for the CIA, as is also done with respect to other governmental agencies dealing in confidential areas.

The respondent's claim is that without detailed information on CIA expenditures—and hence its activities—he cannot intelligently follow the actions of Congress or the Executive, nor can he properly fulfill his obligations as a member of the electorate in voting for candidates seeking national office.

While we can hardly dispute that this respondent has a genuine interest in the use of funds and that his interest may be prompted by his status as a taxpayer, he has not alleged that, as a taxpayer, he is in danger of suffering any particular concrete injury as a result of the operation of this statute.[11]

It can be argued that if respondent is not permitted to litigate this issue, no one can do so. In a very real sense, the absence of any particular individual or class to litigate these claims gives support to the argument that the subject matter is committed to the surveillance of Congress, and ultimately to the political process. Any other conclusion would mean that the Founding Fathers intended to set up something in the nature of an Athenian democracy or a New England town meeting to oversee the conduct of the National Government by means of lawsuits in federal courts. The Constitution created a representative Government with the representatives directly responsible to their constituents at stated periods of two, four, and six years; that the Constitution does not afford a judicial remedy does not, of course, completely disable the citizen who is not satisfied with the "ground rules" established by the Congress for reporting expenditures of the Executive Branch. Lack of standing within the narrow confines of Art. III jurisdiction does not impair the right to assert his views in the political forum or at the polls. Slow, cumbersome, and unresponsive though the traditional electoral process may be thought at times, our system provides for changing members of the political branches when dissatisfied citizens convince a sufficient number of their fellow electors that elected representatives are delinquent in performing duties committed to them.

As our society has become more complex, our numbers more vast, our lives more varied, and our resources more strained, citizens increasingly request the intervention of the courts on a greater variety of issues than at any period of our national development. The acceptance of new categories of judicially cognizable injury has not eliminated the basic principle that to invoke judicial power the claimant must have a "personal stake in the outcome," or a "particular, concrete injury," or "a direct injury," in short, something more than "generalized grievances." Respondent has failed to meet these fundamental tests; accordingly, the judgment of the Court of Appeals is reversed.

---

11. Although we need not reach or decide precisely what is meant by "a regular Statement and Account," it is clear that Congress has plenary power to exact any reporting and accounting it considers appropriate in the public interest. It is therefore open to serious question whether the Framers of the Constitution ever imagined that general directives to the Congress or the Executive would be subject to enforcement by an individual citizen. While the available evidence is neither qualitatively nor quantitatively conclusive, historical analysis of the genesis of cl. 7 suggests that it was intended to permit some degree of secrecy of governmental operations. The ultimate weapon of enforcement available to the Congress would, of course, be the "power of the purse." Independent of the statute here challenged by respondent, Congress could grant standing to taxpayers or citizens, or both, limited, of course, by the "cases" and "controversies" provisions of Art. III.

Not controlling, but surely not unimportant, are nearly two centuries of acceptance of a reading of cl. 7 as vesting in Congress plenary power to spell out the details of precisely when and with what specificity Executive agencies must report the expenditure of appropriated funds and to exempt certain secret activities from comprehensive public reporting.

Mr. Justice POWELL, concurring.

Relaxation of standing requirements is directly related to the expansion of judicial power. It seems to me inescapable that allowing unrestricted taxpayer or citizen standing would significantly alter the allocation of power at the national level, with a shift away from a democratic form of government. I also believe that repeated and essentially head-on confrontations between the life tenured branch and the representative branches of government will not, in the long run, be beneficial to either. The public confidence essential to the former and the vitality critical to the latter may well erode if we do not exercise self-restraint in the utilization of our power to negative the actions of the other branches. We should be ever mindful of the contradictions that would arise if a democracy were to permit general oversight of the elected branches of government by a nonrepresentative, and in large measure insulated, judicial branch. Moreover, the argument that the Court should allow unrestricted taxpayer or citizen standing underestimates the ability of the representative branches of the Federal Government to respond to the citizen pressure that has been responsible in large measure for the concurrent drift toward expanded standing. Indeed, taxpayer or citizen advocacy, given its potentially broad base, is precisely the type of leverage that in a democracy ought to be employed against the branches that were intended to be responsive to public attitudes about the appropriate operation of government.

Mr. Justice DOUGLAS, dissenting.

I would affirm the judgment of the Court of Appeals on the "standing" issue.

Respondent in the present case claims that he has a right to "a regular statement and account" of receipts and expenditures of public moneys for the Central Intelligence Agency. History shows that the curse of government is not always venality; secrecy is one of the most tempting coverups to save regimes from criticism. As the Court of Appeals said:

> "The Framers of the Constitution deemed fiscal information essential if the electorate was to exercise any control over its representatives and meet their new responsibilities as citizens of the Republic; and they mandated publication, although stated in general terms, of the Government's receipts and expenditures. Whatever the ultimate scope and extent of that obligation, its elimination generates a sufficient, adverse interest in a taxpayer." Ibid. (Footnote omitted.)

Whatever may be the merits of the underlying claim, it seems clear that the taxpayer in the present case is not making a generalized complaint about the operation of Government. He does not even challenge the constitutionality of the Central Intelligence Agency Act. He only wants to know the amount of tax money exacted from him that goes into CIA activities. Secrecy of the Government acquires new sanctity when his claim is denied. Secrecy has, of course, some constitutional sanction. Article I, § 5, cl. 3, provides that "Each House shall keep a Journal of its Proceedings, and from time to time publish the same, excepting such Parts as may in their Judgment require Secrecy. . . ."

But the difference was great when it came to an accounting of public money. Secrecy was the evil at which Art. I, § 9, cl. 7, was aimed. At the Convention, Mason took the initiative in moving for an annual account of public expenditures. Madison suggested it be "from time to time" because it was thought that requiring publication at fixed intervals might lead to no publication at all. Indeed under the Articles of Confederation "[a] punctual compliance being often impossible, the practice ha[d] ceased altogether."

During the Maryland debates on the Constitution, McHenry said: "[T]he People who give their Money ought to know in what manner it is expended[.]" In the Virginian debates Mason expressed his belief that while some matters might require secrecy (e.g., ongoing diplomatic negotiations and military operations) "he did not conceive that the receipts and expenditures of the public money ought ever to be concealed. The people, he affirmed, had a right to know the expenditures of their money." In New York Livingston said: "Will not the representatives . . . consider it as essential to their popularity, to gratify their constituents with full and frequent statements of the public accounts? There can be no doubt of it."

From the history of the clause it is apparent that the Framers inserted it in the Constitution to give the public knowledge of the way public funds are expended. No one has a greater "personal stake" in policing this protective measure than a taxpayer. Indeed, if a taxpayer may not raise the question, who may do so? The Court states that discretion to release information is in the first instance "committed to the surveillance of Congress," and that the right of the citizenry to information under Art. I, § 9 cl. 7, cannot be enforced directly, but only through the "(s)low cumbersome, and unresponsive" electoral process. One has only to read constitutional history to realize that statement would shock Mason and Madison. Congress of course has discretion; but to say that it has the power to read the clause out of the Constitution when it comes to one or two or three agencies is astounding. That is the bare-bones issue in the present case. Does Art. I, § 9, cl. 7, of the Constitution permit Congress to withhold "a regular Statement and Account" respecting any agency it chooses? Respecting all federal agencies? What purpose, what function is the clause to perform under the Court's construction? The electoral process already permits the removal of legislators for any reason. Allowing their removal, at the polls for failure to comply with Art. I, § 9, cl. 7, effectively reduces that clause to a nullity, giving it no purpose at all.

The sovereign in this Nation is the people, not the bureaucracy. The statement of accounts of public expenditures goes to the heart of the problem of sovereignty. If taxpayers may not ask that rudimentary question, their sovereignty becomes an empty symbol and a secret bureaucracy is allowed to run our affairs.

The resolution of that issue has not been entrusted to one of the other coordinate branches of government—the test of the "political question" under *Baker v. Carr*. The question is "political" if there is "a textually demonstrable constitutional commitment of the issue to a coordinate political department[.]" The mandate runs to the Congress and to the agencies it creates to make "a regular Statement and Account of the Receipts and Expenditures of all public Money." The beneficiary — as is abundantly clear from the constitutional history — is the public. The public cannot intelligently know how to exercise the franchise unless it has a basic knowledge concerning at least the generality of the accounts under every head of government. No greater crisis in confidence can be generated than today's decision. Its consequences are grave because it relegates to secrecy vast operations of government and keeps the public from knowing what secret plans concerning this Nation or other nations are afoot. The fact that the result is serious does not, of course, make the issue "justiciable." But resolutions of any doubts or ambiguities should be toward protecting an individual's stake in the integrity of constitutional guarantees rather than turning him away without even a chance to be heard.

I would affirm the judgment below.

Mr. Justice STEWART, with whom Mr. Justice MARSHALL joins, dissenting.

Richardson did not bring this action asking a court to invalidate a federal statute on the ground that it was beyond the delegated power of Congress to enact or that it contravened some constitutional prohibition. Richardson's claim is of an entirely different order.

Seeking a determination that the Government owes him a duty to supply the information he has requested, the respondent contends that the Statement and Account Clause gives him a right to receive the information and burdens the Government with a correlative duty to supply it. Courts of law exist for the resolution of such right-duty disputes. When a party is seeking a judicial determination that a defendant owes him an affirmative duty, it seems clear to me that he has standing to litigate the issue of the existence vel non of this duty once he shows that the defendant has declined to honor his claim. If the duty in question involved the payment of a sum of money, I suppose that all would agree that a plaintiff asserting the duty would have standing to litigate the issue of his entitlement to the money upon a showing that he had not been paid. I see no reason for a different result when the defendant is a Government official and the asserted duty relates not to the payment of money, but to the disclosure of items of information.

On the merits, I presume that the Government's position would be that the Statement and Account Clause of the Constitution does not impose an affirmative duty upon it; that any such duty does not in any event run to Richardson; that any such duty is subject to legislative qualifications, one of which is applicable here; and that the question involved is political and thus not justiciable. Richardson might ultimately be thrown out of court on any one of these grounds, or some other. But to say that he might ultimately lose his lawsuit certainly does not mean that he had no standing to bring it.

NOTE AND QUESTION

It is hornbook law that an individual does not have standing to sue for a generalized grievance, i.e., one in which it is impossible to differentiate between potential litigants on the basis of their alleged injury. Thus, a generalized grievance is different than a mass tort, in which the injuries (although suffered by many people) are susceptible to individualization. Which national security issues are generalized grievances and which are not?

III. FRICTIONS *WITHIN* BRANCHES OF THE FEDERAL GOVERNMENT

Generally speaking, the concept of separation of powers in American legal theory parallels the divisions made in the Constitution between the legislature, executive, and judiciary. But what of the separation of powers *within* a particular branch of government?

Given the multifarious and sometimes conflicting policies that agencies pursue, it is not surprising that there is sometimes friction between them. Indeed, this may be the case even when they would seem to be acting in concert toward a common goal.

Friction Point: Getting to Yes

For example, as noted above, Congress has excepted from its prohibition on naturalization by reason of membership in the Communist Party or advocacy of communism anyone who, *inter alia*, "is determined by the Director of Central Intelligence, in consultation with the Secretary of Defense when Department of Defense activities are relevant to the determination, and with the concurrence of the Attorney General and the Secretary of Homeland Security, to have made a contribution to the national security or to the national intelligence mission of the United States." 8 U.S.C. § 1424(e)(4).[20] Notice that the "determination" belongs to the CIA Director, who would seem the logical choice if the exception is to allow the intelligence community to reward double agents brought in from the cold. Although the Director need only decide in certain instances "in consultation" (but not necessarily agreement) with the Secretary of Defense, the Director must obtain "the concurrence" of the Attorney General and the Secretary of Homeland Security. Why? In what instances would their disagreement be the desirable outcome? Is the concurrence of three high-ranking officials an example of intra-branch separation of powers?

---

20. This provision was added by § 306 of the Intelligence Authorization Act for Fiscal Year 2000, Pub. L. No. 106-120, 113 Stat. 1606, Dec. 3, 1999, and slightly revised by § 373 of the Intelligence Authorization Act for Fiscal Year 2004, Pub. L. No. 108-177, 117 Stat. 2628, Dec. 13, 2003.

Friction Point: The Intelligence Community

Or consider the following example. The Terrorist Screening Center (TSC) is a multi-agency office, housed in and administered by the FBI. Its task is to create and manage the nation's various terrorist watchlists. It does so by creating one large Terrorist Screening Database out of information acquired from many different federal, state, and foreign sources and then using it to develop more specialized terrorist watchlists, such as the "No-Fly List" for use by the Transportation Security Administration within the Department of Homeland Security. The lists are based on "nominations" of individuals that different agencies, based on their own intelligence, think should be watchlisted. In 2007, a memorandum of understanding (MOU) was signed by five cabinet officials (State, Treasury, Justice, Defense, and Homeland Security) and five high-ranking officials from the Intelligence Community (the Director of National Intelligence, FBI Director, Director of the National Counterterrorism Center, CIA Director, and Acting Director of the Terrorist Screening Center). The MOU concerned "redress procedures," or how these agencies would interact to respond to individuals who complain about terrorist watchlists. Consider one section, on "deconfliction," i.e., disagreements between these agencies about what to do:

> In the event of a multi-agency nomination where the nominating and/or originating agencies do not agree on what recommendation should be made on a specific redress matter, TSC will request that the agencies consult with one another and share appropriate information about the watchlisted individual in an attempt to provide a joint recommendation to TSC. If the nominating/originating agencies cannot agree to a joint recommendation, TSC (or other agency with the legal authority to make the decision) will make the final determination considering the information provided by each agency.[21]

What does all that actually mean? Who, exactly, is in charge? What is the potential veto power of an agency that disagrees with the TSC? Do these procedures reflect concerns that resonate with the doctrine of separation of powers? In the first years after the attacks of September 11, 2001, the No-Fly List was often used as much as an investigative tool by the FBI as it was used as a security tool by the TSA. Does intra-branch coordination create conditions in which "ambition must be made to counteract ambition" in the same way, or with the same effects, that inter-branch separation of powers structures do?

Friction Point: The Armed Forces and the CIA

Perhaps the most well-known friction point of particular salience to national security issues is that between the Department of Defense, which is responsible for the management of the country's armed forces, and the Central Intelligence Agency, a

---

21. Section 4(C)(v), Memorandum of Understanding on Terrorist Watchlist Redress Procedures, attachment to letter from Leonard C. Boyle, Director Terrorist Screening Center, to Carol E. Dinkins, Chairwoman Privacy and Civil Liberties Oversight Board, and Frances Fragos Townsend, Assistant to the President for Homeland Security and Counterterrorism, Sept. 28, 2007.

civilian organization created in 1947 that is charged with responsibility for intelligence collection, counter-intelligence, and covert action. The former finds its authorizations in Title 10 of the United States Code; the latter finds its governing law in Title 50. Yet, especially post-9/11, the CIA increasingly conducted operations using armed force (e.g., drone strikes, proxy forces, or even its own officers), while the Pentagon expanded its intelligence-gathering networks, sometimes "without the knowledge of the ambassadors and CIA station chiefs in various countries, causing turf battles." *See* Robert Chesney, *Military-Intelligence Convergence and the Law of the Title 10/Title 50 Debate*, 5 J. NAT'L SEC. L. & POL'Y 539, 576 (2012) (citing Eric Schmitt & Thom Shanker, COUNTERSTRIKE: THE UNTOLD STORY OF AMERICA'S SECRET CAMPAIGN AGAINST AL QAEDA 259 (2011)). Just how serious a concern are such "turf battles"? Should anyone outside the fractious bureaucracies care?

IV. FRICTIONS BETWEEN FEDERAL AND STATE AUTHORITIES

To what extent does the federal structure of the United States (unique in the world at the time of the Founding) create friction between state and federal authority for national security? Urging the thirteen colonial states to remain unified, John Jay argued that "weakness and divisions at home, would invite dangers from abroad; and that nothing would tend more to secure us from them than Union, strength, and good Government within ourselves." THE FEDERALIST NO. 5. But how *much* union is necessary? How much division should be tolerated, or even encouraged, in such a diverse nation, now spanning a continent?

The Constitution itself limits the reach of individual states into the realm of foreign affairs and national security. These restrictions are found in Article I, § 10. Note how several of the restrictions on the sovereignty of the states parallel the grant of legislative power to the national legislature:

> No State shall enter into any Treaty, Alliance, or Confederation; [or] grant Letters of Marque and Reprisal. . . .
>
> No State shall, without the Consent of the Congress, lay any Imposts or Duties on Imports or Exports, except what may be absolutely necessary for executing it's inspection Laws: and the net Produce of all Duties and Imposts, laid by any State on Imports or Exports, shall be for the Use of the Treasury of the United States; and all such Laws shall be subject to the Revision and Controul of the Congress.
>
> No State shall, without the Consent of Congress, lay any Duty of Tonnage, keep Troops, or Ships of War in time of Peace, enter into any Agreement or Compact with another State, or with a Foreign Power, or engage in War, unless actually invaded, or in such imminent Danger as will not admit of delay.

How does (how should) the Constitution avoid the fate that Jay feared for an America divided into separate states or rival confederacies, in which "envy and jealousy would soon extinguish confidence and affection, and the partial interests of each confederacy, instead of the general interests of all America, would be the only objects of their policy and pursuits"? THE FEDERALIST NO. 5.

Crosby v. National Foreign Trade Council
530 U.S. 363 (2000)

Justice SOUTER delivered the opinion of the Court.

The issue is whether the Burma law of the Commonwealth of Massachusetts, restricting the authority of its agencies to purchase goods or services from companies doing business with Burma, is invalid under the Supremacy Clause of the National Constitution owing to its threat of frustrating federal statutory objectives. We hold that it is.

In June 1996, Massachusetts adopted "An Act Regulating State Contracts with Companies Doing Business with or in Burma (Myanmar)." The statute generally bars state entities from buying goods or services from any person (defined to include a business organization) identified on a "restricted purchase list" of those doing business with Burma. Although the statute has no general provision for waiver or termination of its ban, it does exempt from boycott any entities present in Burma solely to report the news, or to provide international telecommunication goods or services, or medical supplies.

In September 1996, three months after the Massachusetts law was enacted, Congress passed a statute imposing a set of mandatory and conditional sanctions on Burma. First, it imposes three sanctions directly on Burma. It bans all aid to the Burmese Government except for humanitarian assistance, counter-narcotics efforts, and promotion of human rights and democracy. The statute instructs United States representatives to international financial institutions to vote against loans or other assistance to or for Burma and it provides that no entry visa shall be issued to any Burmese Government official unless required by treaty or to staff the Burmese mission to the United Nations. These restrictions are to remain in effect "[u]ntil such time as the President determines and certifies to Congress that Burma has made measurable and substantial progress in improving human rights practices and implementing democratic government."

Second, the federal Act authorizes the President to impose further sanctions subject to certain conditions. He may prohibit "United States persons" from "new investment" in Burma, and shall do so if he determines and certifies to Congress that the Burmese Government has physically harmed, rearrested, or exiled Daw Aung San Suu Kyi (the opposition leader selected to receive the Nobel Peace Prize), or has committed "large-scale repression of or violence against the Democratic opposition."

Third, the statute directs the President to work to develop "a comprehensive, multilateral strategy to bring democracy to and improve human rights practices and the quality of life in Burma." [The] Act authorizes the President "to waive, temporarily or permanently, any sanction [under the federal Act] . . . if he determines and certifies to Congress that the application of such sanction would be contrary to the national security interests of the United States."

Respondent National Foreign Trade Council (Council) is a nonprofit corporation representing companies engaged in foreign commerce; 34 of its members were on the Massachusetts restricted purchase list in 1998. The Council argued that the state law unconstitutionally infringed on the federal foreign affairs power, violated the Foreign Commerce Clause, and was preempted by the federal Act. [T]he District Court permanently enjoined enforcement of the state Act, holding that it "unconstitutionally impinge[d] on the federal government's exclusive authority to regulate foreign affairs." The United States Court of Appeals for the First Circuit affirmed on three independent grounds. It found the state Act unconstitutionally interfered with the foreign affairs power of the National Government; violated the dormant Foreign Commerce Clause; and was preempted by the congressional Burma Act.

A fundamental principle of the Constitution is that Congress has the power to preempt state law. Even without an express provision for preemption, we have found that state law must yield to a congressional Act in at least two circumstances. When Congress intends federal law to "occupy the field," state law in that area is preempted. And even if Congress has not occupied the field, state law is naturally preempted to the extent of any conflict with a federal statute. We will find preemption where it is impossible for a private party to comply with both state and federal law, and where "under the circumstances of [a] particular case, [the challenged state law] stands as an obstacle to the accomplishment and execution of the full purposes and objectives of Congress."

Applying this standard, we see the state Burma law as an obstacle to the accomplishment of Congress's full objectives under the federal Act.[8] We find that the state law undermines the intended purpose and "natural effect" of at least three provisions of the federal Act, that is, its delegation of effective discretion to the President to control economic sanctions against Burma, its limitation of sanctions solely to United States persons and new investment, and its directive to the President to proceed diplomatically in developing a comprehensive, multilateral strategy toward Burma.

First, Congress clearly intended the federal Act to provide the President with flexible and effective authority over economic sanctions against Burma. This express investiture of the President with statutory authority to act for the United States in imposing sanctions with respect to the Government of Burma, augmented by the flexibility to respond to change by suspending sanctions in the interest of national security, recalls Justice Jackson's observation in *Youngstown Sheet & Tube Co. v. Sawyer* (1952): "When the President acts pursuant to an express or implied authorization of Congress, his authority is at its maximum, for it includes all that he possesses in his own right plus all that Congress can delegate." See also *id.* (noting that the President's power in the area of foreign relations is least restricted by Congress and citing *United States v. Curtiss-Wright Export Corp.* (1936)). Within the sphere defined by Congress, then, the statute has placed the President in a position with as much discretion to exercise economic leverage against Burma, with an eye toward national

---

8. We add that we have already rejected the argument that a State's "statutory scheme . . . escapes pre-emption because it is an exercise of the State's spending power rather than its regulatory power."

security, as our law will admit. And it is just this plenitude of Executive authority that we think controls the issue of preemption here.

Quite simply, if the Massachusetts law is enforceable the President has less to offer and less economic and diplomatic leverage as a consequence. In *Dames & Moore v. Regan* (1981), we used the metaphor of the bargaining chip to describe the President's control of funds valuable to a hostile country; here, the state Act reduces the value of the chips created by the federal statute.

The State has set a different course, and its statute conflicts with federal law at a number of points by penalizing individuals and conduct that Congress has explicitly exempted or excluded from sanctions. While the state Act differs from the federal in relying entirely on indirect economic leverage through third parties with Burmese connections, it otherwise stands in clear contrast to the congressional scheme in the scope of subject matter addressed.

As with the subject of business meant to be affected, so with the class of companies doing it: the state Act's generality stands at odds with the federal discreteness. The Massachusetts law directly and indirectly imposes costs on all companies that do any business in Burma, save for those reporting news or providing international telecommunications goods or services, or medical supplies. It sanctions companies promoting the importation of natural resources controlled by the Government of Burma, or having any operations or affiliates in Burma. The state Act thus penalizes companies with pre-existing affiliates or investments, all of which lie beyond the reach of the federal Act's restrictions on "new investment" in Burmese economic development. The state Act, moreover, imposes restrictions on foreign companies as well as domestic, whereas the federal Act limits its reach to United States persons.

The conflicts are not rendered irrelevant by the State's argument that there is no real conflict between the statutes because they share the same goals and because some companies may comply with both sets of restrictions. The fact of a common end hardly neutralizes conflicting means, and the fact that some companies may be able to comply with both sets of sanctions does not mean that the state Act is not at odds with achievement of the federal decision about the right degree of pressure to employ.

Finally, the state Act is at odds with the President's intended authority to speak for the United States among the world's nations in developing a "comprehensive, multilateral strategy to bring democracy to and improve human rights practices and the quality of life in Burma." Congress called for Presidential cooperation with members of ASEAN and other countries in developing such a strategy directed the President to encourage a dialogue between the Government of Burma and the democratic opposition and required him to report to the Congress on the progress of his diplomatic efforts. As with Congress's explicit delegation to the President of power over economic sanctions, Congress's express command to the President to take the initiative for the United States among the international community invested him with the maximum authority of the National Government, cf. *Youngstown Sheet & Tube Co.*, in harmony with the President's own constitutional powers, U.S. Const.,

Art. II, § 2, cl. 2 ("[The President] shall have Power, by and with the Advice and Consent of the Senate, to make Treaties" and "shall appoint Ambassadors, other public Ministers and Consuls"); § 3 ("[The President] shall receive Ambassadors and other public Ministers"). This clear mandate and invocation of exclusively national power belies any suggestion that Congress intended the President's effective voice to be obscured by state or local action.

Again, the state Act undermines the President's capacity, in this instance for effective diplomacy. It is not merely that the differences between the state and federal Acts in scope and type of sanctions threaten to complicate discussions; they compromise the very capacity of the President to speak for the Nation with one voice in dealing with other governments. We need not get into any general consideration of limits of state action affecting foreign affairs to realize that the President's maximum power to persuade rests on his capacity to bargain for the benefits of access to the entire national economy without exception for enclaves fenced off willy-nilly by inconsistent political tactics.[17] When such exceptions do qualify his capacity to present a coherent position on behalf of the national economy, he is weakened, of course, not only in dealing with the Burmese regime, but in working together with other nations in hopes of reaching common policy and "comprehensive" strategy. Cf. *Dames & Moore.*

[T]he Executive has consistently represented that the state Act has complicated its dealings with foreign sovereigns and proven an impediment to accomplishing objectives assigned it by Congress. Assistant Secretary of State Larson, for example, has directly addressed the mandate of the federal Burma law in saying that the imposition of unilateral state sanctions under the state Act "complicate[s] efforts to build coalitions with our allies" to promote democracy and human rights in Burma. This point has been consistently echoed in the State Department: "While the [Massachusetts sanctions on Burma] were adopted in pursuit of a noble goal, the restoration of democracy in Burma, these measures also risk shifting the focus of the debate with our European Allies away from the best way to bring pressure against the State Law and Order Restoration Council (SLORC) to a potential WTO dispute over its consistency with our international obligations. Let me be clear. We are working with Massachusetts in the WTO dispute settlement process. But we must be honest in saying that the threatened WTO case risks diverting United

---

17. Such concerns have been raised by the President's representatives in the Executive Branch. See Testimony of Under Secretary of State Eizenstat before the Trade Subcommittee of the House Ways and Means Committee ("[U]nless sanctions measures are well conceived and coordinated, so that the United States is speaking with one voice and consistent with our international obligations, such uncoordinated responses can put the U.S. on the political defensive and shift attention away from the problem to the issue of sanctions themselves"). We have expressed similar concerns in our cases on foreign commerce and foreign relations. cf. The Federalist No. 80, pp. 535-536 (J. Cooke ed. 1961) (A. Hamilton) ("[T]he peace of the WHOLE ought not to be left at the disposal of a PART. The union will undoubtedly be answerable to foreign powers for the conduct of its members").

States' and Europe's attention from focusing where it should be — on Burma." Eizenstat testimony.[22]

This evidence in combination is more than sufficient to show that the state Act stands as an obstacle in addressing the congressional obligation to devise a comprehensive, multilateral strategy.

Our discussion in [a prior case] of the limited weight of evidence of formal diplomatic protests, risk of foreign retaliation, and statements by the Executive does not undercut the point. [Then] we had the question of the preemptive effect of federal tax law on state tax law with discriminatory extraterritorial effects. We found the reactions of foreign powers and the opinions of the Executive irrelevant in fathoming congressional intent because Congress had taken specific actions rejecting the positions both of foreign governments and the Executive. Here, however, Congress has done nothing to render such evidence beside the point. In consequence, statements of foreign powers necessarily involved in the President's efforts to comply with the federal Act, indications of concrete disputes with those powers, and opinions of senior National Government officials are competent and direct evidence of the frustration of congressional objectives by the state Act. Although we do not unquestioningly defer to the legal judgments expressed in Executive Branch statements when determining a federal Act's preemptive character, we have never questioned their competence to show the practical difficulty of pursuing a congressional goal requiring multinational agreement. We have, after all, not only recognized the limits of our own capacity to "determin[e] precisely when foreign nations will be offended by particular acts," but consistently acknowledged that the "nuances" of "the foreign policy of the United States . . . are much more the province of the Executive Branch and Congress than of this Court." In this case, repeated representations by the Executive Branch supported by formal diplomatic protests and concrete disputes are more than sufficient to demonstrate that the state Act stands in the way of Congress's diplomatic objectives.

The State's remaining argument is unavailing. The State points out that Congress has repeatedly declined to enact express preemption provisions aimed at state and local sanctions, and it calls our attention to the large number of such measures passed against South Africa in the 1980's, which various authorities cited have thought were not preempted. The State stresses that Congress was aware of the state Act in 1996, but did not preempt it explicitly when it adopted its own Burma statute. The State would have us conclude that Congress's continuing failure to enact express preemption implies approval, particularly in light of occasional instances of express preemption of state sanctions in the past.

The argument is unconvincing on more than one level. A failure to provide for preemption expressly may reflect nothing more than the settled character

---

22. The United States, in its brief as amicus curiae, continues to advance this position before us. See Brief for United States as Amicus Curiae 8-9, and n.7, 34-35. This conclusion has been consistently presented by senior United States officials.

of implied preemption doctrine that courts will dependably apply, and in any event, the existence of conflict cognizable under the Supremacy Clause does not depend on express congressional recognition that federal and state law may conflict. The State's inference of congressional intent is unwarranted here, therefore, simply because the silence of Congress is ambiguous. Since we never ruled on whether state and local sanctions against South Africa in the 1980's were preempted or otherwise invalid, arguable parallels between the two sets of federal and state Acts do not tell us much about the validity of the latter.

Because the state Act's provisions conflict with Congress's specific delegation to the President of flexible discretion, with limitation of sanctions to a limited scope of actions and actors, and with direction to develop a comprehensive, multilateral strategy under the federal Act, it is preempted, and its application is unconstitutional, under the Supremacy Clause.

NOTES AND QUESTIONS

1. The district court and Court of Appeals found the state law unconstitutionally "impinge[d]" or "interfered" with the foreign affairs powers of the national government. But the Supreme Court chose to resolve the case on preemption grounds. Why decide the case on one ground instead of the other? Wouldn't the former opinion be simpler and shorter to write, requiring no more than citation to *Youngstown*, *Curtiss-Wright*, and *Dames & Moore*?

2. Justices Scalia and Thomas joined only the judgment of the Court, not Justice Souter's opinion. They argued that the frequent references to extra-statutory sources, such as statements by members of Congress and executive branch officials and alternative legislative proposals considered but rejected were not only irrelevant sources of legislative intent ("The *only* reliable indication of *that* intent—the only thing we know for sure can be attributed to *all* of them—is the words of the bill that they voted to make law.") but also "harmful, since it tells future litigants that, even when a statute is clear on its face, and its effects clear upon the record, statements from the legislative history may help (and presumably harm) the case." But neither of the concurring Justices express any opinion about the use by Justice Souter of evidence of foreign reaction to the dueling state and federal laws. What's the difference?

V. COMPARATIVE SEPARATION OF POWERS

How do lawyers in other countries value the separation of government powers? As a concluding exercise, consider two views of the concept. Each was given at different ABA-sponsored events that occurred less than a year apart, in 2007–2008, and were published together. They have been slightly edited to obscure their time and place. Do not look at the citations on the bottom of the page before quizzing yourself about them. Write down on a piece of scrap paper what sort of country you imagine the author of each excerpt inhabits. Is that country a democracy or a dictatorship? Is it an established sovereign state or a struggling one? Is it an ethnically or religiously plural society or a more homogenous one? The excerpts have been slightly edited to obscure these facts. Do any of them matter to the success or failure of, the value or indifference about, the separation of powers as a governing concept?

Here is the first excerpt:

> And in this context the cause that the lawyers of ███████ have been fighting for becomes more and more relevant.
>
> The importance is that this is a terrorist war zone. Therefore, the existence of an independent and functioning judiciary is quite crucial to the prosecution of this form of war, which President Bush dubbed as a "War on Terror." The implication is evident. Without an independent judiciary, a contestant cannot win this form of war.
>
> I praise the judicial system in the USA. It is fiercely independent, and its Judiciary has challenged its Executive over Guantanamo Bay and over detention without trial. It is simple. An independent judicial system has to be provided in this theater of war. It is the people in that area that matter.[22]

This author concluded that "no democracy can survive without an independent judiciary. No strong and stable Parliament can be constructed on the debris or ruins of an independent judicial edifice."[23]

Now consider the view of the second author, recounting a series of judicial opinions in his country's history:

> In times of war Courts tend to be particularly diffident about questioning steps taken by the Executive in the interests of national security. In the infamous case of ████████████████████████████ [our highest judicial body] held that the [minister] could not be required to provide any justification for his exercise of the right to detain a man without trial because he believed that this was necessary because of the man's hostile associations. The diffidence persisted in ███████ even after the war.
>
> In 1977 the [minister] served a deportation notice on a Mr. Hosenball, a United States Citizen working as a journalist on the ground that he had sought and obtained for publication information harmful to the security of ███████ ███████. When the [minister] refused to provide any details of this allegation Mr.

---

22. Aitzaz Ahsan, *The Preservation of the Rule of Law in Times of Strife*, 43 Int'l Law. 73, 74 (2009). The author, "of Grays' Inn Barrister-at-Law, is a Senior Advocate in Pakistan, leader of the Lawyers' Movement, former President of the Supreme Court Bar Association, and former MP, Minister of Interior, Law and Justice, Leader of the House and Leader of the Opposition in the Senate of Pakistan. He remains actively in practice a Senior Advocate in the Supreme Court of Pakistan." *Id.* at 73, n.a1.

23. *Id.* at 76.

Hosenball sought judicial review of the decision. This was refused. This is what the [court] had to say:

> There is a conflict here between the interests of national security on the one hand and the freedom of the individual on the other. The balance between these two is not for a court of law. It is for the [minister]. He is the person entrusted by Parliament with the task. In some parts of the world national security has on occasions been used as an excuse for all sorts of infringements of individual liberty. But not in ██████. Both during the wars and after them, successive Ministers have discharged their duties to the complete satisfaction of the people at large.[24]

This author reached quite a different conclusion than the one above:

> Deference to the Executive has not, I believe, been a notable feature of American jurisprudence.
>
> The difference between the two jurisdictions is, of course, that in America the rights of the individual are embodied in and protected by a written Constitution. The U.S. Supreme Court has jurisdiction to protect those rights to the extent of striking down legislation that is unconstitutional.
>
> In the ██████████ the Constitution is largely unwritten. Parliament is supreme and the Courts cannot refuse to give effect to legislation on the ground that it is unconstitutional.[25]

What role does the separation of governmental powers play in national security? Is it essential that power be separated at all? What deference should a judicial power give to the political branches in times of war or national security crises?

---

24. The Rt. Hon the Lord Phillips of Worth Matravers, *Impact of Terrorism on the Rule of Law*, 43 Int'l Law. 13, 13-14 (2009). The author "read law at King's College, Cambridge and was called to the Bar in 1962. He was appointed a Queen's Counsel in 1978 and became a High Court Judge in the Queen's Bench Division in 1987. He was a Lord Justice of Appeal from 1995 to 1999 when he was appointed to the House of Lords as a Lord of Appeal in Ordinary. In 2000 he became Master of the Rolls and Head of Civil Justice in England and Wales and in 2005 Lord Chief Justice for England and Wales. In 2008 he took over from Lord Bingham as Senior Law Lord in the Judicial House of Lords. He is now the President to be of the new Supreme Court of the United Kingdom." *Id.*

25. *Id.* at 14. As the author notes, however, the Human Rights Act of 1998 imposed on judges a duty to consider whether a statute is incompatible with the European Convention on Human Rights.

ASSESSMENT QUESTIONS

1. What did Justice Brandeis mean when he described the effect of the doctrine of separation of powers to be the "inevitable friction" created between the three branches of government? In his view, is this a positive or a negative result?

2. Do arguments to interpret clauses in the Constitution as they were understood at the time of their adoption tend to limit or expand the national security powers of government?

3. What is the difference between "inherent" and "implied" powers? To which branch of federal government is the distinction most frequently important in debates about national security authorities?

ASSESSMENT ANSWERS

1. This question examines the theory behind the separation of powers. The point of the doctrine is not to make government more efficient. In fact, the point is just the opposite. By creating competing institutions with overlapping authorities, government action is harder to undertake. The history of competition between parliaments and monarchs provides empirical support for the way institutional design that deliberately creates "friction" between government bodies may promote liberty. Supporters of constitutions with so-called emergency powers clauses that may be triggered by a national security crisis necessarily prioritize efficiency over friction for short periods of time. Justice Brandeis would not support such exceptions to the doctrine, which he perceived as creating structures that yielded positive results.

2. There is no necessary tendency in either direction. Sometimes, an interpretation focused on the original meaning of a provision may augment power (e.g., the interpretation of the Appropriations Clause by successive attorneys General). On the other hand, those who argue that the original meaning of the verb "to declare" in the Declare War Clause meant only "to notify" would diminish the congressional role vis-à-vis the executive branch in this area.

3. The distinction between inherent and implied powers comes up most frequently in the national security context with regard to the executive branch. Proponents of "inherent" powers, often referencing the difference between the Vesting Clauses in Article I and Article II, argue that the Constitution endows the President with all of the powers "inherent" in (i.e., naturally part of the meaning of) executive authority. This view typically accords more power to the executive

than a view of "implied" powers, which are those that seem to naturally follow from express textual provisions. The Necessary and Proper Clause may be advanced in support of implied powers, but not inherent powers. "Emergency" executive powers to act in a crisis tend to be defended on the basis of inherent, rather than implied, executive power.

CHAPTER 4

Government Interaction

I. INTRODUCTION

The Constitution and its drafting history provide the starting point for understanding the exercise of national security powers but certainly not the endpoint. While the text of the Constitution includes provisions related to national security, the general nature of many of these provisions coupled with the inherent uncertainties and variables associated with national security presents a consistent challenge to those seeking to identify the scope of constitutionally vested authority in this realm of vital policy making. Adding to this complexity is the reality that the Founders diffused power between the three branches of the new federal government they perfected. As a result, reference to constitutional text often leads to more questions than answers in this realm of government action.

Further complicating matters is the reality that judicial decisions addressing national security powers have been far less common than those addressing other aspects of national power. Nonetheless, the handful of cases touching on national security powers decided by the Supreme Court are considered especially significant in this field, precisely because such decisions are few and far between. Indeed, the impact of these decisions arguably transcend their precedential value (although this value is certainly significant), providing what is best understood as a national security legal framework informs and guides the development of national security policy and resolution of national security conflicts. Indeed, the significance of these seminal decisions led former State Department Legal Advisor and Yale Law School Dean Harold Hongju Koh to characterize this amalgam of constitutional text and national security jurisprudence as a "national security constitution."[1]

---

1. *See* Harold Hongju Koh, The National Security Constitution (1990).

As you read through these important decisions, consider the role of legal advisors to both the executive and legislative branches of government. How do these decisions inform assessments of constitutional authority in the realm of national security policy making and execution, the risks of pressing powers into areas of uncertain allocation, and the consequence of crossing into a lane allocated to a coordinate branch?

II. A BROAD CONCEPTION OF EXECUTIVE FOREIGN AFFAIRS POWERS

Like all lawyers, national security legal advisors seek the strongest source of authority to support the advice they provide to their client and the positions they take when the decision of their client is challenged or contested. Because in the context of national security decision-making authority provided by express provisions of the Constitution, statutes or treaties are frequently insufficient to conclusively resolve issues of executive branch authority, these advisors will often invoke judicial precedent they believe supports an expansive interpretation of inherent executive power. Perhaps the most commonly cited decision in support of such broad authority grew out of an historically obscure effort by President Franklin D. Roosevelt to influence events in South America.

> The Constitution vests Congress with the authority to make law. Congress normally exercises that authority by enacting a bill, which is then presented to the President for signature or veto. If vetoed, Congress must then muster a two-thirds majority of both houses to override the veto and enact the bill into law. But when the law Congress seeks to enact is legislation to address foreign policy issues, it will often designate the legislation as a joint resolution. Like a bill, a joint resolution is then presented to the President for signature or veto, and if vetoed may be enacted by congressional override. And importantly, like a bill enacted into law, a joint resolution, once enacted, has the force and effect of any other public law. In contrast, a concurrent resolution is not subject to presentment and veto and therefore does not have the force and effect of a public law.

During the 1930s, a war occurred in a region of Bolivia called the Chaco.[2] In an effort to bring an end to hostilities, Congress, working with the President, enacted a joint resolution that provided criminal penalties for the sale of certain

---

2. *See* Chaco War. 2016. *Encyclopædia Britannica Online*. Retrieved Feb. 15, 2016, from http://www.britannica.com/event/Chaco-War.

weapons to groups engaged in this conflict. However, Congress did not list what weapons fell within the scope of the criminal sanctions established by the law. Instead, the joint resolution empowered President Roosevelt to designate, by executive order, prohibited items. The President did so and the government then prosecuted Curtiss-Wright Export Corporation for violation of the joint resolution based on an allegation it sold weapons listed in the President's executive order.

Following conviction, Curtiss-Wright appealed, asserting that Congress has unconstitutionally delegated its lawmaking authority when it authorized the President to decide what weapons fell within the scope of the joint resolution.

BACKGROUND

United States v. Curtiss-Wright Export Corporation
299 U.S. 304 (1936)

Bolivians train anti-air gun on Paraguayan airplane on May 24, 1934. The Chaco War was fought over the Chaco Boreal wilderness. Everett Collection Historical/Alamy.

THE CHACO WAR IN A NUTSHELL

The war was fought between Paraguay and Bolivia. Both countries were (and are) landlocked. Each desired access to the Paraguay River. To add fuel to the fire, the disputed territory—known as the Chaco Boreal—was rumored at the time to hold massive unexplored reserves of oil. International oil companies in pursuit of their own interests exploited increasing tensions between the two countries, as did arms manufacturers eager to supply each side with weapons. War broke out in June 1932. The war lasted three years and claimed the lives of over 100,000 soldiers. A cease-fire was negotiated in June 1935. Following the war, the Chaco Boreal was determined to contain negligible reserves of oil.

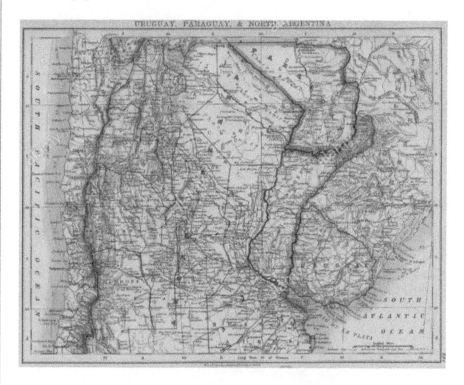

Pre-Chaco War Borders. Chile. 1906 map. Antiqua Print Gallery/Alamy.

Sources: Charles A. Lofgren, *United States v. Curtiss-Wright Export Corporation: An Historical Reassessment*, 83 YALE L.J. 1 (1973); Ryan Lindsay, "The Chaco War," ICE Case Study #48, at http ://www .american.edu/ted/ice/chaco.htm.

THE CRIMINAL CASE IN A NUTSHELL

The Curtiss-Wright Export Corporation, two other companies, and four corporate officers were indicted in the U.S. District Court for the Southern District of New York. The charge was conspiracy to sell aircraft machine guns to Bolivia, in violation of President Roosevelt's proclamation. The defendants challenged the indictment, *inter alia*, on constitutional grounds. The District Court sustained this challenge. A direct appeal to the Supreme Court followed.

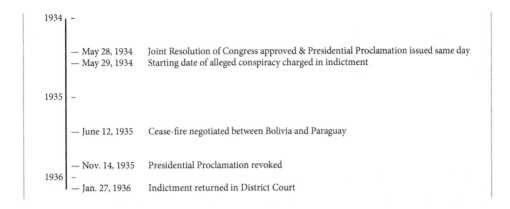

1934	—	
	— May 28, 1934	Joint Resolution of Congress approved & Presidential Proclamation issued same day
	— May 29, 1934	Starting date of alleged conspiracy charged in indictment
1935	—	
	— June 12, 1935	Cease-fire negotiated between Bolivia and Paraguay
	— Nov. 14, 1935	Presidential Proclamation revoked
1936	—	
	— Jan. 27, 1936	Indictment returned in District Court

As you read the Supreme Court's opinion resolving this appeal, try to identify the holding. What was the "narrowest ground" to resolve the appeal? Is that ground a particularly useful aspect of the opinion to invoke in support of broad presidential foreign affairs powers? Or does Justice Sutherland's opinion offer a more useful weapon in the battle to claim presidential primacy in this realm of government activity? If so, how far should the concept of "foreign affairs" extend?

United States v. Curtiss-Wright Export Corp.
299 U.S. 304 (1936)

Mr. Justice SUTHERLAND delivered the opinion of the Court.

On January 27, 1936, an indictment was returned in the court below, the first count of which charges that appellees, beginning with the 29th day of May, 1934, conspired to sell in the United States certain arms of war, namely fifteen machine guns, to Bolivia, a country then engaged in armed conflict in the Chaco, in violation of the Joint Resolution of Congress approved May 28, 1934, and the provisions of a proclamation issued on the same day by the President of the United States pursuant to authority conferred by § 1 of the resolution. In pursuance of the conspiracy, the commission of certain overt acts was alleged, details of which need not be stated. The Joint Resolution follows:

> *Resolved by the Senate and House of Representatives of the United States of America in Congress assembled*, That if the President finds that the prohibition of the sale of arms and munitions of war in the United States to those countries now engaged in armed conflict in the Chaco may contribute to the reestablishment of peace between those countries, and if after consultation with the governments of other American Republics and with their cooperation, as well as that of such other governments as he may deem necessary, he makes proclamation to that effect, it shall be unlawful to sell, except under such limitations and exceptions as the President prescribes, any arms or munitions of war in any place in the United States to the countries now engaged in that armed conflict, or to any person, company, or association acting in the interest of either country, until otherwise ordered by the President or by Congress.

Sec. 2. Whoever sells any arms or munitions of war in violation of section 1 shall, on conviction, be punished by a fine not exceeding $10,000 or by imprisonment not exceeding two years, or both.

The President's proclamation, after reciting the terms of the Joint Resolution, declares:

Now, therefore, I, Franklin D. Roosevelt, President of the United States of America, acting under and by virtue of the authority conferred in me by the said joint resolution of Congress, do hereby declare and proclaim that I have found that the prohibition of the sale of arms and munitions of war in the United States to those countries now engaged in armed conflict in the Chaco may contribute to the reestablishment of peace between those countries, and that I have consulted with the governments of other American Republics and have been assured of the cooperation of such governments as I have deemed necessary as contemplated by the said joint resolution; and I do hereby admonish all citizens of the United States and every person to abstain from every violation of the provisions of the joint resolution above set forth, hereby made applicable to Bolivia and Paraguay, and I do hereby warn them that all violations of such provisions will be rigorously prosecuted. . . .

Appellees severally demurred to the first count of the indictment on the grounds (1) that it did not charge facts sufficient to show the commission by appellees of any offense against any law of the United States. The points urged in support of the demurrers were, first, that the joint resolution effects an invalid delegation of legislative power to the executive.

The court below sustained the demurrers upon the first point. The government appealed. It is contended that by the Joint Resolution, the going into effect and continued operation of the resolution was conditioned (a) upon the President's judgment as to its beneficial effect upon the reestablishment of peace between the countries engaged in armed conflict in the Chaco; (b) upon the making of a proclamation, which was left to his unfettered discretion, thus constituting an attempted substitution of the President's will for that of Congress; (c) upon the making of a proclamation putting an end to the operation of the resolution, which again was left to the President's unfettered discretion; and (d) further, that the extent of its operation in particular cases was subject to limitation and exception by the President, controlled by no standard. In each of these particulars, appellees urge that Congress abdicated its essential functions and delegated them to the Executive.

Whether, if the Joint Resolution had related solely to internal affairs it would be open to the challenge that it constituted an unlawful delegation of legislative power to the Executive, we find it unnecessary to determine. The whole aim of the resolution is to affect a situation entirely external to the United States, and falling within the category of foreign affairs. The determination which we are called to make, therefore, is whether the Joint Resolution, as applied to that situation, is vulnerable to attack under the rule that forbids a delegation of the law-making power. In other words, assuming (but not deciding) that the challenged delegation, if it were confined to internal affairs, would be invalid, may it nevertheless be sustained on the ground that its exclusive aim is to afford a remedy for a hurtful condition within foreign territory?

It will contribute to the elucidation of the question if we first consider the differences between the powers of the federal government in respect of foreign or external affairs and those in respect of domestic or internal affairs. That there are differences between them, and that these differences are fundamental, may not be doubted.

The two classes of powers are different, both in respect of their origin and their nature. The broad statement that the federal government can exercise no powers except those specifically enumerated in the Constitution, and such implied powers as are necessary and proper to carry into effect the enumerated powers, is categorically true only in respect of our internal affairs. In that field, the primary purpose of the Constitution was to carve from the general mass of legislative powers *then possessed by the states* such portions as it was thought desirable to vest in the federal government, leaving those not included in the enumeration still in the states. *Carter v. Carter Coal Co.,* 298 U.S. 238, 294. That this doctrine applies only to powers which the states had, is self evident. And since the states severally never possessed international powers, such powers could not have been carved from the mass of state powers but obviously were transmitted to the United States from some other source. During the colonial period, those powers were possessed exclusively by and were entirely under the control of the Crown. By the Declaration of Independence, "the Representatives of the United States of America" declared the United (not the several) Colonies to be free and independent states, and as such to have "full Power to levy War, conclude Peace, contract Alliances, establish Commerce and to do all other Acts and Things which Independent States may of right do."

As a result of the separation from Great Britain by the colonies acting as a unit, the powers of external sovereignty passed from the Crown not to the colonies severally, but to the colonies in their collective and corporate capacity as the United States of America. Even before the Declaration, the colonies were a unit in foreign affairs, acting through a common agency—namely the Continental Congress, composed of delegates from the thirteen colonies. That agency exercised the powers of war and peace, raised an army, created a navy, and finally adopted the Declaration of Independence. Rulers come and go; governments end and forms of government change; but sovereignty survives. A political society cannot endure without a supreme will somewhere. Sovereignty is never held in suspense. When, therefore, the external sovereignty of Great Britain in respect of the colonies ceased, it immediately passed to the Union. *See Penhallow v. Doane,* 3 Dall. 54, 80-81. That fact was given practical application almost at once. The treaty of peace, made on September 23, 1783, was concluded between his Brittanic Majesty and the "United States of America."

The Union existed before the Constitution, which was ordained and established among other things to form "a more perfect Union." Prior to that event, it is clear that the Union, declared by the Articles of Confederation to be "perpetual," was the sole possessor of external sovereignty and in the Union it remained without change save in so far as the Constitution in express terms qualified its exercise. The Framers' Convention was called and exerted its powers upon the irrefutable postulate that though the states were several their people in respect of foreign affairs were one. . . .

It results that the investment of the federal government with the powers of external sovereignty did not depend upon the affirmative grants of the Constitution. The powers to declare and wage war, to conclude peace, to make treaties, to maintain diplomatic relations with other sovereignties, if they had never been mentioned in the Constitution, would have vested in the federal government as necessary concomitants of nationality. Neither the Constitution nor the laws passed in pursuance of it have any force in foreign territory unless in respect of our own citizens; and operations of the nation in such territory must be governed by treaties, international understandings and compacts, and the principles of international law. As a member of the family of nations, the right and power of the United States in that field are equal to the right and power of the other members of the international family. Otherwise, the United States is not completely sovereign. The power to acquire territory by discovery and occupation, the power to expel undesirable aliens, the power to make such international agreements as do not constitute treaties in the constitutional sense, none of which is expressly affirmed by the Constitution, nevertheless exist as inherently inseparable from the conception of nationality. This the court recognized, and in each of the cases cited found the warrant for its conclusions not in the provisions of the Constitution, but in the law of nations. . . .

Not only, as we have shown, is the federal power over external affairs in origin and essential character different from that over internal affairs, but participation in the exercise of the power is significantly limited. In this vast external realm, with its important, complicated, delicate and manifold problems, the President alone has the power to speak or listen as a representative of the nation. He *makes* treaties with the advice and consent of the Senate; but he alone negotiates. Into the field of negotiation the Senate cannot intrude; and Congress itself is powerless to invade it. As Marshall said in his great argument of March 7, 1800, in the House of Representatives, "The President is the sole organ of the nation in its external relations, and its sole representative with foreign nations." Annals, 6th Cong., col. 613. The Senate Committee on Foreign Relations at a very early day in our history (February 15, 1816), reported to the Senate, among other things, as follows:

> The President is the constitutional representative of the United States with regard to foreign nations. He manages our concerns with foreign nations and must necessarily be most competent to determine when, how, and upon what subjects negotiation may be urged with the greatest prospect of success. For

his conduct he is responsible to the Constitution. The committee consider this responsibility the surest pledge for the faithful discharge of his duty. They think the interference of the Senate in the direction of foreign negotiations calculated to diminish that responsibility and thereby to impair the best security for the national safety. The nature of transactions with foreign nations, moreover, requires caution and unity of design, and their success frequently depends on secrecy and dispatch. U.S. Senate, Reports, Committee on Foreign Relations, vol. 8, p. 24.

It is important to bear in mind that we are here dealing not alone with an authority vested in the President by an exertion of legislative power, but with such an authority plus the very delicate, plenary and exclusive power of the President as the sole organ of the federal government in the field of international relations—a power which does not require as a basis for its exercise an act of Congress, but which, of course, like every other governmental power, must be exercised in subordination to the applicable provisions of the Constitution. It is quite apparent that if, in the maintenance of our international relations, embarrassment—perhaps serious embarrassment—is to be avoided and success for our aims achieved, congressional legislation which is to be made effective through negotiation and inquiry within the international field must often accord to the President a degree of discretion and freedom from statutory restriction which would not be admissible were domestic affairs alone involved. Moreover, he, not Congress, has the better opportunity of knowing the conditions which prevail in foreign countries, and especially is this true in time of war. He has his confidential sources of information. He has his agents in the form of diplomatic, consular and other officials. Secrecy in respect of information gathered by them may be highly necessary, and the premature disclosure of it productive of harmful results. Indeed, so clearly is this true that the first President refused to accede to a request to lay before the House of Representatives the instructions, correspondence and documents relating to the negotiation of the Jay Treaty—a refusal the wisdom of which was recognized by the House itself, and has never since been doubted. . . .

. . .

When the President is to be authorized by legislation to act in respect of a matter intended to affect a situation in foreign territory, the legislator properly bears in mind the important consideration that the form of the President's action or, indeed, whether he shall act at all—may well depend, among other things, upon the nature of the confidential information which he has or may thereafter receive, or upon the effect which his action may have upon our foreign relations. This consideration, in connection with what we have already said on the subject, discloses the unwisdom of requiring Congress in this field of governmental power to lay down narrowly definite standards by which the President is to be governed. As this court said in *Mackenzie v. Hare*, 239 U.S. 299, 239 U.S. 311,

> "As a government, the United States is invested with all the attributes of sovereignty. As it has the character of nationality, it has the powers of nationality,

especially those which concern its relations and intercourse with other countries. *We should hesitate long before limiting or embarrassing such powers.*" (Italics supplied.)

In the light of the foregoing observations, it is evident that this court should not be in haste to apply a general rule which will have the effect of condemning legislation like that under review as constituting an unlawful delegation of legislative power. The principles which justify such legislation find overwhelming support in the unbroken legislative practice which has prevailed almost from the inception of the national government to the present day.

. . . A legislative practice such as we have here, evidenced not by only occasional instances, but marked by the movement of a steady stream for a century and a half of time, goes a long way in the direction of proving the presence of unassailable ground for the constitutionality of the practice, to be found in the origin and history of the power involved, or in its nature, or in both combined. . . .

Mr. Justice MCREYNOLDS does not agree. . . .

Mr. Justice STONE took no part in the consideration or decision of this case.

CURTISS-WRIGHT IN CONTEXT

Curtiss-Wright was not decided in a vacuum. The Court had very recently struck down several pieces of New Deal legislation as unconstitutional, notably on Commerce Clause grounds and under the nondelegation doctrine. Three examples:

1. *Panama Refining Co. v. Ryan*, 293 U.S. 388, was decided on January 7, 1935. In this case—popularly known as the "hot oil" case—the Court held that an executive order to regulate interstate shipments of oil under the National Industrial Recovery Act of 1933 (NIRA) violated the nondelegation doctrine.
2. *Schechter Poultry Corp. v. United States*, 295 U.S. 495, was decided approximately six months later, on May 27, 1935. In this case—the "sick chicken" case—the Court held that NIRA was also unconstitutional under the nondelegation doctrine because it granted private parties acting in trade associations the power to issue industry-wide standards and codes of fair competition. Violation of these codes was a misdemeanor offense.
3. *Carter v. Carter Coal Co.*, 298 U.S. 238, was decided on May 18, 1936. The Court struck down the Bituminous Coal Conservation Act of 1935 as an unconstitutional assertion of the Commerce Clause power and as an unconstitutional delegation of legislative powers to fix hours and wages in the nation's coal industry.

Carter Coal was decided approximately six months before *Curtiss-Wright*. Justice Sutherland delivered the opinion of the Court in both cases. In *Carter Coal*, Justice Sutherland wrote:

> The proposition, often advanced and as often discredited, that the power of the federal government inherently extends to purposes affecting the Nation as a whole with which the states severally cannot deal or cannot adequately deal, and the related notion that Congress, entirely apart from those powers delegated by the Constitution, may enact laws to promote the general welfare, have never been accepted but always definitely rejected by this court. Mr. Justice Story, as early as 1816, laid down the cardinal rule, which has ever since been followed — that the general government "can claim no powers which are not granted to it by the constitution, and the powers actually granted, must be such as are expressly given, or given by necessary implication."

Id. at 291-92. Further along in that opinion, Justice Sutherland wrote:

> It is no longer open to question that the general government, unlike the states, possesses no inherent power in respect of the internal affairs of the states; and emphatically not with regard to legislation. *The question in respect of the inherent power of that government as to the external affairs of the Nation and in the field of international law is a wholly different matter which it is not necessary now to consider.*

Id. at 295 (citation omitted) (emphasis added).

NOTES AND QUESTIONS

1. It should be obvious why *Curtiss-Wright* is so often cited by proponents of expansive presidential authority over any issue related to foreign affairs. Is such citation based on the Court's holding? Does the Court provide any guidance on assessing what qualifies as "foreign affairs" for purposes of presidential powers? If not, how should this term be interpreted?

2. The Court's decision emphasized the logic of Congress affording the President greater flexibility when dealing with issues in the realm of foreign affairs. Do you think the Court's "foreign affairs" emphasis was appropriate for this case? After all, this was a prosecution in the United States of a U.S. person from a U.S. company (descended, incidentally, from the Wright brothers' original company!), and all the alleged misconduct occurred in the United States. And the joint resolution avoids use of foreign policy tools directed at the states involved, instead of at the domestic sales.

3. Many government actions impact both foreign and domestic affairs. Indeed, Curtiss-Wright was challenging a domestic criminal accusation. Might it be

logical to consider issues running across a spectrum from purely domestic to purely foreign affairs, with where the issue falls along that spectrum impacting the deference to presidential authority?

4. What logic supported the Court's conclusion that legislation focused primarily on foreign affairs should be interpreted more deferentially in favor of executive implementation than legislation focused primarily on domestic affairs?

5. Was it necessary for the Court to analyze the nature of presidential foreign affairs powers in order to decide the issue presented? If so, why?

6. Do you think the Court would have upheld the criminal conviction if it had been based exclusively on an executive order issued by the President? In other words, could the President have imposed a criminal consequence for violating an executive order without a legislative foundation? If not, could the President have done anything based on his constitutional authority to prohibit weapons sales?

7. Could Congress have used a concurrent resolution (instead of a joint resolution) to delegate the authority to the President to invoke a criminal sanction? If not, why not?

8. The Court noted that the President has "the power to make such international agreements as do not constitute treaties in the constitutional sense. . . ." Do you think the Constitution imposes any limits on such agreements?

III. WAR, STEEL, AND THE SIGNIFICANCE OF CONSTITUTIONAL TURF

On June 25, 1950, North Korean military forces launched a massive surprise attack on South Korea, determined to reunite the two Koreas under one communist government. In a fortuitous twist of fate the attack began while the Soviet Union was boycotting the United Nations Security Council in protest over the refusal of the Council to oust Taiwan (Nationalist China) from the permanent seat on the Council belonging to China and award the seat to the People's Republic of China. With no Soviet veto to block a Security Council authorization for member states to come to South Korea's aid with military force, the Security Council enacted Resolution 84 on July 7, 1950.

The United States had commenced combat operations in response to the North Korean aggression even before the Security Council enacted the authorization. Acting pursuant to the Charter's collective self-defense provision (Article 51), President Truman committed U.S. forces to action in this first major incident of the emerging Cold War turning hot. Although Congress neither declared war nor enacted a specific statutory authorization for the U.S. military action, it did enact a range of laws that provided the President with the personnel and the resources to wage the war. One of these laws provided for procurement of weapons and ammunition to sustain the war, imposing on President Truman an ostensible obligation to implement this military procurement program.

Labor disputes in U.S. steel mills, which eventually culminated in a strike effectively shutting down steel production, presented a problem for President Truman's military obligations. Pursuant to the Taft-Hartley Labor Relations Act, efforts to end the strike through mediation failed. The authority provided to the President by Taft-Hartley was, however, limited, as Congress had rejected including a provision granting the President authority to seize industry to restore production should mediation efforts fail.

As a result of the strike, the President concluded that defense procurement was placed in jeopardy. Seemingly caught between a requirement to fulfill the procurement program objectives and the limits of labor dispute settlement authority included in Taft-Hartley, President Truman invoked an amalgam of constitutional and statutory authorities to seize the steel mills, place them under the control of the Secretary of Commerce, and bring an end to the strike by granting concessions to labor. His executive order provided:

Exec. Order No. 10340, 17 Fr 3139
DIRECTING THE SECRETARY OF COMMERCE TO TAKE POSSESSION OF AND OPERATE THE PLANTS AND FACILITIES OF CERTAIN STEEL

April 8, 1952

WHEREAS on December 16, 1950, I proclaimed the existence of a national emergency which requires that the military, naval, air, and civilian defenses of this country be strengthened as speedily as possible to the end that we may be able to repel any and all threats against our national security and to fulfill our responsibilities in the efforts being made throughout the United Nations and otherwise to bring about a lasting peace; and

WHEREAS American fighting men and fighting men of other nations of the United Nations are now engaged in deadly combat with the forces of aggression in Korea, and forces of the United States are stationed elsewhere overseas for the purpose of participating in the defense of the Atlantic Community against aggression; and

WHEREAS the weapons and other materials needed by our armed forces and by those joined with us in the defense of the free world are produced to a great extent in this country, and steel is an indispensable component of substantially all of such weapons and materials; and

. . .

WHEREAS a controversy has arisen between certain companies in the United States producing and fabricating steel and the elements thereof and certain of their workers represented by the United Steel Workers of America, CIO, regarding terms and conditions of employment; and

WHEREAS a work stoppage would immediately jeopardize and imperil our national defense and the defense of those joined with us in resisting aggression, and would add to the continuing danger of our soldiers, sailors, and airmen engaged in combat in the field; and

WHEREAS in order to assure the continued availability of steel and steel products during the existing emergency, it is necessary that the United States take possession of and operate the plants, facilities, and other property of the said companies as hereinafter provided:

NOW, THEREFORE, by virtue of the authority vested in me by the Constitution and laws of the United States, and as President of the United States and Commander in Chief of the armed forces of the United States, it is hereby ordered as follows:

1. The Secretary of Commerce is hereby authorized and directed to take possession of all or such of the plants, facilities, and other property of the companies named in the list attached hereto, or any part thereof, as he may deem necessary in the interests of national defense; and to operate or to arrange for the operation thereof and to do all things necessary for, or incidental to, such operation.

   . . .

3. The Secretary of Commerce shall determine and prescribe terms and conditions of employment under which the plants, facilities, and other properties possession of which is taken pursuant to this order shall be operated. The Secretary of Commerce shall recognize the rights of workers to bargain collectively through representatives of their own choosing and to engage in concerted activities for the purpose of collective bargaining, adjustment of grievances, or other mutual aid or protection, provided that such activities do not interfere with the operation of such plants, facilities, and other properties.

4. Except so far as the Secretary of Commerce shall otherwise provide from time to time, the managements of the plants, facilities, and other properties possession of which is taken pursuant to this order shall continue their functions, including the collection and disbursement of funds in the usual and ordinary course of business in the names of their respective companies and by means of any instrumentalities used by such companies.

Harry S. Truman
The White House,
April 8, 1952.

List

American Bridge Company 525 William Penn Place Pittsburgh, PA
American Steel & Wire Co. of New Jersey Rockefeller Building Cleveland, OH
Columbia Steel Company Russ Building San Francisco, CA
Consolidated Western Steel Corporation Los Angeles, CA
Geneva Steel Company Salt Lake City, Utah
Gerrard Steel Strapping Company 2915 W. 47th Street Chicago 32, IL
National Tube Company 525 William Penn Place Pittsburgh, PA
Oil Well Supply Company 2001 North Lamar Street Dallas, Texas
Tennessee Coal, Iron & Railroad Company Fairfield, Alabama
United States Steel Company 525 William Penn Place Pittsburgh, PA
United States Steel Corporation 71 Broadway New York 6, New York
United States Steel Products Company 30 Rockefeller Plaza New York, NY
United States Steel Supply Company 208 South La Salle Street Chicago, IL
Virginia Bridge Company Roanoke, Virginia
Alan Wood Steel Company and Subsidiaries Conshohocken, Pennsylvania
American Chain and Cable Co., Inc., 929 Connecticut Avenue Bridgeport 2, CT
American Chain and Cable Company Monessen, Pennsylvania
Armco Steel Corporation 703 Curtis Street Middletown, Ohio
Armco Drainage & Metal Products, Inc. 703 Curtis Street Middletown, OH
Atlantic Steel Company P. O. Box 1714 Atlanta, Georgia
Babcock and Wilcox Tube Company Beaver Falls, Pennsylvania
Borg-Warner Corporation 310 S. Michigan Avenue Chicago 4, Illinois
Continental Copper and Steel Industries, Incorporated Braeburn, Pennsylvania
Continental Steel Corporation West Markland Avenue Kokomo, Indiana
Copperweld Steel Company Glassport, Pennsylvania
Detroit Steel Corporation 1025 South Oakwood Avenue Detroit 9, Michigan
Eastern Stainless Steel Corporation Baltimore 3, Maryland
Firth Sterling Steel and Carbide Corporation Demmler Road McKeesport, PA
Follansbee Steel Corporation 3rd and Liberty Avenue Pittsburgh 22, PA
Granite City Steel Company 20th Street and Madison Avenue Granite City, IL
Great Lakes Steel Corporation Tecumseh Road Ecorse, Detroit 18, Michigan
Hanna Furnace Corporation Ecorse, Detroit 18, Michigan
Harrisburg Steel Corporation 10th and Herr Streets Harrisburg, PA
Boiardi Steel Company Milton, Pennsylvania
Heppenstall Company 4620 Hatfield Street Pittsburgh, Pennsylvania
Inland Steel Company 38 S. Dearborn Street Chicago 3, Illinois
Joseph T. Ryerson & Son, Incorporated 2558 W. 16th Street Chicago 80, IL
Interlake Iron Corporation 1900 Union Commerce Building Cleveland 14, OH
Pacific States Steel Corporation Lathan Square Building Oakland 12, CA
Pittsburgh Coke & Chemical Company 1905 Grant Building Pittsburgh 19, PA
H. K. Porter Company, Incorporated 1932 Oliver Building Pittsburgh 22, PA
Buffalo Steel Division H. K. Porter Co., Inc., Fillmore Avenue Tonawanda, NY
Joslyn Manufacturing & Supply Company 20 N. Wacker Drive Chicago 6, IL

Joslyn Pacific Company 5100 District Boulevard Los Angeles 11, CA
Latrobe Electric Steel Company Latrobe, Pennsylvania
E. J. Lavino & Company 1528 Walnut Street Philadelphia, Pennsylvania
Lukens Steel Company S. First Avenue Coatesville, Pennsylvania
McLouth Steel Corporation 300 S. Livernois Detroit 17, Michigan
Newport Steel Corporation Ninth and Lowell Streets Newport, Kentucky
Northwest Steel Rolling Mills, Inc., 4315 9th Street N. W. Seattle, WA
Northwestern Steel & Wire Company Sterling, Illinois
Reeves Steel Manufacturing Company 137 Iron Avenue Dover, Ohio
John A. Roebling's Sons Co., 640 South Broad Street Trenton, NJ
Rotary Electric Steel Company Box 90 Detroit 20, Michigan
Sheffield Steel Corporation Sheffield Station Kansas City 3, Missouri
Shenango-Penn Mold Company 812 Oliver Building Pittsburgh 30, PA
Shenango Furnace Company 812 Oliver Building Pittsburgh 30, PA
Stanley Works 195 Lake Street New Britain, Connecticut
Universal Cyclops Steel Corporation Station Street Bridgeville, PA
Vanadium-Alloys Steel Company Latrobe, Pennsylvania
Vulcan Crucible Steel Company 1 Main Street Aliquippa, PA
Wheeling Steel Corporation 1134 Market Street Wheeling, WV
Woodward Iron Company Woodward, Alabama
Allegheny Ludlum Steel Corporation Oliver Building Pittsburgh 22, PA
Bethlehem Steel Company 701 East 3rd Street Bethlehem, Pennsylvania
Bethlehem Pacific Coast Steel Corp., 20th & Illinois Streets San Francisco, CA
Bethlehem Supply Company of California Los Angeles, California
Bethlehem Supply Company Tulsa, Oklahoma
Buffalo Tank Corp., Lackawanna, NY, Charlotte, NC, Dunellen, NJ
Dundalk Company Sparrows Point, Maryland
A. M. Byers Company 717 Liberty Avenue Pittsburgh 30, PA
Colorado Fuel & Iron Corporation 575 Madison Avenue New York 22, NY
Claymont Steel Corporation Claymont, Delaware
Crucible Steel Company Oliver Building Pittsburgh 22, Pennsylvania
Jones & Laughlin Steel Corp., Third Avenue and Ross Street Pittsburgh 30, PA
J. & L. Steel Barrel Company 3711 Sepviva Street Philadelphia 37, Pennsylvania
National Supply Company 1400 Grant Building Pittsburgh 30, Pennsylvania
Pittsburgh Steel Company 1600 Grant Building Pittsburgh 19, Pennsylvania
Johnson Steel & Wire Company, Incorporated 53 Wiser Avenue Worcester 1, MA
Republic Steel Corporation Republic Building Cleveland 1, Ohio
Truscon Steel Company 1315 Albert Street Youngstown, Ohio
Rheem Manufacturing Company Russ Building San Francisco 4, California
Sharon Steel Corporation S. Irvine Avenue Sharon, Pennsylvania
Valley Mould & Iron Corporation Hubbard, Ohio
Youngstown Sheet & Tube Company 44 Central Square Youngstown 1, Ohio
Emsco Derrick & Equipment Company 6811 S. Alameda Street Los Angeles 1, CA

Unsurprisingly, the owners of the steel mills challenged the seizure as an unconstitutional taking. The District Court agreed, granting an injunction against the President and Secretary of Commerce. Six Justices of the Supreme Court agreed with the District Court and struck down the seizure. In his opinion for the Court, Justice Hugo Black offered a quite simple textual basis for the decision: Congress, not the President, is vested with lawmaking authority, and only Congress could act to authorize a seizure of property, because only Congress can authorize just compensation. While each Justice concurring agreed with Justice Black's ultimate conclusion that the President had exceeded his constitutional authority, they reached that conclusion through much more nuanced assessments of constitutional power.

Perhaps no judicial decision has had a more profound impact on national security practice than *Youngstown Sheet & Tube Co. v. Sawyer*, commonly known as *The Steel Seizure Case*. Some scholars continue to insist that this decision had nothing to do with national security and/or foreign affairs, but was simply about a domestic taking. It is indeed uncontroverted that the precise issue that brought the case before the Supreme Court did involve the constitutionality of a domestic taking. However, as you read the concurring and dissenting opinions, consider how the broader geo-strategic context, coupled with the President's asserted authority for the taking and the Court's approach to resolving the issue, warrant the stature that has been accorded to this decision.

As you read the following opinions, consider several important questions. Did any other Justice view the issue through Justice Black's straightforward textualist lens? Why were the dissenting Justices willing to endorse the taking? Was it based on exclusive presidential power or did they believe the President was acting to execute congressional will? Why was it so significant for each of the Justices in the majority that Congress had considered, but rejected, a request to include seizure authority within Taft-Hartley? Do you have the sense that the majority Justices were skeptical that the nation confronted a genuine emergency even though the President had made that assertion in his executive order? How might the conclusion that the nation was in fact in the midst of a genuine emergency have altered the lineup of Justices in the opinion?

WHAT WERE PRESIDENT TRUMAN'S STATUTORY OPTIONS?

As the labor dispute worsened between the steelworkers' union and major steel companies, President Truman had a few statutory options to consider. Because of the Korean War, Congress had granted Truman the power to regulate wages and prices. This complicated the contract negotiations. Steelworkers demanded a significant raise in wages, but the steel companies resisted without a government promise to cover their expenses by raising steel prices. Strike threatened when different government agencies (Wage Stabilization Board and Office of Price Stabilization) could not agree on balancing wage and price changes.

Labor Management Relations Act	Selective Service Act	Defense Production Act
a.k.a. "Taft-Hartley Act" Sets forth Nat'l Labor Rel. Bd. rights/ procedures, provides basics of unfair labor practices, labor organizations, etc. If potential strike could result in national emergency, Act sets forth procedure to follow. Gov't could seek court order enjoining strike for 80 days ("cooling-off period"). If strike still likely, President required to submit report and recommendation to Congress re: how to prevent nat'l emergency. Injunction, as a rule, requires court finding of: —irreparable injury; —no adequate legal remedy; —likelihood of victory on merits; —balancing of the equities.	Section 18 authorized president to place orders for defense materials with any manufacturer, so long as procurement already authorized by Congress. Manufacturer's failure to fill order within specified time would permit President to seize possession of property and operate it to ensure timely production of materials. Government must pay just compensation for the seizure. Truman Administration concerned about applicability where failure to fill order due to labor dispute. Also, this approach disfavored because of lengthy procedures required by the Act: First, time-consuming to place orders, especially since DoD did not buy raw steel but end products made from steel. Second, unclear whether must wait for specified time period to fill order to pass before seizing property, but probably only then could President issue executive order for seizure.	Title II gives President power to requisition property if he determines that its use is "needed for the national defense." But this sounds deceptively simple. Actually quite difficult and lengthy process: must start condemnation proceedings, which involve court filings and deposit of anticipated just compensation. This would be extremely costly in case of steel mills. Further, unclear whether power could be used to avoid labor dispute. This was the Truman Administration's least favored option. Title IV grants President power to set discretionary wage and price controls to prevent inflation and stabilize cost of living. Title V authorizes President to initiate voluntary conferences to settle labor disputes, so long as no conflict with Taft-Hartley Act. Under this statute, Truman established an Economic Stabilization Agency and a Wage Stabilization Board.

Sources: Maeva Marcus, Truman and the Steel Seizure Case (1994); William Rehnquist, The Supreme Court (2001).

Youngstown Sheet & Tube Co. v. Sawyer
(The Steel Seizure Case)
343 U.S. 579 (1952)

Mr. Justice BLACK delivered the opinion of the Court.

We are asked to decide whether the President was acting within his constitutional power when he issued an order directing the Secretary of Commerce to take possession of and operate most of the Nation's steel mills. The mill owners argue that the President's order amounts to lawmaking, a legislative function which the Constitution has expressly confided to the Congress and not to the President. The Government's position is that the order was made on findings of the President that his action was necessary to avert a national catastrophe which would inevitably result from a stoppage of steel production, and that in meeting this grave emergency the President was acting within the aggregate of his constitutional powers as the Nation's Chief Executive and the Commander in Chief of the Armed Forces of the United States. . . .

. . . The Secretary immediately issued his own possessory orders, calling upon the presidents of the various seized companies to serve as operating managers for the United States. They were directed to carry on their activities in accordance with regulations and directions of the Secretary. The next morning the President sent a message to Congress reporting his action. . . . Twelve days later he sent a second message. . . . Congress has taken no action.

Obeying the Secretary's orders under protest, the companies brought proceedings against him in the District Court. . . . Holding against the Government on all points, the District Court on April 30 issued a preliminary injunction restraining the Secretary from "continuing the seizure and possession of the plants . . . and from acting under the purported authority of Executive Order 10340."

. . . The President's power, if any, to issue the order must stem either from an act of Congress or from the Constitution itself. There is no statute that expressly authorizes the President to take possession of property as he did here. Nor is there any act of Congress to which our attention has been directed from which such a power can fairly be implied. Indeed, we do not understand the Government to rely on statutory authorization for this seizure. There are two statutes which do authorize the President to take both personal and real property under certain conditions.

However, the Government admits that these conditions were not met and that the President's order was not rooted in either of the statutes. The Government refers to the seizure provisions of one of these statutes (§ 201(b) of the Defense Production Act) as "much too cumbersome, involved, and time-consuming for the crisis which was at hand."

Moreover, the use of the seizure technique to solve labor disputes in order to prevent work stoppages was not only unauthorized by any congressional enactment; prior to this controversy, Congress had refused to adopt that method of settling labor disputes. When the Taft-Hartley Act was under consideration in 1947, Congress rejected an amendment which would have authorized such governmental seizures in cases of emergency. Apparently it was thought that the technique of seizure, like that of compulsory arbitration, would interfere with the process of collective bargaining. Consequently, the plan Congress adopted in that Act did not provide for seizure under any circumstances. Instead, the plan sought to bring about settlements by use of the customary devices of mediation, conciliation, investigation by boards of inquiry, and public reports. In some instances temporary injunctions were authorized to provide cooling-off periods.

All this failing, unions were left free to strike after a secret vote by employees as to whether they wished to accept their employers' final settlement offer.

It is clear that if the President had authority to issue the order he did, it must be found in some provision of the Constitution. And it is not claimed that express constitutional language grants this power to the President. The contention is that presidential power should be implied from the aggregate of his powers under the Constitution. Particular reliance is placed on provisions in Article II which say that "The executive Power shall be vested in a President . . ."; that "he shall take Care that the Laws be faithfully executed"; and that he "shall be Commander in Chief of the Army and Navy of the United States."

The order cannot properly be sustained as an exercise of the President's military power as Commander in Chief of the Armed Forces. The Government attempts to do so by citing a number of cases upholding broad powers in military commanders engaged in day-to-day fighting in a theater of war. Such cases need not concern us here. Even though "theater of war" be an expanding concept, we cannot with faithfulness to our constitutional system hold that the Commander in Chief of the Armed Forces has the ultimate power as such to take possession of private property in order to keep labor disputes from stopping production. This is a job for the Nation's lawmakers, not for its military authorities.

Nor can the seizure order be sustained because of the several constitutional provisions that grant executive power to the President. In the framework of our Constitution, the President's power to see that the laws are faithfully executed refutes the idea that he is to be a lawmaker. The Constitution limits his functions in the lawmaking process to the recommending of laws he thinks wise and the vetoing of laws he thinks bad. And the Constitution is neither silent nor equivocal about who shall make laws which the President is to execute. The first section of the first article says that "All legislative Powers herein granted shall be vested in a Congress of the United States. . . ." After granting many powers to the Congress, Article I goes on to provide that Congress may "make all Laws which shall be necessary and proper for carrying into Execution the foregoing Powers, and all other Powers vested by this Constitution in the Government of the United States, or in any Department or Officer thereof."

The President's order does not direct that a congressional policy be executed in a manner prescribed by Congress—it directs that a presidential policy be executed in a manner prescribed by the President. The preamble of the order itself, like that of many statutes, sets out reasons why the President believes certain policies should be adopted, proclaims these policies as rules of conduct to be followed, and again, like a statute, authorizes a government official to promulgate additional rules and regulations consistent with the policy proclaimed and needed to carry that policy into execution. The power of Congress to adopt such public policies as those proclaimed by the order is beyond question. It can authorize the taking of private property for public use. It can make laws regulating the relationships between employers and employees, prescribing rules designed to settle labor disputes, and fixing wages and working conditions in certain fields of our economy. The Constitution does not subject this lawmaking power of Congress to presidential or military supervision or control.

It is said that other Presidents without congressional authority have taken possession of private business enterprises in order to settle labor disputes. But even if this be true, Congress has not thereby lost its exclusive constitutional authority to make laws necessary and proper to carry out the powers vested by the Constitution "in the Government of the United States, or any Department or Officer thereof."

The Founders of this Nation entrusted the lawmaking power to the Congress alone in both good and bad times. It would do no good to recall the historical events, the fears of power and the hopes for freedom that lay behind their choice. Such a review would but confirm our holding that this seizure order cannot stand.

The judgment of the District Court is affirmed.

Mr. Justice FRANKFURTER, concurring. . . . The issues before us can be met, and therefore should be, without attempting to define the President's powers comprehensively. . . .

. . . We must therefore put to one side consideration of what powers the President would have had if there had been no legislation whatever bearing on the authority asserted by the seizure, or if the seizure had been only for a short, explicitly temporary period, to be terminated automatically unless Congressional approval were given. These and other questions, like or unlike, are not now here.

. . . No room for doubt remains that the proponents as well as the opponents of the bill which became the Labor Management Relations Act of 1947 clearly understood that as a result of that legislation the only recourse for preventing a shutdown in any basic industry, after failure of mediation, was Congress. . . .

. . . Previous seizure legislation had subjected the powers granted to the President to restrictions of varying degrees of stringency. Instead of giving him even limited powers, Congress in 1947 deemed it wise to require the President, upon failure of attempts to reach a voluntary settlement, to report to Congress if he deemed the power of seizure a needed shot for his locker. The President could not ignore the specific limitations of prior seizure statutes. No more could he act in disregard of the limitation put upon seizure by the 1947 Act.

It cannot be contended that the President would have had power to issue this order had Congress explicitly negated such authority in formal legislation. Congress has expressed its will to withhold this power from the President as though it had said so in so many words. The authoritatively expressed purpose of Congress to disallow such power to the President and to require him, when in his mind the occasion arose for such a seizure, to put the matter to Congress and ask for specific authority from it, could not be more decisive if it had been written into . . . the Labor Management Relations Act of 1947. . . .

. . . The utmost that the Korean conflict may imply is that it may have been desirable to have given the President further authority, a freer hand in these matters. Absence of authority in the President to deal with a crisis does not imply want of power in the Government. Conversely the fact that power exists in the Government does not vest it in the President. The need for new legislation does not enact it. Nor does it repeal or amend existing law. . . .

It is one thing to draw an intention of Congress from general language and to say that Congress would have explicitly written what is inferred, where Congress has not addressed itself to a specific situation. It is quite impossible, however, when Congress did specifically address itself to a problem, as Congress did to that of seizure, to find secreted in the interstices of legislation the very grant of power which Congress consciously withheld. To find authority so explicitly withheld is not merely to disregard in a particular instance the clear will of Congress. It is to disrespect the whole legislative process and the constitutional division of authority between President and Congress. . . .

To be sure, the content of the three authorities of government is not to be derived from an abstract analysis. The areas are partly interacting, not wholly disjointed. The Constitution is a framework for government. Therefore the way the framework has consistently operated fairly establishes that it has operated according to its true nature. Deeply embedded traditional ways of conducting government cannot supplant the Constitution or legislation, but they give meaning to the words of a text or supply them. It is an inadmissibly narrow conception of American constitutional law to confine it to the words of the Constitution and to disregard the gloss which life has written upon them. In short, a systematic, unbroken, executive practice, long pursued to the knowledge of the Congress and never before questioned, engaged in by Presidents who have also sworn to uphold the Constitution, making as it were such exercise of power part of the structure of our government, may be treated as a gloss on "executive Power" vested in the President by § 1 of Art. II. . . .

. . . In the *Midwest Oil* [236 U.S. 459 (1915)] case, lands which Congress had opened for entry were, over a period of 80 years and in 252 instances, and by Presidents learned and unlearned in the law, temporarily withdrawn from entry so as to enable Congress to deal with such withdrawals. No remotely comparable practice can be vouched for executive seizure of property at a time when this country was not at war, in the only constitutional way in which it can be at war. It would pursue the irrelevant to reopen the controversy over the constitutionality of some acts of Lincoln during the Civil War. . . . Suffice it to say that he seized railroads in territory where armed hostilities had already interrupted the movement of troops to the beleaguered Capital, and his order was ratified by the Congress.

The only other instances of seizures are those during the periods of the first and second World Wars. In his eleven seizures of industrial facilities, President Wilson acted, or at least purported to act, under authority granted by Congress. Thus his seizures cannot be adduced as interpretations by a President of his own powers in the absence of statute.

Down to the World War II period, then, the record is barren of instances comparable to the one before us. Of twelve seizures by President Roosevelt prior to the enactment of the War Labor Disputes Act in June, 1943, three were sanctioned by existing law, and six others were effected after Congress, on December 8, 1941, had declared the existence of a state of war. In this case, reliance on the powers that flow from declared war has been commendably disclaimed by the Solicitor General. Thus the list of executive assertions of the power of seizure in circumstances comparable to the present reduces to three in the six-month period from June to December of 1941. We need not split hairs in comparing those actions to the one before us, though much might be said by way of differentiation. Without passing on their validity, as we are not called upon to do, it suffices to say that these three isolated instances do not add up, either in number, scope, duration or contemporaneous legal justification, to the kind of executive construction of the Constitution revealed in the *Midwest Oil* case. Nor do they come to us sanctioned by long-continued acquiescence of Congress giving decisive weight to a construction by the Executive of its powers. . . .

Mr. Justice DOUGLAS, concurring. . . . The legislative nature of the action taken by the President seems to me to be clear. When the United States takes over an industrial plant to settle a labor controversy, it is condemning property. The seizure of the plant is a taking in the constitutional sense. . . .

But there is a duty to pay for all property taken by the Government. The command of the Fifth Amendment is that no "private property be taken for public use, without just compensation." . . .

The President has no power to raise revenues. That power is in the Congress by Article I, Section 8 of the Constitution. . . . The branch of government that has the power to pay compensation for a seizure is the only one able to authorize a seizure or make lawful one that the President has effected. . . .

Stalemates may occur when emergencies mount and the Nation suffers for lack of harmonious, reciprocal action between the White House and Capitol Hill. That is a risk inherent in our system of separation of powers. The tragedy of such stalemates might be avoided by allowing the President the use of some legislative authority. The Framers with memories of the tyrannies produced by a blending of executive and legislative power rejected that political arrangement. Some future generation may, however, deem it so urgent that the President have legislative authority that the Constitution will be amended. We could not sanction the seizures and condemnations of the steel plants in this case without reading Article II as giving the President not only the power to execute the laws but to make some. . . .

Mr. Justice Jackson, concurring in the judgment and opinion of the Court.

. . . A judge, like an executive adviser, may be surprised at the poverty of really useful and unambiguous authority applicable to concrete problems of executive power as they actually present themselves. Just what our forefathers did envision, or would have envisioned had they foreseen modern conditions, must be divined from materials almost as enigmatic as the dreams Joseph was called upon to interpret for Pharaoh. A century and a half of partisan debate and scholarly speculation yields no net result but only supplies more or less apt quotations from respected sources on each side of any question. They largely cancel each other. And court decisions are indecisive because of the judicial practice of dealing with the largest questions in the most narrow way.

The actual art of governing under our Constitution does not and cannot conform to judicial definitions of the power of any of its branches based on isolated clauses or even single Articles torn from context. While the Constitution diffuses power the better to secure liberty, it also contemplates that practice will integrate the dispersed powers into a workable government. It enjoins upon its branches separateness but interdependence, autonomy but reciprocity.

Presidential powers are not fixed but fluctuate, depending upon their disjunction or conjunction with those of Congress. We may well begin by a somewhat over-simplified grouping of practical situations in which a President may doubt, or others may challenge, his powers, and by distinguishing roughly the legal consequences of this factor of relativity.

1. When the President acts pursuant to an express or implied authorization of Congress, his authority is at its maximum, for it includes all that he possesses in his own right plus all that Congress can delegate.[2] In these circumstances, and in these only, may he be said (for what it may be worth) to personify the federal sovereignty. If his act is held unconstitutional under these circumstances, it usually means that the Federal Government as an undivided whole lacks power. A seizure executed by the President pursuant to an Act of Congress would be supported by the strongest of presumptions and the widest latitude of judicial interpretation, and the burden of persuasion would rest heavily upon any who might attack it.

2. When the President acts in absence of either a congressional grant or denial of authority, he can only rely upon his own independent powers, but there is a

---

2. It is in this class of cases that we find the broadest recent statements of presidential power, including those relied on here. *United States v. Curtiss-Wright Corp.*, 299 U.S. 304, involved, not the question of the President's power to act without congressional authority, but the question of his right to act under and in accord with an Act of Congress. . . .

That case does not solve the present controversy. It recognized internal and external affairs as being in separate categories, and held that the strict limitation upon congressional delegations of power to the President over internal affairs does not apply with respect to delegations of power in external affairs. It was intimated that the President might act in external affairs without congressional authority, but not that he might act contrary to an Act of Congress. . . .

zone of twilight in which he and Congress may have concurrent authority, or in which its distribution is uncertain. Therefore, congressional inertia, indifference or quiescence may sometimes, at least as a practical matter, enable, if not invite, measures on independent presidential responsibility. In this area, any actual test of power is likely to depend on the imperatives of events and contemporary imponderables rather than on abstract theories of law.

3. When the President takes measures incompatible with the expressed or implied will of Congress, his power is at its lowest ebb, for then he can rely only upon his own constitutional powers minus any constitutional powers of Congress over the matter. Courts can sustain exclusive presidential control in such a case only by disabling the Congress from acting upon the subject. Presidential claim to a power at once so conclusive and preclusive must be scrutinized with caution, for what is at stake is the equilibrium established by our constitutional system.

Into which of these classifications does this executive seizure of the steel industry fit? It is eliminated from the first by admission, for it is conceded that no congressional authorization exists for this seizure. That takes away also the support of the many precedents and declarations, which were made in relation, and must be confined, to this category.

Can it then be defended under flexible tests available to the second category? It seems clearly eliminated from that class because Congress has not left seizure of private property an open field but has covered it by three statutory policies inconsistent with this seizure. . . .

This leaves the current seizure to be justified only by the severe tests under the third grouping, where it can be supported only by any remainder of executive power after subtraction of such powers as Congress may have over the subject. In short, we can sustain the President only by holding that seizure of such strike-bound industries is within his domain and beyond control by Congress. Thus, this Court's first review of such seizures occurs under circumstances which leave presidential power most vulnerable to attack and in the least favorable of possible constitutional postures.

I did not suppose, and I am not persuaded, that history leaves it open to question, at least in the courts, that the executive branch, like the Federal Government as a whole, possesses only delegated powers. The purpose of the Constitution was not only to grant power, but to keep it from getting out of hand. However, because the President does not enjoy unmentioned powers does not mean that the mentioned ones should be narrowed by a niggardly construction. Some clauses could be made almost unworkable, as well as immutable, by refusal to indulge some latitude of interpretation for changing times. I have heretofore, and do now, give to the enumerated powers the scope and elasticity afforded by what seem to be reasonable, practical implications instead of the rigidity dictated by a doctrinaire textualism.

The Solicitor General seeks the power of seizure in three clauses of the Executive Article, the first reading, "The executive Power shall be vested in a President of the United States of America." Lest I be thought to exaggerate,

I quote the interpretation which his brief puts upon it: "In our view, this clause constitutes a grant of all the executive powers of which the Government is capable." If that be true, it is difficult to see why the forefathers bothered to add several specific items, including some trifling ones.[9] . . .

. . . I cannot accept the view that this clause is a grant in bulk of all conceivable executive power but regard it as an allocation to the presidential office of the generic powers thereafter stated.

The clause on which the Government next relies is that "The President shall be Commander in Chief of the Army and Navy of the United States. . . ." These cryptic words have given rise to some of the most persistent controversies in our constitutional history. Of course, they imply something more than an empty title. But just what authority goes with the name has plagued presidential advisers who would not waive or narrow it by nonassertion yet cannot say where it begins or ends. It undoubtedly puts the Nation's armed forces under presidential command.

Hence, this loose appellation is sometimes advanced as support for any presidential action, internal or external, involving use of force, the idea being that it vests power to do anything, anywhere, that can be done with an army or navy.

That seems to be the logic of an argument tendered at our bar — that the President having, on his own responsibility, sent American troops abroad derives from that act "affirmative power" to seize the means of producing a supply of steel for them. To quote, "Perhaps the most forceful illustration of the scope of Presidential power in this connection is the fact that American troops in Korea, whose safety and effectiveness are so directly involved here, were sent to the field by an exercise of the President's constitutional powers." Thus, it is said, he has invested himself with "war powers."

I cannot foresee all that it might entail if the Court should indorse this argument. Nothing in our Constitution is plainer than that declaration of a war is entrusted only to Congress. Of course, a state of war may in fact exist without a formal declaration. But no doctrine that the Court could promulgate would seem to me more sinister and alarming than that a President whose conduct of foreign affairs is so largely uncontrolled, and often even is unknown, can vastly enlarge his mastery over the internal affairs of the country by his own commitment of the Nation's armed forces to some foreign venture. I do not, however, find it necessary or appropriate to consider the legal status of the Korean enterprise to discountenance argument based on it.

Assuming that we are in a war *de facto*, whether it is or is not a war *de jure*, does that empower the Commander in Chief to seize industries he thinks necessary to supply our army? The Constitution expressly places in Congress power "to raise and *support* Armies" and "to *provide* and *maintain* a Navy." (Emphasis

---

9. ". . . He may require the Opinion, in writing, of the principal Officer in each of the executive Departments, upon any Subject relating to the Duties of their respective Offices. . . ." U.S. Const., Art. II, § 2. He ". . . shall Commission all the Officers of the United States." U.S. Const., Art. II, § 3. Matters such as those would seem to be inherent in the Executive if anything is.

supplied.) This certainly lays upon Congress primary responsibility for supplying the armed forces. Congress alone controls the raising of revenues and their appropriation and may determine in what manner and by what means they shall be spent for military and naval procurement. I suppose no one would doubt that Congress can take over war supply as a Government enterprise. On the other hand, if Congress sees fit to rely on free private enterprise collectively bargaining with free labor for support and maintenance of our armed forces, can the Executive, because of lawful disagreements incidental to that process, seize the facility for operation upon Government-imposed terms?

There are indications that the Constitution did not contemplate that the title Commander in Chief *of the Army and Navy* will constitute him also Commander in Chief of the country, its industries and its inhabitants. He has no monopoly of "war powers," whatever they are. While Congress cannot deprive the President of the command of the army and navy, only Congress can provide him an army or navy to command. It is also empowered to make rules for the "Government and Regulation of land and naval Forces," by which it may to some unknown extent impinge upon even command functions.

That military powers of the Commander in Chief were not to supersede representative government of internal affairs seems obvious from the Constitution and from elementary American history. Time out of mind, and even now in many parts of the world, a military commander can seize private housing to shelter his troops. Not so, however, in the United States, for the Third Amendment says, "No Soldier shall, in time of peace be quartered in any house, without the consent of the Owner, nor in time of war, but in a manner to be prescribed by law." Thus, even in war time, his seizure of needed military housing must be authorized by Congress. It also was expressly left to Congress to "provide for calling forth the Militia to execute the Laws of the Union, suppress Insurrections and repel Invasions. . . ." Such a limitation on the command power, written at a time when the militia rather than a standing army was contemplated as the military weapon of the Republic, underscores the Constitution's policy that Congress, not the Executive, should control utilization of the war power as an instrument of domestic policy. Congress, fulfilling that function, has authorized the President to use the army to enforce certain civil rights. On the other hand, Congress has forbidden him to use the army for the purpose of executing general laws except when *expressly* authorized by the Constitution or by Act of Congress.

While broad claims under this rubric often have been made, advice to the President in specific matters usually has carried overtones that powers, even under this head, are measured by the command functions usual to the topmost officer of the army and navy. Even then, heed has been taken of any efforts of Congress to negative his authority.

We should not use this occasion to circumscribe, much less to contract, the lawful role of the President as Commander in Chief. I should indulge the widest latitude of interpretation to sustain his exclusive function to command the instruments of national force, at least when turned against the outside world for the security of our society. But, when it is turned inward, not because of rebellion but because of a lawful economic struggle between industry and labor, it should have no such indulgence. His command power is not such an absolute as might be implied from that office in a militaristic system but is subject to limitations consistent with a constitutional Republic whose law and policy-making branch is a representative Congress. The purpose of lodging dual titles in one man was to insure that the civilian would control the military, not to enable the military to subordinate the presidential office. No penance would ever expiate the sin against free government of holding that a President can escape control of executive powers by law through assuming his military role. What the power of command may include I do not try to envision, but I think it is not a military prerogative, without support of law, to seize persons or property because they are important or even essential for the military and naval establishment.

The third clause in which the Solicitor General finds seizure powers is that "he shall take Care that the Laws be faithfully executed. . . ." That authority must be matched against words of the Fifth Amendment that "No person shall be . . . deprived of life, liberty or property, without due process of law. . . ." One gives a governmental authority that reaches so far as there is law, the other gives a private right that authority shall go no farther. These signify about all there is of the principle that ours is a government of laws, not of men, and that we submit ourselves to rulers only if under rules.

The Solicitor General lastly grounds support of the seizure upon nebulous, inherent powers never expressly granted but said to have accrued to the office from the customs and claims of preceding administrations. The plea is for a resulting power to deal with a crisis or an emergency according to the necessities of the case, the unarticulated assumption being that necessity knows no law. . . . The appeal . . . that we declare the existence of inherent powers *ex necessitate* to meet an emergency asks us to do what many think would be wise, although it is something the forefathers omitted. They knew what emergencies were, knew the pressures they engender for authoritative action, knew, too, how they afford a ready pretext for usurpation. We may also suspect that they suspected that emergency powers would tend to kindle emergencies. Aside from suspension of the privilege of the writ of habeas corpus in time of rebellion or invasion, when the public safety may require it, they made no express provision for exercise of extraordinary authority because of a crisis.[19] I do not think we rightfully may so amend their work, and, if we could, I am not convinced it would be wise to do so, although many modern nations have forthrightly recognized that war and economic crises may upset the normal balance between liberty and authority. . . .

In the practical working of our Government we already have evolved a technique within the framework of the Constitution by which normal executive powers may be considerably expanded to meet an emergency. Congress may and has granted extraordinary authorities which lie dormant in normal times

---

19. I exclude, as in a very limited category by itself, the establishment of martial law.

but may be called into play by the Executive in war or upon proclamation of a national emergency. . . .

In view of the ease, expedition and safety with which Congress can grant and has granted large emergency powers, certainly ample to embrace this crisis, I am quite unimpressed with the argument that we should affirm possession of them without statute. Such power either has no beginning or it has no end. If it exists, it need submit to no legal restraint. I am not alarmed that it would plunge us straightway into dictatorship, but it is at least a step in that wrong direction.

As to whether there is imperative necessity for such powers, it is relevant to note the gap that exists between the President's paper powers and his real powers. The Constitution does not disclose the measure of the actual controls wielded by the modern presidential office. That instrument must be understood as an Eighteenth-Century sketch of a government hoped for, not as a blueprint of the Government that is. Vast accretions of federal power, eroded from that reserved by the States, have magnified the scope of presidential activity. Subtle shifts take place in the centers of real power that do not show on the face of the Constitution.

Executive power has the advantage of concentration in a single head in whose choice the whole Nation has a part, making him the focus of public hopes and expectations. In drama, magnitude and finality his decisions so far overshadow any others that almost alone he fills the public eye and ear. No other personality in public life can begin to compete with him in access to the public mind through modern methods of communications. By his prestige as head of state and his influence upon public opinion he exerts a leverage upon those who are supposed to check and balance his power which often cancels their effectiveness.

Moreover, rise of the party system has made a significant extraconstitutional supplement to real executive power. No appraisal of his necessities is realistic which overlooks that he heads a political system as well as a legal system. Party loyalties and interests, sometimes more binding than law, extend his effective control into branches of government other than his own and he often may win, as a political leader, what he cannot command under the Constitution. Indeed, Woodrow Wilson, commenting on the President as leader both of his party and of the Nation, observed, "If he rightly interpret the national thought and boldly insist upon it, he is irresistible. . . . His office is anything he has the sagacity and force to make it." I cannot be brought to believe that this country will suffer if the Court refuses further to aggrandize the presidential office, already so potent and so relatively immune from judicial review, at the expense of Congress.

But I have no illusion that any decision by this Court can keep power in the hands of Congress if it is not wise and timely in meeting its problems. A crisis that challenges the President equally, or perhaps primarily, challenges Congress. If not good law, there was worldly wisdom in the maxim attributed to Napoleon that "The tools belong to the man who can use them." We may say that power to legislate for emergencies belongs in the hands of Congress, but only Congress itself can prevent power from slipping through its fingers. . . .

. . . With all its defects, delays and inconveniences, men have discovered no technique for long preserving free government except that the Executive be under the law, and that the law be made by parliamentary deliberations.

Such institutions may be destined to pass away. But it is the duty of the Court to be last, not first, to give them up.

Mr. Justice BURTON, concurring in both the opinion and the judgment of the Court. . . . In the case before us, Congress authorized a procedure which the President declined to follow. Instead, he followed another procedure which he hoped might eliminate the need for the first. Upon its failure, he issued an executive order to seize the steel properties in the face of the reserved right of Congress to adopt or reject that course as a matter of legislative policy.

This brings us to a further crucial question. Does the President, in such a situation, have inherent constitutional power to seize private property which makes congressional action in relation thereto unnecessary? We find no such power available to him under the present circumstances. The present situation is not comparable to that of an imminent invasion or threatened attack. We do not face the issue of what might be the President's constitutional power to meet such catastrophic situations. Nor is it claimed that the current seizure is in the nature of a military command addressed by the President, as Commander-in-Chief, to a mobilized nation waging, or imminently threatened with, total war. . . .

Mr. Justice CLARK, concurring in the judgment of the Court.

. . . The limits of presidential power are obscure. However, Article II, no less than Article I, is part of "a constitution intended to endure for ages to come, and, consequently, to be adapted to the various *crises* of human affairs." Some of our Presidents, such as Lincoln, "felt that measures otherwise unconstitutional might become lawful by becoming indispensable to the preservation of the Constitution through the preservation of the nation." Others, such as Theodore Roosevelt, thought the President to be capable, as a "steward" of the people, of exerting all power save that which is specifically prohibited by the Constitution or the Congress. In my view—taught me not only by the decision of Mr. Chief Justice Marshall in *Little v. Barreme*, but also by a score of other pronouncements of distinguished members of this bench—the Constitution does grant to the President extensive authority in times of grave and imperative national emergency. In fact, to my thinking, such a grant may well be necessary to the very existence of the Constitution itself. As Lincoln aptly said, "[is] it possible to lose the nation and yet preserve the Constitution?" In describing this authority I care not whether one calls it "residual," "inherent," "moral," "implied," "aggregate," "emergency," or otherwise. I am of the conviction that those who have had the gratifying experience of being the President's lawyer have used one or more of these adjectives only with the utmost of sincerity and the highest of purpose.

I conclude that where Congress has laid down specific procedures to deal with the type of crisis confronting the President, he must follow those procedures in meeting the crisis; but that in the absence of such action by Congress, the President's independent power to act depends upon the gravity of the situation confronting the nation. I cannot sustain the seizure in question because here, as in *Little v. Barreme*, Congress had prescribed methods to be followed by the President in meeting the emergency at hand.

Mr. Chief Justice VINSON, with whom Mr. Justice REED and Mr. Justice MINTON join, dissenting. . . .

Those who suggest that this is a case involving extraordinary powers should be mindful that these are extraordinary times. A world not yet recovered from the devastation of World War II has been forced to face the threat of another and more terrifying global conflict. . . .

For almost two full years, our armed forces have been fighting in Korea, suffering casualties of over 108,000 men. Hostilities have not abated. The "determination of the United Nations to continue its action in Korea to meet the aggression" has been reaffirmed. Congressional support of the action in Korea has been manifested by provisions for increased military manpower and equipment and for economic stabilization, as hereinafter described. . . .

. . . Even ignoring for the moment whatever confidential information the President may possess as "the Nation's organ for foreign affairs," the uncontroverted affidavits in this record amply support the finding that "a work stoppage would immediately jeopardize and imperil our national defense.". . .

Focusing now on the situation confronting the President on the night of April 8, 1952, we cannot but conclude that the President was performing his duty under the Constitution to "take Care that the Laws be faithfully executed"—a duty described by President Benjamin Harrison as "the central idea of the office."

The President reported to Congress the morning after the seizure that he acted because a work stoppage in steel production would immediately imperil the safety of the Nation by preventing execution of the legislative programs for procurement of military equipment. And, while a shutdown could be averted by granting the price concessions requested by plaintiffs, granting such concessions would disrupt the price stabilization program also enacted by Congress. Rather than fail to execute either legislative program, the President acted to execute both.

Much of the argument in this case has been directed at straw men. We do not now have before us the case of a President acting solely on the basis of his own notions of the public welfare. Nor is there any question of unlimited executive power in this case. The President himself closed the door to any such claim when he sent his Message to Congress stating his purpose to abide by any action of Congress, whether approving or disapproving his seizure action. Here, the President immediately made sure that Congress was fully informed of the temporary action he had taken only to preserve the legislative programs from destruction until Congress could act.

The absence of a specific statute authorizing seizure of the steel mills as a mode of executing the laws—both the military procurement program and the anti-inflation program—has not until today been thought to prevent the President from executing the laws. Unlike an administrative commission confined to the enforcement of the statute under which it was created, or the head of a department when administering a particular statute, the President is a constitutional officer charged with taking care that a "mass of legislation" be executed. Flexibility as to mode of execution to meet critical situations is a matter of practical necessity. . . .

Whatever the extent of Presidential power on more tranquil occasions, and whatever the right of the President to execute legislative programs as he sees fit without reporting the mode of execution to Congress, the single Presidential purpose disclosed on this record is to faithfully execute the laws by acting in an emergency to maintain the status quo, thereby preventing collapse of the legislative programs until Congress could act. The President's action served the same purposes as a judicial stay entered to maintain the status quo in order to preserve the jurisdiction of a court. . . .

In *United States v. Midwest Oil Co.*, this Court approved executive action where, as here, the President acted to preserve an important matter until Congress could act—even though his action in that case was contrary to an express statute. In this case, there is no statute prohibiting the action taken by the President in a matter not merely important but threatening the very safety of the Nation. Executive inaction in such a situation, courting national disaster, is foreign to the concept of energy and initiative in the Executive as created by the Founding Fathers. The Constitution was itself "adopted in a period of grave emergency. . . . While emergency does not create power, emergency may furnish the occasion for the exercise of power." The Framers knew, as we should know in these times of peril, that there is real danger in Executive weakness. There is no cause to fear Executive tyranny so long as the laws of Congress are being faithfully executed. Certainly there is no basis for fear of dictatorship when the Executive acts, as he did in this case, only to save the situation until Congress could act. . . .

NOTES AND QUESTIONS

1. How many Justices do you think would have ruled in favor of the President had Congress not considered and rejected including seizure authority in the Taft-Hartley Act?
2. Why do you think Justice Frankfurter begins his concurrence by noting, "The issues before us can be met, and therefore should be, without attempting to define the President's powers comprehensively"?
3. What do you think Justice Frankfurter was suggesting when he noted, "No remotely comparable practice can be vouched for executive seizure of property

at a time when this country was not at war, in the only constitutional way in which it can be at war"?

4. What was the significance of Justice Frankfurter's comparison of the assertion of authority for seizing the steel mills with presidential action addressed in the *Midwest Oil* case?

5. Assuming Justice Frankfurter's test for identifying a historical practice "gloss" on constitutional power is satisfied, can Congress "strip" that gloss away with a statute?

6. Justice Jackson showed little sympathy for the President in his opinion. Do you think the "message" he was obviously trying to send with his concurrence was directed mainly at the executive branch?

7. Is there a commonality between Justice Frankfurter's historical practice focus and Justice Jackson's three-tier methodology? If so, how would you describe it?

8. President Truman asserted the existence of a national emergency to justify his action. How many Justices do you feel accepted that assertion? How many explicitly or implicitly rejected it? How much deference should a court give to such presidential assertions?

ASSESSMENT QUESTIONS

1. Briefly describe relevant factors in assessing the existence of a "historical gloss" that might support an exercise of executive power.

ASSESSMENT ANSWERS

1. This concept was best articulated by Justice Frankfurter in *Youngstown*. According to his concurring opinion, the authority asserted by the executive must be consistent with a longstanding executive practice, known to Congress and never before questioned. When such evidence exists, it, according to Justice Frankfurter, reflects an inter-branch understanding of how the Constitution actually allocates power. In *Youngstown*, Justice Frankfurter rejected the assertion of a historically based constitutional seizure authority after including with his opinion a highly detailed appendix analyzing every industry seizure in the nation's history. That appendix is a visual demonstration of the degree of specificity and detail that should be applied to any historical practice analysis.

CHAPTER 5

The "National Security Constitution" and Foreign Affairs

I. IRAN, HOSTAGES, AND ANOTHER TAKING: THE EVOLUTION OF THREE TIERS

On November 4, 1979, Iranian students supporting the Iranian Islamic Revolution stormed the U.S. Embassy and took the Embassy staff as hostages. The Iranian government breached its obligation to protect the Embassy and, after the invasion, to secure the release of the hostages. Among the many responsive measures implemented by the United States, President Carter invoked the International Emergency Economic Powers Act (IEEPA) and ordered all Iranian assets in U.S. banks frozen. During this same period, a number of U.S. commercial interests initiated lawsuits against the government of Iran to recover losses resulting from expropriation of assets in Iran and breaches of contracts. Pursuant to regulations issued by the Department of Treasury, these litigants could apply for licenses for pre-judgment attachments of Iranian assets frozen pursuant to the IEEPA order.

With Algiers acting as an intermediary, the United States negotiated an agreement for release of the hostages. Unsurprisingly, Iran sought access to its financial resources frozen pursuant to the IEEPA order. Pursuant to what was designated as the Algiers Accords, President Carter agreed to nullify all claims against Iran — to include all pre-judgment attachments — and to nullify all claims pending in U.S. courts against Iran, and to redirect those claims into binding international arbitration. Pursuant to this agreement, President Carter issued Executive Order No. 12,294 directing:

> [termination of] all legal proceedings in United States courts involving claims of United States persons and institutions against Iran and its state enterprises, to nullify all attachments and judgments obtained therein, to prohibit all further litigation based on such claims, and to bring about the termination of such claims through binding arbitration.[1]

---

1. Exec. Order No. 12,294, 46 Fed. Reg. 14,111 (Feb. 24, 1981).

On the day President Reagan took office, Iran released the hostages. President Reagan then issued executive orders to implement the attachment and claims nullification provision in the agreement.

As a result of these orders, the Treasury Department nullified the pre-judgment attachment of Iranian assets secured by Dames & Moore, and the federal district court dismissed the Dames & Moore lawsuit. Dames & Moore then challenged both the President's constitutional authority to nullify the attachment and to terminate the claim against Iran. The Supreme Court would ultimately conclude that the President had acted constitutionally.

Prior to the Iranian revolution, Dames & Moore Export Corporation, headquartered in Los Angeles, engaged in substantial commerce with Iran. While negotiations were ongoing to secure release of the hostages, Dames & Moore won a $3.8 million judgment against Iran. But Dames & Moore was not the only U.S. company impacted by the settlement agreement and claim nullification. According to the *New York Times*:

> Before the hostage crisis ended on Jan. 20, more than 400 American companies had filed breach-of-contract suits totaling $3 billion to $4 billion against Iran. They obtained court orders of attachment, or liens, against Iranian funds deposited in this country as guarantees that they would be available to satisfy any judgments.[2]

While reading the Court's decision, consider two important questions. First, how did the rationale for upholding the attachment nullification differ from the rationale for upholding the claim termination? Second, how did Justice Rehnquist, who had been Justice Jackson's clerk when *Youngstown* was decided, propose a more nuanced application of Jackson's three-tier model for assessing the constitutionality of presidential actions in the realm of foreign affairs?

Dames & Moore v. Regan
453 U.S. 654 (1981)

Justice REHNQUIST delivered the opinion of the Court. . . .

On November 4, 1979, the American Embassy in Tehran was seized and our diplomatic personnel were captured and held hostage. In response to that crisis, President Carter, acting pursuant to the International Emergency Economic Powers Act, 50 U.S.C. §§ 1701-1706 (1976 ed., Supp. III) (hereinafter IEEPA), declared a national emergency on November 14, 1979,[1] and blocked the removal or transfer of "all property and interests in property of the Government of Iran, its instrumentalities and controlled entities and the

---

2. Linda Greenhouse, *High Court Rules Pact on Hostages with Iran Is Legal*, July 3, 1981.

1. Title 50 U.S.C. § 1701(a) (1976 ed., Supp. III) states that the President's authority under the Act "may be exercised to deal with any unusual and extraordinary threat, which has its source in whole or substantial part outside the United States, to the national security, foreign policy, or economy of the United States, if the President declares a national emergency with respect to such threat." Petitioner does not challenge President Carter's declaration of a national emergency.

Central Bank of Iran which are or become subject to the jurisdiction of the United States...." Exec. Order No. 12170, 3 C.F.R. 457 (1980), note following 50 U.S.C. § 1701 (1976 ed., Supp. III).[2] ...

[Pursuant to the Order, the Secretary of Treasury promulgated regulations nullifying attachments of Iranian assets on or after November 14, 1979, unless licensed by the Treasury Department. The department subsequently licensed pre-judgment attachments in judicial proceedings against Iran. Dames & Moore sued Iranian descendants for breach of contract and obtained pre-judgment attachment of Iranian assets.

Thereafter, the American hostages were released pursuant to an agreement obligating the United States to terminate all legal proceedings in U.S. courts involving claims of U.S. nationals against Iran, to nullify all attachments and judgments therein, to terminate such claims through binding arbitration, and to transfer U.S.-held Iranian assets to foreign banks for the satisfaction of any arbitration awards rendered against Iran. President Carter issued a series of executive orders implementing this agreement and "nullif[ying]" all non-Iranian interests in Iranian assets acquired after his initial blocking order. President Reagan subsequently ratified the Carter orders.

Meanwhile, Dames & Moore was granted summary judgment on its claim against the Iranian defendants, but the district court vacated all pre-judgment attachments and stayed further proceedings in light of the executive orders discussed above. Dames & Moore then filed an action in the district court to prevent enforcement of the executive orders and Treasury Department regulations implementing the agreement with Iran on the grounds that they were beyond the statutory and constitutional powers of the executive.]

Although we have in the past found and do today find Justice Jackson's classification [in *The Steel Seizure Case*, 343 U.S. at 635-38] of executive actions into three general categories analytically useful, we should be mindful of Justice Holmes' admonition, quoted by Justice Frankfurter in [that case at 343 U.S. at 597] that "[t]he great ordinances of the Constitution do not establish and divide fields of black and white." *Springer v. Philippine Islands*, 277 U.S. 189, 209 (1928) (dissenting opinion). Justice Jackson himself recognized that his three categories represented "a somewhat over-simplified grouping," and it is doubtless the case that executive action in any particular instance falls, not neatly in one of three pigeonholes, but rather at some point along a spectrum running from explicit congressional authorization to explicit congressional prohibition. This is particularly true as respects cases such as the one before us, involving responses to international crises the nature of which Congress can hardly have been expected to anticipate in any detail.

---

2. Title 50 U.S.C. § 1702(a)(1)(B) (1976 ed., Supp. III) empowers the President to "investigate, regulate, direct and compel, nullify, void, prevent or prohibit, any acquisition, holding, withholding, use, transfer, withdrawal, transportation, importation or exportation of, or dealing in, or exercising any right, power, or privilege with respect to, or transactions involving, any property in which any foreign country or a national thereof has any interest...."

In nullifying post-November 14, 1979, attachments and directing those persons holding blocked Iranian funds and securities to transfer them to the Federal Reserve Bank of New York for ultimate transfer to Iran, President Carter cited five sources of express or inherent power. The Government, however, has principally relied on § 203 of the IEEPA as authorization for these actions. [The Court concluded that this statute expressly authorized the nullification of the attachments and the transfer of assets.] . . .

. . . [T]here remains the question of the President's authority to suspend claims pending in American courts. Such claims have, of course, an existence apart from the attachments which accompanied them. In terminating these claims through Executive Order No. 12294, the President purported to act under authority of both the IEEPA and 22 U.S.C. § 1732, the so-called "Hostage Act."

We conclude that although the IEEPA authorized the nullification of the attachments, it cannot be read to authorize the suspension of the claims. The claims of American citizens against Iran are not in themselves transactions involving Iranian property or efforts to exercise any rights with respect to such property. An in personam lawsuit, although it might eventually be reduced to judgment and that judgment might be executed upon, is an effort to establish liability and fix damages and does not focus on any particular property within the jurisdiction. The terms of the IEEPA therefore do not authorize the President to suspend claims in American courts. This is the view of all the courts which have considered the question.

The Hostage Act, passed in 1868, provides:

> Whenever it is made known to the President that any citizen of the United States has been unjustly deprived of his liberty by or under the authority of any foreign government, it shall be the duty of the President forthwith to demand of that government the reasons of such imprisonment; and if it appears to be wrongful and in violation of the rights of American citizenship, the President shall forthwith demand the release of such citizen, and if the release so demanded is unreasonably delayed or refused, the President shall use such means, not amounting to acts of war, as he may think necessary and proper to obtain or effectuate the release; and all the facts and proceedings relative thereto shall as soon as practicable be communicated by the President to Congress. Rev. Stat. § 2001, 22 U.S.C. § 1732.

We are reluctant to conclude that this provision constitutes specific authorization to the President to suspend claims in American courts. Although the broad language of the Hostage Act suggests it may cover this case, there are several difficulties with such a view. The legislative history indicates that the Act was passed in response to a situation unlike the recent Iranian crisis. Congress in 1868 was concerned with the activity of certain countries refusing to recognize the citizenship of naturalized Americans traveling abroad, and repatriating such citizens against their will. These countries were not interested in returning the citizens in exchange for any sort of ransom. This also explains the reference in the Act to imprisonment "in violation of the rights of American citizenship." Although the Iranian hostage-taking violated international law and common decency, the hostages were not seized out of any refusal to recognize their American citizenship—they were seized precisely *because of* their American citizenship. The legislative history is also somewhat ambiguous on the question whether Congress contemplated Presidential action such as that involved here or rather simply reprisals directed against the offending foreign country and *its* citizens.

Concluding that neither the IEEPA nor the Hostage Act constitutes specific authorization of the President's action suspending claims, however, is not to say that these statutory provisions are entirely irrelevant to the question of the validity of the President's action. We think both statutes highly relevant in the looser sense of indicating congressional acceptance of a broad scope for executive action in circumstances such as those presented in this case. . . . [T]he IEEPA delegates broad authority to the President to act in times of national emergency with respect to property of a foreign country. The Hostage Act similarly indicates congressional willingness that the President have broad discretion when responding to the hostile acts of foreign sovereigns. As Senator Williams, draftsman of the language eventually enacted as the Hostage Act, put it:

> If you propose any remedy at all, you must invest the Executive with some discretion, so that he may apply the remedy to a case as it may arise. As to England or France he might adopt one policy to relieve a citizen imprisoned by either one of those countries; as to the Barbary powers, he might adopt another policy; as to the islands of the ocean, another. With different countries that have different systems of government he might adopt different means. Cong. Globe, 40th Cong., 2d Sess., 4359 (1868).

Proponents of the bill recognized that it placed a "loose discretion" in the President's hands, *id.*, at 4238 (Sen. Stewart), but argued that "[s]omething must be intrusted to the Executive" and that "[the] President ought to have the power to do what the exigencies of the case require to rescue [a] citizen from imprisonment." *Id.*, at 4233, 4357 (Sen. Williams). An original version of the Act, which authorized the President to suspend trade with a foreign country and even arrest citizens of that country in the United States in retaliation, was rejected because "there may be a great variety of cases arising where other and different means would be equally effective, and where the end desired could be accomplished without resorting to such dangerous and violent measures." *Id.*, at 4233 (Sen. Williams).

Although we have declined to conclude that the IEEPA or the Hostage Act directly authorizes the President's suspension of claims for the reasons noted, we cannot ignore the general tenor of Congress' legislation in this area in trying to determine whether the President is acting alone or at least with the acceptance of Congress. As we have noted, Congress cannot anticipate and legislate with regard to every possible action the President may find it necessary to take or every possible situation in which he might act. Such failure of Congress specifically to delegate authority does not, "especially . . . in the areas of foreign policy and national security," imply "congressional disapproval" of action taken by the Executive. *Haig v. Agee*, [453 U.S. 280 (1981)], at 291. On the contrary, the enactment of legislation closely related to the question of the President's authority in a particular case which evinces legislative intent to accord the President broad discretion may be considered to "invite" "measures on independent presidential responsibility," *Youngstown*, 343 U.S., at 637 (Jackson, J., concurring). At least this is so where there is no contrary indication of legislative intent and when, as here, there is a history of congressional acquiescence in conduct of the sort engaged in by the President. It is to that history which we now turn.

Not infrequently in affairs between nations, outstanding claims by nationals of one country against the government of another country are "sources of friction" between the two sovereigns. *United States v. Pink*, 315 U.S. 203, 225 (1942). To resolve these difficulties, nations have often entered into agreements settling the claims of their respective nationals. As one treatise writer puts it, international agreements settling claims by nationals of one state against the government of another "are established international practice reflecting traditional international theory." L. Henkin, *Foreign Affairs and the Constitution* 262 (1972). Consistent with that principle, the United States has repeatedly exercised its sovereign authority to settle the claims of its nationals against foreign countries. Though those settlements have sometimes been made by treaty, there has also been a longstanding practice of settling such claims by executive agreement without the advice and consent of the Senate.[8] . . . It is clear that the practice of settling claims continues today. Since 1952, the President has entered into at least 10 binding settlements with foreign nations, including an $80 million settlement with the People's Republic of China.

Crucial to our decision today is the conclusion that Congress has implicitly approved the practice of claim settlement by executive agreement. This is best demonstrated by Congress' enactment of the International Claims Settlement Act of 1949, 22 U.S.C. § 1621 *et seq.* (1976 ed. and Supp. IV). The Act had two purposes: (1) to allocate to United States nationals funds received in the course of an executive claims settlement with Yugoslavia, and (2) to provide a procedure whereby funds resulting from future settlements could be distributed. To achieve these ends Congress created the International Claims Commission, now the Foreign Claims Settlement Commission, and gave it jurisdiction to make final and binding decisions with respect to claims by United States nationals against settlement funds. By creating a procedure to implement future settlement agreements, Congress placed its stamp of approval on such agreements. Indeed, the legislative history of the Act observed that the United

---

8. At least since the case of the "Wilmington Packet" in 1799, Presidents have exercised the power to settle claims of United States nationals by executive agreement. In fact, during the period of 1817-1917, "no fewer than eighty executive agreements were entered into by the United States looking toward the liquidation of claims of its citizens." W. McClure, *International Executive Agreements* 53 (1941).

States was seeking settlements with countries other than Yugoslavia and that the bill contemplated settlements of a similar nature in the future.

Over the years Congress has frequently amended the International Claims Settlement Act to provide for particular problems arising out of settlement agreements, thus demonstrating Congress' continuing acceptance of the President's claim settlement authority. . . . As with legislation involving other executive agreements, Congress did not question the fact of the settlement or the power of the President to have concluded it. . . . Finally, the legislative history of the IEEPA further reveals that Congress has accepted the authority of the Executive to enter into settlement agreements. Though the IEEPA was enacted to provide for some limitation on the President's emergency powers, Congress stressed that "[n]othing in this act is intended . . . to interfere with the authority of the President to [block assets], or to impede the settlement of claims of U.S. citizens against foreign countries." S. Rep. No. 95-466, p. 6 (1977), U.S. Code Cong. Admin. News, 1977, pp. 4540, 4544; 50 U.S.C. § 1706(a)(1) (1976 ed., Supp. III).[10]

In addition to congressional acquiescence in the President's power to settle claims, prior cases of this Court have also recognized that the President does have some measure of power to enter into executive agreements without obtaining the advice and consent of the Senate. In *United States v. Pink*, 315 U.S. 203 (1942), for example, the Court upheld the validity of the Litvinov Assignment, which was part of an Executive Agreement whereby the Soviet Union assigned to the United States amounts owed to it by American nationals so that outstanding claims of other American nationals could be paid. The Court explained that the resolution of such claims was integrally connected with normalizing United States' relations with a foreign state:

> "Power to remove such obstacles to full recognition as settlement of claims of our nationals . . . certainly is a modest implied power of the President. . . . No such obstacle can be placed in the way of rehabilitation of relations between this country and another nation, unless the historic conception of the powers and responsibilities . . . is to be drastically revised." *Id.*, at 229-230. . . .

Just as importantly, Congress has not disapproved of the action taken here. Though Congress has held hearings on the Iranian Agreement itself, Congress has not enacted legislation, or even passed a resolution, indicating its displeasure

---

10. Indeed, Congress has consistently failed to object to this longstanding practice of claim settlement by executive agreement, even when it has had an opportunity to do so. In 1972, Congress entertained legislation relating to congressional oversight of such agreements. But Congress took only limited action, requiring that the text of significant executive agreements be transmitted to Congress. 1 U.S.C. § 112b. In *Haig v. Agee*, [453 U.S. 280,] we noted that "[d]espite the longstanding and officially promulgated view that the Executive has the power to withhold passports for reasons of national security and foreign policy, Congress in 1978, 'though it once again enacted legislation relating to passports, left completely untouched the broad rule-making authority granted in the earlier Act.'" Ante, at 301, quoting *Zemel v. Rusk*, 381 U.S. 1, 12 (1965). Likewise in this case, Congress, though legislating in the area, has left "untouched" the authority of the President to enter into settlement agreements. . . .

with the Agreement. Quite the contrary, the relevant Senate Committee has stated that the establishment of the Tribunal is "of vital importance to the United States." S. Rep. No. 97-71, p. 5 (1981).[13] We are thus clearly not confronted with a situation in which Congress has in some way resisted the exercise of Presidential authority.

Finally, we re-emphasize the narrowness of our decision. We do not decide that the President possesses plenary power to settle claims, even as against foreign governmental entities. As the Court of Appeals for the First Circuit stressed, "[t]he sheer magnitude of such a power, considered against the background of the diversity and complexity of modern international trade, cautions against any broader construction of authority than is necessary." *Chas. T. Main Int'l, Inc. v. Khuzestan Water & Power Authority*, 651 F.2d [800], at 814. But where, as here, the settlement of claims has been determined to be a necessary incident to the resolution of a major foreign policy dispute between our country and another, and where, as here, we can conclude that Congress acquiesced in the President's action, we are not prepared to say that the President lacks the power to settle such claims. . . .

The judgment of the District Court is accordingly affirmed. . . .

[The opinion of Justice Powell, concurring in part and dissenting in part, is omitted.]

NOTES AND QUESTIONS

1. Do you think the Court could have resolved the case by relying on the plain terms of the Hostage Act? What do you think might have motivated the Court to adopt the interpretation of the Hostage Act that failed to resolve the issue?
2. Like *Youngstown*, the *Dames & Moore* Court concluded that while Congress had provided legislation closely related to the issue before the Court, it had not explicitly addressed that issue. What difference in that legislation explains the two different outcomes?
3. Both *Dames & Moore* and *Youngstown* involved an alleged taking of a property interest without due process of law. The *Youngstown* majority acknowledged the foreign affairs aspect of the case but focused primarily on its domestic implications. Did you feel the *Dames & Moore* majority adopted an analogous approach to this case? If not, how do you think that influenced the outcome?

---

13. Contrast congressional reaction to the Iranian Agreements with congressional reaction to a 1973 Executive Agreement with Czechoslovakia. There the President sought to settle over $105 million in claims against Czechoslovakia for $20.5 million. Congress quickly demonstrated its displeasure by enacting legislation requiring that the Agreement be renegotiated. Though Congress has shown itself capable of objecting to executive agreements, it has rarely done so and has not done so in this case.

II. THE ENDURING INFLUENCE OF *CURTISS-WRIGHT* AND *YOUNGSTOWN*

Both *Curtiss-Wright* and *Youngstown* emphasized the significance of longstanding practice to assess the allocation of authority between Congress and the President, especially in the realm of foreign relations. The next case illustrates the significance of an intersection of foreign affairs authority and longstanding practice as it relates to denying a U.S. citizen a passport.

Haig v. Agee
453 U.S. 280 (1981)

BURGER, C.J., delivered the opinion of the Court, in which STEWART, WHITE, BLACKMUN, POWELL, REHNQUIST, and STEVENS, JJ., joined. BLACKMUN, J., filed a concurring opinion, *post*, 453 U.S. 310. BRENNAN, J., filed a dissenting opinion, in which MARSHALL, J., joined, *post*, 453 U.S. 310.

Chief Justice BURGER delivered the opinion of the Court.

The question presented is whether the President, acting through the Secretary of State, has authority to revoke a passport on the ground that the holder's activities in foreign countries are causing or are likely to cause serious damage to the national security or foreign policy of the United States.

I

A

Philip Agee, an American citizen, currently resides in West Germany. From 1957 to 1968, he was employed by the Central Intelligence Agency. He held key positions in the division of the Agency that is responsible for covert intelligence gathering in foreign countries. In the course of his duties at the Agency, Agee received training in clandestine operations, including the methods used to protect the identities of intelligence employees and sources of the United States overseas. He served in undercover assignments abroad and came to know many Government employees and other persons supplying information to the United States. The relationships of many of these people to our Government are highly confidential; many are still engaged in intelligence gathering.

In 1974, Agee called a press conference in London to announce his "campaign to fight the United States CIA wherever it is operating." He declared his intent "to expose CIA officers and agents and to take the measures necessary to drive them out of the countries where they are operating."

Since 1974, Agee has, by his own assertion, devoted consistent effort to that program, and he has traveled extensively in other countries in order to carry it out. To identify CIA personnel in a particular country, Agee goes to the target country and consults sources in local diplomatic circles whom he knows from his prior service in the United States Government. He recruits collaborators and trains them in clandestine techniques designed to expose the "cover" of CIA employees and sources. Agee and his collaborators have repeatedly and publicly identified individuals and organizations located in foreign countries as undercover CIA agents, employees, or sources. The record reveals that the identifications divulge classified information, violate Agee's express contract not to make any public statements about Agency matters without prior clearance by the Agency, have prejudiced the ability of the United States to obtain intelligence, and have been followed by episodes of violence against the persons and organizations identified.

In December, 1979, the Secretary of State revoked Agee's passport and delivered an explanatory notice to Agee in West Germany. The notice states in part:

> "The Department's action is predicated upon a determination made by the Secretary under the provisions of [22 CFR] Section 51.70(b)(4) that your activities abroad are causing or are likely to cause serious damage to the national security or the foreign policy of the United States. The reasons for the Secretary's determination are, in summary, as follows: Since the early 1970's, it has been your stated intention to conduct a continuous campaign to disrupt the intelligence operations of the United States. In carrying out that campaign you have traveled in various countries (including, among others, Mexico, the United Kingdom, Denmark, Jamaica, Cuba, and Germany), and your activities in those countries have caused serious damage to the national security and foreign policy of the United States. Your stated intention to continue such activities threatens additional damage of the same kind."

The notice also advised Agee of his right to an administrative hearing and offered to hold such a hearing in West Germany on 5 days' notice.

Agee at once filed suit against the Secretary. He alleged that the regulation invoked by the Secretary, 22 CFR § 51.70(b)(4) (1980), has not been authorized by Congress and is invalid; that the regulation is impermissibly overbroad; that the revocation prior to a hearing violated his Fifth Amendment right to procedural due process; and that the revocation violated a Fifth Amendment liberty interest in a right to travel and a First Amendment right to criticize Government policies. He sought declaratory and injunctive relief, and he moved for summary judgment on the question of the authority to promulgate the regulation and on the constitutional claims. For purposes of that motion, Agee conceded the Secretary's factual averments and his claim that Agee's activities were causing or were likely to cause serious damage to the national security or foreign policy of the United States. The District Court held that the regulation exceeded the statutory powers of the Secretary under the Passport Act of 1926, 22 U.S.C. § 211a, granted summary judgment for Agee, and ordered the Secretary to restore his passport. . . .

B

A divided panel of the Court of Appeals affirmed. It held that the Secretary was required to show that Congress had authorized the regulation either by an express delegation or by implied approval of a "substantial and consistent" administrative practice, *Zemel v. Rusk*, 381 U.S. 1, 381 U.S. 12 (1965). The court found no express statutory authority for the revocation. It perceived only one other case of actual passport revocation under the regulation since it was promulgated, and only five other instances prior to that in which passports were actually denied "even arguably for national security or foreign policy reasons." 203 U.S. App. D.C. at 5152, 629 F.2d at 886. The Court of Appeals took note of the Secretary's reliance on "a series of statutes, regulations, proclamations, orders and advisory opinions dating back to 1856," but declined to consider those authorities, reasoning that "the criterion for establishing congressional assent by inaction is the actual imposition of sanctions, and not the mere assertion of power." *Id.* at 52-53, 629 F.2d at 86-87. The Court of Appeals held that it was not sufficient that "Agee's conduct may be considered by some to border on treason," since "[w]e are bound by the law as we find it." *Id.* at 53, 629 F.2d at 87. The court also regarded it as material that most of the Secretary's authorities dealt with powers of the Executive Branch "during time of war or national emergency" or with respect to persons "engaged in criminal conduct." *Id.* at 52, 629 F.2d at 86.

We granted certiorari *sub nom. Muskie v. Agee*, 449 U.S. 818 (1980), and stayed the judgment of the Court of Appeals until our disposition of the case on the grant of certiorari.

II

The principal question before us is whether the statute authorizes the action of the Secretary pursuant to the policy announced by the challenged regulation.

A

1

Although the historical background that we develop later is important, we begin with the language of the statute. . . . The Passport Act of 1926 provides in pertinent part:

> "The Secretary of State may grant and issue passports, and cause passports to be granted, issued, and verified in foreign countries by diplomatic representatives of the United States . . . under such rules as the President shall designate and prescribe for and on behalf of the United States, and no other person shall grant, issue, or verify such passports."

22 U.S.C. § 211a (1976 ed., Supp. IV). This language is unchanged since its original enactment in 1926.

The Passport Act does not, in so many words, confer upon the Secretary a power to revoke a passport. Nor, for that matter, does it expressly authorize denials of passport applications. Neither, however, does any statute expressly limit those powers. It is beyond dispute that the Secretary has the power to deny a passport for reasons not specified in the statutes. For example, in *Kent v. Dulles*, 357 U.S. 116 (1958), the Court recognized congressional acquiescence in Executive policies of refusing passports to applicants "participating in illegal conduct, trying to escape the toils of the law, promoting passport frauds, or otherwise engaging in conduct which would violate the laws of the United States." *Id.* at 357 U.S. 127. In *Zemel*, the Court held that "the weightiest considerations of national security" authorized the Secretary to restrict travel to Cuba at the time of the Cuban missile crisis. 381 U.S. at 381 U.S. 16. Agee concedes that, if the Secretary may deny a passport application for a certain reason, he may revoke a passport on the same ground.

2

Particularly in light of the "broad rulemaking authority granted in the [1926] Act," *Zemel*, 381 U.S. at 381 U.S. 12, a consistent administrative construction of that statute must be followed by the courts "unless there are compelling indications that it is wrong." *E. I. du Pont de Nemours & Co. v. Collins*, 432 U.S. 46, 432 U.S. 55 (1977), quoting *Red Lion Broadcasting Co. v. FCC*, 395 U.S. 367, 395 U.S. 381 (1969); see *Zemel*, supra, at 381 U.S. 11. This is especially so in the areas of foreign policy and national security, where congressional silence is not to be equated with congressional disapproval. [Footnote 21] In *United States v. Curtiss-Wright Export Corp.*, 299 U.S. 304 (1936), the volatile nature of problems confronting the Executive in foreign policy and national defense was underscored:

> "In this vast external realm, with its important, complicated, delicate and manifold problems, the President alone has the power to speak or listen as a representative of the nation. . . . As Marshall said in his great argument of March 7, 1800, in the House of Representatives, 'The President is the sole organ of the nation in its external relations, and its sole representative with foreign nations.'"

Id. at 299 U.S. 319.

Applying these considerations to statutory construction, the *Zemel* Court observed:

> "[B]ecause of the changeable and explosive nature of contemporary international relations, and the fact that the Executive is immediately privy to information which cannot be swiftly presented to, evaluated by, and acted upon by the legislature, *Congress—in giving the Executive authority over matters of foreign affairs—must of necessity paint with a brush broader than that it customarily wields in domestic areas.*"

381 U.S. at 381 U.S. 17 (emphasis supplied). Matters intimately related to foreign policy and national security are rarely proper subjects for judicial intervention. In *Harisiades v. Shaughnessy*, 342 U.S. 580 (1952), the Court observed that matters relating "to the conduct of foreign relations . . . are so exclusively entrusted to the political branches of government as to be largely immune from judicial inquiry or interference." *Id.* at 342 U.S. 589; *accord, Chicago & Southern Air Lines, Inc. v. Waterman S.S. Corp.*, 333 U.S. 103, 333 U.S. 111 (1948).

B

1

A passport is, in a sense, a letter of introduction in which the issuing sovereign vouches for the bearer and requests other sovereigns to aid the bearer. 3 G. Hackworth, Digest of International Law § 268, p. 499 (1942). Very early, the Court observed:

> "[A passport] is a document, which, from its nature and object, is addressed to foreign powers; purporting only to be a request, that the bearer of it may pass safely and freely; and is to be considered rather in the character of a political document, by which the bearer is recognised, in foreign countries, as an American citizen; and which, by usage and the law of nations, is received as evidence of the fact."

Urtetiqui v. D'Arcy, 9 Pet. 692, 34 U.S. 698 (1835).

With the enactment of travel control legislation making a passport generally a requirement for travel abroad, a passport took on certain added characteristics. Most important for present purposes, the only means by which an American can lawfully leave the country or return to it — absent a Presidentially granted exception — is with a passport. *See* 8 U.S.C. § 1185(b) (1976 ed., Supp. IV). As a travel control document, a passport is both proof of identity and proof of allegiance to the United States. Even under a travel control statute, however, a passport remains, in a sense, a document by which the Government vouches for the bearer and for his conduct.

The history of passport controls since the earliest days of the Republic shows congressional recognition of Executive authority to withhold passports on the basis of substantial reasons of national security and foreign policy. Prior to 1856, when there was no statute on the subject, the common perception was that the issuance of a passport was committed to the sole discretion of the Executive, and that the Executive would exercise this power in the interests of the national security and foreign policy of the United States. This derived from the generally accepted view that foreign policy was the province and responsibility of the Executive. From the outset, Congress endorsed not only the underlying premise of Executive authority in the areas of foreign policy and national security, but also its specific application to the subject of passports. Early Congresses enacted statutes expressly recognizing the Executive authority with respect to passports.

The first Passport Act, adopted in 1856, provided that the Secretary of State "shall be authorized to grant and issue passports . . . under such rules as the President shall designate and prescribe for and on behalf of the United States. . . ." § 23, 11 Stat. 60. This broad and permissive language worked no change in the power of the Executive to issue passports, nor was it intended to do so. The Act was passed to centralize passport authority in the Federal Government, and specifically in the Secretary of State. In all other respects, the 1856 Act "merely confirmed an authority already possessed and exercised by the Secretary of State. This authority was ancillary to his broader authority to protect American citizens in foreign countries, and was necessarily incident to his general authority to conduct the foreign affairs of the United States under the Chief Executive." Senate Committee on Government Operations, Reorganization of the Passport Functions of the Department of State, 86th Cong., 2d Sess., 13 (Comm. Print 1960).

The President and the Secretary of State consistently construed the 1856 Act to preserve their authority to withhold passports on national security and foreign policy grounds. . . .

. . . Executive Orders issued between 1907 and 1917 cast no doubt on this position. This policy was enforced in peacetime years to deny passports to citizens whose conduct abroad was "likely to embarrass the United States" or who were "disturbing, or endeavoring to disturb, the relations of this country with the representatives of foreign countries."

By enactment of the first travel control statute in 1918, Congress made clear its expectation that the Executive would curtail or prevent international travel by American citizens if it was contrary to the national security. The legislative history reveals that the principal reason for the 1918 statute was fear that "renegade Americans" would travel abroad and engage in "transference of important military information" to persons not entitled to it. The 1918 statute left the power to make exceptions exclusively in the hands of the Executive, without articulating specific standards. Unless the Secretary had power to apply national security criteria in passport decisions, the purpose of the Travel Control Act would plainly have been frustrated.

Against this background, and while the 1918 provisions were still in effect, Congress enacted the Passport Act of 1926. The legislative history of the statute is sparse. However, Congress used language which is identical in pertinent part to that in the 1856 statute (*supra* at 453 U.S. 294), as amended, and the legislative history clearly shows congressional awareness of the Executive policy. There is no evidence of any intent to repudiate the longstanding administrative construction. Absent such evidence, we conclude that Congress, in 1926, adopted the longstanding administrative construction of the 1856 statute. *See Lorillard v. Pons*, 434 U.S. 575, 434 U.S. 580-581 (1978).

The Executive construed the 1926 Act to work no change in prior practice, and specifically interpreted it to authorize denial of a passport on grounds of national security or foreign policy. Indeed, by an unbroken line of Executive Orders, regulations, instructions to consular officials, and notices to passport holders, the President and the Department of State left no doubt that likelihood of damage to national security or foreign policy of the United States was the single most important criterion in passport decisions. The regulations are instructive. The 1952 version authorized denial of passports to citizens engaged in activities which would violate laws designed to protect the security of the United States "[i]n order to promote the national interest by assuring that the conduct of foreign relations shall be free from unlawful interference."

17 Fed. Reg. 8013 (1952). The 1956 amendment to this regulation provided that a passport should be denied to any person whose

> "activities abroad would: (a) violate the laws of the United States;(b) be prejudicial to the orderly conduct of foreign relations; or (c) otherwise be prejudicial to the interests of the United States." 22 CFR § 51.136 (1958).

This regulation remained in effect continuously until 1966.

This history of administrative construction was repeatedly communicated to Congress, not only by routine promulgation of Executive Orders and regulations, but also by specific presentations, including 1957 and 1966 reports by the Department of State explaining the 1956 regulation and a 1960 Senate Staff Report which concluded that "the authority to issue or withhold passports has, by precedent and law, been vested in the Secretary of State as a part of his responsibility to protect American citizens traveling abroad, and what he considered to be the best interests of the Nation."

In 1966, the Secretary of State promulgated the regulations at issue in this case. 22 CFR §§ 51.70(b)(4), 51.71(a) (1980). Closely paralleling the 1956 regulation, these provisions authorize revocation of a passport where

> "[t]he Secretary determines that the national's activities abroad are causing or are likely to cause serious damage to the national security or the foreign policy of the United States."

2

Zemel recognized that congressional acquiescence may sometimes be found from nothing more than silence in the face of an administrative policy. 381 U.S. at 381 U.S. 11; *see Udall v. Tallman*, 380 U.S. 1, 380 U.S. 118 (1965); *Norwegian Nitrogen Co. v. United States*, 288 U.S. 294, 288 U.S. 313 (1933); *Costanzo v. Tillinghast*, 287 U.S. 341, 287 U.S. 345 (1932). Here, however, the inference of congressional approval "is supported by more than mere congressional inaction." *Zemel*, 381 U.S. at 381 U.S. 11-12. Twelve years after the promulgation of the regulations at issue and 22 years after promulgation of the similar 1956 regulation, Congress enacted the statute making it unlawful to travel abroad without a passport even in peacetime. 8 U.S.C. § 1185(b) (1976 ed., Supp. IV). Simultaneously, Congress amended the Passport Act of 1926 to provide that, "unless authorized by law," in the absence of war, armed hostilities, or imminent danger to travelers, a passport may not be geographically restricted. Title 8 U.S.C. § 1185(b) (1976 ed., Supp. IV) must be read *in pari materia* with the Passport Act. *Zemel, supra,* at 381 U.S. 11-12; *see* 2A C. Sands, Sutherland on Statutory Construction § 51.0, p. 299 (4th ed. 1973); *cf. Erlenbaugh v. United States*, 409 U.S. 239, 409 U.S. 243-244 (1972). [Footnote 49]

The 1978 amendments are weighty evidence of congressional approval of the Secretary's interpretation, particularly that in the 1966 regulations. Despite the longstanding and officially promulgated view that the Executive had the power to withhold passports for reasons of national security and foreign policy, Congress, in 1978, "though it once again enacted legislation relating to passports, left completely untouched the broad rulemaking authority granted in the earlier Act." *Zemel, supra*, at 381 U.S. 12; *accord, NLRB v. Bell Aerospace Co.*, 416 U.S. 267, 416 U.S. 274-275 (1974).

3

Agee argues that the only way the Executive can establish implicit congressional approval is by proof of longstanding and consistent *enforcement* of the claimed power: that is, by showing that many passports were revoked on national security and foreign policy grounds. . . .

A necessary premise for Agee's contention is that there were frequent occasions for revocation, and that the claimed Executive power was exercised in only a few of those cases. However, if there were no occasions — or few — to call the Secretary's authority into play, the absence of frequent instances of enforcement is wholly irrelevant. The exercise of a power emerges only in relation to a factual situation, and the continued validity of the power is not diluted simply because there is no need to use it.

The history is clear that there have been few situations involving substantial likelihood of serious damage to the national security or foreign policy of the United States as a result of a passport holder's activities abroad, and that, in the cases which have arisen, the Secretary has consistently exercised his power to withhold passports. Perhaps the most notable example of enforcement of the administrative policy, which surely could not have escaped the attention of Congress, was the 1948 denial of a passport to a Member of Congress who sought to go abroad to support a movement in Greece to overthrow the existing government. Another example was the 1954 revocation of a passport held by a man who was supplying arms to groups abroad whose interests were contrary to positions taken by the United States. In 1970, the Secretary revoked passports of two persons who sought to travel to the site of an international airplane hijacking. *See also* Note, 61 Yale L.J. 170, 174-176 (1952).

The Secretary has construed and applied his regulations consistently, and it would be anomalous to fault the Government because there were so few occasions to exercise the announced policy and practice. Although a pattern of actual enforcement is one indicator of Executive policy, it suffices that the Executive has "openly asserted" the power at issue. *Zemel*, 381 U.S. at 381 U.S. 9; *see id.* at 381 U.S. 10.

. . .

Agee also contends that the statements of Executive policy are entitled to diminished weight because many of them concern the powers of the Executive in wartime. However, the statute provides no support for this argument. History eloquently attests that grave problems of national security and foreign policy are by no means limited to times of formally declared war.

4

. . .

We hold that the policy announced in the challenged regulations is "sufficiently substantial and consistent" to compel the conclusion that Congress has approved it. *See Zemel*, 381 U.S. at 381 U.S. 12.

III

Agee also attacks the Secretary's action on three constitutional grounds: first, that the revocation of his passport impermissibly burdens his freedom to travel; second, that the action was intended to penalize his exercise of free speech and deter his criticism of Government policies and practices; and third, that failure to accord him a prerevocation hearing violated his Fifth Amendment right to procedural due process.

In light of the express language of the passport regulations, which permits their application only in cases involving likelihood of "serious damage" to national security or foreign policy, these claims are without merit.

Revocation of a passport undeniably curtails travel, but the freedom to travel abroad with a "letter of introduction" in the form of a passport issued by the sovereign is subordinate to national security and foreign policy considerations; as such, it is subject to reasonable governmental regulation. The Court has made it plain that the freedom to travel outside the United States must be distinguished from the right to travel within the United States. This was underscored in *Califano v. Aznavorian*, 439 U.S. 170, 176 (1978):

> "Aznavorian urges that the freedom of international travel is basically equivalent to the constitutional right to interstate travel, recognized by this Court for over 100 years. . . . But this Court has often pointed out the crucial difference between the freedom to travel internationally and the right of interstate travel. "'The constitutional right of interstate travel is virtually unqualified, United States v. Guest, 383 U. S. 745, 757-758 (1966); Griffin v. Breckenridge, 403 U. S. 88, 105-106 (1971). By contrast the "right" of international travel has been considered to be no more than an aspect of the "liberty" protected by the Due Process Clause of the Fifth Amendment. As such this "right," the Court has held, can be regulated within the bounds of due process.' (Citations omitted.) Califano v. Torres, 435 U. S. 1, 4 n. 6."

It is "obvious and unarguable" that no governmental interest is more compelling than the security of the Nation. *Aptheker v. Secretary of State*, 378 U.S., at 509; accord *Cole v. Young*, 351 U.S. 536, 546 (1956); see *Zemel, supra*, at 13-17. Protection of the foreign policy of the United States is a governmental interest of great importance, since foreign policy and national security considerations cannot neatly be compartmentalized.

Measures to protect the secrecy of our Government's foreign intelligence operations plainly serve these interests. . . .

Not only has Agee jeopardized the security of the United States, but he has also endangered the interests of countries other than the United States thereby creating serious problems for American foreign relations and foreign policy. Restricting Agee's foreign travel, although perhaps not certain to prevent all of Agee's harmful activities, is the only avenue open to the Government to limit these activities.

Assuming, arguendo, that First Amendment protections reach beyond our national boundaries, Agee's First Amendment claim has no foundation. The revocation of Agee's passport rests in part on the content of his speech: specifically, his repeated disclosures of intelligence operations and names of intelligence personnel. Long ago, however, this Court recognized that "[n]o one would question but that a government might prevent actual obstruction to its recruiting service or the publication of the sailing dates of transports or the number and location of troops." *Near v. Minnesota ex rel. Olson*, 283 U.S. 697, 716 (1931), citing Z. Chafee, Freedom of Speech 10 (1920). Agee's disclosures, among other things, have the declared purpose of obstructing intelligence operations and the recruiting of intelligence personnel. They are clearly not protected by the Constitution. The mere fact that Agee is also engaged in criticism of the Government does not render his conduct beyond the reach of the law.

To the extent the revocation of his passport operates to inhibit Agee, "it is an inhibition of *action*," rather than of speech. *Zemel*, 381 U.S., at 16-17 (emphasis supplied). Agee is as free to criticize the United States Government as he was when he held a passport—always subject, of course, to express limits on certain rights by virtue of his contract with the Government.[61]

On this record, the Government is not required to hold a prerevocation hearing. . . . [W]hen there is a substantial likelihood of "serious damage" to national security or foreign policy as a result of a passport holder's activities in foreign countries, the Government may take action to ensure that the holder may not exploit the sponsorship of his travels by the United States. "[W]hile the Constitution protects against invasions of individual rights, it is not a suicide pact." *Kennedy v. Mendoza-Martinez*, 372 U.S. 144, 160 (1963). The Constitution's due process guarantees call for no more than what has been accorded here: a statement of reasons and an opportunity for a prompt postrevocation hearing.

We reverse the judgment of the Court of Appeals and remand for further proceedings consistent with this opinion.

Reversed and remanded.

NOTES AND QUESTIONS

1. The deaths of several CIA operatives were attributed to Agee's overseas efforts to reveal their identities. Why didn't the United States government simply ask a European ally to arrest Agee for extradition to the United States? A clue may be found in the oral argument in the case, during which Solicitor General Wade

---

61. See *Snepp v. United States, supra.*

McCree acknowledged that Agee's conduct, however reprehensible, "may not be punishable, we're not contending that it's punishable here."

When asked by the Court what would happen if Agee returned to the United States, General McCree replied, "He would not get out again." Should it matter that the government wished to use passport revocation to prevent or punish conduct that Congress apparently had not considered when enacting the relevant legislation? Does that put this case into Justice Jackson's third category? Justice Rehnquist wrote that "[t]he Passport Act does not, in so many words, confer upon the Secretary a power to revoke a passport. Nor, for that matter, does it expressly authorize denials of passport applications. Neither, however, does any statute expressly limit those powers. It is beyond dispute that the Secretary has the power to deny a passport for reasons not specified in the statutes." How similar or different is the reasoning in this case to the reasoning found in the *Youngstown* opinions of Justices Black, Frankfurter, and Jackson?

2. In *Little v. Barreme* (discussed in detail in Chapter 7), the Court gave a strict interpretation to a statute authorizing seizure of vessels "bound or sailing to" French ports or dependencies, rejecting as unauthorized any seizure of American ships sailing "from" such places. This was so, even though the Court recognized that "if only vessels sailing to a French port could be seized on the high seas, that the law would be very often evaded" and that the executive branch's broader "to-and-from" interpretation was "much better calculated to give it effect." Yet, in *Haig v. Agee*, the Court found that "congressional acquiescence may sometimes be found from nothing more than silence in the face of an administrative policy." Was it then just a matter of *timing* that determined that Captain Little was liable for exceeding statutory authorization but Secretary of State Haig could exceed the literal boundaries of the passport laws? Alternatively, could it be that the view of the executive branch's inherent authorities relevant to congressional roles in foreign affairs have shifted *sub silentio* over time? Which is the better approach to statutory interpretation in these Quasi-War and Cold War contexts?

3. The Court notes that the nature of the passport has changed dramatically over time notwithstanding the use of the same word to describe what shifted from a "letter of introduction" addressed to a foreign power to a license of "travel control" that is "the only means by which an American can lawfully leave the country or return to it—absent a Presidentially granted exception[.]" What weight should judicial precedents have when passports and travel have changed so much? What "lessons of history" (to borrow from Chapter 2) should be considered in evaluating the relevancy of older, but not overruled, sources of authority?

In *Haig v. Agee*, as in *Dames & Moore*, the Court concluded that President Reagan had acted consistently with the will of Congress. But what if they had reached the opposite conclusion? Would the President prevail simply because the action at issue involved foreign affairs? Decisions related to the U.S. relationship with other nations obviously falls within the scope of "foreign affairs." But such decisions often implicate constitutional powers vested in both the President and Congress. For example, the President may decide that providing foreign economic or military aid to another nation will make an important contribution to U.S. national security, but only Congress is vested with the constitutional authority to appropriate funds to support such an initiative.

In many situations, however, the line between presidential and congressional authority and the limits imposed by the Constitution on the exercise of authority by either branch will be less clear. In such a situation, the Court may have to decide the extent to which Congress may limit the President's prerogative. The next case provides an example. It also calls into question the precedential significance of Justice Sutherland's invocation of the "sole organ" language as it relates to the scope of the President's inherent foreign affairs powers.

Zivotofsky v. Kerry
576 U.S. 1059 (2015)

Justice KENNEDY delivered the opinion of the Court.

A delicate subject lies in the background of this case. That subject is Jerusalem. Questions touching upon the history of the ancient city and its present legal and international status are among the most difficult and complex in international affairs. In our constitutional system these matters are committed to the Legislature and the Executive, not the Judiciary. As a result, in this opinion the Court does no more, and must do no more, than note the existence of international debate and tensions respecting Jerusalem. Those matters are for Congress and the President to discuss and consider as they seek to shape the Nation's foreign policies.

The Court addresses two questions to resolve the interbranch dispute now before it. First, it must determine whether the President has the exclusive power to grant formal recognition to a foreign sovereign. Second, if he has that power, the Court must determine whether Congress can command the President and his Secretary of State to issue a formal statement that contradicts the earlier recognition. The statement in question here is a congressional mandate that allows a United States citizen born in Jerusalem to direct the President and Secretary of State, when issuing his passport, to state that his place of birth is "Israel."

I

A

Jerusalem's political standing has long been, and remains, one of the most sensitive issues in American foreign policy, and indeed it is one of the most delicate issues in current international affairs. In 1948, President Truman formally recognized Israel in a signed statement of "recognition." See Statement by the President Announcing Recognition of the State of Israel, Public Papers of the Presidents, May 14, 1948, p. 258 (1964). That statement did not recognize Israeli sovereignty over Jerusalem. Over the last 60 years, various actors have sought to assert full or partial sovereignty over the city, including Israel, Jordan, and the Palestinians. Yet, in contrast to a consistent policy of formal recognition of Israel, neither President Truman nor any later United States President has issued an official statement or declaration acknowledging any country's sovereignty over Jerusalem. Instead, the Executive Branch has maintained that " 'the status of Jerusalem . . . should be decided not unilaterally but in consultation with all concerned.' " . . .

The President's position on Jerusalem is reflected in State Department policy regarding passports and consular reports of birth abroad. Understanding that passports will be construed as reflections of American policy, the State Department's Foreign Affairs Manual instructs its employees, in general, to record the place of birth on a passport as the "country [having] present sovereignty over the actual area of birth." Dept. of State, 7 Foreign Affairs Manual (FAM) § 1383.4 (1987). If a citizen objects to the country listed as sovereign by the State Department, he or she may list the city or town of birth rather than the country. See *id.*, § 1383.6. The FAM, however, does not allow citizens to list a sovereign that conflicts with Executive Branch policy. See generally *id.*, § 1383. Because the United States does not recognize any country as having sovereignty over Jerusalem, the FAM instructs employees to record the place of birth for citizens born there as "Jerusalem." *Id.*, § 1383.5-6 (emphasis deleted).

In 2002, Congress passed the Act at issue here, the Foreign Relations Authorization Act, Fiscal Year 2003, 116 Stat. 1350. Section 214 of the Act is titled "United States Policy with Respect to Jerusalem as the Capital of Israel." *Id.*, at 1365. The subsection that lies at the heart of this case, § 214(d), addresses passports. That subsection seeks to override the FAM by allowing citizens born in Jerusalem to list their place of birth as "Israel." Titled "Record of Place of Birth as Israel for Passport Purposes," § 214(d) states "[f]or purposes of the registration of birth, certification of nationality, or issuance of a passport of a United States citizen born in the city of Jerusalem, the Secretary shall, upon the request of the citizen or the citizen's legal guardian, record the place of birth as Israel." *Id.*, at 1366.

When he signed the Act into law, President George W. Bush issued a statement declaring his position that § 214 would, "if construed as mandatory rather than advisory, impermissibly interfere with the President's constitutional authority to formulate the position of the United States, speak for the Nation in international affairs, and determine the terms on which recognition is given to foreign states." . . .

B

In 2002, petitioner Menachem Binyamin Zivotofsky was born to United States citizens living in Jerusalem. App. 24-25. In December 2002, Zivotofsky's mother visited the American Embassy in Tel Aviv to request both a passport and a consular report of birth abroad for her son. *Id.*, at 25. She asked that his place of birth be listed as " 'Jerusalem, Israel.' " *Ibid.* The Embassy clerks explained that, pursuant to State Department policy, the passport would list only "Jerusalem." *Ibid.* Zivotofsky's parents objected and, as his guardians, brought suit on his behalf in the United States District Court for the District of Columbia, seeking to enforce § 214(d).

Pursuant to § 214(d), Zivotofsky claims the right to have "Israel" recorded as his place of birth in his passport. . . . As a result, the Court addresses Zivotofsky's passport arguments and need not engage in a separate analysis of the validity of § 214(d) as applied to consular reports of birth abroad.

After Zivotofsky brought suit, the District Court dismissed his case, reasoning that it presented a nonjusticiable political question and that Zivotofsky lacked standing. App. 28-39. The Court of Appeals for the District of Columbia Circuit reversed on the standing issue, *Zivotofsky v. Secretary of State,* 444 F.3d 614, 617-619 (2006), but later affirmed the District Court's political question determination. See *Zivotofsky* v. *Secretary of State,* 571 F.3d 1227, 1228 (2009).

This Court granted certiorari, vacated the judgment, and remanded the case. Whether § 214(d) is constitutional, the Court held, is not a question reserved for the political branches. In reference to Zivotofsky's claim the Court observed "the Judiciary must decide if Zivotofsky's interpretation of the statute is correct, and whether the statute is constitutional" — not whether Jerusalem is, in fact, part of Israel. *Zivotofsky v. Clinton, supra,* at ___ (slip op., at 7).

On remand the Court of Appeals held the statute unconstitutional. It determined that "the President exclusively holds the power to determine whether to recognize a foreign sovereign," 725 F.3d, at 214, and that "section 214(d) directly contradicts a carefully considered exercise of the Executive branch's recognition power." *Id.,* at 217.

This Court again granted certiorari.

II

. . .

In this case the Secretary contends that § 214(d) infringes on the President's exclusive recognition power by "requiring the President to contradict his recognition position regarding Jerusalem in official communications with foreign sovereigns." [The Court then explained that because the State Department policy contradicted the statute, it should only be sustained if the power at issue is exclusively vested in the President.]

To determine whether the President possesses the exclusive power of recognition the Court examines the Constitution's text and structure, as well as precedent and history bearing on the question.

A

Recognition is a "formal acknowledgement" that a particular "entity possesses the qualifications for statehood" or "that a particular regime is the effective government of a state." Restatement (Third) of Foreign Relations Law of the United States § 203, Comment *a,* p. 84 (1986). . . . It may also be implied — for example, by concluding a bilateral treaty or by sending or receiving diplomatic agents. *Ibid.*; I. Brownlie, Principles of Public International Law 93 (7th ed. 2008) (Brownlie).

Legal consequences follow formal recognition. Recognized sovereigns may sue in United States courts, see *Guaranty Trust Co. v. United States*, 304 U.S. 126, 137 (1938), and may benefit from sovereign immunity when they are sued, see *National City Bank of N. Y. v. Republic of China*, 348 U.S. 356, 358-359 (1955). The actions of a recognized sovereign committed within its own territory also receive deference in domestic courts under the act of state doctrine. See *Oetjen v. Central Leather Co.*, 246 U.S. 297, 302-303 (1918). Recognition at international law, furthermore, is a precondition of regular diplomatic relations. 1 Moore § 27, at 72. Recognition is thus "useful, even necessary," to the existence of a state. *Ibid.*

Despite the importance of the recognition power in foreign relations, the Constitution does not use the term "recognition," either in Article II or elsewhere. The Secretary asserts that the President exercises the recognition power based on the Reception Clause, which directs that the President "shall receive Ambassadors and other public Ministers." Art. II, § 3. As Zivotofsky notes, the Reception Clause received little attention at the Constitutional Convention. See Reinstein, Recognition: A Case Study on the Original Understanding of Executive Power, 45 U. Rich. L. Rev. 801, 860-862 (2011). In fact, during the ratification debates, Alexander Hamilton claimed that the power to receive ambassadors was "more a matter of dignity than of authority," a ministerial duty largely "without consequence." The Federalist No. 69, p. 420 (C. Rossiter ed. 1961).

At the time of the founding, however, prominent international scholars suggested that receiving an ambassador was tantamount to recognizing the sovereignty of the sending state. . . . It is a logical and proper inference, then, that a Clause directing the President alone to receive ambassadors would be understood to acknowledge his power to recognize other nations.

This in fact occurred early in the Nation's history when President Washington recognized the French Revolutionary Government by receiving its ambassador. See A. Hamilton, Pacificus No. 1, in The Letters of Pacificus and Helvidius 5, 13-14 (1845) (reprint 1976) (President "acknowledged the republic of France, by the reception of its minister"). After this incident the import of the Reception Clause became clear—causing Hamilton to change his earlier view. He wrote that the Reception Clause "includes th[e power] of judging, in the case of a revolution of government in a foreign country, whether the new rulers are competent organs of the national will, and ought to be recognised, or not." See *id.*, at 12; see also 3 J. Story, Commentaries on the Constitution of the United States § 1560, p. 416 (1833) ("If the executive receives an ambassador, or other minister, as the representative of a new nation . . . it is an acknowledgment of the sovereign authority *de facto* of such new nation, or party"). As a result, the Reception Clause provides support, although not the sole authority, for the President's power to recognize other nations.

The inference that the President exercises the recognition power is further supported by his additional Article II powers. It is for the President, "by and with the Advice and Consent of the Senate," to "make Treaties, provided two thirds of the Senators present concur." Art. II, § 2, cl. 2. In addition, "he shall nominate, and by and with the Advice and Consent of the Senate, shall appoint Ambassadors" as well as "other public Ministers and Consuls." *Ibid.*

As a matter of constitutional structure, these additional powers give the President control over recognition decisions. At international law, recognition may be effected by different means, but each means is dependent upon Presidential power. In addition to receiving an ambassador, recognition may occur on "the conclusion of a bilateral treaty," or the "formal initiation of diplomatic relations," including the dispatch of an ambassador. Brownlie 93; see also 1 Moore § 27, at 73. The President has the sole power to negotiate treaties, see *United States v. Curtiss-Wright Export Corp.*, 299 U.S. 304, 319 (1936), and the Senate may not conclude or ratify a treaty without Presidential action. The President, too, nominates the Nation's ambassadors and dispatches other diplomatic agents. Congress may not send an ambassador without his involvement. Beyond that, the President himself has the power to open diplomatic channels simply by engaging in direct diplomacy with foreign heads of state and their ministers. The Constitution thus assigns the President means to effect recognition on his own initiative. Congress, by contrast, has no constitutional power that would enable it to initiate diplomatic relations with a foreign nation. Because these specific Clauses confer the recognition power on the President, the Court need not consider whether or to what extent the Vesting Clause, which provides that the "executive Power" shall be vested in the President, provides further support for the President's action here. Art. II, § 1, cl. 1.

The text and structure of the Constitution grant the President the power to recognize foreign nations and governments. The question then becomes whether that power is exclusive. The various ways in which the President may unilaterally effect recognition—and the lack of any similar power vested in Congress—suggest that it is. So, too, do functional considerations. Put simply, the Nation must have a single policy regarding which governments are legitimate in the eyes of the United States and which are not. Foreign countries need to know, before entering into diplomatic relations or commerce with the United States, whether their ambassadors will be received; whether their officials will be immune from suit in federal court; and whether they may initiate lawsuits here to vindicate their rights. These assurances cannot be equivocal.

Recognition is a topic on which the Nation must " 'speak . . . with one voice.' " *American Ins. Assn. v. Garamendi*, 539 U.S. 396, 424 (2003) (quoting *Crosby v. National Foreign Trade Council*, 530 U.S. 363, 381 (2000)). That voice must be the President's. Between the two political branches, only the Executive has the characteristic of unity at all times. And with unity comes the ability to exercise, to a greater degree, "[d]ecision, activity, secrecy, and dispatch." The Federalist No. 70, p. 424 (A. Hamilton). The President is capable, in ways Congress is not, of engaging in the delicate and often secret diplomatic contacts that may lead to a decision on recognition. See, *e.g.*, *United States v. Pink*, 315 U.S. 203, 229 (1942). He is also better positioned to take the decisive, unequivocal action necessary to recognize other states at international law. 1 Oppenheim's International Law § 50, p. 169 (R. Jennings & A. Watts eds., 9th ed. 1992) (act of recognition must "leave no doubt as to the intention to grant it"). These qualities explain why the Framers listed the traditional avenues of recognition—receiving ambassadors, making treaties, and sending ambassadors—as among the President's Article II powers.

As described in more detail below, the President since the founding has exercised this unilateral power to recognize new states—and the Court has endorsed the practice. See *Banco Nacional de Cuba v. Sabbatino*, 376 U.S. 398, 410 (1964); *Pink, supra,* at 229; *Williams* v. *Suffolk Ins. Co.,* 13 Pet. 415, 420 (1839). Texts and treatises on international law treat the President's word as the final word on recognition. See, *e.g.*, Restatement (Third) of Foreign Relations Law § 204, at 89 ("Under the Constitution of the United States the President has exclusive authority to recognize or not to recognize a foreign state or government"); see also L. Henkin, Foreign Affairs and the U.S. Constitution 43 (2d ed. 1996) ("It is no longer questioned that the President does not merely perform the ceremony of receiving foreign ambassadors but also determines whether the United States should recognize or refuse to recognize a foreign government"). In light of this authority all six judges who considered this case in the Court of Appeals agreed that the President holds the exclusive recognition power. See 725 F.3d, at 214 ("[W]e conclude that the President exclusively holds the power to determine whether to recognize a foreign sovereign"); *Zivotofsky*, 571 F.3d, at 1231 ("That this power belongs solely to the President has been clear from the earliest days of the Republic"); *id.*, at 1240 (Edwards, J., concurring) ("The Executive has exclusive and unreviewable authority to recognize foreign sovereigns").

It remains true, of course, that many decisions affecting foreign relations—including decisions that may determine the course of our relations with recognized countries—require congressional action. Congress may "regulate Commerce with foreign Nations," "establish an uniform Rule of Naturalization," "define and punish Piracies and Felonies committed on the high Seas, and Offences against the Law of Nations," "declare War," "grant Letters of Marque and Reprisal," and "make Rules for the Government and Regulation of the land and naval Forces." U.S. Const., Art. I, § 8. In addition, the President cannot make a treaty or appoint an ambassador without the approval of the Senate. Art. II, § 2, cl. 2. The President, furthermore, could not build an American Embassy abroad without congressional appropriation of the necessary funds. Art. I, § 8, cl. 1. Under basic separation-of-powers principles, it is for the Congress to enact the laws, including "all Laws which shall be necessary and proper for carrying into Execution" the powers of the Federal Government. § 8, cl. 18.

In foreign affairs, as in the domestic realm, the Constitution "enjoins upon its branches separateness but interdependence, autonomy but reciprocity." *Youngstown*, 343 U.S., at 635 (Jackson, J., concurring). Although the President alone effects the formal act of recognition, Congress' powers, and its central role in making laws, give it substantial authority regarding many of the policy determinations that precede and follow the act of recognition itself. If Congress disagrees with the President's recognition policy, there may be consequences. Formal recognition may seem a hollow act if it is not accompanied by the dispatch of an ambassador, the easing of trade restrictions, and the conclusion of treaties. And those decisions require action by the Senate or the whole Congress.

In practice, then, the President's recognition determination is just one part of a political process that may require Congress to make laws. The President's exclusive recognition power encompasses the authority to acknowledge, in a formal sense, the legitimacy of other states and governments, including their territorial bounds. Albeit limited, the exclusive recognition power is essential to the conduct of Presidential duties. The formal act of recognition is an executive power that Congress may not qualify. If the President is to be effective in negotiations over a formal recognition determination, it must be evident to his counterparts abroad that he speaks for the Nation on that precise question.

A clear rule that the formal power to recognize a foreign government subsists in the President therefore serves a necessary purpose in diplomatic relations. All this, of course, underscores that Congress has an important role in other aspects of foreign policy, and the President may be bound by any number of laws Congress enacts. In this way ambition counters ambition, ensuring that the democratic will of the people is observed and respected in foreign affairs as in the domestic realm. See The Federalist No. 51, p. 322 (J. Madison).

B

No single precedent resolves the question whether the President has exclusive recognition authority and, if so, how far that power extends. In part that is because, until today, the political branches have resolved their disputes over questions of recognition. The relevant cases, though providing important instruction, address the division of recognition power between the Federal Government and the States, see, *e.g., Pink*, 315 U.S. 203, or between the courts and the political branches, see, *e.g., Banco Nacional de Cuba*, 376 U.S., at 410 — not between the President and Congress. As the parties acknowledge, some isolated statements in those cases lend support to the position that Congress has a role in the recognition process. In the end, however, a fair reading of the cases shows that the President's role in the recognition process is both central and exclusive.

During the administration of President Van Buren, in a case involving a dispute over the status of the Falkland Islands, the Court noted that "when the executive branch of the government" assumes "a fact in regard to the sovereignty of any island or country, it is conclusive on the judicial department." *Williams*, 13 Pet., at 420. Once the President has made his determination, it "is enough to know, that in the exercise of his constitutional functions, he has decided the question. Having done this under the responsibilities which belong to him, it is obligatory on the people and government of the Union." *Ibid.*

Later, during the 1930's and 1940's, the Court addressed issues surrounding President Roosevelt's decision to recognize the Soviet Government of Russia. In *United States v. Belmont*, 301 U.S. 324 (1937), and *Pink*, 315 U.S. 203, New York state courts declined to give full effect to the terms of executive agreements the President had concluded in negotiations over recognition of the Soviet regime. In particular the state courts, based on New York public policy, did not treat assets that had been seized by the Soviet Government as property of Russia and declined to turn those assets over to the United States. The Court stated that it "may not be doubted" that "recognition, establishment of diplomatic relations, . . . and agreements with respect thereto" are "within the competence of the President." *Belmont*, 301 U.S., at 330. In these matters, "the Executive ha[s] authority to speak as the sole organ of th[e] government." *Ibid*. The Court added that the President's authority "is not limited to a determination of the government to be recognized. It includes the power to determine the policy which is to govern the question of recognition." *Pink*, *supra*, at 229; see also *Guaranty Trust Co.*, 304 U.S., at 137-138 (The "political department['s] . . . action in recognizing a foreign government and in receiving its diplomatic representatives is conclusive on all domestic courts"). Thus, New York state courts were required to respect the executive agreements.

It is true, of course, that *Belmont* and *Pink* are not direct holdings that the recognition power is exclusive. Those cases considered the validity of executive agreements, not the initial act of recognition. The President's determination in those cases did not contradict an Act of Congress. And the primary issue was whether the executive agreements could supersede state law. Still, the language in *Pink* and *Belmont*, which confirms the President's competence to determine questions of recognition, is strong support for the conclusion that it is for the President alone to determine which foreign governments are legitimate.

Banco Nacional de Cuba contains even stronger statements regarding the President's authority over recognition. There, the status of Cuba's Government and its acts as a sovereign were at issue. As the Court explained, "Political recognition is exclusively a function of the Executive." 376 U.S., at 410. Because the Executive had recognized the Cuban Government, the Court held that it should be treated as sovereign and could benefit from the "act of state" doctrine. See also *Baker v. Carr*, 369 U.S. 186, 213 (1962) ("[I]t is the executive that determines a person's status as representative of a foreign government"); *National City Bank of N.Y.*, 348 U.S., at 358 ("The status of the Republic of China in our courts is a matter for determination by the Executive and is outside the competence of this Court"). As these cases illustrate, the Court has long considered recognition to be the exclusive prerogative of the Executive.

The Secretary now urges the Court to define the executive power over foreign relations in even broader terms. He contends that under the Court's precedent the President has "exclusive authority to conduct diplomatic relations," along with "the bulk of foreign-affairs powers." Brief for Respondent 18, 16. In support of his submission that the President has broad, undefined powers over foreign affairs, the Secretary quotes *United States v. Curtiss-Wright*

Export Corp., which described the President as "the sole organ of the federal government in the field of international relations." 299 U.S., at 320. This Court declines to acknowledge that unbounded power. A formulation broader than the rule that the President alone determines what nations to formally recognize as legitimate—and that he consequently controls his statements on matters of recognition—presents different issues and is unnecessary to the resolution of this case.

The *Curtiss-Wright* case does not extend so far as the Secretary suggests. In *Curtiss-Wright*, the Court considered whether a congressional delegation of power to the President was constitutional. Congress had passed a joint resolution giving the President the discretion to prohibit arms sales to certain militant powers in South America. The resolution provided criminal penalties for violation of those orders. *Id.*, at 311-312. The Court held that the delegation was constitutional, reasoning that Congress may grant the President substantial authority and discretion in the field of foreign affairs. *Id.*, at 315-329. Describing why such broad delegation may be appropriate, the opinion stated:

> "In this vast external realm, with its important, complicated, delicate and manifold problems, the President alone has the power to speak or listen as a representative of the nation. He *makes* treaties with the advice and consent of the Senate; but he alone negotiates. Into the field of negotiation the Senate cannot intrude; and Congress itself is powerless to invade it. As Marshall said in his great argument of March 7, 1800, in the House of Representatives, 'The President is the sole organ of the nation in its external relations, and its sole representative with foreign nations.' [10 Annals of Cong.] 613." *Id.*, at 319.

This description of the President's exclusive power was not necessary to the holding of *Curtiss-Wright*—which, after all, dealt with congressionally authorized action, not a unilateral Presidential determination. Indeed, *Curtiss-Wright* did not hold that the President is free from Congress' lawmaking power in the field of international relations. The President does have a unique role in communicating with foreign governments, as then-Congressman John Marshall acknowledged. See 10 Annals of Cong. 613 (1800) (cited in *Curtiss-Wright, supra*, at 319). But whether the realm is foreign or domestic, it is still the Legislative Branch, not the Executive Branch, that makes the law.

In a world that is ever more compressed and interdependent, it is essential the congressional role in foreign affairs be understood and respected. For it is Congress that makes laws, and in countless ways its laws will and should shape the Nation's course. The Executive is not free from the ordinary controls and checks of Congress merely because foreign affairs are at issue. See, *e.g., Medellín v. Texas*, 552 U.S. 491, 523-532 (2008); *Youngstown*, 343 U.S., at 589; *Little v. Barreme*, 2 Cranch 170, 177-179 (1804); Glennon, Two Views of Presidential Foreign Affairs Power: *Little v. Barreme* or *Curtiss-Wright*? 13 Yale J. Int'l L. 5, 19-20 (1988); cf. *Dames & Moore v. Regan*, 453 U.S. 654, 680-681 (1981). It is not for the President alone to determine the whole content of the Nation's foreign policy.

That said, judicial precedent and historical practice teach that it is for the President alone to make the specific decision of what foreign power he will recognize as legitimate, both for the Nation as a whole and for the purpose of making his own position clear within the context of recognition in discussions and negotiations with foreign nations. Recognition is an act with immediate and powerful significance for international relations, so the President's position must be clear. Congress cannot require him to contradict his own statement regarding a determination of formal recognition.

Zivotofsky's contrary arguments are unconvincing. The decisions he relies upon are largely inapposite. This Court's cases do not hold that the recognition power is shared. *Jones v. United States*, 137 U.S. 202 (1890), and *Boumediene v. Bush*, 553 U.S. 723 (2008), each addressed the status of territories controlled or acquired by the United States—not whether a province ought to be recognized as part of a foreign country. See also *Vermilya-Brown Co. v. Connell*, 335 U.S. 377, 380 (1948) ("[D]etermination of [American] sovereignty over an area is for the legislative and executive departments"). And no one disputes that Congress has a role in determining the status of United States territories. See U.S. Const., Art. IV, § 3, cl. 2 (Congress may "dispose of and make all needful Rules and Regulations respecting the Territory or other Property belonging to the United States"). Other cases describing a shared power address the recognition of Indian tribes—which is, similarly, a distinct issue from the recognition of foreign countries. See *Cherokee Nation v. Georgia*, 5 Pet. 1 (1831).

To be sure, the Court has mentioned both of the political branches in discussing international recognition, but it has done so primarily in affirming that the Judiciary is not responsible for recognizing foreign nations. . . . This is consistent with the fact that Congress, in the ordinary course, does support the President's recognition policy, for instance by confirming an ambassador to the recognized foreign government. Those cases do not cast doubt on the view that the Executive Branch determines whether the United States will recognize foreign states and governments and their territorial bounds.

C

Having examined the Constitution's text and this Court's precedent, it is appropriate to turn to accepted understandings and practice. In separation-of-powers cases this Court has often "put significant weight upon historical practice." *NLRB v. Noel Canning*, 573 U.S. ___, ___ (2014) (slip op., at 6) (emphasis deleted). Here, history is not all on one side, but on balance it provides strong support for the conclusion that the recognition power is the President's alone. As Zivotofsky argues, certain historical incidents can be interpreted to support the position that recognition is a shared power. But the weight of historical evidence supports the opposite view, which is that the formal determination of recognition is a power to be exercised only by the President.

. . .

From the first Administration forward, the President has claimed unilateral authority to recognize foreign sovereigns. For the most part, Congress has acquiesced in the Executive's exercise of the recognition power [the Court then reviewed historic examples of recognition by Presidents].

. . .

This history confirms the Court's conclusion in the instant case that the power to recognize or decline to recognize a foreign state and its territorial bounds resides in the President alone. For the most part, Congress has respected the Executive's policies and positions as to formal recognition. At times, Congress itself has defended the President's constitutional prerogative. Over the last 100 years, there has been scarcely any debate over the President's power to recognize foreign states. In this respect the Legislature, in the narrow context of recognition, on balance has acknowledged the importance of speaking "with one voice." *Crosby*, 530 U.S., at 381. The weight of historical evidence indicates Congress has accepted that the power to recognize foreign states and governments and their territorial bounds is exclusive to the Presidency.

III

As the power to recognize foreign states resides in the President alone, the question becomes whether § 214(d) infringes on the Executive's consistent decision to withhold recognition with respect to Jerusalem. See *Nixon v. Administrator of General Services*, 433 U.S. 425, 443 (1977) (action unlawful when it "prevents the Executive Branch from accomplishing its constitutionally assigned functions").

Section 214(d) requires that, in a passport or consular report of birth abroad, "the Secretary shall, upon the request of the citizen or the citizen's legal guardian, record the place of birth as Israel" for a "United States citizen born in the city of Jerusalem." 116 Stat. 1366. That is, § 214(d) requires the President, through the Secretary, to identify citizens born in Jerusalem who so request as being born in Israel. But according to the President, those citizens were not born in Israel. As a matter of United States policy, neither Israel nor any other country is acknowledged as having sovereignty over Jerusalem. In this way, § 214(d) "directly contradicts" the "carefully calibrated and longstanding Executive branch policy of neutrality toward Jerusalem." 725 F.3d, at 217, 216.

If the power over recognition is to mean anything, it must mean that the President not only makes the initial, formal recognition determination but also that he may maintain that determination in his and his agent's statements. This conclusion is a matter of both common sense and necessity. If Congress could command the President to state a recognition position inconsistent with his own, Congress could override the President's recognition determination. Under international law, recognition may be effected by "written or oral declaration of the recognizing state." 1 Moore § 27, at 73. In addition an act of recognition must "leave no doubt as to the intention to grant it." 1 Oppenheim's International Law § 50, at 169. Thus, if Congress could alter the President's statements on matters of recognition or force him to contradict them, Congress in effect would exercise the recognition power.

As Justice Jackson wrote in *Youngstown*, when a Presidential power is "exclusive," it "disabl[es] the Congress from acting upon the subject." 343 U.S., at 637-638 (concurring opinion). Here, the subject is quite narrow: The Executive's exclusive power extends no further than his formal recognition determination. But as to that determination, Congress may not enact a law that directly contradicts it. This is not to say Congress may not express its disagreement with the President in myriad ways. For example, it may enact an embargo, decline to confirm an ambassador, or even declare war. But none of these acts would alter the President's recognition decision.

If Congress may not pass a law, speaking in its own voice, that effects formal recognition, then it follows that it may not force the President himself to contradict his earlier statement. That congressional command would not only prevent the Nation from speaking with one voice but also prevent the Executive itself from doing so in conducting foreign relations.

Although the statement required by § 214(d) would not itself constitute a formal act of recognition, it is a mandate that the Executive contradict his prior recognition determination in an official document issued by the Secretary of State. See *Urtetiqui v. D'Arcy*, 9 Pet. 692, 699 (1835) (a passport "from its nature and object, is addressed to foreign powers" and "is to be considered . . . in the character of a political document"). As a result, it is unconstitutional. This is all the more clear in light of the longstanding treatment of a passport's place-of-birth section as an official executive statement implicating recognition. See 725 F.3d, at 224 (Tatel, J., concurring). The Secretary's position on this point has been consistent: He will not place information in the place-of-birth section of a passport that contradicts the President's recognition policy. See 7 FAM § 1383. If a citizen objects to the country listed as sovereign over his place of birth, then the Secretary will accommodate him by listing the city or town of birth rather than the country. See *id.*, § 1383.6. But the Secretary will not list a sovereign that contradicts the President's recognition policy in a passport. Thus, the Secretary will not list "Israel" in a passport as the country containing Jerusalem.

The flaw in § 214(d) is further underscored by the undoubted fact that that the purpose of the statute was to infringe on the recognition power—a power the Court now holds is the sole prerogative of the President. The statute is titled "United States Policy with Respect to Jerusalem as the Capital of Israel." § 214, 116 Stat. 1365. The House Conference Report proclaimed that § 214 "contains four provisions related to the recognition of Jerusalem as Israel's capital." H. R. Conf. Rep. No. 107-671, p. 123 (2002). And, indeed, observers interpreted § 214 as altering United States policy regarding Jerusalem—which led to protests across the region. See *supra*, at 4. From the face of § 214, from the legislative history, and from its reception, it is clear that Congress wanted to express its displeasure with the President's policy by, among other things, commanding the Executive to contradict his own, earlier stated position on Jerusalem. This Congress may not do.

It is true, as Zivotofsky notes, that Congress has substantial authority over passports. See *Haig v. Agee*, 453 U.S. 280 (1981); *Zemel v. Rusk*, 381 U.S. 1 (1965); *Kent v. Dulles*, 357 U.S. 116 (1958). The Court does not question the power of Congress to enact passport legislation of wide scope. In *Kent v. Dulles*, for example, the Court held that if a person's " 'liberty' " to travel "is to be regulated" through a passport, "it must be pursuant to the law-making functions of the Congress." See *id.*, at 129. Later cases, such as *Zemel v. Rusk* and *Haig v. Agee*, also proceeded on the assumption that Congress must authorize the grounds on which passports may be approved or denied. See *Zemel, supra*, at 7-13; *Haig, supra*, at 289-306. This is consistent with the extensive lawmaking power the Constitution vests in Congress over the Nation's foreign affairs.

The problem with § 214(d), however, lies in how Congress exercised its authority over passports. It was an improper act for Congress to "aggrandiz[e] its power at the expense of another branch" by requiring the President to contradict an earlier recognition determination in an official document issued by the Executive Branch. *Freytag v. Commissioner*, 501 U.S. 868, 878 (1991). To allow Congress to control the President's communication in the context of a formal recognition determination is to allow Congress to exercise that exclusive power itself. As a result, the statute is unconstitutional.

*   *   *

In holding § 214(d) invalid the Court does not question the substantial powers of Congress over foreign affairs in general or passports in particular. This case is confined solely to the exclusive power of the President to control recognition determinations, including formal statements by the Executive Branch acknowledging the legitimacy of a state or government and its territorial bounds. Congress cannot command the President to contradict an earlier recognition determination in the issuance of passports.

The judgment of the Court of Appeals for the District of Columbia Circuit is Affirmed.

NOTES AND QUESTIONS

1. Which precedent proved more valuable for the Secretary's argument, *Curtiss-Wright* or *Youngstown*?
2. Why do you think the Court rejected the broad reading of *Curtiss-Wright* advanced by the Secretary of State?
3. Note that when President Bush signed the bill into law that included the provision at issue in *Zivotofsky* he included a statement indicating he considered the provision unconstitutional. This type of "signing statement" is not uncommon. Is it a back-door version of the line item veto held unconstitutional in *Clinton v. City of New York*, 524 U.S. 417 (1998)? If not, what function does it serve?

III. THE "TIER THREE" LIMITS ON COMMANDER-IN-CHIEF ACTION IN RESPONSE TO ENEMY WAR CRIMES

In the wake of the tragic terrorist attacks of September 11, 2001, President Bush issued a Military Order directing the Secretary of Defense to establish a military detention facility at Guantanamo Bay, Cuba. This facility was to be used to detain "unlawful alien enemy combatants" captured during what President Bush indicated in the order was an "armed conflict" between the United States, the Taliban, and al Qaeda. The Military Order also directed the Secretary of Defense to establish a military commission to try captured enemy combatants for violations of the laws and customs of war they allegedly committed.

The United States had not used a military commission to prosecute captured enemy belligerents for alleged war crimes since the years immediately following World War II. In the intervening decades, the evidentiary and procedural character of U.S. military trials had evolved substantially, to include enactment of the Uniform Code of Military Justice, best understood as the U.S. military criminal code. That statute, along with the numerous subsequent amendments and procedures adopted by the President to implement the law, sought to achieve a range of important goals, not least of which was to ensure that U.S. servicemembers subjected to military criminal prosecution receive fundamentally fair process; process that is generally analogous to that used for trials in federal district courts.

Pursuant to the U.C.M.J. and longstanding tradition, the court-martial is the forum used to prosecute U.S. personnel accused of violating military law, while the forum traditionally used to prosecute captured enemy personnel for alleged war crimes is called a military commission. The U.C.M.J., however, authorized use of *either* tribunal to prosecute alleged enemy war criminals, vesting the General Court-Martial with jurisdiction over *any* person who, by the law of war, is subject to trial by military tribunal. In any event, in an apparent effort to ensure the fundamental fairness of either military criminal tribunal, Congress included the following provision in the U.C.M.J. to ensure a general symmetry between the process used for both the court-martial and the military commission:

10 U.S. Code § 836. Art. 36. President may prescribe rules
(a) Pretrial, trial, and post-trial procedures, including modes of proof, for cases arising under this chapter triable in courts-martial, military commissions and other military tribunals, and procedures for courts of inquiry, may be prescribed by the President by regulations which shall, so far as he considers practicable, apply the principles of law and the rules of evidence generally recognized in the trial of criminal cases in the United States district courts, but which may not, except as provided in chapter 47A of this title, be contrary to or inconsistent with this chapter.

(b) All rules and regulations made under this article shall be uniform insofar as practicable, except insofar as applicable to military commissions established under chapter 47A of this title.

While the Secretary of Defense might have implemented the Military Order by directing trial by the well-established general court-martial, he chose instead to order trial by a military commission at Guantanamo. The military commission was *not* established to determine who could be detained. It was instead a criminal tribunal, established to adjudicate allegations of war crimes committed in the context of this armed conflict and adjudge criminal penalties, to include, when appropriate, the death penalty. The Secretary established all the procedures for these military criminal trials, implementing the President's order that they be "full and fair."

Critics, and more significantly the first detainees subjected to trial by this court, argued the procedures provided for nothing close to a "full and fair" trial.

The Secretary of Defense assigned a group of military attorneys (JAG officers) to represent detainees accused of offenses for trial before the military commission. The counsel detailed to represent Salim Hamdan (a detainee who served as Osama bin Laden's driver and was alleged to have been a member of the conspiracy to conduct the September 11th attacks), along with Georgetown Law School Professor Neal Katyal, challenged the process established by the Secretary in a petition for writ of habeas corpus. After Hamdan's challenge was rejected by the D.C. Circuit Court of Appeals, the case found itself at the Supreme Court. The Supreme Court rejected the President's claim of plenary authority to dictate the procedures used by the military commission, in part because these procedures did not comply with Article 36 the Uniform Code of Military Justice. While the *Hamdan* decision will be considered in greater detail in Chapter 10, consider how Justice Jackson's *Youngstown* opinion provided the framework for Justice Kennedy's resolution of the issue:

> Trial by military commission raises separation-of-powers concerns of the highest order. Located within a single branch, these courts carry the risk that offenses will be defined, prosecuted, and adjudicated by executive officials without independent review. Concentration of power puts personal liberty in peril of arbitrary action by officials, an incursion the Constitution's three-part system is designed to avoid. It is imperative, then, that when military tribunals are established, full and proper authority exists for the Presidential directive. . . .
>
> . . .
>
> These structural differences between the military commissions and courts-martial — the concentration of functions, including legal decision making, in a single executive official; the less rigorous standards for composition of the tribunal; and the creation of special review procedures in place of institutions created and regulated by Congress — remove safeguards that are important to the fairness of the proceedings and the independence of the court. Congress has prescribed these guarantees for courts-martial; and no evident practical need explains the departures here. For these reasons the commission cannot be considered regularly constituted under United States law and thus does not satisfy Congress' requirement that military commissions conform to the law of war.
>
> Apart from these structural issues, moreover, the basic procedures for the commissions deviate from procedures for courts-martial, in violation of § 836(b). As the Court explains, the Military Commission Order abandons the detailed Military Rules of Evidence, which are modeled on the Federal Rules of Evidence in conformity with § 836(a)'s requirement of presumptive compliance with district-court rules. . . .
>
> In sum, as presently structured, Hamdan's military commission exceeds the bounds Congress has placed on the President's authority in §§ 836 and 821 of the UCMJ. Because Congress has prescribed these limits, Congress can change them, requiring a new analysis consistent with the Constitution and other governing laws. At this time, however, we must apply the standards Congress has provided. By those standards the military commission is deficient.

In light of the conclusion that the military commission here is unauthorized under the UCMJ, I see no need to consider several further issues addressed in the plurality opinion by Justice Stevens and the dissent by Justice Thomas.

NOTES AND QUESTIONS

1. What "tier" from Justice Jackson's *Youngstown* concurrence did the issue addressed by Justice Kennedy seem to fall into?
2. Do you think the trial of captured enemy personnel in a war for the war crimes they allegedly committed is a function of military command? If so, why did Justice Kennedy reject the President's authority to order the use of this military commission to try Hamdan?
3. Assume the Uniform Code of Military Justice did not address procedures for military commissions. How would this assumption influence your application of Justice Jackson's analytical methodology to this case?

ASSESSMENT QUESTIONS

1. Briefly explain the relationship between Justice Jackson's *Youngstown* opinion and Justice Kennedy's opinion in *Hamdan v. Rumsfeld*.

2. Both *Youngstown Sheet & Tube Co. v. Sawyer* and *Dames & Moore v. Regan* involved a "taking" of a property interest pursuant to an executive order issued by the President. In *Youngstown*, the Court struck down the taking, whereas in *Dames & Moore*, the Court upheld the taking. What explains these disparate outcomes?

ASSESSMENT ANSWERS

1. Justice Kennedy first concluded that the military commission procedure implemented pursuant to Military Order Number 1, issued by President Bush, was incompatible with the Uniform Code of Military Justice. This essentially placed the issue in Justice Jackson's "lowest ebb" of executive power. And, as Justice Jackson indicated, the exercise of executive power in such situations can only be sustained if it is based on exclusive constitutional authority, for doing so will validate a presidential action that directly contradicts the will of Congress. Justice Kennedy then rejected the assertion that the Commander-in-Chief authority of Article II vested President Bush with plenary power to establish procedures for trial by military commission. Instead, these trials and procedures implicated not only the Commander-in-Chief power, but also the power vested in Congress "to make rules for the government and regulation of the land and naval forces"; and to "make rules concerning captures on land and water." Because sustaining the commission procedure would in effect nullify this congressional authority, Justice Kennedy concluded the procedures were unconstitutional.

2. In *Youngstown Sheet & Tube Co. v. Sawyer*, the Court interpreted prior legislation as indicating congressional opposition to the taking. In contrast, in *Dames & Moore v. Regan*, the Court interpreted prior legislation to either not address the issue (the Hostage Act), or to actually suggest congressional support for the action (IEEPA). What seemed especially significant is that the Court seemed to be far more permissive in interpreting these statutes in *Dames* because the issue was predominately related to foreign affairs. In contrast, the *Youngstown* majority treated the issue as predominately domestic in nature, with a secondary or peripheral foreign affairs element.

CHAPTER 6

International Law and National Security

I. TREATY FORMATION

A. Making, Ratifying, and Implementing

Article II, § 2, Cl. 2 of the Constitution provides: "The President . . . shall have Power, by and with the Advice and Consent of the Senate, to make Treaties, provided two thirds of the Senators present concur. . . ." What, however, does "make" treaties involve? Consider the following extract from a Senate Foreign Relations Committee Report entitled "Treaties and Other International Agreements: The Role of the Senate":

> Treaties are a serious legal undertaking both in international and domestic law. Internationally, once in force, treaties are binding on the parties and become part of international law. Domestically, treaties to which the United States is a party are equivalent in status to Federal legislation, forming part of what the Constitution calls "the supreme Law of the Land."
>
> . . .
>
> The Constitution states that the President "shall have Power, by and with the Advice and Consent of the Senate, to make Treaties, provided two-thirds of the Senators present concur." The Convention that drafted the Constitution did not spell out more precisely what role it intended for the Senate in the treatymaking process. Most evidence suggests that it intended the sharing of the treaty power to begin early, with the Senate helping to formulate instructions to negotiators and acting as a council of advisers to the President during the negotiations, as well as approving each treaty entered into by the United States. The function of the Senate was both to protect the rights of the states and to serve as a check against the President's taking excessive or undesirable actions through treaties. The Presidential function in turn

was to provide unity and efficiency in treatymaking and to represent the national interest as a whole.[1]

The constitutional allocation of treaty power was an obvious measure to limit the plenary authority of the nation's executive to bind the nation to international agreements, as indicated by this same Senate Report:

> The requirement for the Senate's advice and consent gives the Senate a check over all international agreements submitted to it as treaties. The Senate may refuse to give its approval to a treaty or do so only with specified conditions, reservations, or understandings. In addition, the knowledge that a treaty must be approved by a two-thirds majority in the Senate may influence the content of the document before it is submitted. . . .[2]

The power to make treaties is generally understood as a power inherent in the sovereign character of a nation. As was explained in the previous chapter, Justice Sutherland emphasized this point in his opinion for the Supreme Court in *United States v. Curtiss-Wright Export Corp.*, where he concluded on behalf of the Court that the allocation of treaty power (and other foreign affairs powers) reflects a limitation of power inherent in the sovereign character of the nation, as opposed to the federal government's exercise of domestic powers, which are derived exclusively from the powers granted to the government by the states.

A treaty, therefore, is an international agreement that is "made" in accordance with the constitutionally mandated process: The President negotiates the agreement and by signing the treaty indicates U.S. intention to become bound. However, the treaty is not "made" until the agreement is "ratified" by the United States, which the President may do only after obtaining the requisite Senate advice and consent. At that point, the President is constitutionally authorized to *ratify* the treaty — the action that indicates to the other treaty parties that the United States is bound by the agreement. In this sense, the President "makes" the treaty but the treaty may only bind the nation to the agreement with Senate advice and consent. As the Senate Report explains:

> The treaty clause of the Constitution does not contain the word ratification, which refers to the formal act by which a nation affirms its willingness to be bound by a specific treaty. From the beginning, the formal act of ratification has been performed by the President acting "by and with the advice and consent of the Senate."

---

1. S. Rep. No. 106-71, at 1-2 (2001).
2. *Id.*

The President ratifies the treaty, but, only after receiving the advice and consent of the Senate.[3]

NOTES AND QUESTIONS

1. Note that while the Constitution requires the President to obtain Senate advice and consent as a condition precedent to ratifying any treaty, it is the President and not the Senate that actually ratifies treaties. What if the Senate were to provide advice and consent to ratify a treaty but the President chose not to do so? May the Senate compel ratification?

2. Ratification indicates the United States is bound by the treaty. But the advice and consent/ratification process may take years, and in some cases even decades. What consequence, if any, flows from the signature of a treaty prior to formal ratification? Consider the Vienna Convention on the Law of Treaties, the so-called treaty on treaties (which the United States has never ratified but considers to reflect customary international law). This treaty provides: "'Ratification,' 'acceptance,' 'approval' and 'accession' mean in each case the international act so named whereby a State establishes on the international plane its consent to be bound by a treaty"; and that "[a] State is obliged to refrain from acts which would defeat the object and purpose of a treaty when: (a) It has signed the treaty or has exchanged instruments constituting the treaty subject to ratification, acceptance or approval, until it shall have made its intention clear not to become a party to the treaty. . . ." Do these two provisions, taken together, mean that a president's decision to sign a treaty functionally binds the United States to terms of the treaty prior to obtaining Senate advice and consent and subsequent ratification?

Once a treaty is ratified, it is, as the Senate Report notes, supreme law of the land. However, whether the treaty is immediately enforceable in our domestic courts will depend on whether any given provision is considered "self-executing." Consider the Senate Report's discussion of this important concept:

> Under the Constitution, a treaty, like a Federal statute, is part of the "supreme Law of the Land." Self-executing treaties, those that do not require implementing legislation, automatically become effective as domestic law immediately upon entry into force. Other treaties do not become effective as domestic law until implementing legislation is enacted, and then technically it is the legislation, not the treaty unless incorporated into the legislation, that is the law of the land.
>
> Sometimes it is not clear on the face of a treaty whether it is self-executing or requires implementing legislation. Some treaties expressly call for implementing legislation or deal with subjects clearly requiring congressional action, such as the

---

3. *Id.* at 2.

appropriation of funds or enactment of domestic penal provisions. The question of whether or not a treaty requires implementing legislation or is self-executing is a matter of interpretation largely by the executive branch or, less frequently, by the courts. On occasion, the Senate includes an understanding in the resolution of ratification that certain provisions are not self-executing or that the President is to exchange or deposit the instrument of ratification only after implementation legislation has been enacted. When a treaty is deemed self-executing, it overrides any conflicting provision of the law of an individual signatory state. If a treaty is in irreconcilable conflict with a Federal law, the one executed later in time prevails, although courts generally try to harmonize domestic and international obligations whenever possible.

. . .

A treaty's effectiveness as domestic law of the United States does not result automatically upon its entry into force on the international level but occurs only where the instrument is "self-executing," that is, where it operates without any necessity for implementing legislation. The classic exposition of this principle is provided by Chief Justice Marshall in *Foster v. Neilson*:

> Our constitution declares a treaty to be the law of the land. It is, consequently, to be regarded in courts of justice as equivalent to an act of the legislature, whenever it operates of itself, without the aid of any legislative provision. But when the terms of the stipulation import a contract, when either of the parties engages to perform a particular act, the treaty addresses itself to the political, not the judicial department; and the legislature must execute the contract, before it can become a rule for the Court.

S. Rep. No. 106-71, at 4, 72-73 (2001).

The following cases address the significance of the self-execution assessment.

Background

Article 92 of the United Nations Charter established the International Court of Justice (ICJ). The ICJ has two means of jurisdiction. First, a U.N. member nation may consent generally to jurisdiction on any question arising under a treaty or general international law. In the alternative, a nation may consent to ICJ jurisdiction over a specific category of cases or disputes pursuant to a treaty. The United States initially consented to general ICJ jurisdiction. However, on October 7, 1985, the United States terminated that consent. Nonetheless, the United States was still subject to the specific jurisdiction of the ICJ pursuant to the Vienna Convention on Consular Relations (Vienna Convention) and its Optional Protocol Concerning the Compulsory Settlement of Disputes to the Vienna Convention (Optional Protocol) ratified in 1969.

On June 24, 1993, José Ernesto Medellín (a Mexican citizen) and several other gang members raped and murdered two teenage girls in Houston, Texas. Medellín was arrested five days later. Though Medellín's *Miranda* warnings were read to him and he waived those rights prior to his confession, local authorities did not advise him of his right to contact the Mexican consulate under the terms of the Vienna

Convention. Medellín was subsequently convicted of rape and capital murder and sentenced to death. He appealed his conviction, arguing that his right to consular notification provided by the Vienna Convention was violated. The Texas Court of Criminal Appeals upheld the conviction, and Medellín then filed a habeas corpus petition in federal district court asserting that he was being deprived of his liberty in violation of a treaty of the United States, one of the bases for invoking federal habeas corpus jurisdiction. But because Medellín procedurally defaulted on this issue by failing to raise it at trial, the federal court dismissed his petition. The Fifth Circuit affirmed.

Around the same time, Mexico brought an action against the United States in the ICJ asserting that the United States had failed to notify fifty-one Mexican citizens (including Medellín) of their Vienna Convention consular rights. In the *Case Concerning Avena and Other Mexican Nationals (Mexico v. United States)*, 2004 I.C.J. 12 (Judgment of Mar. 31) (*Avena*), the ICJ ruled that the fifty-one Mexican nationals were entitled to review and reconsideration of their convictions and sentences in U.S. courts. In response, the United States then withdrew from the Optional Protocol thereby terminating this specific consent to ICJ jurisdiction.

Armed with the ICJ decision Medellín petitioned for certiorari to the United States Supreme Court once again seeking to overturn his conviction due to a violation of the Convention. The Court granted the petition. However, before the Supreme Court heard the case President Bush invoked his Article II authority to interpret international law and, based on the ICJ judgment, issued a Memorandum to the U.S. Attorney General that essentially required States to review the convictions and sentences of foreign nationals who had not been advised of their Vienna Convention rights. The Supreme Court then dismissed Medellín's pending case in anticipation of review by the Texas courts. Based on the President's Memorandum Medellín filed a habeas corpus petition in Texas court, but the Texas Court of Criminal Appeals dismissed Medellín's the petition on the same grounds as it did when Medellín first filed for habeas corpus relief. At that point the U.S. Supreme Court again granted certiorari.

Medellín v. Texas
552 U.S. 491 (2008)

Chief Justice ROBERTS delivered the opinion of the Court.

. . . We granted certiorari to decide two questions. First, is the ICJ's judgment in *Avena* directly enforceable as domestic law in a state court in the United States? Second, does the President's Memorandum independently require the States to provide review and reconsideration of the claims of the 51 Mexican nationals named in *Avena* without regard to state procedural default rules? We conclude that neither *Avena* nor the President's Memorandum constitutes directly enforceable federal law that pre-empts state limitations on the filing of successive habeas petitions. We therefore affirm the decision below.

. . .

Medellín first contends that the ICJ's judgment in *Avena* constitutes a "binding" obligation on the state and federal courts of the United States. He argues that "by virtue of the Supremacy Clause, the treaties requiring compliance with the *Avena* judgment are already the 'Law of the Land' by which all state and federal courts in this country are 'bound.'" Reply Brief for Petitioner 1. Accordingly, Medellín argues, *Avena* is a binding federal rule of decision that pre-empts contrary state limitations on successive habeas petitions.

No one disputes that the *Avena* decision—a decision that flows from the treaties through which the United States submitted to ICJ jurisdiction with respect to Vienna Convention disputes—constitutes an international law obligation on the part of the United States. But not all international law obligations automatically constitute binding federal law enforceable in United States courts. The question we confront here is whether the *Avena* judgment has automatic *domestic* legal effect such that the judgment of its own force applies in state and federal courts.

This Court has long recognized the distinction between treaties that automatically have effect as domestic law, and those that—while they constitute international law commitments—do not by themselves function as binding federal law. The distinction was well explained by Chief Justice Marshall's opinion in *Foster v. Neilson*, 2 Pet. 253, 315, 7 L. Ed. 415 (1829), overruled on other grounds, *United States v. Percheman*, 7 Pet. 51, 8 L. Ed. 604 (1833), which held that a treaty is "equivalent to an act of the legislature," and hence self-executing, when it "operates of itself without the aid of any legislative provision." *Foster*, *supra*, at 314. When, in contrast, "[treaty] stipulations are not self-executing they can only be enforced pursuant to legislation to carry them into effect." *Whitney v. Robertson*, 124 U.S. 190, 194, 8 S. Ct. 456, 31 L. Ed. 386 (1888). In sum, while treaties "may comprise international commitments . . . they are not domestic law unless Congress has either enacted implementing statutes or the treaty itself conveys an intention that it be 'self-executing' and is ratified on these terms." *Igartua-De La Rosa v. United States*, 417 F.3d 145, 150 (C.A.1 2005) (en banc) (Boudin, C.J.).

A treaty is, of course, "primarily a compact between independent nations." *Head Money Cases*, 112 U.S. 580, 598, 5 S. Ct. 247, 28 L. Ed. 798 (1884). It ordinarily "depends for the enforcement of its provisions on the interest and the honor of the governments which are parties to it." *Ibid.*; see also The Federalist No. 33, p. 207 (J. Cooke ed. 1961) (A. Hamilton) (comparing laws that individuals are "bound to observe" as "the *supreme law* of the land" with "a mere treaty, dependent on the good faith of the parties"). "If these [interests] fail, its infraction becomes the subject of international negotiations and reclamations. . . . It is obvious that with all this the judicial courts have nothing to do and can give no redress." *Head Money Cases, supra,* at 598, 112 U.S. 580. Only "[i]f the treaty contains stipulations which are self-executing, that is, require no legislation to make them operative, [will] they have the force and effect of a legislative enactment." *Whitney, supra,* at 194, 8 S. Ct. 456.

Medellín and his *amici* nonetheless contend that the Optional Protocol, United Nations Charter, and ICJ Statute supply the "relevant obligation" to give the *Avena* judgment binding effect in the domestic courts of the United States. Reply Brief for Petitioner 5-6. Because none of these treaty sources creates binding federal law in the absence of implementing legislation, and because it is uncontested that no such legislation exists, we conclude that the *Avena* judgment is not automatically binding domestic law.

. . .

A

The interpretation of a treaty, like the interpretation of a statute, begins with its text. *Air France v. Saks,* 470 U.S. 392, 396-397, 105 S. Ct. 1338, 84 L. Ed. 2d 289 (1985). Because a treaty ratified by the United States is "an agreement among sovereign powers," we have also considered as "aids to its interpretation" the negotiation and drafting history of the treaty as well as "the postratification understanding" of signatory nations. *Zicherman v. Korean Air Lines Co.,* 516 U.S. 217, 226, 116 S. Ct. 629, 133 L. Ed. 2d 596 (1996); see also *United States v. Stuart,* 489 U.S. 353, 365-366, 109 S. Ct. 1183, 103 L. Ed. 2d 388 (1989); *Choctaw Nation v. United States,* 318 U.S. 423, 431-432, 63 S. Ct. 672, 87 L. Ed. 877 (1943).

As a signatory to the Optional Protocol, the United States agreed to submit disputes arising out of the Vienna Convention to the ICJ. The Protocol provides: "Disputes arising out of the interpretation or application of the [Vienna] Convention shall lie within the compulsory jurisdiction of the International Court of Justice." Art. I, 21 U.S.T., at 326. Of course, submitting to jurisdiction and agreeing to be bound are two different things. A party could, for example, agree to compulsory nonbinding arbitration. Such an agreement would require the party to appear before the arbitral tribunal without obligating the party to treat the tribunal's decision as binding. See, *e.g.,* North American Free Trade Agreement, U.S.-Can.-Mex., Art. 2018(1), Dec. 17, 1992, 32 I.L.M. 605, 697 (1993) ("On receipt of the final report of [the arbitral panel requested by a Party to the agreement], the disputing Parties shall agree on the resolution of the dispute, which normally shall conform with the determinations and recommendations of the panel").

The most natural reading of the Optional Protocol is as a bare grant of jurisdiction. It provides only that "[d]isputes arising out of the interpretation or application of the [Vienna] Convention shall lie within the compulsory jurisdiction of the International Court of Justice" and "may accordingly be brought before the [ICJ] . . . by any party to the dispute being a Party to the present Protocol." Art. I, 21 U.S.T., at 326. The Protocol says nothing about the effect of an ICJ decision and does not itself commit signatories to comply with an ICJ judgment. The Protocol is similarly silent as to any enforcement mechanism.

The obligation on the part of signatory nations to comply with ICJ judgments derives not from the Optional Protocol, but rather from Article 94 of the United Nations Charter—the provision that specifically addresses the effect of ICJ decisions. Article 94(1) provides that "[e]ach Member of the United Nations *undertakes to comply* with the decision of the [ICJ] in any case to which it is a party." 59 Stat. 1051 (emphasis added). The Executive Branch contends that the phrase "undertakes to comply" is not "an acknowledgement that an ICJ decision will have immediate legal effect in the courts of U.N. members," but rather "a commitment on the part of U.N. members to take future action through their political branches to comply with an ICJ decision." Brief for United States as *Amicus Curiae* in *Medellín I*, O.T. 2004, No. 04-5928, p. 34.

We agree with this construction of Article 94. The Article is not a directive to domestic courts. It does not provide that the United States "shall" or "must" comply with an ICJ decision, nor indicate that the Senate that ratified the U.N. Charter intended to vest ICJ decisions with immediate legal effect in domestic courts. Instead, "[t]he words of Article 94 . . . call upon governments to take certain action." *Committee of United States Citizens Living in Nicaragua v. Reagan*, 859 F.2d 929, 938 (C.A.D.C. 1988) (quoting *Diggs v. Richardson*, 555 F.2d 848, 851 (C.A.D.C. 1976); internal quotation marks omitted). See also *Foster*, 2 Pet., at 314, 315 (holding a treaty non-self-executing because its text— "'all . . . grants of land . . . shall be ratified and confirmed'"—did not "act directly on the grants" but rather "pledge[d] the faith of the United States to pass acts which shall ratify and confirm them"). In other words, the U.N. Charter reads like "a compact between independent nations" that "depends for the enforcement of its provisions on the interest and the honor of the governments which are parties to it." *Head Money Cases*, 112 U.S., at 598, 5 S. Ct. 247.

The remainder of Article 94 confirms that the U.N. Charter does not contemplate the automatic enforceability of ICJ decisions in domestic courts. Article 94(2)—the enforcement provision—provides the sole remedy for non-compliance: referral to the United Nations Security Council by an aggrieved state. 59 Stat. 1051.

The U.N. Charter's provision of an express diplomatic—that is, nonjudicial—remedy is itself evidence that ICJ judgments were not meant to be enforceable in domestic courts. See *Sanchez-Llamas*, 548 U.S., at 347, 126 S. Ct. 2669. And even this "quintessentially *international* remed[y]," *id.*, at 355, 126 S. Ct. 2669, is not absolute. First, the Security Council must "dee[m] necessary" the issuance of a recommendation or measure to effectuate the judgment. Art. 94(2), 59 Stat. 1051. Second, as the President and Senate were undoubtedly aware in subscribing to the U.N. Charter and Optional Protocol, the United States retained the unqualified right to exercise its veto of any Security Council resolution.

This was the understanding of the Executive Branch when the President agreed to the U.N. Charter and the declaration accepting general compulsory ICJ jurisdiction. See, *e.g.*, The Charter of the United Nations for the Maintenance of International Peace and Security: Hearings before the Senate Committee on Foreign Relations, 79th Cong., 1st Sess., 124-125 (1945) ("[I]f a state fails to perform its obligations under a judgment of the [ICJ], the other party may have recourse to the Security Council"); id., at 286 (statement of Leo Pasvolsky, Special Assistant to the Secretary of State for International Organizations and Security Affairs) ("[W]hen the Court has rendered a judgment and one of the parties refuses to accept it, then the dispute becomes political rather than legal. It is as a political dispute that the matter is referred to the Security Council"). . . .

If ICJ judgments were instead regarded as automatically enforceable domestic law, they would be immediately and directly binding on state and federal courts pursuant to the Supremacy Clause. Mexico or the ICJ would have no need to proceed to the Security Council to enforce the judgment in this case. Noncompliance with an ICJ judgment through exercise of the Security Council veto — always regarded as an option by the Executive and ratifying Senate during and after consideration of the U.N. Charter, Optional Protocol, and ICJ Statute — would no longer be a viable alternative. There would be nothing to veto. In light of the U.N. Charter's remedial scheme, there is no reason to believe that the President and Senate signed up for such a result.

In sum, Medellín's view that ICJ decisions are automatically enforceable as domestic law is fatally undermined by the enforcement structure established by Article 94. His construction would eliminate the option of noncompliance contemplated by Article 94(2), undermining the ability of the political branches to determine whether and how to comply with an ICJ judgment. Those sensitive foreign policy decisions would instead be transferred to state and federal courts charged with applying an ICJ judgment directly as domestic law. And those courts would not be empowered to decide whether to comply with the judgment — again, always regarded as an option by the political branches — any more than courts may consider whether to comply with any other species of domestic law. This result would be particularly anomalous in light of the principle that "[t]he conduct of the foreign relations of our Government is committed by the Constitution to the Executive and Legislative — 'the political' — Departments." *Oetjen v. Central Leather Co.*, 246 U.S. 297, 302, 38 S. Ct. 309, 62 L. Ed. 726 (1918).

The ICJ Statute, incorporated into the U.N. Charter, provides further evidence that the ICJ's judgment in *Avena* does not automatically constitute federal law judicially enforceable in United States courts. Art. 59, 59 Stat. 1062. To begin with, the ICJ's "principal purpose" is said to be to "arbitrate particular disputes between national governments." *Sanchez-Llamas, supra,* at 355, 126 S. Ct. 2669 (citing 59 Stat. 1055). Accordingly, the ICJ can hear disputes only between nations, not individuals. . . .

Medellín argues that because the *Avena* case involves him, it is clear that he—and the 50 other Mexican nationals named in the *Avena* decision—should be regarded as parties to the *Avena* judgment. Brief for Petitioner 21-22. But cases before the ICJ are often precipitated by disputes involving particular persons or entities, disputes that a nation elects to take up as its own. . . . That has never been understood to alter the express and established rules that only nation-states may be parties before the ICJ, Art. 34, 59 Stat. 1059, and—contrary to the position of the dissent, post, at 1387—that ICJ judgments are binding only between those parties, Art. 59, 59 Stat. 1062.

It is, moreover, well settled that the United States' interpretation of a treaty "is entitled to great weight." *Sumitomo Shoji America, Inc. v. Avagliano*, 457 U.S. 176, 184-185, 102 S. Ct. 2374, 72 L. Ed. 2d 765 (1982); see also *El Al Israel Airlines, Ltd. v. Tsui Yuan Tseng*, 525 U.S. 155, 168, 119 S. Ct. 662, 142 L. Ed. 2d 576 (1999). The Executive Branch has unfailingly adhered to its view that the relevant treaties do not create domestically enforceable federal law. See Brief for United States as *Amicus Curiae* 4, 27-29.

The pertinent international agreements, therefore, do not provide for implementation of ICJ judgments through direct enforcement in domestic courts, and "where a treaty does not provide a particular remedy, either expressly or implicitly, it is not for the federal courts to impose one on the States through lawmaking of their own." *Sanchez-Llamas*, 548 U.S., at 347, 126 S. Ct. 2669.

. . .

. . . We do not suggest that treaties can never afford binding domestic effect to international tribunal judgments—only that the U.N. Charter, the Optional Protocol, and the ICJ Statute do not do so. And whether the treaties underlying a judgment are self-executing so that the judgment is directly enforceable as domestic law in our courts is, of course, a matter for this Court to decide. See *Sanchez-Llamas, supra*, at 353-354, 126 S. Ct. 2669.

* * *

B. Treaties: Rules for Conflicts

The line between a self-executing and a non-self-executing treaty provision may often be blurry, but most treaty provisions like the one at issue in *Medellín* are phrased in terms that suggest they are non-self-executing. To "fulfill the contract" Congress may enact implementing legislation. But what is the result when Congress enacts a law that modifies or perhaps even contradicts the terms of the treaty?

In *Whitney v. Robertson*, plaintiff sugar importers claimed that a treaty between the United States and San Domingo provided for the duty-free importing of sugar. The collector of the port disagreed, treating the sugars as dutiable articles pursuant to subsequent acts of Congress. The Supreme Court affirmed the ruling in the port collector's favor, noting:

> If the treaty contains stipulations which are self-executing . . . [it shall have the] force and effect of a legislative enactment. Congress may modify such provisions, so far as they bind the United States, or supersede them altogether. By the constitution,

a treaty is placed on the same footing, and made of like obligation, with an act of legislation. Both are declared by that instrument to be the supreme law of the land, and no superior efficacy is given to either over the other. When the two relate to the same subject, the courts will always endeavor to construe them so as to give effect to both, if that can be done without violating the language of either; but, *if the two are inconsistent, the one last in date will control the other:* provided, always, the stipulation of the treaty on the subject is self-executing.[4]

The next case illustrates application of this "last-in-time" principle.

Background

Diggs v. Shultz arose out of a conflict between a treaty agreement and an act of Congress, and how that conflict affected the importation of metallurgical chromite from Southern Rhodesia. In 1966, the U.N. Security Council adopted a resolution directing that all member states impose an embargo on trade with Southern Rhodesia. In compliance, the President issued two executive orders invoking statutes that established criminal sanctions for embargo violations. In 1971, however, Congress adopted the Byrd Amendment, an addition to the Strategic and Critical Materials Stock Piling Act that disallowed the President the ability to prohibit or regulate the importation of strategic materials, so long as the nation or area of import was not listed as a Communist-dominated area.

Since Southern Rhodesia was not a Communist-controlled country, the Byrd Amendment reopened trade between the United States and Southern Rhodesia. The Office of Foreign Assets Control, upon the President's direction, issued to the corporate appellees in this case a General License authorizing the importation of various materials from Southern Rhodesia, and they began importation. In response, the appellants allege that the Byrd Amendment did not and could not authorize the issuance of such a license contrary to the nation's treaty obligations. They sought to enjoin further importation, and, among other things, wish to declare the General License null and void.

Diggs v. Shultz
470 F.2d 461 (1972)

McGOWAN, Circuit Judge:

This is an appeal from the dismissal by the District Court of a complaint seeking declaratory and injunctive relief in respect of the importation of metallurgical chromite from Southern Rhodesia. The gravamen of this action was an asserted conflict between (1) the official authorization of such importation by the United States, and (2) the treaty obligations of the United States under the United Nations Charter. . . .

. . .

---

4. *Whitney v. Robertson*, 124 U.S. 190, 191 (1888) (emphasis added).

III

The District Court . . . reasoned as follows: It is settled constitutional doctrine that Congress may nullify, in whole or in part, a treaty commitment. Congress, by the Byrd Amendment in 1971, acted to abrogate one aspect of our treaty obligations under the U.N. Charter, that is to say, our continued participation in the economic sanctions taken against Southern Rhodesia. The considerations underlying that step by Congress present issues of political policy which courts do not inquire into. Thus, appellants' quarrel is with Congress, and it is a cause which can be pursued only at the polls and not in the courts.

In this court appellants do not seriously contest the first of these propositions, namely, the constitutional power of Congress to set treaty obligations at naught. They seek, rather, to show that, in the Byrd Amendment, Congress did not really intend to compel the Executive to end United States observance of the Security Council's sanctions, and that, therefore, it is the Executive which is, without the essential shield of Congressional dispensation, violating a treaty engagement of this country. Appellants point out in this regard that the Byrd Amendment does not in terms require importation from Southern Rhodesia, but leaves open two alternative courses of action. The statute says the President may not ban importation from Rhodesia of materials classified as critical and strategic unless importation from Communist countries is also prohibited. Instead of permitting resumption of trade with Rhodesia, the President, so it is said, could (1) have banned importation of these materials from Communist nations as well as from Rhodesia, or (2) have taken steps to have these materials declassified, thereby taking them in either case out of the scope of the Byrd Amendment.

Citing the canon of construction that a statute should, if possible, be construed in a manner consistent with treaty obligations, appellants argue that the Byrd Amendment, although discretionary on its face, should be construed to compel the President to take one or the other of these two steps as a means of escape from the necessity of breaching the U.N. Charter. But these alternatives raise questions of foreign policy and national defense as sensitive as those involved in the decision to honor or abrogate our treaty obligations.[5] To attempt to decide whether the President chose properly among the three alternatives confronting him "would be, not to decide a judicial controversy, but to assume a position of authority over the governmental acts of another and coequal department, an authority which plainly we do not possess." *Frothingham v. Mellon*, 262 U.S. 447, 489, 43 S. Ct. 597, 601, 67 L. Ed. 1078 (1923).

We think that there can be no blinking the purpose and effect of the Byrd Amendment. It was to detach this country from the U.N. boycott of Southern Rhodesia in blatant disregard of our treaty undertakings. The legislative record shows that no member of Congress voting on the measure was under any doubt about what was involved then; and no amount of statutory interpretation now can make the Byrd Amendment other than what it was as presented to the Congress, namely, a measure which would make—and was intended to make—the United States a certain treaty violator. The so-called options given to the President are, in reality, not options at all. In any event, they are in neither case alternatives which are appropriately to be forced upon him by a court.

Under our constitutional scheme, Congress can denounce treaties if it sees fit to do so, and there is nothing the other branches of government can do about it. We consider that this is precisely what Congress has done in this case; and therefore the District Court was correct to the extent that it found the complaint to state no tenable claim in law.

Diggs and *Whitney* indicate that a later-in-time statute will be given priority over a prior treaty. This rule is necessary to address a conflict between treaties and statutes as both these sources of law are enumerated in Article IV, Cl. 2 of the Constitution, which provides:

> This Constitution, and the Laws of the United States which shall be made in Pursuance thereof; and all Treaties made, or which shall be made, under the Authority of the United States, shall be the supreme Law of the Land; and the Judges in every State shall be bound thereby, any Thing in the Constitution or Laws of any State to the Contrary notwithstanding.

In some cases, a similar conflict may arise between a statute (or perhaps even a treaty) and a rule of customary international law. However, because unlike a treaty, customary international law is not referenced in Article VI, the statute or treaty should be given priority even if it predates the emergence of the rule of custom.

Of course, in any situation involving an *apparent* conflict between domestic law and international law, application of these conflict resolution principles will turn on how a court interprets both the statute and the treaty or rule of custom: If the two sources of law can be interpreted in a way that avoids a conflict, both may be given effect. The next case, although addressing a potential conflict between a statute and a rule of customary international law (or the law of nations), illustrates this important first step in addressing such a potential conflict.

The next case illustrates a cannon of statutory construction relied on by courts to, when possible, reconcile domestic and international law.

Murray v. The Schooner Charming Betsy
2 Cranch 64, 6 U.S. 64 (1804)

Chief Justice MARSHALL delivered the opinion of the Court.

The Charming Betsy was an American built vessel, belonging to citizens of the United States, and sailed from Baltimore, under the name of the Jane, on the 10th of April 1800, with a cargo of flour for St. Bartholomew's; she was sent out for the purpose of being sold. The cargo was disposed of at St. Bartholomew's; but finding it impossible to sell the vessel at that place, the captain proceeded with her to the island of St. Thomas, where she was disposed of to Jared Shattuck, who changed her name to that of the Charming Betsy, and having put on board her a cargo consisting of American produce, cleared her out as a Danish vessel for the island of Guadaloupe.

On her voyage she was captured by a French privateer, and eight hands were put on board for the purpose of taking her into Guadaloupe as a prize. She was afterwards recaptured by Captain Murray, commander of the Constellation frigate, and carried into Martinique. It appears that the captain of the Charming Betsy was not willing to be taken into that island; but when there, he claimed to have his vessel and cargo restored, as being the property of Jared Shattuck, a Danish burgher.

Jared Shattuck was born in the United States, but had removed to the island of St. Thomas while an infant, and was proved to have resided there ever since the year 1789 or 1790. He had been accustomed to carry on trade as a Danish subject, had married a wife and acquired real property in the island, and also taken the oath of allegiance to the crown of Denmark in 1797.

Considering him as an American citizen who was violating the law prohibiting all intercourse between the United States, and France or its dependencies, or the sale of the vessel as a mere cover to evade that law, captain Murray sold the cargo of the Charming Betsy, which consisted of American produce, in Martinique, and brought the vessel into the port of Philadelphia, where she was libeled under what is termed the non-intercourse law. The vessel and cargo were claimed by the consul of Denmark as being the bona fide property of a Danish subject.

This cause came on to be heard before the judge for the district of Pennsylvania, who declared the seizure to be illegal, and that the vessel ought to be restored and the proceeds of the cargo paid to the claimant or his lawful agent, together with costs, and such damages as should be assessed by the clerk of the court. . . .

. . .

To this report an account is annexed, in which the damages, without particularizing the items on which the estimate was formed, were stated at 14,930 dollars 30 cents.

. . .

1st. Is the Charming Betsy subject to seizure and condemnation for having violated a law of the United States? . . .

The libel claims this forfeiture under the act passed in February 1800, further to suspend the commercial intercourse between the United States and France and the dependencies thereof.

That act declares "that all commercial intercourse," &c. It has been very properly observed, in argument, that the building of vessels in the United States, for sale to neutrals in the islands, is, during war, a profitable business, which congress cannot be intended to have prohibited, unless that intent be manifested by express words or a very plain and necessary implication.

It has also been observed that an act of congress ought never to be construed to violate the law of nations, if any other possible construction remains, and consequently can never be construed to violate neutral rights, or to affect neutral commerce, further than is warranted by the law of nations as understood in this country.

These principles are believed to be correct, and they ought to be kept in view in construing the act now under consideration.

* * *

[The Court went on to conclude that the seizure was not authorized by the Act of Congress, because, *inter alia*, interpreting the statute to permit seizure of such a vessel would be inconsistent with the law of nations rules related to the rights of neutral vessels.]

NOTES AND QUESTIONS

1. How would you describe the interpretive rule established by this decision?
2. The *Charming Betsy* case did not consider treaty law, but instead the law of nations (the predecessor term for customary international law). Why would a precedent related to customary international law be regarded as establishing an interpretive rule applicable to treaties?
3. What is the rationale that supports the *Charming Betsy* interpretive canon?
4. Does the Court's opinion apply only to situations where a judicial decision requires harmonization between a statute and international law? Or does it stand for the much broader proposition that courts should always consider international law when interpreting domestic statutes, even if the issue before the court does not implicate international law? Consider the Ninth Circuit Court of Appeals decision in *Serra v. Lappin*, 600 F.3d 1191 (2010). In that case, the court rejected the assertion that federal law related to prisoner employment and compensation should be interpreted in a manner that accorded with international law:

> The *Charming Betsy* canon is not an inviolable rule of general application, but a principle of interpretation that bears on a limited range of cases. Mindful that "Congress has the power to legislate beyond the limits posed by international law," . . . we do not review federal law for adherence to the law of nations with the same rigor that we apply when we must review statutes for adherence to the Constitution. We invoke the *Charming Betsy* canon only where conformity with the law of nations is relevant to considerations of international comity. . . .

Courts, like Justice Marshall in the *Charming Betsy*, are understandably hesitant to interpret a later in time statute in conflict with an international law obligation (whether in the form of a treaty or customary international law) for the obvious reason that it will indicate a U.S. law is in conflict with international law. Courts will therefore endeavor to "harmonize" later in time statutes with treaties. As the Senate Report notes:

> In the event of a conflict between a self-executing treaty and a Federal statute, it is well-settled that legal primacy will be accorded the measure which is later

in time. It is precisely because such a conflict will require a ruling that nullifies the effect of the earlier in time provision that courts will endeavor to harmonize the respective international and domestic obligations if possible. As the Supreme Court explained in *Whitney v. Robertson*:

> By the Constitution a treaty is placed on the same footing, and made of like obligation, with an act of legislation. Both are declared by that instrument to be the supreme law of the land, and no superior efficacy is given to either over the other. When the two relate to the same subject, the courts will always endeavor to construe them so as to give effect to both, if that can be done without violating the language of either; but if the two are inconsistent, the one last in date will control the other, provided always the stipulation of the treaty on the subject is self-executing. If the country with which the treaty is made is dissatisfied with the action of the legislative department, it may present its complaint to the executive head of the government and take such other measures as it may deem essential for the protection of its interests. The courts can afford no redress. Whether the complaining nation has just cause or our country was justified in its legislation, are not matters for judicial cognizance.

S. Rep. No. 106-71, (2001), pp. 75-76 (citing *Whitney v. Robinson*, 124 U.S. 581, 594 (1888)).

The interpretive principles addressed above focus on the relationship between international law and statutes. But what about the relationship between treaties and the provisions of the Constitution itself, to include the Bill of Rights? Both the Constitution and treaties are included within the terms of the Supremacy Clause. But as the following opinion confirms, the Constitution is truly the "first among equals."

A SHORT PRIMER ON WHO IS SUBJECT TO MILITARY CRIMINAL JURISDICTION

In 1950, Congress enacted the Uniform Code of Military Justice. This law, which is still in force, established a military criminal justice system pursuant to Congress's express constitutional authority "to make Rules for the Government and Regulation of the land and naval Forces." This statute included procedural rules, the "punitive articles" — the crimes applicable to individuals subject to military law — and (importantly for this case) defined the individuals subject to this military criminal code.

Article 2 of the UCMJ is the in personam jurisdiction article, and defines *who* is subject to the UCMJ ("to the Code"). Unsurprisingly, the first category of individuals subject to the Code are members of the armed forces, but this list is much longer. Through Article 2, Congress included within the scope of military criminal jurisdiction other categories of individuals, such as prisoners of war in U.S. military custody, retired members of the armed forces, and individuals attending U.S. military academies. In Article 2(11), Congress also included *any* person, military or civilian, who was subject to U.S. military jurisdiction as the result of any international agreement.

This provision was a deliberate effort to vest U.S. military criminal courts—courts-martial—with jurisdiction over civilians who accompany the armed forces when they are stationed abroad, such as family members and civilian employees of the armed forces. Congress knew that it was common practice (as it remains to this day) for the United States to enter into international agreements with "host" nations for these military and civilian personnel that establish rights and obligations for these forces when stationed in another country. Known as status of forces agreements, or SOFAs, these agreements almost always include provisions allowing the United States to exercise criminal jurisdiction over these individuals while they are assigned and living in the territory of the host nation.

Following World War II, the United States entered into SOFAs with both the United Kingdom and Japan. Each of these international agreements granted the United States authority to exercise criminal jurisdiction over members of the U.S. armed forces and accompanying civilian personnel. This meant that civilians accompanying the armed forces, such as family members, became subject to the UCMJ by operation of Article 2(11), because the international agreements made them subject to U.S. jurisdiction. Thus, U.S. citizens with only an incidental relationship to the armed forces could, as the result of the intersection of the UCMJ and international agreements, be tried by courts-martial, military criminal courts that lack all the attributes of Article III criminal courts.

Reid v. Covert
354 U.S. 1 (1957)

[Mrs. Covert killed her husband, a sergeant in the United States Air Force, at an airbase in England, as did Mrs. Smith, a civilian spouse of a service-member in Japan. Both defendants were civilians and U.S. citizens; both were subject to UCMJ jurisdiction by terms of a status of forces agreement (an international agreement between the United States and the "host" or "receiving" nation); both were charged with murder in violation of the UCMJ, and tried and convicted by general court-martial. Each challenged the constitutionality of their convictions through writs of habeas corpus asserting that trial by a military criminal court—a court that did not afford them trial by a jury of their peers or indictment by grand jury—violated their Fifth and Sixth Amendment rights. The U.S. District Court granted the petitions and this appeal followed, both cases being consolidated.]

Mr. Justice BLACK announced the judgment of the Court and delivered an opinion, in which THE CHIEF JUSTICE, Mr. Justice DOUGLAS, and Mr. Justice BRENNAN join.

I

At the beginning we reject the idea that when the United States acts against citizens abroad it can do so free of the Bill of Rights. The United States is entirely a creature of the Constitution. Its power and authority have no other source. It can only act in accordance with all the limitations imposed by the Constitution. When the Government reaches out to punish a citizen who is abroad, the shield which the Bill of Rights and other parts of the Constitution provide to protect his life and liberty should not be stripped away just because he happens to be in another land. . . .

. . .

II

At the time of Mrs. Covert's alleged offense, an executive agreement was in effect between the United States and Great Britain which permitted United States' military courts to exercise exclusive jurisdiction over offenses committed in Great Britain by American servicemen or their dependents. For its part, the United States agreed that these military courts would be willing and able to try and to punish all offenses against the laws of Great Britain by such persons. In all material respects, the same situation existed in Japan when Mrs. Smith killed her husband. Even though a court-martial does not give an accused trial by jury and other Bill of Rights protections, the Government contends that article 2(11) of UCMJ, insofar as it provides for the military trial of dependents accompanying the armed forces in Great Britain and Japan, can be sustained as legislation which is necessary and proper to carry out the United States' obligations under the international agreements made with those countries. The obvious and decisive answer to this, of course, is that no agreement with a foreign nation can confer power on the Congress, or on any other branch of Government, which is free from the restraints of the Constitution.

Article VI, the Supremacy Clause of the Constitution, declares:

> "This Constitution, and the Laws of the United States which shall be made in Pursuance thereof; and all Treaties made, or which shall be made, under the Authority of the United States, shall be the supreme Law of the Land. . . ."

There is nothing in this language which intimates that treaties and laws enacted pursuant to them do not have to comply with the provisions of the Constitution. Nor is there anything in the debates which accompanied the drafting and ratification of the Constitution which even suggests such a result. These debates as well as the history that surrounds the adoption of the treaty provision in Article VI make it clear that the reason treaties were not limited to those made in "pursuance" of the Constitution was so that agreements made by the United States under the Articles of Confederation, including the important peace treaties which concluded the Revolutionary War, would remain in effect. It would be manifestly contrary to the objectives of those who created the Constitution, as well as those who were responsible for the Bill of Rights — let alone alien to our entire constitutional history and tradition — to construe Article VI as permitting the United States to exercise power under an international agreement without observing constitutional prohibitions. In effect, such construction would permit amendment of that document in a manner not sanctioned by Article V. The prohibitions of the Constitution were designed to apply to all branches of the National Government and they cannot be nullified by the Executive or by the Executive and the Senate combined.

There is nothing new or unique about what we say here. This Court has regularly and uniformly recognized the supremacy of the Constitution over a treaty. For example, in *Geofroy v. Riggs*, 133 U.S. 258, 267, 10 S. Ct. 295, 297, 33 L. Ed. 642, it declared:

> "The treaty power, as expressed in the constitution, is in terms unlimited except by those restraints which are found in that instrument against the action of the government or of its departments, and those arising from the nature of the government itself and of that of the States. It would not be contended that it extends so far as to authorize what the constitution forbids, or a change in the character of the government or in that of one of the States, or a session of any portion of the territory of the latter, without its consent."

This Court has also repeatedly taken the position that an Act of Congress, which must comply with the Constitution, is on a full parity with a treaty, and that when a statute which is subsequent in time is inconsistent with a treaty, the statute to the extent of conflict renders the treaty null. It would be completely anomalous to say that a treaty need not comply with the Constitution when such an agreement can be overridden by a statute that must conform to that instrument.

There is nothing in *State of Missouri v. Holland*, 252 U.S. 416, 40 S. Ct. 382, 64 L. Ed. 641, which is contrary to the position taken here. There the Court carefully noted that the treaty involved was not inconsistent with any specific provision of the Constitution. The Court was concerned with the Tenth Amendment which reserves to the States or the people all power not delegated to the National Government. To the extent that the United States can validly make treaties, the people and the States have delegated their power to the National Government and the Tenth Amendment is no barrier.

In summary, we conclude that the Constitution in its entirety applied to the trials of Mrs. Smith and Mrs. Covert. Since their court-martial did not meet the requirements of Art. III, § 2, or the Fifth and Sixth Amendments we are compelled to determine if there is anything within the Constitution which authorizes the military trial of dependents accompanying the armed forces overseas.

C. Treaty Interpretation: The Role of Courts

Implementation of a treaty will often involve executive branch interpretation. This executive interpretation function is arguably even more significant in relation to treaties than it is to domestic laws as most treaties implicate the broad presidential authority in the realm of international relations and foreign affairs. However, these interpretations may trigger legal disputes. When these disputes are inter-state, diplomacy will be the normal modality for resolution. But when these disputes implicate individual rights, our courts may be called upon to resolve them. Such cases will most likely arise when the government or some other party seeks to enforce the terms of the treaty domestically and in so doing asks a court to give the treaty domestic effect. In such a situation, while the President's interpretation may be persuasive, it will not be treated as binding on the courts, a point emphasized by Chief Justice Roberts in *Medellín v. Texas* (page 200 *supra*):

> . . . When the President asserts the power to "enforce" a non-self-executing treaty by unilaterally creating domestic law, he acts in conflict with the implicit understanding of the ratifying Senate. His assertion of authority, insofar as it is based on the pertinent non-self-executing treaties, is therefore within Justice Jackson's third category, not the first or even the second. . . .
>
> . . .
>
> None of this is to say, however, that the combination of a non-self-executing treaty and the lack of implementing legislation precludes the President from acting to comply with an international treaty obligation. It is only to say that the Executive cannot unilaterally execute a non-self-executing treaty by giving it domestic effect. That is, the non-self-executing character of a treaty constrains the President's ability to comply with treaty commitments by unilaterally making the treaty binding on domestic courts.

The next case illustrates the judicial role in treaty interpretation. Additionally, it indicates that the Court will have the final say on treaty interpretation, even when the President's interpretation is an exercise of his (or her) constitutional Commander-in-Chief power in a time of armed conflict.

Background

Following the September 11, 2001 attacks, Congress passed a joint resolution authorizing the President to use all necessary and appropriate force against those nations, organizations, or persons he determined planned, authorized, committed, or aided in the September 11 attacks. As noted in Chapter 5, anticipating the capture of individuals falling within the scope of this authorization—what at the time was characterized as the "War on Terror"—President Bush, exercising his authority as chief executive and Commander in Chief, issued Military Order Number 1. This order directed the Secretary of Defense to establish a detention facility at the U.S. Navy Base in Guantanamo Bay, Cuba, to detain "unlawful alien enemy combatants" at that facility, and to establish a military tribunal to try these detainees for violations of the laws and customs of war. During operations in Afghanistan, Salim Ahmed Hamdan, a Yemeni national, was captured by Northern Alliance forces and turned over to the U.S. military. In June 2002, Hamdan was transported to the detention facility in Guantanamo Bay, Cuba, where he was deemed subject to the Military Order of November 13, 2001 and therefore eligible for trial by military commission. Hamdan's military-appointed counsel filed demands for charges and a speedy trial pursuant to the Uniform Code of Military Justice (UCMJ). However, because Hamdan was subject to the jurisdiction of the military commission established pursuant to Military Order Number 1, these demands were denied on the grounds that the UCMJ did not apply to him or the proceedings. The following year, Hamdan was charged with conspiring with al Qaeda to commit the offense of "attacking civilians; attacking civilian objects; murder by an unprivileged belligerent; and terrorism."

Before trial, Hamdan challenged the commission's legality through habeas and mandamus petitions. Hamdan conceded that he was subject to trial by court-martial pursuant to the UCMJ (which establishes jurisdiction over *any person* who is subject to trial for violations of the laws and customs of war), but asserted that the procedures established for his trial by military commission violated the four Geneva Conventions of 1949, specially Article 3 common to all four of these treaties the United States ratified in 1955; specifically the obligation to provide "regularly constituted court affording all the judicial guarantees which are recognized as indispensable by civilized peoples," which Hamdan asserted applied to him as he was captured in the context of a "non-international armed conflict." (Hamdan also asserted that the procedures violated the UCMJ, which requires courts-martial procedures to apply to trial by military commission unless impracticable, and that the military commission lacked authority to try him because neither congressional Act nor the common law of war supported trial by this commission for conspiracy.) The government responded, *inter alia*, that Article 3 of the Geneva Conventions was inapplicable to Hamdan or his military commission, because, pursuant to presidential interpretation, that treaty provision applied only to non-international armed conflicts occurring in United States territory (the territory of the High Contracting Party), and was inapplicable to non-international armed conflicts of "international" scope, such as the armed conflict against al Qaeda. The district court granted Hamdan's habeas and mandamus petitions, but the Court of Appeals, adopting the President's interpretation of Article 3 (in an opinion authored by current Chief Justice John Roberts), reversed. The Supreme Court granted certiorari. The Chief Justice recused himself because of his involvement in the case before the D.C. Circuit.

Hamdan v. Rumsfeld
548 U.S. 557 (2006)

Justice STEVENS announced the judgment of the Court and delivered the opinion of the Court with respect to Parts I through IV, Parts VI through VI-D-iii, Part VI-D-v, and Part VII, and an opinion with respect to Parts V and VI-D-iv, in which Justice SOUTER, Justice GINSBURG, and Justice BREYER join.

. . .

For the reasons that follow, we conclude that the military commission convened to try Hamdan lacks power to proceed because its structure and procedures violate both the UCMJ and the Geneva Conventions. Four of us also conclude, see Part V, *infra*, that the offense with which Hamdan has been charged is not an "offens[e] that by . . . the law of war may be tried by military commissions." 10 U.S.C. § 821.

. . .

II

. . . As an alternative to its holding that Hamdan could not invoke the Geneva Conventions at all [because the Court of Appeals concluded they were not self-executing], the Court of Appeals concluded that the Conventions did not in any event apply to the armed conflict during which Hamdan was captured. The court accepted the Executive's assertions that Hamdan was captured in connection with the United States' war with al Qaeda and that that war is distinct from the war with the Taliban in Afghanistan. It further reasoned that the war with al Qaeda evades the reach of the Geneva Conventions. See 415 F.3d, at 41-42. We, like Judge Williams, disagree with the latter conclusion.

The conflict with al Qaeda is not, according to the Government, a conflict to which the full protections afforded detainees under the 1949 Geneva Conventions apply because Article 2 of those Conventions (which appears in all four Conventions) renders the full protections applicable only to "all cases of declared war or of any other armed conflict which may arise between two or more of the High Contracting Parties." 6 U.S.T., at 3318. Since Hamdan was captured and detained incident to the conflict with al Qaeda and not the conflict with the Taliban, and since al Qaeda, unlike Afghanistan, is not a "High Contracting Party" — i.e., a signatory of the Conventions, the protections of those Conventions are not, it is argued, applicable to Hamdan.

We need not decide the merits of this argument because there is at least one provision of the Geneva Conventions that applies here even if the relevant conflict is not one between signatories. Article 3, often referred to as Common Article 3 because, like Article 2, it appears in all four Geneva Conventions, provides that in a "conflict not of an international character occurring in the territory of one of the High Contracting Parties, each Party to the conflict shall be bound to apply, as a minimum," certain provisions protecting "[p]ersons taking no active part in the hostilities, including members of armed forces who have laid down their arms and those placed *hors de combat* by . . . detention." *Ibid.* One such provision prohibits "the passing of sentences and the carrying out of executions without previous judgment pronounced by a regularly constituted court affording all the judicial guarantees which are recognized as indispensable by civilized peoples." *Id.*, at 3320.

The Court of Appeals thought, and the Government asserts, that Common Article 3 does not apply to Hamdan because the conflict with al Qaeda, being "'international in scope,'" does not qualify as a "'conflict not of an international character.'" 415 F.3d, at 41. That reasoning is erroneous. The term "conflict not of an international character" is used here in contradistinction to a conflict between nations. So much is demonstrated by the "fundamental logic [of] the Convention's provisions on its application." *Id.*, at 44 (Williams, J., concurring). Common Article 2 provides that "the present Convention shall apply to all cases of declared war or of any other armed conflict which may arise between two or more of the High Contracting Parties." 6 U.S.T., at 3318 (Art. 2, ¶ 1). High Contracting Parties (signatories) also must abide by all terms of the Conventions vis-à-vis one another even if one party to the conflict is a nonsignatory "Power," and must so abide vis-à-vis the nonsignatory if "the latter accepts and applies" those terms. *Ibid.* (Art. 2, ¶ 3). Common Article 3, by contrast, affords some minimal protection, falling short of full protection under the Conventions, to individuals associated with neither a signatory nor even a nonsignatory "Power" who are involved in a conflict "in the territory of" a signatory. The latter kind of conflict is distinguishable from the conflict described in Common Article 2 chiefly because it does not involve a clash between nations (whether signatories or not). In context, then, the phrase "not of an international character" bears its literal meaning. See, *e.g.*, J. Bentham, Introduction to the Principles of Morals and Legislation 6, 296 (J. Burns & H. Hart eds. 1970) (using the term "international law" as a "new though not inexpressive appellation" meaning "betwixt nation and nation"; defining "international" to include "mutual transactions between sovereigns as such"); Int'l Comm. of Red Cross, Commentary on the Additional Protocols to the Geneva Conventions of 12 August 1949, p. 1351 (1987) ("[A] non-international armed conflict is distinct from an international armed conflict because of the legal status of the entities opposing each other").

Although the official commentaries accompanying Common Article 3 indicate that an important purpose of the provision was to furnish minimal protection to rebels involved in one kind of "conflict not of an international character," *i.e.*, a civil war, see GCIII Commentary 36-37, the commentaries also make clear "that the scope of application of the Article must be as wide as possible," *id.*, at 36. In fact, limiting language that would have rendered Common Article 3 applicable "especially [to] cases of civil war, colonial conflicts, or wars of religion," was omitted from the final version of the Article, which coupled broader scope of application with a narrower range of rights than did earlier proposed iterations. See *id.*, at 42-43.

III

Common Article 3, then, is applicable here and, as indicated above, requires that Hamdan be tried by a "regularly constituted court affording all the judicial guarantees which are recognized as indispensable by civilized peoples." 6 U.S.T., at 3320 (Art. 3, ¶ 1(*d*)). While the term "regularly constituted court" is not specifically defined in either Common Article 3 or its accompanying commentary, other sources disclose its core meaning. The commentary accompanying a provision of the Fourth Geneva Convention, for example, defines " 'regularly constituted' " tribunals to include "ordinary military courts" and "definitely exclud[e] all special tribunals." GCIV Commentary 340 (defining the term "properly constituted" in Article 66, which the commentary treats as identical to "regularly constituted"); see also *Yamashita*, 327 U.S., at 44, 66 S. Ct. 340 (Rutledge, J., dissenting) (describing military commission as a court "specially constituted for the particular trial"). And one of the Red Cross' own treatises defines "regularly constituted court" as used in Common Article 3 to mean "established and organised in accordance with the laws and procedures already in force in a country." Int'l Comm. of Red Cross, 1 Customary Int'l Humanitarian Law 355 (2005); see also GCIV Commentary 340 (observing that "ordinary military courts" will "be set up in accordance with the recognized principles governing the administration of justice").

The Government offers only a cursory defense of Hamdan's military commission in light of Common Article 3. See Brief for Respondents 49-50. As

Justice Kennedy explains, that defense fails because "[t]he regular military courts in our system are the courts-martial established by congressional statutes." *Post*, at 2803 (opinion concurring in part). At a minimum, a military commission "can be 'regularly constituted' by the standards of our military justice system only if some practical need explains deviations from court-martial practice." *Post*, at 2804. As we have explained, see Part VI-C, *supra*, no such need has been demonstrated here.

IV

Inextricably intertwined with the question of regular constitution is the evaluation of the procedures governing the tribunal and whether they afford "all the judicial guarantees which are recognized as indispensable by civilized peoples." 6 U.S.T., at 3320 (Art. 3, ¶ 1(*d*)). Like the phrase "regularly constituted court," this phrase is not defined in the text of the Geneva Conventions. But it must be understood to incorporate at least the barest of those trial protections that have been recognized by customary international law. Many of these are described in Article 75 of Protocol I to the Geneva Conventions of 1949, adopted in 1977 (Protocol I). Although the United States declined to ratify Protocol I, its objections were not to Article 75 thereof. Indeed, it appears that the Government "regard[s] the provisions of Article 75 as an articulation of safeguards to which all persons in the hands of an enemy are entitled." Taft, The Law of Armed Conflict After 9/11: Some Salient Features, 28 Yale J. Int'l L. 319, 322 (2003). Among the rights set forth in Article 75 is the "right to be tried in [one's] presence." Protocol I, Art. 75(4)(e).

We agree with Justice Kennedy that the procedures adopted to try Hamdan deviate from those governing courts-martial in ways not justified by any "evident practical need," *post*, at 2805, and for that reason, at least, fail to afford the requisite guarantees. See *post*, at 2804-2808. We add only that, as noted in Part VI-A, *supra*, various provisions of Commission Order No. 1 dispense with the principles, articulated in Article 75 and indisputably part of the customary international law, that an accused must, absent disruptive conduct or consent, be present for his trial and must be privy to the evidence against him. See §§ 6(B)(3), (D). That the Government has a compelling interest in denying Hamdan access to certain sensitive information is not doubted. Cf. *post*, at 2848-2849 (Thomas, J., dissenting). But, at least absent express statutory provision to the contrary, information used to convict a person of a crime must be disclosed to him.

V

Common Article 3 obviously tolerates a great degree of flexibility in trying individuals captured during armed conflict; its requirements are general ones, crafted to accommodate a wide variety of legal systems. But *requirements* they are nonetheless. The commission that the President has convened to try Hamdan does not meet those requirements.

VII

. . . [I]n undertaking to try Hamdan and subject him to criminal punishment, the Executive is bound to comply with the rule of law that prevails in this jurisdiction.

The judgment of the Court of Appeals is reversed, and the case is remanded for further proceedings.

D. Treaty Termination

As noted above, Congress may enact a later in time statute that prevails over a prior treaty obligation (at least domestically). But what if it is the President who determines it is in the nation's best interests to nullify a treaty obligation? Does the President's inherent foreign affairs power allow him to do so unilaterally? Or does terminating a treaty require, by implication, the same Senate approval that is required to enter into the treaty?

In *Goldwater v. Carter*, 617 F.2d 697 (D.C. Cir. 1979), a group of members of Congress and senators, including Senator Barry Goldwater, challenged the constitutionality of President Carter's unilateral termination of the Sino-American Mutual Defense Treaty, by which the United States pledged to defend the Republic of China (Taiwan)—an action taken by President Carter as part of a broader foreign policy strategy associated with the restoration of diplomatic relations with the People's Republic of China. The district court initially dismissed the suit for lack of standing, but then granted appeal on an amended complaint. Sitting *en banc*, the Court of Appeals for the D.C. Circuit upheld the President's action and rejected the argument that treaties must be terminated in the same manner by which they are approved: with the advice and consent of the Senate. The court noted, *inter alia*, that Goldwater's theory that the Senate advice and consent role implied a role in treaty termination had not been applied in similar circumstances, such as the removal of ambassadors or other executive officials that are appointed by the President with the advice and consent of the Senate. According to the court:

> The Constitution specifically confers no power of treaty termination on either the Congress or the Executive. We note, however, that the powers conferred upon Congress in Article I of the Constitution are specific, detailed, and limited, while the powers conferred upon the President by Article II are generalized in a manner that bespeaks no such limitation upon foreign affairs powers . . . . The President is the constitutional representative of the United States with respect to external affairs. It is significant that the treaty power appears in Article II of the Constitution, relating to the executive branch, and not in Article I, setting forth the powers of the legislative branch. It is the President as Chief Executive who is given the constitutional authority to enter into a treaty; and even after he has obtained the consent of the Senate it is for him to decide whether to ratify a treaty and put it into effect. Senatorial confirmation of a treaty concededly does not obligate the President to go forward with a treaty if he concludes that it is not in the public interest to do so.
>
> Thus, in contrast to the lawmaking power, the constitutional initiative in the treaty-making field is in the President, not Congress. It would take an unprecedented feat of judicial construction to read into the Constitution an absolute

condition precedent of congressional or Senate approval for termination of all treaties, similar to the specific one relating to initial approval. And it would unalterably
affect the balance of power between the two Branches laid down in Articles I and II.

If we were to hold that under the Constitution a treaty could only be terminated
by exactly the same process by which it was made, we would be locking the United
States into all of its international obligations, even if the President and two-thirds
of the Senate minus one firmly believed that the proper course for the United States
was to terminate a treaty.

The Supreme Court then directed the District Court to dismiss the action pursuant to the political question doctrine (*Goldwater v. Carter*, 444 U.S. 996 (1979)).
According to the Court:

> ... [W]hile the Constitution is express as to the manner in which the Senate shall
> participate in the ratification of a treaty, it is silent as to that body's participation in
> the abrogation of a treaty. In this respect the case is directly analogous to *Coleman,
> supra*. As stated in *Dyer v. Blair*, 390 F. Supp. 1291, 1302 (N.D. Ill. 1975) (three-judge
> court):
>> "A question that might be answered in different ways for different amend-
>> ments must surely be controlled by political standards rather than standards
>> easily characterized as judicially manageable."
>
> In light of the absence of any constitutional provision governing the ter-
> mination of a treaty, and the fact that different termination procedures may
> be appropriate for different treaties (see, *e.g.*, n.1, *infra*), the instant case in my
> view also "must surely be controlled by political standards."

II. OTHER SOURCES OF INTERNATIONAL OBLIGATION

A. Is Customary International Law U.S. Law?

International law is not always established by international agreements, such as
treaties. Customary international law includes a wide range of rules and norms that
impact almost every aspect of international relations. A 1979 U.S. Department of
the Army Pamphlet entitled "The Law of Peace" provides a useful explanation of
customary international law:

> Until fairly recently, custom had been, quantitatively, the primary source of inter-
> national law, a position now assumed by international agreements. Notwithstanding
> this fact, however, custom still exists as an important and vital source of interna-
> tional jurisprudence. This results partially from the fact that it is through custom
> that treaties are interpreted. Of greater importance, however, is the fact that many
> of the legal concepts contained in such treaties can be considered as binding on even
> nonparties, if these agreements are deemed to be merely a codification of already
> existing customary international law. . . . Though custom is often viewed as a some-
> what nebulous legal source, this need not be the case. Custom arises when a clear
> and continuous habit of doing certain actions has grown up under the conviction

that these actions are, according to international law, obligatory. It is state practice accepted as law between states. . . . [5]

Unlike treaties, there is no reference to customary international law (what the Founders characterized as the "law of nations" in other constitutional provisions) in the Supremacy Clause of the Constitution. Does this mean customary international law plays no role as a source of authority in the United States?

The Supreme Court's decision in *The Paquete Habana* (175 U.S. 677 (1900)) is often cited in response to this question. That case arose out of the seizure of a Spanish ship by the U.S. Navy during the Spanish-American War. The *Paquete Habana* was a fishing sloop crewed by three Cubans, including the boat master, who had a fishing license from the Spanish government. She left Havana on March 25, 1898, for a fishing voyage at the western end of Cuba, within the territorial waters of Spain. On the return voyage back to Havana, she was captured by the United States gunboat *Castine* conducting operations as part of the U.S. blockade of Cuba. Until stopped by the blockading squadron, the crew had no knowledge of the existence of the war (Spanish-American War) or of any blockade. There were no munitions on board the sloop and at no point did the crew attempt to flee the blockade or resist at the time of the capture.

The *Paquete Habana* was brought back to Key West, where it was sold as prize of war for $490. Her owner then appealed the sale, citing the customary international law tradition that fishing vessels are deemed exempt from capture during war time. The Supreme Court identified the issue in the case: Was the *Paquete Habana* subject to seizure and disposition as prize of war? Or was the United States bound to respect the "law of nations" rule exempting coastal fishing vessels from this capture and disposition authority? The answer to this question turned on the status of what today is called customary international law in U.S. courts. According to the opinion:

> International law is part of our law, and must be ascertained and administered by the courts of justice of appropriate jurisdiction as often as questions of right depending upon it are duly presented for their determination. For this purpose, where there is no treaty and no controlling executive or legislative act or judicial decision, resort must be had to the customs and usages of civilized nations, and, as evidence of these, to the works of jurists and commentators who by years of labor, research, and experience have made themselves peculiarly well acquainted with the subjects of which they treat. Such works are resorted to by judicial tribunals, not for the speculations of their authors concerning what the law ought to be, but for trustworthy evidence of what the law really is.

The Paquete Habana is accordingly cited for the proposition that customary international law "is part of" U.S. law. But it seems relatively clear that the Court's opinion indicated that while this may be true, it becomes controlling only in the absence of treaty or statute, or perhaps even an executive order. In that case, the

---

5. U.S. Dep't of Defense, Pam. 27-161-1, Law of Peace Vol. 1 para. 1-6(c) Sept. 1979.

Court viewed customary international law as a source of law constraining the authority of the Navy and by implication the nation. But the following decision by the D.C. Circuit Court of Appeals suggests this might not always be the case, especially when Congress has enacted closely related legislation providing broad authority to the President.

Background

Ghaleb Nassar Al-Bihani, a former brigade cook for a unit of foreign volunteers that travelled to Afghanistan to assist the Taliban in defending their regime from the Northern Alliance, was held at the U.S. detention facility at Guantanamo Bay, Cuba. Al-Bihani's habeas petition was denied by the U.S. District Court for the District of Columbia, which found that the government had legal authority to detain any person who fell within the scope of detention authority implicitly authorized by Congress in the Authorization for Use of Military Force (AUMF).

Al-Bihani appealed, asserting *inter alia* that because he had volunteered to support the *Taliban government*, and because that government had long ceased to exist as the result of the Coalition victory in the initial phase of operations in Afghanistan, his continued detention was no longer lawful. Al-Bihani could not cite any treaty rule directly on point but argued instead that customary international law required a detaining power to repatriate all belligerent detainees at the end of hostilities. The D.C. Circuit rejected Al-Bihani's theory, stating that Congress left no indication that the customary international laws of war restricted the President's war powers under the AUMF. The court further noted that international laws of war are binding on U.S. courts only when they have been implemented through domestic law, treaty, or policy. Al-Bihani then petitioned for a rehearing en banc.

A majority of judges concurred with the conclusion that customary international law does not qualify or constrain statutory authority. This view is reflected in the concurring opinions of Judges Brown and Kavanaugh. Judge Williams dissented, arguing that the majority mischaracterized the relationship between customary international law and domestic legal authority.

Al-Bihani v. Obama
619 F.3d 1 (D.C. Cir. 2010)

SENTELLE, Chief Judge, and GINSBURG, HENDERSON, ROGERS, TATEL, GARLAND, and GRIFFITH, Circuit Judges, concurring in the denial of rehearing en banc:

We decline to en banc this case to determine the role of international law-of-war principles in interpreting the AUMF because, as the various opinions issued in the case indicate, the panel's discussion of that question is not necessary to the disposition of the merits. *See Al-Bihani v. Obama*, 590 F.3d 866, 871, 873-74 (D.C. Cir. 2010) (panel opinion); *id.* at 883-85 (Williams, J., concurring in the judgment); *Al-Bihani v. Obama*, No. 09-5051, slip op. at 1 (D.C. Cir. Aug. 31, 2010) (Kavanaugh, J., concurring in the denial of rehearing en banc); *see also* Gov't's Resp. to Pet. for Reh'g and Reh'g En Banc at 1-2 (stating that the dispute over the role of the law of war does not "change[ ] the outcome").

BROWN, Circuit Judge, concurring in the denial of rehearing en banc:

I sense, then, something more significant than a narrow concern over dictum or deference at work in the seven-member concurrence. There is in the scholarly community an intuition that domestic statutes do not stand on their own authority, but rather rest against the backdrop of international norms. This intuition has taken many argumentative forms, some more emphatic than others. For instance, there are those scholars who believe domestic statutes are merely suggestive wordings to which courts can and should append international legal norms, regardless of congressional intent. Others are more shy, imparting to Congress a general intent to legislate in conformity with international law and therefore reasoning that all statutes, unless containing a clear statement otherwise, should be read by courts to incorporate international legal norms. However this intuition is phrased, perhaps the majority of judges on this court are apprehensive about unambiguously rejecting it. So, even though the panel decision foreclosed the idea, the short concurrence may represent a wish to leave open a possibility—however slight—that domestic statutes are in fact subordinate to an overarching international legal order.

If that is their wish, it is a curious one. The idea that international norms hang over domestic law as a corrective force to be implemented by courts is not only alien to our caselaw, but an aggrandizement of the judicial role beyond the Constitution's conception of the separation of powers. *See United States v. Yunis*, 924 F.2d 1086, 1091 (D.C. Cir. 1991) ("[T]he role of judges . . . is to enforce the Constitution, laws, and treaties of the United States, not to conform the law of the land to norms of customary international law."). That aggrandizement is clear in the more extreme scholarly opinions calling for courts to ignore congressional intent in favor of international norms. And it is only slightly better disguised in the superficially restrained claims that Congress intends to conform its actions with global ideals, and that a clear statement is required if courts are to be prevented from reading international law into statutory text. Traditional clear statement rules are justified on the basis of preserving statutes against possible nullification by a constitutional value, keeping both Congress and the judiciary within their constitutional capacities. However, a demand that Congress clearly enunciate the inapplicability of international norms is not premised on any constitutional value; nothing in the Constitution compels the domestic incorporation of international law. Instead, what such a demand protects is a policy preference, imputing to Congress a general posture toward international restrictions and erecting the highest interpretive hurdle to the legitimate prerogative of Congress to legislate apart from them. This is a restrained search for legislative "intent" only in the most Orwellian sense—one that grants judges license to usurp the legislative role and dictate to Congress what it is supposed to think. Surprisingly, proponents of this idea actually claim it guards the separation of powers. *See* Wuerth, *supra*, at 349-50. But if that is the case, then the cure is truly worse than the disease.

I see much of this scholarly idea in Judge Williams' separate opinion.

. . .

This sprint into judicial immodesty cannot be redeemed by Judge Williams' argument that international law parallels traditional tools of statutory interpretation, and that by turning to it for substantive meaning courts are only divining the intent of Congress. I am unaware of *any* federal judicial opinion—and Judge Williams cites none—that has ever before characterized international discourse as a traditional tool of statutory interpretation on par with legislative history, usage in other domestic statutes and cases, or dictionary definitions. The varied process by which international law is made—through treaty, tribunal decision, and the constant churn of state practice and *opinio juris*—shares few, if any, of the qualities that give the traditional sources of interpretation their authority. Courts turn to legislative history because it comes from the mouths of legislators and therefore arguably sheds light on their intentions and understandings. Courts examine the usage of terms in other statutes and judicial decisions because our law is a closed and coherent system that strives for internal consistency. And courts consult dictionaries for the same reason most people do: our law, like the rest of our society, is dependent on language's technical meaning among American English speakers. On none of these grounds can the use of international law be justified.

. . .

There is no indication that the AUMF placed any international legal limits on the President's discretion to prosecute the war and, in light of the challenge our nation faced after September 11, 2001, that makes eminent sense. Confronted with a shadowy, non-traditional foe that succeeded in bringing a war to our doorstep by asymmetric means, it was (and still is) unclear how international law applies in all respects to this new context. The prospect is very real that some tradeoffs traditionally struck by the laws of war no longer make sense. That Congress wished the President to retain the discretion to recalibrate the military's strategy and tactics in light of circumstances not contemplated by our international obligations is therefore sensible, and reflects the traditional sovereign prerogative to violate international law or terminate international agreements. *See Garcia-Mir v. Meese*, 788 F.2d 1446, 1455 (11th Cir. 1986) ("[T]he power of the President to disregard international law in service of domestic needs is reaffirmed."); Restatement (Third) of the Foreign Relations Law of the United States § 339 (describing power of the President to suspend or terminate international agreements).

The only way a court could reach the opposite conclusion is to go beyond the AUMF's text, freeing it—as Judge Williams suggests—to appeal to an international meta-narrative, one activated whenever a legal issue touches on matters that strike the judge as transnational in flavor. Judges act prudently when they consciously forego opportunities for policymaking. Therefore, ignoring the text and plain meaning of a statute to privilege a more creative interpretation is the antithesis of prudence. And, in a time of war, it has the inconvenient effect of upending more than a century of our jurisprudence based on an understanding as old as the Republic: that the "conduct of foreign relations of our government is committed by the Constitution to the executive and legislative . . . departments," not to the judiciary. *Oetjen v. Cent. Leather Co.*, 246 U.S. 297, 302, 38 S. Ct. 309, 62 L. Ed. 726 (1918).

The only proper judicial role in this case is the truly modest route taken by the panel opinion in *Al-Bihani*. We read "necessary and appropriate" [the grant of authority in the AUMF to the President to use "necessary and appropriate force" in response to the September 11th terrorist attacks] in its traditional sense, taking Congress at its word that the President is to have wide discretion. This is a modest course because the President retains the leeway to implement his authority as broadly or narrowly as he believes appropriate — consistent with international law or not — and the legislature, in turn, may add whatever limits or constraints it deems wise as the war progresses. This ensures that wartime decisions will be informed by the expertise of the political branches, stated in a clear fashion, and that the decisionmakers will be accountable to the electorate.

None of those benefits accrue if the conduct of the military is subject to judicial correction based on norms of international discourse. Such an approach would place ultimate control of the war in the one branch insulated from both the battlefield and the ballot box. That would add further illegitimacy to the unpredictable and ad hoc rules judges would draw from the primordial stew of treaties, state practice, tribunal decisions, scholarly opinion, and foreign law that swirls beyond our borders. It is no comfort to the military to say, as Judge Williams does, that courts will only apply international rules they deem to possess the qualities of serious reason, evenhandedness, and practicality. Those are not judicially manageable standards. Those are buzzwords, the pleasing sound of which nearly lulls the mind into missing the vision of judicial supremacy at the heart of Judge Williams' opinion.

KAVANAUGH, Circuit Judge, concurring in the denial of rehearing en banc:

Al-Bihani's invocation of international law raises two fundamental questions. First, are international-law norms automatically part of domestic U.S. law? Second, even if international-law norms are not automatically part of domestic U.S. law, does the 2001 AUMF incorporate international-law principles as judicially enforceable limits on the President's wartime authority under the AUMF? The answer to both questions is no.

First, international-law norms are not domestic U.S. law in the absence of action by the political branches to codify those norms. Congress and the President can and often do incorporate international-law principles into domestic U.S. law by way of a statute (or executive regulations issued pursuant to statutory authority) or a self-executing treaty. When that happens, the relevant international-law principles become part of the domestic U.S. law that federal courts must enforce, assuming there is a cognizable cause of action and the prerequisites for federal jurisdiction are satisfied. But in light of the Supreme Court's 1938 decision in *Erie Railroad Co. v. Tompkins*, 304 U.S. 64, 58 S. Ct. 817, 82 L. Ed. 1188 (1938), which established that there is no federal general common law, international-law norms are not enforceable in federal courts unless the political branches have incorporated the norms into domestic U.S. law. None of the international-law norms cited by Al-Bihani has been so incorporated into domestic U.S. law.

Second, the 2001 AUMF does not expressly or impliedly incorporate judicially enforceable international-law limits on the President's direction of the war against al Qaeda and the Taliban. In authorizing the President to employ force, the AUMF authorizes the President to command the U.S. military to kill, capture, and detain the enemy, as Commanders in Chief traditionally have done in waging wars throughout American history. Congress enacted the AUMF with knowledge that the U.S. Constitution and other federal statutes would limit the President's conduct of the war. But neither the AUMF's text nor contemporaneous statements by Members of Congress suggest that Congress intended to impose judicially enforceable *international-law* limits on the President's authority under the AUMF.

. . .

Before proceeding to the analysis of these issues, I emphasize three overarching points about the position advanced in this separate opinion.

First, this opinion recognizes and reinforces the traditional roles of Congress, the President, and the Judiciary in national-security-related matters — roles enduringly articulated in Justice Jackson's separate opinion in *Youngstown Sheet & Tube Co. v. Sawyer*, 343 U.S. 579, 72 S. Ct. 863, 96 L. Ed. 1153 (1952). Courts enforce constitutionally permissible constraints imposed *by Congress* on the President's war powers. *See Hamdan v. Rumsfeld*, 548 U.S. 557, 126 S. Ct. 2749, 165 L. Ed. 2d 723 (2006); *Youngstown*, 343 U.S. at 634-655, 72 S. Ct. 863 (Jackson, J., concurring); *see generally* David J. Barron & Martin S. Lederman, *The Commander in Chief at the Lowest Ebb — Framing the Problem, Doctrine, and Original Understanding*, 121 Harv. L. Rev. 689, 761-66 (2008). So, too, courts enforce judicially manageable limits imposed *by the U.S. Constitution* on the President's war powers. *See Boumediene v. Bush*, 553 U.S. 723, 128 S. Ct. 2229, 171 L. Ed. 2d 41 (2008); *Hamdi*, 542 U.S. 507, 124 S. Ct. 2633. But courts may not interfere with the President's exercise of war powers based on international-law norms that the political branches have not seen fit to enact into domestic U.S. law.

Second, the limited authority of the Judiciary to rely on international law to restrict the American war effort does not imply that the political branches should ignore or disregard international-law norms. The principles of the international laws of war (and of international law more generally) deserve the respect of the United States. Violating international-law norms and breaching international obligations may trigger serious consequences, such as subjecting the United States to sanctions, undermining U.S. standing in the world community, or encouraging retaliation against U.S. personnel abroad. Therefore, Congress and the President are often well-advised to take account of international-law principles when considering potential legislation or treaties. And even when international-law norms have not been incorporated into domestic U.S. law, the Executive Branch, to the extent permissible under its constitutional and statutory authority, is often wise to pay close attention to those norms as a matter of sound policy, international obligation, or effective foreign relations. *See, e.g.*, Harold Hongju Koh, Legal Adviser, U.S. Department of State, The Obama Administration and International Law: Address at the Annual Meeting of the American Society of International Law (Mar. 25, 2010); John B. Bellinger III, Legal Adviser, U.S. Department of State, Testimony Before the Senate Committee on Foreign Relations (April 15, 2008), *reprinted in part in* Digest of United States Practice In International Law 2008, at 887-88 (Elizabeth R. Wilcox ed.); Letter from Gen. Colin L. Powell to Sen. John McCain (Sept. 13, 2006), *reprinted at* 152 Cong. Rec. S10,412 (daily ed. Sept. 28, 2006).

But in our constitutional system of separated powers, it is for Congress and the President—not the courts—to determine in the first instance whether and how the United States will meet its international obligations. When Congress and the President have chosen not to incorporate international-law norms into domestic U.S. law, bedrock principles of judicial restraint and separation of powers counsel that courts respect that decision.

Third, consistent with that constitutional division of authority, Congress has enacted a significant body of legislation to prohibit certain wartime actions by the Executive and military that contravene American values. For example, Congress has adopted a detailed and extensive Uniform Code of Military Justice, which governs many aspects of military conduct. *See* 10 U.S.C. §§ 801-946. Congress also has passed separate laws banning genocide and war crimes, including laws criminalizing grave breaches of the Geneva Conventions (such as rape, torture, and murder). *See, e.g.*, 18 U.S.C. §§ 1091, 2441. In addition, acting pursuant to congressional authorization, the Executive Branch has promulgated numerous legally binding rules that regulate wartime conduct of the military. *See, e.g.*, Enemy Prisoners of War, Retained Personnel, Civilian Internees and Other Detainees, Army Reg. 190-8, § 1-1(b) (Oct. 1, 1997). Those laws, along with many other statutes and regulations, together constitute a comprehensive body of domestic U.S. laws of war.

In his thoughtful opinion in connection with the denial of rehearing, Judge Williams says that it "would be an odd member of Congress who supposed that in authorizing the use of military force he was embracing uses equivalent to *all* such uses that have ever occurred: think Nanking 1937-38; Katyn 1940; Lidice 1942; My Lai 1968." Williams Op. at 54. I agree entirely with Judge Williams on that point, but not because I believe Congress intended for U.S. courts to enforce international-law norms against the Executive. Rather, when Congress authorized war in 2001, it did so knowing that domestic U.S. law already prohibited a variety of improper wartime conduct. Judge Williams' worrisome hypotheticals are thus already taken care of—by the domestic U.S. laws of war—and do not support his suggestion that the AUMF incorporates international-law norms. Notably, Judge Williams points to no examples of violations of international law that would be contrary to fundamental American values but that are not already independently prohibited by domestic U.S. law. There is a good deal of overlap between the international laws of war and domestic

U.S. laws regulating war. When there is divergence, however, Congress and the President—not the courts—have the authority in the first instance to decide whether and how to conform U.S. law to international law.

I

Four categories of law are relevant to this case: federal statutes; self-executing treaties made by the President with the concurrence of two-thirds of the Senate; non-self-executing treaties made by the President with the concurrence of two-thirds of the Senate; and customary international law.

Those four categories do not share the same status in U.S. law. As I will explain, statutes and self-executing treaties are domestic U.S. law and thus enforceable in U.S. courts. By contrast, non-self-executing treaties and customary international law are not domestic U.S. law. *See Medellín v. Texas*, 552 U.S. 491, 128 S. Ct. 1346, 170 L. Ed. 2d 190 (2008); *Sosa v. Alvarez-Machain*, 542 U.S. 692, 124 S. Ct. 2739, 159 L. Ed. 2d 718 (2004). Only when international-law principles are incorporated into a statute or a self-executing treaty do they become domestic U.S. law enforceable in U.S. courts.

In this case, none of the purported international-law principles cited by Al-Bihani has been incorporated into a statute or self-executing treaty. Those principles are therefore not part of the domestic law of the United States and, on their own, do not authorize a U.S. court to order Al-Bihani's release from U.S. military detention.

. . .

II

Even though none of the international-law sources Al-Bihani relies on is part of domestic U.S. law, Al-Bihani and amici alternatively argue that courts must nonetheless apply international-law principles in resolving cases under the 2001 Authorization for Use of Military Force, Pub. L. No. 107-40, 115 Stat. 224. In particular, Al-Bihani and amici contend that we should interpret the AUMF as incorporating international-law principles that limit the President's authority under the AUMF to wage war against al Qaeda and the Taliban.

On its face, this is a radical argument. Al-Bihani and amici would have the Federal Judiciary limit the scope of the President's war-making authority—*not* based on the Constitution and *not* based on express language in a statute or self-executing treaty, but rather based on international-law norms that have never been enacted into domestic U.S. law by American lawmakers.

For the reasons set forth at length below, the argument advanced by Al-Bihani and amici lacks merit: Congress has broadly authorized the President to wage war against al Qaeda and the Taliban. Neither the AUMF's text nor its legislative history suggests that Congress intended international-law principles to limit the scope of that congressional authorization. Congress often incorporates international-law principles into federal law; it did not do so here. Courts must respect that decision. Congress has also enacted a vast body of domestic

U.S. laws of war. But Congress has provided no indication that it wants courts to freelance and go beyond Congress's direction by imposing international-law limits on the Executive. Moreover, the *Charming Betsy* canon of statutory construction does not authorize courts to read international-law limitations into the authority granted to the President by the AUMF. The Supreme Court's decision in *Hamdi v. Rumsfeld*, 542 U.S. 507, 124 S. Ct. 2633, 159 L. Ed. 2d 578 (2004), similarly does not support Al-Bihani's submission.

* * *

To sum up on *Charming Betsy*: The canon exists to the extent it supports applying the presumption against extraterritorial application of federal statutes. Beyond that, after *Erie* and particularly after *Sosa* and *Medellín*, it is not appropriate for courts to use the *Charming Betsy* canon to alter interpretation of federal statutes to conform them to norms found in non-self-executing treaties and customary international law, which Congress has not chosen to incorporate into domestic U.S. law. In the alternative, even if one disagrees with that broader proposition and concludes that use of the *Charming Betsy* canon is appropriate in some such cases, it should not be invoked against the Executive Branch, which has the authority to weigh international-law considerations when interpreting the scope of ambiguous statutes. And even if one also disagrees with that, it is not appropriate for courts to narrow a congressional authorization of war based on international-law norms that are not part of domestic U.S. law.

. . .

WILLIAMS, Senior Circuit Judge:

Judge Kavanaugh, I think, fails to adequately distinguish between treatment of international law norms as "judicially enforceable limits" on Presidential authority, *id.* at 9, or as "domestic U.S. law," *id.* at 13, and use of such norms as a "basis for courts to alter their interpretation of federal statutes," *id.* at 32. By "alter their interpretation," I take Judge Kavanaugh to mean (as I said above) for a court to allow international law to persuade it to adopt a narrower interpretation of the President's authority than it would otherwise have chosen. I will assume that Judge Kavanaugh is correct as to the impropriety of the stronger use of international law (treating it as "domestic law"), but I believe him incorrect on the weaker (allowing it to affect a court's statutory interpretation).

Courts use a wide range of information outside the words of a statute to find those words' meaning. This reflects the simple truth that the question of a word's meaning is an empirical one: what have persons in the relevant community actually meant when using the words that appear in a statute? Among the most obvious outside sources to resolve that question are legislative history, usage in other laws and in judicial decisions, and dictionaries. Courts use all three incessantly. Dictionaries, of course, are only scholars' claims as to how people have historically used the words in question. Because military conflict is commonly an international phenomenon, words relating to such conflict are used in international discourse, of which international law is a subset. That international law has a normative element is nothing special; virtually all laws do — yet laws represent widely known public uses of language that legislatures often repackage in novel combinations and contexts. It would be an odd member of Congress who supposed that in authorizing the use of military force he was embracing uses equivalent to all such uses that have ever occurred: think Nanking 1937-38; Katyn 1940; Lidice 1942; My Lai 1968. More generally, it seems improbable that in authorizing the use of all "necessary and appropriate force" Congress could have contemplated employment of methods clearly and unequivocally condemned by international law.

Judge Kavanaugh agrees with that conclusion, but argues that we infer such limits on Congress's grant of power simply from penalties or prohibitions in domestic law. See *id.* at 31. He is surely correct that this is *one* source for finding limits on an authorization of military force, but that does not make it the only legitimate source of such limits. In some circumstances, Judge Kavanaugh's "domestic U.S. law of war," *id.* at 30-31 n.14, may have relatively little to say on a question that international practice has addressed for centuries. It obviously seemed so to the Supreme Court in *Hamdi v. Rumsfeld*, 542 U.S. 507, 518-21, 124 S. Ct. 2633, 159 L. Ed. 2d 578 (2004), where the plurality looked to international norms on the question of whom the President may detain pursuant to the AUMF, and for how long.

Before *Erie R.R. Co. v. Tompkins*, 304 U.S. 64, 58 S. Ct. 817, 82 L. Ed. 1188 (1938), U.S. courts undoubtedly used international law to help resolve cases. See Kavanaugh Op. at 17. It appears to have been uncontroversial for international law to serve not only as a species of federal general common law, binding absent contrary domestic law, see *id.* at 17-18, but also as a source of interpretive guidance regarding statutes passed by Congress, see, e.g., *Brown v. United States*, 8 Cranch 110, 124-28, 3 L. Ed. 504 (1814) (Marshall, C.J.) (interpreting the domestic legal effects of a U.S. declaration of war in part by reference to international norms, along with constitutional principles and domestic statutes). To dispute that commonsensical understanding, after all, requires defending the unlikely view that international law — unlike other known binding laws — offered no useful information whatsoever regarding the meaning of new laws on similar subjects. In Judge Kavanaugh's view, *Erie* effectively proscribed use of international law as "enforceable" U.S. law. See Kavanaugh Op. at 17-18. But that landmark case left intact the pre-existing alternative role of international law as a store of information regarding the sense of words Congress enacts into laws governing international matters — a role that never depended on international law's being a form of federal general common law (which *Erie* famously banished). *Erie* hardly requires that every last source of information regarding the meaning of words in statutes be an enacted law; if it does, federal courts have been disobeying its command for more than seven decades.

Even Judge Kavanaugh appears to acknowledge that international law may in some circumstances properly shape a court's interpretation of a federal statute. If I understand him correctly, though, he accepts reliance on international law to *expand* the meaning of a statutory grant of executive authority but never to *contract* it (the benchmark being the reading the court would otherwise have reached). See Kavanaugh Op. at 43; *id.* at 44 n.23. Use of international law as a one-way ratchet seems to me illogical. As Curtis Bradley and Jack Goldsmith put it in *Congressional Authorization and the War on Terrorism*, if the international laws of war "can inform the powers that Congress has implicitly granted to the President in the AUMF, they logically can inform the boundaries of such powers." 118 Harv. L. Rev. 2047, 2094 (2005). To whatever extent the international laws of war shed light on what the AUMF lets the President do, they shed light in all directions, not just one. If international law supports finding a grant of the "X" power (a power that by hypothesis the court would not otherwise have found), it must support some inquiry into what "X" means.

NOTES AND QUESTIONS

1. Do you think the judges who rejected Al-Bihani's assertion that he was protected by customary international law believed customary international law was irrelevant to presidential decisions related to the conduct of war? Or were they focused more precisely on the judicial enforceability of such norms as a constraint on the President? Why might a president comply with customary international law constraints even if she concluded they were not judicially enforceable?

2. In *Hamdi v. Rumsfeld*, Hamdi challenged the government's legal authority to detain him as an enemy belligerent based on the assertion he had been fighting with and alongside the Taliban. The government responded, *inter alia*, that detention of captured enemy belligerents was justified pursuant to the law of war principle of military necessity. Four members of the Court, joined by Justice Thomas, concluded that the authority to use "necessary and appropriate force" included within the same AUMF at issue in *Al-Bihani* implicitly authorized detention of enemy belligerents like Hamdi because by authorizing necessary force, Congress had, in effect, incorporated the customary "principles" of the international laws of war:

   > In light of these principles, it is of no moment that the AUMF does not use specific language of detention. Because detention to prevent a combatant's return to the battlefield is a fundamental incident of waging war, in permitting the use of "necessary and appropriate force," Congress has clearly and unmistakably authorized detention in the narrow circumstances considered here.

   How can this conclusion be reconciled with the *Al-Bihani* conclusion that these same principles in no way qualify the authority granted to the President by the AUMF?

3. Following the *Al-Bihani* decision, the Department of Justice indicated it did not necessarily agree that customary international law did not restrict the President's wartime authority. However, because it determined the conflict that *Al-Bihani* was associated with had not in fact terminated, it did not believe he was entitled to repatriation.

4. In *Sosa v. Alvarez-Machain*, 542 U.S. 692 (2004), the Supreme Court considered whether customary international law provides a cause of action under the Alien Tort Statute, a law that grants federal courts "original jurisdiction of any civil action by an alien for a tort only, committed in violation of the law of nations. . . . " § 1350. The Court concluded that norms of customary international law may provide a cause of action, but only in the absence of contrary statute and only for those norms of customary international law that are so universally accepted as to be analogous to the prohibition against piracy that existed at the time of the Founding. Specifically, the Court noted:

> The second inference to be drawn from the history is that Congress intended the ATS to furnish jurisdiction for a relatively modest set of actions alleging violations of the law of nations. Uppermost in the legislative mind appears to have been offenses against ambassadors, see *id.*, at 118; violations of safe conduct were probably understood to be actionable, *ibid.*, and individual actions arising out of prize captures and piracy may well have also been contemplated. *Id.*, at 113-114. But the common law appears to have understood only those three of the hybrid variety as definite and actionable, or at any rate, to have assumed only a very limited set of claims. As Blackstone had put it, "offences against this law [of nations] are principally incident to whole states or nations," and not individuals seeking relief in court. 4 Commentaries 68.
>
> . . .
>
> . . . All Members of the Court agree that § 1350 is only jurisdictional. We also agree, or at least Justice Scalia does not dispute, *post*, at 2, 7, that the jurisdiction was originally understood to be available to enforce a small number of international norms that a federal court could properly recognize as within the common law enforceable without further statutory authority. Justice Scalia concludes, however, that two subsequent developments should be understood to preclude federal courts from recognizing any further international norms as judicially enforceable today, absent further congressional action. As described before, we now tend to understand common law not as a discoverable reflection of universal reason but, in a positivistic way, as a product of human choice. And we now adhere to a conception of limited judicial power first expressed in reorienting federal diversity jurisdiction, see *Erie R. Co. v. Tompkins*, 304 U.S. 64 (1938), that federal courts have no authority to derive "general" common law.
>
> Whereas Justice Scalia sees these developments as sufficient to close the door to further independent judicial recognition of actionable international norms, other considerations persuade us that the judicial power should be exercised on the understanding that the door is still ajar subject to vigilant doorkeeping, and thus open to a narrow class of international norms today. *Erie* did not in terms bar any judicial recognition of new substantive rules, no matter what the circumstances, and post-*Erie* understanding has identified limited enclaves in which federal courts may derive some substantive law in a common law way. For two centuries we have affirmed that the domestic law of the United States recognizes the law of nations. See, *e.g.*, *Sabbatino*, 376 U.S., at 423 ("[I]t is, of course, true that United States courts apply international law as a part of our own in appropriate circumstances") [footnote 18]; *The Paquete Habana*, 175 U.S., at 700 ("International law is part of our law, and must be ascertained and administered by the courts of justice of appropriate jurisdiction, as often as questions of right

depending upon it are duly presented for their determination"); *The Nereide*, 9 Cranch 388, 423 (1815) (Marshall, C.J.) ("[T]he Court is bound by the law of nations which is a part of the law of the land"); see also *Texas Industries, Inc. v. Radcliff Materials, Inc.*, 451 U.S. 630, 641 (1981) (recognizing that "international disputes implicating . . . our relations with foreign nations" are one of the "narrow areas" in which "federal common law" continues to exist). It would take some explaining to say now that federal courts must avert their gaze entirely from any international norm intended to protect individuals.

Does the *Sosa* Court's explanation of the relationship between customary international law norms and the *Erie* doctrine seem consistent or inconsistent with *Al-Bihani*?

B. Statutory Codification of Customary International Law

Recall that Article I vests Congress with authority "To define and punish Piracies and Felonies committed on the high Seas, and Offences against the Law of Nations." In so doing, must Congress constantly update such statutes to keep apace with developments in customary international law? Or does the codification of international law offenses imply congressional intent that the statutory definition evolve as international law evolves? The following opinion addresses this question.

United States v. Dire
680 F.3d 446 (4th Cir. 2012)

KING, Circuit Judge:

In the early morning hours of April 1, 2010, on the high seas between Somalia and the Seychelles (in the Indian Ocean off the east coast of Africa), the defendants Abdi Wali Dire, Gabul Abdullahi Ali, Abdi Mohammed Umar, Abdi Mohammed Gurewardher, and Mohammed Modin Hasan imprudently launched an attack on the USS Nicholas, having confused that mighty Navy frigate for a vulnerable merchant ship. The defendants, all Somalis, were swiftly apprehended and then transported to the Eastern District of Virginia, where they were convicted of the crime of piracy, as proscribed by 18 U.S.C. § 1651, plus myriad other criminal offenses. In this appeal, the defendants challenge their convictions and life plus-eighty-year sentences on several grounds, including that their fleeting and fruitless strike on the Nicholas did not, as a matter of law, amount to a § 1651 piracy offense. As explained below, we reject their contentions and affirm.

I.

A.

According to the trial evidence, the USS Nicholas was on a counter-piracy mission in the Indian Ocean when, lit to disguise itself as a merchant vessel, it encountered the defendants shortly after midnight on April 1, 2010. The Nicholas was approached by an attack skiff operated by defendant Hasan and also carrying defendants Dire and Ali, while defendants Umar and Gurewardher remained with a larger mother-ship some distance away. From their posts on the Nicholas, crew members could see by way of night-vision devices that Hasan was armed with a loaded rocket-propelled grenade launcher (commonly referred to as an "RPG"), and that Dire and Ali carried AK-47 assault rifles.

The captain of the USS Nicholas, Commander Mark Kesselring, directed his gunners to man their stations and prepare to fire, and ordered his unarmed personnel inside the skin of the ship for safety. When the defendants' attack skiff was within sixty feet of the Nicholas's fantail (its lowest and thus most accessible point), Dire and Ali discharged the first shots bursts of rapid, auto-matic fire from their AK-47s aimed at the Nicholas and meant to attain its sur-render. The Nicholas's crew responded in kind, resulting in an exchange of fire that lasted less than thirty seconds. Bullets from Dire and Ali's AK-47s struck the Nicholas near two of its crew members, but the defendants' brief attack was (thankfully) casualty-free. Dire, Ali, and Hasan then turned their skiff and fled, with the Nicholas in pursuit.

During the chase, sailors on the USS Nicholas observed a flashing light on the horizon [—] a beacon from Umar and Gurewardher to lead the attack skiff back to the mothership. Commander Kesselring, however, managed to keep the Nicholas between the defendants' two vessels to thwart the attempted reunion. Meanwhile, Dire, Ali, and Hasan threw various items from the skiff overboard into the Indian Ocean, discarding the RPG, the AK-47s, and a ladder that would have enabled them to board the Nicholas. About thirty minutes into the pursuit, the Nicholas captured the three defendants in the skiff. Thereafter, the Nicholas chased and captured the two defendants in the mothership. A sus-pected second attack skiff, which had appeared on radar but did not close on the Nicholas, was never found.

. . . [O]n April 4, 2010, during questioning aboard the Nicholas, the defen-dants separately confessed to participating willingly in a scheme to hijack a merchant vessel, and they provided details about their operation.

B.

The grand jury in the Eastern District of Virginia returned a six-count indictment against the defendants on April 20, 2010, and a fourteen-count superseding indictment (the operative "Indictment") on July 7, 2010. . . . The Indictment identified the Eastern District of Virginia as the proper venue under 18 U.S.C. § 3238, which provides that "[t]he trial of all offenses begun or committed upon the high seas . . . shall be in the district in which the offender, or any one of two or more joint offenders, is arrested or is first brought."

At the conclusion of an eleven-day trial, conducted between November 9 and 24, 2010, the jury returned separate verdicts of guilty against all defendants on all counts. . . .

II.

In these consolidated appeals, the defendants first contend that their ill-fated attack on the USS Nicholas did not constitute piracy under 18 U.S.C. § 1651, which provides in full:

> *Whoever, on the high seas, commits the crime of piracy as defined by the law of nations, and is afterwards brought into or found in the United States, shall be imprisoned for life.*

According to the defendants, the crime of piracy has been narrowly defined for purposes of § 1651 as robbery at sea, i.e., seizing or otherwise robbing a vessel. Because they boarded the Nicholas only as captives and indisputably took no property, the defendants contest their convictions on Count One, as well as the affixed life sentences.

A.

The defendants' piracy contention is one that they unsuccessfully presented at multiple stages of the district court proceedings. Prior to their trial, the defendants moved to dismiss Count One under Rule 12 of the Federal Rules of Criminal Procedure. By its published opinion of October 29, 2010, the district court denied relief, premised on its determination that the Indictment "set forth facts that are sufficient, if proven true, to constitute the crime of piracy as defined by the law of nations, in violation of 18 U.S.C. § 1651." *United States v. Hasan*, 747 F. Supp. 2d 599, 602 (E.D. Va. 2010) ("*Hasan I*"). In so ruling, the court concluded contrary to the defendants' posited robbery requirement that piracy as defined by § 1651's incorporated law of nations encompasses, inter alia, acts of violence committed on the high seas for private ends. *See id.* at 640-42. . . .

1.

The *Hasan I* opinion was issued on the heels of the August 17, 2010 published opinion in *United States v. Said*, 757 F. Supp. 2d 554 (E.D. Va. 2010) (Jackson, J.), wherein a different judge of the Eastern District of Virginia essentially took these defendants' view of the piracy offense by recognizing a robbery element. Like these defendants, the *Said* defendants have been charged with piracy under 18 U.S.C. § 1651 for attacking but not seizing or otherwise robbing a United States Navy ship. *See Said*, 757 F. Supp. 2d at 556-57 (describing indictment's allegations that, around 5:00 A.M. on April 10, 2010, *Said* defendants fired at least one shot on USS Ashland from skiff in Gulf of Aden). The *Said* court granted the defendants' pretrial motion, pursuant to Federal Rule of Criminal Procedure 12, to dismiss the piracy count from the indictment because no taking of property was alleged. *Id.* at 556.

As the *Said* court recognized, article I of the Constitution accords Congress the power "[t]o define and punish Piracies and Felonies committed on the high Seas, and Offences against the Law of Nations." U.S. Const. art. I, § 8, cl. 10 (the "Define and Punish Clause"). In its present form, the language of

18 U.S.C. § 1651 can be traced to an 1819 act of Congress, which similarly provided, in pertinent part:

> *That if any person or persons whatsoever, shall, on the high seas, commit the crime of piracy, as defined by the law of nations, and such offender or offenders, shall afterwards be brought into or found in the United States, every such offender or offenders shall, upon conviction thereof, . . . be punished. . . .*

See Act of Mar. 3, 1819, ch. 77, § 5, 3 Stat. 510, 513-14 (the "Act of 1819"). Whereas today's mandatory penalty for piracy is life imprisonment, however, the Act of 1819 commanded punishment "with death." *Id.* at 514. Examining the Act of 1819 in its *United States v. Smith* decision of 1820, the Supreme Court recognized:

> There is scarcely a writer on the law of nations, who does not allude to piracy, as a crime of a settled and determinate nature; and whatever may be the diversity of definitions, in other respects, all writers concur, in holding, that robbery, or forcible depredations upon the sea, *animo furandi*, is piracy. . . .

Invoking the principle that a court "must interpret a statute by its ordinary meaning at the time of its enactment," the *Said* court deemed *Smith* to be the definitive authority on the meaning of piracy under 18 U.S.C. § 1651. . . . The *Said* court noted that it was the first court since the 1800s to be tasked with "interpreting the piracy statute . . . as it applies to alleged conduct in international waters." *Id.* at 558. Looking to courts that have addressed the piracy statute post-*Smith* in other contexts, the *Said* court concluded that "the discernible definition of piracy as 'robbery or forcible depredations committed on the high seas' under § 1651 has remained consistent and has reached a level of concrete consensus in United S[t]ates law." *Id.* at 560.

The *Said* court also reviewed the legislative history of § 1651 and detected no congressional modifications to *Smith*'s definition of piracy. . . .

Additionally, the *Said* court discerned support for a static definition of piracy under § 1651 from the existence of the statute criminalizing an attack to plunder a vessel, 18 U.S.C. § 1659, which provides:

> *Whoever, upon the high seas or other waters within the admiralty and maritime jurisdiction of the United States, by surprise or open force, maliciously attacks or sets upon any vessel belonging to another, with an intent unlawfully to plunder the same, or to despoil any owner thereof of any moneys, goods, or merchandise laden on board thereof, shall be fined under this title or imprisoned not more than ten years, or both.*

The court perceived that, because § 1659 targets "exactly the conduct charged against [the *Said* defendants] of shooting at the USS Ashland with an AK-47 rifle," it would be rendered redundant by extending the meaning of piracy under § 1651 to include that same violent conduct. . . .

Finally, although the *Said* court acknowledged contemporary international law sources defining piracy to encompass the *Said* defendants' violent conduct, the court deemed such sources to be too "unsettled" to be authoritative. *See*

Said, 757 F. Supp. 2d at 563-66. The court further determined that relying on those international law sources would violate due process, explaining that, if "the definition of piracy [were adopted] from the[ ] debatable international sources whose promulgations evolve over time, defendants in United States courts would be required to constantly guess whether their conduct is proscribed by § 1651[,] render[ing] the statute unconstitutionally vague." *Id.* at 566. Thereby undeterred from employing the "clear and authoritative" definition in *Smith* "of piracy as sea robbery," the court dismissed the piracy count from the *Said* indictment. *Id.* at 567.

2.

Here, the district court took a different tack, as laid out in its sweeping *Hasan I* opinion denying these defendants' pretrial motion to dismiss the Count One piracy charge from their Indictment. That is, the court focused on piracy's unusual status as a crime defined by the law of nations and subject to universal jurisdiction.

a.

The district court began by recognizing that, "[f]or centuries, pirates have been universally condemned as *hostis humani generis*—enemies of all mankind because they attack vessels on the high seas, and thus outside of any nation's territorial jurisdiction, . . . with devastating effect to global commerce and navigation." *Hasan I*, 747 F. Supp. 2d at 602. The court then turned its attention to the Define and Punish Clause, and specifically the potential "double redundancy [presented] by pairing 'Piracies' with 'Felonies committed on the high Seas' and 'Offences against the Law of Nations,' the latter two categories being broader groupings of offenses within which piracy was already included." *Id.* at 605 (quoting U.S. Const. art. I, § 8, cl. 10).

The district court perceived that, by nonetheless including "Piracies" in the Define and Punish Clause, the Framers distinguished that crime from "Felonies committed on the high Seas" and "Offences against the Law of Nations" [—] a sensible distinction to make in light of what would have been known to the Framers: "that piracy on the high seas was a unique offense because it permitted nations to invoke universal jurisdiction, such that any country could arrest and prosecute pirates in its domestic courts, irrespective of the existence of a jurisdictional nexus." . . .

With that history in mind, the district court recognized that the Define and Punish Clause "accords to Congress the special power of criminalizing piracy in a manner consistent with the exercise of universal jurisdiction." *Hasan I*, 747 F. Supp. 2d at 605. The court further recognized, however, that Congress encountered early difficulties in criminalizing "general piracy" (that is, piracy in contravention of the law of nations), rather than solely "municipal piracy" (i.e., piracy in violation of United States law). *See id.* at 606. On the one hand, "[w]hile municipal piracy is flexible enough to cover virtually any overt act Congress chooses to dub piracy, it is necessarily restricted to those acts that have a jurisdictional nexus with the United States." . . . Importantly, though, "because it is created by international consensus, general piracy is restricted in substance to those offenses that the international community agrees constitute piracy." *Id.*

The district court elucidated that, in the absence of federal common law power to apply the law of nations, "Congress had to enact a municipal law that adequately embodied the international crime of piracy," requiring legislation "that was broad enough to incorporate the definition of piracy under the law of nations (and, in so doing, invoke universal jurisdiction) but narrow enough to exclude conduct that was beyond the scope of that definition." *Hasan I,* 747 F. Supp. 2d at 610. Congress's first effort in that regard, a 1790 act, proved unsuccessful. *See id.* at 612 (discussing Act of Apr. 30, 1790, ch. 9, § 8, 1 Stat. 112 (the "Act of 1790")). By Chief Justice Marshall's 1818 decision in *United States v. Palmer,* the Supreme Court ruled that because the wording of the Act of 1790 evidenced an intent to criminalize "offences against the United States, not offences against the human race[,]" the Act did not "authorize the courts of the Union to inflict its penalties on persons who are not citizens of the United States, nor sailing under their flag, nor offending particularly against them." 16 U.S. (3 Wheat.) 610, 631, 4 L. Ed. 471 (1818). The *Palmer* decision thus announced the Act of 1790's failure to define piracy as a universal jurisdiction crime.

Within a year of *Palmer,* as the district court recounted, "Congress passed the Act of 1819 to make clear that it wished to proscribe not only piratical acts that had a nexus to the United States, but also piracy as an international offense subject to universal jurisdiction." . . . In key part, both § 1651 and the Act of 1819 proscribe piracy simply "as defined by the law of nations." . . .

b.

The district court in *Hasan I* astutely traced the meaning of "piracy" under the law of nations, from the time of the Act of 1819 to the modern era and the crime's codification at 18 U.S.C. § 1651. The court commenced with the Supreme Court's 1820 decision in *United States v. Smith,* relating that Justice Story easily concluded that "the Act of 1819 'sufficiently and constitutionally' defined piracy by expressly incorporating the definition of piracy under the law of nations." *See Hasan I,* 747 F. Supp. 2d at 616 (quoting *Smith,* 18 U.S. (5 Wheat.) at 162). The district court also recounted that . . . "whatever may be the diversity of definitions, in other respects, all writers concur, in holding, that robbery, or forcible depredations upon the sea, *animo furandi,* is piracy." . . .

Having noted that "[n]o other Supreme Court decision since *Smith* has directly addressed the definition of general piracy," and recognizing the necessity of looking to foreign sources to determine the law of nations, the district court then focused on case law from other countries [the court then summarized the *Hasan I* court's review of decisions from the U.K. and Kenya considering whether robbery is an essential element of piracy] . . . .

As detailed in *Hasan I*, "there are two prominent international agreements that have directly addressed, and defined, the crime of general piracy." *See* 747 F. Supp. 2d at 618. The first of those treaties is the Geneva Convention on the High Seas (the "High Seas Convention"), which was adopted in 1958 and ratified by the United States in 1961 . . . . Under the High Seas Convention,

[p]iracy consists of any of the following acts:
(1) Any illegal acts of violence, detention or any act of depredation, committed for private ends by the crew or the passengers of a private ship or a private aircraft, and directed:
(a) On the high seas, against another ship or aircraft, or against persons or property on board such ship or aircraft;
(b) Against a ship, aircraft, persons or property in a place outside the jurisdiction of any State;
(2) Any act of voluntary participation in the operation of a ship or of an aircraft with knowledge of facts making it a pirate ship or aircraft;
(3) Any act of inciting or of intentionally facilitating an act described in sub-paragraph 1 or subparagraph 2 of this article.

Geneva Convention on the High Seas, art. 15, *opened for signature* Apr. 29, 1958, 13 U.S.T. 2312, 450 U.N.T.S. 11 (entered into force Sept. 30, 1962).

The second pertinent treaty is the United Nations Convention on the Law of the Sea (the "UNCLOS"), which has amassed 162 parties since 1982 albeit not the United States, which has not ratified the UNCLOS "but has recognized that its baseline provisions reflect customary international law." . . . Relevant here, the UNCLOS provides that

[p]iracy consists of any of the following acts:
(a) any illegal acts of violence or detention, or any act of depredation, committed for private ends by the crew or the passengers of a private ship or a private aircraft, and directed:
(i) on the high seas, against another ship or aircraft, or against persons or property on board such ship or aircraft;
(ii) against a ship, aircraft, persons or property in a place outside the jurisdiction of any State;
(b) any act of voluntary participation in the operation of a ship or of an aircraft with knowledge of facts making it a pirate-ship or aircraft;
(c) any act of inciting or of intentionally facilitating an act described in subparagraph (a) or (b).

U.N. Convention on the Law of the Sea, art. 101, *opened for signature* Dec. 10, 1982, 1833 U.N.T.S. 397 (entered into force Nov. 16, 1994). Upon comparing the High Seas Convention with the UNCLOS, the district court in *Hasan I* recognized that the latter treaty "defines piracy in exactly the same terms as the [former agreement], with only negligible stylistic changes." *See* 747 F. Supp. 2d at 620. The court also observed that the UNCLOS "represents the most recent international statement regarding the definition . . . of piracy." *Id.*

c.

Turning to the contentions of the parties herein, the district court related the defendants' position "that the authoritative definition of piracy under the law of nations, and thus within the meaning of 18 U.S.C. § 1651, is provided by the Supreme Court's decision in *Smith.*" *Hasan I,* 747 F. Supp. 2d at 620-21. According to the defendants, because their Indictment did not allege "that they committed any actual robbery on the high seas," the Count One piracy charge had to be dismissed. *Id.* at 621. For its part, however, the government defended Count One on the premise "that *Smith* neither foreclosed the possibility that piracy included conduct other than robbery nor precluded the possibility that the definition of piracy under the law of nations might later come to include conduct other than robbery." *Id.* In response, the district court recognized that "if the definition of piracy under the law of nations can evolve over time, such that the modern law of nations must be applied, rather than any recitation of the state of the law in the early Nineteenth Century," the court need not determine "[w]hether *Smith* was limited to its facts and not intended to be exhaustive, or whether its description of piracy was exhaustive but only represented the definition of piracy accepted at that time by the international community." *Id.* at 622. The court then embarked on the relevant analysis.

First, the district court interpreted 18 U.S.C. § 1651 as an unequivocal demonstration of congressional intent "to incorporate . . . any subsequent developments in the definition of general piracy under the law of nations." *Hasan I,* 747 F. Supp. 2d at 623. The court rationalized:

> The plain language of 18 U.S.C. § 1651 reveals that, in choosing to define the international crime of piracy by [reference to the "law of nations"], Congress made a conscious decision to adopt a flexible but at all times sufficiently precise definition of general piracy that would automatically incorporate developing international norms regarding piracy. Accordingly, Congress necessarily left it to the federal courts to determine the definition of piracy under the law of nations based on the international consensus at the time of the alleged offense.

Id. (citing *Ex parte Quirin,* 317 U.S. 1, 29-30, 63 S. Ct. 2, 87 L. Ed. 3 (1942), where the Supreme Court reiterated its 1820 ruling in *Smith* that "[a]n Act of Congress punishing 'the crime of piracy, as defined by the law of nations' is an appropriate exercise of its constitutional authority to 'define and punish' the offense, since it has adopted by reference the sufficiently precise definition of international law" (citations omitted)). The district court further gleaned that Congress intended to adopt "a flexible definition for general piracy" from the history of § 1651 . . . . Thus, according to the court, the Act of 1819's simple incorporation of the law of nations made sense, because it relieved Congress of "having to revise the general piracy statute continually to mirror the international consensus definition." *Id.* As written, the Act of 1819, and now 18 U.S.C. § 1651, "automatically incorporate[ ]" advancements "in the definition of general piracy under the law of nations." *Id.*

"Having concluded that Congress's proscription of 'piracy as defined by the law of nations' in 18 U.S.C. § 1651 necessarily incorporates modern developments in international law," the district court next endeavored to "discern the definition of piracy under the law of nations at the time of the alleged offense in April 2010." . . . Engaging in that analysis, the court concluded:

> As of April 1, 2010, the law of nations, also known as customary international law, defined piracy to *include* acts of violence committed on the high seas for private ends without an actual taking. More specifically, . . . the definition of general piracy under modern customary international law is, at the very least, reflected in Article 15 of the 1958 High Seas Convention and Article 101 of the 1982 UNCLOS.

. . .

In the course of its discussion of the High Seas Convention and the UNCLOS, the district court recognized that "'[t]reaties are proper evidence of customary international law because, and insofar as, they create legal obligations akin to contractual obligations on the States parties to them.'" *Hasan I,* 747 F. Supp. 2d at 633 (quoting *Kiobel v. Royal Dutch Petroleum Co.,* 621 F.3d 111, 137 (2d Cir. 2010)). According to the court, "[w]hile all treaties shed some light on the customs and practices of a state, 'a treaty will only constitute sufficient proof of a norm of customary international law if an overwhelming majority of States have ratified the treaty, and those States uniformly and consistently act in accordance with its principles.'" *Id.* (emphasis omitted) (quoting *Kiobel,* 621 F.3d at 137). "In this regard," the court emphasized, "it is also important to understand that a treaty can either 'embod[y] or create[ ] a rule of customary international law,' and such a rule 'applies beyond the limited subject matter of the treaty and *to nations that have not ratified it.*'" *Id.* (alterations in original) (quoting *Kiobel,* 621 F.3d at 138). With those principles in mind, the court recognized:

> There were 63 states parties to the High Seas Convention as of June 10, 2010, including the United States, and there were 161 states parties to UNCLOS (including the European Union) as of October 5, 2010, including Somalia. The 161 states parties to UNCLOS represent the "overwhelming majority" of the 192 Member States of the United Nations, and the 194 countries recognized by the United States Department of State. UNCLOS's definition of piracy therefore represents a widely accepted norm, followed out of a sense of agreement (or, in the case of the states parties, treaty obligation), that has been recognized by an overwhelming majority of the world.

The status of UNCLOS as representing customary international law is enhanced by the fact that the states parties to it include all of the nations bordering the Indian Ocean on the east coast of Africa, where the incident in the instant case is alleged to have taken place: South Africa, Mozambique, Tanzania, Kenya, and Somalia. . . .

The district court further observed "that UNCLOS does not represent the first time that acts of violence have been included in the definition of general piracy." *Hasan I,* 747 F. Supp. 2d at 635. Rather, even accepting that "actual robbery on the high seas" was once an essential element of general piracy, "the view that general piracy does not require an actual robbery on the sea has certainly gained traction since the Nineteenth Century, as evidenced by [intervening case law], the Harvard Draft Convention on Piracy, the High Seas Convention, and UNCLOS." *Id.* The court took especial note of Kenya's recent reliance on the UNCLOS to define general piracy in the 2006 *Republic v. Ahmed* case, concluding:

> This actual state practice by Kenya, the country currently most involved in prosecuting piracy, as well as the active support of such practice by other nations, which continue to bring other alleged pirates to Kenya for prosecution, is indicative of the fact that the definition of piracy contained in the High Seas Convention and UNCLOS have attained the status of a binding rule of customary international law.

Hasan I, 747 F. Supp. 2d at 636. Additionally, the court recognized that "[c]ontemporary scholarly sources . . . appear to agree that the definition of piracy in UNCLOS represents customary international law." . . .

Significantly, the district court rejected the defendants' contention—endorsed by the *Said* court [—] that the piracy statute, 18 U.S.C. § 1651, "cannot be read to include mere acts of violence committed in an effort to rob another vessel on the high seas, because doing so would render . . . superfluous" the attack-to-plunder-a-vessel statute, 18 U.S.C. § 1659. *See Hasan I,* 747 F. Supp. 2d at 637. The court in *Hasan I* articulated that, although the defendants were "correct in their assertion that reading § 1651 to include acts of violence without an actual taking would render punishable as general piracy acts that also fall within § 1659," the defendants defectively ignored "the distinct jurisdictional scopes provided by § 1651 and § 1659." *Id.* That is, "[w]hile § 1659 applies only to acts by United States citizens or foreign nationals 'set[ting] upon' U.S. citizens or U.S. ships, § 1651 provides for the prosecution of general piracy (as opposed to municipal piracy) with the ability to invoke universal jurisdiction. Therefore, 18 U.S.C. § 1659 is not superfluous." *Id.* (second alteration in original).

The *Hasan I* opinion further rejected the *Said*-approved theory "that applying the contemporary customary international law definition of general piracy violates fundamental due process protections." . . . According to *Hasan I,* "§ 1651's express incorporation of the definition of piracy provided by 'the law of nations,' which is today synonymous with customary international law, provides fair warning of what conduct is proscribed by the statute." . . .

d.

. . .

The district court concluded that defendants Ali and Dire were adequately charged in Count One . . . .

3.

Faithful to its *Hasan I* opinion, the district court instructed the jury on Count One, over the defendants' objection, that the Law of Nations defines the crime of piracy to [include] any of the three following actions:

(A) any illegal acts of violence or detention or any act of depredation committed for private ends on the high seas or a place outside the jurisdiction of any state by the crew or the passengers of a private ship and directed against another ship or against persons or property on board such ship; or

(B) any act of voluntary participation in the operation of a ship with knowledge of facts making it a pirate ship; or

(C) any act of inciting or of intentionally facilitating an act described in (A) or (B) above.

. . . The court also specified "that an assault with a firearm as alleged in the indictment in this case, if proven beyond a reasonable doubt, is an illegal act of violence." *Id.* at 19. The jury found each of the defendants guilty of the Count One piracy offense by a general verdict.

. . .

B.

On appeal, the defendants maintain that the district court erred with respect to Count One . . . .

Simply put, we agree with the conception of the law outlined by the court below. Indeed, we have carefully considered the defendants' appellate contentions endorsed by the amicus curiae brief submitted on their behalf, yet remain convinced of the correctness of the trial court's analysis.

The crux of the defendants' position is now, as it was in the district court, that the definition of general piracy was fixed in the early Nineteenth Century, when Congress passed the Act of 1819 first authorizing the exercise of universal jurisdiction by United States courts to adjudicate charges of "piracy as defined by the law of nations." . . .

The defendants would have us believe that, since the *Smith* era, the United States' proscription of general piracy has been limited to "robbery upon the sea." But that interpretation of our law would render it incongruous with the modern law of nations and prevent us from exercising universal jurisdiction in piracy cases. . . . At bottom, then, the defendants' position is irreconcilable with the noncontroversial notion that Congress intended in § 1651 to define piracy as a universal jurisdiction crime. In these circumstances, we are constrained to agree with the district court that § 1651 incorporates a definition of piracy that changes with advancements in the law of nations.

We also agree with the district court that the definition of piracy under the law of nations, at the time of the defendants' attack on the USS Nicholas and continuing today, had for decades encompassed their violent conduct. . . . Because the district court correctly applied the UNCLOS definition of piracy as customary international law, we reject the defendants' challenge to their Count One piracy convictions, as well as their mandatory life sentences.

C. Executive Agreements

Executive agreements are another source of international obligation not refer-enced in the Supremacy Clause. Unlike treaties, executive agreements are not sub-ject to the advice and consent requirement; but like treaties they purport to bind the United States to obligations with other nations pursuant to international law. A Congressional Research Service Report provides the following explanation of executive agreements:

> The great majority of international agreements that the United States enters into are not treaties but executive agreements—agreements entered into by the executive branch that are not submitted to the Senate for its advice and consent. Congress generally requires notification upon the entry of such an agreement. Executive agreements are not specifically discussed in the Constitution, but they nonetheless have been considered valid international compacts under Supreme Court jurisprudence and as a matter of historical practice. Although the United States has entered international compacts by way of executive agreement since the earliest days of the Republic, executive agreements have been employed much more frequently since the World War II era. In recent years, the State Department has begun making available on its website the text of executive agreements recently entered by the United States. Adding these agreements to earlier State Department estimates, it would appear that over 18,500 executive agreements have been con-cluded by the United States since 1789 (more than 17,300 of which were concluded since 1939), compared to roughly 1,100 treaties that have been ratified by the United States. However, this estimate seems likely to undercount the number of executive agreements entered by the United States. While the precise number of unreported executive agreements is unknown, there is likely a substantial number of agreements (mainly dealing with "minor or trivial undertakings") that are not included in these figures.
>
> There are three types of prima facie legal executive agreements: (1) congressional-executive agreements, in which Congress has previously or retroactively authorized an international agreement entered into by the Executive; (2) executive agreements made pursuant to an earlier treaty, in which the agreement is authorized by a rat-ified treaty; and (3) sole executive agreements, in which an agreement is made pursuant to the President's constitutional authority without further congressional authorization. The Executive's authority to enter the agreement is different in each case. . . .
>
> In the case of congressional-executive agreements, the "constitutional-ity . . . seems well established." Unlike in the case of treaties, where only the Senate plays a role in approving the agreement, both houses of Congress are involved in the authorizing process for congressional executive agreements. Congressional authori-zation of such agreements takes the form of a statute which must pass both houses of Congress. Historically, congressional-executive agreements have been made for a wide variety of topics, ranging from postal conventions to bilateral trade to military assistance. . . .
>
> Agreements made pursuant to treaties are also well-established as legitimate, though controversy occasionally arises as to whether the agreement was actually imputed by the treaty in question. Since the earlier treaty is the "Law of the Land," the power to enter into an agreement required or contemplated by the treaty lies fairly clearly within the President's executive function.

Sole executive agreements rely on neither treaty nor congressional authority to provide for their legal basis. The Constitution may confer limited authority upon the President to promulgate such agreements on the basis of his foreign affairs power. If the President enters into an executive agreement pursuant to and dealing with an area where he has clear, exclusive constitutional authority—such as an agreement to recognize a particular foreign government for diplomatic purposes—the agreement is legally permissible regardless of Congress's opinion on the matter. If, however, the President enters into an agreement and his constitutional authority over the agreement's subject matter is unclear, a reviewing court may consider Congress's position in determining whether the agreement is legitimate. If Congress has given its implicit approval to the President entering the agreement, or is silent on the matter, it is more likely that the agreement will be deemed valid. When Congress opposes the agreement and the President's constitutional authority to enter the agreement is ambiguous, it is unclear if or when such an agreement would be given effect. The Litvinov Assignment, under which the Soviet Union purported to assign to the United States claims to American assets in Russia that had previously been nationalized by the Soviet Union, is an example of a sole executive agreement.[6]

The following Supreme Court decision provides insight into the legal effect of such agreements.

Background

First Russian Insurance Co., which was organized under the former Empire of Russia, opened a New York branch in 1907. Following the Russian Revolution, the Russian government issued orders in 1918 and 1919 that nationalized the insurance business, including First Russian. The government thereby acquired all properties, wherever situated, and absolved all debt of such companies and canceled all property rights of company shareholders. The New York Branch of First Russian continued operations until 1925, when the Supreme Court of New York ordered the Superintendent of Insurance, Louis H. Pink, to take possession of the branch's assets to resolve claims of U.S. creditors. After paying all U.S. creditors, Pink was left in control of an excess balance of over one million dollars. The court then ordered Pink to make subsequent payments to certain foreign creditors.

On November 16, 1933, the United States recognized the Union of Soviet Socialist Republics as the de jure government of Russia. Incident to that recognition the United States and the USSR entered into what was known as the Litvinov Assignment, which required all remaining claims against the USSR to be settled through a claims commission. The U.S. government then brought an action in New York seeking to take control of the remaining assets in Pink's control. The New York court held that the prior decision of the state court should be respected, and that the United States's recognition of the Litvinov Assignment in no way terminated those prior orders. That order was affirmed on appeal.

In 1939, the New York Court of Appeals decided *Moscow Fire Ins. Co. v. Bank of New York & Trust Co.*, a case involving analogous circumstances. The U.S. Supreme

---

6. Michael John Garcia, Cong. Research Serv., RL32528, Int'l Law and Agreements: Their Effect upon U.S. Law 4-6 (Feb. 18, 2015).

Court reviewed the decision and affirmed the New York high court's holding rejecting federal government efforts to take control of assets. Pink, relying on this decision, then moved to dismiss the claims against him by the United States. The New York Supreme Court, Appellate Division, ordered a dismissal of the claims and the Court of Appeals affirmed. The U.S. Supreme Court granted the petition for certiorari.

United States v. Pink
315 U.S. 203 (1942)

Mr. Justice DOUGLAS delivered the opinion of the Court.

. . .

The New York Court of Appeals held in the Moscow case that the Russian decrees in question had no extraterritorial effect. If that is true, it is decisive of the present controversy. For the United States acquired under the Litvinov Assignment only such rights as Russia had. *Guaranty Trust Co. v. United States*, 304 U.S. 126, 143, 58 S. Ct. 785, 793, 82 L. Ed. 1224. If the Russian decrees left the New York assets of the Russian insurance companies unaffected, then Russia had nothing here to assign. But that question of foreign law is not to be determined exclusively by the state court. [The Court then determined that the Russian Decree nationalizing the insurance industry had extraterritorial effect and included the assets of the First Russian Insurance Co., New York Branch.]

. . . One primary issue raised . . . is whether under our constitutional system New York law can be allowed to stand in the way [of the Litvinov Assignment]. . . .

At the outset it should be noted that, so far as appears, all creditors whose claims arose out of dealings with the New York branch have been paid. . . . The contest here is between the United States and creditors of the Russian corporation who, we assume, are not citizens of this country and whose claims did not arise out of transactions with the New York branch. The United States is seeking to protect not only claims which it holds but also claims of its nationals. H. Rep. No. 865, 76th Cong., 1st Sess. Such claims did not arise out of transactions with this Russian corporation; they are, however, claims against Russia or its nationals. The existence of such claims and their non-payment had for years been one of the barriers to recognition of the Soviet regime by the Executive Department. . . . Settlement of all American claims against Russia was one method of removing some of the prior objections to recognition based on the Soviet policy of nationalization. The Litvinov Assignment was not only part and parcel of the new policy of recognition (id., p. 13); it was also the method adopted by the Executive Department for alleviating in this country the rigors of nationalization. Congress tacitly recognized that policy . . . it authorized the appointment of a Commissioner to determine the claims of American nationals against the Soviet Government. Joint Resolution of August 4, 1939, 53 Stat. 1199.

If the President had the power to determine the policy which was to govern the question of recognition, then the Fifth Amendment does not stand in the way of giving full force and effect to the Litvinov Assignment. . . . There is no reason why it may not through such devices as the Litvinov Assignment make itself and its nationals whole from assets here before it permits such assets to go abroad in satisfaction of claims of aliens made elsewhere and not incurred in connection with business conducted in this country. The fact that New York has marshaled the claims of the foreign creditors here involved and authorized their payment does not give them immunity from that general rule.

If the priority had been accorded American claims by treaty with Russia, there would be no doubt as to its validity. *Cf. Santovincenzo v. Egan, supra.* The same result obtains here. The powers of the President in the conduct of foreign relations included the power, without consent of the Senate, to determine the public policy of the United States with respect to the Russian nationalization decrees. "What government is to be regarded here as representative of a foreign sovereign state is a political rather than a judicial question, and is to be determined by the political department of the government." *Guaranty Trust Co. v. United States, supra,* 304 U.S. page 137, 58 S. Ct. page 791, 82 L. Ed. 1224. That authority is not limited to a determination of the government to be recognized. It includes the power to determine the policy which is to govern the question of recognition. Objections to the underlying policy as well as objections to recognition are to be addressed to the political department and not to the courts. . . . [T]his Court in the *Belmont* case recognized that the Litvinov Assignment was an international compact which did not require the participation of the Senate. It stated (301 U.S. pages 330, 331, 57 S. Ct. pages 760, 761, 81 L. Ed. 1134): "There are many such compacts, of which a protocol, a modus vivendi, a postal convention, and agreements like that now under consideration are illustrations." . . . Power to remove such obstacles to full recognition as settlement of claims of our nationals (Levitan, Executive Agreements, 35 Ill. L. Rev. 365, 382-385) certainly is a modest implied power of the President who is the "sole organ of the federal government in the field of international relations." *United States v. Curtiss-Wright Corp.,* supra, 299 U.S. page 320, 57 S. Ct. page 221, 81 L. Ed. 225. Effectiveness in handling the delicate problems of foreign relations requires no less. Unless such a power exists, the power of recognition might be thwarted or seriously diluted. No such obstacle can be placed in the way of rehabilitation of relations between this country and another nation, unless the historic conception of the powers and responsibilities of the President in the conduct of foreign affairs (*see* Moore, Treaties and Executive Agreements, 20 Pol. Sc. Q. 385, 403-417) is to be drastically revised. It was the judgment of the political department that full recognition of the Soviet Government required the settlement of all outstanding problems including the claims of our nationals. Recognition and the Litvinov Assignment were interdependent. We would usurp the executive function if we held that that decision was not final and conclusive in the courts.

. . . A treaty is a "Law of the Land" under the supremacy clause, Art. VI, Cl. 2, of the Constitution. Such international compacts and agreements as the Litvinov Assignment have a similar dignity. *United States v. Belmont,* supra, 301 U.S. page 331, 57 S. Ct. page 761, 81 L. Ed. 1134. *See* Corwin, The President, Office & Powers (1940), pp. 228-240.

It is of course true that even treaties with foreign nations will be carefully construed so as not to derogate from the authority and jurisdiction of the States of this nation unless clearly necessary to effectuate the national policy. . . . But state law must yield when it is inconsistent with or impairs the policy or provisions of a treaty or of an international compact or agreement. *See Nielsen v. Johnson*, 279 U.S. 47, 49 S. Ct. 223, 73 L. Ed. 607. Then the power of a State to refuse enforcement of rights based on foreign law which runs counter to the public policy of the forum (*Griffin v. McCoach*, 313 U.S. 498, 506, 61 S. Ct. 1023, 1027, 85 L. Ed. 1481, 134 A.L.R. 1462) must give way before the superior Federal policy evidenced by a treaty or international compact or agreement. *Santovincenzo v. Egan, supra*; *United States v. Belmont, supra*.

. . .

The action of New York in this case amounts in substance to a rejection of a part of the policy underlying recognition by this nation of Soviet Russia. Such power is not accorded a State in our constitutional system. . . .

We hold that the right to the funds or property in question became vested in the Soviet Government as the successor to the First Russian Insurance Co.; that this right has passed to the United States under the Litvinov Assignment; and that the United States is entitled to the property as against the corporation and the foreign creditors.

Executive agreements are commonly used by the United States to enter into international commitments. *Pink* indicates they will normally be given the same effect as a treaty for purposes of domestic litigation. But as they are not subject to Senate advice and consent, isn't there a risk that the President may enter into commitments Congress might never be aware of? To protect against such risk, Congress enacted a statute requiring all such agreements be reported to it by the Department of State. Known as the Case-Zablocki Act, this law provides in part that

> the Secretary of State shall transmit to the Congress the text of any international agreement (including the text of any oral international agreement, which agreement shall be reduced to writing), other than a treaty, to which the United States is a party as soon as practicable after such agreement has entered into force with respect to the United States but in no event later than sixty days thereafter. However, any such agreement the immediate public disclosure of which would, in the opinion of the President, be prejudicial to the national security of the United States shall not be so transmitted to the Congress but shall be transmitted to the Committee on Foreign Relations of the Senate and the Committee on International Relations of the House of Representatives under an appropriate injunction of secrecy to be removed only upon due notice from the President.
>
> Any department or agency of the United States Government which enters into any international agreement on behalf of the United States shall transmit to the Department of State the text of such agreement not later than twenty days after such agreement has been signed.

NOTES AND QUESTIONS

1. If executive agreements are not included within the Supremacy Clause, how are they reconciled with inconsistent treaties or statutes?
2. Can you see the logical connection between the absence of any mention of executive agreements in the Supremacy Clause and the Case-Zablocki statutory congressional "notification" requirement?
3. Do you think the President is ever required to secure congressional authorization for or approval of an executive agreement? Might the nature of the agreement influence your answer?

ASSESSMENT QUESTIONS

1. General Manuel Noriega was the chief of the Panamanian Defense Forces (PDF) and de facto ruler of Panama in 1989. The United States conducted a major military attack against Panama. The state objectives were to protect the Panama Canal, protect the 30,000 plus U.S. nationals living in Panama, destroy the PDF, and capture General Noriega so he could be brought to the United States to stand trial for outstanding narcotics trafficking indictments. After his capture, Noriega was in fact brought to trial in the Southern District of Florida. The trial court concluded that Noriega qualified as a prisoner of war pursuant to the Third Geneva Convention. Article 108 of this treaty, ratified by the United States in 1955, provides:

   > Sentences pronounced on prisoners of war after a conviction has become duly enforceable, shall be served in the same establishments and under the same conditions as in the case of members of the armed forces of the Detaining Power. . . . Furthermore, they shall be entitled to receive and despatch correspondence, to receive at least one relief parcel monthly, to take regular exercise in the open air, to have the medical care required by their state of health, and the spiritual assistance they may desire. . . .

   Noriega was convicted and sentenced to forty years' confinement. Noriega claimed he was entitled to the benefits of Article 108. If you were the judge presiding over his trial, would you conclude Article 108 is self-executing? Why or why not?

2. Continuing from the prior question, Noriega was granted a sentence reduction, but when he completed his sentence, the United States sought to extradite him to France to stand trial for corruption charges related to his use of French banks and real estate to cover his ill-gotten gains while in Panama. Noriega sought to block extradition by invoking other articles of the Third Geneva Convention, including Article 118, which provides: "Prisoners of war shall be released and repatriated without delay after the cessation of active hostilities," and Article 12, which Noriega argued prohibited transfer to another detaining power by extradition to stand trial for a criminal offense. The government responded that Noriega was barred from invoking *any* provision of the Geneva Convention as a claim of right in a U.S. court based on Article 5 of the Military Commissions Act of 2006, which provided:

   > No person may invoke the Geneva Conventions or any protocols thereto in any habeas corpus or other civil action or proceeding to which the United States, or . . . agent of the United States is a party as a source of rights in any court of the United States or its States or territories.

   If a reviewing court determines that the articles invoked by Noriega are self-executing, should the court consider granting relief based on those articles?

3. In 1997, the United States ratified the International Covenant on Civil and Political Rights (ICCPR). This human rights treaty includes a provision prohibiting criminal trial by any tribunal that is not sufficiently impartial, with a requirement that any tribunal be presided over by a judicial officer of sufficient impartiality. You are an attorney working for a firm retained by the family of an alien enemy combatant, pending trial by military commission. The Military Commissions Act of 2006 (as amended in 2009) includes the following provision:

> **§948j. Military judge of a military commission**
> (a) Detail of Military Judge. — A military judge shall be detailed to each military commission under this chapter. The Secretary of Defense shall prescribe regulations providing for the manner in which military judges are so detailed to military commissions. The military judge shall preside over each military commission to which such military judge has been detailed.

Your senior partner is convinced that allowing the Secretary of Defense to detail the judge for military commissions violates the ICCPR. She tasks you to analyze how a federal court is likely to respond to a lawsuit seeking an injunction against trial of your client's son based on this provision of the ICCPR. How would you respond?

ASSESSMENT ANSWERS

1. Article 108 is probably best understood as self-executing. The language of the article imposes an immediate obligation to provide certain benefits for prisoners of war, and does not speak in terms of a commitment to take future action to implement the obligation. Furthermore, providing access to correspondence, receipt of relief packages, and open air exercise does not seem to implicate powers exclusively vested in Congress that would necessitate implementing legislation. The obligation to provide medical care, however, may be considered an indication that the article is non-self-executing, because provision of such medical care requires expenditure of federal funds, thereby implicating congressional authority.

2. No. Even if these treaty articles were considered self-executing when the treaty was ratified, the subsequent congressional statute prevails over the prior treaty. Congress has plenary authority to enact U.S. law that is inconsistent with international law, even a treaty ratified by the United States. This "later in time" rule means that the provision of the Military Commissions Act prohibiting invoking the Geneva Convention as a source of a right in U.S. court prevails even if the treaty articles are considered self-executing (which they almost certainly are).

3. The court is unlikely to grant an injunction. First, pursuant to the *Charming Betsy* principle, the court will strive to reconcile the treaty obligation with the subsequent statute. This is because courts should presume that Congress did not intend to enact domestic law that violates international law. However, even if the court concludes that the military judge provision of the Military Commissions Act violates the obligations imposed by the ICCPR, it will conclude that the later in time statute prevails over the prior treaty obligation.

WAR POWERS AND MILITARY FORCE

CHAPTER 7

War Powers

I. WAR POWERS: INTERTWINED NATIONAL SECURITY POWERS

As noted in Chapter 1, enhancing the nation's capacity to engage in "common defense" was a significant motivation for adopting the new Constitution in 1787. While the new national charter did indeed include a number of provisions to accomplish this objective, it also left many questions unanswered. The Constitution vested Congress with a number of enumerated powers related to war, not the least of which was the power to declare war. But the President was vested with the "executive power" of the nation and designated the Commander in Chief of the armed forces. What was clear, therefore, was that only Congress could declare war, and only the President could exercise the command authority as the nation's "top general." But lying between these two obvious conclusions were many questions: Could Congress authorize hostilities short of a declared war? Could Congress authorize limited war—limited in terms of duration, objectives, means, or perhaps geography? Could anything less than express congressional authorization for war be treated by the President as implied authorization? Could the President initiate hostilities short of a declared war on his own initiative? Could Congress force the President to terminate a war he initiated, or perhaps one that he was waging pursuant to congressional authorization? And finally, what role, if any, could the judiciary play in resolving disputes related to war powers?

These and other war powers questions have arisen periodically throughout the nation's history. In most cases, issues related to the nation's war powers have been resolved through cooperation between the two political branches, avoiding the type of constitutional impasse that would necessitate judicial interpretation of the mosaic of war powers provisions embedded in the Constitution. However, this political cooperation has been significantly influenced by a number of important judicial decisions addressing the constitutional allocation and exercise of war powers.

A. Congress's War Authorization Powers

Article I, § 8 of the Constitution vested Congress with the power "[t]o declare War, grant Letters of Marque and Reprisal, and make Rules concerning Captures on Land and Water." But the same constitutional article vests Congress with the authority "[t]o make all Laws which shall be necessary and proper for carrying into Execution the foregoing Powers, and all other Powers vested by this Constitution in the Government of the United States, or in any Department or Officer thereof." It is therefore beyond dispute that Congress may declare war, but what is the significance of a declaration of war, and is it the only method by which Congress may authorize war?

Several decisions early in the nation's history provide important insight into these questions. The context for these decisions was what is known as the "Quasi War" between the United States and France, an ongoing series of naval engagements between U.S. and French forces between 1798 and 1800. During this period, France and the United Kingdom were engaged in an ongoing war on both land and sea. The United States declared its neutrality, an obvious disappointment to the French, considering they had provided substantial military support to the colonies during the war for independence. This disappointment was exacerbated when the United States refused to pay the debt incurred during the Revolution on the grounds that it was owed to the French monarchy, and not the new French Republic. In response, French naval forces engaged in deprivations against U.S. shipping, including seizing U.S. ships and impressing their crews into military service.

The new nation faced the significant challenge of protecting its interests without being drawn into a full-scale war. The following cases all address the authority of U.S. naval ships to seize vessels on the high seas pursuant to the *jus belli* (a term that is generally understood to denote what is today known as the law of armed conflict or international humanitarian law—the law that regulates the conduct of military operations during armed conflicts).

The term "prize" refers to the status of captured enemy ships and cargo during what prior to 1949 was termed a war, and subsequent to 1949 is termed an international armed conflict. The *jus belli* provides belligerents with authority to both capture and dispose of enemy vessels, be they military or civilian, as "prize." A **prize court** adjudicates the validity of the claim of prize, ensuring that the ship was in fact subject to capture. Traditionally, the prize court may order destruction of the ship, or more commonly sale of the ship and its contents, with the proceeds allocated to the capturing forces. But if the court determines that the capture was improper—either because the ship was that of a neutral state, or because the ship was not captured from an enemy during a time of war—the court will order return of the ship to the owner. Pursuant to its enumerated authority to "make rules concerning captures on land and water," Congress has enacted statutes that authorize prize disposition. Today, 10 U.S.C. §§ 7651-7681 provides the district courts with original jurisdiction over any prize claim, although such actions almost never occur in the context of modern warfare. However, this was not always the case, as the following cases indicate.

Bas v. Tingy
4 U.S. (4 Dall.) 37 (1800)

[This case involved an appeal by the original American owner of the ship *Eliza* from an order by the district court disposing of the *Eliza* as prize. The *Eliza* had been captured from the French by the U.S. Navy ship *Ganges* after the *Eliza* had itself been captured by the French more than ninety-six hours earlier. The district court awarded the captain of the *Ganges* one-half the value of the *Eliza*, pursuant to a statute that allocated one-half of the value of any American ship recaptured from the "enemy" to the crew of the capturing U.S. Navy ship. The ship's owner contested this allocation, asserting that a prior statute allocating one-eighth the value of any vessel recaptured from the French (with no indication it was recaptured from the "enemy") controlled the disposition as it was improper to consider France an "enemy" of the United States.]

. . .

The controversy involved a consideration of the following sections in two acts of Congress: by an Act of 28 June, 1798, 4 vol. 154, § 2, it is declared

> "That whenever any vessel the property of or employed by any citizen of the United States or person resident therein or any goods or effects belonging to any such citizen or resident shall be recaptured by any public armed vessel of the United States, the same shall be restored to the former owner or owners upon due proof, he or they paying and allowing, as and for salvage to the recaptors, one-eighth part of the value of such vessel, goods, and effects, free from all deduction and expenses."

By an Act of 2 March, 1799, 4 vol. 472, it is declared

> "That for the ships or goods belonging to the citizens of the United States or to the citizens or subjects of any nation in amity with the United States, if retaken from the enemy within twenty-four hours, the owners are to allow one-eighth part of the whole value for salvage, . . . and if above ninety-six hours one-half all of which is to be paid without any deduction whatsoever. . . ."

The Judges delivered their opinions *seriatim* in the following manner:

MOORE, Justice.

This case depends on the construction of the act for the regulation of the navy. It is objected, indeed, that the act applies only to future wars, but its provisions are obviously applicable to the present situation of things, and there is nothing to prevent an immediate commencement of its operation.

It is, however, more particularly urged that the word "enemy" cannot be applied to the French, because the section in which it is used, is confined to such a state of war, as would authorize a recapture of property belonging to a nation in amity with the United States, and such a state of war, it is said, does not exist between America and France. A number of books have been cited to furnish a glossary on the word enemy; yet our situation is so extraordinary that I doubt whether a parallel case can be traced in the history of nations.

But if words are the representatives of ideas, let me ask by what other word the idea of the relative situation of America and France could be communicated, than by that of hostility, or war? And how can the characters of the parties engaged in hostility or war be otherwise described than by the denomination of enemies? It is for the honor and dignity of both nations, therefore, that they should be called enemies, for it is by that description alone that either could justify or excuse the scene of bloodshed, depredation, and confiscation which has unhappily occurred, and surely Congress could only employ the language of the act of June 13, 1798, towards a nation whom she considered as an enemy.

. . .

The only remaining objection offered on behalf of the plaintiff in error supposes that because there are no repealing or negative words, the last law must be confined to future cases in order to have a subject for the first law to regulate. But if two laws are inconsistent (as, in my judgment, the laws in question are), the latter is a virtual repeal of the former, without any express declaration on the subject.

On these grounds I am clearly of opinion that the decree of the circuit court ought to be affirmed.

Washington, Justice.

It is admitted on all hands that the defendant in error is entitled to some compensation, but the plaintiff in error contends that the compensation should be regulated by the Act of 28 June 1798, 4 vol. 154, § 2, which allows only one-eighth for salvage, while the defendant in error refers his claim to the Act of 2 March (*ibid.* 456, § 7), which makes an allowance of one-half, upon a recapture from the enemy, after an adverse possession of ninety-six hours.

If the defendant's claim is well founded, it follows that the latter law must virtually have worked a repeal of the former, but this has been denied for a variety of reasons:

1st. Because the former law relates to recaptures from the French, and the latter law relates to recaptures from the enemy, and it is said that "the enemy" is not descriptive of France or of her armed vessels according to the correct and technical understanding of the word.

The decision of this question must depend upon another, which is whether, at the time of passing the Act of Congress of 2 March, 1799, there subsisted a state of war between the two nations? It may, I believe, be safely laid down that every contention by force between two nations in external matters, under the authority of their respective governments, is not only war, but public war. If it be declared in form, it is called solemn and is of the perfect kind; because one whole nation is at war with another whole nation, and all the members of the nation declaring war, are authorized to commit hostilities against all the members of the other, in every place, and under every circumstance. In such a war, all the members act under a general authority, and all the rights and consequences of war attach to their condition.

But hostilities may subsist between two nations more confined in its nature and extent, being limited as to places, persons, and things, and this is more properly termed imperfect war; because not solemn, and because those who are authorized to commit hostilities, act under special authority, and can go no further than to the extent of their commission. Still, however, it is public war, because it is an external contention by force between some of the members of the two nations, authorized by the legitimate powers. It is a war between the two nations, though all the members are not authorized to commit hostilities such as in a solemn war, where the government restrain the general power.

Now if this be the true definition of war, let us see what was the situation of the United States in relation to France. In March, 1799, Congress had raised an army, stopped all intercourse with France, dissolved our treaty, built and equipped ships of war, and commissioned private armed ships, enjoining the former, and authorizing the latter, to defend themselves against the armed ships of France, to attack them on the high seas, to subdue and take them as prize, and to recapture armed vessels found in their possession. Here, then, let me ask what were the technical characters of an American and French armed vessel combating on the high seas with a view the one to subdue the other and to make prize of his property? They certainly were not friends, because there was a contention by force; nor were they private enemies, because the contention was external, and authorized by the legitimate authority of the two governments. If they were not our enemies, I know not what constitutes an enemy.

2d. But secondly it is said that a war of the imperfect kind is more properly called acts of hostility, or reprisal, and that Congress did not mean to consider the hostility subsisting between France and the United States, as constituting a state of war.

In support of this position it has been observed that in no law prior to March, 1799, is France styled our enemy, nor are we said to be at war. This is true, but neither of these things was necessary to be done, because as to France, she was sufficiently described by the title of the French Republic, and as to America, the degree of hostility meant to be carried on was sufficiently described without declaring war or declaring that we were at war. Such a declaration by Congress might have constituted a perfect state of war, which was not intended by the government.

. . .

. . . Another reason has been assigned by the defendant's counsel why the former law is not to be regarded as repealed by the latter, to-wit: that a subsequent affirmative general law cannot repeal a former affirmative special law, if both may stand together. This ground is not taken, because such an effect involves an indecent censure upon the legislature for passing contradictory laws, since the censure only applies where the contradiction appears in the same law, and it does not follow that a provision which is proper at one time may not be improper at another when circumstances are changed, but the ground of argument is that a change ought not to be presumed. Yet if there is sufficient evidence of such a change in the legislative will, and the two laws are in collision, we are forced to presume it.

What then is the evidence of legislative will? In fact and in law, we are at war: an American vessel fighting with a French vessel, to subdue and make her prize, is fighting with an enemy accurately and technically speaking, and if this be not sufficient evidence of the legislative mind, it is explained in the same law. The sixth and the ninth sections of the act speak of prizes, which can only be of property taken at sea from an enemy *jure belli*, and the 9th section speaks of prizes as taken from an enemy, in so many words, alluding to prizes which had been previously taken; but no prize could have been then taken except from France; prizes taken from France were therefore taken from the enemy. This, then, is a legislative interpretation of the word "enemy," and if the enemy as to prizes, surely they preserve the same character as to recaptures. Besides, it may be fairly asked, why should the rate of salvage be different in such a war as the present, from the salvage in a war more solemn or general? And it must be recollected that the occasion of making the law of March, 1799, was not only to raise the salvage, but to apportion it to the hazard in which the property retaken was placed, a circumstance for which the former salvage law had not provided.

The two laws, upon the whole, cannot be rendered consistent unless the court could wink so hard as not to see and know that in fact, in the view of Congress, and to every intent and purpose, the possession by a French armed vessel of an American vessel was the possession of an enemy, and therefore, in my opinion, the decree of the circuit court ought to be affirmed.

CHASE, Justice.

. . . Congress is empowered to declare a general war, or Congress may wage a limited war, limited in place, in objects, and in time. If a general war is declared, its extent and operations are only restricted and regulated by the *jus belli*, forming a part of the law of nations, but if a partial war is waged, its extent and operation depend on our municipal laws.

What, then, is the nature of the contest subsisting between American and France? In my judgment it is a limited partial war. Congress has not declared war in general terms, but Congress has authorized hostilities on the high seas by certain persons in certain cases. There is no authority given to commit hostilities on land, to capture unarmed French vessels, nor even to capture French armed vessels lying in a French port, and the authority is not given indiscriminately to every citizen of America against every citizen of France; but only to citizens appointed by commissions or exposed to immediate outrage and violence. So far it is unquestionably a partial war; but nevertheless it is a public war, on account of the public authority from which it emanates.

. . .

The acts of Congress have been analyzed to show that a war is not openly denounced against France, and that France is nowhere expressly called the enemy of America, but this only proves the circumspection and prudence of the legislature. Considering our national prepossessions in favor of the French Republic, Congress had an arduous task to perform, even in preparing for necessary defense, and just retaliation. As the temper of the people rose, however, in resentment of accumulated wrongs, the language and the measures of the government became more and more energetic and indignant; though hitherto the popular feeling may not have been ripe for a solemn declaration of war; and an active and powerful opposition in our public councils, has postponed, if not prevented that decisive event, which many thought would have best suited the interest, as well as the honor of the United States. The progress of our contest with France, indeed, resembles much the progress of our revolutionary contest, in which, watching the current of public sentiment, the patriots of that day proceeded, step by step, from the supplicatory language of petitions for a redress of grievances, to the bold and noble declaration of national independence.

Having, then, no hesitation in pronouncing, that a partial war exists between America and France, and that France was an enemy within the meaning of the act of March 1799, my voice must be given for affirming the decree of the circuit court.

PATERSON, Justice.

As the case appears on the record and has been accurately stated by the counsel and by the judges who have delivered their opinions, it is not necessary to recapitulate the facts. My opinion shall be expressed in a few words. The United States and the French republic are in a qualified state of hostility. An imperfect war, or a war, as to certain objects, and to a certain extent, exists between the two nations, and this modified warfare is authorized by the constitutional authority of our country. It is a war *quo ad hoc*. As far as Congress tolerated and authorized the war on our part, so far may we proceed in hostile operations. It is a maritime war; a war at sea as to certain purposes. The national armed vessels of France attack and capture the national armed vessels of the United States, and the national armed vessels of the United States are expressly authorized and directed to attack, subdue, and take the national armed vessels of France, and also to recapture American vessels. It is therefore a public war between the two nations, qualified, on our part, in the manner prescribed by the constitutional organ of our country. In such a state of things, it is scarcely necessary to add that the term "enemy," applies; it is the appropriate expression, to be limited in its signification, import, and use, by the qualified nature and operation of the war on our part. The word "enemy" proceeds the full length of the war, and no further. Besides, the intention of the legislature as to the meaning of this word "enemy" is clearly deducible from the act for the government of the navy, passed 2 March, 1799. This act embraces the past, present, and future, and contains passages, which point the character of enemy at the French, in the most clear and irresistible manner. I shall select one paragraph—namely that which refers to prizes taken by our public vessels anterior to the passing of the latter act. The word "prizes" in this section can apply to the French, and the French only. This is decisive on the subject of legislative intention.

By the Court:

Let the decree of the circuit court be affirmed.

NOTES AND QUESTIONS

1. At least one scholar has dismissed the significance of *Bas v. Tingy* on the basis that it was not a "war powers" case, but instead a "capture" case. Does the focal point of the analysis appear to turn on Congress's power to authorize disposition of captured ships, or on whether a state of war existed between the United States and France?

2. According to the Court, what are the two methods Congress may utilize to authorize "public" war with another nation?

3. How would you explain the difference between a declared war and a congressionally authorized war short of a declared war?

4. Why, according to Justice Chase, might Congress choose to authorize war short of a declared war?

5. *Bas v. Tingy*, with its various opinions written in close proximity to the ratification of the Constitution, seems to indicate that Congress is vested with a range of war authorization options. Declaring war is obviously one of these options. What limits, if any, did the Court indicate would bind the President were Congress to declare war?

> Throughout the nation's history, Congress has authorized hostilities, or "war," by both declarations of war and statutory authorizations short of declarations. Both types of authorization take the form of joint resolutions. A joint resolution is passed by both houses of Congress, and presented to the President for signature. Accordingly, it has the force and effect of a statute enacted by Congress. It differs from a concurrent resolution, which is passed by a majority of both houses of Congress but is *not* presented to the President for signature or veto. Since 1787, only five conflicts have been authorized by a formal declaration of war: the War of 1812, the Mexican-American War, the Spanish-American War, World War I, and World War II. In contrast, Congress has provided statutory authority for conflicts short of formal declarations of war at least seven times. Since 1945, when Congress has provided express statutory authority for a "war" or conflict, it has done so by a joint resolution for the use of military force, commonly referred to as an "AUMF."

According to *Bas v. Tingy*, a declaration of war legally "perfects" a conflict on the international plane. But a declaration of war will also have a potentially important domestic effect as a manifestation of the government's commitment to mobilize the full power of the nation to the end of victory. In *Lichter v. United States*, 334 U.S.

742 (1948), the Supreme Court rejected a challenge to a federal statute authorizing the renegotiation of government contracts by the President in order to recover "excessive" profits (the Renegotiation Act). The contractors argued that the Act exceeded Congress's lawmaking authority, and that the vague definition of what qualified as "excessive" violated the nondelegation doctrine.

The Supreme Court first concluded that because the Act was a measure intended to contribute to the accomplishment of victory in a declared war, it was "necessary and proper" legislation and therefore within Congress's lawmaking power. The Court then concluded that the delegation of authority to essentially define "excessive" did not violate the nondelegation doctrine. On both issues, the declaration of war was a vital foundation for the congressional action. Indeed, the Court specifically indicated that but for the declaration of war, the vague definition of "excessive" may very well have violated the nondelegation doctrine. However, the Court emphasized that the objective of victory in a declared war must influence the interpretation of the scope of other constitutional powers:

> A constitutional power implies a power of delegation of authority under it sufficient to effect its purposes. This power is especially significant in connection with constitutional war powers under which the exercise of broad discretion as to methods to be employed may be essential to an effective use of its war powers by Congress. . . . [I]t is of the highest importance that the fundamental purposes of the Constitution be kept in mind and given effect in order that, through the Constitution, the people of the United States may in time of war as in peace bring to the support of those purposes the full force of their united action. In time of crisis nothing could be more tragic and less expressive of the intent of the people than so to construe their Constitution that by its own terms it would substantially hinder rather than help them in defending their national safety.[1]

To emphasize the impact of a declaration of war on the assessment of other constitutional powers, the Court then cited a speech by Honorable Charles E. Hughes, of New York, on "War Powers Under the Constitution" (September 5, 1917, 42 A.B.A. Rep. 232, 238-39, 247-48):

> The power to wage war is the power to wage war successfully. The framers of the constitution were under no illusions as to war. They had emerged from a long struggle which had taught them the weakness of a mere confederation, and they had no hope that they could hold what they had won save as they established a Union which could fight with the strength of one people under one government entrusted with the common defence. In equipping the National Government with the needed authority in war, they tolerated no limitations inconsistent with that object, as they realized that the very existence of the Nation might be at stake and that every resource of the people must be at command. . . .

Bas v. Tingy indicated that Congress could choose between authorizing war by declaration, or providing a more "tailored" statutory authorization. Justice Washington indicated that in so doing, "hostilities may subsist between two nations

---

1. *Lichter v. United States*, 334 U.S. 742, 778-79 (1948).

more confined in its nature and extent, being limited as to places, persons, and things. . . ." And, as the Court noted, this is precisely how Congress chose to gradually escalate the authority to use military force in response to the French. Does this suggest that Congress may limit the President's authority to execute military action by authorizing "limited" war? The next case, also arising out of the Quasi War, offers the view of Chief Justice John Marshall on this important question.

Little v. Barreme
6 U.S. (2 Cranch) 170 (1804)

[Like *Bas v. Tingy*, this case also arose out of a prize proceeding following the seizure of a ship named *The Flying Fish* by a U.S. naval ship, the *Boston*, during the Quasi War. Captain Little was the commander of the *Boston*, and seized the ship because he suspected it was American and was engaged in illicit trade with the French. Congress had enacted a statute authorizing the seizure of American ships traveling *to* French ports, but the statute provided no authority to seize American ships traveling *from* French ports. However, the Secretary of the Navy had issued instructions to the fleet to seize American ships on suspicion of commerce with the French, which included ships traveling to or from French ports. Pursuant to this order, Captain Little seized the *Flying Fish*, learning only later that the ship was in fact Danish. The district court ordered return of the *Flying Fish*, relying on the statute to conclude that the seizure had not been authorized. The district court did not, however, award damages to the ship's owner. On appeal, the circuit court reversed that portion of the opinion and ordered Captain Little to pay damages to the owner of the *Flying Fish* for the unlawful seizure. The Supreme Court then considered the case.]

Mr. Chief Justice MARSHALL delivered the opinion of the Court.

. . .

During the hostilities between the United States and France, an act for the suspension of all intercourse between the two nations was annually passed. That under which the *Flying Fish* was condemned declared every vessel owned, hired, or employed wholly or in part by an American which should be employed in any traffic or commerce with or for any person resident within the jurisdiction or under the authority of the French Republic, to be forfeited together with her cargo, the one-half to accrue to the United States and the other to any person or persons, citizens of the United States, who will inform and prosecute for the same.

The fifth section of this act authorizes the President of the United States to instruct the commanders of armed vessels

> "to stop and examine any ship or vessel of the United States on the high sea which there may be reason to suspect to be engaged in any traffic or commerce contrary to the true tenor of the act, and if upon examination it should appear that such ship or vessel is bound or sailing to any or place within the territory of the French Republic or her dependencies, it is rendered lawful to seize such vessel and send her into the United States for adjudication."

It is by no means clear that the President of the United States, whose high duty it is to "take care that the laws be faithfully executed," and who is commander in chief of the armies and navies of the United States, might not, without any special authority for that purpose, in the then existing state of things, have empowered the officers commanding the armed vessels of the United States to seize and send into port for adjudication American vessels which were forfeited by being engaged in this illicit commerce. But when it is observed that the general clause of the first section of the "act, which declares that such vessels may be seized, and may be prosecuted in any district or circuit court, which shall be holden within or for the district where the seizure shall be made," obviously contemplates a seizure within the United States, and that the fifth section gives a special authority to seize on the high seas, and limits that authority to the seizure of vessels bound or sailing to a French port, *the legislature seem to have prescribed that the manner in which this law shall be carried into execution, was to exclude a seizure of any vessel not bound to a French port* (emphasis added). Of consequence, however, strong the circumstances might be which induced Captain Little to suspect the *Flying Fish* to be an American vessel, they could not excuse the detention of her, since he would not have been authorized to detain her had she been really American.

It was so obvious that if only vessels sailing to a French port could be seized on the high seas, that the law would be very often evaded that this act of Congress appears to have received a different construction from the executive of the United States—a construction much better calculated to give it effect.

A copy of this act was transmitted by the Secretary of the Navy to the captains of the armed vessels, who were ordered to consider the fifth section as a part of their instructions. The same letter contained the following clause:

> "A proper discharge of the important duties enjoined on you arising out of this act will require the exercise of a sound and an impartial judgment. You are not only to do all that in you lies to prevent all intercourse, whether direct or circuitous, between the ports of the United States and those of France or her dependencies, where the vessels are apparently as well as really American and protected by American papers only, but you are to be vigilant that vessels or cargoes really American, but covered by Danish or other foreign papers, and bound to or from French ports, do not escape you."

These orders, given by the executive under the construction of the act of Congress made by the department to which its execution was assigned, enjoin the seizure of American vessels sailing from a French port. Is the officer who obeys them liable for damages sustained by this misconstruction of the act, or will his orders excuse him? If his instructions afford him no protection, then the law must take its course, and he must pay such damages as are legally awarded against him; if they excuse an act not otherwise excusable, it would then be necessary to inquire whether this is a case in which the probable cause which existed to induce a suspicion that the vessel was American, would excuse the captor from damages when the vessel appeared in fact to be neutral.

I confess the first bias of my mind was very strong in favor of the opinion that though the instructions of the executive could not give a right, they might yet excuse from damages. I was much inclined to think that a distinction ought to be taken between acts of civil and those of military officers, and between proceedings within the body of the country and those on the high seas. That implicit obedience which military men usually pay to the orders of their superiors, which indeed is indispensably necessary to every military system, appeared to me strongly to imply the principle that those orders, if not to perform a prohibited act, ought to justify the person whose general duty it is to obey them, and who is placed by the laws of his country in a situation which in general requires that he should obey them. I was strongly inclined to think that where, in consequence of orders from the legitimate authority, a vessel is seized with pure intention, the claim of the injured party for damages would be against that government from which the orders proceeded, and would be a proper subject for negotiation. But I have been convinced that I was mistaken, and I have receded from this first opinion. I acquiesce in that of my brethren, which is that the instructions cannot change the nature of the transaction or legalize an act which without those instructions would have been a plain trespass.

It becomes therefore unnecessary to inquire whether the probable cause afforded by the conduct of the *Flying Fish* to suspect her of being an American, would excuse Captain Little from damages for having seized and sent her into port, since had she actually been an American, the seizure would have been unlawful.

Captain Little, then, must be answerable in damages to the owner of this neutral vessel, and as the account taken by order of the circuit court is not objectionable on its face, and has not been excepted to by counsel before the proper tribunal, this Court can receive no objection to it.

There appears then to be no error in the judgment of the circuit court, and it must be

Affirmed with costs.

NOTES AND QUESTIONS

1. It seems surprising that the Supreme Court would uphold a damages award against a Navy captain who followed the orders he received from the Secretary of the Navy. What does this suggest about Congress's power to restrict the manner in which the President executes a war?

2. What did Justice Marshall suggest when he noted that it was not "clear" that absent the statutory limitation on seizures, the President, through an order, might have provided lawful authority for the seizure?

3. If, as both *Bas* and *Little* suggest, Congress may impose limits on the geography, means, and duration of war, is there any point at which a President might be constitutionally justified in ignoring such limits?

4. If Congress authorizes war with no such limit, perhaps even by declaring war, is there any other limit on the President's authority to execute the war? If so, what is its source?

B. Responsive Military Action

In all of the cases considered thus far, Congress enacted legislative authority to respond to attacks on the United States territory or citizens. At least in the case of the attack on Pearl Harbor, there is no doubt that U.S. forces began fighting against the Japanese the moment of the attack, before Congress was able to respond with a declaration of war. When the nation is the victim of such an attack, or perhaps even when the President assesses such an attack as imminent, must Congress provide express statutory authority to meet the challenge? The next case provides a relatively clear answer to this question.

The Civil War was in fact a rebellion by a confederation of Southern states that sought to secede from the Union. In response, President Lincoln invoked the Insurrection Act to call forth the militia of the loyal states in order to fill the ranks of the Army. Until the Cold War, the United States maintained a very small standing regular Army, relying instead on "federalizing" the state militia (what is today the National Guard) to bolster the ranks of this small force when necessary. The first Congress provided express statutory authority for this action in the Insurrection Act, which implemented Congress's vested Article I authority to "provide for calling forth the Militia to execute the Laws of the Union, suppress Insurrections and repel Invasions. . . ." President Lincoln, therefore, certainly had statutory authority—at least implicit—for his decision to use the federal armed forces to "suppress" the rebellion. (Lincoln's Attorney General Edward Bates noted that "[t]he duty to suppress the insurrection, being obvious and imperative, the two acts of Congress, of 1795 and 1807, come to his aid, and furnish the physical force which he needs, to suppress the insurrection and execute the laws. Those two acts authorize the President to employ, for that purpose, the Militia, the Army and the Navy." *Letter from Edward Bates to Abraham Lincoln* (July 5, 1861) in Abraham Lincoln Papers, Series 1, General Correspondence, at 2-3 (1833-1916).) What was more complicated, however, was whether the President was authorized to utilize powers triggered by a state of war without a congressional war authorization.

The Prize Cases
67 U.S. (2 Black) 635 (1862)

[Once again, a judicial challenge to the disposition of a ship captured as prize would provide the catalyst for the Court to assess constitutional allocation of war powers. As part of the military response to the Southern insurrection, President Lincoln ordered, by proclamation, a blockade of Southern ports. The proclamation invoked the "law of nations" (what is today called customary international law) as a source of authority for the blockade. Pursuant to that legal authority, the proclamation ordered the capture and disposition as prize of ships violating the blockade. This led ship owners to challenge the prize dispositions as unconstitutional deprivations of property.]

Mr. Justice GRIER. . . .

Had the President a right to institute a blockade? . . .

The right of prize and capture has its origin in the "*jus belli*," and is governed and adjudged under the law of nations [the predecessor term for customary international law]. To legitimate the capture of a neutral vessel or property on the high seas, a war must exist *de facto*, and the neutral vessel must have a knowledge or notice of the intention of one of the parties belligerent to use this mode of coercion against a port, city, or territory, in possession of the other.

Let us enquire whether, at the time this blockade was instituted, a state of war existed which would justify a resort to these means of subduing the hostile force. . . .

By the Constitution, Congress alone has the power to declare a national or foreign war. It cannot declare war against a State, or any number of States, by virtue of any clause in the Constitution. The Constitution confers on the President the whole Executive power. He is bound to take care that the laws be faithfully executed. He is Commander-in-chief of the Army and Navy of the United States, and of the militia of the several States when called into the actual service of the United States. He has no power to initiate or declare a war either against a foreign nation or a domestic State. But by the Acts of Congress of February 28th, 1795, and 3d of March, 1807, he is authorized to call out the militia and use the military and naval forces of the United States in case of invasion by foreign nations, and to suppress insurrection against the government of a State or of the United States.

If a war be made by invasion of a foreign nation, the President is not only authorized but bound to resist force by force. He does not initiate the war, but is bound to accept the challenge without waiting for any special legislative authority. And whether the hostile party be a foreign invader, or States organized in rebellion, it is none the less a war, although the declaration of it be "*unilateral.*" Lord Stowell (1 Dodson, 247) observes, "It is not the less a war on *that account*, for war may exist without a declaration on either side. It is so laid down by the best writers on the law of nations. A declaration of war by one country only, is not a mere challenge to be accepted or refused at pleasure by the other." . . .

This greatest of civil wars . . . sprung forth suddenly from the parent brain, a Minerva in the full panoply of *war*. The President was bound to meet it in the shape it presented itself, without waiting for Congress to baptize it with a name; and no name given to it by him or them could change the fact. . . .

Whether the President in fulfilling his duties, as Commander-in-chief, in suppressing an insurrection, has met with such armed hostile resistance, and a civil war of such alarming proportions as will compel him to accord to them the character of belligerents, is a question to be decided *by him*, and this Court must be governed by the decisions and acts of the political department of the Government to which this power was entrusted. "He must determine what degree of force the crisis demands." The proclamation of blockade is itself official and conclusive evidence to the Court that a state of war existed. . . .

If it were necessary to the technical existence of a war, that it should have a legislative sanction, we find it in almost every act passed at the extraordinary session of the Legislature of 1861, which was wholly employed in enacting laws to enable the Government to prosecute the war with vigor and efficiency. And finally, in 1861, we find Congress "*ex majore cautela*" . . . passing an act "approving, legalizing, and making valid all the acts, proclamations, and orders of the President, &c., as if they had been *issued and done under the previous express authority* and direction of the Congress of the United States."

Without admitting that such an act was necessary under the circumstances, it is plain that if the President had in any manner assumed powers which it was necessary should have the authority or sanction of Congress, that on the well known principle of law, "*omnis ratihabitio retrotrahitur et mandato equiparatur,*" [ratifications relate back to and are the equivalent of prior authority] this ratification has operated to perfectly cure the defect. . . .

On this first question therefore we are of the opinion that the President had a right, *jure belli*, to institute a blockade of ports in possession of the States in rebellion, which neutrals are bound to regard. . . .

Mr. Justice NELSON, dissenting [in an opinion in which Chief Justice TANEY and Justices CATRON and CLIFFORD concurred].

. . . [B]efore this insurrection against the established Government can be dealt with on the footing of a civil war, within the meaning of the law of nations and the Constitution of the United States, and which will draw after it belligerent rights, it must be recognized or declared by the war-making power of the Government. No power short of this can change the legal status of the Government or the relations of its citizens from that of peace to a state of war, or bring into existence all those duties and obligations of neutral third parties growing out of a state of war. . . .

. . . [W]e find there that to constitute a civil war . . . it must be recognized or declared by the sovereign power of the State, and which sovereign power by our Constitution is lodged in the Congress of the United States—civil war, therefore, under our system of government, can exist only by an act of Congress, which requires the assent of two of the great departments of the Government, the Executive and Legislative. . . .

. . . But we are asked, what would become of the peace and integrity of the Union in case of an insurrection at home or invasion from abroad if this power could not be exercised by the President in the recess of Congress, and until that body could be assembled?

The framers of the Constitution fully comprehended this question, and provided for the contingency. . . . The Constitution declares that Congress shall have power "to provide for calling forth the militia to execute the laws of the Union, suppress insurrections, and repel invasions." Another clause, "that the President shall be Commander-in-chief of the Army and Navy of the United States, and of the militia of the several States when called into the actual service of United States"; and, again, "He shall take care that the laws shall be faithfully executed." Congress passed laws on this subject in 1792 and 1795. 1 United States Laws, pp. 264, 424 [the Insurrection Acts]. . . .

The Acts of 1795 and 1805 did not, and could not under the Constitution, confer on the President the power of declaring war against a State of this Union, or of deciding that war existed, and upon that ground authorize the capture and confiscation of the property of every citizen of the State whenever it was found on the waters. . . . Congress alone can determine whether war exists or should be declared; and until they have acted, no citizen of the State can be punished in his person or property, unless he has committed some offence against a law of Congress passed before the act was committed, which made it a crime, and defined the punishment. . . .

. . . [T]he President had no power to set on foot a blockade under the law of nations, and . . . the capture of the vessel and cargo in this case, and in all cases before us in which the capture occurred before the 13th of July, 1861 [the date on which Congress first authorized a naval blockade of the Confederacy], for breach of blockade, or as enemies' property, are illegal and void, and . . . the decrees of condemnation should be reversed and the vessel and cargo restored.

NOTES AND QUESTIONS

1. According to the dissent, what was the President's authority to respond to the armed rebellion by the Southern states, and what was the precise source of that authority?

2. Why did the dissent conclude that the seizure of ships was unlawful prior to July 13, 1861?

3. According to the majority, what "situation" empowers the President to invoke the laws of war to justify his actions?

4. Why did the majority reach a different conclusion than the dissent as to the legality of the seizures prior to July 13, 1861?

5. Wasn't the majority's reliance on the President's blockade proclamation to bolster the conclusion that a war de facto existed circular?

6. Based on this decision, how would you explain the scope of the President's authority to use military force absent an express congressional use of force authorization?

7. Following the infamous terrorist attacks of September 11, 2001, the White House ordered the Department of Defense to scramble U.S. Air Force fighter jets. The pilots were issued orders to shoot down any commercial airliners that entered New York or Washington, D.C. airspace. If they had been compelled to do so, and the family members of passengers killed as a result filed suit against the United States for an unconstitutional deprivation of life in violation of due process, how do you think a court might assess the legality of the action?

8. The majority was obviously hesitant to second-guess the President's judgment that wartime measures were necessary to respond to the hostile threat that had been "thrust" upon the nation. Does this indicate that there is no limit to the

deference granted to the President to make such judgments? If there is a limit, how could a court identify the line between valid and invalid invocations of what might be called the "defensive" war power vested in the President? Would it ever be appropriate for a court to make this judgment? If not, how is the nation protected from a President invoking the *Prize Cases* authority as a pretext for committing the nation to a war?

Beginning with the Cold War with the Soviet Union, and continuing today in places like South Korea, the United States maintains robust "forward deployed" military units—units that are permanently based on the territory of an ally, or are deployed to "hot spots" to demonstrate U.S. resolve. These forces are obviously intended to deter aggression against U.S. allies, but their presences at the proverbial "tip of the spear" also signal to allies and potential enemies that aggression against the ally will immediately embroil U.S. military forces in hostilities. A classic illustration of such a forward deployed unit was the Berlin Brigade, a U.S. Army combat unit stationed in West Berlin for decades. No one seriously expected this unit, which numbered approximately 5,000, to be more than a "speed bump" to a Soviet offensive against Western Europe, nor that it could prevent the Soviets from capturing West Berlin. But the unit's presence in the heart of the German Democratic Republic (East Germany) made it virtually impossible for the Soviets to launch such an attack without immediately engaging in hostilities against U.S. forces. Does the presence of such forces clarify the President's constitutional authority to immediately order military action in support of an ally subjected to a military attack?

C. The Rescue Power

Non-Combatant Evacuation Operation (NEO) is the Department of Defense term for military missions to rescue and/or evacuate U.S. and other personnel from other countries where they may be at risk. NEOs may be "permissive" or "non-permissive." A permissive NEO is executed with the consent of the state where the evacuation occurs; a non-permissive NEO is a euphemism for a rescue/evacuation without consent of the state where it occurs, conducted by force if necessary. In short, non-permissive NEOs may involve "fighting in and fighting out." Traditionally, NEOs, whether permissive or non-permissive, are executed at the direction of the President.

But is the President vested with inherent constitutional authority to commit U.S. armed forces to imminent or actual hostilities to rescue Americans abroad? For example, in 1975 President Ford ordered a large-scale military attack on Cambodian military personnel and installations in order to rescue a U.S. merchant ship and its crew, the *Mayaguez*, even though Congress had voted to prohibit expending funds for any military action in Southeast Asia. The following legal analysis related to Operation Eagle Claw, the 1980 failed U.S. mission to rescue Americans held hostage in Iran, reflects the longstanding view that historical practice supports such authority.

Memorandum Opinion for the Attorney General
(February 12, 1980)[2]

This responds to your request for our review of certain questions regarding the effect of the War Powers Resolution on the President's power to use military force without special congressional authorization and related issues. We have considered the President's existing power to employ the armed forces in any of three distinct kinds of operations: (1) deployment abroad at some risk of engagement — for example, the current presence of the fleet in the Persian Gulf region; (2) a military expedition to rescue the hostages or to retaliate against Iran if the hostages are harmed; (3) an attempt to repel an assault that threatens our vital interests in that region. We believe that the President has constitutional authority to order all of the foregoing operations.

We also conclude that the War Powers Resolution, 50 U.S.C. §§ 1541-1548, has neither the purpose nor the effect of modifying the President's power in this regard. The Resolution does, however, impose procedural requirements of consultation and reporting on certain presidential actions, which we summarize. The Resolution also provides for the termination of the use of the armed forces in hostilities within 60 days or sooner if directed by a concurrent resolution of Congress. We believe that Congress may terminate presidentially initiated hostilities through the enactment of legislation, but that it cannot do so by means of a legislative veto device such as a concurrent resolution.

I. The President's Constitutional Authority to Employ the Armed Forces

The centrally relevant constitutional provisions are Article II, § 2, which declares that "the President shall be Commander in Chief of the Army and Navy of the United States," and Article I, § 8, which grants Congress the power "To declare War." Early in our constitutional history, it perhaps could have been successfully argued that the Framers intended to confine the President to directing the military forces in wars declared by Congress.[1] Even then, however, it was clear that the Framers contemplated that the President might use force to repel sudden invasions or rebellions without first seeking congressional approval.[2]

In addition to the Commander-in-Chief Clause, the President's broad foreign policy powers support deployment of the armed forces abroad.[3] The

---

2. *See* Presidential Power to Use the Armed Forces Abroad Without Statutory Authorization, 4A Op. O.L.C. 185, 187 (1980).

1. Hamilton, in The Federalist No. 69, disparaged the President's power as that of "first General and Admiral" of the Nation, contrasting it to that of the British king, who could declare war and raise and regulate armies.

2. See M. Farrand, The Records of the Federal Convention of 1787, 318-19 (1911). Other presidential actions, such as protecting American lives and property abroad and defending our allies, were not directly considered by the Framers. This is understandable: the military needs of the 18th century probably did not require constitutional authority for immediate presidential action in case of an attack on an ally.

3. See generally *United States v. Curtiss-Wright Export Corp.*, 299 U.S. 304 (1936).

President also derives authority from his duty to "take Care that the Laws be faithfully executed,"[4] for both treaties and customary international law are part of our law and Presidents have repeatedly asserted authority to enforce our international obligations[5] even when Congress has not enacted implementing legislation.

We believe that the substantive constitutional limits on the exercise of these inherent powers by the President are, at any particular time, a function of historical practice and the political relationship between the President and Congress. Our history is replete with instances of presidential uses of military force abroad in the absence of prior congressional approval. This pattern of presidential initiative and congressional acquiescence may be said to reflect the implicit advantage held by the executive over the legislature under our constitutional scheme in situations calling for immediate action. Thus, constitutional practice over two centuries, supported by the nature of the functions exercised and by the few legal benchmarks that exist, evidences the existence of broad constitutional power.[6]

The power to deploy troops abroad without the initiation of hostilities is the most clearly established exercise of the President's general power as a matter of historical practice. Examples of such actions in the past include the use of the Navy to "open up" Japan, and President Johnson's introduction of the armed forces into the Dominican Republic in 1965 to forestall revolution.

Operations of rescue and retaliation have also been ordered by the President without congressional authorization even when they involved hostilities. Presidents have repeatedly employed troops abroad in defense of American lives and property. A famous early example is President Jefferson's use of the Navy to suppress the Barbary pirates. Other instances abound, including protection of American citizens in China during the Boxer Rebellion in 1900, and the use of troops in 1916 to pursue Pancho Villa across the Mexican border. Recent examples include the Danang sealift during the collapse of Vietnam's defenses (1975); the evacuation of Phnom Penh (Cambodia, 1975); the evacuation of Saigon (1975); the Mayaguez incident (1975); evacuation of civilians during the civil war in Lebanon (1976); and the dispatch of forces to aid American victims in Guyana (1978).

This history reveals that purposes of protecting American lives and property and retaliating against those causing injury to them are often intertwined.

---

4. See *In re Neagle*, 135 U.S. 1 (1890) (broad view of inherent presidential power to enforce constitutional as well as statutory provisions).

5. It should be observed, however, that treaties may not modify the basic allocation of powers in our constitutional scheme. *Reid v. Covert*, 354 U.S. 1 (1957). Mutual defense treaties are generally not self-executing regarding the internal processes of the signatory powers. Similarly, customary international law, which includes authority for reasonable reprisals in response to another country's breach of international obligation, probably does not confer authority on the President beyond the warrant of necessity.

6. In other contexts, the Supreme Court has recognized the validity of longstanding presidential practices never expressly authorized by Congress but arguably ratified by its silence. See *United States v. Midwest Oil Co.*, 236 U.S. 459 (1915) (withdrawal of public lands from private acquisition).

In *Durand v. Hollins*, 8 F. Cas. 111 (No. 4186) (C.C.S.D.N.Y. 1860), the court upheld the legality of the bombardment of a Nicaraguan town which was ordered because the local authorities refused to pay reparations for an attack by a mob on the United States Consul. Policies of deterrence seem to have eroded any clear distinction between cases of rescue and retaliation.

Thus, there is much historical support for the power of the President to deploy troops without initiating hostilities and to direct rescue and retaliation operations even where hostilities are a certainty. There is precedent as well for the commitment of United States armed forces, without prior congressional approval or declaration of war, to aid an ally in repelling an armed invasion, in President Truman's response to the North Korean invasion of South Korea.[7] But clearly such a response cannot be sustained over time without the acquiescence, indeed the approval, of Congress, for it is Congress that must appropriate the money to fight a war or a police action. While Presidents have exercised their authority to introduce troops into Korea and Vietnam[8] without prior congressional authorization, those troops remained only with the approval of Congress.

In April 1980, President Carter informed Congress of casualties resulting from a crash between a helicopter and a C-130 aircraft during their attempted withdrawal from the aborted mission to rescue U.S. hostages in Iran on April 24, 1980.[3] Lloyd Cutler, Counsel to President Carter, opined that the President had not violated the War Powers Resolution of 1973 by ordering a rescue operation in Iran without consulting Congress. President Carter's Legal Counsel, Lloyd Cutler, offered a similar interpretation of the President's constitutional authority:

Legal Opinion of May 9, 1980, by Lloyd Cutler, Counsel to Former President Carter, on War Powers Consultation Relative to the Iran Rescue Mission[4]

1. In my opinion, the President's decision to use the armed forces in an attempt to rescue the American hostages in Iran, without consulting Congress before taking this action, was a lawful exercise of his constitutional powers

---

7. Although support for this introduction of our armed forces into a "hot" war could be found in the U.N. Charter and a Security Council resolution, the fact remains that this commitment of substantial forces occurred without congressional approval.

8. The substantial American military presence in Vietnam before the Tonkin Gulf Resolution was known to and supported by Congress. See, e.g., *Mora v. McNamara*, 387 F.2d 862 (1967).

3. *See* Report dated April 26, 1980, from Former President Jimmy Carter to Hon. Thomas P. O'Neill, Jr., Speaker of the House of Representatives, in Compliance with Section 4(a) of the War Powers Resolution, Relative to the Aborted Rescue Attempt in Iran, reprinted in *Subcomm. on Int'l Security and Scientific Affairs of the House Comm. on Foreign Affairs*, 98th Cong., 1st Sess., THE WAR POWERS RESOLUTION, RELEVANT DOCUMENTS, CORRESPONDENCE AND REPORTS 47-49 (1983).

4. *See* Legal Opinion of May 9, 1980, by Lloyd Cutler, Counsel to Former President Carter, on War Powers Consultation Relative to the Iran Rescue Mission, reprinted in *Subcomm. on Int'l Security and Scientific Affairs of the House Comm. on Foreign Affairs*, 98th Cong., 1st Sess., THE WAR POWERS RESOLUTION, RELEVANT DOCUMENTS, CORRESPONDENCE AND REPORTS 50 (1983).

as President and Commander-in-Chief, and did not violate the War Powers Resolution of 1973.

2. The President's constitutional power to use the armed forces to rescue Americans illegally detained abroad is clearly established. *In re Neagle*, 135 U.S. 1, *Durand v. Hollings*, 8 Fed. Cases 111. This power was expressly recognized in the Senate version of the War Powers Resolution, and is not negated by the final version of the Resolution, especially where, as here, those to be rescued include United States Marines.

3. His inherent constitutional power to conduct this kind of rescue operation, which depends on total surprise, includes the power to act before consulting Congress, if the President concludes, as he did in this case, that to do so would unreasonably endanger the success of the operation and the safety of those to be rescued.

4. Section 3 of the War Powers Resolution does require consulting with Congress "in every possible instance" before introducing United States Armed Forces into "hostilities or into situations where imminent involvement in hostilities is clearly indicated by the circumstances." In this case, the first stage of the operation—introducing the rescue team into Iran during the night of April 24—did not involve any hostilities. The rescue effort itself was not to be initiated before the following night, and could have been aborted before any involvement in hostilities was "clearly indicated," and this is in fact what occurred.

5. In any event, Section 8(d)(1) of the War Powers Resolution provides that nothing in it "is intended to alter the constitutional authority of the Congress or of the President." If Section 3 were read to require prior consultation in these precise circumstances—where the President has inherent constitutional authority to conduct a rescue operation dependent on surprise and reasonable ground to believe that prior consultation would unreasonably endanger the success of the operation and the safety of those to be rescued—this would raise grave issues as to the constitutionality of Section 3. Since statutes and joint resolutions are to be read where possible in a manner that does not raise such grave constitutional issues, Section 3 and Section 8(d)(1), read together, should not be construed to require prior consultation under the precise circumstances of this case. *Eastern Railroad Conference v. Noerr*, 365 U.S. 127 (1961); *California v. Arizona*, 440 U.S. 59 (1979).

Both of the opinions related to the Iran hostage rescue cited *In re Neagle*. This case had nothing to do with rescuing Americans abroad. In response to a concern that a disgruntled litigant was planning to attack Supreme Court Justice Field while he was in California performing his function as a Circuit Judge, the Attorney General detailed a U.S. Marshal, David Neagle, to accompany the Justice to provide personal protection. The threat materialized when a man named Terry attempted to kill Justice Field. Neagle, executing his assigned duty, prevented the attack by shooting and killing Terry. California authorities then arrested Neagle on a charge of criminal homicide. Neagle filed a petition for a writ of habeas corpus in U.S. District Court, which provided for release so long as he was acting pursuant to the "laws" of the United States.

His case reached the Supreme Court on the question of whether Neagle was acting pursuant to a law of the United States when he executed the mission assigned to him by the President. According to the opinion:

> It is urged . . . that the party seeking the benefit of the writ of habeas corpus must in this connection show that he is "in custody for an act done or omitted in pursuance of a law of the United States," [which] makes it necessary that, upon this occasion, it should be shown that the act for which Neagle is imprisoned as done by virtue of an act of Congress. It is not supposed that any special act of Congress exists which authorizes the marshals or deputy marshals of the United States in express terms to accompany the judges of the Supreme Court through their circuits, and act as a bodyguard to them, to defend them against malicious assaults against their persons. But we are of opinion that this view of the statute is an unwarranted restriction of the meaning of a law designed to extend in a liberal manner the benefit of the writ of habeas corpus to persons imprisoned for the performance of their duty. And we are satisfied that, if it was the duty of Neagle, under the circumstances, a duty which could only arise under the laws of the United States, to defend Mr. Justice Field from a murderous attack upon him, he brings himself within the meaning of the section we have recited. This view of the subject is confirmed by the alternative provision, that he must be in custody "for an act done or omitted in pursuance of a law of the United States or of an order, process, or decree of a court or judge thereof, or is in custody in violation of the Constitution or of a law or treaty of the United States." . . .
>
> Where, then, are we to look for the protection which we have shown Judge Field was entitled to when engaged in the discharge of his official duties? Not to the courts of the United States, because, as has been more than once said in this court, in the division of the powers of government between the three great departments, executive, legislative and judicial, the judicial is the weakest for the purposes of self-protection and for the enforcement of the powers which it exercises. . . .
>
> The legislative branch of the government can only protect the judicial officers by the enactment of laws for that purpose, and the argument we are now combating assumes that no such law has been passed by Congress.
>
> If we turn to the executive department of the government, we find a very different condition of affairs. The Constitution, section 3, Article 2, declares that the President "shall take care that the laws be faithfully executed," and he is provided with the means of fulfilling this obligation by his authority to commission all the officers of the United States, and, by and with the advice and consent of the Senate, to appoint the most important of them and to fill vacancies. He is declared to be commander-in-chief of the army and navy of the United States. The duties which are thus imposed upon him he is further enabled to perform by the recognition in the Constitution, and the creation by acts of Congress, of executive departments . . . and thus he is enabled to fulfill the duty of his great department, expressed in the phrase that "he shall take care that the laws be faithfully executed."
>
> Is this duty limited to the enforcement of acts of Congress or of treaties of the United States according to their *express terms*, or does it include the rights, duties and obligations growing out of the Constitution itself, our international

relations, and all the protection implied by the nature of the government under the Constitution?

The Court then concluded,

> We cannot doubt the power of the President to take measures for the protection of a judge of one of the courts of the United States who, while in the discharge of the duties of his office, is threatened with a personal attack which may probably result in his death. . . .

Two Justices dissented, concluding that because the President cannot make law, his order did not qualify as law for purposes of the federal habeas corpus statute. However, *all* members of the Court seemed to agree that the President is vested with inherent constitutional authority to rescue Americans who are endangered abroad. As the majority noted:

> One of the most remarkable episodes in the history of our foreign relations, and which has become an attractive historical incident, is the case of Martin Koszta, a native of Hungary, who, though not fully a naturalized citizen of the United States, had in due form of law made his declaration of intention to become a citizen. While in Smyrna, he was seized by command of the Austrian consul general at that place, and carried on board the Hussar, an Austrian vessel, where he was held in close confinement. Captain Ingraham, in command of the American sloop of war St. Louis, arriving in port at that critical period, and ascertaining that Koszta had with him his naturalization papers, demanded his surrender to him, and was compelled to train his guns upon the Austrian vessel before his demands were complied with. It was, however, to prevent bloodshed, agreed that Koszta should be placed in the hands of the French consul subject to the result of diplomatic negotiations between Austria and the United States. The celebrated correspondence between Mr. Marcy, Secretary of State, and Chevalier Hulsemann, the Austrian minister at Washington, which arose out of this affair and resulted in the release and restoration to liberty of Koszta, attracted a great deal of public attention, and the position assumed by Mr. Marcy met the approval of the country and of Congress, who voted a gold medal to Captain Ingraham for his conduct in the affair. Upon what act of Congress then existing can anyone lay his finger in support of the action of our government in this matter?

The dissent distinguished this incident because it involved an exercise of foreign affairs. But the consensus among all members of the Court that the rescue of Martin Koszta resulted from an exercise of inherent executive authority explains the significance of this precedent in relation to rescue operations.

NOTES AND QUESTIONS

1. Who decides at what point a non-permissive NEO is necessary? If the answer is the President, is there any check on use of the rescue power as a pretext to launch a war that would otherwise require congressional approval?
2. How does the President's vested authority as Commander in Chief intersect with the apparent inherent "rescue" power? Is the President vested with plenary

authority to determine the means of executing a rescue operation? Does this allow the President to use a robust military attack to completely neutralize the capability of a nation's military forces when he determines that doing so is necessary to effectively protect the endangered Americans?

3. If a President were to determine that a large population of U.S. nationals was in danger of serious harm in another nation, and that evacuation was simply not feasible due to the numbers involved, would *Neagle* provide authority for a forcible military intervention into that state with operations conducted to ensure the safety of this population?

4. Notice that the Department of Justice analysis indicates that "there is much historical support for the power of the President to deploy troops without initiating hostilities and to direct rescue *and retaliation* operations even where hostilities are a certainty." Should operations of rescue be equated with those of retaliation? Does the inherent authority to use military force to rescue Americans abroad necessarily equate to an inherent authority to order military action to "punish" an opponent? Remember that Article I of the Constitution vests Congress with the authority to grant Letters of Reprisal. That alone calls into question the Department of Justice Conclusion. Recall also that the Charter of the United Nations recognizes a very limited authority for a state to use military force absent U.N. Security Council authorization: the inherent right of self-defense. This further complicates the question because many of the examples relied on to support the Department of Justice conclusion predated the U.S. ratification of the U.N. Charter.

Indeed, the most commonly cited authority for this assertion is *Durand v. Hollins*, 8 F. Cas. 111 (C.C.S.D.N.Y. 1860) (No. 4186). In that case, the district court concluded that a U.S. Navy Captain acted lawfully when he carried out his orders to use military force in response to an affront to a U.S. diplomat and an attack on U.S. property in what is now Nicaragua. The incident grew out of a dispute between a U.S.-sponsored transportation company and a competitor in the City of Greytown along the Nicaraguan coast. Greytown officials did not comply with Captain Hollins's request for an apology, and Hollins then ordered his ship to bombard the city. An American citizen injured in the attack then sued Hollins. The district court dismissed the lawsuit, finding that Hollins acted lawfully as the subordinate agent of the President, and that:

> As the executive head of the nation, the president is made the only legitimate organ of the general government, to open and carry on correspondence or negotiations with foreign nations, in matters concerning the interests of the country or of its citizens. It is to him, also, the citizens abroad must look for protection of person and of property, and for the faithful execution of the laws existing and intended for their protection. For this purpose, the whole executive power of the country is placed in his hands, under the constitution . . . .
>
> Now, as it respects the interposition of the executive abroad, for the protection of the lives or property of the citizen, the duty must, of necessity, rest in the discretion of the president . . . .
>
> The question whether it was the duty of the president to interpose for the protection of the citizens at Greytown against an irresponsible and marauding

community that had established itself there, was a public political question, in which the government, as well as the citizens whose interests were involved, was concerned, and which belonged to the executive to determine; and his decision is final and conclusive, and justified the defendant in the execution of his orders given through the secretary of the navy.

If the U.N. Charter had been in force at the time of this incident, how would you have advised a President who sought to punish the "Greytown mob" for the affront to a U.S. diplomat?

5. As explained later in this chapter, the War Powers Resolution, enacted over President Nixon's veto in 1973, makes no reference to the rescue power as a legal basis for a President to commit U.S. armed forces into hostilities or a situation indicating imminent hostilities. Accordingly, were a President to consider the War Powers Resolution binding, he or she would be obligated to secure express congressional authorization for any such military action.

In 1975, President Ford ordered a military attack against military forces and installations in Cambodia as part of an operation to rescue the American ship *SS Mayaguez*, which had been seized by Cambodia (*see* Christopher J. Lamb, *The Mayaguez Crisis, Mission Command, and Civil-Military Relations*, Joint History Office, Office of the Chairman of the Joint Chiefs of Staff Washington, DC (2018)). Although the President notified Congress of the action after it was conducted, he did not seek any pre-attack authorization. The congressional reaction was overwhelmingly favorable, with many legislators praising the President's decisive action (*see* Congressional Record, Vol. 121, No. 78 (May 15, 1975)). If you were a presidential advisor, how would this incident and congressional reaction impact your assessment of whether the President is vested with inherent "rescue" authority?

II. WAR IN THE AUTHORIZATION "TWILIGHT ZONE"

The decisions considered thus far provide signposts for assessing war powers: Congress may declare war; authorize war with statutes short of a declaration; and even place limits on the scope, duration, and objectives of war. The President, in turn, is vested with inherent power to respond to attacks "thrust upon the nation," and to use military force to rescue Americans abroad. But lying between these two extremes is a wide array of potential war-making decisions, situations where the President seeks to initiate hostilities without seeking express congressional authorization, or perhaps continue or expand hostilities that had previously been authorized after the authorization was revoked. This is not an uncommon situation, especially when the scale of the military operation is assessed as minor, at least at inception.

As Justice Jackson noted in his *Youngstown* concurrence:

> But I have no illusion that any decision by this Court can keep power in the hands of Congress if it is not wise and timely in meeting its problems. A crisis that challenges the President equally, or perhaps primarily, challenges Congress. If not

good law, there was worldly wisdom in the maxim attributed to Napoleon that "The tools belong to the man who can use them." We may say that power to legislate for emergencies belongs in the hands of Congress, but only Congress itself can prevent power from slipping through its fingers. . . .[5]

In the context of war powers, what then is the constitutional significance of congressional *inaction* in the face of presidential action? No conflict in our nation's history spawned more judicial consideration of this issue than the Vietnam War. Although the Supreme Court never waded into these murky waters, several district and circuit court decisions offer valuable insight into how such situations should be assessed constitutionally. As you consider these decisions, focus not only on why these courts rejected arguments that persecution of the war was unconstitutional, but also what they suggest would have been the outcome had Congress clearly and unequivocally demanded a termination of the conflict.

During the war in Vietnam federal courts adjudicated a number of service-member challenges to the legality of deployment orders. This may seem odd on the surface—why would the courts entertain a lawsuit by a member of the military seeking to prevent enforcement of an order issued by a superior commander to deploy to war? But members of the armed forces are still citizens entitled to due process. Like the owner of a steel mill who believes a presidentially ordered seizure of his property violates due process because the President lacked constitutional authority to issue the order, so too a service-member could argue that he will be denied the "process due" if his life is deprived in the course of fighting a war the President did not have constitutional authority to wage. In such a situation, there would be virtually no place to turn other than the courts for a service-member who sought to vindicate his right to due process.

Early in the Vietnam War, several courts invoked the political question doctrine to dismiss service-member-initiated lawsuits challenging the constitutionality of the Vietnam War. These courts concluded that because war-making decisions were vested by the Constitution in the political branches of government, the courts had no role in assessing this issue. As the war progressed, the application of this doctrine became more nuanced: Courts began to treat the question of whether Congress played a role in authorizing the war as justiciable, treating mutual participation in war authorization as a constitutional requirement subject to judicial scrutiny. Pursuant to this more nuanced approach, the political question was not the broad question of how war is authorized, but instead the more focused question of whether the evidence demonstrated that congressional support was constitutionally sufficient. Thus, although courts dismissed these later cases based on the political question doctrine, this more precise framing of the relevant political question implicitly indicated a requirement for congressional support for presidential war power decisions.

The first example of this, *Berk v. Laird*, 429 F.2d 302 (2d Cir. 1970), involved an Army enlistee's challenge to orders sending him to Vietnam. The district court

---

5. *Youngstown Sheet & Tube Co. v. Sawyer*, 343 U.S. 579, 654 (1952) (Jackson, J. concurring).

denied his request for a preliminary injunction against the Secretary of Defense and those subordinate officers who signed his orders. The circuit court affirmed and specifically addressed the issue of constitutional distribution of war power.

The government sought dismissal based on the political question doctrine. The court responded that the case did not call for judicial "second guessing" of a presidential decision "to commit armed forces to action." Instead, the precise issue was whether the courts "have the power to make the particular kind of constitutional decision involving the division of powers between legislative and executive branches." The court then rejected the government assertion that, absent a declaration of war, the scope of the President's constitutional authority as Commander in Chief is as broad and unitary as his power over foreign affairs in general, noting that the government argument would essentially nullify the war authorization powers vested in Congress. Concluding that the Declaration Clause was intended to preclude unilateral executive war making, the court held that the executive and legislative branches shared the constitutional authority to commit the United States to war. Accordingly, the Constitution required participation by both of these branches in any such decision.

The *Berk* court then considered whether Congress had in fact participated in the decision to wage war in Vietnam, and concluded that the Tonkin Gulf Resolution (Pub. L. No. 88-408, 88th Cong., August 7, 1964) and other indications of implied congressional support provided sufficient evidence of this requisite congressional participation. But the court then concluded that the question of how Congress chose to manifest support for the conflict was a political question. For the *Berk* court, whether the manner of support was constitutionally sufficient involved a "lack of judicially discoverable and manageable standards." Thus, while ascertaining whether Congress was in fact supporting the war was not a political question, the question of what constitutes sufficient congressional participation in the decision to wage war was.

The next case involved two Army enlistees who asserted that the Constitution required "an express and explicit congressional authorization of the Vietnam hostilities," the absence of which rendered their orders to war unconstitutional. To support this argument, they asserted that "because military appropriations lacked an explicit authorization for particular hostilities, they could not, as a matter of law, be considered sufficient."

Orlando v. Laird

443 F.2d 1039 (2d Cir.), *cert. denied*, 404 U.S. 869 (1971)

ANDERSON, J.

Shortly after receiving orders to report for transfer to Vietnam, Pfc. Malcolm A. Berk and Sp. E5 Salvatore Orlando, enlistees in the United States Army, commenced separate actions in June, 1970, seeking to enjoin the Secretary of Defense, the Secretary of the Army and the commanding officers, who signed their deployment orders, from enforcing them. The plaintiffs-appellants contended that these executive officers exceeded their constitutional authority by ordering them to participate in a war not properly authorized by Congress.

. . . [I]n *Berk v. Laird*, 429 F.2d 302 (2nd Cir. 1970) . . . [w]e held that the war declaring power of Congress, enumerated in Article I, section 8, of the Constitution, contains a "discoverable standard calling for *some* mutual participation by Congress," and directed that *Berk* be given an opportunity "to provide a method for resolving the question of when specified joint legislative-executive action is sufficient to authorize various levels of military activity," and thereby escape application of the political question doctrine to his claim that congressional participation has been in this instance, insufficient. . . .

It is the appellants' position that the sufficiency of congressional authorization is a matter within judicial competence because that question can be resolved by "judicially discoverable and manageable standards" dictated by the congressional power "to declare War." See *Baker v. Carr*, 369 U.S. 186 (1962); *Powell v. McCormack*, 395 U.S. 486 (1969). They interpret the constitutional provision to require an express and explicit congressional authorization of the Vietnam hostilities though not necessarily in the words, "We declare that the United States of America is at war with North Vietnam." In support of this construction they point out that the original intent of the clause was to place responsibility for the initiation of war upon the body most responsive to popular will and argue that historical developments have not altered the need for significant congressional participation in such commitments of national resources. They further assert that, without a requirement of express and explicit congressional authorization, developments committing the nation to war, as a *fait accompli*, became the inevitable adjuncts of presidential direction of foreign policy, and, because military appropriations and other war-implementing enactments lack an explicit authorization of particular hostilities, they cannot, as a matter of law, be considered sufficient.

Alternatively, appellants would have this court find that, because the President requested accelerating defense appropriations and extensions of the conscription laws after the war was well under way, Congress was, in effect, placed in a strait jacket and could not freely decide whether or not to enact this legislation, but rather was compelled to do so. For this reason appellants claim that such enactments cannot, as a factual matter, be considered sufficient congressional approval or ratification.

The Government on the other hand takes the position that the suits concern a non-justiciable political question; that the military action in South Vietnam was authorized by Congress in the "Joint Resolution to Promote the Maintenance of Internal Peace and Security in Southeast Asia" (the Tonkin Gulf Resolution) considered in connection with the Seato Treaty; and that the military action was authorized and ratified by congressional appropriations expressly designated for use in support of the military operations in Vietnam.

We held in the first *Berk* opinion that the constitutional delegation of the war-declaring power to the Congress contains a discoverable and manageable standard imposing on the Congress a duty of mutual participation in the prosecution of war. Judicial scrutiny of that duty, therefore, is not foreclosed by the political question doctrine. *Baker v. Carr*, *supra*; *Powell v. McCormack*, *supra*. As we see it, the test is whether there is any action by the Congress sufficient to authorize or ratify the military activity in question. The evidentiary materials produced at the hearings in the district court clearly disclose that this test is satisfied.

The Congress and the Executive have taken mutual and joint action in the prosecution and support of military operations in Southeast Asia from the beginning of those operations. The Tonkin Gulf Resolution, enacted August 10, 1964 (repealed December 31, 1970) was passed at the request of President Johnson and, though occasioned by specific naval incidents in the Gulf of Tonkin, was expressed in broad language which clearly showed the state of mind of the Congress and its intention fully to implement and support the military and naval actions taken by and planned to be taken by the President at that time in Southeast Asia, and as might be required in the future "to prevent further aggression." Congress has ratified the executive's initiatives by appropriating billions of dollars to carry out military operations in Southeast Asia[2] and by extending the Military Selective Service Act with full knowledge that persons conscripted under that Act had been, and would continue to be, sent to Vietnam. Moreover, it specifically conscripted manpower to fill "the substantial induction calls necessitated by the current Vietnam buildup."[3]

There is, therefore, no lack of clear evidence to support a conclusion that there was an abundance of continuing mutual participation in the prosecution of the war. Both branches collaborated in the endeavor, and neither could long maintain such a war without the concurrence and cooperation of the other.

Although appellants do not contend that Congress can exercise its war declaring power only through a formal declaration, they argue that congressional

---

2. In response to the demands of the military operations the executive during the 1960s ordered more and more men and material into the war zone; and congressional appropriations have been commensurate with each new level of fighting. Until 1965, defense appropriations had not earmarked funds for Vietnam. In May of that year President Johnson asked Congress for an emergency supplemental appropriation "to provide our forces [then numbering 35,000] with the best and most modern supplies and equipment." 111 Cong. Rec. 9283 (May 4, 1965). Congress appropriated $700 million for use "upon determination by the President that such action is necessary in connection with military activities in Southeast Asia." Pub. L. 89-18, 79 Stat. 109 (1965). Appropriation acts in each subsequent year explicitly authorized expenditures for men and material sent to Vietnam. The 1967 appropriations act, for example, declared Congress' "firm intention to provide all necessary support for members of the Armed Forces of the United States fighting in Vietnam" and supported "the efforts being made by the President of the United States ... to prevent an expansion of the war in Vietnam and to bring that conflict to an end through a negotiated settlement...." Pub. L. 90-5, 81 Stat. 5 (1967).

3. In H. Rep. No. 267, 90th Cong., 1st Sess. 38 (1967), in addition to extending the conscription mechanism, Congress continued a suspension of the permanent ceiling on the active duty strength of the Armed Forces, fixed at 2 million men, and replaced it with a secondary ceiling of 5 million. The House Report recommending extension of the draft concluded that the permanent men power limitations "are much lower than the currently required strength." The Report referred to President Johnson's selective service message which said ... that without the draft we cannot realistically expect to meet our present commitments or the requirements we can now foresee and that volunteers alone could be expected to man a force of little more than 2.0 million. "The present number of personnel on active duty is about 3.3 million and it is scheduled to reach almost 3.5 million by June, 1968 if the present conflict is not concluded by then." H. Rep. No. 267, 90th Cong., 1st Sess. 38, 41 (1967).

authorization cannot, as a matter of law, be inferred from military appropriations or other war-implementing legislation that does not contain an express and explicit authorization for the making of war by the President. Putting aside for a moment the explicit authorization of the Tonkin Gulf Resolution, we disagree with appellants' interpretation of the declaration clause for neither the language nor the purpose underlying that provision prohibits an inference of the fact of authorization from such legislative action as we have in this instance. The framers' intent to vest the war power in Congress is in no way defeated by permitting an inference of authorization from legislative action furnishing the manpower and materials of war for the protracted military operation in Southeast Asia.

The choice, for example, between an explicit declaration on the one hand and a resolution and war-implementing legislation, on the other, as the medium for expression of congressional consent involves "the exercise of a discretion demonstrably committed . . . to the legislature," *Baker v. Carr, supra* at 211, and therefore, invokes the political question doctrine.

Such a choice involves an important area of decision making in which, through mutual influence and reciprocal action between the President and the Congress, policies governing the relationship between this country and other parts of the world are formulated in the best interests of the United States. If there can be nothing more than minor military operations conducted under any circumstances, short of an express and explicit declaration of war by Congress, then extended military operations could not be conducted even though both the Congress and the President were agreed that they were necessary and were also agreed that a formal declaration of war would place the nation in a posture in its international relations which would be against its best interests. For the judicial branch to enunciate and enforce such a standard would be not only extremely unwise but also would constitute a deep invasion of the political question domain. As the Government says, "decisions regarding the form and substance of congressional enactments authorizing hostilities are determined by highly complex considerations of diplomacy, foreign policy and military strategy inappropriate to judicial inquiry." It would, indeed, destroy the flexibility of action which the executive and legislative branches must have in dealing with other sovereigns. What has been said and done by both the President and the Congress in their collaborative conduct of the military operations in Vietnam implies a consensus on the advisability of not making a formal declaration of war because it would be contrary to the interests of the United States to do so. The making of a policy decision of that kind is clearly within the constitutional domain of those two branches and is just as clearly not within the competency or power of the judiciary.

Beyond determining that there has been some mutual participation between the Congress and the President, which unquestionably exists here, with action by the Congress sufficient to authorize or ratify the military activity at issue, it is clear that the constitutional propriety of the means by which Congress has chosen to ratify and approve the protracted military operations in Southeast

Asia is a political question. The form which congressional authorization should take is one of policy, committed to the discretion of the Congress and outside the power and competency of the judiciary, because there are no intelligible and objectively manageable standards by which to judge such actions. *Baker v. Carr, supra,* 369 U.S. at 217; *Powell v. McCormack, supra,* 395 U.S. at 518....

The judgments of the district court are *affirmed.*

[The concurring opinion of Kaufman, J., is omitted.]

The *Orlando* court relied heavily on the Tonkin Gulf Resolution as evidence of congressional support for the Vietnam War. But what if Congress seeks to bring a conflict it expressly authorized to an end; will repeal of the express authorization necessitate a contrary conclusion? This issue became ripe when, in early 1971, Congress enacted a law that repealed the resolution. In *DaCosta v. Laird,* 448 F.2d 1368 (2d Cir. 1971), the Second Circuit then faced a constitutional challenge to the war when a draftee sought to prevent enforcement of deployment orders to Vietnam. Emphasizing the Second Circuit's prior holding in *Orlando* that the Tonkin Gulf Resolution served as substantial evidence of congressional authorization for the war, the soldier argued that this constitutionally requisite support no longer existed.

The court, however, refused to treat the repeal as sufficient evidence that Congress no longer supported the war. Instead, it found evidence of support in defense appropriations and selective service authorizations. Characterizing the repeal as a means of "winding down" the war, the court held that how the President and Congress chose to cooperate in ending a war was as much a political question as how they chose to cooperate in authorizing a war. Based on what it concluded was evidence of satisfactory inter-branch cooperation, the court dismissed the challenge. The court indicated, however, that "if the executive were now escalating the prolonged struggle instead of decreasing it, additional supporting action by the legislative branch over what is presently afforded, might well be required[.]" 448 F.2d at 1370.

But this suggestion that an escalation might necessitate a different outcome created an equally complex question: What is the line between an unconstitutional escalation and a constitutional "tactical surge" consistent with congressional will that a war be brought to an expeditious end? President Nixon forced this issue when, on May 8, 1972, he announced his decision to mine major North Vietnamese ports and to substantially escalate the bombing campaign against North Vietnam. The President's asserted justification for this major escalation in attacks against North Vietnam was the need to deny the enemy the capability to continue to wage war in order to compel concessions at stalled peace negotiations.

DaCosta once again sought an injunction to halt the war in Southeast Asia (*DaCosta v. Laird,* 471 F.2d 1146 (2d Cir. 1973)). Armed with evidence of this escalation, and relying on the "now escalating" language in the opinion dismissing his first challenge, he asserted that the President unilaterally and unconstitutionally escalated the war.

The Second Circuit once again dismissed the action as a political question. Unlike prior decisions, the court did not regard the case as an attack on the constitutionality of the war. Instead, it framed the issue in the following terms:

> We are called upon to decide the very specific question whether the Secretary of Defense, the Secretaries of the Army, Navy, and Air Force, and the Commander of American military forces in Vietnam, may implement the directive of the President of the United States, announced on May 8, 1972, ordering the mining of the ports and harbors of North Vietnam and the continuation of air and naval strikes against military targets located in that battle-scarred land. The appellant seeks a declaratory judgment that the military operations undertaken pursuant to that directive are unlawful in the absence of explicit Congressional authorization, and asks for what he terms "appropriate equitable relief."[6]

Accordingly, the court focused on whether "the President's conduct has so altered the course of hostilities in Vietnam as to make the war as it is currently pursued different from the war which we held in *Orlando* and *DaCosta* to have been constitutionally ratified and authorized[.]" 471 F.2d at 1154. It then clarified the meaning of the "now escalating" language, upon which the appellant relied. According to the court, this language "implied, of course, that litigants raising such a claim had a responsibility to present to the court a manageable standard which would allow for proper judicial resolution of the issue." The court concluded it was required to dismiss the challenge because the judiciary lacked the ability to resolve the issue absent such standards. According to the court:

> The difficulty we face in attempting to decide this case is compounded by a lack of discoverable and manageable judicial standards. Judge Dooling [who decided the case for the district court] believed that the case could be resolved by simply inquiring whether the actions taken by the President were a foreseeable part of the continued prosecution of the war. That test, it seems to us, is superficially appealing but overly simplistic. Judges, deficient in military knowledge, lacking vital information upon which to assess the nature of battlefield decisions, and sitting thousands of miles from the field of action, cannot reasonably or appropriately determine whether a specific military operation constitutes an "escalation" of the war or is merely a new tactical approach within a continuing strategic plan.[7]

Nonetheless, the court refused to abandon its previous indication that a large-scale escalation would, as a constitutional matter, require additional congressional support. Unfortunately for DaCosta, the court also reemphasized the significance of what it concluded was continued congressional support for the war:

> Having previously determined, in accordance with our duty, that the Vietnamese war has been constitutionally authorized by the mutual participation of Congress and the President, we must recognize that those two coordinate branches of government — the Executive by military action and the Congress, by not cutting off the appropriations that are the wherewithal for such action — have

---

6. *Da Costa v. Laird*, 471 F.2d 1146 (2d Cir. 1973).
7. *Id.* at 1155.

taken a position that it is not within our power, even if it were our wish, to alter by judicial decree.[8]

The *Orlando/DaCosta* rationale seems to place Congress in a proverbial Catch-22 once a conflict has been initiated: It can either provide needed support for the forces in the field and risk having that support treated as an endorsement of the conflict, or withdraw that support and in so doing place the forces themselves at risk. This leads to an important question: If providing resources to support a conflict indicates implicit support for the conflict, will efforts to carefully "wind down" that support imply sufficient opposition to a conflict to require it to terminate? *Holtzman v. Schlesinger*, below, offers insight into how a court might treat this question.

NOTES AND QUESTIONS

1. Is there an intersection between Justice Jackson's "three tier" model for assessing presidential powers and the *Orlando* court's reasoning?
2. If this is an appropriate standard for assessing whether a president is constitutionally authorized to initiate and/or sustain a "non-defensive" war, is there any point at which the President would not be authorized to engage in such action?
3. Is Congress ever precluded or prevented from exercising its constitutional authority to demand a termination of a war, whether "perfect" or "imperfect"? Is it possible for a President to authorize and prosecute combat operations with such secrecy that Congress has no knowledge or notice? If the answer is no, would you advise a president to treat what Justice Jackson characterized as congressional "inertia, indifference or quiescence" as an indication of at least implied support for the conflict?
4. Consider the following quote from Judge Dooling, who rejected Orlando's challenge to the legality of the Vietnam conflict at the district court level, 317 F. Supp. 1013, 1019 (E.D.N.Y. 1970), as it relates to the question of how to interpret uncertain congressional reactions to presidential war-making initiatives:

> It is passionately argued that none of the acts of the Congress which have furnished forth the sinew of war in levying taxes, appropriating the nation's treasure and conscripting its manpower in order to continue the Vietnam conflict can amount to authorizing the combat activities because the Constitution contemplates express authorization taken without the coercions exerted by illicit seizures of the initiative by the presidency. But it is idle to suggest that the Congress is so little ingenious or so inappreciative of its powers, including the power of impeachment, that it cannot seize policy and action initiatives at will, and halt course of action from which it wishes the national power to be withdrawn. Political expediency may have counseled the Congress's choice of the particular forms and modes by which it has united with the presidency in prosecuting the Vietnam combat activities, but the reality of the collaborative action of the executive and the legislative required by the Constitution has been present from the earliest stages.

---

8. *Id.* at 1157.

Holtzman v. Schlesinger
484 F.2d 1307 (2d Cir. 1973)

Mulligan, J.

This is an appeal from a judgment of the United States District Court [granting the plaintiff Air Force bomber pilots and Congresswoman Holtzman declaratory relief] . . . that "there is no existing Congressional authority to order military forces into combat in Cambodia or to release bombs over Cambodia, and that military activities in Cambodia by American armed forces are unauthorized and unlawful. . . ." The order further enjoined and restrained the named defendants and their officers, agents, servants, employees and attorneys "from participating in any way in military activities in or over Cambodia or releasing any bombs which may fall in Cambodia." . . .

We fail to see how the present challenge involving the bombing in Cambodia is in any significant manner distinguishable from the situation discussed by Judge Kaufman in *DaCosta v. Laird* [*DaCosta III*]. . . . If we were incompetent to judge the significance of the mining and bombing of North Vietnam's harbors and territories, we fail to see our competence to determine that the bombing of Cambodia is a "basic change" in the situation and that it is not a "tactical decision" within the competence of the President. . . .

The court below and our dissenting Brother assume that since American ground forces and prisoners have been removed and accounted for, Congressional authorization has ceased as determined by virtue of the so-called Mansfield Amendment, Pub. L. 92-156, 85 Stat. 430, § 601 [calling on the President to terminate hostilities in Southeast Asia as soon as possible]. The fallacy of this position is that we have no way of knowing whether the Cambodian bombing furthers or hinders the goals of the Mansfield Amendment. . . . Moreover, although § 601(a)(1) of the Amendment urges the President to remove all military forces contingent upon release of American prisoners, it also in § 601(a)(2) urges him to negotiate for an immediate cease fire by all parties in the hostilities in *Indo-China*. (Emphasis added). In our view, the return and repatriation of American troops only represents the beginning and not the end of the inquiry as to whether such a basic change has occurred that the Executive at this stage is suddenly bereft of power and authority. That inquiry involves diplomatic and military intelligence which is totally absent in the record before us, and its digestion in any event is beyond judicial management. . . .

Since the argument that continuing Congressional approval was necessary, was predicated upon a determination that the Cambodian bombing constituted a basic change in the war not within the tactical discretion of the President and since that is a determination we have found to be a political question, we have not found it necessary to dwell at length upon Congressional participation. . . . We cannot resist however commenting that the most recent expression of Congressional approval by appropriation, the Joint Resolution Continuing Appropriations for Fiscal 1974 (Pub. L. 93-52), enacted into law July 1, 1973, contains the following provision:

> Sec. 108. Notwithstanding any other provision of law, on or after August 15, 1973, no funds herein or heretofore appropriated may be obligated or expended

to finance directly or indirectly combat activities by United States military forces in or over or from off the shores of North Vietnam, South Vietnam, Laos or Cambodia.

Assuming arguendo that the military and diplomatic issues were manageable and that we were obliged to find some participation by Congress, we cannot see how this provision does not support the proposition that the Congress has approved the Cambodian bombing. The statute is facially clear.... It is [nevertheless] urged that since the Constitution entrusts the power to declare war to a majority of the Congress, the veto exercised makes it possible for the President to thwart the will of Congress by holding one-third plus one of the members of either House....

We cannot agree that the Congress was "coerced" by the President's veto. There was unquestionably a Congressional impasse resulting from the desire of a majority of Congress to stop bombing immediately and the desire of the President that his discretion be unfettered by an arbitrarily selected date. Instead of an acute constitutional confrontation, as Senator Javits noted an "agreement" was reached. (119 Cong. Rec. S12561 (daily ed. June 29, 1973))....

While the Constitution vests the war declaring authority in the Congress, the Founding Fathers also conferred the veto power upon the President. (Art. I, § 7, cl. 2). The suggestion that the veto power is impotent with respect to an authority vested solely in Congress by the Constitution is unsupported by any citation of authority and is hardly persuasive. It of course assumes here that the Cambodian bombing constitutes a new war requiring a new declaration and that it is not part of the extrication of a long suffering nation from an Indo-China war lasting for several years. This again in our view is the nucleus of the issue and we have no way of resolving that question particularly here on a motion for summary judgment....

The judgment is reversed and the case is remanded with instructions to dismiss the complaint. The mandate shall issue forthwith.

OAKES, J. (dissenting).

... Has Congress ratified or authorized the bombing in Cambodia by appropriations acts or otherwise? ...

... [A]n argument could be made that congressional authorization of appropriations with knowledge of our "presence" in Cambodia was ratification. But for authorization on the part of Congress by way of an appropriation to be effective, the congressional action must be based on a knowledge of the facts. *Greene v. McElroy*, 360 U.S. 474 (1959) (appropriation to Defense Department for security program did not ratify procedure denying right of an individual to confront witnesses). I am aware of only one instance in which it has previously been argued that a war was illegal as a result of Congress being misinformed as to the underlying facts surrounding American participation in that war. While the argument was unique and unsuccessful to boot, however, time has vindicated it, I believe....

And here, incredibly enough, it appears that neither the American people nor the Congress, at the time it was voting appropriations in aid of the war in Vietnam, were given the facts pertaining to our bombing in Cambodia. Recent disclosures have indicated that Air Force B-52 bombers were secretly attacking Cambodia in 1969, 1970 and even later while the United States was publicly proclaiming respect for Cambodian neutrality. . . .

. . .

We come then to the effect of the legislation, following upon a presidential veto of an immediate prohibition against the use of funds to bomb in Cambodia, adopted as a compromise this July 1st: the Continuing Appropriations Act for Fiscal Year 1974, Pub. L. No. 93-52, 93rd Cong. 2nd Sess. (July 1, 1973) which expressly provided that " . . . on or after August 15, 1973, no funds herein or heretofore appropriated may be obligated or expended to finance directly or indirectly combat activities by United States military forces in or over or from off the shores of North Vietnam, South Vietnam, Laos or Cambodia." § 108. . . .

It can be argued that Congress could, if it had so desired, cut off the funds for bombing Cambodia immediately by overriding the Presidential veto. This was indeed championed by those voting against the ultimate compromise Resolution. But it does not follow that those who voted in favor of the Resolution were thereby putting the Congressional stamp of approval on the bombing continuation. While the Resolution constituted a recognition that Executive power was being exercised, it did not constitute a concession that such exercise was rightful, lawful or constitutional. . . .

. . . Congress[,] as I see it, took the only practical way out. It acknowledged the reality of the Executive's exercise of power even while it disputed the Executive's authority for that exercise. It agreed to a final cut-off date as the best practical result but never conceded the legality or constitutionality of interim exercise.

Thus the Resolution of July 1, 1973 cannot be the basis for legalization of otherwise unlawful Executive action. We are talking here about the separate branches of government, and in doing so we must distinguish between the exercise of power on the one hand and authorization for such exercise on the other. That the Executive Branch had the power to bomb in Cambodia, there can be no doubt; it did so, and indeed is continuing to do so. Whether it had the constitutional authority for its action is another question. . . .

Interestingly, this case generated a rare opportunity for two Supreme Court Justices to offer at least some insight into how they might have addressed this type of war powers dispute. After the district court granted the plaintiff's requested injunction, the Second Circuit granted the government's request to stay the injunction pending resolution of the appeal. The plaintiffs then requested that Justice Marshall dissolve the stay in his capacity as a Circuit Justice. Although Justice Marshall indicated his belief that the lawsuit was not barred by the political question doctrine, he did not dissolve the stay. He concluded that because a plausible interpretation of the facts might show continued congressional support for the bombing, which would allow the government to prevail on appeal, dissolution was inappropriate. He did, however, emphasize what he considered the critical need for some congressional role in the decision to wage war: "As a matter of substantive constitutional law, it seems likely that the President may not wage war without some form of congressional approval—except, perhaps in the case of pressing emergency or when the President is in the process of extricating himself from a war which Congress once authorized."

The plaintiffs then applied to Justice Douglas, in his capacity as a Circuit Justice, for the same relief that had been denied by Justice Marshall. Justice Douglas ordered dissolution. He noted the unusual nature of the request following the denial by Justice Marshall; however, he concluded he was not bound by Justice Marshall's decision. He justified his re-imposition of the injunction by focusing on the potential loss of life facing the pilots, equating the case to a capital case because of the possible deprivation of life without due process that might result from obeying an unconstitutional presidential order. Notably, like Justice Marshall, Justice Douglas emphasized his belief that the President did not possess unilateral constitutional authority to make war:

> The question of justiciability does not seem to be substantial. In the *Prize Cases*, decided in 1863, the Court entertained a complaint involving the constitutionality of the Civil War. In my time we held that President Truman in the undeclared Korean War had no power to seize the steel mills in order to increase war production. The *Prize Cases* and the *Youngstown* case involved the seizure of property. But the Government conceded on oral argument that property is no more important than life under our Constitution. . . . Property is important, but if President Truman could not seize it in violation of the Constitution, I do not see how any President can take "life" in violation of the Constitution.

For Justice Douglas, the constitutional grant of war declaration authority to Congress, coupled with doubtful congressional support for the bombing of Cambodia, indicated the plaintiffs might ultimately prevail.

The government returned to Justice Marshall the following day with a request to re-impose the stay. Justice Marshall, noting that the Second Circuit had scheduled expedited hearing of the appeal, granted the government request. The Second Circuit then issued a decision on the government appeal on August 8, 1973, effectively terminating the case. *See* Geoffrey S. Corn, *Presidential War Power: Do the Courts Offer Any Answers?*, 157 MIL. L. REV. 180, 244-49 (1998).

NOTES AND QUESTIONS

1. Based on this decision, what might qualify as an unconstitutional expansion or escalation of an otherwise authorized war?

2. Do decisions like *Holtzman* and *DaCosta* suggest why Presidents Bush and Obama both characterized their increase of forces in Iraq and Afghanistan, respectively, as "surges"?

3. How could a senator or member of Congress concerned about the loss of legislative power to restrain presidential war-making decisions prevent future outcomes similar to those of the Vietnam decisions?

III. ENTER THE WAR POWERS RESOLUTION

The conflict in Southeast Asia produced a myriad of significant consequences on the nation, not least of which was a Congress energized to reclaim what it perceived as its legitimate constitutional role in war-making decisions. This led Congress to enact, over President Nixon's veto, the War Powers Act (because it was a joint resolution, it is often called the War Powers Resolution or WPR). The text of this law follows.

War Powers Resolution
50 U.S.C. §§ 1541-1548 (2000)

Resolved by the Senate and the House of Representatives of the United States of America in Congress assembled,

Section 1. Short Title.
This joint resolution may be cited as the "War Powers Resolution."

Section 2. Purpose and Policy.
(a) It is the purpose of this joint resolution to fulfill the intent of the framers of the Constitution of the United States and insure that the collective judgment of both the Congress and the President will apply to the introduction of United States Armed Forces into hostilities, or into situations where imminent involvement in hostilities is clearly indicated by the circumstances, and to the continued use of such forces in hostilities or in such situations.

(b) Under article I, section 8, of the Constitution, it is specifically provided that the Congress shall have the power to make all laws necessary and proper for carrying into execution, not only its own powers but also all other powers vested by the Constitution in the Government of the United States, or in any department or officer thereof.

(c) The constitutional powers of the President as Commander-in-Chief to introduce United States Armed Forces into hostilities, or into situations where imminent involvement in hostilities is clearly indicated by the circumstances, are exercised only pursuant to (1) a declaration of war, (2) specific statutory authorization, or (3) a national emergency created by attack upon the United States, its territories or possessions, or its armed forces.

Section 3. Consultation
The President in every possible instance shall consult with Congress before introducing United States Armed Forces into hostilities or into situation where imminent involvement in hostilities is clearly indicated by the circumstances, and after every such introduction shall consult regularly with the Congress until United States Armed Forces are no longer engaged in hostilities or have been removed from such situations.

Section 4. Reporting

(a) In the absence of a declaration of war, in any case in which United States Armed Forces are introduced—

(1) into hostilities or into situations where imminent involvement in hostilities is clearly indicated by the circumstances;

(2) into the territory, airspace or waters of a foreign nation, while equipped for combat, except for deployments which relate solely to supply, replacement, repair, or training of such forces; or

(3) in numbers which substantially enlarge United States Armed Forces equipped for combat already located in a foreign nation; the president shall submit within 48 hours to the Speaker of the House of Representatives and to the President pro tempore of the Senate a report, in writing, setting forth—

(A) the circumstances necessitating the introduction of United States Armed Forces;

(B) the constitutional and legislative authority under which such introduction took place; and

(C) the estimated scope and duration of the hostilities or involvement.

(b) The President shall provide such other information as the Congress may request in the fulfillment of its constitutional responsibilities with respect to committing the Nation to war and to the use of United States Armed Forces abroad.

(c) Whenever United States Armed Forces are introduced into hostilities or into any situation described in subsection (a) of this section, the President shall, so long as such armed forces continue to be engaged in such hostilities or situation, report to the Congress periodically on the status of such hostilities or situation as well as on the scope and duration of such hostilities or situation, but in no event shall he report to the Congress less often than once every six months.

Section 5. Congressional Action

(a) Each report submitted pursuant to section 4(a)(1) shall be transmitted to the Speaker of the House of Representatives and to the President pro tempore of the Senate on the same calendar day. Each report so transmitted shall be referred to the Committee on Foreign Affairs of the House of Representatives and to the Committee on Foreign Relations of the Senate for appropriate action. If, when the report is transmitted, the Congress has adjourned sine die or has adjourned for any period in excess of three calendar days, the Speaker of the House of Representatives and the President pro tempore of the Senate, if they deem it advisable (or if petitioned by at least 30 percent of the membership of their respective Houses) shall jointly request the President to convene Congress in order that it may consider the report and take appropriate action pursuant to this section.

(b) Within sixty calendar days after a report is submitted or is required to be submitted pursuant to section 4(a)(1), whichever is earlier, the President shall terminate any use of United States Armed Forces with respect to which such report was submitted (or required to be submitted), unless the Congress (1) has declared war or has enacted a specific authorization for such use of United States Armed Forces, (2) has extended by law such sixty-day period, or (3) is physically unable to meet as a result of an armed attack upon the United States. Such sixty-day period shall be extended for not more than an additional thirty days if the President determines and certifies to the Congress in writing that unavoidable military necessity respecting the safety of United States Armed Forces requires the continued use of such armed forces in the course of bringing about a prompt removal of such forces.

(c) Notwithstanding subsection (b), at any time that United States Armed Forces are engaged in hostilities outside the territory of the United States, its possessions and territories without a declaration of war or specific statutory authorization, such forces shall be removed by the President if the Congress so directs by concurrent resolution.

[Sections 6 and 7, Congressional Priority Procedures for Joint Resolution or Bill, and for Concurrent Resolution, respectively, provide for expedited consideration of such legislative measures to approve the President's actions under Section 5(b) or disapprove them under Section 5(c).]

Section 8. Interpretation of Joint Resolution

(a) Authority to introduce United States Armed Forces into hostilities or into situations wherein involvement in hostilities is clearly indicated by the circumstances shall not be inferred—

(1) from any provision of law (whether or not in effect before the date of the enactment of this joint resolution), including any provision contained in any appropriation Act, unless such provision specifically authorizes the introduction of United States Armed Forces into hostilities or into such situations and stating that it is intended to constitute specific statutory authorization within the meaning of this joint resolution; or

(2) from any treaty heretofore or hereafter ratified unless such treaty is implemented by legislation specifically authorizing the introduction of United States Armed Forces into hostilities or into such situations and stating that it is intended to constitute specific statutory authorization within the meaning of this joint resolution.

(b) Nothing in this joint resolution shall be construed to require any further specific statutory authorization to permit members of United States Armed Forces to participate jointly with members of the armed forces of one or more foreign countries in the headquarters operations of high-level military commands which were established prior to the date of enactment of this joint resolution and pursuant to the United Nations Charter or any treaty ratified by the United States prior to such date.

(c) For purposes of this joint resolution, the term "introduction of United States Armed Forces" includes the assignment of member of such armed forces to command, coordinate, participate in the movement of, or accompany the regular or irregular military forces of any foreign country or government when such military forces are engaged, or there exists an imminent threat that such forces will become engaged, in hostilities.

(d) Nothing in this joint resolution—

(1) is intended to alter the constitutional authority of the Congress or of the President, or the provision of existing treaties; or

(2) shall be construed as granting any authority to the President with respect to the introduction of United States Armed Forces into hostilities or into situations wherein involvement in hostilities is clearly indicated by the circumstances which authority he would not have had in the absence of this joint resolution.

Section 9. Separability Clause

If any provision of this joint resolution or the application thereof to any person or circumstance is held invalid, the remainder of the joint resolution and the application of such provision to any other person or circumstance shall not be affected thereby.

President Nixon vetoed the WPR, and no President since then has considered the law constitutional. In his veto message, President Nixon asserted what he believed were a number of constitutional flaws with the law, to include how the law

> would attempt to take away, by a mere legislative act, authorities which the President has properly exercised under the Constitution for almost 200 years. One of its provisions would automatically cut off certain authorities after sixty days unless the Congress extended them. Another would allow the Congress to eliminate certain authorities merely by the passage of a concurrent resolution—an action which does not normally have the force of law, since it denies the President his constitutional role in approving legislation. I believe that both these provisions are unconstitutional. The only way in which the constitutional powers of a branch of the Government can be altered is by amending the Constitution—and any attempt to make such alterations by legislation alone is clearly without force.

The President also objected to the "termination by inaction" consequence of the law:

> I am particularly disturbed by the fact that certain of the President's constitutional powers as Commander in Chief of the Armed Forces would terminate automatically under this resolution 60 days after they were invoked. No overt Congressional action would be required to cut off these powers—they would disappear automatically unless the Congress extended them. In effect, the Congress is here attempting to increase its policy-making role through a provision which requires it to take absolutely no action at all.
>
> In my view, the proper way for the Congress to make known its will on such foreign policy questions is through a positive action, with full debate on the merits of the issue and with each member taking the responsibility of casting a yes or no vote after considering those merits .... I do not, however, believe that the

Congress can responsibly contribute its considered, collective judgment on such grave questions without full debate and without a yes or no vote. Yet this is precisely what the joint resolution would allow. It would give every future Congress the ability to handcuff every future President merely by doing nothing . . . .[9]

Ironically, post-WPR practice, to include the influence of judicial decisions addressing war powers, seems to have validated both President Nixon's objections and his view that congressional inaction is insufficient to fulfill its constitutional war powers function.

No President since the law's enactment has considered it constitutional, and two have ordered the continuation of "offensive" combat operations beyond sixty days with no express statutory authorization (President Clinton's order to conduct combat operations against Serbia to force an end to ethnic cleansing in Kosovo and President Obama's order to provide combat air and missile support to the NATO campaign to prevent humanitarian crisis in Libya). Nonetheless, every President has submitted reports on deployments to Congress, although they are always characterized as being submitted "consistent with" the law, a deliberate term indicating the President does not consider the reporting requirements binding. According to a Congressional Research Service report titled "The War Powers Resolution: Concepts and Practice" (updated March 8, 2019):

> From 1975 through March 2017, Presidents have submitted 168 reports as the result of the War Powers Resolution, but only one, the 1975 Mayaguez seizure, cited Section 4(a)(1), which triggers the 60-day withdrawal requirement, and in this case the military action was completed and U.S. armed forces had disengaged from the area of conflict when the report was made. The reports submitted by the President since enactment of the War Powers Resolution cover a range of military activities, from embassy evacuations to full-scale combat military operations, such as the Persian Gulf conflict, and the 2003 war with Iraq, the intervention in Kosovo, and the anti-terrorism actions in Afghanistan . . . .

If inter-branch cooperation in war powers decisions enhances the legitimacy and effectiveness of such operations, perhaps the WPR has had a positive effect even with all its uncertainties and potential constitutional flaws.

NOTES AND QUESTIONS

1. How is the so-called sixty-day clock triggered? Who has the ultimate say on what constitutes a situation of imminent hostilities? What happens if the President's position is that a military operation does not trigger the War Powers Resolution, and Congress fails to react with a majority vote to the contrary?
2. It is commonly asserted that the WPR provides the President authority to commit U.S. armed forces to hostilities for sixty days. Is this accurate?
3. If the WPR does not provide such authority, does it perhaps "tolerate" such commitments?

---

9. War Powers Act Veto Message, Richard Nixon, The White House, October 24, 1973.

4. In *INS v. Chadha*, the Supreme Court struck down as unconstitutional the so-called legislative veto—a concurrent resolution that revokes authority delegated to the executive branch by statute. In his dissenting opinion, Justice White noted that the decision ostensibly invalidated the concurrent resolution section of the WPR. In his concurring opinion, Justice Powell expressed his view that Justice White's concern might have been unjustified. Is there a way to reconcile *Chadha* with the continued validity of § 5(c) of the WPR?

5. Should the WPR be understood as a rebuttal to the "implied authorization" vein that ran through all the Vietnam-era judicial decisions? If so, is it legitimate that one session of Congress enacts a law that prohibits future Congresses from adopting the same method of "implied" war authorization? What answer does footnote 26 from Judge Harold Greene's decision in *Dellums v. Bush*, below, suggest? (Judge Greene dismissed, on ripeness grounds, a lawsuit by a group of legislators contesting President George H.W. Bush's constitutional authority to initiate hostilities in what would become the first Gulf War in 1990: "It might be that these legislators are content to follow some of the historical patterns, including those involving the hostilities in Vietnam and Korea where there was no declaration of war, or that they deem the consultations had in recent months and weeks between the Executive and congressional leaders to constitute adequate compliance with Article I, § 8, Cl. 11 of the Constitution.")

6. The WPR was certainly responsive to the Vietnam War, and perhaps more precisely on the concern that the President might again in the future initiate small-scale military action that eventually draws the nation into the quagmire of a major war. Should the very low risk of so-called boots on the ground (ground combat operations) and casualties justify excluding a military action from the WPR?

7. Note that the WPR did not include "rescue" in § 2(c). In 1975, President Ford ordered a combined air/sea/ground attack against Cambodian communist forces to rescue the U.S. ship *Mayaguez* and its crew. Since that time, other presidents have also ordered military actions to rescue Americans, including President Reagan's order to invade Grenada in 1983. Does this suggest that the WPR's omission of rescue is constitutionally invalid?

8. All presidents have submitted reports to congressional leaders as called for in § 4. These reports always indicated they are submitted "consistent with" and not "in accordance with" the WPR. Is this terminology significant? What benefit does a president potentially derive from submitting reports even with this terminology?

IV. SO WHAT TRIGGERS THE WAR POWERS RESOLUTION?

Notice that § 5 of the WPR indicates that the sixty days begins to run when the President submits a report pursuant to § 4(a)(1) or *when such a report is required*, meaning that the clock might start running even if the President fails to submit such a report. Notice also that § 4(a)(1) requires such a report whenever the President introduces U.S. armed forces "into hostilities or into situations where imminent involvement in hostilities is clearly indicated by the circumstances."

There is, however, no definition of hostilities, much less "situations where imminent involvement in hostilities is clearly indicated by the circumstances." It is easy to imagine that a president and Congress might have very different interpretations of these terms in relation to a wide range of military operations. For example, a president might conclude that a deployment of U.S. armed forces is necessary to reduce tensions or deter a potential aggressor and thereby avert hostilities. But Congress might perceive such a deployment as falling squarely within the scope of § 4(a)(1). After sixty days there would likely be members of Congress asserting the President is obligated to terminate the operation pursuant to § 5(b), but it is highly unlikely the President would agree. And notice that § 5(b) requires no affirmative action by Congress to require such termination but instead functions automatically.

One solution to the uncertainty over what qualifies as a situation of hostilities or imminent hostilities might be to turn to the courts. But as the following Congressional Research Service report summary of judicial decisions indicates, a court is unlikely to resolve such a dispute due to the inherent ambiguity of these terms coupled with the foreign relations and national security implications of such judicial resolution.

War Powers Litigation Initiated by Members of Congress Since the Enactment of the War Powers Resolution
Michael John Garcia, Legislative Attorney, February 17, 2012

El Salvador

In the 1982 case of *Crockett v. Reagan*, 16 Senators and 13 House Members asked a federal district court to declare that military aid supplied to the government of El Salvador by President Reagan usurped Congress's war powers under the Constitution and violated the War Powers Resolution and the Foreign Assistance Act. In particular, the lawmakers charged that the unreported dispatch of at least 56 members of the U.S. Armed Forces as military advisers to war-racked El Salvador constituted a violation of the Resolution. The Reagan Administration moved to dismiss the action on the grounds the suit involved a political question, and the district court granted the motion. The U.S. Court of Appeals for the District of Columbia affirmed.

Examining the categories of political questions set forth by the Supreme Court in *Baker v. Carr*, the trial court rejected the Administration's arguments that judicial resolution was inappropriate because it would interfere with executive discretion in the foreign affairs field or because the suit involved the apportionment of power between the executive and legislative branches. However, it concluded, judicial resolution was inappropriate because there were no "judicially discoverable and manageable standards for resolution" of the case:

> The questions as to the nature and extent of the United States' presence in El Salvador and whether a report under the WPR is mandated because our forces have been subject to hostile fire or are taking part in the war effort

are appropriate for congressional, not judicial, investigation. Further, in order to determine the application of the 60-day provision, the Court would be required to decide at exactly what point in time U.S. forces had been introduced into hostilities or imminent hostilities, and whether that situation continues to exist. This inquiry would be even more inappropriate for the judiciary. The Court lacks the resources and expertise (which are accessible to the Congress) to resolve disputed questions of fact concerning the military situation in El Salvador.

The trial court contrasted the situation in El Salvador with the conflict in Vietnam, noting that the latter conflict had persisted for seven years, resulted in more than 1 million deaths (including over 50,000 Americans), and involved the expenditure of $100 billion. In El Salvador, the court noted, the American military personnel were relatively few in number and had suffered no casualties. Accordingly, the court concluded, the question of whether U.S. forces had been introduced into hostilities in El Salvador was less obvious than Vietnam, and "[t]he subtleties of fact-finding in this situation should be left to the political branches."

The court declined to speculate about the kind of congressional actions that might give rise to a judicially manageable issue, noting simply that "Congress has taken absolutely no action that could be interpreted to have that effect." However, it did state that "were Congress to pass a resolution to the effect that a report was required under the WPR, or to the effect that the forces should be withdrawn, and the President disregarded it, a constitutional impasse appropriate for judicial resolution would be presented."

On appeal the U.S. Court of Appeals for the District of Columbia affirmed the dismissal in a brief per curiam opinion "for the reasons stated by the District Court." The Supreme Court subsequently denied a petition of certiorari to review the decision.

Nicaragua

In *Sanchez-Espinoza v. Reagan* in 1983, 12 Members of the House of Representatives, 12 Nicaraguan citizens, and two United States citizens sued for damages, injunctive relief, and a declaration that President Reagan and other executive officials violated various federal statutes, including the War Powers Resolution, by supporting paramilitary operations designed to overthrow the government of Nicaragua. A federal district court dismissed the litigation as raising nonjusticiable political questions, and the U.S. Court of Appeals for the District of Columbia again affirmed.

. . .

In accord with the *Crockett* decision, the district court held that resolution of the issue raised by the congressional plaintiffs called for fact-finding that exceeded the court's competence. In political question terms, the court said that resolution of the issue raised by the lawmakers was difficult if not impossible because of the lack of "judicially discoverable and manageable standards." According to the court, the circumstances before it were even more egregious than those in *Crockett* since "the covert activities of CIA operatives in Nicaragua and Honduras are perforce even less judicially discoverable than the level of participation by U.S. military personnel in hostilities in El Salvador. In addition, the court stated, in light of the wide differences between the President and Congress concerning Nicaraguan policy, "[a] second reason for finding this matter non-justiciable is the impossibility of our undertaking independent resolution without expressing a lack of the respect due coordinate branches of government." . . .

Grenada

In *Conyers v. Reagan*, 11 Members of the House challenged the President Reagan's use of force in Grenada as an executive usurpation of Congress's war powers under the Constitution. The federal district court dismissed the action on the basis of the doctrine of equitable/remedial discretion, which counsels the courts to refrain from hearing cases brought by congressional plaintiffs who can obtain substantial relief by legislative action . . . .

The justiciability obstacles to WPR litigation are indeed daunting, especially for congressional plaintiffs. If the courts refuse to resolve the question of whether a report was required pursuant to § 4(a)(1) and the President persists in the view that a report is not required and that § 5(b) is not only unconstitutional but inapplicable, then it would appear to require congressional action that invokes both provisions. But that requirement undermines the presumption at the core of the WPR: that committing U.S. forces to hostilities or situations of imminent hostilities is unauthorized absent express congressional authorization and that therefore congressional *inaction* must be treated as opposition. Hence the requirement to terminate operations after sixty days absent express authorization.

This intersection of statutory ambiguity, presidential interpretation, and judicial avoidance raises the question of whether the WPR has any genuine effect in relation to presidential decisions to commit U.S. armed forces into situations of hostilities or imminent hostilities. If Congress must act affirmatively to prevent or force the President to terminate such an operation, what is the value of the WPR? In this regard, it is interesting to recall Judge Greene's opinion in *Dellums v. Bush* included in Chapter 3. Judge Greene seems to have had no difficulty concluding the scale of the deployment to Saudi Arabia and the Persian Gulf in response to the Iraqi invasion of Kuwait indicated hostilities were imminent. Yet nowhere in the opinion did the court address the WPR. Instead, Judge Greene relied heavily on the fact that the then sitting Congress had taken no affirmative action to oppose the march toward war, a clear indication he was unwilling to treat congressional inaction as evidence of such opposition. Consider how footnote 26 of the opinion appears to completely dismiss the impact of § 5(b) and the WPR "inaction requires termination" effect:

> It might be that these legislators are content to follow some of the historical patterns, including those involving the hostilities in Vietnam and Korea where there

was no declaration of war, or that they deem the consultations had in recent months and weeks between the Executive and congressional leaders to constitute adequate compliance with Article I, Section 8, Clause 11 of the Constitution.

This seemed to be an endorsement of the exact implied consent theory the WPR seems to have been adopted to invalidate. Footnote 27 then suggested, with no consideration of the WPR, that Congress must act affirmatively to prevent or terminate presidential action believed to exceed constitutional authority; and that legislators frustrated with congressional inaction should address that frustration through the lawmaking process, and not in court:

> The plaintiffs argue that "Congress cannot, and should not, be able to read the War Powers Clause out of the Constitution by failure to act." However, plaintiffs are not entitled to receive relief from action or non-action of their colleagues in Congress through a suit for an injunction against the President.

The opinion also suggested that *if* Congress were to act affirmatively to prohibit presidential initiation of offensive military action *and* the President were to ignore Congress, a justiciable issue would arise. But note how even this aspect of the opinion appears to ignore the WPR. If Congress must enact law to prohibit a president from initiating offensive hostilities or accept the risk that by not doing so the President will have free hand, what is the value of the WPR?

Recall also that the ripeness doctrine provided the legal rationale for Judge Greene's dismissal of the lawsuit in *Dellums*. This is aligned with both of these footnotes, as the absence of affirmative congressional action to constrain President Bush indicated that the two branches of government had not reached a "constitutional loggerhead" and therefore there was no ripe constitutional issue for the court to resolve. But again, isn't that exactly what the WPR purports to create by characterizing congressional inaction as unambiguous evidence of congressional opposition to a presidential deployment of U.S. armed forces into hostilities or situations of imminent hostilities?

Dellums v. Bush was decided before the Supreme Court decided *Raines v. Byrd*, 521 U.S. 811 (1997), in which the Court established the standard for "legislative standing." According to the Court, the prior decision in *Coleman v. Miller*, 307 U.S. 433 (1939), stood for the "proposition that legislators whose votes would have been sufficient to defeat (or enact) a specific legislative act have standing to sue if that legislative action goes into effect (or does not go into effect), on the ground that their votes have been completely nullified." *Raines v. Byrd*, 521 U.S. 811, 823.

This test for legislator standing would present a new barrier to challenging presidential war-making decisions in 1999. That year, President Clinton ordered the U.S. armed forces to lead a NATO air campaign against Serbia. The operation was authorized by the NATO member states in order to force President Slobodan Milosevic to terminate what the United Nations Security Council and NATO concluded was a genocide against the Muslim population in the Serbian province of Kosovo. Because of Russian opposition, the United Nations Security Council never authorized military action against Serbia, although it did enact a number of resolutions condemning Serbian violence in Kosovo.

President Clinton neither sought nor received express statutory authorization for the mission. Like so many other conflicts, what the United States and NATO thought would be a short campaign dragged out as the result of Serbian resistance and refusal to submit to NATO demands that it withdraw its military forces from Kosovo. This resulted in the first combat operation after enactment of the War Powers Resolution (a federal statute) that lasted more than sixty days. This duration was significant, because pursuant to the terms of this law, the President is required to terminate any operation that exceeds sixty days unless Congress expressly authorizes the military operation or votes to authorize a thirty-day extension. Congress did neither in the case of this air campaign.

When the operation exceeded sixty days, Representative Tom Campbell, joined by other legislators, sought declaratory relief from the U.S. District Court for the District of Columbia, on the dual theory that the continued prosecution of hostilities violated both the War Powers Resolution and the Constitution. The Court of Appeals for the District of Columbia would ultimately invoke *Raines v. Byrd* to dismiss the case.

In *Campbell v. Clinton* (203 F.3d 19 (D.C. Cir. 2000)), the Court of Appeals for the D.C. Circuit dismissed the lawsuit seeking declaratory relief that the President's continued prosecution of the air campaign violated both the War Powers Resolution and the U.S. Constitution. The court began the opinion by highlighting the record of congressional action in relation to the campaign:

> On March 24, 1999, President Clinton announced the commencement of NATO air and cruise missile attacks on Yugoslav targets. Two days later he submitted to Congress a report, "consistent with the War Powers Resolution," detailing the circumstances necessitating the use of armed forces, the deployment's scope and expected duration, and asserting that he had "taken these actions pursuant to [his] authority . . . as Commander in Chief and Chief Executive." On April 28, Congress voted on four resolutions related to the Yugoslav conflict: It voted down a declaration of war 427 to 2 and an "authorization" of the air strikes 213 to 213, but it also voted against requiring the President to immediately end U.S. participation in the NATO operation and voted to fund that involvement. The conflict between NATO and Yugoslavia continued for 79 days, ending on June 10 with Yugoslavia's agreement to withdraw its forces from Kosovo and allow deployment of a NATO-led peacekeeping force. Throughout this period Pentagon, State Department, and NATO spokesmen informed the public on a frequent basis of developments in the fighting.

Based on the fact that Congress had not enacted any law to prohibit continued prosecution of the campaign, the court concluded that the legislators lacked standing because they could not establish that their votes had been completely nullified by the President. Interestingly there was almost no mention of the War Powers Act and the undeniable fact that the campaign exceeded the sixty-day grace period with no express statutory authorization. In this sense, it seems that the court interpreted the "vote nullification" requirement for legislative standing to apply to a vote by the legislators seeking judicial relief, and not a nullification of a law enacted by a prior Congress. Specifically, the court noted:

In this case, Congress certainly could have passed a law forbidding the use of U.S. forces in the Yugoslav campaign; indeed, there was a measure—albeit only a concurrent resolution—introduced to require the President to withdraw U.S. troops. Unfortunately, however, for those congressmen who, like appellants, desired an end to U.S. involvement in Yugoslavia, this measure was defeated by a 139 to 290 vote. Of course, Congress always retains appropriations authority and could have cut off funds for the American role in the conflict. Again there was an effort to do so but it failed; appropriations were authorized. And there always remains the possibility of impeachment should a President act in disregard of Congress' authority on these matters.

. . .

Appellants' constitutional claim stands on no firmer footing. Appellants argue that the War Powers Clause of the Constitution proscribes a President from using military force except as is necessary to repel a sudden attack. But they also argue that the WPR "implements" or channels congressional authority under the Constitution. It may well be then that since we have determined that appellants lack standing to enforce the WPR there is nothing left of their constitutional claim. Assuming, however, that appellants' constitutional claim should be considered separately, the same logic dictates they do not have standing to bring such a challenge. That is to say Congress has a broad range of legislative authority it can use to stop a President's war making . . . and therefore under *Raines* congressmen may not challenge the President's war-making powers in federal court.

NOTES AND QUESTIONS

1. In footnote 26 of the Dellums opinion, Judge Greene expressed his view that the power to declare war necessarily implies the power to prohibit war, and that if Congress asserts that power and the President ignores Congress, only judicial intervention can ensure respect for the Constitution. Was Judge Greene's assertion that only a court can enforce congressional will overbroad? Doesn't Congress possess the authority to do so?

2. What is the constitutional and practical significance, if any, of a majority vote in both the House of Representatives and the Senate *against* authorizing hostilities? For example, imagine Congress votes down an Authorization to Use Military Force. Does this expression of majority opposition to hostilities prohibit the President from ordering military action? This certainly seemed to be what Judge Greene had in mind in his *Dellums* opinion. But would a lawsuit to "enforce" such a vote be justiciable? If not, what could Congress do to enforce the implicit prohibition?

3. If, as the D.C. Circuit concluded, legislative standing requires Congress to pass a law prohibiting military action that the President ignores, thereby "totally nullifying" legislator votes, has the standing doctrine functionally nullified the value of the War Powers Resolution? If the legislative standing doctrine requires Congress to enact a law prohibiting military action, what value does the WPR serve?

4. Are there any potential plaintiffs who might have standing to seek judicial enforcement of the WPR even in the face of congressional inaction?

V. AN EXPANDING VIEW OF INHERENT PRESIDENTIAL WAR POWERS

A. Libya

In 1969, Muammar Qadhafi seized power in Libya following a military revolt against the then reigning monarchy. His sponsorship of terrorism, efforts to arm his forces with weapons of mass destruction, expansive claims of territorial sovereignty on the high seas, and other policies led to substantial tension—and at times outright conflict—with the United States. However, between 2003 and 2008 Qadhafi's compliance with international policies regarding weapons of mass destruction and terrorism led to the lifting of sanctions, allowing for businesses to reengage with the country. Despite the resulting economic revitalization of the Libyan economy, political reform was still nonexistent. But political change in neighboring Tunisia and Egypt helped bring long-simmering Libyan reform debates to the boiling point in January and early February 2011.

These events triggered an uprising in mid-February 2011 that quickly spiraled out of Qadhafi's control. Violent reprisals by regime forces led to a rapid escalation by opposition forces. In February and March 2011, the Qadhafi regime began using substantial military force against civilians to quash unrest, sparking international outcry. On March 17, the United Nations Security Council (UNSC) adopted Resolution 1973 (UNSCR) authorizing NATO member states to use force in Libya to protect Libyan civilians. Shortly thereafter NATO (including U.S.) military forces began carrying out operations and air strikes against regime targets in order to dismantle any formal resistance. UNSCR 1973 declared a no-fly zone over Libyan airspace, as well as enforcement measures regarding the UNSCR 1970 arms embargo against Libya. By March 28, U.S. and coalition forces effectively neutralized all regime military capabilities and focused on non-official targets violating UNSCR 1973. U.S. participation in these operations was limited almost exclusively to air and missile operations with no introduction of U.S. ground forces into Libya.

According to the Obama Administration, the President exercised constitutional authority to commit U.S. military forces to this U.N. Security Council–authorized operation because he could reasonably determine that such use of force was in the national interest. Citing both the President's Commander-in-Chief and foreign affairs powers, the President's lawyers advised, and he concluded, that he was vested with constitutional authority to commit U.S. armed forces to hostilities in defense of national interests, absent prior congressional approval. According to the Office of Legal Counsel:

> The President's constitutional authority to commit forces abroad absent congressional approval, as supported by express textual interpretation, the doctrine of separation of powers, and centuries of precedent and jurisprudence, have shown acceptable instances of presidential initiative operating within the workable boundaries of our constitutional scheme. See Am. Ins. Ass'n v. Garamendi, 539 U.S. 396, 414 (2003). See Youngstown Sheet & Tube Co., 343 U.S. at 635-36 n.2 (Jackson, J.,

concurring) (noting President's constitutional power to "act in external affairs without congressional authority").

The reporting mechanisms within the War Powers Resolution presupposes an independent authority of the President to respond to imminent hostilities without prior authorization. However, the President's Article II powers potentially do not grant him authority to take national security actions that would in and of themselves constitute a war and thus abdicate Congress of their Article I powers. Yet simultaneously, a clear and obvious distinction must be made between actions constituting war and the contours of every other possible military engagement. This distinction should be based on a fact specific assessment covering the anticipated nature, scope, and duration of the potential military operation. See Haiti Deployment, 18 Op. O.L.C. at 179.

Based on the foregoing precedents, the President's ability to intervene in Libya requires assessing two questions: 1) are there sufficiently important national security interests requiring US military operations in Libya, and 2) do such operations constitute a war requiring congressional declaration.

At the current juncture, it can be determined based on all available intelligence that there are two key national security interests at stake regarding US intervention in Libya: preserving regional stability and supporting the UNSC's credibility and effectiveness. These two national security interests are well within the understanding of the President's responsibilities and would justify the use of military force in Libya.

The Libyan government's action are a clear threat to regional stability, peace, and security. Further violence and destabilization of the region will only frustrate counterterrorism initiatives among other ambitions and campaigns in the region. Additionally, such actions by the Libyan government are similar to prior actions by governments in the former Yugoslavia and Haiti which saw presidential intervention absent congressional approval. Finally, such chaos will lead to a worsening humanitarian crisis and refugee problems only complicating US strategies as well as compromising the security of neighboring states. The US also has a serious commitment to the international mission and integrity of the UNSC. By abandoning such commitments, the ability of the UNSC to be taken seriously as a credible entity will falter. *See* Military Forces in Somalia, 16 Op. O.L.C. at 12.

The deployment and response strategies anticipated by the US also do not come within the context of an Article I war in terms of scope, duration, and intensity. *See* Proposed Bosnia Deployment, 19 Op. O.L.C. at 334 (reaching conclusion based on specific "circumstances"); Haiti Deployment, 18 Op. O.L.C. at 178 (same). President Obama determined that the US military will be limited to airstrikes and other support missions avoiding the need for intense and prolonged engagements or other occupational missions. There will not be any need for ground troops.

Accordingly, President Obama could rely on his constitutional power to safeguard the national interest by directing the anticipated military operations in Libya—which were limited in their nature, scope, and duration—without prior congressional authorization.[10]

---

10. Authority to Use Military Force in Libya (Slip Opinion), DOJ OLC (April 1, 2011). https://www.justice.gov/sites/default/files/olc/opinions/2011/04/31/authority-military-use-in-libya_0.pdf

B. Syria

Since March of 2011, Syria was gripped by violent opposition to the Syrian regime led by President Assad—violence that evolved into a full-scale civil war. Early in the conflict, it became clear the Syrian armed forces used chemical weapons. In response, President Obama prepared to take military action, but this action was averted when Syria promised to remove or destroy all such weapons.

In 2018, it became apparent that Syria had breached its disarmament commitment and had once again used chemical weapons. In response, on April 14, 2018, President Trump announced that he had ordered air and missile attacks against Syrian military targets as part of a coalition response that included similar action by the United Kingdom and France.

The legal basis for this operation tracked closely with that relied on by President Obama when he ordered U.S. operations against Libya. According to the Office of Legal Counsel, the President, as Commander in Chief and chief executive, had the constitutional authority to deploy the military to protect vital national interests without seeking prior authorization from Congress. Specifically, the opinion concluded:

> On April 13, 2018, the President directed the United States military to launch airstrikes against three facilities associated with the chemical-weapons capability of the Syrian Arab Republic ("Syria"). The President's direction was consistent with many others taken by prior Presidents, who have deployed our military forces in limited engagements without seeking the prior authorization of Congress. This deeply rooted historical practice, acknowledged by courts and Congress, reflects the well-established division of war powers under our Constitution. Prior to the Syrian operation, you requested our advice on the President's authority. Before the strikes occurred, we advised that the President could lawfully direct them because he had reasonably determined that the use of force would be in the national interest and that the anticipated hostilities would not rise to the level of a war in the constitutional sense. This memorandum explains the bases for our conclusion.
>
> The President's Article II powers grants him the constitutional authority to oversee the deployment of US military personnel in the defense of national interests abroad. . . . *See Fleming v. Page*, 50 U.S. (9 How.) 603, 615 (1850) . . .
>
> Examples of such deployments absent congressional approval include: Washington's offensives against the Wabash Indians in 1790, Jefferson's directives against the Barba[r]y pirates, Truman's defense of South Korea, Kennedy's introduction of forces into South Vietnam, Reagan's retaliatory strikes in Libya, HW Bush's introduction of troops into Somalia, Clinton's actions in Bosnia, Haiti, Kosovo, Sudan, and Afghanistan, W Bush's intervention in Haiti, and Obama's airstrikes in Libya and Yemen. From all over the world, Presidents have acted, and Congress has accepted or ratified the President's use of the military, to advance our national interests. It is undeniable at this current period that the President does in fact have the constitutional authority to commit troops abroad for the purpose of safeguarding vital national security interests. *See* Somalia Deployment, 16 Op. O.L.C. at 9.
>
> Although "[t]he limits of the President's power as Commander in Chief are nowhere defined in the Constitution," we have recognized "a negative implication from the fact that the power to declare war is committed to Congress." Cambodian Sanctuaries, 1 Op. O.L.C. Supp. at 325. The Constitution reserves to Congress the

power to "declare War," U.S. Const. art. I, § 8, cl. 11, and the authority to fund military operations, id. art. I, § 8, cl. 12. This was a deliberate choice of the Founders, who sought to prevent the President from bringing the Nation into a full-scale war with-out the authorization of Congress. . . . These powers further oblige the President to seek congressional approval prior to contemplating military action that would bring the Nation into a war.

Not every military operation, however, rises to the level of a war. Rather, "the historical practice of military action without congressional approval precludes any suggestion that Congress's authority to declare war covers every military engagement, however limited, that the President initiates." Libya Deployment at *8.

. . .

Based on the foregoing precedents, the President's ability to intervene in Syria with airstrikes requires assessing two questions: 1) are there sufficiently important national security interests requiring US military operations in Syria, and 2) do such operations constitute a war requiring congressional declaration.

. . . [11]

Each of these military actions involved committing U.S. armed forces into situations of hostilities, yet in each case the President acted pursuant to an assertion of inherent constitutional authority that superseded the requirements of the War Powers Resolution. Note that in neither situation did President Obama or President Trump assert an imminent threat to U.S. territory or armed forces. Instead, the asserted trigger for the exercise of inherent constitutional authority was a threat to U.S. *national interests.* And, while each President acknowledged that this inherent authority did not allow the President to commit the nation to a "war," their use of limited military capabilities with the accordant avoidance of commitment of ground forces led them to conclude the actions fell well outside the scope of that term, at least in the constitutional sense. And consider this articulation of the Office of Legal Counsel interpretation of the War Powers Resolution included in a footnote to the Syria air strike legal opinion:

> The War Powers Resolution does not constitute an affirmative source of authority for the President to introduce U.S. forces into hostilities, 50 U.S.C. § 1547(d)(2), but it also is not "intended to alter the constitutional authority . . . of the President." Id. § 1547(d)(1). By seeking to require the cessation of hostilities within sixty days, absent congressional authorization, the statute assumes that the President has the authority to authorize such engagements. The statute begins with a statement of purpose and policy that identifies a narrow set of engagements that the President may direct without congressional authorization. Id. § 1541(c). Yet we have recognized that this policy statement neither affirmatively limits presidential authority nor constitutes an exhaustive list of the circumstances in which the President may use military force to protect important national interests. See, e.g., Overview of the War Powers Resolution, 8 Op. O.L.C. 271, 274 (1984); see also Authority of the President Under Domestic and International Law to Use Military Force Against

---

11. April 2018 Airstrikes Against Syrian Chemical-Weapons Facilities (Slip Opinion), DOJ OLC (May 31, 2018) https://www.justice.gov/olc/opinion/file/1067551/download

Iraq, 26 Op. O.L.C. 143, 159-61 (2002) (summarizing the Executive Branch's long-standing constitutional concerns with the War Powers Resolution).[12]

Consider how this notion of authority to commit U.S. forces not only into situations where hostilities are likely, but into actual armed hostilities, represents a substantial expansion of inherent presidential authority to initiate hostilities. Consider also how avoiding compliance with the War Powers Resolution—or any effort to obtain congressional authorization—based on a "no ground troops"/limited involvement argument might have been perceived by those who enacted that law. Wasn't this the theory asserted by Presidents Kennedy and Johnson early in the Vietnam conflict? Wasn't the War Powers Resolution intended to prevent presidents from involving the nation in what *they* thought was a limited conflict because of the inability to ever predict with certainty how such a commitment might evolve?

Yet it seems equally important to consider congressional reaction to events such as those in Libya and Syria. Indeed, the Libyan air campaign—like that ordered by President Clinton against Serbia—continued beyond the sixty-day "grace" period in the War Powers Resolution with no express congressional authorization. What impact might congressional acquiescence to events such as these have on presidential assessments of their inherent constitutional authority in the future?

Congress Imposes a New War Powers Reporting Requirement[13]
Section 1264, National Defense Authorization Act for Fiscal Year 2018, Pub. L. No. 115-91 (2017) ("NDAA for FY 2018"), as amended by Section 1261, National Defense Authorization Act for Fiscal Year 2020, Pub. L. No. 116-92 (2019) ("NDAA for FY 2020")

A healthy democracy requires transparency from its political branches, both in order for its electorate to hold its elected representatives accountable, and for elected legislators to make informed decisions regarding shared war powers, national security programs, etc. While presidential administrations are often leery to share their legal and policy justifications with the public, President Barack Obama, after years of high-level public speeches by members of his administration outlining the legal framework for American use of force abroad, in 2016 issued an unclassified document titled "Report On The Legal and Policy Frameworks Guiding The U.S. Use of Military Force and Related National Security Operations."

Congress took note, and in Section 1264 of the Fiscal Year 2018 National Defense Authorization Act (NDAA), as amended by Section 1261 of the

---

12. April 2018 Airstrikes Against Syrian Chemical-Weapons Facilities (Slip Opinion), DOJ OLC (May 31, 2018), at page 7, n. 2, https://www.justice.gov/olc/opinion/file/1067551/download.

13. Special thanks to Professor Rachel VanLandingham for this contribution.

Fiscal Year 2020 NDAA, required such an initial report from the Trump Administration. Congress also mandated updates from the executive branch whenever the executive branch's legal and policy justifications for such national security actions changed, and in 2020 further established a requirement for an annual such report.

Specifically, Section 1264, as amended, mandates an annual report "on the legal and policy frameworks for the United States' use of military force and related national security operations" by March 1 of each year as well as notification "[n]ot later than 30 days after the date on which a change is made to the legal and policy frameworks . . . including the legal, factual, and policy justification for such change."

While Section 1264 permits a classified annex to the annual report and change notices, the report and notifications themselves must not be classified, and must "be made available to the public at the same time it is submitted" to Congress, and this "[t]he unclassified portion . . . shall, at a minimum, include each change made to the legal and policy frameworks during the preceding year and the legal, factual, and policy justifications for such changes[.]"

NOTES AND QUESTIONS

1. Why would Congress impose a new statutory reporting requirement on the President when the WPR already requires such a report?

2. Considering the background for enactment of the WPR—most notably the perception that the nation was incrementally drawn into a major conflict in Vietnam by presidents who insisted each escalation was limited and sufficient—do the more recent WPR avoidance theories seem consistent with the motivation for the law? Wasn't Congress specifically focused on preventing what a president perceived as a "low risk" military action from spiraling into a conflict Congress will be compelled to support?

ASSESSMENT QUESTIONS

1. You are a staff attorney for the Senate Armed Services Committee. The Chairman wants to assert the constitutional validity of the concurrent resolution provision of the War Powers Resolution. What answer below is the best argument to support the assertion that this provision is a constitutional means of requiring the President to terminate a military action she launched without express congressional authorization, even prior to the termination of the sixty-day clock?

2. How would you argue that the War Powers Resolution, although generally constitutional, is inapplicable to drone and cyber operations?

3. Why is the sixty-day clock in the War Powers Resolution often criticized as illogical?

ASSESSMENT ANSWERS

1. As the result of the Supreme Court's holding in *INS v. Chadha*, 462 U.S. 919 (1983), concurrent resolutions are generally assumed to be ineffective in compelling any action, and are merely an expression of congressional opinion. However, *Chadha* involved the use of a concurrent resolution to revoke or withdraw authority that had been previously delegated to the President by statute. In that context, the Court's holding was essentially that "what Congress giveth by statute, Congress must take away by statute." In contrast, the concurrent resolution provision of the War Powers Resolution does not necessarily involve revoking a previously delegated war-making authority. Accordingly, there may be a basis to distinguish the effect of *this* concurrent resolution from the concurrent resolution held unconstitutional in *Chadha*. In this context, Congress is not revoking or withdrawing a delegation; it is instead expressing its unwillingness, by majority of both houses, to support a conflict initiated by the President.

2. By emphasizing that these military capabilities do not result in placing U.S. military personnel into situations of hostilities or situations where the imminence of hostilities are clearly indicated by the circumstances, a president may assert that the use of such capabilities falls outside the intended scope of the WPR. While it will be difficult to dispute the fact that the use of "stand-off" capabilities will certainly be perceived by adversaries as acts of hostilities, these emerging tools in the combat arsenal open the door for arguments that their use does not implicate the congressional concerns that motivated enactment of the WPR: that presidents possessed too much power to drag the nation into an unwanted war. When the nature of the capability does not expose U.S. forces to the immediate consequences of hostilities, the risk of unexpected escalation is diminished. This is *an* argument, but concededly a dubious one. Indeed, it is important to recall that the War Powers Resolution was a response to the Vietnam conflict, which

began with very limited use of U.S. airpower. What that conflict (and many others) seems to indicate is that it is impossible to predict how conflicts will evolve, which is precisely why Congress enacted the law.

3. From a practical perspective, critics condemn this provision because it signals to U.S. adversaries a "termination date" for U.S. military action, thereby providing them an incentive to resist for that duration. From a legal perspective, the provision seems incoherent—how can the President possess constitutional authority to commit U.S. forces into hostilities on days one to sixty, but no authority on day sixty-one? From the President's perspective, either the commitment is constitutional at inception, and remains constitutional after day sixty, or is unconstitutional from inception, in which case Congress should act to terminate the commitment on day one.

CHAPTER 8

The Use of Military Force

I. AUTHORITY TO USE MILITARY FORCE: THE UNITED NATIONS CHARTER PARADIGM

A. Prohibition Against Use of Military Force

"War" may be a pragmatic concept for those impacted by hostilities, but it has always been a term with specific international legal meaning. According to a 2010 International Law Association report on the Use of Force:

> In Oppenheim's classic definition, war was "a contention between two or more States through their armed forces, for the purpose of overpowering each other and imposing such conditions of peace as the victor pleases." During the period when many legal scholars and states contended that the resort to force was unregulated, a declaration of war had considerable legal significance, such as bringing into operation not only the laws of war, as IHL was then known, but also the institution of neutrality and validating the exercise of belligerent rights. The United Nations Charter, however, prohibits all use of force except in self-defence or with Security Council authorisation. After the adoption of the Charter, governments and jurists began to abandon the use of the term "war."

In the immediate aftermath of World War I, the community of nations attempted to build a legal architecture to prevent nations from resorting to war in the future, most notably through the adoption of the 1928 Kellogg-Briand Pact (General Treaty for Renunciation of War as an Instrument of National Policy), and creation of the League of Nations. While World War II exposed the insufficiency of these efforts, the war crimes trials that followed that war solidified the international legal prohibitions against waging a war of aggression in violation of international law established during the inter-war years.

Even before World War II ended, however, the victorious allies initiated the process to create a much more effective mechanism to achieve the objective of limiting resort to force as a means of national policy. These efforts culminated in the creation of the United Nations, an international organization based on a treaty, the Charter of the United Nations. In the very first provision of the Charter of the United Nations, Article 1 provides that the new organization created by the treaty was intended

> [t]o maintain international peace and security, and to that end: to take effective collective measures for the prevention and removal of threats to the peace, and for the suppression of acts of aggression or other breaches of the peace, and to bring about by peaceful means, and in conformity with the principles of justice and international law, adjustment or settlement of international disputes or situations which might lead to a breach of the peace. . . .

Article 2(3) of the Charter establishes that "all Members shall settle their international disputes by peaceful means in such a manner that international peace and security, and justice, are not endangered." This is perhaps the most important principle established in the Charter, reflecting a collective rejection of the use of military force by states as a means to advance their sovereign interests. Complementing this obligation is a prohibition against using military force. This prohibition is codified in Article 2(4) of the Charter, which established what is perhaps the most significant rule imposed on states by international law related to the permissible use of military force as an instrument of international relations: the presumptive prohibition against such use or threatened use of force:

> All Members shall refrain in their international relations from the threat or use of force against the territorial integrity or political independence of any state, or in any other manner inconsistent with the Purposes of the United Nations.

As this language emphasizes, unlike the Kellogg-Briand Pact the U.N. Charter prohibits *any* use or threat of force that is "inconsistent with the Purposes of the United Nations." Accordingly, whether a particular use or threatened use of force qualifies as a "war" within the meaning of international law is no longer central to assessing compliance with how international law regulates the legality of a nation's resort to the use of military force (or threat to do so) as a means of solving a dispute or advancing a national security interest. What matters is whether the action qualifies as a use or threatened use of force within the meaning of the U.N. Charter. This much broader concept of military actions subject to international legal regulation was deliberate and intended to prevent States from sidestepping international legal limits on the use of force by characterizing a given action as something other than war.

The United States is not only a party to the Charter of the United Nations (granted advice and consent by a Senate vote of 89-2 on July 28, 1945), but is also a permanent member of the Security Council. Accordingly, the United States, like all other nations, is prohibited from using or threatening a use of military force to achieve national security objectives unless that use complies with the Charter. This, in turn, implicates the two justifications for a lawful use of military force by members of the community of nations: action to enforce a Security Council mandate, or action in individual or collective self-defense.

B. Security Council Authorization

In order to empower the new United Nations organization with meaningful authority to respond to the type of breaches of international law that led to World War II, the Charter vested the Security Council with what is best understood as "enforcement" authority. Pursuant to Chapter VII of the Charter, the UNSC may authorize member states to take military action in response to an act of aggression, breach of the peace, or a threat to international peace and security. While the UNSC may authorize non-forceful measures to address such situations (such as quarantines, embargoes, travel restrictions, etc.), it is not required to exhaust these means as a prerequisite to authorizing the use of force. Of course, because each of the permanent members of the UNSC (the United States, United Kingdom, France, Russia, and China) are vested by the Charter with the power to veto any UNSC resolution, support or acquiescence by each member is necessary for adoption of any enforcement resolution. However, if adopted, the resolution will normally expressly authorize member states to use "all necessary means"—including the use of military force—to restore international peace and security. Such a resolution provides international legal authority for the use of military force.

The following UNSC Resolution provides an example:

Resolution 678 (1990)
of 29 November 1990

The Security Council,

Recalling, and reaffirming its resolutions 660 (1990) of 2 August (1990), 661 (1990) of 6 August 1990, 662 (1990) of 9 August 1990, 664 (1990) of 18 August 1990, 665 (1990) of 25 August 1990, 666 (1990) of 13 September 1990, 667 (1990) of 16 September 1990, 669 (1990) of 24 September 1990, 670 (1990) of 25 September 1990, 674 (1990) of 29 October 1990 and 677 (1990) of 28 November 1990.

Noting that, despite all efforts by the United Nations, Iraq refuses to comply with its obligation to implement resolution 660 (1990) and the above-mentioned subsequent relevant resolutions, in flagrant contempt of the Security Council,

Mindful of its duties and responsibilities under the Charter of the United Nations for the maintenance and preservation of international peace and security,

Determined to secure full compliance with its decisions,

Acting under Chapter VII of the Charter,

1. *Demands* that Iraq comply fully with resolution 660 (1990) and all subsequent relevant resolutions, and decides, while maintaining all its decisions, to allow Iraq one final opportunity, as a pause of goodwill, to do so;

2. *Authorizes* Member States co-operating with the Government of Kuwait, unless Iraq on or before 15 January 1991 fully implements, as set forth in paragraph 1 above, the foregoing resolutions, to use all necessary means to uphold and implement resolution 660 (1990) and all subsequent relevant resolutions and to restore international peace and security in the area;

3. *Requests* all States to provide appropriate support for the actions undertaken in pursuance of paragraph 2 of the present resolution;

4. *Requests* the States concerned to keep the Security Council regularly informed on the progress of actions undertaken pursuant to paragraphs 2 and 3 of the present resolution;

5. *Decides* to remain seized of the matter.

In 2002, the United States sought a new "all necessary means" resolution pursuant to Chapter VII to authorize what would eventually become Operation Iraqi Freedom, the 2003 invasion of Iraq. Secretary of State Colin Powell made a highly publicized presentation to the Security Council presenting what the United States and the United Kingdom considered compelling evidence that Saddam Hussein's regime represented a serious threat to international peace and security. Other permanent members of the UNSC, most notably France and Russia, were not persuaded that the situation justified military action to oust the Hussein regime, essentially ensuring that no such new authorization would be adopted by the UNSC.

Undeterred, the United States moved ahead with its plan to oust Hussein by military action, leading ultimately to the March 2003 invasion. While it was widely assumed that the United States considered the action justified pursuant to the international legal right to act in self-defense against an imminent threat, the actual asserted legal justification for the invasion was the 1990 UNSCR that authorized the first Gulf War, and the subsequent Security Council Resolutions requiring that Iraq fully comply with all post-conflict disarmament and inspection obligations imposed by the UNSC. The United States took the position that because Iraq was in material breach of these compliance obligations, the authority to conduct military action provided by Security Council Resolution 678 was in effect resurrected.

NOTES AND QUESTIONS

1. Note that nothing in UNSCR 678 qualified the authority it granted in a way that would prohibit such invocation, or suggested that it was invalid for the United States to rely on this existing UNSC authority. If other members of the UNSC, or of the international community, consider this resurrection of a decade-old use of force authorization invalid, what recourse is available to them?

2. UNSC invocation of Chapter VII enforcement authority has not been limited to military actions. The Security Council has used this authority to respond to

a range of international incidents and problems. What limit, if any, is there on the UNSC's prerogative to characterize a crisis as a "threat to international peace and security," thereby triggering its power to authorize enforcement actions by member states? Can the mass exodus of migrants from one country seeking refuge in another country qualify, justifying military action to depose a tyrannical regime and use a long-duration military presence to establish a "safe and secure" environment? Is impunity for serious violations of the laws and customs of war in the context of a purely internal armed conflict (a civil war) a threat to international peace and security, justifying Chapter VII action to establish a "war crimes" tribunal with non-consensual jurisdiction over citizens of the warring state?

3. Article 43 of the U.N. Charter provided for member states to make military forces available to the UNSC through standing agreements, in effect providing the UNSC with an "on call" military force to respond to threats to international peace and security. This has never proved to be effective. Instead, when the UNSC authorizes military action pursuant to Chapter VII, it will call upon member states to contribute to the effort. Normally, the UNSC will know beforehand that certain member states—usually permanent members of the UNSC—will provide the forces and resources to implement the resolution.

Chapter VI of the U.N. Charter provides the UNSC with authority to authorize measures short of enforcement measures to contribute to the "pacific settlement" of disputes. These measures will often involve the use of military forces, but unlike Chapter VII authorizations, such forces will not (normally) be authorized to engage in hostilities other than acting in self-defense. These so-called peacekeeping operations are symbolized by the ubiquitous "blue helmet"—the indication that military forces operating under U.N. mandate are performing non-combat missions. Chapter VI peacekeeping missions can range from monitoring cease-fires, separation of forces, providing humanitarian assistance, election monitoring, and a range of other missions. Some Chapter VI missions have been ongoing for decades.

The United States routinely contributes military forces to Chapter VI peacekeeping missions. Because these missions are by definition not "enforcement" actions, they will rarely involve the types of military activities that would be viewed by the President or Congress as "combat" missions or missions involving U.S. forces in "hostilities." Accordingly, Presidents have routinely authorized such missions as an exercise of their inherent foreign affairs power without seeking express congressional approval.

These missions are not, however, without risk, and U.S. forces participating in them will normally be equipped and prepared to use a robust range of combat power. U.S. forces participating in such missions always retain the inherent right to use force to defend themselves or their units. Should a presidential decision to commit U.S. forces to such a Chapter VI mission, for example, the decades-long U.S. participation in the Multi-National Force and Observers mission in the Sinai, require congressional approval or compliance with the War Powers Resolution? In 1945,

Congress enacted the United Nations Participation Act (UNPA). Section 6 of the UNPA provides:

> The President is authorized to negotiate a special agreement or agreements with the Security Council which shall be subject to the approval of the Congress by appropriate Act or joint resolution providing for the numbers and types of armed forces, their degree of readiness and general location, and the nature of facilities and assistance, including rights of passage, to be made available to the Security Council on its call for the purpose of maintaining international peace and security in accordance with article 43 of said Charter. The President shall not be deemed to require the authorization of the Congress to make available to the Security Council on its call in order to take action under article 42 of said Charter and pursuant to such special agreement or agreements the armed forces, facilities, or assistance provided for therein:
>
> > Provided . . . nothing herein contained shall be construed as an authorization to the President by the Congress to make available to the Security Council for such purpose armed forces, facilities, or assistance in addition to the forces, facilities, and assistance provided for in such special agreement or agreements.

Notice that by requiring congressional approval of any Article 43 agreement, Congress essentially relied on the Article 43 "force provision" mechanism to ensure it had a say in if and when U.S. armed forces could be committed to military action as the result of a Chapter VII authorization. However, none of the military actions conducted pursuant to such authorizations since that time have involved the use of U.S. armed forces made available to the UNSC by an Article 43 agreement. Based on your understanding of the President's constitutional authority to commit U.S. armed forces to hostilities, what significance, if any, should be attributed to the UNPA?

NOTES AND QUESTIONS

1. While there is little debate over the legality of using military force when authorized by a Chapter VII UNSCR, debate can arise over the permissible scope of such use. For example, President George H.W. Bush was widely criticized for not continuing the 1991 combat operation to oust Iraqi forces from Kuwait into a full-scale invasion of Iraq to oust Saddam Hussein from power. The President defended his decision to halt combat operations on the basis that the objectives of UNSCR 678 had been achieved. In contrast, although Russia supported the 2011 UNSCR authorizing use of military force in Libya to establish a no-fly zone and protect civilians from a humanitarian disaster, Russia later objected to what it considered an unauthorized expansion of combat operations by NATO for the purpose of ousting the Qadhafi regime from Libya.

2. Article 2(4) of the U.N. Charter prohibits states from the threat or use of force "against the territorial integrity or political independence of any state, or in any other manner inconsistent with the Purposes of the United Nations." What if one state, like the United States, obtained consent from another state to use force in its territory? Would that violate Article 2(4)? It would seem that if the objective of the

prohibition is to contribute to peace among states, consent would render the use of force consistent with the Charter. But what if the United States sought to use force in the territory of another state against a non-state actor operating in that territory without consent, but disavowed any effort to interfere with the political independence of the state and used either air power only, or a short duration raid into the state's territory? Would the nature of the non-state objective support a plausible claim that the use of force did not violate Article 2(4)? Consider the U.S. mission to capture or kill Osama bin Laden in Pakistan. If you were advising the President on compliance with the U.N. Charter, could you make a credible argument that the mission would not be inconsistent with Article 2(4)?

3. What recourse, if any, exists to respond to an unjustified expansion of UNSCR authorized military operations? In June of 1950, UNSCR 84 authorized member states to come to the aid of South Korea in response to what the UNSC determined was an act of aggression by North Korea (the USSR was absent from the UNSC vote on that resolution because it was boycotting the UNSC because of its refusal to recognize the People's Republic of China as the proper representative of China in the United Nations). The Resolution indicated that force could be used "as may be necessary to repel the armed attack and restore international peace and security to the area." After halting the North Korean military onslaught at the southern tip of the Korean peninsula, United Nations forces, commanded by U.S. General Douglas MacArthur, launched a counter-offensive that progressed all the way to the North Korean/Chinese border. Was this operation properly within the scope of the UNSCR authorization? Could the United States have lawfully attacked the People's Republic of China with nuclear weapons after China entered the conflict in North Korea pursuant to the UNSCR?

C. Article 51: Force in Self-Defense

Security Council action pursuant to Chapter VII is not the exclusive source of international legal authority for use of military force codified in the U.N. Charter. Article 51 is an equally, if not more important source of such authority, providing:

> Nothing in the present Charter shall impair the inherent right of individual or collective self-defence if an armed attack occurs against a Member of the United Nations, until the Security Council has taken measures necessary to maintain international peace and security. Measures taken by Members in the exercise of this right of self-defence shall be immediately reported to the Security Council and shall not in any way affect the authority and responsibility of the Security Council under the present Charter to take at any time such action as it deems necessary in order to maintain or restore international peace and security.

This Charter's recognition of the "inherent right of self-defense" permits states to use military force to defend themselves and also to collectively defend other victim states. Like the concept of self-defense in criminal law, this inherent right is a right of pure necessity: The right arises only when absolutely necessary; the right terminates when the threat has been neutralized and self-defense is no longer necessary; and only those measures necessary to reduce the threat may be used. Thus, like criminal law self-defense and defense of others, Article 51 self-defense is triggered only by an actual or imminent *unlawful* threat; justifies only those measures that are necessary and proportionate in response; and terminates once the threat is neutralized.

Each of the following requirements must be satisfied before a state or states legitimately invoke the right of individual or collective self-defense: unlawful attack or imminent threat of unlawful attack, necessary means of response, proportionate response, and present immense complexities in actual implementation. When is a threat imminent? How much force is truly necessary in response? When is a use of force considered excessive in relation to the threat? At what point does the right of self-defense terminate because a threat has been neutralized? Of course, in the criminal law context, juries will often be the final judges of whether the elements of self-defense were properly applied, an aspect of self-defense law that is completely inapposite to the inter-state relations context. However, Article 51, in an obvious recognition that it is the UNSC that is ultimately responsible for measures to restore international peace and security, requires any state that exercises the right of individual or collective self-defense to "immediately" notify the UNSC, enabling the UNSC to essentially pass judgment on the assertion of the right through either action or inaction in response.

The United States has invoked the Article 51 right of individual and collective self-defense many times. These invocations, like those of other nations, can be fraught with controversy. Two of the most controversial issues are when a threat becomes sufficiently "imminent" to trigger the right of self-defense, and whether that threat can be the result of non-state actors. While Article 51 was adopted at a time when the "threat focus" was predominately, if not exclusively, the conduct of other states, today many states consider non-state threats capable of triggering Article 51 authority. Consider the following U.S. submission to the UNSC following the attacks of September 11, 2001.

September 11, 2001: Attack on America
Letter of John Negroponte to the President of the Security Council, October 7, 2001

The Representative of the United States of America to the United Nations October 7, 2001

Mr. President:

In accordance with Article 51 of the Charter of the United Nations, I wish, on behalf of my Government, to report that the United States of America, together with other States, has initiated actions in the exercise of its inherent right of individual and collective self-defense following armed attacks that were carried out against the United States on September 11, 2001.

On September 11, 2001, the United States was the victim of massive and brutal attacks in the states of New York, Pennsylvania, and Virginia. These attacks were specifically designed to maximize the loss of life; they resulted in the death of more than five thousand persons, including nationals of 81 countries, as well as the destruction of four civilian aircraft, the World Trade Center towers and a section of the Pentagon. Since September 11, my Government has obtained clear and compelling information that the Al-Qaeda organization, which is supported by the Taliban regime in Afghanistan, had a central role in the attacks. There is still much we do not know. Our inquiry is in its early stages. We may find that our self-defense requires further actions with respect to other organizations and other States.

The attacks on September 11, 2001, and the ongoing threat to the United States and its nationals posed by the Al-Qaeda organization have been made possible by the decision of the Taliban regime to allow the parts of Afghanistan that it controls to be used by this organization as a base of operation. Despite every effort by the United States and the international community, the Taliban regime has refused to change its policy. From the territory of Afghanistan, the Al-Qaeda organization continues to train and support agents of terror who attack innocent people throughout the world and target United States nationals and interests in the United States and abroad.

In response to these attacks, and in accordance with the inherent right of individual and collective self-defense, United States armed forces have initiated actions designed to prevent and deter further attacks on the United States. These actions include measures against Al-Qaeda terrorist training camps and military installations of the Taliban regime in Afghanistan. In carrying out these actions, the United States will continue its humanitarian efforts to alleviate the suffering of the people of Afghanistan. We are providing them with food, medicine and supplies.

I ask that you circulate the text of the present letter as a document of the Security Council.

Sincerely,
John D. Negroponte

On September 18, 2012, Harold Koh, then serving as the Legal Advisor to the Secretary of State, gave a speech in which he addressed the U.S. interpretation of what "triggers" the inherent right of self-defense under the U.N. Charter. Koh stated, "To cite just one example of this, the United States has for a long time taken the position that the inherent right of self-defense potentially applies against any illegal use of force. In our view, there is no threshold for a use of deadly force to qualify as an 'armed attack' that may warrant a forcible response." Harold Hongju Koh, *International Law in Cyberspace*, U.S. Dep't of State (Sept. 18, 2012), http://www.state.gov/s/l/releases/remarks/197924.htm.

This interpretation is not necessarily consistent with the views of other states, which believe that there is distinction between a use of force in violation of Article 2(4) and an "armed attack" triggering the Article 51 right of self-defense. This distinction was recognized by the International Court of Justice when, in 1986, it decided *The Case Concerning Military and Paramilitary Activities in and Against Nicaragua*

(*Nicaragua v. United States of America*). Nicaragua alleged that the United States had engaged in acts of aggression against it. In response the United States argued that its actions were justified as measures of collective self-defense to protect El Salvador from Nicaraguan aggression in the form of supporting leftist rebels engaged in a civil war against the El Salvadoran government. This required the court to consider whether Nicaragua's support for the FMLN rebels qualified as an "armed attack" triggering the right of individual and collective self-defense. On this point, the court concluded:

> As regards certain particular aspects of the principle in question, it will be necessary to distinguish the most grave forms of the use of force (those constituting an armed attack) from other less grave forms. In determining the legal rule which applies to these latter forms, the Court can again draw on the formulations contained in the Declaration on Principles of International Law concerning Friendly Relations and Co-operation among States in accordance with the Charter of the United Nations (General Assembly resolution 2625 (XXV), referred to above). As already observed, the adoption by States of this text affords an indication of their *opinio juris* as to customary international law on the question. Alongside certain descriptions which may refer to aggression, this text includes others which refer only to less grave forms of the use of force. In particular, according to this resolution:

>> "Every State has the duty to refrain from the threat or use of force to violate the existing international boundaries of another State or as a means of solving international disputes, including territorial disputes and problems concerning frontiers of States.

>> . . .

>> States have a duty to refrain from acts of reprisal involving the use of force.

>> . . .

>> Every State has the duty to refrain from any forcible action which deprives peoples referred to in the elaboration of the principle of equal rights and self-determination of that right to self- determination and freedom and independence.

>> Every State has the duty to refrain from organizing or encouraging the organization of irregular forces or armed bands, including mercenaries, for incursion into the territory of another State.

>> Every State has the duty to refrain from organizing, instigating, assisting or participating in acts of civil strife or terrorist acts in another State or acquiescing in organized activities within its territory directed towards the commission of such acts, when the acts referred to in the present paragraph involve a threat or use of force." *Military and Paramilitary Activities in and against Nicaragua (Nicar. v. U.S.)*, 1986 I.C.J. 14, 101 (June 27).

These disparate interpretations of the inherent right of self-defense raise an important national security question: Is a responsive use of force consistent with international law whenever another state violates Article 2(4), or must there be some level of intensity of the violation in order to rise to the level of an "armed attack" triggering the right to use force in response? Koh's speech reflects the U.S. interpretation, although in many situations the President may refrain from exercising the legal right based on policy considerations. For an excellent discussion of this complex question of international law, see Michael N. Schmitt, *International Law in Cyberspace: The Koh Speech and Tallinn Manual Juxtaposed*, 54 HARV. INT'L L.J. 13 (2012).

NOTES AND QUESTIONS

1. If non-state groups can present a threat sufficient to trigger the right of self-defense, what about individual actors? Could the United States be justified in invoking Article 51 in response to a cyber-threat posed by one individual?

2. The U.S. interpretation of the Article 51 right of self-defense applies to non-state threats, but there is not universal agreement on this point. In fact, the International Court of Justice concluded that Article 51 did not apply to non-state threats in two post–September 11th decisions. In the "Wall" case, the ICJ rejected Israel's invocation of the right of self-defense as a legal basis to build the barrier wall between Israel and the occupied West Bank, concluding that the threats posed by Palestinian militants could not trigger Article 51. In *Congo v. Uganda*, the ICJ rejected Uganda's invocation of Article 51 to justify military intervention into the Congo to neutralize rebel forces that threatened Uganda. Nonetheless, other states, such as Israel, the United Kingdom, and many other NATO allies seem to align themselves with the U.S. interpretation. For example, the United Kingdom notified the UNSC of its participation in military action against al Qaeda in Afghanistan following the September 11th attacks, specifically indicating that

> [t]he United Kingdom has military assets engaged in operations against targets we know to be involved in the operation of terror against the United States of America, the United Kingdom and other countries around the world, as part of a wider international effort. These forces have now been employed in exercise of the inherent right of individual and collective self-defence, recognised in Article 51, following the terrorist outrage of 11 September, to avert the continuing threat of attacks from the same source. This military action . . . is directed against Usama Bin Laden's Al Qaida terrorist organisation and the Taliban regime that is supporting it.[1]

In fact, even the UNSC seemed to recognize a right of self-defense in response to the September 11th attacks, when on September 12, 2001, it adopted UNSCR 1368, which began with the following language:

> Reaffirming the principles and purposes of the Charter of the United Nations,
> Determined to combat by all means threats to international peace and security caused by terrorist acts,
> Recognizing the inherent right of individual or collective self-defence in accordance with the Charter,

---

1. Letter from Stewart Eldon, Chargé d'Affaires, UK Mission to the U.N. in New York, to the President of the Security Council, S/2001/947, 7 October 2001.

Why would these indications of "state practice" suggest a broader scope of Article 51 authority than the ICJ seemed willing to recognize?

3. As a result of the rise of ISIS and its terror activities throughout Europe, the view that Article 51 applies to threats posed by non-state groups has gained support. The United Kingdom, Germany, Belgium, France, and Denmark (to name a few) have submitted notice to the Security Council invoking Article 51 as the basis for military action against ISIS.

4. The issue of "what or who" may be defended can also raise complexities. Is the right of self-defense limited to defending national territory? Does it extend to military forces deployed abroad? The United States has a longstanding practice of deploying military forces, sometimes on an ad hoc basis but also in relatively permanent status, outside the United States to demonstrate U.S. resolve in the face of potential threats to the United States, allies, or even freedom of navigation. These forces are sometimes euphemistically called "tripwire" forces, suggesting that any attack against them will trigger U.S. military response. Is this "tripwire" concept more than pragmatic? Can you see a linkage to international legal authority to use military force?

5. Does the Article 51 right of self-defense extend to protecting citizens in another country from threats posed by that country or by forces in that country when host-nation authorities are unwilling or unable to protect U.S. citizens? The United States has periodically invoked this "defense of national" theory to justify what are called "nonpermissive noncombatant evacuation operations," military operations to force entry into the territory of another country in order to assemble and evacuate U.S. nationals. But what if the population of U.S. nationals is so extensive that evacuation is not a safe option to protect them? Does Article 51 justify "taking down" a government and its armed forces in order to protect these individuals? In 1989, the United States invaded Panama in order to neutralize the capabilities of the Panamanian Defense Forces and oust General Manuel Noriega from his position of leadership of the nation and the PDF. According to a GAO Report, defense of nationals pursuant to Article 51 provided one of the legal justifications invoked by the United States for the invasion:

> The invasion was viewed by the State Department as a necessary and proportionate response to the threat that General Noriega posed to the United States. According to the State Department, the Panamanian National Assembly, at Noriega's urging, had declared that a state of war existed between the United States and Panama. The following day, on December 16, 1989, a U.S. Marine officer was killed, reportedly without justification, by Panama Defense Forces personnel. Further, a U.S. naval officer and his wife allegedly were unlawfully detained and physically abused by Panama Defense Forces personnel. The State Department attributed these acts to Noriega and his subordinates and claimed that these acts were done in a climate of aggression that jeopardized American lives and interests. Under these circumstances and after the exhaustion of other avenues, including political and economic sanctions, the administration believed that the United States had the right to use force to protect itself.[2]

---

2. General Accounting Office, Panama: Issues Relating to the U.S. Invasion, Rep. No. NSIAD-91-174FS (Apr. 24, 1991), http://www.gao.gov/assets/90/89061.pdf.

If defense of nationals is justified pursuant to Article 51, at what point would a full-scale invasion become an "excessive" use of military force?

D. Self-Defense Against Whom, When and Where?

Another complex issue related to invoking the right of self-defense is the point at which a threat triggers that right. The inclusion of non-state threats, such as terrorist groups and perhaps even cyber-threats, within the scope of the Article 51 right has exacerbated this complexity, because unlike conventional state military threats, it is much more difficult to assess when attack by such threats is about to occur. The following excerpt from a Congressional Research Service Report summarizes how the United States interprets the right of self-defense to apply to transnational non-state threats.

<hr>

Congressional Research Service Memorandum
Legal Issues Related to the Lethal Targeting of U.S. Citizens Suspected of Terrorist Activities

* * *

Self Defense Under International Law

Even outside the context of an armed conflict, sovereign states retain the right to self defense in the event of an armed attack. The law governing the resort to force, frequently known by its Latin term *jus ad bellum*, is related to but separate from the law governing the use of force, *jus in bello*. Prior to World War II, states were recognized as having a sovereign right to use military force against other states to vindicate any number of wrongs. In drafting the U.N. Charter, member states sought to reduce the incidence of war by curtailing the rights of states to use force against one another.

Although Article 2(4) of the U.N. Charter generally prohibits member states from using or threatening to use force "against the territorial integrity or political independence of any state," Article 51 preserves the "inherent right of individual or collective self-defence if an armed attack occurs against a Member of the United Nations, until the Security Council has taken measures necessary to maintain international peace and security." Read literally, Article 51's articulation of the right seems to preclude a state's use of force until *after* an armed attack has already commenced and not merely on the threat of any use of force, but some authorities regard the right as encompassing the previously existing inherent right of self-defense under customary international law, which many likewise regard as including a right to preemptive (or "anticipatory") self-defense in the event of an imminent attack.

The classic formulation of the right to use force in self-defense on the territory of a foreign state was set forth by Secretary of State Daniel Webster in connection with the famous *Caroline* incident. In 1837 British troops attacked a private American ship, the *Caroline*, while it was moored for the night on the New York side of the Niagara River, asserting that the ship was being used to provide supplies to insurrectionists against British rule in Canada who were based on an island on the Canadian side of the river. The United States protested this "extraordinary outrage" and demanded an apology and reparations.

In the course of the ensuing diplomatic exchanges with the British Government, Secretary of State Daniel Webster asserted that an intrusion into the territory of another state can be justified as an act of self-defense only in those "cases in which the necessity of that self-defence is instant, overwhelming, and leaving no choice of means and no moment for deliberation." Moreover, he wrote that even if justified, the use of defensive force must be proportional to the threat, "since the act, justified by the necessity of self-defence, must be limited by that necessity, and kept clearly within it." The three conditions of necessity, proportionality, and immediacy (or imminence) are widely regarded as establishing the grounds for invoking the right to resort to force extraterritorially.

The United States has used force in self-defense to respond to terrorist attacks in the past, and also has asserted the right to use force in anticipation of an imminent attack. The right to use force in self-defense, and even the actual use of force justified under the circumstances, do not necessarily indicate the existence of an armed conflict. For example, the United States in 1986 used force against Libya in response to a terrorist attack against American personnel in Berlin, but neither Libya nor the United States seems to have regarded the circumstances as amounting to an armed conflict. Likewise, the use of force against suspected terrorist targets in Afghanistan and Sudan in response to the bombing of U.S. embassies in Africa does not appear to have been regarded at the time as giving rise to a situation of armed conflict so as to bring the law of war into operation in those places.

If the state on whose territory force is to be used gives its consent, there is no violation of article 2(4) of the UN Charter and therefore no need to invoke a theory of self-defense. Another possibility for resolving a conflict of sovereignty in order to justify the use of force without consent on the territory of another state which did not itself initiate an armed attack is to justify intervention on the basis that the invaded or injured state is "unable or unwilling" to remove the threat emanating from its territory. It has been suggested that the right to intervene militarily in such cases stems from the obligation of neutrality during wars between states, but for peacetime purposes, where an incursion or threat does not amount to an "armed attack" within the meaning of the UN Charter, the right may be an extension of the concept of "self-help" in international law, which in theory did not survive the adoption of the UN Charter insofar as it involves the use of force. In present-day application, it is not clear whether the "unwilling or unable" test is understood to be a separate test from the *Caroline* test, an additional consideration (for example, an element of necessity), or a substitute for one of the factors, perhaps immediacy in the case of a continuing threat.

If an armed attack on the part of a non-state armed group gives rise to a State's right of self-defense, it remains to be considered what rules govern the resulting use of force on the part of the state. Some argue that the necessity, proportionality, and immediacy requirements to justify the resort to force also provide an adequate framework to govern its use. Others, however, believe that the legal framework applicable under the law of war applies in the event hostilities meet the threshold to be considered an armed conflict, or that the legal framework applicable to peacetime law enforcement operations applies in the event they do not.

As noted above, the ICJ has twice rejected claims that Article 51 applied to non-state threats. For a majority of Judges, only threats from States implicated the inherent right of self-defense. This is not consistent with the U.S. interpretation. On this question, consider the following excerpt from Judge Buergenthal's separate opinion in the Israel "Wall" decision and how the Judge highlights both the complexity of this issue and why the practice of states like the United States and Israel may be modifying the traditional understanding of this right.

Declaration of Judge Buergenthal

4. . . . I accept that the Palestinian people have the right to self-determination and that it is entitled to be fully protected. But assuming without necessarily agreeing that this right is relevant to the case before us and that it is being violated, Israel's right to self-defence, if applicable and legitimately invoked, would nevertheless have to preclude any wrongfulness in this regard. See Article 21 of the International Law Commission's Articles on Responsibility of States for Internationally Wrongful Acts, which declares: "The wrongfulness of an act of a State is precluded if the act constitutes a lawful measure of self-defence taken in conformity with the Charter of the United Nations."

5. Whether Israel's right of self-defence is in play in the instant case depends, in my opinion, on an examination of the nature and scope of the deadly terrorist attacks to which Israel proper is being subjected from across the Green Line and the extent to which the construction of the wall, in whole or in part, is a necessary and proportionate response to these attacks. As a matter of law, it is not inconceivable to me that some segments of the wall being constructed on Palestinian territory meet that test and that others do not. But to reach a conclusion either way, one has to examine the facts bearing on that issue with regard to the specific segments of the wall, their defensive needs and related topographical considerations.

Since these facts are not before the Court, it is compelled to adopt the to me legally dubious conclusion that the right of legitimate or inherent self-defence is not applicable in the present case. The Court puts the matter as follows:

> "Article 51 of the Charter . . . recognizes the existence of an inherent right of self-defence in the case of armed attack by one State against another State. However, Israel does not claim that the attacks against it are imputable to a foreign State. The Court also notes that Israel exercises control in the Occupied Palestinian Territory and that, as Israel itself states, the threat which it regards as justifying the construction of the wall originates within, and not outside, that territory. The situation is thus different from that contemplated by Security Council resolutions 1368 (2001) and 1373 (2001), and therefore Israel could not in any event invoke those resolutions in support of its claim to be exercising a right of self-defence. Consequently, the Court concludes that Article 51 of the Charter has no relevance in this case." (Para. 139.)

6. There are two principal problems with this conclusion. The first is that the United Nations Charter, in affirming the inherent right of self-defence, does not make its exercise dependent upon an armed attack by another State, leaving aside for the

moment the question whether Palestine, for purposes of this case, should not be and is not in fact being assimilated by the Court to a State. Article 51 of the Charter provides that "Nothing in the present Charter shall impair the inherent right of individual or collective self-defence if an armed attack occurs against a Member of the United Nations. . . ." Moreover, in the resolutions cited by the Court, the Security Council has made clear that "international terrorism constitutes a threat to international peace and security" while "*reaffirming* the inherent right of individual or collective self-defence as recognized by the Charter of the United Nations as reiterated in resolution 1368 (2001)" (Security Council resolution 1373 (2001)). In its resolution 1368 (2001), adopted only one day after the 11 September 2001 attacks on the United States, the Security Council invokes the right of self-defence in calling on the international community to combat terrorism. In neither of these resolutions did the Security Council limit their application to terrorist attacks by State actors only, nor was an assumption to that effect implicit in these resolutions. In fact, the contrary appears to have been the case. (See Thomas Franck, "Terrorism and the Right of Self-Defense," *American Journal of International Law*, Vol. 95, 2001, pp. 839-840.)[3]

Both the actions and official statements by the United States clearly adopt the broader interpretation of Article 51 reflected in Judge Buergenthal's opinion. On April 1, 2016, Brian Egan, the Legal Advisor for the Department of State, delivered an important speech to the 110th Annual Meeting of the American Society for International Law (the full text of the speech, including all of the extracts below, is reprinted in the U.S. Naval War College International Law Studies, Brian Egan, *International Law, Legal Diplomacy, and the Counter-ISIL Campaign: Some Observations*, 92 INT'L L. STUD. 235 (2016)). Egan carefully and clearly articulated the U.S. government's legal basis for conducting military operations against ISIS in both Iraq and Syria. In the speech, Egan reconfirmed that the United States considers the Article 51 right of individual and collective self-defense to extend to non-state transnational threats. Specifically, Egan noted:

> To say a few more words about self-defense: First, the inherent right of individual and collective self-defense recognized in the U.N. Charter is not restricted to threats posed by States. Nor is the right of self-defense on the territory of another State against non-State actors, such as ISIL, something that developed after 9/11. To the contrary, for at least the past two hundred years, States have invoked the right of self-defense to justify taking action on the territory of another State against non-State actors. As but one example, the oft-cited Caroline incident involved the use of force by the United Kingdom in self-defense against a non-State actor located in the United States. Although the precise wording of the justification for the exercise of self-defense against non-State actors may have varied, the acceptance of this right has remained the same.
>
> Under the jus ad bellum, a State may use force in the exercise of its inherent right of self-defense not only in response to armed attacks that have occurred, but also in response to imminent ones before they occur.

---

3. Legal Consequences of the Construction of a Wall in the Occupied Palestinian Territory (Advisory Opinion), International Court of Justice, 9 July 2004, 43 ILM 1009 (Separate Declaration of Judge Buergenthal).

When considering whether an armed attack is imminent under the jus ad bellum for purposes of the initial use of force against a particular non-State actor, the United States analyzes a variety of factors, including those identified by Sir Daniel Bethlehem in the enumeration he set forth in the American Journal of International Law — the ASIL's own in-house publication — in 2012. These factors include the nature and immediacy of the threat; the probability of an attack; whether the anticipated attack is part of a concerted pattern of continuing armed activity; the likely scale of the attack and the injury, loss, or damage likely to result therefrom in the absence of mitigating action; and the likelihood that there will be other opportunities to undertake effective action in self-defense that may be expected to cause less serious collateral injury, loss, or damage. The absence of specific evidence of where an attack will take place or of the precise nature of an attack does not preclude a conclusion that an armed attack is imminent for purposes of the exercise of the right of self-defense, provided that there is a reasonable and objective basis for concluding that an armed attack is imminent.

Mr. Egan then emphasized that once it is engaged in an ongoing armed conflict, the United States is not obligated to make a new self-defense assessment as a predicate to every military action against the enemy:

In the view of the United States, once a State has lawfully resorted to force in self-defense against a particular armed group following an actual or imminent armed attack by that group, it is not necessary as a matter of international law to reassess whether an armed attack is imminent prior to every subsequent action taken against that group, provided that hostilities have not ended.

Mr. Egan also pushed back against the perception that the nature of non-state enemies who operate transnationally essentially results in a "global war on terrorism." To the contrary, Egan explained that when members of an enemy group in an ongoing armed conflict are located outside areas of active combat operations, determining that they are lawful targets is only the first step in the attack legality analysis. The second step must assess whether the United States is permitted to conduct the attack in the sovereign territory of the nation where they are found. At this point, the "unable or unwilling" test may become decisive:

I'd also like to say a few words on how State sovereignty and consent factor into the international legal analysis when considering the use of force. President Obama has made clear that "America cannot take strikes wherever we choose; our actions are bound by consultations with partners, and respect for state sovereignty." This is true of our operations against ISIL as it has been true in our non-international armed conflict against al Qa'ida and associated forces.

Indeed, under the jus ad bellum, the international legal basis for the resort to force in self-defense on another State's territory takes into account State sovereignty. . . . In other words, international law not only requires a State to analyze whether it has a legal basis for the use of force against a particular non-State actor — which I'll call the "against whom" question — but also requires a State to analyze whether it has a legal basis to use force against that non-State actor in a particular location — which I'll call the "where" question.

It is with respect to this "where" question that international law requires that States must either determine that they have the relevant government's consent or, if they must rely on self-defense to use force against a non-State actor on another State's territory, determine that the territorial State is "unable or unwilling" to address the threat posed by the non-State actor on its territory. . . .

In some cases, international law does not require a State to obtain the consent of the State on whose territory force will be used. In particular, there will be cases in which there is a reasonable and objective basis for concluding that the territorial State is unwilling or unable to effectively confront the non-State actor in its territory so that it is necessary to act in self-defense against the non-State actor in that State's territory without the territorial State's consent. . . .

The unable or unwilling standard is not a license to wage war globally or to disregard the borders and territorial integrity of other States. Indeed, this legal standard does not dispense with the importance of respecting the sovereignty of other States. To the contrary, applying the standard ensures that the sovereignty of other States is respected. Specifically, applying the standard ensures that force is used on foreign territory without consent only in those exceptional circumstances in which a State cannot or will not take effective measures to confront a non-State actor that is using its territory as a base for attacks and related operations against other States. With respect to the "unable" prong of the standard, inability perhaps can be demonstrated most plainly, for example, where a State has lost or abandoned effective control over the portion of its territory from which the non-State actor is operating. This is the case with respect to the situation in Syria. By September 2014, the Syrian government had lost effective control of much of eastern and northeastern Syria, with much of that territory under ISIL's control.

Mr. Egan left no doubt about two important aspects of the U.S. interpretation of Article 51 self-defense. First, the right applies to threats posed by non-state groups, to include terrorist groups. Second, the "unable or unwilling" test is viewed as justifying acts of self-defense in the sovereign territory of other nations without violating Article 2(4) of the U.N. Charter. You should ponder how the United States might react if another nation, perhaps Mexico, were to execute an armed attack without consent on U.S. territory based on a determination that the United States was "unwilling" to effectively deal with a non-state actor operating out of its territory.

NOTES AND QUESTIONS

1. The U.S. interpretation that transnational terrorist groups may pose an imminent threat to the United States has been central to the legal theory relied on by both Presidents Obama and Bush (and perhaps even Clinton) to authorize lethal military attacks against terrorist operatives. It is not, however, without controversy. While there is almost universal agreement that the Article 51 right of self-defense is triggered not only by an actual armed attack, but also by an imminent armed attack, the meaning of armed attack and imminence remains one of the controversial international legal questions. Should the unconventional nature of a potential threat, especially when emanating from a non-state

group, influence the meaning of imminence? Consider the following excerpt from a report prepared by a group of international law experts:

4. A state may use force in self-defence against a threatened attack only if that attack is "imminent"

There is a risk of abuse of the doctrine of anticipatory self-defence, and it needs to be applied in good faith and on the basis of sound evidence. But the criterion of imminence must be interpreted so as to take into account current kinds of threat and it must be applied having regard to the particular circumstances of each case. The criterion of imminence is closely related to the requirement of necessity.

- Force may be used only when any further delay would result in an inability by the threatened state effectively to defend against or avert the attack against it.
- In assessing the imminence of the attack, reference may be made to the gravity of the attack, the capability of the attacker, and the nature of the threat, for example if the attack is likely to come without warning.
- Force may be used only on a proper factual basis and after a good faith assessment of the facts.

The concept of "imminence" reflects the *Caroline* formulation of "instant, overwhelming, leaving no choice of means, and no moment for deliberation." In the context of contemporary threats imminence cannot be construed by reference to a temporal criterion only, but must reflect the wider circumstances of the threat.

There must exist a circumstance of irreversible emergency. Whether the attack is "imminent" depends upon the nature of the threat and the possibility of dealing effectively with it at any given stage. Factors that may be taken into account include: the *gravity* of the threatened attack—whether what is threatened is a catastrophic use of WMD; *capability*—for example, whether the relevant state or terrorist organisation is in possession of WMD, or merely of material or component parts to be used in its manufacture; and the *nature* of the attack—including the possible risks of making a wrong assessment of the danger. Other factors may also be relevant, such as the geographical situation of the victim state, and the past record of attacks by the state concerned.

The criterion of imminence requires that it is believed that any further delay in countering the intended attack will result in the inability of the defending state effectively to defend itself against the attack. In this sense, necessity will determine imminence: it must be necessary to act before it is too late. There is a question as to whether "imminence" is a separate criterion in its own right, or simply part of the criterion of "necessity" properly understood. As an additional criterion however it serves to place added emphasis on the fact that a forcible response in these circumstances lies at the limits of an already exceptional legal category, and therefore requires a correspondingly high level of justification.

To the extent that a doctrine of "pre-emption" encompasses a right to respond to threats which have not yet crystallized but which might materialise at some time in the future, such a doctrine (sometimes called "preventive defence") has no basis in international law. A fatal flaw in the so-called doctrine of prevention is that it excludes by definition any possibility of an *ex post facto* judgment of lawfulness by the very fact that it aims to deal in advance with threats that have not yet materialised.

Each case will necessarily turn on its own facts. A forceful action to disrupt a terrorist act being prepared in another state might, depending upon the circumstances, be legitimate; force to attack a person who may in the future contemplate such activity is not. While the possession of WMD without a hostile intent to launch an attack does not in itself give rise to a right of self-defence, the difficulty of determining intent and the catastrophic consequences of making an error will be relevant factors in any determination of "imminence" made by another state.

The determination of "imminence" is in the first place for the relevant state to make, but it must be made in good faith and on grounds which are capable of objective assessment. Insofar as this can reasonably be achieved, the evidence should be publicly demonstrable. Some kinds of evidence cannot be reasonably produced, whether because of the nature or source, or because it is the product of interpretation of many small pieces of information. But evidence is fundamental to accountability, and accountability to the rule of law. The more far-reaching, and the more irreversible its external actions, the more a state should accept (internally as well as externally) the burden of showing that its actions were justifiable on the facts. And there should be proper internal procedures for the assessment of intelligence and appropriate procedural safeguards.[4]

Does the U.S. interpretation seem consistent with this interpretation of imminence? Consider the U.S. attack that killed Iranian General Soleimani in 2020. Soon after the attack President Trump and others in his administration made public statements indicating that the attack was authorized based on intelligence that General Soleimani was not only responsible for the recent attack on the U.S. embassy in Iraq, but was also planning other imminent attacks against U.S. facilities (embassies) and personnel in the region. According to an unclassified report provided by the Trump Administration to Congress pursuant to § 1264 of the National Defense Authorization Act of 2018 (as amended):

> At the President's direction, United States Armed Forces conducted an air strike in Iraq on January 2, 2020, killing Qassem Soleimani, leader of Iran's Islamic Revolutionary Guard Corps-Qods Force, a designated foreign terrorist organization. The President directed this action in response to an escalating series of attacks in preceding months by Iran and Iran-backed militias on United States forces and interests in the Middle East region. The purposes of this action were to protect United States personnel, to deter Iran from conducting or supporting further attacks against United States forces and interests, to degrade Iran's and Qods Force-backed militias' ability to conduct attacks, and to end Iran's strategic escalation of attacks on, and threats to United States interests.[5]

But this Notice suggests the threat might not have been as imminent as first suggested, omitting the word "imminent" from the explanation of why the attack was launched:

---

4. Elizabeth Wilmshurst, *International Law: Principles of International Law on the Use of Force by States in Self-Defence*, Chatham House 8-9 (October 2005), https://www.chathamhouse.org/sites/files/chathamhouse/public/Research/International%20Law/ilpforce.doc.

5. *See Notice on the Legal and Policy Frameworks Guiding the United States' Use of Military Force and Related National Security Operations, available at* https://www.justsecurity.org/wp-content/uploads/2020/02/notice-on-the-legal-and-policy-frameworks-guiding-the-united-states-use-of-military-force-and-related-national-security-operations.pdf

Iran's past and recent activities, coupled with intelligence at the time of the air strike, indicated that Iran's Qods Force posed a threat to the United States in Iraq, and the air strike against Soleimani was intended to protect United States personnel and deter future Iranian attack plans against United States forces and interests in Iraq and threats emanating from Iraq.

Nonetheless, the Notice closed by emphasizing the U.S. view that the action fell squarely within the scope of Article 51 of the U.N. Charter:

> As a matter of international law, the strike targeting Soleimani in Iraq was taken in United States national self-defense, as recognized in Article 51 of the United Nations Charter, in response to a series of escalating armed attacks that Iran and Iraq supported militias had already conducted against the United States. The United States reported the air strike to the United Nations Security Council on January, 2020, in accordance with Article 51 of the United Nations Charter. Although the threat of further attack existed, recourse to the inherent right of self-defense was justified sufficiently by the series of attacks that preceded the January 2 strike.

So what exactly did this last paragraph mean? Was the Trump Administration conceding that there was no intelligence that Soleimani was directing *another* imminent attack when the U.S. attack was launched? Notice that the final sentence, like the earlier provision, omits the word "imminent" when it refers to "further attacks." Was the administration asserting that the prior attacks attributable to Soleimani justified the U.S. attack even without intelligence indicating he was at that time planning another imminent attack? If so, that would represent a troubling conflation of the right of self-defense with unlawful reprisal. While that line is often difficult to identify, especially as prior acts of aggression will logically inform the assessment of when a *subsequent* armed attack is imminent, a use of armed force in reprisal or revenge for prior attacks does not fall within the scope of the inherent right of self-defense. For more on the difference between self-defense and reprisal, see Geoffrey Corn & Rachel VanLandingham, *Lawful Self-Defense vs. Revenge Strikes: Scrutinizing Iran and U.S. Uses of Force Under International Law*, Just Security, Jan. 8, 2020, *available at* https://www.justsecurity.org/67970/lawful-self-defense-vs-revenge-strikes-scrutinizing-iran-and-u-s-uses-of-force-under-international-law/.

2. Article 51 includes not only the right of individual self-defense, but also collective self-defense. This was a logical inclusion in the Charter, enabling collective response to aggression even if absent UNSC authorization, thereby protecting less powerful states from more powerful aggressors. May the United States invoke this collective self-defense authority without a request for assistance from the defended state? Or must the United States await such a request before taking action pursuant to this authority? In *Nicaragua v. United States* (the Paramilitaries case), the ICJ rejected a U.S. argument that its covert actions against Nicaragua and support for the Nicaraguan Contra rebels were justified as actions in collective self-defense of El Salvador, because Nicaragua was supporting leftist rebels (the FMLN) trying to overthrow the El Salvadoran government. The ICJ concluded that even assuming Nicaragua's support for the FMLN

qualified as armed aggression against El Salvador (an assertion it ultimately rejected), invocation of the right of collective self-defense was contingent on an assertion of self-defense or a request for assistance from the protected state. With no evidence of such an assertion or request from El Salvador, the ICJ concluded the United States could not rely on this authority. Why might a state be hesitant to formally request such assistance but nonetheless favor U.S. military action in support of its interests?

3. As a permanent member of the UNSC, the United States is able to veto any resolution condemning or criticizing a U.S. invocation of Article 51. Does this mean that the United States is free to stretch the meaning of self-defense beyond widely accepted meaning in order to justify military action? What factors do you think might influence U.S. interpretations of Article 51?

II. THE LEGAL REGULATION OF ARMED CONFLICT

A. Sources and Contours

International law, as explained above, establishes when a state may lawfully resort to the use of military force. Once military force is employed, international law also plays a vital role in regulating the conduct of military operations. This branch of the *jus belli* (laws of war) is generally known as the *jus in bello*, and is as old as international law itself. These "laws and customs of war" originally were purely customary in nature, but over time many of these rules have been codified in multi-lateral treaties. Whether treaty or customary law, U.S. armed forces must comply with any rule considered binding by the United States, and will often endeavor to comply with other rules even if not technically binding, especially when conducting coalition operations with partners who are bound by treaty obligations inapplicable to the United States.

Conflict regulation is generally divided along two broad functional lines: rules that regulate the conduct of hostilities (the methods (tactics) and means (weapons) of warfare), and rules that protect the interests of victims of war—individuals who take no part in hostilities (like most civilians) or individuals who are "out of the fight" due to capture, wounds, or sickness. The protection of war victims is the primary focus of the four Geneva Conventions of 1949, each of which is devoted to the protection of a distinct category of war victims (the wounded and sick; the wounded, sick, and shipwrecked at sea; prisoners of war; and civilians under the control of an enemy). Conduct of hostilities regulation was originally codified in the Regulations Annexed to the Hague Convention IV of 1899 and then 1907 and evolved primarily as customary international law.

In 1977, two treaties developed to supplement the 1949 Geneva Conventions, Additional Protocols I and II, came into force. Additional Protocol I updated the rules for the protection of war victims, and codified many of the customary rules regulating the conduct of hostilities. Almost all this law, however, applied only to inter-state conflicts, what the Geneva Conventions defined as "international armed conflict." The 1949 Conventions included only one article—Article 3, common to all four Geneva Conventions—to regulate "non-international" armed conflicts, although Additional Protocol II updated this very minimal law. Today, many other treaties regulate weapons and tactics, such as the Chemical Weapons Convention and the Convention on Certain Conventional Weapons.

Accordingly, determining what rules regulate U.S. military operations depends on several considerations. First, will the operation qualify as an "armed conflict" triggering applicability of this body of international law? Second, if so, will the armed conflict be international (inter-state), bringing into force all of the rules; or will it be non-international, bringing into force a less comprehensive legal regime? Finally, is the United States bound by a particular international law rule as a matter of treaty obligation or because the United States considers the rule customary international law? It is beyond question, however, that *if and when* a rule of international law is applicable to military operations, U.S. forces must comply with that (or those) rules. Consider the following excerpt from the Foreword to the Department of Defense Law of War Manual, published in 2015 after an extensive drafting process that specifically considered the challenges of contemporary military conflicts:

> The law of war is of fundamental importance to the Armed Forces of the United States. The law of war is part of who we are. George Washington, as Commander in Chief of the Continental Army, agreed with his British adversary that the Revolutionary War would be "carried on agreeable to the rules which humanity formed" and "to prevent or punish every breach of the rules of war within the sphere of our respective commands." During the Civil War, President Lincoln approved a set of "Instructions for the Government of the Armies of the United States in the Field," which inspired other countries to adopt similar codes for their armed forces, and which served as a template for international codifications of the law of war.
>
> . . .
>
> The law of war is a part of our military heritage, and obeying it is the right thing to do. But we also know that the law of war poses no obstacle to fighting well and prevailing. Nations have developed the law of war to be fundamentally consistent with the military doctrines that are the basis for effective combat operations. For example, the self-control needed to refrain from violations of the law of war under the stresses of combat is the same good order and discipline necessary to operate cohesively and victoriously in battle. Similarly, the law of war's prohibitions on torture and unnecessary destruction are consistent with the practical insight that such actions ultimately frustrate rather than accomplish the mission.
>
> This manual reflects many years of labor and expertise, on the part of civilian and military lawyers from every Military Service. It reflects the experience of this Department in applying the law of war in actual military operations, and it will help us remember the hard learned lessons from the past. Understanding our duties imposed by the law of war and our rights under it is essential to our service in the nation's defense.

Compliance with this body of law, what the United States today refers to as the law of armed conflict (LOAC), but more commonly known as international humanitarian law (IHL) is, as noted in the above extract, central to the success and legitimacy of U.S. military operations. But when is the law applicable to such operations?

From a common sense perspective, the answer might seem simple: when our armed forces are involved in "wars" or perhaps "armed conflicts."

B. The Trigger: What Is Armed Conflict?

But when does a particular situation, or military operation, qualify as such? This is a critical question for a range of reasons, to include not only regulation of conduct, but also international criminal accountability. The following excerpt from the Department of Defense Law of War Manual provides insight into how this question is analyzed. As you read this except, keep in mind that the term "war" seems to be used in the pragmatic sense and not as a legal term, meaning a state of hostilities that brings into force the international law of war. As the excerpt highlights, the critical question for assessing whether the law of armed conflict is applicable to a given situation is not whether the situation qualifies as a "war," but whether it qualifies as an "armed conflict."

From the Department of Defense Law of War Manual
(June 2015 (Updated December 2016))

3.4 WHEN *JUS IN BELLO* RULES APPLY

Jus in bello treaties often provide that they apply in cases of "declared war or of any other armed conflict," even if the state of war is not recognized by them. This standard has also been understood to result in the application of the customary law of war.

A case of "declared war or any other armed conflict" for the purpose of determining whether parties must comply with *jus in bello* rules may be understood as arising in two ways: (1) when a party intends to conduct hostilities; or (2) when parties are actually conducting hostilities. "War," "hostilities," and "armed conflict" may be defined differently for other legal purposes.

3.4.2 *Act-Based Test for Applying* Jus in Bello *Rules. Jus in bello* rules apply when parties are actually conducting hostilities, even if the war is not declared or if the state of war is not recognized by them. The *de facto* existence of an armed conflict is sufficient to trigger obligations for the conduct of hostilities.

The United States has interpreted "armed conflict" in Common Article 2 of the 1949 Geneva Conventions [defining "international" armed conflict] to include "any situation in which there is hostile action between the armed forces of two parties, regardless of the duration, intensity or scope of the fighting."

3.3.1 *International Armed Conflict and Non-International Armed Conflict.* The law of war treats situations of "war," "hostilities," or "armed conflict" differently based on the legal status of parties to the conflict. If two or more States oppose one another, then this type of armed conflict is known as an "international armed conflict" because it takes place between States. However, a state of war can exist when States are not on opposite sides of the conflict. These other types of conflict are described as "not of an international character" or "non-international armed conflict." For example, two non-State armed groups warring against one another or States warring against non-State armed groups may be described as "non-international armed conflict," even if international borders are crossed in the fighting. . . .

. . .

3.4.1.2 *Non-State Armed Groups with the Intention of Conducting Hostilities.* A non-State armed group, such as a rebel group, might also intend to conduct hostilities. Non-State armed groups are similarly bound by the restrictions in the law of war for the conduct of hostilities when they intend to conduct hostilities. However, in contrast to States, non-State armed groups lack *competent authority.* Thus, there would not be a basis for non-State armed groups to claim the permissions that may be viewed as inherent in parts of the law of war. For example, members of a non-State group may be subject to prosecution under a State's domestic law for their participation in hostilities against it.

. . .

3.4.2.2 *Distinguishing Armed Conflict from Internal Disturbances and Tensions.* In assessing whether de facto hostilities exist for the purpose of applying *jus in bello* restrictions, situations of internal disturbances and tensions, such as riots, isolated and sporadic acts of violence, and other acts of a similar nature do not amount to armed conflict.

Any hostile action between the armed forces of different States (*i.e.,* international armed conflict) may readily be distinguished from an "internal disturbance or tension." However, it has been more difficult to distinguish "armed conflict not of an international character" from "internal disturbances or tensions."

"Armed conflict not of an international character" for the purpose of applying the obligations in Common Article 3 of the 1949 Geneva Conventions was not specifically defined in those conventions. There has been a range of views on what constitutes an "armed conflict not of an international character" for this purpose. The intensity of the conflict and the organization of the parties are criteria that have been assessed to distinguish between non-international armed conflict and "internal disturbances and tensions." A variety of factors have been considered in assessing these criteria and in seeking to distinguish between armed conflict and internal disturbances and tensions.

A helpful rule of thumb may be that where parties are, in fact, engaged in activities that the law of war contemplates (e.g., detention of enemy military personnel without criminal charge, bombardment of military objectives), those activities are subject to the law of war.

A determination by the United States that it is engaged in an "armed conflict," whether international (inter-state) or non-international (against a non-state organized armed group), is profoundly significant because it brings into force a body of law normally inapplicable to protect national security interests. That law includes numerous humanitarian constraints, but also provides authority to use force as a measure of first resort against any individuals assessed as being members of enemy armed forces or members of the belligerent wing of an organized armed group (unless those individuals have been captured or disabled by wounds or sickness). Furthermore, unlike a use of force in a law enforcement operation, these individuals are not protected by any proportionality limitation, meaning U.S. armed forces are not legally obligated to employ the least-harmful measures to subdue such individuals (for more on this, see Geoffrey Corn, Laurie Blank, Eric Jensen & Chris Jenks, *Belligerent Targeting and the Invalidity of a Least Harmful Means Rule*, 9 INT'L L. STUD. 536 (2013)).

The following extract from a Department of Justice Memorandum on the legality of lethal attack against U.S. citizens associated with al Qaeda highlights why crossing this line is so legally significant. That U.S. citizen was Anwar al-Aulaqi, assessed by the United States as an al Qaeda militant, teacher, and recruiter, most notably known for directing Umar Farouk Abdulmutallab to blow up a U.S. commercial transatlantic flight with an underwear bomb in 2009 (the attack failed and Abdulmutallab was sentenced by a federal court to life in prison).

On September 30, 2011, Anwar al-Aulaqi was killed in a drone strike in northern Yemen.

From the Memorandum for the Attorney General

. . . Based on the combination of facts presented to us, we conclude that DoD would carry out its operation as part of the non-international armed conflict between the United States and al-Qaida, and thus that on those facts the operation would comply with international law so long as DoD would conduct it in accord with the applicable laws of war that govern targeting in such a conflict.

In *Hamdan v. Rumsfeld*, the Supreme Court held that the United States is engaged in a non-international armed conflict with al-Qaida. In so holding, the Court rejected the argument that non-international armed conflicts are limited to civil wars and other internal conflicts between a state and an internal non-state armed group that are confined to the territory of the state itself; it held instead that a conflict between a transnational non-state actor and a nation, occurring outside that nation's territory, is an armed conflict "not of an international character" because it is not a "clash between nations."

Here, unlike in *Hamdan*, the contemplated DoD operation would occur in Yemen, a location that is far from the most active theater of combat between the United States and al-Qaida. That does not affect our conclusion, however, that the combination of facts present here would make the DoD operation in Yemen part of the non-international armed conflict with al-Qaida. To be sure, *Hamdan* did not directly address the geographic scope of the non-international armed conflict between the United States and al-Qaida that the Court recognized, other than to implicitly hold that it extended to Afghanistan, where Hamdan was apprehended. The Court did, however, specifically reject the argument that non-international armed conflicts are necessarily limited to internal conflicts. The Common Article 3 term "conflict not of an international character," the Court explained, bears its "literal meaning"—namely, that it is a conflict that "does not involve a clash between nations." The Court referenced the statement in the 1949 ICRC Commentary on the Additional Protocols to the Geneva Conventions that a non-international armed conflict "is distinct from an international armed conflict because of the legal status of the entities opposing each other[.]" The Court explained that this interpretation—that the nature of the conflict depends at least in part on the status of the parties, rather than simply on the locations in which they fight—in turn accords with the view expressed in the commentaries to the Geneva Conventions that "the scope of application" of Common Article 3, which establishes basic protections that govern conflicts not of an international character, "must be as wide as possible."

Invoking the principle that for purposes of international law an armed conflict generally exists only when there is "protracted armed violence between governmental authorities and armed groups," some commentators have suggested that the conflict between the United States and al-Qaida cannot extend to nations outside Afghanistan in which the level of hostilities is less intense or prolonged than in Afghanistan itself. There is little judicial or other authoritative precedent that speaks directly to the question of the geographic scope of a non-international armed conflict in which one of the parties is a transnational, non-state actor and where the principal theater of operations is not within the territory of the nation that is a party to the conflict. Thus, in considering this issue, we must look to principles and statements from analogous contexts, recognizing that they were articulated without consideration of the particular factual circumstances of the sort of conflict at issue here.

In looking for such guidance, we have not come across any authority for the proposition that when one of the parties to an armed conflict plans and executes operations from a base in a new nation, an operation to engage the enemy in that location can never be part of the original armed conflict—and thus subject to the laws of war governing that conflict—unless and until the hostilities become sufficiently intensive and protracted within that new location. . . . [W]e think the determination of whether a particular operation would be part of an ongoing armed conflict for purposes of international law requires consideration of the particular facts and circumstances present in each case. Such an inquiry may be particularly appropriate in a conflict of the sort here, given that the parties to it include transnational non-state organizations that are dispersed and that thus may have no single site serving as their base of operations.

We also find some support for this view in an argument the United States made to the International Criminal Tribunal for Yugoslavia (ICTY) in 1995. To be sure, the United States was there confronting a question, and a conflict, quite distinct from those we address here. Nonetheless, in that case the United States argued that in determining *which* body of humanitarian law applies in a particular conflict, "the conflict must be considered as a whole," and that "it is artificial and improper to attempt to divide it into isolated segments, either geographically or chronologically, in an attempt to exclude the application of [the relevant] rules." . . .

For present purposes, in applying the more context-specific approach to determining whether an operation would take place within the scope of a particular armed conflict, it is sufficient that the facts as they have been represented to us here, in combination, support the judgment that DoD's operation in Yemen would be conducted as part of the non-international armed conflict between the United States and al-Qaida. Specifically, DoD proposes to target a leader of AQAP, an organized enemy force that is either a component of al-Qaida or that is a co-belligerent of that central party to the conflict and engaged in hostilities against the United States as part of the same comprehensive armed conflict, in league with the principal enemy. . . .

[Later portions of the Attorney General's memorandum are found on page 338, *infra*.]

C. Regulating the Conduct of Hostilities: "Targeting" Law

When the political leadership of the United States decides that the United States is engaged in an armed conflict, it indicates U.S. armed forces will be authorized to use the full range of their lethal combat power to bring an enemy into submission or otherwise produce strategic outcomes favorable to the nation. It is therefore axiomatic that armed conflict will involve consequential decisions on who, what, when, where, and how to attack enemy forces and their resources. The law of armed conflict, or LOAC, provides a legal framework that guides these "targeting" decisions. This framework was largely customary in nature until 1977, when many of the rules were codified in a treaty that supplemented the four Geneva Conventions of 1949: Additional Protocol I. While the United States is not a party to this treaty, the United States considers almost all of the "targeting" rules codified in this treaty as customary international law and incorporates them into military directives, manuals, and rules of engagement.

The following excerpt summarizes the most significant of these LOAC rules, treated by the United States as applicable to any armed conflict, whether international or non-international in character.

National Security Law in the News: A Guide for Journalists, Scholars, and Policymakers[6]
Chapter 6: The Laws of War Regulating the Use of Force
By Geoffrey S. Corn and Laurie R. Blank

* * *

Core LOAC Principles: The Foundation of Conflict Regulation

As reflected in the preamble to the 1899 Hague Convention IV, one of the first multilateral international agreements regulating armed conflict, the LOAC in many ways rests on the "desire to diminish the evils of war":

---

6. Footnotes have been omitted from this excerpt but are available in the original text.

[I]n cases not covered by the attached regulations, the belligerents remain under the protection and the rule of the principles of the laws of nations as derived from the usages established among civilized people, the laws of humanity and the dictates of the public conscience.

Known as the Martens clause, this statement provides additional support for the proposition that no conflict can be permitted to fall outside the regulation of the foundational principles of the laws of war. These principles provide the foundation for and add meaning to more specific treaty rules. After more than a century of codifying customary rules in the form of treaties, today there is an extensive body of treaty law regulating armed conflict. These treaties fall into two broad categories: The Hague tradition and the Geneva tradition.

The Hague tradition focuses on the regulation of the means (weapons and ammunition) and methods (tactics) of warfare: for example, prohibiting certain types of weapons (like chemical or biological weapons) and defining who and what qualifies as a legitimate target in warfare. The Geneva tradition focuses on the protection of war victims—individuals who are not actively participating in hostilities but are negatively impacted by armed conflict. Thus, each of the four Geneva Conventions of 1949 is devoted to the protection of a distinct category of war victim (the wounded and sick in the field; the wounded, sick, and shipwrecked at sea; prisoners of war; and civilians under the control of an enemy power).

Understanding the core principles upon which the entire LOAC regulatory regime is built will illuminate the framework of conflict regulation. Indeed, for U.S. armed forces (and the armed forces of many other nations), these principles extend even beyond the context of armed conflict to guide the planning and execution of other types of military operations (such as peacekeeping missions). While General William T. Sherman's notorious statement that "war is hell" no longer reflects the moral underpinnings of the LOAC, it has and will always reflect the reality of the battlefield. The LOAC's principles thus provide the proverbial azimuth points that guide warriors through the moral abyss of mortal combat. Effective training is the foundation for success in combat; training that must prepare combatants not only for the difficult task of inflicting violence on demand, but also for the equally difficult task of doing so within the limits of the law developed to regulate hostilities and mitigate the suffering associated with war.

Military Necessity: The First Principle of Authority

Military necessity "justifies those measures not forbidden by international law which are indispensable for securing the complete submission of the enemy as soon as possible." Accordingly, military necessity supplies the authority to employ those measures necessary to bring an enemy to submission, including the application of deadly combat power, and to capture and detain enemy personnel until the end of hostilities or until they no longer present a threat. However, the principle also provides an essential constraint on the authority of armed forces. Military necessity therefore reflects a balance between the authority to inflict harm and the obligation to limit suffering that lies at the very core of combat regulation. This balance is reflected in Napoleon's great maxim, "in politics and war alike, every injury done to the enemy, even though permitted by the rules, is excusable only so far as it is absolutely necessary; everything beyond that is criminal."

Critically, military necessity does not justify departures from the LOAC. Up through World War II, some nations viewed military necessity as a "trump card" for all other humanitarian constraints. A German doctrine called *Kriegsraison* asserted that war could justify any measures—even in violation of the laws of war—when the necessities of any particular situation purportedly justified it. However, "[w]ar crimes trials after World War II clearly rejected this view. Military necessity cannot justify actions absolutely prohibited by law, as the means to achieve military victory are not unlimited. Armed conflict must be carried on within the limits set by International Law."

Humanity: The First Principle of Constraint

The principle of humanity provides an essential counter-balance to the authority associated with defeating an enemy in armed conflict. In practice, the principle of humanity provides the foundation for two critical limits on the authority to inflict suffering in the context of armed conflict: first, the prohibition against subjecting an opponent to superfluous injury or unnecessary suffering (injury or suffering beyond that which is necessary to bring about the opponent's prompt submission); and second, the obligation to ensure the humane treatment of any person (even a captured enemy) who is no longer or never was actively participating in armed hostilities. The LOAC fully synchronizes the principles of humanity and military necessity by excluding from the measures justified by military necessity anything that violates the principle of humanity.

This principle is the central focus of the four Geneva Conventions of 1949 and is implemented through numerous LOAC treaty provisions. These include the prohibition against the use of any type of coercion against a prisoner of war or civilian internee; the obligation to search for and collect the wounded and sick and ensure that priority of medical care is based solely on medical considerations; the obligation to search for and collect the shipwrecked at sea; the obligation to provide notice of capture of enemy personnel to the enemy state through a neutral intermediary; the obligation to facilitate the efforts of neutral relief agencies; the extensive immunities from attack afforded to places engaged in medical functions; and even the obligation to maintain and record the location of interment of the enemy dead.

Common Article 3 extended the principle of humanity to non-international armed conflicts in 1949, leading to a general symmetry in the application of the principle of humanity to both inter-state and intra-state armed conflicts. This symmetry is consistent with the universally accepted view that humane treatment is a fundamental principle found at the very core of the Geneva tradition of protecting victims of war in all situations of hostilities.

The principle of humanity also protects participants in hostilities, but to a much more limited extent, prohibiting the use of weapons or tactics that cause unnecessary suffering. However, it is essential to note that inherent within this protection is the assumption that war involves the infliction of substantial necessary suffering. What then is the scope of this protection? It really comes down to one word: superfluous. War—military necessity to be more precise—justifies the infliction of suffering on an opponent, but only that amount of suffering necessary to subdue an enemy force. Today, this concept prohibits parties engaged in hostilities from inflicting superfluous injury or unnecessary suffering on their battlefield opponents—injuries that exceed those necessary for bringing about prompt submission. In this regard, it is critical to understand that "prompt submission" applies to the enemy force in the corporate sense, not individual enemy soldiers. Accordingly, it is not impermissible to employ overwhelming combat power at the decisive place and time of battle to overwhelm enemy forces in order to influence the overall capacity of the enemy writ large. This principle does, however, prohibit armed forces from employing "weapons, projectiles and material, and methods of warfare of a nature to cause superfluous injury or unnecessary suffering."

Over time, it has become apparent that reaching consensus on what weapons and tactics violate this prohibition is extremely difficult. As a result, the modern trend has been to identify particular weapon systems—such as chemical and biological weapons and antipersonnel mines—and develop treaties for the exclusive purpose of prohibiting their production, stockpile, or use (the United States did not join the antipersonnel landmine ban, however, based on the determination that technology of our self-neutralizing landmines sufficiently mitigated the risk of collateral casualties and because of the perceived operational importance of being able to utilize this weapon in future conflicts).

Distinction

The principle of distinction requires that combatants always differentiate between lawful objects of attack and all other persons, places, and things in the battle space. Pursuant to this principle, combat power may be deliberately directed only against lawful objects of attack. This principle therefore operates to protect innocent individuals and their property (i.e., individuals and property not actively contributing to enemy military operations) from being made the deliberate object of attack, and ensures that the application of combat power is restricted to targets that contribute to the submission of an opponent's military capability.

In operational terms, the principle of distinction enables commanders to determine what is and is not a lawful target. A target is a person, place, or thing made the object of attack by a military force. The target selection and engagement process begins with the military mission. Operational planners then determine how to best leverage the capabilities of their military units to achieve the effects deemed necessary to accomplish the mission, including destruction, neutralization, denial, harassment, and disruption. Distinction thus mandates that only targets that are lawful military objectives can be attacked.

The principle of distinction thus rests on two presumptions: military personnel, equipment, and facilities are lawful objects of attack; all other persons, places, or things are immune from attack. However, neither of these presumptions is conclusive. A member of the enemy armed forces who surrenders is no longer the lawful object of attack for the obvious reason that disabling him by attack is no longer justified by military necessity. A civilian who takes up arms and engages in hostilities against military forces is no longer immune from attack for the equally obvious reason that disabling that civilian is necessary in order to protect allied forces. These presumptions demonstrate that distinction is unquestionably derived from the concept of military necessity. Because the law presumes that deliberately inflicting death or destruction on civilians or civilian property does not contribute to this objective, distinction prohibits combatants from making civilians or civilian property the deliberate objects of attack unless and until they engage in conduct that supports rebutting this presumption of immunity. Analogous rebuttable presumptions apply to places and things, like a hospital being improperly used by enemy forces to launch attacks. Compliance with the principle of distinction obviously requires a definition of what constitutes a lawful military objective. The rule of military objective provides this definition by establishing targets that may be made the lawful objects of attack:

> Attacks shall be limited strictly to military objectives. In so far as objects are concerned, military objectives are limited to those objects which by their nature, location, purpose or use make an effective contribution to military action and whose total or partial destruction, capture or neutralization, in the circumstances ruling at the time, offers a definite military advantage.

Determining whether places or things are, or are not, lawful objects of attack requires a case-by-case analysis of these key factors — nature, location, use and purpose — based on the mission, enemy, troops available, terrain, time, and presence of civilians.

A second, and equally important aspect of distinction is that persons who are fighting (whether soldiers, organized armed groups or others) must distinguish themselves from innocent civilians. Like the prohibition on deliberately targeting civilians, this obligation is central to the LOAC's fundamental goal of protecting civilians in the course of armed conflict. To this end, the LOAC prohibits perfidy, which is when an individual launches an attack while leading the enemy to believe he or she (the attacker) is protected from attack. In other words, an individual cannot pretend to be inoffensive and then attack — such as a suicide bombing by an individual dressed as a local civilian.

Similarly, the LOAC requires that parties to a conflict refrain from locating military objectives in densely populated or civilian areas. As part of this analysis, Article 51 of Additional Protocol I provides that "[t]he presence or movements of the civilian population or individual civilians shall not be used to render certain points or areas immune from military operations, in particular in attempts to shield military objectives from attacks or to shield, favour or impede military operations." Pursuant to this rule, the presence of civilians in or around what qualifies as a military objective does not "immunize" the thing or area from attack. Instead, the operational decision-maker is obligated to analyze the legality of the attack pursuant to the complimentary prohibition against engaging in indiscriminate attacks, and assess whether the expected harm to civilians, or civilian property, will be excessive in relation to the concrete and direct military advantage anticipated (commonly referred to as the proportionality analysis and discussed in greater detail below).

Proportionality

The almost inevitable presence of civilians and civilian property in areas of armed hostilities has produced an ever-increasing risk that the effects of combat operations will extend beyond lawful military objectives and impact these civilians and their property. Because of this reality, it is universally recognized that the principle of military objective is insufficient to provide adequate protection for civilians from the harmful effects of hostilities. During the twentieth century, hundreds of thousands of civilians became victims of war, not as the result of a decision to deliberately target them, but as the result of the collateral effects of attacks on lawful military objectives.

The principle of proportionality responds to this reality. Legality of attack is not automatic even after determining that a person, place, or thing satisfies the military objective test. The principle of proportionality imposes an obligation on combatants to refrain from attacks on targets that qualify as lawful military objectives when the expected loss of life and damage to property will be excessive in relation to the *concrete and direct* military advantage anticipated to be gained.

Proportionality is not a separate legal standard as such, but provides a means by which military commanders can balance military necessity against the protection of non-combatants in circumstances when they believe an attack is likely to cause incidental damage to civilian personnel or property. However, it is important to note that an attack does not become indiscriminate when the collateral damage or incidental injury is slightly greater than the military advantage anticipated (as is suggested by the term "disproportionate"), but only when those effects are excessive.

The principle of proportionality requires commanders to balance the anticipated effects of an attack. The two critical components of this balance are the anticipated military advantage to be gained by attacking a lawful target, and the expected collateral damage and incidental injury to civilians and civilian property. There are no established numerical equations or ratios for applying this rule, which by its very nature requires case-by-case analysis of the key factors of Mission, Enemy, Troops, Terrain, Time, and Civilians. Any critique regarding application of this rule must be based on this reality and must therefore be made through the subjective perspective of the commander at the time the targeting decision was made. All facts and circumstances available to the commander, including the pressures of time and the proverbial "fog of war," must be considered when rendering an objective assessment of the validity of a targeting decision.

. . .

In the same speech by the Department of State Legal Advisor referenced earlier in the chapter, Mr. Egan also emphasized U.S. commitment to international law regulating armed conflict, the *jus in bello*, and that this commitment extended to all armed conflicts, no matter the nature of the enemy. Mr. Egan noted that the United States considers the armed conflict against ISIS to be "non-international" in nature, and then summarized the key rules of international law applicable to our operations in that conflict:

> The rules applicable in NIACs [non-international armed conflicts] have received close scrutiny since the September 11 attacks within the U.S. Government, in our courts in the context of ongoing litigation concerning detention and military commission prosecutions, and in the expanding and ever more sophisticated treatment that these issues receive in academia. I would like to clarify briefly some of the rules that the United States is bound to comply with as a matter of international law in the conduct of hostilities during NIACs. In particular, I'd like to spend a few minutes walking through some of the targeting rules that the United States regards as customary international law applicable to all parties in a NIAC:
>
> ▪ First, parties must distinguish between military objectives, including combatants, on the one hand, and civilians and civilian objects on the other. Only military objectives, including combatants, may be made the object of attack.
> ▪ Insofar as objects are concerned, military objectives are those objects which by their nature, location, purpose or use make an effective contribution to military action and whose total or partial destruction, capture or neutralization, in the circumstances ruling at the time, offers a definite military advantage. The United States has interpreted this definition to include objects that make an effective contribution to the enemy's war-fighting or war-sustaining capabilities.
> ▪ Feasible precautions must be taken in conducting an attack to reduce the risk of harm to civilians, such as, in certain circumstances, warnings to civilians before bombardments.
> ▪ Customary international law also specifically prohibits a number of targeting measures in NIACs. First, attacks directed against civilians or civilian objects as such are prohibited. Additionally, indiscriminate attacks, including but not limited to attacks using inherently indiscriminate weapons, are prohibited.
> ▪ Attacks directed against specifically protected objects such as cultural property and hospitals are also prohibited unless their protection has been forfeited.
> ▪ Also prohibited are attacks that violate the principle of proportionality—that is, attacks against combatants or other military objectives that are expected to cause incidental harm to civilians that would be excessive in relation to the concrete and direct military advantage anticipated.
> ▪ Moreover, acts or threats of violence the primary purpose of which is to spread terror among the civilian population are prohibited.

Brian Egan, *International Law, Legal Diplomacy, and the Counter-ISIL Campaign: Some Observations*, 92 Int'l L. Stud. 235, 242-43 (2016).

DIRECT PARTICIPATION IN HOSTILITIES VERSUS
STATUS-BASED TARGETING

While civilians enjoy immunity from attack, they lose such protection from direct attack in both international and non-international armed conflicts when they "directly participate in hostilities." The determination of what constitutes such participation has taken on great significance in modern armed conflicts, due to both the increasing use of civilian contractors, and to the practice of non-state armed groups who both fail to distinguish themselves from civilians and choose to engage in operations in civilian urban centers.

Regarding non-state armed groups: To be identified as targetable by opposing forces during a NIAC, individuals must either be assessed as engaging in direct participation in hostilities (DPH), or as a someone who has attained the status of membership in the non-state armed group. This latter, status-based targeting authority based on membership (versus conduct at the time of attack) is drawn by analogy to states' armed forces in IACs, and the LOAC's recognition that members of such forces are presumptively military objectives based purely on that status — due to the member's agency relationship to the state. Even the ICRC has acknowledged the LOAC legality of such status-based targeting of members of non-state armed groups in NIACs, though its recommended analysis of how to determine said membership (through a restrictive so-called continuous combat function assessment based on regular DPH conduct) remains unaccepted as law, given that group membership can also be based on other approaches, most importantly functional ones.

In contrast to membership, the contours of the other legal basis for making a person an object of attack during armed conflict — direct participation in hostilities — are clearer, though by no means without controversy. Essentially, a civilian directly participates in hostilities when he is acting like a belligerent operative and hence trying to cause harm to the enemy, such as by taking up arms against the enemy. Easy examples include a civilian planting an improvised explosive device on behalf of an armed group who is party to an armed conflict, or running up to a military base during an occupation and setting up a rocket launcher to lob rockets onto the base. Other activities that are classically considered DPH also include re-supplying troops on the front line, engaging in intelligence collection near military operations, acting as a lookout on behalf of armed forces, etc.

However, civilians engaged in general war-sustaining activities, such as working in a munitions factory far from the front lines, are not considered to be directly participating in hostilities, though of course the factory itself is a lawful military objective and its civilian workers exposed to targeting effects. Whether a certain activity constitutes direct participation in hostilities is a highly contextual one. For further discussion and analysis, see the DOD Law of War Manual, § 5.8, which states that "[t]aking a direct part in hostilities extends beyond merely engaging in combat and also includes certain acts that are an integral part of combat operations or that effectively and substantially contribute to an adversary's ability to conduct or sustain combat operations."

D. Rules of Engagement

DISTINGUISHING BETWEEN LAW AND POLICY: UNDERSTANDING RULES OF ENGAGEMENT

No understanding of the LOAC and how it impacts the planning and execution of military operations would be complete without an examination of the relationship between this law and rules of engagement, commonly referred to as ROE. Although the LOAC and ROE are inextricably connected, they are not synonymous, but are instead two distinct sources of operational regulation.

As defined in U.S. military doctrine, ROE are "directives issued by competent military authority that delineate the circumstances and limitations under which United States forces will initiate and/or continue combat engagement with other forces encountered." In other words, ROE are intended to give operational and tactical military leaders greater control over the execution of combat operations by subordinate forces. The history of warfare is replete with examples of what have essentially been ROE. The Battle of Bunker Hill provides an excellent example of such use. Captain William Prescott imposed a limitation on the use of combat power by his forces in the form of the directive, "don't shoot until you see the whites of their eyes." Given his limited resources against a much larger and better-equipped foe, he used this tactical control measure to maximize the effect of his firepower. This example of what was, in effect, a ROE is remembered to this day for one primary reason — it enabled the colonial militia to maximize enemy casualties.

Contemporary military operations increasingly manifest the operational necessity for similar constraints on the otherwise lawful scope of the use of force authority. As a result, ROE have become a key aspect of modern warfare and a key component of mission planning for U.S. and many other armed forces. In preparation for military operations, the President and/or Secretary of Defense personally review and approve the ROE, ensuring they meet the military and political objectives. Ideally, ROE represent the confluence of three important factors: operational requirements, national policy, and the LOAC.

It is particularly important to note that while ROE are not coterminous with the LOAC, they must be completely consistent with it. In other words, while some aspects of the LOAC do not impact a mission's ROE, all ROE must comply with this law . . . it is common for the authority provided by the ROE to be more limited than the LOAC's parameters. For example, in order to provide greater protection against collateral injury to civilians, the ROE may require that the engagement of a clearly defined military objective in a populated area is authorized only when the target is under direct observation. This is a fundamental principle and key to the proper formation and application of ROE. In fact, the preeminent U.S. ROE order explicitly directs U.S. forces that they "will comply with the Law of Armed Conflict during military operations involving armed conflict, no matter how the conflict may be characterized under international law, and will comply with the principles and spirit of the Law of Armed Conflict during all other operations." Note that this directive applies to any "armed conflict," and not only to international armed conflicts.

To illustrate the interaction between ROE and the law of armed conflict, consider a ROE provision that allows a soldier to kill an enemy. Although this provision is completely appropriate, it does not implicitly include the authority to kill an enemy who is surrendering because such conduct would violate the law of armed conflict. Similarly, if the ROE allows for a pilot to destroy a bridge with a bomb, it does not relieve the pilot of his responsibility to terminate the attack if she believes it will violate the principle of proportionality, as explained above. ROE will also often contain provisions that remind soldiers that they can only engage the enemy, or other individuals, that engage in defined conduct endangering soldiers or others. In this way, ROE ensures compliance with the laws of war.

Appreciating this interrelationship is therefore vital to understanding why the violation of a constraint imposed by a specific ROE, or even customarily imposed by ROE, does not *ipso facto* establish violation of the LOAC. To assess that apparent discrepancy, it is necessary to determine whether the ROE constraint was coterminous with the LOAC, or more restrictive than the scope of permissible authority established by the LOAC. In contemporary military operations, it is common for ROE to be more restrictive than the LOAC in order to satisfy policy considerations related to the application of combat power.

E. Legal Status of Captured Enemy Operatives: Who Receives Combatant Immunity Versus Criminal Prosecution?

The law of armed conflict also regulates the treatment of individuals who do not participate in hostilities, or who can no longer participate due to wounds, sickness, or capture. In very general terms, dealing with such individuals implicates four broad areas of legal concern: the authority to detain both captured enemy personnel and civilians who pose a threat to U.S. forces; the process required to justify detention; the treatment of detainees and other individuals subject to the control of U.S. forces; and the authority to criminally punish captured individuals for pre-capture misconduct.

Detention of captured enemy belligerents implicates complex issues of both detention authority and detention process, both of which are addressed in Chapter 11. Sometimes, however, the United States will seek to prosecute a captured enemy operative for violations of domestic and/or international law committed prior to capture. These individuals may invoke the concept of "combatant immunity" to block such prosecution. When this immunity is applicable to an enemy captive is thus an important national security issue. Consider the excerpt below, and then the court's ruling in the case of John Walker Lindh, the "American Taliban."

National Security Law in the News: A Guide for Journalists, Scholars, and Policymakers[7]
Chapter 6: The Laws of War Regulating the Use of Force
By Geoffrey S. Corn and Laurie R. Blank

The LOAC categorizes persons in international armed conflict as combatants or civilians. Combatants have the right to participate in hostilities and—as a result—are lawful targets of attack at all times, except when wounded or detained. Upon capture, combatants enjoy POW status. The principle of combatant immunity is based on the premise that because soldiers fight as agents of their respective states, it is unjust to subject them to criminal liability for executing their duty so long as they do so in compliance with the LOAC. Accordingly, if captured by an enemy, the enemy state may not criminally prosecute such prisoners for their lawful pre-capture conduct, even when that conduct was harmful to the capturing state. As General Telford Taylor stated at Nuremberg,

> War consists largely of acts that would be criminal if performed in time of peace—killing, wounding, kidnapping, destroying or carrying off other people's property. Such conduct is not regarded as criminal if it takes place in the course of war, because the state of war lays a blanket of immunity over the warriors.

For soldiers, this is perhaps the most important benefit associated with the status of prisoner of war (POW). However, only individuals who qualify as "privileged belligerents"—individuals legally entitled to participate in armed conflict pursuant to the laws and customs of war—are combatants and may claim combatant immunity (sometimes referred to as the combatants' privilege). A privileged belligerent is a person who qualifies for status as a POW upon capture. There are several critical requirements that must be met to qualify for POW status and the accordant combatant immunity. First, combatant immunity only applies in international armed conflict, because the Third Geneva Convention Relative to the Treatment of Prisoners of War only applies in such conflicts. Second, only individuals fighting under state authority may qualify for POW status. Thus, members of the regular armed forces of a state are combatants. Members of regular militia belonging to a state party to the conflict may qualify for POW (combatant) status if they satisfy four criteria. These four criteria, incorporated into the Geneva POW Convention and derived from treaties dating back to 1899, are:

1. being commanded by a person responsible for his subordinates;
2. having a fixed distinctive sign recognizable at a distance;
3. carrying arms openly; and
4. conducting their operations in accordance with the laws and customs of war.

Members of insurgent groups or other non-state groups are never entitled to combatant immunity because they do not operate pursuant to state authority.

---

7. Footnotes have been omitted from this excerpt but are available in the original text.

Captured enemy belligerent personnel who fail to meet these requirements are not POWs, although in U.S. practice they will nonetheless be detained to prevent their return to hostilities. In addition, because they are not POWs they are not protected by combatant immunity and may be prosecuted for their pre-capture wartime conduct. It is also important to note that combatant immunity is not absolute and extends only to wartime conduct that complies with the LOAC. Wartime conduct in violation of the LOAC subjects the individual to war crimes liability, even when the individual qualifies as a POW.

The following opinion illustrates the criminal liability consequence for an individual captured by the United States during an armed conflict classified as a belligerent who fails to qualify for POW status. As the opinion notes, the status of such captives is determined pursuant to the Geneva Convention Relative to the Treatment of Prisoners of War, which provides in Article 4:

A. Prisoners of war, in the sense of the present Convention, are persons belonging to one of the following categories, who have fallen into the power of the enemy:

(1) Members of the armed forces of a Party to the conflict as well as members of militias or volunteer corps forming part of such armed forces.

(2) Members of other militias and members of other volunteer corps, including those of organized resistance movements, belonging to a Party to the conflict and operating in or outside their own territory, even if this territory is occupied, provided that such militias or volunteer corps, including such organized resistance movements, fulfil the following conditions:

(a) that of being commanded by a person responsible for his subordinates;

(b) that of having a fixed distinctive sign recognizable at a distance;

(c) that of carrying arms openly;

(d) that of conducting their operations in accordance with the laws and customs of war.

(3) Members of regular armed forces who profess allegiance to a government or an authority not recognized by the Detaining Power.

As you read the opinion, consider two questions. First, did Lindh's claim to POW status turn on the determination by President Bush that the Taliban fought on behalf of Afghanistan? Second, is there a plausible argument that Lindh qualifies as a POW even if he and his unit failed to satisfy the four conditions of Article 4A(2)?

United States v. Lindh

212 F. Supp. 2d 541 (E.D. Va. 2002)

MEMORANDUM OPINION

ELLIS, District Judge.

John Phillip Walker Lindh ("Lindh") is an American citizen who, according to the ten-count Indictment filed against him in February 2002, joined certain foreign terrorist organizations in Afghanistan and served these organizations there in combat against Northern Alliance and American forces until his capture in November 2001. In seven threshold motions, Lindh sought dismissal of certain counts of the Indictment on a variety of grounds, including lawful combatant immunity and selective prosecution. . . .

I.

The Indictment's allegations may be succinctly summarized. In mid-2001, Lindh attended a military training camp in Pakistan run by Harakat ul-Mujahideen ("HUM"), a terrorist group dedicated to an extremist view of Islam. After receiving several weeks of training, Lindh informed HUM officials that "he wished to fight with the Taliban in Afghanistan." Indictment. p. 6, ¶ 5. Thus, in May or June 2001, he traveled from Pakistan into Afghanistan "for the purpose of taking up arms with the Taliban," eventually arriving at a Taliban recruiting center in Kabul, Afghanistan—the Dar ul-Anan Headquarters of the Mujahideen. Indictment, p. 7, ¶ 6. On his arrival, Lindh presented a letter of introduction from HUM and advised Taliban personnel "that he was an American and that he wanted to go to the front lines to fight." Indictment, p. 7, ¶ 7.

While at the Dar ul-Anan Headquarters, Lindh agreed to receive additional and extensive military training at an al Qaeda training camp. He made this decision "knowing that America and its citizens were the enemies of Bin Laden and al-Qaeda and that a principal purpose of al-Qaeda was to fight and kill Americans." . . .

When Lindh completed his training at al Farooq in July or August 2001, he traveled to Kabul, Afghanistan, where he was issued an AKM rifle "with a barrel suitable for long range shooting." Indictment, p. 8, ¶ 16. Armed with this rifle, Lindh, together with approximately 150 non-Afghani fighters, traveled from Kabul to the front line at Takhar, located in Northeastern Afghanistan, where the entire unit was placed under the command of an Iraqi named Abdul Hady. Lindh's group was eventually divided into smaller groups that fought in shifts against Northern Alliance troops in the Takhar trenches, rotating every one to two weeks. . . . [I]t is specifically alleged that Lindh remained with his fighting group from October to December 2001, "after learning that United States military forces and United States nationals had become directly engaged in support of the Northern Alliance in its military conflict with Taliban and al Qaeda forces." Indictment, p. 9, ¶ 21.

In November 2001, Lindh . . . surrendered to Northern Alliance troops. On November 24, 2001, he and the other captured Taliban fighters were transported to . . . Qala-i-Janghi (QIJ) prison compound. The following day, November 25, Lindh was interviewed by two Americans—Agent Johnny Micheal Spann from the Central Intelligence Agency (CIA) and another government employee. Later that day, it is alleged that Taliban detainees in the QIJ compound attacked Spann and the other employee, overpowered the guards, and armed themselves. Spann was shot and killed in the course of the uprising and Lindh, after being wounded, retreated with other detainees to a basement area of the QIJ compound. The uprising at QIJ was eventually suppressed on December 1, 2001, at which time Lindh and other Taliban and al Qaeda fighters were taken into custody by Northern Alliance and American forces.

[Lindh was charged in Count 1 of a ten-count indictment with conspiracy to murder U.S. nationals, government employees, and military personnel in Afghanistan following the 9/11 attacks.]

III.

Lindh claims that Count One of the Indictment should be dismissed because, as a Taliban soldier, he was a lawful combatant entitled to the affirmative defense of lawful combatant immunity.

Lawful combatant immunity, a doctrine rooted in the customary international law of war, forbids prosecution of soldiers for their lawful belligerent acts committed during the course of armed conflicts against legitimate military targets. Belligerent acts committed in armed conflict by enemy members of the armed forces may be punished as crimes under a belligerent's municipal law only to the extent that they violate international humanitarian law or are unrelated to the armed conflict. This doctrine has a long history, which is reflected in part in various early international conventions, statutes and documents. But more pertinent, indeed controlling, here is that the doctrine also finds expression in the Geneva Convention Relative to the Treatment of Prisoners of War, Aug. 12, 1949. 6 U.S.T. 3316, 75 U.N.T.S. 135 ("GPW"), to which the United States is a signatory. Significantly, Article 87 of the GPW admonishes that combatants "may not be sentenced . . . to any penalties except those provided for in respect of members of the armed forces of the said Power who have committed the same acts." GPW, art. 87. Similarly, Article 99 provides that "[n]o prisoner of war may be tried or sentenced for an act which is not forbidden by the law of the Detaining Power or by international law, in force at the time the said act was committed." GPW, art. 99. These Articles, when read together, make clear that a belligerent in a war cannot prosecute the soldiers of its foes for the soldiers' lawful acts of war.

The inclusion of the lawful combatant immunity doctrine as a part of the GPW is particularly important here given that the GPW, insofar as it is pertinent here, is a self-executing treaty to which the United States is a signatory. It follows from this that the GPW provisions in issue here are a part of American law and thus binding in federal courts under the Supremacy Clause. . . .

Importantly, this lawful combatant immunity is not automatically available to anyone who takes up arms in a conflict. Rather, it is generally accepted that this immunity can be invoked only by members of regular or irregular armed forces who fight on behalf of a state and comply with the requirements for lawful combatants. Thus, it is well-established that

> the law of war draws a distinction between the armed forces and the peaceful populations of belligerent nations and also between those who are lawful and unlawful combatants. Lawful combatants are subject to capture and detention as prisoners of war by opposing military forces. Unlawful combatants are likewise subject to capture and detention, but in addition they are subject to trial and punishment by military tribunals for acts which render their belligerency unlawful.

> *Ex Parte Quirin,* 317 U.S. 1, 30-31, 63 S. Ct. 2, 87 L. Ed. 3 (1942) (footnote omitted).

The GPW also reflects this distinction between lawful and unlawful combatants, with only the former eligible for immunity from prosecution. *See* GPW, art. 87, 99. Thus, the question presented here is whether Lindh is a lawful combatant entitled to immunity under the GPW.

The starting point in the analysis of Lindh's immunity claim is recognition that the President has unequivocally determined that Lindh, as a member of the Taliban, is an unlawful combatant and, as such, may not invoke lawful combatant immunity. On February 7, 2002, the White House announced the President's decision, as Commander-in-Chief, that the Taliban militia were unlawful combatants pursuant to GPW and general principles of international law, and, therefore, they were not entitled to POW status under the Geneva Conventions. This presidential determination, according to the government, is significant, indeed decisive, because the President, as the "Commander in Chief of the Army and Navy of the United States," has broad constitutional power to issue such a determination. Moreover, in the current conflict, he has also been "authorized" by Congress "to use all necessary and appropriate force against those nations, organizations, or persons he determines planned, authorized, committed, or aided the terrorist attacks that occurred on September 11, 2001, or harbored such organizations or persons." Authorization for Use of Military Force, Pub. L. No. 107-40, § 2, 115 Stat. 224 (2001). Thus, the government argues, the decision of the President to use force against the Taliban and al Qaeda, as endorsed by Congress, represents the exercise of the full extent of his constitutional presidential authority. It follows, the government contends, that the President's determination that Taliban members are unlawful combatants was made pursuant to his constitutional Commander-in-Chief and foreign affairs powers and is therefore not subject to judicial review or second guessing because it involves a quintessentially nonjusticiable political question.

This argument, while not without appeal, is ultimately unpersuasive. Because the consequence of accepting a political question argument is so significant—judicial review is completely foreclosed—courts must subject such arguments to searching scrutiny, for it is central to the rule of law in our constitutional system that federal courts must, in appropriate circumstances, review or second guess, and indeed sometimes even trump, the actions of the other governmental branches. At a minimum, this scrutiny requires careful consideration of whether the circumstances that trigger the application of the political question doctrine are present here. Thus, it is difficult to see, except at the highest level of abstraction, a textually demonstrable constitutional commitment regarding this issue. Moreover, it is difficult to see why the application of the GPW's lawful combatant immunity doctrine to Lindh's case involves a lack of judicially discoverable and manageable standards. Indeed, the contrary appears to be true. The presence of any remaining factors is also doubtful. To sum up briefly then, while it may be argued that some of the triggering circumstances for a political question are present to some degree here, others plainly are not and thus the government's political question argument is ultimately unpersuasive. Understandably and appropriately, therefore, courts have recognized that treaty interpretation does not implicate the political question doctrine and is not a subject beyond judicial review.

This, however, does not end the analysis, for it remains important to determine the precise nature of judicial review that is appropriate here, including, in particular, what, if any, respect or effect should be afforded the President's determination that Lindh and the Taliban are not lawful combatants entitled to lawful combatant immunity. The answer to this question may be found both in settled caselaw and in sound principle. Thus, courts have long held that treaty interpretations made by the Executive Branch are entitled to some degree of deference. . . .

It is important to recognize that the deference here is appropriately accorded not only to the President's interpretation of any ambiguity in the treaty, but also to the President's application of the treaty to the facts in issue. Again, this is warranted given the President's special competency in, and constitutional responsibility for, foreign affairs and the conduct of overseas military operations. . . . [T]he appropriate deference is to accord substantial or great weight to the President's decision regarding the interpretation and application of the GPW to Lindh, provided the interpretation and application of the treaty to Lindh may be said to be reasonable and not contradicted by the terms of the treaty or the facts. It is this proviso that is the focus of the judicial review here of the President's determination that Lindh is an unlawful combatant under the GPW.

The GPW sets forth four criteria an organization must meet for its members to qualify for lawful combatant status:

i. the organization must be commanded by a person responsible for his subordinates;
ii. the organization's members must have a fixed distinctive emblem or uniform recognizable at a distance;
iii. the organization's members must carry arms openly; and
iv. the organization's members must conduct their operations in accordance with the laws and customs of war.

See GPW, art. 4(A)(2). Nor are these four criteria unique to the GPW: they are also established under customary international law and were also included in the Hague Regulations of 1907. *See* Hague Convention Respecting the Laws and Customs of War on Land, Oct. 18, 1907, 36 Stat. 2277, T.S. No. 539 (Hague Regulations).

In the application of these criteria to the case at bar, it is Lindh who bears the burden of establishing the affirmative defense that he is entitled to lawful combatant immunity, *i.e.*, that the Taliban satisfies the four criteria required for lawful combatant status outlined by the GPW. On this point, Lindh has not carried his burden; indeed, he has made no persuasive showing at all on this point. For this reason alone, it follows that the President's decision denying Lindh lawful combatant immunity is correct. In any event, a review of the available record information leads to the same conclusion. Thus, it appears that the Taliban lacked the command structure necessary to fulfill the first criterion, as it is manifest that the Taliban had no internal system of military command or discipline. . . .

Similarly, it appears the Taliban typically wore no distinctive sign that could be recognized by opposing combatants; they wore no uniforms or insignia and were effectively indistinguishable from the rest of the population. The requirement of such a sign is critical to ensure that combatants may be distinguished from the non-combatant, civilian population. Accordingly, Lindh cannot establish the second criterion.

Next, although it appears that Lindh and his cohorts carried arms openly in satisfaction of the third criterion for lawful combatant status, it is equally apparent that members of the Taliban failed to observe the laws and customs of war. *See* GPW, art. 4(A)(2). Thus, because record evidence supports the conclusion that the Taliban regularly targeted civilian populations in clear contravention of the laws and customs of war, Lindh cannot meet his burden concerning the fourth criterion.

In sum, the President's determination that Lindh is an unlawful combatant and thus ineligible for immunity is controlling here (i) because that determination is entitled to deference as a reasonable interpretation and application of the GPW to Lindh as a Taliban; (ii) because Lindh has failed to carry his burden of demonstrating the contrary; and (iii) because even absent deference, the Taliban falls far short when measured against the four GPW criteria for determining entitlement to lawful combatant immunity.

. . .

NOTES AND QUESTIONS

1. Notice that Lindh asserted, and the government conceded, he was a member of the Taliban armed forces. On that basis alone wasn't he entitled to Prisoner of War status and the accordant combatant immunity? Go back and look at paragraph 4A(1) of the Geneva Prisoner of War Convention cited in the case. Does that paragraph require compliance with the "four criteria" relied on by the court to deny his status?

2. Notice also that the key treaty provision establishing prisoner of war status and the accordant combatant immunity is Article 4 of the Geneva Prisoner of War Convention. That article applies *only* in the context of an international armed conflict. As a result, because Lindh was associated with the Taliban while it was the government of Afghanistan fighting the United States, he was able to assert the immunity. But his al Qaeda counterparts could not because the United States considered its armed conflict with al Qaeda to be "non-international" in nature.

3. The Department of Defense Law of War Manual reflects the same approach to belligerent status and combatant immunity qualification adopted by the *Lindh* court:

> 4.4.3 *Combatants—Legal Immunity from a Foreign State's Domestic Law.* International law affords combatants a special legal immunity from the domestic

law of the enemy State for their actions done in accordance with the law of war. This legal immunity is sometimes called the "combatant's privilege" or "combatant immunity." This means that a combatant's "killing, wounding, or other warlike acts are not individual crimes or offenses," if they are done under military authority and are not prohibited by the law of war. Similarly, a combatant's warlike acts done under military authority and in accordance with the law of war also do not create civil liability.

Combatants lack legal immunity from an enemy State's domestic law for acts that are prohibited by the law of war. Also, combatants lack legal immunity from an enemy State's domestic law while engaging in spying or sabotage. Combatants, however, must receive a fair and regular trial before any punishment.

. . .

4.6.1.1 *GPW 4A(2) Conditions Required on a Group Basis.* The armed group, as a whole, must fulfill these conditions for its members to be entitled to the privileges of combatant status. For example, if a member of an armed group met these requirements, but the armed group did not, that member would not be entitled to the privileges of combatant status. . . .

. . .

4.6.1.3 *Application of GPW 4A(2) Conditions to the Armed Forces of a State.* The text of the GPW does not expressly apply the conditions in Article 4A(2) of the GPW to the armed forces of a State. Thus, under the GPW, members of the armed forces of a State receive combatant status (including its privileges and liabilities) by virtue of their membership in the armed forces of a State. Nonetheless, the GPW 4A(2) conditions were intended to reflect attributes of States' armed forces. If an armed force of a State systematically failed to distinguish itself from the civilian population and to conduct its operations in accordance with the law of war, its members should not expect to receive the privileges afforded lawful combatants. Similarly, members of the armed forces engaged in spying or sabotage forfeit their entitlement to the privileges of combatant status if captured while engaged in those activities.

4. It is important to remember that prisoner of war qualification does not result in *absolute* immunity from prosecution by the detaining power. Combatant immunity extends only to conduct that is lawful pursuant to the law of armed conflict. Indeed, there may be occasions when the United States seeks to prosecute a captive for crimes that fall outside the scope of combatant immunity: crimes that predated the conflict or for war crimes committed during the armed conflict. Combatant immunity would not prohibit such prosecutions. Combatant immunity only protects the "privileged belligerent" (a belligerent qualified for prisoner of war status) from criminal sanction for *lawful* conduct related to the international armed conflict. A war crime prosecution is based on the allegation that the captive committed *unlawful* conduct during an armed conflict: an act or omission in violation of the law of armed conflict. Accordingly, that criminal act or omission falls beyond the scope of combatant immunity. This also means that combatant immunity has no application to acts or omissions committed outside the context of the armed conflict.

Consider the trial and conviction of General Manuel Noriega, captured after the United States invaded Panama in 1989. Noriega was brought to trial for various federal criminal offenses related to narcotics trafficking. All of the alleged crimes occurred *prior to* the armed conflict. Noriega claimed POW status and the trial court issued an order granting him that status. But the same court also concluded that his POW status in no way barred prosecution for *pre-conflict* criminal offenses against U.S. domestic law. Noriega was subsequently convicted and served approximately twenty years in U.S. prison, although he retained his POW status for the duration of his incarceration and was, in accordance with the Geneva POW Convention, granted certain privileges not available to other inmates. *See* Geoffrey S. Corn & Sharon G. Finegan, *America's Longest Held Prisoner of War: Lessons Learned from the Capture, Prosecution, and Extradition of General Manuel Noriega*, 71 LA. L. REV. 1111 (2011).

F. Treatment of Detainees (Regardless Whether Civilian or Belligerent)

Treatment standards applicable to individuals detained by U.S. armed forces are important not only from a purely humanitarian perspective, but also from a strategic perspective. Incidents such as the detainee abuse at Abu Ghraib prison in Iraq and the harsh interrogation methods (what many believe was torture) of al Qaeda detainees authorized by senior members of the Bush Administration negatively impacted U.S. credibility on many fronts. The LOAC provides different "packages" of detainee rights depending on the status of the detainee, with prisoners of war and civilian internees granted the most comprehensive protections. However, as the following excerpt explains, "humane treatment" is the imperative baseline treatment standard for *any* detainee, no matter what status that individual is entitled to pursuant to the Geneva Conventions. The excerpt also explains how U.S. deviation from this baseline treatment standard was corrected in the years following the September 11th attacks.

The Law of Armed Conflict: An Operational Approach[8]
Chapter 10: Detention *By Geoffrey S. Corn et al.*

* * *

C. Treatment in Non-International Armed Conflict

Individuals *hors de combat* (out of combat) detained in the context of non-international armed conflict must, in accordance with Common Article 3, be treated humanely, without any adverse distinction. Although not intended to be exhaustive, Common Article 3 explicitly prohibits the following:

---

8. Footnotes have been omitted from this excerpt but are available in the original text.

(a) violence to life and person, in particular murder of all kinds, mutilation, cruel treatment and torture;

(b) taking of hostages;

(c) outrages upon personal dignity, in particular, humiliating and degrading treatment;

(d) the passing of sentences and the carrying out of executions without previous judgment pronounced by a regularly constituted court affording all the judicial guarantees which are recognized as indispensable by civilized peoples.

AP II, the treaty that supplemented Common Article 3, also explicitly prohibits certain conduct: violence to the life, health, and physical or mental well-being of detained persons; collective punishment; acts of terrorism; rape, enforced prosecution and any form of indecent assault; slavery and the slave trade; pillage; and threats to commit the foregoing acts (Art. 4). But there is precious little guidance as to treatment in either Common Article 3 or AP II.

The only treatment standards for detainees in Common Article 3 were indirect, by nature. Common Article 3 provided for medical care for wounded and sick and oversight by the ICRC, subject to the consent of the state party. Like the prohibitions noted above, AP II also elaborated upon the minimum "humane treatment" standards of Common Article 3. Article 5 of AP II provides guidance as to "persons whose liberty has been restricted." Like the civilian internees, non-international armed conflict detainees must be given sufficient food and drinking water to maintain health and hygiene, and must be protected "against the rigors of the climate and the dangers of armed conflict." They must be allowed to receive individual or collective relief, practice their religion and receive spiritual assistance, and benefit from the same work standards as the local civilian population. Non-international armed conflict detainees should be segregated between men and women. They should be allowed to send and receive letters and cards (with censorship, as required), provided medical examinations, and protected from the dangers of armed conflict. Finally, penal prosecutions cannot violate the extensive due process provisions discussed above, in Article 75 of AP I, or the similar provisions in Article 6 of AP II.

VI. Interrogation

A. Interrogation in International Armed Conflict

POWs are also protected from any sort of cruelty or maltreatment in the course of interrogation, pursuant to Article 17 of the Prisoner of War Convention:

Every prisoner of war, when questioned on the subject, is bound to give only his surname, first names and rank, date of birth, and army, regimental, personal or serial number, or failing this, equivalent information. If he willfully infringes this rule, he may render himself liable to a restriction of the privileges accorded to his rank or status. . . . No physical or mental torture, nor any other form of coercion, may be inflicted or prisoners of war to secure from them information of any kind whatsoever. Prisoners of war who refuse to answer may not be threatened, insulted, or exposed to unpleasant or disadvantageous treatment of any kind.

These proscriptions are clear and unequivocal. They do not prohibit the interrogation of POWs, nor do they require any sort of "*Miranda* warnings" be provided to enemy combatants. But they do prohibit involuntary statements, induced by any form of coercion or torture. And the provision banning "disadvantageous treatment of any kind" prevents interrogators from denying the standard of treatment applicable to all POWs to induce prisoners to provide information. Providing positive incentives for POW cooperation is, however, in no way prohibited. In fact, the ICRC Commentary to Art. 17 acknowledges that such practice is both customary and permissible.

The Civilian Convention protects civilian internees from the types of physical suffering or torture prohibited against POWs (Art. 32); in addition, no "physical or moral coercion shall be exercised against protected persons, in particular to obtain information from them or from third parties" (Art. 31). This provision and a ban on reprisals against civilians, captives, and the taking of hostages prevent the use of other civilians as leverage to induce civilian internees to provide information.

Finally, coercive or abusive interrogation techniques would also violate the humane treatment mandate reflected in Common Article 3 as extended to international armed conflict explicitly by Art. 75 of AP I. Accordingly, while POWs and civilian internees are expressly protected from such techniques by specific provisions of the Prisoner of War Convention and Civilian Convention (respectively), even a detainee who does not qualify for such status is protected from these techniques by the baseline humanitarian protections of the LOAC.

B. Interrogation in NIAC

Common Article 3 protects detainees subject to interrogation during a non-international armed conflict. As noted above (and throughout this text), this critically important LOAC provision prohibits violence to life and person, mutilation, cruel treatment and torture, hostage taking, and outrages upon personal dignity, including humiliating and degrading treatment. AP II adds proscriptions against violence to the health and physical or mental well-being of detained persons, any form of indecent assault, and threats to commit the foregoing acts. These proscriptions establish limitations on interrogation methods utilized during non-international armed conflict (in reality any armed conflict): insurgencies, civil wars, and transnational armed conflicts. Most of these prohibitions need no elaboration or definition, but "outrages upon personal dignity" or "humiliating and degrading treatment" are less susceptible to easy definitions. For most professional armed forces, there is nothing especially remarkable about these limitations. Indeed, as will be explained below, imposing humanitarian limitations on permissible interrogation techniques has been a consistent feature of U.S. military practice for decades, if not centuries.

C. Historical Limitations on Interrogation

The standard for interrogation embraced by the U.S. Army throughout the post-World War II era is based on the Prisoner of War Convention prohibitions against POW coercion, as well as the proscriptions on assaults, cruel treatment, torture and threats included in the Prisoner of War Convention, the Civilian Convention, and the UCMJ. In large measure a result of the debates surrounding "enhanced interrogation techniques" adopted for use against al Qaeda and Taliban detainees at the inception of the war on terror, the Army field manual on interrogation that implements this protective standard has attained both iconic and statutory status. Field manuals establish Army doctrine, which is essentially a "how to" guide for subordinate forces developed after careful assessment of "best practices" developed over time. The interrogation FM provided doctrinal guidance to Army interrogators for decades (including those in Panama in 1989), and adopted the Prisoner of War Convention standard prohibiting the use of coercion during interrogation, also prohibiting mistreatment of all other detainees. The 1987 version of the field manual also expanded on the prohibition against the use of force against detainees and proscribed "brainwashing, mental torture, or any other form of mental coercion, to include drugs." The current version of this FM, modified in the face of allegations that U.S. military advisors condoned torture of prisoners during the civil war in El Salvador in the early 1980's, added the requirement that U.S. military advisors eschew "brutal methods" used by host country forces, remove themselves from the scene, and report in accordance with theater command directives.

Another important source of authority related to NIAC interrogation arose out of the insurgency in Nicaragua that occurred at the same time U.S. advisors were operating in El Salvador. In *Military and Paramilitary Activities in and Against Nicaragua* (the *Nicaragua* case), the International Court of Justice (ICJ) analyzed, *inter alia*, LOAC standards related to interrogation during non-international armed conflict. The Court considered the legality of providing advice on how to conduct coercive interrogation contained in manuals allegedly provided by the United States to *contra* rebels. The Court concluded that the methods in these manuals were contrary to standards of customary "international humanitarian law [LOAC]." The ICJ noted that Common Article 3 was the "minimum yardstick" of conduct for military activities conducted during a NIAC. It also found that, under general principles of humanitarian law, the United States was bound to

> ... refrain from encouragement of persons or groups engaged in the conflict in Nicaragua to commit violations of common Article 3 of the four Geneva Conventions of 12 August 1949. The manual on "Psychological Operations in Guerrilla Warfare," for the publication and dissemination of which the United States is responsible, advises certain acts which cannot but be regarded as contrary to that article.

The *Nicaragua* decision really just confirmed the practice of U.S. forces. There is no indication that the interrogation methods in the manuals provided to the *contras* the ICJ assessed were ever utilized by the U.S. military. The decision did, however, have an important impact by confirming the customary international law status of the Common Article 3 humane treatment mandate, bolstering the Army FM approach to extending humanitarian protections to any detainee subject to interrogation. Universal application of this standard continued, especially after the largely conventional 1991 Persian Gulf War involving hundreds of thousands of U.S. forces engaged in an IAC in Kuwait and southern Iraq. Detainee protection, and by implication limitations on interrogation techniques, was enhanced by several revisions of the U.S. Army Regulation for detention during the 1990's. The 1997 version of this regulation (AR 190-8), which as explained above applies to all military services, added several of the protections afforded by Article 75 of AP I and Article 4-6 of AP II. Accordingly, this joint service regulation — a source of binding authority within the military — provides equivalent "minimum humane treatment" standards consistent with those of Common Article 3, AP I, and AP II. The mandate of this regulation, still in effect today, provides:

1-5. General protection policy

a. U.S. policy, relative to the treatment of EPW [Enemy Prisoners of War], Civilian Internee and RP [Retained Persons] in the custody of the U.S. Armed Forces, is as follows:

(1) All persons captured, detained, interned, or otherwise held in U.S. Armed Forces custody during the course of conflict will be given humanitarian care and treatment from the moment they fall into the hands of U.S. forces until final release or repatriation.

(2) All persons taken into custody by U.S. forces will be provided with the protections of the GPW until some other legal status is determined by competent authority.

(3) The punishment of EPW, CI and RP known to have, or suspected of having, committed serious offenses will be administered IAW due process of law and under legally constituted authority per the GPW, GC, the Uniform Code of Military Justice and the Manual for Courts Martial.

(4) The inhumane treatment of EPW, CI, RP is prohibited and is not justified by the stress of combat or with deep provocation. Inhumane treatment is a serious and punishable violation under international law and the Uniform Code of Military Justice (UCMJ).

b. All prisoners will receive humane treatment without regard to race, nationality, religion, political opinion, sex, or other criteria.

The following acts are prohibited: murder, torture, corporal punishment, mutilation, the taking of hostages, sensory deprivation, collective punishments, execution without trial by proper authority, and all cruel and degrading treatment.

c. All persons will be respected as human beings. They will be protected against all acts of violence to include rape, forced prostitution, assault and theft, insults, public curiosity, bodily injury, and reprisals of any kind. They will not be subjected to medical or scientific experiments. This list is not exclusive. EPW/RP [Enemy Prisoners of War/Retained Persons] are to be protected from all threats or acts of violence.

Like U.S. military interrogation manuals of this same period, the minimum humane treatment standards for all detainees eschewed maltreatment and coercive interrogation techniques under all circumstances, irrespective of the legal status of the detainee. Events following September 11th, 2001 would, however, expose that policy is ultimately malleable.

D. Interrogation in the War on Terror

It was only during the war on terror that interrogation standards were relaxed for "unlawful combatants" seized shortly after September 11, and then only for a brief period. The determination to obtain timely and accurate intelligence from captured terrorists drove this alteration of treatment standards from the fall of 2001 to late 2008. Ultimately, the Supreme Court, legislation, and policy developments restored traditionally followed LOAC standards for military's treatment and interrogation of detainees. In the interim, the military (with substantial policy direction from the leadership of the U.S. Department of Defense, the U.S. Department of Justice's Office of Legal Counsel (OLC), and the White House) essentially abandoned its longstanding reliance on LOAC treaties and principles as the base-line for the treatment of detained terrorists, in favor of a narrowly drawn legal position that allowed the U.S. government to selectively use aggressive interrogation and treatment techniques that did not comport with these time-tested standards.

The military legal community at every level resisted this deviation from the traditional application of LOAC standards to all detainees in all operational contexts. However, investigations conducted in response to detainee abuse at the U.S. detention facility in Abu Ghraib, Iraq concluded that some of the aggressive interrogation techniques adopted for unlawful combatants detained at Guantanamo migrated to other theaters of operations and resulted in mistreatment of detainees in several instances (despite the efforts of many Judge Advocates in the chain of command).

This deviation from the traditional LOAC-based approach to detainee treatment and interrogation began when President Bush issued Military Order Number 1 on November 13, 2001 (ostensibly styled as a military order instead of an executive order to emphasize exercise of commander in chief authority). That order mandated the following treatment of captured al Qaeda terrorists responsible for the attacks on September 11, those who "aided and abetted," and those who "knowingly harbored" them (to include Taliban detainees):

Any individual subject to this order shall be —

(a) Detained at an appropriate location designated by the Secretary of Defense outside or within the United States,

(b) Treated humanely, without any adverse distinction based on race, color, religion, gender, birth, wealth, or any similar criteria,

(c) Afforded adequate food, drinking water, shelter, clothing, and medical treatment,

(d) Allowed the free exercise of religion, consistent with the requirements of such detention,

(e) And detained in accordance with such other conditions as the Secretary of Defense may prescribe.

The order seems to adopt a Common Article 3 humane treatment standard. However, a subsequent determination made by President Bush indicated that the humane treatment mandated by this order was in fact not analogous to the minimum standards of Common Article 3 and paragraph 1-5 of Army Regulation 190-8. On 7 February 2002 President Bush issued a memorandum specifically addressing treatment of captured Taliban and al Qaeda detainees. This memorandum included the President's determination that detainees captured during the war against al Qaeda and the Taliban did not qualify as POWs. As a result they were not protected by the Prisoner of War Convention, but instead should be treated "humanely and, to the extent appropriate and consistent with military necessity, in a manner consistent with the principles of Geneva." This memorandum was preceded and followed by memoranda from the Department of Justice Office of Legal Counsel and the White House Counsel, all of which justified this position and exploited the relaxed standards to provide a legal justification for harsh interrogation techniques. Some of these techniques were then adopted by the U.S. interrogators for limited application at Guantanamo Bay and in Afghanistan.

In August of 2002, John Yoo, a Deputy Assistant Attorney General at OLC (writing for his immediate superior, Jay Bybee), provided an opinion to the General Counsel of the Department of Defense (DoD General Counsel, William Haynes) on legally permissible interrogation techniques. This infamous "Torture Memorandum," later repudiated by Yoo's successors, provided broad latitude for the conduct of harsh interrogations. Yoo's opinion excluded unlawful combatant detainees from any LOAC protections, and concluded any violation of U.S. domestic law criminalizing torture (10 USC § 2340A, the Torture Statute) requires proof of specific intent to violate the law, which would presumably not be present for U.S. officials that relied on his opinion. In addition, Yoo concluded the "severe pain and suffering" provision of the Torture Statute requires "serious physical injury so severe that death, organ failure, or permanent damage resulting in a loss of significant body function will likely result" or "severe mental pain" which exists only if there is "lasting psychological harm, such as seen in mental disorders like post-traumatic stress disorder." Finally, Yoo posited that both "necessity" and "self-defense" would legally justify use of torture to determine key details of an impending al Qaeda threat to national security. Because of the quasi-judicial function of the OLC (establishing the legal standards for the Executive Branch), this legal opinion, coupled with the President's prior findings and other classified legal opinions on specified techniques, laid the foundation for proposed interrogation techniques for use by civilian internee and military interrogators that were facially inconsistent with the Geneva Conventions and the "minimum humane treatment" mandate of Common Article 3.

The Department of Defense subsequently considered a list of such techniques proposed for use at Guantanamo by a JAG officer assigned to provide legal advice to the detention facility commander. The request included three categories of techniques, each increasingly more aggressive: Category I included yelling at the detainee, techniques of deception, and false flag (interrogators claiming to be from a harsh allied regime); Category II included stress positions, use of false documents, and up to 30 days of isolation, deprivation of auditory stimuli, prolonged interrogations, removal of comfort items (including religious items), changing hot rations to MRE's, removal of clothing, forced grooming, and exploitation of detainee phobias (e.g., fear of dogs); Category III would include use of scenarios threatening death to him or his family, exposure to cold weather or water, use of dripping water to induce "misperception of suffocation" (water-boarding), and use of "mild, non-injurious physical contact." Military law of war experts involved in this study heavily criticized the proposal. Nonetheless, despite objections from the military services, the DOD General Counsel recommended approval of several restricted techniques (which did not include Category III techniques of water-boarding or death threats, but did include "mild, non-injurious physical contact"), to be carefully controlled and personally approved by the Secretary of Defense.

These techniques, approved by the Secretary of Defense in December 2002, were withdrawn in January 2003 after Alberto Mora, the General Counsel of the Navy, threatened to prepare a formal memorandum of non-concurrence for the DOD General Counsel after he was made aware of detainee abuse at Guantanamo (a Naval Base subject to his legal oversight). Shortly thereafter, the DOD General Counsel convened a panel of legal experts to conduct another review the interrogation techniques; but the committee was told to confine their legal analysis to the contours of a re-issued Yoo memorandum on the applicability of the law of war and humane treatment standards. On April 16, 2003, less than two weeks after the Working Group completed its report, the Secretary of Defense authorized the use of 24 specific interrogation techniques at Guantanamo. While the authorization included such techniques as dietary manipulation, environmental manipulation, and sleep adjustment, it was silent on many of the more aggressive techniques in the original request. Secretary Rumsfeld's authorization did, however, indicate that "if, in your view, you require additional interrogation techniques for a particular detainee, you should provide me, via the Chairman of the Joint Chiefs of Staff, a written request describing the proposed technique, recommended safeguards, and the rationale for applying it with an identified detainee."

The techniques approved on 2 December 2002 were transmitted to Guantanamo for use only at that facility. However, the movement of interrogators between facilities at Guantanamo and others in Iraq and Afghanistan resulted in use of these techniques without authorization in these other operational theaters. The end result of this process contributed to abuses at all three locations. At least one Guantanamo detainee, Mohammed Al Qahtani (the alleged "twentieth hijacker"), was subjected to sleep deprivation for weeks on end, stripped naked, harassed by military working dogs and loud music, made to wear a leash and told to perform dog tricks. Detainees in Afghanistan and Iraq suffered similar abuses.

Soldiers who conducted interrogations at the U.S. detention facility at Bagram Air Base in Afghanistan also claimed they had been authorized to provide "punishment blows" to detainees who were not cooperating with the interrogation. When their abusive interrogation resulted in the death of the taxi driver (Nabibullah) and several other detainees, they were tried and convicted by court-martial. Soldiers who engaged in criminal misconduct by using unauthorized interrogation techniques or committing aggravated assault or murder, was never linked directly to the policies adopted by the Secretary of Defense (something defense attorneys made every effort to establish; but the abuse resulted, at least in part, "from misinterpretation of law or policy" and "confusion about what techniques were permitted," all of which began with these policies.

All of the investigations of the abuses at Abu Ghraib that evaluated the involvement of the chain of command in the scandal, including the overarching Schlesinger Report, resulted in the same conclusion. The first investigation, regarding alleged military police misconduct and conducted by Major General Antonio Taguba, concluded that there were numerous incidents of "sadistic, blatant, and wanton criminal abuses intentionally inflicted on several detainees from October to December 2003"; and recommended criminal liability for soldiers who engaged in such misconduct. Major General George Fay, who investigated the involvement of military intelligence interrogators, concluded that "most of the violent or sexual abuse occurred separately from interrogations and was not caused by uncertainty about law or policy. Soldiers knew they were violating approved techniques and procedures." He also found that the Commander of the Joint Intelligence Center (JIC) at Abu Ghraib, Colonel Thomas Pappas (assisted by Captain Wood, who had previously worked at Bagram), consented to "clothing removal and the use of dogs" without proper authorization from higher headquarters; but those actions did not cause the violent or sexual abuse at Abu Ghraib.

The military's use of "enhanced interrogation techniques" (with one exception, a carefully prescribed "separation technique") ceased after exposure of the detainee abuse at Abu Ghraib. Congress intervened in 2005 when it passed the Detainee Treatment Act (DTA). The DTA proscribed torture, but also permitted certain techniques that pass a Fifth Amendment substantive due process test, which is based on balancing the importance of the governmental interest with the nature of the method used by government agents, prohibiting only conduct that "shocks the conscience." Incorporating this due process test in the context of a dire threat to national security[,] because the law was interpreted as being consistent with the Yoo Memoranda, it had little effect on interrogation policy.

Ultimately, it was a Supreme Court decision unrelated to interrogation that resurrected the LOAC-based detainee treatment standard. In *Hamdan v. Rumsfeld*, the Court considered the legality of trying an al Qaeda detainee by a military commission established pursuant to President Bush's Military Order Number 1. Resolution of this issue led the Court to consider applicability of Common Article 3 to unlawful combatants captured in the transnational armed conflict with al Qaeda. A majority of justices rejected the Bush administration interpretation of Geneva applicability, and concluded that Common Article 3 applied in any armed conflict that does not qualify as an IAC. The implication of this decision on the interrogation debate was immediately clear: Because the Court interpreted Common Article 3 to apply to the armed conflict with al Qaeda, even unlawful combatants were protected by this baseline humane treatment obligation.

Immediately following the *Hamdan* decision, Undersecretary for Defense Gordon England issued a memorandum to all elements of the Department of Defense confirming that all existing DoD orders, policies, orders and doctrine comply with Common Article 3 (other than the commission procedures that the *Hamdan* Court found in violation), and directing that all DoD personnel adhere to the humane treatment standards of Common Article 3. This memorandum reconfirmed the "minimum humane treatment policy" of the Department of Defense Law of War Directive (2311.01E). The pre-September 11 practice of full compliance with all provisions of Common Article 3 and the General Protection Policy in paragraph 1-5 of AR 190-8, is, as a result, once again controlling. Further, on 6 September 2006 the Army released a revised field manual for interrogation operations, FM 2-22.3. This new interrogation manual elevated the standards from Common Article 3's "minimum humane treatment standards" to the more protective standard of the Prisoner of War Convention, Article 17, requiring compliance with the most protective international armed conflict standard during the interrogation of any detainee. Congress endorsed this more protective approach by including in the DTA a provision indicating that the Army field manual techniques are the exclusive techniques permitted for use by U.S. interrogators.

The debate over the harsh interrogation techniques authorized for use against unlawful combatants, the process that led to that authorization, and responsibility for subsequent abuses continues to this day. Did these techniques qualify as torture? Should senior government officials, to include President Bush, be held accountable for criminal violations? Why were the concerns of military legal advisors dismissed? These are all important questions, but ultimately beyond the scope of this chapter. What is clearly within the scope, however, is the transcendent lesson learned from this brief but significant deviation from the traditional approach of extending LOAC treatment standards to all detainees. It has never been established that an unbroken chain of orders and supervisory responsibility linked the abuses at Abu Ghraib to Secretary Rumsfeld's authorization for use of harsh interrogation techniques.

That authorization stands, however, as a clear leadership failure and, at a minimum, establishes moral responsibility for the corrosion of standards applied at Guantanamo, Bagram, and Abu Ghraib. Interpreting the LOAC to justify abusive treatment of wartime detainees perverted the underlying principles of the Conventions and distorted the logic of conflict regulation. It also produced a corrosive effect on subordinates who were empowered to make their own value judgments on whether a detainee in Iraq or Afghanistan was morally worthy of humane treatment. This is not a judgment soldiers should ever be entitled to make. Instead, offsetting the instincts generated by the brutality of armed conflict necessitates constant emphasis on the principle of humanity [and] must permeate all military policies and orders.

Military leaders have long understood this imperative, which was central to the Department of Defense policy of extending LOAC principles to all detention operations. Restoration with enhancement of this core ethos is perhaps the one beneficial outcome of the brief but significant deviation from this tradition. Contrary to the opinions relied on by Secretary Rumsfeld to authorize harsh interrogation techniques, no person subject to the absolute control of the military should be excluded from humanitarian protections—military necessity cannot justify "whatever it takes" to extract information from detainees. From the Lieber Code's categorical prohibition against the use of torture to extract information from prisoners (adopted at a time when the nation faced perhaps the greatest challenge ever to its survival), to the development of Common Article 3, AP II, and Article 75 of AP I, to the adoption of the Department of Defense Law of War Directive and the extension of humane treatment to all military operations, U.S. military practice and international law have continuously evolved to stress the importance of this baseline treatment standard.

NOTES AND QUESTIONS

1. The 2015 Department of Defense Law of War Manual provides the following explanation of the principle of military necessity:

> 2.2.1 *Military Necessity as a Justification. Military necessity* justifies actions, such as destroying and seizing persons and property. Thus, *military necessity* underlies law of war concepts that explain when persons and property may be the object of attack, *e.g.*, the concepts of "taking a direct part in hostilities" and "military objective." *Military necessity* may justify not only violence and destruction, but also alternative means of subduing the enemy. For example, military necessity may justify the capture of enemy persons, or non-forcible measures, such as propaganda and intelligence-gathering. . . .
>
> 2.2.2 Military Necessity and Law of War Rules.
>
> 2.2.2.1 *Military Necessity Does Not Justify Actions Prohibited by the Law of War.* Military necessity does not justify actions that are prohibited by the law of war. From the late 19th Century through World War II, Germany asserted that *military* necessity could override specific law of war rules (*Kriegsraeson geht vor Kriegsmanier*—"necessity in war overrules the manner of warfare"). This view was strongly criticized. Post-World War II war crimes tribunals rejected it as well. *Military necessity* cannot justify departures from the law of war because States have crafted the law of war specifically with war's exigencies in mind. In devising law of war rules, States considered military requirements. Thus, prohibitions on conduct in the law of war may be understood to reflect

States' determinations that such conduct is militarily unnecessary *per se*. The fact that law of war rules are formulated specifically with military requirements in mind has played an important part in the doctrine that the law of war is the *lex specialis* governing armed conflict.

Does this explain why military necessity may not be invoked as a legal justification for torture or other harsh interrogation techniques?

2. How would you explain the humane treatment obligation to a junior ranking soldier responsible for interrogating a captured enemy belligerent? Is it enough to simply tell her she must treat the detainee humanely?

3. Does the discussion of military necessity make any reference to the consequences of an enemy's complete disregard of *its* obligation to treat captured U.S. personnel humanely? What if they are routinely tortured, or even summarily executed? If this does not impact the nature of the U.S. obligation, how can this be explained?

ASSESSMENT QUESTIONS

1. You are the legal advisor for a U.S. military command in Afghanistan that captured a member of an al Qaeda militia group fighting with the Taliban. He is designated an unprivileged enemy belligerent. The commander is convinced the detainee has information about the location of an al Qaeda safe house used for the production and assembly of improvised explosive devices that are then distributed to suicide bombers. The commander wants to use harsh interrogation techniques, including physical abuse, to compel the detainee to provide the location of the safe house. The interrogators assured the commander that the physical abuse they plan on using will not amount to torture. How would you respond to this proposed interrogation plan?

2. The United States learns that a high-level ISIS commander is located in a safe house in an area of Syria completely under ISIS control. The President is provided intelligence that establishes that this commander is responsible for the planning and direction of past and future ISIS terrorist attacks directed against U.S. military personnel in Turkey, and civilians in the United States. In fact, two such attacks were recently thwarted when FBI agents raided terrorist safe houses in New York and Los Angeles. The President is presented with a plan whereby U.S. special forces will conduct a raid into the area to capture or kill the commander. Explain if and why this military action would be consistent with international law.

3. Continuing from the prior question, U.S. special forces conduct the raid. During the raid, U.S. forces unexpectedly encountered Syrian Army forces at a forward operating base they established deep inside Syria. The Syrian patrol attacked the U.S. forces, and during the firefight two U.S. soldiers were killed. The U.S. forces captured two Syrian soldiers. The U.S. forces also captured the ISIS commander. All three captured personnel are transported to the United States; all three are brought to trial in federal district court on charges of murder and attempted murder of U.S. citizens abroad. The U.S. Attorney prosecuting the cases anticipates each defendant will move to dismiss the indictments based on a claim of combatant immunity. Will these motions be successful?

ASSESSMENT ANSWERS

1. Advise the commander that she may not approve this interrogation plan. This detainee is not a prisoner of war because the armed conflict with al Qaeda, a non-state group, cannot qualify as an international armed conflict triggering the prisoner of war provisions of the Third Geneva Convention. However, pursuant to *Hamdan v. Rumsfeld*, any armed conflict that does not qualify as "international" within the meaning of the Geneva Conventions is, "in contradistinction,"

an armed conflict not of an international character falling within the scope of Common Article 3 of the Geneva Conventions. Common Article 3 prohibits not only torture, but cruel, inhumane, or degrading treatment of any enemy belligerent detainee. Accordingly, this proposed interrogation plan is unlawful.

2. This military action will be justified based on the U.S. interpretation of the inherent right of self-defense codified in Article 51 of the Charter of the United Nations. This right is triggered by an actual or imminent armed attack against the United States. The intelligence supports the conclusion that the threat posed by this commander is imminent. A raid to capture or kill him is both necessary and proportionate. The United States interprets this right to apply not only to threats from other states, but also from non-state groups such as ISIS (although the President should be advised that there is no universal consensus on applicability of the right of self-defense to non-state threats, and that the International Court of Justice has rejected such claims). Because Syria is "unwilling or unable" to respond to this threat, the United States will conclude that it has a right of self-help action. The United States should notify the U.N. Security Council of this action once it is completed.

3. Combatant immunity provides immunity for lawful or privileged belligerents in armed conflict for their lawful military actions. It prevents lawful or privileged belligerents from being prosecuted and punished by a state that captures them for the harm caused during the armed conflict, so long as their conduct complied with the laws and customs of war (international humanitarian law). The ISIS commander will not be successful in invoking combatant immunity for two reasons. First, because he is a member of a non-state belligerent group, he cannot qualify as a privileged or lawful belligerent. This is because to so qualify, an individual must qualify for prisoner of war status, and that status is limited to individuals who fight on behalf of a state (members of the regular armed forces or associated militia or volunteer groups). Second, even if he could qualify as a lawful/privileged belligerent, his complicity in plots to attack U.S. civilians would violate the international humanitarian law/law of war principle of distinction, and would still be subject to criminal sanction. The two Syrian soldiers will be successful in asserting combatant immunity. They are members of the Syrian Army, and were captured following hostilities with U.S. special forces. Even though limited in duration, that encounter qualified as an international armed conflict, and as members of an enemy state's armed forces, they qualify as prisoners of war. The two U.S. soldiers were killed during the firefight, which was a lawful act of war. Therefore these two prisoners of war may not be prosecuted for these killings.

PART III

CRIME AND NATIONAL SECURITY

CHAPTER 9

Criminal Investigations and National Security

I. INTRODUCTION

The use of criminal sanctions as a tool in the national security arsenal often implicates the authority of the United States to extend its laws abroad and important constitutional rights established to limit the exercise of government power in the pursuit of criminal justice. Most notably, it implicates the Fourth Amendment prohibition against unreasonable searches, the Fifth Amendment prohibition against coercive interrogations, the *Miranda* rule created to protect the privilege against compelled self-incrimination, and the right to a fair trial guaranteed by the Sixth Amendment. Understanding the applicability of each of these constitutional protections in the national security context is essential to an effective leverage of the nation's criminal power.

II. EXTENDING U.S. CRIMINAL JURISDICTION BEYOND U.S. BORDERS

"Long arm" statutes extend U.S. criminal law to conduct and individuals outside the territory of the United States.[1] These statutes provide federal prosecutors with the jurisdiction needed to leverage the nation's criminal laws to protect a wide range of national security interests. But the extension of domestic criminal laws beyond national borders always creates a risk of intruding upon the sovereignty of other states. To balance potentially competing sovereign interests, international law developed certain principles of jurisdiction. These principles serve the interests of the international community by mitigating the risk that such extensions will

---

1. 18 U.S.C. § 2332a (use of weapons of mass destruction); 18 U.S.C. § 2332f (making it a crime to bomb public places where the victim is a United States national); 18 U.S.C. § 2339C (making it a crime to finance terrorism outside of the United States).

produce disputes between states by establishing the conditions or situations that justify, from an international law perspective, these invocations of national criminal jurisdiction. The following opinion illustrates how these principles inform decisions challenging the validity of asserted U.S. criminal jurisdiction.

United States v. Yousef
327 F.3d 56 (2d Cir. 2003)

INTRODUCTION

Defendants-appellants Ramzi Yousef, Eyad Ismoil, and Abdul Hakim Murad appeal from judgments of conviction entered in the United States District Court for the Southern District of New York (Kevin Thomas Duffy, Judge) on April 13, June 2, and June 15, 1998, respectively. Judge Duffy presided over two separate jury trials. In the first trial, Yousef, Murad, and Wali Khan Amin Shah were tried on charges relating to a conspiracy to bomb United States commercial airliners in Southeast Asia. In the second trial, Yousef and Ismoil were tried for their involvement in the February 1993 bombing of the World Trade Center in New York City. Yousef, Ismoil, and Murad now appeal from their convictions, asserting a number of claims. Yousef and Ismoil also appeal from the District Court's denial of several of their post-judgment motions. In reviewing these claims, we view the evidence in the light most favorable to the Government, as required by *Jackson v. Virginia*, 443 U.S. 307, 319, 99 S. Ct. 2781, 61 L. Ed. 2d 560 (1979).

GENERAL BACKGROUND

I. WORLD TRADE CENTER BOMBING

The conspiracy to bomb the World Trade Center began in the Spring of 1992, when Yousef met Ahmad Mohammad Ajaj at a terrorist training camp on the border of Afghanistan and Pakistan. After formulating their terrorist plot, Yousef and Ajaj traveled to New York together in September 1992. In Ajaj's luggage, he carried a "terrorist kit" that included, among other things, bomb-making manuals. After Yousef and Ajaj arrived at John F. Kennedy International Airport, inspectors of the Immigration and Naturalization Service ("INS") discovered the "terrorist kit" in Ajaj's luggage and arrested him. Although Yousef was also stopped, he and Ajaj did not disclose their connection to one another, and INS officials allowed Yousef to enter the United States.

Once in New York, Yousef began to put together the manpower and the supplies that he would need to carry out his plan to bomb the World Trade Center. . . .

On February 26, 1993, Yousef and Ismoil drove a bomb-laden van onto the B-2 level of the parking garage below the World Trade Center. They then set the bomb's timer to detonate minutes later. At approximately 12:18 P.M. that day, the bomb exploded, killing six people, injuring more than a thousand others, and causing widespread fear and more than $500 million in property damage.

Soon after the bombing, Yousef and Ismoil fled from the United States. Yousef and Ismoil were indicted for their participation in the bombing on March 31, 1993 and August 8, 1994, respectively. Yousef was captured in Pakistan nearly two years after the bombing, and Ismoil was arrested in Jordan a little over two years after the attack. Both were returned to the United States to answer the charges in the indictment.

II. Airline Bombing

A year and a half after the World Trade Center bombing, Yousef entered Manila, the capital of the Philippines, under an assumed name. By September 1994, Yousef had devised a plan to attack United States airliners. According to the plan, five individuals would place bombs aboard twelve United States-flag aircrafts that served routes in Southeast Asia. The conspirators would board an airliner in Southeast Asia, assemble a bomb on the plane, and then exit the plane during its first layover. As the planes continued on toward their next destinations, the timebombs would detonate. Eleven of the twelve flights targeted were ultimately destined for cities in the United States.

Yousef and his co-conspirators performed several tests in preparation for the airline bombings. In December 1994, Yousef and Wali Khan Amin Shah placed one of the bombs they had constructed in a Manila movie theater. The bomb exploded, injuring several patrons of the theater. Ten days later, Yousef planted another test bomb under a passenger's seat during the first leg of a Philippine Airlines flight from Manila to Japan. Yousef disembarked from the plane during the stopover and then made his way back to Manila. During the second leg of the flight, the bomb exploded, killing one passenger, a Japanese national, and injuring others.

The plot to bomb the United States-flag airliners was uncovered in January 1995, only two weeks before the conspirators intended to carry it out. Yousef and Murad were burning chemicals in their Manila apartment and accidentally caused a fire. . . . Philippine police arrived at the apartment, where they discovered chemicals and bomb components, a laptop computer on which Yousef had set forth the aircraft bombing plans, and other incriminating evidence. Philippine authorities arrested Murad and Shah, though Shah escaped and was not recaptured until nearly a year later. Yousef fled the country, but was captured in Pakistan the next month.

. . .

[The court sentenced Yousef for each conviction for a total period of confinement that amounted to life in prison. Yousef appealed, raising a number of issues.]

DISCUSSION

I. Assertion of Extraterritorial Jurisdiction over Defendants Yousef and Murad

Yousef contends that the Government exceeded its authority by trying him in the United States for his conduct in the aircraft bombing case. In particular, he asserts that the charges alleged in Counts Twelve, Thirteen, Fourteen and Nineteen should be dismissed because 18 U.S.C. § 32 cannot be applied to conduct outside the United States. . . .

A. Jurisdiction to Prosecute Defendants' Extraterritorial Conduct Under Federal Law

1. Applicable Law

It is beyond doubt that, as a general proposition, Congress has the authority to "enforce its laws beyond the territorial boundaries of the United States." *EEOC v. Arabian Am. Oil Co.*, 499 U.S. 244, 248, 111 S. Ct. 1227, 113 L. Ed. 2d 274 (1991). Although there is a presumption that Congress does not intend a statute to apply to conduct outside the territorial jurisdiction of the United States . . . [a]s long as Congress has indicated its intent to reach such conduct, a United States court is "bound to follow the Congressional direction unless this would violate the due process clause of the Fifth Amendment." *United States v. Pinto-Mejia*, 720 F.2d 248, 259 (2d Cir. 1983) (internal quotation marks omitted). Moreover, the presumption against extraterritorial application does not apply to those "criminal statutes which are, as a class, not logically dependent on their locality for the Government's jurisdiction." *United States v. Bowman*, 260 U.S. 94, 98, 43 S. Ct. 39, 67 L. Ed. 149 (1922).

In determining whether Congress intended a federal statute to apply to overseas conduct, "an act of Congress ought never to be construed to violate the law of nations if any other possible construction remains." *McCulloch v. Sociedad Nacional de Marineros de Honduras*, 372 U.S. 10, 21, 83 S. Ct. 671, 9 L. Ed. 2d 547 (1963) (internal quotation marks omitted). Nonetheless, in fashioning the reach of our criminal law, "Congress is not bound by international law." *Pinto-Mejia*, 720 F.2d at 259. "If it chooses to do so, it may legislate with respect to conduct outside the United States, in excess of the limits posed by international law." *Id.; see also United States v. Quemener*, 789 F.2d 145, 156 (2d Cir. 1986); *United States v. Allen*, 760 F.2d 447, 454 (2d Cir. 1985).

2. Counts Thirteen and Fourteen

Counts Thirteen and Fourteen charged Yousef, Murad and Shah with violating 18 U.S.C. § 32(a). Count Thirteen alleged that they attempted to damage aircraft in the special aircraft jurisdiction of the United States and civil aircraft operated in foreign air commerce, in violation of § 32(a)(1) and (7). Count Fourteen charged them with violating § 32(a)(2) and (7) by attempting to place a bomb on such aircraft in Count Fourteen.

Section 32(a)(1) prohibits damaging "any aircraft in the special aircraft jurisdiction of the United States" or "any civil aircraft used, operated, or employed in interstate, overseas, or foreign air commerce." Section 32(a)(2) makes it a crime to place a destructive device on board any such aircraft if it would be likely to endanger the aircraft's safety. Section 32(a)(7) prohibits an attempt or conspiracy to do anything forbidden under § 32(a).

The text of the applicable federal statutes makes it clear that Congress intended § 32(a) to apply extraterritorially. Under 49 U.S.C. § 46501(2)(A) the "special aircraft jurisdiction of the United States" is defined to include any "civil aircraft of the United States" while that aircraft is in flight. "Civil aircraft of the United States," in turn, is defined in 49 U.S.C. § 40102(a)(17) as "an aircraft registered under Chapter 441" of Title 49, which requires registration of any United States-flag aircraft. *See* 49 U.S.C. §§ 44101-44103. Accordingly, § 32(a) covers any United States-flag aircraft while in flight, wherever in the world it may be. In addition, Congress defined "foreign air commerce" to cover "the transportation of passengers or property by aircraft . . . between a place in the United States and a place outside the United States." 49 U.S.C. § 40102(a)(22).

The District Court was correct to hold that the twelve aircraft targeted in the instant case fell within [a statutory definition] of aircraft protected by United States law. The relevant aircraft were all United States-flag aircraft targeted while in flight, and were therefore in "the special aircraft jurisdiction of the United States." 18 U.S.C. § 32(a)(1). Furthermore, all but one of the aircraft targeted in the conspiracy charged in Counts Thirteen and Fourteen were civil aircraft carrying passengers destined for the United States, and were therefore "civil aircraft used, operated, or employed in . . . overseas, or foreign air commerce." . . . Accordingly, it was proper for the District Court to exercise jurisdiction over the extraterritorial crimes charged in Counts Thirteen and Fourteen.

3. Count Twelve

In Count Twelve, the defendants were charged with violating 18 U.S.C. § 371 by conspiring to place bombs on board aircraft and destroy aircraft, in violation of 18 U.S.C. § 32(a)(1) and (2). The District Court concluded that, because it had jurisdiction over the substantive crimes charged—including attempted destruction of aircraft in the special aircraft jurisdiction of the United States—it also had derivative jurisdiction over the conspiracy charges. *United States v. Yousef*, 927 F. Supp. 673, 682 (S.D.N.Y. 1996).

We agree. Indeed, this conclusion is a simple application of the rule enunciated by the Supreme Court as long ago as 1922 in *Bowman*, that Congress is presumed to intend extraterritorial application of criminal statutes where the nature of the crime does not depend on the locality of the defendants' acts and where restricting the statute to United States territory would severely diminish the statute's effectiveness. *See Bowman*, 260 U.S. at 98, 43 S. Ct. 39. . . . In the instant case, if Congress intended United States courts to have jurisdiction over the substantive crime of placing bombs on board the aircraft at issue, it is reasonable to conclude that Congress also intended to vest in United States courts the requisite jurisdiction over an extraterritorial conspiracy to commit that crime. . . .

4. Count Nineteen

In Count Nineteen, Yousef alone was charged with violating 18 U.S.C. § 32(b)(3) for placing a bomb on a civil aircraft registered in another country.

Specifically, Yousef was charged with planting a bomb on board a Philippine Airlines flight traveling from the Philippines to Japan on December 11, 1994. The aircraft was a civil aircraft registered in the Philippines.

There is no dispute that Congress intended § 32(b) to apply to attacks on non-United States-flag aircraft. The statute applies expressly to placing a bomb on aircraft registered in other countries while in flight, no matter where the attack is committed, and provides for jurisdiction over such extraterritorial crimes whenever, *inter alia*, "an offender is afterwards found in the United States." 18 U.S.C. § 32(b).

The court then rejected Yousef's argument that he was not "found" within the United States because he was brought to the United States against his will to answer for the indictment.

B. Exercise of United States Extraterritorial Jurisdiction and Customary International Law

On appeal, Yousef challenges the District Court's jurisdiction over Counts Twelve through Nineteen of the indictment by arguing that customary international law does not provide a basis for jurisdiction over these counts and that United States law is subordinate to customary international law and therefore cannot provide a basis for jurisdiction.[24] *See* Yousef Br. at 136-37, 141-48. He particularly contests the District Court's conclusion that customary international law permits the United States to prosecute him under the so-called universality principle for the bombing of Philippine Airline Flight 434 charged in Count Nineteen. Yousef claims that, absent a universally agreed-upon definition of "terrorism" and an international consensus that terrorism is a subject matter over which universal jurisdiction may be exercised, the United States cannot rest jurisdiction over him for this "terrorist" act *either* on the

---

24. Customary international law is comprised of those practices and customs that States view as obligatory and that are engaged in or otherwise acceded to by a preponderance of States in a uniform and consistent fashion. Ian Brownlie, *Principles of Public International Law* 5-7 (5th ed. 1999). *See also* Restatement (Third) § 102(2) (stating that customary international law "results from . . . [the] consistent practice of states followed by them from a sense of legal obligation"). Customary international law recognizes five bases on which a State may exercise criminal jurisdiction over a citizen or non-citizen for acts committed outside of the prosecuting State. These five well-recognized bases of criminal jurisdiction are: (1) the "objective territorial principle," which provides for jurisdiction over conduct committed outside a State's borders that has, or is intended to have, a substantial effect within its territory; (2) the "nationality principle," which provides for jurisdiction over extraterritorial acts committed by a State's own citizen; (3) the "protective principle," which provides for jurisdiction over acts committed outside the State that harm the State's interests; (4) the "passive personality principle," which provides for jurisdiction over acts that harm a State's citizens abroad; and (5) the "universality principle," which provides for jurisdiction over extraterritorial acts by a citizen or non-citizen that are so heinous as to be universally condemned by all civilized nations. *See generally In re Marc Rich & Co.*, 707 F.2d 663, 666 (2d Cir. 1983) (citing *Introductory Comment to Research on International Law, Part II, Draft Convention on Jurisdiction with Respect to Crime*, 29 Am. J. Int'l L. 435, 445 (Supp. 1935)); *United States v. Pizzarusso*, 388 F.2d 8, 10-11 (2d Cir. 1968); *see also Tel-Oren v. Libyan Arab Republic*, 726 F.2d 774, 781 n.7 (D.C. Cir. 1984) (Edwards, J., concurring); *United States v. Marino-Garcia*, 679 F.2d 1373, 1380-83 & nn.13-16 (11th Cir. 1982).

universality principle or on any United States positive law, which, he claims, necessarily is subordinate to customary international law.

Yousef's arguments fail. First, irrespective of whether customary international law provides a basis for jurisdiction over Yousef for Counts Twelve through Nineteen, United States law provides a separate and complete basis for jurisdiction over each of these counts and, contrary to Yousef's assertions, United States law is not subordinate to customary international law or necessarily subordinate to treaty-based international law and, in fact, may conflict with both. Further contrary to Yousef's claims, customary international law *does* provide a substantial basis for jurisdiction by the United States over each of these counts, although not (as the District Court held) under the universality principle.

While the District Court correctly held that jurisdiction was proper over each count, and we affirm the substance of its rulings in full, we hold that the District Court erred in partially grounding its exercise of jurisdiction over Count Nineteen. . . .

We conclude, instead, that jurisdiction over Count Nineteen was proper, first, under domestic law, 18 U.S.C. § 32; second, under the *aut dedere aut punire* ("extradite or prosecute") jurisdiction created by the Montreal Convention, as implemented in 18 U.S.C. § 32 (destruction of aircraft) and 49 U.S.C. § 46502 (aircraft piracy); and third, under the *protective* principle of the customary international law of criminal jurisdiction.

1. Bases of Jurisdiction over the Counts Charged

a. Relationship Between Domestic and International Law in Yousef's Prosecution

Jurisdiction over Yousef on Counts Twelve through Nineteen was based on 18 U.S.C. § 32. Yousef argues that this statute cannot give rise to jurisdiction because his prosecution thereunder conflicts with established principles of customary international law. Yousef's argument fails because, while customary international law may inform the judgment of our courts in an appropriate case, it cannot alter or constrain the making of law by the political branches of the government as ordained by the Constitution. . . .

While it is permissible for United States law to conflict with customary international law, where legislation is susceptible to multiple interpretations, the interpretation that does not conflict with "the law of nations" is preferred. *Murray v. Charming Betsy*, 6 U.S. (2 Cranch) 64, 118, 2 L. Ed. 208 (1804). . . .

If a statute makes plain Congress's intent (instead of employing ambiguous or "general" words), then Article III courts, which can overrule Congressional enactments only when such enactments conflict with the Constitution, *see, e.g., Sinclair Refining Co. v. Atkinson*, 370 U.S. 195, 215, 82 S. Ct. 1328, 8 L. Ed. 2d 440 (1962) (stating that, "[i]n dealing with problems of interpretation and application of federal statutes, we have no power to change deliberate choices of legislative policy that Congress has made within its constitutional powers"). . . . It also is established that Congress "may legislate with respect to conduct outside the United States, in excess of the limits posed by international law." *United States v. Pinto-Mejia*, 720 F.2d 248, 259 (2d Cir. 1983). . . .

2. Jurisdiction over Counts Twelve Through Eighteen

Jurisdiction over Counts Twelve through Eighteen is straight-forward, and we affirm both the District Court's finding of jurisdiction and its reasoning. United States domestic law provides a complete basis for jurisdiction over the conduct charged in these counts, independent of customary international law. Nevertheless, contrary to Yousef's claims, jurisdiction is consistent with three of the five principles of customary international law criminal jurisdiction — the objective, protective, and passive personality principles, described at note 24, *ante.*

First, jurisdiction over Counts Twelve through Eighteen is consistent with the "passive personality principle" of customary international jurisdiction because each of these counts involved a plot to bomb United States-flag aircraft that would have been carrying United States citizens and crews and that were destined for cities in the United States. Moreover, assertion of jurisdiction is appropriate under the "objective territorial principle" because the purpose of the attack was to influence United States foreign policy and the defendants intended their actions to have an effect — in this case, a devastating effect — on and within the United States. Finally, there is no doubt that jurisdiction is proper under the "protective principle" because the planned attacks were intended to affect the United States and to alter its foreign policy.

3. Jurisdiction over Count Nineteen

a. The District Court's Holding and Yousef's Challenges on Appeal

Count Nineteen, the bombing of Philippine Airlines Flight 434, appears to present a less straight-forward jurisdictional issue because the airplane that was bombed was not a United States-flag aircraft, it was flying between two destinations outside of the United States, and there is no evidence that any United States citizens were aboard the flight or were targets of the bombing. The District Court nevertheless concluded that jurisdiction over Yousef for the offenses charged in Count Nineteen was proper, *inter alia*, under the principle of "universal jurisdiction." *Yousef*, 927 F. Supp. at 681-82.

Yousef makes a two-part argument on appeal challenging the District Court's holding with respect to the Court's jurisdiction over Count Nineteen. First, he claims that the District Court erred in holding that the universality principle provides jurisdiction over Count Nineteen. He bases this claim on the argument that, if his placing the bomb on the Philippine Airlines plane constituted terrorism, then jurisdiction under the universality principle is improper because terrorism is not universally condemned by the community of States and, therefore, is not subject to universal jurisdiction under customary international law. Yousef Br. at 143-48. Second, he argues that because customary international law does not provide for the punishment of terrorist acts under the universality principle, such failure precludes or invalidates United States laws that provide for the prosecution of such acts that occur extraterritorially. *See id.* at 139-141, 148 (arguing that jurisdiction over Count Nineteen cannot exist apart from a jurisdictional basis supplied by customary international law).

In light of the District Court's conclusion that Yousef's prosecution for the acts charged in Count Nineteen was proper under the universality principle, and in light of Yousef's arguments both that the universality principle does not provide jurisdiction over terrorist acts and that this failure precludes United States law from proscribing such acts, we (i) first present the District Court's holding as to its jurisdiction over this count, (ii) examine whether the District Court correctly concluded that the universality principle provides for jurisdiction over the acts charged in Count Nineteen, and (iii) examine whether the universality principle provides for jurisdiction over "terrorist" acts. We hold that the District Court erred as a matter of law in relying upon the universality principle as a basis for jurisdiction over the acts charged in Count Nineteen and further hold that customary international law currently does not provide for the prosecution of "terrorist" acts under the universality principle, in part due to the failure of States to achieve anything like consensus on the definition of terrorism. However . . . we hold that Yousef's conduct charged in Count Nineteen—regardless of whether it is termed "terrorist"—constitutes the core conduct proscribed by the Montreal Convention and its implementing legislation. Accordingly, Yousef's prosecution and conviction on this Count is both consistent with and required by the United States' treaty obligations and domestic laws. We therefore reject Yousef's claim that jurisdiction over Count Nineteen was lacking and affirm the substance of the District Court's ruling.

i. The District Court's Opinion

In holding that it could exercise universal jurisdiction over Yousef for Count Nineteen, the District Court stated:

> "The issue of exercising extraterritorial jurisdiction over a criminal prosecution based on universal jurisdiction was also discussed in *United States v. Yunis*, [924 F.2d 1086 (D.C. Cir. 1991)]." . . .

The *Yunis* court did not decide that universal jurisdiction was insufficient as the sole basis for jurisdiction under the Antihijacking Act. . . .

Endorsing the exercise of universal jurisdiction in the prosecution of an aircraft-related crime, the [*Yunis*] court stated that "aircraft hijacking may well be one of the few crimes so clearly condemned under the law of nations that states may assert universal jurisdiction to bring offenders to justice, even when the state has no territorial connection to the hijacking and its citizens are not involved." *Id.* [at 1092].

The court in *Yunis* cited to the Restatement (Third) of the Foreign Relations Law to support exercise of universal jurisdiction in a criminal prosecution related to crimes involving aircraft. Section 404 [of the Restatement (Third)] states, "[a] state has jurisdiction to define and prescribe punishment for certain offenses recognized by the community of nations as of universal concern, such as piracy, slave trade, attacks on or hijacking of aircraft, genocide, war crimes, and perhaps certain acts of terrorism, even where none of the other bases of jurisdiction indicated in §402 is present." Restatement (Third) § 404 (1987). *Yousef*, 927 F. Supp. at 681 (additional internal citations omitted) (emphasis removed).

The District Court then added:

> The disregard for human life which would accompany the placing of a bomb aboard an airplane with the intent for that bomb to explode while the airplane is in flight and fully occupied with people, or otherwise sabotaging that plane, is at least as heinous a crime of international concern as hijacking a plane. *Id.* at 682.

The District Court thus held, relying on *Yunis*, the Restatement (Third), and its own analogy between "the placing of a bomb aboard an airplane" and other "heinous" crimes that support universal jurisdiction, that the United States on this ground alone could exercise universal jurisdiction to prosecute "aircraft-related crime." *Id.* at 681-82. . . . Drawing an analogy between aircraft hijacking and Yousef's act of placing a bomb aboard an aircraft, the District Court concluded that the acts charged in Count Nineteen are considered "by the United States and the international community to be 'Offenses against the Law of Nations'" that support the exercise of universal jurisdiction over Yousef. *Id.* (internal citation omitted in original).

In relying primarily on the Restatement (Third) (and its incorporation into *Yunis*) and in expanding the scope of universal jurisdiction to new offenses by judicial analogy to its traditional subjects, the District Court erred, first, in its use of the sources of authority from which a court may discern the content of customary international law and, second, in its conclusion that universal jurisdiction may be expanded by judicial analogy to the crimes that currently are subject to jurisdiction under the universality principle. We address these points in turn. . . .

[The court first explained why reliance on the Restatement was misplaced because the Restatement is an insufficient source of authority for the conclusion that aircraft terrorism fell within the scope of the universality principle.]

iii. The Universality Principle Provides for Jurisdiction over Only a Limited Set of Acts Violating the Law of Nations

The District Court erred in holding that the universality principle provides a basis for jurisdiction over Yousef for the acts charged in Count Nineteen because the universality principle permits jurisdiction over only a limited set of crimes that cannot be expanded judicially, as discussed in full below. . . .

The universality principle permits a State to prosecute an offender of any nationality for an offense committed outside of that State and without contacts to that State, but only for the few, near-unique offenses uniformly recognized by the "civilized nations" as an offense against the "Law of

Nations." The strictly limited set of crimes subject to universal jurisdiction cannot be expanded by drawing an analogy between some new crime such as placing a bomb on board an airplane and universal jurisdiction's traditional subjects. . . .

Unlike those offenses supporting universal jurisdiction under customary international law — that is, piracy, war crimes, and crimes against humanity — that now have fairly precise definitions and that have achieved universal condemnation, "terrorism" is a term as loosely deployed as it is powerfully charged. . . . Judge Harry T. Edwards of the District of Columbia Circuit stated eighteen years ago in *Tel-Oren v. Libyan Arab Republic*, 726 F.2d 774 (D.C. Cir. 1984), that "[w]hile this nation unequivocally condemns all terrorist acts, that sentiment is not universal. Indeed, the nations of the world are so divisively split on the legitimacy of such aggression as to make it impossible to pinpoint an area of harmony or consensus." *Id.* at 795 (Edwards, J., concurring). Similarly, Judge Robert H. Bork stated in his opinion in *Tel-Oren* that the claim that a defendant "violated customary principles of international law against terrorism[] concerns an area of international law in which there is little or no consensus and in which the disagreements concern politically sensitive issues. . . . [N]o consensus has developed on how properly to define 'terrorism' generally." *Id.* at 806-07 (Bork, J., concurring).

Finally, in a third concurring opinion, Judge Roger Robb found the question of assigning culpability for terrorist acts to be "non-justiciable" and outside of the competency of the courts as inextricably linked with "political question[s]." *Id.* at 823 (Robb, J., concurring). Judge Robb stated that

> [I]nternational "law," or the absence thereof, renders even the search for the least common denominators of civilized conduct in this area [defining and punishing acts of terrorism] an impossible-to-accomplish judicial task. Courts ought not to engage in it when that search takes us towards a consideration of terrorism's place in the international order. Indeed, when such a review forces us to dignify by judicial notice the most outrageous of the diplomatic charades that attempt to dignify the violence of terrorist atrocities, we corrupt our own understanding of evil. *Id.*

We regrettably are no closer now than eighteen years ago to an international consensus on the definition of terrorism or even its proscription; the mere existence of the phrase "state-sponsored terrorism" proves the absence of agreement on basic terms among a large number of States that terrorism violates public international law. Moreover, there continues to be strenuous disagreement among States about what actions do or do not constitute terrorism, nor have we shaken ourselves free of the cliché that "one man's terrorist is another man's freedom fighter." We thus conclude that the statements of Judges Edwards, Bork, and Robb remain true today, and that terrorism — unlike piracy, war crimes, and crimes against humanity — does not provide a basis for universal jurisdiction.

b. Jurisdiction Is Proper Under United States Laws Giving Effect to Its Obligations Under the Montreal Convention

While it is true, as Yousef asserts, that the District Court erred in concluding that the universality principle conferred jurisdiction over the crimes charged in Count Nineteen, Yousef's claim that principles of customary international law constrain Congress's power to enact laws that proscribe extraterritorial conduct is simply wrong. . . .

[The court then concluded that jurisdiction over this count was proper as an exercise of congressional authority to implement the obligations established by the Montreal Convention through a criminal statute. The court then explained why jurisdiction over count 19 was proper as an exercise of congressional authority to implement the obligations established by the Montreal Convention through a criminal statute.] . . .

In the following opinion, the Court adopts a "split decision" on the extraterritorial application of a federal criminal statute, concluding that at least for one offense the government failed to carry its burden of rebutting the presumption of non-extraterritorial application.

United States v. Sota

United States Court of Appeals for the District of Columbia Circuit
December 16, 2019, Argued; January 21, 2020, Decided
No. 17-3091 Consolidated with 17-3092

WILLIAMS, Senior Circuit Judge: According to a longstanding canon of statutory interpretation, our courts presume that American laws do not apply outside of the United States—unless Congress directs otherwise. Here two criminal defendants attacked a pair of American law enforcement officers in Mexico, killing one and wounding the other; they now argue that the canon requires us to set aside three of the ensuing convictions for each defendant.

After apprehension and extradition to the United States, the defendants stood trial in the District of Columbia, and a jury convicted each on four counts: two counts under 18 U.S.C. § 1114, which criminalizes the killing of an officer or employee of the United States; one count under 18 U.S.C. § 924(c) for using a firearm while committing a crime of violence; and one count under 18 U.S.C. § 1116, which criminalizes the killing of certain persons protected under international law. In this appeal, the defendants argue that § 1114 and § 924(c) do not apply extraterritorially; they don't contest their convictions under § 1116.

The defendants are correct about § 1114, which has a purely domestic scope, but not about § 924(c), which can apply to conduct overseas. We thus vacate their convictions under § 1114 and remand their cases for a limited resentencing.

* * *

In recent years the Supreme Court has applied the canon with increased clarity and insistence. See, e.g., *RJR Nabisco, Inc. v. European Cmty.*, 136 S. Ct.

2090, 195 L. Ed. 2d 476 (2016); *Kiobel v. Royal Dutch Petroleum Co.*, 569 U.S. 108, 133 S. Ct. 1659, 185 L. Ed. 2d 671 (2013); *Morrison v. Nat'l Australia Bank Ltd.*, 561 U.S. 247, 130 S. Ct. 2869, 177 L. Ed. 2d 535 (2010). The canon "rests on the perception that Congress ordinarily legislates with respect to domestic, not foreign, matters." *Morrison*, 561 U.S. at 255. The presumption also "serves to avoid the international discord that can result when U.S. law is applied to conduct in foreign countries." *RJR Nabisco*, 136 S. Ct. at 2100.

But the presumption against extraterritorial application is just a presumption. It can be overcome when Congress "has affirmatively and unmistakably instructed that the statute will" apply abroad. *Id.*

We address first 18 U.S.C. § 1114, then *id.* § 924(c), and finally a sentence enhancement under *id.* § 924(j)(1).

1. Section 1114 provides for the punishment of anyone who

> . . . kills or attempts to kill any officer or employee of the United States or of any agency in any branch of the United States Government (including any member of the uniformed services) while such officer or employee is engaged in or on account of the performance of official duties . . . .

18 U.S.C. § 1114. On its face, § 1114 does not speak to extraterritorial application one way or the other, thus leaving the presumption against extraterritoriality unrebutted.

In a number of ways the context reinforces the case against extraterritorial application of § 1114. Nearby § 1116 criminalizes killing a U.S. officer or employee who is otherwise "entitled pursuant to international law to special protection against attack upon his person, freedom, or dignity." *Id.* § 1116(b)(4)(B). And § 1116 explicitly applies to conduct beyond our borders. See *id.* § 1116(c) (delineating the statute's express extraterritorial scope). Here, as in *United States v. Thompson*, 921 F.3d 263, 266 (D.C. Cir. 2019), Congress's explicit provision for extraterritorial jurisdiction in one provision (§ 1116) militates against inferring any such application for a closely related and nearby provision with no such signal (§ 1114).

(In this case, one of the American law enforcement officers—Agent Victor Avila—possessed diplomatic status, entitling him to protection under § 1116. The other—Agent Jaime Zapata—was only stationed in Mexico temporarily and apparently did not have diplomatic status. Recall that the jury found both defendants guilty under § 1116 for the attempted killing of Avila.)

Strengthening the inference from § 1116 against extraterritorial application of § 1114 is that Congress gave both provisions their current form in a single statute, the Antiterrorism and Effective Death Penalty Act of 1996 ("AEDPA"). . . . Most notably, AEDPA revised the portion of § 1116 providing for § 1116's extraterritorial application but inserted no similar provision into § 1114. See AEDPA §§ 721, 727.

AEDPA also modified § 1114, but not, so far as we see, in a way that assists the government. Before AEDPA, § 1114 contained a long list of discrete categories of protected U.S. agents working for dozens of U.S. agencies—the list occupies a column and a half of fine print in the United States Code. See 18 U.S.C. § 1114 (1994). As a result of AEDPA, by contrast, § 1114 generically protects "any officer or employee of the United States or of any agency in any branch of the United States Government." 18 U.S.C. § 1114; AEDPA § 727 (amending § 1114 to its current form). The government correctly notes that some employees in some of the categories specifically protected under the pre-AEDPA § 1114 would have commonly been working overseas, specifically "any security officer of the Department of State or the Foreign Service." The government would have us infer extraterritorial scope in the current, expanded and generalized version of § 1114 from the old § 1114's (supposedly obvious) extraterritorial applications.

But it's far from obvious that the innumerable categories used in the prior version of § 1114 covered a material number of individuals whose work would occur only (or even largely) overseas. Even security officers for the Department of State and Foreign Service perform quite a range of *domestic* tasks, as well as work overseas. . . . Accordingly, we cannot see either the pre-AEDPA's § 1114 protections for multiple separate categories of employees, nor AEDPA's switch to generic terms, as conveying any direction to apply the statute to conduct overseas.

Similarly, the government sees significance in current § 1114's parenthetical, "(including any member of the uniformed services)." 18 U.S.C. § 1114. But at the time Congress passed AEDPA, around 85% of U.S. military personnel were stationed at home, so we can't infer anything from the group's inclusion in § 1114. . . .

The government rests primarily on *United States v. Bowman*, 260 U.S. 94, 43 S. Ct. 39, 67 L. Ed. 149 (1922). There the Supreme Court permitted the extraterritorial application of a statute outlawing conspiracy to defraud the government of the United States, including, under a recent amendment, a "corporation in which the United States of America is a stockholder." . . .

The Court acknowledged the general rule that if a statute is intended to include offenses "committed outside of the strict territorial jurisdiction [of the United States], it is natural for Congress to say so in the statute, and failure to do so will negative the purpose of Congress in this regard." . . .

In this court's most recent discussion of *Bowman* we rested our finding that Congress intended extraterritorial application largely on the great likelihood that the outlawed conduct would occur abroad. In *United States v. Delgado-Garcia*, 374 F.3d 1337, 1346, 362 U.S. App. D.C. 512 (D.C. Cir. 2004), we upheld extraterritorial application of a statute criminalizing the inducement of and assistance with unauthorized entry into the United States, observing, "It is natural to expect that a statute that protects the borders of the United States, unlike ordinary domestic statutes, would reach those outside the borders." *Id.* at 1345.

The government eschews the idea that *Bowman* and following cases such as *Delgado-Garcia* truly depend on the high probability that the criminalized conduct would occur abroad, and instead urges us to read *Bowman* as a broad rule that "criminal statutes that protect the United States government from harm should not be construed" to apply only within the United States. See Appellee's Br. 15. But such an analysis requires treating almost all the discussion in *Bowman* and *Delgado-Garcia* as surplusage and would purport to rebut the presumption against extraterritoriality in broad swaths of the U.S. Code.

Finally, the government argues that AEDPA, in reenacting § 1114, implicitly adopted the Eleventh Circuit's decision in *United States v. Benitez*, 741 F.2d 1312, 1317 (11th Cir. 1984), finding the section applicable extraterritorially. But while we presume that Congress knows of "well-settled judicial construction," *United States v. Davis*, 139 S. Ct. 2319, 2331, 204 L. Ed. 2d 757 (2019), a lone appellate case hardly counts. . . .

We acknowledge that since AEDPA the Second Circuit has joined the Eleventh Circuit in finding § 1114 applicable abroad. See *United States v. Siddiqui*, 699 F.3d 690, 701 (2d Cir. 2012) (following the court's prior decision in *United States v. Al Kassar*, 660 F.3d 108, 118 (2d Cir. 2011)). But neither of those circuits addressed the striking differences between § 1114 and its neighbor § 1116 or grappled with the Supreme Court's recent admonitions regarding the presumption against extraterritoriality.

Because § 1114 does not apply extraterritorially, we must vacate the portion of the defendants' convictions based on that statute.

2. 18 U.S.C. § 924(c) renders criminal the use of a firearm "in relation to any crime of violence or drug trafficking crime." All agree that attempted murder under § 1116 qualifies as "a crime of violence" and that the defendants used a firearm. But that in itself isn't enough to establish that *§ 924(c)* applies overseas—even where its application depends upon a crime of violence that (like § 1116) indisputably applies abroad.

Section 924(c) belongs to a genus of statute that imposes liability only if a defendant commits a predicate crime. In *RJR Nabisco*, the Supreme Court faced a similar scheme established by the Racketeer Influenced and Corrupt Organizations Act ("RICO"). The Court made clear that for RICO to apply to conduct overseas, an absolute minimum is that "the predicates alleged in a particular case themselves apply extraterritorially." As noted, § 1116 satisfies that criterion.

But *RJR Nabisco* insisted on more: affirmative evidence of congressional intent that the umbrella crime itself (RICO there, § 924(c) here) should apply to conduct overseas. The Court found such evidence in RICO's explicit listing of named predicate offenses that each provided explicitly for extraterritorial application, including, for example, 18 U.S.C. § 351(i) (incorporated into RICO by 18 U.S.C. § 1961(1)(G)); 18 U.S.C. § 1957(d)(2) (incorporated into RICO by *id.* § 1961(1)(B)). See *RJR Nabisco*, 136 S. Ct. at 2101-02 (invoking these and similar predicate crimes).

Section 924(c) defines a crime of violence in generic terms as a felony which "has as an element the use, attempted use, or threatened use of physical force against the person or property of another." *Id.* § 924(c)(3)(A). We assume that such incorporation of a mass of crimes of violence, of which we may assume only a handful reflect a congressional intent of application abroad, would not satisfy *RJR Nabisco*. But § 924(c) also includes drug trafficking crimes as predicate offenses (or at least § 924(c)'s analogy to RICO's predicate offenses), see 18 U.S.C. § 924(c)(2), and specifically enumerates 46 U.S.C. § 70503. In the latter, subsection (a) identifies forbidden drug-trafficking conduct and subsection (b) specifies that (a) "applies even though the act is committed outside the territorial jurisdiction of the United States." Following *RJR Nabisco*, we believe these predicates provide the necessary textual indication that Congress meant § 924(c) to apply overseas "to the extent that the predicates alleged in a particular case themselves apply extraterritorially." 136 S. Ct. at 2101. . . .

Because we vacate the defendants' convictions under § 1114, we remand their cases for a limited resentencing in which the district court may determine whether to modify its sentence in light of our vacatur. See *United States v. Blackson*, 709 F.3d 36, 40, 404 U.S. App. D.C. 206 (D.C. Cir. 2013).

So ordered.

NOTES AND QUESTIONS

1. What is the "presumptive" scope of federal criminal statutes?
2. What impact does the alignment, or lack thereof, between the scope of a federal criminal statute and customary international law have on the weight of this presumption?
3. Piracy is often cited as an example of conduct that falls within the scope of the universality principle of international law. May a U.S. Attorney charge an individual with the crime of piracy by alleging a violation of international law? Or does Congress have to proscribe piracy as a violation of federal criminal law? Does Congress have the authority to transform a violation of international law into a violation of federal criminal law?
4. May Congress include a nationality limit in the definition of a crime falling within the scope of the universality principle? War crimes are generally considered to fall within the scope of universal jurisdiction. The War Crimes Act, 18 U.S.C. § 2241, established federal criminal jurisdiction over certain war crimes. The statute provides:

> (a) Offense.—Whoever, whether inside or outside the United States, commits a war crime, in any of the circumstances described in subsection (b), shall be fined under this title or imprisoned for life or any term of years, or both, and if death results to the victim, shall also be subject to the penalty of death.
>
> (b) Circumstances.—The circumstances referred to in subsection (a) are that the person committing such war crime or the victim of such war crime is a member of the Armed Forces of the United States or a national of the United States (as defined in section 101 of the Immigration and Nationality Act).

Is this consistent with the principle of universal jurisdiction?

5. If, as the *Yousef* court notes, Congress may always extend U.S. criminal law extra-territorially, what logically explains why a court will "presume" Congress did not intend a statute to conflict with customary international law?

6. Is a "clear statement" of extraterritorial applicability in the text of a criminal statute the only justification for concluding it was intended to apply extraterritorially?

7. What explains the "split decision" by the *Sota* court in relation to the two statutory provisions it considered? What does this suggest about the weight of the presumption of non-extraterritorial applicability of criminal statutes?

8. What action might Congress take in order to ensure that § 1114 applied extra-territorially in the future?

INTERNATIONAL ABDUCTION AND CRIMINAL JURISDICTION

At one point in *Yousef*, the court noted that "in February 2012, following additional motion practice—including a failed attempt to have the indictment dismissed on the ground that the government's conduct in transferring him to the United States was improper. . . ." This indicates that Yousef sought to dismiss the indictment based on the manner in which he was brought into U.S. jurisdiction. The court also noted, "Yousef obtained a conditional release from prison in Honduras. Although Yousef disputes the government's version of exactly what happened next, his freedom was short-lived. He was almost immediately detained and transported from Honduras to the Southern District of New York." Does this suggest Yousef may have been brought to the United States against his will, perhaps even after being abducted by U.S. government agents?

The United States has and will almost certainly continue to utilize such tactics—abducting a suspect abroad and bringing him against his will to the United States to stand trial—to bring individuals to justice. When this occurs, the defendant will often seek to challenge the exercise of jurisdiction by alleging the illegality of the manner in which he or she was brought before the court. However, even when a defendant is able to establish illegal abduction, it is rare this will result in any relief.

In response to such challenges, U.S. courts apply what is known as the "*Ker-Frisbie*" doctrine, which mirrors an international law doctrine known as *male captus, bene detentus*: Jurisdiction of a national court is not affected by the manner or methods by which a defendant is brought before the court. In U.S. practice, this doctrine is based on two Supreme Court decisions, *Ker v. Illinois*, 119 U.S. 436 (1886), and *Frisbie v. Collins*, 342 U.S. 519 (1952). In *Ker*, the defendant was kidnapped in Peru and brought back to the United States. The Court held that "such forcible abduction is no sufficient reason why the party should not answer when brought within the jurisdiction of the court which has the right to try him for such an offence, and presents no valid objection to his trial in such court." In *Frisbie*, a defendant abducted in Ohio and then brought to Michigan to stand trial made a due process challenge to the exercise of jurisdiction. Applying the *Ker* principle, the Court rejected the challenge upheld Frisbie's conviction. Nor does the fact that the United States has an extradition treaty with the nation impact this principle, as reflected in *United States v. Alvarez-Machain*,

504 U.S. 655 (1992). In that case, the defendant was abducted in Mexico with the collusion of the Drug Enforcement Agency, and then brought to the United States. The Court rejected the argument that due process required dismissal of the indictment because allowing such practices would effectively nullify the extradition treaty with Mexico.

At least one circuit has carved a narrow exception out of the *Ker-Frisbie* doctrine. In *United States v. Toscanino*, 500 F.2d 267 (2d Cir. 1974), the defendant appealed his narcotics conviction. Toscanino asserted on appeal that the court acquired jurisdiction over him unlawfully through the conduct of American agents who kidnapped him in Uruguay. However, not only did he allege he was kidnapped, he also alleged the U.S. agents used illegal electronic surveillance and tortured him. The Second Circuit Court of Appeals reversed his conviction and remanded his case to the district court to consider whether the methods used to bring him before the court were so outrageous that they "shock the conscience." The opinion relied on *Rochin v. California*, 342 U.S. 165 (1952), decided the same Term as *Ker*, in which the Court noted:

> Regard for the requirements of the Due Process Clause "inescapably imposes upon this Court an exercise of judgment upon the whole course of the proceedings (resulting in a conviction) in order to ascertain whether they offend those canons of decency and fairness which express the notions of justice of English-speaking peoples even toward those charged with the most heinous offenses."
>
> Applying these general considerations to the circumstances of the present case, we are compelled to conclude that the proceedings by which this conviction was obtained do more than offend some fastidious squeamishness or private sentimentalism about combatting crime too categorically. This is conduct that shocks the conscience. . . .

For the *Toscanino* court, this decision indicated that while *Ker* tolerated international abduction, the methods used during the abduction could necessitate due process–based dismissal. According to the opinion:

> In light of these developments we are satisfied that the *Ker-Frisbie* rule cannot be reconciled with the Supreme Court's expansion of the concept of due process, which now protects the accused against pretrial illegality by denying to the government the fruits of its exploitation of any deliberate and unnecessary lawlessness on its part. . . . Faced with a conflict between the two concepts of due process, the one being the restricted version found in *Ker-Frisbie* and the other the expanded and enlightened interpretation expressed in more recent decisions of the Supreme Court, we are persuaded that to the extent that the two are in conflict, the *Ker-Frisbie* version must yield. Accordingly we view due process as now requiring a court to divest itself of jurisdiction over the person of a defendant where it has been acquired as the result of the government's deliberate, unnecessary and unreasonable invasion of the accused's constitutional rights.

The so-called *Toscanino* exception has, however, rarely been effectively invoked. An interesting example of a court rejecting a *Toscanino* argument is *United States v. Noriega*, where the trial and appeals courts both concluded that the invasion of Panama and capture of General Noriega did not "shock the conscience." According to the Eleventh Circuit opinion, "Noriega also sought the dismissal of the indictment against him on the ground that the manner in which he was brought before the district court (i.e., through a military invasion) was so unconscionable as to constitute a violation of substantive due process." The court then concluded that the due process claim "falls squarely within the [Supreme Court's] *Ker-Frisbie* doctrine, which holds that a defendant cannot defeat personal jurisdiction by asserting the illegality of the procurement of his presence," and that "Noriega has not alleged that the government mistreated him personally, and thus, he cannot come within the purview of the caveat to *Ker-Frisbie* recognized by the Second Circuit in *United States v. Toscanino*, 500 F.2d 267 (2d Cir. 1974), were this court inclined to adopt such an exception."

III. THE BILL OF RIGHTS—THE "WHERE, WHEN, AND WHO" OF PROTECTION

The Bill of Rights provides essential protection for individuals against government investigatory efforts, questioning, and use of criminal prosecutions. Although originally adopted to restrain only federal government power, most of these rights apply to the states through the Due Process Clause of the Fourteenth Amendment. But do they also apply to U.S. citizens and/or other nationals outside the United States? Or do the protections cease at the borders, allowing the federal government to conduct investigations and prosecutions outside the nation without concern for these rights?

Recall the Supreme Court's ruling in *Reid v. Covert* addressed in Chapter 6 that the Constitution's protections are supreme and cannot be modified by a statute even when that statute implements a treaty. The issue in that case was whether trial of U.S. citizens by courts-martial violated the rights protected by the Sixth Amendment. The Court's affirmative answer to that question addressed in Chapter 6 was based on the conclusion that the protections afforded by the Sixth Amendment applied extraterritorially to the two military spouses involved in the case, one living in the United Kingdom and the other in Japan. While this might seem an obvious conclusion today, it was not so obvious at that time. Indeed, the analysis that led to this conclusion was an important aspect of the decision. Consider the following framing of the issue in the opinion:

> These cases raise basic constitutional issues of the utmost concern. They call into question the role of the military under our system of government. They involve the power of Congress to expose civilians to trial by military tribunals, under military regulations and procedures, for offenses against the United States thereby depriving them of trial in civilian courts, under civilian laws and procedures and with all the safeguards of the Bill of Rights. . . .
>
> The two cases were consolidated and argued last Term and a majority of the Court, with three Justices dissenting and one reserving opinion, held that

military trial of Mrs. Smith and Mrs. Covert for their alleged offenses was constitutional. 351 U.S. 470, 76 S. Ct. 886, 100 L. Ed. 1342; 351 U.S. 487, 76 S. Ct. 880, 100 L. Ed. 1352. The majority held that the provisions of Article III and the Fifth and Sixth Amendments which require that crimes be tried by a jury after indictment by a grand jury did not protect an American citizen when he was tried by the American Government in foreign lands for offenses committed there and that Congress could provide for the trial of such offenses in any manner it saw fit so long as the procedures established were reasonable and consonant with due process. . . .

After noting the Court granted petition for rehearing, the plurality concluded:

At the beginning we reject the idea that when the United States acts against citizens abroad it can do so free of the Bill of Rights. The United States is entirely a creature of the Constitution. Its power and authority have no other source. It can only act in accordance with all the limitations imposed by the Constitution. When the Government reaches out to punish a citizen who is abroad, the shield which the Bill of Rights and other parts of the Constitution provide to protect his life and liberty should not be stripped away just because he happens to be in another land. This is not a novel concept. To the contrary, it is as old as government. . . .

In summary, we conclude that the constitution in its entirety applied to the trials of Mrs. Smith and Mrs. Covert. Since their court-martial did not meet the requirements of Art. III, § 2 or the Fifth and Sixth Amendments we are compelled to determine if there is anything *within* the Constitution which authorizes the military trial of dependents accompanying the armed forces overseas.

Note that only a plurality of the Court agreed on this assertion of extraterritorial applicability of the Bill of Rights. Justice Harlan concurred in the result, but was unwilling to agree with the breadth of the conclusion, focusing instead on the fact that both citizens faced capital punishment in their military trials:

I cannot agree with the sweeping proposition that a full Article III trial, with indictment and trial by jury, is required in every case for the trial of a civilian dependent of a serviceman overseas. . . . I need not go into details, beyond stating that except for capital offenses, such as we have here, to which, in my opinion, special considerations apply, I am by no means ready to say that Congress' power to provide for trial by court-martial of civilian dependents overseas is limited by Article III and the Fifth and Sixth Amendments. Where, if at all, the dividing line should be drawn among cases not capital, need not now be decided. . . .

So far as capital cases are concerned, I think they stand on quite a different footing than other offenses. In such cases the law is especially sensitive to demands for that procedural fairness which inheres in a civilian trial where the judge and trier of fact are not responsive to the command of the convening authority. I do not concede that whatever process is "due" an offender faced with a fine or a prison sentence necessarily satisfies the requirements of the Constitution in a capital case. . . .

Nonetheless, *Reid* is often cited to support the proposition that the Bill of Rights is not territorially restricted but follows U.S. citizens wherever they are subjected to the power of the federal government. As the next case indicates, the analysis is more complex *vis-à-vis* aliens.

United States v. Verdugo-Urquidez
494 U.S. 259 (1990)

Chief Justice REHNQUIST delivered the opinion of the Court.

The question presented by this case is whether the Fourth Amendment applies to the search and seizure by United States agents of property that is owned by a nonresident alien and located in a foreign country. We hold that it does not.

Respondent Rene Martin Verdugo-Urquidez is a citizen and resident of Mexico. He is believed by the United States Drug Enforcement Agency (DEA) to be one of the leaders of a large and violent organization in Mexico that smuggles narcotics into the United States. Based on a complaint charging respondent with various narcotics-related offenses, the Government obtained a warrant for his arrest on August 3, 1985. In January 1986, Mexican police officers, after discussions with United States marshals, apprehended Verdugo-Urquidez in Mexico and transported him to the United States Border Patrol station in Calexico, California. There, United States marshals arrested respondent and eventually moved him to a correctional center in San Diego, California, where he remains incarcerated pending trial.

Following respondent's arrest, Terry Bowen, a DEA agent assigned to the Calexico DEA office, decided to arrange for searches of Verdugo-Urquidez's Mexican residences located in Mexicali and San Felipe. Bowen believed that the searches would reveal evidence related to respondent's alleged narcotics trafficking activities and his involvement in the kidnaping and torture-murder of DEA Special Agent Enrique Camarena Salazar (for which respondent subsequently has been convicted in a separate prosecution. See *United States v. Verdugo-Urquidez*, No. CR-87-422-ER (CD Cal., Nov. 22, 1988)). Bowen telephoned Walter White, the Assistant Special Agent in charge of the DEA office in Mexico City, and asked him to seek authorization for the search from the Director General of the Mexican Federal Judicial Police (MFJP). After several attempts to reach high ranking Mexican officials, White eventually contacted the Director General, who authorized the searches and promised the cooperation of Mexican authorities. Thereafter, DEA agents working in concert with officers of the MFJP searched respondent's properties in Mexicali and San Felipe and seized certain documents. In particular, the search of the Mexicali residence uncovered a tally sheet, which the Government believes reflects the quantities of marijuana smuggled by Verdugo-Urquidez into the United States.

The District Court granted respondent's motion to suppress evidence seized during the searches, concluding that the Fourth Amendment applied to the searches and that the DEA agents had failed to justify searching respondent's premises without a warrant. A divided panel of the Court of Appeals for the Ninth Circuit affirmed. 856 F.2d 1214 (1988). It cited this Court's decision in *Reid v. Covert*, 354 U.S. 1 (1957), which held that American citizens tried by United States military authorities in a foreign country were entitled to the protections of the Fifth and Sixth Amendments, and concluded that "[t]he Constitution imposes substantive constraints on the federal government, even when it operates abroad." 856 F.2d, at 1218. Relying on our decision in *INS v. Lopez-Mendoza*, 468 U.S. 1032 (1984), where a majority of Justices assumed that illegal aliens in the United States have Fourth Amendment rights, the Ninth Circuit majority found it "difficult to conclude that Verdugo-Urquidez lacks these same protections." 856 F.2d, at 1223. It also observed that persons in respondent's position enjoy certain trial-related rights, and reasoned that "[i]t would be odd indeed to acknowledge that Verdugo-Urquidez is entitled to due process under the fifth amendment, and to a fair trial under the sixth amendment, . . . and deny him the protection from unreasonable searches and seizures afforded under the fourth amendment." *Id.*, at 1224. Having concluded that the Fourth Amendment applied to the searches of respondent's properties, the court went on to decide that the searches violated the Constitution because the DEA agents failed to procure a search warrant. Although recognizing that "an American search warrant would be of no legal validity in Mexico," the majority deemed it sufficient that a warrant would have "substantial constitutional value in this country" because it would reflect a magistrate's determination that there existed probable cause to search and would define the scope of the search. *Id.*, at 1230.

. . . Before analyzing the scope of the Fourth Amendment, we think it significant to note that it operates in a different manner than the Fifth Amendment, which is not at issue in this case. The privilege against self-incrimination guaranteed by the Fifth Amendment is a fundamental trial right of criminal defendants. See *Malloy v. Hogan*, 378 U.S. 1 (1964). Although conduct by law enforcement officials prior to trial may ultimately impair that right, a constitutional violation occurs only at trial. *Kastigar v. United States*, 406 U.S. 441, 453 (1972). The Fourth Amendment functions differently. It prohibits "unreasonable searches and seizures" whether or not the evidence is sought to be used in a criminal trial, and a violation of the Amendment is "fully accomplished" at the time of an unreasonable governmental intrusion. *United States v. Calandra*, 414 U.S. 338, 354 (1974); *United States v. Leon*, 468 U.S. 897, 906 (1984). For purposes of this case, therefore, if there were a constitutional violation, it occurred solely in Mexico. Whether evidence obtained from respondent's Mexican residences should be excluded at trial in the United States is a remedial question separate from the existence *vel non* of the constitutional violation. *Calandra, supra*, at 354; *Leon, supra*, at 906.

The Fourth Amendment provides:

"The right of the people to be secure in their persons, houses, papers, and effects, against unreasonable searches and seizures, shall not be violated, and no Warrants shall issue, but upon probable cause, supported by Oath or affirmation, and particularly describing the place to be searched, and the persons or things to be seized."

That text, by contrast with the Fifth and Sixth Amendments, extends its reach only to "the people." Contrary to the suggestion of *amici curiae* that the Framers used this phrase "simply to avoid [an] awkward rhetorical redundancy," Brief for American Civil Liberties Union et al. as *Amici Curiae* 12, n.4, "the people" seems to have been a term of art employed in select parts of the Constitution. The Preamble declares that the Constitution is ordained and established by "the people of the United States." The Second Amendment protects "the right of the people to keep and bear Arms," and the Ninth and Tenth Amendments provide that certain rights and powers are retained by and reserved to "the people." See also U.S. Const., Amdt. 1 ("Congress shall make no law . . . abridging . . . *the right of the people* peaceably to assemble") (emphasis added); Art. I, § 2, cl. 1 ("The House of Representatives shall be composed of Members chosen every second Year *by the people* of the several States") (emphasis added). While this textual exegesis is by no means conclusive, it suggests that "the people" protected by the Fourth Amendment, and by the First and Second Amendments, and to whom rights and powers are reserved in the Ninth and Tenth Amendments, refers to a class of persons who are part of a national community or who have otherwise developed sufficient connection with this country to be considered part of that community. See *United States ex rel. Turner v. Williams*, 194 U.S. 279, 292 (1904) (Excludable alien is not entitled to First Amendment rights, because "[h]e does not become one of the people to whom these things are secured by our Constitution by an attempt to enter forbidden by law"). The language of these Amendments contrasts with the words "person" and "accused" used in the Fifth and Sixth Amendments regulating procedure in criminal cases.

What we know of the history of the drafting of the Fourth Amendment also suggests that its purpose was to restrict searches and seizures which might be conducted by the United States in domestic matters. . . . The driving force behind the adoption of the Amendment, as suggested by Madison's advocacy, was widespread hostility among the former colonists to the issuance of writs of assistance empowering revenue officers to search suspected places for smuggled goods, and general search warrants permitting the search of private houses, often to uncover papers that might be used to convict persons of libel. See *Boyd v. United States*, 116 U.S. 616, 625-626 (1886). The available historical data show, therefore, that the purpose of the Fourth Amendment was to protect the people of the United States against arbitrary action by their own

Government; it was never suggested that the provision was intended to restrain the actions of the Federal Government against aliens outside of the United States territory.

The global view taken by the Court of Appeals of the application of the Constitution is also contrary to this Court's decisions in the Insular Cases, which held that not every constitutional provision applies to governmental activity even where the United States has sovereign power. See, e.g., *Balzac v. Porto Rico*, 258 U.S. 298 (1922) (Sixth Amendment right to jury trial inapplicable in Puerto Rico); *Ocampo v. United States*, 234 U.S. 91 (1914) (Fifth Amendment grand jury provision inapplicable in Philippines); *Dorr v. United States*, 195 U.S. 138 (1904) (jury trial provision inapplicable in Philippines); *Hawaii v. Mankichi*, 190 U.S. 197 (1903) (provisions on indictment by grand jury and jury trial inapplicable in Hawaii); *Downes v. Bidwell*, 182 U.S. 244 (1901) (Revenue Clauses of Constitution inapplicable to Puerto Rico). In *Dorr*, we declared the general rule that in an unincorporated territory — one not clearly destined for statehood — Congress was not required to adopt "a system of laws which shall include the right of trial by jury, and that the Constitution does not, without legislation and of its own force, *carry such right to territory so situated*." 195 U.S., at 149 (emphasis added). Only "fundamental" constitutional rights are guaranteed to inhabitants of those territories. *Id.* at 148; *Balzac, supra*, at 312-313; see *Examining Board of Engineers, Architects and Surveyors v. Flores de Otero*, 426 U.S. 572, 599, n.30 (1976). If that is true with respect to territories ultimately governed by Congress, respondent's claim that the protections of the Fourth Amendment extend to aliens in foreign nations is even weaker. And certainly, it is not open to us in light of the Insular Cases to endorse the view that every constitutional provision applies wherever the United States Government exercises its power.

Indeed, we have rejected the claim that aliens are entitled to Fifth Amendment rights outside the sovereign territory of the United States. In *Johnson v. Eisentrager*, 339 U.S. 763 (1950), the Court held that enemy aliens arrested in China and imprisoned in Germany after World War II could not obtain writs of habeas corpus in our federal courts on the ground that their convictions for war crimes had violated the Fifth Amendment and other constitutional provisions. The *Eisentrager* opinion acknowledged that in some cases constitutional provisions extend beyond the citizenry; "[t]he alien . . . has been accorded a generous and ascending scale of rights as he increases his identity with our society." *Id.*, at 770. But our rejection of extraterritorial application of the Fifth Amendment was emphatic:

> "Such extraterritorial application of organic law would have been so significant an innovation in the practice of governments that, if intended or apprehended, it could scarcely have failed to excite contemporary comment. Not one word can be cited. No decision of this Court supports such a view. Cf. *Downes v. Bidwell*, 182 U.S. 244 [(1901)]. None of the learned commentators on our

Constitution has even hinted at it. The practice of every modern government is opposed to it." *Id.*, at 784.

If such is true of the Fifth Amendment, which speaks in the relatively universal term of "person," it would seem even more true with respect to the Fourth Amendment, which applies only to "the people."

To support his all-encompassing view of the Fourth Amendment, respondent points to language from the plurality opinion in *Reid v. Covert*, 354 U.S. 1 (1957). *Reid* involved an attempt by Congress to subject the wives of American servicemen to trial by military tribunals without the protection of the Fifth and Sixth Amendments. The Court held that it was unconstitutional to apply the Uniform Code of Military Justice to the trials of the American women for capital crimes. Four Justices "reject[ed] the idea that when the United States acts *against citizens* abroad it can do so free of the Bill of Rights." *Id.*, at 5 (emphasis added). The plurality went on to say:

> "The United States is entirely a creature of the Constitution. Its power and authority have no other source. It can only act in accordance with all the limitations imposed by the Constitution. When the Government reaches out to punish a *citizen* who is abroad, the shield which the Bill of Rights and other parts of the Constitution provide to protect his life and liberty should not be stripped away just because he happens to be in another land." *Id.*, at 5-6 (emphasis added; footnote omitted).

Respondent urges that we interpret this discussion to mean that federal officials are constrained by the Fourth Amendment wherever and against whomever they act. But the holding of *Reid* stands for no such sweeping proposition: it decided that United States citizens stationed abroad could invoke the protection of the Fifth and Sixth Amendments. The concurrences by Justices Frankfurter and Harlan in *Reid* resolved the case on much narrower grounds than the plurality and declined even to hold that United States citizens were entitled to the full range of constitutional protections in all overseas criminal prosecutions. *See id.*, at 75 (Harlan, J., concurring in result) ("I agree with my brother Frankfurter that . . . we have before us a question analogous, ultimately, to issues of due process; one can say, in fact, that the question of which specific safeguards of the Constitution are appropriately to be applied in a particular context overseas can be reduced to the issue of what process is 'due' a defendant in the particular circumstances of a particular case"). Since respondent is not a United States citizen, he can derive no comfort from the *Reid* holding.

For better or for worse, we live in a world of nation-states in which our Government must be able to "functio[n] effectively in the company of sovereign nations." *Perez v. Brownell*, 356 U.S. 44, 57 (1958). Some who violate our laws may live outside our borders under a regime quite different from that which obtains in this country. . . . The judgment of the Court of Appeals is accordingly
  Reversed.

NOTES AND QUESTIONS

1. *Reid v. Covert* is often invoked for the proposition that "the Bill of Rights follows Americans abroad." Is this an accurate characterization of the decision?
2. Almost all constitutional rights related to criminal investigation and prosecution have been "incorporated" through the Due Process Clause of the Fourteenth Amendment to apply to the states (exceptions include the grand jury requirement, the unanimous verdict requirement in non-capital cases, and the twelve-person jury in non-capital cases). These "incorporation" decisions are based on the Supreme Court's determination that each of these rights is "fundamental" in nature. Do these decisions impact the applicability of these rights outside the United States?
3. The *Verdugo* majority concluded that the "timing" of a constitutional violation indicates the Fourth Amendment is not implicated when prosecutors introduce evidence against an alien who was seized outside the United States by U.S. agents. Does this "time framing" also support the same outcome if the defendant is a U.S. citizen or national?
4. The Court rejected Verdugo's argument that *Reid v. Covert* supported extending the Fourth Amendment to the search of his residence in Mexico. Was it necessary for the majority to emphasize Justice Harlan's dissent in *Reid* to support this rejection?
5. If you were asked to render an opinion on the applicability of the Fourth Amendment's reasonableness requirement to a search or seizure abroad, how would you respond in light of *Verdugo* and *Reid*? What if the question was whether the FBI was restricted by the *Miranda* rule derived from the Fifth Amendment, or whether an alien could move to exclude a confession procured by actual coercion at the hands of U.S. agents?

IV. NATIONAL SECURITY, CRIMINAL INVESTIGATIONS, AND THE BILL OF RIGHTS

Reid and *Verdugo* turned on the applicability of constitutional protections to individuals outside the United States. While aliens with no connection to the United States are not protected by the Fourth Amendment, these decisions indicate that this is the exception, and not the rule. In most situations, government investigatory and surveillance activities will be subject to constitutional limitations. The contours of these constitutional criminal procedure rules will therefore often be an important consideration in assessing the legality of national security–related investigations.

A. The Fourth Amendment's Reasonableness Requirement

The Fourth Amendment prohibits "unreasonable" seizures or searches and requires that warrants be supported by probable cause. A seizure or search will be deemed reasonable when it is conducted pursuant to a properly issued warrant, or pursuant to an established exception to the warrant and/or probable cause requirement. But this "reasonableness" requirement is only implicated by U.S government action (when a private party or a foreign government acting independently obtains evidence and provides it to the U.S. government, this does not implicate the Fourth Amendment) that amounts to a seizure or a search.

In *United States v. Karo*, 468 U.S. 705 (1984), the Supreme Court held that property is seized within the meaning of the Fourth Amendment only when government action results in a "meaningful interference with a possessory interest." When government agents take possession of property, this is obviously a seizure. However, if government agents attach something to property, for example, a beeper or a GPS device, this is not a seizure so long as the individual is unaware of the placement, as it will not interfere with the use of the property.

It is more common to question whether government action qualifies as a search will arise during the course of an investigation. If so, and the search is directed against an individual who may invoke the protection of the Fourth Amendment, it must be reasonable. While it may seem that whenever government agents "look" for something they are "searching," this is both overbroad and underinclusive. A search within the meaning of the Fourth Amendment is defined by *where* the government agent looks for or gains access to the information.

Until 2012, the test for what qualified as a search triggering the reasonableness requirement of the Fourth Amendment was whether government agents intruded upon a reasonable expectation of privacy. That test originated in the Court's landmark decision of *Katz v. United States*, 389 U.S. 347 (1967). In that case, the Court held that use of a listening device to monitor the conversation in a phone booth was a search because Katz demonstrated a subjective expectation of privacy by closing the door and it was an expectation society recognized as legitimate or reasonable. The Court's subsequent expectation of privacy jurisprudence established a touchstone for assessing when government efforts to find something intruded on a reasonable expectation of privacy: whether the "thing" had been knowingly exposed to the public. If so, there was no such expectation and "looking" did not qualify as "searching."

However, in *United States v. Jones*, 565 U.S. 400 (2012), the Supreme Court clarified the controlling test for assessing when government action qualifies as a search. In that case, police attached a GPS device to the undercarriage of the suspect's vehicle *while it was in a public parking lot* and then monitored the vehicle's movements on public roads. Jones moved to suppress all the data from the GPS, arguing it amounted to a search. The trial court rejected that argument (with the exception of GPS data while the car was in his garage) because the car was knowingly exposed to the public and therefore neither the placement of the GPS device nor the monitoring required police to intrude upon a reasonable expectation of privacy.

The Supreme Court reached a different conclusion, but not based on reasonable expectation of privacy analysis. Instead, the Court clarified that the *Katz* test was never intended to supersede the protection provided by the text of the Fourth

Amendment, but instead was a supplement to that protection. The Court then concluded that the text of the Amendment always treated a physical trespass against an enumerated protection — persons, home, papers, or effects — for the purpose of gathering evidence as a search. Accordingly, when police committed a trespass against Jones's effect (his car) for the purpose of gathering evidence, *that* was a Fourth Amendment search. As a result, it was irrelevant that Jones exposed his car to the public in the parking lot, because the reasonable expectation of privacy test is a *supplement* and not a *substitute* for the textual trespass test. According to the majority opinion:

> The Government contends that the *Harlan* standard shows that no search occurred here, since Jones had no "reasonable expectation of privacy" in the area of the Jeep accessed by Government agents (its underbody) and in the locations of the Jeep on the public roads, which were visible to all. But we need not address the Government's contentions, because Jones's Fourth Amendment rights do not rise or fall with the *Katz* formulation. At bottom, we must "assur[e] preservation of that degree of privacy against government that existed when the Fourth Amendment was adopted." *Kyllo*, supra, at 34, 121 S. Ct. 2038. As explained, for most of our history the Fourth Amendment was understood to embody a particular concern for government trespass upon the areas ("persons, houses, papers, and effects") it enumerates. *Katz* did not repudiate that understanding. Less than two years later the Court upheld defendants' contention that the Government could not introduce against them conversations between *other* people obtained by warrantless placement of electronic surveillance devices in their homes. The opinion rejected the dissent's contention that there was no Fourth Amendment violation "unless the conversational privacy of the homeowner himself is invaded." *Alderman v. United States*, 394 U.S. 165, 176, 89 S. Ct. 961, 22 L. Ed. 2d 176 (1969). "[W]e [do not] believe that *Katz*, by holding that the Fourth Amendment protects persons and their private conversations, was intended to withdraw any of the protection which the Amendment extends to the home...." *Id.*, at 180, 89 S. Ct. 961.

Notice how the Court never reached the question of whether the actual GPS surveillance of the car qualified as a search because the trespass to emplace the GPS resolved that question. But several Justices raised suggested that the reasonable expectation of privacy test might need to be reconsidered to address the question of whether extensive technology-enabled surveillance of a citizen even on the public roads should qualify as a search. For example, in her concurring opinion Justice Sotomayor indicated:

> I join the Court's opinion because I agree that a search within the meaning of the Fourth Amendment occurs, at a minimum, "[w]here, as here, the Government obtains information by physically intruding on a constitutionally protected area." ...
>
> ... As Justice Alito incisively observes, the same technological advances that have made possible nontrespassory surveillance techniques will also affect the *Katz* test by shaping the evolution of societal privacy expectations. *Post*, at 962-963. Under that rubric, I agree with Justice Alito that, at the very least, "longer term GPS monitoring in investigations of most offenses impinges on expectations of privacy."
>
> ...

More fundamentally, it may be necessary to reconsider the premise that an individual has no reasonable expectation of privacy in information voluntarily disclosed to third parties. *E.g., Smith*, 442 U.S., at 742, 99 S. Ct. 2577; *United States v. Miller*, 425 U.S. 435, 443, 96 S. Ct. 1619, 48 L. Ed. 2d 71 (1976). This approach is ill suited to the digital age, in which people reveal a great deal of information about themselves to third parties in the course of carrying out mundane tasks.

Justice Sotomayor concluded her concurring opinion by indicating that "resolution of these difficult questions in this case is unnecessary, however, because the Government's physical intrusion on Jones' Jeep supplies a narrower basis for decision."

It is difficult to overstate the potential impact of treating access to "third party" records as a Fourth Amendment search. Because such access has long been understood as falling outside the scope of the Fourth Amendment, federal agents engaged in criminal and national security investigations may access such information without having to establish probable cause and obtain a warrant. Instead, a subpoena, issued based on a determination that there is a reasonable basis to believe the information is relevant to an investigation (a much lower standard than probable cause), will often be used to obtain such information. But as Justice Sotomayor noted in *Jones*, the assumption that access to third-party records does not qualify as a search subject to the presumptive warrant requirement of the Fourth Amendment seems ill-suited to the digital age. The next case suggests the seed she planted may be taking root.

Carpenter v. United States
138 S. Ct. 2206 (2018), 585 U.S. ___, No. 16-402 (June 22, 2018)

Chief Justice ROBERTS delivered the opinion of the Court.

This case presents the question whether the Government conducts a search under the Fourth Amendment when it accesses historical cell phone records that provide a comprehensive chronicle of the user's past movements.

I

A

There are 396 million cell phone service accounts in the United States — for a Nation of 326 million people. Cell phones perform their wide and growing variety of functions by connecting to a set of radio antennas called "cell sites." Although cell sites are usually mounted on a tower, they can also be found on light posts, flagpoles, church steeples, or the sides of buildings. Cell sites typically have several directional antennas that divide the covered area into sectors.

Cell phones continuously scan their environment looking for the best signal, which generally comes from the closest cell site. Most modern devices, such as smartphones, tap into the wireless network several times a minute whenever their signal is on, even if the owner is not using one of the phone's features. Each time the phone connects to a cell site, it generates a time-stamped record known as cell-site location information (CSLI). The precision of this information depends on the size of the geographic area covered by the cell site. The greater the concentration of cell sites, the smaller the coverage area. As data usage from cell phones has increased, wireless carriers have installed more cell sites to handle the traffic. That has led to increasingly compact coverage areas, especially in urban areas.

Wireless carriers collect and store CSLI for their own business purposes, including finding weak spots in their network and applying "roaming" charges when another carrier routes data through their cell sites. In addition, wireless carriers often sell aggregated location records to data brokers, without individual identifying information of the sort at issue here. While carriers have long retained CSLI for the start and end of incoming calls, in recent years phone companies have also collected location information from the transmission of text messages and routine data connections. Accordingly, modern cell phones generate increasingly vast amounts of increasingly precise CSLI.

B

In 2011, police officers arrested four men suspected of robbing a series of Radio Shack and (ironically enough) T-Mobile stores in Detroit. One of the men confessed that, over the previous four months, the group (along with a rotating cast of getaway drivers and lookouts) had robbed nine different stores in Michigan and Ohio. The suspect identified 15 accomplices who had participated in the heists and gave the FBI some of their cell phone numbers; the FBI then reviewed his call records to identify additional numbers that he had called around the time of the robberies.

Based on that information, the prosecutors applied for court orders under the Stored Communications Act to obtain cell phone records for petitioner Timothy Carpenter and several other suspects. That statute, as amended in 1994, permits the Government to compel the disclosure of certain telecommunications records when it "offers specific and articulable facts showing that there are reasonable grounds to believe" that the records sought "are relevant and material to an ongoing criminal investigation." 18 U.S.C. § 2703(d). Federal Magistrate Judges issued two orders directing Carpenter's wireless carriers—MetroPCS and Sprint—to disclose "cell/site sector [information] for [Carpenter's] telephone[ ] at call origination and at call termination for incoming and outgoing calls" during the four-month period when the string of robberies occurred. . . . Altogether the Government obtained 12,898 location points cataloging Carpenter's movements—an average of 101 data points per day.

Carpenter was charged with six counts of robbery and an additional six counts of carrying a firearm during a federal crime of violence. . . . Carpenter moved to suppress the cell-site data provided by the wireless carriers. He argued that the Government's seizure of the records violated the Fourth Amendment because they had been obtained without a warrant supported by probable cause. The District Court denied the motion. . . . App. to Pet. for Cert. 38a-39a.

At trial . . . FBI agent Christopher Hess offered expert testimony about the cell-site data. . . . Hess produced maps that placed Carpenter's phone near four of the charged robberies. In the Government's view, the location records clinched the case: They confirmed that Carpenter was "right where the . . . robbery was at the exact time of the robbery." App. 131 (closing argument). Carpenter was convicted . . . and sentenced to more than 100 years in prison.

The Court of Appeals for the Sixth Circuit affirmed. 819 F.3d 880 (2016). The court held that Carpenter lacked a reasonable expectation of privacy in the location information collected by the FBI because he had shared that information with his wireless carriers. . . . [T]he court concluded that the resulting business records are not entitled to Fourth Amendment protection. *Id.*, at 888 (quoting *Smith v. Maryland*, 442 U.S. 735, 741 (1979)).

We granted certiorari. 582 U.S. ___ (2017).

II

A

The Fourth Amendment protects "[t]he right of the people to be secure in their persons, houses, papers, and effects, against unreasonable searches and seizures." The "basic purpose of this Amendment," our cases have recognized, "is to safeguard the privacy and security of individuals against arbitrary invasions by governmental officials." . . .

For much of our history, Fourth Amendment search doctrine was "tied to common-law trespass" and focused on whether the Government "obtains information by physically intruding on a constitutionally protected area." *United States v. Jones*, 565 U.S. 400, 405, 406, n.3 (2012). More recently, the Court has recognized that "property rights are not the sole measure of Fourth Amendment violations." *Soldal v. Cook County*, 506 U.S. 56, 64 (1992). In *Katz v. United States*, 389 U.S. 347, 351 (1967), we established that "the Fourth Amendment protects people, not places," and expanded our conception of the Amendment to protect certain expectations of privacy as well. When an individual "seeks to preserve something as private," and his expectation of privacy is "one that society is prepared to recognize as reasonable," we have held that official intrusion into that private sphere generally qualifies as a search . . . .

. . . [O]ur cases have recognized some basic guideposts. First, that the Amendment seeks to secure "the privacies of life" against "arbitrary power." *Boyd v. United States*, 116 U.S. 616, 630 (1886). Second, and relatedly, that a central aim of the Framers was "to place obstacles in the way of a too permeating police surveillance." *United States v. Di Re*, 332 U.S. 581, 595 (1948).

We have kept this attention to Founding-era understandings in mind when applying the Fourth Amendment to innovations in surveillance tools. As technology has enhanced the Government's capacity to encroach upon areas normally guarded from inquisitive eyes, this Court has sought to "assure[ ] preservation of that degree of privacy against government that existed when the Fourth Amendment was adopted." *Kyllo v. United States,* 533 U.S. 27, 34 (2001). . . .

B

The case before us involves the Government's acquisition of wireless carrier cell-site records revealing the location of Carpenter's cell phone whenever it made or received calls. This sort of digital data—personal location information maintained by a third party—does not fit neatly under existing precedents. Instead, requests for cell-site records lie at the intersection of two lines of cases, both of which inform our understanding of the privacy interests at stake.

The first set of cases addresses a person's expectation of privacy in his physical location and movements. In *United States v. Knotts,* 460 U.S. 276 (1983), we considered the Government's use of a "beeper" to aid in tracking a vehicle through traffic. Police officers in that case planted a beeper in a container of chloroform before it was purchased by one of Knotts's co-conspirators. The officers (with intermittent aerial assistance) then followed the automobile carrying the container from Minneapolis to Knotts's cabin in Wisconsin, relying on the beeper's signal to help keep the vehicle in view. The Court concluded that the "augment[ed]" visual surveillance did not constitute a search because "[a] person traveling in an automobile on public thoroughfares has no reasonable expectation of privacy in his movements from one place to another." *Id.,* at 281, 282. Since the movements of the vehicle and its final destination had been "voluntarily conveyed to anyone who wanted to look," Knotts could not assert a privacy interest in the information obtained. *Id.,* at 281.

This Court in Knotts, however, was careful to distinguish between the rudimentary tracking facilitated by the beeper and more sweeping modes of surveillance. . . . Significantly, the Court reserved the question whether "different constitutional principles may be applicable" if "twenty-four hour surveillance of any citizen of this country [were] possible." *Id.,* at 283-284.

Three decades later, the Court considered more sophisticated surveillance of the sort envisioned in *Knotts* and found that different principles did indeed apply. In *United States v. Jones,* FBI agents installed a GPS tracking device on Jones's vehicle and remotely monitored the vehicle's movements for 28 days. The Court decided the case based on the Government's physical trespass of the vehicle. 565 U.S., at 404-405. At the same time, five Justices agreed that related privacy concerns would be raised by, for example, "surreptitiously activating a stolen vehicle detection system" in Jones's car to track Jones himself, or conducting GPS tracking of his cell phone. *Id.,* at 426, 428 (Alito, J., concurring in judgment); *id.,* at 415 (Sotomayor, J., concurring). Since GPS monitoring of a vehicle tracks "every movement" a person makes in that vehicle, the concurring Justices concluded that "longer term GPS monitoring in investigations of most offenses impinges on expectations of privacy"—regardless whether those movements were disclosed to the public at large. *Id.*, at 430 (opinion of Alito, J.); *id.*, at 415 (opinion of Sotomayor, J.).

In a second set of decisions, the Court has drawn a line between what a person keeps to himself and what he shares with others. We have previously held that "a person has no legitimate expectation of privacy in information he voluntarily turns over to third parties." *Smith*, 442 U.S., at 743-744. That remains true "even if the information is revealed on the assumption that it will be used only for a limited purpose." *United States v. Miller*, 425 U.S. 435, 443 (1976). As a result, the Government is typically free to obtain such information from the recipient without triggering Fourth Amendment protections.

This third-party doctrine largely traces its roots to *Miller*. While investigating Miller for tax evasion, the Government subpoenaed his banks, seeking several months of canceled checks, deposit slips, and monthly statements. The Court rejected a Fourth Amendment challenge to the records collection. For one, Miller could "assert neither ownership nor possession" of the documents; they were "business records of the banks." *Id.*, at 440. For another, the nature of those records confirmed Miller's limited expectation of privacy, because the checks were "not confidential communications but negotiable instruments to be used in commercial transactions," and the bank statements contained information "exposed to [bank] employees in the ordinary course of business." *Id.*, at 442. The Court thus concluded that Miller had "take[n] the risk, in revealing his affairs to another, that the information [would] be conveyed by that person to the Government." *Id.*, at 443.

Three years later, *Smith* applied the same principles in the context of information conveyed to a telephone company. The Court ruled that the Government's use of a pen register—a device that recorded the outgoing phone numbers dialed on a landline telephone—was not a search. Noting the pen register's "limited capabilities," the Court "doubt[ed] that people in general entertain any actual expectation of privacy in the numbers they dial." . . . When Smith placed a call, he "voluntarily conveyed" the dialed numbers to the phone company by "expos[ing] that information to its equipment in the ordinary course of business." *Id.*, at 744 (internal quotation marks omitted). Once again, we held that the defendant "assumed the risk" that the company's records "would be divulged to police." *Id.*, at 745.

III

The question we confront today is how to apply the Fourth Amendment to a new phenomenon: the ability to chronicle a person's past movements through the record of his cell phone signals. Such tracking partakes of many of the qualities of the GPS monitoring we considered in *Jones*. Much like GPS tracking of a vehicle, cell phone location information is detailed, encyclopedic, and effortlessly compiled.

At the same time, the fact that the individual continuously reveals his location to his wireless carrier implicates the third-party principle of *Smith* and *Miller*. But while the third-party doctrine applies to telephone numbers and bank records, it is not clear whether its logic extends to the qualitatively different category of cell-site records. After all, when *Smith* was decided in 1979, few could have imagined a society in which a phone goes wherever its owner goes, conveying to the wireless carrier not just dialed digits, but a detailed and comprehensive record of the person's movements.

We decline to extend *Smith* and *Miller* to cover these novel circumstances. Given the unique nature of cell phone location records, the fact that the information is held by a third party does not by itself overcome the user's claim to Fourth Amendment protection. Whether the Government employs its own surveillance technology as in *Jones* or leverages the technology of a wireless carrier, we hold that an individual maintains a legitimate expectation of privacy in the record of his physical movements as captured through CSLI. The location information obtained from Carpenter's wireless carriers was the product of a search.

A

A person does not surrender all Fourth Amendment protection by venturing into the public sphere. To the contrary, "what [one] seeks to preserve as private, even in an area accessible to the public, may be constitutionally protected." *Katz*, 389 U.S., at 351-352. A majority of this Court has already recognized that individuals have a reasonable expectation of privacy in the whole of their physical movements. *Jones*, 565 U.S., at 430 (Alito, J., concurring in judgment); *id.*, at 415 (Sotomayor, J., concurring). Prior to the digital age, law enforcement might have pursued a suspect for a brief stretch, but doing so "for any extended period of time was difficult and costly and therefore rarely undertaken." *Id.*, at 429 (opinion of Alito, J.). For that reason, "society's expectation has been that law enforcement agents and others would not—and indeed, in the main, simply could not—secretly monitor and catalogue every single movement of an individual's car for a very long period." *Id.*, at 430.

Allowing government access to cell-site records contravenes that expectation. . . . Mapping a cell phone's location over the course of 127 days provides an all-encompassing record of the holder's whereabouts. As with GPS information, the time-stamped data provides an intimate window into a person's life, revealing not only his particular movements, but through them his "familial, political, professional, religious, and sexual associations." . . .

In fact, historical cell-site records present even greater privacy concerns than the GPS monitoring of a vehicle we considered in *Jones*. . . . While individuals regularly leave their vehicles, they compulsively carry cell phones with them all the time. . . . Accordingly, when the Government tracks the location of a cell phone it achieves near perfect surveillance, as if it had attached an ankle monitor to the phone's user.

Moreover, the retrospective quality of the data here gives police access to a category of information otherwise unknowable. . . . Unlike with the GPS device in *Jones*, police need not even know in advance whether they want to follow a particular individual, or when.

Whoever the suspect turns out to be, he has effectively been tailed every moment of every day for five years, and the police may—in the Government's view—call upon the results of that surveillance without regard to the constraints of the Fourth Amendment. Only the few without cell phones could escape this tireless and absolute surveillance.

. . .

Accordingly, when the Government accessed CSLI from the wireless carriers, it invaded Carpenter's reasonable expectation of privacy in the whole of his physical movements.

B

The Government's primary contention to the contrary is that the third-party doctrine governs this case. In its view, cell-site records are fair game because they are "business records" created and maintained by the wireless carriers. The Government (along with Justice Kennedy) recognizes that this case features new technology, but asserts that the legal question nonetheless turns on a garden-variety request for information from a third-party witness. . . .

The Government's position fails to contend with the seismic shifts in digital technology that made possible the tracking of not only Carpenter's location but also everyone else's, not for a short period but for years and years. . . . There is a world of difference between the limited types of personal information addressed in *Smith* and *Miller* and the exhaustive chronicle of location information casually collected by wireless carriers today. The Government thus is not asking for a straightforward application of the third-party doctrine, but instead a significant extension of it to a distinct category of information.

Neither does the second rationale underlying the third-party doctrine— voluntary exposure—hold up when it comes to CSLI. Cell phone location information is not truly "shared" as one normally understands the term. . . . [A] cell phone logs a cell-site record by dint of its operation, without any affirmative act on the part of the user beyond powering up. . . . As a result, in no meaningful sense does the user voluntarily "assume[ ] the risk" of turning over a comprehensive dossier of his physical movements. *Smith*, 442 U.S., at 745.

We therefore decline to extend *Smith* and *Miller* to the collection of CSLI. Given the unique nature of cell phone location information, the fact that the Government obtained the information from a third party does not overcome Carpenter's claim to Fourth Amendment protection. The Government's acquisition of the cell-site records was a search within the meaning of the Fourth Amendment.

* * *

Our decision today is a narrow one. We do not express a view on matters not before us: real-time CSLI or "tower dumps" (a download of information on all the devices that connected to a particular cell site during a particular interval). We do not disturb the application of *Smith* and *Miller* or call into question conventional surveillance techniques and tools, such as security cameras. Nor do we address other business records that might incidentally reveal location information. Further, our opinion does not consider other collection techniques involving foreign affairs or national security. . . .

. . .

This is certainly not to say that all orders compelling the production of documents will require a showing of probable cause. The Government will be able to use subpoenas to acquire records in the overwhelming majority of investigations. We hold only that a warrant is required in the rare case where the suspect has a legitimate privacy interest in records held by a third party.

. . .

The judgment of the Court of Appeals is reversed, and the case is remanded for further proceedings consistent with this opinion.

It is so ordered.

NOTES AND QUESTIONS

1. Notice how the *Carpenter* opinion seems to minimize the trespass aspect of *United States v. Jones* and emphasize the pervasive surveillance the GPS facilitated. Is the Court signaling a broader skepticism about government exploitation of technology to conduct surveillance?
2. The Court also emphasized the limited scope of the decision and that it was not overruling the third-party doctrine. What then were the key considerations in distinguishing CSLI from a pen register obtained from the phone company?
3. What do you think the Court was suggesting when it noted that it did not "consider other collection techniques involving foreign affairs or national security"? What "other" collection techniques do you think the Court had in mind?

B. National Security Surveillance and the Warrant Requirement

It is clear that many government surveillance activities, even when conducted for national security purposes, will implicate the Fourth Amendment's reasonableness requirement. What is or is not reasonable, however, will often be dictated by applicability of Supreme Court–established exceptions to the warrant and/or probable cause requirement. The next case considers the validity of a government-asserted "national security" exception.

United States v. United States District Court
407 U.S. 297 (1972)

Mr. Justice POWELL delivered the opinion of the Court.

The issue before us is an important one for the people of our country and their Government. It involves the delicate question of the President's power, acting through the Attorney General, to authorize electronic surveillance in internal security matters without prior judicial approval. Successive Presidents for more than one-quarter of a century have authorized such surveillance in varying degrees, without guidance from the Congress or a definitive decision of this Court. This case brings the issue here for the first time. Its resolution is a matter of national concern, requiring sensitivity both to the Government's right to protect itself from unlawful subversion and attack and to the citizen's right to be secure in his privacy against unreasonable Government intrusion.

This case arises from a criminal proceeding in the United States District Court for the Eastern District of Michigan, in which the United States charged three defendants with conspiracy to destroy Government property in violation of 18 U.S.C. § 371. One of the defendants, Plamondon, was charged with the dynamite bombing of an office of the Central Intelligence Agency in Ann Arbor, Michigan.

During pretrial proceedings, the defendants moved to compel the United States to disclose certain electronic surveillance information and to conduct a hearing to determine whether this information "tainted" the evidence on which the indictment was based or which the Government intended to offer at trial. In response, the Government filed an affidavit of the Attorney General, acknowledging that its agents had overheard conversations in which Plamondon had participated. The affidavit also stated that the Attorney General approved the wiretaps to gather intelligence information deemed necessary to protect the nation from attempts of domestic organizations to attack and subvert the existing structure of the Government. The logs of the surveillance were filed in a sealed exhibit for *in camera* inspection by the District Court.

On the basis of the Attorney General's affidavit and the sealed exhibit, the Government asserted that the surveillance was lawful, though conducted without prior judicial approval, as a reasonable exercise of the President's power (exercised through the Attorney General) to protect the national security. The District Court held that the surveillance violated the Fourth Amendment, and ordered the Government to make full disclosure to Plamondon of his overheard conversations, 321 F. Supp. 1074 (E.D. Mich. 1971).

The Government then filed in the Court of Appeals for the Sixth Circuit a petition for a writ of mandamus to set aside the District Court order, which was stayed pending final disposition of the case. After concluding that it had jurisdiction, that court held that the surveillance was unlawful, and that the

District Court had properly required disclosure of the overheard conversations, 444 F.2d 651 (1971). We granted certiorari, 403 U.S. 930.

I

Title III of the Omnibus Crime Control and Safe Streets Act, 18 U.S.C. §§ 2510-2520, authorizes the use of electronic surveillance for classes of crimes carefully specified in 18 U.S.C. § 2516. Such surveillance is subject to prior court order. Section 2518 sets forth the detailed and particularized application necessary to obtain such an order, as well as carefully circumscribed conditions for its use. The Act represents a comprehensive attempt by Congress to promote more effective control of crime while protecting the privacy of individual thought and expression. Much of Title III was drawn to meet the constitutional requirements for electronic surveillance enunciated by this Court in *Berger v. New York*, 388 U.S. 41 (1967), and *Katz v. United States*, 389 U.S. 347 (1967).

Together with the elaborate surveillance requirements in Title III, there is the following proviso, 18 U.S.C. § 2511(3):

> "Nothing contained in this chapter or in section 605 of the Communications Act of 1934 (48 Stat. 1143; 47 U.S.C. 605) shall limit the constitutional power of the President to take such measures as he deems necessary to protect the Nation against actual or potential attack or other hostile acts of a foreign power, to obtain foreign intelligence information deemed essential to the security of the United States, or to protect national security information against foreign intelligence activities. *Nor shall anything contained in this chapter be deemed to limit the constitutional power of the President to take such measures as he deems necessary to protect the United States against the overthrow of the Government by force or other unlawful means, or against any other clear and present danger to the structure or existence of the Government.* The contents of any wire or oral communication intercepted by authority of the President in the exercise of the foregoing powers may be received in evidence in any trial hearing, or other proceeding only where such interception was reasonable, and shall not be otherwise used or disclosed except as is necessary to implement that power." (Emphasis supplied.)

The Government relies on § 2511(3). It argues that, "in excepting national security surveillances from the Act's warrant requirement, Congress recognized the President's authority to conduct such surveillances without prior judicial approval." Brief for United States 7, 28. The section thus is viewed as a recognition or affirmance of a constitutional authority in the President to conduct warrantless domestic security surveillance such as that involved in this case.

We think the language of § 2511(3), as well as the legislative history of the statute, refutes this interpretation. The relevant language is that: "Nothing contained in this chapter . . . shall limit the constitutional power of the President to take such measures as he deems necessary to protect . . ." against the dangers specified. At most, this is an implicit recognition that the President does have certain powers in the specified areas. Few would doubt this, as the section refers—among other things—to protection "against actual or potential attack or other hostile acts of a foreign power." But so far as the use of the President's electronic surveillance power is concerned, the language is essentially neutral.

Section 2511(3) certainly confers no power, as the language is wholly inappropriate for such a purpose. It merely provides that the Act shall not be interpreted to limit or disturb such power as the President may have under the Constitution. In short, Congress simply left presidential powers where it found them. . . .

. . . Where the Act authorizes surveillance, the procedure to be followed is specified in § 2518. Subsection (1) thereof requires application to a judge of competent jurisdiction for a prior order of approval, and states in detail the information required in such application. Subsection (3) prescribes the necessary elements of probable cause which the judge must find before issuing an order authorizing an interception. Subsection (4) sets forth the required contents of such an order. Subsection (5) sets strict time limits on an order. Provision is made in subsection (7) for "an emergency situation" found to exist by the Attorney General (or by the principal prosecuting attorney of a State) "with respect to conspiratorial activities threatening the national security interest." In such a situation, emergency surveillance may be conducted "if an application for an order approving the interception is made . . . within forty-eight hours." If such an order is not obtained, or the application therefor is denied, the interception is deemed to be a violation of the Act.

In view of these and other interrelated provisions delineating permissible interceptions of particular criminal activity upon carefully specified conditions, it would have been incongruous for Congress to have legislated with respect to the important and complex area of national security in a single brief and nebulous paragraph. . . . We therefore think the conclusion inescapable that Congress only intended to make clear that the Act simply did not legislate with respect to national security surveillances.

The legislative history of § 2511(3) supports this interpretation. . . .

. . . The [legislative record] indicates that nothing in § 2511(3) was intended to expand or to contract or to define whatever presidential surveillance powers existed in matters affecting the national security. If we could accept the Government's characterization of § 2511(3) as a congressionally prescribed exception to the general requirement of a warrant, it would be necessary to consider the question of whether the surveillance in this case came within the exception, and, if so, whether the statutory exception was itself constitutionally valid. But viewing § 2511(3) as a congressional disclaimer and expression of neutrality, we hold that the statute is not the measure of the executive authority asserted in this case. Rather, we must look to the constitutional powers of the President.

II

It is important at the outset to emphasize the limited nature of the question before the Court. This case raises no constitutional challenge to electronic surveillance as specifically authorized by Title III of the Omnibus

Crime Control and Safe Streets Act of 1968. Nor is there any question or doubt as to the necessity of obtaining a warrant in the surveillance of crimes unrelated to the national security interest. *Katz v. United States*, 389 U.S. 347 (1967); *Berger v. New York*, 388 U.S. 41 (1967). Further, the instant case requires no judgment on the scope of the President's surveillance power with respect to the activities of foreign powers, within or without this country. The Attorney General's affidavit in this case states that the surveillances were "deemed necessary to protect the nation from attempts of *domestic organizations* to attack and subvert the existing structure of Government" (emphasis supplied). There is no evidence of any involvement, directly or indirectly, of a foreign power.

Our present inquiry, though important, is therefore a narrow one. It addresses a question left open by *Katz*, *supra*, at 389 U.S. 358 n.23:

> "Whether safeguards other than prior authorization by a magistrate would satisfy the Fourth Amendment in a situation involving the national security. . . ."

The determination of this question requires the essential Fourth Amendment inquiry into the "reasonableness" of the search and seizure in question, and the way in which that "reasonableness" derives content and meaning through reference to the warrant clause. *Coolidge v. New Hampshire*, 403 U.S. 443, 403 U.S. 473-484 (1971).

We begin the inquiry by noting that the President of the United States has the fundamental duty, under Art. II, § 1, of the Constitution, to "preserve, protect and defend the Constitution of the United States." Implicit in that duty is the power to protect our Government against those who would subvert or overthrow it by unlawful means. In the discharge of this duty, the President — through the Attorney General — may find it necessary to employ electronic surveillance to obtain intelligence information on the plans of those who plot unlawful acts against the Government. The use of such surveillance in internal security cases has been sanctioned more or less continuously by various Presidents and Attorneys General since July, 1946. . . .

Though the Government and respondents debate their seriousness and magnitude, threats and acts of sabotage against the Government exist in sufficient number to justify investigative powers with respect to them. The covertness and complexity of potential unlawful conduct against the Government and the necessary dependency of many conspirators upon the telephone make electronic surveillance an effective investigatory instrument in certain circumstances. The marked acceleration in technological developments and sophistication in their use have resulted in new techniques for the planning, commission, and concealment of criminal activities. It would be contrary to the public interest for Government to deny to itself the prudent and lawful employment of those very techniques which are employed against the Government and its law-abiding citizens.

It has been said that "[t]he most basic function of any government is to provide for the security of the individual and of his property." *Miranda v. Arizona*, 384 U.S. 436, 384 U.S. 539 (1966) (White, J., dissenting). And unless Government safeguards its own capacity to function and to preserve the security of its people, society itself could become so disordered that all rights and liberties would be endangered. As Chief Justice Hughes reminded us in *Cox v. New Hampshire*, 312 U.S. 569, 312 U.S. 574 (1941):

> "Civil liberties, as guaranteed by the Constitution, imply the existence of an organized society maintaining public order without which liberty itself would be lost in the excesses of unrestrained abuses."

But a recognition of these elementary truths does not make the employment by Government of electronic surveillance a welcome development—even when employed with restraint and under judicial supervision. There is, understandably, a deep-seated uneasiness and apprehension that this capability will be used to intrude upon cherished privacy of law-abiding citizens. We look to the Bill of Rights to safeguard this privacy. Though physical entry of the home is the chief evil against which the wording of the Fourth Amendment is directed, its broader spirit now shields private speech from unreasonable surveillance. *Katz v. United States, supra; Berger v. New York, supra; Silverman v. United States*, 365 U.S. 505 (1961). Our decision in *Katz* refused to lock the Fourth Amendment into instances of actual physical trespass. Rather, the Amendment governs "not only the seizure of tangible items, but extends as well to the recording of oral statements . . . without any 'technical trespass under . . . local property law.'" *Katz, supra*, at 389 U.S. 353. That decision implicitly recognized that the broad and unsuspected governmental incursions into conversational privacy which electronic surveillance entails necessitate the application of Fourth Amendment safeguards.

National security cases, moreover, often reflect a convergence of First and Fourth Amendment values not present in cases of "ordinary" crime. Though the investigative duty of the executive may be stronger in such cases, so also is there greater jeopardy to constitutionally protected speech. . . . The danger to political dissent is acute where the Government attempts to act under so vague a concept as the power to protect "domestic security." Given the difficulty of defining the domestic security interest, the danger of abuse in acting to protect that interest becomes apparent. Senator Hart addressed this dilemma in the floor debate on § 2511(3):

> "As I read it—and this is my fear—we are saying that the President, on his motion, could declare—name your favorite poison—draft dodgers, Black Muslims, the Ku Klux Klan, or civil rights activists to be a clear and present danger to the structure or existence of the Government."

The price of lawful public dissent must not be a dread of subjection to an unchecked surveillance power. Nor must the fear of unauthorized official eavesdropping deter vigorous citizen dissent and discussion of Government action in private conversation. For private dissent, no less than open public discourse, is essential to our free society.

III

As the Fourth Amendment is not absolute in its terms, our task is to examine and balance the basic values at stake in this case: the duty of Government to protect the domestic security, and the potential danger posed by unreasonable surveillance to individual privacy and free expression. If the legitimate need of Government to safeguard domestic security requires the use of electronic surveillance, the question is whether the needs of citizens for privacy and free expression may not be better protected by requiring a warrant before such surveillance is undertaken. We must also ask whether a warrant requirement would unduly frustrate the efforts of Government to protect itself from acts of subversion and overthrow directed against it.

Though the Fourth Amendment speaks broadly of "unreasonable searches and seizures," the definition of "reasonableness" turns, at least in part, on the more specific commands of the warrant clause. Some have argued that "[t]he relevant test is not whether it is reasonable to procure a search warrant, but whether the search was reasonable," *United States v. Rabinowitz*, 339 U.S. 56, 339 U.S. 66 (1950). This view, however, overlooks the second clause of the Amendment. The warrant clause of the Fourth Amendment is not dead language. Rather, it has been

> "a valued part of our constitutional law for decades, and it has determined the result in scores and scores of cases in courts all over this country. It is not an inconvenience to be somehow 'weighed' against the claims of police efficiency. It is, or should be, an important working part of our machinery of government, operating as a matter of course to check the 'well-intentioned but mistakenly overzealous executive officers' who are a part of any system of law enforcement." *Coolidge v. New Hampshire*, 403 U.S. at 403 U.S. 481.

See also United States v. Rabinowitz, supra, at 339 U.S. 68 (Frankfurter, J., dissenting); *Davis v. United States*, 328 U.S. 582, 328 U.S. 604 (1946) (Frankfurter, J., dissenting).

Over two centuries ago, Lord Mansfield held that common law principles prohibited warrants that ordered the arrest of unnamed individuals who the officer might conclude were guilty of seditious libel. "It is not fit," said Mansfield, "that the receiving or judging of the information should be left to the discretion of the officer. The magistrate ought to judge; and should give certain directions to the officer." *Leach v. Three of the King's Messengers*, 19 How. St. Tr. 1001, 1027 (1765).

Lord Mansfield's formulation touches the very heart of the Fourth Amendment directive: that, where practical, a governmental search and seizure should represent both the efforts of the officer to gather evidence of wrongful acts and the judgment of the magistrate that the collected evidence is sufficient to justify invasion of a citizen's private premises or conversation. Inherent in the concept of a warrant is its issuance by a "neutral and detached magistrate." *Coolidge v. New Hampshire, supra*, at 403 U.S. 453; *Katz v. United States, supra*, at 389 U.S. 356. The further requirement of "probable cause" instructs the magistrate that baseless searches shall not proceed. These Fourth Amendment freedoms cannot properly be guaranteed if domestic security surveillances may be conducted solely within the discretion of the Executive Branch. The Fourth Amendment does not contemplate the executive officers of Government as neutral and disinterested magistrates. Their duty and responsibility are to enforce the laws, to investigate, and to prosecute. *Katz v. United States, supra*, at 389 U.S. 359-360 (Douglas, J., concurring). But those charged with this investigative and prosecutorial duty should not be the sole judges of when to utilize constitutionally sensitive means in pursuing their tasks. The historical judgment, which the Fourth Amendment accepts, is that unreviewed executive discretion may yield too readily to pressures to obtain incriminating evidence and overlook potential invasions of privacy and protected speech.

It may well be that, in the instant case, the Government's surveillance of Plamondon's conversations was a reasonable one which readily would have gained prior judicial approval. But this Court "has never sustained a search upon the sole ground that officers reasonably expected to find evidence of a particular crime and voluntarily confined their activities to the least intrusive means consistent with that end." *Katz, supra*, at 389 U.S. 356-357. The Fourth Amendment contemplates a prior judicial judgment, not the risk that executive discretion may be reasonably exercised. . . . Prior review by a neutral and detached magistrate is the time-tested means of effectuating Fourth Amendment rights. *Beck v. Ohio*, 379 U.S. 89, 379 U.S. 96 (1964).

It is true that there have been some exceptions to the warrant requirement. *Chimel v. California*, 395 U.S. 752 (1969); *Terry v. Ohio*, 392 U.S. 1 (1968); *McDonald v. United States*, 335 U.S. 451 (1948); *Carroll v. United States*, 267 U.S. 132 (1925). But those exceptions are few in number, and carefully delineated. . . .

The Government argues that the special circumstances applicable to domestic security surveillances necessitate a further exception to the warrant requirement. It is urged that the requirement of prior judicial review would obstruct the President in the discharge of his constitutional duty to protect domestic security. We are told further that these surveillances are directed primarily to the collecting and maintaining of intelligence with respect to subversive forces, and are not an attempt to gather evidence for specific criminal prosecutions. It is said that this type of surveillance should not be subject to traditional warrant requirements which were established to govern investigation of criminal activity, not ongoing intelligence gathering. Brief for United States 15-16, 23-24; Reply Brief for United States 2-3. The Government further insists that courts "as a practical matter would have neither the knowledge nor the techniques necessary to determine whether there was probable cause to believe that surveillance was necessary to protect national security." These security problems, the Government contends, involve "a large number of complex and subtle factors" beyond the competence of courts to evaluate. Reply Brief for United States 4.

As a final reason for exemption from a warrant requirement, the Government believes that disclosure to a magistrate of all or even a significant portion of the information involved in domestic security surveillances "would create serious potential dangers to the national security and to the lives of informants and agents. . . . Secrecy is the essential ingredient in intelligence gathering; requiring prior judicial authorization would create a greater 'danger of leaks . . . because, in addition to the judge, you have the clerk, the stenographer and some other officer like a law assistant or bailiff who may be apprised of the nature' of the surveillance." Brief for United States 24-25.

But we do not think a case has been made for the requested departure from Fourth Amendment standards. The circumstances described do not justify complete exemption of domestic security surveillance from prior judicial scrutiny. Official surveillance, whether its purpose be criminal investigation or ongoing intelligence gathering, risks infringement of constitutionally protected privacy of speech. Security surveillances are especially sensitive because of the inherent vagueness of the domestic security concept, the necessarily broad and continuing nature of intelligence gathering, and the temptation to utilize such surveillances to oversee political dissent. We recognize, as we have before, the constitutional basis of the President's domestic security role, but we think it must be exercised in a manner compatible with the Fourth Amendment. In this case, we hold that this requires an appropriate prior warrant procedure.

We cannot accept the Government's argument that internal security matters are too subtle and complex for judicial evaluation. Courts regularly deal with the most difficult issues of our society. . . . If the threat is too subtle or complex for our senior law enforcement officers to convey its significance to a court, one may question whether there is probable cause for surveillance.

Nor do we believe prior judicial approval will fracture the secrecy essential to official intelligence gathering. The investigation of criminal activity has long involved imparting sensitive information to judicial officers who have respected the confidentialities involved. Judges may be counted upon to be especially conscious of security requirements in national security cases. . . . Whatever security dangers clerical and secretarial personnel may pose can be minimized by proper administrative measures, possibly to the point of allowing the Government itself to provide the necessary clerical assistance.

Thus, we conclude that the Government's concerns do not justify departure in this case from the customary Fourth Amendment requirement of judicial approval prior to initiation of a search or surveillance. Although some added burden will be imposed upon the Attorney General, this inconvenience is justified in a free society to protect constitutional values. Nor do we think the Government's domestic surveillance powers will be impaired to any significant degree. A prior warrant establishes presumptive validity of the surveillance and will minimize the burden of justification in post-surveillance judicial review. By no means of least importance will be the reassurance of the public generally that indiscriminate wiretapping and bugging of law-abiding citizens cannot occur.

IV

We emphasize, before concluding this opinion, the scope of our decision. As stated at the outset, this case involves only the domestic aspects of national security. We have not addressed, and express no opinion as to, the issues which may be involved with respect to activities of foreign powers or their agents. Nor does our decision rest on the language of § 2511(3) or any other section of Title III of the Omnibus Crime Control and Safe Streets Act of 1968. That Act does not attempt to define or delineate the powers of the President to meet domestic threats to the national security.

Moreover, we do not hold that the same type of standards and procedures prescribed by Title III are necessarily applicable to this case. We recognize that domestic security surveillance may involve different policy and practical considerations from the surveillance of "ordinary crime." The gathering of security intelligence is often long range and involves the interrelation of various sources and types of information. The exact targets of such surveillance may be more difficult to identify than in surveillance operations against many types of crime specified in Title III. Often, too, the emphasis of domestic intelligence gathering is on the prevention of unlawful activity or the enhancement of the Government's preparedness for some possible future crisis or emergency. Thus, the focus of domestic surveillance may be less precise than that directed against more conventional types of crime.

Given these potential distinctions between Title III criminal surveillances and those involving the domestic security, Congress may wish to consider protective standards for the latter which differ from those already prescribed for specified crimes in Title III. Different standards may be compatible with the Fourth Amendment if they are reasonable both in relation to the legitimate need of Government for intelligence information and the protected rights of our citizens. For the warrant application may vary according to the governmental interest to be enforced and the nature of citizen rights deserving protection. . . .

. . . We do not attempt to detail the precise standards for domestic security warrants any more than our decision in *Katz* sought to set the refined requirements for the specified criminal surveillances which now constitute Title III. We do hold, however, that, prior judicial approval is required for the type of domestic security surveillance involved in this case, and that such approval may be made in accordance with such reasonable standards as the Congress may prescribe.

V

As the surveillance of Plamondon's conversations was unlawful, because conducted without prior judicial approval, the courts below correctly held that *Alderman v. United States*, 394 U.S. 165 (1969), is controlling, and that it requires disclosure to the accused of his own impermissibly intercepted conversations. . . .

Affirmed.

NOTES AND QUESTIONS

1. What was the precise nature of the asserted "national security" exception to the warrant requirement rejected by the Court?
2. Why did the Court suggest the outcome would likely have been different had the target of the government surveillance been an agent of a foreign power?
3. Was the Court's suggested modified warrant process directed toward foreign intelligence surveillance, or the type of "domestic dissident" surveillance addressed in this case?
4. Based on this decision, would you say there is a "national security" exception to the warrant requirement? If so, when will it apply?

Congress subsequently acted on the Court's suggestion to develop a specialized surveillance authorization process for certain national security investigations. However, contrary to the Court's suggested focus — the type of domestic dissident surveillance that occurred in the *Keith* case — Congress imposed this new authorization process on *foreign intelligence* surveillance in the Foreign Intelligence Surveillance Act. This law will be addressed in greater detail in Chapter 12. Congress has never responded to the Court's "invitation" to adopt a similarly tailored surveillance authorization process for investigations similar to that in *Keith*. Thus, the Court's invitation to create a tailored process for the surveillance it held fell within the Fourth Amendment warrant requirement became the basis for imposing a warrant-type authorization requirement on the type of surveillance the Court suggested fell outside that requirement.

C. The Fifth Amendment, *Miranda*, and Terrorist Interrogation

Government agents obviously seek to question suspects and other witnesses to gather information during the course of national security investigations. When these suspects and/or witnesses are abroad, the questioning will sometimes be conducted by U.S. agents or sometimes by foreign agents with or without involvement of U.S. agents. When the U.S. government seeks to introduce such statements as evidence in criminal trials, a defendant may seek exclusion based on the Fifth Amendment voluntariness test or the *Miranda* warning and waiver requirement.

As you will probably remember from a different course, *Miranda v. Arizona*, 384 U.S. 436 (1966), and its progeny require police to inform suspects subjected to custodial interrogation of their "Miranda" rights and obtain a knowing and voluntary waiver of those rights as a precondition to using any statements in the prosecution case-in-chief. The Supreme Court has not, however, ruled on whether this *Miranda* warning and waiver requirement is applicable outside the territorial jurisdiction of the United States. Nonetheless, a number of lower federal courts faced with this question have held the requirement applies no matter where the interrogation takes place (*see, e.g., United States v. Dire*, 680 F.3d 446 (4th Cir. 2012); *In re Terrorist Bombings of U.S. Embassies in E. Afr.*, 552 F.3d 177 (2d Cir. 2008); *United States v. Hassan*, 747 F. Supp. 2d 642 (E.D. Va. 2010); *United States v. Karake*, 443

F. Supp. 2d 8 (D.D.C. 2006); *United States v. Bin Laden*, 132 F. Supp. 2d 168, 168 (S.D.N.Y. 2001)).

The following opinion addresses a range of issues that arise in these situations, explaining applicability of both the Fifth Amendment due process "voluntariness" doctrine and the *Miranda* doctrine to such situations.

United States v. Abu Ali
528 F.3d 210 (4th Cir. 2008)

WILKINSON, MOTZ, and TRAXLER, Circuit Judges:

Ahmed Omar Abu Ali was convicted by a jury of nine criminal counts arising from his affiliation with an al-Qaeda terrorist cell located in Medina, Saudi Arabia, and its plans to carry out a number of terrorist acts in this country. He was sentenced by the district court to 360 months imprisonment and 360 months of supervised release following imprisonment. Abu Ali appeals his convictions and the government cross-appeals his sentence. For the following reasons, we affirm the conviction, but we vacate and remand for purposes of resentencing.

Unlike some others suspected of terrorist acts and designs upon the United States, Abu Ali was formally charged and tried according to the customary processes of the criminal justice system. Persons of good will may disagree over the precise extent to which the formal criminal justice process must be utilized when those suspected of participation in terrorist cells and networks are involved. There should be no disagreement, however, that the criminal justice system does retain an important place in the ongoing effort to deter and punish terrorist acts without the sacrifice of American constitutional norms and bedrock values. As will be apparent herein, the criminal justice system is not without those attributes of adaptation that will permit it to function in the post-9/11 world. These adaptations, however, need not and must not come at the expense of the requirement that an accused receive a fundamentally fair trial. In this case, we are satisfied that Abu Ali received a fair trial, though not a perfect one, and that the criminal justice system performed those functions which the Constitution envisioned for it. The three of us unanimously express our conviction that this is so in this opinion, which we have jointly authored.

Some differences do exist, however, among the panel members. Judge Wilkinson and Judge Traxler join in the opinion in its entirety. Judge Motz dissents (in footnote 6) from the majority's holding that the interrogation of Abu Ali on June 15, 2003, did not constitute a joint venture between law enforcement officers of Saudi Arabia and those of the United States. Judge Motz likewise dissents from Section VII of the panel's opinion, which directs that the case be remanded to the district court for the purposes of resentencing.

[The court explained how Abu Ali, an American citizen, became involved with al Qaeda operatives in Saudi Arabia over the course of several years, and ultimately became involved in planning to conduct terrorist attacks in the United States. The court noted that "according to Abu Ali, he met with al-Faq'asi on six separate occasions to plan such terrorist operations within the United States. In the course of these meetings, Abu Ali suggested assassinations or kidnappings of members of the United States Senate, the United States Army, and the Bush Administration, a plan to rescue the prisoners at Guantanamo Bay, and plans to blow up American warplanes on United States bases and at United States ports, similar to the USS Cole operation." Abu Ali then progressed to training for terrorist operations, including being provided resources to carry out such operations.]

On May 6, 2003, Saudi authorities discovered a large stash of weapons and explosives in Riyadh, Saudi Arabia, which was suspected to be intended for use in terrorist activities within that country. The following day, the Saudi government published a list of the 19 most wanted individuals in connection with terrorist activity. The list included al-Faq'asi and Sultan Jubran [Abu Ali's contacts]. According to Abu Ali, after the list was published, al-Faq'asi told him that the villa location would be changed and Abu Ali was taken to a farm where he stayed for several days.

Six days later, on May 12, 2003, al-Qaeda carried out a number of suicide bombings in Riyadh, killing approximately 34 people including 9 Americans. That night, Abu Ali and the other cell members performed guard duty at the cell's safehouses. After the bombings, Abu Ali and a number of the others moved to a second villa in an al-Iskan neighborhood where they stayed for three days, although Abu Ali did not spend the night in the villa with the others. According to Abu Ali, the villa contained "a dimly-lit room that contained wires and cell phones, . . . machine guns, ammunition, a pistol and a hand grenade." Later, the group moved back to the farm, where Abu Ali continued his training in explosives and forgery. He received lessons from Majid (Mohammad Salem al-Ghamdi) on forging and removing seals, altering photos, and removing visas, and received lessons from al-Faq'asi on explosives, making explosives, and compounds. Another man, Umar al-Hakmi, provided lessons on fuses and wiring.

On May 26 and 27, 2003, authorities with the Saudi Mabahith received orders to raid several suspected terrorist safe houses in Medina, including the safe house in the Al-Azhari villa where Abu Ali had received training. Among the evidence retrieved during the search of one safe house was an English translation of an American pilot's radio transmission and a paper with Abu Ali's additional alias names of "Hani" and "Hanimohawk" written on it. The authorities also recovered a number of automatic rifles and guns, ammunition, fertilizer, hand grenades, cell phones which were being converted to explosives, as well as computers, cameras, walkie-talkies, and laminating equipment for identification cards. A number of members of the al-Faq'asi terrorist cell were arrested during the raids, including al-Ghamdi, who had trained Abu Ali, and Sheikh Nasser, who had given Abu Ali the blessing for the presidential assassination. Al-Faq'asi and Sultan Jubran, disguised in women's clothing, escaped.

During subsequent questioning by the Saudi authorities, al-Ghamdi informed the Mabahith that one of their members was a student at the

University of Medina of either American or European background who went by the alias "Reda" or "Ashraf." Further investigative efforts resulted in the photo identification of Abu Ali as the American or European member of the cell.

On June 8, 2003, Abu Ali was arrested by the Mabahith at the Islamic University in Medina and his dormitory room was searched. Among the items found there were a GPS device, jihad literature, a walkie talkie, a United States passport, a Jordanian passport and identification card, a Nokia cellular telephone, a telephone notebook containing al-Qahtani's name, and literature on jihad. Abu Ali was then flown from Medina to Riyadh, where he was interrogated by the Mabahith. Although he initially denied involvement with the al-Faq'asi cell, he confessed when the Mabahith officers addressed him with his alias names of "Reda" and "Ashraf." Specifically, Abu Ali confessed to his affiliation with al-Qaeda and, in particular, the Medina cell headed by al-Faq'asi. According to Abu Ali, he joined the al-Qaeda cell "to prepare and train for an operation inside the [United States]," including an "intention to prepare and train to kill the [United States] President." In addition to written confessions, the Mabahith obtained a videotaped confession in which Abu Ali admitted his affiliation with the Medina cell and its plans to conduct terrorist operations within the United States, including the plan to assassinate President Bush and to destroy airliners destined to this country.

Following Abu Ali's arrest by the Saudi authorities, the FBI was notified of his suspected involvement in the al-Qaeda cell in Saudi Arabia and advised that the cell was planning on conducting terrorism operations in the United States. Although the FBI requested access to Abu Ali, the Mabahith denied the request. On June 15, 2003, the Mabahith allowed the FBI to supply proposed questions, but later rejected the list and the breadth of the inquiry sought. Ultimately, the Mabahith only agreed to ask Abu Ali six of those questions and to allow the FBI officers to observe his responses through a one-way mirror. Abu Ali was asked whether he was tasked to assassinate the President (as had been reported by the Mabahith to the FBI), when he arrived in Saudi Arabia, whether he knew of any planned terrorist attacks against American, Saudi, or Western interests, whether he was recruited by any terrorist organization, whether he had used false passports, and the nature of his father's position in the Embassy. Other than consular contact, the United States was denied all access to Abu Ali until September of 2003.

In the meantime, on June 16, 2003, the FBI obtained and executed a search warrant at Abu Ali's home in Virginia. Among the items found there, the agents discovered a printout of the buddy list of email addresses from MSN Hotmail account Ahmedabuali@hotmail.com, which contained an address of abumuslim99@hotmail.com for al-Qahtani, an address book containing the name of al-Qahtani, a two-page article praising the 9/11 attacks in this country, a handguns magazine addressed to Abu Ali which contained a feature article on methods for the concealed carrying of handguns, and an email message from an unknown individual to Abu Ali discussing opportunities for Muslim fighters in the conflict between Muslim rebels and Russians in Chechnya.

B.

On February 3, 2005, a federal grand jury returned an indictment against Abu Ali. The Saudi officials surrendered Abu Ali to United States authorities and he was flown back to the United States on February 21, 2005. He had his initial appearance before the United States magistrate judge the following day. . . .

. . . On October 25, 2005, the district court rejected Abu Ali's subsequent attempts to . . . suppress the introduction of his various statements and confession made to the Saudi Mabahith, *see United States v. Abu Ali*, 395 F. Supp. 2d 338 (E.D. Va. 2005), and trial commenced before the jury on October 31, 2005.

On November 22, 2005, Abu Ali was convicted of all charges. He was subsequently sentenced to 360 months imprisonment to be followed by a term of 360 months of supervised release. Abu Ali appeals his convictions and his sentence on a number of grounds and the government cross-appeals the sentence.

II.

It is undisputed that during Abu Ali's time in Saudi custody, he was repeatedly interrogated, but never given either a probable cause determination or *Miranda* warnings, *see Miranda v. Arizona*, 384 U.S. 436, 86 S. Ct. 1602, 16 L. Ed. 2d 694 (1966). It is also undisputed that the district court admitted into evidence at trial inculpatory statements and confessions elicited during this custodial interrogation. Abu Ali contends that the court erred in permitting the jury to consider these statements and confessions, because (1) he was never brought before a judicial officer for a probable cause determination, (2) he was never given *Miranda* warnings, and (3) his statements were allegedly involuntary. We address each purported basis for exclusion in turn.

[In Part A, the court considered and rejected Abu Ali's assertion that his detention by Saudi authorities without a U.S. probable cause determination violated the Fourth Amendment.]

B.

1.

We next consider Abu Ali's *Miranda* challenge. Generally, statements made by a defendant held in United States custody and questioned by law enforcement officers without receiving *Miranda* warnings are inadmissible at trial in this country. *See New York v. Quarles*, 467 U.S. 649, 654, 104 S. Ct. 2626, 81 L. Ed. 2d 550 (1984). But because the United States cannot dictate the protections provided to criminal suspects by foreign nations and one of the principal purposes of the exclusionary rule—deterrence of unlawful police activity—is absent when foreign agents direct an interrogation, a different rule applies to statements elicited by foreign officials. *See United States v. Martindale*, 790 F.2d 1129, 1132 (4th Cir. 1986) ("[T]he exclusionary rule has little or no effect upon the conduct of foreign police."). Thus, voluntary statements obtained from a defendant by foreign law enforcement officers, even without *Miranda* warnings, generally are admissible. *See United States v. Yousef*, 327 F.3d 56, 145 (2d Cir. 2003); *Kilday v. United States*, 481 F.2d 655, 656 (5th Cir. 1973).

Notwithstanding this distinction, United States law enforcement officials may not intentionally evade the requirements of *Miranda* by purposefully delegating interrogation duties to foreign law enforcement officers and then having the fruits of the interrogation admitted at trial in the United States. *See, e.g., United States v. Maturo*, 982 F.2d 57, 61 (2d Cir. 1992); *cf. Anderson*, 318 U.S. at 356, 63 S. Ct. 599 ("There was a working arrangement between the federal officers and [a local sheriff] . . . [therefore, the fact that the federal officers themselves were not formally guilty of illegal conduct does not affect the admissibility of the evidence which they secured improperly through collaboration with state officers."). For this reason, two exceptions have developed to the general rule that voluntary statements obtained by foreign officials during a custodial interrogation without benefit of *Miranda* warnings are admissible. Namely, such statements will not be admissible if obtained by foreign officials (1) engaged in a joint venture with, or (2) acting as agents of, United States law enforcement officers. *See, e.g., United States v. Heller*, 625 F.2d 594, 599 (5th Cir. 1980); *see also Maturo*, 982 F.2d at 61.

Abu Ali contends that his answers to an interrogation on June 15, 2003 should not have been admitted into evidence because that interrogation constituted a "joint venture" between his Saudi interrogators and United States law enforcement officers, and his Saudi interrogators acted as the agents of United States law enforcement on that day, posing questions prepared by the FBI and asked at its behest. The district court considered and rejected both claims in denying Abu Ali's pre-trial motion to suppress, holding admissible all of his statements to the Mabahith.

Abu Ali does not dispute the court's factual finding that the United States was not involved in his interrogation prior to June 15th, or in his handwritten confession or the July 24th videotaped reading of that confession and that, therefore, United States officials had no duty to ensure that he received *Miranda* warnings on those occasions. Thus, he only challenges the failure to provide *Miranda* warnings with respect to the statements taken on June 15, 2003, and argues that the June 15th violation tainted his later statements.

2.

As mentioned earlier, prior to its June 15th interrogation of Abu Ali, the Saudi Mabahith allowed United States law enforcement officers to propose questions to be asked of the defendant. The FBI supplied a list of questions, and, on June 15th, the Mabahith asked Abu Ali six of the questions submitted. However, the Saudis rejected a majority of the questions proposed by the FBI, and asked a number of their own questions during the interrogation. Furthermore, although no FBI or other United States agents were present in the interrogation room on June 15th or had any direct contact with Abu Ali, FBI and Secret Service agents did observe Abu Ali and his interrogator through a one-way mirror during the questioning, and a Saudi official consulted with the observing United States agents at the end of the interview. After properly recounting these facts, the district court concluded that they did not constitute a "joint venture" between Saudi interrogators and United States law enforcement officers.

The "joint venture" doctrine provides that "statements elicited during overseas interrogation by foreign police in the absence of *Miranda* warnings must be suppressed whenever United States law enforcement agents actively participate in questioning conducted by foreign authorities." *Yousef*, 327 F.3d at 145; *see also Heller*, 625 F.2d at 599 ("[I]f American officials participated in the foreign search or interrogation . . . the exclusionary rule should be invoked."); *Pfeifer v. U.S. Bureau of Prisons*, 615 F.2d 873, 877 (9th Cir. 1980) ("Under the joint venture doctrine, evidence obtained through activities of foreign officials, in which federal agents substantially participated and which violated the accused's Fifth Amendment or *Miranda* rights, must be suppressed in a subsequent trial in the United States.").

Only a few cases illuminate what constitutes "active" or "substantial" participation. *See Yousef*, 327 F.3d at 144-46 (finding no active participation when there was no evidence that the United States had "encouraged, requested, or participated in [suspect's] interrogation or written statement" and United States agents did not receive any statement from foreign authorities until after suspect was in United States custody); *Heller*, 625 F.2d at 599-600 & n.7 (finding no joint venture when American law enforcement was only "peripheral[ly]" involved in suspect's arrest, *Mirandized* the suspect when questioning him, and did not exchange information with British authorities regarding separate un-*Mirandized* interrogation of suspect by the British); *Pfeifer*, 615 F.2d at 877 (finding no substantial participation when an American Drug Enforcement Agency (D.E.A.) agent was present during interrogation, but there was no evidence that the agent instigated any questioning or took any part in it); *United States v. Emery*, 591 F.2d 1266, 1268 (9th Cir. 1978) (finding substantial participation when American D.E.A. agents contacted Mexican officials about suspected drug activity, coordinated the relevant surveillance, supplied personnel in the sting operation, signaled appropriate time to arrest suspects, and were present at suspect's interrogation); *United States v. Trenary*, 473 F.2d 680, 682 (9th Cir. 1973) (finding no joint venture when American customs officer, who never identified himself as an American agent, translated questions asked by Mexican police officers).

Although few in number, these cases do permit us to derive one general rule: mere presence at an interrogation does not constitute the "active" or "substantial" participation necessary for a "joint venture," *see Pfeifer*, 615 F.2d at 877, but coordination and direction of an investigation or interrogation does, *see Emery*, 591 F.2d at 1268; *see also Pfeifer*, 615 F.2d at 877 & n.3 (implying that had U.S. officials participated in the suspect's questioning the court might face a different case). A majority of the court would affirm the district court's holding that the June 15th interrogation was not a joint venture and so there was no *Miranda* violation. One judge believes that the June 15th interrogation was a joint venture in which United States law enforcement officials violated Abu Ali's *Miranda* rights.

[In Part B.3, the court concluded that even if Abu Ali's confession had been improperly admitted, the error was harmless.]

C.

Abu Ali next claims that all of his statements and confessions while in Saudi custody should have been suppressed as involuntary. The district court rejected this argument, finding that the government had "demonstrated by a 'preponderance of the evidence' that any incriminating statements" made by Abu Ali while in Saudi custody in June and July, 2003, were "voluntary" and so admissible at trial. *Abu Ali*, 395 F. Supp. 2d at 342.

When *Miranda* warnings are unnecessary, as in the case of an interrogation by foreign officials, we assess the voluntariness of a defendant's statements by asking whether the confession is "the product of an essentially free and unconstrained choice by its maker." *Culombe v. Connecticut*, 367 U.S. 568, 602, 81 S. Ct. 1860, 6 L. Ed. 2d 1037 (1961). If it is, "it may be used against him." *Id.* at 602, 81 S. Ct. 1860. But, if the defendant's "will has been overborne and his capacity for self-determination critically impaired, the use of his confession offends due process." *Id.*; *see also Schneckloth v. Bustamonte*, 412 U.S. 218, 225-26, 93 S. Ct. 2041, 36 L. Ed. 2d 854 (1973). The government acknowledges that "[t]he crucial inquiry is whether [Abu Ali's] will has been 'overborne,'" and maintains that it was not; Abu Ali, of course, contends that it was.

In evaluating whether a defendant's will has been overborne, courts must assess the totality of the circumstances, taking into account characteristics of the accused, and details of the interrogation. . . .

[The court then summarized the evidence relied on by the district court to conclude that Abu Ali's confession was voluntary.]

. . . Initially, the court properly recognized that "torture, and evidence obtained thereby, have no place in the American system of justice." *Abu Ali*, 395 F. Supp. 2d at 380. But, based on its evaluations of "the credibility of the witnesses," and "the quality of the evidence presented," *id.* at 374, the district court found itself "left with lingering questions concerning the credibility of Mr. Abu Ali and his claim that he was tortured," *id.* at 378. The court credited the testimony of the Saudi Arresting Officer and the Lieutenant Colonel (the Warden at the Medina detention facility where Abu Ali was held for two days following his arrest) that no Saudi official used coercive interrogation techniques on Abu Ali. The court found that the Lieutenant Colonel's testimony that Abu Ali was never abused was believable while Abu Ali's contrary testimony "raise[d] questions that bear on the defendant's credibility." *Id.* at 373.

. . . The district court largely rested its legal conclusion that Abu Ali's statements were voluntary on its factual findings concerning his claims of torture and abuse. Our thorough review of the record provides no basis for finding clear error in any of those findings. This, however, does not end our inquiry. We must evaluate the voluntariness of Abu Ali's confessions *de novo*, looking to the totality of the circumstances to determine whether his will was "overborne." *See Schneckloth*, 412 U.S. at 225, 93 S. Ct. 2041.

NOTES AND QUESTIONS

1. What is the principal rationale for limiting the *Miranda* warning and waiver requirement to "joint venture" interrogations?
2. Does the court's proposed test for when *Miranda* warnings and waiver are required during foreign interrogations effectively prevent U.S. agents from avoiding the requirement by relying on foreign agents?
3. In *Colorado v. Connelly*, the Supreme Court held that "official action" that produces coercion was an essential requirement for finding a violation of due process. The Court later relied on this "official action" requirement in *Perry v. New Hampshire* when it rejected a due process challenge to an identification made as the result of unnecessarily suggestive procedures because the procedures were not orchestrated by the police. How can the *Abu Ali* court's assumption that due process voluntariness provides a basis to suppress a confession procured by foreign government agents be reconciled with this "official action" requirement?

D. *Miranda* and the Public Safety Exception

When a suspect is subjected to custodial interrogation by U.S. agents or in a situation where foreign questioning is imputed to U.S. agents, *Miranda* requires a warning and waiver as a precondition to use of the statement against the suspect in the prosecution's case-in-chief. In most situations, a national security motive for the questioning has no impact on this requirement; in other words, there is no recognized national security or foreign intelligence *Miranda* exception.

The Supreme Court has, however, recognized what is known as the "public safety" exception to the *Miranda* warning and waiver requirement. In *New York v. Quarles*, 467 U.S. 649 (1984), the Supreme Court held that spontaneous police questioning of a suspect who the officer had just arrested, in order to locate a pistol, fell outside the *Miranda* requirement. The Court based its holding on the conclusion that the questioning in this type of situation was not motivated by an effort to build a case against the suspect, and therefore the situation did not implicate the underlying concerns of inherent coercion central to the *Miranda* decision. The Court seemed to emphasize two reasons why this type of questioning did not pose a significant risk of inherent coercion: First, the motive was not to gather evidence, but instead to protect the officer or others from an imminent threat; and second, the spontaneous nature of the questioning indicated that the officer did not have the opportunity to calculate methods to subtly coerce the suspect.

This exception has obvious relevance to questioning suspected terrorists. While foiling a terrorist threat may obviously implicate a legitimate public safety concern, this type of questioning may not necessarily be spontaneous as was the question in *Quarles*. The following ruling suggests a prioritization of the objective public safety motive over spontaneity.

United States v. Abdulmutallab

011 WL 4345243 (E.D. Mich. 2011)
Opinion and Order Denying Defendant's Motion to Suppress Statements
Made at the University of Michigan Hospital

Nancy G. Edmunds, District Judge

At an evidentiary hearing held on September 14 and 15, 2011, this matter came before the Court on Defendant's motion to suppress statements made at the University of Michigan Hospital. Defendant's motion raises two separate issues: (1) whether Defendant's statements to federal agents at the University of Michigan Hospital on December 25, 2009 were voluntary, and (2) whether the circumstances present at the time of this questioning fall within the public safety exception to *Miranda* recognized by the Supreme Court in *New York v. Quarles*, 467 U.S. 649, 104 S. Ct. 2626, 81 L. Ed. 2d 550 (1984). The answer to both is yes. Because the Court finds the government's witnesses to be credible and for the reasons stated more fully below, Defendant's motion is DENIED.

I. FACTS—EVIDENTIARY HEARING

On December 25, 2009, when Northwest Delta Flight 253 landed, U.S. Customs and Border Protection officers met the plane at the gate, having been advised of an incident on board the plane. They quickly determined that Defendant's burns were far too extensive to have been caused by firecrackers. After assessing the severity of Defendant's burns, U.S. Customs officers transported Defendant to the U of M Hospital for treatment and informed the FBI's Joint Terrorism Task Force of the situation.

Defendant arrived at the hospital about 12:25 P.M. and received treatment for his burns, including 50 micrograms of the pain killer fentanyl that was administered through an IV at 2:00 P.M. Defendant was then transferred to the hospital's burn unit, where his treatment was continued. Between 2:30 P.M. and 3:00 P.M., his primary care nurse, R.N. Julia Longenecker, administered incremental doses of fentanyl through an IV for a total of 300 micrograms to relieve pain while Defendant's burn wounds were scrubbed. After the scrubbing, Defendant's wounds were dressed, and he was transferred to a room across the hall. The R.N. testified that she monitored Defendant's medical condition during this time. All the medical data and her observations confirmed that Defendant's reaction to the painkiller was normal and that he was tolerating the drug well. She also monitored his mental alertness and testified that he was not confused or "high" at any time. Rather, he was very lucid, alert, gave appropriate responses to verbal commands, and was "orientated times 3"—meaning that he knew who he was, where he was, and when/what time it was—throughout and after his burn scrubbing and dressing treatment.

Around 3:35 P.M., after he was moved to a room, Defendant was questioned by FBI Special Agent Timothy Waters. Other federal agents were present, including FBI Special Agent Peissig, and U.S. Customs Officer Steigerwald. Before the 3:35 interview began, Special Agent Waters had learned from U.S. Customs and Border Protection Officer Steigerwald that Defendant had admitted that he had detonated an explosive device hidden in his underwear while on Flight 253 and that he was acting on behalf of al-Qaeda. He had also learned from other federal agents that an explosive device similar to the one used by Defendant had been used previously, although not on a plane. He also knew that the explosive device had no mechanical devices associated with it and was thus problematic because it could defeat airport security and, indeed, had done so in this instance. Mindful of Defendant's self-proclaimed association with al-Qaeda and knowing the group's past history of large, coordinated plots and attacks, the agents feared that there could be additional, imminent aircraft attacks in the United States and elsewhere in the world. For these reasons, Agent Waters questioned Defendant for about 50 minutes without first advising him of his *Miranda* rights.

During that interview, Agent Waters testified, as R.N. Longenecker had, that Defendant appeared at all times during the questioning to be alert and lucid. Defendant told him that he was not in pain, that he felt fine, and that he understood that the agents needed to ask him some questions. There was no evidence that Defendant was reluctant to answer questions, that he was confused or having trouble understanding the questions. He knew where he was, why he was there, and what had happened and when. Defendant had no trouble understanding or speaking English. Agent Waters asked Defendant where he traveled, when he had traveled, how, and with whom; the details of the explosive device; the details regarding the bomb-maker, including where Defendant had received the bomb; his intentions in attacking Flight 253; and who else might be planning an attack. Every question sought to identify any other potential attackers and to prevent another potential attack. Defendant answered, providing information that helped the agents to determine where to go next and investigate if anyone else might be planning to or was already in the process of carrying a similar device on an aircraft. At the end of the interview, once they received the public safety information, the agents turned their attention to immediately sharing the information with law enforcement and intelligence agencies worldwide.

II. ANALYSIS

[In Part A, the court rejected the defendant's assertion that his statement was coerced and therefore involuntary in violation of due process.]

B. QUARLES EXCEPTION

Defendant argues that his statements to the federal agents on December 25, 2009 at U of M Hospital should be suppressed because the federal agents failed to first advise him of his *Miranda* rights. The Court disagrees. The circumstances present at the time of Defendant's questioning fall within the public safety exception to *Miranda* recognized in *Quarles*, 467 U.S. at 657. The Sixth Circuit has applied the *Quarles* exception. See *United States v. Talley*, 275 F.3d 560, 564 (6th Cir. 2001) (applying the *Quarles* public safety exception).

The federal courts have extended the logic of *Quarles* to the questioning of terrorism suspects. See *Khalil*, 214 F.3d at 121. In *Khalil*, the district court determined that the *Quarles* exception to *Miranda* applied when, after a raid on the defendant's apartment where he was injured, officers questioned the defendant at the hospital "about the construction and stability of the bombs" discovered in his apartment and included within the *Quarles* exception the defendant's response to the officer's inquiry "whether he had intended to kill himself in detonating the bombs." *Id.* On appeal, the defendant challenged the district court's "ruling only insofar as the court failed to suppress" his response to the question about his intent to kill himself, arguing "that question was unrelated to the matter of public safety." *Id.* The Second Circuit resolved the issue as follows:

> We are inclined to disagree, given that [the defendant]'s vision as to whether or not he would survive his attempt to detonate the bomb had the potential for shedding light on the bomb's stability. In any event, even if we were to take a different view as to the relevance of that question, we would conclude that the admission of [the defendant's] response at trial was, at worst, harmless error. *Id; see also In re Terrorist Bombings of U.S. Embassies in E. Africa*, 552 F.3d 177, 203 n.19, 204 (2d Cir. 2008) (assuming *Quarles* would apply to exigent circumstances in a terrorism case).

In light of the testimony provided at the evidentiary hearing, the logic of *Quarles* extends to the questioning of Defendant, a terrorism suspect at the time of his December 25, 2009 questioning. The agents' questions were intended to shed light on the obvious public safety concerns in this case and were "necessary to secure . . . the safety of the public[.]" *Quarles*, 467 U.S. at 659. Defendant was asked where he traveled, when he had traveled, how, and with whom; the details of the explosive device; the details regarding the bomb-maker, including where Defendant had received the bomb; his intentions in attacking Flight 253; who else might be planning an attack; whether he associated with, lived with, or attended the same mosque with others who had a similar mind-set as Defendant about jihad, martyrdom, support for al-Qaeda, and a desire to attack the United States by using a similar explosive device on a plane, and what these individuals looked like—all in an attempt to discover whether Defendant had information about others who could be on planes or about to board planes with explosive devices similar to the one Defendant used because, based upon his training, experience, and knowledge of earlier al-Qaeda attacks, this was not a solo incident and the potential for a multi-prong attack existed even if Defendant was unaware of any specific additional planned attack.

Special Agent Waters reiterated that, before he interviewed Defendant, he was aware that defendant claimed to be acting on behalf of al-Qaeda. The agents were also well aware that on September 11, 2001, al-Qaeda operatives hijacked four airplanes in an attack on the United States that killed almost 3,000 people. Mindful of Defendant's self-proclaimed association with al-Qaeda and knowing the group's past history of large, coordinated plots and attacks, the agents logically feared that there could be additional, imminent aircraft attacks in the United States and elsewhere in the world. Defendant was asked questions that sought to identify any other attackers or other potentially imminent attacks — information that could be used in conjunction with other U.S. government information to identify and disrupt such imminent attacks before they could occur. The agents limited their questioning to approximately 50 minutes, at which time they had sufficient information to address the threat to public safety. The agents then concluded their interview and immediately passed that information on to other law enforcement and intelligence agencies worldwide, further underscoring that it was obtained for purposes of public safety, to deal with other possible threats.

The circumstances present at the time of Defendant's questioning fall within the public safety exception to *Miranda* recognized in *Quarles*. Accordingly, the fact that he was questioned by federal agents at U of M Hospital on December 25, 2009 before receiving *Miranda* warnings does not warrant suppression of his challenged statements. Doing so here was fully justified.

III. CONCLUSION

For the above-stated reasons, Defendant's motion to suppress is DENIED.

NOTES AND QUESTIONS

1. Abdulmutallab pled guilty and was sentenced to four consecutive life sentences plus fifty years.
2. In *Quarles*, Justice O'Connor dissented because she did not consider a "public safety" carve-out consistent with the *Miranda* opinion. However, she also emphasized that because the Court had previously characterized *Miranda* as a "prophylactic" rule that "sweeps more broadly" than the Fifth Amendment itself, she did not believe it prohibited such questioning without a warning. In her view, *Miranda* has no prohibitory effect on questioning but instead only produces an evidentiary consequence when police fail to obtain a valid waiver. Thus she believed police must make a choice in such situations: prioritize public safety over use of a confession as evidence and question without a warning; or prioritize the admissibility of any statement and comply with *Miranda*.
3. During President Obama's Administration, Attorney General Eric Holder testified before Congress that he supported a law that would authorize extended questioning of terrorist suspects without a *Miranda* warning. Do you think such a law would be treated by a federal court as controlling for purposes of assessing the admissibility of a confession obtained by such a suspect? If Justice

O'Connor was correct to emphasize in *Quarles* that the only consequence of a *Miranda* violation is inadmissibility of the confession in the prosecution case-in-chief (and she was), then why would such a law be necessary? Is it possible the Obama Administration was hoping that such a law might trigger a legal challenge that would produce a Supreme Court decision that expanded the public safety exception?

4. If you were advising FBI agents about to interrogate a suspected terrorist, what factors would you focus on to determine whether to recommend dispensing with *Miranda* warnings based on the public safety exception?

ASSESSMENT QUESTIONS

1. Tarik Hasan is a Kuwaiti citizen who is also a resident alien living in the United States six months each year. He has been in the United States for one month. Hasan is indicted for, *inter alia*, violating the following federal statute:

   Unlawful Possession or Use of a Weapon of Mass Destruction
   Whoever knowingly possesses or intentionally uses a weapon of mass destruction (defined as a chemical, nuclear, biological, or radioactive weapon) in the context of an armed conflict or in support of terrorism shall be confined for no less than 20 years.

   The indictment is based on evidence obtained from Hasan's computer in his residence in Kuwait. A joint FBI/Kuwait Police team cooperating in the investigation searched the computer. The FBI agents did not have a warrant to search the residence, nor did they obtain approval from the Attorney General. The indictment alleges that while engaged in hostilities in Syria, Hasan was in possession of a deadly chemical agent intended for use against the Syrian armed forces in the event those forces employed chemical weapons against dissident forces, although the weapon was never used.

   Hasan files two motions. The first seeks dismissal of the charge based on an assertion that the statute should not be interpreted to apply extraterritorially. The second seeks suppression of the computer evidence based on an assertion that the search of his residence was unreasonable. How should the court rule on these motions?

2. U.S. FBI agents abduct Defendant from Argentina. Defendant is a non-resident alien indicted for a terrorism-related conspiracy. Defendant alleges that prior to his abduction by the FBI and transport to the United States, he was held in Argentine police custody and questioned extensively without any *Miranda* warning or waiver. He does not allege the FBI agents questioned him, but the government concedes the agents observed the interrogation. His defense counsel learns that the U.S. Attorney intends to offer the confession made to the Argentine police against the defendant at trial. Defense counsel moves to (1) suppress the confession based on a *Miranda* violation; and (2) dismiss the indictment based on the fact that Defendant was abducted and brought to the United States. How should the court rule on these motions?

3. The Chemical Weapons Implementation Act, 18 U.S.C. § 229, provides as follows:

   (a) Unlawful Conduct.— ... it shall be unlawful for any person knowingly —

   (1) to develop, produce, otherwise acquire, transfer directly or indirectly, receive, stockpile, retain, own, possess, or use, or threaten to use, any chemical weapon; or

(2) to assist or induce, in any way, any person to violate paragraph (1), or to attempt or conspire to violate paragraph (1).

. . .

The United States indicts an ISIS commander for a violation of this statute, and alleges that he was an accomplice to the use of mustard gas against Kurdish forces in Iraq. He moves to dismiss the indictment. What theory of international jurisdiction would you invoke as a U.S. Attorney in response to this motion to dismiss?

ASSESSMENT ANSWERS

1. The court should deny the motion to dismiss because the presumption of non-extraterritorial applicability of the federal statute is rebutted, and deny the motion to suppress because the defendant is not protected by the Fourth Amendment.

2. The court should deny both motions. The motion to suppress should be denied because there is no evidence that the FBI agents were involved in a joint venture with the Argentine police, and their observation of the interrogation is insufficient to trigger the *Miranda* requirement. The motion to dismiss should be denied based on the *Ker-Frisbie* doctrine, as there is no indication FBI conduct "shocked the conscience."

3. You would invoke the universality principle. War crimes are violations of international law considered to fall within the scope of universal jurisdiction. By defining this war crime as a violation of federal criminal law, it is reasonable to infer Congress intended the offense to run consistently with the scope of universal jurisdiction. Even though the defendant, his victims, and his conduct are not connected to the United States, the statute should be interpreted to apply to him based on this inference absent an indication Congress did not intend the statute to apply to this extraterritorial conduct.

CHAPTER 10

Prosecuting National Security Crimes

I. GENERAL OVERVIEW

The use of criminal sanctions is an essential component of an effective national security strategy. Criminal prosecution serves several important functions. Successful prosecution of crimes that threaten national security incapacitates wrongdoers, disrupts plots to undermine and harm vital U.S. national security interests, and deters future criminal wrongdoing. This chapter examines the principal criminal statutes enacted by Congress to protect national security, including treason, seditious conspiracy, and the material support to terrorism statutes. The chapter will review the constitutional challenges to prosecution under these criminal provisions, which implicate several important constitutional rights, such as the First Amendment rights of freedom of speech, association, and religion, the Fifth Amendment rights of fair notice and the void-for-vagueness and overbreadth doctrines, and the constitutional prohibition of *ex post facto* laws. Prosecution for espionage is discussed in Chapter 13, Protecting Sensitive Information, and punishment for willful violations of U.S. economic sanctions is covered in Chapter 15, Economic Powers and National Security. However, since prosecutors rely heavily on the material support statutes to prosecute suspected terrorists, their financial sponsors, and aiders and abettors, this chapter places special emphasis on the scope and application of the material support statutes, and legal challenges to prosecution under these provisions. Finally, the chapter will explore the option of prosecuting suspected terrorists before a military tribunal, and whether conspiracy to commit war crimes and material support for terrorism may be lawfully tried before a military tribunal.

II. NATIONAL SECURITY CRIMES

A. Treason

Treason punishes "levying war" against the United States or "adhering" to its enemies, giving them "aid and comfort." U.S. Const., Art. III, § 3.[1] Treason is the most serious national crime, which is punishable by death. *See* 18 U.S.C. § 2381. However, historically, the United States has been reluctant to prosecute persons for treason. Since 1789, there have been only thirty domestic treason trials. *See* Erin Creegan, *National Security Crime*, 3 HARV. NAT'L SEC. J. 373, 379 (2012). For example, after the 1794 Whiskey Rebellion, President George Washington pardoned all the members of the rebellion. *Id.* at 380. Following the Civil War, not a single member of the leadership of the Confederacy was tried and punished for treason. *Id.* There are a few cases from the World War II era charging U.S. nationals with aiding and abetting the enemy by broadcasting over the radio propaganda meant to demoralize U.S. soldiers. *Id.* at 378. More recently, John Walker Lindh, a United States citizen, captured on the battlefield in Afghanistan fighting for the Taliban, was not prosecuted for treason, but less serious crimes. Finally, one of the few treason indictments was brought against Adam Gadahn, a U.S. citizen and notorious members of al Qaeda. He was indicted for treason and providing material support to a foreign terrorist organization.[2] What explains the limited number of treason indictments in the history of the United States?

The crime of treason has three main elements. First, one may commit treason by levying war or rebelling against the United States, or, alternatively, by supporting an enemy of the United States. Second, treason requires proof of the specific intent to betray one's country. A person must owe allegiance to the United States in order to betray the country, but citizenship is not the only form of allegiance. Third, there must be an "overt act" directed at the objective of treason. The overt act requirement ensures that someone is not prosecuted for treason to repress peaceful political opposition. Further, treason can be proven in only one of two ways. The first is testimony by two eyewitnesses to the same overt act. U.S. Const., Art. III, § 3. Evidence of one witness each to two separate overt acts will not do. The second is a confession given in open court. *Id.* A confession to a law enforcement officer would not satisfy the constitutional requirement. Does the high bar posed by the constitutional requirements to convict for treason explain

---

1. The statutory prohibition on treason appears at 18 U.S.C. § 2381, adding to the Constitution:

   Whoever, owing allegiance to the United States, levies war against them or adheres to their enemies, giving them aid and comfort within the United States or elsewhere, is guilty of treason and shall suffer death, or shall be imprisoned not less than five years and fined under this title but not less than $10,000; and shall be incapable of holding any office under the United States.

2. In January 2015, Adam Gadahn was killed in a drone strike. *See Adam Gadahn, American Mouthpiece for al Qaeda, Killed*, CNN (Apr. 23, 2015).

why the United States has been reluctant to prosecute for treason? The following cases explore many of the legal issues and defenses that arise in treason prosecutions.

Cramer v. United States
325 U.S. 1 (1945)

Mr. Justice JACKSON delivered the opinion of the Court.

Anthony Cramer, the petitioner, stands convicted of violating Section 1 of the Criminal Code, which provides: "Whoever, owing allegiance to the United States, levies war against them or adheres to their enemies, giving them aid and comfort within the United States or elsewhere, is guilty of treason."

Cramer owed allegiance to the United States. A German by birth, he had been a resident of the United States since 1925 and was naturalized in 1936. Prosecution resulted from his association with two of the German saboteurs who in June 1942 landed on our shores from enemy submarines to disrupt industry in the United States and whose cases was considered in *Ex parte Quirin*, 317 U.S. 1 (1942). One of those, spared from execution, appeared as a government witness on the trial of Cramer. He testified that Werner Thiel and Edward Kerling were members of that sabotage crew, detailed their plot, and described their preparations for its consummation. . . .

There was no evidence, and the Government makes no claim, that he had foreknowledge that the saboteurs were coming to this country or that he came into association with them by prearrangement. Cramer, however, had known intimately the saboteur Werner Thiel while the latter lived in this country. They had worked together, roomed together, and jointly had ventured in a small and luckless delicatessen enterprise. Thiel early and frankly avowed adherence to the National Socialist movement in Germany; he foresaw the war and returned in 1941 for the purpose of helping Germany. Cramer did not do so. How much he sympathized with the doctrines of the Nazi Party is not clear. He became at one time, in Indiana, a member and officer of the Friends of New Germany, which was a predecessor of the Bund. However, he withdrew in 1935 before it became the Bund. He says there was some swindle about it that he did not like and also that he did not like their drilling and "radical activities." In 1936 he made a trip to Germany, attended the Olympic games, and saw some of the Bundsmen from this country who went there at that time for conferences with Nazi Party officials. There is no suggestion that Cramer while there had any such associations. He does not appear to have been regarded as a person of that consequence. His friends and associates in this country were largely German. His social life in New York City, where he recently had lived, seems to have been centered around Kolping House, a German-Catholic recreational center.

Cramer retained a strong affection for his fatherland. He corresponded in German with his family and friends there. Before the United States entered the war he expressed strong sympathy with Germany in its conflict with other European powers. Before the attack upon Pearl Harbor, Cramer openly opposed participation by this country in the war against Germany. He refused to work on war materials. He expressed concern about being drafted into our army and "misused" for purposes of "world conquest." There is no proof, however, except for the matter charged in the indictment, of any act or utterance disloyal to this country after we entered the war.

Coming down to the time of the alleged treason, the main facts, as related on the witness stand by Cramer, are not seriously in dispute. He was living in New York; and in response to a cryptic note left under his door, which did not mention Thiel, he went to the Grand Central Station. There Thiel appeared. Cramer had supposed that Thiel was in Germany, knowing that he had left the United States shortly before the war to go there. Together they went to public places and had some drinks. Cramer denies that Thiel revealed his mission of sabotage. Cramer said to Thiel that he must have come to America by submarine, but Thiel refused to confirm it, although his attitude increased Cramer's suspicion. Thiel promised to tell later how he came to this country. Thiel asked about a girl who was a mutual acquaintance and whom Thiel had engaged to marry previous to his going to Germany. Cramer knew where she was, and offered to and did write to her to come to New York, without disclosing in the letter that Thiel had arrived. Thiel said that he had in his possession about $3,600, but did not disclose that it was provided by the German Government, saying only that one could get money in Germany if he had the right connections. Thiel owed Cramer an old debt of $200. He gave Cramer his money belt containing some $3,600, from which Cramer was to be paid. Cramer agreed to and did place the rest in his own safe-deposit box, except a sum which he kept in his room in case Thiel should want it quickly.

After the second of these meetings Thiel and Kerling, who was present briefly at one meeting, were arrested. Cramer's expectation of meeting Thiel later and of bringing him and his fiancee together was foiled. Shortly thereafter Cramer was arrested, tried, and found guilty. The trial judge at the time of sentencing said:

> "I shall not impose the maximum penalty of death. It does not appear that this defendant Cramer was aware that Thiel and Kerling were in possession of explosives or other means for destroying factories and property in the United States or planned to do that. From the evidence it appears that Cramer had no more guilty knowledge of any subversive purposes on the part of Thiel or Kerling than a vague idea that they came here for the purpose of organizing pro-German propaganda and agitation. If there were any proof that they had confided in him what their real purposes were, or that he knew or believed what they really were, I should not hesitate to impose the death penalty."

Cramer's case raises questions as to application of the constitutional provision that "Treason against the United States shall consist only in levying War against them, or in adhering to their Enemies, giving them Aid and Comfort. No person shall be convicted of Treason unless on the Testimony of two Witnesses to the same overt Act, or on Confession in open Court."

Cramer's contention may be well stated in words of Judge Learned Hand in *United States v. Robinson*:

> "Nevertheless a question may indeed be raised whether the prosecution may lay as an overt act a step taken in execution of the traitorous design, innocent in itself, and getting its treasonable character only from some covert and undeclared intent. It is true that in prosecutions for conspiracy under our federal statute it is well settled that any step in performance of the conspiracy is enough, though it is innocent except for its relation to the agreement. I doubt very much whether that rule has any application to the case of treason, where the requirement affected the character of the pleading and proof, rather than accorded a season of repentance before the crime should be complete. Lord Reading in his charge in *Casement's Case* uses language which accords with my understanding: 'Overt acts are such acts as manifest a criminal intention and tend towards the accomplishment of the criminal object. They are acts by which the purpose is manifested and the means by which it is intended to be fulfilled.'"

The Government, however, contends for, and the court below has affirmed, this conviction upon a contrary principle. It said: "We believe in short that no more need be laid for an overt act of treason than for an overt act of conspiracy.... Hence we hold the overt acts relied on were sufficient to be submitted to the jury, even though they perhaps may have appeared as innocent on their face." A similar conclusion was reached in *United States v. Fricke*; it is: "An overt act in itself may be a perfectly innocent act standing by itself; it must be in some manner in furtherance of the crime."

As lower courts thus have taken conflicting positions, or, where the issue was less clearly drawn, have dealt with the problem ambiguously, we granted certiorari....

. . .

III.

Historical materials aid interpretation chiefly in that they show two kinds of dangers against which the framers were concerned to guard the treason offense: (1) perversion by established authority to repress peaceful political opposition; and (2) conviction of the innocent as a result of perjury, passion, or inadequate evidence. The first danger could be diminished by closely circumscribing the kind of conduct which should be treason—making the constitutional definition exclusive, making it clear, and making the offense one not susceptible of being inferred from all sorts of insubordinations. The second danger lay in the manner of trial and was one which would be diminished mainly by procedural requirements—mainly but not wholly, for the hazards of trial also would be diminished by confining the treason offense to kinds of conduct susceptible of reasonably sure proof. The concern uppermost in the framers' minds, that mere mental attitudes or expressions should not be treason, influenced both definition of the crime and procedure for its trial. In the proposed Constitution the first sentence of the treason article undertook to define the offense; the second, to surround its trial with procedural safeguards....

Treason of adherence to an enemy was old in the law. It consisted of breaking allegiance to one's own king by forming an attachment to his enemy. Its scope was comprehensive, its requirements indeterminate. It might be predicated on intellectual or emotional sympathy with the foe, or merely lack of zeal in the cause of one's own country. That was not the kind of disloyalty the framers thought should constitute treason. They promptly accepted the proposal to restrict it to cases where also there was conduct which was "giving them aid and comfort."

"Aid and comfort" was defined by Lord Reading in the Casement trial comprehensively, as ". . . an act which strengthens or tends to strengthen the enemies of the King in the conduct of a war against the King, that is in law the giving of aid and comfort" and "an act which weakens or tends to weaken the power of the King and of the country to resist or to attack the enemies of the King and the country . . . is . . . giving of aid and comfort." Lord Reading explained it, as we think one must, in terms of an "act." It is not easy, if indeed possible, to think of a way in which "aid and comfort" can be "given" to an enemy except by some kind of action. Its very nature partakes of a deed or physical activity as opposed to a mental operation.

Thus the crime of treason consists of two elements: adherence to the enemy and rendering him aid and comfort. A citizen intellectually or emotionally may favor the enemy and harbor sympathies or convictions disloyal to this country's policy or interest, but so long as he commits no act of aid and comfort to the enemy, there is no treason. On the other hand, a citizen may take actions which do aid and comfort the enemy—making a speech critical of the government or opposing its measures, profiteering, striking in defense plants or essential work, and the hundred other things which impair our cohesion and diminish our strength—but if there is no adherence to the enemy in this, if there is no intent to betray, there is no treason.

Having thus by definition made treason consist of something outward and visible and capable of direct proof, the framers turned to safeguarding procedures of trial and ordained that "No Person shall be convicted of Treason unless on the Testimony of two Witnesses to the same overt Act, or on Confession in open Court." This repeats in procedural terms the concept that thoughts and attitudes alone cannot make a treason. It need not trouble us that we find so dominant a purpose emphasized in two different ways. But does the procedural requirement add some limitation not already present in the definition of the crime, and if so, what?

While to prove giving of aid and comfort would require the prosecution to show actions and deeds, if the Constitution stopped there, such acts could be inferred from circumstantial evidence. This the framers thought would not do. So they added what in effect is a command that the overt acts must be established by direct evidence, and the direct testimony must be that of two witnesses instead of one. In this sense the overt act procedural provision adds something, and something important, to the definition.

Our problem begins where the Constitution ends. That instrument omits to specify what relation the indispensable overt act must sustain to the two elements of the offense as defined: viz., adherence and giving aid and comfort. It requires that two witnesses testify to the same overt act, and clearly enough the act must show something toward treason, but what? Must the act be one of giving aid and comfort? If so, how must adherence to the enemy, the disloyal state of mind, be shown?

The defendant especially challenges the sufficiency of the overt acts to prove treasonable intention. Questions of intent in a treason case are even more complicated than in most criminal cases because of the peculiarity of the two different elements which together make the offense. Of course the overt acts of aid and comfort must be intentional as distinguished from merely negligent or undesigned ones. Intent in that limited sense is not in issue here. But to make treason the defendant not only must intend the act, but he must intend to betray his country by means of the act. It is here that Cramer defends. The issue is joined between conflicting theories as to how this treacherous intention and treasonable purpose must be made to appear.

Bearing in mind that the constitutional requirement in effect is one of direct rather than circumstantial evidence, we must give it a reasonable effect in the light of its purpose both to preserve the offense and to protect citizens from its abuse. What is designed in the mind of an accused never is susceptible of proof by direct testimony. If we were to hold that the disloyal and treacherous intention must be proved by the direct testimony of two witnesses, it would be to hold that it is never provable. It seems obvious that adherence to the enemy, in the sense of a disloyal state of mind, cannot be, and is not required to be, proved by deposition of two witnesses.

Since intent must be inferred from conduct of some sort, we think it is permissible to draw usual reasonable inferences as to intent from the overt acts. The law of treason, like the law of lesser crimes, assumes every man to intend the natural consequences which one standing in his circumstances and possessing his knowledge would reasonably expect to result from his acts. . . .

While of course it must be proved that the accused acted with an intention and purpose to betray or there is no treason, we think that in some circumstances at least the overt act itself will be evidence of the treasonable purpose and intent. But that still leaves us with exceedingly difficult problems. How decisively must treacherous intention be made manifest in the act itself? Will a scintilla of evidence of traitorous intent suffice? Or must it be sufficient to convince beyond reasonable doubt? Or need it show only that treasonable intent was more probable than not? Must the overt act be appraised for legal sufficiency only as supported by the testimony of two witnesses, or may other evidence be thrown into the scales to create inferences not otherwise reasonably to be drawn or to reinforce those which might be drawn from the act itself?

It is only overt acts by the accused which the Constitution explicitly requires to be proved by the testimony of two witnesses. It does not make other common-law evidence inadmissible nor deny its inherent powers of persuasion. It does not forbid judging by the usual process by which the significance of conduct often will be determined by facts which are not acts. . . .

Environment illuminates the meaning of acts, as context does that of words. What a man is up to may be clear from considering his bare acts by themselves; often it is made clear when we know the reciprocity and sequence of his acts with those of others, the interchange between him and another, the give and take of the situation.

It would be no contribution to certainty of judgment, which is the object of the provision, to construe it to deprive a trial court of the aid of testimony under the ordinary sanctions of verity, provided, of course, resort is not had to evidence of less than the constitutional standard to supply deficiencies in the constitutional measure of proof of overt acts. For it must be remembered that the constitutional provision establishes a minimum of proof of incriminating acts, without which there can be no conviction, but it is not otherwise a limitation on the evidence with which a jury may be persuaded that it ought to convict. The Constitution does not exclude or set up standards to test evidence which will show the relevant acts of persons other than the accused or their identity or enemy character or other surrounding circumstances. Nor does it preclude any proper evidence of non-incriminating facts about a defendant, such for example as his nationality, naturalization, and residence.

From duly proven overt acts of aid and comfort to the enemy in their setting, it may well be that the natural and reasonable inference of intention to betray will be warranted. The two-witness evidence of the acts accused, together with common-law evidence of acts of others and of facts which are not acts, will help to determine which among possible inferences as to the actor's knowledge, motivation, or intent are the true ones. But the protection of the two-witness rule extends at least to all acts of the defendant which are used to draw incriminating inferences that aid and comfort have been given.

The controversy before us has been waged in terms of intentions, but this, we think, is the reflection of a more fundamental issue as to what is the real function of the overt act in convicting of treason. The prisoner's contention that it alone and on its face must manifest a traitorous intention, apart from an intention to do the act itself, would place on the overt act the whole burden of establishing a complete treason. On the other hand, the Government's contention that it may prove by two witnesses an apparently commonplace and insignificant act and from other circumstances create an inference that the act was a step in treason and was done with treasonable intent really is a contention that the function of the overt act in a treason prosecution is almost zero. It is obvious that the function we ascribe to the overt act is significant chiefly because it measures the two-witness rule protection to the accused and its handicap to the prosecution. If the overt act or acts must go all the way to make out the complete treason, the defendant is protected at all points by the two-witness requirement. If the act may be an insignificant one, then the constitutional safeguards are shrunken so as to be applicable only at a point where they are least needed.

The very minimum function that an overt act must perform in a treason prosecution is that it show sufficient action by the accused, in its setting, to sustain a finding that the accused actually gave aid and comfort to the enemy. Every act, movement, deed, and word of the defendant charged to constitute treason must be supported by the testimony of two witnesses. The two-witness principle is to interdict imputation of *incriminating acts* to the accused by circumstantial evidence or by the testimony of a single witness. The prosecution cannot rely on evidence which does not meet the constitutional test for overt acts to create any inference that the accused did other acts or did something more than was shown in the overt act, in order to make a giving of aid and comfort to the enemy. The words of the Constitution were chosen, not to make it hard to prove merely routine and everyday acts, but to make the proof of acts that convict of treason as sure as trial processes may. When the prosecution's case is thus established, the Constitution does not prevent presentation of corroborative or cumulative evidence of any admissible character either to strengthen a direct case or to rebut the testimony or inferences on behalf of defendant. The Government is not prevented from making a strong case; it is denied a conviction on a weak one. . . .

IV.

The indictment charged Cramer with adhering to the enemies of the United States, giving them aid and comfort, and set forth ten overt acts. The prosecution withdrew seven, and three were submitted to the jury. The overt acts which present the principal issue are alleged in the following language:

> "1. Anthony Cramer, the defendant herein, on or about June 23, 1942, at the Southern District of New York and within the jurisdiction of this Court, did meet with Werner Thiel and Edward John Kerling, enemies of the United States, at the Twin Oaks Inn at Lexington Avenue and 44th Street, in the City and State of New York, and did confer, treat, and counsel with said Werner Thiel and Edward John Kerling for a period of time for the purpose of giving and with intent to give aid and comfort to said enemies, Werner Thiel and Edward John Kerling.
> "2. Anthony Cramer, the defendant herein, on or about June 23, 1942, at the Southern District of New York and within the jurisdiction of this Court, did accompany, confer, treat, and counsel with Werner Thiel, an enemy of the United States, for a period of time at the Twin Oaks Inn at Lexington Avenue and 44th Street, and at Thompson's Cafeteria on 42nd Street between Lexington and Vanderbilt Avenues, both in the City and State of New York, for the purpose of giving and with intent to give aid and comfort to said enemy, Werner Thiel."

It appeared upon the trial that at all times involved in these acts Kerling and Thiel were under surveillance of the Federal Bureau of Investigation. By direct testimony of two or more agents it was established that Cramer met Thiel and Kerling on the occasions and at the places charged and that they drank together and engaged long and earnestly in conversation. This is the sum of the overt acts as established by the testimony of two witnesses. There is no two-witness proof of what they said nor in what language they conversed. There is no showing that Cramer gave them any information whatever of value to their mission or indeed that he had any to give. No effort at secrecy is shown, for they met in public places. Cramer furnished them no shelter, nothing that can be called sustenance or supplies, and there is no evidence that he gave them encouragement or counsel, or even paid for their drinks. . . .

The shortcomings of the overt act submitted are emphasized by contrast with others which the indictment charged but which the prosecution withdrew for admitted insufficiency of proof. It appears that Cramer took from Thiel for safekeeping a money belt containing about $3,600, some $160 of which he held in his room concealed in books for Thiel's use as needed. An old indebtedness of Thiel to Cramer of $200 was paid from the fund, and the rest Cramer put in his safe-deposit box in a bank for safekeeping. All of this was at Thiel's request. That Thiel would be aided by having the security of a safe-deposit box for his funds, plus availability of smaller amounts, and by being relieved of the risks of carrying large sums on his person — without disclosing his presence or identity to a bank — seems obvious. The inference of intent from such act is also very different from the intent manifest by drinking and talking together. Taking what must have seemed a large sum of money for safekeeping is not a usual amenity of social intercourse. That such responsibilities are undertaken and such trust bestowed without the scratch of a pen to show it, implies some degree of mutuality and concert from which a jury could say that aid and comfort was given and was intended. If these acts had been submitted as overt acts of treason, and we were now required to decide whether they had been established as required, we would have a quite different case. . . . But this transaction was not proven as the Government evidently hoped to do when the indictment was obtained. The overt acts based on it were expressly withdrawn from the jury, and Cramer has not been convicted of treason on account of such acts. We cannot sustain a conviction for the acts submitted on the theory that, even if insufficient, some unsubmitted ones may be resorted to as proof of treason. . . .

The Government contends that outside of the overt acts, and by lesser degree of proof, it has shown a treasonable intent on Cramer's part in meeting and talking with Thiel and Kerling. But if it showed him disposed to betray, and showed that he had opportunity to do so, it still has not proved in the manner required that he did any acts submitted to the jury as a basis for conviction which had the effect of betraying by giving aid and comfort. To take the intent for the deed would carry us back to constructive treasons. . . .

Most damaging is the testimony of Norma Kopp, a friend of Cramer's and one with whom, if she is to be believed, he had been most indiscreetly confidential. Her testimony went considerably beyond that of the agents of the Federal Bureau of Investigation as to admissions of guilty knowledge of Thiel's hostile mission and of Cramer's sympathy with it. To the extent that his conviction rests upon such evidence, and it does to an unknown but considerable extent, it rests upon the uncorroborated testimony of one witness not without strong emotional interest in the drama of which Cramer's trial was a part. Other evidence relates statements by Cramer before the United States was at war with

Germany. At the time they were uttered, however, they were not treasonable. To use pre-war expressions of opposition to entering a war to convict of treason during the war is a dangerous procedure at best. . . . Another class of evidence consists of admissions to agents of the Federal Bureau of Investigation. They are, of course, not "confessions in open court." The Government does not contend and could not well contend that admission made out of court, if otherwise admissible, can supply a deficiency in proof of the overt act itself.

V.

The Government has urged that our initial interpretation of the treason clause should be less exacting, lest treason be too hard to prove and the Government disabled from adequately combating the techniques of modern warfare. But the treason offense is not the only nor can it well serve as the principal legal weapon to vindicate our national cohesion and security. . . . Congress repeatedly has enacted prohibitions of specific acts thought to endanger our security and the practice of foreign nations with defense problems more acute than our own affords examples of others.

The framers' effort to compress into two sentences the law of one of the most intricate of crimes gives a superficial appearance of clarity and simplicity which proves illusory when it is put to practical application. There are few subjects on which the temptation to utter abstract interpretative generalizations is greater or on which they are more to be distrusted. The little clause is packed with controversy and difficulty. The offense is one of subtlety, and it is easy to demonstrate lack of logic in almost any interpretation by hypothetical cases, to which real treasons rarely will conform. The protection of the two-witness requirement, limited as it is to overt acts, may be wholly unrelated to the real controversial factors in a case. . . . Although nothing in the conduct of Cramer's trial evokes it, a repetition of Chief Justice Marshall's warning can never be untimely:

> "As there is no crime which can more excite and agitate the passions of men than treason, no charge demands more from the tribunal before which it is made, a deliberate and temperate inquiry. Whether this inquiry be directed to the fact or to the law, none can be more solemn, none more important to the citizen or to the government; none can more affect the safety of both.
>
> ". . . It is, therefore, more safe, as well as more consonant to the principles of our constitution, that the crime of treason should not be extended by construction to doubtful cases; and that crimes not clearly within the constitutional definition, should receive such punishment as the legislature in its wisdom may provide." *Ex parte Bollman*, 4 Cranch 75, 125, 127.

. . . Certainly the treason rule, whether wisely or not, is severely restrictive. . . . The provision was adopted not merely in spite of the difficulties it put in the way of prosecution but because of them. And it was not by whim or by accident, but because one of the most venerated of that venerated group considered that "prosecutions for treason were generally virulent." Time has not made the accusation of treachery less poisonous, nor the task of judging one charged with betraying the country, including his triers, less susceptible to the influence of suspicion and rancor. The innovations made by the forefathers in the law of treason were conceived in a faith such as Paine put in the maxim that "He that would make his own liberty secure must guard even his enemy from oppression; for if he violates this duty he establishes a precedent that will reach himself." We still put trust in it.

We hold that overt acts 1 and 2 are insufficient as proved to support the judgment of conviction, which accordingly is *Reversed.*

NOTES AND QUESTIONS

1. There are two kinds of dangers against which the Framers were seeking to guard in defining and punishing treason. What are those dangers? How does Article III, § 3 of the Constitution address those concerns?
2. The Court states: "Certainly the treason rule, whether wisely or not, is severely restrictive." What is the justification for imposing these restrictions and evidentiary hurdles on prosecution for treason?
3. Why did the Court find that overt acts 1 and 2 of the indictment were insufficient to support a conviction for treason?
4. What is the nature of the overt act required to convict for treason? Must the overt act for treason be criminal in nature? Is the overt act requirement similar to the overt act requirement for conspiracy? Must the overt act be one of providing aid and comfort to the enemy?
5. The crime of treason prohibits levying war against the United States or adhering to the country's enemies and rendering them "aid and comfort." Does political advocacy—making a speech critical of U.S. foreign policy and supporting the goals of a foreign terrorist organization such as ISIS—constitute "aid and comfort" to the enemy? What about soliciting others to fight with ISIS in Syria? Would words alone ever constitute treason?
6. The mens rea requirement for treason has two aspects. First, the overt acts of providing aid and comfort to the enemy must be intentional, not merely negligent or accidental. Second, the defendant must intend to betray his country by means of such acts. Must the defendant's treasonous intent be proven by the testimony of two witnesses? May the purpose to betray be inferred from the overt act required to prove treason?
7. While the Constitution requires that overt acts by the accused be proven by the testimony of two witnesses, is other incriminating evidence required to be supported by the testimony of two witnesses?
8. What is the function of the overt act requirement? The Court states:

> The very minimum function that an overt act must perform in a treason prosecution is that it show sufficient action by the accused, in its setting, to sustain a finding that the accused actually gave aid and comfort to the enemy. . . . The prosecution cannot rely on evidence which does not meet the constitutional test for overt acts to create any inference that the accused did other acts or did

something more than was shown in the overt acts, in order to make a giving of aid and comfort to the enemy.[3]

What exactly does this mean? What limitations are imposed on the admissibility of evidence in a trial for treason? Does the Constitution prevent the presentation of corroborative or cumulative evidence to strengthen the government's case-in-chief or rebut testimony on behalf of the defendant?

9. The Court discussed other overt acts by the defendant that were expressly withdrawn from the jury. Are those overt acts sufficient to support a conviction for treason?

Kawakita v. United States
343 U.S. 717 (1952)

Mr. Justice DOUGLAS delivered the opinion of the Court.

Petitioner, a national both of the United States and of Japan, was indicted for treason, the overt acts relating to his treatment of American prisoners of war. He was convicted of treason after a jury trial and the judgment of conviction was affirmed. . . . The case is here on certiorari. . . .

First. The important question that lies at the threshold of the case relates to expatriation. Petitioner was born in this country in 1921 of Japanese parents who were citizens of Japan. He was thus a citizen of the United States by birth (Amendment XIV, § 1) and, by reason of Japanese law, a national of Japan.

In 1939 shortly before petitioner turned 18 years of age he went to Japan with his father to visit his grandfather. He traveled on a United States passport; and to obtain it he took the customary oath of allegiance. In 1940 he registered with an American consul in Japan as an American citizen. Petitioner remained in Japan, his father returning to this country. In March, 1941, he entered Meiji University and took a commercial course and military training. In April, 1941, he renewed his United States passport, once more taking the oath of allegiance to the United States. During this period he was registered as an alien with the Japanese police. When war was declared, petitioner was still a student at Meiji University. He became of age in 1942 and completed his schooling in 1943, at which time it was impossible for him to return to the United States. In 1943 he registered in the Koseki, a family census register. Petitioner did not join the Japanese Army nor serve as a soldier. Rather, he obtained employment as an interpreter with the Oeyama Nickel Industry Co., Ltd., where he worked until Japan's surrender. He was hired to interpret communications between the Japanese and the prisoners of war who were assigned to work at the mine and in the factory of this company. The treasonable acts for which he was convicted involved his conduct toward American prisoners of war.

---

3. *Cramer*, 325 U.S. at 34-35.

In December, 1945, petitioner went to the United States consul at Yokohama and applied for registration as an American citizen. He stated under oath that he was a United States citizen and had not done various acts amounting to expatriation. He was issued a passport and returned to the United States in 1946. Shortly thereafter he was recognized by a former American prisoner of war, whereupon he was arrested, and indicted, and tried for treason.

Petitioner defended at his trial on the ground that he had renounced or abandoned his United States citizenship and was expatriated. Congress has provided by § 401 of the Nationality Act of 1940, 54 Stat. 1137, 1168, as amended, 8 U.S.C. § 801, that a national of the United States may lose his nationality in certain prescribed ways. It provides in relevant part,

> "A person who is a national of the United States, whether by birth or naturalization, shall lose his nationality by:
>
> "(a) Obtaining naturalization in a foreign state . . . ; or
>
> "(b) Taking an oath or making an affirmation or other formal declaration of allegiance to a foreign state; or
>
> "(c) Entering, or serving in, the armed forces of a foreign state unless expressly authorized by the laws of the United States, if he has or acquires the nationality of such foreign state; or
>
> "(d) Accepting, or performing the duties of, any office, post, or employment under the government of a foreign state or political subdivision thereof for which only nationals of such state are eligible. . . ."

Petitioner asks us to hold as a matter of law that he had expatriated himself by his acts and conduct beginning in 1943. He places special emphasis on the entry of his name in the Koseki. Prior to that time he had been registered by the police as an alien. There is evidence that after that time he was considered by Japanese authorities as a Japanese and that he took action which might give rise to the inference that he had elected the Japanese nationality: he took a copy of the Koseki to the police station and had his name removed as an alien; he changed his registration at the University from American to Japanese and his address from California to Japan; he used the Koseki entry to get a job at the Oeyama camp; he went to China on a Japanese passport; he accepted labor draft papers from the Japanese government; he faced the east each morning and paid his respects to the Emperor.

The difficulty with petitioner's position is that the implications from the acts, which he admittedly performed, are ambiguous. He had a dual nationality, a status long recognized in the law. *Perkins v. Elg*, 307 U.S. 325, 344-349. The concept of dual citizenship recognizes that a person may have and exercise rights of nationality in two countries and be subject to the responsibilities of both. The mere fact that he asserts the rights of one citizenship does not without more mean that he renounces the other. . . . From this it would appear that the registration may have been nothing more than the disclosure of a fact theretofore not made public.

Conceivably it might have greater consequences. In other settings it might be the equivalent of "naturalization" within the meaning of § 401(a) of the Act or the making of "an affirmation or other formal declaration of allegiance" to Japan within the meaning of § 401(b). Certainly it was relevant to the issue of expatriation. But we cannot say as a matter of law that it was a renunciation of petitioner's American citizenship. . . .

As we have said, dual citizenship presupposes rights of citizenship in each country. It could not exist if the assertion of rights or the assumption of liabilities of one were deemed inconsistent with the maintenance of the other. For example, when one has a dual citizenship, it is not necessarily inconsistent with his citizenship in one nation to use a passport proclaiming his citizenship in the other. Hence the use by petitioner of a Japanese passport on his trip to China, his use of the Koseki entry to obtain work at the Oeyama camp, the bowing to the Emperor, and his acceptance of labor draft papers from the Japanese government might reasonably mean no more than acceptance of some of the incidents of Japanese citizenship made possible by his dual citizenship.

Those acts, to be sure, were colored by various other acts and statements of petitioner. He testified for example that he felt no loyalty to the United States from about March, 1943, to late 1945. There was evidence that he boasted that Japan was winning and would win the war, that he taunted American prisoners of war with General MacArthur's departure from the Philippines, that he expressed his hatred toward things American and toward the prisoners as Americans. That was in 1943 and 1944. This attitude continued into 1945, although in May or June, 1945, shortly before Japan's surrender, he was saying he did not care "which way the war goes because I am going back to the States anyway."

On December 31, 1945, he applied for registration as an American citizen, and in that connection he made an affidavit in which he stated that he had been "temporarily residing" in Japan since August 10, 1939; that he came to Japan to study Japanese; that he possessed dual nationality from birth but that his name was not entered in the census register until March 8, 1943; and that he had "never been naturalized, taken an oath of allegiance, or voted as a foreign citizen or subject, or in any way held myself out as such. . . ."

If petitioner were to be believed in December, 1945, he never once renounced his American citizenship. If what petitioner now says were his thoughts, attitudes, and motives in 1943 and 1944 and in part of 1945, he did intend to renounce his American citizenship. If the latter version were believed by the jury, the signing of the family register, and the changing of his registration at the police station and at the University would assume different significance; those acts might then readily suggest the making of a declaration of allegiance to Japan within the meaning of § 401(b). If, on the other hand, petitioner were to be believed when in 1945 he stated he had not done acts by which he renounced his American citizenship, then the Koseki incident and the changes in his police and University registration could reasonably be taken as amounting to no more than a public declaration of an established and pre-existing fact, viz. his Japanese nationality. We think, in other words, that the question whether petitioner had renounced his American citizenship was on this record peculiarly for the jury to determine. The charge was that the jury must be satisfied beyond a reasonable doubt that during the period specified in the indictment, petitioner was an American citizen. We cannot say there was insufficient evidence for that finding.

Petitioner concedes he did not enter the armed services of Japan within the meaning of § 401(c) of the Act but claims that during his tour of duty at the Oeyama camp he was "serving in" the Japanese armed services within the statutory meaning of those words. . . .

The Oeyama Nickel Industry Co., Ltd., was a private company, organized for profit. It was engaged in producing metals used for war under contracts with the Japanese government. In 1944 it was designated by the Japanese government as a munitions corporation and under Japanese law civilian employees were not allowed to change or quit their employment without the consent of the government. The company's mine and factory were manned in part by prisoners of war. They lived in a camp controlled by the Japanese army. Though petitioner took orders from the military, he was not a soldier in the armed services; he wore insignia on his uniform distinguishing him as nonmilitary personnel; he had no duties to perform in relation to the prisoners, except those of an interpreter. His employment was as an interpreter for the Oeyama Nickel Industry Co., Ltd., a private company. The regulation of the company by the Japanese government, the freezing of its labor force, the assignment to it of prisoners of war under military command were incidents of a war economy. But we find no indication that the Oeyama Company was nationalized or its properties seized and operated by the government. The evidence indicates that it was a part of a regimented industry; but it was an organization operating for private profit under private management. We cannot say that petitioner's status as an employee of a private company was changed by that regimentation of the industry. . . .

Second. Petitioner contends that a person who has a dual nationality can be guilty of treason only to the country where he resides, not to the other country which claims him as a national. More specifically, he maintains that while petitioner resided in Japan he owed his paramount allegiance to that country and was indeed, in the eyes of our law, an alien enemy.

The argument in its broadest reach is that treason against the United States cannot be committed abroad or in enemy territory, at least by an American with a dual nationality residing in the other country which claims him as a national. The definition of treason, however, contained in the Constitution contains no territorial limitation. "Treason against the United States, shall consist only in levying War against them, or in adhering to their Enemies, giving them Aid and Comfort. . . ." Art. III, § 3. A substitute proposal containing some territorial limitations was rejected by the Constitutional Convention. . . . We must therefore reject the suggestion that an American citizen living beyond the territorial limits of the United States may not commit treason against them. . . .

. . . An American who has a dual nationality may find himself in a foreign country when it wages war on us. The very fact that he must make a livelihood there may indirectly help the enemy nation. In these days of total war manpower becomes critical and everyone who can be placed in a productive position increases the strength of the enemy to wage war. Of course, a person caught in that predicament can resolve the conflict of duty by openly electing one nationality or the other and becoming either an alien enemy of the country where he resides or a national of it alone. Yet, so far as the existing law of this country is concerned, he need not make that choice but can continue his dual citizenship. . . . Of course, an American citizen who is also a Japanese national living in Japan has obligations to Japan necessitated by his residence there. There might conceivably be cases where the mere nonperformance of the acts complained of would be a breach of Japanese law. He may have employment which requires him to perform certain acts. The compulsion may come from the fact that he is drafted for the job or that his conduct is demanded by the laws of Japan. He may be coerced by his employer or supervisor or by the force of circumstances to do things which he has no desire or heart to do. That was one of petitioner's defenses in this case. Such acts—if done voluntarily and willfully—might be treasonable. But if done under the compulsion of the job or the law or some other influence, those acts would not rise to the gravity of that offense. The trial judge recognized the distinction in his charge when he instructed the jury to acquit petitioner if he did not do the acts willingly or voluntarily "but so acted only because performance of the duties of his employment required him to do so or because of other coercion or compulsion." In short, petitioner was held accountable by the jury only for performing acts of hostility toward this country which he was not required by Japan to perform. . . .

Third. Article III, § 3 of the Constitution provides, "Treason against the United States, shall consist only in levying War against them, or in adhering to their Enemies, giving them Aid and Comfort. No Person shall be convicted of Treason unless on the Testimony of two Witnesses to the same overt Act, or on Confession in open Court."

So far as material here, the crime thus consists of two elements—adhering to the enemy; and giving him aid and comfort. See *Cramer v. United States*, 325 U.S. 1, 29 (1945). One may think disloyal thoughts and have his heart on the side of the enemy. Yet if he commits no act giving aid and comfort to the enemy, he is not guilty of treason. He may on the other hand commit acts which do give aid and comfort to the enemy and yet not be guilty of treason, as for example where he acts impulsively with no intent to betray. Two witnesses are required not to the disloyal and treacherous intention but to the same overt act.

The jury found petitioner guilty of eight overt acts. . . . Each of these related to his treatment of American prisoners of war at the Oeyama camp. These prisoners were mostly from Bataan and were in weakened condition on their arrival. All were below normal weight; many of them were suffering from disease; most of them were unfit for work. They were assigned to work either in the factory or at the mine of the Oeyama Company. They were under the supervision of the Japanese army. Petitioner was a civilian interpreter, as we have said. There was evidence that he had no authority and no duties, as respects the prisoners, except as an interpreter. Yet the record shows a long, persistent, and continuous course of conduct directed against the American prisoners and going beyond any conceivable duty of an interpreter.

After the American prisoners arrived, the Japanese authorities raised the quota of ore which they were expected to produce each day. The quota had been between 120 and 165 carloads a day; now it was increased to 200. A part of petitioner's conduct was swearing at the prisoners, beating them, threatening them, and punishing them for not working faster and harder, for failing to fill their quotas, for resting, and for slowing down.

There were two overt acts in this category. Overt act (a) as alleged in the indictment and developed at the trial was that in May, 1945, petitioner kicked a prisoner named Toland who was ill, because he slowed down in lifting pieces of ore rocks from the tracks at the factory to keep the tracks clear. Toland had suffered a dizzy spell and slowed down. Petitioner told him to get to work and thereupon kicked him, causing him to fall flat and to cut his face and hand. Another prisoner wanted to pick Toland up; but petitioner would not let him. Overt act (j) as alleged in the indictment and developed at the trial was that in May, 1945, petitioner struck a prisoner named Armellino, who was weak and emaciated, in order to make him carry more lead. Armellino had been carrying only one bucket of lead. Petitioner thereupon struck him, causing him to fall. When he got up, petitioner forced him to carry two buckets, pushing him along.

Each of these acts was aimed at getting more work out of the prisoners — work that produced munitions of war for the enemy, or so the jury might have concluded. The increased efforts charged in overt acts (a) and (j) were small; the contribution to the war effort of the enemy certainly was minor, not crucial. . . . It is the nature of the act that is important. The act may be unnecessary to a successful completion of the enemy's project; it may be an abortive attempt; it may in the sum total of the enemy's effort be a casual and unimportant step. But if it gives aid and comfort to the enemy at the immediate moment of its performance, it qualifies as an overt act within the constitutional standard of treason. As Chief Justice Marshall said in *Ex parte Bollman*, 4 Cranch 75, 126, "If war be actually levied, . . . all those who perform any part, however minute, or however remote from the scene of action, and who are actually leagued in the general conspiracy, are to be considered as traitors." These two overt acts, if designed to speed up Japan's war production, plainly gave aid and comfort to the enemy in the constitutional sense.

Overt act (b) . . . was that one Grant, an American prisoner, had been seen by a Japanese sentry coming out of the Red Cross storeroom with a package of cigarettes. He was thereupon thrown into a cesspool by a Japanese sergeant, ordered out, and knocked back repeatedly. While Grant was in the cesspool, petitioner hit him over the head with a wooden pole or sword, told him to squat down, and tried to force him to sit in the water. When Grant was taken from the pool, he was blue, his teeth were chattering, and he could not straighten up.

Overt act (c) . . . was that in December, 1944, petitioner and Japanese guards lined up about 30 American prisoners and, as punishment for making articles of clothing out of blankets, struck them and forced them to strike each other. Petitioner hit prisoners who, he thought, did not hit each other hard enough.

Overt act (d) . . . was that petitioner imposed cruelty on O'Connor, an American prisoner, who was sick and had stolen Red Cross supplies. He was knocked into the cesspool by Japanese soldiers and then repeatedly hit and thrown back into the pool by them and by petitioner, with the result that O'Connor temporarily lost his reason.

Overt act (g) . . . was that in July or August, 1945, a Japanese sergeant compelled a work detail of American prisoners, who had returned early, to run around a quadrangle. Petitioner forced two of the Americans, who were unable to run fast because of illness, to run the course an additional four and six times respectively. . . .

Overt act (i) . . . was that in December, 1944, petitioner ordered one Carter, an American prisoner of war, to carry a heavy log up an ice-covered slope at the mine. When Carter slipped, fell, and was injured, petitioner although he knew Carter was badly hurt and needed attention delayed his removal back to camp for approximately five hours.

Overt act (k) . . . was that in the spring or summer of 1945 petitioner participated in the inhuman punishment of one Shaffer, an American prisoner of war. Shaffer was forced to kneel on bamboo sticks on a platform with a bamboo stick inside the joints of his knees, and to keep his arms above his head holding a bucket of water and later a log. When Shaffer became tired and bent his elbows, petitioner would strike him. When Shaffer leaned over and spilled some water, petitioner would take the bucket, throw the water on Shaffer, and have the bucket refilled. Then Shaffer was required to hold up a log. It fell on him, causing a gash. After the wound was treated, petitioner placed bamboo sticks on the ground and once more made Shaffer kneel on them and go through the same performance.

As we have said, petitioner was not required by his employment to inflict punishment on the prisoners. His duties regarding the prisoners related solely to the role of interpreter. His acts of cruelty toward the prisoners were over and beyond the call of duty of his job, or so the jury might have found. We cannot say as a matter of law that petitioner did these acts under compulsion. He seeks, however, to find protection under Japanese municipal law. It is difficult to see how that argument helps petitioner. The source of the law of treason is the Constitution. If an American citizen is a traitor by the constitutional definition, he gains no immunity because the same acts may have been unlawful under the law of the country where the acts were performed. Treason is a separate offense; treason can be committed by one who scrupulously observes the laws of other nations; and his acts may be nonetheless treasonable though the same conduct amounts to a different crime. . . .

The jury found that each of the six overt acts of cruelty actually gave aid and comfort to the enemy. We agree. . . . They were acts which showed more than sympathy with the enemy, more than a lack of zeal in the American cause, more than a breaking of allegiance to the United States. They showed conduct which actually promoted the cause of the enemy. They were acts which tended to strengthen the enemy and advance its interests. These acts in their setting would help make all the prisoners fearful, docile, and subservient. Because of these punishments the prisoners would be less likely to be troublesome; they would need fewer guards; they would require less watching. . . . All of the overt acts tended to strengthen Japan's war efforts; all of them encouraged the enemy and advanced its interests.

Petitioner contends that the overt acts were not sufficiently proved by two witnesses. Each witness who testified to an overt act was, however, an eyewitness of the commission of that act. They were present and saw or heard that to which they testified. In some instances there was a variance as to details. Thus overt act (b) was testified to by thirteen witnesses. They did not all agree as to the exact date when the overt act occurred, whether in April, May, or June, 1945. But they all agreed that it did take place, that Grant was the victim, and that it happened between 3 and 6 o'clock in the afternoon; and most of them agreed that petitioner struck Grant. The Court of Appeals concluded, and we agree, that the disagreement among the witnesses was not on what took place but on collateral details. "While two witnesses must testify to the same act, it is not required that their testimony be identical." *Haupt v. United States, supra*, p. 640. There is no doubt that as respects each of the eight overt acts the witnesses were all talking about the same incident and were describing the same conduct on petitioner's part.

Fourth. Petitioner challenges the sufficiency of the evidence to show the second element in the crime of treason—adhering to the enemy. The two-witness requirement does not extend to this element. *Cramer v. United States, supra*, p. 31. Intent to betray must be inferred from conduct. It may be inferred from the overt acts themselves (*Cramer v. United States, supra*, p. 31), from the defendant's own statements . . . and from his own professions of loyalty to Japan.

Evidence of what petitioner said during this period concerning the war effort and his professions of loyalty, if believed by the jury, leaves little doubt of his traitorous intent. "It looks like MacArthur took a run-out powder on you boys"; "The Japanese were a little superior to your American soldiers"; "You Americans don't have no chance. We will win the war." "Well, you guys needn't be interested in when the war will be over because you won't go back; you will stay here and work. I will go back to the States because I am an American citizen"; "We will kill all you prisoners right here anyway, whether you win the war or lose it. You will never get to go back to the States"; "I will be glad when all of the Americans is dead, and then I can go home and live happy." These are some of the statements petitioner made aligning himself with the Japanese cause. . . .

If the versions of petitioner's words and conduct at the Oeyama camp, testified to by the various witnesses, were believed, the traitorous intent would be shown by overwhelming evidence. . . . The issue of intent to betray, like the citizenship issue, was plainly one for the jury to decide. We would have to reject all the evidence adverse to petitioner and accept as the truth his protestations when the shadow of the hangman's noose was on him in order to save him from the finding that he did have the intent to betray. That finding of the jury was based on its conclusion that what he did was done willingly and voluntarily and not because the duty of his office or any coercion compelled him to do it. The finding that he had an uncoerced and voluntary purpose was amply supported by the evidence. Therefore the second element of the crime of treason was firmly established.

. . . The trial judge imposed the death sentence. The argument is that that sentence was so severe as to be arbitrary. It was, however, within the statutory limits. . . . The flagrant and persistent acts of petitioner gave the trial judge such a leeway in reaching a decision on the sentence that we would not be warranted in interfering. *Affirmed.*

NOTES AND QUESTIONS

1. Petitioner Kawakita claimed that he renounced or abandoned his United States citizenship and therefore did not owe allegiance to the United States. What acts did petitioner maintain demonstrated renunciation of his United States citizenship? Why did the Court reject his renunciation defense?

2. Petitioner maintained that a person who has dual nationality can be guilty of treason only to the country where Kawakita resides, not to the other country that claims him as a national. More specifically, he argued that "treason against the United States cannot be committed abroad or in enemy territory, at least by an American with a dual nationality residing in the other country which claims him as a national." Does treason contain a territorial limitation?

3. What are the legal consequences of dual nationality? Does a person who retains dual citizenship owe allegiance to both countries?

4. The jury found Petitioner guilty of eight overt acts involving mistreatment of American prisoners of war. How did Petitioner's conduct provide aid and comfort to the enemy?

5. Should it be a defense to treason that Petitioner's conduct was lawful under the law of the country where the overt acts were performed?

6. Does the two-witness rule require that the witnesses agree on the details of the overt acts? While two witnesses must testify to the same act, must their testimony be identical?

7. The Court held that Petitioner's intent to betray the United States was firmly established. Do you agree? What evidence proves Petitioner's traitorous intent?

8. The crime of treason requires proof of two elements—adhering to the enemy and giving him aid and comfort. Does the two-witness rule apply to the first element—adhering to the enemy? May intent to betray be inferred from the overt acts themselves? From other conduct?

B. Seditious Conspiracy

Seditious conspiracy is prohibited by 18 U.S.C. § 2384 and punishable by up to twenty years in prison. The statute was enacted in response to the American civil war. It proscribes two or more persons who "conspire to overthrow, put down, or to destroy by force the Government of the United States, or to levy war against them, or to oppose by force the authority thereof, or by force to prevent, hinder, or delay the execution of any law of the United States, or by force to seize, take, or possess any property of the United States contrary to the authority thereof." 18 U.S.C. § 2384. The statute closely tracks conduct proscribed by treason. However, there are several important differences regarding proof of treason and seditious conspiracy. Seditious conspiracy does not require allegiance to the United States, nor proof of the same overt act by the testimony of two witnesses. Are international terrorists who commit a terrorist attack in the United States guilty of seditious conspiracy, but not guilty of treason? Does such an attack constitute a conspiracy "to destroy by force the Government of the United States" or "oppose by force the authority thereof?" The following cases examine the elements of seditious conspiracy and the principal differences between seditious conspiracy and treason.

United States v. Rodriguez
803 F.2d 318 (7th Cir. 1986)

BAUER, Chief Judge.

Defendant Jose Rodriguez was convicted of conspiracy to oppose by force the authority of the United States government in violation of Title 18, U.S.C. § 2384. On appeal the defendant presents four principal arguments. First, he argues that the seditious conspiracy statute violates the treason clause of the Constitution. Second, he argues that he was selected for prosecution on impermissible grounds. Third, he argues that the district court erred in admitting video tape and false identification evidence. Fourth, he argues that the district court incorrectly instructed the jury on the elements of seditious conspiracy. We disagree with all four arguments and affirm the judgment of conviction.

I.

Jose Rodriguez is a member of the FALN, an armed clandestine terrorist organization seeking independence for Puerto Rico. The FALN has claimed responsibility for the use of force, terror and violence, including the construction and planting of explosive devices at banks, stores, office buildings and government buildings in the Chicago area.

With court authorization, the government planted hidden cameras and microphones at two FALN safe-houses. A five month electronic surveillance followed. On April 17, 1983, Jose Rodriguez and FALN member Alberto Rodriguez met at the safe-house apartment located at 1135 West Lunt and discussed FALN activities including the following: (1) breaking out currently incarcerated FALN members from state and federal prisons; (2) the acquisition of sets of false identification; (3) the desirability of using code names; (4) methods of avoiding law enforcement surveillance; and (5) the sharing of funds by one FALN group with others around the country.

Within a month of this meeting, Jose Rodriguez applied for a Chicago public library card in the name of Benjamin Santiago, a twenty-year-old retarded deaf mute under his care at La Casita, a home for young mentally retarded patients. He used the library card and Santiago's birthdate and social security number to obtain an Illinois driver's license.

On June 29, 1983, government agents arrested Jose Rodriguez, Edwin Cortes, Alejanderina Torres, and Alberto Rodriguez for conspiracy to bomb a Marine Training Center located at 3040 West Foster Avenue, and the Army Reserve Training Center located at 6230 North Kedzie Avenue.

At trial, the evidence showed that Jose Rodriguez was a member of the conspiracy and that his intended role was to drive his co-conspirators to the bombing sites.

Jose Rodriguez was convicted of seditious conspiracy after a five week trial. He received a suspended sentence and was placed on five years' probation. This appeal followed.

II.

Jose Rodriguez argues that Section 2384 is unconstitutional on its face and as applied to this case, because it conflicts with the treason clause in Article III, Section 3 of the Constitution. He argues that Section 2384 is merely a "constructive treason" statute that dispenses with the constitutional requirement of an overt act or the testimony of two witnesses in open court to the same overt act. We disagree and hold that Section 2384 does not conflict with the treason clause. Section 2384 protects a different governmental interest and proscribes a different crime.

Treason, a more limited offense than the offense of seditious conspiracy, *Cramer v. United States*, 325 U.S. 1, 8-22 (1944), is the most serious national crime and is punishable by death. It can only be committed by someone owing allegiance to the United States and it consists only of levying war against the United States for giving aid and comfort to its enemies. The reason for the restrictive definition is apparent from the historical backdrop of the treason clause. The framers of the Constitution were reluctant to facilitate such prosecutions because they were well aware of abuses, and they themselves were traitors in the eyes of England.

In contrast, Section 2384 has no requirement of the duty of loyalty, fidelity or allegiance to the United States. Unlike treason, seditious conspiracy does not extend beyond United States jurisdictional boundaries. It does not contemplate the presence of an enemy foreign state or an actual war. Finally, Section 2384 requires at least two persons to commit the offense.

The purpose of Section 2384 also distinguishes it from the treason clause. Congress enacted Section 2384 to help the government cope with and fend off urban terrorism. It protects a different interest than that contemplated by the framers of the Constitution in the 18th century with regard to levying war. Section 2384 provides a vehicle for the government to make arrests before a conspiracy ripens into a violent situation. The government's interest in thwarting such plans and in safeguarding public security is unquestioned. Because Section

2384 proscribes a different crime and protects a different governmental interest, we find that Section 2384 does not conflict with the treason clause.

. . .

Finally, Rodriguez argues that the district court improperly took judicial notice of the authority of the United States over Puerto Rico. He contends that it was error to instruct the jury that the United States has authority over Puerto Rico and exclude his evidence on the unlawfulness of that authority. We disagree. The court properly took judicial notice of United States authority over Puerto Rico, and this authority is not subject to dispute. The court may take judicial notice of the United States Constitution and Statutes. *Downes v. Bidwell*, 182 U.S. 244 (1901). . . .

. . .

Affirmed.

United States v. Rahman
189 F.3d 88 (2d Cir. 1999)

INTRODUCTION

These are appeals by ten defendants convicted of seditious conspiracy and other offenses arising out of a wide-ranging plot to conduct a campaign of urban terrorism. Among the activities of some or all of the defendants were rendering assistance to those who bombed the World Trade Center, *see United States v. Salameh*, 152 F.3d 88 (2d Cir. 1998) (affirming convictions of all four defendants), planning to bomb bridges and tunnels in New York City, murdering Rabbi Meir Kahane, and planning to murder the President of Egypt. We affirm the convictions of all the defendants. . . .

BACKGROUND

Defendants-Appellants Sheik Omar Abdel Rahman [and others appeal the verdict against them] following a nine-month jury trial in the United States District Court for the Southern District of New York (Michael B. Mukasey, District Judge).

The defendants were convicted of the following: seditious conspiracy (all defendants); soliciting the murder of Egyptian President Hosni Mubarak and soliciting an attack on American military installations (Abdel Rahman); conspiracy to murder Mubarak (Abdel Rahman); bombing conspiracy (all defendants found guilty except Nosair and El-Gabrowny); attempted bombing (Hampton-El, Amir, Fadil, Khallafalla, Elhassan, Saleh, and Alvarez); two counts of attempted murder and one count of murder in furtherance of a racketeering enterprise (Nosiar). . . .

I. The Government's Case

At trial, the Government sought to prove that the defendants and others joined in a seditious conspiracy to wage a war of urban terrorism against the

United States and forcibly to oppose its authority. . . . The Government alleged that members of the conspiracy (acting alone or in concert) took the following actions, among others, in furtherance of the group's objectives: the attempted murder of Hosni Mubarak; the provision of assistance to the bombing of the World Trade Center in New York City on February 26, 1993; and the Spring 1993 campaign of attempted bombings of buildings and tunnels in New York City. In addition, some members of the group were allegedly involved in the murder of Rabbi Meir Kahane by defendant Nosair.

The Government adduced evidence at trial showing the following: Abdel Rahman, a blind Islamic scholar and cleric, was the leader of the seditious conspiracy, the purpose of which was "jihad," in the sense of a struggle against the enemies of Islam. . . . Abdel Rahman's role in the conspiracy was generally limited to overall supervision and direction of the membership, as he made efforts to remain a level above the details of individual operations. However, as a cleric and the group's leader, Abdel Rahman was entitled to dispense "*fatwas*," religious opinions on the holiness of an act, to the members of the group sanctioning proposed courses of conduct and advising them whether the acts would be in furtherance of *jihad*.

According to his speeches and writings, Abdel Rahman perceived the United States as the primary oppressor of Muslims worldwide, active in assisting Israel to gain power in the Middle East. . . . Abdel Rahman also considered the secular Egyptian government of Mubarak to be an oppressor. . . . Holding these views, Abdel Rahman believed that *jihad* against Egypt and the United States is mandated by the Qur'an. Formation of a *jihad* army made up of small "divisions" and "battalions" to carry out this *jihad* was therefore necessary, according to Abdel Rahman, in order to beat back these oppressors of Islam including the United States.

. . .

DISCUSSION

I. CONSTITUTIONAL CHALLENGES

A. Seditious Conspiracy Statute and the Treason Clause

Defendant Nosair (joined by other defendants) contends that his conviction for seditious conspiracy, in violation of 18 U.S.C. § 2384, was illegal because it failed to satisfy the requirements of the Treason Clause of the U.S. Constitution, Art. III, § 3.

Article III, Section 3 provides, in relevant part:

> Treason against the United States, shall consist only in levying War against them, or in adhering to their Enemies, giving them Aid and Comfort. No Person shall be convicted of Treason unless on the Testimony of two Witnesses to the same overt Act, or on Confession in open Court.

The seditious conspiracy statute provides:

> If two or more persons in any State or Territory, or in any place subject to the jurisdiction of the United States, conspire to overthrow, put down or to destroy

by force the Government of the United States, or to levy war against them, or to oppose by force the authority thereof, or by force to prevent, hinder or delay the execution of any law of the United States, or by force to seize, take, or possess any property of the United States contrary to the authority thereof, they shall each be fined under this title or imprisoned not more than twenty years, or both.

18 U.S.C. § 2384.

Nosair contends that because the seditious conspiracy statute punishes conspiracy to "levy war" against the United States without a conforming two-witness requirement, the statute is unconstitutional. He further claims that because his conviction for conspiracy to levy war against the United States was not based on the testimony of two witnesses to the same overt act, the conviction violates constitutional standards.

It is undisputed that Nosair's conviction was not supported by two witnesses to the same overt act. Accordingly the conviction must be overturned if the requirement of the Treason Clause applies to this prosecution for seditious conspiracy.

The plain answer is that the Treason Clause does not apply to the prosecution. The provisions of Article III, Section 3 apply to prosecutions for "treason." Nosair and his co-appellants were not charged with treason. Their offense of conviction, seditious conspiracy under Section 2384, differs from treason not only in name and associated stigma, but also in its essential elements and punishment. . . .

At the time of the drafting of the Constitution [ ], treason was punishable not only by death, but by an exceptionally cruel method of execution designed to enhance the suffering of the traitor. *See* 4 William Blackstone, *Commentaries* (observing that the punishment for treason is "terrible" in that the traitor is "hanged by the neck, then cut down alive," that "his entrails [are then] taken out, and burned, while he is yet alive," "that his head [is] cut off," and that his "body [is then] divided into four parts"). In contrast, lesser subversive offenses were penalized by noncapital punishments or less brutal modes of execution. *See id.* at *94-*126. The Framers may have intended to limit the applicability of the most severe penalties—or simply the applicability of capital punishment for alleged subversion—to instances of levying war against, or adhering to enemies of, the United States. . . . Today treason continues to be punishable by death, while seditious conspiracy commands a maximum penalty of twenty years imprisonment.

In recognition of the potential for political manipulation of the treason charge, the Framers may have formulated the Treason Clause as a protection against promiscuous resort to this particularly stigmatizing label, which carries such harsh consequences. It is thus possible to interpret the Treason Clause as applying only to charges denominated as "treason."

The Supreme Court has identified but not resolved the question whether the clause applies to offenses that include all the elements of treason but are not branded as such. *Compare Ex Parte Quirin*, 317 U.S. 1, 38 (1942) (suggesting, in *dictum*, that citizens could be tried for an offense against the law of war that included all the elements of treason), *with Cramer v. United States*, 325 U.S. 1, 45 (1945) (noting in *dictum* that it did not "intimate that Congress could dispense with [the] two-witness rule merely by giving the same offense [of treason] another name.") The question whether a defendant who engaged in subversive conduct might be tried for a crime involving all the elements of treason, but under a different name and without the constitutional protection of the Treason Clause, therefore remains open. And we need not decide it in this case, because the crime of which Nosair was convicted differs significantly from treason, not only in name and punishment, but also in definition.

Seditious conspiracy by levying war includes no requirement that the defendant owe allegiance to the United States, an element necessary to conviction of treason. Nosair nevertheless maintains that "[t]he only distinction between the elements of seditious conspiracy under the levy war prong and treason by levying war is that the former requires proof of a conspiracy while the latter requires proof of the substantive crime." *Reply Brief for Nosair* at 9. Noting that the requirement of allegiance appears explicitly in the treason statute, but not in the Treason Clause, Nosair suggests that allegiance to the United States is not an element of treason within the contemplation of the Constitution. He concludes that, for constitutional purposes, the elements constituting seditious conspiracy by levying war and treason by levying war are identical, and consequently that prosecutions for seditious conspiracy by levying war must conform to the requirements of the Treason Clause.

The argument rests on a false premise. The Treason Clause does not, as Nosair supposes, purport to specify the elements of the crime of treason. Instead, in addition to providing evidentiary safeguards, the Clause restricts the conduct that may be deemed treason to "levying war" against the United States and "adhering to their Enemies, giving them Aid and Comfort." It does not undertake to define the constituent elements of the substantive crime.

Moreover, any acceptable recitation of the elements of treason must include the breach of allegiance. The concept of allegiance betrayed is integral to the term "treason," and has been since well before the drafting of the Constitution. *See* 3 Holdsworth, *History of English Law* 287 (noting that "the idea of treachery" has been part of the treason offense since the reign of Edward III). In both "its common-law and constitutional definitions the term 'treason' imports a breach of allegiance." *Green's Case*, 8 Ct. Cl. 412, 1872 WL 5731 (1872). Treason "imports a betraying." *Id.* (quoting 3 *Tomlin's Law Dictionary* 637). Blackstone, too, noted that treason, "in it's [*sic*] very name . . . imports a betraying, treachery or breach of faith." 4 Blackstone, *supra*, at *75. Early on, our Supreme Court recognized that "[t]reason is a breach of allegiance, and can be committed by him only who owes allegiance." *United States v. Wiltberger*, 18 U.S. (5 Wheat.) 76, 97, 5 L. Ed. 37 (1820) (Marshall, C.J.). Nor is there any doubt that the delegates to the Constitutional Convention "used [the term 'treason'] to express the central concept of betrayal of allegiance." Hurst, *supra*, at 415.

Nosair's suggestion that the statutory definition of treason added the requirement of allegiance is mistaken. The reference to treason in the constitutional clause necessarily incorporates the elements of allegiance and betrayal that are essential to the concept of treason. The functions of the Clause are to limit the crime of treason to betrayals of allegiance that are substantial, amounting to levying war or giving comfort to enemies, and to require sufficiently reliable evidence. Treason, in other words, may not be found on the basis of mere mutterings of discontent, or relatively innocuous opposition. The fact that the Treason Clause imposes its requirements without mentioning the requirement of allegiance is not a basis for concluding that treason may be prosecuted without allegiance being proved. That any conviction for treason under the laws of the United States requires a betrayal of allegiance is simply implicit in the term "treason." Nosair was thus tried for a different, and lesser, offense than treason. We therefore see no reasonable basis to maintain that the requirements of the Treason Clause should apply to Nosair's prosecution.

B. Seditious Conspiracy Statute and the First Amendment

Abdel Rahman, joined by the other appellants, contends that the seditious conspiracy statute, 18 U.S.C. § 2384, is an unconstitutional burden on free speech and the free exercise of religion in violation of the First Amendment. First, Abdel Rahman argues that the statute is facially invalid because it criminalizes protected expression and that it is overbroad and unconstitutionally vague. Second, Abdel Rahman contends that his conviction violated the First Amendment because it rested solely on his political views and religious practices.

1. Facial Challenge

a. Restraint on Speech

. . .

As Section 2384 proscribes "speech" only when it constitutes an agreement to use force against the United States, Abdel Rahman's generalized First Amendment challenge to the statute is without merit. Our court has previously considered and rejected a First Amendment challenge to Section 2384. *See United States v. Lebron*, 222 F.2d 531, 536 (2d Cir. 1955). Although *Lebron*'s analysis of the First Amendment issues posed by Section 2384 was brief, the panel found the question was squarely controlled by the Supreme Court's then-recent decision in *Dennis v. United States*, 341 U.S. 494 (1951). In *Dennis*, the Court upheld the constitutionality of the Smith Act, which made it a crime to advocate, or to conspire to advocate, the overthrow of the United States government by force or violence. *See* 18 U.S.C. § 2385; *Dennis*, 341 U.S. at 494. The *Dennis* Court concluded that, while the "element of speech" inherent in Smith Act convictions required that the Act be given close First Amendment scrutiny, the Act did not impermissibly burden the expression of protected speech, as it was properly "directed at advocacy [of overthrow of the government by force], not discussion." *See id.* at 502.

After *Dennis*, the Court broadened the scope of First Amendment restrictions on laws that criminalize subversive advocacy. It remains fundamental that while the state may not criminalize the expression of views—even including the view that violent overthrow of the government is desirable—it may nonetheless outlaw encouragement, inducement, or conspiracy to take violent action. Thus, in *Yates v. United States*, 354 U.S. 298, 318 (1957), *overruled in part on other grounds, Burks v. United States*, 437 U.S. 1, 7 (1978), the Court interpreted the Smith Act to prohibit only the advocacy of concrete violent action, but not "advocacy and teaching of forcible overthrow as an abstract principle, divorced from any effort to instigate action to that end." And in *Brandenburg v. Ohio*, 395 U.S. 444, 447 (1969) (per curiam), the Court held that a state may proscribe subversive advocacy only when such advocacy is directed towards, and is likely to result in, "imminent lawless action."

The prohibitions of the seditious conspiracy statute are much further removed from the realm of constitutionally protected speech than those at issue in *Dennis* and its progeny. To be convicted under Section 2384, one must conspire to *use* force, not just to *advocate* the use of force. We have no doubt that this passes the test of constitutionality.

Our view of Section 2384's constitutionality also finds support in a number of the Supreme Court's more recent First Amendment decisions. These cases make clear that a line exists between expressions of belief, which are protected by the First Amendment, and threatened or actual uses of force, which are not. *See Wisconsin v. Mitchell*, 508 U.S. 476, 484 (1993) ("A physical assault is not . . . expressive conduct protected by the First Amendment"); *R.A.V. v. City of St. Paul*, 505 U.S. 377, 388 (1992) ("[T]hreats of violence are outside the First Amendment"); *NAACP v. Claiborne Hardware Co.*, 458 U.S. 886, 916 (1982) ("The First Amendment does not protect violence"); *Watts v. United States*, 394 U.S. 705, 707 (1969) (Congress may outlaw threats against President, provided that "[w]hat is a threat [is] distinguished from what is constitutionally protected speech."). . . .

b. Vagueness and Overbreadth

Abdel Rahman also contends that Section 2384 is overbroad and void for vagueness.

(i) *Overbreadth.* A law is overbroad, and hence void, if it "does not aim specifically at evils within the allowable area of State control, but, on the contrary, sweeps within its ambit other activities that . . . constitute an exercise of freedom of speech or of the press." *Thornhill v. Alabama*, 310 U.S. 88, 97 (1940). Particularly when conduct and not speech is involved, to void the statute the overbreadth must be "real [and] substantial . . . judged in relation to the statute's plainly legitimate sweep." *Broadrick v. Oklahoma*, 413 U.S. 601, 613 (1973); *see also City Council of Los Angeles v. Taxpayers for Vincent*, 466 U.S. 789, 799-800 & 800 n.19 (1984). . . .

Abdel Rahman argues that Section 2384 is overbroad because Congress could have achieved its public safety aims "without chilling First Amendment rights" by punishing only "substantive acts involving bombs, weapons, or other violent acts." Abdel Rahman Br. at 67. One of the beneficial purposes of the conspiracy law is to permit arrest and prosecution before the substantive crime has been accomplished. The Government, possessed of evidence of conspiratorial planning, need not wait until buildings and tunnels have been bombed and people killed before arresting the conspirators. Accordingly, it is well established that the Government may criminalize certain preparatory steps towards criminal action, even when the crime consists of the use of conspiratorial or exhortatory words. Because Section 2384 prohibits only conspiratorial agreement, we are satisfied that the statute is not constitutionally overbroad.

(ii) *Vagueness.* Abdel Rahman also challenges the statute for vagueness. A criminal statute, particularly one regulating speech, must "define the criminal offense with sufficient definiteness that ordinary people can understand what conduct is prohibited and in a manner that does not encourage arbitrary and discriminatory enforcement." *Kolender v. Lawson*, 461 U.S. 352, 357 (1983). . . . Abdel Rahman argues that Section 2384 does not provide "fair warning" about what acts are unlawful, leaving constitutionally protected speech vulnerable to criminal prosecution.

There is indeed authority suggesting that the word "seditious" does not sufficiently convey what conduct it forbids to serve as an essential element of a crime. *See Keyishian v. Board of Regents*, 385 U.S. 589, 598 (1967) (noting that "dangers fatal to First Amendment freedoms inhere in the word 'seditious,'" and invalidating law that provided, *inter alia*, that state employees who utter "seditious words" may be discharged). But the word "seditious" does not appear in the prohibitory text of the statute; it appears only in the caption. The terms of the statute are far more precise. The portions charged against Abdel Rahman and his co-defendants—conspiracy to levy war against the United States and to oppose by force the authority thereof—do not involve terms of such vague meaning. Furthermore, they unquestionably specify that agreement *to use force* is an essential element of the crime. Abdel Rahman therefore cannot prevail on the claim that the portions of Section 2384 charged against him criminalize mere expressions of opinion, or are unduly vague.

2. Application of Section 2384 to Abdel Rahman's Case

Abdel Rahman also argues that he was convicted not for entering into any conspiratorial agreement that Congress may properly forbid, but "solely for his religious words and deeds" which, he contends, are protected by the First Amendment. In support of this claim, Abdel Rahman cites the Government's use in evidence of his speeches and writings.

There are two answers to Abdel Rahman's contention. The first is that freedom of speech and of religion do not extend so far as to bar prosecution of one who uses a public speech or a religious ministry to commit crimes. Numerous crimes under the federal criminal code are, or can be, committed by speech alone. As examples: Section 2 makes it an offense to "counsel[]," "command[]," "induce[]" or "procure[]" the commission of an offense against the United

States. 18 U.S.C. § 2(a). Section 371 makes it a crime to "conspire . . . to commit any offense against the United States." 18 U.S.C. § 371. Section 373, with which Abdel Rahman was charged, makes it a crime to "solicit[], command[], induce[], or otherwise endeavor[] to persuade" another person to commit a crime of violence. 18 U.S.C. §373(a). . . . All of these offenses are characteristically committed through speech. Notwithstanding that political speech and religious exercise are among the activities most jealously guarded by the First Amendment, one is not immunized from prosecution for such speech-based offenses merely because one commits them through the medium of political speech or religious preaching. Of course, courts must be vigilant to insure that prosecutions are not improperly based on the mere expression of unpopular ideas. But if the evidence shows that the speeches crossed the line into criminal solicitation, procurement of criminal activity, or conspiracy to violate the laws, the prosecution is permissible.

The evidence justifying Abdel Rahman's conviction for conspiracy and solicitation showed beyond a reasonable doubt that he crossed this line. His speeches were not simply the expression of ideas; in some instances they constituted the crime of conspiracy to wage war on the United States under Section 2384 and solicitation of attack on the United States military installations, as well as of the murder of Egyptian President Hosni Mubarak under Section 373.

For example:

Abdel Rahman told Salem he "should make up with God . . . by turning his rifle's barrel to President Mubarak's chest, and kill[ing] him." Tr. 4633.

On another occasion, speaking to Abdo Mohammed Haggag about murdering President Mubarak during his visit to the United States, Abdel Rahman told Haggag, "Depend on God. Carry out this operation. It does not require a fatwa. . . . You are ready in training, but do it. Go ahead." Tr. 10108.

The evidence further showed that Siddig Ali consulted with Abdel Rahman about the bombing of the United Nations Headquarters, and Abdel Rahman told him, "Yes, it's a must, it's a duty." Tr. 5527-29.

On another occasion, when Abdel Rahman was asked by Salem about bombing the United Nations, he counseled against it on the ground that it would be "bad for Muslims," Tr. 6029, but added that Salem should "find a plan to destroy or to bomb or to . . . inflict damage to the American Army." Tr. 6029-30.

Words of this nature—ones that instruct, solicit, or persuade others to commit crimes of violence—violate the law and may be properly prosecuted regardless of whether they are uttered in private, or in a public speech, or in administering the duties of a religious ministry. The fact that his speech or conduct was "religious" does not immunize him from prosecution under generally-applicable criminal statutes.

. . .

We reject Abdel Rahman's claim that his conviction violated his rights under the First Amendment.

D. Sufficiency of the Evidence

. . .

2. *Abdel Rahman*

Abdel Rahman argues that the evidence presented by the Government was insufficient to support a conviction for any of the counts with which he was charged. Abdel Rahman asserts that he had limited contact with most of the other defendants, that he was physically incapable, due to his blindness, of participating in the "operational" aspects of the conspiracies, and that there was little direct evidence of his knowledge of many of the events in question. We find Abdel Rahman's claims unavailing.

a. Seditious Conspiracy and Bombing Conspiracy

To support a conviction for seditious conspiracy under 18 U.S.C. § 2384, the Government must demonstrate that: (1) in a State, or Territory, or place subject to the jurisdiction of the United States, (2) two or more persons conspired to "levy war against" or "oppose by force the authority of" the United States government, and (3) that the defendant was a member of the conspiracy. 18 U.S.C. § 2384.

First, we find ample evidence in the record to support the jury's finding that there was indeed a conspiracy to "levy war" against the United States. Over the course of the trial, the jury was presented with considerable evidence of a conspiracy. The evidence included the fact that many of the defendants in this case, as well as many the World Trade Center defendants, participated in military training exercises the purpose of which was to train members to carry out *jihad* "operations." Tr. 6496-97. Appellant Nosair murdered Kahane in 1990, assisted by Salameh (who had been present at the training sessions). Among Nosair's possessions, the Government found notebooks describing "war" on the enemies of Islam and the manner of prosecuting such, including "exploding . . . their high world buildings," as well as manuals on guerilla warfare tactics and explosives. Tr. 3963.

Salameh, Yousef, and Abouhalima, the bombers of the World Trade Center, had considerable phone contact and/or direct contact with El-Gabrowny, Nosair, and Abdel Rahman in the weeks leading up to the bombing. Siddig Ali assisted Abouhalima's flight from the United States following the bombing. Abdel Rahman also encouraged Salem to murder Mubarak and issued a *fatwa* calling for the murder. In accordance with this call to duty, Siddig Ali plotted to assassinate Mubarak in March of 1993. The Abdelganis, Saleh, Elhassan, Hampton-El, and Alvarez engaged in a plot to bomb the Lincoln and Holland Tunnels and the United Nations. They purchased fuel, fertilizers, and timers and actively sought detonators. They had begun construction of the explosives when they were arrested. Each of these acts was connected by myriad contacts between the defendants. These illustrative acts, coupled with other evidence presented at trial, convince us that there is ample evidence to support the jury's conclusion that there was a conspiracy to "levy war" on the United States, and that the conspiracy contemplated the use of force.

As to Abdel Rahman's individual claim, there is also sufficient evidence to support the conclusion that he was in fact a member of the conspiracy. While there is no evidence that Abdel Rahman personally participated in the performance of the conspiracy, when conspiracy is charged, the Government is not required to show that the defendant personally performed acts in its furtherance: it is sufficient for the defendant to join in the illegal agreement. The evidence showed that Abdel Rahman was in constant contact with other members of the conspiracy, that he was looked to as a leader, and that he accepted that role and encouraged his co-conspirators to engage in violent acts against the United States.

Abdel Rahman discussed the results of the paramilitary training with Abouhalima and Nosair, and encouraged his followers to conduct *jihad*, including acts of violence, against the United States. During a visit to Nosair at Attica, Nosair instructed Shinawy to seek a *fatwa* from Abdel Rahman regarding a plan to bomb various targets. Siddig Ali reported to Abdel Rahman concerning the resumed paramilitary training. Abdel Rahman encouraged Salem to conduct *jihad* by killing Mubarak and issued a *fatwa* for Mubarek's death. Abdel Rahman made numerous calls overseas, including calls to a number in Pakistan that was inscribed in a bombing manual carried by convicted World Trade Center bomber Yousef. Abdel Rahman also had frequent contact with other members of the conspiracy including El-Gabrowny, Abouhalima, and Salameh in the weeks leading up to the World Trade Center bombing.

Siddig Ali told Salem that Abdel Rahman had referred to the spring 1993 bombing campaign as a "must" and a "duty." Siddig Ali also told Salem that he was free to discuss the plot with Abdel Rahman, but to do so in general terms so as to keep Abdel Rahman insulated. Although Abdel Rahman did advise against making the United Nations a bombing target because that would be bad for Muslims, he advised Salem to seek a different target (U.S. military installations) for the bombings, and to plan for them carefully. In that same conversation, he also warned Salem to be careful around Siddig Ali, who he suspected was a traitor. Abdel Rahman then sought out the traitor in his group, having a long discussion with Salem and Siddig Ali over who was the traitor. This evidence shows that a reasonable trier of fact could have found that Abdel Rahman was a member of the conspiracy and that he was in fact its leader. . . .

[The court found sufficient evidence to support the other criminal charges against Abdel Rahman and criminal counts against the other members of the conspiracy.] AFFIRMED.

NOTES AND QUESTIONS

1. What are the elements required to convict for seditious conspiracy? What are the principal differences between seditious conspiracy and treason? Is it easier for the government to prove seditious conspiracy or treason? What is the essential element that distinguishes treason from seditious conspiracy? Is seditious conspiracy a lesser included offense of treason? Does the Double Jeopardy

Clause prohibit prosecution and punishment for both treason and seditious conspiracy?

2. Why did the court reject Abdel Rahman's claim that the seditious conspiracy statute imposes an unconstitutional burden on free speech and the free exercise of religion? Does the statute punish expressions of belief?

3. Abdel Rahman argued that 18 U.S.C. § 2384 is overbroad and void for vagueness. Why did the court reject these constitutional claims? Does the seditious conspiracy statute "define the criminal offense with sufficient definiteness that ordinary people can understand what conduct is prohibited and in a manner that does not encourage arbitrary and discriminatory enforcement"? *Kolender v. Lawson*, 461 U.S. 352, 357 (1983).

4. The court stated that "[t]he question whether a defendant who engaged in subversive conduct might be tried for a crime involving all the elements of treason, but under a different name and without the constitutional protection of the Treason Clause" remains an open question. If Congress enacted such a statute, would it be unconstitutional? How should this issue be resolved?

5. Did the bombing of the Alfred P. Murrah Federal Building in Oklahoma City on April 19, 1995, by Timothy McVeigh and Terry Nichols constitute a violation of the seditious conspiracy statute? Was the bombing an act of urban terrorism proscribed by the statute?

C. Espionage

Criminal prosecution under the Espionage Act, 18 U.S.C. §§ 793-798, is discussed in Chapter 13, Protecting Sensitive Information.

D. Economic Sanctions

Criminal prosecution for a willful violation of the International Emergency Economic Powers Act, 50 U.S.C. § 1705(c), is discussed in Chapter 15, Economic Powers and National Security.

E. Terrorism

Providing Material Support or Resources to Foreign Terrorists

International terrorism poses a serious threat to United States national security. To combat the threat of terrorism, Congress enacted the material support statutes, 18 U.S.C. §§ 2339A and 2339B.[4] The material support statutes are preventive measures that "criminalize not the terrorist attacks themselves, but aid that makes the attacks more likely to occur." *Holder v. Humanitarian Law Project*, 561 U.S. 1, 35 (2010). More specifically, §§ 2339A and 2339B punish the provision of "material

---

4. The general discussion of the material support statutes is taken in large part from JIMMY GURULÉ & GEOFFREY S. CORN, PRINCIPLES OF COUNTER-TERRORISM LAW 257-58 (2011).

support or resources," including money, weapons, explosives, housing, transportation, training, personnel, expert advice and assistance, and services to foreign terrorists or foreign terrorist organizations. Congress recognized that "[c]utting off 'material support or resources' from terrorist organizations deprives them of the means with which to carry out acts of terrorism and potentially leads to their demise." *Humanitarian Law Project v. Mukasey*, 52 F.3d 916, 931 (9th Cir. 2009), *overturned on other grounds, Holder v. Humanitarian Law Project*, 561 U.S. 1 (2010).

Section 2339A makes it a crime to provide "material support or resources" "knowing or intending" that they are to be used to commit violent crimes enumerated in the statute. Section 2339B, on the other hand, punishes whoever knowingly provides "material support or resources" to a "foreign terrorist organization" (FTO). To violate this provision, a person must have knowledge that the organization is a designated terrorist organization, or that the organization has engaged or engages in terrorist activity. 18 U.S.C. § 2339B(a)(1). Section 2339B is aimed at depriving foreign terrorist groups of funding and other resources. The prohibition is based on a finding by Congress that terrorist organizations "are so tainted by their criminal conduct that any contribution to such an organization facilitates that conduct."[5]

Prosecutions under 18 U.S.C. §§ 2339A and 2339B have been challenged on constitutional grounds. Defendants maintain that the definition of "material support or resources" to an FTO is unconstitutionally vague and violates freedom of speech and association under the First Amendment. Defendants also claim that in the absence of proof that the defendant acted with the specific intent to further the terrorist organization's criminal activities, § 2339B violates the Due Process Clause. Finally, defendants argue that the inability to collaterally attack the validity of an organization's designation as an FTO in § 2339B criminal proceeding deprives them of the right of due process. The following cases examine the principal constitutional challenges to the material support statutes.

FEDERAL TERRORISM-RELATED STATUTES

Other federal statutes punishing terrorist-related activity include:

- aircraft sabotage (18 U.S.C. § 32)
- crimes against internationally protected persons (18 U.S.C. §§ 112, 878, 116, 1201(a)(4))
- hostage-taking (18 U.S.C. § 1203)
- terrorist acts abroad against U.S. nationals (18 U.S.C. § 2332)
- acts of terrorism transcending national boundaries (18 U.S.C. § 2332b)
- conspiracy within the United States to murder, kidnap, or maim persons or to damage property overseas (18 U.S.C. § 956)

---

5. Antiterrorism and Effective Death Penalty Act of 1996, Pub. L. No. 104-132, § 301(a)(7), 110 Stat. 1247 note following 18 U.S.C. § 2339B (Findings and Purpose).

- financing terrorism (18 U.S.C. § 2339C)
- receiving military-style training from a foreign terrorist organization (18 U.S.C. § 2339D)
- use of biological, nuclear, chemical or other weapons of mass destruction (18 U.S.C. §§ 175, 831, 2332a)
- harboring or concealing terrorists (18 U.S.C. § 2339)
- terrorist bombing (18 U.S.C. § 2332f)

a. The Designation of Foreign Terrorist Organizations

United States v. Afshari
412 F.3d 1071 (9th Cir. 2005)

KLEINFELD, Circuit Judge.

FACTS

The issue here is the constitutionality of the crime charged in the indictment, that from 1997 to 2001, Rahmani and others knowingly and willfully conspired to provide material support to the Mujahedin-e Khalq ("MEK"), a designated terrorist organization, in violation of 18 U.S.C. § 2339B(a)(1).

According to the indictment, the defendants solicited charitable contributions at the Los Angeles International Airport for the "Committee for Human Rights," gave money and credit cards to the MEK, and wired money from the "Committee for Human Rights" to an MEK bank account in Turkey. They did all this after participating in a conference call with an MEK leader, in which they learned that the State Department had designated the MEK as a foreign terrorist organization. The MEK leader told them to continue to provide material support despite the designation. According to the indictment in this case, the money they sent to the MEK amounted to at least several hundred thousand dollars.

The MEK was founded in the 1960's as an Iranian Marxist group seeking to overthrow the regime then ruling Iran. It participated in various terrorist activities against the Iranian regime and against the United States, including the taking of American embassy personnel as hostages in 1979. After the Iranian regime fell and was replaced by a clerical, rather than a Marxist, regime, MEK members fled to France. They later settled in Iraq, along the Iranian border. There they carried out terrorist activities with the support of Saddam Hussein's regime, as well as, if the indictment is correct, the money that the defendants sent them. . . .

The district court dismissed the indictment on the ground that the terrorist designation statute was unconstitutional. We review de novo, and reverse.

ANALYSIS

I. CHALLENGING THE DESIGNATION

8 U.S.C. § 1189(a)(1) sets out a carefully articulated scheme for designating foreign terrorist organizations. To make the designation, the Secretary has to make specific findings that "the organization is a foreign organization"; that "the organization engages in terrorist activity (as defined in 8 U.S.C. § 1182(a)(3)(B))"; and that "the terrorist activity of the organization threatens the security of United States nationals or the national security of the United States."

The Secretary of State's designation is only the beginning. The Secretary also must furnish the congressional leadership advance notification of the designation and the factual basis for it, which Congress can reject. The designation is published in the Federal Register. The designated organization is entitled to judicial review of the Secretary's action in the United States Court of Appeals for the District of Columbia. That court may set aside the designation for the ordinary administrative law reasons, such as that the designation is "arbitrary, capricious, an abuse of discretion, or otherwise not in accordance with law." That court may also set aside a designation for several other reasons, including that the designation is "contrary to constitutional right, power, privilege, or immunity." Congress or the Secretary can revoke a designation. Among the concrete incentives that a designated organization has to contest the designation is that the Secretary of the Treasury may require American financial institutions to block all financial transactions involving its assets.

. . .

II. DUE PROCESS CLAIM

The statute assigns criminal penalties to one who "knowingly provides material support or resources to a foreign terrorist organization, or attempts or conspires to do so." The statutory phrase "terrorist organization" is a term of art, defined by Congress as "an organization designated as a terrorist organization" under 8 U.S.C. § 1189(a)(1). The defendants' central argument is that § 2339B denies them their constitutional rights because it prohibits them from collaterally attacking the designation of a foreign terrorist organization. . . .

The specific section that is at issue here is 8 U.S.C. § 1189(a)(8), which states in relevant part:

> If a designation . . . has become effective . . . a defendant in a criminal action or an alien in a removal proceeding shall not be permitted to raise any question concerning the validity of the issuance of such designation or redesignation as a defense or an objection at any trial or hearing.

The defendants are right that § 1189(a)(8) prevents them from contending, in defense of the charges against them under 18 U.S.C. § 2339B, that the designated terrorist organization is not really terrorist at all. No doubt Congress was well aware that some might claim that "one man's terrorist is another man's freedom fighter." Congress clearly chose to delegate policymaking authority to the President and Department of State with respect to designation of terrorist organizations, and to keep such policymaking authority out of the hands of United States Attorneys and juries. Under § 2339B, if defendants provide material support for an organization that has been designated a terrorist organization under § 1189, they commit the crime, and it does not matter whether the designation is correct or not.

The question then, is whether due process prohibits a prosecution under § 2339B when the predicate designation was obtained in an unconstitutional manner or is otherwise erroneous. In *Lewis v. United States*, 445 U.S. 55, 100 (1980), the Supreme Court held that a prior conviction could properly be used as a predicate for a subsequent conviction for a felon in possession of a firearm, even though it had been obtained in violation of the Sixth Amendment right to counsel. The Court held that it was proper to prohibit a collateral attack on the predicate during the criminal hearing because the felon-in-possession statute made no exception "for a person whose outstanding felony conviction ultimately might turn out to be invalid for any reason." *Id*. at 62. The Court noted that the prohibition on collateral attack was proper because a convicted felon could challenge the validity of the conviction before he purchased his firearm.

The defendants attempt to distinguish *Lewis* from this § 2339B prosecution because the defendant in *Lewis* had the ability to challenge his predicate, whereas here the defendants themselves are prohibited from challenging the designation. But this does not change the principle that a criminal proceeding may go forward, even if the predicate was in some way unconstitutional, so long as a sufficient opportunity for judicial review of the predicate exists. Here there was such an opportunity, which the MEK took advantage of each time it was designated a foreign terrorist organization.

The defendants also attempt to distinguish *Lewis* by relying on *United States v. Mendoza-Lopez*, 481 U.S. 828 (1987). In that case, the Supreme Court held that a prosecution under 8 U.S.C. § 1326 for illegal reentry does not comport with due process if there is no judicial review of whether the predicate deportation proceeding violated the alien's rights. It is not at all clear from *Mendoza-Lopez* that the Supreme Court meant that the due process problem is in the *later* proceeding. The Court held that "where a determination made in an administrative proceeding is to play a critical role in the subsequent imposition of a criminal sanction, there must be *some* meaningful review of the administrative proceeding." *Id*. at 837-38 (emphasis in original). Nothing in *Mendoza-Lopez* appears to require that this review be had by the defendant in the subsequent criminal proceeding.

Furthermore, it is obvious in *Lewis* and *Mendoza-Lopez* that the opportunity to seek review would be in the hands of the defendants themselves because it was *their* rights at issue in the hearing that created the predicate in the later criminal proceeding. But here, the defendants' rights were not directly violated in the earlier designation proceeding. The predicate designation was against the MEK, not the defendants. Section 1189 provides for the organizations to seek review of the predicate designation, and that review was had in this case.

Therefore, due process does not require another review of the predicate by the court adjudicating the instant § 2339B criminal proceeding. . . . Congress has explicitly provided that the D.C. Circuit is the arbiter of the constitutionality of any designation under § 1189. Thus, there is no constitutional need for the defendants to challenge the predicate designation in this proceeding.

As we noted in another case where we rejected a defendant's right to challenge an export listing in a subsequent criminal proceeding, the defendants' argument here "is analogous to one by a defendant in a drug possession case that his conviction cannot stand because no specific showing has been made that the drug is a threat to society. . . . [A] showing that the drug possessed by the individual defendant has a 'detrimental effect on the general welfare' [is not] an element of the offense." Likewise, the element of the crime that the prosecutor must prove in a § 2339B case is the predicate fact that a particular organization *was* designated at the time the material support was given, not whether the government made a correct designation. . . .

. . .

REVERSED.

NOTES AND QUESTIONS

1. The U.S. Court of Appeals for the District of Columbia has exclusive jurisdiction to review FTO designations. *See* 8 U.S.C. § 1189(c)(3). The appellate court may review the Secretary of State's findings that the entity is a "foreign" organization and that it engages in "terrorist activity." *See People's Mojahedin Org. of Iran v. Department of State*, 327 F.3d 1238, 1240-41 (D.C. Cir. 2003). However, whether the organization "threatens the security of United States nationals or the national security of the United States" is a nonjusticiable question. *Id.* In *People's Mojahedin Org. of Iran v. Department of State*, the D.C. Circuit stated that "[s]uch questions concerning the foreign policy decisions of the Executive Branch present political judgments, decisions of a kind for which the Judiciary has neither aptitude, facilities nor responsibilities and have long been held to belong in the domain of political power not subject to judicial intrusion or inquiry." *Id.*

2. The D.C. Circuit may set aside an FTO designation if it finds it to be "(1) arbitrary, capricious, an abuse of discretion, or otherwise not in accordance with the law; (2) contrary to constitutional right, power, privilege, or immunity; (3) in excess of statutory jurisdiction, authority, or limitation, or short of statutory right; (4) lacking substantial support in the administrative record taken as a whole or in classified information submitted to the court; or (5) not in accord with the procedures required by law." *United States v. Taleb-Jedi*, 566 F. Supp. 2d 157, 163 (E.D.N.Y. 2008) (citing 8 U.S.C. § 1189(c)(3)(A)-(E)).

3. The courts unequivocally hold that the relevant element of 18 U.S.C. § 2339B is the *fact* of an organization's designation as an FTO, not the *validity* of the designation. *See, e.g., United States v. Chandia*, 514 F.3d 365, 371 (4th Cir. 2008); *United States v. Afshari*, 412 F.3d 1071, 1076 (9th Cir. 2005); *United States*

v. Hammoud, 381 F.3d 316, 331 (4th Cir. 2004); *United States v. Warsame*, 537 F. Supp. 2d 1005, 1021 (D. Minn. 2008).

FOREIGN TERRORIST ORGANIZATIONS

"Foreign Terrorist Organizations (FTOs) are foreign organizations that are designated by the Secretary of State in accordance with § 219 of the Immigration and Nationality Act (INA), as amended. FTO designations play a critical role in our fight against terrorism and are an effective means of curtailing support for terrorist activities and pressuring groups to get out of the terrorism business."

Foreign Terrorist Organizations, Bureau of Counterterrorism, U.S. Dep't of State, *available at* www.state.gov/j/ct/rls/other/des/123085.htm.

The Secretary of State has designated sixty-nine foreign entities as FTOs, including al Qaeda; al Qaeda in the Arabian Peninsula; al Qaeda in the Islamic Maghreb, Islamic State of Iraq and the Levant (ISIL) (formerly known as al Qaeda in Iraq); al Shabaab; Ansar al-Islam; Ansar al-Sharia in Benghazi; al-Nusrah Front; Boko Haram; HAMAS; Hizballah; Palestinian Liberation Front; Palestinian Islamic Jihad; Revolutionary Armed Forces of Colombia (FARC), and the Islamic Revolutionary Guard Corps (IRGC), among others.

Id.

---

b. Legal Challenges

Holder v. Humanitarian Law Project
561 U.S. 1 (2010)

Chief Justice ROBERTS delivered the opinion of the Court.

I

This litigation concerns 18 U.S.C. § 2339B, which makes it a federal crime to "knowingly provid[e] material support or resources to a foreign terrorist organization." Congress has amended the definition of "material support or resources" periodically, but at present it is defined as follows:

> "[T]he term 'material support or resources' means any property, tangible or intangible, or service, including currency or monetary instruments or financial securities, financial services, lodging, training, expert advice or assistance, safehouses, false documentation or identification, communications equipment, facilities, weapons, lethal substances, explosives, personnel (1 or more individuals who may be or include oneself), and transportation, except medicine or religious materials." § 2339A(b)(1); see also § 2339B(g)(4).

The authority to designate an entity a "foreign terrorist organization" rests with the Secretary of State. 8 U.S.C. §§ 1189(a)(1), (d)(4). She may, in consultation with the Secretary of the Treasury and the Attorney General, so designate an organization upon finding that it is foreign, engages in "terrorist activity" or "terrorism," and thereby "threatens the security of United States nationals or the national security of the United States." §§ 1189(a)(1), (d)(4). "'[N]ational security' means the national defense, foreign relations, or economic interests of the United States." § 1189(d)(2)....

In 1997, the Secretary of State designated 30 groups as foreign terrorist organizations. Two of those groups are the Kurdistan Workers' Party (also known as the Partiya Karkeran Kurdistan, or PKK) and the Liberation Tigers of Tamil Eelam (LTTE). The PKK is an organization founded in 1974 with the aim of establishing an independent Kurdish state in southeastern Turkey. The LTTE is an organization founded in 1976 for the purpose of creating an independent Tamil state in Sri Lanka. The District Court in this action found that the PKK and the LTTE engage in political and humanitarian activities. The Government has presented evidence that both groups have also committed numerous terrorist attacks, some of which have harmed American citizens. The LTTE sought judicial review of its designation as a foreign terrorist organization; the D.C. Circuit upheld that designation. See *People's Mojahedin Organization of Iran v. Dept. of State*, 182 F.3d 17, 18-19, 25 (1999). The PKK did not challenge its designation.

Plaintiffs in this litigation are two U.S. citizens and six domestic organizations: the Humanitarian Law Project (HLP) (a human rights organization with consultative status to the United Nations); Ralph Fertig (the HLP's president, and a retired administrative law judge); Nagalingam Jeyalingam (a Tamil physician, born in Sri Lanka and a naturalized U.S. citizen); and five nonprofit groups dedicated to the interests of persons of Tamil descent. In 1998, plaintiffs filed suit in federal court challenging the constitutionality of the material-support statute, § 2339B. Plaintiffs claimed that they wished to provide support for the humanitarian and political activities of the PKK and the LTTE in the form of monetary contributions, other tangible aid, legal training, and political advocacy, but that they could not do so for fear of prosecution under § 2339B.

As relevant here, plaintiffs claimed that the material-support statute was unconstitutional on two grounds: First, it violated their freedom of speech and freedom of association under the First Amendment, because it criminalized their provision of material support to the PKK and the LTTE, without requiring the Government to prove that plaintiffs had a specific intent to further the unlawful ends of those organizations. Second, plaintiffs argued that the statute was unconstitutionally vague....

In IRTPA, Congress clarified the mental state necessary to violate § 2339B, requiring knowledge of the foreign group's designation as a terrorist organization or the group's commission of terrorist acts. § 2339B(a)(1). Congress also added the term "service" to the definition of "material support or resources," § 2339A(b)(1), and defined "training" to mean "instruction or teaching designed to impart a specific skill, as opposed to general knowledge," §2339A(b)(2). It also defined "expert advice or assistance" to mean "advice or assistance derived from scientific, technical or other specialized knowledge." § 2339A(b)(3). Finally, IRTPA clarified the scope of the term "personnel" by providing:

> "No person may be prosecuted under [§ 2339B] in connection with the term 'personnel' unless that person has knowingly provided, attempted to provide, or conspired to provide a foreign terrorist organization with 1 or more individuals (who may be or include himself) to work under that terrorist organization's direction or control or to organize, manage, supervise, or otherwise direct the operation of that organization. Individuals who act entirely independently of the foreign terrorist organization to advance its goals or objectives shall not be considered to be working under the foreign terrorist organization's direction and control." § 2339B(h).

Shortly after Congress enacted IRTPA, the en banc Court of Appeals issued an order in plaintiffs' first action. 393 F.3d 902, 903 (C.A.9 2004). The en banc court affirmed the rejection of plaintiffs' First Amendment claims for the reasons set out in the Ninth Circuit's panel decision in 2000. See *ibid.* In light of IRTPA, however, the en banc court vacated the panel's 2003 judgment with respect to vagueness, and remanded to the District Court for further proceedings in plaintiffs' second action (relating to "expert advice or assistance") also remanded in light of IRTPA. See 380 F. Supp. 2d, at 1139.

The District Court consolidated the two actions on remand. See *ibid.* The court also allowed plaintiffs to challenge the new term "service." See *id.*, at 1151, n.24. The parties moved for summary judgment, and the District Court granted partial relief to plaintiffs on vagueness grounds. See *id.*, at 1156.

The Court of Appeals affirmed once more. 552 F.3d 916, 933 (C.A.9 2009). The court first rejected plaintiffs' claim that the material-support statute would violate due process unless it were read to require a specific intent to further the illegal ends of a foreign terrorist organization. See *id.*, at 926-927. The Ninth Circuit also held that the statute was not overbroad in violation of the First Amendment. See *id.*, at 931-932. As for vagueness, the Court of Appeals noted that plaintiffs had not raised a "facial vagueness challenge." *Id.*, at 929, n.6. The court held that, as applied to plaintiffs, the terms "training," "expert advice or assistance" (when derived from "other specialized knowledge"), and "service" were vague because they "continue[d] to cover constitutionally protected advocacy," but the term "personnel" was not vague because it "no longer criminalize[d] pure speech protected by the First Amendment." *Id.*, at 929-931.

The Government petitioned for certiorari, and plaintiffs filed a conditional cross-petition. We granted both petitions.

II

Given the complicated 12-year history of this litigation, we pause to clarify the questions before us. Plaintiffs challenge § 2339B's prohibition on four types of material support—"training," "expert advice or assistance," "service," and "personnel." They raise three constitutional claims. First, plaintiffs claim that § 2339B violates the Due Process Clause of the Fifth Amendment because these four statutory terms are impermissibly vague. Second, plaintiffs claim that § 2339B violates their freedom of speech under the First Amendment. Third, plaintiffs claim that § 2339B violates their First Amendment freedom of association.

Plaintiffs do not challenge the above statutory terms in all their applications. Rather, plaintiffs claim that § 2339B is invalid to the extent it prohibits them from engaging in certain specified activities. With respect to the HLP and Judge Fertig, those activities are: (1) "train[ing] members of [the] PKK on how to use humanitarian and international law to peacefully resolve disputes"; (2) "engag[ing] in political advocacy on behalf of Kurds who live in Turkey"; and (3) "teach[ing] PKK members how to petition various representative bodies such as the United Nations for relief." 552 F.3d, at 921, n.1; see 380 F. Supp. 2d, at 1136. With respect to the other plaintiffs, those activities are: (1) "train[ing] members of [the] LTTE to present claims for tsunami-related aid to mediators and international bodies"; (2) "offer[ing] their legal expertise in negotiating peace agreements between the LTTE and the Sri Lankan government"; and (3) "engag[ing] in political advocacy on behalf of Tamils who live in Sri Lanka." 552 F.3d, at 921, n.1; see 380 F. Supp. 2d, at 1137. . . .

III

Plaintiffs claim, as a threshold matter, that we should affirm the Court of Appeals without reaching any issues of constitutional law. They contend that we should interpret the material-support statute, when applied to speech, to require proof that a defendant intended to further a foreign terrorist organization's illegal activities. That interpretation, they say, would end the litigation because plaintiffs' proposed activities consist of speech, but plaintiffs do not intend to further unlawful conduct by the PKK or the LTTE.

We reject plaintiffs' interpretation of § 2339B because it is inconsistent with the text of the statute. Section 2339B(a) prohibits "knowingly" providing material support. It then specifically describes the type of knowledge that is required: "To violate this paragraph, a person must have knowledge that the organization is a designated terrorist organization . . . , that the organization has engaged or engages in terrorist activity . . . , or that the organization has engaged or engages in terrorism. . . ." *Ibid.* Congress plainly spoke to the necessary mental state for a violation of § 2339B, and it chose knowledge about the organization's connection to terrorism, not specific intent to further the organization's terrorist activities.

Plaintiffs' interpretation is also untenable in light of the sections immediately surrounding § 2339B, both of which do refer to intent to further terrorist activity. See § 2339A(a) (establishing criminal penalties for one who "provides material support or resources . . . knowing or intending that they are to be used in preparation for, or in carrying out, a violation of" statutes prohibiting violent terrorist acts); § 2339C(a)(1) (setting criminal penalties for one who "unlawfully and willfully provides or collects funds with the intention that such funds be used, or with the knowledge that such funds are to be used, in full or in part, in order to carry out" other unlawful acts). Congress enacted

§ 2339A in 1994 and § 2339C in 2002. Yet Congress did not import the intent language of those provisions into § 2339B, either when it enacted § 2339B in 1996, or when it clarified § 2339B's knowledge requirement in 2004.

. . .

IV

We turn to the question whether the material-support statute, as applied to plaintiffs, is impermissibly vague under the Due Process Clause of the Fifth Amendment. "A conviction fails to comport with due process if the statute under which it is obtained fails to provide a person of ordinary intelligence fair notice of what is prohibited, or is so standardless that it authorizes or encourages seriously discriminatory enforcement." *United States v. Williams*, 553 U.S. 285, 304 (2008). We consider whether a statute is vague as applied to the particular facts at issue, for "[a] plaintiff who engages in some conduct that is clearly proscribed cannot complain of the vagueness of the law as applied to the conduct of others." *Hoffman Estates v. Flipside, Hoffman Estates, Inc.*, 455 U.S. 489, 455 (1982). We have said that when a statute "interferes with the right of free speech or of association, a more stringent vagueness test should apply." *Id.*, at 499. "But 'perfect clarity and precise guidance have never been required even of regulations that restrict expressive activity.'" *Williams, supra*, at 304 (quoting *Ward v. Rock Against Racism*, 491 U.S. 781, 794 (1989)). . . .

Under a proper analysis, plaintiffs' claims of vagueness lack merit. Plaintiffs do not argue that the material-support statute grants too much enforcement discretion to the Government. We therefore address only whether the statute "provide[s] a person of ordinary intelligence fair notice of what is prohibited." *Williams*, 553 U.S., at 304.

As a general matter, the statutory terms at issue here are quite different from the sorts of terms that we have previously declared to be vague. We have in the past "struck down statutes that tied criminal culpability to whether the defendant's conduct was 'annoying' or 'indecent' — wholly subjective judgments without statutory definitions, narrowing context, or settled legal meanings." *Id.* at 306; *see also Papachristou v. Jacksonville*, 405 U.S. 156, n.1 (1972) (holding vague an ordinance that punished "vagrants," defined to include "rogues and vagabonds," "persons who use juggling," and "common night walkers" (internal quotation marks omitted)). Applying the statutory terms in this action —"training," "expert advice or assistance," "service," and "personnel" — does not require similarly untethered, subjective judgments.

Congress also took care to add narrowing definitions to the material-support statute over time. These definitions increased the clarity of the statute's terms. See § 2339A(b) ("'training' means instruction or teaching designed to impart a specific skill, as opposed to general knowledge"); § 2339A(b)(3) ("'expert advice or assistance' means advice or assistance derived from scientific, technical or other specialized knowledge"); § 2339B(h) (clarifying the scope of "personnel"). And the knowledge requirement of the statute further reduces any potential for vagueness, as we have held with respect to other statutes containing a similar requirement. See *Hill v. Colorado*, 530 U.S. 703, 732 (2000); *Posters 'N' Things, Ltd. v. United States*, 511 U.S. 513, 523, 526 (1994); *see also Hoffman Estates*, 455 U.S., at 499. . . .

Most of the activities in which plaintiffs seek to engage readily fall within the scope of the terms "training" and "expert advice or assistance." Plaintiffs want to "train members of [the] PKK on how to use humanitarian and international law to peacefully resolve disputes," and "teach PKK members how to petition various representative bodies such as the United Nations for relief." 552 F.3d, at 921, n.1. A person of ordinary intelligence would understand that instruction on resolving disputes through international law falls within the statute's definition of "training" because it imparts a "specific skill," not "general knowledge." § 2339A(b)(2). Plaintiffs' activities also fall comfortably within the scope of "expert advice or assistance": A reasonable person would recognize that teaching the PKK how to petition for humanitarian relief before the United Nations involves advice derived from, as the statute puts it, "specialized knowledge." § 2339A(b)(3). In fact, plaintiffs themselves have repeatedly used the terms "training" and "expert advice" throughout this litigation to describe their own proposed activities, demonstrating that these common terms readily and naturally cover plaintiffs' conduct. . . .

Plaintiffs also contend that they want to engage in "political advocacy" on behalf of Kurds living in Turkey and Tamils living in Sri Lanka. 552 F.3d, at 921, n.1. They are concerned that such advocacy might be regarded as "material support" in the form of providing "personnel" or "service[s]," and assert that the statute is unconstitutionally vague because they cannot tell.

As for "personnel," Congress enacted a limiting definition in IRTPA that answers plaintiffs' vagueness concerns. Providing material support that constitutes "personnel" is defined as knowingly providing a person "to work under that terrorist organization's direction or control or to organize, manage, supervise, or otherwise direct the operation of that organization." § 2339B(h). The statute makes clear that "personnel" does not cover *independent* advocacy: "Individuals who act entirely independently of the foreign terrorist organization to advance its goals or objectives shall not be considered to be working under the foreign terrorist organization's direction and control." *Ibid.*

"[S]ervice" similarly refers to concerted activity, not independent advocacy. . . . Context confirms that ordinary meaning here. The statute prohibits providing a service "*to* a foreign terrorist organization." § 2339B(a)(1) (emphasis added). The use of the word "to" indicates a connection between the service and the foreign group. We think a person of ordinary intelligence would understand that independently advocating for a cause is different from providing a service to a group that is advocating for that cause.

V

A

We next consider whether the material-support statute, as applied to plaintiffs, violates the freedom of speech guaranteed by the First Amendment.

Both plaintiffs and the Government take extreme positions on this question. Plaintiffs claim that Congress has banned their "pure political speech." *E.g.*, Brief for Plaintiffs 2, 25, 43. It has not. Under the material-support statute, plaintiffs may say anything they wish on any topic. They may speak and write freely about the PKK and LTTE, the governments of Turkey and Sri Lanka, human rights, and international law. They may advocate before the United Nations. As the Government states: "The statute does not prohibit independent advocacy or expression of any kind." Brief for Government 13. Section 2339B also "does not prevent [plaintiffs] from becoming members of the PKK and LTTE or impose any sanction on them for doing so." *Id.*, at 60. Congress has not, therefore, sought to suppress ideas or opinions in the form of "pure political speech." Rather, Congress has prohibited "material support," which most often does not take the form of speech at all. And when it does, the statute is carefully drawn to cover only a narrow category of speech to, under the direction of, or in coordination with foreign groups that the speaker knows to be terrorist organizations. . . .

B

The First Amendment issue before us is more refined than either plaintiffs or the Government would have it. It is not whether the Government may prohibit pure political speech, or may prohibit material support in the form of conduct. It is instead whether the Government may prohibit what plaintiffs want to do—provide material support to the PKK and LTTE in the form of speech.

Everyone agrees that the Government's interest in combating terrorism is an urgent objective of the highest order. Plaintiffs' complaint is that the ban on material support, applied to what they wish to do, is not "necessary to further that interest." *Ibid.* The objective of combating terrorism does not justify prohibiting their speech, plaintiffs argue, because their support will advance only the legitimate activities of the designated terrorist organizations, not their terrorism. *Id.*, at 51-52.

Whether foreign terrorist organizations meaningfully segregate support of their legitimate activities from support of terrorism is an empirical question. When it enacted § 2339B in 1996, Congress made specific findings regarding the serious threat posed by international terrorism. See AEDPA §§ 301(a)(1)-(7), 110 Stat. 1247, note following 18 U.S.C. § 2339B (Findings and Purpose). One of those findings explicitly rejects plaintiffs' contention that their support would not further the terrorist activities of the PKK and LTTE: "[F]oreign organizations that engage in terrorist activity are so tainted by their criminal conduct that *any contribution to such an organization* facilitates that conduct." § 301(a)(7) (emphasis added). . . .

Material support meant to "promot[e] peaceable, lawful conduct," Brief for Plaintiffs 51, can further terrorism by foreign groups in multiple ways. "Material support" is a valuable resource by definition. Such support frees up other resources within the organization that may be put to violent ends. It also importantly helps lend legitimacy to foreign terrorist groups—legitimacy that makes it easier for those groups to persist, to recruit members, and to raise funds — all of which facilitate more terrorist attacks. . . .

Money is fungible, and "[w]hen foreign terrorist organizations that have a dual structure raise funds, they highlight the civilian and humanitarian ends to which such moneys could be put." McKune Affidavit, App. 134, ¶ 9. But "there is reason to believe that foreign terrorist organizations do not maintain legitimate *financial* firewalls between those funds raised for civil, nonviolent activities, and those ultimately used to support violent, terrorist operations." *Id.*, at 135, ¶ 12. Thus, "[f]unds raised ostensibly for charitable purposes have in the past been redirected by some terrorist groups to fund the purchase of arms and explosives." *Id.*, at 134, ¶ 10. . . . There is evidence that the PKK and the LTTE, in particular, have not "respected the line between humanitarian and violent activities." McKune Affidavit, App. 135, ¶ 13 (discussing PKK); see *id.*, at 134 (LTTE).

The dissent argues that there is "no natural stopping place" for the proposition that aiding a foreign terrorist organization's lawful activity promotes the terrorist organization as a whole. But Congress has settled on just such a natural stopping place: The statute reaches only material support coordinated with or under the direction of a designated foreign terrorist organization. Independent advocacy that might be viewed as promoting the group's legitimacy is not covered. . . .

C.

In analyzing whether it is possible in practice to distinguish material support for a foreign terrorist group's violent activities and its nonviolent activities, we do not rely exclusively on our own inferences drawn from the record evidence. We have before us an affidavit stating the Executive Branch's conclusion on that question. The State Department informs us that "[t]he experience and analysis of the U.S. government agencies charged with combating terrorism strongly suppor[t]" Congress's finding that all contributions to foreign terrorist organizations further their terrorism. McKune Affidavit, App. 133, ¶ 8. . . . In the Executive's view: "Given the purposes, organizational structure, and clandestine nature of foreign terrorist organizations, it is highly likely that any material support to these organizations will ultimately inure to the benefit of their criminal, terrorist functions — regardless of whether such support was ostensibly intended to support non-violent, non-terrorist activities." McKune Affidavit, App. 133, ¶ 8.

That evaluation of the facts by the Executive, like Congress's assessment, is entitled to deference. This litigation implicates sensitive and weighty interests of national security and foreign affairs. . . . We have noted that "neither the Members of this Court nor most federal judges begin the day with briefings that may describe new and serious threats to our Nation and its people." *Boumediene v. Bush*, 553 U.S. 723, 797 (2008). It is vital in this context "not to substitute . . . our own evaluation of evidence for a reasonable evaluation by the Legislative Branch." *Rostker v. Goldberg*, 453 U.S. 57, 68 (1981).

Our precedents, old and new, make clear that concerns of national security and foreign relations do not warrant abdication of the judicial role. We do not defer to the Government's reading of the First Amendment, even when such interests are at stake. We are one with the dissent that the Government's "authority and expertise in these matters do not automatically trump the Court's own obligation to secure the protection that the Constitution grants to individuals." *Post*, at 2743. But when it comes to collecting evidence and drawing factual inferences in this area, "the lack of competence on the part of the courts is marked," *Rostker, supra*, at 65, and respect for the Government's conclusions is appropriate.

One reason for that respect is that national security and foreign policy concerns arise in connection with efforts to confront evolving threats in an area where information can be difficult to obtain and the impact of certain conduct difficult to assess. . . . In this context, conclusions must often be based on informed judgment rather than concrete evidence, and that reality affects what we may reasonably insist on from the Government. The material-support statute is, on its face, a preventive measure—it criminalizes not terrorist attacks themselves, but aid that makes the attacks more likely to occur. The Government, when seeking to prevent imminent harms in the context of international affairs and national security, is not required to conclusively link all the pieces in the puzzle before we grant weight to its empirical conclusions. See *Zemel v. Rusk*, 381 U.S., at 17 ("[B]ecause of the changeable and explosive nature of contemporary international relations, . . . Congress . . . must of necessity paint with a brush broader than that it customarily wields in domestic areas"). . . .

At bottom, plaintiffs simply disagree with the considered judgment of Congress and the Executive that providing material support to a designated foreign terrorist organization—even seemingly benign support—bolsters the terrorist activities of that organization. That judgment, however, is entitled to significant weight, and we have persuasive evidence before us to sustain it. Given the sensitive interests in national security and foreign affairs at stake, the political branches have adequately substantiated their determination that, to serve the Government's interest in preventing terrorism, it was necessary to prohibit providing material support in the form of training, expert advice, personnel, and services to foreign terrorist groups, even if the supporters meant to promote only the groups' nonviolent ends. . . .

All this is not to say that any future applications of the material-support statute to speech or advocacy will survive First Amendment scrutiny. It is also not to say that any other statute relating to speech and terrorism would satisfy the First Amendment. In particular, we in no way suggest that a regulation of independent speech would pass constitutional muster, even if the Government were to show that such speech benefits foreign terrorist organizations. We also do not suggest that Congress could extend the same prohibition on material support at issue here to domestic organizations. We simply hold that, in prohibiting the particular forms of support that plaintiffs seek to provide to foreign terrorist groups, § 2339B does not violate the freedom of speech.

VI

Plaintiffs' final claim is that the material-support statute violates their freedom of association under the First Amendment. Plaintiffs argue that the statute criminalizes the mere fact of their associating with the PKK and the LTTE, thereby running afoul of decisions like *De Jonge v. Oregon*, 299 U.S. 353 (1937), and cases in which we have overturned sanctions for joining the Communist Party, see, *e.g., Keyishian v. Board of Regents of Univ. of State of N.Y.*, 385 U.S. 589 (1967); *United States v. Robel*, 389 U.S. 258 (1967).

The Court of Appeals correctly rejected this claim because the statute does not penalize mere association with a foreign terrorist organization. As the Ninth Circuit put it: "The statute does not prohibit being a member of one of the designated groups or vigorously promoting and supporting the political goals of the group. . . . What [§ 2339B] prohibits is the act of giving material support. . . ." 205 F.3d, at 1133. Plaintiffs want to do the latter. Our decisions scrutinizing penalties on simple association or assembly are therefore inapposite. . . .

. . .

The Preamble to the Constitution proclaims that the people of the United States ordained and established that charter of government in part to "provide for the common defence." As Madison explained, "[s]ecurity against foreign danger is . . . an avowed and essential object of the American Union." The Federalist No. 41, p. 269 (J. Cooke ed. 1961). We hold that, in regulating the particular forms of support that plaintiffs seek to provide to foreign terrorist organizations, Congress has pursued that objective consistent with the limitations of the First and Fifth Amendments.

The judgment of the United States Court of Appeals for the Ninth Circuit is affirmed in part and reversed in part, and the cases are remanded for further proceedings consistent with this opinion.

NOTES AND QUESTIONS

1. The Court held that the material support statute does not violate freedom of speech. The Court reasoned that the material support statute does not prohibit "independent advocacy" of any kind, nor prevent or punish someone from becoming a member of a foreign terrorist organization. *Holder v. Humanitarian Law Project*, 561 U.S. at 26. The Court declared that "the statute is carefully drawn to cover only a narrow category of speech to, under the direction of, or in coordination with foreign groups that the speaker knows to be terrorist organizations." *Id.* The critical question left unresolved by the Court is what degree of direction or coordination is sufficient to move the conduct from "independent advocacy," which is protected speech under the First Amendment, to material support, which is punishable under the statute.

2. The Court rejected plaintiffs' claim that the material support statute violates their freedom of association under the First Amendment. *Id.* at 39. The Court

stated that the statute does not penalize mere association with a foreign terrorist organization (FTO), including being a member of one of the designated terrorist groups, or vigorously promoting and supporting the ideological goals of the group. *Id.*

3. Should it be a crime for an ISIS sympathizer to solicit and encourage others to join ISIS in Syria, or make monetary contributions to support ISIS's goal of establishing a caliphate? Does this conduct constitute attempt to provide material support to an FTO? While the material support statute punishes attempt and conspiracy to provide material support to an FTO, the statute does not criminalize solicitation and incitement. Should solicitation and incitement to provide material support to international terrorists be prohibited under the statute?

4. The Court stated that "service" refers to "concerted activity," not independent advocacy. The statute prohibits providing a service "to a foreign terrorist organization." 18 U.S.C. § 2339B(a)(1). According to the Court, the use of the word "to" indicates a connection between the service and the terrorist organization. How much direction or coordination is necessary for an activity to constitute a "service"? Would any communication with a member of the terrorist organization be sufficient? With a leader? Must the "relationship" have formal elements, such as an employment or contractual relationship? What about a relationship with an intermediary? *See Holder v. Humanitarian Law Project*, 561 U.S. at 25.

5. The material support statute punishes a wide range of activities involving an FTO. *See e.g., United States v. Hammoud*, 381 F.3d 316, 331 (4th Cir. 2004) (upholding defendant's conviction for violating § 2339B for making a monetary donation to Hizballah, a designated FTO); *United States v. Abu-Jihaad*, 600 F. Supp. 2d 362, 401 (D. Conn. 2009) (holding that defendant provided "training" to al Qaeda by teaching English at an al Qaeda medical clinic in Afghanistan to assist nurses in reading English-language medicine labels); *United States v. Warsame*, 537 F. Supp. 2d 1005, 1018 (D. Minn. 2008) (attending an al Qaeda training camp constitutes the provision of "personnel" to an FTO); *United States v. Shah*, 474 F. Supp. 2d 497-98 (S.D.N.Y. 2007) (upholding the application of the term "personnel" to a doctor who provided medical support to members of al Qaeda).

6. The Court held that the material support statute does not require proof that the defendant intended to further the foreign terrorist organization's illegal activities. *Id.* at 16. It is a violation of the material support statute, for example, if the defendant provided material support to a foreign terrorist organization with the intent to support the humanitarian activities of the foreign group.

7. Congress made specific findings regarding the serious threat posed by international terrorism. Congress found that "foreign terrorist organizations that engage in terrorist activity are so tainted by their criminal conduct that any contribution to such an organization facilitates that conduct." *See* AEDPA §§ 301(a)(1)-(7), 110 Stat. 1247, note following 18 U.S.C. § 2339B (Findings and Purpose). What is the justification for banning material support to a terrorist organization intended to "promote peaceable, lawful conduct"?

8. The Supreme Court found that the material support statute, as applied to plaintiffs, was not impermissibly vague under the Due Process Clause of the

Fifth Amendment. The Court stated that "Congress . . . took care to add narrowing definitions to the material-support statute over time. These definitions increased the clarity of the statute's terms." *Holder v. Humanitarian Law Project*, 561 U.S. at 21. Do you agree? Do the statutory definitions of "training," 18 U.S.C. § 2339A(b)(2), and "expert advice or assistance," § 2339A(b)(3), provide a person of ordinary intelligence fair notice of what is prohibited under the statute?

PROSECUTIONS UNDER THE MATERIAL SUPPORT STATUTES

The material support statutes, 18 U.S.C. § 2339A and § 2339B, have become far and away the most commonly used statutes by the U.S. Department of Justice to combat international terrorism, with 87.5 percent of all federal terrorism cases involving material support charges. *See* CENTER ON LAW AND SECURITY, NEW YORK UNIVERSITY SCHOOL OF LAW, TEN YEARS LATER: TERRORIST TRIAL REPORT CARD: 2001-2011 (2011).

United States v. Dhirane
896 F.3d 295 (4th Cir. 2018)

NIEMEYER, Circuit Judge:

Following a bench trial, the district court found Muna Osman Jama and Hinda Osman Dhirane guilty of conspiracy to provide and of providing on numerous occasions material support to al-Shabaab, a designated foreign terrorist organization, in violation of 18 U.S.C. § 2339B. The defendants, naturalized American citizens who were born in Somalia, collected money from members of online chat rooms and transmitted the funds to co-conspirators in Somalia and Kenya to assist al-Shabaab's terrorist activities in the Horn of Africa. The district court sentenced Jama to 144 months' imprisonment and Dhirane to 132 months' imprisonment.

On appeal, the defendants contend (1) that the district court erred in denying their motion to suppress evidence obtained pursuant to warrants issued under the Foreign Intelligence Surveillance Act ("FISA"), arguing that the evidence was obtained unconstitutionally in light of FISA's *ex parte* and *in camera* judicial review process; [and] (2) that the district court applied an incorrect legal standard to conclude that two co-conspirators in Somalia and Kenya, to whom the defendants transmitted monies, were "part of" al-Shabaab. . . .

For the reasons that follow, we affirm.

I

In 2008, the U.S. Department of State designated al-Shabaab a foreign terrorist organization under § 219 of the Immigration and Nationality Act, 8 U.S.C. § 1189. At that time and continuing through the events of this case, al-Shabaab was engaged in terrorist activities in the Horn of Africa region, principally in Somalia.

In the period from 2011 to 2013, the defendants participated in an online chat room composed of members of the Somali diaspora in the United States and around the world. Participants generally discussed current events concerning Somalia, including al-Shabaab's activities there, and, on various occasions, al-Shabaab leaders and representatives would speak to the group and solicit support, including financial support, for their terrorist activities. During that time, the defendants also participated in a smaller, private chat room known as the "Group of Fifteen." Only those participants from the larger chat room who had been or who could be persuaded to become committed supporters of al-Shabaab were invited to join. The Group of Fifteen conversed confidentially approximately once or twice a month, where members pledged to make periodic payments ranging from $50 to $200 in support of al-Shabaab's operations. The defendants kept track of those commitments and contributed money themselves. They also arranged for representatives or persons associated with al-Shabaab to speak to the Group of Fifteen and solicit support, including financial resources, for al-Shabaab's activities.

As the money was collected, the defendants transmitted it to persons involved with al-Shabaab either on "the Nairobi side," referring to the geographical area around Nairobi, Kenya, or "the Hargeisa side," referring to the geographical area around Hargeisa, Somalia. Defendant Jama "personally solicited contributions" from the Group of Fifteen, "monitored whether the individual members had satisfied their monthly commitments," and saw to it that the sums were "successfully transmitted to and received by [al-Shabaab] contacts," both on the Nairobi side and the Hargeisa side. And defendant Dhirane played a similar role, mostly for the Hargeisa side. The monies sent to the Nairobi side were transmitted principally to a woman named Fardowsa Jama Mohamed, who used the funds to operate two safehouses in Nairobi for al-Shabaab fighters. The monies sent to the Hargeisa side were transmitted principally to a woman named Barira Hassan Abdullahi, described as a financial organizer on behalf of al-Shabaab, who used the funds to purchase vehicles and other supplies for al-Shabaab fighters in the Golis Mountains just north of Hargeisa. . . .

In June 2014, the defendants, along with others—including Mohamed and Abdullahi—were indicted and charged with one count of conspiracy to provide material support to al-Shabaab, a designated foreign terrorist organization, and both defendants were charged with 20 substantive counts of providing material support in the form of money to al-Shabaab—one count for each transmission of money—all in violation of 18 U.S.C. § 2339B(a)(1). . . .

The defendants waived their right to a jury trial, and the district court conducted a bench trial beginning in July 2016. During trial, the defendants argued that they provided monies exclusively for the purpose of procuring medicine and medical services for al-Shabaab members, which they claimed fell within the "medicine" exception to "material support" as used in 18 U.S.C. § 2339B. *See id.* § 2339A(b)(1). At the conclusion of trial, the court found both defendants guilty of conspiracy, Jama guilty of all substantive counts, and Dhirane guilty of those substantive counts covering conduct that occurred after she joined the conspiracy, acquitting her on the remaining counts. The court issued a written opinion dated November 4, 2016, providing its findings of fact and addressing the various legal issues that had been presented at trial.

The court found as facts that the defendants were "ardent, committed, and active supporters of [al-Shabaab]"; that they knew that al-Shabaab was a designated foreign terrorist organization and was engaging in terrorist activities; and that they knew that it was unlawful to provide support to that organization. The court found further that the defendants played a prominent role in the Group of Fifteen chat room, arranging for representatives of or persons associated with al-Shabaab to solicit funds from members of the chat room and then organizing the collection of those funds and their transmission to Kenya and Somalia. It found that the defendants transmitted the funds mostly to co-conspirator Mohamed on the Nairobi side and co-conspirator Abdullahi on the Hargeisa side for the specific purpose of supporting al-Shabaab's activities in those areas. Mohamed, it found, operated two safehouses in Nairobi, one for providing medical care and treatment to injured al-Shabaab soldiers and the other as a staging ground for al-Shabaab's military operations. Abdullahi, it found, received the monies in Hargeisa and used them to provide transportation, trucks, and other support services to al-Shabaab soldiers. The court found generally that the defendants, as part of their fundraising activities, had access to al-Shabaab leaders and to nonpublic information pertaining to al-Shabaab's financial needs, including for its military activities. In this regard, the court found specifically that these defendants coordinated "to some degree their fundraising" with respect to the specific military activities of al-Shabaab. In sum, the court found that the defendants "understood, intended, and planned that, when they provided money to [Mohamed, Abdullahi, and others], they provided money to [al-Shabaab]."

. . .

III

For their main argument on appeal, the defendants contend that the district court, in the course of its opinion after trial, erred by "redefin[ing] an element of § 2339B," without any legal support, when it defined "a foreign terrorist organization" as used in the statute to include any person "engaged in significant activity on behalf of [a foreign terrorist organization] relative to [its] goals and objectives" and developed a list of non-exclusive factors to determine if someone met that definition. They argue that with this broadened definition of "organization," the court concluded that co-conspirators Mohamed and Abdullahi, to whom the defendants sent money, were part of al-Shabaab. This was, the defendants maintain, critical to the finding of guilt, because they claimed at trial that Mohamed and Abdullahi were independent of any foreign terrorist organization and that therefore the defendants' transmission of funds to them was not "to a foreign terrorist organization. . . ."

In its written opinion finding the defendants guilty, the district court began with its factual findings. It then applied § 2339B to the facts. In applying the statute, however, the court seemed to assume, as the defendants had argued, that the transmission of monies by the defendants for use by al-Shabaab could only satisfy the elements of the statute if the monies were transmitted to persons — here, Mohamed and Abdullahi — who were "*part of* al-Shabaab." The court's discussion was in response to the defendants' particular argument for acquittal — that Mohamed and Abdullahi, to whom the defendants transmitted the monies, were "independent of" al-Shabaab and that the monies paid to them were "for purposes the Defendants believed were lawful," thus insulating them from criminal liability as they "did not intend to deliver these funds to [al-Shabaab] or anyone who could be considered part of [al-Shabaab]." As the court thus understood its task, it was looking for a standard "to determine whether someone [was] sufficiently *acting for or on behalf of* [a foreign terrorist organization] *to be deemed a part of* the [foreign terrorist organization]." When looking for the substance of that standard, however, the court observed:

> There is surprisingly little case law concerning by what standard to determine whether a particular individual is sufficiently associated with [a foreign terrorist organization] to constitute the organization itself.

Therefore, the court, on its own, developed a seven-part balancing test from analogous sources to determine whether Mohamed and Abdullahi, "to whom the defendants delivered their funds[,] were *part of* [al-Shabaab]." The court then applied the test to the facts and concluded that both Mohamed and Abdullahi, as well as the defendants, were indeed *part of* al-Shabaab. . . .

The district court's adoption of a test to determine whether someone was *part of* a foreign terrorist organization for purposes of § 2339B was, we conclude, unnecessary and resulted from a misunderstanding of what § 2339B required in the context of this case. Section 2339B does not require that persons such as Mohamed and Abdullahi be *part of* a foreign terrorist organization, nor does it require that the defendants themselves be *part of* the organization. The statute prohibits *anyone* from knowingly providing or attempting to provide material support or resources to a foreign terrorist organization. As § 2339B provides:

> Whoever knowingly provides material support or resources to a foreign terrorist organization, or attempts or conspires to do so, shall be [punished]. . . . To violate this paragraph, a person must have knowledge that the organization is a designated terrorist organization . . . has engaged or engages in terrorist activity . . . or that the organization has engaged or engages in terrorism.

The statute defines "material support or resources" to include, among other things, "any property," "currency," "safehouses," "facilities," or "transportation," but it excludes "medicine or religious materials." 18 U.S.C. §§ 2339B(a)(1), 2339B(g)(4), 2339A(b)(1). Accordingly, to prove a violation, the government must establish that a defendant (1) knowingly provided or attempted or conspired to provide material support (2) to a foreign terrorist organization (3) that the defendant knew had been designated a foreign terrorist organization or had engaged in terrorism. *See Holder v. Humanitarian Law Project*, 561 U.S. 1, 16-17 (2010) (clarifying that the requisite "mental state" required to violate § 2339B is "knowledge about the organization's connection to terrorism, not specific intent to further the organization's terrorist activities").

Thus, determining that Mohamed and Abdullahi, to whom monies were transmitted, were part of al-Shabaab was not necessary to finding that the defendants had provided or attempted to provide material support to al-Shabaab. Soliciting money to satisfy al-Shabaab's expressed needs, collecting that money, and then transmitting it to individuals in Africa who were associated with al-Shabaab for the sole purpose of funding al-Shabaab's activities violated § 2339B. And while such an attempt alone is all that is necessary — *see Humanitarian Law Project*, 561 U.S. at 30 (noting that even "working in coordination with" a designated terrorist organization "serves to legitimize and further their terrorist means") — in this case the monies actually went to maintain safehouses for al-Shabaab militants and to acquire trucks, transportation, and other support services for the militants. As the court found, the monies reached the defendants' intended objects and accomplished the intended purpose of assisting al-Shabaab. That undoubtedly fulfills the elements of the prohibited conduct.

The defendants' argument that support given to assist a terrorist organization might thereafter have been used to purchase medical equipment or supplies was therefore irrelevant. The defendants were charged with providing *money*, not medical supplies, and in particular money that they had solicited and collected with the stated purpose that it would be sent to support al-Shabaab and its various activities. As the Supreme Court has observed in this context, even material support given to a terrorist organization to promote "peaceable" or "lawful" conduct furthers terrorism as it "frees up other resources within the organization that may be put to violent ends." *Humanitarian Law Project*, 561 U.S. at 30; *see also id.* at 32 (noting that providing material support to terrorist groups in any form "also furthers terrorism by straining the United States' relationship with its allies and undermining cooperative efforts between nations to prevent terrorist attacks"). "Money," the Court observed, "is fungible." *Id.* at 31. There was thus no need for the district court to respond to the defendants' assertion that at least some of the money they sent was used for medical supplies.

Yet, while the district court's development and application of its multifactor test was unnecessary, its factual findings nonetheless amply satisfied each element of the offense. The court began by finding that al-Shabaab was designated as a foreign terrorist organization, that it "had engaged and was engaging in terrorist activities at the time of the events involved in this case," and that the defendants knew of these facts. It also found that the defendants were "ardent, committed, and active supporters of [al-Shabaab]." Indeed, it found that the defendants were "involved in arranging for representatives or persons associated with [al-Shabaab] to speak to [their] chat room . . . during which time these [al-Shabaab] members solicited support, including financial resources." The court found further that the defendants, as members of the chat room, were "committed to providing financial contributions approximately monthly for the benefit of [al-Shabaab]" and that "[t]his money was delivered to persons involved in [al-Shabaab's] operations." In particular, it found that Jama "personally solicited contributions," "monitored whether the individual members had satisfied their monthly commitments and whether those sums had been successfully transmitted to and received by [al-Shabaab] contacts," and served "in the nature of an enforcer by following up with those . . . who had not paid their monthly commitments." Dhirane, the court found, came to play a similar role. The court found that the defendants "associated and coordinated with other supporters of [al-Shabaab], including Codefendant Mohamed . . . and Codefendant Abdullahi." "All of these other individuals," it found, "were actively involved in arranging for and facilitating support for [al-Shabaab]." Finally, the court found that neither Mohamed nor Abdullahi was involved with or was using the money for any entity other than al-Shabaab and that the defendants knew this.

In short, the defendants engaged, over a lengthy period of time, in collecting monies for the purpose of providing material support to al-Shabaab, which they knew was a terrorist group engaged in military activities, and then in sending those monies to individuals they knew were associated with al-Shabaab and involved in providing it with various resources and support. That conduct constitutes the provision of or at least the attempt to provide material support to al-Shabaab in the form of money. And these facts, which the defendants do not challenge on appeal, amply satisfy each of the elements for a conviction under § 2339B. Thus, while we do not subscribe to the analysis conducted by the district court in response to the defendants' position that the court had to find the co-conspirators to be *part of* the subject terrorist organization, we conclude that the court appropriately found both defendants guilty of violating § 2339B. We therefore affirm.

NOTES AND QUESTIONS

1. The material support statute punishes providing material support or resources, directly or indirectly, to an FTO. In the traditional case, if the defendant knowingly provides material support to an FTO, knowing that the organization engages in acts of terrorism, such conduct violates the statute. This is an example of directly providing material support to an FTO. However, in *Dhirane* the court held that § 2339B does not require that the recipients of the material support be *part of* an FTO, nor does it require that the defendants themselves be *part of* the organization. Thus, if a person donates money to an organization associated with an FTO and that organization subsequently transfers the funds to the FTO, he or she could be convicted of violating the material support statute. This would constitute the indirect provision of material support to an FTO. Moreover, even if the government cannot trace the funds from the intermediary recipient to the FTO, the defendant would be liable of attempt to provide material support to an FTO. However, it appears that in the indirect provision of material support context the defendant must have the intent to benefit an FTO. For example, if a person provides monetary support to a charity associated with an FTO and the charity transfers the funds to an FTO, in

the absence of specific intent to benefit the FTO, would the defendant donor be liable under the material support statute? On the other hand, if the donor had "reason to believe" that the charity would use the funds to benefit the FTO, or intended the charity to do so, would the donor violate the material support statute?

2. The *Dhirane* case highlights the scope and breadth of the material support statute. Even if a monetary donation given to an organization associated with an FTO never reached the FTO, the defendant could be convicted of attempt to provide material support to an FTO. However, to support a conviction under an attempt theory, the government would have to prove that the defendant acted with the intent to violate the material support statute and his actions satisfied the dangerous close proximity test or constituted a "substantial step" strongly corroborative of the actor's criminal purpose under the Model Penal Code. *See* MPC § 5.01(1)(c) and (2).

3. The agreement to collect and provide money to an FTO could support a charge of conspiracy to violate the material support statute. Furthermore, under the *Pinkerton* doctrine the members of the conspiracy could be vicariously liable for any substantive transfer of funds to an FTO, assuming the money was transferred by a member of the conspiracy and during the conspiracy. *Pinkerton v. United States*, 328 U.S. 640 (1946). Since the object of the conspiracy was to provide financial support to an FTO, the transfer of funds would also be reasonably foreseeable and in furtherance of the conspiracy, satisfying the other *Pinkerton* requirements. *Id.*

4. While § 2339B penalizes the provision of *material* support or resources to an FTO, the term "material" is not synonymous with "substantial" or "significant." In other words, the provision of even *de minimis* support to an FTO could sustain a violation of the statute. For example, in *Dhirane* the defendants were collecting monthly donations ranging from $50 to $200. Even a $50 donation to al-Shabaab, a designated FTO, is a violation of the material support statute if committed with the requisite scienter.

United States v. Mehanna
735 F.3d 32 (1st Cir. 2013)

Terrorism is the modern-day equivalent of the bubonic plague: it is an existential threat. Predictably, then, the government's efforts to combat terrorism through the enforcement of the criminal laws will be fierce. Sometimes, those efforts require a court to patrol the fine line between vital national security concerns and forbidden encroachments on constitutionally protected freedoms of speech and association. This is such a case. . . .

I. OVERVIEW

This appeal has its genesis in an indictment returned by a federal grand jury sitting in the District of Massachusetts. In its final form, the indictment charged the defendant with four terrorism-related counts and three counts premised on allegedly false statements. The terrorism-related counts included one count of conspiracy to provide material support to al-Qa'ida (count 1); one count of conspiracy to provide material support to terrorists knowing or intending its use to be in violation of 18 U.S.C. §§ 956 and 2332 (count 2); one count of providing and attempting to provide material support to terrorists, knowing and intending its use to be in violation of 18 U.S.C. §§ 956 and 2332 (count 3); and one count of conspiracy to kill persons in a foreign country (count 4). The remaining counts included one count of conspiracy to make false statements as part of a conspiracy to commit an offense against the United States (count 5) and two counts of knowingly and willfully making false statements to federal officers (counts 6 and 7). *See* 18 U.S.C. §§ 371, 1001. . . .

Counts 1 through 3 (the conspiracy and material support charges) were based on two separate clusters of activities. The first cluster centered on the defendant's travel to Yemen. We briefly describe that trip.

In 2004, the defendant, an American citizen, was 21 years old and living with his parents in Sudbury, Massachusetts. On February 1, he flew from Boston to the United Arab Emirates with his associates, Kareem Abuzahra and Ahmad Abousamra. Abuzahra returned to the United States soon thereafter but the defendant and Abousamra continued on to Yemen in search of a terrorist training camp. They remained there for a week but were unable to locate a camp. The defendant then returned home, while Abousamra eventually reached Iraq.

The second cluster of activities was translation-centric. In 2005, the defendant began to translate Arab-language materials into English and post his translations on a website — at-Tibyan — that comprised an online community for those sympathetic to al-Qa'ida and Salafi-Jihadi perspectives. Website members shared opinions, videos, texts, and kindred materials in online forums. At least some offerings that the defendant translated constituted al-Qa'ida-generated media and materials supportive of al-Qa'ida and/or jihad. . . .

The district court refused to grant judgment of acquittal on any of the seven counts. The jury convicted the defendant on all of them, and the district court imposed a 210-month term of immurement. . . .

III. THE TERRORISM-RELATED COUNTS

. . .

A. SUFFICIENCY OF THE EVIDENCE

. . . To put the defendant's sufficiency challenge into a workable perspective, it is helpful to trace the anatomy of the four terrorism charges. Count 1 charges the defendant with conspiring to violate 18 U.S.C. § 2339B, which proscribes "knowingly provid[ing] material support or resources to a foreign terrorist organization." *Id.* § 2339B(a)(1). To satisfy the intent requirement of section 2339B, a defendant must have "knowledge about the organization's connection to terrorism." *Holder v. Humanitarian Law Project* (*HLP*), 561 U.S. 1, 16-17 (2010). A specific intent to advance the organization's terrorist activities is not essential. . . .

In this case, the defendant does not dispute that al-Qa'ida was and is a foreign terrorist organization (FTO). Nor could he credibly do so. *See* Redesignation of Foreign Terrorist Organizations, 68 Fed. Reg. 56,860, 56,862 (Oct. 2, 2003). . . . By like token, the record leaves no doubt that the defendant was aware of al-Qa'ida's status.

Count 2 charges the defendant with conspiring to violate 18 U.S.C. § 2339A, which proscribes "provid[ing] material support or resources . . . , knowing or intending that they are to be used in preparation for, or in carrying out," certain other criminal activities. *Id.* § 2339A(a). The intent requirement under section 2339A differs somewhat from the intent requirement under section 2339B: to be guilty under section 2339A, the defendant must have "provide[d] support or resources *with the knowledge or intent* that such resources be used to commit specific violent crimes." *United States v. Stewart*, 590 F.3d 93, 113 (2d Cir. 2009) (emphasis in original). Thus, "the mental state in section 2339A extends both to the support itself, and to the underlying purposes for which the support is given." *Id.* at 113 n.18. As adapted to the circumstances of this case, the government had to prove that the defendant had the specific intent to provide material support, knowing or intending that it would be used in a conspiracy to kill persons abroad. *See* 18 U.S.C. §§ 956, 2332.

Count 3 is closely related to count 2. It charges the defendant with violating, or attempting to violate, 18 U.S.C. § 2339A. The district court instructed the jury that it could find the defendant guilty on count 3 under theories of direct liability, attempt, aiding and abetting, or agency. Because the parties' arguments on appeal target the attempt theory, we focus our attention there.

Material support is defined identically for purposes of sections 2339A and 2339B. Such support may take various forms, including (as arguably pertinent here) the provision of "service[s]" or "personnel." 18 U.S.C. §§ 2339A(b)(1), 2339B(g)(4). With respect to the Yemen trip, the government accused the defendant of conspiring to provide himself as an al-Qa'ida recruit (count 1); knowing or intending the use of this material support in a conspiracy to kill persons abroad (count 2); and attempting to provide this support, knowing or intending that it would be used in such a conspiracy (count 3). . . .

We turn next to the government's proof. In gauging the sufficiency of that proof, we start with the Yemen trip and the cluster of activities surrounding it.

The defendant asserts that this trip cannot bear the weight of his convictions on any of the four terrorism-related counts because the record shows nothing more than that he went to Yemen to pursue Islamic studies. The government counters that the evidence reflects a far more sinister purpose. The salient question — at least with respect to the first three terrorism-related counts — is whether the record, viewed in the light most agreeable to the verdict, supports a finding that the defendant conspired to provide or attempted to provide himself and others as recruits (and, thus, as material support) for al-Qa'ida's terrorist aims.

The government's evidence of the defendant's specific intent with respect to his Yemen trip included his own actions, discussions with others, coconspirator statements, and materials that the defendant either kept on his computer or shared on the Internet. The defendant contends that this evidence, in the aggregate, showed nothing more than his participation in activities protected by the First Amendment (e.g., discussing politics and religion, consuming media related to those topics, and associating with certain individuals and groups) and, thus, could not support a finding of guilt. . . . But the defendant is looking at the evidence through rose-colored glasses. We think it virtually unarguable that rational jurors could find that the defendant and his associates went abroad to enlist in a terrorist training camp.

On this point, the defendant's own statements are highly probative. His coconspirators testified that the defendant persistently stated his belief that engaging in jihad was "a duty upon a Muslim if he's capable of performing it," and that this duty included committing violence. The evidence further showed that, following United States intervention in Iraq, the defendant concluded "that America was at war with Islam," and saw American "soldiers as being valid targets."

Acting upon these views, the defendant and his associates—as early as 2001—discussed seeking out a terrorist training camp. Following these discussions, the defendant expressed interest in receiving military-type training in order to participate in jihad. The defendant made clear that he wished to engage in jihad if he "ever had the chance" and that he and his associates "would make a way to go." Together, they "discussed the different ways people could get into Iraq, the different training camps. . . ."

Coconspirator testimony shined a bright light on the defendant's intent. This testimony made pellucid that the defendant and his comrades traveled to Yemen "for the purpose of finding a terrorist training camp" and "[e]ventually . . . get[ting] into Iraq." The defendant's particular interest in Iraq was because it was "an area that was being attacked." He took the position that "there was an obligation for Muslims to stand up and fight against invasion of Iraq and the U.S. forces in Iraq."

The defendant attempts to characterize these remarks as mere political speech. The jury, however, was entitled to draw a different inference: that the defendant's comments were evidence of the formation and implementation of a scheme to go abroad, obtain training, join with al-Qa'ida, and wage war against American soldiers fighting in Iraq. . . .

We note that the defendant and his associates purchased round-trip airline tickets. In the travelers' own words, however, the return portions were for use "[i]f things didn't work out," as well as to avoid raising the sort of suspicion often associated with one-way ticketing. And Abuzahra testified at trial that, notwithstanding the return ticket, he did not expect to return to the United States because "[t]he purpose of . . . going was to basically fight in a war. . . ."

There was more. The evidence showed that the defendant and his associates had a plan of action for their arrival in Yemen. Abousamra had obtained the name of a contact there "who was going to get them to a military training camp." When the men traveled to Yemen, they carried a piece of paper that contained the contact's name.

To be sure, the Yemen trip did not bear fruit. Once there, the defendant learned to his evident dismay that training camps no longer existed in the area and "that it was nearly impossible for anybody to get any training" there. The contact in Yemen fizzled, telling the defendant and Abousamra that "all that stuff is gone ever since the planes hit the twin towers." It is consistent with the government's theory of the case, however, that the defendant, when confronted with this news, expressed disappointment that he had "left [his] life behind" based on faulty information.

The government's case is strengthened by evidence that the defendant and his associates engaged in a cover up that continued long after the defendant's return from Yemen. The record reflects that the defendant and his associates repeatedly discussed how to align their stories and mislead federal investigators (in point of fact, they formulated cover stories for their Yemen trip even before the trip began). To facilitate the cover up, the defendant and his cohorts attempted to obscure their communications by using code words such as "peanut butter," "peanut butter and jelly," or "PB & J" for jihad and "culinary school" for terrorist training. Relatedly, the defendant encouraged an associate to install an "encryptor" on his computer in order to make it "much harder for [the FBI] to" monitor their online communications. . . .

The defendant's communication with his "best friend," Daniel Maldonado, further evinced his determination to engage in jihad. In December of 2006, Maldonado telephoned the defendant from Somalia. During this call, the two discussed the logistics needed for the defendant to join Maldonado in Somalia, including transportation and travel documents. Maldonado said that he was "in a culinary school" and "mak[ing] peanut butter and jelly." Maldonado testified that this was code language, familiar to the defendant, denoting that Maldonado was in a terrorist training camp and engaged in jihad.

Percipient witnesses testified that the defendant watched jihadi videos with his associates for the purpose of "gain[ing] inspiration from the[m]" and "becom[ing] like a mujahid." These videos depicted events such as Marines being killed by explosives, suicide bombings, and combat scenes glorifying the mujahideen. The defendant was "jubilant" while watching them.

In a similar vein, the record is shot through with evidence of the defendant's rabid support for al-Qa'ida, his "love" for Osama bin Laden, his admiration of the September 11 hijackers, and his conviction that the September 11 attacks were justified and a "happy" occasion. . . .

The evidence we have summarized sufficed to ground a finding, beyond a reasonable doubt, that the defendant traveled to Yemen with the specific intent of providing material support to al-Qa'ida, knowing or intending that this support would be used in a conspiracy to kill persons abroad. It likewise sufficed to ground a finding that the defendant attempted to provide such material support, knowing or intending that it would be used in a conspiracy to kill persons abroad. Finally, it sufficed to ground a finding that the defendant, while in the United States, conspired with others in a plan to kill persons abroad. The evidence was, therefore, ample to convict on the four terrorism-related counts.

B. The Defendant's Rejoinders

Despite the obvious logic of the government's position and the wealth of evidence that supports it, the defendant labors to undermine the four terrorism-related convictions. His efforts take two different directions—one a frontal assault and the other an end run. We address each in turn.

1. *Scholarly Pursuits.* The defendant argues that the only reasonable interpretation of his Yemen trip and the activities surrounding it is an innocent one: he sojourned to Yemen solely for the purpose of studying there. He describes himself as a devoted scholar of Islam and asserts that he visited Yemen, specifically, because the purest form of Arabic is spoken there. In support, he reminds us that he toured a school while in the country. . . .

We readily agree that the record contains some evidence supporting the defendant's alternative narrative. Yet, that evidence does not eclipse the plethora of proof pointing in the opposite direction. When all was said and done, the jury heard and rejected the defendant's innocent explanation of the events that occurred. It was plainly entitled to do so.

To gain a conviction, the government need not "eliminat[e] every possible theory consistent with the defendant's innocence." *United States v. Noah*, 130 F.3d 490, 494 (1st Cir. 1997). It is the jury's role—not that of the Court of Appeals—to choose between conflicting hypotheses, especially when such choices depend on the drawing of inferences and elusive concepts such as motive and intent. *See id.*

2. *The Alternative Theory of Guilt.* The defendant's second rejoinder represents an attempt to change the trajectory of the debate. He points out that the indictment identifies his translations as culpable activity; that the government introduced copious evidence in support of a theory of guilt based on the translations; that it argued this theory to the jury; and that the jury returned a general verdict. Building on this platform, he argues that even if the evidence of the Yemen trip is sufficient to ground his terrorism-related convictions, those convictions cannot stand because they may have been predicated on protected First Amendment speech. . . .

When it comes to the argument that the defendant makes here—that one of two possible grounds for the general verdict is suspect—the classification of the specific error makes all the difference. If "a mistake about the law" underlies the argument, reversal may be necessary. *Griffin v. United States*, 502 U.S. 46, 59 (1991); *see Yates v. United States*, 354 U.S. 298, 312 (1957); *Stromberg v. California*, 283 U.S. 359, 367-68 (1931). Such a "legal error" occurs, for instance, when "jurors have been left the option of relying upon a legally inadequate theory" by the trial court's charge. *Griffin*, 502 U.S. at 59. If, however, "a mistake concerning the weight or the factual import of the evidence" underlies the argument, the verdict must be upheld as long as the evidence is adequate to support one of the government's alternative theories of guilt. *Id.*

With this short primer in place, we turn to the defendant's asseveration that the district court committed legal error in charging the jury with respect to his translations. At first blush, this asseveration is counter-intuitive because the court below evinced a keen awareness of the First Amendment issues implicated here. Pertinently, the court instructed:

> Now, this is important. Persons who act independently of a foreign terrorist organization to advance its goals or objectives are not considered to be working under the organization's direction or control. A person cannot be convicted under this statute when he's acting entirely independently of a foreign terrorist organization. That is true even if the person is advancing the organization's goals or objectives. Rather, for a person to be guilty under this count, a person must be acting in coordination with or at the direction of a designated foreign terrorist organization, here, as alleged in Count 1, al Qa'ida.
>
> You need not worry about the scope or effect of the guarantee of free speech contained in the First Amendment to our Constitution. According to the Supreme Court, this statute already accommodates that guarantee by punishing only conduct that is done in coordination with or at the direction of a foreign terrorist organization. Advocacy that is done independently of the terrorist organization and not at its direction or in coordination with it does not violate the statute.
>
> Put another way, activity that is proven to be the furnishing of material support or resources to a designated foreign terrorist organization under the statute is not activity that is protected by the First Amendment; on the other hand, as I've said, independent advocacy on behalf of the organization, not done at its direction or in coordination with it, is not a violation of the statute.

The defendant assigns error to these instructions in three respects. He says that they (i) fail to define the term "coordination"; (ii) incorrectly direct the jury not to consider the First Amendment; and (iii) should have been replaced by a set of instructions that he unsuccessfully proffered to the district court. . . .

Although we agree that coordination can be a critical integer in the calculus of material support, the defendant's first assignment of instructional error is simply wrong. While the district court did not use the phrase "is defined as," it nonetheless defined the term "coordination" functionally. It explained to the jury in no fewer than three different ways that independent advocacy for either an FTO or an FTO's goals does not amount to coordination. This distinction, which the court accurately characterized as "important," went to the heart of the matter.

Moreover, the district court's instructions harmonize with the text of the material support statute, which reads: "Individuals who act entirely independently of the [FTO] to advance its goals or objectives shall not be considered to be working under the [FTO]'s direction and control." 18 U.S.C. § 2339B(h). The context made clear that the government's "translations-as-material-support" theory was premised on the concept that the translations comprised a "service," which is a form of material support within the purview of the statute. *See id.* §§ 2339A(b)(1), 2339B(g)(4). The *HLP* Court explained that "service," as material support, "refers to concerted activity, not independent advocacy." 130 S. Ct. at 2721. The instructions given to the jury embraced this construct.

In sum, the district court's instructions captured the essence of the controlling decision in *HLP*, where the Court determined that otherwise-protected speech rises to the level of criminal material support only if it is "in coordination with foreign groups that the speaker knows to be terrorist organizations." *Id.* at 2723. If speech fits within this taxonomy, it is not protected. *See id.* at 2722-26. This means that "advocacy performed in coordination with, or at the direction of," an FTO is not shielded by the First Amendment. *Id.* at 2722. The district court's instructions tracked the contours of this legal framework. The court appropriately treated the question of whether enough coordination existed to criminalize the defendant's translations as factbound and left that question to the jury. . . . We discern no error.

The second assignment of instructional error is no more robust. The defendant contends that the court below erroneously foreclosed his argument that his activities were constitutionally protected by telling the jury: "You need not worry about the scope or effect of the guarantee of free speech contained in the First Amendment to our Constitution."

This contention is futile. The very next sentence of the instructions makes the district court's purpose pellucid: "According to the Supreme Court, this statute already accommodates that guarantee by punishing only conduct that is done in coordination with or at the direction of a foreign terrorist organization." The instructions, read in context, did not tell the jury to blind itself to the protections of the First Amendment. Instead, they appropriately advised the jury that the material support statute, as well as the instructions the district court gave regarding that statute, already accounted for those protections. . . .

The defendant's third assignment of instructional error calumnizes the district court for failing to give his proffered instructions on the interaction of the material support statutes and the prophylaxis afforded by the First Amendment. We will reverse a trial court's refusal to give a proffered jury instruction only if the proffered instruction is substantively correct, not otherwise covered in substance in the court's charge, and of sufficient import that its omission seriously affects the defendant's ability to present his defense.

In the case at hand, the defendant's proffered instructions were not substantively correct but, rather, contained legally flawed propositions. There is nothing to be gained by citing book and verse. A single illustration suffices.

The proffered instruction stated: "the person [providing the alleged support] must have a direct connection to the group [FTO] and be working directly with the group [FTO] for it to be a violation of the statute." Contrary to the tenor of this statement, a direct link is neither required by statute nor mandated by *HLP.* . . .

The proffered instructions stated: "[m]ere association with terrorists or a terrorist organization is not sufficient to meet the element of 'in coordination with.'" What the district court told the jury is perfectly consistent with this language. That ends the matter: a defendant has a right to an instruction on his theory of the case, but he has no right to insist that the trial court parrot his preferred wording. *See, e.g., United States v. DeStefano*, 59 F.3d 1, 2-3 (1st Cir. 1995); *McGill*, 953 F.2d at 12.

The bottom line is that the defendant's assault on the district court's jury instructions is without merit. And, having eliminated the defendant's claims of legal error, we are left only with his claim that the jury's finding of "coordination" lacked sufficient supporting evidence.

As noted above, that inquiry is foreclosed by *Griffin*. We already have determined that the cluster of activities surrounding the defendant's Yemen trip supplied an independently sufficient evidentiary predicate for the convictions on the terrorism-related counts. The defendant's translation-related activities were tendered to the jury only as an alternative basis for those convictions. Even if that proof is factually insufficient, *Griffin* dictates that we affirm based on the government's Yemen theory.

It makes no difference that the absence of facts showing coordination with al-Qa'ida might have resulted in constitutionally protected conduct. The dividing line that the Supreme Court drew in *Griffin* was based on the distinct roles of judge and jury in our system of justice, not the presence vel non of constitutional issues. We entrust trial judges with the grave responsibility of giving juries a proper view of the law, and when they fail to do so, reversal may be warranted because "there is no reason to think that [jurors'] own intelligence and expertise will save them from that error." *Griffin*, 502 U.S. at 59. . . .

That brings down the final curtain. We have found the defendant's claims of legal error with respect to his translation activities wanting, and we have no occasion to examine the factual sufficiency of those activities as a basis for his terrorism-related convictions. Even if the government's translation-as-material-support theory were factually insufficient, we would not reverse: the defendant's convictions on the affected counts are independently supported by the mass of evidence surrounding the Yemen trip and, under *Griffin*, we need go no further. . . .

Affirmed.

NOTES AND QUESTIONS

1. The court states that the intent requirement under § 2339A differs from the scienter requirement under § 2339B. To be guilty under § 2339A, the defendant must provide "material support or resources" with what mens rea? What is the mens rea required to support a conviction under § 2339B? Is it easier to convict a defendant under § 2339A or § 2339B?

2. The term "material support or resources" is defined identically for purposes of §§ 2339A and 2339B and includes many different forms of prohibited support and assistance. What forms of material support did Mehanna purportedly provide al Qaeda?

3. Section 2339B is broad in scope. Under the statute, a defendant may be guilty under theories of direct liability, attempt, aiding and abetting, and conspiracy. *See* 18 U.S.C. § 2339B. In *Mehanna*, the district court instructed the jury that it could find the defendant guilty under what theories of liability?

4. The government maintained that Mehanna's trip to Yemen constituted an attempt to provide *personnel* to al Qaeda. Section 2339B(h) provides:

> No person may be prosecuted under this section in connection with the term "personnel" unless that person has knowingly provided, attempted to provide, or conspired to provide a foreign terrorist organization with 1 or more individuals (who may include himself) to work under that terrorist organization's direction or control. . . . Individuals who act entirely independently of the foreign terrorist organization to advance its goals or objectives shall not be considered to be working under the foreign terrorist direction and control.

The statute makes clear that "personnel" does not cover independent advocacy. Do the facts in *Mehanna* support a violation of the material support statute under a theory of personnel?

5. Did Mehanna's translation of documents and materials supportive of al Qaeda and jihad constitute a violation of the material support statutes? What form of material support did the translation-related activities constitute?

6. Do the translation activities of Mehanna involve protected free speech under the First Amendment? Was Mehanna acting independently of a foreign terrorist organization when he performed the translation activities? Was Mehanna acting "in coordination" with al Qaeda? What level of "coordination" is required to support a conviction under the material support statute?

7. The district court gave the jury the following instruction: "A person cannot be convicted under this statute when he's acting entirely independently of a foreign terrorist organization. That is true even if the person is advancing the organization's goals or objectives." However, if the defendant acts entirely independently of a foreign terrorist organization but acts with the intent to advance the organization's goals and objectives, could he be convicted under a theory of aiding and abetting acts of terrorism?

8. Mehanna traveled to Yemen "for the purpose of finding a terrorist training camp." Had the defendant been successful and received military-type training from al Qaeda, he would have violated 18 U.S.C. § 2339D. Section 2339D punishes receiving military-type training from any organization designated by the Secretary of State as a foreign terrorist organization. To violate the statute, the defendant must have knowledge that the organization is a designated foreign terrorist organization or has engaged or engages in terrorist activity. *Id.* Upon conviction, a defendant may be sentenced to a term of imprisonment for ten years.

c. Attempt to Provide Material Support to a Foreign Terrorist Organization

United States v. Farhane
34 F.3d 127 (2d Cir. 2011)

REENA RAGGI, Circuit Judge:

Defendant Rafiq Sabir, whose birth name is Rene Wright, is a United States citizen and licensed physician who, in May 2005, swore an oath of allegiance to al Qaeda and promised to be on call to treat wounded members of that terrorist organization in Saudi Arabia. Convicted after a jury trial in the United States District Court for the Southern District of New York . . . of conspiring to provide and actually providing or attempting to provide material support to a terrorist organization in violation of 18 U.S.C. § 2339B, and sentenced to a 300-month term of incarceration, Sabir now challenges his conviction on various grounds. . . .

A. 2001: THE INITIAL FBI INVESTIGATION INTO CO-DEFENDANT TARIK SHAH

Defendant Rafiq Sabir is a New York licensed physician, trained at Columbia University, who specializes in emergency medicine. In 2001, the Federal Bureau of Investigation began investigating Sabir's longtime friend Tarik Shah for the possible transfer of money to insurgents in Afghanistan. As part of that investigation, an FBI confidential informant known as "Saeed" cultivated a relationship with Shah, in the course of which Shah was recorded speaking openly about his commitment to *jihad* (holy war) in order to establish *Sharia* (Islamic law) and about his wish to provide "deadly and dangerous" martial arts training to *mujahideen* (*jihad* warriors). During these conversations, Shah repeatedly identified Sabir as his "partner."

B. 2004: SHAH OFFERS TO SUPPORT AL QAEDA

On March 3, 2004, Saeed and Shah traveled to Plattsburgh, New York, where Saeed introduced Shah to Ali Soufan, an undercover FBI agent posing as a recruiter for al Qaeda. In a series of recorded meetings with Agent Soufan, Shah detailed his martial arts expertise and offered to travel abroad to train al Qaeda combatants. Shah also told Soufan about Sabir, "an emergency room doctor" who had been his "trusted friend[ ]" for more than 25 years. Explaining that he knew Sabir's "heart," Shah proposed that the two men join al Qaeda as "a pair, me and a doctor." At a subsequent meeting with Saeed, Shah reported that he had spoken in person with Sabir about this plan. . . .

C. 2005: SHAH AND SABIR SWEAR ALLEGIANCE TO AL QAEDA AND ATTEMPT TO PROVIDE MATERIAL SUPPORT

For most of the time between May 2004 and May 2005, Sabir was out of the United States, working at a Saudi military hospital in Riyadh. On May 20,

2005, during a visit to New York, Sabir met with Saeed and Agent Soufan at Shah's Bronx apartment. Sabir told Soufan that he would soon be returning to Riyadh. He expressed interest in meeting with *mujahideen* operating in Saudi Arabia and agreed to provide medical assistance to any who were wounded. He suggested that he was ideally situated to provide such assistance because he would have a car in Riyadh and "carte blanche" to move freely about the city.

To ensure that Shah and Sabir were, in fact, knowingly proffering support for terrorism, Soufan stated that the purpose of "our war, . . . our *jihad*" is to "[e]xpel the infidels from the Arabian peninsula," and he repeatedly identified "Sheikh Osama" (in context a clear reference to Osama bin Laden) as the leader of that effort. Shah quickly agreed to the need for war to "[e]xpel the Jews and the Christians from the Arabian Peninsula," while Sabir observed that those fighting such a war were "striving in the way of Allah" and "most deserving" of his help.

To permit *mujahideen* needing medical assistance to contact him in Riyadh, Sabir provided Soufan with his personal and work telephone numbers. When Shah and Soufan noted that writing down this contact information might create a security risk, Sabir encoded the numbers using a code provided by Soufan.

Sabir and Shah then participated in *bayat*, a ritual in which each swore an oath of allegiance to al Qaeda, promising to serve as a "soldier of Islam" and to protect "brothers on the path of *Jihad*" and "the path of al Qaeda." The men further swore obedience to "the guardians of the pledge," whom Soufan expressly identified as "Sheikh Osama," *i.e.*, Osama bin Laden, and his second in command, "Doctor Ayman Zawahiri."

D. Prosecution and Conviction

Shah and Sabir were arrested on May 28, 2005, and thereafter indicted in the Southern District of New York on charges that between October 2003 and May 2005, they (1) conspired to provide material support or resources to the terrorist organization al Qaeda, *see* 18 U.S.C. § 2339B; and (2) provided or attempted to provide such support, *see id.* §§ 2339B, 2. . . . The two counts used identical language to describe three types of material support that defendants provided, attempted to provide, or conspired to provide:

> (i) one or more individuals (including themselves) to work under al Qaeda's direction and control and to organize, manage, supervise, and otherwise direct the operation of al Qaeda, (ii) instruction and teaching designed to impart a special skill to further the illegal objectives of al Qaeda, and (iii) advice and assistance derived from scientific, technical and other specialized knowledge to further the illegal objectives of al Qaeda.

The two counts further alleged that Shah would provide "martial arts training and instruction for jihadists," while Sabir would provide "medical support to wounded jihadists," both defendants "knowing that al Qaeda had engaged and engages in terrorist activity" and "terrorism."

After Shah pleaded guilty on April 4, 2007, to Count One of the indictment, trial against Sabir commenced on April 24. On May 21, 2007, the jury found

Sabir guilty on both the conspiratorial and substantive charges against him, and, on November 28, 2007, the district court sentenced him principally to 300 months' incarceration. This appeal followed.

II. DISCUSSION

1. The Statutory Framework

... Title 18 U.S.C. § 2339B(a)(1) imposes criminal liability on anyone who "knowingly provides material support or resources to a foreign terrorist organization, or attempts or conspires to do so." The statute expressly conditions liability on a person having knowledge that the relevant organization is a "designated terrorist organization" or "has engaged or engages in terrorist activity" or "terrorism" consistent with various specified provisions of law. 18 U.S.C. § 2339B(a)(1); *see Holder v. Humanitarian Law Project*, 130 S. Ct. 2705, 2709 (2010) (holding that "knowledge about the organization's connection to terrorism, not specific intent to further the organization's terrorist activities," is mental state required to prove violation of § 2339B).

In identifying the "material support or resources" whose provision to a designated terrorist organization is proscribed, § 2339B references the definition of that term "in section 2339A (including the definitions of 'training' and 'expert advice or assistance' in that section)." *Id.* § 2339B(g)(4). Section 2339A states, in pertinent part:

> (1) the term "material support or resources" means any property, tangible or intangible, or service, including currency or monetary instruments or financial securities, financial services, lodging, training, expert advice or assistance, safehouses, false documentation or identification, communications equipment, facilities, weapons, lethal substances, explosives, personnel (1 or more individuals who may be or include oneself), and transportation, except medicine or religious materials;
> (2) the term "training" means instruction or teaching designed to impart a specific skill, as opposed to general knowledge; and
> (3) the term "expert advice or assistance" means advice or assistance derived from scientific, technical or other specialized knowledge.

Id. § 2339A(b).

With respect to the provision of "personnel," § 2339B limits liability to persons who have "knowingly provided, attempted to provide, or conspired to provide a foreign terrorist organization with 1 or more individuals (who may be or include himself) to work under that terrorist organization's direction or control or to organize, manage, supervise, or otherwise direct the operation of that organization." *Id.* § 2339B(h). The statute states that "[i]ndividuals who act entirely independently of the foreign terrorist organization to advance its goals or objectives shall not be considered to be working under the foreign terrorist organization's direction and control." *Id.*

...

B. The Trial Evidence Was Sufficient to Support Sabir's Conviction

Sabir contends that the evidence was insufficient to support his conviction. . . . A defendant raising a sufficiency challenge bears a heavy burden because a reviewing court must consider the totality of the evidence in the light most favorable to the prosecution and uphold the conviction if "*any* rational trier of fact could have found the essential elements of the crime beyond a reasonable doubt." *Jackson v. Virginia*, 443 U.S. 307, 319 (1979) (emphasis in original). . . . Applying these principles to Sabir's case, we reject his sufficiency challenge as without merit.

. . .

4. Count Two: Attempt

Equally meritless is Sabir's argument that the evidence was insufficient to support his conviction for attempting to provide material support to a known foreign terrorist organization. A conviction for attempt requires proof that a defendant (a) had the intent to commit the object crime and (b) engaged in conduct amounting to a substantial step towards its commission. *See, e.g., United States v. Yousef*, 327 F.3d 56, 134 (2d Cir. 2003).

a. Intent

Sabir does not challenge the sufficiency of the evidence establishing his intent to provide material support to a foreign terrorist organization. Nor could he. In addition to Sabir's statements already quoted in this opinion . . . which constitute powerful evidence of the requisite intent, the following transcript excerpts from the May 20, 1995 meeting further support this element.

After Sabir advised that his work in a Riyadh military hospital would put him in Saudi Arabia for two years, Agent Soufan stated that Sabir could help al Qaeda "[a]s a doctor . . . as a Mujahid." GX 906T at 19. Sabir not only signaled assent, he emphasized a need to "feel sure within myself that if I make a certain move, that move is going to be effective." *Id.* To provide that assurance, Agent Soufan clarified how a doctor could be helpful to al Qaeda's pursuit of *jihad*. He stated that Osama bin Laden himself had told Soufan that "we need doctors if they are trusted." *Id.* at 32. Soufan explained that "brothers" sometimes get "hurt with a bullet" during "training" and in "operation[s]." *Id.* at 48-49. Because they cannot "go to a hospital," the organization needs "doctor brothers . . . to protect them . . . [to] keep the other brothers healthy." *Id.* at 49. Sabir readily agreed to provide that support, stating, "Let me give you another number," whereupon he supplied his personal mobile telephone number, which, with Soufan's assistance, he rendered into code. *Id.* at 48-50. Sabir understood that the purpose of the code was to conceal the fact that he was working for al Qaeda. . . . He also understood that the coded number would be provided to a trusted al Qaeda operative, who would identify himself as "Mus'ab" when contacting Sabir on behalf of a wounded jihadist. Sabir responded to this information, "*God willing.*" *Id.* at 87.

Still later in the conversation, when Agent Soufan emphasized to Sabir that he could decline to treat *mujahideen* if he was not committed to al Qaeda's goals, Sabir made plain that he had no reservations about using his medical expertise to support al Qaeda: "I will [do what]ever I can do for the sake of God. . . . This is my job . . . the best I can do is to benefit those people . . . who are striving in the way of Allah. . . . [T]hese are the ones that are most deserving of the help." *Id.* at 66. When Soufan further stated that it was difficult to take *mujahideen* to a hospital for treatment, Sabir emphasized that his military identification allowed him to travel freely around Saudi Arabia, thereby suggesting that he could go to the injured person. . . .

With evidence of his intent thus clearly established, Sabir focuses his sufficiency challenge on the "substantial step" element of attempt.

b. Substantial Step

(1) The "Substantial Step" Requirement Expands Attempt Beyond the Common Law

The "substantial step" requirement for attempt derives from the American Law Institute's Model Penal Code, which in the early 1960s sought to "widen the ambit of attempt liability." *United States v. Ivic*, 700 F.2d 51, 66 (2d Cir. 1983) (Friendly, J.) (citing Model Penal Code § 5.01(1)(c) (Proposed Official Draft 1962)), *overruled on other grounds by National Org. for Women, Inc. v. Scheidler*, 510 U.S. 249, 254-55, 262 (1994). Previously, at common law, attempt had been limited to conduct close to the completion of the intended crime. . . . By requiring proof only of a "substantial step" in furtherance of the intended crime, the Model Code ushered in a broader view of attempt.

This court effectively adopted the Model Code's formulation of attempt in *United States v. Stallworth*, 543 F.2d 1038, 1040-41 (2d Cir. 1976). The *Stallworth* defendants were arrested when their planned armed robbery was "in progress" and "[a]ll that stood between [them] and success was a group of F.B.I. agents and police officers." *Id.* at 1041. As such evidence would have demonstrated attempt even under the common law, the significance of the case rests not on its facts but on the court's approving citation to the Model Code's identification of a range of conduct—not always proximate to the desired criminal end—that might nevertheless constitute a substantial step when "strongly corroborative of the firmness of the defendant's criminal intent." *Id.* at 1040 & n.5. . . . Thus, a "substantial step" must be "something more than mere preparation, yet may be less than the last act necessary before the actual commission of the substantive crime." *United States v. Manley*, 632 F.2d 978, 987 (2d Cir. 1980). It is conduct "'planned to culminate'" in the commission of the substantive crime being attempted. *United States v. Ivic*, 700 F.2d at 66 (quoting Model Penal Code § 5.01(c) (Proposed Official Draft 1962)).

(2) Identifying a Substantial Step by Reference to the Crime Being Attempted

While the parameters of the substantial step requirement are simply stated, they do not always provide bright lines for application. This is not surprising;

the identification of a substantial step, like the identification of attempt itself, is necessarily a matter "'of degree,'" *United States v. Coplon*, 185 F.2d 629, 633 (2d Cir. 1950) (L. Hand, J.) (quoting *Commonwealth v. Peaslee*, 177 Mass. at 272, 59 N.E. at 56), that can vary depending on "'the particular facts of each case'" viewed in light of the crime charged, *United States v. Ivic*, 700 F.2d at 66 (quoting *United States v. Manley*, 632 F.2d at 988). . . . An act that may constitute a substantial step towards the commission of one crime may not constitute such a step with respect to a different crime. . . . Thus, substantial-step analysis necessarily begins with a proper understanding of the crime being attempted.

For example, in *United States v. Delvecchio*, 816 F.2d 859 (2d Cir. 1987), a case frequently cited as illustrative of actions insufficient to demonstrate attempt, the substantive crime at issue was possession of a large quantity of heroin. We held that a substantial step to commit that crime was not established by proof that defendants had met with suppliers, agreed on terms, and provided their beeper numbers. Such evidence, at most, established a "verbal agreement," which, "without more, is insufficient as a matter of law to support an attempt[ed possession] conviction." *Id.* at 862. In so concluding, we noted that what was missing was any act to effect possession, such as acquisition, or attempted acquisition, of the purchase money, or travel to the agreed-on purchase site. *See id.*

The crime here at issue, however, is of a quite different sort. Sabir was charged with attempting to provide material support for terrorism. Whereas an attempt to possess focuses on a defendant's efforts to acquire, an attempt to provide focuses on his efforts to supply, a distinction that necessarily informs an assessment of what conduct will manifest a substantial step towards the charged objective. Thus, while an agreement to purchase drugs from a supplier is not a substantial step sufficient to convict for attempted *possession*, *see id.* at 862, such an agreement to acquire might constitute a substantial step when the crime at issue is attempted *distribution*, *see United States v. Rosa*, 11 F.3d 315, 340 (2d Cir. 1993). . . .

Further important to a substantial-step assessment is an understanding of the underlying conduct proscribed by the crime being attempted. The conduct here at issue, material support to a foreign terrorist organization, is different from drug trafficking and any number of activities (*e.g.*, murder, robbery, fraud) that are criminally proscribed because they are inherently harmful. The material support statute criminalizes a range of conduct that may not be harmful in itself but that may assist, even indirectly, organizations committed to pursuing acts of devastating harm. Thus, as the Supreme Court recently observed, the very focus of the material support statute is "preventative" in that it "criminalizes not terrorist attacks themselves, but aid that makes the attacks more likely to occur." *Holder v. Humanitarian Law Project*, 130 S. Ct. at 2728. Accordingly, while a substantial step to commit a robbery must be conduct planned clearly to culminate in that particular harm, a substantial step towards the provision of material support need not be planned to culminate in actual terrorist harm, but only in support—even benign support—for an organization committed to such harm. *See generally id.* at 2724 (discussing Congress's finding that designated foreign terrorist organizations "'are so tainted by their criminal conduct that *any contribution to such an organization* facilitates that conduct'" (quoting AEDPA § 301(a)(7), 110 Stat. at 1247) (emphasis in *Humanitarian Law Project*).)

(3) The Evidence Manifests a Substantial Step Towards the Provision of Material Support in the Form of Personnel

The indictment charged Sabir with attempting to supply al Qaeda with material support in three of the forms proscribed in 18 U.S.C. § 2339A(b)(1): "personnel, training, and expert advice and assistance." We conclude that the evidence was sufficient to support Sabir's conviction for attempting to provide material support in the form of personnel—specifically, himself—to work for al Qaeda as a doctor on-call to treat wounded jihadists in Saudi Arabia. *See United States v. McCourty*, 562 F.3d 458, 471 (2d Cir. 2009) (recognizing that when theories of liability are pleaded in conjunctive, defendant may be found guilty on proof of any one theory). . . . By coming to meet with a purported al Qaeda member on May 20, 1995; by swearing an oath of allegiance to al Qaeda; by promising to be on call in Saudi Arabia to treat wounded al Qaeda members; and by providing private and work contact numbers for al Qaeda members to reach him in Saudi Arabia whenever they needed treatment, Sabir engaged in conduct planned to culminate in his supplying al Qaeda with personnel, thereby satisfying the substantial step requirement.

(4) The Dissent's Mistaken View of the Substantial Step Requirement

(a) Sabir Did More Than Express a Radical Idea When He Produced Himself as a Doctor Sworn to Work Under the Direction of al Qaeda

In dissent, Chief Judge Dearie asserts that by upholding Sabir's attempt conviction on the record evidence, we approve punishing a defendant for radical thoughts rather than criminal deeds. We do no such thing. Sabir's words and actions on May 20, 1995, did more than manifest radical sympathies. . . . By attending the May 20, 2005 meeting and committing to work under al-Qaeda's direction and control as an on-call doctor, Sabir physically produced the very personnel to be provided as material support for the terrorist organization: himself. . . .

Viewed in this context, Sabir's oath of allegiance to al Qaeda evidenced more than "mere membership" in that terrorist organization. *Holder v. Humanitarian Law Project*, 130 S. Ct. at 2719 (holding that § 2339B does not criminalize "mere membership" in designated terrorist organization; it prohibits providing "material support" to that group). Sabir's purpose in swearing *bayat* was to formalize his promise to work as a doctor under the organization's direction and control. That is most certainly evidence of a crime: the charged crime of attempting to provide material support to terrorism in the form of personnel. *See* 18 U.S.C. § 2339B(h) (clarifying that what is proscribed is the provision of personnel "to work under" the "direction or control" of a terrorist organization). Further, by providing his contact numbers, Sabir took a step essential to provide al Qaeda with personnel in the form of an on-call doctor: he provided the means by which *mujahideen* in Riyadh could reach that doctor at any time, day or night, that they needed emergency treatment. From the totality of these facts, a reasonable jury could have concluded that on May 20, 2005, Sabir crossed the line from simply professing radical beliefs or joining a radical organization to attempting a crime, specifically, Sabir's provision of himself as personnel to work under the direction and control of al Qaeda.

> (b) The Provision of Personnel and the Subsequent Provision of Expert Services by Such Personnel Are Distinct Forms of Material Support

Chief Judge Dearie submits that the time and distance to be traveled by Sabir before he actually provided any medical treatment to al Qaeda warriors was too great to permit a jury to find that his actions constituted a substantial step towards commission of the charged crime. *See* Dissenting Op., *post* at [178, 179-80]. This mistakenly equates the provision of *personnel* to a terrorist organization with the subsequent provision of *services* by that personnel, a misapprehension that pervades the dissent and informs its conclusion that Sabir stands guilty "for an offense that he did not commit." *Id.* at [183]. While it may frequently be the case that a defendant who intends to provide a terrorist organization with personnel also intends for the personnel to provide the organization with services, § 2339A(b)(1) specifically recognizes "personnel" and "services" — particularly services in the form of "expert advice and assistance," such as medical treatment — as distinct types of material support. Thus, even if the provision (or attempted provision) of these two forms of material support may be simultaneous in some cases, it may not be in others. For that reason, evidence sufficient to demonstrate a substantial step towards the provision of personnel may not always be sufficient to demonstrate a substantial step towards the personnel's provision of services. Whether or not Sabir's May 20, 2005 actions were a substantial step in the provision of expert medical services to terrorists, we conclude that they were a substantial step in the provision of Sabir himself as personnel.

To illustrate, assume that, instead of offering himself as an on-call doctor to al Qaeda, Sabir had recruited a doctor who was, in all respects, identically situated to himself. Assume further that Sabir then brought that doctor to a meeting in New York where the doctor swore allegiance to al Qaeda, promised a supposed al Qaeda member that he would work as an on-call doctor for the organization, and gave the member contact numbers so that wounded jihadists in Saudi Arabia could reach the doctor when necessary. Even the dissent concedes that such evidence would be sufficient to prove Sabir "guilty of attempting to provide personnel," although the recruited doctor would not provide actual medical services until sometime in the future and after he traveled from New York to Saudi Arabia. Dissenting Op., *post* at [179]. Because Sabir would be guilty of attempting to provide personnel in the circumstances hypothesized, we think it necessarily follows that he is equally guilty on the record facts. He is guilty of attempting to provide himself as personnel to al Qaeda on May 20, 2005, even if he is not yet guilty of attempting to provide medical services to that organization.

In concluding otherwise, Chief Judge Dearie submits that the recruiter in the hypothetical "has done something. He has provided a service to the organization." *Id.* By contrast, he submits that Sabir "has done nothing more than conspire." *Id.* at 179. We disagree. Section 2339(B) criminalizes providing personnel through self-recruitment (*i.e.*, volunteering oneself to serve under the direction of a terrorist organization) no less than through recruitment (securing another person to serve under such direction). By volunteering himself as an on-call doctor for al Qaeda, Sabir rendered, or attempted to render, that organization as much of a service in producing personnel as the recruiter who solicited a doctor for that purpose. To hold otherwise would be to apply a different standard of sufficiency to the provision of personnel depending on whether the person being provided is oneself or another, a distinction for which there is no support in a statute that equally proscribes the provision of oneself or another to work under the direction of a terrorist organization.

Chief Judge Dearie suggests that a constitutional concern arises when a defendant is prosecuted for providing himself rather than a third party as personnel because in the former circumstance a defendant "'could be punished for, in effect, providing [himself] to speak out in support of the program or principles of a foreign terrorist organization, an activity protected by the First Amendment. . . .'" The Supreme Court, however, has now held otherwise, explaining that the material support statute leaves persons free to engage in "independent advocacy," proscribing only conduct "directed to, coordinated with, or controlled by foreign terrorist groups." *Holder v. Humanitarian Law Project*, 130 S. Ct. at 2728; *see id.* at 2721 (observing that § 2339B "makes clear that 'personnel' does not cover *independent* advocacy" (emphasis in original)).

Here, there is no question that Sabir was providing himself to work under the direction and control of al Qaeda—the jury heard him solemnly swear to do so. By dismissing this evidence as "insubstantial" and "immaterial," and demanding proof of a greater level of "engagement, activity or compliance" to support conviction, our dissenting colleague persists in conflating the provision of personnel with the provision of services by that personnel. While the latter form of material support may require proof of particular engagement or activity, the former focuses on submission to the direction and control of a terrorist organization.

The importance of the distinction we draw between the evidence necessary to prove a defendant's provision of personnel to a terrorist organization and that personnel's subsequent provision of services to the organization reaches beyond this case. Experience teaches that terrorist organizations frequently recruit persons into their ranks at times and places removed from any service they might render. Thus, someone who supplies suicide bombers or pilots or chemists or doctors or simple foot soldiers to a terrorist organization may reasonably be understood to provide the organization with material support in the form of personnel when the recruited individuals pledge to work under the direction of the organization, even though they may not be called upon to render any particular service for months, years, or at all. By the same reasoning, when a person supplies himself as the bomber or pilot or doctor sought by the terrorist organization, he provides—or certainly attempts to provide—material support in the form of personnel as soon as he pledges to work under the direction of the organization. In both circumstances, the organization acquires an important asset, reserve personnel, which can facilitate its planning of future terrorism objectives. . . . Thus, even if Sabir needed to return to Riyadh before he could provide actual medical services to members of al Qaeda—something he planned to do within two weeks, his actions on May 20, 2005, constituted a substantial step clearly intended to culminate in supplying himself as personnel to work under the direction of that terrorist organization.

. . .

The judgment of conviction is AFFIRMED.

NOTES AND QUESTIONS

1. The *Farhane* case demonstrates the broad reach of the material support statute, 18 U.S.C. § 2339B. The statute is essentially an aiding and abetting statute. However, the government is not required to prove that the aider and abettor shared the intent of the principal or intended to further the terrorist objectives of the foreign terrorist organization. A person is criminally liable if he knowingly provides material support or resources to an FTO with knowledge that the organization has been designated as an FTO, or knowing that the organization engages or has engaged in terrorist-related activities irrespective of the defendant's intent. Further, under the material support statute, the defendant may be found guilty under theories of direct liability, attempt, or conspiracy. Therefore, someone who attempts or conspires to provide material support to an FTO but actually fails to assist the terrorist group is criminally liable under the statute.

2. Sabir was charged with attempt to supply al Qaeda with material support in the form of personnel, training, and expert advice and assistance. The court affirmed Sabir's conviction for attempt to provide material support in the form of personnel—himself—to work for al Qaeda as a doctor on call to treat wounded jihadists. The court held that Sabir possessed the requisite intent and his conduct constituted a "substantial step" toward the provision of personnel to al Qaeda. Proof of a substantial step requires evidence that is "strongly corroborative of the firmness of the defendant's criminal intent." *United States v. Farhane*, 634 F.3d at 147; *see also* Model Penal Code § 5.01(1)(c). What evidence strongly corroborates Sabir's intent to join al Qaeda as an on-call doctor?

3. At common law, attempt is limited to conduct close to the completion of the intended crime. To constitute attempt, the suspect's conduct must "carry the project forward within dangerous proximity to the criminal end to be attained." *Farhane*, 634 F.3d at 146 (quoting *People v. Werblow*, 148 N.Y. 55, 69, 148 N.E. 786, 789 (1935)). In a jurisdiction that follows the common law and adopts the

"dangerous proximity" test, did Sabir's conduct constitute an attempt to provide material support in the form of personnel to al Qaeda?

4. In *United States v. Delvecchio*, 816 F.2d 859 (2d Cir. 1987), the court held that the evidence was insufficient to support a conviction for attempt to possess a large quantity of heroin. The court held that a substantial step to commit that crime was not established by proof that defendants met with drug suppliers, agreed on terms, and exchanged their beeper numbers. Should the court in *Farhane* have reached the same result? Didn't Sabir's conduct merely involve meetings and conversations about joining al Qaeda?

5. Sabir was found guilty on both the conspiratorial and substantive charges against him, including attempt to provide "expert advice or assistance" in the form of medical services to al Qaeda. The term "expert advice or assistance" means "advice or assistance derived from scientific, technical or other specialized knowledge." 18 U.S.C. § 2339A(b)(3). However, because the Second Circuit Court of Appeals found that the evidence was sufficient to convict Sabir under a theory of attempt to provide personnel (himself) to al Qaeda, the court failed to consider whether the evidence was sufficient to support a conviction for attempting to provide material support in the form of "expert advice or assistance." Does Sabir's conduct constitute a "substantial step" to support a conviction for attempt to provide "expert advice or assistance" to al Qaeda in the form of medical assistance?

6. The statutory definition of "material support or resources" explicitly exempts "medicine or religious materials." 18 U.S.C. § 2339A(b)(1). Thus, providing medicine and religious materials to an FTO is not prohibited under the statute. The question arises whether the medicine exception also exempts the provision of medical services. In *Farhane*, Sabir maintained that the material support statute was unconstitutionally vague because the statute did not provide a person of ordinary intelligence adequate notice of whether the exemption for medicine included medical treatment by a doctor. The court rejected Sabir's unconstitutional vagueness argument, reasoning:

> In the context of a statute focused on things that might be *provided* to support a terrorist organization, "medicine" is reasonably understood as a substance or preparation rather than as an art or science. "Providing medicine" is how common usage refers to the prescription of a substance or preparation to treat a patient. . . . By contrast, "practicing medicine" is how common usage describes Sabir's proposed activity, i.e., employing the art or science of medicine to treat a patient. . . . Where the word "provide" is used to describe the latter activity, reference ordinarily is made to "medical care," or "medical treatment," rather than to "medicine" alone. . . .
>
> Moreover, Congress's intent to have the medicine exception in § 2339A(b)(1) reach no further than substances or preparations that might be provided to a terrorist organization is stated with particular clarity in the statute's legislative history. . . .
>
> In short, context, common usage, and legislative history combine to serve on both individuals and law enforcement officers the notice required by due process that the medicine exception identified in § 2339A(b)(1) shields only those who provide substances qualifying as medicine to terrorist organizations. Other

medical support, such as volunteering to serve as an on-call doctor for a terrorist organization constitutes a provision of personnel and/or scientific assistance proscribed by law.[6]

7. Chief Judge Dearie filed a dissenting opinion arguing that Sabir was being punished for "radical thoughts rather than criminal deeds." *Id.* at 149. Do you agree? Does the evidence merely demonstrate Sabir's support for al Qaeda and the terror group's goals and ideology? Chief Judge Dearie stated that "the time and distance to be traveled by Sabir before he actually provided any medical treatment to al Qaeda warriors was too great to permit a jury to find that his actions constituted a substantial step towards commission of the charged crime." *Id.* at 150. Do you agree?

III. THE MILITARY TRIBUNAL PROSECUTION OPTION

"A military commission is a military criminal court historically created out of necessity to fill a jurisdictional gap or to provide battlefield commanders a forum to hold captured enemy personnel accountable for . . . violations of the laws and customs of war." JIMMY GURULÉ & GEOFFREY S. CORN, PRINCIPLES OF COUNTER-TERRORISM LAW 151 (2011). Used by American military commanders since the inception of our nation, military commissions have historically addressed three distinct situations. First, they have served as a substitute for civilian criminal courts during martial law when those courts were not functioning. *Id.* at 152. Second, they have been used to prosecute allegations of criminal misconduct by persons residing in enemy territory under the control of the U.S. military during periods of belligerent occupation. *Id.* Third, military commission have been used as a forum to adjudicate allegations of violations of the laws of war by members of the U.S. military and captured enemy combatants. *Id.*

Shortly following the terrorist attacks of September 11, 2001, Congress adopted a joint resolution authorizing the President to "use all necessary and appropriate force against those nations, organizations, or persons he determines planned, authorized, committed or aided the terrorist attacks . . . in order to prevent any future attacks of international terrorism against the United States by such nations, organizations or persons." Authorization for Use of Military Force (AUMF), 115 Stat. 224, note following 50 U.S.C. § 1541 (2000 ed., Suppl. III). On November 13, 2001, President George W. Bush, acting in his capacity as Commander in Chief, and pursuant to the AUMF, issued a comprehensive military order intended to govern the "Detention, Treatment, and Trial of Certain Non-Citizens in the War Against Terrorism." 6 Fed. Reg. 57833. Persons subject to the military order include any non-citizen for whom the President determines "there is reason to believe" that he (1) "is or was" a member of al Qaeda or (2) has engaged or participated in terrorist activities aimed at or harmful to the United States. *Id.* at 57834. Under the Military Order, any such individual "shall, when tried, be tried by a military commission for any and all offenses triable by military commission that such individual is alleged to have committed. . . ." *Ibid.*

---

6. *United States v. Farhane*, 634 F.3d at 142-43.

The military commission created by the Defense Department pursuant to this order resurrected the trial process used during and in the aftermath of World War II, but not since 1950 when Congress enacted the Uniform Code of Military Justice (UCMJ). The UCMJ sought to more closely align military criminal procedure with civilian criminal procedure, and, as the *Hamdan* opinion will show, included military commissions within the scope of that objective. However, the resurrection of a military commission model from the 1940s for use in the context of the so-called War on Terrorism has been highly controversial. Critics maintain that the judicial procedures afforded persons tried by military commission are substantially less favorable than process provided to U.S. service-members tried by courts-martial. Further, these procedures violate the UCMJ and fair trial requirements of Common Article 3 of the 1949 Geneva Conventions. Equally controversial is the assertion of war crimes jurisdiction to try foreign terrorists. Several important legal issues are implicated. First, is the United States engaged in an "armed conflict" with al Qaeda and related terrorist organizations that justifies war crimes allegations and trial by military commission? If so, when did the conflict begin? Did the armed conflict begin on September 11, 2001? Second, are members of al Qaeda and associated terrorist organizations "enemy combatants," who may in time of war be tried by military commission, or civilians who should be tried for terrorism offenses in civilian courts? Third, if such persons are subject to military commission jurisdiction, does the armed conflict against al Qaeda fall within the scope of Common Article 3 of the four Geneva Conventions, or was this "new" type of conflict uncontemplated by that baseline humanitarian provision? Fourth, what offenses qualify as violations of the law of war in this "new" type of armed conflict, which may be tried by military commission? Does the court have jurisdiction over conspiracy to commit war crimes? Is material support terrorism, a crime defined by 18 U.S.C. § 2339B, a war crime subject to trial before a military commission? Finally, may solicitation of war crimes be tried by military commission? These and other important related questions are examined in the following cases.

UNIFORM CODE OF MILITARY JUSTICE

The Uniform Code of Military Justice was enacted by Congress in 1950 to unify the Army and Navy Articles of War into one comprehensive military code for U.S. armed forces. The "Code" includes provisions establishing who is subject to the law, offenses applicable to these individuals, procedural and evidentiary rules for trial and appeal, and the jurisdiction of different types of military tribunals. The most common military tribunal used is the court-martial. The Code establishes the jurisdiction of three types of courts-martial: summary, special, and general. The general courts-martial, or GCM, is vested by Article 18 of the Code with jurisdiction to try any person "subject to the Code" for any offense made criminal by the Code. Article 2 establishes who is subject to the Code, most obviously members of the armed forces, but also civilians accompanying the force in the field during contingency operations and declared wars, cadets and midshipmen, retired members of the armed forces, and prisoners of war *after* they fall into U.S. custody. These individuals, therefore, may be tried for violations of the offenses enumerated in the Code. However, Article 18 also vests the GCM with jurisdiction to try "*any person* who, by the law of war, is subject to trial by military tribunal." Unlike persons "subject to the code," this jurisdictional grant does not permit such individuals to be charged with and prosecuted for violations of the Code (U.S. domestic law), but only for violations of international law applicable to them at the time of their offense. Thus, Congress chose to vest the GCM with authority to hold a captured enemy accountable for his *pre-capture* violation of the international law of war by using the GCM as the forum to adjudicate an accusation of commission of a war crime.

Prior to 1916, however, GCM jurisdiction was limited to members of the armed forces. Up to that time, the military commission was an alternate military tribunal used to try the captured enemy for violations of the laws and customs of war (war crimes). In the 1916 version of the Articles of War, Congress added jurisdiction over such offenders and offenses to the GCM. However, while Article 15 of the Articles of War provided this grant of jurisdiction to the GCM, it did not deprive military commissions of concurrent jurisdiction over the same. This concurrent jurisdiction scheme was incorporated into the UCMJ: Article 18 vests the GCM with jurisdiction over *both* persons subject to the Code for violations of the Code, *and* for any other individual who is subject to trial by military tribunal for violating the law of war; Article 21 indicates that this latter grant of jurisdiction does not deprive military commission of jurisdiction over the same. Thus, assuming the United States captures an individual who, prior to capture, committed a violation of the law of war, either of these forums may be used to prosecute the offense. However, unlike a member of the U.S. armed forces, the individual cannot be charged with a violation of the Code, because prior to capture he was not subject to that criminal law. Instead, the government must allege and prove a war crime.

On November 13, 2001, President Bush issued Military Order Number 1, directing the Secretary of Defense to establish a detention facility at the U.S. naval base at Guantanamo Bay, Cuba to detain captured alien unlawful combatants. The order also directed the Secretary of Defense to establish a military commission to try these captives for violations of the laws of war.

Hamdan: A Continuum of Issues

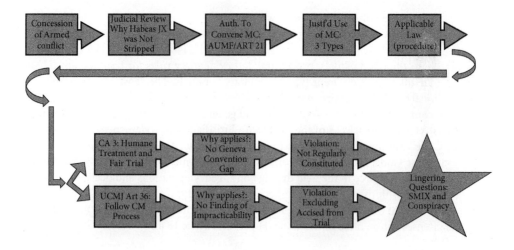

Hamdan v. Rumsfeld
548 U.S. 557 (2006)

Justice STEVENS announced the judgment of the Court and delivered the opinion of the Court with respect to Parts I through IV, Parts VI through VI-D-iii, Part VI-D-v, and Part VII, and an opinion with respect to Parts V and VI-D-iv, in which Justice SOUTER, Justice GINSBURG, and Justice BREYER join. . . .

For the reasons that follow, we conclude that the military commission convened to try Hamdan lacks the power to proceed because its structure and procedures violate both the UCMJ and the Geneva Conventions. Four of us also conclude, see Part V, *infra*, that the offense with which Hamdan has been charged is not an "offens[e] that by . . . the law of war may be tried by military commissions." 10 U.S.C. § 821.

[In an omitted portion of the opinion, the Court rejected the government's argument that it lacked jurisdiction. Hamdan's petition for habeas corpus was filed pursuant to the federal habeas corpus statute, based on the Court's 2004 decision in *Rasul v. Bush* holding that the U.S. base in Guantanamo fell with the reach of this statute. However, in 2005, in a section of the Detainee Treatment Act, Congress amended the federal habeas statute to explicitly exclude the detainees at Guantanamo from its scope. The government argued that as a result the Court lacked jurisdiction to consider Hamdan's petition. The Court concluded, however, that Congress did not intend for the habeas-stripping provision to apply retroactively to petitions that were already pending at the time it enacted the Detainee Treatment Act.]

I.

On September 11, 2001, agents of the al Qaeda terrorist organization hijacked commercial airplanes and attacked the World Trade Center in New York City and the national headquarters of the Department of Defense in Arlington, Virginia. Nearly 3,000 civilians were killed.

Congress responded by adopting a Joint Resolution authorizing the President to "use all necessary and appropriate force against those nations, organizations, or persons he determines planned, authorized, committed, or aided the terrorist attacks . . . in order to prevent any future acts of international terrorism against the United States by such nations, organizations or persons." Authorization for Use of Military Force (AUMF), 115 Stat. 224, note following 50 U.S.C. § 1541 (2000 ed., Supp. III). Acting pursuant to the AUMF, and having determined that the Taliban regime had supported al Qaeda, the President ordered the Armed Forces of the United States to invade Afghanistan. In the ensuing hostilities, hundreds of individuals, Hamdan among them, were captured and eventually detained at Guantanamo Bay.

On November 13, 2001, while the United States was still engaged in active combat with the Taliban, the President issued a comprehensive military order intended to govern the "Detention, Treatment, and Trial of Certain Non-Citizens in the War Against Terrorism," 66 Fed. Reg. 57833 (hereinafter November 13 Order or Order). Those subject to the November 13 Order include any noncitizen for whom the President determines "there is reason to believe" that he or she (1) "is or was" a member of al Qaeda or (2) has engaged or participated in terrorist activities aimed at or harmful to the United States. *Id.*, at 57834. Any such individual "shall, when tried, be tried by military commission for any and all offenses triable by military commission that such individual is alleged to have committed, and may be punished in accordance with the penalties provided under applicable law, including life imprisonment or death." *Ibid.* . . .

On July 3, 2003, the President announced his determination that Hamdan and five other detainees at Guantanamo Bay were subject to the November 13 Order and thus triable by military commission. . . . Not until July 13, 2004, after Hamdan had commenced this action in the United States District Court for the Western District of Washington, did the Government finally charge him with the offense for which, a year earlier, he had been deemed eligible for trial by military commission.

The charging document, which is unsigned, contains 13 numbered paragraphs. The first two paragraphs recite the asserted bases for the military commission's jurisdiction—namely, the November 13 Order and the President's July 3, 2003, declaration that Hamdan is eligible for trial by military commission. The next nine paragraphs, collectively entitled "General Allegations," describe al Qaeda's activities from its inception in 1989 through 2001 and identify Usama bin Laden as the group's leader. Hamdan is not mentioned in these paragraphs.

Only the final two paragraphs, entitled "Charge: Conspiracy," contain allegations against Hamdan. Paragraph 12 charges that "from on or about February 1996 to on or about November 24, 2001," Hamdan "willfully and knowingly joined an enterprise of persons who shared a common criminal purpose and conspired and agreed with [named members of al Qaeda] to commit the following offenses triable by military commission: attacking civilians; attacking civilian objects; murder by an unprivileged belligerent; and terrorism." App. to Pet. for Cert. 65a. . . .

Paragraph 13 lists four "overt acts" that Hamdan is alleged to have committed sometime between 1996 and November 2001 in furtherance of the "enterprise and conspiracy": (1) he acted as Usama bin Laden's "bodyguard and personal driver," "believ[ing]" all the while that bin Laden "and his associates were involved in" terrorist acts prior to and including the attacks of September 11, 2001; (2) he arranged for transportation of, and actually transported, weapons used by al Qaeda members and by bin Laden's bodyguards (Hamdan among them); (3) he "drove or accompanied [U]sama bin Laden to various al Qaida-sponsored training camps, press conferences, or lectures," at which bin Laden encouraged attacks against Americans; and (4) he received weapons training at al Qaeda-sponsored camps. *Id.*, at 65a-67a.

On November 8, 2004, however, the District Court granted Hamdan's petition for habeas corpus and stayed the commission's proceedings. It concluded that the President's authority to establish military commissions extends only to "offenders or offenses triable by military [commission] under the law of war,"

344 F. Supp. 2d, at 158; that the law of war includes the Geneva Convention (III) Relative to the Treatment of Prisoners of War, Aug. 12, 1949, [1955] 6 U.S.T. 3316, T.I.A.S. No. 3364 (Third Geneva Convention); that Hamdan is entitled to the full protections of the Third Geneva Convention until adjudged, in compliance with that treaty, not to be a prisoner of war; and that, whether or not Hamdan is properly classified as a prisoner of war, the military commission convened to try him was established in violation of both the UCMJ and Common Article 3 of the Third Geneva Convention because it had the power to convict based on evidence the accused would never see or hear. 344 F. Supp. 2d, at 158-172.

The Court of Appeals for the District of Columbia Circuit reversed. . . . On the merits, the panel rejected the District Court's [ ] conclusion that Hamdan was entitled to relief under the Third Geneva Convention. All three judges agreed that the Geneva Conventions were not "judicially enforceable," 415 F.3d, at 38, and two thought that the Conventions did not in any event apply to Hamdan, *id.*, at 40-42; but see *id.*, at 44 (Williams, J., concurring). In other portions of its opinion, the court concluded that our decision in *Quirin* foreclosed any separation-of-powers objection to the military commission's jurisdiction, and held that Hamdan's trial before the contemplated commission would violate neither the UCMJ nor U.S. Armed Forces regulations intended to implement the Geneva Conventions. 415 F.3d, at 38, 42-43.

On November 7, 2005, we granted certiorari to decide whether the military commission convened to try Hamdan has authority to do so, and whether Hamdan may rely on the Geneva Conventions in these proceedings.

. . .

IV.

The military commission, a tribunal neither mentioned in the Constitution nor created by statute, was born of military necessity. Though foreshadowed in some respects by earlier tribunals like the Board of General Officers that General Washington convened to try British Major John André for spying during the Revolutionary War, the commission "as such" was inaugurated in 1847. As commander of occupied Mexican territory, and having available to him no other tribunal, General Winfield Scott that year ordered the establishment of both " '*military commissions*' " to try ordinary crimes committed in the occupied territory and a "*council of war*" to try offenses against the law of war. Winthrop 832 (emphasis in original).

When the exigencies of war next gave rise to a need for use of military commissions, during the Civil War, the dual system favored by General Scott was not adopted. Instead, a single tribunal often took jurisdiction over ordinary crimes, war crimes, and breaches of military orders alike. As further discussed below, each aspect of that seemingly broad jurisdiction was in fact supported by a separate military exigency. Generally, though, the need for military commissions during this period — as during the Mexican War — was driven largely by the then very limited jurisdiction of courts-martial: "The *occasion* for the military commission arises principally from the fact that the jurisdiction of the court-martial proper, in our law, is restricted by statute almost exclusively to members of the military force and to certain specific offences defined in a written code." *Id.*, at 831 (emphasis in original).

Exigency alone, of course, will not justify the establishment and use of penal tribunals not contemplated by Article I, § 8, and Article III, § 1, of the Constitution unless some other part of that document authorizes a response to the felt need. And that authority, if it exists, can derive only from the powers granted jointly to the President and Congress in time of war.

The Constitution makes the President the "Commander in Chief" of the Armed Forces, Art. II, § 2, cl. 1, but vests in Congress the powers to "declare War . . . and make Rules concerning Captures on Land and Water," Art. I, § 8, cl. 11, to "raise and support Armies," *id.*, cl. 12, to "define and punish . . . Offences against the Law of Nations," *id.*, cl. 10, and "To make Rules for the Government and Regulation of the land and naval Forces," *id.*, cl. 14. The interplay between these powers was described by Chief Justice Chase in the seminal case of *Ex parte Milligan*:

> "The power to make the necessary laws is in Congress; the power to execute in the President. Both powers imply many subordinate and auxiliary powers. Each includes all authorities essential to its due exercise. But neither can the President, in war more than in peace, intrude upon the proper authority of Congress, nor Congress upon the proper authority of the President. . . . Congress cannot direct the conduct of campaigns, nor can the President, or any commander under him, without the sanction of Congress, institute tribunals for the trial and punishment of offences, either of soldiers or civilians, unless in cases of a controlling necessity, which justifies what it compels, or at least insures acts of indemnity from the justice of the legislature." 4 Wall., at 139-140.

We have no occasion to revisit *Quirin*'s controversial characterization of Article of War 15 as congressional authorization for military commissions. Contrary to the Government's assertion, however, even *Quirin* did not view the authorization as a sweeping mandate for the President to "invoke military commissions when he deems them necessary." Rather, the *Quirin* Court recognized that Congress had simply preserved what power, under the Constitution and the common law of war, the President had had before 1916 to convene military commissions—with the express condition that the President and those under his command comply with the law of war.

The Government would have us dispense with the inquiry that the *Quirin* Court undertook and find in either the AUMF or the DTA specific, overriding authorization for the very commission that has been convened to try Hamdan. Neither of these congressional Acts, however, expands the President's authority to convene military commissions. First, while we assume that the AUMF activated the President's war powers, and that those powers include the authority to convene military commissions in appropriate circumstances, there is nothing in the text or legislative history of the AUMF even hinting that Congress intended to expand or alter the authorization set forth in Article 21 of the UCMJ.

Likewise, the DTA cannot be read to authorize this commission. Although the DTA, unlike either Article 21 or the AUMF, was enacted after the President had convened Hamdan's commission, it contains no language authorizing that tribunal or any other at Guantanamo Bay. The DTA obviously "recognize[s]" the existence of the Guantanamo Bay commissions in the weakest sense because it references some of the military orders governing them and creates limited judicial review of their "final decision[s]," DTA § 1005(e)(3), 119 Stat. 2743. But the statute also pointedly reserves judgment on whether "the Constitution and laws of the United States are applicable" in reviewing such decisions and whether, if they are, the "standards and procedures" used to try Hamdan and other detainees actually violate the "Constitution and laws." *Ibid.*

Together, the UCMJ, the AUMF, and the DTA at most acknowledge a general Presidential authority to convene military commissions in circumstances where justified under the "Constitution and laws," including the law of war. Absent a more specific congressional authorization, the task of this Court is, as it was in *Quirin*, to decide whether Hamdan's military commission is so justified.

V.

The common law governing military commissions may be gleaned from past practice and what sparse legal precedent exists. Commissions historically have been used in three situations. First, they have substituted for civilian courts at times and in places where martial law has been declared. Their use in these circumstances has raised constitutional questions, see *Duncan v. Kahanamoku*, 327 U.S. 304 (1946); *Milligan*, 4 Wall., at 121-122, but is well recognized. Second, commissions have been established to try civilians "as part of a temporary military government over occupied enemy territory or territory regained from an enemy where civilian government cannot and does not function." *Duncan*, 327 U.S., at 314. Illustrative of this second kind of commission is the one that was established, with jurisdiction to apply the German Criminal Code, in occupied Germany following the end of World War II. See *Madsen v. Kinsella*, 343 U.S. 341, 356 (1952).

The third type of commission, convened as an "incident to the conduct of war" when there is a need "to seize and subject to disciplinary measures those enemies who in their attempt to thwart or impede our military effort have violated the law of war," *Quirin*, 317 U.S., at 28-29, has been described as "utterly different" from the other two. Not only is its jurisdiction limited to offenses cognizable during time of war, but its role is primarily a factfinding one — to determine, typically on the battle-field itself, whether the defendant has violated the law of war. The last time the U.S. Armed Forces used the law-of-war military commission was during World War II. In *Quirin*, this Court sanctioned President Roosevelt's use of such a tribunal to try Nazi saboteurs captured on American soil during the War. 317 U.S. 1. And in *Yamashita*, we held that a military commission had jurisdiction to try a Japanese commander for failing to prevent troops under his command from committing atrocities in the Philippines. 327 U.S. 1.

Quirin is the model the Government invokes most frequently to defend the commission convened to try Hamdan. That is both appropriate and unsurprising. Since Guantanamo Bay is neither enemy-occupied territory nor under martial law, the law-of-war commission is the only model available. At the same time, no more robust model of executive power exists; *Quirin* represents the high-water mark of military power to try enemy combatants for war crimes.

The classic treatise penned by Colonel William Winthrop, whom we have called "the 'Blackstone of Military Law,'" *Reid v. Covert*, 354 U.S. 1, 19, n.38 (1957) (plurality opinion), describes at least four preconditions for exercise of jurisdiction by a tribunal of the type convened to try Hamdan. First, "[a] military commission, (except where otherwise authorized by statute), can legally assume jurisdiction only of offences committed within the field of the command of the convening commander." Winthrop 836. The "field of the command" in these circumstances means the "theatre of war." *Ibid.* Second, the offense charged "must have been committed within the period of the war." *Id.*, at 837. No jurisdiction exists to try offenses "committed either before or after the war." *Ibid.* Third, a military commission not established pursuant to martial law or an occupation may try only "[i]ndividuals of the enemy's army who have been guilty of illegitimate warfare or other offences in violation of the laws of war" and members of one's own army "who, in time of war, become chargeable with crimes or offences not cognizable, or triable, by the criminal courts or under the Articles of war." *Id.*, at 838. Finally, a law-of-war commission has jurisdiction to try only two kinds of offense: "Violations of the laws and usages of war cognizable by military tribunals only," and "[b]reaches of military orders or regulations for which offenders are not legally triable by court-martial under the Articles of war." *Id.*, at 839.

All parties agree that Colonel Winthrop's treatise accurately describes the common law governing military commissions, and that the jurisdictional limitations he identifies were incorporated in Article of War 15 and, later, Article 21 of the UCMJ. . . . The question is whether the preconditions designed to ensure that a military necessity exists to justify the use of this extraordinary tribunal have been satisfied here.

The charge against Hamdan, described in detail in Part I, *supra*, alleges a conspiracy extending over a number of years, from 1996 to November 2001. All but two months of that more than 5-year-long period preceded the attacks of September 11, 2001, and the enactment of the AUMF—the Act of Congress on which the Government relies for exercise of its war powers and thus for its authority to convene military commissions. Neither the purported agreement with Usama bin Laden and others to commit war crimes, nor a single overt act, is alleged to have occurred in a theater of war or on any specified date after September 11, 2001. None of the overt acts that Hamdan is alleged to have committed violates the law of war.

These facts alone cast doubt on the legality of the charge and, hence, the commission; as Winthrop makes plain, the offense alleged must have been committed both in a theater of war and *during*, not before, the relevant conflict.

But the deficiencies in the time and place allegations also underscore—indeed are symptomatic of—the most serious defect of this charge: The offense it alleges is not triable by law-of-war military commission.

There is no suggestion that Congress has, in exercise of its constitutional authority to "define and punish . . . Offences against the Law of Nations," U.S. Const., Art. I, § 8, cl. 10, positively identified "conspiracy" as a war crime. As we explained in *Quirin*, that is not necessarily fatal to the Government's claim of authority to try the alleged offense by military commission; Congress, through Article 21 of the UCMJ, has "incorporated by reference" the common law of war, which may render triable by military commission certain offenses not defined by statute. 317 U.S., at 30. When, however, neither the elements of the offense nor the range of permissible punishments is defined by statute or treaty, the precedent must be plain and unambiguous. To demand any less would be to risk concentrating in military hands a degree of adjudicative and punitive power in excess of that contemplated either by statute or by the Constitution. . . .

The crime of "conspiracy" has rarely if ever been tried as such in this country by any law-of-war military commission not exercising some other form of jurisdiction, and does not appear in either the Geneva Conventions or the Hague Conventions—the major treaties on the law of war. Winthrop explains that under the common law governing military commissions, it is not enough to intend to violate the law of war and commit overt acts in furtherance of that intention unless the overt acts either are themselves offenses against the law of war or constitute steps sufficiently substantial to qualify as an attempt.

The Government cites three sources that it says show otherwise. First, it points out that the Nazi saboteurs in *Quirin* were charged with conspiracy. See Brief for Respondents 27. Second, it observes that Winthrop at one point in his treatise identifies conspiracy as an offense "prosecuted by military commissions." *Ibid.* (citing Winthrop 839, and n.5). Finally, it notes that another military historian, Charles Roscoe Howland, lists conspiracy "'to violate the laws of war by destroying life or property in aid of the enemy'" as an offense that was tried as a violation of the law of war during the Civil War. On close analysis, however, these sources at best lend little support to the Government's position and at worst undermine it. By any measure, they fail to satisfy the high standard of clarity required to justify the use of a military commission.

That the defendants in *Quirin* were charged with conspiracy is not persuasive, since the Court declined to address whether the offense actually qualified as a violation of the law of war—let alone one triable by military commission. The *Quirin* defendants were charged with the following offenses:

> "[I.] Violation of the law of war.
>
> . . .
>
> "[IV.] Conspiracy to commit the offenses alleged in charges [I, II, and III]."
> 317 U.S., at 23.

The Government, defending its charge, argued that the conspiracy alleged "con-stitute[d] an additional violation of the law of war." *Id.*, at 15. The saboteurs disagreed; they maintained that "[t]he charge of conspiracy cannot stand if the other charges fall." *Id.*, at 8. The Court, however, declined to resolve the dispute. It concluded, first, that the specification supporting Charge I adequately alleged a "violation of the law of war" that was not "merely colorable or without foun-dation." *Id.*, at 36. The facts the Court deemed sufficient for this purpose were that the defendants, admitted enemy combatants, entered upon U.S. territory in time of war without uniform "for the purpose of destroying property used or useful in prosecuting the war." That act was "a hostile and warlike" one. *Id.*, at 36, 37. The Court was careful in its decision to identify an overt, "complete" act. Responding to the argument that the saboteurs had "not actually commit-ted or attempted to commit any act of depredation or entered the theatre or zone of active military operations" and therefore had not violated the law of war, the Court responded that they had actually "passed our military and naval lines and defenses or went behind those lines, in civilian dress and with hostile purpose." *Id.*, at 38. "The offense was complete when with that purpose they entered — or, having so entered, they remained upon — our territory in time of war without uniform or other appropriate means of identification." *Ibid.*

Turning to the other charges alleged, the Court explained that "[s]ince the first specification of Charge I sets forth a violation of the law of war, we have no occasion to pass on the adequacy of the second specification of Charge I, or to construe the 81st and 82nd Articles of War for the purpose of ascertaining whether the specifications under Charges II and III allege violations of those Articles or whether if so construed they are constitutional." *Id.*, at 46. No men-tion was made at all of Charge IV — the conspiracy charge.

If anything, *Quirin* supports Hamdan's argument that conspiracy is not a violation of the law of war. Not only did the Court pointedly omit any discus-sion of the conspiracy charge, but its analysis of Charge I placed special empha-sis on the *completion* of an offense; it took seriously the saboteurs' argument that there can be no violation of a law of war — at least not one triable by mil-itary commission — without the actual commission of or attempt to commit a "hostile and warlike act." *Id.*, at 37-38.

That limitation makes eminent sense when one considers the necessity from whence this kind of military commission grew: The need to dispense swift jus-tice, often in the form of execution, to illegal belligerents captured on the bat-tlefield. The same urgency would not have been felt vis-à-vis enemies who had done little more than agree to violate the laws of war. . . . The *Quirin* Court acknowledged as much when it described the President's authority to use law-of-war military commissions as the power to "seize and subject to disciplinary measures those enemies *who in their attempt to thwart or impede our military effort* have violated the law of war." 317 U.S., at 28-29 (emphasis added).

Winthrop and Howland are only superficially more helpful to the Government. Howland, granted, lists "conspiracy by two or more to violate the laws of war by destroying life or property in aid of the enemy" as one of over

20 "offenses against the laws and usages of war" "passed upon and punished by military commissions." Howland 1070-1071. But while the records of cases that Howland cites following his list of offenses against the law of war support inclusion of the other offenses mentioned, they provide no support for the inclusion of conspiracy as a violation of the law of war. See *id.* Winthrop, apparently recognizing as much, excludes conspiracy of any kind from his own list of offenses against the law of war. . . .

. . .

Finally, international sources confirm that the crime charged here is not a recognized violation of the law of war. As observed above, see *supra*, at 603-604, none of the major treaties governing the law of war identifies conspiracy as a violation thereof. And the only "conspiracy" crimes that have been recognized by international war crimes tribunals . . . are conspiracy to commit genocide and common plan to wage aggressive war, which is a crime against the peace and requires for its commission actual participation in a "concrete plan to wage war." 1 Trial of the Major War Criminals Before the International Military Tribunal: Nuremberg, 14 November 1945-1 October 1946, p. 225 (1947). . . . The International Military Tribunal at Nuremberg, over the prosecution's objections, pointedly refused to recognize as a violation of the law of war conspiracy to commit war crimes, see, *e.g., id.,* at 469, and convicted only Hitler's most senior associates of conspiracy to wage aggressive war. As one prominent figure from the Nuremberg trials has explained, members of the Tribunal objected to recognition of conspiracy as a violation of the law of war on the ground that "[t]he Anglo-American concept of conspiracy was not part of European legal systems and arguably not an element of the internationally recognized laws of war." T. Taylor, Anatomy of the Nuremberg Trials: A Personal Memoir 36 (1992). . . .

In sum, the sources that the Government . . . rely upon to show that conspiracy to violate the law of war is itself a violation of the law of war in fact demonstrate quite the opposite. Far from making the requisite substantial showing, the Government has failed even to offer a "merely colorable" case for inclusion of conspiracy among those offenses cognizable by law-of-war military commission. Because the charge does not support the commission's jurisdiction, the commission lacks authority to try Hamdan.

VI.

Whether or not the Government has charged Hamdan with an offense against the law of war cognizable by military commission, the commission lacks the power to proceed. The UCMJ conditions the President's use of military commissions on compliance not only with the American common law of war, but also with the rest of the UCMJ itself, insofar as applicable, and with the "rules and precepts of the law of nations." *Quirin,* 317 U.S. at 28 — including, *inter alia,* the four Geneva Conventions signed in 1949. See *Yamashita,* 327 U.S., at 20-21, 23-24. The procedures that the Government has decreed will govern Hamdan's trial by commission violated these laws.

A.

[The Court held that the criminal procedures afforded persons tried before the President's military commission violated the uniformity principle reflected in Article 36 of the UCMJ, 10 U.S.C. § 836. The Court stated: "We agree with Justice Kennedy that the procedures adopted to try Hamdan deviate from those governing courts-martial in ways not justified by any 'evident practical need' . . . and for that reason . . . fail to afford the requisite guarantees."]

. . .

D.

The procedures adopted to try Hamdan also violate the Geneva Conventions. The Court of Appeals dismissed Hamdan's Geneva Convention challenge on three independent grounds: (1) the Geneva Conventions are not judicially enforceable; (2) Hamdan in any event is not entitled to their protections; and (3) even if he is entitled to their protections . . . abstention is appropriate. . . .

ii.

. . .

The conflict with al Qaeda is not, according to the Government, a conflict to which the full protections afforded detainees under the 1949 Geneva Conventions apply because Article 2 of those Conventions . . . renders the full protections applicable only to "all cases of declared war or of any other armed conflict which may arise between two or more of the High Contracting Parties." 6 U.S.T., at 3318. Since Hamdan was captured and detained incident to the conflict with al Qaeda and not the conflict with the Taliban, and since al Qaeda, unlike Afghanistan, is not a "High Contracting Party" — *i.e.*, a signatory of the Conventions, the protections of those Conventions are not, it is argued, applicable to Hamdan.

We need not decide the merits of this argument because there is at least one provision of the Geneva Conventions that applies here even if the relevant conflict is not one between signatories. Article 3, often referred to as Common Article 3 because, like Article 2, it appears in all four Geneva Conventions, provides that in a "conflict not of an international character occurring in the territory of one of the High Contracting Parties, each Party to the conflict shall be bound to apply as a minimum, certain provisions protecting "[p]ersons taking no active part in the hostilities, including members of armed forces who have laid down their arms and those placed hors de combat by . . . detention." *Ibid*. One such provision prohibits "the passing of sentences and the carrying out of executions without previous judgment pronounced by regularly constituted court affording all the judicial guarantees which are recognized as indispensable by civilized peoples." *Ibid*.

The Court of Appeals thought, and the Government asserts, that Common Article 3 does not apply to Hamdan because the conflict with al Qaeda being " 'international in scope,' " does not qualify as a " 'conflict not of an international character.'" That reasoning is erroneous. The term "conflict not of an international character" is used here in contradistinction to a conflict between nations. So much is demonstrated by the "fundamental logic [of] the Convention's provisions on its application." 415 F.3d 33, 44 (D.C. Cir.) (Williams, J., concurring). Common Article 2 provides that "the present Convention shall apply to all cases of declared war or of any other armed conflict which may arise between two or more of the High Contracting Parties." 6 U.S.T., at 3318 (Art. 2, ¶ 1). High Contracting Parties (signatories) also must abide by all terms of the Conventions vis-à-vis the nonsignatory if "the latter accepts and applies" those terms. *Ibid.* (Art. 2, ¶ 3). Common Article 3, by contrast, affords some minimal protection, falling short of full protection under the Conventions, to individuals associated with neither a signatory nor even a nonsignatory "Power" who are involved in a conflict "in the territory of" a signatory. The latter kind of conflict is distinguishable from the conflict described in Common Article 2 chiefly because it does not involve a clash between nations. . . . In context, then, the phrase "not of an international character" bears its literal meaning. See J. Bentham, Introduction to the Principles of Morals and Legislation 6, 296 (J. Burns & H. Hart eds. 1970) (using the term "international law" as a "new though not inexpressive appellation" meaning "betwixt nation and nation": defining "international" to include "mutual transactions between sovereigns as such"). . . .

iii.

Common Article 3, then, is applicable here and, as indicated above, requires that Hamdan be tried by a "regularly constituted court affording all the judicial guarantees which are recognized as indispensable by civilized peoples." [The Court then concluded that the court-martial served as the ideal example of a fair and "regularly constituted" tribunal, and therefore significant deviation from court-martial procedures violated the U.S. obligation imposed by Common Article 3.]

The judgment of the Court of Appeals is reversed, and the case is remanded for further proceedings.

THE CHIEF JUSTICE took no part in the consideration or decision of this case.

Justice KENNEDY, with whom Justice SOUTER, Justice GINSBURG, and Justice BREYER join as to Parts I and II, concurring in part.

. . .

I

Assuming the President has authority to establish a special military commission to try Hamdan, the commission must satisfy Common Article 3's requirement of a "regularly constituted court affording all the judicial guarantees which are recognized as indispensable by civilized peoples," 6 U.S.T., at

3320. The terms of this general standard are yet to be elaborated and further defined, but Congress has required compliance with it by referring to the "law of war" in § 821. The Court correctly concludes that the military commission here does not comply with this provision.

Common Article 3's standard of a "regularly constituted court affording all the judicial guarantees which are recognized as indispensable by civilized peoples," *ibid.*, supports, at the least, a uniformity principle similar to that codified in § 836(b). The concept of a "regularly constituted court" providing "indispensable" judicial guarantees requires consideration of the system of justice under which the commission is established, though no doubt certain minimum standards are applicable. . . .

The regular military courts in our system are the courts-martial established by congressional statutes. Acts of Congress confer on those courts the jurisdiction to try "any person" subject to war crimes prosecution. 10 U.S.C. § 818. As the Court explains, moreover, while special military commissions have been convened in previous armed conflicts — a practice recognized in § 821 — those military commissions generally have adopted the structure and procedure of courts-martial. Today, moreover, § 836(b) — which took effect after the military trials in the World War II cases . . . codifies this presumption of uniformity at least as to "[p]retrial, trial, and post-trial procedures." Absent more concrete statutory guidance, this historical and statutory background — which suggests that some practical need must justify deviations from the court-martial model — informs the understanding of which military courts are "regularly constituted" under United States law. . . .

At a minimum a military commission like the one at issue — a commission specially convened by the President to try specific persons without express congressional authorization — can be "regularly constituted" by the standards of our military justice system only if some practical need explains deviations from court-martial practice.

II.

Against this background, the Court is correct to conclude that the military commission the President has convened to try Hamdan is unauthorized.

To begin with, the structure and composition of the military commission deviate from conventional court-martial standards. Although these deviations raise questions about the fairness of the trial, no evident practical need explains them.

In sum, as presently structured, Hamdan's military commission exceeds the bounds Congress has placed on the President's authority in Articles 36 and 21 of the UCMJ, 10 U.S.C. §§ 836, 821. Because Congress has prescribed these limits, Congress can change them, requiring a new analysis consistent with the Constitution and other governing laws. At this time, however, we must apply the standards Congress has provided. By those standards the military commission is deficient.

III.

In light of the conclusion that the military commission here is unauthorized under the UCMJ, I see no need to consider several further issues addressed in the plurality opinion.

There should be reluctance, furthermore, to reach unnecessarily the question whether, as the plurality seems to conclude, *ante*, at 633, Article 75 of Protocol I to the Geneva Conventions is binding law notwithstanding the earlier decision by our Government not to accede to the Protocol. I likewise see no need to address the validity of the conspiracy charge against Hamdan — an issue addressed at length in Part V of Justice Stevens' opinion and in Part II-C of Justice Thomas' dissent. In light of the conclusion that the military commissions at issue are unauthorized, Congress may choose to provide further guidance in this area. Congress, not the Court, is the branch in the better position to undertake the "sensitive task of establishing a principle not inconsistent with the national interest or with international justice." *Banco Nacional de Cuba v. Sabbatino*, 376 U.S. 398, 428 (1964).

NOTES AND QUESTIONS

1. The military commission established to prosecute Hamdan was authorized by Military Order Number 1, "Detention, Treatment, and Trial of Certain Non-Citizens in the War Against Terrorism," 66 Fed. Reg. 57833 (Nov. 13, 2001). Who is subject to prosecution before a military tribunal established under the November 13 Order? May U.S. citizens and foreign nationals fighting for al Qaeda or ISIS be prosecuted by military commission?

2. The Court avoided the question of whether President Bush was vested with inherent constitutional authority to order use of a military commission under the circumstances of the case. The Court did so by interpreting Article 21 of the UCMJ as a congressional authorization for such use. Review the language of Article 21 cited in the opinion, which indicates that by vesting the general court-martial with jurisdiction over war crimes, the UCMJ did not deprive military commissions of concurrent jurisdiction over these same offenses and offenders. But if a military commission has concurrent jurisdiction over such offenses, what is the source of that jurisdiction? Does Article 21 read as a delegation of authority? Or was Congress perhaps acknowledging an authority that already existed? If the latter, what was the source of the authority?

3. What is the constitutional authority to establish a military commission? *See Hamdan v. Rumsfeld*, 548 U.S. at 591-92. Do the President and Congress share this authority?

4. The indictment against Hamdan alleged that he "willfully and knowingly joined an enterprise of persons who shared a common criminal purpose and conspired and agreed with [named members of al Qaeda] to commit the following offenses triable by military commission: attacking civilians; attacking civilian objects; murder by an unprivileged belligerent; and terrorism." Is terrorism a war crime, a violation of the laws and usages of war?

5. The Court states that historically military commissions have been used in three situations. What are they? What type of military commission was created pursuant to Military Order Number 1, "Detention, Treatment, and Trial of Certain Non-Citizens in the War Against Terrorism"? What is the purpose of this type of military commission?

6. The Court identified four preconditions for exercise of jurisdiction by a military tribunal of the type convened to try Hamdan. Are those preconditions satisfied with respect to Hamdan? The Court states that the offense charged "must have been committed within the period of war." No jurisdiction exists to try offenses "committed either before or after the war." When did the armed conflict with al Qaeda begin? Is the armed conflict with al Qaeda still ongoing? How will we be able to determine whether the armed conflict has ended?

7. The Court stated that "Congress, through Article 21 of the UCMJ, has 'incorporated by reference' the common law of war, which may render triable by military commission certain offenses not defined by statute." *Hamdan v. Rumsfeld*, 584 U.S. at 601. What is the "common law of war"? What crimes are considered violations of the laws of war? Is there uniform agreement in the international community regarding what crimes constitute violations of the laws of war?

8. The Court was divided on whether conspiracy to commit war crimes is an offense proscribed under the "law of war." Seven Justices opined on the conspiracy question and split four to three in contrasting opinions written by Justice Stevens and Justice Thomas. Justice Kennedy did not address the conspiracy charge, and Chief Justice Roberts did not take part in the case. Justice Stevens's plurality opinion concluded that conspiracy was not a law of war offense under 10 U.S.C. § 821, but qualified that conclusion by emphasizing Congress had not enumerated conspiracy as a crime subject to trial by military commission. *See* 548 U.S. 600-12. Justice Thomas's opinion concluded that conspiracy was a law of war offense under § 821. *See id.* at 697-706. What authority did the government cite in support of its position that conspiracy is a violation of the laws of war? Why did Justice Stevens reject the government's arguments?

9. In response to the *Hamdan* decision, Congress enacted the Military Commissions Act of 2006 (2006 MCA), Pub. L. No. 109-366, 120 Stat. 2600, codified at chapter 47a of title 10, U.S. Code, which amended the statutory procedures governing military commissions to cure the flaws identified in *Hamdan*. Among other things, the 2006 MCA exempts a military commission established under the Act from the uniformity requirement of 10 U.S.C. § 836. As a result, the procedures afforded persons tried before a military commission may deviate from courts-martial practice. However, whether a military commission established under the 2006 MCA violates Common Article 3 of the Geneva Conventions remains an open issue.

10. In an omitted portion of the decision, Justice Thomas dissented from the majority's conclusion that the procedures established for trial by military

commission violated Common Article 3's "fair and regularly constituted" tribunal obligation. According to Justice Thomas, when Common Article 3 was added to the Geneva Conventions in 1949, the intent was to prohibit the summary trials that were so notorious in civil wars like the civil war in Spain from 1936-1939. Justice Thomas believed that the procedures established for military commission trials went far beyond the minimalist requirement of Common Article 3, even if they did not mirror procedures for trial by court-martial. Considering the historical motivation for Common Article 3, do you think that Justice Thomas's interpretation was more appropriate than that adopted by the majority?

11. Responding to proposals by President Obama to enhance the procedures of the military commission, Congress passed the Military Commissions Act of 2009 (2009 MCA). Evidentiary issues were addressed in the new Act. The 2009 MCA extended the exclusionary rule for statements obtained by torture to any statement obtained by torture or cruel, inhuman, or degrading treatment, *see* 10 U.S.C. § 948r(a), and established voluntariness as the standard of admissibility of statements generally. *Id.* § 948r(d). The Act also limited hearsay evidence to certain exceptions, and imposed a burden on the prosecution to establish reliability as a predicate to admissibility. Compulsory process and discovery rights were also enhanced. Finally, individuals subject to trial by military commission are no longer designated as "unlawful enemy combatants." Instead, the term "unprivileged enemy belligerent" is used, which includes an individual (other than a privileged belligerent) who

   (A) has engaged in hostilities against the United States or its coalition partners;
   (B) has purposely and materially supported hostilities against the United States or its coalition partners; or
   (C) was a part of Al Qaeda at the time of the alleged offense under [chapter 7A of title 10, U.S. Code].[7]

   What factors are probative to establish that the defendant is "part of" al Qaeda?

12. The MCA of 2009 provides jurisdiction to military commissions to try alien unprivileged belligerents for terrorism, providing material support for terrorism, and conspiracy. Are terrorism, providing material support for terrorism and conspiracy to commit war crimes offenses against the laws of war?

13. The 2006 MCA cured many of the procedural defects at issue in *Hamdan*, and the 2009 MCA conclusively prohibits use of statements obtained by coercion (not merely torture). However, one procedural issue that remains contentious is whether the fruits of inadmissible coerced statements may be used at trial. Would the use of such evidence violate Common Article 3?

---

7. *Id.* § 948a(7)(B).

MILITARY COMMISSIONS ACT OF 2006

"Congress heeded the Court's holding when it enacted the Military Commissions Act of 2006. The procedures enacted by the Act were intended to not only resurrect the commissions, but to ensure that future trials would be conducted consistent with the requirements of domestic and international law. The MCA indicates that '[t]he procedures for military commissions set forth in this Chapter are based upon the procedures for trial by general courts-martial under Chapter 47 of this title (Uniform Code of Military Justice).' The Act further asserts that 'a military commission established under this chapter is a regularly constituted court affording all the necessary "judicial guarantees which are recognized as indispensable by civilized peoples" for purposes of common Article 3 of the Geneva Conventions.' While this assertion is not necessarily accepted by all critics ... it does indicate that the United States now accepts Common Article 3 as the applicable standard for procedural fairness for trial by military commission."

JIMMY GURULÉ & GEOFFREY S. CORN, PRINCIPLES OF COUNTER-TERRORISM LAW 171 (2011).

Bahlul v. United States

840 F.3d 757 (D.C. Cir. 2016) (en banc)

PER CURIAM:

Bahlul is a member of al Qaeda who assisted Osama bin Laden in planning the September 11, 2001, attacks on the United States. Bahlul was convicted by a U.S. military commission of the offense of conspiracy to commit war crimes, among other offenses. The U.S. Court of Military Commission Review affirmed Bahlul's conviction.

In a prior en banc decision, we recounted the facts and considered Bahlul's Ex Post Facto Clause objection to the conspiracy conviction. Applying plain error review, we concluded that the Ex Post Facto Clause did not preclude the conspiracy charge against Bahlul. *See Al Bahlul v. United States*, 767 F.3d 1 (D.C. Cir. 2014) (en banc).

In this en banc case, Bahlul argues that Articles I and III of the Constitution bar Congress from making conspiracy an offense triable by military commission, because conspiracy is not an offense under the international law of war.

We affirm the judgment of the U.S. Court of Military Commission Review upholding Bahlul's conspiracy conviction. Six judges—Judges Henderson, Brown, Griffith, Kavanaugh, Millett, and Wilkins—have voted to affirm. Three judges—Judges Rogers, Tatel, and Pillard—dissent.

Of the six-judge majority, four judges (Judges Henderson, Brown, Griffith, and Kavanaugh) would affirm because they conclude that, consistent with Articles I and III of the Constitution, Congress may make conspiracy to commit war crimes an offense triable by military commission. They would uphold Bahlul's conspiracy conviction on that basis.

Judge Millett would apply plain error review and affirm Bahlul's conviction under that standard of review. She would not reach the question of whether Congress may make inchoate conspiracy an offense triable by military commission.

Judge Wilkins would affirm because he concludes that the particular features of Bahlul's conviction demonstrate that Bahlul was not convicted of an inchoate conspiracy offense. He further concludes that Bahlul's conviction complies with the Constitution because the particular features of Bahlul's conviction have sufficient roots in international law. He therefore would not reach the question of whether Congress may make inchoate conspiracy an offense triable by military commission.

Judges Rogers, Tatel, and Pillard have filed a Joint Dissent. They conclude that Article III of the Constitution bars Congress from making inchoate conspiracy an offense triable by a law-of-war military commission. . . .

We affirm the judgment of the U.S. Court of Military Commission Review upholding Bahlul's conspiracy conviction.

KAREN LeCRAFT HENDERSON, Circuit Judge, concurring:

I join the Court's judgment affirming Bahlul's conspiracy conviction. I do so for the reasons stated in my dissent in *Al Bahlul v. United States*, 792 F.3d 1, 27-72 (D.C. Cir. 2015) (since vacated). I incorporate by reference thereto that previously published opinion as my concurrence here.

KAVANAUGH, Circuit Judge, with whom Circuit Judges BROWN and GRIFFITH join, concurring:

Pursuant to congressional authorization, Presidents throughout U.S. history have employed military commissions to try enemy war criminals for conspiracy to commit war crimes. That history includes the two most significant U.S. military commission trials: the 1865 military commission trial of the Confederate conspirators who plotted to kill President Lincoln and the 1942 military commission trial of the Nazi conspirators who secretly entered the United States during World War II and planned to attack U.S. infrastructure and military facilities.

In the wake of al Qaeda's attacks on the United States on September 11, 2001, Congress has twice passed laws (signed by President Bush in 2006 and President Obama in 2009) expressly reaffirming that military commissions may try unlawful enemy combatants for conspiracy to commit war crimes. Pursuant to those express congressional authorizations, President Bush and later President Obama have employed military commissions to try alleged al Qaeda war criminals for the offense of conspiracy to commit war crimes. Indeed, Khalid Sheikh Mohammad, one of the alleged masterminds of the September 11th attacks, faces a conspiracy charge in his pending military commission trial. Several other al Qaeda members likewise have been charged with conspiracy before U.S. military commissions.

Bahlul is an al Qaeda member who worked closely with Osama bin Laden in plotting al Qaeda's September 11th attacks on the United States. In December 2001, Bahlul was captured in Pakistan. In 2008, he was tried and convicted before a U.S. military commission of conspiracy to commit war crimes.

Citing Article I and Article III of the Constitution, Bahlul argues that Congress may establish military commissions only for offenses under the *international* law of war. Bahlul further argues (and the Government concedes) that conspiracy is not an offense under the international law of war. Therefore, Bahlul contends that he may not be tried for conspiracy before a U.S. military commission.

On its face, Bahlul's argument is extraordinary. It would incorporate international law into the U.S. Constitution as a judicially enforceable constraint on Congress and the President. As a matter of U.S. constitutional law, the wartime decisions of Congress and the President to try unlawful enemy combatants before military commissions would be subject to the dictates of foreign nations and the international community, as embodied in international law.

The Government responds that, under the Constitution, Congress may establish military commissions to try, at a minimum, (i) international law of war offenses *and* (ii) offenses that are not international law of war offenses but have historically been tried by U.S. military commissions. As the Government points out, conspiracy has historically been tried by U.S. military commissions.

This case therefore raises one central legal question: Under the U.S. Constitution, may Congress establish military commissions to try unlawful enemy combatants for the offense of conspiracy to commit war crimes, even if conspiracy is not an offense under the international law of war? The answer is yes. We know that from the text and original understanding of the Constitution; the structure of the Constitution; landmark Supreme Court precedent; longstanding congressional practice, as reflected in venerable and contemporary federal statutes; and deeply rooted Executive Branch practice, from the 1800s to the present.

I

We first address the Article I issue. Bahlul acknowledges that Congress possesses authority under Article I to establish military commissions to try war crimes. But he contends that military commissions may try only *international* law of war offenses. Bahlul further argues (and the Government concedes) that conspiracy is not an international law of war offense. Therefore, Bahlul says he may not be tried by military commission for conspiracy.

Contrary to Bahlul's argument, Article I of the Constitution does not impose international law as a limit on Congress's authority to make offenses triable by military commission. That is apparent from five sources of law: the text and original understanding of Article I, the overall structure of the Constitution, landmark Supreme Court precedent, longstanding federal statutes, and deeply rooted U.S. military commission practice.

First, the text and original understanding of Article I demonstrate that international law does not impose a limit on Congress's authority to make offenses triable by military commission.

The premise of Bahlul's Article I argument is that Congress's *sole* source of constitutional authority to make offenses triable by military commission is the

Define and Punish Clause of Article I. That Clause grants Congress authority to "define and punish . . . Offences against the Law of Nations." U.S. CONST. art. I, § 8, cl. 10. Bahlul argues that the "law of nations" is a synonym for international law, and further contends that conspiracy is not an offense under the international law of war. Therefore, according to Bahlul, Congress lacks power under Article I, Section 8 to make conspiracy an offense triable by military commission.

We need not decide the scope of the Define and Punish Clause in this case. That is because the premise of Bahlul's Article I argument is flawed. Regardless of the scope of the Define and Punish Clause, an issue we do not decide, Congress's Article I authority to establish military commissions—including its authority to determine which crimes may be tried by military commission—does not derive exclusively from that Clause.

Rather, the war powers clauses in Article I, Section 8—including the Declare War Clause and the Captures Clause, together with the Necessary and Proper Clause—supply Congress with ample authority to establish military commissions and make offenses triable by military commission. And the Declare War Clause and the other war powers clauses in Article I do not refer to international law or otherwise impose international law as a constraint on Congress's authority to make offenses triable by military commission.

As the Supreme Court has long recognized, a congressional authorization of war pursuant to the Declare War Clause is understood "by universal agreement and practice" to encompass all of the traditional incidents of war—including the power to kill, capture, and detain enemy combatants, and most relevant here, the power to try unlawful enemy combatants by military commission for war crimes. *Hamdi v. Rumsfeld*, 542 U.S. 507, 518 (2004) (binding opinion of O'Connor, J.); *see also Hamdan v. Rumsfeld*, 548 U.S. 557, 593-94 (2006); *In re Yamashita*, 327 U.S. 1, 11-12 (1946). As Colonel William Winthrop, described by the Supreme Court as the "Blackstone of Military Law," *Reid v. Covert*, 354 U.S. 1, 19 n.38 (1957) (plurality opinion), summarized it: "[I]n general, it is those provisions of the Constitution which empower Congress to 'declare war' and 'raise armies,' and which, in authorizing the initiation of *war*, authorize the employment of all necessary and proper agencies for its due prosecution, from which this tribunal derives its original sanction. . . . The commission is simply an instrumentality for the more efficient execution of the war powers vested in Congress and the power vested in the President as Commander-in-chief in war." WILLIAM WINTHROP, MILITARY LAW AND PRECEDENTS 831 (rev. 2d ed. 1920). So too, Justice Story explained that Congress's power to make substantive and procedural rules for military commissions is a "natural incident to the preceding powers to make war, to raise armies, and to provide and maintain a navy." 3 JOSEPH STORY, COMMENTARIES ON THE CONSTITUTION OF THE UNITED STATES § 1192 (1833).

In short, it would be textually and historically inaccurate to deem the Define and Punish Clause, whatever its scope, as the *sole* source of Congress's authority here. The Declare War Clause and the other war powers clauses in Article

I authorize Congress to establish military commissions and make offenses triable by military commission. And those clauses do not refer to international law or otherwise impose international law as a constraint on Congress's authority to make offenses triable by military commission. By their terms, therefore, those clauses do not confine U.S. military commissions to trying only international law of war offenses.

Second, the overall structure of the Constitution strongly reinforces the conclusion that international law does not impose a limit on Congress's authority to make offenses triable by military commission.

The Framers of the Constitution paid careful attention to the allocation of war powers between the national government and the states, and within the national government. The Framers assigned the national government — in particular, Congress and the President — the authority to make wartime decisions on behalf of the United States. The Framers assigned that power to the national government in part because the inability to wage war effectively had been one of the key weaknesses of the Articles of Confederation, and the Framers sought to fix that flaw.

What matters most for present purposes is that the Framers certainly did not purport to afford foreign nations (acting through the international law of war or otherwise) any constitutional authority over the wartime decisions of the United States, such as the determination of which war crimes may be prosecuted by U.S. military commissions. It would be a historical anomaly to conclude that "We the People of the United States" gave foreign or international bodies the power to constrain U.S. war-making authority in that way. Yet that would be the necessary consequence of the argument put forward by Bahlul and the joint dissent. They would incorporate international law into the U.S. Constitution as a *judicially enforceable constraint* on the wartime decisions of the Congress and the President. *As a matter of U.S. constitutional law*, Congress and the President would be subject to the dictates of the international community, a community that at any given time may be unsupportive of or even hostile to U.S. national security interests.

Put simply, the argument advanced by Bahlul and the joint dissent does not comport with the Constitution's structure. The Constitution does not give foreign nations (acting through the international law of war or otherwise) a de facto veto over Congress's determination of which war crimes may be tried by U.S. military commissions.

Third, consistent with the Constitution's text and structure, landmark Supreme Court precedent likewise supports the conclusion that Congress's authority to establish offenses triable by military commission is not confined by international law.

The Supreme Court's leading constitutional decision regarding military commissions is *Ex Parte Quirin*. There, the Supreme Court ruled that use of military commissions to try war crimes was constitutionally permissible. In doing so, the Court emphasized that U.S. military commissions have long been authorized by Congress, and the Court noted in particular that military commissions have long tried the offense of spying. *See Ex Parte Quirin*, 317 U.S. 1, 41-42 & n.14 (1942). But spying was not and has never been an offense under the international law of war. The Court nonetheless relied on and approved of trying spying offenses by military commission. *Quirin* is admittedly a difficult decision to decipher. But the Supreme Court's reliance on spying, a non-international-law-of-war offense, as an offense triable by military commission at least suggests—even if it does not conclusively show—that Congress has authority under Article I to make offenses triable by military commission even if those offenses are not war crimes under the international law of war.

The Court in *Quirin* did not say that military commissions are constitutionally permitted only for international law of war offenses. Nor did any later Supreme Court case hold that military commissions are constitutionally permitted only for international law of war offenses. One would have expected the Court at some point to say as much if the Court actually thought as much.

An amicus brief nonetheless argues that the *Quirin* Court thought that international law was a constitutional constraint on Congress but that the *Quirin* Court believed, albeit mistakenly, that spying was an international law of war offense. *See* National Institute of Military Justice Amicus Br. at 14 n.6. The joint dissent agrees. That argument lacks foundation. To begin with, the Supreme Court never said anything to the effect that Congress's *constitutional* authority to make offenses triable by military commission is constrained by the international law of war. Moreover, the idea that the Court actually thought spying was an international law offense necessarily assumes that the *Quirin* Court—with Justices such as Harlan Fiske Stone, Felix Frankfurter, Robert Jackson, and Hugo Black—was ignorant of the content of international law. We cannot plausibly make such an assumption. There is no indication in the opinion or historical record that the *Quirin* Court actually believed that spying was an international law of war offense. Nor do any later Supreme Court cases suggest as much. On the contrary, the *Quirin* Court cited authorities that indicated that spying was *not* an international law of war offense.

Fourth, when we interpret the Constitution, especially the provisions related to the separation of powers, the historical practice of the Legislative and Executive Branches matters. *See Zivotofsky v. Kerry*, ____ U.S. ____, 135 S. Ct. 2076, 2091 (2015) ("In separation-of-powers cases this Court has often put significant weight upon historical practice."); *NLRB v. Noel Canning*, ____ U.S. ____, 134 S. Ct. 2550, 2560 (2014) ("[L]ongstanding practice of the government can inform our determination of what the law is."); *The Pocket Veto Case*, 279 U.S. 655, 689 (1929) ("Long settled and established practice is a consideration of great weight in a proper interpretation of constitutional provisions . . . .").

In this case, turning first to the Legislative Branch, Congress's longstanding practice strongly supports the conclusion that international law is not a constitutional constraint on Congress's authority to make particular crimes triable by military commission. From the earliest days of the Republic, Congress has gone beyond international law in specifying the offenses that may be tried by military commission. Beginning in 1776, the Continental Congress codified the offense of spying—a non-international-law offense—as a crime triable by military tribunal. *See* Resolution of the Continental Congress (Aug. 21, 1776), *in* 5 Journals of the Continental Congress 1774-1789, at 693 (Worthington Chauncey Ford ed. 1906) [hereinafter "Journals"] (authorizing trial by military court of "all persons, not members of, nor owing allegiance to, any of the United States of America . . . who shall be found lurking as spies"). Likewise, in September 1776, Congress authorized trial by military tribunal for another non-international-law offense: aiding the enemy. *See* Articles of War (Sept. 20, 1776), *in* 5 Journals, at 799. In 1789, after the Constitution was ratified, the First Congress adopted the same Articles of War that had been promulgated by the Continental Congress, including the offenses of spying and aiding the enemy. *See* Act of Sept. 29, 1789, ch. 25, § 4, 1 Stat. 95, 96 (1789). Again in 1806, Congress updated those provisions and, in doing so, was careful to preserve the offenses of spying and aiding the enemy as crimes triable by military tribunal. *See* Articles of War of 1806, ch. 20, arts. 56, 57, § 2, 2 Stat. 359, 366, 371 (1806). Both of those prohibitions remain on the books today. *See* 10 U.S.C. §§ 950t(26), 950t(27). Congress has made those two crimes triable by military commission even though they are *not* international law of war offenses.

Congress's practice of going beyond international law has continued to the present. As recently as 2006 and 2009, Congress enacted new laws making several non-international-law offenses, such as solicitation and material support for terrorism, triable by military commission. *See* Military Commissions Act of 2006, Pub. L. No. 109-366, 120 Stat. 2600, 2630; Military Commissions Act of 2009, Pub. L. No. 111-84, 123 Stat. 2574, 2611. . . .

Fifth, in addition to the historical practice in Congress, the historical practice in the Executive Branch demonstrates that international law is not a constraint on which offenses may be tried by military commissions. Indeed, perhaps the most telling factor when considering this constitutional question is the deeply rooted history of U.S. military commission trials of the offense of conspiracy, which is not and has never been an offense under the international law of war.

The two most important military commission precedents in U.S. history—the trials of the Lincoln conspirators and the Nazi saboteurs—were trials for the offense of conspiracy.

Consider the trial of the Lincoln conspirators. After seeking the advice of the Attorney General, President Andrew Johnson decided to try the Lincoln conspirators by military commission rather than by criminal trial in civilian court. The Lincoln conspirators were expressly charged with and convicted of *conspiracy*—in that case, conspiracy to violate the law of war by killing the President and Commander in Chief of the Union Army, Abraham Lincoln. Indeed, conspiracy was the *only* offense charged against them. After an extensive multi-week trial that gripped the Nation and after vigorous argument about the facts and the commission's jurisdiction, numerous conspirators were convicted of conspiracy.

The joint dissent tries to cast doubt on whether the Lincoln conspirators were actually tried for conspiracy. There is no doubt. Consider what a contemporary court said in response to a habeas petition filed by three of the Lincoln conspirators: "[T]he prisoners are guilty of the charge on which they were convicted—of a conspiracy to commit the military crime which one of their number did commit, and some of them of more or less participation." *Ex parte Mudd*, 17 F. Cas. 954 (S.D. Fla. 1868). . . .

Consider also the military commission trial of the eight Nazi saboteurs who had been selected to execute Operation Pastorius—Adolf Hitler's plan to destroy America's war industries and facilities—and secretly entered the United States during World War II. The defendants were expressly charged with and convicted of *conspiracy*, as well as of other offenses. Attorney General of the United States Francis Biddle, who would later represent the United States as a judge at Nuremberg, personally prosecuted the case before the military commission. President Franklin Roosevelt reviewed and approved all of the convictions. The defendants filed habeas corpus petitions to block the proceedings as unconstitutional. The Supreme Court affirmed the legality of the trial, and in doing so, did not disturb the conspiracy charge. *See Quirin*, 317 U.S. at 46. . . .

[I]n the two most significant U.S. wars of the last 200 years—the Civil War and World War II—as well as in the current war against al Qaeda and its associated forces, the U.S. has employed military commissions. And the *most important* military commission trials during those wars were trials for conspiracy, which is not an international law of war offense. That historical and contemporary practice cannot be airbrushed out of the picture. Prosecuting conspiracy and other non-international-law-of-war offenses is not at the periphery of U.S. military commission history and practice. Prosecuting conspiracy and other non-international-law-of-war offenses lies at the core of U.S. military commission history and practice. . . .

In short, the text and original understanding of the Constitution; the structure of the Constitution; landmark Supreme Court precedent; the deeply rooted historical practice of the Legislative Branch, as seen in federal statutes; and the longstanding practice of the Executive Branch, as seen in U.S. military commission practice stretching back over two centuries, all point decisively to the same conclusion: The war powers clauses of Article I of the Constitution do not impose international law as a constraint on Congress's authority to establish offenses triable by military commission.

II

Bahlul also contends that Article III of the U.S. Constitution confines U.S. military commissions to international law of war offenses.

This iteration of Bahlul's argument begins with the premise that Article III vests the judicial power in Article III courts and requires crimes to be tried by jury, not before military commissions. Based solely on the text of Article III,

Bahlul might have a point. But the Supreme Court has long recognized an exception to Article III for military commissions to try enemy war crimes.

Exceptions to Article III, including the exception for military commissions, are established and interpreted in light of historical practice. . . .

In this context, if historical practice demonstrates that an offense is triable by U.S. military commission, that history resolves the Article III issue. As explained in Part I of this opinion, the history of U.S. military commissions trying non-international-law-of-war offenses is extensive and dates from the beginning of the Republic. That historical practice therefore amply demonstrates that Article III is not a barrier to U.S. military commission trials of non-international-law-of-war offenses, including the offense of conspiracy to commit war crimes.

Notwithstanding that history, Bahlul says that *Quirin* already considered the military commission exception to Article III and limited the exception to international law of war offenses.

Bahlul's reading of *Quirin* is incorrect. In *Quirin*, the Nazi saboteur defendants claimed that they had a right under Article III to be tried by jury in an Article III federal court and therefore could not be tried by military commission. At some length, the *Quirin* Court specifically considered and rejected the defendants' Article III objection. *See Quirin*, 317 U.S. at 38-45. The Court explained that Article III did not "enlarge the then existing right to a jury trial" beyond the right as it existed at common law. *Id.* at 39. Because the common law did not preclude trial by military commission for war crimes, Article III "cannot be taken to have extended the right to demand a jury to trials by military commission, or to have required that offenses against the law of war not triable by jury at common law be tried only in the civil courts." *Id.* at 40. . . .

The Supreme Court's analysis in *Quirin* is instructive for present purposes because, as noted above, the offense of spying on which the *Quirin* Court relied to answer the Article III objection was not (and is not) an offense under the international law of war. It thus makes little sense to read *Quirin* as barring military commission trials of non-international-law-of-war offenses when *Quirin*, in rejecting a jury trial objection to military commissions, expressly relied on a longstanding statute making spying—a *non*-international-law-of-war offense—triable by military commission. . . .

In short, Article III does not limit U.S. military commissions to international law of war offenses or otherwise foreclose trial of the offense of conspiracy to commit war crimes before U.S. military commissions.

All of that said, the Constitution does not grant Congress unlimited authority to designate crimes as triable by military commission. At oral argument, the Government stated that the charges must at least involve an enemy combatant who committed a proscribed act during or in relation to hostilities against the United States. In general, if an offense is an international law of war offense *or* has historically been tried by U.S. military commission, that is *sufficient* to uphold Congress's constitutional authority to make the offense triable by military commission. . . .

But is one of those conditions *necessary*? In other words, what if an offense is neither an international law of war offense nor historically rooted in U.S. military commission practice? Consider a hypothetical new statute that makes cyber-attacks by enemy forces a war crime triable by military commission. *Quirin* stated that Article III does "not restrict whatever authority was conferred by the Constitution to try offenses against the law of war by military commission," and does not bar "the practice of trying, before military tribunals without a jury, offenses committed by enemy belligerents against the law of war." *Quirin*, 317 U.S. at 45, 41. Perhaps that language suggests that Article III permits what Article I authorizes with respect to which enemy war crimes may be tried by U.S. military commission. But we need not answer that hypothetical in this case and need not define with precision the outer limits of the Constitution in this context, other than to say that international law is not such a limit. Wherever one might ultimately draw the outer boundaries of Congress's authority to establish offenses triable by military commission, the historically rooted offense of conspiracy to commit war crimes is well within those limits. An enemy of the United States who engages in a conspiracy to commit war crimes—in Bahlul's case, by plotting with Osama bin Laden to murder thousands of American civilians—may be tried by a U.S. military commission for conspiracy to commit war crimes.

III

In light of the importance of this case, and the serious and passionate arguments advanced by the joint dissent, we close with a few additional responses to points made by the joint dissent.

First, in reaching its conclusion, the joint dissent relies in part on *Hamdan v. Rumsfeld*, 548 U.S. 557 (2006). That reliance is misplaced. As relevant here, *Hamdan* was a statutory case interpreting the phrase "law of war" in 10 U.S.C. § 821. Nowhere did the Supreme Court ever say (or even hint) that the *United States Constitution* imposed international law as a limit on what offenses may be tried by U.S. military commissions. The joint dissent's citations to *Hamdan* therefore do not support its *constitutional* position.

In fact, the *Hamdan* decision and its aftermath only highlight the extraordinary nature of the joint dissent's position. In *Hamdan*, the Court confronted but ultimately did not resolve the question of whether the relevant statute in effect at the time, 10 U.S.C. § 821, barred military commission trials of alleged war criminals *for conspiracy*. But four of the Justices in the majority expressly invited Congress to clarify the scope of military commission power. *Hamdan*, 548 U.S. at 636 (Breyer, J., concurring, joined by Kennedy, Souter, and Ginsburg, JJ.); *id.* at 653 (Kennedy, J., concurring in part, joined in relevant part by Souter, Ginsburg, and Breyer, JJ.). In response to the Justices' invitation, Congress and the President promptly enacted new legislation to make crystal clear that conspiracy is an offense triable by military commission. Military Commissions Act of 2006 (expressly authorizing trials before military commissions for conspiracy offenses). . . .

Second, the joint dissent says: "It is not international law, however, that constrains Congress's authority here—it is Article III." Dissenting Op. at 827-28. That sentence glides over the key question. The question is whether Article III (or Article I) incorporates international law as a constraint on U.S. military commissions. The joint dissent says yes. But the constitutional text and structure, Supreme Court precedents, and deeply rooted U.S. history tell us that the answer is no.

Of course, the consistent U.S. history is the consistent U.S. history for a reason. As explained above, the consequences for the United States of *judicially* incorporating international law into the U.S. Constitution would be deeply problematic and run afoul of our most fundamental constitutional principles and traditions. International law often embodies a majority or consensus view of nations. Does the United States Constitution really allow foreign nations, through the guise of international law, to set *constitutional* limits *enforceable in U.S. courts* against the U.S. war effort? Under Bahlul's argument, and under the theory advanced by the joint dissent, the answer would be yes. We think not. We see no basis in U.S. law, precedent, or history—not to mention, common sense—for that position. To paraphrase Justice Jackson, the Constitution is not "a suicide pact." *Terminiello v. Chicago*, 337 U.S. 1, 37 (1949) (Jackson, J., dissenting).

To be sure, the Judiciary plays a critical role in enforcing constitutional and statutory limits in justiciable wartime cases, and this Court must not hesitate (and has not hesitated) in doing so, even when the consequences are significant. But in this case, neither Article I nor Article III confines Congress to international law of war offenses when Congress establishes war crimes triable by military commission.

To be clear, we take no position on the *policy* question of whether the U.S. Government should use military commissions to try the offense of conspiracy or other non-international-law-of-war offenses, or indeed whether the Government should use military commissions at all. That policy decision belongs first to Congress and the President in the legislative process, and then to the President in the exercise of his or her Commander-in-Chief power. . . . International law is important, and the political branches have good reason to adhere to international law when determining what offenses will be tried before U.S. military commissions. But international law has its own enforcement mechanisms. The federal courts are not roving enforcers of international law. And the federal courts are not empowered to smuggle international law into the U.S. Constitution and then wield it as a club against Congress and the President in wartime.

Third, the joint dissent seeks to explain away the history and practice of U.S. military commissions. But that effort is entirely unpersuasive.

In the face of the deeply rooted U.S. history and practice of trying conspiracy offenses by military commission, the joint dissent had two options. It could discount the importance of history to the constitutional analysis, and try to explain that the constitutional text and structure matter most here. The joint dissent did not choose that approach, no doubt because the constitutional text and structure also show what the history shows: that international law is not a constraint on Congress when Congress determines which offenses may be tried by military commission.

Alternatively, the joint dissent could attack the history head-on on the theory that the history does not actually show what it seems to show. That is the route that the joint dissent chose. But it does not work. Consider all of the contortions the joint dissent has to make in attempting to wriggle out of the history. First, faced with the historical fact that Congress since the Founding has consistently made non-international-law offenses triable by military commission, the joint dissent unconvincingly posits that those Congresses all mistakenly believed that those offenses actually were international law offenses (even though they were not and even though there is no persuasive evidence that Congress thought they were). Second, faced with the historical fact that the Executive Branch's two most important military commissions in the history of the country were trials of conspiracy offenses, which are not international law offenses, the joint dissent implausibly suggests that the Lincoln case was not really a conspiracy case (even though it plainly was), and it notes that the conspiracy charges against the eight Nazis at issue in *Quirin* were never directly reviewed by a court (even though the relevant point is that the military commission trial of the Nazis for conspiracy remains a central part of Executive Branch historical practice). Third, faced with the fact that the Supreme Court relied on a non-international-law offense, spying, in its landmark *Quirin* decision upholding military commissions, the joint dissent seeks to sweep that inconvenient snippet under the rug by suggesting that the Court mistakenly believed that spying was an international law offense (even though there is no persuasive evidence that the Court actually thought as much).

The bottom line here is that the history matters, the history is overwhelming, and the history devastates the joint dissent's position.

Fourth, in justifying its position, the joint dissent posits a hypothetical of non-U.S.-citizens living together in an apartment in Virginia with pipe bombs, al Qaeda propaganda, and a map of the Washington Metro. The joint dissent says it would be "dangerous" to apprehend such a group and then try them for conspiracy before a military commission. We are mystified by the joint dissent's apparent belief that this is a helpful hypothetical for its position. We take it that the point of the hypothetical is to suggest that military commissions should not be used to try non-citizen enemy terrorists who are (i) captured in the United States (ii) before they commit their planned attacks. Of course, the current war has no such neat geographical boundaries. And neither did World War II, for that matter. After all, the Nazi saboteurs were captured in the United States before their planned attacks on U.S. facilities. They were then prosecuted before U.S. military commissions. And if Mohamed Atta and his fellow attackers had been captured on the night of September 10, 2001, in Portland, Maine, and elsewhere, and then tried before congressionally authorized U.S. military commissions for conspiracy, we certainly would not have characterized that scenario as "dangerous."

Fifth, the joint dissent insists that the mission of the military is to defeat enemies on the battlefield, not to punish enemy wrongdoers. The dissent's effort to define U.S. military strategy in that way is both legally and factually flawed. As the Supreme Court has long recognized, including in landmark cases such as *Hamdi*, war is waged not only by killing enemy combatants, but also by surveilling, capturing, and detaining enemy forces, and by trying unlawful enemy combatants for war crimes. And in the current war, the modus operandi of the enemy is to target citizens; to frighten, unsettle, disrupt, and demoralize; to make normal peaceful life impossible and carnage routine. In response to the enemy's tactics, two Congresses and two Presidents—like their predecessors throughout U.S. history—have determined that employing military commissions to try unlawful enemy combatants for their war crimes is an important part of the overall war effort. The Constitution assigns that question of military strategy to Congress and the President, not to the joint dissenters.

Sixth, and relatedly, in seeking to minimize the consequences of its theory, the joint dissent suggests that military commissions are not essential to the U.S. war effort because the U.S. Government can simply try al Qaeda war criminals in federal courts, including for conspiracy to commit war crimes. With all respect, the joint dissent has no business making such a statement. It has no basis to express such confidence and no relevant expertise on that question of wartime strategy. Unlike the joint dissenters, Presidents Bush and Obama, as well as the two Congresses in 2006 and 2009, determined that the ordinary federal court process is not suitable for trying certain enemy war criminals. The only question for us as judges is one of law: whether the U.S. Constitution permits that policy choice by Congress and the President. If the answer were no, then we would enforce the Constitution. But here, the answer is yes.

. . .

We vote to affirm Bahlul's conviction for conspiracy to commit war crimes.

NOTES AND QUESTIONS

1. What is the actual holding in *Bahlul*? Nine judges decided the case. However, only four judges held that international law does not impose a limitation on Congress's authority to make offenses triable by military commission.

2. Judge Kavanaugh (now Supreme Court Justice Kavanaugh) maintains that international law does not impose a limit on Congress's authority to make offenses triable by military commission. He cites five sources of law to support his argument. What sources of law does Judge Kavanaugh rely? Which of these five sources of law do you find most persuasive? Which of these five sources of law do you find least persuasive?

3. Judge Kavanaugh maintains that the war powers clauses in Article I, § 8—including the Declare War Clause and Captures Clause, together with the Necessary and Proper Clause—supply Congress with ample authority to establish military commissions and make offenses triable by military commissions, including inchoate conspiracy to commit war crimes. Do you find Kavanaugh's arguments persuasive? Do the 1949 Geneva Conventions impose a limit on Congress's war powers, including the treatment and prosecution of alleged war criminals?

4. Judge Kavanaugh concedes that the Constitution does not grant Congress unlimited authority to designate crimes as triable by military commission. What are the limitations imposed on Congress's authority in this context? Based on these limitations, can Congress lawfully designate material support for terrorism as an offense triable by military commission? What are the outer limits of Congress's authority to make crimes triable by military commission?

5. The dissent argues that military commissions are not essential to the U.S. war effort because the government can simply try al Qaeda and other terrorist war criminals in federal court. Traditionally, military tribunals are born of military necessity. *See Hamdan v. Rumsfeld*, 548 U.S. 557 (2006). What is the military necessity for the use of military commissions to try suspected foreign terrorists today?

6. In her concurring opinion, Judge Henderson affirms Bahlul's conviction for the reasons she provided in her dissent in *Al Bahlul v. United States*, 792 F.3d 1, 27-72 (D.C. Cir. 2015) (since vacated). Like Judges Kavanaugh, Brown, and Griffith, Judge Henderson concludes that Congress has the authority to make conspiracy to commit war crimes an offense triable by military commission. Within Article I, Judge Henderson identifies three areas of the Constitution from which Congress derives its power to try enemy combatants by military commission: the Define and Punish Clause, the Necessary and Proper Clause, and Congress's Article I war powers, including the power to conduct war in all of its "incidents." *Id.* at 42-55. Within Article III, Judge Henderson points to the long-time historical use of military commissions for war crime prosecutions—an exception to the Judicial Power Clause—as a constitutional basis for its use. *Id.* at 63-64. Henderson would distinguish *Bahlul* from other national security cases such as *Quirin*, *Hamdan*, and *Yamashita* in finding that the actions of Congress and the President satisfy Justice Jackson's first category of his *Youngstown* framework. *Id.* at 52. Here, Congress exercised its Article I power to enumerate conspiracy as a law-of-war offense by enacting the Military Commissions Act of 2006, which subsequently gave the President the necessary congressional approval to try perpetrators for conspiracy by military commission.

7. In a separate concurring opinion Judge Millett analyzed the issue solely from a procedural standpoint and would review Bahlul's constitutional challenges only for plain error. *Bahlul v. United States*, 840 F.3d 757, 778-80 (D.C. Cir. 2016) (en banc). Millet argued that since Bahlul failed to raise any Article III objections during trial, he could not raise them on appeal without violating fundamental procedural protections such as the contemporaneous-objection requirement.

Hence for Judge Millett, it was not necessary for the court to reach the more substantive question of whether inchoate conspiracy is an offense triable by military commission. According to Millett, Bahlul did not simply waive his right to appeal any legal challenges but forfeited it when he intentionally chose not to raise constitutional objections at trial. *Id.* at 784. On those grounds, Judge Millett found that Bahlul's conviction did not plainly exceed Congress's power under Article I's Define and Punish Clause or offend Article III's assignment of judicial power to the federal courts.

8. In his concurrence, Judge Wilkins affirmed Bahlul's conviction but for different reasons. He argued that "Bahlul's conviction shares little in common with . . . the features of inchoate conspiracy, and instead bears a close kinship to a conviction under a *Pinkerton* theory, which does not offend the Constitution." *Bahlul v. United States*, 840 F.3d at 801. Under a *Pinkerton* theory, a member to a conspiracy can be vicariously liable if the substantive offense is reasonably foreseeable and committed in furtherance of the conspiracy's objectives. *Id.* Judge Wilkins found that the government "proved all of the *Pinkerton* elements beyond a reasonable doubt." *Id.* at 803. Furthermore, Judge Wilkins equated Bahlul's criminal liability under *Pinkerton* with the joint criminal enterprise (JCE) doctrine, a recognized theory of vicarious liability under international law. There are three forms of JCE. The third variant occurs when there is "a common purpose to commit a crime where one of the perpetrators commits an act which, while outside the common purpose, is nevertheless a natural and foreseeable consequence of the effecting of that common purpose." *Id.* at 803 (quoting *Prosecutor v. Vasiljevic*, Case No. IT-98-3-A, Judgment, ¶ 99 (Int'l Crim. Trib. for the Former Yugoslavia, Feb. 25, 2004). Judge Wilkins found that JCE III is "essentially the *Pinkerton* doctrine," and "[b]ecause the factual elements that were proven during Bahlul's prosecution were indistinguishable from a theory recognized under international law, it does not offend the Constitution." *Id.* at 804.

However, it should be noted that JCE III is a very controversial theory of criminal liability under international law. The critics of JCE III maintain that it is unfair to hold someone vicariously liable for a crime he did not commit nor intend. For example, the Rome Statute of the International Criminal Court, Article 25(3)(d), rejects JCE III liability. Article 25(3)(d) requires proof that the accused committed an act that "contributes to the commission or attempted commission of such a crime by a group of persons acting with a common purpose." Furthermore, such contribution must be intentional and "made with the aim of furthering the criminal activity or criminal purpose of the group" or made "in the knowledge of the intention of the group to commit the crime." Under the statute, merely entering into an agreement to commit an unlawful act is insufficient to hold the accused vicariously liable for every crime committed by a member of the conspiracy that is reasonably foreseeable. In 2010, a Cambodian Tribunal rejected JCE III liability with respect to crimes against humanity and war crimes committed in Cambodia between 1975 and 1979. *See Prosecutor v. Ieng Thirith, Ieng Sary and Khieu Samphan*, Criminal Case File

No. 002/19-09-2007-ECCC/OCIJ (PTC38), Decision on the Appeals Against the Co-Investigative Judges Order on Joint Criminal Enterprise (JCE) (ECCC May 20, 2010). *See also* Cóman Kenny, *Jurisprudence Continues to Evolve: The ECCC's Revision of Common Purpose Liability*, 16 J. Int'l Crim. Just. 623, 633 (2018) (in 2003, the International Criminal Tribunal for the Former Yugoslavia unanimously held that a person accused of committing genocide could not be convicted of a specific intent crime pursuant to JCE III because of insufficient connection between moral culpability and the mode of liability); Natalia Perova, *Stretching the Joint Criminal Enterprise Doctrine to the Extreme: When Culpability and Liability Do Not Match*, 16 J. Int'l Crim. Just. 761, 788-90 (2016) (argues that the level of culpability does not match the degree of punishment under JCE III and that the application of JCE III is especially problematic with respect to specific intent crimes because the mens rea standard is lowered from proof of a specific intent (*dolus specialis*) to advertent recklessness (*dolus eventualis*)); Jens David Ohlin, *Joint Intentions to Commit International Crimes*, 11 Chi. J. Int'l L. 693, 753 (2011) (argues that JCE III for specific intent crimes should be eliminated altogether because the doctrine is not able to distinguish between criminal defendants who merely exhibit recklessness from those who directly intend the consequences of their criminal participation, thus ultimately raising questions about fairness and legality).

ASSESSMENT QUESTIONS

1. Treason differs from the offense of seditious conspiracy in several important respects. Which of the following statements are correct?
   a. Treason can only be committed by someone owing allegiance to the United States.
   b. Seditious conspiracy has a requirement of duty of loyalty or allegiance to the United States.
   c. Treason and seditious conspiracy extend beyond United States jurisdictional boundaries.
   d. Treason requires the testimony of two witnesses to the same overt act.
   e. Seditious conspiracy requires at least two persons to commit the offense.
   f. Seditious conspiracy proscribes a different crime and protects a different governmental interest than treason.
   g. Only a, d, e, and f are correct.
   h. Only a, d, and e are correct.

2. True or False: Because the seditious conspiracy statute punishes conspiracy to "levy war" against the United States without a confirming two-witness requirement, the statute is unconstitutional.

3. True or False: The seditious conspiracy statute is overbroad because Congress could have achieved its public safety aims without chilling First Amendment rights by punishing only substantive acts such as bombing, the provision of weapons, or other related violent acts.

4. Which of the following statements about the material support statutes, 18 U.S.C. §§ 2339A and B, are correct?
   a. The provision of material support intended to promote the non-violent activities of a foreign terrorist organization is not punishable under 18 U.S.C. § 2339B.
   b. Section 2339B prohibits being a member of a foreign terrorist organization, such as al Qaeda or ISIS, or vigorously promoting and supporting the political goals of the group.
   c. Independent advocacy that lends legitimacy and support to a foreign terrorist organization is punishable under 18 U.S.C. § 2339B.
   d. Section 2339A requires proof that the provision of material support or resources was done "knowing or intending" that they are to be used to carry out a statutorily enumerated violent crime.
   e. To sustain a conviction under § 2339B, the government only has to prove that the defendant acted with knowledge that the organization is a designated "foreign terrorist organization," or the organization has engaged or engages in terrorist activity.
   f. All of the above.

    g. Only a, d, and e are correct.

    h. Only d and e are correct.

5. True or False: Inchoate conspiracy to commit war crimes is an offense triable before a military commission?

ASSESSMENT ANSWERS

1. The correct answer is g. Statements a, d, e, and f are correct. Statement a is correct because the treason statute, 18 U.S.C. § 2381, limits treason to those persons "owing allegiance to the United States." The seditious conspiracy statute does not include a requirement of loyalty or allegiance to the United States and therefore is incorrect. Therefore, statement b is wrong. Statement c is incorrect. In *Kawakita v. United States*, 343 U.S. 717 (1952), the Court rejected the defendant's argument that treason cannot be committed abroad or in enemy territory, stating that "we . . . therefore reject the suggestion that an American citizen living beyond the territorial limits of the United States may not commit treason. . . ." Moreover, in *United States v. Rodriguez*, 803 F.2d 318 (7th Cir. 1986), the court stated: "Unlike treason, seditious conspiracy does not extend beyond United States territorial boundaries."

    Statement d is correct. Article III, § 3 provides: "No Person shall be convicted of Treason unless on the Testimony of two Witnesses to the same overt Act, or on Confession in open Court." Statement e is also correct because seditious conspiracy requires proof of a conspiratorial agreement between two or more persons. Finally, statement f is correct because the seditious conspiracy statute was enacted by Congress to "fend off urban terrorism," while treason protects a different interest, "levying war." In *Rodriguez*, the court added that § 2384 "provides a vehicle for the government to make arrests before a conspiracy ripens into a violent situation."

2. The statement is false. This argument was expressly rejected in *United States v. Rahman*, 189 F.3d 8 (2d Cir. 1999), where the court stated that seditious conspiracy is a distinct and separate offense from treason. The court stated that seditious conspiracy "differs from treason not only in name and associated stigma, but also in its essential elements."

3. The statement is false. This argument was rejected by the court in *Rahman*. The court stated: "[I]t is well established that the Government may criminalize certain preparatory steps towards criminal action, even when the crime consists of the use of conspiratorial or exhortatory words."

4. The correct answer is h. Statements d and e correctly state the mens rea requirements for conviction under 18 U.S.C. §§ 2339A and 2339B. Statement a is incorrect. In *Holder v. Humanitarian Law Project*, 561 U.S. 1 (2010), the Court rejected the plaintiffs' argument that § 2339B requires intent to further the goals of the terrorist organization. The Court held: "Congress plainly spoke to the necessary mental state for a violation of § 2339B, and it chose knowledge about

the organization's connection to terrorism, not specific intent to further the organization's terrorist activities."

Statement b is incorrect because the Court explicitly stated: "The statute does not prohibit being a member of one of the designated groups or vigorously promoting and supporting the political goals of the group. . . . What [§ 2339B] prohibits is the act of giving material support. . . ." Finally, statement c is wrong because the Court in *Humanitarian Law Project* held that the statute does not criminalize "independent" political advocacy. Instead, the statute only punishes political advocacy if the defendant is acting in coordination with or under the direction and control of a designated FTO.

5. Whether conspiracy to commit war crimes is an offense triable by military commission remains an open question. While the en banc court in *Bahlul v. United States* affirmed Bahlul's conviction for conspiracy, only a plurality of four judges upheld Congress's authority to make conspiracy a war crime triable by military commission.

CHAPTER 11

Preventive Detention

The previous chapter explored the power of the state to deprive a person of liberty through the operation of the criminal justice system. But whether civilian or military, such processes are *ex post*, i.e., detention *follows* sufficient proof of a past offense and usually serves as punishment for a criminal conviction. Even pretrial detention anticipates an impending process to judge alleged criminal conduct. This chapter asks a different set of questions, those concerning *ex ante* detention for reasons *other* than punishment. This is what is meant by the phrase "preventive detention," the deprivation of liberty to prevent some perceived threat from occurring in the first place, including *future* crimes that may be thought possible of prediction.[1] We will explore these questions, as before, in both civilian and military contexts.

I. SOURCES OF AUTHORITY FOR DETENTION

The Constitution does not expressly grant either the President or the Congress a detention power. To the extent a detention regime may be established, the power to do so is derived from the exercise of enumerated powers together with the Necessary and Proper Clause, Art. I, § 8, cl. 18. For example, Congress may enact a criminal

---

1. It is important to note the important distinction between a *future* crime predicted on the basis of past conduct or characteristics of the would-be perpetrator and so-called inchoate offenses. An inchoate offense is a completed crime (such as attempt or conspiracy or incitement) that is subject to criminal sanction because the completed action is considered to be so grave as to be worthy of punishment. "A principal feature of these crimes is that they are committed even though the substantive offence is not successfully consummated. An attempt fails, a conspiracy comes to nothing, words of incitement are ignored — in all these instances, there may be liability for the inchoate crime." *Inchoate*, BLACK'S LAW DICTIONARY 830 (9th ed. 2009) (quoting ANDREW ASHWORTH, PRINCIPLES OF CRIMINAL LAW 395 (1991)). The discussion in this chapter is about crimes closer to those imagined by Philip K. Dick in his 1956 short story, *The Minority Report*.

statute in furtherance of its commerce or spending powers. *See, e.g., Sabri v. United States*, 541 U.S. 600, 605 (2004) (upholding federal criminal statute "proscribing bribery of state, local, and tribal officials of entities that receive at least $10,000 in federal funds" as a valid exercise of Congress's powers under the Spending Clause and Necessary and Proper Clause); *Gonzales v. Raich*, 545 U.S. 1, 27 (2005) (upholding federal criminalization of the intra-state cultivation of marijuana as part of a "comprehensive regulatory regime" in furtherance of Congress's Commerce Clause power). Recall the authority Congress conferred on the President to issue a finding that would have the effect of criminalizing the export of arms and munitions of war, upheld in *United States v. Curtiss-Wright Export Corp.*, 299 U.S. 304, 318 (1936). This was an assertion of the power of Congress "to regulate Commerce with foreign Nations," and, as the Court found (perhaps more controversially), that "the investment of the federal government with the powers of external sovereignty did not depend upon the affirmative grants of the Constitution."

Where, then, is the power to incarcerate those convicted of breaking these laws? That power comes from the Necessary and Proper Clause, too. It is at one remove, as it were, a power suited to furthering the ends pursued in the exercise of those enumerated powers in the first instance. *United States v. Comstock*, 560 U.S. 126, 137 (2010) ("Neither Congress' power to criminalize conduct, nor its power to imprison individuals who engage in that conduct, nor its power to enact laws governing prisons and prisoners, is explicitly mentioned in the Constitution. But Congress nonetheless possesses broad authority to do each of those things in the course of 'carrying into Execution' the enumerated powers 'vested by' the 'Constitution in the Government of the United States,' Art. I, § 8, cl. 18—authority granted by the Necessary and Proper Clause."). Thus, Congress may build the prisons, hire the guards, and provide for other means that are broadly considered "necessary" (in the sense of "calculated to produce" or "convenient" or "useful") to achieve the constitutionally permissible end. The elasticity of the Necessary and Proper Clause has been demonstrated to stretch even so far as the maintenance of a "federal civil-commitment statute [that] authorizes the Department of Justice to detain a mentally ill, sexually dangerous federal prisoner beyond the date the prisoner would otherwise be released." *Id.* at 129.

But there are limits to this elasticity. The Necessary and Proper Clause, it must be remembered, has two parts. The famous mandate in *McCulloch v. Maryland* that "the end be legitimate" is immediately followed by the requirement that the means "are not prohibited" by some other part of the Constitution. 4 Wheat. (17 U.S.) 316, 421 (1819). In the criminal context, obvious restrictions on Congress's power are found in the prohibitions against bills of attainder and *ex post facto* laws (Art. I, § 9), the search and seizure requirements of the Fourth Amendment, the Double Jeopardy Clause of the Fifth Amendment, the fair trial guarantees of the Sixth Amendment, and the prohibitions on excessive bail and fines, and on cruel and unusual punishments in the Eighth Amendment. In criminal as well as non-criminal contexts, the Due Process Clause is an obvious impediment to arbitrary detention. This Clause will feature in many of the cases discussed in this chapter.

Of course, the power to criminalize conduct is only one form of detention. Detention in the context of national security raises additional constitutional issues. The source of such authority is not necessarily clear.[2]

In *Hamdi v. Rumsfeld*, discussed in detail in Chapter 1, Justice O'Connor found the authority to detain enemy combatants, regardless of citizenship, to be a lesser version of the authority to kill them — "a fundamental incident of waging war." But to the extent that such powers are derived (as *Curtiss-Wright* might have it) from "powers of external sovereignty [that do] not depend upon the affirmative grants of the Constitution," constitutional *restrictions* still remain. Thus, Justice Scalia, dissenting, answered Justice O'Connor by noting a constitutional distinction: "That captivity may be consistent with the principles of international law does not prove that it also complies with the restrictions that the Constitution places on the American Government's treatment of its own citizens." *Hamdi v. Rumsfeld*, 542 U.S. 507, 574, n.5 (2004).

Similarly, those who discern "inherent" powers in the executive branch, especially with regard to national security, must still grapple with express constitutional prohibitions on the exercise of such power. Recall, for example, the colloquy between Judge David Pine and Assistant Attorney General Baldridge in the district court hearing that preceded *The Steel Seizure Case*. As Maeva Marcus recounted: "What would happen to you if the President ordered Secretary Sawyer to put you in jail right now and have you executed tomorrow? Judge Pine asked. Would the court be unable to protect you? Baldridge floundered for an answer until Judge Pine observed: 'On the question of the deprivation of your rights you have the Fifth Amendment; that is what protects you.'" MAEVA MARCUS, TRUMAN AND THE STEEL SEIZURE CASE: THE LIMITS OF PRESIDENTIAL POWER 117 (1994).

II. PREVENTIVE DETENTION IN HISTORICAL PERSPECTIVE

American history provides plenty of examples of government assertion of the power to detain an individual for purposes other than enforcement of the criminal

---

2. For example, some have pointed to the Captures Clause in Article I, § 8, Cl. 11 ("[The Congress shall have Power To] make Rules concerning Captures on Land and Water") as a seemingly obvious textual commitment of a detention power. What else could captures mean? Since its insertion in the Constitution did not generate recorded debate, a range of options is possible (assuming that the original meaning of the term should completely control its current use):

> "Rules concerning Captures" could mean rules for determining what (or whom) precisely is subject to capture by whom or it might mean procedural rules governing the disposition and treatment of captures. Giving Congress the first kind of power — to determine what (or whom) may be taken — could, if the power includes control over the actions of the public armed forces, make inroads on what is frequently believed to fall exclusively within the commander-in-chief power: tactical and combat decisions.

Ingrid Wuerth, *The Captures Clause*, 76 CHI. L. REV. 1683, 1686-87 (2009). Wuerth ultimately concludes that the Clause reaches only things (not people), and only certain kinds of things at that — goods removable from seized vessels. From the perspective of constitutional law, would it be tolerable to repurpose the Clause with different meaning?

laws. Many such cases occurred during the Civil War. The opinion below is one of a series of World War II–era opinions describing, and in this case upholding, a particularly odious policy: detention on the basis of race. Note that although Justice Black wished to limit the issue presented to the narrow question of Fred Korematsu's criminal conviction for violating an exclusion order, the dissenters considered the larger detention program, of which this was a part, to be equally relevant.

Korematsu v. United States
323 U.S. 214 (1944)

Mr. Justice BLACK delivered the opinion of the Court.

The petitioner, an American citizen of Japanese descent, was convicted in a federal district court for remaining in San Leandro, California, a "Military Area," contrary to Civilian Exclusion Order No. 34 of the Commanding General of the Western Command, U.S. Army, which directed that after May 9, 1942, all persons of Japanese ancestry should be excluded from that area. No question was raised as to petitioner's loyalty to the United States. The Circuit Court of Appeals affirmed, and the importance of the constitutional question involved caused us to grant certiorari.

It should be noted, to begin with, that all legal restrictions which curtail the civil rights of a single racial group are immediately suspect. That is not to say that all such restrictions are unconstitutional. It is to say that courts must subject them to the most rigid scrutiny. Pressing public necessity may sometimes justify the existence of such restrictions; racial antagonism never can.

In the instant case prosecution of the petitioner was begun by information charging violation of an Act of Congress, of March 21, 1942, which provides that "... whoever shall enter, remain in, leave, or commit any act in any military area or military zone prescribed, under the authority of an Executive order of the President, by the Secretary of War, or by any military commander designated by the Secretary of War, contrary to the restrictions applicable to any such area or zone or contrary to the order of the Secretary of War or any such military commander, shall, if it appears that he knew or should have known of the existence and extent of the restrictions or order and that his act was in violation thereof, be guilty of a misdemeanor and upon conviction shall be liable to a fine of not to exceed $5,000 or to imprisonment for not more than one year, or both, for each offense."

Exclusion Order No. 34, which the petitioner knowingly and admittedly violated was one of a number of military orders and proclamations, all of which were substantially based upon Executive Order No. 9066. That order, issued after we were at war with Japan, declared that "the successful prosecution of the war requires every possible protection against espionage and against sabotage to national-defense material, national-defense premises, and national-defense utilities. . . ."

One of the series of orders and proclamations, a curfew order, which like the exclusion order here was promulgated pursuant to Executive Order No. 9066, subjected all persons of Japanese ancestry in prescribed West Coast military areas to remain in their residences from 8 P.M. to 6 A.M. As is the case with the exclusion order here, that prior curfew order was designed as a "protection against espionage and against sabotage." In *Hirabayashi v. United States*, we sustained a conviction obtained for violation of the curfew order. The *Hirabayashi* conviction and this one thus rest on the same 1942 Congressional Act and the same basic executive and military orders, all of which orders were aimed at the twin dangers of espionage and sabotage.

The 1942 Act was attacked in the *Hirabayashi* case as an unconstitutional delegation of power; it was contended that the curfew order and other orders on which it rested were beyond the war powers of the Congress, the military authorities and of the President, as Commander in Chief of the Army; and finally that to apply the curfew order against none but citizens of Japanese ancestry amounted to a constitutionally prohibited discrimination solely on account of race. To these questions, we gave the serious consideration which their importance justified. We upheld the curfew order as an exercise of the power of the government to take steps necessary to prevent espionage and sabotage in an area threatened by Japanese attack.

In the light of the principles we announced in the *Hirabayashi* case, we are unable to conclude that it was beyond the war power of Congress and the Executive to exclude those of Japanese ancestry from the West Coast war area at the time they did. True, exclusion from the area in which one's home is located is a far greater deprivation than constant confinement to the home from 8 P.M. to 6 A.M. Nothing short of apprehension by the proper military authorities of the gravest imminent danger to the public safety can constitutionally justify either. But exclusion from a threatened area, no less than curfew, has a definite and close relationship to the prevention of espionage and sabotage. The military authorities, charged with the primary responsibility of defending our shores, concluded that curfew provided inadequate protection and ordered exclusion. They did so, as pointed out in our *Hirabayashi* opinion, in accordance with Congressional authority to the military to say who should, and who should not, remain in the threatened areas.

In this case the petitioner challenges the assumptions upon which we rested our conclusions in the *Hirabayashi* case. He also urges that by May 1942, when Order No. 34 was promulgated, all danger of Japanese invasion of the West Coast had disappeared.

[W]e cannot reject as unfounded the judgment of the military authorities and of Congress that there were disloyal members of that population, whose number and strength could not be precisely and quickly ascertained. We cannot say that the war-making branches of the Government did not have ground for believing that in a critical hour such persons could not readily be isolated and separately dealt with, and constituted a menace to the national defense and safety, which demanded that prompt and adequate measures be taken to guard against it.

Like curfew, exclusion of those of Japanese origin was deemed necessary because of the presence of an unascertained number of disloyal members of the group, most of whom we have no doubt were loyal to this country. It was because we could not reject the finding of the military authorities that it was impossible to bring about an immediate segregation of the disloyal from the loyal that we sustained the validity of the curfew order as applying to the whole group. In the instant case, temporary exclusion of the entire group was rested by the military on the same ground. The judgment that exclusion of the whole group was for the same reason a military imperative answers the contention that the exclusion was in the nature of group punishment based on antagonism to those of Japanese origin. That there were members of the group who retained loyalties to Japan has been confirmed by investigations made subsequent to the exclusion. Approximately five thousand American citizens of Japanese ancestry refused to swear unqualified allegiance to the United States and to renounce allegiance to the Japanese Emperor, and several thousand evacuees requested repatriation to Japan.

We uphold the exclusion order as of the time it was made and when the petitioner violated it. In doing so, we are not unmindful of the hardships imposed by it upon a large group of American citizens. But hardships are part of war, and war is an aggregation of hardships. All citizens alike, both in and out of uniform, feel the impact of war in greater or lesser measure. Citizenship has its responsibilities as well as its privileges, and in time of war the burden is always heavier.

[T]he military authorities had already determined that the evacuation should be effected by assembling together and placing under guard all those of Japanese ancestry, at central points, designated as "assembly centers," in order "to insure the orderly evacuation and resettlement of Japanese voluntarily migrating from military area No. 1 to restrict and regulate such migration." Civilian Restrictive Order No. 1 provided for detention of those of Japanese ancestry in assembly or relocation centers. It is now argued that . . . we must treat these separate orders as one and inseparable; that, for this reason, if detention in the assembly or relocation center would have illegally deprived the petitioner of his liberty, the exclusion order and his conviction under it cannot stand.

We are thus being asked to pass at this time upon the whole subsequent detention program in both assembly and relocation centers, although the only issues framed at the trial related to petitioner's remaining in the prohibited area in violation of the exclusion order. Had petitioner here left the prohibited area and gone to an assembly center we cannot say either as a matter of fact or law, that his presence in that center would have resulted in his detention in a relocation center. Some who did report to the assembly center were not sent to relocation centers, but were released upon condition that they remain outside the prohibited zone until the military orders were modified or lifted. This illustrates that they pose different problems and may be governed by different principles. The lawfulness of one does not necessarily determine the lawfulness of the others.

Since the petitioner has not been convicted of failing to report or to remain in an assembly or relocation center, we cannot in this case determine the validity of those separate provisions of the order. It is sufficient here for us to pass upon the order which petitioner violated. To do more would be to go beyond the issues raised, and to decide momentous questions not contained within the framework of the pleadings or the evidence in this case. It will be time enough to decide the serious constitutional issues which petitioner seeks to raise when an assembly or relocation order is applied or is certain to be applied to him, and we have its terms before us.

Some of the members of the Court are of the view that evacuation and detention in an Assembly Center were inseparable. After May 3, 1942, the date of Exclusion Order No. 34, Korematsu was under compulsion to leave the area not as he would choose but via an Assembly Center. The Assembly Center was conceived as a part of the machinery for group evacuation. The power to exclude includes the power to do it by force if necessary. And any forcible measure must necessarily entail some degree of detention or restraint whatever method of removal is selected. But whichever view is taken, it results in holding that the order under which petitioner was convicted was valid.

It is said that we are dealing here with the case of imprisonment of a citizen in a concentration camp solely because of his ancestry, without evidence or inquiry concerning his loyalty and good disposition towards the United States. Our task would be simple, our duty clear, were this a case involving the imprisonment of a loyal citizen in a concentration camp because of racial prejudice. Regardless of the true nature of the assembly and relocation centers—and we deem it unjustifiable to call them concentration camps with all the ugly connotations that term implies—we are dealing specifically with nothing but an exclusion order. To cast this case into outlines of racial prejudice, without reference to the real military dangers which were presented, merely confuses the issue. Korematsu was not excluded from the Military Area because of hostility to him or his race. He was excluded because we are at war with the Japanese Empire, because the properly constituted military authorities feared an invasion of our West Coast and felt constrained to take proper security measures, because they decided that the military urgency of the situation demanded that all citizens of Japanese ancestry be segregated from the West Coast temporarily, and finally, because Congress, reposing its confidence in this time of war in our military leaders—as inevitably it must—determined that they should have the power to do just this. There was evidence of disloyalty on the part of some, the military authorities considered that the need for action was great, and time was short. We cannot—by availing ourselves of the calm perspective of hindsight—now say that at that time these actions were unjustified.

Affirmed.

Mr. Justice FRANKFURTER, concurring.

I join in the opinion of the Court, but should like to add a few words of my own.

The provisions of the Constitution which confer on the Congress and the President powers to enable this country to wage war are as much part of the Constitution as provisions looking to a nation at peace. And we have had recent occasion to quote approvingly the statement of former Chief Justice Hughes that the war power of the Government is "the power to wage war successfully." Therefore, the validity of action under the war power must be judged wholly in the context of war. That action is not to be stigmatized as lawless because like action in times of peace would be lawless. . . . To recognize that military orders are "reasonably expedient military precautions" in time of war and yet to deny them constitutional legitimacy makes of the Constitution an instrument for dialetic subtleties not reasonably to be attributed to the hard-headed Framers, of whom a majority had had actual participation in war. If a military order such as that under review does not transcend the means appropriate for conducting war, such action by the military is as constitutional as would be any authorized action by the Interstate Commerce Commission within the limits of the constitutional power to regulate commerce. And being an exercise of the war power explicitly granted by the Constitution for safeguarding the national life by prosecuting war effectively, I find nothing in the Constitution which denies to Congress the power to enforce such a valid military order by making its violation an offense triable in the civil courts. To find that the Constitution does not forbid the military measures now complained of does not carry with it approval of that which Congress and the Executive did. That is their business, not ours.

Mr. Justice ROBERTS.

I dissent, because I think the indisputable facts exhibit a clear violation of Constitutional rights.

This is not a case of keeping people off the streets at night as was *Hirabayashi v. United States*, nor a case of temporary exclusion of a citizen from an area for his own safety or that of the community, nor a case of offering him an opportunity to go temporarily out of an area where his presence might cause danger to himself or to his fellows. On the contrary, it is the case of convicting a citizen as a punishment for not submitting to imprisonment in a concentration camp, based on his ancestry, and solely because of his ancestry, without evidence or inquiry concerning his loyalty and good disposition towards the United States. If this be a correct statement of the facts disclosed by this record, and facts of which we take judicial notice, I need hardly labor the conclusion that Constitutional rights have been violated.

The Government's argument, and the opinion of the court, in my judgment, erroneously divide that which is single and indivisible and thus make the case appear as if the petitioner violated a Military Order, sanctioned by Act of Congress, which excluded him from his home, by refusing voluntarily to leave and, so, knowingly and intentionally, defying the order and the Act of Congress.

The petitioner, a resident of San Leandro, Alameda County, California, is a native of the United States of Japanese ancestry who, according to the uncontradicted evidence, is a loyal citizen of the nation.

A chronological recitation of events will make it plain that the petitioner's supposed offense did not, in truth, consist in his refusal voluntarily to leave the area which included his home in obedience to the order excluding him therefrom. Critical attention must be given to the dates and sequence of events.

December 8, 1941, the United States declared war on Japan.

February 19, 1942, the President issued Executive Order No. 9066, which provided that certain Military Commanders might, in their discretion, "prescribe military areas" and define their extent, "from which any or all persons may be excluded, and with respect to which, the right of any person to enter, remain in, or leave shall be subject to whatever restrictions" the "Military Commander may impose in his discretion."

February 20, 1942, Lieutenant General DeWitt was designated Military Commander of the Western Defense Command embracing the westernmost states of the Union,—about one-fourth of the total area of the nation.

March 2, 1942, General DeWitt promulgated Public Proclamation No. 1, which recites that the entire Pacific Coast is "particularly subject to attack, to attempted invasion . . . and, in connection therewith, is subject to espionage and acts of sabotage." It states that "as a matter of military necessity" certain military areas and zones are established known as Military Areas Nos. 1 and 2. [Subsequent] orders required that if any person of Japanese, German or Italian ancestry residing in Area No. 1 desired to change his habitual residence he must execute and deliver to the authorities a Change of Residence Notice.

March 21, 1942, Congress enacted that anyone who knowingly "shall enter, remain in, leave, or commit any act in any military area or military zone pre-scribed . . . by any military commander . . . contrary to the restrictions appli-cable to any such area or zone or contrary to the order of . . . any such military commander" shall be guilty of a misdemeanor. This is the Act under which the petitioner was charged.

March 24, 1942, General DeWitt instituted the curfew for certain areas within his command, by an order the validity of which was sustained in *Hirabayashi v. United States.*

March 27, 1942, by Proclamation No. 4, the General recited that "it is nec-essary, in order to provide for the welfare and to insure the orderly evacuation and resettlement of Japanese *voluntarily migrating* from Military Area No. 1 to restrict and regulate such migration"; and ordered that, as of March 29, 1942, "all alien Japanese and persons of Japanese ancestry who are within the limits of Military Area No. 1, be and they are hereby prohibited from leaving that area for any purpose until and to the extent that a future proclamation or order of this headquarters shall so permit or direct."[5]

No order had been made excluding the petitioner from the area in which he lived. By Proclamation No. 4 he was, after March 29, 1942, confined to the limits of Area No. 1. If the Executive Order No. 9066 and the Act of Congress meant what they said, to leave that area, in the face of Proclamation No. 4, would be to commit a misdemeanor.

May 3, 1942, General DeWitt issued Civilian Exclusion Order No. 34 pro-viding that, after 12 o'clock May 8, 1942, all persons of Japanese ancestry, both alien and non-alien, were to be excluded from a described portion of Military Area No. 1, which included the County of Alameda, California. The order required a responsible member of each family and each individual living alone to report, at a time set, at a Civil Control Station for instructions to go to an Assembly Center, and added that any person failing to comply with the

---

5. The italics in the quotation are mine. The use of the word "voluntarily" exhibits a grim irony probably not lost on petitioner and others in like case. Either so, or its use was a disingenuous attempt to camouflage the compulsion which was to be applied.

provisions of the order who was found in the described area after the date set would be liable to prosecution under the Act of March 21, 1942. It is important to note that the order, by its express terms, had no application to persons within the bounds "of an established Assembly Center pursuant to instructions from this Headquarters. . . ." The obvious purpose of the orders made, taken together, was to drive all citizens of Japanese ancestry into Assembly Centers within the zones of their residence, under pain of criminal prosecution.

In the dilemma that he dare not remain in his home, or voluntarily leave the area, without incurring criminal penalties, and that the only way he could avoid punishment was to go to an Assembly Center and submit himself to military imprisonment, the petitioner did nothing.

June 12, 1942, an Information was filed in the District Court for Northern California charging a violation of the Act of March 21, 1942, in that petitioner had knowingly remained within the area covered by Exclusion Order No. 34. [The] petitioner was tried under a plea of not guilty and convicted. Sentence was suspended and he was placed on probation for five years. We know, however, in the light of the foregoing recitation, that he was at once taken into military custody and lodged in an Assembly Center. We further know that, on March 18, 1942, the President had promulgated Executive Order No. 9102 establishing the War Relocation Authority under which so-called Relocation Centers, a euphemism for concentration camps, were established pursuant to cooperation between the military authorities of the Western Defense Command and the Relocation Authority, and that the petitioner has been confined either in an Assembly Center, within the zone in which he had lived or has been removed to a Relocation Center.

The Government has argued this case as if the only order outstanding at the time the petitioner was arrested and informed against was Exclusion Order No. 34 ordering him to leave the area in which he resided, which was the basis of the information against him. That argument has evidently been effective. The opinion refers to the *Hirabayashi* case, supra, to show that this court has sustained the validity of a curfew order in an emergency. The argument then is that exclusion from a given area of danger, while somewhat more sweeping than a curfew regulation, is of the same nature, — a temporary expedient made necessary by a sudden emergency. This, I think, is a substitution of an hypothetical case for the case actually before the court. I might agree with the court's disposition of the hypothetical case.[8] The liberty of every American citizen freely to come and to go must frequently, in the face of sudden danger, be temporarily limited or suspended. The civil authorities must often resort to the expedient of excluding citizens temporarily from a locality. The drawing of fire lines in the case of a conflagration, the removal of persons from the area where a pestilence has broken out, are familiar examples. If the exclusion worked by Exclusion Order No. 34 were of that nature the *Hirabayashi* case

---

8. My agreement would depend on the definition and application of the terms "temporary" and "emergency." No pronouncement of the commanding officer can, in my view, preclude judicial inquiry and determination whether an emergency ever existed and whether, if so, it remained, at the date of the restraint out of which the litigation arose.

would be authority for sustaining it. But the facts . . . show that the exclusion was but a part of an over-all plan for forceable detention.

We cannot shut our eyes to the fact that had the petitioner attempted to violate Proclamation No. 4 and leave the military area in which he lived he would have been arrested and tried and convicted for violation of Proclamation No. 4. The two conflicting orders, one which commanded him to stay and the other which commanded him to go, were nothing but a cleverly devised trap to accomplish the real purpose of the military authority, which was to lock him up in a concentration camp. The only course by which the petitioner could avoid arrest and prosecution was to go to that camp according to instructions to be given him when he reported at a Civil Control Center. We know that is the fact. Why should we set up a figmentary and artificial situation instead of addressing ourselves to the actualities of the case?

I would reverse the judgment of conviction.

Mr. Justice MURPHY, dissenting.

This exclusion of "all persons of Japanese ancestry, both alien and non-alien," from the Pacific Coast area on a plea of military necessity in the absence of martial law ought not to be approved. Such exclusion goes over "the very brink of constitutional power" and falls into the ugly abyss of racism.

In dealing with matters relating to the prosecution and progress of a war, we must accord great respect and consideration to the judgments of the military authorities who are on the scene and who have full knowledge of the military facts. The scope of their discretion must, as a matter of necessity and common sense, be wide. And their judgments ought not to be overruled lightly by those whose training and duties ill-equip them to deal intelligently with matters so vital to the physical security of the nation.

At the same time, however, it is essential that there be definite limits to military discretion, especially where martial law has not been declared. Thus, like other claims conflicting with the asserted constitutional rights of the individual, the military claim must subject itself to the judicial process of having its reasonableness determined and its conflicts with other interests reconciled.

The judicial test of whether the Government, on a plea of military necessity, can validly deprive an individual of any of his constitutional rights is whether the deprivation is reasonably related to a public danger that is so "immediate, imminent, and impending" as not to admit of delay and not to permit the intervention of ordinary constitutional processes to alleviate the danger. Civilian Exclusion Order No. 34, banishing from a prescribed area of the Pacific Coast "all persons of Japanese ancestry, both alien and non-alien," clearly does not meet that test.

It must be conceded that the military and naval situation in the spring of 1942 was such as to generate a very real fear of invasion of the Pacific Coast, accompanied by fears of sabotage and espionage in that area. The military command was therefore justified in adopting all reasonable means necessary to combat these dangers. In adjudging the military action taken in light of the then apparent dangers, we must not erect too high or too meticulous standards; it is necessary only that the action have some reasonable relation to the removal of the dangers of invasion, sabotage and espionage. But the exclusion, either temporarily or permanently, of all persons with Japanese blood in their veins has no such reasonable relation. And that relation is lacking because the exclusion order necessarily must rely for its reasonableness upon the assumption that all persons of Japanese ancestry may have a dangerous tendency to commit sabotage and espionage and to aid our Japanese enemy in other ways. It is difficult to believe that reason, logic or experience could be marshalled in support of such an assumption.

That this forced exclusion was the result in good measure of this erroneous assumption of racial guilt rather than bona fide military necessity is evidenced by the Commanding General's Final Report on the evacuation from the Pacific Coast area.[1] In it he refers to all individuals of Japanese descent as "subversive," as belonging to "an enemy race" whose "racial strains are undiluted," and as constituting "over 112,000 potential enemies . . . at large today" along the Pacific Coast.[2] In support of this blanket condemnation of all persons of Japanese descent, however, no reliable evidence is cited to show that such individuals were generally disloyal, or had generally so conducted themselves in this area as to constitute a special menace to defense installations or war industries, or had otherwise by their behavior furnished reasonable ground for their exclusion as a group.

Justification for the exclusion is sought, instead, mainly upon questionable racial and sociological grounds not ordinarily within the realm of expert military judgment, supplemented by certain semi-military conclusions drawn from an unwarranted use of circumstantial evidence. Individuals of Japanese ancestry are condemned because they are said to be "a large, unassimilated, tightly knit racial group, bound to an enemy nation by strong ties of race, culture, custom and religion."[4] It is intimated that many of these individuals deliberately resided "adjacent to strategic points," thus enabling them "to carry

---

1. Final Report, Japanese Evacuation from the West Coast, 1942, by Lt. Gen. J.L. De Witt. This report is dated June 5, 1943, but was not made public until January, 1944.

2. Further evidence of the Commanding General's attitude toward individuals of Japanese ancestry is revealed in his voluntary testimony on April 13, 1943, in San Francisco before the House Naval Affairs Subcommittee to Investigate Congested Areas:

> I don't want any of them (persons of Japanese ancestry) here. They are a dangerous element. There is no way to determine their loyalty. The west coast contains too many vital installations essential to the defense of the country to allow any Japanese on this coast. . . . The danger of the Japanese was, and is now — if they are permitted to come back — espionage and sabotage. It makes no difference whether he is an American citizen, he is still a Japanese. American citizenship does not necessarily determine loyalty. . . . But we must worry about the Japanese all the time until he is wiped off the map. Sabotage and espionage will make problems as long as he is allowed in this area. . . .

4. Final Report, p. vii; see also pp. 9, 17. To the extent that assimilation is a problem, it is largely the result of certain social customs and laws of the American general public. Studies demonstrate that persons of Japanese descent are readily susceptible to integration in our society if given the opportunity. The failure to accomplish an ideal status of assimilation, therefore, cannot be charged to the refusal of these persons to become Americanized or to their loyalty to Japan. And the retention by some persons of certain customs and religious practices of their ancestors is no criterion of their loyalty to the United States.

into execution a tremendous program of sabotage on a mass scale should any considerable number of them have been inclined to do so."[9]

The main reasons relied upon by those responsible for the forced evacuation, therefore, do not prove a reasonable relation between the group characteristics of Japanese Americans and the dangers of invasion, sabotage and espionage. The reasons appear, instead, to be largely an accumulation of much of the misinformation, half-truths and insinuations that for years have been directed against Japanese Americans by people with racial and economic prejudices — the same people who have been among the foremost advocates of the evacuation.[12] A military judgment based upon such racial and sociological considerations is not entitled to the great weight ordinarily given the judgments based upon strictly military considerations.

The military necessity which is essential to the validity of the evacuation order thus resolves itself into a few intimations that certain individuals actively aided the enemy, from which it is inferred that the entire group of Japanese Americans could not be trusted to be or remain loyal to the United States. No one denies, of course, that there were some disloyal persons of Japanese descent on the Pacific Coast who did all in their power to aid their ancestral land. Similar disloyal activities have been engaged in by many persons of German, Italian and even more pioneer stock in our country. But to infer that examples of individual disloyalty prove group disloyalty and justify discriminatory action against the entire group is to deny that under our system of law individual guilt is the sole basis for deprivation of rights. Moreover, this inference, which is at the very heart of the evacuation orders, has been used in support of the abhorrent and despicable treatment of minority groups by the dictatorial tyrannies which this nation is now pledged to destroy. To give constitutional sanction to that inference in this case, however well-intentioned may have been the military command on the Pacific Coast, is to adopt one of the cruelest of the rationales used by our enemies to destroy the dignity of the individual and to encourage and open the door to discriminatory actions against other minority groups in the passions of tomorrow.

---

9. Final Report, p. 10 see also pp. vii, 9, 15-17. This insinuation, based purely upon speculation and circumstantial evidence, completely overlooks the fact that the main geographic pattern of Japanese population was fixed many years ago with reference to economic, social and soil conditions. Limited occupational outlets and social pressures encouraged their concentration near their initial points of entry on the Pacific Coast. That these points may now be near certain strategic military and industrial areas is no proof of a diabolical purpose on the part of Japanese Americans.

12. Special interest groups were extremely active in applying pressure for mass evacuation. See House Report No. 2124 (77th Cong., 2d Sess.) 154-6; McWilliams, Prejudice, 126-8 (1944). Mr. Austin E. Anson, managing secretary of the Salinas Vegetable Grower-Shipper Association, has frankly admitted that "We're charged with wanting to get rid of the Japs for selfish reasons. We do. It's a question of whether the white man lives on the Pacific Coast or the brown men. They came into this valley to work, and they stayed to take over. . . . They undersell the white man in the markets. . . . They work their women and children while the white farmer has to pay wages for his help. If all the Japs were removed tomorrow, we'd never miss them in two weeks, because the white farmers can take over and produce everything the Jap grows. And we don't want them back when the war ends, either." Quoted by Taylor in his article "The People Nobody Wants," 214 SAT. EVE. POST 24, 66 (May 9, 1942).

No adequate reason is given for the failure to treat these Japanese Americans on an individual basis by holding investigations and hearings to separate the loyal from the disloyal, as was done in the case of persons of German and Italian ancestry. [DeWitt's report] asserted merely that the loyalties of this group "were unknown and time was of the essence." Yet nearly four months elapsed after Pearl Harbor before the first exclusion order was issued; nearly eight months went by until the last order was issued; and the last of these "subversive" persons was not actually removed until almost eleven months had elapsed. Leisure and deliberation seem to have been more of the essence than speed. And the fact that conditions were not such as to warrant a declaration of martial law adds strength to the belief that the factors of time and military necessity were not as urgent as they have been represented to be.

Moreover, there was no adequate proof that the Federal Bureau of Investigation and the military and naval intelligence services did not have the espionage and sabotage situation well in hand during this long period. Nor is there any denial of the fact that not one person of Japanese ancestry was accused or convicted of espionage or sabotage after Pearl Harbor while they were still free,[15] a fact which is some evidence of the loyalty of the vast majority of these individuals and of the effectiveness of the established methods of combatting these evils.

I dissent, therefore, from this legalization of racism. Racial discrimination in any form and in any degree has no justifiable part whatever in our democratic way of life. It is unattractive in any setting but it is utterly revolting among a free people who have embraced the principles set forth in the Constitution of the United States. All residents of this nation are kin in some way by blood or culture to a foreign land. Yet they are primarily and necessarily a part of the new and distinct civilization of the United States. They must accordingly be treated at all times as the heirs of the American experiment and as entitled to all the rights and freedoms guaranteed by the Constitution.

Mr. Justice JACKSON, dissenting.

Korematsu was born on our soil, of parents born in Japan. The Constitution makes him a citizen of the United States by nativity and a citizen of California by residence. No claim is made that he is not loyal to this country. There is no suggestion that apart from the matter involved here he is not law-abiding and well disposed. Korematsu, however, has been convicted of an act not commonly a crime. It consists merely of being present in the state whereof he is a citizen, near the place where he was born, and where all his life he has lived.

A citizen's presence in the locality, however, was made a crime only if his parents were of Japanese birth. Had Korematsu been one of four—the others being, say, a German alien enemy, an Italian alien enemy, and a citizen of American-born ancestors, convicted of treason but out on parole—only Korematsu's presence would have violated the order. The difference between their innocence

---

15. The Final Report, p. 34, makes the amazing statement that as of February 14, 1942, "The very fact that no sabotage has taken place to date is a disturbing and confirming indication that such action will be taken." Apparently, in the minds of the military leaders, there was no way that the Japanese Americans could escape the suspicion of sabotage.

and his crime would result, not from anything he did, said, or thought, different than they, but only in that he was born of different racial stock.

Now, if any fundamental assumption underlies our system, it is that guilt is personal and not inheritable. If Congress in peace-time legislation should enact such a criminal law, I should suppose this Court would refuse to enforce it.

But the "law" which this prisoner is convicted of disregarding is not found in an act of Congress, but in a military order. Neither the Act of Congress nor the Executive Order of the President, nor both together, would afford a basis for this conviction. It rests on the orders of General DeWitt. And it is said that if the military commander had reasonable military grounds for promulgating the orders, they are constitutional and become law, and the Court is required to enforce them. There are several reasons why I cannot subscribe to this doctrine.

It would be impracticable and dangerous idealism to expect or insist that each specific military command in an area of probable operations will conform to conventional tests of constitutionality. When an area is so beset that it must be put under military control at all, the paramount consideration is that its measures be successful, rather than legal. The armed services must protect a society, not merely its Constitution. The very essence of the military job is to marshal physical force, to remove every obstacle to its effectiveness, to give it every strategic advantage. Defense measures will not, and often should not, be held within the limits that bind civil authority in peace. No court can require such a commander in such circumstances to act as a reasonable man; he may be unreasonably cautious and exacting. Perhaps he should be. But a commander in temporarily focusing the life of a community on defense is carrying out a military program; he is not making law in the sense the courts know the term. He issues orders, and they may have a certain authority as military commands, although they may be very bad as constitutional law.

But if we cannot confine military expedients by the Constitution, neither would I distort the Constitution to approve all that the military may deem expedient. This is what the Court appears to be doing, whether consciously or not. I cannot say, from any evidence before me, that the orders of General DeWitt were not reasonably expedient military precautions, nor could I say that they were. But even if they were permissible military procedures, I deny that it follows that they are constitutional. If, as the Court holds, it does follow, then we may as well say that any military order will be constitutional and have done with it.

The limitation under which courts always will labor in examining the necessity for a military order are illustrated by this case. How does the Court know that these orders have a reasonable basis in necessity? No evidence whatever on that subject has been taken by this or any other court. There is sharp controversy as to the credibility of the DeWitt report. So the Court, having no real evidence before it, has no choice but to accept General DeWitt's own unsworn, self-serving statement, untested by any cross-examination, that what he did was reasonable. And thus it will always be when courts try to look into the reasonableness of a military order.

In the very nature of things military decisions are not susceptible of intelligent judicial appraisal. They do not pretend to rest on evidence, but are made on information that often would not be admissible and on assumptions that could not be proved. Information in support of an order could not be disclosed to courts without danger that it would reach the enemy. Neither can courts act on communications made in confidence. Hence courts can never have any real alternative to accepting the mere declaration of the authority that issued the order that it was reasonably necessary from a military viewpoint.

Much is said of the danger to liberty from the Army program for deporting and detaining these citizens of Japanese extraction. But a judicial construction of the due process clause that will sustain this order is a far more subtle blow to liberty than the promulgation of the order itself. A military order, however unconstitutional, is not apt to last longer than the military emergency. Even during that period a succeeding commander may revoke it all. But once a judicial opinion rationalizes such an order to show that it conforms to the Constitution, or rather rationalizes the Constitution to show that the Constitution sanctions such an order, the Court for all time has validated the principle of racial discrimination in criminal procedure and of transplanting American citizens. The principle then lies about like a loaded weapon ready for the hand of any authority that can bring forward a plausible claim of an urgent need. A military commander may overstep the bounds of constitutionality, and it is an incident. But if we review and approve, that passing incident becomes the doctrine of the Constitution. There it has a generative power of its own, and all that it creates will be in its own image. Nothing better illustrates this danger than does the Court's opinion in this case.

It argues that we are bound to uphold the conviction of Korematsu because we upheld one in *Hirabayashi v. United States* when we sustained these orders in so far as they applied a curfew requirement to a citizen of Japanese ancestry. I think we should learn something from that experience.

In that case we were urged to consider only that curfew feature, that being all that technically was involved, because it was the only count necessary to sustain Hirabayashi's conviction and sentence. We yielded, and the Chief Justice guarded the opinion as carefully as language will do. He said: "We decide only the issue as we have defined it — we decide only that the curfew order as applied, and at the time it was applied, was within the boundaries of the war power." However, in spite of our limiting words we did validate a discrimination of the basis of ancestry for mild and temporary deprivation of liberty. Now the principle of racial discrimination is pushed from support of mild measures to very harsh ones, and from temporary deprivations to indeterminate ones. And the precedent which it is said requires us to do so is *Hirabayashi*. The Court is now saying that in *Hirabayashi* we did decide the very things we there said we were not deciding. Because we said that these citizens could be made to stay in their homes during the hours of dark, it is said we must require them to leave home entirely; and if that, we are told they may also be taken into custody for deportation; and if that, it is argued they may also be held for some undetermined time in detention camps. How far the principle of this case would be extended before plausible reasons would play out, I do not know.

I should hold that a civil court cannot be made to enforce an order which violates constitutional limitations even if it is a reasonable exercise of military authority. The courts can exercise only the judicial power, can apply only law, and must abide by the Constitution, or they cease to be civil courts and become instruments of military policy.

Of course the existence of a military power resting on force, so vagrant, so centralized, so necessarily heedless of the individual, is an inherent threat to liberty. But I would not lead people to rely on this Court for a review that seems to me wholly delusive. The military reasonableness of these orders can only be determined by military superiors. If the people ever let command of the war power fall into irresponsible and unscrupulous hands, the courts wield no power equal to its restraint. The chief restraint upon those who command the physical forces of the country, in the future as in the past, must be their responsibility to the political judgments of their contemporaries and to the moral judgments of history.

My duties as a justice as I see them do not require me to make a military judgment as to whether General DeWitt's evacuation and detention program was a reasonable military necessity. I do not suggest that the courts should have attempted to interfere with the Army in carrying out its task. But I do not think they may be asked to execute a military expedient that has no place in law under the Constitution. I would reverse the judgment and discharge the prisoner.

NOTES AND QUESTIONS

1. Justice Black notes that "the importance of the constitutional question involved caused us to grant certiorari" in this case. But precisely what was the question? Justice Black, in his opinion for the Court, insists that "[i]t is sufficient here for us to pass upon the order which petitioner violated," and *not* evaluate the constitutionality of "the whole subsequent detention program in both assembly and relocation centers," because "[t]o do more would be to go beyond the issues raised, and to decide momentous questions not contained within the framework of the pleadings or the evidence in this case." But Justice Roberts, dissenting, calls this a false division of the issues: "Why should we set up a figmentary and artificial situation instead of addressing ourselves to the actualities of the case?"

2. On the thirty-fourth anniversary of the issuance of Executive Order 9066, President Gerald R. Ford issued a proclamation "that all authority conferred by Executive Order 9066 terminated upon the issuance of Proclamation 2714, which formally proclaimed the cessation of hostilities of World War II on December 31, 1946." He acknowledged the anniversary as "a sad day in American history" and noted the displacement of over "one hundred thousand persons of Japanese ancestry" as a "setback to fundamental American principles" and called upon the nation to affirm "that we have learned from the tragedy of that long-ago experience forever to treasure liberty and justice for each individual American, and resolve that this kind of action shall never again be repeated." Proclamation 4417, Feb. 19, 1976. A formal apology and

compensation ($20,000) was not approved by Congress until 1988, when only approximately half of those subject to internment remained alive. Payment did not begin until 1990, when Congress finally appropriated the funds. Six years earlier, a federal court granted Fred Korematsu's petition for a writ of coram nobis to overturn his conviction, *inter alia*, because of evidence presented that the government committed a fraud on the Supreme Court: "[T]here is substantial support in the record that the government deliberately omitted relevant information and provided misleading information in papers before the court." *Korematsu v. United States*, 584 F. Supp. 1406, 1419-20 (N.D. Cal. 1984) ("Was the court misled by any omissions or distortions in concluding that the other branches' decisions had a reasonable basis in fact? Omitted from the reports presented to the courts was information possessed by the Federal Communications Commission, the Department of the Navy, and the Justice Department which directly contradicted General DeWitt's statements. Thus, the court had before it a selective record.")

3. Justice Black applies "the most rigid scrutiny" to the exclusion order but nevertheless upholds it. Justice Murphy reached the opposite conclusion after stating that the judicial test "is whether the deprivation is reasonably related" to a sufficient public danger. An assessment of the "reasonableness" of government action typically generates a fairly low and deferential standard of review. Are they evaluating the same issues? Do they consider the same facts to be relevant, or even to be facts?

4. Justice Jackson seems ambivalent about the Court's role in evaluating General DeWitt's orders. What exactly would he have the Court decide, or not decide, when a military order is at the root of an issue before the Court? What would be the effect, for Korematsu and those similarly situated to him, of a narrower holding?

5. If deference is the necessary posture of the Court toward the military because, as Justice Jackson wrote, "[t]he chief restraint . . . must be their responsibility to the political judgments of their contemporaries and to the moral judgments of history," how should we assess that restraint? In a book written a few years before 9/11, Chief Justice Rehnquist was neither indulgent nor apologetic about those restraints in the context of the *Korematsu* case itself:

> The role of General DeWitt, the commander of the west coast military department, was not one to encourage a nice calculation of the costs in civil liberties as opposed to the benefits to national security. Contributing to this attitude would have been the news that General Walter Short, the army commander in Hawaii, and Admiral Husband E. Kimmel, the navy commander there, were both summarily removed from their commands ten days after Pearl Harbor because of their failure to anticipate the Japanese surprise attack. DeWitt was surely going to err on the side of caution in making his calculations.
>
> DeWitt and his associates did not at first recommend evacuation of the Issei [first-generation Japanese immigrants] and Nisei [second-generation Japanese immigrants]. The principal proponents of that idea in its early stages were three California officials — the state's Governor and Attorney General, and the Mayor of Los Angeles — and the congressional delegations of the three west coast

states. Public opinion should not be the determining factor in making a military appraisal, but it is bound to occur to those engaged in that task that their names will very likely be "Mudd" if they reject a widely popular security measure that in retrospect will prove to have been necessary.

The United States prides itself on a system in which the civilian heads of the service departments are supreme over the military chiefs, so one might expect that [Secretary of War] Henry Stimson and [Assistant Secretary of War] John McCloy would have made a more careful evaluation of the evacuation proposal than they appear to have done. Far from the west coast, they would be expected to have a more detached view than the commander on the scene. But here too there seems to have been a tendency to feel that concern for civil liberties was not their responsibility. There is even more of this feeling in Roosevelt's perfunctory approval of the plan in response to a telephone call from Stimson. [Attorney General] Biddle's protests proved to be futile even at the highest levels of government, in part because no significant element of public opinion opposed the relocation. The American Civil Liberties Union, for example, which filed briefs in the Supreme Court supporting both *Hirabayashi* and *Korematsu* when those cases were argued, was noticeably silent at the time that the program was put into operation.[3]

Has *Korematsu*'s infamous holding, arguably a member of the "anti-canon" of Supreme Court cases that are regarded with the least respect in many quarters, increased the level of "restraint" to be expected from political and civil authorities?

6. In a case announced the same day as *Korematsu*, Sacramento resident Mitsuye Endo's petition for a writ of habeas corpus was granted and she was released from an internment camp in Topaz, Utah, after more than two years of involuntary detention. *Ex parte Endo*, 323 U.S. 283 (1944). The government conceded Endo to be "a loyal and law-abiding citizen. They make no claim that she is detained on any charge or that she is even suspected of disloyalty. Moreover, they do not contend that she may be held any longer in the Relocation Center." *Id.* at 294-95. Her continued detention was defended, in part, on the grounds that state politicians "refused to be responsible for maintenance of law and order unless evacuees brought into their States were kept under constant military surveillance" and to prevent "dangerously disorderly migration of unwanted people to unprepared communities." *Id.* at 295, 297. Thus, the government argued it needed to continue to detain Endo as part of the final stages of its evacuation program and that the government could exercise this authority "for controlling situations created by the exercise of the powers expressly conferred for protection against espionage and sabotage." *Id.* at 297. The Supreme Court freed Endo while leaving the constitutionality of the federal program responsible for her detention intact: "We are of the view that Mitsuye Endo should be given her liberty. In reaching that conclusion we do not come to the underlying constitutional issues which have been argued.

---

3. WILLIAM H. REHNQUIST, ALL THE LAWS BUT ONE: CIVIL LIBERTIES IN WARTIME 204 (1998).

For we conclude that, whatever power the [civilian administrative agency known as the] War Relocation Authority may have to detain other classes of citizens, it has no authority to subject citizens who are concededly loyal to its leave procedure." *Id.* The case was decided eight months before the surrender of Japan. Is that a coincidence?

7. Dissenting from what he calls the Court's validation of racial discrimination in the military orders and criminal process that followed from them, Justice Jackson wrote: "The principle then lies about like a loaded weapon ready for the hand of any authority that can bring forward a plausible claim of an urgent need." This echoes a rule followed by the nineteenth-century Russian playwright Anton Chekhov: "Don't place a loaded gun on the stage if no one intends to shoot it." Letter to A.S. Lazerev, Nov. 1, 1889. Was Justice Jackson's warning justified?

8. According to the 9/11 Commission:

> Beginning on September 11, Immigration and Naturalization Service agents working in cooperation with the FBI began arresting individuals for immigration violations whom they encountered while following up leads in the FBI's investigation of the 9/11 attacks. Eventually, 768 aliens were arrested as "special interest" detainees. Some (such as Zacarias Moussaoui) were actually in INS custody before 9/11; most were arrested after. Attorney General John Ashcroft told us that he saw his job in directing this effort as "risk minimization," both to find out who had committed the attacks and to prevent a subsequent attack. Ashcroft ordered all special interest immigration hearings closed to the public, family members, and press; directed government attorneys to seek denial of bond until such time as they were "cleared" of terrorist connections by the FBI and other agencies; and ordered the identity of the detainees kept secret. INS attorneys charged with prosecuting the immigration violations had trouble getting information about the detainees and any terrorist connections; in the chaos after the attacks, it was very difficult to reach law enforcement officials, who were following up on other leads. The clearance process approved by the Justice Department was time-consuming, lasting an average of about 80 days.
>
> We have assessed this effort to detain aliens of "special interest." The detainees were lawfully held on immigration charges. Records indicate that 531 were deported, 162 were released on bond, 24 received some kind of immigration benefits, 12 had their proceedings terminated, and 8—one of whom was Moussaoui—were remanded to the custody of the U.S. Marshals Service. The inspector general of the Justice Department found significant problems in the way the 9/11 detainees were treated. In response to a request about the counterterrorism benefits of the 9/11 detainee program, the Justice Department cited six individuals on the special interest detainee list, noting that two (including Moussaoui) were linked directly to a terrorist organization and that it had obtained new leads helpful to the investigation of the 9/11 terrorist attacks. A senior al Qaeda detainee has stated that U.S. government efforts after the 9/11 attacks to monitor the American homeland, including review of Muslims' immigration files and deportation of nonpermanent residents, forced al Qaeda to operate less freely in the United States.[4]

---

4. The 9/11 Commission Report: Final Report of the National Commission on Terrorist Attacks upon the United States 327-38 (2004) (footnotes omitted).

However, as one scholar noted, a focus on the average length of detention could obscure some important details. "Of the 762 people detained in the months after 9/11 on immigration violations, more than 200 would spend from 51 to 100 days in jail, while another 175 would spend up to 150 days in jail. More than 125 would be held longer, some for a year or more. And not a single one of the detainees was ever charged with terrorism or a terrorist-related offense." EDWARD ALDEN, THE CLOSING OF THE AMERICAN BORDER 98 (2009). Were these immigration sweeps justified? Are they distinguishable from the reasoning used to detain Japanese and Japanese-Americans during World War II?

9. Is *Korematsu* still a valid precedent? The district court that overturned Fred Korematsu's conviction nevertheless held that "the Supreme Court's decision stands as the law of this case and for whatever precedential value it may still have." *Korematsu v. United States*, 584 F. Supp. 1406, 1420 (N.D. Cal. 1984).

Did *Trump v. Hawaii*, 138 S. Ct. 2392 (2018), overrule *Korematsu*? Justice Sotomayor, dissenting, noted the "stark parallels between the reasoning of this case and that of *Korematsu*." *Id.* at 2447. In both cases, she argued, "the Government invoked an ill-defined national-security threat to justify an exclusionary policy of sweeping proportion," the order "was rooted in dangerous stereotypes," "the Government was unwilling to reveal its own intelligence agencies' views of the alleged security concerns to the very citizens it purported to protect," and "there was strong evidence that impermissible hostility and animus motivated the Government's policy." *Id.* She concluded that the majority in *Trump v. Hawaii* had overruled *Korematsu*, but argued that "[b]y blindly accepting the Government's misguided invitation to sanction a discriminatory policy motivated by animosity toward a disfavored group, all in the name of a superficial claim of national security, the Court redeploys the same dangerous logic underlying *Korematsu* and merely replaces one 'gravely wrong' decision with another." *Id.* at 2448.

Was even Justice Sotomayor reading too charitably the majority opinion in *Trump v. Hawaii*, which upheld a presidential proclamation suspending entry of aliens from selected countries? Chief Justice Roberts, writing for the Court, stated that although "*Korematsu* has nothing to do with this case," the Court would take "the opportunity to make express what is already obvious: *Korematsu* was gravely wrong the day it was decided, has been overruled in the court of history, and – to be clear – 'has no place in law under the Constitution'." *Id.* at 2423 (quoting Justice Jackson, dissenting, in *Korematsu*). "The forcible relocation of U.S. citizens to concentration camps, solely and explicitly on the basis of race, is objectively unlawful and outside the scope of Presidential authority." *Id.* Why didn't the Chief Justice write, in the formulaic terms that the Court uses to overrule cases, that *Korematsu* "should be, and hereby is, overruled"? Was a narrow door left open for national security emergencies of the future? Is detention of citizens that is *not* "solely and explicitly" on the basis of race "objectively unlawful"?

10. Consider this letter, by the Mayor of Roanoke, Virginia, written at the height of a debate concerning the U.S. role in the Syrian refugee crisis. Is this an example of Jackson's/Chekhov's loaded gun? How many errors can you find in it?

DAVID A. BOWERS
Mayor

CITY OF ROANOKE
OFFICE OF THE MAYOR
215 CHURCH AVENUE, S.W., SUITE 452
ROANOKE, VIRGINIA 24011-1594
TELEPHONE: (540) 853-2444
FAX: (540) 853-1145

STATEMENT OF MAYOR DAVID A. BOWERS

November 18, 2015

Roanoke is a welcoming city and America is the melting pot of the world, and right and successful we have been at both.

However, since the recent terrorist bombing of the Russian airliner, the attacks in Paris and now with the murderous threats to our nation's capital, I am convinced that it is presently imprudent to assist in the relocation of Syrian refugees to our part of Virginia.

Thus, today, I'm requesting that all Roanoke Valley governments and non-governmental agencies suspend and delay any further Syrian refugee assistance until these serious hostilities and atrocities end, or at the very least until regarded as under control by U.S. authorities, and normalcy is restored.

I'm reminded that President Franklin D. Roosevelt felt compelled to sequester Japanese foreign nationals after the bombing of Pearl Harbor, and it appears that the threat of harm to America from Isis now is just as real and serious as that from our enemies then.

I further want to assure our citizens that Roanoke's law enforcement and public safety agencies are and will be prepared to the best of their ability to assure our citizens that everything is and will be done to protect Roanokers from harm and danger from this present scourge upon the earth.

In this regard, at least for awhile into the future, it seems to me to be better safe than sorry.

Sincerely,

David A. Bowers
Mayor

III. THE DICHOTOMY BETWEEN PUNITIVE AND PREVENTIVE DETENTION

Before a magistrate may issue a warrant for an arrest, the Fourth Amendment requires a showing by a law enforcement officer of probable cause to believe that a person has committed a crime. Similarly, a warrantless arrest also requires that the arresting officer have probable cause for such an action to remain outside the category of "unreasonable searches and seizures" forbidden by the Fourth Amendment.

But neither that legal standard nor those procedures constitute the universe of ways that the state may detain or search a person. The classic "stop-and-frisk" (a.k.a. the "Terry stop") is one such example. If a police officer is "able to point to specific and articulable facts which, taken together with rational inferences from those facts, reasonably warrant" his or her suspicion of possibly criminal behavior, that officer may briefly detain the person and even conduct a search (a "frisk") for purposes of the officer's safety. *Terry v. Ohio*, 392 U.S. 1 (1968). How long the stop may last turns out to be a relative term based on context: "[A]n investigative detention must be temporary and last no longer than is necessary to effectuate the purpose of the stop." *Florida v. Royer*, 460 U.S. 491 (1983); *but compare Rodriguez v. United States*, 135 S. Ct. 1609 (2015) (seven- or eight-minute delay after traffic stop to allow for drug dog sniff unrelated to the purpose of the stop unlawful if it was "prolonged beyond the time reasonably required to complete the mission of issuing a ticket for the violation" and "not independently supported by individualized suspicion" of criminal activity) *with United States v. Richards*, 500 F.2d 1025 (9th Cir. 1974) (gunpoint stop and roughly hour-long detention did not constitute arrest requiring probable cause because appellant's "implausible and evasive responses to these questions indicated that something was awry and created even more reason for the investigation being pursued further").

Such stops, based on individualized suspicion that falls short of probable cause, are by their nature intended to be "brief," and therefore very unlikely to rise to the level of "indefinite" detention. However, a long line of cases has upheld other exceptions to traditional Fourth Amendment requirements on the grounds of "administrative inspections" and "regulatory searches." These are deemed permissible even without any individualized probable cause so long as their reasonableness is based on neutral criteria. So-called safety inspections to further building or health codes, searches at the nation's borders (which include airports and transportation hubs far from any geographical border), and certain kinds of checkpoints (e.g., immigration, drunk-driving prevention) are all permitted both without probable cause and without a focus on any particular individual.

Such detentions and searches, occurring as they do in the course of police operations, tend to be relatively short in duration. The prospect for much more substantial periods of imprisonment may be found in various statutes. Consider two examples.

A. Pretrial Detention on Grounds of Future Dangerousness

The Bail Reform Act of 1984 permitted detention before trial if, after a hearing requiring written findings of fact supported by clear and convincing evidence, a judicial officer found that "no condition or combination of conditions will reasonably assure the appearance of the person as required and the safety of any other person and the community." The Act provided the person facing detention a wide array of procedural protections, including rights to counsel, to present evidence, and to cross-examination. With various amendments over the years, these components of the Act remain in place, permitting detention before trial on grounds of future dangerousness. *See* 18 U.S.C. § 3142(e)-(j).

In *United States v. Salerno*, 481 U.S. 739 (1987), the Supreme Court upheld the Act against constitutional challenges under the Fifth Amendment and the Eighth Amendment. The case concerned two men: Anthony Salerno, whom the government argued was the head of the Genovese crime family, and Vincent Cafaro, also arrested and charged in the indictment as a "captain" in the family. The government wanted the two detained before trial and the lower court agreed: "The activities of a criminal organization such as the Genovese Family do not cease with the arrest of its principals and their release on even the most stringent of bail conditions. . . . When business as usual involves threats, beatings, and murder, the present danger such people pose in the community is self-evident."

The Second Circuit found that the statute violated substantive due process. One member of the panel, Judge Feinberg, dissented and posed a terrorism hypothetical: "[I]f a member of a terrorist organization is indicted for blowing up an airliner for political reasons and there is clear and persuasive evidence that the defendant will do so again if not confined, it is not self-evident to me that society must nevertheless immediately release him on bail until he is tried." *United States v. Salerno*, 794 F.2d 64, 77 (2d Cir. 1986). At oral argument, Solicitor General Charles Fried referenced the point and Justice Scalia asked the first question from the bench about it: "But in fact, General Fried, to go back to your terrorist example, had the same situation, except he isn't arrested for a past offense yet; he has just gone around saying, I am going to blow up an airline. Now, you acknowledge that in that situation, this legislation would not apply. There would be no way to detain the individual unless and until he commits an offense for which he's arrested. That's what causes . . . that's what produces the argument that there has to be some punitive element to this detention." General Fried agreed: "This is a statute which is intended to be ancillary to . . . it is clearly auxiliary to . . . the normal working of the criminal process. . . . This is not . . . this is not a free standing attempt to supplant or to have a predictive regime replace the normal criminal law. The criminal charge is there. And this is a way of dealing with a problem in the interim. It's not an independent way of getting at dangerous people."

Writing for the Court, Chief Justice Rehnquist rejected the argument that the statute violated substantive due process as punishment before trial, holding that "the Government's regulatory interest in community safety can, in appropriate circumstances, outweigh an individual's liberty interest." This interest was compelling enough, he concluded, also to reject the claim that the Excessive Bail Clause of the

Eighth Amendment was violated by what amounted to setting bail "at an infinite amount for reasons not related to the risk of flight." There was nothing in the text of that clause, Rehnquist observed, that "limits permissible Government considerations solely to questions of flight." The only substantive limit prohibited "excessive" bail, which must be judged against the evil sought to be prevented.

What else might be so compelling a government interest? Chief Justice Rehnquist noted, *inter alia*, "in times of war or insurrection, when society's interest is at its peak, the Government may detain individuals whom the government believes to be dangerous. Even outside the exigencies of war, we have found that sufficiently compelling governmental interests can justify detention of dangerous persons. Thus, we have found no absolute constitutional barrier to detention of potentially dangerous resident aliens pending deportation proceedings. We have also held that the government may detain mentally unstable individuals who present a danger to the public and dangerous defendants who become incompetent to stand trial."

Justice Marshall dissented, finding the protections of substantive due process and prohibition on excessive bail broader than conceived by the majority and not avoidable by characterizing detention as regulatory rather than punitive. Illustrating his point, Justice Marshall offered a hypothetical:

> But let us suppose that a defendant is indicted and the Government shows by clear and convincing evidence that he is dangerous and should be detained pending a trial, at which trial the defendant is acquitted. May the Government continue to hold the defendant in detention based upon its showing that he is dangerous? The answer cannot be yes, for that would allow the Government to imprison someone for uncommitted crimes based upon "proof" not beyond a reasonable doubt. The result must therefore be that once the indictment has failed, detention cannot continue. But our fundamental principles of justice declare that the defendant is as innocent on the day before his trial as he is on the morning after his acquittal. Under this statute an untried indictment somehow acts to permit a detention, based on other charges, which after an acquittal would be unconstitutional. The conclusion is inescapable that the indictment has been turned into evidence, if not that the defendant is guilty of the crime charged, then that left to his own devices he will soon be guilty of something else.

Finally, Justice Marshall referred back to what he called "the peculiar facts of this case." Although both Salerno and Cafaro were detained on a finding of their danger to the community, "[n]o response or appearance of counsel was filed on behalf of respondent Cafaro" in response to the Solicitor General's petition for certiorari. Only Salerno responded. That was because shortly before the SG's petition, Cafaro began cooperating with the government's investigation. In Marshall's view, this change spoke volumes:

> There is a connection between the peculiar facts of this case and the evident constitutional defects in the statute which the Court upholds today. Respondent Cafaro was originally incarcerated for an indeterminate period at the request of the Government, which believed (or professed to believe) that his release imminently threatened the safety of the community. That threat apparently vanished,

from the Government's point of view, when Cafaro agreed to act as a covert agent of the Government. There could be no more eloquent demonstration of the coercive power of authority to imprison upon prediction, or of the dangers which the almost inevitable abuses pose to the cherished liberties of a free society.

Throughout the world today there are men, women, and children interned indefinitely, awaiting trials which may never come or which may be a mockery of the word, because their governments believe them to be "dangerous." Our Constitution, whose construction began two centuries ago, can shelter us forever from the evils of such unchecked power. Over 200 years it has slowly, through our efforts, grown more durable, more expansive, and more just. But it cannot protect us if we lack the courage, and the self-restraint, to protect ourselves.

In a footnote to his opinion in *Salerno*, Chief Justice Rehnquist wrote: "We intimate no view as to the point at which detention in a particular case might become excessively prolonged, and therefore punitive, in relation to Congress' regulatory goal." Fourteen years later, the Court considered a habeas petition from Kestutis Zadvydas, an alien whose admission to the United States as a child was revoked in adulthood after numerous criminal convictions. In such a case, Congress required his detention pending removal for up to ninety days; in case of delay, another statute provided that such persons "may" be detained or subject to supervised release. But when no country would accept him (he was born in a displaced persons camp in 1948 and had no clear citizenship), Zadvydas sought release from what he claimed to be the prospect of indefinite detention. The government argued that "whether to continue to detain such an alien and, if so, in what circumstances and for how long" was subject only to the discretion of the Attorney General. The Supreme Court, in a five-four opinion by Justice Breyer, took a narrower view of executive discretion, even as seemingly authorized by statute:

> A statute permitting indefinite detention of an alien would raise a serious constitutional problem. [T]his Court has said that government detention violates [the Due Process] Clause unless the detention is ordered in a criminal proceeding with adequate procedural protections, see *United States v. Salerno*, 481 U.S. 739, 746 (1987), or, in certain special and "narrow" nonpunitive "circumstances," where a special justification, such as harm-threatening mental illness, outweighs the "individual's constitutionally protected interest in avoiding physical restraint."
>
> The proceedings at issue here are civil, not criminal, and we assume that they are nonpunitive in purpose and effect. There is no sufficiently strong special justification here for indefinite civil detention — at least as administered under this statute. The statute, says the Government, has two regulatory goals: "ensuring the appearance of aliens at future immigration proceedings" and "[p]reventing danger to the community." But by definition the first justification — preventing flight — is weak or nonexistent where removal seems a remote possibility at best. . . . The second justification — protecting the community — does not necessarily diminish in force over time. But we have upheld preventive detention based on dangerousness only when limited to specially dangerous individuals and subject to strong procedural protections.
>
> The civil confinement here at issue is not limited, but potentially permanent. The provision authorizing detention does not apply narrowly to "a small segment

of particularly dangerous individuals," say, suspected terrorists, but broadly to aliens ordered removed for many and various reasons, including tourist visa violations.

Zadvydas v. Davis, 533 U.S. 678, 690-91 (2001) (internal citations omitted). The Court found that "[t]he serious constitutional problem arising out of a statute that, in these circumstances, permits an indefinite, perhaps permanent, deprivation of human liberty without any such protection is obvious." *Id.* at 692. The Court deftly distinguished or avoided concerns that, in its view, would call for deference to the political branches, emphasizing that "we leave no unprotected spot in the Nation's armor. Neither do we consider terrorism or other special circumstances where special arguments might be made for forms of preventive detention and for heightened deference to the judgments of the political branches with respect to matters of national security." *Id.* at 695-96 (citation and quotation marks omitted). The Court instructed judges hearing such petitions to determine "whether the detention in question exceeds a period reasonably necessary to secure removal" with a rebuttable presumption that six months would be the outer limit of such a period. *Id.* at 699, 701. Justice Scalia, dissenting, would have placed no temporal limit on the executive's power to detain such a person: "A criminal alien under final order of removal who allegedly will not be accepted by any other country in the reasonably foreseeable future claims a constitutional right of supervised release into the United States. This claim can be repackaged as freedom from 'physical restraint' or freedom from 'indefinite detention,' but it is at bottom a claimed right of release into this country by an individual who concededly has no legal right to be here. There is no such constitutional right." *Id.* at 702-03.

B. Detention as a Material Witness

Another statute that may be used to detain an individual without a finding of probable cause of criminal conduct is found at 18 U.S.C. § 3144:

> If it appears from an affidavit filed by a party that the testimony of a person is material in a criminal proceeding, and if it is shown that it may become impracticable to secure the presence of the person by subpoena, a judicial officer may order the arrest of the person and treat the person in accordance with the provisions of section 3142 of this title [concerning "release or detention of a defendant pending trial"]. No material witness may be detained because of inability to comply with any condition of release if the testimony of such witness can adequately be secured by deposition, and if further detention is not necessary to prevent a failure of justice. Release of a material witness may be delayed for a reasonable period of time until the deposition of the witness can be taken pursuant to the Federal Rules of Criminal Procedure.

Professor David Cole described a dramatic change in the use of the material witness law after September 11, 2001:

> This is an extraordinary power, used only sparingly before September 11, because it authorizes the incarceration of persons who are charged with no crime, based solely on a *prediction* about their reluctance to testify. Since September 11, however, the Justice Department has aggressively exploited the material witness law, not for its legitimate purpose of ensuring that reluctant witnesses are available for trial, but for preventive detention of persons who could not otherwise be held. As [Attorney

General John] Ashcroft himself admitted at an October 31, 2001, press conference, "Aggressive detention of lawbreakers and material witnesses is vital to preventing, disrupting, or delaying new attacks. It is difficult for a person in jail or under detention to murder innocent people or to aid or abet in terrorism." The government has locked up people as material witnesses without ever bringing them before a grand jury or a criminal trial to testify, has held them under harsh conditions more befitting a suspect than a witness, and has interrogated them at length in custody. A study by the *Washington Post* identified forty-four people who had been held as material witnesses in the first fourteen months of the September 11 investigation, almost half of whom had not testified in any proceeding.[5]

Among those subject to material witness warrants prior to their designation as enemy combatants were Ali al-Marri and Jose Padilla, whose cases are discussed in more detail below. First, consider this case.

Ashcroft v. al-Kidd
563 U.S. 731 (2011)

Justice SCALIA delivered the opinion of the Court.

The federal material-witness statute authorizes judges to "order the arrest of [a] person" whose testimony "is material in a criminal proceeding . . . if it is shown that it may become impracticable to secure the presence of the person by subpoena." Material witnesses enjoy the same constitutional right to pretrial release as other federal detainees, and federal law requires release if their testimony "can adequately be secured by deposition, and if further detention is not necessary to prevent a failure of justice."

Because this case arises from a motion to dismiss, we accept as true the factual allegations in Abdullah al-Kidd's complaint. The complaint alleges that, in the aftermath of the September 11th terrorist attacks, then-Attorney General John Ashcroft authorized federal prosecutors and law enforcement officials to use the material-witness statute to detain individuals with suspected ties to terrorist organizations. It is alleged that federal officials had no intention of calling most of these individuals as witnesses, and that they were detained, at Ashcroft's direction, because federal officials suspected them of supporting terrorism but lacked sufficient evidence to charge them with a crime.

It is alleged that this pretextual detention policy led to the material-witness arrest of al-Kidd, a native-born United States citizen. FBI agents apprehended him in March 2003 as he checked in for a flight to Saudi Arabia. Two days earlier, federal officials had informed a Magistrate Judge that, if al-Kidd boarded his flight, they believed information "crucial" to the prosecution of Sami Omar al-Hussayen would be lost. Al-Kidd remained in federal custody for 16 days and on supervised release until al-Hussayen's trial concluded 14 months later. Prosecutors never called him as a witness.

---

5. DAVID COLE, ENEMY ALIENS: DOUBLE STANDARDS AND CONSTITUTIONAL FREEDOMS IN THE WAR ON TERRORISM 36-37 (2003) (footnotes omitted).

In March 2005, al-Kidd filed this *Bivens* action to challenge the constitutionality of Ashcroft's alleged policy; he also asserted several other claims not relevant here against Ashcroft and others. Ashcroft filed a motion to dismiss based on absolute and qualified immunity, which the District Court denied. A divided panel of the United States Court of Appeals for the Ninth Circuit affirmed, holding that the Fourth Amendment prohibits pretextual arrests absent probable cause of criminal wrongdoing, and that Ashcroft could not claim qualified or absolute immunity.

The Fourth Amendment protects "[t]he right of the people to be secure in their persons, houses, papers, and effects, against unreasonable searches and seizures." An arrest, of course, qualifies as a "seizure" of a "person" under this provision, and so must be reasonable under the circumstances. Al-Kidd does not assert that Government officials would have acted unreasonably if they had used a material-witness warrant to arrest him for the purpose of securing his testimony for trial. He contests, however (and the Court of Appeals here rejected), the reasonableness of using the warrant to detain him as a suspected criminal.

Fourth Amendment reasonableness is predominantly an objective inquiry. We ask whether the circumstances, viewed objectively, justify the challenged action. If so, that action was reasonable *whatever* the subjective intent motivating the relevant officials. This approach recognizes that the Fourth Amendment regulates conduct rather than thoughts; and it promotes evenhanded, uniform enforcement of the law.

Two limited exceptions to this rule are our special-needs and administrative-search cases, where actual motivations do matter. The Government seeks to justify the present arrest on the basis of a properly issued judicial warrant—so that the special-needs and administrative-inspection cases cannot be the basis for a purpose inquiry here.

A warrant based on individualized suspicion in fact grants more protection against the malevolent and the incompetent than existed in most of our cases eschewing inquiries into intent. [We have] declined to probe the motives behind seizures supported by probable cause but lacking a warrant approved by a detached magistrate. [We have also] applied an objective standard to warrantless searches justified by a lesser showing of reasonable suspicion. We review even some suspicionless searches for objective reasonableness. If concerns about improper motives and pretext do not justify subjective inquiries in those less protective contexts, we see no reason to adopt that inquiry here.

Al-Kidd would read our cases more narrowly. He asserts that we ignore subjective intent only when there exists "probable cause to believe that a violation of law has occurred"—which was not the case here. That is a distortion. [We have unanimously] held that we would not look behind an objectively reasonable traffic stop to determine whether racial profiling or a desire to investigate other potential crimes was the real motive. In the course of our analysis, we dismissed [in that case, petitioner] Whren's reliance on our inventory-search and administrative-inspection cases by explaining that those cases do not "endors[e] the principle that ulterior motives can invalidate police conduct that is justifiable on the basis of probable cause to believe that a violation of law has occurred." But to say that ulterior motives do *not* invalidate a search that is legitimate because of probable cause to believe a crime has occurred is not to say that it *does* invalidate all searches that are legitimate for other reasons.

Because al-Kidd concedes that individualized suspicion supported the issuance of the material-witness arrest warrant; and does not assert that his arrest would have been unconstitutional absent the alleged pretextual use of the warrant; we find no Fourth Amendment violation.[3] Efficient and evenhanded application of the law demands that we look to whether the arrest is objectively justified, rather than to the motive of the arresting officer.

. . .

We hold that an objectively reasonable arrest and detention of a material witness pursuant to a validly obtained warrant cannot be challenged as unconstitutional on the basis of allegations that the arresting authority had an improper motive. Because Ashcroft did not violate clearly established law, we need not address the more difficult question whether he enjoys absolute immunity. The judgment of the Court of Appeals is reversed, and the case is remanded for further proceedings consistent with this opinion.

It is so ordered.

Justice KAGAN took no part in the consideration or decision of this case.

Justice KENNEDY, with whom Justice GINSBURG, Justice BREYER, and Justice SOTOMAYOR join as to Part I, concurring.

The Court's holding is limited to the arguments presented by the parties and leaves unresolved whether the Government's use of the Material Witness Statute in this case was lawful. Under the statute, a Magistrate Judge may issue a warrant to arrest someone as a material witness upon a showing by affidavit that "the testimony of a person is material in a criminal proceeding" and "that it may become impracticable to secure the presence of the person by subpoena." The scope of the statute's lawful authorization is uncertain. For example, a law-abiding citizen might observe a crime during the days or weeks before a scheduled flight abroad. It is unclear whether those facts alone might allow police to obtain a material witness warrant on the ground that it "may become impracticable" to secure the person's presence by subpoena. The question becomes more difficult if one further assumes the traveler would be willing to testify if asked; and more difficult still if one supposes that authorities delay obtaining or executing the warrant until the traveler has arrived at the airport. These possibilities resemble the facts in this case.

---

3. The concerns of Justices Ginsburg and Sotomayor about the validity of the warrant in this case are beside the point. Al-Kidd does not claim that Ashcroft is liable because the FBI agents failed to obtain a valid warrant. He takes the validity of the warrant as a given, and argues that his arrest nevertheless violated the Constitution because it was motivated by an illegitimate purpose. His separate Fourth Amendment and statutory claims against the FBI agents who sought the material-witness warrant, which are the focus of both concurrences, are not before us.

In considering these issues, it is important to bear in mind that the Material Witness Statute might not provide for the issuance of warrants within the meaning of the Fourth Amendment's Warrant Clause. The typical arrest warrant is based on probable cause that the arrestee has committed a crime; but that is not the standard for the issuance of warrants under the Material Witness Statute. If material witness warrants do not qualify as "Warrants" under the Fourth Amendment, then material witness arrests might still be governed by the Fourth Amendment's separate reasonableness requirement for seizures of the person. Given the difficulty of these issues, the Court is correct to address only the legal theory put before it, without further exploring when material witness arrests might be consistent with statutory and constitutional requirements.

Justice GINSBURG, with whom Justice BREYER and Justice SOTOMAYOR join, concurring in the judgment.

I agree with the Court that no "clearly established law" renders Ashcroft answerable in damages for the abuse of authority al-Kidd charged. But I join Justice Sotomayor in objecting to the Court's disposition of al-Kidd's Fourth Amendment claim on the merits; as she observes, that claim involves novel and trying questions that will "have no effect on the outcome of th[is] case."

In addressing al-Kidd's Fourth Amendment claim against Ashcroft, the Court assumes at the outset the existence of a *validly obtained* material witness warrant. That characterization is puzzling.[1] Is a warrant "validly obtained" when the affidavit on which it is based fails to inform the issuing Magistrate Judge that "the Government has no intention of using [al-Kidd as a witness] at [another's] trial," and does not disclose that al-Kidd had cooperated with FBI agents each of the several times they had asked to interview him?

Casting further doubt on the assumption that the warrant was validly obtained, the Magistrate Judge was not told that al-Kidd's parents, wife, and children were all citizens and residents of the United States. In addition, the affidavit misrepresented that al-Kidd was about to take a one-way flight to Saudi Arabia, with a first-class ticket costing approximately $5,000; in fact, al-Kidd had a round-trip, coach-class ticket that cost $1,700.[2] Given these omissions and misrepresentations, there is strong cause to question the Court's opening

---

1. Nowhere in al-Kidd's complaint is there any concession that the warrant gained by the FBI agents was validly obtained.

2. Judicial officers asked to issue material witness warrants must determine whether the affidavit supporting the application shows that "the testimony of a person is material in a criminal proceeding" and that "it may become impracticable to secure the presence of the person by subpoena." 18 U.S.C. § 3144. Even if these conditions are met, issuance of the warrant is discretionary. Al-Kidd's experience illustrates the importance of vigilant exercise of this checking role by the judicial officer to whom the warrant application is presented.

The affidavit used to secure al-Kidd's detention was spare; it did not state with particularity the information al-Kidd purportedly possessed, nor did it specify how al-Kidd's knowledge would be material to Sami Omar al-Hussayen's prosecution. As to impracticability, the affidavit contained only this unelaborated statement: "It is believed that if Al-Kidd travels to Saudi Arabia, the United States Government will be unable to secure his presence at trial via subpoena." Had the Magistrate Judge insisted on more concrete showings of materiality and impracticability, al-Kidd might have been spared the entire ordeal.

assumption—a valid material-witness warrant—and equally strong reason to conclude that a merits determination was neither necessary nor proper.

I also agree with Justice Kennedy that al-Kidd's treatment presents serious questions, unaddressed by the Court, concerning "the [legality of] the Government's use of the Material Witness Statute in this case." In addition to the questions Justice Kennedy poses, and even if the initial material witness classification had been proper, what even arguably legitimate basis could there be for the harsh custodial conditions to which al-Kidd was subjected: Ostensibly held only to secure his testimony, al-Kidd was confined in three different detention centers during his 16 days' incarceration, kept in high-security cells lit 24 hours a day, strip-searched and subjected to body-cavity inspections on more than one occasion, and handcuffed and shackled about his wrists, legs, and waist.

However circumscribed al-Kidd's *Bivens* claim against Ashcroft may have been, his remaining claims against the FBI agents who apprehended him invite consideration of the issues Justice Kennedy identified. His challenges to the brutal conditions of his confinement have been settled. But his ordeal is a grim reminder of the need to install safeguards against disrespect for human dignity, constraints that will control officialdom even in perilous times.

Justice SOTOMAYOR, with whom Justice GINSBURG and Justice BREYER join, concurring in the judgment.

I concur in the Court's judgment reversing the Court of Appeals because I agree with the majority's conclusion that Ashcroft did not violate clearly established law. I cannot join the majority's opinion, however, because it unnecessarily "resolve[s] [a] difficult and novel questio[n] of constitutional . . . interpretation that will 'have no effect on the outcome of the case.'"

Whether the Fourth Amendment permits the pretextual use of a material witness warrant for preventive detention of an individual whom the Government has no intention of using at trial is, in my view, a closer question than the majority's opinion suggests. Although the majority is correct that a government official's subjective intent is generally irrelevant in determining whether that officer's actions violate the Fourth Amendment, none of our prior cases recognizing that principle involved prolonged detention of an individual without probable cause to believe he had committed any criminal offense. We have never considered whether an official's subjective intent matters for purposes of the Fourth Amendment in that novel context, and we need not and should not resolve that question in this case. All Members of the Court agree that, whatever the merits of the underlying Fourth Amendment question, Ashcroft did not violate clearly established law.

The majority's constitutional ruling is a narrow one premised on the existence of a "valid material-witness warran[t]," —a premise that, at the very least, is questionable in light of the allegations set forth in al-Kidd's complaint. Based on those allegations, it is not at all clear that it would have been "impracticable to secure [al-Kidd's] presence . . . by subpoena" or that his testimony could not "adequately be secured by deposition." 18 U.S.C. § 3144; see First Amended Complaint in No. 05-093-EJL, ¶ 55 ("Mr. al-Kidd would have complied with a subpoena had he been issued one or agreed to a deposition"). Nor is it clear that the affidavit supporting the warrant was sufficient; its failure to disclose that the Government had no intention of using al-Kidd as a witness at trial may very well have rendered the affidavit deliberately false and misleading. The majority assumes away these factual difficulties, but in my view, they point to the artificiality of the way the Fourth Amendment question has been presented to this Court and provide further reason to avoid rendering an unnecessary holding on the constitutional question.

I also join Part I of Justice Kennedy's concurring opinion. As that opinion makes clear, this case does not present an occasion to address the proper scope of the material witness statute or its constitutionality as applied in this case. Indeed, nothing in the majority's opinion today should be read as placing this Court's imprimatur on the actions taken by the Government against al-Kidd.

NOTE

Many detainees received no compensation of any kind for their incarceration as material witnesses. Brandon Mayfield, a lawyer jailed under the material witness statute for two weeks following his mistaken identification from partial fingerprints taken at the scene of the March 2004 Madrid bombings, received a $2 million settlement that came with a formal apology from the Department of Justice. Eric Lichtblau, *U.S. Will Pay $2 Million to Lawyer Wrongly Jailed*, N.Y. Times, Nov. 30, 2008, at A18.

IV. DETENTION IN WARTIME: THE POST-9/11 CHOICE BETWEEN MILITARY AND CIVILIAN DETENTION REGIMES

As will be recalled from the second part of Chapter 8, U.S. views on the legal regulation of armed conflict draw on international, constitutional, statutory, and regulatory sources. The law of armed conflict was developed over many years and from the desire to reduce the horror of war to the shortest duration and least degree and volume of human misery possible. Like all law, it resulted from the accretion of past experience. This produced particular tensions in the U.S. military response to the attacks of September 11, 2001. The response, until at least 2008 when the Supreme Court announced its opinion in *Boumediene*, was at odds with longstanding U.S. practice, the experience of its military lawyers, and the understanding of many respected authorities in the international legal community.

This divergence, and its practical effects, was best summarized by this short passage:

> Prior to [September 11, 2001, U.S. military] lawyers applied an "either/or" law-triggering paradigm that dictated when the law of armed conflict (LOAC) applied to U.S. operations: either those operations involved hostilities against the armed forces of another State so as to qualify as international armed conflicts, or they involved hostilities against insurgent forces within a State on whose behalf the United States had intervened, thereby falling into the alternative category of internal armed conflict.

Derived from common articles 2 and 3 of the 1949 Geneva Conventions, this law-triggering paradigm was a genuine article of faith for U.S. military lawyers. . . .

These lawyers and the forces they supported were [equally] well versed in military operations that fell outside these inter/intra state armed conflict paradigms. . . . Based on this methodology, when U.S. forces first "hit the ground" in Afghanistan, operational legal advisors, like their predecessors in Panama and Somalia, followed this "default" approach and advised their commanders to comply with the LOAC [as a matter of policy, not as a requirement of law] as if they were involved in an international armed conflict.

[Soon after their arrival in Afghanistan, however, U.S.] commanders were directed to halt the practice of treating captured personnel "as if" they were prisoners of war, because a new status had been adopted for these detainees: "unlawful enemy combatant." This characterization was created to denote a detained enemy operative who did not qualify for status as a prisoner of war and who would therefore not be entitled to claim the benefit of LOAC protections. . . .

With regard to execution of combat operations, this incongruity [of relying on LOAC as the legal basis *only* for the use of force against al-Qaeda, *not* to regulate detention] had little impact due to the military practice of following LOAC principles during all operations as a matter of policy. However, as the United States began to capture and detain alleged terrorist operatives, it became quickly apparent that the inapplicability of LOAC obligations would be a key component to the development of detainee treatment and interrogation policies.[6]

The decision to fight a war justified by a body of law that was not invoked (indeed, deemed not relevant) to regulate all of its conduct led to some of the worst abuses and shameful episodes of this continuing struggle with an adversary that seemed to defy categorization under that existing law.

A. Debating the Choice Between War and Crime

There is no question that detention is authorized in wartime. But the purpose of such detention is not punitive; rather, it is to prevent continued participation in an armed conflict. Consequently, the duration of one's confinement is a function of the continuing state of that armed conflict. Similarly, this purpose also constrains to whom such detention authority may be applied. In sharp distinction from detention under the criminal law, the baseline rule for detention under the law of armed conflict is a determination of one's general status. For example, and again as a general rule, detention is limited to those who are members of an opposing military force; if one's status is that of a civilian, not a combatant, detention authority is much more limited.

One can thus see that military detention does not serve the same purposes, and is not justified by the same legal theories, that support incarceration as part of a system of criminal justice or even detention for administrative or other special needs. Generally speaking, civilian detention regimes are based on one's conduct (commission of a crime), not status (with very limited exceptions, e.g., quarantine). Detention is generally punitive and its duration set in advance (again, with limited exceptions).

---

6. Geoffrey S. Corn, *Triggering the Law of Armed Conflict?,* in The War on Terror and the Laws of War 33-36 (Corn et al. eds., 2d ed. 2015) (footnotes omitted).

Scholars and practitioners debate whether a civilian or military detention regime is the optimal choice for the post-9/11 world. As a matter of law, the United States considers its actions against al Qaeda, ISIS, and other non-state actors to be responses to non-international armed conflicts and considers those who fight as members of those organizations to be without combatant immunity, the "privilege" not to be prosecuted for violent acts that if committed outside of the context of war would be crimes against persons (including, most obviously, murder) and property. Indeed, Title 18 of the United States Code contains numerous terrorism-related offenses that carry steep terms of imprisonment (as well as the possibility of capital punishment). In addition, unprivileged belligerents may be prosecuted for their acts against U.S. armed forces, in which case the forum may not be a United States court but a military commission with different procedures, protections, and penalties. But *must* prosecution follow capture? Here are two views on the question.

Bruce Ackerman, *The Emergency Constitution*
113 Yale L.J. 1029 (2004)

Our legal tradition provides us with two fundamental concepts — war and crime — to deal with our present predicament. Neither fits.

A. War?

The "war on terrorism" has paid enormous political dividends for President Bush, but that does not make it a compelling legal concept. War is traditionally defined as a state of belligerency between sovereigns. The wars with Afghanistan and Iraq were wars; the struggle against Osama bin Laden and al Qaeda is not.[3] The selective adaptation of doctrines dealing with war predictably leads to sweeping incursions on fundamental liberties. It is one thing for President Roosevelt to designate a captured American citizen serving in the German army as an "enemy combatant" and try him without standard scrutiny by the civilian courts; it is quite another for President Bush to do the same thing for suspected members of al Qaeda.

The difference is obvious and fundamental: Only a very small percentage of the human race is composed of recognized members of the German military, but anybody can be suspected of complicity with al Qaeda. This means that all of us are, in principle, subject to executive detention once we treat the "war on terrorism" as if it were the legal equivalent of the war against Germany.

War between sovereign states also comes to an end; some decisive act of capitulation, armistice, or treaty takes place for all the world to see. But this will not happen in the war against terrorism. Even if bin Laden is caught, tried, and convicted, it will not be clear whether al Qaeda has survived. Even if this network disintegrates, it will likely morph into other terrorist groups. Al Qaeda is already collaborating with Hezbollah,

---

3. Traditional definitions hold that a state of warfare exists when "states through the medium of their armed forces, such forces being under a regular command, wearing uniform or such other identifiable marks as to make them recognisable at a distance . . . conduct[] their hostilities in accordance with the international rules of armed conflict." L.C. Green, THE CONTEMPORARY LAW OF ARMED CONFLICT 54-55 (2d ed. 2000). . . . The ongoing crisis of definition posed by the existence of guerrilla and terrorist groups is the subject of much recent scholarship. . . .

for example, and how will anybody determine where one group ends and the other begins? There are more than six billion people in the world—more than enough to supply terrorist networks with haters, even if the West does nothing to stir the pot. So if we choose to call this a war, it will be endless. This means that we not only subject everybody to the risk of detention by the Commander in Chief, but we subject everybody to the risk of endless detention.

If the President is allowed to punish, as well as to detain, the logic of war-talk leads to the creation of a full-blown alternative system of criminal justice for terrorism suspects. This system is already emerging in the military, and we are beginning to argue about the way it should be constructed: How little evidence suffices to justify how much detention? Can detainees ever get in touch with civilian lawyers? Can these lawyers ever scrutinize the evidence, or must it remain secret?

These are important questions, but it is even more important to challenge the war-talk that makes the entire enterprise seem plausible. The only legal language presently available for making this critique—the language of the criminal law—is not entirely persuasive. But it is powerful.

B. Crime?

For the criminal law purist, the "war on terrorism" is merely a metaphor without decisive legal significance, more like the "war on drugs" or the "war on crime" than the war against Nazi Germany. Al Qaeda is a dangerous conspiracy, but so is the Mafia, whose activities lead to the deaths of thousands through drug overdoses and gangland murders. Conspiracy is a serious crime, and crime fighters have special tools to deal with it. But nobody supposes that casual talk of a "war on crime" permits us to sweep away the entire panoply of criminal protections built up over the centuries. Why is the "war on terrorism" any different?

Recall too the experience of the Cold War. There was pervasive talk of a Communist conspiracy—and in contrast to al Qaeda, the shadowy cells of grim-faced plotters were supported by a great superpower commanding massive armies with nuclear weapons. American presidents also had substantial evidence of links between domestic Communist cells and the Soviet GRU, which was a military organization.[11] For decades, we were only minutes away from an incident that could lead to nuclear holocaust. From a legal point of view, domestic Communist cells were virtually front-line troops in something very close to a classic war between sovereign states.

Yet no president ever suspended the normal operation of the criminal law by calling domestic Communists "enemy combatants."[12] The Communist conspiracy was

---

11. Throughout much of the Cold War, there were two main Soviet intelligence-gathering operations. One was the KGB and its many predecessor organizations. The other was the GRU, the Chief Directorate for Intelligence of the Red Army's General Staff. GRU officers interacted with members of the Comintern, which supervised the Communist Party of the United States, and also supervised Communist Party agents within the U.S. government. . . .

12. This presidential restraint is especially noteworthy since statutory authority could have been stretched to support such actions. *See* Emergency Detention Act of 1950, Pub. L. No. 81-831, tit. II, §§ 102-103, 64 Stat. 1019, 1021 (repealed 1971) (authorizing the detention, during an "Internal Security Emergency," of persons for whom there was a "reasonable ground" to believe that they would "probably" commit, or conspire to commit, espionage or sabotage). The repeal of these provisions makes it far more difficult to sustain President Bush's actions to detain American citizens as "enemy combatants," especially in light of the Code provision accompanying the repeal. *See* 18 U.S.C. § 4001(a) (2000). . . .

treated as a Communist conspiracy; the accused were provided all the traditional protections of the criminal law. If Cold War anxieties did not overwhelm us, why should war-talk justify extraordinary military measures against small bands of terrorists who cannot rely on the massive assistance of an aggressive superpower?

These are powerful questions that provide a crucial context for questioning the remarkable success of the present administration in persuading the public that wartime emergency measures are appropriate responses to our present predicaments. . . .

Despite the excessive rhetoric and repressive practices, there is one distinctive feature of our present situation that distinguishes it from the scares of the past. Begin with the criminal law purist's normative benchmarks: the traditional legal response to the Mafia and other wide-ranging conspiracies. The purist rightfully emphasizes that the criminal law has managed to contain antisocial organizations within tolerable limits without the need for arbitrary police-state measures. Nonetheless, the reassurance such analogies offer is distinctly limited.

Even the most successful organized crime operations lack the overweening pretensions of the most humble terrorist cell. Mafiosi are generally content to allow government officials to flaunt their symbols of legitimacy so long as gangsters control the underworld. Whatever else is happening in Palermo, the mayor's office is occupied by the duly elected representative of the Italian Republic. But the point of a terrorist bomb is to launch a distinctly political challenge to the government. The deaths caused by terrorists may be smaller in number than those caused by the drug-dealing Mafia. Nevertheless, terrorists' challenge to political authority is greater. The only way to meet this challenge is for the government to demonstrate to its terrified citizens that it is taking steps to act decisively against the blatant assault on its sovereign authority.

The political dimension of the terrorist threat makes the lessons from the McCarthy era more relevant, but once again there is a difference. For all the McCarthyite talk of the Red Menace, the danger remained abstract to ordinary people. While the Cuban Missile Crisis brought us to the brink of World War III, it did not conclude with an event, like the toppling of the Twin Towers, that dramatized America's incapacity to defend its frontiers.

The risk of nuclear devastation during the Cold War might well have been much larger than the terrorist danger today. But we were lucky, and the threat of nuclear holocaust remained a threat. In contrast, the changing technological balance in favor of terrorists means that events like September 11 will recur at unpredictable intervals, each shattering anew the ordinary citizen's confidence in the government's capacity to fend off catastrophic breaches of national security.

Paradoxically, the relative weakness of terrorists compared to the Communist conspiracy only exacerbates the political problems involved in an effective response. If the Cold War threat of nuclear annihilation had been realized, it would have meant the end of civilization as we know it. The survivors would have been obliged to build a legitimate government from the ground up. This will not be true in the new age of terrorism. It may only be a matter of time before a suitcase A-bomb obliterates a major American city, but there will be nothing like a Soviet-style rocket assault leading to the destruction of all major cities simultaneously. Despite the horror, the death, and the pain, American government will survive the day after the tragedy. And it will be obliged to establish — quickly — that it has not been thoroughly demoralized by the lurking terrorist underground.

C. Reassurance

So neither of the standard legal rubrics is really adequate. The rhetoric of war does express the shattering affront to national sovereignty left in the aftermath of a successful terrorist attack. But when translated from politics to law, it threatens all of us with indefinite detention without the traditional safeguards developed over centuries of painful struggle. The rubric of the criminal law has proved itself adequate (with ongoing fine-tunings) to protect fundamental rights while handling serious criminal conspiracies, but only within a social context that presupposes broad-ranging confidence in the government's general capacity to discharge its sovereign functions. When this premise is called into question by a successful terrorist attack, a distinctive interest comes into play.

Call it the *reassurance function*: When a terrorist attack places the state's effective sovereignty in doubt, government must act visibly and decisively to demonstrate to its terrorized citizens that the breach was only temporary, and that it is taking aggressive action to contain the crisis and to deal with the prospect of its recurrence. Most importantly, my proposal for an emergency constitution authorizes the government to detain suspects without the criminal law's usual protections of probable cause or even reasonable suspicion. Government may well assert other powers in carrying out the reassurance function, but in developing my argument, I shall be focusing on the grant of extraordinary powers of detention as the paradigm.

My aim is to design a constitutional framework for a temporary state of emergency that enables government to discharge the reassurance function without doing long-term damage to individual rights.

Easier said than done.

. . .

By comparison, William H. Taft IV (whose memo to Attorney General Gonzales regarding the Geneva Conventions was discussed in Chapter 2), preferred a law-of-war baseline for thinking about the right legal paradigm rather than civilian criminal law and criminal procedure approaches. The terrorists that the United States was fighting, he said, were not analogous to organized crime families like the Mafia, triads, or other groups that challenged the state only to the extent that it interfered with their corrupt or criminal projects. Rather, although a terrorist organization such as Al Qaeda is not a sovereign state,

> nor is it simply the Red Brigades or even the IRA or the Basque movement, with their specific goals to change the policy of a single national state. Al Qaeda's program addresses itself directly to the conduct of national governments around the world. Its methods, moreover, are the methods of war, and the scale and international character of its activity are similarly familiar to us only in war. . . .
>
> Because under the law of war it is not necessary to provide detained persons with lawyers, advise them of their rights to remain silent or charge them with any crime — they may not, after all, have committed one — they are more likely to provide vital intelligence information than would be the case in a law enforcement setting. The law of war, which traditionally has immunized lawful combatants for acts that in other contexts would be criminal, recognizes that a belligerent's interest in gaining intelligence may outweigh his interest in prosecuting individual members of the opposing force for criminal acts — apart, of course, for war crimes, which present a special case. [T]he law of war recognizes that it is not necessary to charge a detained person with a crime to keep him off the battlefield while hostilities

continue. Preventing his further participation in the conflict will, presumably, hasten its end and could significantly reduce the risk of additional casualties to our population. Such preventive detention obviously has no place in our concept of criminal law enforcement, but it has long been accepted in the law of war. . . .

A third advantage of applying the law of war to [fighting international terrorism] is that it embodies an established set of rules for the conduct of our own troops.[7]

Taft was not advocating a wholesale adoption of the law of war as the legal paradigm, but as a starting point. He also recognized important ways that such a body of law might need to adapt to the particulars of counter-terrorism: "[T]his war varies in important respects from the state-against-state wars for which the law of war was designed . . . ." Among other points, he noted the need for greater care in determining who qualified as "the enemy" and assessing when those detained should be released.

NOTES AND QUESTIONS

1. Ackerman and Taft both claim the War on Terror (as it was called when they wrote these articles) could go on indefinitely. But why aren't terrorists like pirates or members of the Mafia? The United States has a long history of applying the law enforcement paradigm to those "wars," even if they don't end in the way that "traditional" wars have done.

2. Are you persuaded by Ackerman's argument to distinguish the Cold War from the War on Terror?

3. What advantages does Taft advance in favor of the war paradigm over the law enforcement approach? Are these differences grounded in the practicalities of fighting terrorists or in legal theory? Should it matter?

4. John Phillip Walker Lindh is an American citizen who was captured by the Northern Alliance in Afghanistan in November 2001 and transferred to U.S. military custody. In February 2002, he was transported to the United States and charged with multiple federal criminal offenses including conspiracy to murder U.S. nationals, including military and government personnel, in Afghanistan after September 11 (in violation of 18 U.S.C. § 2332(b)(2)) and conspiracy to provide, and the actual provision of, material support to multiple foreign terrorist organizations (18 U.S.C. § 2339B). *United States v. Lindh*, 212 F. Supp. 2d 541, 547 (E.D. Va. 2002). Why not detain him as an enemy combatant for the duration of hostilities? Could the United States have both detained him as an enemy combatant *and* prosecuted him in an Article III court for violating federal laws?

B. Military Detention Under LOAC and the Constitution

Legal questions concerning military detention have been resolved by the federal judiciary along two broad dividing lines. The first division is between the few cases concerning U.S. citizens and the much larger set concerning non-U.S. citizens. The

---

7. William H. Taft IV, *War Not Crime*, in THE TORTURE DEBATE IN AMERICA 223 (Karen J. Greenberg ed., 2006).

second division splits each of these categories into military detention that begins with capture by the military outside the United States and military detention that begins with a law enforcement arrest inside the United States followed by transfer of custody to the Department of Defense.[8]

Thus, as the timeline on the next page illustrates, four separate tracks have emerged in the post-9/11 case law concerning military detention.

A brief summary of these four "tracks" is helpful in advance of a more in-depth look, below.

Most detainees designated as "enemy combatants" and held in the custody of the armed forces have been non-U.S. citizens. All except one of these individuals were seized *outside* the United States. Many were held in detention facilities built at the Naval Station located at Guantanamo Bay, Cuba. Others were held closer to the theater of military operations in which they were captured, such as prisons at Bagram Air Force Base in Afghanistan and detention facilities in U.S.-occupied Iraq.

The sole non-citizen held as an "enemy combatant" after his seizure *inside* the United States is Ali al-Marri, a Qatari national. After more than six years in solitary confinement in the Naval Consolidated Brig in Charleston, South Carolina, al-Marri was transferred back into the custody of the Department of Justice in 2009 and processed through the federal criminal justice system.

Similarly, only one U.S. citizen has been held as an "enemy combatant" after his seizure inside the United States, Jose Padilla. He, too, was held at the Naval Consolidated Brig and, after four years in solitary confinement, Padilla was transferred back into the custody of the Department of Justice and processed through the federal criminal justice system.

---

8. There are, of course, many other topics and approaches to organizing a discussion under this heading. For example, what should be made of perceived divergence between the body of public international law known as the law of armed conflict and detention authority invoked under U.S. constitutional or statutory law? *See, e.g., Al-Bihani v. Obama*, 590 F.3d 866 (2010). What degree of precision must Congress give to terms that purport to establish the bounds of detention authority granted the armed forces? *See, e.g.*, Christopher Jenks, *Civil Liberties and the Indefinite Detention of U.S. Citizens*, 2 HARV. J.L. & PUB. POL'Y — FEDERALIST EDITION 173 (2014). How should one resolve "boundary" questions about the circumstances in which the law of armed conflict applies in contexts not always clearly imagined by its precedents and founding sources, and yet perhaps important for constitutional and statutory analysis? As one very perceptive scholar in this field notes:

> It is not that people disagree about the test for LOAC's field of application, at least not when stated in abstract terms. . . . But once we move to apply this test to a particular fact pattern, we quickly discover that the room for disagreements is substantial. [Regarding a state party confronted with a non-state actor, the] general outlines of the test appear settled, but the agreement does not extend to the granular level, let alone to the proper application and results in particular cases. First, it is entirely unclear just where the line lies between the level of intensity at which violence remains a matter of civil disorder or criminality and the level at which it earns the title "armed conflict." . . . Assuming that one overcomes these obstacles, a separate boundary issue involving LOAC then arises: Are there geographic constraints with respect to *where* LOAC may apply?

Robert M. Chesney, *Beyond the Battlefield, Beyond Al Qaeda: The Destabilizing Legal Architecture of Counterterrorism*, 112 MICH. L. REV. 163, 166 (2013).

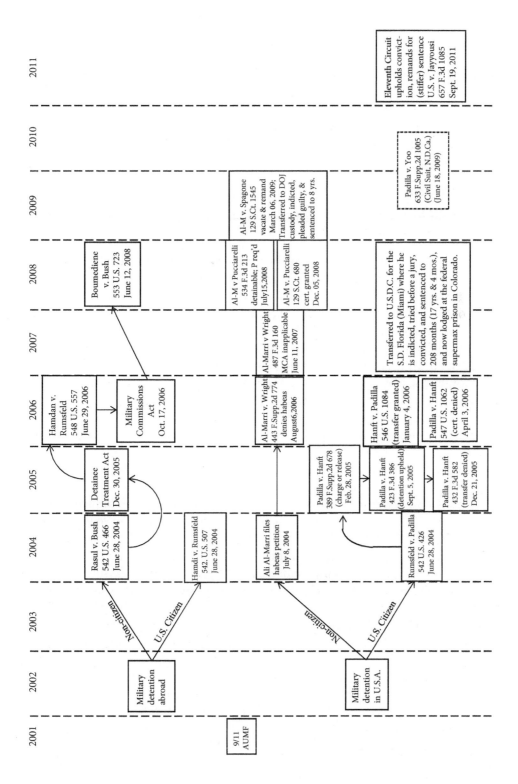

2001 2002 2003 2004 2005 2006 2007 2008 2009 2010 2011

9/11
AUMF

Military
detention
abroad

Non-citizen

U.S. Citizen

Rasul v. Bush
542 U.S. 466
June 28, 2004

Hamdi v. Rumsfeld
542. U.S. 507
June 28, 2004

Detainee
Treatment Act
Dec. 30, 2005

Hamdan v.
Rumsfeld
548 U.S. 557
June 29, 2006

Military
Commissions
Act
Oct. 17, 2006

Boumediene
v. Bush
553 U.S. 723
June 12, 2008

Military
detention
in U.S.A.

Non-citizen

U.S. Citizen

Ali Al-Marri files
habeas petition
July 8, 2004

Rumsfeld v. Padilla
542 U.S. 426
June 28, 2004

Padilla v. Hanft
389 F.Supp.2d 678
(charge or release)
Feb. 28, 2005

Padilla v. Hanft
423 F.3d 386
(detention upheld)
Sept. 5, 2005

Padilla v. Hanft
432 F.3d 582
(transfer denied)
Dec. 21, 2005

Al-Marri v. Wright
443 F.Supp.2d 774
denies habeas
August6,2006

Hanft v. Padilla
546 U.S. 1084
(transfer granted)
January 4, 2006

Padilla v. Hanft
547 U.S. 1062
(cert. denied)
April 3, 2006

Al-Marri v Wright
487 F.3d 160
MCA inapplicable
June 11, 2007

Al-M v Pucciarelli
534 F.3d 213
detainable; P req'd
July15,2008

Al-M. v. Pucciarelli
129 S.Ct. 680
cert. granted
Dec. 05, 2008

Al-M v. Spagone
129 S.Ct. 1545
vacate & remand
March 06, 2009;
[Transferred to DOJ
custody, indicted,
pleaded guilty, &
sentenced to 8 yrs.

Transferred to U.S.D.C. for the
S.D. Florida (Miami) where he
is indicted, tried before a jury,
convicted, and sentenced to
208 months (17 yrs. & 4 mos.),
and now lodged at the federal
supermax prison in Colorado.

Padilla v. Yoo
633 F.Supp.2d 1005
(Civil Suit, N.D.Ca.)
(June 18, 2009)

Eleventh Circuit
upholds convict-
ion, remands for
(stiffer) sentence
U.S. v. Jayyousi
657 F.3d 1085
Sept. 19, 2011

The remaining category, a U.S. citizen seized *outside* the United States as an enemy combatant and then brought to the United States (again, to the Naval Consolidated Brig), was famously the case of Yaser Esam Hamdi. Because so much of the law concerning the other three categories was developed in the shadow of Hamdi's case, it was discussed at length in Chapter 1.

As you read about these cases, ask yourself what the court identifies as (and, if you disagree, what you think should be) the salient factual distinctions among these cases. What common features do they all share?

1. Citizens

a. Capture Outside the United States: Lindh and Hamdi, . . . and Doe (Alsheikh)

In the years immediately following the September 11th attacks, two cases appeared in the Article III courts concerning U.S. citizens captured abroad in the fight against al Qaeda and the Taliban. It is worth comparing them. The first is that of John Phillip Walker Lindh, mentioned above and in Chapter 8, who was captured in November 2001 in Afghanistan by Afghan soldiers for the Northern Alliance. Following a plea agreement, Lindh was sentenced in a criminal proceeding in federal court to twenty years' imprisonment for supplying services to the Taliban and for the use of explosives in the commission of a felony. A federal district court judge rejected Lindh's claim to be a lawful combatant entitled to immunity for his actions, holding *inter alia* that the President's determination to the contrary was entitled to deference. It is worth noting, however, that the initial position of the Justice Department was that the President's decision was not subject to any judicial review at all because it presented a political question. This position was rejected by the district court. *United States v. Lindh*, 212 F. Supp. 2d 541, 555 (E.D. Va. 2002).

The second case is that of Yaser Esam Hamdi. This case was examined in detail in Chapter 1. Hamdi was not convicted of, or even charged with, any federal crimes. The government sought to hold him for an indefinite period of time as an enemy combatant. In her plurality opinion announcing the judgment of the Court, Justice O'Connor held that "a citizen-detainee seeking to challenge his classification as an enemy combatant must receive notice of the factual basis of his classification, and a fair opportunity to rebut the Government's factual assertions before a neutral decisionmaker." This holding rejected the government's argument that, at most, courts should review the executive's classification under an extremely deferential standard of review requiring only that the government provide "some evidence" (which a court should assume to be accurate) that the executive's basis for detention was a legitimate one. Holding to the contrary, Justice O'Connor observed, "[W]e necessarily reject the Government's assertion that separation of powers principles mandate a heavily circumscribed role for the courts in such circumstances."

Those circumstances, as Justice Scalia noted in a dissent joined by Justice Stevens, "must surely be rare." That prediction turned out to be generally true. More than fifteen years passed before another U.S. citizen was held abroad by the U.S. military as an enemy combatant kept from any civilian criminal process. When the United States sought to transfer him to the custody of another country, the following case arose.

Doe v. Mattis
928 F.3d 1 (D.C. Cir. 2019)

SRINIVASAN, Circuit Judge:

In September 2017, Syrian Democratic Forces encountered Doe at a screening point on an active battlefield in Syrian territory controlled by ISIL. Doe surrendered, informed the Syrian Democratic Forces that he was an American citizen, and asked to speak to U.S. officials. The Syrian Democratic Forces transferred Doe to the custody of U.S. military forces in the region. The military reached a preliminary determination that Doe is an enemy combatant, and has detained him at a U.S. facility in Iraq.

The military's preliminary determination that Doe is an enemy combatant is based on evidence that he is a member or substantial supporter of ISIL [a designated terrorist group responsible for killing thousands]. The evidence against Doe includes the following: the circumstances of his surrender, his statements upon surrender and during detention, and records of his ISIL membership.

In October 2017, the American Civil Liberties Union Foundation, acting on Doe's behalf, petitioned the district court for a writ of habeas corpus. The petition asserts that the military's existing authority to engage in armed conflict does not extend to ISIL, that the military thus lacks legal authority to detain an alleged member of ISIL, and that, as a result, the government must either prosecute Doe in an Article III court or release him. In addition to those legal arguments, Doe contends as a factual matter that he is not an ISIL combatant.

The district court determined that the ACLU had standing to bring the action on Doe's behalf. The court ordered the government to give the ACLU access to Doe to ascertain whether he wanted to continue the action. On January 5, 2018, the ACLU informed the court that Doe wanted to continue pursuing the habeas petition with the ACLU representing him. The ACLU then asked for an order barring the government from transferring Doe to another country until the court decided the merits of his petition.

On January 23, the district court granted Doe's request in part. The court entered a preliminary injunction requiring the government to provide 72 hours' notice before transferring Doe to any other country.

The government appealed. [But on April 16, 2018, the government communicated to the district court its] intent to transfer Doe to the custody of Country B in 72 hours. Doe moved for a preliminary injunction or temporary restraining order to block the proposed transfer.

On April 19, 2018, the district court granted the preliminary injunction, barring the government "from transferring [Doe] from U.S. custody." The government appealed the second injunction to this court.

II.

A.

[T]he relevant question is whether, in the circumstances of this case, involuntarily transferring Doe to Country B would be unlawful. We hold that it would be.

a.

A fundamental attribute of United States citizenship is a "right to . . . remain in this country" and "to return" after leaving. *Mandoli v. Acheson*, 344 U.S. 133, 139 (1952). That right is implicated when the government seeks to forcibly transfer an American citizen from the United States to a foreign country. To effect such a transfer, the government must both (i) demonstrate that a treaty or statute authorizes the transfer, and (ii) give the citizen an opportunity to challenge the factual basis for the transfer. *Valentine v. United States ex rel. Neidecker*, 299 U.S. 5, 9 (1936).

The government's first argument in this case, though, is that a citizen loses both of those protections the instant he leaves U.S. territory. When a citizen sets foot outside the United States, the government says, the Executive can forcibly transfer him to the custody of any country having a "legitimate sovereign interest" in him. The transfer, the government emphasizes, would be "total." Following the citizen's transfer, then, he would be fully—and irrevocably—subject to the power of the foreign sovereign now holding him.

The government's contention that it possesses that kind of transfer authority over an American citizen is centrally predicated on *Munaf v. Geren*, 553 U.S. 674 (2008), which is itself predicated on *Wilson v. Girard*, 354 U.S. 524 (1957). We disagree with the government's understanding of those decisions.

In *Wilson*, William Girard, a U.S. soldier stationed in Japan, was accused by Japan of committing a homicide in its territory. The Army agreed to relinquish Girard to Japanese custody for pretrial detention. Girard filed a habeas petition, and the district court issued a preliminary injunction prohibiting the transfer. The Supreme Court vacated the order and allowed the handover of Girard to Japanese custody.

The Court began by recognizing that, as a general matter, a "sovereign nation has exclusive jurisdiction to punish offenses against its laws committed within its borders." Japan had voluntarily surrendered that prerogative in a security agreement with the United States that governed the treatment of U.S. soldiers stationed in Japan. But the agreement permitted the United States to cede back to Japan the authority to prosecute a service member in a given instance. In Girard's case, the United States had done just that. So the question, the Court said, was whether there was any "constitutional or statutory barrier" to the Executive (i) waiving the United States's jurisdiction and (ii) transferring Girard to Japan to face criminal prosecution. Finding no such barrier, the Court sanctioned Girard's transfer to Japanese custody.

Munaf involved two American citizens who voluntarily traveled to Iraq and allegedly committed crimes while there. A multinational military coalition identified the two citizens as security risks, and they were held by U.S. military forces in Iraq "[p]ending their criminal prosecution for those offenses" in Iraqi courts. Both of the citizens filed habeas petitions, asserting (i) that the Executive lacked the power to transfer them to Iraq's custody for criminal proceedings, and (ii) that transferring them thus would violate the Due Process Clause. The Court rejected their arguments and allowed the military to relinquish them to Iraqi custody.

Relying on *Wilson*, the Court emphasized that a country has a "sovereign right to 'punish offenses against its laws committed within its borders.'" The Executive thus could transfer the petitioners to Iraqi custody without violating the Due Process Clause.

In both *Munaf* and *Wilson*, the authority of the Executive to transfer U.S. citizens had no roots in any military authority over enemy combatants under the law of war. *Wilson*[,] after all, concerned "the peacetime actions of a [U.S.] serviceman," not the wartime actions of an enemy combatant. In *Munaf*, meanwhile, it is true that the alleged crimes involved insurgent acts committed in a time of war, for which both suspects had been designated "security internees" and one had been deemed an enemy combatant. But the Court's recognition of the Executive's power to transfer the two men did not depend on those designations or on the nature of the alleged crimes. [T]he Court in *Munaf* observed that "[t]hose who commit crimes within a sovereign's territory may be transferred to that sovereign's government for prosecution" even if the "crime at issue" is an inherently non-war offense like "embezzlement."

Munaf and *Wilson* do not suggest a general prerogative on the part of the Executive to seize any American citizen voluntarily traveling abroad for forcible transfer to any country with some legitimate sovereign interest in her. Those cases did not involve a citizen forcibly transferred from one foreign country they voluntarily visited to the custody of another foreign country. The petitioners in *Munaf* had "voluntarily traveled" to Iraq, and the petitioner in *Wilson*, an Army specialist, was stationed in Japan. They were "therefore subject to the territorial jurisdiction of [those] sovereign[s], not of the United States."

The government is surely correct that a sovereign's prescriptive jurisdiction — its power to regulate conduct — extends to persons located beyond its borders. But the fact that a foreign country may have prescriptive jurisdiction over an American citizen who is outside its territory hardly means that, as long as the citizen is somewhere else abroad, the Executive has power to seize her and deliver her to that foreign country.

Indeed, we know of no instance — in the history of the United States — in which the government has forcibly transferred an American citizen from one foreign country to another. (That includes the case of Amir Meshal, in which the government ardently denied a citizen's allegations that foreign officials, who had moved him from Kenya, to Somalia, to Ethiopia, were acting at the United States's behest.)

To that end, the absence of even a single known example of the unilateral power the Executive claims here is illuminating. Indeed, we are unaware of any involuntary transfer of a U.S. citizen from one foreign country to another even pursuant to a treaty or statute. There is all the more reason, then, to proceed with considerable caution before recognizing such a power as a unilateral (although apparently never-before-exercised) prerogative of the Executive.

The implications of the government's reading of *Munaf* and *Wilson* amplify the reasons to reject it. Consider, for example, a U.S. citizen who becomes a journalist, travels to Thailand for a multi-year assignment, and, on returning to the United States, writes articles critical of the Thai King that are alleged to play some role in sparking demonstrations in Thailand. Thailand might well argue that she falls within its prescriptive jurisdiction. And its arguments would have force if, for instance, she underpaid her Thai taxes while there, or her articles were deemed to have had a "substantial effect" within Thailand. *See* Restatement (Fourth) of the Foreign Relations Law of the United States §§ 211 & cmt. f, 213 (Draft No. 2, 2016).

If the government were right about *Munaf* and *Wilson*, then the moment the journalist stepped outside the United States, the Executive would have unilateral power to apprehend her and forcibly transfer her to Thailand if she were accused of violating Thai law. (Incidentally, there is a good reason to think the U.S.-Thai extradition treaty would not apply in that instance, given that it covers only "persons found in the territory of one of the Contracting Parties." Extradition Treaty, U.S.-Thai., art. 1, Dec. 14, 1983, S. Treaty Doc. No. 98-16.) By the government's logic, then, alleged breaches of the Thai tax code would authorize a forcible transfer. So too would alleged violations of Thailand's lèse-majesté statute — under which anyone who "defames, insults, or threatens the [Thai] King . . . shall be punished with imprisonment of three to fifteen years."

Thailand's mere desire to have one of its citizens back cannot give the Executive the unilateral authority to forcibly transfer an American there, just because she steps outside the United States. After all, a dual citizen "is entitled to all the rights and privileges of [U.S.] citizenship." *Perkins v. Elg*, 307 U.S. 325, 349 (1939). That includes the "right to return to and remain" in the United States after having left. *Mandoli* (1952).

The government emphasizes that, on the facts of this case, Doe is not just any citizen who traveled someplace abroad and is suspected of conduct like tax evasion. Rather, he went to an active battlefield; and Country B, a "coalition partner[ ] in an ongoing armed conflict" against ISIL, has, the government says, "an obvious and legitimate interest in taking custody of" him.

Those circumstances, however, do not give the Executive transfer power under *Munaf* and *Wilson* that it would otherwise lack. *Munaf* and *Wilson*, as explained, do not rest on the military's authority under the law of war. That a country may have an especially important interest in a citizen — including by reason of her allegedly hostile actions against the country's interests in a time of war — does not affect that conclusion.

b.

We now take up the latter facet of the government's claim of authority to transfer Doe: that it can do so pursuant to the Executive's wartime powers under the law of war. We conclude that the Executive does generally possess authority under the law of war to transfer an enemy combatant to the custody of an ally in the conflict. But that authority, we hold, could potentially support a transfer of Doe only if the government (i) demonstrates that it is legally authorized to use military force against ISIL, and (ii) affords Doe an adequate opportunity to challenge the Executive's factual determination that he is an ISIL combatant.

The starting point for our analysis is the Supreme Court's decision in *Hamdi v. Rumsfeld*, 542 U.S. 507 (2004). (Because the plurality in *Hamdi* issued the controlling opinion, which our court has treated as binding, we will treat the plurality opinion as that of the Court for purposes of this opinion.) There, the Court spoke directly to the military's authority over an American citizen under the law of war. The case involved Yaser Esam Hamdi, who, like Doe, was captured on a foreign battlefield, where the government alleged he had fought with the Taliban against the United States. Hamdi, again like Doe, was a dual citizen of the United States and Saudi Arabia.

[See Chapter 1 for the facts and holding in *Hamdi*.]

[Is] the Executive's transfer authority (this case) on par with its detention authority (*Hamdi*) as a fundamental incident of waging war? [I]f so, is the Executive's exercise of transfer authority against a U.S. citizen subject to the same conditions attending the exercise of detention authority against a U.S. citizen? In other words, do transfer authority over citizens and detention authority over citizens essentially rise or fall together? We conclude they do.

First, the military possesses settled wartime authority under the law of war to transfer enemy combatants to allied countries. That power, in the words of *Hamdi*, is "a fundamental incident of waging war," such that the Executive generally has the authority to transfer when it has legal authorization to engage in hostilities.

Even if transfers of alien combatants have been a regular feature of warfare, does the traditional authority to transfer enemy combatants extend to a U.S. citizen? On this score, the historical evidence is sparse. As noted, we know of no instance in which the Executive has forcibly transferred a citizen from one foreign country to another; and that includes wartime transfers of enemy combatants.

Hamdi, however, instructs that a traditional military power over enemy combatants in wartime should generally be assumed to encompass American citizens. The Court reasoned that a citizen, "no less than an alien," can be a part of an enemy force. For that proposition, the Court relied on its decision in *Ex parte Quirin*, 317 U.S. 1 (1942), in which it had upheld the military trial of a U.S. citizen for his unlawful belligerency in support of the enemy in World War II.

Following the approach set out in *Hamdi*, we similarly see no basis for excluding a citizen—at least as a categorical matter—from the Executive's wartime authority to transfer enemy combatants.

[But] having determined that the Executive has authority to transfer enemy combatants under the law of war, and that there is no blanket exemption from that power for U.S. citizens, we now assess whether *Hamdi*'s conditions on the exercise of detention authority equally govern any exercise of transfer authority. Those conditions, again, are that the Executive have legal authority to use military force against the relevant enemy (here, ISIL), and that the citizen be afforded the process laid out in *Hamdi* for challenging the factual determination that he is an enemy combatant.

In considering whether transfer should be subject to those conditions, an initial point bears noting: the transfer of a citizen to another country's custody, unlike continued detention of that citizen, is irrevocable. Once the Executive relinquishes custody of an American citizen to another country, our government, and our laws—including our law's habeas guarantee, which a detainee can use to seek relief from detention over time—would be unavailable to her, perhaps in perpetuity. Decisions about the duration and conditions of her custody, and about the availability to her of a means of challenging her confinement, would be entirely up to the detaining sovereign.

Given that transfers involve fundamental liberty interests, we see no basis for concluding that, for the transfer of a citizen (as opposed to the detention of a citizen), the Executive need not satisfy the *Hamdi* conditions.

[Furthermore,] *Hamdi* itself rejects the notion that it could "make a determinative constitutional difference" if an American citizen were detained overseas rather than in the United States. The Court understood that any such conclusion would "create[ ] a perverse incentive" to hold American citizens abroad. . . . [*S*]*ee also Al Bahlul v. United States*, 767 F.3d 1, 65 n.3 (D.C. Cir. 2014) (Kavanaugh, J., concurring in the judgment in part and dissenting in part) ("As a general matter, the U.S. Constitution applies to U.S. citizens worldwide and to non-U.S. citizens within the 50 states and the District of Columbia[.]"). There is no basis for thinking that a citizen relinquishes her right to bring a legal challenge to her detention—or, equivalently, to her transfer—if she is detained in (or transferred from) a foreign country.

Consider the implications if there were, in fact, an asymmetry between transfer and detention, such that the Executive could transfer a U.S. citizen to another country without meeting the *Hamdi* conditions. With regard to legal authority, the military could irrevocably transfer a citizen thought to be an enemy combatant even if judicial review would have revealed that the Executive lacked lawful authority to use military force against the particular enemy. In that event, detainees in U.S. custody—and thus protected by U.S. law—would need to be released or criminally charged. But for those who had already been transferred to another country, an American court could not order their return or grant them comparable relief.

With regard to a factual-basis challenge, the *Hamdi* Court sought to "meet the goal of ensuring that the errant tourist, embedded journalist, or local aid worker has a chance to prove military error." The procedural guarantees prescribed by the Court were intended to guard against an undue risk of an erroneous military determination. But if the transfer of a citizen could be accomplished without affording her those protections, a risk of error thought unacceptable for continued detention would be present for an irrevocable transfer to another country. An "errant tourist" might then be protected against detention but unable to avoid an irrevocable transfer to another country's custody.

The government, in that respect, relies on its having made a "good-faith determination, supported by extensive record evidence, that [Doe] is an enemy combatant." We do not doubt the government's good faith. Nor do we discount the importance of the need to avoid unduly burdening the Executive's prosecution of a war, which concerned the *Hamdi* Court as well. But in *Hamdi*, one point on which eight Justices agreed was that, in the case of an American citizen, the government's good-faith determination that he is an enemy combatant is not enough to justify his detention for the duration of a conflict. We find the same to be true of an irrevocable transfer to another country's custody.

In that regard, it is instructive to consider the implications of the government's argument here for the facts of *Hamdi* itself. Upon holding that the government's continued detention of Hamdi was contingent on his having a meaningful opportunity to challenge the factual basis for his detention, the Court remanded the matter so that the government could conduct the fact-finding process the Court had outlined. That process would result in a determination of whether Hamdi was a person against whom military force could be applied.

Under the government's argument here, though, the Executive, rather than grant Hamdi that process following remand, could have simply avoided it by choosing instead to forcibly and irrevocably transfer him to the custody of another country (pursuant to its authority under the 2001 AUMF). True, the government eventually did in fact transfer Hamdi to Saudi Arabia—but with his consent, not over his objection (and after he renounced his American citizenship). There is, of course, a vast difference between a voluntary transfer and an involuntary one. As to the latter, we do not believe the *Hamdi* Court would have countenanced Hamdi's forcible transfer to another country unless he were first afforded the process the Court held he was constitutionally due.

The government's final argument on this score is that transfer without process is permissible if effected in conjunction with "initial capture[ ] on the battlefield." But while *Hamdi* allows for temporary detention without process attending "initial capture," a citizen can be released if there ends up being an insufficient factual basis to continue detention. Transfer may be different because it, by nature, is not temporary.

In addition, there would be no citizenship-based limit on transfer unless there were reason to know that a person is a citizen. Here, at any rate, the Executive decided to transfer Doe—and reached an agreement to do so—several months after his capture. This transfer decision, then, was not a battlefield judgment. For those reasons, the Executive cannot transfer Doe at this stage unless he receives the process required by *Hamdi*.

c.

In light of the above analysis, can the Executive involuntarily transfer Doe to Country B? We conclude it cannot, at least as things stand now. We take up the two strands of the government's argument in order.

We first address whether the Executive can forcibly transfer Doe to Country B based on the general transfer authority recognized in *Munaf* and *Wilson*. That authority, as we have explained, does not encompass the forcible transfer of a citizen from one foreign country to the custody of another foreign country. Insofar as the transfer of Doe to Country B would be an inter-country transfer, it falls outside of *Munaf* and *Wilson*.

The government contends that the transfer nonetheless should be allowed because Doe is a dual citizen of the United States and Country B (Saudi Arabia). As a result, the government emphasizes, Country B has an especially strong interest in accepting custody over Doe: the interest in repatriating one of its own nationals in order to attempt to rehabilitate him consistent with its own laws and practices.

To that end, the government notes that a country always has prescriptive jurisdiction over its own nationals, including when they are abroad. And by carrying out the transfer, the government urges, the United States also would further its own interest in maintaining constructive relations with an ally in the military efforts against ISIL (which would, among other benefits, allow for productive discussions with Country B about the transfer of additional combatants in the future).

We do not doubt the weight of Country B's sovereign interests in (and prescriptive jurisdiction over) Doe based on all of those considerations, including, in particular, his Saudi citizenship. Nor do we question the Executive's assessment of Country B's interests. But the strength of Country B's interests in Doe as a Saudi citizen does not diminish the force of Doe's rights as a U.S. citizen: here, the right to resist the Executive's forcible seizure and transfer of him to the custody of another country. After all, "dual citizenship presupposes rights of citizenship in each country." And the limits on unilateral Executive authority ultimately "protect the individual."

We now turn to whether the forcible transfer of Doe to Country B can be supported by the Executive's wartime authority over enemy combatants under the law of war. That authority, as we have explained, encompasses transfers of enemy combatants to an allied country. But before the Executive could exercise that transfer power against Doe, the two *Hamdi* conditions would need to be met.

The first condition is a determination that the Executive has legal authority to wage war against ISIL. "For wartime military transfers," we have said, "Article II and the relevant Authorization to Use Military Force generally give the Executive legal authority to transfer." Second, Doe would need to be afforded a meaningful chance to rebut the government's factual assertion that he is an ISIL combatant, per the requirements set out in *Hamdi*.

Neither condition has been met at this point. Until those conditions are satisfied, the Executive lacks power under the law of war to transfer Doe to Country B on the basis of his status as an alleged ISIL combatant.

* * *

Our disposition will constrain the government's ability to transfer an American citizen believed to be an enemy combatant more than the government would like. That is an important consideration in this case in light of the deference owed to military judgments in wartime. But "such cases," — *i.e.*, those in which "a United States citizen [is] captured in a foreign combat zone" — "must surely be rare." *Hamdi* (Scalia, J., dissenting) (formatting altered).

In those rare cases, the constraints on the Executive could, in theory, discourage the Executive from taking custody of a suspected enemy combatant known to be an American citizen. That was equally true, though, of the Supreme Court's decision in *Hamdi*, which established constraints on the Executive's treatment of U.S. citizens captured on a foreign battlefield. We adhere to that decision and apply it to military transfers, consistent with our precedent.

The *Hamdi* Court believed it "unlikely" that its decision would have a "dire impact on the central functions of warmaking." At the same time, the Court thought it "vital" that it "not give short shrift to the values that this country holds dear or to the privilege that is American citizenship." We follow the Court's guidance today.

It is so ordered.

KAREN LeCRAFT HENDERSON, Circuit Judge, dissenting:

A reader, having just reviewed the majority opinion, might well be thinking it declares a lead-pipe result. *Caveat lector.* The opinion treats all but silently the judiciary's dispositively downsized role in the theater of war. The majority affirms a preliminary injunction (Order) that ventures well beyond the district court's limited authority. The Order blocks our military from transferring a battlefield captive, petitioner John Doe, to a country that has a sovereign interest in him based on his citizenship there. The district court does not find — because there is no evidence — that Doe will be mistreated if transferred. Instead, the point of the Order is to ensure that Doe can challenge his custody in the hope of winning release therefrom on his own terms. The Order is without precedent.

I. BACKGROUND

Doe is a citizen of Saudi Arabia. He is also a citizen of the United States but has not lived here since 2006 and has not visited since 2014.[2]

In July 2014, Doe voluntarily traveled to Syria to join the Islamic State of Iraq and the Levant, a terrorist organization better known as ISIS.

Starting in or about March 2015, Doe attended ISIS training in Syria with fellow recruits. At the training site, he swore allegiance to Abu Hafs al-Maghrebi, who acted on behalf of ISIS's leader, Abu Bakr al-Baghdadi. ISIS assigned Doe

---

2. Doe was born in the United States. When he was ten years old, he moved to Saudi Arabia and became a citizen there. He returned to the United States for college but moved back to Saudi Arabia two years later. Before taking up with ISIS, Doe owned businesses in Saudi Arabia, got married there and fathered a daughter there. Members of his extended family still live there.

to be a fighter in the Zarqawi Brigade, a military unit that "guard[ed] the front lines" in Syria. There, Doe procured fuel for ISIS vehicles, handled funds for ISIS expenses and performed other administrative tasks. He was later assigned to guard the gate of an ISIS oil field and then to monitor personnel who worked on ISIS's heavy equipment.

On or about September 11, 2017, Syrian Democratic Forces captured him on an active battlefield as he tried to escape Syria into Turkey. He was carrying thumb drives that contained ISIS personnel spreadsheets as well as "military style handbooks" about techniques for interrogation, handling weapons and building bombs. Doe told his captors he had been walking for two days. ISIS controlled all of the territory within a two-day walk. Doe's physical appearance was "typical of an [ISIS] devotee." And, indeed, he expressly identified himself as "daesh," another name for ISIS. Claiming American citizenship, he said he "wanted to speak to the Americans" and "turn himself in."

Because Doe claimed American citizenship, the Syrian Democratic Forces transferred him "to U.S. forces stationed in Iraq," within the same theater of combat as his capture. During custodial interrogation, Doe admitted that he attended ISIS training and "became an active member of ISIS." Based on those admissions and other facts, the Executive Branch has concluded that he is an enemy combatant.

II. ANALYSIS

1. Law of Detention and Transfer

a. Extended Detention in *Hamdi*

Yaser Hamdi, an American citizen, allegedly took up arms with the Taliban before September 11, 2001 and remained with his unit afterward. Later in 2001, a coalition of our allies captured him in an active combat zone in Afghanistan. They transferred him to the United States military, which in turn sent him to Guantanamo Bay and later to stateside naval brigs. With no apparent intention of transferring him to another country, the government claimed the authority to detain him indefinitely as an enemy combatant.

Faced with that claim of authority—to *detain* Hamdi without charge "for the duration of the particular conflict in which [he was] captured"—the Supreme Court agreed that a 2001 congressional enactment supplied the authority if Hamdi was in fact an enemy combatant. The Court turned, then, to "the question of what process is constitutionally due to a citizen who disputes his enemy-combatant status." Balancing the competing interests under *Mathews v. Eldridge*, 424 U.S. 319 (1976), the Court concluded "that a citizen-detainee seeking to challenge his classification as an enemy combatant must receive notice of the factual basis for his classification, and a fair opportunity to rebut the Government's factual assertions before a neutral decisionmaker."

Importantly, however, the Court emphasized "that initial captures on the battlefield need not receive the process we have discussed" and that such "process is due only when the determination is made to *continue to hold* those who have been seized." (emphasis altered). Moreover, the Court repeatedly made plain that its due process analysis applies only to detention. The Court's analysis mentioned the concept of sovereign-to-sovereign transfer only once and only in passing. Even then, it equated transfer with repatriation or release, not continued detention.

b. Transfer in *Munaf*

Acting under a United Nations resolution, a coalition force of 26 countries took Shawqi Omar and Mohammad Munaf into military custody for their "serious hostile acts" in Iraq. I focus here on Omar. He was a citizen of the United States and Jordan. He was "believed to have provided aid to" al Qaeda. He was held in Iraq "in the immediate physical custody of American soldiers." A tribunal of three American military officers concluded that he was an enemy combatant. A coalition review board reached the same conclusion. The coalition later "decided to refer" Omar to Iraqi criminal court "for criminal proceedings."

Members of Omar's family filed a habeas petition on his behalf. They asserted that Omar was an "innocent civilian[ ] . . . unlawfully detained by the United States in violation of the Due Process Clause." As here, the United States decided to relinquish custody to another country. As here, the district court "issued a preliminary injunction barring transfer in order to preserve its jurisdiction to entertain the habeas petition." As here, no criminal charges were pending in the receiving country when the court issued the preliminary injunction. As here, this Court upheld the preliminary injunction on the theory that it "properly preserve[d]" the district court's jurisdiction "to test the lawfulness of . . . extrajudicial detention."

The Supreme Court vacated this Court's decision and the preliminary injunction itself. I recognize that the Supreme Court's *holding* was narrow: the Court concluded that district courts cannot "exercise their habeas jurisdiction to enjoin our Armed Forces from transferring individuals detained within another sovereign's territory to that sovereign's government for criminal prosecution." But the Court's *reasoning* swept more broadly. Because it weighs heavily against the Order here, I discuss it in detail.

The Court observed that, "at its core," habeas is directed at "unlawful executive detention," the "typical remedy" for which is "release." In the Court's view, the atypical remedy of blocking Omar's transfer to Iraq was "not appropriate." The Court emphasized that habeas "is governed by equitable principles," which means that "prudential concerns, such as comity and the orderly administration of criminal justice, may require a federal court to forgo the exercise of its habeas corpus power." And the Court concluded that comity — specifically, respect for Iraq's sovereign interest in prosecuting crimes committed within Iraq's borders, even by citizens of the United States — prevented the district court from enjoining Omar's transfer.

In a passage my colleagues downplay, the Court found further support for its conclusion in separation of powers principles. Even in peacetime, the Court noted, "the Constitution allows the Executive to transfer American citizens to foreign authorities for criminal prosecution." The Court remarked on how "strange" it would be "to hold that the Executive lacks that same authority where, as here, the detainees were captured by our Armed Forces for engaging in serious hostile acts against an ally in what the Government refers to as 'an active theater of combat.'" "Such a conclusion," the Court cautioned, "would implicate . . . concerns about unwarranted judicial intrusion into the Executive's ability to conduct military operations abroad."

Finally, the Court rejected Omar's contention that "the Government may not transfer a citizen" to another country "without legal authority" in the form of "a treaty or statute." Omar had relied on *Valentine v. United States ex rel. Neidecker*, 299 U.S. 5 (1936), which the Court found "readily distinguishable" because "[i]t involved the extradition of an individual from the United States." The Court acknowledged that, in the context of extradition from the territorial United States, the government cannot "'seize [a fugitive criminal] and surrender him to a foreign power'" absent authority conferred by "a pertinent constitutional or legislative provision." "But Omar . . . voluntarily traveled to Iraq" and was "captured and already detained" there. Because he was not within the territorial jurisdiction of the United States, *Valentine* was inapposite.

2. Application to Doe's Transfer

Under the foregoing framework, Doe has not shown—in fact, cannot show—that he will likely succeed on the merits.

a. As Judge Brown recognized in *Omar*, "we must first [ask] *in what sense*" a putative transferee "must be likely to succeed." (Brown, J., dissenting in part). The Supreme Court answered that question in *Munaf*: we look to whether he will likely succeed on "the merits of [his] habeas petition."

Here, Doe's habeas petition challenges his detention *at the hands of the Executive Branch*. Doe therefore cannot succeed on the merits of his habeas petition *unless* he remains "detained by the United States." And he will not remain detained by the United States if the district court has improperly blocked the government from relinquishing custody to Saudi Arabia.

b. To repeat, habeas "at its core" is aimed at "unlawful executive detention," not at a transfer that ends it. Accordingly, if it is ever "appropriate," as a matter of "equitable principles," to enjoin a captive's transfer from Executive Branch custody simply to allow him to challenge that soon-to-be-erstwhile custody, such relief ought to be reserved for the most "extreme case" of Executive Branch malfeasance. Doe's case is by no means extreme in that sense. Indeed, it tracks *Munaf* in two crucial respects.

First, as in *Munaf*, the receiving country here has a facially strong—for that matter, all but undisputed—interest in the transfer. Granted, the *particular* interest here is slightly different from that in *Munaf*. There, the Court relied on Iraq's "sovereign right to prosecute Omar and Munaf for crimes committed on its soil." Here, by contrast, Doe did not (as far as the record discloses) commit crimes within the receiving country's territory and he has not (to date) been charged with any offense there. But the difference in the two cases is not as stark as Doe would have it: recall that Omar had not been charged with a crime in Iraq before the district court issued the preliminary injunction, or even before this Court issued a decision. More to the point, focusing on a receiving country's interest in prosecuting territorial offenses misses the ocean for the boat: in the habeas context, *comity* is why the prosecutorial interest matters.

Comity is "[c]ourtesy" towards "the laws and usages" of another nation. By definition, it counsels "mutual recognition of legislative, executive, and judicial acts" that go well beyond prosecutorial prerogatives. In some cases, then, comity weighs against blocking a captive's transfer even if the receiving country claims no immediate interest in prosecuting him for a territorial offense.

Perhaps the most obvious case is one like Doe's, in which the captive is a citizen of the receiving country. Customary international law recognizes a state's "sovereign[ ] interest in retaining control over its nationals and residents, wherever they may be."

Second, the separation of powers considerations highlighted in *Munaf* also apply here. When "'adjudicating issues inevitably entangled in the conduct of our international relations,'" a court is "to proceed 'with . . . circumspection.'" Far from circumspect, the Order upends the Executive Branch's decision to relinquish Doe to a country the district court acknowledges is a "strategic ally."

c. Doe argues that *Hamdi* justifies the intrusion. He contends that, absent an applicable extradition treaty, the government cannot transfer him unless it "can lawfully detain [him] as an enemy combatant in the first place." It follows, in his view, that the district court can appropriately block his transfer in order to review the government's "unilateral and untested assertion" that he is a detainable enemy combatant. To hold otherwise, he says, would wrongly deprive him of the due process protections to which *Hamdi* entitles him.

I disagree. For starters, the Supreme Court in *Munaf* did not read *Hamdi* the way Doe does. Omar was merely "*alleged* to have committed hostile or warlike acts in Iraq." Based on those alleged hostile acts, military authorities decided that Omar was an enemy combatant. The Court did not hold that a federal judge had to review that determination as a prerequisite to transfer, whether as a matter of "positive legal authority" or due process. To the contrary, the Court concluded that it was "not appropriate" to block Omar's transfer for the sake of ensuring he could litigate, via habeas, his claim that he was an "innocent civilian[ ] . . . unlawfully detained by the United States in violation of the Due Process Clause."

Notably, the Court in *Munaf* cited *Hamdi* only once, for the proposition that "[h]abeas is at its core a remedy for unlawful executive *detention*." (emphasis added). Conversely, as mentioned above, the Court in *Hamdi* invoked the concept of sovereign-to-sovereign transfer only once, equating it with repatriation or release rather than detention. Reading the cases together, I can only conclude that detention and transfer are not flipsides of the same coin but two entirely different currencies. *Hamdi*, in short, does not apply to Doe's transfer. It is a case about detention potentially "for the duration of the relevant hostilities." To reiterate, the Court excepted "initial captures on the battlefield" from "the process we have discussed," emphasizing that such "process is due only when the determination is made to *continue to hold* those who have been seized." (emphasis altered).

The end result is the judicial equivalent of mission creep. After today, a habeas court is authorized to review not only a decision to "*continue*" Executive Branch custody of a citizen captured abroad on an active battlefield, *Hamdi*, but also—extraordinarily—a decision to *discontinue* it. Indeed, if the captive's next friend gets to the courthouse quickly enough, nearly any Executive decision about the captive will be subject to judicial review. Doe makes no showing—much less a *clear* showing—that *Hamdi* reserves so little breathing room for the military's on-the-ground judgment.

d. [Doe] claims that *Valentine* forbids the government to relinquish him to another country absent "positive legal authority" set forth in a statute or extradition treaty. But *Valentine* involved "fugitive criminal[s]" apprehended in the United States. In that "very narrow" context, the Supreme Court required a "statute or treaty confer[ring] the power" to extradite.

Doe bears no resemblance to the fugitives in *Valentine*. He voluntarily traveled abroad to an active war zone. He was captured on a foreign battlefield by foreign military forces. He admitted affiliation with a terrorist organization the United States is combatting militarily. And he was taken at his own request into United States military custody within the same theater of combat. Nothing in *Valentine* indicates that extradition rules apply to such a person any more than the laws of war apply to a fugitive criminal apprehended in the United States. Moreover, because Doe has the burden of persuasion, I think it significant that—despite numerous armed conflicts since 1936—he cites no case that has ever applied *Valentine* to the wartime transfer of a battlefield captive abroad.

Doe is similarly mistaken in suggesting that *Wilson v. Girard* requires "positive legal authority" for his transfer.

Girard, an American serviceman in Japan, was alleged to have killed a Japanese national there. Because he did so, arguably in performance of his duties, [a bilateral Status of Forces Agreement between the United States and Japan] "seemed to give [him] a right to be tried by an American military tribunal, not a Japanese court." But the Executive Branch "decided not to exercise . . . jurisdiction." Per the Agreement, it notified the Japanese government that it intended to transfer Girard to Japanese custody for trial in a Japanese court. In turn, the Japanese government indicted him. Girard petitioned for habeas relief and a district court here in the United States enjoined his transfer. Far from requiring affirmative authority for the transfer, the Supreme Court vacated the injunction because the Court discerned "no constitutional or statutory *barrier*" to the transfer (emphasis added). "In the absence of such encroachments," the Court deferred to the "wisdom" of the political branches. The Court apparently saw nothing of relevance in *Valentine*, which it nowhere mentioned.

Doe nevertheless reads *Wilson* to hold that "a treaty satisfied the requirement of positive legal authority for the transfer." He misunderstands the Status of Forces Agreement. The Agreement's mere procedural requirements—to give Japan's interests "consideration" and to promptly "notify" Japan when the United States "decide[d] *not* to exercise jurisdiction," *Wilson* (emphasis added)—were hardly "authority" for a transfer, let alone the sort of "positive legal authority" that Doe demands here.

e. Doe suggests the foregoing analysis cannot possibly be correct because, as he sees it, it gives the Executive Branch license to run roughshod over the rights of American citizens with no judicial check. None of this is so.

When someone in Executive Branch custody files a habeas petition, the federal courts ensure that the Executive handles him "in accordance with law," including due process. But there are limits to a habeas court's equitable power, even if the petitioner is a citizen. I have explained why, in my view, considerations of comity and separation of powers preclude the Order here. Especially important to me are Doe's voluntary travel abroad to a war zone during active hostilities; his capture on a foreign battlefield by foreign military forces; his admitted affiliation with a terrorist organization the United States is combatting militarily; the Executive Branch's resulting good-faith determination that Doe is an enemy combatant; Doe's continued presence in the same active theater of combat as his capture; and the receiving country's facially compelling interest in his transfer.

If these facts differed, the prudential considerations might differ and the district court might have equitable authority to block a transfer.

* * *

To borrow an understatement, the Order is "not appropriate." I would vacate it. Accordingly, I respectfully dissent.

NOTES AND QUESTIONS

1. Was *Hamdi* the appropriate precedent to follow in this case? Was its holding expanded or simply followed by the majority? Should *Hamdi* be limited to detention, not transfer, authority? The dissent argues that *Munaf* was the right precedent to follow. Assess the similarities and differences in the facts presented by *Hamdi*, *Munaf*, and *Doe*. Recall the facts of John Walker Lindh's capture and detention. Under facts similar to those in Lindh's case, would *Doe v. Mattis* prevent transfer of custody to Afghan authorities?

2. The D.C. Circuit was considering the government's appeal of two preliminary injunctions issued by the district court. Four factors were balanced by that court in issuing its orders. The first two consider the likelihood for the party seeking the injunctive relief of (1) success on the merits of the action (the focus of the excerpts above); and (2) irreparable harm in the absence of an injunction. The remaining two consider the balance of equities between the parties and whether an injunction is in the public interest. In considering the appeal, the district court's determinations are generally reviewed for abuse of discretion; legal conclusions are reviewed *de novo*.

3. How should irreparable harm be characterized? The government argued that transferring Doe *out* of U.S. custody granted him the very relief a successful habeas petition necessarily would provide: freedom from detention from the U.S. government. Judge Srinivasan (joined by Judge Wilkins) concluded that position "cannot be correct. It would mean that any habeas petitioner objecting to a planned extradition of him would be unable to demonstrate irreparable injury if he were extradited. . . . [T]ransfer to a foreign country's custody necessarily ends U.S. custody; but the transfer itself is a harm that cannot be remedied." Judge Henderson, dissenting, concluded that "Doe has no *cognizable interest* in pursuing his petition once he is released from the very custody he challenges." (Emphasis in original.) She found little practical difference between a transfer to Iraqi or Saudi Arabian custody (what the government sought to do) and release from detention *in situ* (the remedy Doe sought, acknowledging that the United States could notify those authorities of his release). Under *Doe v. Mattis*, could the United States release Doe from U.S. custody (with no transfer to the custody of another authority) but deny him a valid passport or place him on a terrorist watchlist? *See* Jeffrey Kahn, *Doe v. Mattis and the Right of Citizens to Return to the United States*, LAWFARE, Aug. 13, 2018.

4. The *Doe* majority found the last two factors—balancing the equities and assessing the public interest—also in Doe's interest. The court's interference in military judgments and foreign relations were outweighed by Doe's "most elemental of liberty interests," citing *Hamdi*. Judge Henderson warned of a perverse incentive created by the court's holding: "What if our military had known before taking custody of Doe that it would not be permitted to relinquish him to an ally with a facially strong interest in him unless it first litigated—in distant courts, for months, if not years, on end—the ability to do so? Would our commanders in the field have declined custody, leaving a citizen to the actions of other countries or, even worse, to the chaos of the battlefield? It seems to me that today's result gives the military an incentive to avoid custody when possible, especially if it is not immediately clear in the heat of combat that the captive is a U.S. citizen. And I doubt that the innocent American citizen who finds himself on a foreign battlefield could fare better than in the custody of our military."

5. *Doe v. Mattis* was decided on May 7, 2018, and re-issued with redacted material removed on June 28, 2019. In the interim, Doe's identity was revealed to be Abdulrahman Ahmad Alsheikh, and he was released to Bahrain, where he joined his wife and daughter. *See* Charlie Savage, Rukmini Callmachi & Eric Schmitt, *American ISIS Suspect Is Freed After Being Held More Than a Year*, N.Y. TIMES, Oct. 29, 2018. Alsheikh no longer possesses a valid U.S. passport, but retains his citizenship. Compare this conclusion to the final dispositions for Hamdi and Lindh.

6. Why didn't the U.S. seek en banc review or petition for a writ of certiorari to the Supreme Court? Would continued detention while the habeas petition moved to the merits stage risk a judicial determination of the applicability of the 2001 and 2002 AUMFs to U.S. military action against ISIL/ISIS?

b. Capture Inside the United States: Padilla

On June 10, 2002, Attorney General John Ashcroft announced via satellite from meetings he was attending in Moscow that "[w]e have captured a known terrorist who was exploring a plan to build and explode a radiological dispersion device, or 'dirty bomb,' in the United States." James Risen & Philip Shenon, *U.S. Says It Halted Qaeda Plot to Use Radioactive Bomb*, N.Y. TIMES, June 10, 2002. The arrest had occurred a month earlier at O'Hare International Airport. Two days later, Secretary of Defense Rumsfeld gave a press briefing at which he explained: "[W]e are not interested in trying him at the moment; we are not interested in punishing him at the moment. We are interested in finding out what he knows. Here is a person who unambiguously was interested in radiation weapons and terrorist activity, and was in league with al Qaeda. Now our job, as responsible government officials, is to do everything possible to find out what that person knows, and see if we can't help our country or other countries." News Briefing, Department of Defense (June 12, 2002), 2002 WL 22026773.

The suspect, Jose Padilla, was arrested on a sealed material witness warrant, transported to New York, and detained in the custody of the Department of Justice. Padilla was appointed counsel, who moved to vacate the material witness warrant. Shortly before a hearing on the motion before then Judge Michael Mukasey, the Justice Department contacted the court *ex parte* to request that the material witness warrant be vacated, which Judge Mukasey ordered. The Justice Department further informed the court that President Bush had designated Padilla an "enemy combatant" and that Padilla would be transferred to the custody of the Department of Defense and transported to the Consolidated Naval Brig in South Carolina. Padilla's counsel was informed two days later at the previously scheduled hearing.

There then ensued four years of habeas litigation. The first round produced a lengthy opinion by Chief Judge Mukasey, in which he relied on a sealed declaration, undisclosed to Padilla's counsel, by Michael Mobbs (the same Defense Department official on whom the *Hamdi* Court relied). In that opinion, Judge Mukasey determined that Padilla was still entitled to access to his counsel. Judge Mukasey also relied on Secretary Rumsfeld's comments, quoted above, which he found to show the Secretary's familiarity with Padilla's detention and "his personal involvement in the handling of Padilla's case." *Padilla ex rel. Newman v. Bush*, 233 F. Supp. 2d 564, 574 (S.D.N.Y. 2002). Judge Mukasey ruled that "the court will examine only whether the President had some evidence to support his finding that Padilla was an enemy combatant, and whether that evidence has been mooted by events subsequent to his detention." *Id.* at 610.

The Supreme Court ended Padilla's first habeas attempt in mid-2004, finding that he had improperly filed his petition naming Secretary Rumsfeld in the Southern District of New York, from which district he was transferred to military custody, rather than South Carolina, where he was lodged in the naval brig under custody of Commander Marr. *Rumsfeld v. Padilla*, 542 U.S. 426 (2004). The case was dismissed without prejudice and Padilla started again in South Carolina. There, the district court granted his petition and directed his release, *Padilla v. Hanft*, 389 F. Supp. 2d 678, 691 (D.S.C. 2005) ("Simply stated, this is a law enforcement matter, not a military matter. The civilian authorities captured Petitioner just as they should have. At the time that Petitioner was arrested pursuant to the material arrest warrant, any alleged terrorist plans that he harbored were thwarted. From then on, he was available to be questioned—and was indeed questioned—just like any other citizen accused of criminal conduct. This is as it should be."). The Court of Appeals for the Fourth Circuit reversed, upholding his detention. *Padilla v. Hanft*, 423 F.3d 386, 397 (4th Cir. 2005) ("The Congress of the United States, in the Authorization for Use of Military Force Joint Resolution, provided the President all powers necessary and appropriate to protect American citizens from terrorist acts by those who attacked the United States on September 11, 2001. As would be expected, and as the Supreme Court has held, those powers include the power to detain identified and committed enemies such as Padilla, who associated with al Qaeda and the Taliban regime, who took up arms against this Nation in its war against these enemies, and who entered the United States for the avowed purpose of further prosecuting that war by attacking American citizens and targets on our own soil—a power without which, Congress understood, the President could well be unable to protect American citizens from the very kind of savage attack that occurred four years ago almost to the day.").

Three months later, three and a half years into Padilla's detention, and two business days before its brief was due in opposition to Padilla's petition for certiorari to the Supreme Court, the government filed an "emergency application" for an order to transfer Padilla out of military custody and into the custody of federal law enforcement officials in Florida. The government also requested that the appellate court withdraw its opinion. The Court of Appeals rejected the motion "[b]ecause we believe that the transfer of Padilla and the withdrawal of our opinion at the government's request while the Supreme Court is reviewing this court's decision of September 9 would compound what is, in the absence of explanation, at least an appearance that the government may be attempting to avoid consideration of our decision by the Supreme Court, and also because we believe that this case presents an issue of such especial national importance as to warrant final consideration by that court." *Padilla v. Hanft*, 432 U.S. 582, 583 (4th Cir. 2005).

Nevertheless, the Supreme Court granted the transfer, *Hanft v. Padilla*, 546 U.S. 1084 (2006), and denied Padilla's petition for writ of certiorari four months later. This elicited the unusual brief statements below by Justices Kennedy and Ginsburg.

Padilla v. Hanft
547 U.S. 1062 (2006)

The petition for a writ of certiorari is denied. Justice SOUTER and Justice BREYER would grant the petition for a writ of certiorari.

Justice KENNEDY, with whom THE CHIEF JUSTICE and Justice STEVENS join, concurring.
The Court's decision to deny the petition for writ of certiorari is, in my view, a proper exercise of its discretion in light of the circumstances of the case.

The history of petitioner Jose Padilla's detention, however, does require this brief explanatory statement.

Padilla is a United States citizen. Acting pursuant to a material witness warrant issued by the United States District Court for the Southern District of New York, federal agents apprehended Padilla at Chicago's O'Hare International Airport on May 8, 2002. He was transported to New York, and on May 22 he moved to vacate the warrant. On June 9, while that motion was pending, the President issued an order to the Secretary of Defense designating Padilla an enemy combatant and ordering his military detention. The District Court, notified of this action by the Government's *ex parte* motion, vacated the material witness warrant.

Padilla was taken to the Consolidated Naval Brig in Charleston, South Carolina. On June 11, Padilla's counsel filed a habeas corpus petition in the Southern District of New York challenging the military detention. The District Court denied the petition, but the Court of Appeals for the Second Circuit reversed and ordered the issuance of a writ directing Padilla's release. This Court granted certiorari and ordered dismissal of the habeas corpus petition without prejudice, holding that the District Court for the Southern District of New York was not the appropriate court to consider it.

The present case arises from Padilla's subsequent habeas corpus petition, filed in the United States District Court for the District of South Carolina on July 2, 2004. Padilla requested that he be released immediately or else charged with a crime. The District Court granted the petition on February 28, 2005, but the Court of Appeals for the Fourth Circuit reversed that judgment on September 9, 2005. Padilla then filed the instant petition for writ of certiorari.

After Padilla sought certiorari in this Court, the Government obtained an indictment charging him with various federal crimes. The President ordered that Padilla be released from military custody and transferred to the control of the Attorney General to face criminal charges. The Government filed a motion for approval of Padilla's transfer in the Court of Appeals for the Fourth Circuit. The Court of Appeals denied the motion, but this Court granted the Government's subsequent application respecting the transfer. The Government also filed a brief in opposition to certiorari, arguing, among other things, that Padilla's petition should be denied as moot.

The Government's mootness argument is based on the premise that Padilla, now having been charged with crimes and released from military custody, has received the principal relief he sought. Padilla responds that his case was not mooted by the Government's voluntary actions because there remains a possibility that he will be redesignated and redetained as an enemy combatant.

Whatever the ultimate merits of the parties' mootness arguments, there are strong prudential considerations disfavoring the exercise of the Court's certiorari power. Even if the Court were to rule in Padilla's favor, his present custody status would be unaffected. Padilla is scheduled to be tried on criminal charges. Any consideration of what rights he might be able to assert if he were returned to military custody would be hypothetical, and to no effect, at this stage of the proceedings.

In light of the previous changes in his custody status and the fact that nearly four years have passed since he first was detained, Padilla, it must be acknowledged, has a continuing concern that his status might be altered again. That concern, however, can be addressed if the necessity arises. Padilla is now being held pursuant to the control and supervision of the United States District Court for the Southern District of Florida, pending trial of the criminal case. In the course of its supervision over Padilla's custody and trial the District Court will be obliged to afford him the protection, including the right to a speedy trial, guaranteed to all federal criminal defendants. Were the Government to seek to change the status or conditions of Padilla's custody, that court would be in a position to rule quickly on any responsive filings submitted by Padilla. In such an event, the District Court, as well as other courts of competent jurisdiction, should act promptly to ensure that the office and purposes of the writ of habeas corpus are not compromised. Padilla, moreover, retains the option of seeking a writ of habeas corpus in this Court.

That Padilla's claims raise fundamental issues respecting the separation of powers, including consideration of the role and function of the courts, also counsels against addressing those claims when the course of legal proceedings has made them, at least for now, hypothetical. This is especially true given that Padilla's current custody is part of the relief he sought, and that its lawfulness is uncontested.

These are the reasons for my vote to deny certiorari.

Justice GINSBURG, dissenting.

This case, here for the second time, raises a question of profound importance to the Nation: Does the President have authority to imprison indefinitely a United States citizen arrested on United States soil distant from a zone of combat, based on an executive declaration that the citizen was, at the time of his arrest, an "enemy combatant"? It is a question the Court heard, and should have decided, two years ago. Nothing the Government has yet done purports to retract the assertion of executive power Padilla protests.

Although the Government has recently lodged charges against Padilla in a civilian court, nothing prevents the Executive from returning to the road it earlier constructed and defended. A party's voluntary cessation does not make a case less capable of repetition or less evasive of review. Satisfied that this case is not moot, I would grant the petition for certiorari.

NOTES AND QUESTIONS

1. Recall that Judge Mukasey ordered the government to permit Padilla access to his counsel for the limited purpose of submitting facts to support his habeas petition. Three months later, Padilla continued to be held incommunicado with no access to his attorney. Instead, the government submitted an untimely motion for reconsideration of the court's ruling, providing an affidavit by Vice Admiral Lowell E. Jacoby, Director of the Defense Intelligence Agency, to support the argument that "permitting Padilla to consult with counsel could set back by months

the government's efforts to bring psychological pressure to bear upon Padilla in an effort to interrogate him, and could compromise the government's interrogation techniques." *Padilla ex rel. Newman v. Rumsfeld*, 243 F. Supp. 2d 42, 46 (S.D.N.Y. 2003). Jacoby warned that time-sensitive information about the dirty bomb plot could be lost if the court broke the "atmosphere of dependency and trust between the subject and the interrogator" that the intelligence service had taken pains to develop. Should the judge have deferred to the admiral on the need for such intelligence? Why should less deference be accorded the admiral than the President's determination that Padilla was an enemy combatant in the first place?

2. Upon reconsideration, Judge Mukasey upheld his original order:

> The limits of this case warrant mention for another reason as well. The Jacoby Declaration is none too subtle in cautioning this court against going too far in the protection of this detainee's rights, suggesting at one point that permitting Padilla to consult with a lawyer "risks that plans for future attacks will go undetected." More than a match for that are passages in the amicus curiae submissions in this case, where lawyers raise the specter of *Korematsu v. United States* (1944), and call Padilla's detention "a repudiation of the Magna Carta," thereby suggesting that if Padilla does not receive the full panoply of protections afforded defendants in criminal cases, a dictatorship will be upon us, the tanks will have rolled. Those to whom images of catastrophe come that easily might take comfort in recalling that it is a year and a half since September 11, 2001, and Padilla's is not only the first, but also the only case of its kind. There is every reason not only to hope, but also to expect that this case will be just another of the isolated cases, like *Quirin*, that deal with isolated events and have limited application.
>
> Once again, counsel will consult in an effort to agree on the conditions under which Padilla will consult with counsel and, if he chooses, submit facts in response to the Mobbs Declaration. Absent agreement, the court will impose conditions. Lest any confusion remain, this is not a suggestion or a request that Padilla be permitted to consult with counsel, and it is certainly not an invitation to conduct a further "dialogue" about whether he will be permitted to do so. It is a ruling—a determination—that he will be permitted to do so.[9]

Given that so few U.S. citizens have been declared "enemy combatants," is Judge Mukasey on good ground "not only to hope, but also to expect" that these are "isolated cases . . . that deal with isolated events and have limited application"? Or, per Justice Jackson and Anton Chekhov, *supra*, do they sit on the judicial table of precedents like a loaded gun?

3. By way of a coda, in the criminal case in Florida, no mention was made of the initial allegations by Attorney General Ashcroft and Secretary Rumsfeld about a plot to blow up a radioactive "dirty bomb." Padilla was instead convicted of conspiracy to injure property of a foreign government, conspiracy to defraud the United States, and providing material support to terrorists. He was initially sentenced below the recommended federal sentencing guidelines, to seventeen

---

9. *Id.* at 57.

years and four months' imprisonment with credit for his time spent in military custody. At sentencing, the judge said, "There is no evidence that these defendants personally maimed, kidnapped or killed anyone in the United States or elsewhere. There was never a plot to overthrow the United States government." Kirk Semple, *Padilla Gets 17 Years in Conspiracy Case*, N.Y. TIMES, Jan. 23, 2008.

2. Non-Citizens

a. Capture Inside the United States: al-Marri

This category consists of exactly one case. Although fear of "lone wolves" and "sleeper cells" of foreign terrorists within the United States has been an omnipresent fear, to date the United States has asserted authority to detain only one such person as an "enemy combatant" (i.e., outside of the criminal justice system). Many individuals, however, have been arrested and convicted of federal crimes (e.g., material support for a terrorist organization under 18 U.S.C. §§ 2339A or 2339B) in the federal courts.

Ali al-Marri was a Qatari national lawfully admitted into the United States with his family on September 10, 2001, for purposes of graduate study in Illinois. On December 12, 2001, he was arrested on a material witness warrant related to the 9/11 investigation by the U.S. Attorney for the Southern District of New York and detained in New York City. In early 2002, and again in early 2003, he was indicted on various charges related to fraud, counterfeiting, and false statements. Al-Marri succeeded in challenging venue in New York with the result that a new criminal complaint was filed in Illinois. In June 2003, roughly a month before the jury trial scheduled in his case, President Bush designated al-Marri as an enemy combatant. Over the protests of his criminal defense counsel, al-Marri was transferred from Illinois to the control of the Defense Department and detained in the Naval Consolidated Brig in Charleston, South Carolina.

Al-Marri's petition for a writ of habeas corpus was addressed in the shadow of the *Hamdi* and *Padilla* cases that preceded it. The district court found that the President had ample authority in the AUMF to declare him an enemy combatant regardless of the place of capture and that the *Hamdi* Court had devolved on the district courts broad discretion to construct any hearings required by due process: "*Hamdi* indicated that enemy combatant proceedings should be both prudent and incremental [and] that the first increment consists of a simple examination of the available evidence and an opportunity for rebuttal by the detainee [so that the court] can quickly separate out the errant tourist, embedded journalist, or local aid worker." *Al-Marri ex rel. Berman v. Wright*, 443 F. Supp. 2d 774 (D.S.C. 2006) (citation to *Hamdi* and quotation marks omitted). Accepting hearsay evidence in the government's declaration (from a director of the Joint Intelligence Task Force for Combating Terrorism) and presuming it true subject to a burden placed on al-Marri to rebut it with "more persuasive evidence," the court had little difficulty finding the factual predicate for his detention met. (Al-Marri's position was that he "respectfully declines . . . to assume the burden of proving his own innocence, a burden that is unconstitutional, unlawful, and un-American."). *Id.* at 780, 784.

The Fourth Circuit reversed. Initially, a three-judge panel found that the Military Commissions Act (discussed below) did not apply to strip the court of its jurisdiction to hear al-Marri's habeas petition. While acknowledging that the Due Process Clause would not be violated (per *Hamdi*) by military detention of individuals whom the President designated as enemy combatants and who indeed *qualified* as enemy combatants, the court denied that either the AUMF or the President's "inherent" constitutional authority granted him power in this case. First, the panel interpreted the Supreme Court's *Hamdi* opinion and the Fourth Circuit's *Padilla* opinion to hold that "enemy combatant status rests on an individual's affiliation during wartime with the military arm of the enemy government." *Al-Marri ex rel. Berman v. Wright*, 487 F.3d 160, 181 (4th Cir. 2007). Emphasizing the narrowness of those holdings, the panel noted:

> For unlike Hamdi and Padilla, al-Marri is not alleged to have been part of a Taliban unit, not alleged to have stood alongside the Taliban or the armed forces of any other enemy nation, not alleged to have been on the battlefield during the war in Afghanistan, not alleged to have even been in Afghanistan during the armed conflict there, and not alleged to have engaged in combat with United States forces anywhere in the world. . . . [H]ere the Government argues that al-Marri's seizure and indefinite military detention in this country are justified "because he engaged in, and continues to pose a very real threat of carrying out, . . . acts of international terrorism." And instead of seeking judicial deference to decisions of "military officers who are engaged in the serious work of waging battle," *Hamdi*, the Government asks us to defer to the "multi-agency evaluation process" of government bureaucrats in Washington made eighteen months after al-Marri was taken into custody. Neither the holding in *Hamdi* nor that in *Padilla* supports the Government's contentions here.[10]

Finally, having concluded that the AUMF provided no statutory support for the President's designation and detention of al-Marri, the panel rejected any argument that he had inherent power to do so under Article II. Drawing on the *Youngstown* framework, the panel found that Congress had expressly prohibited the indefinite detention of "terrorist aliens" in the USA PATRIOT Act, § 412 of which provided for only short-term detention in the civilian court system. With his power assessed "at its lowest ebb," and al-Marri entitled to the full due process of any other civilian with substantial connections to the United States, the panel found no inherent authority to seize al-Marri "any more than they permit the President to order the military to seize and detain, without criminal process, other terrorists within the United States, like the Unabomber or the perpetrators of the Oklahoma City bombing." *Id.* at 193. A sharply split en banc opinion reversed the panel's decision, narrowly holding that Congress had granted the President power to detain al-Marri as an enemy combatant but that al-Marri had not been given sufficient process to contest the designation. *Al-Marri ex rel. Berman v. Pucciarelli*, 534 F.3d 213 (4th Cir. 2008).

What followed next might have seemed an eerie echo of the dénouement in the *Padilla* case. The Supreme Court granted al-Marri's petition for a writ of certiorari. 555 U.S. 1066 (2008). Three months later, Acting Solicitor General Edwin

---

10. *Id.* at 183 (internal citations omitted).

Kneedler made an application to transfer al-Marri from military custody to the custody of the Department of Justice. The Court granted the application, vacated the judgment below, and remanded the case to the Fourth Circuit instructing that the appeal be dismissed as moot. *Al-Marri v. Spagone*, 555 U.S. 1220 (2009). The change was the result of the presidential election. Two days after his inauguration, President Barack Obama ordered a review of detainees held at Guantanamo Bay and, separately, of al-Marri as the only designated enemy combatant held in the United States. *See* Memorandum for the Attorney General, Review of the Detention of Ali Saleh Kahlah al-Marri, https://www.whitehouse.gov/the-press-office/ReviewoftheDetentionofAliSalehKahlah. On October 29, 2009, al-Marri was sentenced to 100 months in prison following his plea to a charge of conspiring to provide material support to a foreign terrorist organization. According to the plea agreement, al-Marri admitted to having entered into an "agreement with Khalid Sheikh Mohammed to assist al Qaeda operations in the United States."

b. Capture Outside the United States: Rasul, Hamdan, Boumediene, and Beyond

This final track demonstrates more clearly than any of the other three the interplay between the President, Congress, and the Supreme Court. In a series of cases that begins with *Rasul v. Bush*, the Court and the political branches engaged in a dialogue in which each advanced its legal positions through the mechanisms assigned by the Constitution.

Rasul v. Bush, 542 U.S. 466 (2004), was announced on the same day as *Hamdi v. Rumsfeld*. Writing for a slim majority, Justice Stevens's opinion for the Court held that the federal courts had jurisdiction to hear statutory habeas petitions from non-U.S. citizen detainees at Guantanamo Bay who challenged the legality of their detention. Justice Stevens noted that "the United States exercises 'complete jurisdiction and control' over the Guantanamo Bay Naval Base" and that since the habeas statute "draws no distinction between Americans and aliens held in federal custody, there is little reason to think that Congress intended the geographical coverage of the statute to vary depending on the detainee's citizenship." *Id.* at 480-81.

Six months later, Congress responded with the Detainee Treatment Act of 2005, Pub. L. No. 109-148, 119 Stat. 2739. Section 1005(e) provided, with very limited exceptions, that

> no court, justice, or judge shall have jurisdiction to hear or consider (1) an application for a writ of habeas corpus filed by or on behalf of an alien detained by the Department of Defense at Guantanamo Bay, Cuba; or (2) any other action against the United States or its agents relating to any aspect of the detention by the Department of Defense of an alien at Guantanamo Bay, Cuba, who (A) is currently in military custody; or (B) has been determined by the United States Court of Appeals for the District of Columbia Circuit in accordance with the procedures set forth in section 1005(e) of the Detainee Treatment Act of 2005 to have been properly detained as an enemy combatant.

The exceptions concerned the limited power granted exclusively to the Court of Appeals for the District of Columbia Circuit to review the work of the "Combatant Status Review Tribunals" (CSRTs) established to confirm enemy combatant designations and to review the decisions of military commissions established to try law-of-war offenses.

In *Hamdan v. Rumsfeld*, 548 U.S. 557 (2006), a narrow majority held that the Detainee Treatment Act did not deprive the Court of jurisdiction to hear cases pending at the time the statute was enacted. Hamdan, a Yemeni who served as a driver for Osama bin Laden, was detained at Guantanamo Bay as an enemy combatant following his capture in Afghanistan and plans initiated to try him by military commission on a charge of conspiracy "to commit offenses . . . triable by military commission." The Court first denied the President the authority to prosecute conspiracy as a war crime:

> The charge's shortcomings are not merely formal, but are indicative of a broader inability on the Executive's part here to satisfy the most basic precondition—at least in the absence of specific congressional authorization—for establishment of military commissions: military necessity. Hamdan's tribunal was appointed not by a military commander in the field of battle, but by a retired major general stationed away from any active hostilities. Hamdan is charged not with an overt act for which he was caught redhanded in a theater of war and which military efficiency demands be tried expeditiously, but with an agreement the inception of which long predated the attacks of September 11, 2001, and the AUMF. That may well be a crime, but it is not an offense that by the law of war may be tried by military commission. None of the overt acts alleged to have been committed in furtherance of the agreement is itself a war crime, or even necessarily occurred during time of, or in a theater of, war. Any urgent need for imposition or execution of judgment is utterly belied by the record; Hamdan was arrested in November 2001 and he was not charged until mid-2004. These simply are not the circumstances in which, by any stretch of the historical evidence or this Court's precedents, a military commission established by Executive Order under the authority of Article 21 of the UCMJ may lawfully try a person and subject him to punishment.[11]

The Court next found the commissions themselves—created solely on the basis of a military order issued by President Bush[12]—not in compliance with the processes

---

11. *Id.* at 612-13.

12. Military Order of November 13, 2001—Detention, Treatment and Trial of Certain Non-Citizens in the War Against Terrorism, 66 Fed. Reg. 57833 (2001). This order, though styled a "military" order, described a category of people subject to detention that was much broader than the traditional universe of combatants in an armed conflict. Section 2(a) of the order defined as subject to the President's discretion to detain:

> any individual who is not a United States citizen with respect to whom I determine from time to time in writing that:

> (1) there is reason to believe that such individual, at the relevant times,
>   (i) is or was a member of the organization known as al Qaida;
>   (ii) has engaged in, aided or abetted, or conspired to commit, acts of international terrorism, or acts in preparation therefor, that have caused, threaten to cause, or have as their aim to cause, injury to or adverse effects on the United States, its citizens, national security, foreign policy, or economy; or
>   (iii) has knowingly harbored one or more individuals described in subparagraphs (i) or (ii) of subsection 2(a)(1) of this order; and
> (2) it is in the interest of the United States that such individual be subject to this order.

established by Congress in the Uniform Code of Military Justice or with relevant international law. Since Congress had not rescinded or abridged the procedural rules set in the Code in either the AUMF or the Detainee Treatment Act, the President could not override them of his own accord.

Little more than three months later, Congress responded with the Military Commissions Act of 2006, Pub. L. No. 109-366, § 7 120 Stat. 2600. Among other things, the Act amended the federal habeas statute to provide:

> No court, justice, or judge shall have jurisdiction to hear or consider an application for a writ of habeas corpus filed by or on behalf of an alien detained by the United States who has been determined by the United States to have been properly detained as an enemy combatant or is awaiting such determination. (2) Except as provided in paragraphs (2) and (3) of section 1005(e) of the Detainee Treatment Act of 2005 (10 U.S.C. 801 note), no court, justice, or judge shall have jurisdiction to hear or consider any other action against the United States or its agents relating to any aspect of the detention, transfer, treatment, trial, or conditions of confinement of an alien who is or was detained by the United States and has been determined by the United States to have been properly detained as an enemy combatant or is awaiting such determination.

The statute was pellucidly clear as to its effective date: "[This amendment] shall take effect on the date of the enactment of this Act, and shall apply to all cases, without exception, pending on or after the date of the enactment of this Act which relate to any aspect of the detention, transfer, treatment, trial, or conditions of detention of an alien detained by the United States since September 11, 2001." What could be clearer?

The final word on the subject, as was then readily predictable, was delivered by the Supreme Court. *Boumediene v. Bush*, 553 U.S. 723, 738 (2008), acknowledged that the Military Commissions Act "was a direct response to *Hamdan*'s holding that the DTA's jurisdiction-stripping provision had no application to pending cases." The Court then took notice "of the obvious and uncontested fact that the United States, by virtue of its complete jurisdiction and control over [Guantanamo Bay], maintains de facto sovereignty over this territory." *Id.* at 755. This was essential for the Court's conclusion that, whatever jurisdiction over *statutory* habeas rights that Congress had stripped from the Court, the *constitutional* right to habeas corpus extended to the Naval Station there. *Id.* at 771.[13] Since the Military Commissions Act "does not purport to be a formal suspension of the writ; and the Government, in its submissions to us, has not argued that it is," the Court held that the detainees were "entitled to the privilege of habeas corpus to challenge the legality of their detention." *Id.* Finally, the Court concluded that the CSRTs and their judicial review

---

13. The Court made clear, however, that such a determination would need to be made on a case-by-case basis with consideration for such additional factors as "(1) the citizenship and status of the detainee and the adequacy of the process through which that status determination was made; (2) the nature of the sites where apprehension and then detention took place; and (3) the practical obstacles inherent in resolving the prisoner's entitlement to the writ." *Id.* at 766. When detainees at Bagram Air Base in Afghanistan sought to exercise a constitutional right to habeas, the D.C. Circuit rejected the attempt by application of these factors. *Al Maqaleh v. Gates*, 605 F.3d 84 (D.C. Cir. 2010).

process were not an adequate substitute for the exercise of this right. That meant that the Military Commissions Act worked an unconstitutional suspension of the writ of habeas corpus.

What is one to conclude from these cases and procedures? If the line of cases from *Rasul* through *Boumediene* seemed a victory for detainees challenging their detention, that victory proved to be of questionable value. The Supreme Court seemed to make clear that the Court of Appeals for the District of Columbia Circuit would have considerable discretion to review the habeas process unfolding before district court judges. The D.C. Circuit has decided every Guantanamo habeas challenge that has come before it in favor of the government. James A. Schoettler, Jr., *Detention of Combatants and the War on Terror*, in THE WAR ON TERROR AND THE LAWS OF WAR 176 (2d ed. 2015).

In that light, twelve years after *Boumediene* and almost nineteen years after the start of the U.S. war in Afghanistan, consider the following case.

Ali v. Trump
959 F.3d 364 (D.C. Cir. May 15, 2020)

MILLETT, Circuit Judge:

The United States has detained appellant Abdul Razak Ali, an Algerian national, at the Guantanamo Bay Naval Base in Cuba since June 2002. In this appeal, Ali asks the court to hold that the Fifth Amendment's Due Process Clause categorically applies in full to detainees at Guantanamo Bay, and that his ongoing detention violates both the procedural and substantive aspects of the Due Process Clause. Those broad arguments are foreclosed by circuit precedent. To be sure, whether and which particular aspects of the Due Process Clause apply to detainees at Guantanamo Bay largely remain open questions in this circuit. So too does the question of what procedural protections the Suspension Clause requires. But Ali has eschewed any such calibrated or as-applied constitutional arguments in this case. For those reasons, the district court's denial of Ali's petition for a writ of habeas corpus is affirmed.

I

A

Shortly after the September 11, 2001 terrorist attacks, Congress passed the Authorization for Use of Military Force ("AUMF"), [empowering] the President "to use all necessary and appropriate force against those nations, organizations, or persons he determines planned, authorized, committed, or aided the terrorist attacks that occurred on September 11, 2001[.]" This includes the detention of "those who are part of forces associated with Al Qaeda or the Taliban[.]" *Hamdi v. Rumsfeld*, 542 U.S. 507, 516, 518–519 (2004).

Congress subsequently passed the National Defense Authorization Act for Fiscal Year 2012. That Act "affirms that the authority of the President to use all necessary and appropriate force pursuant to the [AUMF] includes the authority for the Armed Forces of the United States to detain covered persons" until "the end of the hostilities authorized by the [AUMF]." The National Defense Authorization Act defines "covered persons" to include those "who planned, authorized, committed, or aided the terrorist attacks that occurred on September 11, 2001, or harbored those responsible for those attacks," or who were "part of or substantially supported al-Qaeda, the Taliban, or associated forces that are engaged in hostilities against the United States or its coalition partners[.]"

B

Ali is an Algerian citizen. He was captured by United States and Pakistani forces in March 2002 during a raid of a four-bedroom guesthouse in Faisalabad, Pakistan. Ali kept troubling company there. At the time of the raid, he was living with the al Qaeda facilitator Abu Zubaydah and several of Zubaydah's compatriots, including four former trainers from a terrorist training camp in Afghanistan, multiple experts in explosives, and an individual who had fought alongside the Taliban. The guesthouse also contained a device typically used to assemble remote bombing devices and documents bearing the designation al Qaeda.

In June 2002, the United States transferred Ali to the Naval Base at Guantanamo Bay. A few years later, Ali filed a petition for habeas corpus in the United States District Court for the District of Columbia challenging his designation and detention as an enemy combatant. The district court denied the petition. Applying a preponderance of the evidence standard, the district court concluded that Ali was a member of Zubaydah's forces, which the district court found was an "associated force" of al Qaeda and the Taliban within the meaning of the AUMF. This court affirmed, concluding that Ali's presence in the "terrorist guesthouse" alongside other terrorist combatants strongly supported the district court's finding that he was an enemy combatant.

On January 11, 2018, Ali joined several other Guantanamo detainees in filing renewed habeas petitions arguing that their continued detention violated the Due Process Clause and the AUMF. The district court subsequently denied Ali's habeas petition.

II

A

The district court's decision that the Due Process Clause is categorically inapplicable to detainees at Guantanamo Bay was misplaced. The Supreme Court's decision in *Boumediene v. Bush*, 553 U.S. 723 (2008), unequivocally held that Guantanamo Bay detainees must be afforded those procedures necessary to ensure "meaningful review" of the lawfulness of their detention. In particular, detainees are constitutionally entitled to "those 'procedural protections'" that are "necessary (i) to 'rebut the factual basis for the Government's assertion that [the detainee] is an enemy combatant'; (ii) to give the prisoner 'a meaningful opportunity to demonstrate that he is being held pursuant to the erroneous application or interpretation of relevant law'; and (iii) to create a record that will support 'meaningful review'" by federal courts.[1]

In identifying those constitutional protections for detainees, the Supreme Court pointed both to the Constitution's guarantee of habeas corpus and the Due Process Clause.

Circuit precedent has not yet comprehensively resolved which "constitutional procedural protections apply to the adjudication of detainee habeas corpus petitions," and whether those "rights are housed" in the Due Process Clause, the Suspension Clause, or both.

In this case, Ali has chosen not to ground any of his claims for procedural protections in the Suspension Clause. So that issue is not before us. Instead, Ali's main argument puts all of his eggs in one constitutional basket. He argues that the Due Process Clause's procedural and substantive requirements apply wholesale, without any qualifications, to habeas corpus petitions filed by all Guantanamo detainees.

That argument sweeps too far.

For starters, the argument is in substantial tension with the Supreme Court's more calibrated approach in *Boumediene*, which tied the constitutional protections afforded to Guantanamo Bay detainees' habeas corpus proceedings to their role in vindicating the constitutional right to the Great Writ and the judicial role in checking Executive Branch overreach. The court stressed that the scope of constitutional protections must "turn on objective factors and practical concerns, not formalism." Yet Ali argues for only a formal and unyielding line.

Ali has abstained from pressing any more gradated or as-applied Due Process Clause argument here. [T]he determination of what constitutional procedural protections govern the adjudication of habeas corpus petitions from Guantanamo detainees should be analyzed on an issue-by-issue basis, applying *Boumediene*'s functional approach. The type of sweeping and global application asserted by Ali fails to account for the unique context and balancing of interests that *Boumediene* requires when reviewing the detention of foreign nationals captured during ongoing hostilities.

B

1

Ali argues that his continued detention for more than seventeen years violates substantive due process. While Ali's detention has been quite lengthy, under binding circuit precedent the Due Process Clause's substantive protections would offer him no help.

---

1. This opinion's references to detainees at Guantanamo Bay and the constitutional protections they enjoy speaks only to foreign national detainees, who compose the Naval Base's current population in detention. We do not address what protections would apply to United States citizens or those with similar legal ties to the United States were they to be detained at Guantanamo Bay.

Among other things, the substantive component of the Due Process Clause "bars certain arbitrary, wrongful government actions regardless of the fairness of the procedures used to implement them." But only government action that is "so egregious, so outrageous, that it may fairly be said to shock the contemporary conscience" qualifies as arbitrary for the purposes of substantive due process.

Ali contends that his ongoing detention violates substantive due process in two ways. First, he argues that his continued detention is driven by a new blanket and punitive policy against releasing detainees and, as such, is "untethered to any ongoing, individualized purpose to detain him." Second, Ali argues that his "[p]erpetual detention" based on an "eighteen-day stay in a guest-house" shocks the conscience. Neither argument succeeds.

First, Ali's detention is long because the armed conflict out of which it arises has been long, continuing to the present day. Given that, Ali's detention still serves the established law-of-war purpose of "prevent[ing] captured individuals from returning to the field of battle and taking up arms once again." *See Hamdi*, 542 U.S. at 518, 521.

Ali does not dispute that hostilities authorized by the AUMF are ongoing. And although the AUMF was initially enacted in 2001, Congress reaffirmed the government's interest in detaining enemy combatants by passing the National Defense Authorization Act in 2011. Whatever subjective motivations Ali might impute to the government, its original and legitimate purpose for detaining him—recognized by the law of war and Supreme Court precedent—persists.

On top of that, Ali has little ground to stand on in claiming that time has dissipated the threat he poses. The Guantanamo Bay Periodic Review Board has specifically reviewed Ali's detention no less than eight times to determine whether his continued detention remains necessary to protect against a significant security threat to the United States. And each time the Periodic Review Board has recommended continued detention because of the threat his release would pose.

In its most recent full review of Ali's detention, the Periodic Review Board "determined that continued law of war detention of the detainee remains necessary to protect against a continuing significant threat to the security of the United States." In reaching this conclusion, the Board "considered the detainee's elevated threat profile as evidenced by his prior roles in Afghanistan and prior association[,] [t]he Board's inability to assess the detainee's current threat level due to the detainee's refusal to participate in meetings with his representative, the lack of submission of any new materials by the detainee and the detainee's decision not to attend the hearing."

And in its most recent review of Ali's case file in January 2020, the Periodic Review Board determined "by consensus" that "no significant question [was] raised as to whether [Ali's] continued detention [was] warranted."[4]

---

4. Because Ali has repeatedly been found to be unsuitable for relief, this case does not present the question of what protections might apply to a detainee whom the Board has determined to be suitable for release, yet who continues to be detained.

Second, the fact that hostilities have endured for a long time, without more, does not render the government's continued detention of Ali a shock to the conscience, in light of the dangers the Periodic Review Board has found to be associated with his release.

Ali attempts to downplay his connection to Zubaydah's force by characterizing it as an "eighteen-day stay in a guesthouse." But that is a long time to be in the company of senior terrorist leaders. Nor does Ali dispute that he was actively studying in their English program while there, acquiring a skill that would have equipped him to harm the United States. Finally, Ali has provided no sound basis for concluding that either his ability or his desire to rejoin opposing forces has diminished.

2

Ali also argues that, as a matter of procedural due process, the extended duration of the government's detention of detainees at Guantanamo Bay requires the government to show, by clear and convincing evidence, that continued detention is necessary to avoid specific, articulable dangers. He further contends that the Due Process Clause precludes the use of hearsay evidence and bars the presumption of regularity with respect to the government's evidence. Circuit precedent forecloses each of those arguments.

To begin with, we have repeatedly held that, to uphold an order of detention, the individual's status as an enemy combatant need only be proved by a preponderance of the evidence. The same holds true for the use of hearsay evidence during habeas corpus and other detention proceedings.

As for the presumption of regularity, it is not at all clear that the presumption has even been used in Ali's case. In any event, this court's cases have also expressly granted a presumption of regularity to certain government evidence.

Ali responds that, despite these precedents, a new balancing under *Mathews v. Eldridge*, 424 U.S. 319 (1976), is necessary because, as his detention drags on, the government's asserted security interest in his continued detention grows weaker while his liberty interest grows stronger. *See Rasul v. Bush*, 542 U.S. 466, 488 (2004) (Kennedy, J., concurring) ("[A]s the period of detention stretches from months to years, the case for continued detention to meet military exigencies becomes weaker."). In other words, according to Ali, a new balancing analysis is in order because any assumption that wartime detention will be temporary "has long since dissipated" given the prolonged hostilities.

That argument does not extract Ali from the force of binding circuit precedent. In developing the procedures applicable to AUMF challenges, this court contemplated that detentions could last for the duration of hostilities. The length for which hostilities might continue was uncertain then and continues to be uncertain now.

Indeed, Ali agrees that, if the hostilities covered by the AUMF were a more traditional type of war that continued for this same length of time, there would be no substantive due process objection to continued detention. Yet Ali cites no authority suggesting that the form of hostilities that enemy combatants undertake changes the law of war's authorization of their continued detention, especially when, as here, the government has found that the threat Ali poses continues.

III

For all of those reasons, the district court's denial of Ali's petition for a writ of habeas corpus is affirmed.

So ordered.

NOTES AND QUESTIONS

1. Senior Circuit Judge A. Raymond Randolph concurred only in the judgment. In his view, "it is 'well established' that the protections of the Fifth Amendment's Due Process Clause 'do not extend to aliens outside the territorial boundaries' of the United States, including those held at Guantanamo Bay." Judge Randolph here cited Zadvydas v. Davis, 533 U.S. 678, 693 (2001). Under this view, officers of the United States (civilian or military) derive their authority from constitutional sources but, their actions concerning non-citizens outside the United States are not constrained by the Constitution. What *does* constrain their range of action in such circumstances? When, if ever, should the Constitution "follow the flag" when U.S. government actors, including military forces, have complete control over a foreign national? Consider that, for European coalition partners subject to the jurisdiction of the European Court of Human Rights, such levels of control have been held to oblige those states to abide by their international legal obligations under the European Convention on Human Rights, including protections against arbitrary deprivation of liberty.

2. Recall Chief Justice Rehnquist's caveat in a footnote to his opinion in *Salerno* (*supra* p. 576): " 'We intimate no view as to the point at which detention in a particular case might become excessively prolonged, and therefore punitive, in relation to Congress' regulatory goal." Is there a point (in the ongoing conflict in Afghanistan? In Ali's lifespan?) when this objection takes hold? On the other hand, Justice Breyer emphasized in *Zadvydas* (*supra* p. 577) that "we leave no unprotected spot in the Nation's armor. Neither do we consider terrorism or other special circumstances where special arguments might be made for forms of preventive detention and for heightened deference to the judgments of the political branches with respect to matters of national security." Finally, consider the view expressed in the plurality opinion in *Hamdi* (*supra* p. 8) that "If the practical circumstances of a given conflict are entirely unlike those of the conflicts that informed the development of the law of war, that understanding may unravel." When *Hamdi* was decided in 2004, the plurality concluded "that is not the situation we face as of this date." How about now?

3. Is the particular "armed conflict" in which Ali was a participant "continuing to the present day," as the court asserts? If the armed conflict with al Qaeda has terminated, or no longer constitutes an armed conflict under international humanitarian law, shouldn't Ali be released from detention? Ali was detained because he "was a member of Zubaydah's forces, which the district court found

was an 'associated force' of al Qaeda and the Taliban within the meaning of the AUMF." What result if "Zubaydah's forces" no longer exist? What evidence would be sufficient to show that an associated force has ceased to be? (Abu Zubaydah has been detained at Guantanamo Bay since 2006.)

4. The appellate court's holding is a narrow one. The court rejected Ali's argument "that the Due Process Clause's procedural and substantive requirements apply wholesale, without any qualifications, to habeas corpus petitions filed by all Guantanamo detainees." What due process issues does this opinion leave unanswered?

5. The court suggests that the length of detention, "without more, does not render the government's detention of Ali a shock to the conscience." What if Ali was subjected to waterboarding or other forms of coerced interrogation while in detention at Gitmo? Would such conduct "shock the conscience" and violate substantive due process?

V. CONCLUDING THOUGHTS

Recall that Yaser Hamdi's release meant that no review procedure was crafted to satisfy his due process rights as a U.S. citizen contesting his designation and detention as an enemy combatant. Nothing in that decision suggested such review was required for alien detainees. However, perhaps in an effort to ward off potential judicial review of those detentions—a prospect that was made very real when the Supreme Court ruled in *Rasul v. Bush* that the federal habeas statute applied to Guantanamo detainees—*non*-U.S. citizen detainees at Guantanamo Bay shortly thereafter found themselves provided two separate review procedures.

The first review procedure is called a "Combatant Status Review Tribunal." It was established by order of the Deputy Secretary of Defense less than ten days after the Supreme Court handed down its *Hamdi* opinion. The CSRT is most easily understood as an "Article 5 like" tribunal of another name (because the CSRT is not assessing prisoner of war status, designating it as a tribunal required by Article 5 of the Third Geneva Convention would have added more confusion to the detention regime). Like an Article 5 tribunal, the CSRT performs a distinct function: determining whether a captive falls into a detainable status. The CSRT is the detainee's "opportunity to contest designation as an enemy combatant." Obviously, no detainee will be brought before a CSRT unless an initial enemy combatant status determination is made at the time of capture. However, it is the CSRT that must validate or reject that initial determination. Assisted by a military officer detailed as the detainee's "personal representative" who has had the chance to review "any reasonably available information," the detainee may appear before a three-member tribunal of commissioned officers who were not themselves involved in the detainee's "apprehension, detention, interrogation, or previous determination of status." At least one member of the tribunal must be a judge advocate (i.e., a military attorney). The CSRT will listen to the detainee (who may remain silent), hear from witnesses "reasonably available," and "consider any information it deems relevant and helpful" to determine "by majority vote whether the detainee is properly detained as an enemy combatant." The tribunal uses a preponderance of the evidence standard with a rebuttable presumption in favor of the government's evidence. Its record is then reviewed by the staff judge advocate who makes a recommendation to the convening authority appointed by the Secretary of the Navy (the Department of Defense lead agent for Guantanamo detention issues).

The second review structure, an "Administrative Review Board," was also established by the Deputy Secretary of Defense, but almost two months *before Hamdi* was decided. The ARB does not determine status, that conclusion having already been made and subsequently reaffirmed by a CSRT. Rather, the ARB was intended to assess "annually the need to continue to detain each enemy combatant during the course of the current and ongoing hostilities." The procedure was adopted "as a matter of policy" rather than out of a sense of legal obligation "to address some unique and unprecedented characteristics of the current conflict." Like a CSRT, an ARB comprised at least three officers, but without the requirement that any of them have legal training (although at least one required experience "in the field of intelligence"). The ARB would "assess whether each enemy combatant remains a threat to the United States and its allies in the ongoing armed conflict against al Qaida and its affiliates and supporters or if there is any other reason that it is in the interest of the United States and its allies for the enemy combatant to remain in the control" of the Department of Defense. With provisions for assistance to the detainee similar to those found in the CSRT context, and with the added option of notice to the detainee's state of nationality for receipt of information relevant to the ARB's function, the ARB would make a written determination to be provided to a "presidentially-appointed Senate-confirmed civilian in the Department of Defense" designated by the Secretary of Defense. That person would then make a determination provided to the Secretary, detainees, and participants in the review process.

On March 7, 2011, President Obama issued Executive Order 13567, which replaced this system with a "Periodic Review Board" process for detainees held at Guantanamo Bay "on the date of this order," who had been "(i) designated for continued law of war detention; or (ii) referred for prosecution, except for those detainees against whom charges are pending or a judgment of conviction has been entered." The stated purpose of the PRB was "solely to establish, as a discretionary matter, a process to review on a periodic basis the executive branch's continued, discretionary exercise of existing detention authority in individual cases." The order anticipated an initial review for each detainee that would be conducted "as soon as possible but no later than 1 year from the date of this order." Subsequent "full" reviews would occur every three years, while "file" reviews occur in six-month increments. The order provided detainees with a personal representative and opportunity to receive written, unclassified summaries intended "to provide adequate notice to the detainee of the reasons for continued detention." Detention would be continued if determined to be "necessary to protect against a significant threat to the security of the United States." A Periodic Review Secretariat has been established in the Department of Defense. *See* http://www.prs.mil/.

When President Obama took the oath of office, 242 individuals remained subject to law-of-war–based detention at Guantanamo Bay. Five years after Executive

Order 13567 was signed, ninety-one individuals remained in detention, forty of whom were yet to receive their first PRB review. Carol Rosenberg, *Guantánamo Limbo: Dozens Still Waiting for First Review Obama Ordered in 2011*, MIAMI HERALD, Mar. 28, 2016. Rosenberg reported a Justice Department attorney's presentation to a federal court that "the process was hampered by the need to create a bureaucracy to handle Obama's executive order and complicated by the participation of multiple agencies in it." A breakdown of statistics for those remaining detainees reveals that as many as 80 percent of the so-called forever prisoners who *had* received the results of at least an initial PRB review as of April 4, 2016, either had been released or cleared for release while awaiting that ultimate result. *See* Guantanamo Periodic Review Board Guide, MIAMI HERALD, www.miamiherald.com/news/nation-world/world/americas/guantanamo/article68333292.html. As of March 2020, the *New York Times* reported that 731 detainees had been transferred and 40 detainees remained. Of the forty remaining in military custody at Guantanamo Bay:

> Seven have been charged, and two convicted, in military commissions, with three more detainees proposed, but no charges referred yet, for trial in that system.
>
> Five remain in LOAC detention but have been recommended for transfer to other countries.
>
> Twenty-three remain in LOAC detention with no recommendation for transfer.

The last change in this data occurred in May 2018. *See The Guantánamo Docket*, N.Y. TIMES, https://www.nytimes.com/interactive/projects/guantanamo (last accessed Mar. 16, 2020).

Finally, the four-track analysis of military detention described in the previous section obscures the blending that sometimes occurs in this conflict between civilian and military, and criminal and preventive, forms of detention. In spring 2011, for example, a Somali national named Ahmed Warsame was captured when U.S. military forces seized his small fishing vessel in the Gulf of Aden. He was detained in the brig of the *U.S.S. Boxer* for two months, during which time he was subject to interrogation; U.S. officials suspected him of membership in at least two designated foreign terrorist organizations, "Al-Shabaab" (a Somali group) and AQAP (or Al Qaeda in the Arabian Peninsula). While his capture was still unreported by either government or private media sources, Warsame (still in the brig of a U.S. Navy vessel) "was read his *Miranda* rights, and after waiving those rights, he spoke to law enforcement agents for several days." *See* Guilty Plea Unsealed in New York Involving Ahmed Warsame, Mar. 25, 2013, https://www.fbi.gov (insert press release title in search box on main page); *see also* Robert M. Chesney, *Beyond the Battlefield, Beyond Al Qaeda: The Destabilizing Legal Architecture of Counterterrorism*, 112 MICH. L. REV. 163, 166 (2013). Only then, upon arrival in New York, was he arraigned before a federal district court judge on charges of providing material support to designated foreign terrorist organizations and other crimes.

What was the basis for Warsame's capture? Was he captured on a "hot battlefield"? Did his citizenship matter? Was the "Warsame Model" a fifth track that selectively combined features of military and criminal law enforcement detention authorities?

ASSESSMENT QUESTIONS

1. Where is detention authority found in the U.S. Constitution?
2. What is meant by the distinction between punitive and preventive detention?
3. How has citizenship, place of seizure, and location of confinement influenced the development of the law governing the choice between military and civilian detention authorities?

ASSESSMENT ANSWERS

1. The Necessary and Proper Clause, in conjunction with other enumerated powers, grants Congress authority to pass criminal laws and create institutions necessary to enforce those laws, including prisons. The Necessary and Proper Clause has also been accepted as a source of authority for certain forms of civil commitment. Other constitutional provisions restrict exercise of this power.
2. As noted, Congress may pass laws criminalizing conduct and punish with periods of incarceration the violation of those laws. That is a punitive sanction based on past conduct. The Supreme Court has also permitted other forms of detention—some of very short duration, others longer—that are not premised on a punitive purpose. One example is the so-called *Terry* stop, from *Terry v. Ohio*. Pretrial detention on grounds of future dangerousness was upheld under limited circumstances in *United States v. Salerno*. A person may also be held as a "material witness" in an ongoing investigation. None of these are punitive detentions, according to the Court. They are meant to prevent some other harm.
3. Most cases of military detention have involved non-U.S. persons captured far from the United States. Their right to petition for a writ of habeas corpus has been upheld when they have been held at Guantanamo Bay, Cuba, but nowhere else to date. Cases concerning U.S. citizens have been very few in number (Lindh, Hamdi, Padilla) as have instances of military detention of non-U.S. persons seized in the United States (al-Marri). Their cases have generated some additional protections, but just as often, have been mooted, presenting no judicial opinion by the Supreme Court and, sometimes, in the lower courts as well.

PART IV

INFORMATION AND NATIONAL SECURITY

CHAPTER 12

Intelligence Exploitation

I. GENERAL OVERVIEW

The collection and analysis of foreign intelligence information is critical to protect national security and conduct foreign relations. The failure to timely collect and share intelligence information across the U.S. intelligence community can have devastating consequences. Post-9/11, the independent National Commission on Terrorist Attacks upon the United States (the "9/11 Commission") concluded that structural barriers to performing joint intelligence work and sharing foreign intelligence information impeded the government's ability to prevent the 9/11 terrorist attacks. The 9/11 Commission found:

> Current security requirements nurture over-classification and excessive compartmentation of information among agencies. Each agency's incentive structure opposes sharing, with risks (criminal, civil, and internal administrative sanctions) but few rewards for sharing information. . . . Agencies uphold a "need-to-know" culture of information protection rather than promoting a "need-to-share" culture of integration.[1]

The Final Report proposed sweeping changes in the intelligence community, including the creation of a National Intelligence Director to manage the national intelligence program and oversee the sharing of intelligence information. *See* FINAL REPORT OF THE NATIONAL COMMISSION ON TERRORIST ATTACKS UPON THE UNITED STATES 411 (2004).

After the report was released, the federal government undertook various reforms. President Bush signed four executive orders in August 2004 that strengthened the intelligence community. In Congress, both the House and Senate

---

1. FINAL REPORT OF THE NATIONAL COMMISSION ON TERRORIST ATTACKS UPON THE UNITED STATES 417 (2004)

passed bills with major amendments to the National Security Act of 1947. After intense negotiations to reconcile the two bills, Congress passed the Intelligence Reform and Terrorism Prevention Act (IRTPA) of 2004, which created the Office of National Intelligence, and the Director of National Intelligence. *See* Pub. L. No. 108-458, § 1061(b), 118 Stat. 3638 (2004). The President signed the bill into law on December 17, 2004.

While collecting foreign intelligence information is essential to protecting national security, the government is not afforded unfettered authority. Instead, the Constitution limits the government's actions. In the Final Report, the 9/11 Commission stated:

> [W]hile protecting our homeland, Americans should be mindful of threats to vital personal and civil liberties. This balancing is no easy task, but we must constantly strive to keep it right. . . . We must find ways of reconciling security with liberty, since the success of one helps protect the other. The choice between security and liberty is a false choice, as nothing is more likely to endanger America's liberties than the success of a terrorist attack at home. Our history has shown us that insecurity threatens liberty. Yet, if our liberties are curtailed, we lose the values that we are struggling to defend.[2]

To achieve the proper balance between national security and civil liberties, the 9/11 Commission recommended the creation of a board within the executive branch to ensure government adherence to defending civil liberties. In 2004, Congress enacted the IRTPA, which created a Privacy and Civil Liberties Oversight Board (PCLOB), within the Executive Office of the President, to "analyze and review actions the executive branch takes to protect the Nation from terrorism, ensuring that the need for such actions is balanced with the need to protect privacy and civil liberties." Privacy and Civil Liberties Oversight Board, REPORT ON THE TELEPHONE RECORDS PROGRAM CONDUCTED UNDER SECTION 215 OF THE USA PATRIOT ACT AND ON THE OPERATIONS OF THE FOREIGN INTELLIGENCE SURVEILLANCE COURT 2 (Jan. 23, 2014). The PCLOB, for example, has been highly critical of the government's bulk collection of telephone metadata program under the Foreign Intelligence Surveillance Act (FISA), 50 U.S.C. §§ 1801 et seq., claiming that the program is unlawful and raises serious concerns under the First and Fourth Amendments of the U.S. Constitution. *Id.* at 10-11.

This chapter examines the collection of foreign intelligence information under the FISA. More specifically, the chapter considers the operation of the FISA court, the warrant application process, and the meaning of key statutory terms such as "foreign power," "agent of a foreign power," and "foreign intelligence information." The chapter also considers the legal challenges to FISA, including claims that FISA orders violate the First and Fourth Amendments of the Constitution.

---

2. *Id.* at 394-95.

II. FOREIGN INTELLIGENCE SURVEILLANCE ACT, 50 U.S.C. §§ 1801 ET SEQ.

A. Statutory Framework

The Foreign Intelligence Surveillance Act (FISA), 50 U.S.C. §§ 1801 et seq., authorizes the collection of foreign intelligence information. Following the terrorist attacks of September 11, 2001, FISA, as amended, has become a critical tool used by the national intelligence community to prevent terrorist attacks and conduct international terrorism investigations. As originally enacted by Congress in 1978, FISA governs the collection of "foreign intelligence information" through the use of electronic surveillance of a "foreign power" and "agents of a foreign power." FISA has been amended to authorize physical searches,[3] the use of pen registers and trap and trace devices,[4] and the seizure of business records and other "tangible things" for the purpose of gathering foreign intelligence information.[5]

Three terms are essential to understanding FISA's scope and application: (1) "foreign intelligence information," (2) "foreign power," and (3) "agent of a foreign power." A "significant purpose" of a FISA order must be to collect "foreign intelligence information." The latter term includes two broad categories of information. Section 1801(e)(1) authorizes the collection of "counter-intelligence" or "protective" foreign intelligence information. Such information relates to the ability of the United States to protect against "(A) actual or potential attack or other grave hostile acts of a foreign power or an agent of a foreign power; (B) sabotage, international terrorism, or the international proliferation of weapons of mass destruction by a foreign power or an agent of a foreign power; or (C) clandestine intelligence activities by an intelligence service or network of a foreign power or agent of a foreign power." 50 U.S.C. § 1801(e)(1)(A)-(C). FISA authorizes electronic surveillance or a physical search to collect information intended to prevent sabotage or an international terrorist attack. The term also includes "positive" foreign intelligence information. Section 1801(e)(2) authorizes the collection of information with respect to a "foreign power or foreign territory" that relates to "the national defense or security of the United States" or "the conduct of the foreign affairs of the United States." Thus, the collection of foreign intelligence information is not limited to preventing a terrorist attack and thwarting foreign spying.

---

3. *See* Intelligence Authorization Act for Fiscal Year 1995, Pub. L. No. 103-359, § 807, 108 Stat. 3423, 3443 (1994) (codified as amended 50 U.S.C. §§ 1821-1829).

4. *See* Intelligence Authorization Act for Fiscal Year 1999, Pub. L. No. 105-271, § 601(2), 112 Stat. 2396 (codified as amended at 50 U.S.C. §§ 1841-1846). Pen registers capture the numbers dialed on a targeted phone line (only the outgoing calls placed from the targeted phone), while trap and trace devices identify the originating number of a call on a targeted telephone line (who called the targeted number). *See* 18 U.S.C. §§ 3127(3)-(4). Such devices do not collect the contents of the telephone communication.

5. *See* USA PATRIOT Act, Pub. L. No. 107-56, 115 Stat. 272 (2001) (codified at 50 U.S.C. § 1861). The term "foreign intelligence information" is defined by 50 U.S.C. § 1801(e).

The target of a FISA order is limited to a "foreign power" or an "agent of a foreign power." The term "foreign power" includes traditional state or state-related entities, such as a foreign government, a faction of a foreign nation, or an entity that is directed and controlled by such foreign government. *Id.* § 1801(a)(1)-(3). The definition of "foreign power" also includes non-state entities such as groups engaged in international terrorism or the international proliferation of weapons of mass destruction. 50 U.S.C. §§ 1801(a)(4), (7). Thus, for example, a foreign terrorist organization such as al Qaeda or the Islamic State of Iraq and Syria (ISIS) is a foreign power under FISA and could be the target of a FISA electronic surveillance order.

The definition of "agent of a foreign power" differs depending on whether the FISA target is a foreign national or "United States person." If the target is a foreign national, "agent of a foreign power" means a person who (A) acts as an officer, employee, or member of a foreign power; (B) acts for or on behalf of a foreign power engaged in clandestine activities in the United States; (C) engages in international terrorism or related activities; (D) engages in the international proliferation of weapons of mass destruction or related activities; or (E) engages in the international proliferation of weapons of mass destruction or related activities on behalf of a foreign power. 50 U.S.C. §§ 1801(b)(1)(A)-(E). However, if the target engages in international terrorism or international proliferation of weapons of mass destruction, there is no requirement of a connection to a foreign power. §§ 1801(b)(1)(C), (D). At the same time, "agent of a foreign power" covers any person, including a United States person, who (A) knowingly engages in clandestine intelligence gathering activities on behalf of a foreign power, (B) engages in such activities at the direction of an intelligence service or network of a foreign power, (C) knowingly engages in sabotage or international terrorism on behalf of a foreign power, (D) knowingly enters the United States under a false or fraudulent identity, on behalf of a foreign power, or (E) aids and abets or conspires with any person to engage in prohibited activities enumerated under the statute. §§ 1801(b)(2)(A)-(E). If the FISA target is a United States person, he must act for or on behalf of a foreign power. Thus, a United States national acting as a "lone wolf" terrorist would not be an agent of a foreign power under FISA.

The purpose of obtaining a FISA warrant substantially differs from that required for a traditional wiretap or search warrant. In a traditional situation, a federal judge may issue an *ex parte* order authorizing electronic surveillance if there is probable cause to believe that an individual is committing, has committed, or is about to commit a criminal offense. 18 U.S.C. § 2518(3)(a). By contrast, FISA requires a showing of probable cause to believe that the intended target is a "foreign power" or "agent of a foreign power," and each of the facilities or places to be searched or at which the electronic surveillance is directed, is being used, or is about to be used, by a "foreign power" or "agent of a foreign power." 50 U.S.C. § 1805(a)(2). Further, a "significant purpose" of the FISA electronic surveillance or physical search order must be to obtain "foreign intelligence information." *Id.* § 1804(a)(6)(B). However, there is no requirement that the information sought is evidence of a crime or intended for criminal prosecution.

In enacting FISA, Congress created two new Article III courts—the Foreign Intelligence Surveillance Court (FISC), and the Foreign Intelligence Surveillance Court of Review (FISCR). The FISA authorizes the Chief Justice of the Supreme Court to designate eleven federal district court judges as members of the FISC, "which shall have jurisdiction to hear applications for and grant orders approving electronic surveillance anywhere in the United States," and, in certain circumstances, in foreign countries. *Id.* § 1803(a). The FISC judges sit on a rotating basis holding classified, *ex parte* proceedings in a secure facility located in the federal courthouse in Washington, D.C. Generally, the FISC hears from only one side—the government. Attorneys from the Department of Justice, Office of Intelligence and Policy Review, appear before the FISC to present applications for FISA warrants. However, the USA FREEDOM Act of 2015 amended FISA to authorize the appointment of at least five individuals to serve as amicus curiae to assist in the consideration of any application for a FISA order or review that presents a novel or significant interpretation of the law unless the court finds that such appointment is not necessary.[6] Finally, rulings of the FISC may be appealed to the FISCR, which consists of three federal district court or circuit court of appeals judges, also designated by the Chief Justice of the Supreme Court.

In 2008, Congress enacted the FISA Amendments Act, 50 U.S.C. § 1881a, which authorizes the electronic surveillance of individuals who are not United States persons and are "reasonably believed" to be located outside of the United States. The statute permits electronic surveillance of such non-U.S. persons using either of two procedures. First, electronic surveillance is authorized upon issuance of an order by the FISC. Second, electronic surveillance may be conducted *without* a court order on a determination by the Attorney General and Director of National Intelligence that exigent circumstances exist and "without immediate implementation of an authorization [of electronic surveillance] intelligence important to the national security of the United States may be lost or not timely acquired and time does not permit the issuance of an order . . . prior to the implementation of such authorization." 50 U.S.C. § 1881a(c)(2). In applying for a FISA order under § 1881a, the government is not required to identify the targets of the requested surveillance or establish probable cause to believe that the target is a foreign power or agent of a foreign power. *Id.* § 1881a(d)(1), (i)(3)(A). The government is also not required to identify the specific facilities or places at which the surveillance will occur. *Id.* § 1881a(d)(1), (g)(4), (i)(3)(A). This is a major departure from § 1805(a)(2), which requires the government to establish probable cause to believe that the target of the surveillance is a foreign power or agent of a foreign power, and that each of the facilities or places where the electronic surveillance will be conducted is being used, or is about to be used, by a foreign power or an agent of a foreign power. Finally, in 2015, Congress enacted the USA FREEDOM Act, Pub. L. No. 114-23, 129 Stat. 268, which imposes strict limitations on the collection of telephone metadata.

---

6. USA FREEDOM Act of 2015, Pub. L. No. 114-23, 129 Stat. 268, § 401, codified at 50 U.S.C. § 1803(i)(1).

FISA APPLICATION PROCESS

"An application for electronic surveillance must also contain a 'certification' by the Assistant to the President for National Security Affairs or a designated executive branch official, such as the Director of the FBI. This official must certify: (1) that the information sought is foreign intelligence information; (2) a 'significant purpose' of the surveillance is to obtain foreign intelligence information; and (3) such information cannot 'reasonably be obtained by normal investigative techniques.' The certification must also designate the type of foreign intelligence information being sought using the categories described in § 1801(c)'s definition of 'foreign intelligence information.' Further, the certifying official must include a statement of the basis for the certification that '(i) the information sought is the type of foreign intelligence information designated; and (ii) such information could not reasonably be obtained by normal investigative techniques.'

Each application must also contain a statement of the means by which the surveillance will be conducted, the period of time for which the electronic surveillance is required, and whether any previous applications have been made to any judges involving any of the persons, facilities, or places specified in the application as well as the action taken on each previous application. Finally, such application must be approved by the Attorney General, the Deputy Attorney General, or upon designation of the Attorney General, the Assistant Attorney General for National Security."

GEOFFREY CORN ET AL., NATIONAL SECURITY LAW — PRINCIPLES AND POLICY 206 (2015).

The critics of FISA maintain that the statutory scheme affords the government unfettered power to seize personal information unrelated to protecting national security. Moreover, they claim that FISA provides insufficient procedural safeguards to prevent the government from encroaching on important civil liberties, including freedom of speech and association, and the ban on unreasonable search and seizure. While plaintiffs have raised numerous legal challenges to FISA, they have been largely unsuccessful in prevailing on their claims. The next section analyzes some of the more prominent legal issues implicated by FISA, beginning with standing. Finally, the chapter examines the constitutionality of the government's bulk collection telephone metadata program.

B. Legal Challenges to FISA

1. Standing

In order to reach the merits of a constitutional challenge to a FISA order, the court must first determine whether plaintiffs have standing to bring such cause of action. To establish standing, an injury must be "concrete, particularized, and actual or imminent; fairly traceable to the challenged action; and redressable by a favorable ruling." *Monsanto Co. v. Geertson Seed Farms*, 561 U.S. 139, 140 (2010). However, because the FISA application process is secretive in nature and generally the government is not required to give notice to the target of a FISA order, plaintiffs have struggled to prove that their telephone and cell phone calls have been monitored by the government. Further, the absence of proof that plaintiffs were the actual target of a FISA order seriously undermines their claims of injury for purposes of establishing standing. In *Clapper v. Amnesty International, USA*, 568 U.S. 398 (2013), respondents challenged the constitutionality of 50 U.S.C. § 1881a. Respondents claimed that they could establish injury in fact because there was an objectively reasonable likelihood that their communications would be intercepted by the government under FISA at some point in the future. In a five-four decision, the Supreme Court disagreed, finding that respondents failed to show that they suffered some actual or threatened injury as a result of the government's conduct, and therefore they lacked standing.

Clapper v. Amnesty International, USA
568 U.S. 398 (2013)

Justice ALITO delivered the opinion of the Court.

Section 702 of the Foreign Intelligence Surveillance Act of 1978, 50 U.S.C. § 1881a (2006 ed., Supp. V), allows the Attorney General and the Director of National Intelligence to acquire foreign intelligence information by jointly authorizing the surveillance of individuals who are not "United States persons" and are reasonably believed to be located outside the United States. Before doing so, the Attorney General and the Director of National Intelligence normally must obtain the Foreign Intelligence Surveillance Court's approval. Respondents are United States persons whose work, they allege, requires them to engage in sensitive international communications with individuals who they believe are likely targets of surveillance under § 1881a. Respondents seek a declaration that § 1881a is unconstitutional, as well as an injunction against § 1881a-authorized surveillance. The question before us is whether respondents have Article III standing to seek this prospective relief.

. . .

I

A

In 1978, after years of debate, Congress enacted the Foreign Intelligence Surveillance Act (FISA) to authorize and regulate certain governmental electronic surveillance of communications for foreign intelligence purposes. In enacting FISA, Congress legislated against the backdrop of our decision in *United States v. United States Dist. Court for Eastern Dist. of Mich.*, 407 U.S. 297 (1972) (*Keith*), in which we explained that the standards and procedures that law enforcement officials must follow when conducting "surveillance of 'ordinary crime'" might not be required in the context of surveillance conducted for domestic national-security purposes. *Id.*, at 322-323. Although the *Keith* opinion expressly disclaimed any ruling "on the scope of the President's surveillance power with respect to the activities of foreign powers," *id.*, at 308, it implicitly suggested that a special framework for foreign intelligence surveillance might be constitutionally permissible.

In constructing such a framework for foreign intelligence surveillance, Congress created two specialized courts. In FISA, Congress authorized judges of the Foreign Intelligence Surveillance Court (FISC) to approve electronic surveillance for foreign intelligence purposes if there is probable cause to believe that "the target of the electronic surveillance is a foreign power or an agent of a foreign power," and that each of the specific "facilities or places at which the electronic surveillance is directed is being used, or is about to be used, by a foreign power or an agent of a foreign power." § 105(a)(3), 92 Stat. 1790; see § 105(b)(1)(A), (b)(1)(B). Additionally, Congress vested the Foreign Intelligence Surveillance Court of Review with jurisdiction to review any denials by the FISC of applications for electronic surveillance.

In the wake of the September 11th attacks, President George W. Bush authorized the National Security Agency (NSA) to conduct warrantless wiretapping of telephone and e-mail communications where one party to the communication was located outside the United States and a participant in "the call was reasonably believed to be a member or agent of al Qaeda or an affiliated terrorist organization," App. to Pet. for Cert. 403a. In January 2007, the FISC issued orders authorizing the Government to target international communications into or out of the United States where there was probable cause to believe that one participant to the communication was a member or agent of al Qaeda or an associated terrorist organization. These FISC orders subjected any electronic surveillance that was then occurring under the NSA's program to the approval of the FISC. After a FISC Judge subsequently narrowed the FISC's authorization of such surveillance, however, the Executive asked Congress to amend FISA so that it would provide the intelligence community with additional authority to meet the challenges of modern technology and international terrorism.

When Congress enacted the FISA Amendments Act of 2008 (FISA Amendments Act), it left much of FISA intact, but it "established a new and independent source of intelligence collection authority, beyond that granted in traditional FISA." 1 Kris & Wilson § 9:11, at 349-350. As relevant here, § 702 of FISA, 50 U.S.C. § 1881a (2006 ed., Supp. V), which was enacted as part of the FISA Amendments Act, supplements pre-existing FISA authority by creating a new framework under which the Government may seek the FISC's authorization of certain foreign intelligence surveillance targeting the communications of non-U.S. persons located abroad. Unlike traditional FISA surveillance, § 1881a does not require the Government to demonstrate probable cause that the target of the electronic surveillance is a foreign power or agent of a foreign power. And, unlike traditional FISA, § 1881a does not require the Government to specify the nature and location of each of the particular facilities or places at which the electronic surveillance will occur.

The present case involves a constitutional challenge to § 1881a. Surveillance under § 1881a is subject to statutory conditions, judicial authorization, congressional supervision, and compliance with the Fourth Amendment. Section 1881a provides that, upon the issuance of an order from the Foreign Intelligence Surveillance Court, "the Attorney General and the Director of National Intelligence may authorize jointly, for a period of up to 1 year . . . , the targeting of persons reasonably believed to be located outside the United States to acquire foreign intelligence information." § 1881a(a). Surveillance under § 1881a may not be intentionally targeted at any person known to be in the United States or any U.S. person reasonably believed to be located abroad. § 1881a(b)(1)-(3); see also § 1801(i). Additionally, acquisitions under § 1881a must comport with the Fourth Amendment. § 1881a(b)(5). Moreover, surveillance under § 1881a is subject to congressional oversight and several types of Executive Branch review.

Section 1881a mandates that the Government obtain the Foreign Intelligence Surveillance Court's approval of "targeting" procedures, "minimization" procedures, and a governmental certification regarding proposed surveillance. § 1881a(a), (c)(1), (i)(2), (i)(3). Among other things, the Government's certification must attest that (1) procedures are in place "that have been approved, have been submitted for approval, or will be submitted with the certification for approval by the [FISC] that are reasonably designed" to ensure that an acquisition is "limited to targeting persons reasonably believed to be located outside" the United States; (2) minimization procedures adequately restrict the acquisition, retention, and dissemination of nonpublic information about unconsenting U.S. persons, as appropriate; (3) guidelines have been adopted to ensure compliance with targeting limits and the Fourth Amendment; and (4) the procedures and guidelines referred to above comport with the Fourth Amendment. § 1881a(g)(2); see § 1801(h).

The Foreign Intelligence Surveillance Court's role includes determining whether the Government's certification contains the required elements. Additionally, the Court assesses whether the targeting procedures are "reasonably designed" (1) to "ensure that an acquisition . . . is limited to targeting persons reasonably believed to be located outside the United States" and (2) to "prevent the intentional acquisition of any communication as to which the sender and all intended recipients are known . . . to be located in the United States." § 1881a(i)(2)(B). The Court analyzes whether the minimization procedures "meet the definition of minimization procedures under section 1801(h) . . ., as appropriate." § 1881a(i)(2)(C). The Court also assesses whether the targeting and minimization procedures are consistent with the statute and the Fourth Amendment.

B

Respondents are attorneys and human rights, labor, legal, and media organizations whose work allegedly requires them to engage in sensitive and sometimes privileged telephone and e-mail communications with colleagues, clients, sources, and other individuals located abroad. Respondents believe that some of the people with whom they exchange foreign intelligence information are likely targets of surveillance under § 1881a. Specifically, respondents claim that they communicate by telephone and e-mail with people the Government "believes or believed to be associated with terrorist organizations," "people located in geographic areas that are a special focus" of the Government's counterterrorism or diplomatic efforts, and activists who oppose governments that are supported by the United States Government. App. to Pet. for Cert. 399a.

Respondents claim that § 1881a compromises their ability to locate witnesses, cultivate sources, obtain information, and communicate confidential information to their clients. Respondents also assert that they "have ceased engaging" in certain telephone and e-mail conversations. *Id.*, at 400a. According to respondents, the threat of surveillance will compel them to travel abroad in order to have in-person conversations. In addition, respondents declare that they have undertaken "costly and burdensome measures" to protect the confidentiality of sensitive communications. *Ibid.*

C

On the day when the FISA Amendments Act was enacted, respondents filed this action seeking (1) a declaration that § 1881a, on its face, violates the Fourth Amendment, the First Amendment, Article III, and separation-of-powers principles and (2) a permanent injunction against the use of § 1881a. Respondents assert what they characterize as two separate theories of Article III standing. First, they claim that there is an objectively reasonable likelihood that their communications will be acquired under § 1881a at some point in the future, thus causing them injury. Second, respondents maintain that the risk of surveillance under § 1881a is so substantial that they have been forced to take costly and burdensome measures to protect the confidentiality of their international communications; in their view, the costs they have incurred constitute present injury that is fairly traceable to § 1881a.

After both parties moved for summary judgment, the District Court held that respondents do not have standing. On appeal, however, a panel of the Second Circuit reversed. The panel agreed with respondents' argument that they have standing due to the objectively reasonable likelihood that their communications will be intercepted at some time in the future. In addition, the panel held that respondents have established that they are suffering "*present* injuries in fact—economic and professional harms—stemming from a reasonable fear of *future* harmful government conduct." The Second Circuit denied rehearing en banc by an equally divided vote.

Because of the importance of the issue and the novel view of standing adopted by the Court of Appeals, we granted certiorari, and we now reverse.

II

. . .

To establish Article III standing, an injury must be "concrete, particularized, and actual or imminent; fairly traceable to the challenged action; and redressable by a favorable ruling." *Monsanto Co. v. Geertson Seed Farms*, 561 U.S. 139,

140 (2010). "Although imminence is concededly a somewhat elastic concept, it cannot be stretched beyond its purpose, which is to ensure that the alleged injury is not too speculative for Article III purposes—that the injury is *certainly* impending." *Summers v. Earth Island Institute*, 555 U.S. 488, 565 (2009). Thus, we have repeatedly reiterated that "threatened injury must be *certainly impending* to constitute injury in fact," and that "[a]llegations of *possible* future injury" are not sufficient. *Whitmore*, 495 U.S. at 158 (emphasis added; internal quotation marks omitted).

III

A

Respondents assert that they can establish injury in fact that is fairly traceable to § 1881a because there is an objectively reasonable likelihood that their communications with their foreign contacts will be intercepted under § 1881a at some point in the future. This argument fails. As an initial matter, the Second Circuit's "objectively reasonable likelihood" standard is inconsistent with our requirement that "threatened injury must be certainly impending to constitute injury in fact." *Whitmore, supra*, at 158. Furthermore, respondents' argument rests on their highly speculative fear that: (1) the Government will decide to target the communications of non-U.S. persons with whom they communicate; (2) in doing so, the Government will choose to invoke its authority under § 1881a rather than utilizing another method of surveillance; (3) the Article III judges who serve on the Foreign Intelligence Surveillance Court will conclude that the Government's proposed surveillance procedures satisfy § 1881a's many safeguards and are consistent with the Fourth Amendment; (4) the Government will succeed in intercepting the communications of respondents' contacts; and (5) respondents will be parties to the particular communications that the Government intercepts. As discussed below, respondents' theory of standing, which relies on a highly attenuated chain of possibilities, does not satisfy the requirement that threatened injury must be certainly impending. Moreover, even if respondents could demonstrate injury in fact, the second link in the above-described chain of contingencies—which amounts to mere speculation about whether surveillance would be under § 1881a or some other authority—shows that respondents cannot satisfy the requirement that any injury in fact must be fairly traceable to § 1881a.

First, it is speculative whether the Government will imminently target communications to which respondents are parties. Section 1881a expressly provides that respondents, who are U.S. persons, cannot be targeted for surveillance under § 1881a. Accordingly, it is no surprise that respondents fail to offer any evidence that their communications have been monitored under § 1881a, a failure that substantially undermines their standing theory. Indeed, respondents do not even allege that the Government has sought the FISC's approval for surveillance of their communications. Accordingly, respondents' theory necessarily rests on their assertion that the Government will target *other individuals*—namely, their foreign contacts.

Yet respondents have no actual knowledge of the Government's § 1881a targeting practices. Instead, respondents merely speculate and make assumptions about whether their communications with their foreign contacts will be acquired under § 1881a. . . . "The party invoking federal jurisdiction bears the burden of establishing" standing—and, at the summary judgment stage, such a party "can no longer rest on . . . 'mere allegations,' but must 'set forth' by affidavit or other evidence 'specific facts.'" *Defenders of Wildlife*, 504 U.S., at 561. Respondents, however, have set forth no specific facts demonstrating that the communications of their foreign contacts will be targeted. Moreover, because § 1881a at most *authorizes*—but does not *mandate* or *direct*—the surveillance that respondents fear, respondents' allegations are necessarily conjectural. Simply put, respondents can only speculate as to how the Attorney General and the Director of National Intelligence will exercise their discretion in determining which communications to target.

Second, even if respondents could demonstrate that the targeting of their foreign contacts is imminent, respondents can only speculate as to whether the Government will seek to use § 1881a-authorized surveillance (rather than other methods) to do so. The Government has numerous other methods of conducting surveillance, none of which is challenged here. Even after the enactment of the FISA Amendments Act, for example, the Government may still conduct electronic surveillance of persons abroad under the older provisions of FISA so long as it satisfies the applicable requirements, including a demonstration of probable cause to believe that the person is a foreign power or agent of a foreign power. The Government may also obtain information from the intelligence services of foreign nations. And, although we do not reach the question, the Government contends that it can conduct FISA-exempt human and technical surveillance programs that are governed by Executive Order 12333. Even if respondents could demonstrate that their foreign contacts will imminently be targeted—indeed, even if they could show that interception of their own communications will imminently occur—they would still need to show that their injury is fairly traceable to § 1881a. But, because respondents can only speculate as to whether any (asserted) interception would be under § 1881a or some other authority, they cannot satisfy the "fairly traceable" requirement.

Third, even if respondents could show that the Government will seek the Foreign Intelligence Surveillance Court's authorization to acquire the communications of respondents' foreign contacts under § 1881a, respondents can only speculate as to whether that court will authorize such surveillance. In the past, we have been reluctant to endorse standing theories that require guesswork as to how independent decisionmakers will exercise their judgment. . . .

We decline to abandon our usual reluctance to endorse standing theories that rest on speculation about the decisions of independent actors. Section 1881a mandates that the Government must obtain the Foreign Intelligence Surveillance Court's approval of targeting procedures, minimization procedures, and a governmental certification regarding proposed surveillance. § 1881a(a), (c)(1), (i)(2), (i)(3). The Court must, for example, determine whether the Government's procedures are "reasonably designed . . . to minimize the acquisition and retention, and prohibit the dissemination, of nonpublicly available information concerning unconsenting United States persons." § 1801(h); see § 1881a(i)(2), (i)(3)(A). And, critically, the Court must also assess whether the Government's targeting and minimization procedures comport with the Fourth Amendment. § 1881a(i)(3)(A).

Fourth, even if the Government were to obtain the Foreign Intelligence Surveillance Court's approval to target respondents' foreign contacts under § 1881a, it is unclear whether the Government would succeed in acquiring the communications of respondents' foreign contacts. And fifth, even if the Government were to conduct surveillance of respondents' foreign contacts, respondents can only speculate as to whether *their own communications* with their foreign contacts would be incidentally acquired.

In sum, respondents' speculative chain of possibilities does not establish that injury based on potential future surveillance is certainly impending or is fairly traceable to § 1881a.

B

Respondents' alternative argument—namely, that they can establish standing based on the measures that they have undertaken to avoid § 1881a-authorized surveillance—fares no better. Respondents assert that they are suffering ongoing injuries that are fairly traceable to § 1881a because the risk of surveillance under § 1881a requires them to take costly and burdensome measures to protect the confidentiality of their communications. Respondents claim, for instance, that the threat of surveillance sometimes compels them to avoid certain e-mail and phone conversations, to "tal[k] in generalities rather than specifics," or to travel so that they can have in-person conversations. Tr. of Oral Arg. 38. The Second Circuit panel concluded that, because respondents are already suffering such ongoing injuries, the likelihood of interception under § 1881a is relevant only to the question whether respondents' ongoing injuries are "fairly traceable" to § 1881a. See 638 F.3d, at 133-134; 667 F.3d, at 180 (opinion of Raggi, J.). Analyzing the "fairly traceable" element of standing under a relaxed reasonableness standard, see 638 F.3d, at 133-134, the Second Circuit then held that "plaintiffs have established that they suffered *present* injuries in fact—economic and professional harms—stemming from a reasonable fear of *future* harmful government conduct," *id.*, at 138.

The Second Circuit's analysis improperly allowed respondents to establish standing by asserting that they suffer present costs and burdens that are based on a fear of surveillance, so long as that fear is not "fanciful, paranoid, or otherwise unreasonable." See *id.*, at 134. This improperly waters down the fundamental requirements of Article III. Respondents' contention that they have standing because they incurred certain costs as a reasonable reaction to a risk of harm is unavailing—because the harm respondents seek to avoid is not certainly impending. In other words, respondents cannot manufacture standing merely by inflicting harm on themselves based on their fears of hypothetical future harm that is not certainly impending. Any ongoing injuries that respondents are suffering are not fairly traceable to § 1881a.

If the law were otherwise, an enterprising plaintiff would be able to secure a lower standard for Article III standing simply by making an expenditure based on a nonparanoid fear. As Judge Raggi accurately noted, under the Second Circuit panel's reasoning, respondents could, "for the price of a plane ticket, . . . transform their standing burden from one requiring a showing of actual or imminent . . . interception to one requiring a showing that their subjective fear of such interception is not fanciful, irrational, or clearly unreasonable." 667 F.3d, at 180 (internal quotation marks omitted). Thus, allowing respondents to bring this action based on costs they incurred in response to a speculative threat would be tantamount to accepting a repackaged version of respondents' first failed theory of standing. . . .

Because respondents do not face a threat of certainly impending interception under § 1881a, the costs that they have incurred to avoid surveillance are simply the product of their fear of surveillance, and our decision in *Laird* makes it clear that such a fear is insufficient to create standing. See 408 U.S., at 10-15. The plaintiffs in *Laird* argued that their exercise of First Amendment rights was being "chilled by the mere existence, without more, of [the Army's] investigative and data-gathering activity." *Id.*, at 10. While acknowledging that prior cases had held that constitutional violations may arise from the chilling effect of "regulations that fall short of a direct prohibition against the exercise of First Amendment rights," the Court declared that none of those cases involved a "chilling effect aris[ing] merely from the individual's knowledge that a governmental agency was engaged in certain activities or from the individual's concomitant fear that, armed with the fruits of those activities, the agency might in the future take some *other* and additional action detrimental to that individual." *Id.*, at 11. Because "[a]llegations of a subjective 'chill' are not an adequate substitute for a claim of specific present objective harm or a threat of specific future harm," *id.*, at 13-14, the plaintiffs in *Laird*—and respondents here—lack standing.

For the reasons discussed above, respondents' self-inflicted injuries are not fairly traceable to the Government's purported activities under § 1881a, and their subjective fear of surveillance does not give rise to standing.

IV

. . .

B

Respondents also suggest that they should be held to have standing because otherwise the constitutionality of § 1881a could not be challenged. It would be wrong, they maintain, to "insulate the government's surveillance activities from meaningful judicial review." Brief for Respondents 60. Respondents' suggestion is both legally and factually incorrect. First, "'[t]he assumption that if respondents have no standing to sue, no one would have standing, is not a reason to find standing.'" *Valley Forge Christian College*, 454 U.S., at 489; *Schlesinger*, 418 U.S., at 227.

Second, our holding today by no means insulates § 1881a from judicial review. As described above, Congress created a comprehensive scheme in which the Foreign Intelligence Surveillance Court evaluates the Government's certifications, targeting procedures, and minimization procedures — including assessing whether the targeting and minimization procedures comport with the Fourth Amendment. § 1881a(a), (c)(1), (i)(2), (i)(3). Any dissatisfaction that respondents may have about the Foreign Intelligence Surveillance Court's rulings — or the congressional delineation of that court's role — is irrelevant to our standing analysis.

Additionally, if the Government intends to use or disclose information obtained or derived from a § 1881a acquisition in judicial or administrative proceedings, it must provide advance notice of its intent, and the affected person may challenge the lawfulness of the acquisition. §§ 1806(c), 1806(e), 1881e(a) (2006 ed. and Supp. V). Thus, if the Government were to prosecute one of respondent-attorney's foreign clients using § 1881a-authorized surveillance, the Government would be required to make a disclosure.

Although the foreign client might not have a viable Fourth Amendment claim, it is possible that the monitoring of the target's conversations with his or her attorney would provide grounds for a claim of standing on the part of the attorney. Such an attorney would certainly have a stronger evidentiary basis for establishing standing than do respondents in the present case. In such a situation, unlike in the present case, it would at least be clear that the Government had acquired the foreign client's communications using § 1881a-authorized surveillance.

Finally, any electronic communications service provider that the Government directs to assist in § 1881a surveillance may challenge the lawfulness of that directive before the FISC. § 1881a(h)(4), (6). Indeed, at the behest of a service provider, the Foreign Intelligence Surveillance Court of Review previously analyzed the constitutionality of electronic surveillance directives issued pursuant to a now-expired set of FISA amendments. See *In re Directives Pursuant to Section 105B of Foreign Intelligence Surveillance Act*, 551 F.3d 1004, 1006-1016 (2008) (holding that the provider had standing and that the directives were constitutional).

. . .

We hold that respondents lack Article III standing because they cannot demonstrate that the future injury they purportedly fear is certainly impending and because they cannot manufacture standing by incurring costs in anticipation of non-imminent harm. We therefore reverse the judgment of the Second Circuit and remand the case for further proceedings consistent with this opinion.

NOTES AND QUESTIONS

1. To establish standing, an injury must be "concrete, particularized, and actual or *imminent*; fairly traceable to the challenged action; and redressable by a favorable ruling." *Monsanto Co. v. Geertson Seed Farms*, 561 U.S. 139, 140 (2010) (emphasis added). In *Amnesty International*, the majority states that "[a]lthough imminence is concededly a somewhat elastic concept, it cannot be stretched beyond its purpose, which is to ensure that the alleged injury is not speculative for Article III purposes—that the injury is *certainly* impending." What does "certainly impending" mean? Were respondents threatened with a "certainly impending" injury? If not, why not?

2. What is the scope of the Court's holding in *Amnesty International*? Generally, to establish standing an injury must be "concrete, particularized, and actual or *imminent*." *Monsanto Co.*, 561 U.S. at 140 (emphasis added). Must plaintiffs prove that they were actually the target of a FISA warrant and suffered injury? Does the majority require proof of actual injury caused by the issuance of a FISA warrant? Because the FISA application process is secretive in nature and generally the government is not required to give notice to the affected person, how difficult will it be to prove standing after *Amnesty International*?

3. *Terrorist finance tracking program.* The courts are divided on whether bank customers have standing to challenge the legality of administrative subpoenas issued by the Treasury Department to the Society for Worldwide Interbank Financial Telecommunication (SWIFT), pursuant to the Terrorist Financing Tracking Program. *See Amidax Trading Group v. S.W.I.F.T. SCRL*, 671 F.3d 140 (2d Cir. 2011) (action was dismissed for lack of standing, plaintiff's alleged injury was merely "hypothetical and conjectural"). *But see Walker v. S.W.I.F.T. SCRL*, 491 F. Supp. 2d 781 (N.D. Ill. 2007) (customers of financial institutions who filed proposed class action against international cooperative consortium that owned database for global banking industry, alleging that consortium violated their constitutional rights when it disclosed certain financial records to U.S. counterterrorism officials, sufficiently alleged standing; "general factual allegations of injury resulting from the defendant's conduct may suffice") (quoting *Lujan v. Defenders of Wildlife*, 504 U.S. 555, 561 (1992)).

4. In *Amnesty International*, Justice Alito, writing for the majority, claims that "even if respondents could show that the Government will seek the Foreign Intelligence Surveillance Court's authorization to acquire the communications of respondents' foreign contacts under § 1881a, respondents can only speculate as to whether that court will authorize such surveillance." How often does the FISC grant the government's application for a FISA order? Annual reports submitted by the government to Congress on the number of warrants issued under FISA reveal that the FISC almost always grants the government's FISA applications. Do these congressional reports undermine the majority's argument that whether the FISC will approve the government's electronic surveillance application is speculative?

5. Does the majority's ruling "insulate the government's surveillance activities from meaningful judicial review"? The majority rejected this claim, stating that if the government intends to use any evidence derived from a FISA warrant in a criminal prosecution, the defendant could seek to suppress the use of the evidence. If

the government intends to use information obtained or derived from electronic surveillance, physical search, or the use of pen registers or trap and trace devices, prior notice must be given to the "aggrieved person" against whom the information is to be used. Upon receipt of such notice, an aggrieved person may seek to suppress the use of the FISA-derived evidence on the grounds that the evidence was unlawfully acquired or the government did not act in conformity with the relevant FISA order. Further, pursuant to 50 U.S.C. §§ 1806(f) (electronic surveillance), 1825(g) (physical search), and 1845(f) (pen register or trap and trace device), the defendant may move to compel disclosure of FISA materials, including the FISA applications, affidavits, court orders, and extensions, as well as any other documents related to the FISA surveillance, search, pen register, or trap and trace order.

However, if the defendant moves to compel disclosure of FISA evidence, the Attorney General may oppose such request by filing an affidavit stating that the disclosure "would harm the national security of the United States." 50 U.S.C. §§ 1806(f), 1825(g), 1845(f). Upon filing such an affidavit, the district court must conduct an *in camera* and *ex parte* review of the FISA warrant application and related materials to determine whether the surveillance was "lawfully authorized and conducted." *Id.* After an *in camera* review, the district court has discretion to disclose portions of the documents "only where such disclosure is necessary to make an accurate determination of the legality of the surveillance [or physical search or use of the pen register or trap and trace device]." *Id.* However, to date, no court has found it necessary to disclose FISA materials to make a determination of the lawfulness of FISA warrant. The courts uniformly hold that FISA's *in camera* review procedures afford a defendant adequate due process. Do you agree? Do the FISA procedures described above afford the aggrieved person "meaningful judicial review"?

"LONE WOLF" TERRORIST

"In 2004, Congress amended FISA to expand the government's authority to conduct electronic surveillance and physical searches of suspected international terrorists. Commonly referred to as the 'lone wolf' amendment, section 6001(a) of the Intelligence Reform and Terrorism Prevention Act (IRTPA), broadened the definition of an 'agent of a foreign power' to include any non-U.S. person who 'engages in international terrorism or activities in preparation therefor. . . .'

Prior to the 'lone wolf' amendment, FISA authorized the FISC to approve applications for physical searches only if probable cause existed to believe that the premises to be searched were owned or controlled by a foreign power or its agent. . . . The 'lone wolf' provision eliminates any need to provide an evidentiary connection between the target of a FISA application and a foreign government or terrorist organization. The proponents of the provision contend that 'the increased self-organization among terror networks has made proving connections to identifiable groups more difficult. Thus, a "lone wolf" provision is necessary to combat terrorists who use a modern organizational structure or who are self-radicalized.'"

JIMMY GURULÉ & GEOFFREY S. CORN, PRINCIPLES OF COUNTER-TERRORISM LAW 217-18 (2011).

2. Fourth Amendment Challenges

Section 215 of the USA PATRIOT Act, codified at 50 U.S.C. § 1861, authorizes the production of business records and other "tangible things" to protect against international terrorism or clandestine intelligence activities. In 2005, Congress amended the statute to require that the FBI's application seeking an order from the FISC include a statement of facts showing that there are reasonable grounds to believe that the tangible things sought are *relevant* to an "authorized investigation," which includes a foreign intelligence, international terrorism, or espionage investigation. *Id.* § 1861(b)(2)(A).[7]

Beginning in 2006, the FBI and NSA relied on § 215 to compel the production of "telephony metadata" of over 300 million Americans. Under the NSA's bulk telephone metadata program, electronic communication service providers are required to turn over "call detail information" created by their subscribers on an ongoing daily basis. "Call detail information" includes "any information that pertains to the transmission of specific telephone calls, including . . . the number called . . . the number from which [a] call was placed and the time, location, or duration of any call." 47 C.F.R. § 64.2003(d) (2012). However, the requested telephone metadata does not include any information about the content of those calls. The NSA collects the telephone metadata of these telecommunication providers, compiles the requested information into a massive database, stores it for five years, and analyzes it.

The government maintains that the bulk collection of telephone metadata is necessary to detect whether known or suspected terrorists are communicating with persons inside the United States. The database is queried using telephone identifiers associated with suspected terrorists or terrorist organizations. The terrorist-related number is run through the telephone metadata base to see whether the number has called or received calls from any of the telephone numbers in the database.

The government and the FISC broadly construed the statutory requirement that the production of tangible things be "relevant" to a terrorism investigation. According to the government, if the requested information could at some point conceivably lead to other information that directly bears on a terrorism investigation, such information is "relevant" for purposes of § 215. Therefore, because the bulk collection of telephone metadata could potentially lead to identifying persons calling or receiving calls from suspected terrorists, all such metadata is "relevant" to a terrorism investigation. Further, the government adopted an expansive construction of the term "authorized investigation," which encompasses the global War on Terrorism. Because the government is investigating al Qaeda and its affiliated members, the collection of telephone metadata is relevant to that "authorized investigation." As a result, the government is not required to prove that the requested telephone records are relevant to a specific terrorism investigation involving identified individuals plotting a specific terrorist attack.

---

7. Editors' Note: On March 15, 2020, section 215, as well as the "lone wolf" and roving wiretap provisions of FISA, expired pursuant to a sunset provision. These provisions were allowed to expire because Congress was unable to reach agreement on a broader set of reforms to FISA. However, these authorities remain available for either investigations open at the time of the expiration or investigations predicated on conduct that predated the sunset date.

The critics of the telephone metadata program maintain that it is unlawful on two grounds. First, the text of § 215 does not support the government's expansive reading of the statute, and therefore the program violates the statute. Second, the collection of bulk telephone metadata on an ongoing, daily basis constitutes an unreasonable seizure in violation of the Fourth Amendment. In *American Civil Liberties Union v. Clapper*, 785 F.3d 787, 821 (2d Cir. 2015), the court rejected the government's expansive reading of § 215, holding that "the text of § 215 cannot bear the weight the government asks us to assign it, and . . . does not authorize the metadata program." However, while the court overturned the government's telephone metadata program on statutory grounds, it failed to decide whether the collection of telephone metadata under FISA violates the Fourth Amendment. The Second Circuit left open the question of whether an individual has a legitimate expectation of privacy in telephone metadata.

In 2015, Congress addressed the statutory violation argument by enacting the USA FREEDOM Act, Pub. L. No. 114-23, 129 Stat. 268. The Act prohibits the NSA's controversial bulk collection of metadata based on a claim that the information is necessary to identify communications between suspected terrorists and persons located in the United States sometime in the future. More specifically, the 2015 amendments require the FBI, in applications for ongoing production of call detail records to protect against international terrorism, to show (1) reasonable grounds to believe that the call detail records are relevant to such investigation; and (2) reasonable articulable suspicion that the "specific selection term" or telephone number being queried is associated with a foreign power or an agent of a foreign power engaged in international terrorism, or related preparatory activities. *Id.* § 101. Under the USA FREEDOM Act, the collection of telephone metadata must be linked to a foreign power or agent of a foreign power engaged in international terrorism or preparatory acts of terrorism.

In *In re Application of the Federal Bureau of Investigation for an Order Requiring the Production of Tangible Things*, Amended Memorandum Opinion, No. BR 12-109, at 9 (FISC, Aug. 29, 2013), the FISC held that the collection of telephone metadata did not violate the Fourth Amendment. Relying on *Smith v. Maryland*, 442 U.S. 735 (1979), the FISC found that there is no reasonable expectation of privacy in telephone metadata. In *Smith*, the Supreme Court articulated the third-party records doctrine, finding that once a person has voluntarily transmitted information to a third party (in this case, a cell phone service provider), the person "has no legitimate expectation of privacy in [the] information. . . ." *Id.* at 744. However, the viability of the third-party records doctrine and its application to the collection of telephone metadata remains an open issue.

In March 2019, complex technical glitches in the bulk telephone metadata program were discovered causing the NSA to shut it down. *Disputed NSA Phone Program Is Shut Down, Aide Says,* N.Y. Times (March 4, 2019). However, there are concerns that NSA could revive the controversial telephone metadata program in the future or collect telephone metadata on a smaller scale raising important Fourth Amendment privacy issues.

a. The Third-Party Records Doctrine

Smith v. Maryland
442 U.S. 735 (1979)

Mr. Justice BLACKMUN delivered the opinion of the Court.

This case presents the question whether the installation and use of a pen register constitutes a "search" within the meaning of the Fourth Amendment, made applicable to the States through the Fourteenth Amendment.

I

On March 5, 1976, in Baltimore, Md., Patricia McDonough was robbed. She gave the police a description of the robber and of a 1975 Monte Carlo automobile she had observed near the scene of the crime. After the robbery, McDonough began receiving threatening and obscene phone calls from a man identifying himself as the robber. On one occasion, the caller asked that she step out on her front porch; she did so, and saw the 1975 Monte Carlo she had earlier described to police moving slowly past her home. On March 16, police spotted a man who met McDonough's description driving a 1975 Monte Carlo in her neighborhood. By tracing the license plate number, police learned that the car was registered in the name of petitioner, Michael Lee Smith.

The next day, the telephone company, at police request, installed a pen register at its central offices to record the numbers dialed from the telephone at petitioner's home. The police did not get a warrant or court order before having the pen register installed. The register revealed that on March 17 a call was placed from petitioner's home to McDonough's phone. On the basis of this and other evidence, the police obtained a warrant to search petitioner's residence. The search revealed that a page in petitioner's phone book was turned down to the name and number of Patricia McDonough; the phone book was seized. Petitioner was arrested, and a six-man lineup was held on March 19. McDonough identified petitioner as the man who had robbed her.

Petitioner was indicted in the Criminal Court of Baltimore for robbery. By pretrial motion, he sought to suppress "all fruits derived from the pen register" on the ground that the police had failed to secure a warrant prior to its installation. The trial court denied the suppression motion, holding that the warrantless installation of the pen register did not violate the Fourth Amendment. Petitioner then waived a jury, and the case was submitted to the court on an agreed statement of facts. The pen register tape (evidencing the fact that a phone call had been made from petitioner's phone to McDonough's phone) and the phone book seized in the search of petitioner's residence were admitted into evidence against him. Petitioner was convicted and was sentenced to six years. He appealed to the Maryland Court of Special Appeals, but the Court of Appeals of Maryland issued a writ of certiorari to the intermediate court in advance of its decision in order to consider whether the pen register evidence had been properly admitted at petitioner's trial. 389 A.2d 858, 860 (1978).

The Court of Appeals affirmed the judgment of conviction, holding that "there is no constitutionally protected reasonable expectation of privacy in the numbers dialed into a telephone system and hence no search within the fourth amendment is implicated by the use of a pen register installed at the central offices of the telephone company." 389 A.2d, at 867. Because there was no "search," the court concluded, no warrant was needed. Three judges dissented, expressing the view that individuals do have a legitimate expectation of privacy regarding the phone numbers they dial from their homes; that the installation of a pen register thus constitutes a "search"; and that, in the absence of exigent circumstances, the failure of police to secure a warrant mandated that the pen register evidence here be excluded. Certiorari was granted in order to resolve indications of conflict in the decided cases as to the restrictions imposed by the Fourth Amendment on the use of pen registers.

II

A

The Fourth Amendment guarantees "[t]he right of the people to be secure in their persons, houses, papers, and effects, against unreasonable searches and seizures." In determining whether a particular form of government-initiated electronic surveillance is a "search" within the meaning of the Fourth Amendment, our lodestar is *Katz v. United States*, 389 U.S. 347 (1967). In *Katz*, Government agents had intercepted the contents of a telephone conversation by attaching an electronic listening device to the outside of a public phone booth. The Court rejected the argument that a "search" can occur only when there has been a "physical intrusion" into a "constitutionally protected area," noting that the Fourth Amendment "protects people, not places." *Id.*, at 351-353. Because the Government's monitoring of Katz' conversation "violated the privacy upon which he justifiably relied while using the telephone booth," the Court held that it "constituted a 'search and seizure' within the meaning of the Fourth Amendment." *Id.*, at 353.

Consistently with *Katz*, this Court uniformly has held that the application of the Fourth Amendment depends on whether the person invoking its protection can claim a "justifiable," a "reasonable," or a "legitimate expectation of privacy" that has been invaded by government action. *E.g., Rakas v. Illinois*, 439 U.S. 128, 143, and n.12 (1978); *id.*, at 150, 151 (concurring opinion); *id.*, at 164 (dissenting opinion). . . . This inquiry, as Mr. Justice Harlan aptly noted in his *Katz* concurrence, normally embraces two discrete questions. The first is whether the individual, by his conduct, has "exhibited an actual (subjective) expectation of privacy," 389 U.S., at 361 — whether, in the words of the *Katz* majority, the individual has shown that "he seeks to preserve [something] as private." *Id.*, at 351. The second question is whether the individual's subjective expectation of privacy is "one that society is prepared to recognize as 'reasonable,' " *id.*, at 361 — whether, in the words of the *Katz* majority, the individual's expectation, viewed objectively, is "justifiable" under the circumstances. *Id.*, at 353.

B

In applying the *Katz* analysis to this case, it is important to begin by specifying precisely the nature of the state activity that is challenged. The activity here took the form of installing and using a pen register. Since the pen register was installed on telephone company property at the telephone company's central offices, petitioner obviously cannot claim that his "property" was invaded or that police intruded into a "constitutionally protected area." Petitioner's claim, rather, is that, notwithstanding the absence of a trespass, the State, as did the Government in *Katz*, infringed a "legitimate expectation of privacy" that petitioner held. Yet a pen register differs significantly from the listening device employed in *Katz*, for pen registers do not acquire the *contents* of communications. This Court recently noted:

> "Indeed, a law enforcement official could not even determine from the use of a pen register whether a communication existed. These devices do not hear sound. They disclose only the telephone numbers that have been dialed—a means of establishing communication. Neither the purport of any communication between the caller and the recipient of the call, their identities, nor whether the call was even completed is disclosed by pen registers." *United States v. New York Tel. Co.*, 434 U.S. 159, 167 (1977).

Given a pen register's limited capabilities, therefore, petitioner's argument that its installation and use constituted a "search" necessarily rests upon a claim that he had a "legitimate expectation of privacy" regarding the numbers he dialed on his phone.

This claim must be rejected. First, we doubt that people in general entertain any actual expectation of privacy in the numbers they dial. All telephone users realize that they must "convey" phone numbers to the telephone company, since it is through telephone-company switching equipment that their calls are completed. All subscribers realize, moreover, that the phone company has facilities for making permanent records of the numbers they dial, for they see a list of their long-distance (toll) calls on their monthly bills. In fact, pen registers and similar devices are routinely used by telephone companies "for the purposes of checking billing operations, detecting fraud and preventing violations of law." *United States v. New York Tel. Co.*, 434 U.S., at 174-175. Electronic equipment is used not only to keep billing records of toll calls, but also "to keep a record of all calls dialed from a telephone which is subject to a special rate structure." *Hodge v. Mountain States Tel. & Tel. Co.*, 555 F.2d 254, 266 (C.A.9 1977) (concurring opinion). Pen registers are regularly employed "to determine whether a home phone is being used to conduct a business, to check for a defective dial, or to check for overbilling." Note, The Legal Constraints upon the Use of the Pen Register as a Law Enforcement Tool, 60 Cornell L. Rev. 1028, 1029 (1975) (footnotes omitted). Although most people may be oblivious to a pen register's esoteric functions, they presumably have some awareness of one common use: to aid in the identification of persons making annoying or obscene calls. Most phone books tell subscribers, on a page entitled "Consumer Information," that the company "can frequently help in identifying to the authorities the origin of unwelcome and troublesome calls." *E.g.*, Baltimore Telephone Directory 21 (1978); District of Columbia Telephone Directory 13 (1978). Telephone users, in sum, typically know that they must convey numerical information to the phone company; that the phone company has facilities for recording this information; and that the phone company does in fact record this information for a variety of legitimate business purposes. Although subjective expectations cannot be scientifically gauged, it is too much to believe that telephone subscribers, under these circumstances, harbor any general expectation that the numbers they dial will remain secret.

Petitioner argues, however, that, whatever the expectations of telephone users in general, he demonstrated an expectation of privacy by his own conduct here, since he "us[ed] the telephone *in his house* to the exclusion of all others." Brief for Petitioner 6 (emphasis added). But the site of the call is immaterial for purposes of analysis in this case. Although petitioner's conduct may have been calculated to keep the *contents* of his conversation private, his conduct was not and could not have been calculated to preserve the privacy of the number he dialed. Regardless of his location, petitioner had to convey that number to the telephone company in precisely the same way if he wished to complete his call. The fact that he dialed the number on his home phone rather than on some other phone could make no conceivable difference, nor could any subscriber rationally think that it would.

Second, even if petitioner did harbor some subjective expectation that the phone numbers he dialed would remain private, this expectation is not "one that society is prepared to recognize as 'reasonable.'" *Katz v. United States*, 389 U.S., at 361. This Court consistently has held that a person has no legitimate expectation of privacy in information he voluntarily turns over to third parties. *E.g.*, *United States v. Miller*, 425 U.S., at 442-444; *Couch v. United States*, 409 U.S., at 335-336; *United States v. White*, 401 U.S., at 752 (plurality opinion); *Hoffa v. United States*, 385 U.S. 293, 302 (1966); *Lopez v. United States*, 373 U.S. 427 (1963). In *Miller*, for example, the Court held that a bank depositor has no "legitimate 'expectation of privacy'" in financial information "voluntarily conveyed to . . . banks and exposed to their employees in the ordinary course of business." 425 U.S., at 442. The Court explained:

> "The depositor takes the risk, in revealing his affairs to another, that the information will be conveyed by that person to the Government. . . . This Court has held repeatedly that the Fourth Amendment does not prohibit the obtaining of information revealed to a third party and conveyed by him to Government authorities, even if the information is revealed on the assumption that it will be used only for a limited purpose and the confidence placed in the third party will not be betrayed." *Id.*, at 443.

Because the depositor "assumed the risk" of disclosure, the Court held that it would be unreasonable for him to expect his financial records to remain private.

This analysis dictates that petitioner can claim no legitimate expectation of privacy here. When he used his phone, petitioner voluntarily conveyed numerical information to the telephone company and "exposed" that information to its equipment in the ordinary course of business. In so doing, petitioner assumed the risk that the company would reveal to police the numbers he dialed. The switching equipment that processed those numbers is merely the modern counterpart of the operator who, in an earlier day, personally completed calls for the subscriber. Petitioner concedes that if he had placed his calls through an operator, he could claim no legitimate expectation of privacy. We are not inclined to hold that a different constitutional result is required because the telephone company has decided to automate.

*   *   *

We therefore conclude that petitioner in all probability entertained no actual expectation of privacy in the phone numbers he dialed, and that, even if he did, his expectation was not "legitimate." The installation and use of a pen register, consequently, was not a "search," and no warrant was required. The judgment of the Maryland Court of Appeals is affirmed.

Carpenter v. United States
138 S. Ct. 2206 (2018)

Chief Justice ROBERTS delivered the opinion of the Court.

This case presents the question whether the Government conducts a search under the Fourth Amendment when it accesses historical cell phone records that provide a comprehensive chronicle of the user's past movements.

I

A

There are 396 million cell phone service accounts in the United States — for a Nation of 326 million people. Cell phones perform their wide and growing variety of functions by connecting to a set of radio antennas called "cell sites." Although cell sites are usually mounted on a tower, they can also be found on light posts, flagpoles, church steeples, or the sides of buildings. Cell sites typically have several directional antennas that divide the covered area into sectors.

Cell phones continuously scan their environment looking for the best signal, which generally comes from the closest cell site. Most modern devices, such as smartphones, tap into the wireless network several times a minute whenever their signal is on, even if the owner is not using one of the phone's features. Each time the phone connects to a cell site, it generates a time-stamped record known as cell-site location information (CSLI). The precision of this information depends on the size of the geographic area covered by the cell site. The greater the concentration of cell sites, the smaller the coverage area. As data usage from cell phones has increased, wireless carriers have installed more cell sites to handle the traffic. That has led to increasingly compact coverage areas, especially in urban areas.

Wireless carriers collect and store CSLI for their own business purposes, including finding weak spots in their network and applying "roaming" charges when another carrier routes data through their cell sites. In addition, wireless carriers often sell aggregated location records to data brokers, without individual identifying information of the sort at issue here. While carriers have long retained CSLI for the start and end of incoming calls, in recent years phone companies have also collected location information from the transmission of text messages and routine data connections. Accordingly, modern cell phones generate increasingly vast amounts of increasingly precise CSLI.

B

In 2011, police officers arrested four men suspected of robbing a series of Radio Shack and (ironically enough) T-Mobile stores in Detroit. One of the men confessed that, over the previous four months, the group (along with a rotating cast of getaway drivers and lookouts) had robbed nine different stores in Michigan and Ohio. The suspect identified 15 accomplices who had participated in the heists and gave the FBI some of their cell phone numbers; the FBI then reviewed his call records to identify additional numbers that he had called around the time of the robberies.

Based on that information, the prosecutors applied for court orders under the Stored Communications Act to obtain cell phone records for petitioner Timothy Carpenter and several other suspects. That statute, as amended in 1994, permits the Government to compel the disclosure of certain telecommunications records when it "offers specific and articulable facts showing that there are reasonable grounds to believe" that the records sought "are relevant and material to an ongoing criminal investigation." 18 U.S.C. § 2703(d). Federal Magistrate Judges issued two orders directing Carpenter's wireless carriers—MetroPCS and Sprint—to disclose "cell/site sector [information] for [Carpenter's] telephone[ ] at call origination and at call termination for incoming and outgoing calls" during the four-month period when the string of robberies occurred. App. to Pet. for Cert. 60a, 72a. The first order sought 152 days of cell-site records from MetroPCS, which produced records spanning 127 days. The second order requested seven days of CSLI from Sprint, which produced two days of records covering the period when Carpenter's phone was "roaming" in northeastern Ohio. Altogether the Government obtained 12,898 location points cataloging Carpenter's movements—an average of 101 data points per day.

Carpenter was charged with six counts of robbery and an additional six counts of carrying a firearm during a federal crime of violence. See 18 U.S.C. §§ 924(c), 1951(a). Prior to trial, Carpenter moved to suppress the cell-site data provided by the wireless carriers. He argued that the Government's seizure of the records violated the Fourth Amendment because they had been obtained without a warrant supported by probable cause. The District Court denied the motion. App. to Pet. for Cert. 38a-39a.

At trial, seven of Carpenter's confederates pegged him as the leader of the operation. In addition, FBI agent Christopher Hess offered expert testimony about the cell-site data. Hess explained that each time a cell phone taps into the wireless network, the carrier logs a time-stamped record of the cell site and particular sector that were used. With this information, Hess produced maps that placed Carpenter's phone near four of the charged robberies. In the Government's view, the location records clinched the case: They confirmed that Carpenter was "right where the . . . robbery was at the exact time of the robbery." App. 131 (closing argument). Carpenter was convicted on all but one of the firearm counts and sentenced to more than 100 years in prison.

The Court of Appeals for the Sixth Circuit affirmed. 819 F.3d 880 (2016). The court held that Carpenter lacked a reasonable expectation of privacy in the location information collected by the FBI because he had shared that information with his wireless carriers. Given that cell phone users voluntarily convey cell-site data to their carriers as "a means of establishing communication," the court concluded that the resulting business records are not entitled to Fourth Amendment protection. *Id.,* at 888 (quoting *Smith v. Maryland,* 442 U.S. 735, 741 (1979)).

We granted certiorari. 582 U.S. ___, 137 S. Ct. 2211 (2017).

II

A

The Fourth Amendment protects "[t]he right of the people to be secure in their persons, houses, papers, and effects, against unreasonable searches and seizures." The "basic purpose of this Amendment," our cases have recognized, "is to safeguard the privacy and security of individuals against arbitrary invasions by governmental officials." *Camara v. Municipal Court of City and County of San Francisco,* 387 U.S. 523, 528 (1967). . . .

Although no single rubric definitively resolves which expectations of privacy are entitled to protection, the analysis is informed by historical understandings "of what was deemed an unreasonable search and seizure when [the Fourth Amendment] was adopted." *Carroll v. United States,* 267 U.S. 132, 149 (1925). On this score, our cases have recognized some basic guideposts. First, that the Amendment seeks to secure "the privacies of life" against "arbitrary power." *Boyd v. United States,* 116 U.S. 616, 630 (1886). Second, and relatedly, that a central aim of the Framers was "to place obstacles in the way of a too permeating police surveillance." *United States v. Di Re,* 332 U.S. 581, 595 (1948).

We have kept this attention to Founding-era understandings in mind when applying the Fourth Amendment to innovations in surveillance tools. As technology has enhanced the Government's capacity to encroach upon areas normally guarded from inquisitive eyes, this Court has sought to "assure [ ] preservation of that degree of privacy against government that existed when the Fourth

Amendment was adopted." *Kyllo v. United States*, 533 U.S. 27, 34 (2001). For that reason, we rejected in *Kyllo* a "mechanical interpretation" of the Fourth Amendment and held that use of a thermal imager to detect heat radiating from the side of the defendant's home was a search. *Id.*, at 35. Because any other conclusion would leave homeowners "at the mercy of advancing technology," we determined that the Government—absent a warrant—could not capitalize on such new sense-enhancing technology to explore what was happening within the home. *Ibid.*

Likewise in *Riley*, the Court recognized the "immense storage capacity" of modern cell phones in holding that police officers must generally obtain a warrant before searching the contents of a phone. 573 U.S., at ___, 134 S. Ct., at 2489. We explained that while the general rule allowing warrantless searches incident to arrest "strikes the appropriate balance in the context of physical objects, neither of its rationales has much force with respect to" the vast store of sensitive information on a cell phone. *Id.*, at ___, 134 S. Ct., at 2484.

B

The case before us involves the Government's acquisition of wireless carrier cell-site records revealing the location of Carpenter's cell phone whenever it made or received calls. This sort of digital data—personal location information maintained by a third party—does not fit neatly under existing precedents. Instead, requests for cell-site records lie at the intersection of two lines of cases, both of which inform our understanding of the privacy interests at stake.

The first set of cases addresses a person's expectation of privacy in his physical location and movements. In *United States v. Knotts*, 460 U.S. 276 (1983), we considered the Government's use of a "beeper" to aid in tracking a vehicle through traffic. Police officers in that case planted a beeper in a container of chloroform before it was purchased by one of Knotts's co-conspirators. The officers (with intermittent aerial assistance) then followed the automobile carrying the container from Minneapolis to Knotts's cabin in Wisconsin, relying on the beeper's signal to help keep the vehicle in view. The Court concluded that the "augment[ed]" visual surveillance did not constitute a search because "[a] person traveling in an automobile on public thoroughfares has no reasonable expectation of privacy in his movements from one place to another." *Id.*, at 281, 282. Since the movements of the vehicle and its final destination had been "voluntarily conveyed to anyone who wanted to look," Knotts could not assert a privacy interest in the information obtained. *Id.*, at 281.

This Court in *Knotts*, however, was careful to distinguish between the rudimentary tracking facilitated by the beeper and more sweeping modes of surveillance. The Court emphasized the "limited use which the government made of the signals from this particular beeper" during a discrete "automotive journey." *Id.*, at 284, 285. Significantly, the Court reserved the question whether "different constitutional principles may be applicable" if "twenty-four hour surveillance of any citizen of this country [were] possible." *Id.*, at 283-284.

Three decades later, the Court considered more sophisticated surveillance of the sort envisioned in *Knotts* and found that different principles did indeed apply. In *United States v. Jones*, FBI agents installed a GPS tracking device on Jones's vehicle and remotely monitored the vehicle's movements for 28 days. The Court decided the case based on the Government's physical trespass of the vehicle. 565 U.S., at 404-405. At the same time, five Justices agreed that related privacy concerns would be raised by, for example, "surreptitiously activating a stolen vehicle detection system" in Jones's car to track Jones himself, or conducting GPS tracking of his cell phone. *Id.*, at 426, 428 (Alito, J., concurring in judgment); *id.*, at 415 (Sotomayor, J., concurring). Since GPS monitoring of a vehicle tracks "every movement" a person makes in that vehicle, the concurring Justices concluded that "longer term GPS monitoring in investigations of most offenses impinges on expectations of privacy"—regardless whether those movements were disclosed to the public at large. *Id.*, at 430 (opinion of Alito, J.); *id.*, at 415 (opinion of Sotomayor, J.).

In a second set of decisions, the Court has drawn a line between what a person keeps to himself and what he shares with others. We have previously held that "a person has no legitimate expectation of privacy in information he voluntarily turns over to third parties." *Smith*, 442 U.S., at 743-744. That remains true "even if the information is revealed on the assumption that it will be used only for a limited purpose." *United States v. Miller*, 425 U.S. 435, 443 (1976). As a result, the Government is typically free to obtain such information from the recipient without triggering Fourth Amendment protections.

This third-party doctrine largely traces its roots to *Miller*. While investigating Miller for tax evasion, the Government subpoenaed his banks, seeking several months of canceled checks, deposit slips, and monthly statements. The Court rejected a Fourth Amendment challenge to the records collection. For one, Miller could "assert neither ownership nor possession" of the documents; they were "business records of the banks." *Id.*, at 440. For another, the nature of those records confirmed Miller's limited expectation of privacy, because the checks were "not confidential communications but negotiable instruments to be used in commercial transactions," and the bank statements contained information "exposed to [bank] employees in the ordinary course of business." *Id.*, at 442. The Court thus concluded that Miller had "take[n] the risk, in revealing his affairs to another, that the information [would] be conveyed by that person to the Government." *Id.*, at 443.

Three years later, *Smith* applied the same principles in the context of information conveyed to a telephone company. The Court ruled that the Government's use of a pen register—a device that recorded the outgoing phone numbers dialed on a landline telephone—was not a search. Noting the pen register's "limited capabilities," the Court "doubt[ed] that people in general entertain any actual expectation of privacy in the numbers they dial." 442 U.S., at 742. Telephone subscribers know, after all, that the numbers are used by the telephone company "for a variety of legitimate business purposes," including routing calls. *Id.*, at 743. And at any rate, the Court explained, such an expectation "is not one that society is prepared to recognize as reasonable." *Ibid.* (internal quotation marks omitted). When Smith placed a call, he "voluntarily conveyed" the dialed numbers to the phone company by "expos[ing] that information to its equipment in the ordinary course of business." *Id.*, at 744 (internal quotation marks omitted). Once again, we held that the defendant "assumed the risk" that the company's records "would be divulged to police." *Id.*, at 745.

III

The question we confront today is how to apply the Fourth Amendment to a new phenomenon: the ability to chronicle a person's past movements through the record of his cell phone signals. Such tracking partakes of many of the qualities of the GPS monitoring we considered in *Jones*. Much like GPS tracking of a vehicle, cell phone location information is detailed, encyclopedic, and effortlessly compiled.

At the same time, the fact that the individual continuously reveals his location to his wireless carrier implicates the third-party principle of *Smith* and *Miller*. But while the third-party doctrine applies to telephone numbers and bank records, it is not clear whether its logic extends to the qualitatively different category of cell-site records. After all, when *Smith* was decided in 1979, few could have imagined a society in which a phone goes wherever its owner goes, conveying to the wireless carrier not just dialed digits, but a detailed and comprehensive record of the person's movements.

We decline to extend *Smith* and *Miller* to cover these novel circumstances. Given the unique nature of cell phone location records, the fact that the information is held by a third party does not by itself overcome the user's claim to Fourth Amendment protection. Whether the Government employs its own surveillance technology as in *Jones* or leverages the technology of a wireless carrier, we hold that an individual maintains a legitimate expectation of privacy in the record of his physical movements as captured through CSLI. The location information obtained from Carpenter's wireless carriers was the product of a search.

A

A person does not surrender all Fourth Amendment protection by venturing into the public sphere. To the contrary, "what [one] seeks to preserve as private, even in an area accessible to the public, may be constitutionally protected." *Katz*, 389 U.S., at 351-352. A majority of this Court has already recognized that individuals have a reasonable expectation of privacy in the whole of their physical movements. *Jones*, 565 U.S., at 430 (Alito, J., concurring in judgment); *id.*, at 415 (Sotomayor, J., concurring). Prior to the digital age, law enforcement might have pursued a suspect for a brief stretch, but doing so "for any extended period of time was difficult and costly and therefore rarely undertaken." *Id.*, at 429 (opinion of Alito, J.). For that reason, "society's expectation has been that law enforcement agents and others would not—and indeed, in the main, simply could not—secretly monitor and catalogue every single movement of an individual's car for a very long period." *Id.*, at 430.

Allowing government access to cell-site records contravenes that expectation. Although such records are generated for commercial purposes, that distinction does not negate Carpenter's anticipation of privacy in his physical location. Mapping a cell phone's location over the course of 127 days provides an all-encompassing record of the holder's whereabouts. As with GPS information, the time-stamped data provides an intimate window into a person's life, revealing not only his particular movements, but through them his "familial, political, professional, religious, and sexual associations." *Id.*, at 415 (opinion of Sotomayor, J.). These location records "hold for many Americans the 'privacies of life.'" *Riley*, 573 U.S., at ___, 134 S. Ct., at 2494-2495 (quoting *Boyd*, 116 U.S., at 630). . . .

In fact, historical cell-site records present even greater privacy concerns than the GPS monitoring of a vehicle we considered in *Jones*. Unlike the bugged container in *Knotts* or the car in *Jones,* a cell phone—almost a "feature of human anatomy," *Riley*, 573 U.S., at ___, 134 S. Ct., at 2484—tracks nearly exactly the movements of its owner. While individuals regularly leave their vehicles, they compulsively carry cell phones with them all the time. A cell phone faithfully follows its owner beyond public thoroughfares and into private residences, doctor's offices, political headquarters, and other potentially revealing locales. See *id.*, at ___, 134 S. Ct., at 2490 (noting that "nearly three-quarters of smart phone users report being within five feet of their phones most of the time, with 12% admitting that they even use their phones in the shower"). . . . Accordingly, when the Government tracks the location of a cell phone it achieves near perfect surveillance, as if it had attached an ankle monitor to the phone's user.

Moreover, the retrospective quality of the data here gives police access to a category of information otherwise unknowable. In the past, attempts to reconstruct a person's movements were limited by a dearth of records and the frailties of recollection. With access to CSLI, the Government can now travel back in time to retrace a person's whereabouts, subject only to the retention policies of the wireless carriers, which currently maintain records for up to five years. Critically, because location information is continually logged for all of the 400 million devices in the United States—not just those belonging to persons who might happen to come under investigation—this newfound tracking capacity runs against everyone. Unlike with the GPS device in *Jones,* police need not even know in advance whether they want to follow a particular individual, or when.

Whoever the suspect turns out to be, he has effectively been tailed every moment of every day for five years, and the police may—in the Government's view—call upon the results of that surveillance without regard to the constraints of the Fourth Amendment. Only the few without cell phones could escape this tireless and absolute surveillance. . . .

Accordingly, when the Government accessed CSLI from the wireless carriers, it invaded Carpenter's reasonable expectation of privacy in the whole of his physical movements.

B

The Government's primary contention to the contrary is that the third-party doctrine governs this case. In its view, cell-site records are fair game because they are "business records" created and maintained by the wireless carriers. The Government (along with Justice Kennedy) recognizes that this case features new technology, but asserts that the legal question nonetheless turns on a garden-variety request for information from a third-party witness. Brief for United States 32-34; *post*, at 2229-2231.

The Government's position fails to contend with the seismic shifts in digital technology that made possible the tracking of not only Carpenter's location but also everyone else's, not for a short period but for years and years. Sprint Corporation and its competitors are not your typical witnesses. Unlike the nosy neighbor who keeps an eye on comings and goings, they are ever alert, and their memory is nearly infallible. There is a world of difference between the limited types of personal information addressed in *Smith* and *Miller* and the exhaustive chronicle of location information casually collected by wireless carriers today. The Government thus is not asking for a straightforward application of the third-party doctrine, but instead a significant extension of it to a distinct category of information.

The third-party doctrine partly stems from the notion that an individual has a reduced expectation of privacy in information knowingly shared with another. But the fact of "diminished privacy interests does not mean that the Fourth Amendment falls out of the picture entirely." *Riley*, 573 U.S., at ___, 134 S. Ct., at 2488. *Smith* and *Miller*, after all, did not rely solely on the act of sharing. Instead, they considered "the nature of the particular documents sought" to determine whether "there is a legitimate 'expectation of privacy' concerning their contents." *Miller*, 425 U.S., at 442. *Smith* pointed out the limited capabilities of a pen register; as explained in *Riley*, telephone call logs reveal little in the way of "identifying information." *Smith*, 442 U.S., at 742; *Riley*, 573 U.S., at ___, 134 S. Ct., at 2493. *Miller* likewise noted that checks were "not confidential communications but negotiable instruments to be used in commercial transactions." 425 U.S., at 442. In mechanically applying the third-party doctrine to this case, the Government fails to appreciate that there are no comparable limitations on the revealing nature of CSLI.

The Court has in fact already shown special solicitude for location information in the third-party context. In *Knotts*, the Court relied on *Smith* to hold that an individual has no reasonable expectation of privacy in public movements that he "voluntarily conveyed to anyone who wanted to look." *Knotts*, 460 U.S., at 281; see *id.*, at 283 (discussing *Smith*). But when confronted with more pervasive tracking, five Justices agreed that longer term GPS monitoring of even a vehicle traveling on public streets constitutes a search. *Jones*, 565 U.S., at 430 (Alito, J., concurring in judgment); *id.*, at 415 (Sotomayor, J., concurring). Justice Gorsuch wonders why "someone's location when using a phone" is sensitive, *post*, at 2262, and Justice Kennedy assumes that a person's discrete movements "are not particularly private," *post*, at 2232. Yet this case is not about "using a phone" or a person's movement at a particular time. It is about a detailed chronicle of a person's physical presence compiled every day, every moment, over several years. Such a chronicle implicates privacy concerns far beyond those considered in *Smith* and *Miller*.

Neither does the second rationale underlying the third-party doctrine—voluntary exposure—hold up when it comes to CSLI. Cell phone location information is not truly "shared" as one normally understands the term. In the first place, cell phones and the services they provide are "such a pervasive and insistent part of daily life" that carrying one is indispensable to participation in modern society. *Riley*, 573 U.S., at ___, 134 S. Ct., at 2484. Second, a cell phone logs a cell-site record by dint of its operation, without any affirmative act on the part of the user beyond powering up. Virtually any activity on the phone generates CSLI, including incoming calls, texts, or e-mails and countless other data connections that a phone automatically makes when checking for news, weather, or social media updates. Apart from disconnecting the phone from the network, there is no way to avoid leaving behind a trail of location data. As a result, in no meaningful sense does the user voluntarily "assume[ ] the risk" of turning over a comprehensive dossier of his physical movements. *Smith*, 442 U.S., at 745.

We therefore decline to extend *Smith* and *Miller* to the collection of CSLI. Given the unique nature of cell phone location information, the fact that the Government obtained the information from a third party does not overcome Carpenter's claim to Fourth Amendment protection. The Government's acquisition of the cell-site records was a search within the meaning of the Fourth Amendment.

*   *   *

Our decision today is a narrow one. We do not express a view on matters not before us: real-time CSLI or "tower dumps" (a download of information on all the devices that connected to a particular cell site during a particular interval). We do not disturb the application of *Smith* and *Miller* or call into question conventional surveillance techniques and tools, such as security cameras. Nor do we address other business records that might incidentally reveal location information. Further, our opinion does not consider other collection techniques involving foreign affairs or national security. As Justice Frankfurter noted when considering new innovations in airplanes and radios, the Court must tread carefully in such cases, to ensure that we do not "embarrass the future." *Northwest Airlines, Inc. v. Minnesota*, 322 U.S. 292, 300 (1944).

IV

Having found that the acquisition of Carpenter's CSLI was a search, we also conclude that the Government must generally obtain a warrant supported by probable cause before acquiring such records. Although the "ultimate measure of the constitutionality of a governmental search is 'reasonableness,' " our cases establish that warrantless searches are typically unreasonable where "a search is undertaken by law enforcement officials to discover evidence of criminal wrongdoing." *Vernonia School Dist. 47J v. Acton*, 515 U.S. 646, 652-653 (1995). Thus, "[i]n the absence of a warrant, a search is reasonable only if it falls within a specific exception to the warrant requirement." *Riley*, 573 U.S., at ___, 134 S. Ct., at 2482. . . .

*   *   *

As Justice Brandeis explained in his famous dissent, the Court is obligated—as "[s]ubtler and more far-reaching means of invading privacy have become available to the Government"—to ensure that the "progress of science" does not erode Fourth Amendment protections. *Olmstead v. United States*, 277 U.S. 438, 473-474 (1928). Here the progress of science has afforded law enforcement a powerful new tool to carry out its important responsibilities. At the same time, this tool risks Government encroachment of the sort the Framers, "after consulting the lessons of history," drafted the Fourth Amendment to prevent. *Di Re*, 332 U.S., at 595.

We decline to grant the state unrestricted access to a wireless carrier's database of physical location information. In light of the deeply revealing nature of CSLI, its depth, breadth, and comprehensive reach, and the inescapable and automatic nature of its collection, the fact that such information is gathered by a third party does not make it any less deserving of Fourth Amendment protection. The Government's acquisition of the cell-site records here was a search under that Amendment.

The judgment of the Court of Appeals is reversed, and the case is remanded for further proceedings consistent with this opinion.

Justice KENNEDY, with whom Justice THOMAS and Justice ALITO join, dissenting.

. . .

III

The Court rejects a straightforward application of *Miller* and *Smith*. It concludes instead that applying those cases to cell-site records would work a "significant extension" of the principles underlying them, *ante*, at 2219, and holds that the acquisition of more than six days of cell-site records constitutes a search, *ante*, at 2217, n.3.

In my respectful view the majority opinion misreads this Court's precedents, old and recent, and transforms *Miller* and *Smith* into an unprincipled and unworkable doctrine. The Court's newly conceived constitutional standard will cause confusion; will undermine traditional and important law enforcement practices; and will allow the cell phone to become a protected medium that dangerous persons will use to commit serious crimes.

. . .

B

. . .

The Court appears, in my respectful view, to read *Miller* and *Smith* to establish a balancing test. For each "qualitatively different category" of information, the Court suggests, the privacy interests at stake must be weighed against the fact that the information has been disclosed to a third party. See *ante*, at 2216, 2219-2220. When the privacy interests are weighty enough to "overcome" the third-party disclosure, the Fourth Amendment's protections apply. See *ante*, at 2220.

That is an untenable reading of *Miller* and *Smith*. As already discussed, the fact that information was relinquished to a third party was the entire basis for concluding that the defendants in those cases lacked a reasonable expectation of privacy. *Miller* and *Smith* do not establish the kind of category-by-category balancing the Court today prescribes.

NOTES AND QUESTIONS

1. What is the scope of the Court's holding in *Carpenter*? Chief Justice Roberts stated that the Court's decision is a "narrow one." Specifically, Roberts stated: "[O]ur opinion does not consider other collection techniques involving foreign affairs or national security." After *Carpenter*, does a person have standing to challenge the NSA's seizure of bulk telephone metadata collected pursuant to a FISA warrant? Telephone metadata includes the numbers called to and from a targeted cell phone and the date and length of the telephone conversations. However, telephone metadata does not include the contents of the telephone conversations. Thus, pursuant to a FISA order the government could identify every cell phone number called by the FISA target as well as every cell phone number that called the FISA target over an extended period of time. After *Carpenter*, does the third-party records doctrine apply, depriving the FISA target of standing? Does the FISA target have a legitimate expectation of privacy in telephone metadata? Is the nature of telephone metadata similar to cell-site records in what they reveal about the person's private life?

    The Court stated that "[t]he third-party doctrine partly stems from the notion that an individual has a reduced expectation of privacy in information knowingly shared with another." Telephone metadata is shared with the cell phone service provider for billing purposes. Is telephone metadata truly "shared" as one normally understands the term? Does the user voluntarily "assume the risk" of turning over his or her telephone metadata to the NSA or FBI?

2. Writing in dissent, Justice Kennedy states that the majority wrongly interprets *Miller* and *Smith* to establish a "balancing test." Do you agree? If so, what competing interests must the court weigh and balance in determining whether the third-party doctrine applies and the person lacks standing?

3. Justices Thomas, Alito, and Gorsuch also dissented and each wrote a separate dissenting opinion. Justice Thomas argued that the majority's decision was flawed in that it did not turn on whose property was searched. Carpenter did not own or create the records seized—rather, the wireless carrier did. Therefore, Carpenter lacked standing to challenge the seizure of cell-site records. Justice Thomas further maintained that the more "fundamental problem" was that the "reasonable expectation of privacy" principle enunciated in *Katz* has "no basis in the text or history of the Fourth Amendment" and should be overruled. Justice Thomas also joined Justice Alito's dissent. Justice Alito dissented on two grounds. First, he wrote that "the Court ignores the basic distinction between an actual search . . . and an order merely requiring

a party to look through its own records and produce specified documents." According to Alito, the latter scenario has few privacy implications and therefore should not be treated as a search under the Fourth Amendment. Second, he stated that allowing a defendant to object to the seizure of a third party's property (cell phone service provider) was "revolutionary." The Fourth Amendment protects an individual's house, papers, and effects from unreasonable search and seizure, not those of others. Thus, the Court's decision is a dramatic departure from the fundamentals of the Fourth Amendment.

Finally, Justice Gorsuch in dissent was critical of *Katz*, *Miller*, and *Smith*. He proposed returning to a more traditional Fourth Amendment approach, focusing on whether the defendant has a property right or interest in the papers and effects subject to search and seizure. Gorsuch stated that "the traditional approach asked if a house, paper or effect was yours under law." He opined that "if a house, paper, or effect is yours, you have a Fourth Amendment interest in its protection," which does not automatically disappear just because you share such property with third parties.

USA FREEDOM ACT

In 2015, Congress enacted the USA FREEDOM Act, Pub. L. No. 114-23, 129 Stat. 268. The Act establishes new procedures for applying for a FISA court order requiring telephone companies to produce telephone call records to the National Security Agency. The new procedures prohibit the FBI from applying for a production order unless a "specific selection term" is used as the basis for the production. For the production on an ongoing basis of call detail records relating to an authorized international terrorism investigation, the selection term must specifically identify an individual, account, or personal device. *See id.* § 103. The Act also requires the FBI to demonstrate the following in its FISA application: (1) reasonable grounds to believe that the call detail records are relevant to an international terrorism investigation; and (2) reasonable articulable suspicion that the specific selection term is associated with a foreign power or an agent of a foreign power engaged in international terrorism or related activities. *See id.* § 101(a)(1)(C)(i)-(ii). Do these procedures properly balance "the paramount interest in protecting the security of our nation . . . with the privacy interests of its citizens in a world where surveillance capabilities are vast and where it is difficult if not impossible to avoid exposing a wealth of information about oneself to those surveillance mechanisms"? *ACLU v. Clapper*, 785 F.3d 787, 826 (2d Cir. 2015).

---

b. Satisfying the Warrant Clause and "Reasonableness" Requirements

A "significant purpose" of a FISA warrant must be to gather "foreign intelligence information." 50 U.S.C. § 1804(a)(6)(B). Therefore, obtaining a FISA warrant to collect *domestic* intelligence information or information solely for the purpose of investigating a criminal offense would fall outside the proper scope of FISA. Prior to the USA PATRIOT Act, several federal courts acknowledged that while Congress viewed arrest and prosecution as one of the possible outcomes of a FISA investigation, surveillance under FISA would be "appropriate only if foreign intelligence surveillance is the government's *primary* purpose." *United States v. Megahey*, 553 F. Supp. 1180, 1189-90 (E.D.N.Y. 1982) (emphasis added), *aff'd sub nom. United States v. Duggan*, 743 F.2d 59, 77 (2d Cir. 1984). In 1995, the Justice Department not only adopted the "primary purpose" requirement, but to avoid running afoul of that restriction it adopted procedures prohibiting the sharing of foreign intelligence information between law enforcement and intelligence officials. The procedures eventually came to be narrowly interpreted by the Department of Justice as erecting a "wall" to prevent FBI intelligence officials from communicating with federal prosecutors regarding ongoing intelligence investigations.

In 2001, Congress amended FISA as part of the USA PATRIOT Act. Among other things, Congress amended FISA to change "the purpose" language in § 1804(a)(7)(B) to a "significant purpose" of the requested surveillance. Thus, if gathering foreign intelligence information is a "significant purpose," another purpose, such as criminal investigation and prosecution, could be primary. Critics of the PATRIOT Act immediately challenged the new provision, claiming that FISA could be abused by law enforcement and used to circumvent the requirements of obtaining a traditional search and seizure warrant based on probable cause to believe that the evidence is connected to criminal activity. Further, the FISA critics argued that FISA warrants violate the Fourth Amendment. They maintain that the FISA procedures fail to satisfy the warrant requirement because such procedures (1) lack a particularity requirement, (2) lack a reasonable durational limit, and (3) fail to provide adequate notice to persons whose communications are intercepted or premises are searched. *In re Sealed Case*, the first case decided by the FISA Court of Review, addresses several of these important issues.

In re Sealed Case
310 F.3d 717 (FISA Ct. Rev. 2002)

PER CURIAM:

This is the first appeal from the Foreign Intelligence Surveillance Court to the Court of Review since the passage of the Foreign Intelligence Surveillance Act (FISA) in 1978. The appeal is brought by the United States from a FISA court surveillance order which imposed certain restrictions on the government. Since the government is the only party to FISA proceedings, we have accepted briefs filed by the American Civil Liberties Union (ACLU) and the National Association of Criminal Defense Lawyers (NACDL) as *amici curiae*.

Not surprisingly this case raises important questions of statutory interpretation, and constitutionality. After a careful review of the briefs filed by the government and *amici*, we conclude that FISA, as amended by the Patriot Act, supports the government's position, and that the restrictions imposed by the FISA court are not required by FISA or the Constitution. We therefore remand for further proceedings in accordance with this opinion.

I.

The court's decision from which the government appeals imposed certain requirements and limitations accompanying an order authorizing electronic surveillance of an "agent of a foreign power" as defined in FISA. . . . The FISA court authorized the surveillance, but imposed certain restrictions, which the government contends are neither mandated nor authorized by FISA. . . . We think it fair to say, however, that the May 17 opinion of the FISA court does not clearly set forth the basis for its decision. It appears to proceed from the assumption that FISA constructed a barrier between counterintelligence/intelligence officials and law enforcement officers in the Executive Branch—indeed, it uses the word "wall" popularized by certain commentators (and journalists) to describe that supposed barrier.

The "wall" emerges from the court's implicit interpretation of FISA. The court apparently believes it can approve applications for electronic surveillance only if the government's objective is *not* primarily directed toward criminal prosecution of the foreign agents for their foreign intelligence activity. But the court neither refers to any FISA language supporting that view, nor does it reference the Patriot Act amendments, which the government contends specifically altered FISA to make clear that an application could be obtained even if criminal prosecution is the primary counter mechanism.

Instead the court relied for its imposition of the disputed restrictions on its statutory authority to approve "minimization procedures" designed to prevent the acquisition, retention, and dissemination within the government of material gathered in an electronic surveillance that is unnecessary to the government's need for foreign intelligence information. 50 U.S.C. § 1801(h).

. . .

The origin of what the government refers to as the false dichotomy between foreign intelligence information that is evidence of foreign intelligence crimes and that which is not appears to have been a Fourth Circuit case decided in 1980. *United States v. Truong Dinh Hung*, 629 F.2d 908 (4th Cir. 1980). That case, however, involved an electronic surveillance carried out prior to the passage of FISA and predicated on the President's executive power. In approving the district court's exclusion of evidence obtained through a warrantless surveillance subsequent to the point in time when the government's investigation became "primarily" driven by law enforcement objectives, the court held that the Executive Branch should be excused from securing a warrant only when "the object of the search or the surveillance is a foreign power, its agents or collaborators," and "the surveillance is conducted 'primarily' for foreign intelligence reasons." *Id.* at 915. Targets must "receive the protection of the warrant requirement if the government is primarily attempting to put together a criminal prosecution." *Id.* at 916. Although the *Truong* court acknowledged that "almost all foreign intelligence investigations are in part criminal" ones, it rejected the government's assertion that "if surveillance is to any degree directed at gathering foreign intelligence, the executive may ignore the warrant requirement of the Fourth Amendment." *Id.* at 915.

Several circuits have followed *Truong* in applying similar versions of the "primary purpose" test, despite the fact that *Truong* was not a FISA decision. (It was an interpretation of the Constitution, in the context of measuring the boundaries of the President's inherent executive authority, and we discuss *Truong's* constitutional analysis at length in Section III of this opinion.) In one of the first major challenges to a FISA search, *United States v. Megahey*, 553 F. Supp. 1180 (E.D.N.Y. 1982), *aff'd sub nom. United States v. Duggan*, 743 F.2d 59 (2d Cir. 1984), the district court acknowledged that while Congress clearly viewed arrest and prosecution as one of the possible outcomes of a FISA investigation, surveillance under FISA would nevertheless be "appropriate only if foreign intelligence surveillance is the Government's primary purpose." *Id.* at 1189-90.

In *Duggan* the court stated that "[t]he requirement that foreign intelligence information be the primary objective of the surveillance is plain," and the district court was correct in "finding that 'the purpose of the surveillance in this case, both initially and throughout, was to secure foreign intelligence information and was not, as [the] defendants assert, directed towards criminal investigation or the institution of a criminal prosecution.'" *Duggan*, 743 F.2d at 77-78 (quoting *Megahey*, 553 F. Supp. at 1190). Yet the court never explained why it apparently read foreign intelligence information to exclude evidence of crimes—endorsing the district court's implied dichotomy—when the statute's definitions of foreign intelligence and foreign agent are actually cast in terms of criminal conduct.

In sum, we think that the FISA as passed by Congress in 1978 clearly did *not* preclude or limit the government's use or proposed use of foreign intelligence information, which included evidence of certain kinds of criminal activity, in a criminal prosecution. . . .

THE PATRIOT ACT AND THE FISA COURT'S DECISION

. . .

III.

Having determined that FISA, as amended, does not oblige the government to demonstrate to the FISA court that its primary purpose in conducting electronic surveillance is *not* criminal prosecution, we are obliged to consider whether the statute as amended is consistent with the Fourth Amendment. The Fourth Amendment provides:

> The right of the people to be secure in their persons, houses, papers, and effects, against unreasonable searches and seizures, shall not be violated, and no Warrants shall issue, but upon probable cause, supported by Oath or affirmation, and particularly describing the place to be searched, and the persons or things to be seized.

Although the FISA court did not explicitly rely on the Fourth Amendment, it at least suggested that this provision was the animating principle driving its statutory analysis. The FISA court indicated that its disapproval of the Attorney General's 2002 Procedures was based on the need to safeguard the "privacy of Americans in these highly intrusive surveillances and searches," which implies the invocation of the Fourth Amendment. The government, recognizing the Fourth Amendment's shadow effect on the FISA court's opinion, has affirmatively argued that FISA is constitutional. . . .

The FISA court expressed concern that unless FISA were "construed" in the fashion that it did, the government could use a FISA order as an improper substitute for an ordinary criminal warrant under Title III. That concern seems to suggest that the FISA court thought Title III procedures are constitutionally mandated if the government has a prosecutorial objective regarding an agent of a foreign power. But in *United States v. United States District Court (Keith)*, 407 U.S. 297, 322 (1972)—in which the Supreme Court explicitly declined to consider foreign intelligence surveillance—the Court indicated that, even with respect to domestic national security intelligence gathering for prosecutorial purposes where a warrant was mandated, Title III procedures were not constitutionally required: "[W]e do not hold that the same type of standards and procedures prescribed by Title III are necessarily applicable to this case. We recognize that domestic security surveillance may involve different policy and practical considerations from the surveillance of 'ordinary crime.'" Nevertheless, in asking whether FISA procedures can be regarded as reasonable under the Fourth Amendment, we think it is instructive to compare those procedures and requirements with their Title III counterparts. Obviously, the closer those FISA procedures are to Title III procedures, the lesser are our constitutional concerns.

COMPARISON OF FISA PROCEDURES WITH TITLE III

It is important to note that while many of FISA's requirements for a surveillance order differ from those in Title III, few of those differences have any constitutional relevance. In the context of ordinary crime, beyond requiring searches and seizures to be reasonable, the Supreme Court has interpreted the warrant clause of the Fourth Amendment to require three elements:

> First, warrants must be issued by neutral, disinterested magistrates. Second, those seeking the warrant must demonstrate to the magistrate their probable cause to believe that "the evidence sought will aid in a particular apprehension or conviction" for a particular offense. Finally, "warrants must particularly describe the 'things to be seized,'" as well as the place to be searched.

Dalia v. United States, 441 U.S. 238, 255 (1979) (citations omitted).

With limited exceptions not at issue here, both Title III and FISA require prior judicial scrutiny of an application for an order authorizing electronic surveillance. 50 U.S.C. § 1805; 18 U.S.C. § 2518. And there is no dispute that a FISA judge satisfies the Fourth Amendment's requirement of a "neutral and detached magistrate." *See United States v. Cavanagh*, 807 F.2d 787, 790 (9th Cir. 1987) (FISA court is a "detached and neutral body"). . . .

The statutes differ to some extent in their probable cause showings. Title III allows a court to enter an *ex parte* order authorizing electronic surveillance if it determines on the basis of the facts submitted in the government's application that "there is probable cause for belief that an individual is committing, has committed, or is about to commit" a specified predicate offense. 18 U.S.C. § 2518(3)(a). FISA by contrast requires a showing of probable cause that the target is a foreign power or an agent of a foreign power. 50 U.S.C. § 1805(a)(3). We have noted, however, that where a U.S. person is involved, an "agent of a foreign power" is defined in terms of criminal activity. Admittedly, the definition of one category of U.S.-person agents of foreign powers—that is, persons engaged in espionage and clandestine intelligence activities for a foreign power—does not necessarily require a showing of an imminent violation of criminal law. *See* 50 U.S.C. § 1801(b)(2)(A) (defining such activities as those which "involve" or "*may* involve" a violation of criminal statutes of the United States). . . .

Turning then to the first of the particularity requirements, while Title III requires probable cause to believe that particular communications concerning the specified crime will be obtained through the interception, 18 U.S.C. § 2518(3)(b), FISA instead requires an official to designate the type of foreign intelligence information being sought, and to certify that the information sought is foreign intelligence information. When the target is a U.S. person, the FISA judge reviews the certification for clear error, but this "standard of review is not, of course, comparable to a probable cause finding by the judge." H. Rep. at 80. Nevertheless, FISA provides additional protections to ensure that only pertinent information is sought. The certification must be made by a national security officer—typically the FBI Director—and must be approved by the Attorney General or the Attorney General's Deputy. Congress recognized that this certification would "assure[ ] written accountability within the Executive Branch" and provide "an internal check on Executive Branch arbitrariness." H. Rep. at 80. In addition, the court may require the government to submit any further information it deems necessary to determine whether or not the certification is clearly erroneous.

With respect to the second element of particularity, although Title III generally requires probable cause to believe that the facilities subject to surveillance are being used or are about to be used in connection with the commission of a crime or are leased to, listed in the name of, or used by the individual committing the crime, 18 U.S.C. § 2518(3)(d), FISA requires probable cause to believe that each of the facilities or places at which the surveillance is directed is being used, or is about to be used, by a foreign power or agent. 50 U.S.C. § 1805(a)(3)(B). In cases where the targeted facilities are not leased to, listed in the name of, or used by the individual committing the crime, Title III requires the government to show a nexus between the facilities and communications regarding the criminal offense. The government does not have to show, however, anything about the target of the surveillance; it is enough that "*an individual*"—not necessarily the target—is committing a crime. 18 U.S.C. §§ 2518(3)(a), (d). . . . On the other hand, FISA requires probable cause to believe the target is an agent of a foreign power (that is, the individual committing a foreign intelligence crime) who uses or is about to use the targeted facility. Simply put, FISA requires less of a nexus between the facility and the pertinent communications than Title III, but more of a nexus between the target and the pertinent communications.

There are other elements of Title III that at least some circuits have determined are constitutionally significant — that is, necessity, duration of surveillance, and minimization. Both statutes have a "necessity" provision, which requires the court to find that the information sought is not available through normal investigative procedures. The statutes also have duration provisions; Title III orders may last up to 30 days, 18 U.S.C. § 2518(5), while FISA orders may last up to 90 days for U.S. persons. 50 U.S.C. § 1805(e)(1). This difference is based on the nature of national security surveillance, which is "often long range and involves the interrelation of various sources and types of information." *Keith*, 407 U.S. at 322. . . . And where Title III requires minimization of what is acquired, as we have discussed, for U.S. persons, FISA requires minimization of what is acquired, retained, and disseminated. The FISA court notes, however, that in practice FISA surveillance devices are normally left on continuously, and the minimization occurs in the process of indexing and logging the pertinent communications. The reasonableness of this approach depends on the facts and circumstances of each case. Less minimization in the acquisition stage may well be justified to the extent the intercepted communications are "ambiguous in nature or apparently involve[ ] guarded or coded language," or "the investigation is focusing on what is thought to be a widespread conspiracy [where] more extensive surveillance may be justified in an attempt to determine the precise scope of the enterprise." *Id.* at 140. Given the targets of FISA surveillance, it will often be the case that intercepted communications will be in code or a foreign language for which there is no contemporaneously available translator, and the activities of foreign agents will involve multiple actors and complex plots.

Amici particularly focus on the differences between the two statutes concerning notice. Title III requires notice to the target (and, within the discretion of the judge, to other persons whose communications were intercepted) once the surveillance order expires. 18 U.S.C. § 2518(8)(d). FISA does not require notice to a person whose communications were intercepted unless the government "intends to enter into evidence or otherwise use or disclose" such communications in a trial or other enumerated official proceedings. 50 U.S.C. § 1806(c). As the government points out, however, to the extent evidence obtained through a FISA surveillance order is used in a criminal proceeding, notice to the defendant is required. Of course, where such evidence is not ultimately going to be used for law enforcement, Congress observed that "[t]he need to preserve secrecy for sensitive counterintelligence sources and methods justifies elimination of the notice requirement." S. Rep. at 12.

Based on the foregoing, it should be evident that while Title III contains some protections that are not in FISA, in many significant respects the two statutes are equivalent, and in some, FISA contains additional protections. Still, to the extent the two statutes diverge in constitutionally relevant areas—in particular, in their probable cause and particularity showings—a FISA order may not be a "warrant" contemplated by the Fourth Amendment. The government itself does not actually claim that it is, instead noting only that there is authority for the proposition that a FISA order is a warrant in the constitutional sense. We do not decide the issue but note that to the extent a FISA order comes close to meeting Title III, that certainly bears on its reasonableness under the Fourth Amendment.

. . .

SUPREME COURT'S SPECIAL NEEDS CASES

The distinction between ordinary criminal prosecutions and extraordinary situations underlies the Supreme Court's approval of entirely warrantless and even suspicionless searches that are designed to serve the government's "special needs, beyond the normal need for law enforcement." *Vernonia School Dist. 47J v. Acton*, 515 U.S. 646, 653 (1995) (quoting *Griffin v. Wisconsin*, 483 U.S. 868, 873 1987) (internal quotation marks omitted)) (random drug-testing of student athletes). Apprehending drunk drivers and securing the border constitute such unique interests beyond ordinary, general law enforcement. *Id.* at 654 (citing *Michigan Dep't of State Police v. Sitz*, 496 U.S. 444 (1990), and *United States v. Martinez-Fuerte*, 428 U.S. 543 (1976)).

A recent case, *City of Indianapolis v. Edmond*, 531 U.S. 32 (2000), is relied on by both the government and *amici*. In that case, the Court held that a highway check point designed to catch drug dealers did not fit within its special needs exception because the government's "primary purpose" was merely "to uncover evidence of ordinary criminal wrongdoing." *Id.* at 41-42. The Court rejected the government's argument that the "severe and intractable nature of the drug problem" was sufficient justification for such a dragnet seizure lacking any individualized suspicion. *Id.* at 42. *Amici* particularly rely on the Court's statement that "the gravity of the threat alone cannot be dispositive of questions concerning what means law enforcement officers may employ to pursue a given purpose." *Id.*

But by "purpose" the Court makes clear it was referring not to a subjective intent, which is not relevant in ordinary Fourth Amendment probable cause analysis, but rather to a programmatic purpose. The Court distinguished the prior check point cases *Martinez-Fuerte* (involving checkpoints less than 100 miles from the Mexican border) and *Sitz* (checkpoints to detect intoxicated motorists) on the ground that the former involved the government's "longstanding concern for the protection of the integrity of the border," *id.* at 38, and the latter was "aimed at reducing the immediate hazard posed by the presence of drunk drivers on the highways." *Id.* at 39. The Court emphasized that it was decidedly not drawing a distinction between suspicionless seizures with a "non-law-enforcement primary purpose" and those designed for law enforcement. *Id.* at 44 n.1. Rather, the Court distinguished general crime control programs and those that have another particular purpose, such as protection of citizens against special hazards or protection of our borders. The Court specifically acknowledged that an appropriately tailored road block could be used "to thwart an imminent terrorist attack." *Id.* at 44. The nature of the "emergency," which is simply another word for threat, takes the matter out of the realm of ordinary crime control.

CONCLUSION

FISA's general programmatic purpose, to protect the nation against terrorists and espionage threats directed by foreign powers, has from its outset been distinguishable from "ordinary crime control." After the events of September 11, 2001, though, it is hard to imagine greater emergencies facing Americans than those experienced on that date.

We acknowledge, however, that the constitutional question presented by this case—whether Congress' disapproval of the primary purpose test is consistent with the Fourth Amendment—has no definitive jurisprudential answer. The Supreme Court's special needs cases involve random stops (seizures) not electronic searches. In one sense, they can be thought of as a greater encroachment into personal privacy because they are not based on any particular suspicion. On the other hand, wiretapping is a good deal more intrusive than an automobile stop accompanied by questioning.

Although the Court in *City of Indianapolis* cautioned that the threat to society is not dispositive in determining whether a search or seizure is reasonable, it certainly remains a crucial factor. Our case may well involve the most serious threat our country faces. Even without taking into account the President's inherent constitutional authority to conduct warrantless foreign intelligence surveillance, we think the procedures and government showings required under FISA, if they do not meet the minimum Fourth Amendment warrant standards, certainly come close. We, therefore, believe firmly, applying the balancing test drawn from *Keith* that FISA as amended is constitutional because the surveillances it authorizes are reasonable.

Accordingly, we reverse the FISA court's orders in this case to the extent they imposed conditions on the grant of the government's applications, vacate the FISA court's Rule 11, and remand with instructions to grant the applications as submitted and proceed henceforth in accordance with this opinion.

NOTES AND QUESTIONS

1. What is the holding in *In re Sealed Case*? Do FISA warrants satisfy the Fourth Amendment Warrants Clause? If so, why? What are the differences and similarities between a FISA surveillance warrant and a Title III surveillance warrant?

2. Do FISA warrants satisfy the Fourth Amendment's reasonableness requirement? If so, why?

3. After passage of the USA PATRIOT Act, can criminal investigation and prosecution be the "primary purpose" of a FISA warrant? If so, is there a substantial risk

that the FBI will seek to obtain a FISA surveillance or physical search warrant to avoid the requirements of a Title III wiretap warrant or traditional search warrant?

4. In *United States v. Abu-Jihad*, 630 F.3d 102 (2d Cir. 2010), the court held that FISA's "significant purpose" requirement was not unconstitutional. The court stated:

> For Fourth Amendment purposes, the critical question is not whether the executive can certify that obtaining foreign intelligence information is its "primary" purpose, but whether it can certify that it is a bona fide purpose of the surveillance. Thus, where the executive in good faith pursues both intelligence and law enforcement purposes, it may apply for surveillance authority under either FISA or Title III, provided it satisfies the particular warrant standards of the statute invoked. A Fourth Amendment concern would arise only if the executive, without a bona fide purpose to obtain foreign intelligence information, tried to secure a warrant under the standards identified in FISA as reasonable for that purpose.[8]

5. The FISC Court of Review discussed but did not decide whether the "special needs" exception applies to the collection of foreign intelligence information. Is the collection of foreign intelligence information "beyond the normal need for law enforcement"? Does it matter whether the "primary purpose" of the FISA electronic surveillance was to gather evidence of a criminal offense, and a "significant purpose" was to collect foreign intelligence information?

6. The USA PATRIOT Act dismantled the "wall" between intelligence and law enforcement personnel erected to ensure that the primary purpose of any FISA surveillance or search was to obtain foreign intelligence information and not evidence of a crime. Congress amended FISA, expressly authorizing federal officers conducting surveillance for the purpose of obtaining foreign intelligence information to coordinate their activities with law enforcement officers. *See* Pub. L. No. 107-56, § 504, 115 Stat. at 291 (codified as amended at 50 U.S.C. § 1806(k)(1)) ("Federal officers who conduct electronic surveillance to acquire foreign intelligence information under this title may consult with Federal law enforcement officers or law enforcement personnel of a State or political subdivision of a State . . . to coordinate efforts to investigate or protect against [*inter alia*, actual or potential attack by a foreign power or agent of a foreign power, sabotage, international terrorism, or other clandestine intelligence activities by a foreign power or agent of a foreign power].").

7. The considerations identified in *United States v. United States District Court (Keith)*, 407 U.S. 297 (1972), distinguishing domestic security surveillance from the surveillance of "ordinary crime" and, therefore, supporting different warrant standards, apply with equal force to foreign intelligence surveillance:

> The gathering of security intelligence is often long range and involves the interrelation of various sources and types of information. The exact targets of such surveillance may be more difficult to identify than in surveillance operations

---

8. *Id.* at 127-28.

against many types of crime specified in Title III. Often, too, the emphasis of domestic intelligence gathering is on the prevention of unlawful activity or the enhancement of the Government's preparedness for some possible future crisis or emergency. Thus, the focus of domestic surveillance may be less precise, than that directed against more conventional types of crime.[9]

Do you agree that different warrant standards should be applied?

THE ENCRYPTION BATTLE

Should the federal government be able to force Apple Inc. to develop software to override a safety feature in an iPhone operating system to assist the government in extracting data that belongs to a suspected terrorist or drug dealer? Newer iPhone operating systems have been designed in such a way that law enforcement cannot bypass the passcode to extract data. Apple Inc. must build software to disable a safety feature that it had built in to protect a phone's encrypted data. The feature deletes data from the phone after ten incorrect tries to guess the password.

The Apple case highlights the tension between the government's legitimate interest in preventing terrorist attacks and protecting national security, and the equally legitimate societal interest in privacy. Apple Inc. General Counsel Bruce Sewell maintains that developing a "backdoor" into the iPhone would set a dangerous precedent, opening up a universe of similar requests to access data on locked iPhones, which could be widely exploited and lead to an expansion of government surveillance, and violate their customers' privacy.

Manhattan District Attorney Cyrus Vance has countered that "[t]echnology companies should not be able to dictate who can access key evidence in criminal investigations." Vance wants Apple to go back to a previous non-encrypted state, prior to iOS 8, which switched on the encryption device. He claims that his office has recovered 175 iPhones that may contain data relevant to criminal investigations that cannot be unlocked.

Should national security concerns trump privacy interests? What is the legal authority for requiring Apple to comply with the government's request? *See FBI, Apple Bringing Fight over Encryption to Capitol Hill*, WASH. POST, Mar. 1, 2016.

United States v. Mohamud
843 F.3d 420 (9th Cir. 2016)

OWENS, Circuit Judge:

Mohamed Osman Mohamud appeals from his conviction for attempting to detonate a large bomb during the annual Christmas Tree Lighting Ceremony in Pioneer Courthouse Square in downtown Portland, Oregon, in violation of 18 U.S.C. § 2332a(a)(2)(A). We have jurisdiction under 28 U.S.C. § 1291, and we affirm.

. . .

---

9. *Id.* at 322.

II. PROCEDURAL HISTORY

A. Indictment and Trial

A one-count indictment charged Mohamud with attempted use of a weapon of mass destruction in violation of 18 U.S.C. § 2332a(a)(2)(A). After several years of pretrial litigation and review of immense discovery (including considerable litigation under the Classified Information Procedures Act, 18 U.S.C. app. 3), trial began in January 2013 and lasted thirteen days. Both sides called numerous witnesses, and the cross-examinations were sharp and thorough.

There was no dispute that Mohamud had tried to blow up Pioneer Courthouse Square while it was filled with people. The spirited (and supportable) defense was entrapment—Mohamud, a teenager with no criminal record, had neither the means nor the intent to commit domestic terrorism until he became involved with the undercover FBI contractor (Bill Smith) and FBI agents (Youssef and Hussein). The government countered that Mohamud's actions before any contact with the FBI—including his *Jihad Recollections* articles—as well as his readiness to commit such a horrific act of violence proved that he had the necessary predisposition to commit the crime. After the close of evidence and argument, the jury returned a guilty verdict, rejecting the entrapment defense.

B. Post-Trial Motions

Mohamud challenged his conviction on numerous grounds. He cited *Sherman v. United States*, 356 U.S. 369 (1958), to argue that the government had entrapped him as a matter of law. Mohamud contended that he had intended to complete college in the United States, and only the FBI's aggressive and coercive actions had led him down the bombing path. The district court rejected that argument, pointing to evidence that before any contact with the FBI, Mohamud: (1) originally planned to wage war in the United States until a dream refocused him on Yemen; (2) wrote articles for *Jihad Recollections* which advised how best to prepare to carry out "jihad" on non-believers; and (3) had lengthy email conversations with men that the FBI believed promoted terrorism. The court also highlighted that Mohamud never showed any reluctance (unlike the defendant in *Sherman*), and only thirteen minutes after meeting Youssef in person, he said that he wanted to become "operational" by using a car bomb.

After the verdict (but before sentencing), the government filed a supplemental notice that it had "offered into evidence or otherwise used or disclosed in proceedings, including at trial" information derived from information collected pursuant to § 702 of the Foreign Intelligence Surveillance Act of 1978 ("FISA"), 50 U.S.C. § 1881a (hereinafter referred to as "§ 702"). Mohamud argued that this late notice warranted suppression of this evidence (and any fruits thereof). The government countered that FISA did not provide for suppression in these circumstances, and in any case, there was no substantial prejudice, as the district court could conduct a post-trial suppression analysis. The district court agreed, finding no misconduct in the late disclosure, and that Mohamud had suffered no prejudice from the delayed disclosure. . . .

Finally, the district court held that § 702 does not violate the Fourth Amendment. The court reasoned that § 702 surveillance does not trigger the Fourth Amendment's warrant requirement because U.S. persons' data is collected only incidentally, but even if it did, no warrant would be required because the foreign intelligence exception would apply. The court then balanced the government's interests in the search against the intrusions on Mohamud's privacy, and held that the § 702 collection here was reasonable under the Fourth Amendment.

. . .

D. Section 702 Collection of Mohamud's Email Communications

1. Legal Background

In 1978, Congress enacted FISA "to authorize and regulate certain governmental electronic surveillance of communications for foreign intelligence purposes." *Clapper v. Amnesty Int'l USA*, 133 S. Ct. 1138, 1143 (2013) (citing 50 U.S.C. § 1801 *et seq.*). To do so, the government must obtain a FISA warrant from the FISC. The FISA Court of Review assesses any denials by the FISC of applications for electronic surveillance.

Thirty years later, Congress enacted § 702 as part of the FISA Amendments Act of 2008. 50 U.S.C. § 1881a. Section 702 "supplements pre-existing FISA authority by creating a new framework under which the Government may seek the FISC's authorization of certain foreign intelligence surveillance targeting the communications of non-U.S. persons located abroad." *Clapper*, 133 S. Ct. at 1144. "Unlike traditional FISA surveillance, § [702] does not require the Government to demonstrate probable cause that the target of the electronic surveillance is a foreign power or agent of a foreign power." *Id.* "And, unlike traditional FISA, § [702] does not require the Government to specify the nature and location of each of the particular facilities or places at which the electronic surveillance will occur." *Id.* Instead, § 702 mandates that the government obtain the FISC's "approval of 'targeting' procedures, 'minimization' procedures, and a governmental certification regarding proposed surveillance." *Id.* at 1145 (quoting 50 U.S.C. § 1881a(a), (c)(1), (i)(2), (i)(3)).

2. No Fourth Amendment Violation

Although § 702 potentially raises complex statutory and constitutional issues, this case does not. As explained below, the initial collection of Mohamud's email communications did not involve so-called "upstreaming" or targeting of Mohamud under § 702, more controversial methods of collecting information. It also did not involve the retention and querying of incidentally collected communications. All this case involved was the targeting of a foreign national under § 702, through which Mohamud's email communications were incidentally collected. Confined to the particular facts of this case, we hold that the § 702 acquisition of Mohamud's email communications did not violate the Fourth Amendment.

At our request post-argument, the government declassified certain facts about Mohamud's surveillance. Through the monitoring of a foreign national's email account, the United States government learned that Mohamud was in contact with that foreign national, who was located overseas. This contact—a limited number of emails between Mohamud and the foreign national—was used to obtain a FISA warrant to surveil Mohamud and his activities. None of these emails was introduced at trial. We permitted the parties to file supplemental briefs to address the facts offered in the post-argument disclosure.

a. No Warrant Required to Intercept Overseas Foreign National's Communications or to Intercept U.S. Person's Communications Incidentally

As a threshold matter, "the Fourth Amendment does not apply to searches and seizures by the United States against a non-resident alien in a foreign country." *United States v. Zakharov*, 468 F.3d 1171, 1179 (9th Cir. 2006) (citing *United States v. Verdugo-Urquidez*, 494 U.S. 259, 274-75 (1990)); *see also Verdugo-Urquidez*, 494 U.S. at 274-75 ("At the time of the search, [respondent] was a citizen and resident of Mexico with no voluntary attachment to the United States, and the place searched was located in Mexico. Under these circumstances, the Fourth Amendment has no application."). Thus, the government's monitoring of the overseas foreign national's email fell outside the Fourth Amendment.

Mohamud argues that under *Verdugo-Urquidez*, the location of the search matters, and that here, the searches took place in the United States. Indeed, the government acknowledges that "collection from service providers under Section 702 takes place within the United States." Yet, as one court put it, "what matters here is the location of the *target*," and not where the government literally obtained the electronic data. *United States v. Hasbajrami*, No. 11-CR-623, 2016 WL 1029500, at *9 n.15 (E.D.N.Y. Mar. 8, 2016) (emphasis in original); *see also* Kris & Wilson, *National Security Investigations & Prosecutions* § 17:3 (2016) ("For non-U.S. person targets, there is no probable-cause requirement; the only thing that matters is [ ]the government's reasonable belief about[ ] the target's location.").

Consistent with *Verdugo-Urquidez* and our precedent, we hold that this particular type of non-upstream collection—where a search was not directed at a U.S. person's communications, though some were incidentally swept up in it—does not require a warrant, because the search was targeted at a non-U.S. person with no Fourth Amendment right.

The FISA Review Court in *In re Directives Pursuant to Section 105B of FISA*, similarly applied this principle, holding that "incidental collections occurring as a result of constitutionally permissible acquisitions do not render those acquisitions unlawful." 551 F.3d 1004, 1015 (FISA Ct. Rev. 2008).

Mohamud and Amici urge us not to apply this "incidental overhear" approach. First, Amici contend that surveillance of U.S. persons' communications under

§ 702 is not "incidental" because the monitoring of communications between foreign targets and U.S. persons was specifically contemplated and to some degree desired. We agree that such communications were anticipated. As the Privacy and Civil Liberties Oversight Board found with respect to PRISM collection, "[t]he collection of communications to and from a target inevitably returns communications in which non-targets are on the other end, some of whom will be U.S. persons. Such 'incidental' collection of communications is not accidental, nor is it inadvertent." PCLOB Report at 82. . . . The fact that the government knew some U.S. persons' communications would be swept up during foreign intelligence gathering does not make such collection any more unlawful in this context than in the Title III or traditional FISA context.

Mohamud and Amici also contend that the "sheer amount of 'incidental' collection" separates § 702 from prior cases where courts have found such collection permissible. We agree with the district court's observation that the most troubling aspect of this "incidental" collection is not whether such collection was anticipated, but rather its volume, which is vast, not *de minimis*. *See* PCLOB Report at 114 ("The term 'incidental' is appropriate because such collection is not accidental or inadvertent, but rather is an anticipated collateral result of monitoring an overseas target. But the term should not be understood to suggest that such collection is infrequent or that it is an inconsequential part of the Section 702 program."). This quantity distinguishes § 702 collection from Title III and traditional FISA interceptions. However, the mere fact that more communications are being collected incidentally does not make it unconstitutional to apply the same approach to § 702 collection, though it does increase the importance of minimization procedures once the communications are collected.

Additionally, Mohamud and Amici contend that prior cases upholding incidental collection involved prior judicial review or a "narrowly drawn exception to the warrant requirement," as opposed to the collection here. *See, e.g., United States v. Kahn*, 415 U.S. 143, 156-57 (1974) (upholding interception of communications of a woman that were incidentally collected under a wiretap order targeting her husband); *United States v. Figueroa*, 757 F.2d 466, 473-75 (2d Cir. 1985) (holding that wiretap order was not made unconstitutional by permitting interception of conversations of "others as yet unknown"). . . . However, the searches in those cases targeted United States citizens and took place within the United States, so a warrant was required for the initial search to be constitutionally permissible. But "the guiding principle behind them applies with equal force here: when surveillance is lawful in the first place—whether it is the domestic surveillance of U.S. persons pursuant to a warrant, or the warrantless surveillance of non-U.S. persons who are abroad—the incidental interception of non-targeted U.S. persons' communications with the targeted persons is also lawful." *Hasbajrami*, 2016 WL 1029500, at *9.

For these reasons, and because the target of the surveillance was a non-U.S. person located outside of the United States at the time of the surveillance, the government was not required to obtain a search warrant to collect

Mohamud's email communications with the overseas foreign national as an incident to its lawful search of the foreign national's email.

b. Collection of Mohamud's Emails Was Reasonable

Assuming that Mohamud had a Fourth Amendment right in the incidentally collected communications, the search at issue was reasonable under the Fourth Amendment.

"Even if a warrant is not required, a search is not beyond Fourth Amendment scrutiny; for it must be reasonable in its scope and manner of execution." *Maryland v. King*, 133 S. Ct. 1958, 1970 (2013). In deciding reasonableness, we examine the totality of the circumstances and weigh "'the promotion of legitimate governmental interests' against 'the degree to which [the search] intrudes upon an individual's privacy.'" *Id.* (quoting *Wyoming v. Houghton*, 526 U.S. 295, 300 (1999)). We agree with the district court that under these circumstances, the search was reasonable under the Fourth Amendment.

i. Government Interest

"[T]he Government's interest in combating terrorism is an urgent objective of the highest order." *Holder v. Humanitarian Law Project*, 561 U.S. 1, 28 (2010). Neither Mohamud nor Amici challenge this. Instead, they argue that (1) the statutory definition of "foreign intelligence information" in § 702 is overbroad because it is not confined to national security information but also includes "the conduct of [ ] foreign affairs"; and (2) even if national security justifies the initial acquisition, it is unreasonable to then retain and later search U.S. persons' § 702-acquired communications without a warrant.

The declassified facts foreclose both arguments. First, as the district court observed, "the discovery in this case all concerned protecting the country from a terrorist threat and did not stray into the broader category of the conduct of foreign affairs." Thus, we need not determine whether the collection of foreign affairs communications is reasonable. Similarly, the second argument is also outside the scope of our review, as no such retention and querying is at issue in this case.

ii. Mohamud's Privacy Interest

The parties agree that Mohamud had some expectation of privacy in his electronic communications, but disagree as to the strength of his interest. The government argues that U.S. persons have a limited expectation of privacy when communicating electronically with non-U.S. persons located outside the United States because of the Fourth Amendment's "third-party" doctrine—that a person's privacy interest is diminished where he or she reveals information to a third party, even in confidence. Mohamud contends that the voluntary disclosure of information to third parties does not reduce the expectation of privacy. The district court determined that under the third-party doctrine, Mohamud had a reduced expectation of privacy in his communications to third parties. We agree.

With respect to a U.S. person's privacy interest, we treat emails as letters. . . . Accordingly, until electronic communications reach the recipient, they retain the same level of privacy interest as if they were still in the home.

But as with letters, "[a] person's reasonable expectation of privacy may be diminished in 'transmissions over the Internet or e-mail that have already arrived at the recipient.'" *United States v. Heckenkamp*, 482 F.3d 1142, 1146 (9th Cir. 2007).

It is true that prior case law contemplates a diminished expectation of privacy due to the risk that the recipient will reveal the communication, not that the government will be monitoring the communication unbeknownst to the third party. . . . While these cases do not address the question of government interception, the communications at issue here had been sent to a third party, which reduces Mohamud's privacy interest at least somewhat, if perhaps not as much as if the foreign national had turned them over to the government voluntarily.

Thus, Mohamud's interest in the privacy of his communications received by the overseas foreign national is diminished.

iii. Privacy Protecting Measures

An important component of the reasonableness inquiry is whether the FISC-approved targeting and minimization measures sufficiently protect the privacy interests of U.S. persons. Targeting and minimization procedures govern, respectively, who may be targeted for surveillance and how intercepted communications are to be retained and disseminated.

In brief, targeting procedures must be "reasonably designed" to "ensure that any acquisition authorized under [the certification] is limited to targeting persons reasonably believed to be located outside the United States" and to "prevent the intentional acquisition of any communication as to which the sender and all intended recipients are known at the time of the acquisition to be located in the United States." 50 U.S.C. § 1881a(d)(1). Among other requirements, minimization procedures must be "reasonably designed" "to minimize the acquisition and retention, and prohibit the dissemination, of nonpublicly available information concerning unconsenting United States persons consistent with the need of the United States to obtain, produce, and disseminate foreign intelligence information." 50 U.S.C. §§ 1801(h)(1), 1881a(e)(1).

After evaluating the protections detailed in § 702 and the classified minimization procedures, the district court concluded that as applied to Mohamud, § 702 is reasonable under the Fourth Amendment. Based on our review of the classified record, we agree that the applicable targeting and minimization procedures, which were followed in practice, sufficiently protected Mohamud's privacy interest.

The government also contends that certain oversight procedures provide an important check on Executive Branch actions. For example, § 702 requires the Attorney General ("AG") and Director of National Intelligence ("DNI") to certify, among other things, that (1) a significant purpose of the acquisition is to obtain foreign intelligence information, (2) they have adopted guidelines to ensure compliance with the statutory limitations in § 702(b), and (3) the targeting and minimization procedures and guidelines are consistent with the Fourth Amendment. 50 U.S.C § 1881a(g)(2)(A).

While Executive Branch certification contributes some degree of further protection, it does not weigh heavily. Typically in the Fourth Amendment context, review from a neutral magistrate is considered the appropriate check on the Executive, which otherwise may be motivated by its interest in carrying out its duties. . . . Under these circumstances, where the only judicial review comes in the form of the FISC reviewing the adequacy of procedures, this type of internal oversight does not provide a robust safeguard. The government notes that in *In re Sealed Case*, 310 F.3d 717, 739 (FISA Ct. Rev. 2002), the FISA Review Court observed that Congress recognized that certification by the AG in the traditional FISA context would "'assure [ ] written accountability within the Executive Branch' and provide 'an internal check on Executive Branch arbitrariness.'" (citation omitted). However, as described above, § 702 differs in important ways from traditional FISA, and a mechanism that might provide additional protections above and beyond those already employed in a traditional FISA context provides far less assurance and accountability in the § 702 context, which lacks those baseline protections.

Accordingly, although we do not place great weight on the oversight procedures, under the totality of the circumstances, we conclude that the applied targeting and minimization procedures adequately protected Mohamud's diminished privacy interest, in light of the government's compelling interest in national security.

In sum, even assuming Mohamud had a Fourth Amendment right in the incidentally collected communications, the search was reasonable. Thus, we hold that the application of § 702 did not violate the Fourth Amendment under the particular facts of this case.

IV. CONCLUSION

Many young people think and say alarming things that they later disavow, and we will never know if Mohamud—a young man with promise—would have carried out a mass attack absent the FBI's involvement. But some "promising" young people—Charles Whitman, Timothy McVeigh, and James Holmes, to name a few from a tragically long list—take the next step, leading to horrific consequences. While technology makes it easier to capture the thoughts of these individuals, it also makes it easier for them to commit terrible crimes. Here, the evidence supported the jury's verdict, and the government's surveillance, investigation, and prosecution of Mohamud were consistent with constitutional and statutory requirements.

AFFIRMED.

NOTES AND QUESTIONS

1. Traditional FISA surveillance warrants require the government to demonstrate probable cause that the target of the electronic surveillance is a foreign power or agent of a foreign power and the targeted facilities are used, or about to be used, by a foreign power or their agents. 50 U.S.C. § 1805(a)(2)(A)-(B). Section 702 of FISA, codified at 50 U.S.C. § 1881a, does not impose these requirements. Instead, a § 1881a application must include a written certification and supporting affidavit under oath to the FISC. *Id.* § 1881a(g)(1)(A). The certification must attest that there are "targeting procedures" in place that are reasonably designed to ensure that the acquisition of foreign intelligence information is limited to a non-U.S. person reasonably believed to be located outside of the United States. *Id.* § 1881a(g)(2)(A)(i). The certification must also attest that the government has "minimization procedures" in place that are reasonably designed to protect against the acquisition, retention, and dissemination of nonpublic information that is not foreign intelligence information. *Id.* § 1881a(g)(2)(A)(ii). For a comprehensive discussion of § 702, see the Report on the Surveillance Program Operated Pursuant to Section 702 of the Foreign Intelligence Surveillance Act, PCLOB (2014).

2. Critics of § 702 fear that it will be abused and used to evade the probable cause requirements imposed on traditional FISA surveillance warrants and used to target non-U.S. persons located outside the United States for the true purpose of surveilling a U.S. person or someone inside the United States. *See* Laura K. Donohue, *Section 702 and the Collection of International Telephone and Internet Content*, 38 Harv. J.L. & Pub. Pol'y, 117 (2015). Is this a valid concern? If so, how can this type of abuse be prevented?

3. The court held that the "incidental" collection of Mohamud's e-mail communications did not violate the Fourth Amendment. Mohamud's e-mails were collected pursuant to a FISA surveillance warrant issued under § 702, which targeted a non-U.S. person reasonably believed to be located outside the United States. The court held that the Fourth Amendment does not apply to searches and seizures against non-U.S. persons in a foreign country, citing *United States v. Verdugo-Urquidez*, 494 U.S. 259, 274-75 (1990). The *Verdugo-Urquidez* case involved the search of a foreign national's residence in Mexico conducted without a search warrant. The Supreme Court rejected Verdugo-Urquidez's claim that the warrantless search violated the Fourth Amendment. The Court held that the Fourth Amendment has no application to a foreign citizen with no voluntary, substantial connections to the United States, where the place searched was located outside the United States. What is the scope of the holding in *Verdugo-Urquidez*? Does the Fourth Amendment apply to FISA surveillance of a non-U.S. person lawfully working or studying in the United States on a visa, while traveling abroad to visit family? Do such persons have sufficient connections to the United States to implicate Fourth Amendment protections?

(4) The court concluded that even if Mohamud had a Fourth Amendment right in the incidentally collected communications, the seizure of his e-mail communications was reasonable under the Fourth Amendment. In deciding reasonableness, the court examined the totality of the circumstances and balanced the legitimate government interests against the defendant's privacy interests. The court concluded that the government's interest in combating terrorism outweighed Mohamud's privacy interest. Applying the court's balancing test, isn't the government's interest in preventing terrorist attacks always going to trump individual privacy concerns? Can you envision a scenario where an individual's privacy interest outweighs the government's counter-terrorism interests?

(5) In finding that the incidental collection of Mohamud's e-mail communications was reasonable under the Fourth Amendment, the court emphasized the privacy protection measures required under 50 U.S.C. § 1881a. What are these privacy protection measures and how do they protect the privacy interests of U.S. persons? At the same time, the court rejected the government's claim that internal oversight procedures provide an important check on executive branch actions. What are the relevant internal oversight procedures? Why didn't the court place great weight on the oversight procedures?

c. Fifth Amendment Due Process — Disclosure of FISA Materials

United States v. Dhirane
896 F.3d 295 (4th Cir. 2018)

NIEMEYER, Circuit Judge:

Following a bench trial, the district court found Muna Osman Jama and Hinda Osman Dhirane guilty of conspiracy to provide and of providing on numerous occasions material support to al-Shabaab, a designated foreign terrorist organization, in violation of 18 U.S.C. § 2339B. The defendants, naturalized American citizens who were born in Somalia, collected money from members of online chat rooms and transmitted the funds to co-conspirators in Somalia and Kenya to assist al-Shabaab's terrorist activities in the Horn of Africa. The district court sentenced Jama to 144 months' imprisonment and Dhirane to 132 months' imprisonment.

On appeal, the defendants contend (1) that the district court erred in denying their motion to suppress evidence obtained pursuant to warrants issued under the Foreign Intelligence Surveillance Act ("FISA"), arguing that the evidence was obtained unconstitutionally in light of FISA's *ex parte* and *in camera* judicial review process; [and] (2) that the district court applied an incorrect legal standard to conclude that two co-conspirators in Somalia and Kenya, to whom the defendants transmitted monies, were "part of" al-Shabaab. . . .

For the reasons that follow, we affirm.

I

In 2008, the U.S. Department of State designated al-Shabaab a foreign terrorist organization under § 219 of the Immigration and Nationality Act, 8 U.S.C. § 1189. At that time and continuing through the events of this case, al-Shabaab was engaged in terrorist activities in the Horn of Africa region, principally in Somalia.

In the period from 2011 to 2013, the defendants participated in an online chat room composed of members of the Somali diaspora in the United States and around the world. Participants generally discussed current events concerning Somalia, including al-Shabaab's activities there, and, on various occasions, al-Shabaab leaders and representatives would speak to the group and solicit support, including financial support, for their terrorist activities. During that time, the defendants also participated in a smaller, private chat room known as the "Group of Fifteen." Only those participants from the larger chat room who had been or who could be persuaded to become committed supporters of al-Shabaab were invited to join. The Group of Fifteen conversed confidentially approximately once or twice a month, where members pledged to make periodic payments ranging from $50 to $200 in support of al-Shabaab's operations. The defendants kept track of those commitments and contributed money themselves. They also arranged for representatives or persons associated with al-Shabaab to speak to the Group of Fifteen and solicit support, including financial resources, for al-Shabaab's activities.

As the money was collected, the defendants transmitted it to persons involved with al-Shabaab either on "the Nairobi side," referring to the geographical area around Nairobi, Kenya, or "the Hargeisa side," referring to the geographical area around Hargeisa, Somalia. Defendant Jama "personally solicited contributions" from the Group of Fifteen, "monitored whether the individual members had satisfied their monthly commitments," and saw to it that the sums were "successfully transmitted to and received by [al-Shabaab] contacts," both on the Nairobi side and the Hargeisa side. And defendant Dhirane played a similar role, mostly for the Hargeisa side. The monies sent to the Nairobi side were transmitted principally to a woman named Fardowsa Jama Mohamed, who used the funds to operate two safehouses in Nairobi for al-Shabaab fighters. The monies sent to the Hargeisa side were transmitted principally to a woman named Barira Hassan Abdullahi, described as a financial organizer on behalf of al-Shabaab, who used the funds to purchase vehicles and other supplies for al-Shabaab fighters in the Golis Mountains just north of Hargeisa.

The government gathered evidence of the defendants' activities through electronic surveillance authorized under FISA. Transcripts of conversations collected during this surveillance showed the defendants and their coconspirators using coded language and sharing advice about how to avoid being caught and what to say if questioned. They also showed the defendants discussing instances where their financial help had assisted fighters in the field. On one occasion, Dhirane described a news report of an attack by al-Shabaab on Somali government troops as an ambush "by our forces," stating, "Thanks to God; let him die. . . . Yes, wonderful; that one will benefit us."

In June 2014, the defendants, along with others—including Mohamed and Abdullahi—were indicted and charged with one count of conspiracy to provide material support to al-Shabaab, a designated foreign terrorist organization, and both defendants were charged with 20 substantive counts of providing material support in the form of money to al-Shabaab—one count for each transmission of money—all in violation of 18 U.S.C. § 2339B(a)(1).

Prior to trial, the government filed a notice of its intent to present evidence gathered during the surveillance that was conducted pursuant to warrants issued under FISA. The defendants filed a joint motion to suppress the evidence, even though they had not reviewed the warrant application and supporting materials due to the fact that they were classified, contending that the information was unlawfully acquired or the surveillance was not made in conformity with an order of authorization or approval, citing 50 U.S.C. §§ 1806(e) and 1825(f). They also requested that their counsel, who possessed a security clearance, be given access to the classified FISA materials. While the district court denied their counsel access to the FISA materials, it nonetheless conducted an *in camera* and *ex parte* review of the materials and thereafter denied the defendants' motion to suppress. The court concluded that there was probable cause to issue the warrants; that the surveillance complied with all applicable procedures; and that nothing in the materials suggested that a false statement or misleading omission had been made to the Foreign Intelligence Surveillance Court that issued the warrants authorizing the surveillance.

The defendants waived their right to a jury trial, and the district court conducted a bench trial beginning in July 2016. During trial, the defendants argued that they provided monies exclusively for the purpose of procuring medicine and medical services for al-Shabaab members, which they claimed fell within the "medicine" exception to "material support" as used in 18 U.S.C. § 2339B. *See id.* § 2339A(b)(1). At the conclusion of trial, the court found both defendants guilty of conspiracy, Jama guilty of all substantive counts, and Dhirane guilty of those substantive counts covering conduct that occurred after she joined the conspiracy, acquitting her on the remaining counts. . . .

The court found as facts that the defendants were "ardent, committed, and active supporters of [al-Shabaab]"; that they knew that al-Shabaab was a designated foreign terrorist organization and was engaging in terrorist activities; and that they knew that it was unlawful to provide support to that organization. The court found further that the defendants played a prominent role in the Group of Fifteen chat room, arranging for representatives of or persons associated with al-Shabaab to solicit funds from members of the chat room and then organizing the collection of those funds and their transmission to Kenya and Somalia. It found that the defendants transmitted the funds mostly to coconspirator Mohamed on the Nairobi side and coconspirator Abdullahi on the Hargeisa side for the specific purpose of supporting al-Shabaab's activities in those areas. Mohamed, it found, operated two safehouses in Nairobi, one for providing medical care and treatment to injured al-Shabaab soldiers and the other as a staging ground for al-Shabaab's military operations. Abdullahi, it found, received the monies in Hargeisa and used them to provide transportation, trucks, and other support services to al-Shabaab soldiers. The court found generally that the defendants, as part of their fundraising activities, had access to al-Shabaab leaders and to nonpublic information pertaining to al-Shabaab's financial needs, including for its military activities. In this regard, the court found specifically that these defendants coordinated "to some degree their fundraising" with respect to the specific military activities of al-Shabaab. In sum, the court found that the defendants "understood, intended, and planned that, when they provided money to [Mohamed, Abdullahi, and others], they provided money to [al-Shabaab]."

. . .

II

The defendants contend first that the statutory framework that allowed the district court to determine *ex parte* and *in camera* the legality of the government's surveillance of them pursuant to the FISA warrants was "fundamentally at odds with our adversary system." They argue that it was contrary to our constitutionally established adversary system to deny their counsel, who possessed the requisite security clearance, access to the warrant applications and supporting materials to assess whether they met statutory requirements and were consistent with the Fourth Amendment. Such a review on behalf of any defendant, they assert, should only be made by the defendant's counsel as an advocate, not by the court. Moreover, they contend that by refusing to allow defense counsel to review the materials, the district court effectively precluded counsel from obtaining a *Franks* hearing. *See Franks v. Delaware*, 438 U.S. 154, 171-72 (1978) (authorizing an adversarial hearing on the validity of a warrant upon a showing of an intentional or reckless falsehood in a warrant affidavit). The defendants make clear, however, that they do not challenge on appeal the conclusions reached by the district court, only the statutory framework that allowed the court to reach those conclusions without the participation of counsel.

The defendants filed a motion to suppress the surveillance evidence before trial, and because the Attorney General filed an affidavit stating that disclosure of the classified materials involved in obtaining the warrants would harm national security, the district court conducted an *ex parte* and *in camera* review of the warrant applications and underlying materials, as provided by FISA. The court found that it was able to adjudicate the legality of the FISA surveillance without the assistance of defense counsel, although the statute provided it with discretion to seek that assistance, and it concluded that the surveillance was properly authorized and lawfully conducted.

In enacting FISA, Congress intended that the procedures provided strike a reasonable balance between the competing interests in protecting individuals' constitutional guarantees and in protecting matters involving national security. The Act provides that when a defendant files a motion to suppress and the Attorney General files "an affidavit under oath that disclosure or an adversary hearing would harm the national security of the United States," the court must review the materials *ex parte* and *in camera* "to determine whether the surveillance of the aggrieved person was lawfully authorized and conducted." 50 U.S.C. § 1806(f); *see also id.* § 1825(g). The Act gives the court authority to disclose the materials to the party moving to suppress, but "only where such disclosure is necessary to make an accurate determination of the legality of the surveillance." *Id.* § 1806(f); *see also id.* § 1825(g).

The government notes that every federal court to have considered the constitutionality of these procedures has concluded that FISA reached a reasonable and therefore constitutional balance of competing interests. And we share that view. It is consistent with the general notion, even in the criminal context, that the right to an adversarial proceeding to determine disputes of fact is not absolute.

Nonetheless, the defendants contend that the FISA structure denied them their constitutionally established right to a *Franks* hearing. In *Franks*, the Supreme Court recognized that a defendant has the right to challenge the veracity of an affidavit made in support of a warrant, but in order to procure an evidentiary hearing on the matter, the defendant must first specifically identify what aspect of the affidavit used by the judicial officer to issue the warrant was allegedly false and must accompany that allegation with an offer of proof. 438 U.S. at 167, 171. FISA similarly provides for court review of a warrant application's veracity and legality and, if the court finds it necessary, a hearing. In conducting its review, however, the court relies on the input of various executive officers and its own review of the relevant materials to decide whether a hearing is necessary. *See* 50 U.S.C. § 1806(e)-(g); *see also Daoud*, 755 F.3d at 484 ("[T]he judge makes the additional determination, based on full access to all classified materials and the defense's proffer of its version of the events, of whether it's possible to determine the validity of the *Franks* challenge without disclosure of any of the classified materials to the defense").

We recognize the benefit that an open, adversarial proceeding could provide, particularly in cases where a falsehood in the affidavit could be more readily identified by the defendant or his counsel than by a court perhaps less familiar with the subject matter. But Congress did not run afoul of the Constitution when it reasoned that the additional benefit of an unconditional adversarial process was outweighed by the Nation's interest in protecting itself from foreign threats. And even then, it took care to mitigate the loss of any such benefit by requiring the involvement of a number of high-ranking executive officials who, subject to additional oversight by the Attorney General, must participate in the FISA-warrant application process. *See* 50 U.S.C. § 1804 (requiring, *inter alia*, (1) that the application be made by a federal officer upon oath or affirmation, (2) that the Attorney General personally approve the application, (3) that a high-ranking executive official certify the application, and (4) that other affidavits or certifications be provided as the judge or Attorney General may demand).

At bottom, we reject the defendants' challenge to the FISA framework and thus to the district court's decision not to disclose the classified FISA materials to the defendants' counsel under that framework, even though, as the defendants repeatedly noted, their counsel had the requisite security clearance.

. . .

The judgments of the district court in convicting and sentencing the defendants are accordingly affirmed.

NOTES AND QUESTIONS

1. What are the procedural requirements for disclosing FISA applications, affidavits, and related materials? Do these procedures substantially disadvantage the defendant or "aggrieved person"? Is the district court in a position to challenge the government's assertion that disclosure of such materials would harm national security? As a result, is the district court always going to defer to the government on its claim that disclosure of FISA material would harm national security?

2. Once the *in camera, ex parte* procedure is triggered, the reviewing court may disclose such materials "only where such disclosure is necessary to make an accurate determination of the legality of the surveillance." 50 U.S.C. §1806(c). Under what circumstances, if any, is the district court likely to disclose FISA materials to the defendant?

3. To date, no court has found it necessary to disclose FISA materials to a defendant seeking to suppress evidence derived from a FISA warrant. Courts uniformly hold that *in camera* review procedures do not deprive a defendant of due process. While defendants are significantly disadvantaged by not being able to review FISA materials needed to effectively challenge a FISA warrant, the courts contend that in devising the procedures that govern disclosure of FISA materials, Congress made a reasonable effort to balance the competing interests in privacy and national security. Do you agree? If a defendant is prohibited from viewing the underlying FISA materials upon which the FISA warrant is based, how can he effectively seek to suppress FISA-derived evidence on the grounds that the evidence was unlawfully acquired, or the electronic surveillance, or physical search was not conducted in conformity with the FISA order?

4. In *United States v. Belfield*, 692 F.2d (D.C. Cir. 1982), the court recognized the dilemma confronting the defendant, but nonetheless found that denying the defendant access to the underlying FISA materials does not violate due process. The court stated:

> We appreciate the difficulties of appellants' counsel in this case. They must argue that the determination of legality is so complex that an adversary hearing with full access to relevant materials is necessary. But without access to the relevant materials their claim of complexity can be given no concreteness. . . . Congress was also aware of these difficulties. But it chose to resolve them through means

other than mandatory disclosure. . . . [I]t cannot be said that this exclusion [of defendants from the process] rises to the level of a constitutional violation.[10]

If defense counsel is not permitted access to the underlying FISA materials, what is he supposed to argue at the hearing on the motion to suppress evidence? In effect, the defendant is wholly dependent on the district court's *in camera* review of the FISA materials. Does this procedure satisfy due process? In essence, does national security trump the defendant's due process rights?

5. FISA requires the government to "notify the aggrieved person and the court" prior to trial when it intends to use at trial evidence "obtained or derived from electronic surveillance" pursuant to FISA. 50 U.S.C. § 1806(c). In *United States v. Mohamud*, 843 F.3d 420 (9th Cir. 2016), discussed *supra*, the government provided notice regarding evidence derived under § 702 *after* the trial concluded. Despite this egregious violation of the FISA notice requirement, the Ninth Circuit held that the district court did not err in denying Mohamud's motion to suppress based on the late FISA notice. The court held that Mohamud failed to demonstrate how the late notice prejudiced him.

III. NATIONAL SECURITY LETTERS

Five statutory provisions require businesses to produce specified records to federal officials conducting national security investigations.[11] These requests for the production of business records, comparable to administrative subpoenas, are known as National Security Letters (NSLs). NSLs differ from FISA orders in several important respects. First, unlike FISA orders, NSLs do not require a court order and are issued by federal government agencies responsible for national security investigations. Second, FISA orders authorize electronic surveillance, physical searches, the installation of pen registers and trap and trace devices, and authorize the production of business records and other tangible things relevant to national security. However, the scope of documents and information that can be obtained by NSLs is more limited. NSLs require the recipient to produce financial records, credit history information, telephone records, or certain information relevant to an investigation of a federal employee for unlawfully disclosing classified information. Finally, NSLs do not require a nexus between the requested records and a foreign power or an agent of a foreign power.

Under each of the NSL statutes, a government official must certify that the purpose of the NSL is to acquire information related to national security concerns. For example, under the Electronic Communications Privacy Act, 18 U.S.C. § 2709(b), the designated senior FBI official must certify that "[the information] sought [is]

---

10. *Id.* at 148.

11. These statutory provisions include: § 114(a)(5) of the Right to Financial Privacy Act (12 U.S.C. § 3414(a)(5)) (financial records); §§ 626 and 627 of the Fair Credit Reporting Act (15 U.S.C. §§ 1681u) (credit history), 1681v (full credit reports); Electronic Communications Privacy Act (18 U.S.C. § 2709) (telephone records); and § 802 of the National Security Act (50 U.S.C. § 436) (information concerning investigation of unlawful disclosure of classified information by a federal employee).

relevant to an authorized investigation to protect against international terrorism or clandestine intelligence activities. . . ." The certification required under the Fair Credit Reporting Act and Right to Financial Privacy Act are quite similar. Finally, the National Security Act requires a certification that the information is sought to conduct "any authorized law enforcement investigation, counterintelligence inquiry, or security determination. . . ."

Each of the NSL statutes contains a nondisclosure or confidentiality requirement. The recipient of the NSL can, however, disclose such information to the extent necessary to comply with the request or to an attorney to obtain legal advice or assistance with respect to the request as long as the recipient informs such persons of the nondisclosure requirement. A breach of the confidentiality requirement committed knowingly and with the intent to obstruct justice is punishable by up to five years in prison, a fine of not more than $250,000 (an organization can be fined up to $500,000), or both.

Section 3511 of Title 18 of the United States Code provides for judicial review of NSLs and the nondisclosure requirement issued under the NSL statutes. The USA FREEDOM Act of 2015 amended the procedures for judicial review. *See* USA FREEDOM Act §§ 502(a) (telephone records), (b) (financial records), (c) (credit reports), (d) (consumer reports), and (e) (investigation of persons with access to classified information). Under the Act, if a recipient of an NSL wishes to have a court review a nondisclosure requirement, the recipient may notify the government or file a petition for judicial review in any district where the NSL was issued. Next, not later than thirty days after the receipt of a notification for judicial review, the government shall apply for an order prohibiting the disclosure of the existence or contents of the relevant NSL request. In the government's application, the Director of the FBI, or other high-ranking designated government official, shall certify that disclosure of the existence of the NSL may result in "(i) a danger to the national security of the United States; (ii) interference with a criminal, counterterrorism, or counterintelligence investigation; (iii) interference with diplomatic relations; or (iv) danger to the life or physical safety of any person." An application may be filed in the district court in which the recipient is doing business or where the authorized investigation is being conducted. Finally, a district court that receives a petition by the NSL recipient or application by the government is required to rule expeditiously on the matter. The district court shall issue a nondisclosure order if the court determines there is "reason to believe" that disclosure of the information subject to the nondisclosure requirement may result in any of the threats to national security set forth in the government's certification.

NOTES AND QUESTIONS

1. It should be noted that the amendments to the procedures for judicial review of NSLs enacted by the USA FREEDOM Act of 2015 were in response to *Doe v. Mukasey*, 549 F.3d 861 (2d Cir. 2008), where the court held that judicial review procedures violated the First Amendment because the government did not bear the burden to seek prompt judicial review of the nondisclosure order.

2. Do NSLs constitute a search and seizure under the Fourth Amendment? If so, is the government required to obtain a search warrant from a federal judge to obtain the requested records?
3. Does the third-party records doctrine apply to the production of records under the NSL statutes? Do the targets of NSL orders have a reasonable expectation of privacy in the records obtained by the government pursuant to NSL orders?
4. Does the "special needs" exception to the Fourth Amendment Warrants Clause apply to records obtained in response to NSL orders? Are the records obtained by NSL orders "beyond the normal need for law enforcement"? *Vernonia School Dist. 47J v. Acton*, 515 U.S. 646, 653 (1995) (quoting *Griffin v. Wisconsin*, 483 U.S. 868, 873 (1987) (internal quotation marks omitted)) (random drug testing of student athletes).

ASSESSMENT QUESTIONS

1. True or False: After *Clapper v. Amnesty International, USA*, 568 U.S. 398 (2013), plaintiffs confront a difficult legal hurdle to establish standing.

2. True or False: Cell phone customers whose telephone metadata is being collected by the NSA have a reasonable expectation of privacy in such data.

3. True or False: Under FISA, if gathering foreign intelligence information is a "significant purpose," another purpose, such as criminal investigation and prosecution, could be the primary purpose.

4. True or False: FISA warrants do not satisfy the Fourth Amendment reasonableness requirement.

5. True or False: The "special needs exception" applies to the collection of foreign intelligence information thereby precluding the requirement of a warrant based on probable cause.

ASSESSMENT ANSWERS

1. The statement is true. In *Clapper v. Amnesty International, USA*, 568 U.S. 398 (2013), Justice Alito, writing for the majority, found that respondents' reasonable belief that they were the target of a FISA electronic surveillance order was insufficient to establish standing. Because the FISA application process is secretive in nature and generally the government is not required to disclose the issuance of a FISA warrant, it will be quite difficult for a party to prove an injury "concrete, particularized, and actual or imminent," required to establish standing.

2. This remains an open issue after *Carpenter*. While the Supreme Court held that Carpenter had a reasonable expectation of privacy in cell site locator information, the Court stated that its opinion "does not consider other collection techniques involving foreign affairs or national security."

3. The statement is true. Prior to the passage of the USA PATRIOT Act in 2001, FISA had been interpreted to require that the primary purpose of the FISA warrant was to collect foreign intelligence information. The PATRIOT Act amended FISA to require that the collection of foreign intelligence information was a "significant purpose," while criminal investigation and prosecution could be the primary purpose.

4. The statement is false. In *In re Sealed Case*, 310 F.3d 717 (FISA Ct. Rev. 2002), the FISA Court of Review strongly intimated that a FISA order satisfies the reasonableness requirement under the Fourth Amendment. The court stated that a

FISA order comes close to meeting the procedural requirements for obtaining a Title III wiretap order, and "that certainly bears on its reasonableness under the Fourth Amendment."

5. The statement is false. In *In re Sealed Case*, the FISC Court of Review discussed, but did not decide, whether the "special needs" exception applies to the collection of foreign intelligence information. The issue would turn on whether the collection of foreign intelligence information in the particular case is "beyond the normal need for law enforcement." If the "primary purpose" of the FISA electronic surveillance was to gather evidence of a crime for criminal prosecution, a "significant purpose" was to collect foreign intelligence information, the requirement that the search was "beyond the normal need for law enforcement" would not be satisfied.

CHAPTER 13

Protecting Sensitive Information

I. OVERVIEW

An open and transparent government is essential to maintaining a vibrant democracy. For democracy to thrive the American people must be informed of the activities of their government. However, "throughout our history, the national defense has required that certain information be maintained in confidence in order to protect our citizens, our democratic institutions, our homeland security, and our interactions with foreign nations." Exec. Order No. 13526, 75 Fed. Reg. 707 (Jan. 5, 2010). The purpose for restricting access to government documents is to prevent this information from being used by foreign nations, entities, and individuals to inflict harm upon the United States or undermine national security interests.

The importance of protecting classified information was dramatically highlighted when WikiLeaks, an organization that describes itself as a "public service designed to protect whistleblowers, journalists, and activists who have sensitive materials to communicate to the public," obtained more than 91,000 classified government documents related to the wars in Afghanistan and Iraq, and other sensitive matters, and posted the majority of these documents on its website. JENNIFER K. ELSEA, CONG. RESEARCH SERV., R41404, CRIMINAL PROHIBITIONS ON THE PUBLICATION OF CLASSIFIED DEFENSE INFORMATION, at 2 (Sept. 19, 2013). A second incident involved the disclosure of classified information by Edward Snowden, a former government contractor, who leaked approximately 58,000 classified files to *The Guardian* newspaper, which disclosed the existence of the National Security Agency's (NSA) bulk "metadata program," which collects the cell phone records (but not the content of those communications) of hundreds of millions of Americans. Jill Lawless, *Guardian: We Have Published 1 Percent of Snowden Leak*, ASSOCIATED PRESS, Dec. 3, 2013. Snowden's critics maintain that the disclosure of the NSA surveillance program has severely compromised U.S. national security, and that he should be criminally prosecuted for treason. *Id.*

This chapter examines the U.S. government's system for classifying and securing national security information, as well as criminal prosecution for disclosure of national defense information prohibited by the Espionage Act of 1917, codified at 18 U.S.C. §§ 793-798. The following section discusses whether the disclosure of classified information to the media should be criminally punished, and whether so-called whistleblowers should be prosecuted for disclosing classified materials revealing government waste, fraud, and abuse. The chapter also considers the disclosure of national security information in civil litigation, including the tension between the government's need for secrecy and the plaintiff's right to pursue a judicial remedy. More specifically, the chapter discusses the *Totten* bar and the state-secrets privilege. Finally, it explores issues surrounding the disclosure of classified information in criminal litigation under the Classified Information Procedures Act (CIPA, 18 U.S.C. App. 3 §§ 1-16, S. Rep. No. 96-823 (1980)). The CIPA attempts to balance the government's interest in protecting national security and the defendant's right to present a defense and receive a fair trial.

II. THE U.S. GOVERNMENT CLASSIFICATION SYSTEM — EXECUTIVE ORDER 13526

The United States government's system for classifying, declassifying, and safeguarding national security information, including information to combat international terrorism, is established by Executive Order 13526. Exec. Order No. 13526, 75 Fed. Reg. 707 (Jan. 5, 2010). Information is classified based upon an assessment of the damage to national security that would result from disclosure of the information. Information may be classified at three levels: Top Secret, Secret, and Confidential. *Id.* § 1.2(a)(1)-(3). If a person holds a Top Secret security clearance, he may handle information up to the level of Top Secret, including Secret and Confidential. However, if a person holds a Secret clearance, such person may have access to Secret and Confidential classified information, but not information classified at the Top Secret level. Information is classified as "Top Secret" if unauthorized disclosure could cause "exceptionally grave damage" to national security. *Id.* § 1-2(a)(1). Information is classified as "Secret" if unauthorized disclosure could cause "serious damage" to national security. *Id.* § 1-2(a)(2). Finally, information is deemed "Confidential" if unauthorized disclosure could "damage" national security. *Id.* § 1-2(a)(3).

The authority to classify information may be exercised by the President, Vice President, or agency heads and officials designated by the President. *Id.* § 1.3(a). Executive Order 13526 limits the type of information that may be classified. Section 1.4 provides that information shall not be classified unless its unauthorized disclosure could reasonably be expected to cause damage to national security, as set forth in § 1.2(a), and it pertains to the following:

(a) Military plans, weapons systems, or operations;
(b) Foreign government information;
(c) Intelligence activities (including covert action), intelligence sources or methods, or cryptology;

(d) Foreign relations or foreign activities of the United States, including confidential sources;

(e) Scientific, technological, or economic matters relating to the national security;

(f) United States Government programs for safeguarding nuclear materials or facilities;

(g) Vulnerabilities or capabilities of systems, installations, infrastructures, projects, plans, or protection services relating to the national security; or

(h) The development, production, or use of weapons of mass destruction.[1]

Information may not remain classified indefinitely. At the time of the original classification, the classification authority is required to establish a specific date or event for declassification. *Id.* § 1.5(a). However, if the original classification authority cannot determine a specific date for declassification, the document shall be marked for declassification ten years from the date of the original classification, unless the classifying authority determines that the sensitivity of the information requires that it remain classified for up to twenty-five years from the date of the original decision. *Id.* § 1.5(b). Finally, except for information that would "clearly and demonstrably" reveal the identity of a confidential human source or human intelligence source, or the key design concepts of weapons of mass destruction, the date for declassification should not exceed twenty-five years. *Id.* § 1.5(a).

While classifying information to protect national security is laudable, there is a danger of government agencies over-classifying information. There is a reasonable risk that information that does not impact national security could be classified to cover up government misconduct, illegal government programs, or to protect governmental agency turf. The over-classification of information undermines government transparency and deprives the American public of information to evaluate the effectiveness of government programs and policy. Should the unauthorized disclosure of classified information to the media be criminally punished? If so, could such prosecutions have a chilling effect on the First Amendment? What about the unauthorized disclosure of information by government employees, so-called whistleblowers, for the purpose of preventing government waste, fraud, and abuse? Should prosecution turn on whether the disclosure of classified information actually harmed national security? These are a few of the important issues that will be examined in the next section on criminal prosecution under the Espionage Act.

III. CRIMINAL PROSECUTION FOR DISCLOSURE OF NATIONAL DEFENSE INFORMATION

A. The Espionage Act

The disclosure of national defense information is prohibited by the Espionage Act of 1917, codified at 18 U.S.C. §§ 793-798. The central statutory provision is 18 U.S.C.

---

1. *Id.* § 1.4(a)-(h).

§ 793, which criminalizes a wide range of activities associated with the possession, receipt, communication, delivery, and transmission of information relating to the "national defense" with "intent or reason to believe" that the information could be "used to the injury of the United States, or to the advantage of any foreign nation." Section 793(a) prohibits entering a U.S.-owned or U.S.-controlled protected place to obtain certain national defense information with "intent or reason to believe that the information is to be used to the injury of the United States, or to the advantage of any nation." Similarly, § 793(b) prohibits individuals with "like intent or reason to believe" from copying, taking, making, or obtaining "any sketch, photograph, photographic negative, blueprint, plan, map, model, instrument, appliance, document, writing, or note of anything *connected with the national defense.*" 18 U.S.C. § 793(b) (emphasis added).

Section 793(c) creates criminal liability for any individual who "receives or obtains or agrees or attempts to receive or obtain from any person, or from any source whatever" various material related to the national defense, if he "know[s] or ha[s] reason to believe, at the time he receives or obtains [the information] . . . that it has been or will be obtained, taken, or disposed of by any person contrary to the provisions of [the Espionage Act]."

Section 793(d) is one of the most important provisions of the Espionage Act. The statute prohibits someone with lawful access to national defense information from willfully communicating, delivering, or transmitting the information to a person not entitled to receive it. Section 793(d) is often used to prosecute the unauthorized disclosure of national defense information to members of the media. Significantly, § 793(d) is not limited to "classic spying" or the disclosure of national defense secrets to an agent of a foreign government, but criminalizes the disclosure to *anyone* not entitled to receive it.

While § 793(d) prohibits someone having "lawful" access to secret information from willfully disclosing it to a person not entitled to receive it, § 793(e) punishes the willful disclosure of documents or information relating to the national defense of the United States by an "unauthorized" possessor. Under § 793(e), it is unlawful for a person having unauthorized possession of defense information who has reason to believe the information could be used to harm national security or benefit any foreign nation, to willfully disclose that information to any person not entitled to receive it. Additionally, § 793(f) covers any person lawfully in possession of national defense information who either permits the information to be removed from where it belongs through "gross negligence" or, having knowledge that the information has been removed or delivered to any unauthorized person, fails to report the incident to his superior.

Another important provision of the Espionage Act is 18 U.S.C. § 794, which criminalizes communicating, delivering, or transmitting "any document, writing, code book, signal book, sketch, photograph, photographic negative, blueprint, plan, map, model, note, instrument, appliance, or information relating to national defense" to any foreign government, or faction or military or naval force within a foreign country, or to any representative, officer, agent or employee of a foreign government. 18 U.S.C. § 794(a). To be convicted under the statute, the accused must act "with intent or reason to believe" that the proscribed materials will be used "to the injury of the United States or to the advantage of a foreign nation." *Id.* A violation of § 794(a) may be punished by death or imprisonment of any terms of years or for life. However, a sentence of death shall not be imposed unless the jury finds that the offense resulted in the identification by a foreign power of an individual acting as an agent of the United States and the death of that individual, or "directly concerned nuclear weaponry, military spacecraft or satellites, early warning systems, or other means of defense or retaliation against large-scale attack; war plan; communications intelligence or cryptographic information; or any other major weapons system or major element of defense strategy." *Id.* A sentence of death is also authorized if, during "time of war," information is communicated to the enemy "with respect to the movement, numbers, description, condition, or disposition of any of the Armed Forces, ships, aircraft, or war materials of the United States." *Id.* § 794(b). Finally, the death sentence is permitted if the information disclosed involved "plans or conduct . . . of any naval or military operations, or with respect to any works or measures undertaken for or connected with, or intended for the fortification or defense of any place, or any other information relating to the public defense, which might be useful to the enemy." *Id.*

The principal focus of criminal litigation has been on the scienter requirements of §§ 793(a)-(d), and claims of vagueness. In the following case, the Supreme Court examines issues of statutory construction and vagueness related to an earlier version of 18 U.S.C §§ 793(b) and 794(a).

RETENTION AND DISCLOSURE OF CLASSIFIED INFORMATION

In March 2015, David H. Petraeus, the former CIA Director and retired four-star Army General, pleaded guilty to one misdemeanor count of retaining classified information, in violation of 18 U.S.C. § 1924. *United States v. Petraeus*, No. 315 CR 47, Plea Agreement (W.D.N.C. Mar. 3, 2015). Section 1924 prohibits the unauthorized removal or retention of classified documents or material by an officer, employee, contractor, or consultant of the United States.

According to court documents, General Petraeus gave his mistress and biographer Paula Broadwell eight notebooks that contained classified information regarding the identities of covert intelligence officers, war strategy, intelligence capabilities, diplomatic discussions at high-level National Security Council meetings, and private meetings with President Obama. These materials had been kept by General Petraeus at his residence, and had been given to Broadwell to assist her in drafting a biography about Petraeus.

Could General Petraeus have been prosecuted under 18 U.S.C. § 793(d) for willfully delivering information relating to the national defense to a person not entitled to receive it? Was Broadwell authorized to receive such information? Did Petraeus have reason to believe that these materials could be used to the injury of the United States or to the advantage of a foreign nation? Broadwell claims that she did not divulge any of the secrets she received from General Petraeus. Does criminal liability depend on whether the unauthorized recipient publicly disclosed the classified information?

1. Materials Related to or Connected with "National Defense"

Gorin v. United States
312 U.S. 19 (1941)

Justice REED delivered the opinion of the Court.

This certiorari brings here a judgment of the Circuit Court of Appeals affirming the sentences of the two petitioners who were convicted of violation of the Espionage Act. As the affirmance turned upon a determination of the scope of the Act and its constitutionality as construed, the petition was allowed because of the questions, important in enforcing this criminal statute.

The joint indictment in three counts charged in the first count violation of section 1(b) by allegations in the words of the statute of obtaining documents "connected with the national defense"; in the second count violation of section 2(a) in delivering and inducing the delivery of these documents to the petitioner, Gorin, the agent of a foreign nation; and in the third count of section 4 by conspiracy to deliver them to a foreign government and its agent, just named. The pertinent statutory provisions appear below.[1] A third party, the

---

1. Espionage Act of June 15, 1917, c. 30, 40 Stat. 217:

"Title 1. Espionage. Section 1. That (a) whoever, for the purpose of obtaining information respecting the national defense with intent or reason to believe that the information to be obtained is to be used to the injury of the United States, or to the advantage of any foreign nation, goes upon, enters, flies over, or otherwise obtains information concerning any vessel, aircraft, work of defense, navy yard, naval station, submarine base, coaling station, fort, battery, torpedo station, dockyard, canal, railroad, arsenal, camp, factory, mine, telegraph, telephone, wireless, or signal station, building, office, or other place connected with the national defense, ... or any place in which any vessel, aircraft, arms, munitions, or other materials or instruments for use in time of war are being made, prepared, repaired, or stored ...; or (b) whoever for the purpose aforesaid, and with like intent or reason to believe, copies, takes, makes, or obtains, or attempts, or induces or aids another to copy, take, make, or obtain, any sketch, photograph, photographic negative, blue print, plan, map, model, instrument, appliance, document, writing, or note of anything connected with the national defense; ... shall be punished by a fine of not more than $10,000, or by imprisonment for not more than two years, or both.

"Sec. 2. (a) Whoever, with intent or reason to believe that it is to be used to the injury of the United States or to the advantage of a foreign nation, communicates, delivers, or transmits, or attempts to, or aids or induces another to, communicate, deliver, or transmit, to any foreign government, or to any faction or party or military or naval force within a foreign country, whether recognized or unrecognized by the United States, or to any representative, officer, agent, employee, subject, or citizen thereof, either directly or indirectly, any document, writing, code book, signal book, sketch, photograph, photographic negative, blue print, plan, map, model, note, instrument, appliance, or information relating to the national defense, shall be punished by imprisonment for not more than twenty years: Provided, That whoever shall violate the provisions of subsection (a) of this section in time of war shall be punished by death or by imprisonment for not more than thirty years; and (b) whoever, in time of war, with intent that the same shall be communicated to the enemy, shall collect, record, publish, or communicate, or attempt to elicit any information with respect to the movement, numbers, description, condition, or disposition of any of the armed forces, ships, aircraft, or war materials of the United States, or with respect to the plans or conduct, or supposed plans or conduct of any naval or military operations, or with respect to any works or measures undertaken for or connected with, or intended for the fortification or defense of any place, or any other information relating to the public defense,

wife of Gorin, was joined in and acquitted on all three counts. The petitioners were found guilty on each count and sentenced to various terms of imprisonment to run concurrently and fines of $10,000 each. The longest term of Gorin is six years and of Salich four years.

The proof indicated that Gorin, a citizen of the Union of Soviet Socialist Republics, acted as its agent in gathering information. He sought and obtained from Salich for substantial pay the contents of over fifty reports relating chiefly to Japanese activities in the United States. These reports were in the files of the Naval Intelligence branch office at San Pedro, California. Salich, a naturalized, Russian-born citizen, had free access to the records as he was a civilian investigator for that office. Speaking broadly the reports detailed the coming and going on the west coast of Japanese military and civil officials as well as private citizens whose actions were deemed of possible interest to the Intelligence Office. Some statements appear as to the movements of fishing boats, suspected of espionage and as to the taking of photographs of American war vessels.

Petitioners object to the convictions principally on the grounds (1) that the prohibitions of the act are limited to obtaining and delivering information concerning the specifically described places and things set out in the act, such as a vessel, aircraft, fort, signal station, code or signal book; and (2) that an interpretation which put within the statute the furnishing of any other information connected with or relating to the national defense than that concerning these specifically described places and things would make the act unconstitutional as violative of due process because of indefiniteness.

The philosophy behind the insistence that the prohibitions of sections 1(b) and 2(a), upon which the indictment is based, are limited to the places and things which are specifically set out in section 1(a) relies upon the traditional freedom of discussion of matters connected with national defense which is permitted in this country. It would require, urge petitioners, the clearest sort of declaration by the Congress to bring under the statute the obtaining and delivering to a foreign government for its advantage of reports generally published and available which deal with food production, the advances of civil aeronautics, reserves of raw materials or other similar matters not directly connected with and yet of the greatest importance to national defense. The possibility of such an interpretation of the terms "connected with" or "relating to" national defense is to be avoided by construing the act so as "to make it a crime only to obtain information as to places and things specifically listed in section 1 as connected with or related to the national defense." Petitioners argue that the

---

which might be useful to the enemy, shall be punished by death or by imprisonment for not more than thirty years. . . .

"Sec. 4. If two or more persons conspire to violate the provisions of sections two or three of this title, and one or more of such persons does any act to effect the object of the conspiracy, each of the parties to such conspiracy shall be punished as in said sections provided in the case of the doing of the act the accomplishment of which is the object of such conspiracy."

statute should not be construed so as to leave to a jury to determine whether an innocuous report on a crop yield is "connected" with the national defense. . . .

An examination of the words of the statute satisfies us that the meaning of national defense in sections 1(b) and 2(a) cannot be limited to the places and things specified in section 1(a). Certainly there is no such express limitation in the later sections. Section 1(a) lays down the test of purpose and intent and then defines the crime as going upon or otherwise obtaining information as to named things and places connected with the national defense. Section 1(b) adopts the same purpose and intent of 1(a) and then defines the crime as copying, taking or picturing certain articles such as models, appliances, documents, and so forth of anything connected with the national defense. None of the articles specified in 1(b) are the same as the things specified in 1(a). Apparently the draftsmen of the act first set out the places to be protected, and included in that connotation ships and planes and then in 1(b) covered much of the contents of such places in the nature of plans and documents. Section 2(a), it will be observed, covers in much the same way the delivery of these movable articles or information to a foreign nation or its agent. If a government model of a new weapon were obtained or delivered there seems to be little logic in making its transfer a crime only when it is connected in some undefined way with the places catalogued under 1(a). It is our view that it is a crime to obtain or deliver, in violation of the intent and purposes specified, the things described in sections 1(b) and 2(a) without regard to their connection with the places and things of 1(a).

In each of these sections the document or other thing protected is required also to be "connected with" or "relating to" the national defense. The sections are not simple prohibitions against obtaining or delivering to foreign powers information which a jury may consider relating to national defense. If this were the language, it would need to be tested by the inquiry as to whether it had double meaning or forced anyone, at his peril, to speculate as to whether certain actions violated the statute. This Court has frequently held criminal laws deemed to violate these tests invalid. *United States v. Cohen Grocery Company*, urged as a precedent by petitioners, points out that the statute there under consideration forbade no specific act, that it really punished acts "detrimental to the public interest when unjust and unreasonable" in a jury's view. In *Lanzetta v. New Jersey* the statute was equally vague. "Any person not engaged in any lawful occupation, known to be a member of any gang . . . who has been convicted at least three times of being a disorderly person or who has been convicted of any crime in this or in any other State, is declared to be a gangster. . . ." We there said that the statute "condemns no act or omission"; that the vagueness is such as to violate due process.

But we find no uncertainty in this statute which deprives a person of the ability to predetermine whether a contemplated action is criminal under the provisions of this law. The obvious delimiting words in the statute are those requiring "intent or reason to believe that the information to be obtained is to be used to the injury of the United States, or to the advantage of any foreign nation." This requires those prosecuted to have acted in bad faith. The sanctions apply only when scienter is established. Where there is no occasion for secrecy, as with reports relating to national defense, published by authority of Congress or the military departments, there can, of course, in all likelihood be no reasonable intent to give an advantage to a foreign government. Finally, we are of the view that the use of the words "national defense" has given them, as here employed, a well understood connotation. They were used in the Defense Secrets Act of 1911. The traditional concept of war as a struggle between nations is not changed by the intensity of support given to the armed forces by civilians or the extension of the combat area. National defense, the Government maintains, "is a generic concept of broad connotations, referring to the military and naval establishments and the related activities of national preparedness." We agree that the words "national defense" in the Espionage Act carry that meaning. Whether a document or report is covered by sections 1(b) or 2(a) depends upon their relation to the national defense, as so defined, not upon their connection with places specified in section 1(a). The language employed appears sufficiently definite to apprise the public of prohibited activities and is consonant with due process.

. . .

Nor do we think it necessary to prove that the information obtained was to be used to the injury of the United States. The statute is explicit in phrasing the crime of espionage as an act of obtaining information relating to the national defense "to be used . . . to the advantage of any foreign nation." No distinction is made between friend or enemy. Unhappily the status of a foreign government may change. The evil which the statute punishes is the obtaining or furnishing of this guarded information, either to our hurt or another's gain. If we accept petitioners' contention that "advantage" means advantage as against the United States, it would be a useless addition, as no advantage could be given our competitor or opponent in that sense without injury to us. . . .

The Circuit Court of Appeals properly refused to consider the errors alleged with respect to the conspiracy count.

Affirmed.

NOTES AND QUESTIONS

1. The Espionage Act has been amended since the *Gorin* case. Gorin was charged with obtaining over fifty reports taken from a Naval Intelligence branch office pertaining to Japanese activities in the United States, in violation of § 1(b) of the Espionage Act, now 18 U.S.C. § 793(b). Salich had lawful possession of those reports and was charged with unlawfully delivering those materials to Gorin, a foreign agent, in violation of § 2(a), now 18 U.S.C. § 794(a). What are the elements required to support a conviction under 18 U.S.C. § 793(b)? What are the elements required to sustain a violation of § 794(a)? What is the mens rea requirement for each statute? What is the principal difference between the two statutes?

2. What is the justification for imposition of the death penalty under § 794(a)?
3. What is the meaning of the term "national defense" for purposes of the Espionage Act? Is the statutory language unconstitutionally vague?
4. Are matters relating to or connected with "national defense" limited to the places and things specified in § 1(a) (now § 793(a))? Are §§ 1(b) (now § 793(b)), and 2(a) (now § 794)) limited to the places and things set forth in § 1(a) (now § 793(a))?
5. Sections 793(b) and 794(a) of the Espionage Act require the government to prove that the defendant acted with "intent or reason to believe that the information to be obtained is to be used to the injury of the United States, or to the advantage of any foreign nation." Is it a violation of the statute to provide public or "open source" information connected to national defense to a hostile nation with the intent to benefit that nation?
6. Does the Espionage Act require proof that the information was to be used to the injury of the United States? Is it a violation of §§ 793(b) or 794(a) if the proscribed material or information is given to a friendly foreign nation such as Israel, where the accused has no intent or reason to believe that the information will be used to the injury of the United States?

The next case involves an analysis of the Espionage Act, 18 U.S.C. §§ 793(d) and (e).

2. Espionage Act Violations Under Sections 793(d) and (e)

United States v. Morison
844 F.2d 1057 (4th Cir. 1988)

The defendant is appealing his conviction under four counts of an indictment for violation of 18 U.S.C. § 641, and of two provisions of the Espionage Act, 18 U.S.C. § 793(d) and (e). The violations of the Espionage Act involved the unauthorized transmittal of certain satellite secured photographs of Soviet naval preparations to "one not entitled to receive them" (count 1) and the obtaining of unauthorized possession of secret intelligence reports and the retaining of them without delivering them to "one entitled to receive" them (count 3). Counts 2 and 4 of the indictment charged violation of the theft provisions of 18 U.S.C. § 641. His defense was essentially that the statutes did not encompass the conduct charged against him and, if they did, the statutes were unconstitutional. . . . We find the claims of error unfounded and affirm the conviction.

I. SUMMARY OF THE FACTS

The defendant was employed at the Naval Intelligence Support Center (NISC) at Suitland, Maryland from 1974 until October, 1984. At the time of the incidents involved in this prosecution, he was assigned as an amphibious and hospital ship and mine warfare analyst in the NISC and as such had been given a security clearance of "Top Secret-Sensitive Compartmented Information."

His work place was in what was described as a "vaulted area," closed to all persons without a Top Secret Clearance. In connection with his security clearance, he had signed a Non-Disclosure Agreement. . . .

For some time prior to the incidents with which this prosecution is concerned, the defendant had been doing certain off-duty work for *Jane's Fighting Ships*, an annual English publication which provided current information on naval operations internationally. Sometime before July, 1984, *Jane's*, which for many years had been publishing *Jane's*, had begun the publication of another periodical on a weekly basis. This new publication was called *Jane's Defence Weekly* and its editor-in-chief was Derek Wood, with an office in London. The defendant had been paid varying amounts for such services as rendered *Jane's* dependent on the value of the information he furnished. This arrangement with *Jane's* had been submitted to and approved by the Navy but subject to the defendant's agreement that he would not obtain and supply any classified information on the U.S. Navy or extract unclassified data on any subject and forward it to *Jane's*. The defendant's off-duty services with *Jane's* had become a subject of some controversy between him and the Navy. As a result, the defendant had become dissatisfied with his employment by the Navy and wished to secure full-time employment with *Jane's*. The defendant began a correspondence with Wood on the prospects for full-time employment with the periodical. He requested an opportunity to interview Wood when the latter was in Washington next.

Wood visited Washington in June, 1984, and, by arrangement, saw the defendant in connection with the latter's request for employment. At that time, Wood discussed with the defendant a report which had appeared in the American press with regard to an explosion that had recently occurred at the Severomorsk Soviet Naval base. Wood expressed the interest of his publication in securing additional details since such an explosion was "a very serious matter." The defendant told Wood that the explosion "was a much larger subject than even they had thought and there was a lot more behind it." The defendant also said he could "provide more material on it" if *Jane's* were interested. . . .

When Wood returned to London a few days later, he received from the defendant "about three typed pages of material background on Severomorsk." A few days later, the defendant transmitted to Wood "two other items on further explosions that had occurred at the site on different dates and also a mention of one particular explosion in East Germany."

The activity of the defendant which led to this prosecution began on July 24, 1984, a few days after the interview of the defendant by Wood and after the defendant had sent Wood the material described in the preceding paragraph. At that time the defendant saw, on the desk of another employee in the vaulted area where he worked, certain glossy photographs depicting a Soviet aircraft carrier under construction in a Black Sea naval shipyard. The photographs, produced by a KH-11 reconnaissance satellite photographing machine, had been given this analyst so that he could analyze and determine the capabilities and capacities of the carrier under construction. The photographs were stamped "Secret" and also had a "Warning Notice: Intelligence Sources or Methods

Involved" imprinted on the borders of the photographs. The defendant later in his confession said he had earlier sent an artist's sketch of a Soviet carrier under construction to *Jane's* and had been paid $200 for his services. When he saw the photographs, the defendant recognized them as satellite photographs of the Soviet ship, taken by a secret method utilized by the Navy in its intelligence operations. Unobserved, he picked the photographs up, secreted them, and, after cutting off the borders of the photographs which recorded the words "Top Secret" and the Warning Notice as well as any indication of their source, mailed them to Derek Wood personally. *Jane's Defence Weekly* published the photographs in its weekly edition a few days later and made the pictures available to other news agencies. One of these photographs was published on August 8, 1984 in the *Washington Post.* When the Navy officers saw the photographs, they began a search and discovered that the photographs had been stolen. An investigation was immediately begun to ascertain the identity of the thief.

When arrested, the defendant repeated his many denials of any connection with the theft of the photographs, though the arresting officer told him they had discovered his fingerprints on the photographs, demonstrating that he was not truthful when he said he had never seen the photographs. . . .

The defendant has appealed his conviction on various claims of error. We find all the claims without merit and affirm the judgment of conviction. . . .

His contentions with respect to the first claim under sections 793(d) and (e) are that his activity as set forth in the two counts of the indictment was not within the literal or intended prohibitions of the relevant statutes and that, if within the prohibition of the statutes, whether read literally or in accord with legislative intent, such statutes are constitutionally invalid for vagueness and overbreadth. . . .

II. THE CONVICTIONS UNDER SECTIONS 793(D) AND (E)

The initial defense of the defendant to his prosecution as stated in Counts 1 and 3 of the indictment (sections 793(d) and (e)), rests on what he conceives to be the meaning and scope of the two espionage statutes he is charged with violating. It is his position that, properly construed and applied, these two subsections of 793 do not prohibit the conduct of which he is charged in those counts. Stated more specifically, it is his view that the prohibitions of these two subsections are to be narrowly and strictly confined to conduct represented "in classic spying and espionage activity" by persons who, in the course of that activity had transmitted "national security secrets to agents of foreign governments with intent to injure the United States." He argued that the conduct of which he is charged simply does not fit within the mold of "classical spying" as that term was defined, since he transmitted the national security secret materials involved in the indictment to a recognized international naval news organization located in London, England, and not to an agent of a foreign power. In short, he leaked to the press; he did not transmit to a foreign government. . . .

Both statutes plainly apply to "whoever" having access to national defense information has under section 793(d) "wilfully communicate[d], deliver[ed] or transmit[ted] . . . to a person not entitled to receive it," or has retained it in violation of section 793(e). The language of the two statutes includes no limitation to spies or to "an agent of a foreign government," either as to the transmitter or the transmittee of the information, and they declare no exemption in favor of one who leaks to the press. It covers "anyone." It is difficult to conceive of any language more definite and clear. . . .

We are convinced . . . that the legislative history will not support the defendant's construction of sections 793(d) and (e). When a statute is a part of a larger Act as these statutes are, the starting point for ascertaining legislative intent is to look to other sections of the Act *in pari materia* with the statute under review. Section 793(d) was a part of the Espionage Act of 1917; section 793, however, is but one section of the Espionage Act of 1917; as equally as important a section of the Act was section 794. . . . The purpose of the drafter was to break down the Act into very specific sections, prescribing separate and distinct offenses or crimes, and providing varying punishments for conviction under each section dependent on the seriousness of each of the offenses. This purpose of the Act was recognized by us in *Boeckenhaupt v. United States,* 392 F.2d 24, 28 (4th Cir. 1968), *cert. denied,* 393 U.S. 896 (1968), and we in that case upheld the power of the Congress so to break down the Espionage Act with separate and distinct sections, covering separate and distinct activities. . . .

It is important, therefore, to ascertain the essential element in each section which made it separate and distinct from the other. Both statutes dealt in common with national defense materials and both statutes define the national interest materials covered by them in substantially the same language. Both prohibit disclosure. The two statutes differ — and this is the critical point to note in analyzing the two statutes — in their identification of the person to whom disclosure is prohibited. In section 793(d) that party to whom disclosure is prohibited under criminal sanction is one "not entitled to receive" the national defense material. Section 794 prohibits disclosure to an "agent . . . [of a] foreign government. . . ." Manifestly, section 794 is a far more serious offense than section 793(d); it covers the act of "classic spying"; and, because of its seriousness, it authorizes a far more serious punishment than that provided for section 793(d). In section 794, the punishment provided is stated to be "punish[ment] by *death* or by imprisonment for any term of years or for life" (Italics added). The punishment for violation of section 793(d) is considerably more lenient: A fine of "not more than $10,000 or imprisoned not more than ten years, or both." In short, section 794 covers "classic spying"; sections 793(d) and (e) cover a much lesser offense than that of "spying" and extends to disclosure to *any* person "not entitled to receive" the information. It follows that, considered in connection with the structure and purposes of the Espionage Act as a whole and with other sections of the Act *in pari materia* with it, section 793(d) was not intended to apply narrowly to "spying" but was intended to apply to disclosure of the secret defense material to *anyone* "not entitled to receive" it, whereas section 794 was to apply narrowly to classic spying.

. . .

It seems abundantly clear from this legislative history that sections 793(d) and (e) were not intended to be restricted in application to "classic spying" but were intended to criminalize the disclosure to anyone "not entitled to receive it." Accordingly, whether we look to the literal language of the statutes themselves, to the structure of the Act of which the sections were a part, or to the legislative history, sections 793(d) and (e) may not be limited in their scope to "classic spying," as the defendant argues. . . .

The legislative record is similarly silent on any Congressional intent in enacting sections 793(d) and (e) to exempt from its application the transmittal of secret military information by a defendant to the press or a representative of the press. Actually, there was little or no discussion of the First Amendment in the legislative record *directly* relating to sections 793(d) and (e) in this connection. . . . There is, however, no evidence whatsoever in the legislative record that the Congress intended to exempt from the coverage of section 793(d) national defense information by a governmental employee, particularly by one who had purloined from the files of the Department such information, simply because he transmitted it to a representative of the press.

But, though he cannot point to anything in the legislative record which intimates that Congress intended to exempt "leaks to the press," as the defendant describes it, he argues that, unless such an exemption is read into these sections they will run afoul of the First Amendment. Actually we do not perceive any First Amendment rights to be implicated here. This certainly is no prior restraint case such as *New York Times v. United States*, 403 U.S. 713 (1971). . . . It is a prosecution under a statute, of which the defendant, who, as an employee in the intelligence service of the military establishment, had been expressly noticed of his obligations by the terms of his letter of agreement with the Navy, is being prosecuted for purloining from the intelligence files of the Navy national defense materials clearly marked as "Intelligence Information" and "Secret" and for transmitting that material to "one not entitled to receive it." And the prosecution premises its prosecution on establishing that he did this knowingly and "wilfully" as evidenced by the manner in which he sought to conceal the "Secret" character of the information and the efforts he had taken to thwart any tracing of the theft to him. We do not think that the First Amendment offers asylum under those circumstances, if proven, merely because the transmittal was to a representative of the press. This conclusion in our view follows from the decision in *Branzburg v. Hayes*, 408 U.S. 665 (1972).

In *Branzburg*, a news reporter had written, and his paper had published, an article describing certain criminal activity by two individuals witnessed by the reporter under a pledge by him that he would protect the identity of the two offenders. A grand jury investigating the criminal activity subpoenaed the reporter in order to examine him on the identity of the two individuals and on their criminal activity. He sought to avoid the process on the ground that it would be a violation of his First Amendment right in news-gathering to require him to expose or identify his informants. He said to deny him protection in this regard would make it extremely difficult, if not impossible, for him to gather news. The Supreme Court denied the plea, and, in the course of so doing, made certain rulings which are pertinent in this connection. The Court, in Justice White's opinion in that case, said at 691-92:

> It would be frivolous to assert—and no one does in these cases—that the First Amendment, in the interest of securing news or otherwise, confers a license on either the reporter or his news sources to violate valid criminal laws. Although stealing documents or private wiretapping could provide newsworthy information, neither reporter nor source is immune from conviction for such conduct, whatever the impact on the flow of news. Neither is immune, on First Amendment grounds, from testifying against the other, before the grand jury or at a criminal trial. . . . To assert the contrary proposition "is to answer it, since it involves in its very statement the contention that the freedom of the press is the freedom to do wrong with impunity and implies the right to frustrate and defeat the discharge of those governmental duties upon the performance of which the freedom of all, including that of the press, depends. . . . It suffices to say that, however complete is the right of the press to state public things and discuss them, that right, as every other right enjoyed in human society, is subject to the restraints which separate right from wrong-doing." *Toledo Newspaper Co. v. United States*, 247 U.S. 402, 419-20 (1918).

United States v. Marchetti, 466 F.2d 1309, 1317 (4th Cir. 1972), though not as directly on point as *Branzburg*, is instructive in this regard. In that case, the United States sought an injunction to prevent a former Central Intelligence Agency [CIA] employee, who had signed a confidentiality agreement not to divulge naval classified information to which he had access from publishing classified CIA information after he left the CIA. The employee contended such a restraint violated his First Amendment rights. We affirmed the granting of the restraint. In so doing, the Court made this statement in response to the employee's First Amendment claim:

> Thus Marchetti retains the right to speak and write about the CIA and its operations, and to criticize it as any other citizen may, but he may not disclose classified information obtained by him during the course of his employment which is not already in the public domain.

Subsequently in *Snepp v. United States*, 444 U.S. 507, 508 (1980), another case which, though not directly on point, is relevant here. There the Supreme Court reviewed the right of the United States to enforce an agreement by a former CIA employee, that he would not "publish . . . any information or material relating to the Agency, its activities . . . without specific prior approval by the Agency." The defendant had violated the agreement by publishing a book with some material relating to the CIA in it without securing CIA prior approval for such publication. The Supreme Court assumed the propriety of the restraint on publication in this agreement.

If *Branzburg*, *Marchetti*, and *Snepp* are to be followed, it seems beyond controversy that a recreant intelligence department employee who had abstracted from the government files secret intelligence information and had wilfully transmitted or given it to one "not entitled to receive it" as did the defendant in this case, is not entitled to invoke the First Amendment as a shield to immunize his act of thievery. To permit the thief thus to misuse the Amendment would be to prostitute the salutary purposes of the First Amendment. Sections 793(d) and (e) unquestionably criminalize such conduct by a delinquent governmental employee and, when applied to a defendant in the position of the defendant here, there is no First Amendment right implicated. . . .

Even though the statutes are not to be confined strictly to "classic" spying and even though they contain no implicit exception in favor of transmittal of secret defense material to the press, the defendant argues that the statutes themselves, are constitutionally infirm for vagueness and overbreadth and the prosecutions under them should be stricken. We, therefore, proceed to address these attacks on the constitutionality of the statutes.

. . . The vagueness doctrine is rooted in due process principles and is basically directed at lack of sufficient clarity and precision in the statute; overbreadth, on the other hand, would invalidate a statute when it "infringe[s] on expression to a degree greater than justified by the legitimate governmental need" which is the valid purpose of the statute. Because of the differences in the two concepts, we discuss them separately in disposing of the defendant's argument, beginning with the defendant's claim of vagueness in sections 793(d) and (e) as applied to him.

It has been repeatedly stated that a statute which "either forbids or requires the doing of an act in terms so vague that men of common intelligence must necessarily guess at its meaning and differ as to its application, violates the first essential of due process of law." *Connally v. General Construction Co., supra*, 269 U.S. at 391. It is sufficient to satisfy requirements of "reasonable certainty," that while "the prohibitions [of a statute] may not satisfy those intent on finding fault at any cost, they are set out in terms that the ordinary person exercising ordinary common sense can sufficiently understand and comply with, without sacrifice to the public interest . . . [and they] will not be struck down as vague, even though marginal cases could be put where doubts might arise." *Arnett v. Kennedy*, 416 U.S. 134, 159 (1974). . . . Finally, the statute must be read in its entirety and all vagueness may be corrected by judicial construction which narrows the sweep of the statute within the range of reasonable certainty.

Applying these standards for measuring a statute for vagueness, we turn to the specific provisions of sections 793(d) and (e) which the defendant would find unconstitutionally vague. He identifies two terms in the statutes which he says are vague within the constitution prohibition. The first of these is the phrase, "relating to the national defense." The defendant concedes that this phrase was assailed as unconstitutionally vague in *United States v. Dedeyan*, 584 F.2d 36, 39 (4th Cir. 1978), a prosecution under section 793(f)(2). In responding to that contention, we stated in *Dedeyan* that the term "relating to the national defense" was not "vague in the constitutional sense." The defendant would distinguish this case from *Dedeyan* because the prosecution there was under subsection (f)(2) which contains a scienter requirement. Subsections

(d) and (e), however, have the same scienter requirement as subsection (f)(2). They prescribe that the prohibited activity must be "wilful." The district judge defined "wilfully" in his jury instructions as follows:

> All four of these counts as I have referred to them in my description of them to you used the word *wilfully*. An act is done *wilfully* if it is done voluntarily and *intentionally* and with the *specific intent to do something that the law forbids. That is to say, with a bad purpose either to disobey or to disregard the law.* With respect to the offenses that are charged in the indictment specific intent must be proved beyond a reasonable doubt before a defendant can be convicted. Specific intent, as that term suggests, requires more than a general intent to engage in a certain conduct. To establish specific intent the government must prove that the defendant knowingly did an act which the law forbids. It is the government's burden to present affirmative evidence of the existence of the required unlawful intent. Again, in determining whether or not the intent existed you may look at all the facts and the circumstances involved in the case. (Italics added)

Moreover, in his instructions, the district judge also gave this definition of "national defense":

> And that term, the term national defense, includes all matters that directly or may reasonably be connected with the defense of the United States against any of its enemies. It refers to the military and naval establishments and the related activities of national preparedness. To prove that the documents or the photographs relate to national defense there are two things that the government must prove. First, it must prove that the disclosure of the photographs would be potentially damaging to the United States or might be useful to an enemy of the United States. Secondly, the government must prove that the documents or the photographs are closely held in that [they] . . . have not been made public and are not available to the general public.

Combining the two instructions, the one on wilfulness and the one defining national defense, the district judge in this case gave precisely the instruction on this vagueness issue that we approved in *United States v. Truong Dinh Hung, supra*, 629 F.2d at 919.

The defendant would, however, argue that the district judge's jury instructions which we find removed any possibility of vagueness in the application of the statutes, actually imparted vagueness into the phrases "related to national defense" and "wilfulness." His argument on the term "related to national defense" is directed at the district judge's instruction that, in order to "prove that the documents or photographs" herein involved "related to national defense," the government must prove "the disclosure of the photographs would be *potentially damaging* to the United States or might be useful to the enemy of the United States." He attacks the use of the phrase "potentially damaging," italicized as above as too indefinite; he contends the word "actual" should have been used, for "potentially." The phrase "potentially damaging" was used by Justice White in his concurring opinion in *United States v. New York Times, supra*, 403 U.S. at 740, and in *Dedeyan* the district judge used the term in his instructions, an instruction we expressly approved on appeal. . . . We find no error in the instruction and, particularly in its use of the word "potentially" in the district court's instruction.

The second point of the defendant goes to the definition of "wilfully" as included in the district court's jury instructions. The defendant asserts that the district court, in its instructions in this regard, had said that "[p]roof of the most laudable motives, or any motive at all, is irrelevant under the statute." In his brief, he gives three record citations in support of his contention on this point. Two of these citations are extracted from the district court's opinion on the defendant's motion to dismiss the indictment herein. In the argument on his motion, the defendant, through his counsel, urged the district court to adopt the definition of "wilfully" as used in *Hartzel v. United States*, 322 U.S. 680, 686 (1944). That was a "pure speech" case and not one which was "in the shadow of the First Amendment" as here. The defendant in that case had written and published a scurrilous pamphlet attacking our allies in World War II and favoring peace with Germany in order to eliminate a war "between whites." He was indicted under the Espionage Act for "wilfully" attempting to "cause insubordination, disloyalty, mutiny or refusal of duty, in the military or naval forces of the United States. . . ." The Supreme Court found the statute under which the defendant was indicted required "a specific intent or evil purpose" to violate the statute. It said: "That word [wilfully], when viewed in the context of a highly penal statute restricting freedom of expression, must be taken to mean *deliberately and with a specific purpose to do the acts proscribed by Congress.*" 322 U.S. at 686. (Italics added) The district court in this case construed the "wilfully" language in *Hartzel* to require "that the prohibited act be done deliberately and with a specific purpose to do that which was proscribed." That is precisely the manner in which *Hartzel* said the instruction should be given and that was the precise instruction that was given in this case. . . .

Moreover, the defendant in this case knew that he was dealing with national defense material which a "foreign government in possession of . . . would be in a position to use it either for itself, in following the movements of the agents reported upon, or as a check upon this country's efficiency in ferreting out foreign espionage." *Gorin v. United States*, 312 U.S. 19, 29 (1941). He was an experienced intelligence officer. He had been instructed on all the regulations concerning the security of secret national defense materials. With the scienter requirement sections 793(d) and (e), bulwarked with the defendant's own expertise in the field of governmental secrecy and intelligence operations, the language of the statutes, "relating to the national security" was not unconstitutionally vague as applied to this defendant and this is especially true, since the trial judge, under proper instructions, left for the jury, as he should have, the determination whether the materials involved met the test for defense material or information and the jury found they did. . . . Further, the materials involved here are alleged in the indictment and were proved at trial to be marked plainly "Secret" and that classification is said in the Classification Order to be properly "applied to information, the unauthorized disclosure of which could reasonably be expected to cause serious damage to the national security." That definition of the material may be considered in reviewing for constitutionality the statute under which a defendant with the knowledge of security classification that the defendant had is charged. We are thus convinced that the statutory language "relating to the national defense," as applied to the defendant, is not constitutionally vague under our prior decisions reviewing section 793.

The defendant would also indict the phrase "entitled to receive" as vague. The defendant finds this phrase vague because it does not spell out exactly who may "receive" such material. However, any omission in the statute is clarified and supplied by the government's classification system provided under 18 U.S.C. App. 1 for the protection of the national security and the district judge so ruled. And courts have recognized the legitimacy of looking to the classification system for fleshing out the phrases such as that in question here.

Under Executive Order [12356], the classification "Secret" . . . was to "be applied to information, the unauthorized disclosure of which reasonably could be expected to cause serious damage to the national security." Those Regulations were well known to the defendant and he had agreed in writing to abide by them. The defendant worked in a vaulted area where, as the district court observed, "even other employees of NISC were not allowed to enter," much less to read or transmit intelligence materials being reviewed therein. Certainly the phrase "not authorized to receive it" was well understood by the defendant. As to him, the statute was not vague in its reference to "one not entitled to receive it."

. . .

Turning to the claim of overbreadth, we note at the outset that, unlike the situation presented by a vagueness claim, the overbreadth doctrine "is an exception to our traditional rules of practice," *Broadrick v. Oklahoma*, 413 U.S. 601, and has not been recognized outside the limited context of the First Amendment. So limited, it is "strong medicine," to be applied "with hesitation and then only as a last resort," and only if the statute cannot be given a narrowing construction to remove the overbreadth. *New York v. Ferber, supra* at 769. Thus, in *McGehee v. Casey*, 718 F.2d at 1146, Judge Wald held that "overbreadth analysis should not be deployed when a limiting construction could save the rule from its constitutional defects.". . .

An authority on the scope of the doctrine has formulated a statement of what he characterizes as the three "fundamental circumstances" under which the doctrine may be applied after discussing the foregoing rules. These circumstances are: "(1) when 'the governmental interest sought to be implemented is too insubstantial, or at least insufficient in relation to the inhibitory effect on first amendment freedoms'; (2) when the means employed bear little relation to the asserted governmental interest; and (3) when the means chosen by the legislature do in fact relate to a substantial governmental interest, but that interest could be achieved by a 'less drastic means' — that is, a method less invasive of free speech interests." Redish, *The Warren Court, the Burger Court and the First Amendment Overbreadth Doctrine*, 78 Nw. U. L. Rev. 1031, 1035 (1983).

Unquestionably, these statutes are expressions of an important and vital governmental interest and have a direct relation to the interests involved here, and are, therefore, without the first and second requirement for the application of the overbreadth doctrine. It is thus plain that the first two circumstances posited by Professor Redish are met; the only "circumstances," under which these statutes could be voided for overbreadth, would be that the substantial governmental interest reflected in the statutes could be achieved by means "less invasive of free speech interests."

It has been said that the court, by narrowing constructions of a statute, may bring the statute within conformity with the rule requiring that it be applied by means "less invasive of free speech interests." The defendant would find a violation of the overbreadth doctrine in the failure of either the statute or in judicial rulings construing and limiting the statute to employ "a method less invasive of free speech interests" than is represented in the terms "national defense" and "one not entitled to receive." So far as any overbreadth in the term "national defense" was concerned, it was reasonably narrowed by the district court in its instructions to confine national defense to matters under the statute which "directly or may reasonably be connected with the defense of the United States," the disclosure of which "would be potentially damaging to the United States or might be useful to an enemy of the United States" and which had been "closely held" by the government and was "not available to the general public." This narrowing of the definition of "national defense" information or material removed any legitimate overbreadth objection to the term. The phrase "to one not entitled to receive" was defined in the legislative history of the statute to mean one "not authorized to receive," as we have already observed, and "not authorized to receive" was clearly covered by the Classification Act, to which we have already referred, because of its classification as "Secret" national defense materials. It follows that there is no overbreadth in the two terms either as they may have been narrowed by court instruction or as fleshed out by the Classification Act.

Having reviewed all of the defendant's claims of error herein and found them without merit, we affirm the judgment of conviction of the defendant herein.

NOTES AND QUESTIONS

1. In *Morison*, the court held that §§ 793(d) and (e) are not limited to "classic spying and espionage activity" by persons who transmit "national security secrets to agents of foreign governments with the intent to injure the United States." What is the reasoning of the court?

2. What must the government prove to sustain a conviction under § 793(d)? What is required to support a violation of § 793(e)? What conduct is prohibited under each statute? How do §§ 793(d) and (e) differ from § 794(a)?

3. In *Morison*, the court found that the phrase "relating to national defense" was not unconstitutionally vague. What was the reasoning of the court?

4. Is the term "entitled to receive" unconstitutionally vague because it doesn't spell out exactly who may "receive" such material? If not, why not?

5. In *Morison*, the court held that the Espionage Act does not recognize an exemption for leaks to the media. The court stated: "Sections 793(d) and (e) unquestionably criminalize such conduct by a delinquent governmental employee and, when applied to a defendant in the position of the defendant here, there is no First Amendment right implicated." Should the Act exempt the disclosure of information to the media that does not harm national security?

6. Does 18 U.S.C. § 793(d) only punish the disclosure of "classified information" to a person not entitled to receive it? Can information be protected from disclosure even if no agency or official has classified it yet? In other words, can information be protected from disclosure based on its nature alone? For example, would information provided to a U.S. State Department official by a foreign government in confidence and later disclosed to a person who does not hold a security clearance support a violation of § 793(d)?

7. When does the overbreadth doctrine apply? Are those circumstances satisfied in *Morison*? Could the purpose of the statute be achieved by means "less invasive of free speech interests"?

8. There are multiple incentives, unrelated to national security, to classify information. Classification is a way for officials to enhance their status or protect an agency's turf. It can also hide embarrassing facts or evidence of misconduct. However, there are no countervailing disincentives, as agencies are not punished for over-classifying. The result is massive over-classification of government documents, a substantial portion of which could safely be released. Doesn't over-classification stifle public discussion and debate? How can over-classification be prevented?

9. Should the Espionage Act provide protection for the knowing release of classified information by whistleblowers? Should the Espionage Act—a statute meant to target spies and traitors—be used to prosecute federal employees who revealed waste, fraud, and abuse? Should whistleblowers be prosecuted for disclosing classified information if the federal employee did not harm or intend to harm national security? Is Edward Snowden, a former government contractor responsible for leaking information about the NSA cell phone bulk metadata program, a whistleblower? Should he be prosecuted under the Espionage Act? If so, under what statutory provision?

REPORTER'S PRIVILEGE

In *United States v. Sterling*, 724 F.3d 482 (4th Cir. 2013), a federal common law claim of reporter's privilege was proffered in an attempt to quash a government subpoena requesting a *New York Times* reporter to testify regarding his source of classified information. The district court granted the motion to quash. However, the Fourth Circuit, basing its decision on *Branzburg v. Hayes*, 408 U.S. 665 (1972), reversed. The court held:

> There is no First Amendment testimonial privilege, absolute or qualified, that protects a reporter from being compelled to testify . . . in a criminal proceeding[ ] about criminal conduct that the reporter personally witnessed or participated in, absent a showing of bad faith, harassment, or other such non-legitimate motive, even though the reporter promised confidentiality to his source.[2]

The court highlighted the difference between civil and criminal cases, stating that in civil cases "the public interest in effective criminal law enforcement is absent," and a qualified reporter's privilege may exist. *Id.* at 497 (citing *Zerilli v. Smith*, 656 F.2d 705, 711-12 (D.C. Cir. 1981)).

3. Preventing the Disclosure of National Security Information in Civil Litigation

a. The *Totten* Bar

Totten v. United States
92 U.S. 105 (1875)

Mr. Justice FIELD delivered the opinion of the court.

This case comes before us on appeal from the Court of Claims. The action was brought to recover compensation for services alleged to have been rendered by the claimant's intestate, William A. Lloyd, under a contract with President Lincoln, made in July, 1861, by which he was to proceed South and ascertain the number of troops stationed at points in the insurrectionary States, procure plans of forts and fortifications, and gain such other information as might be beneficial to the government of the United States, and report the facts to the President; for which services he was to be paid $200 a month.

The Court of Claims finds that Lloyd proceeded, under the contract, within the rebel lines, and remained there during the entire period of the war, collecting, and from time to time transmitting, information to the President; and that, upon the close of the war, he was only reimbursed his expenses. But the court, being equally divided in opinion as to the authority of the President to bind the United States by the contract in question, decided, for the purposes of an appeal, against the claim, and dismissed the petition.

We have no difficulty as to the authority of the President in the matter. He was undoubtedly authorized during the war, as commander-in-chief of the armies of the United States, to employ secret agents to enter the rebel lines and obtain information respecting the strength, resources, and movements of the enemy; and contracts to compensate such agents are so far binding upon the government as to render it lawful for the President to direct payment of the amount stipulated out of the contingent fund under his control. Our objection

---

2. *Sterling*, 724 F.3d at 492.

is not to the contract, but to the action upon it in the Court of Claims. The service stipulated by the contract was a secret service; the information sought was to be obtained clandestinely, and was to be communicated privately; the employment and the service were to be equally concealed. Both employer and agent must have understood that the lips of the other were to be for ever [sic] sealed respecting the relation of either to the matter. This condition of the engagement was implied from the nature of the employment, and is implied in all secret employments of the government in time of war, or upon matters affecting our foreign relations, where a disclosure of the service might compromise or embarrass our government in its public duties, or endanger the person or injure the character of the agent. If upon contracts of such a nature an action against the government could be maintained in the Court of Claims, whenever an agent should deem himself entitled to greater or different compensation than that awarded to him, the whole service in any case, and the manner of its discharge, with the details of dealings with individuals and officers, might be exposed, to the serious detriment of the public. A secret service, with liability to publicity in this way, would be impossible; and, as such services are sometimes indispensable to the government, its agents in those services must look for their compensation to the contingent fund of the department employing them, and to such allowance from it as those who dispense that fund may award. The secrecy which such contracts impose precludes any action for their enforcement. The publicity produced by an action would itself be a breach of a contract of that kind, and thus defeat a recovery.

It may be stated as a general principle, that public policy forbids the maintenance of any suit in a court of justice, the trial of which would inevitably lead to the disclosure of matters which the law itself regards as confidential, and respecting which it will not allow the confidence to be violated. On this principle, suits cannot be maintained which would require a disclosure of the confidences of the confessional, or those between husband and wife, or of communications by a client to his counsel for professional advice, or of a patient to his physician for a similar purpose. Much greater reason exists for the application of the principle to cases of contract for secret services with the government, as the existence of a contract of that kind is itself a fact not to be disclosed.

Judgment affirmed.

Tenet v. Doe
544 U.S. 1 (2005)

Chief Justice REHNQUIST delivered the opinion of the Court.

In *Totten v. United States*, 92 U.S. 105 (1876), we held that public policy forbade a self-styled Civil War spy from suing the United States to enforce its obligations under their secret espionage agreement. Respondents here, alleged former Cold War spies, filed suit against the United States and the Director of the Central Intelligence Agency (CIA), asserting estoppel and due process claims for the CIA's alleged failure to provide respondents with the assistance it had promised in return for their espionage services. Finding that *Totten* did not bar respondents' suit, the District Court and the Court of Appeals for the Ninth Circuit held that the case could proceed. We reverse because this holding contravenes the longstanding rule, announced more than a century ago in *Totten*, prohibiting suits against the Government based on covert espionage agreements.

Respondents, a husband and wife who use the fictitious names John and Jane Doe, brought suit in the United States District Court for the Western District of Washington. According to respondents, they were formerly citizens of a foreign country that at the time was considered to be an enemy of the United States, and John Doe was a high-ranking diplomat for the country. After respondents expressed interest in defecting to the United States, CIA agents persuaded them to remain at their posts and conduct espionage for the United States for a specified period of time, promising in return that the Government "would arrange for travel to the United States and ensure financial and personal security for life." . . . After "carrying out their end of the bargain" by completing years of purportedly high-risk, valuable espionage services, respondents defected (under new names and false backgrounds) and became United States citizens, with the Government's help. The CIA designated respondents with "PL-110" status and began providing financial assistance and personal security.

With the CIA's help, respondent John Doe obtained employment in the State of Washington. As his salary increased, the CIA decreased his living stipend until, at some point, he agreed to a discontinuation of benefits while he was working. Years later, in 1997, John Doe was laid off after a corporate merger. Because John Doe was unable to find new employment as a result of CIA restrictions on the type of jobs he could hold, respondents contacted the CIA for financial assistance. Denied such assistance by the CIA, they claim they are unable to properly provide for themselves. Thus, they are faced with the prospect of either returning to their home country (where they say they face extreme sanctions), or remaining in the United States in their present circumstances.

Respondents assert, among other things, that the CIA violated their procedural and substantive due process rights by denying them support and by failing to provide them with a fair internal process for reviewing their claims. They seek injunctive relief ordering the CIA to resume monthly financial support pending further agency review. They also request a declaratory judgment stating that the CIA failed to provide a constitutionally adequate review process, and detailing the minimal process the agency must provide. Finally, respondents seek a mandamus order requiring the CIA to adopt agency procedures, to give them fair review, and to provide them with security and financial assistance.

The Government moved to dismiss the complaint under Federal Rules of Civil Procedure 12(b)(1) and 12(b)(6), principally on the ground that *Totten* bars respondents' suit. The District Court dismissed some of respondents' claims but denied the Government's *Totten* objection, ruling that the due process claims could proceed. . . .

[On appeal, a] divided panel of the Court of Appeals for the Ninth Circuit affirmed in relevant part. It reasoned that *Totten* posed no bar to reviewing some of respondents' claims . . . subject to the Government's asserting the evidentiary state secrets privilege and the District Court's resolving that issue. Over dissent, the Court of Appeals denied a petition for rehearing en banc. The Government sought review, and we granted certiorari.

In *Totten*, the administrator of William A. Lloyd's estate brought suit against the United States to recover compensation for services that Lloyd allegedly rendered as a spy during the Civil War. Lloyd purportedly entered into a contract with President Lincoln in July 1861 to spy behind Confederate lines on troop placement and fort plans, for which he was to be paid $200 a month. The lower court had found that Lloyd performed on the contract but did not receive full compensation. After concluding with "no difficulty" that the President had the authority to bind the United States to contracts with secret agents, we observed that the very essence of the alleged contract between Lloyd and the Government was that it was secret, and had to remain so:

> "The service stipulated by the contract was a secret service; the information sought was to be obtained clandestinely, and was to be communicated privately; the employment and the service were to be equally concealed. Both employer and agent must have understood that the lips of the other were to be for ever [sic] sealed respecting the relation of either to the matter. This condition of the engagement was implied from the nature of the employment, and is implied in all secret employments of the government in time of war, or upon matters affecting our foreign relations, where a disclosure of the service might compromise or embarrass our government in its public duties, or endanger the person or injure the character of the agent."

Thus, we thought it entirely incompatible with the nature of such a contract that a former spy could bring suit to enforce it.

We think the Court of Appeals was quite wrong in holding that *Totten* does not require dismissal of respondents' claims. That court, and respondents here, reasoned first that *Totten* developed merely a contract rule, prohibiting breach-of-contract claims seeking to enforce the terms of espionage agreements but not barring claims based on due process or estoppel theories. In fact, *Totten* was not so limited: "[P]ublic policy forbids the maintenance of *any suit* in a court of justice, the trial of which would inevitably lead to the disclosure of matters which the law itself regards as confidential." Id., at 107 (emphasis added). . . . No matter the clothing in which alleged spies dress their claims, Totten precludes judicial review in cases such as respondents' where success depends upon the existence of their secret espionage relationship with the Government.

Relying mainly on *United States v. Reynolds*, 345 U.S. 1 (1953), the Court of Appeals also claimed that *Totten* has been recast simply as an early expression of the evidentiary "state secrets" privilege, rather than a categorical bar to their claims. *Reynolds* involved a wrongful-death action brought under the Federal Tort Claims Act, 28 U.S.C. § 1346, by the widows of three civilians who died in the crash of a military B-29 aircraft. In the course of discovery, the plaintiffs sought certain investigation-related documents, which the Government said contained " 'highly secret,' " privileged military information. Id., at 3-4. We recognized "the privilege against revealing military secrets, a privilege which is well established in the law of evidence," id., at 6-7, and we set out a balancing approach for courts to apply in resolving Government claims of privilege, id., at 7-11. We ultimately concluded that the Government was entitled to the privilege in that case.

When invoking the "well established" state secrets privilege, we indeed looked to *Totten*. . . . But that in no way signaled our retreat from *Totten*'s broader holding that lawsuits premised on alleged espionage agreements are altogether forbidden. Indeed, our opinion in *Reynolds* refutes this very suggestion: Citing *Totten* as a case "where the very subject matter of the action, a contract to perform espionage, was a matter of state secret," we declared that such a case was to be "dismissed *on the pleadings without ever reaching the question of evidence*, since it was so obvious that the action should never prevail over the privilege." 345 U.S., at 11, n.26 (emphasis added).

In a later case, we again credited the more sweeping holding in *Totten*, thus confirming its continued validity. See *Weinberger v. Catholic Action of Haw./ Peace Ed. Project*, 454 U.S. 139, 146-147 (1981) (citing *Totten* in holding that "whether or not the Navy has complied with [§ 102(2)(C) of the National Environmental Policy Act of 1969, 83 Stat. 853, 42 U.S.C. § 4332(2)(C)] 'to the fullest extent possible' is beyond judicial scrutiny in this case," where, "[d]ue to national security reasons," the Navy could "neither admit nor deny" the fact that was central to the suit, i.e., "that it propose[d] to store nuclear weapons" at a facility). *Reynolds* therefore cannot plausibly be read to have replaced the categorical *Totten* bar with the balancing of the state secrets evidentiary privilege in the distinct class of cases that depend upon clandestine spy relationships.

. . .

There is, in short, no basis for respondents' and the Court of Appeals' view that the *Totten* bar has been reduced to an example of the state secrets privilege. In a far closer case than this, we observed that if the "precedent of this Court has direct application in a case, yet appears to rest on reasons rejected in some other line of decisions, the Court of Appeals should follow the case which directly controls, leaving to this Court the prerogative of overruling its own decisions." *Rodriguez de Quijas v. Shearson/American Express, Inc.*, 490 U.S. 477, 484 (1989).

We adhere to *Totten*. The state secrets privilege and the more frequent use of in camera judicial proceedings simply cannot provide the absolute protection we found necessary in enunciating the *Totten* rule. The possibility that a suit may proceed and an espionage relationship may be revealed, if the state secrets privilege is found not to apply, is unacceptable: "Even a small chance that some court will order disclosure of a source's identity could well impair intelligence gathering and cause sources to 'close up like a clam.'" *CIA v. Sims*, 471 U.S. 159, 175 (1985). Forcing the Government to litigate these claims would also make it vulnerable to "graymail," i.e., individual lawsuits brought to induce the CIA to settle a case (or prevent its filing) out of fear that any effort to litigate the action would reveal classified information that may undermine ongoing covert operations. And requiring the Government to invoke the privilege on a case-by-case basis risks the perception that it is either confirming or denying relationships with individual plaintiffs.

The judgment of the Court of Appeals is reversed.

Justice STEVENS, with whom Justice GINSBURG joins, concur; Justice SCALIA concurs [separately].

NOTES AND QUESTIONS

1. What is the scope of the Court's holding in *Totten*? The Court stated that "public policy forbids the maintenance of any suit in a court of justice, the trial of which would inevitably lead to the disclosure of matters which the law itself regards as confidential, and respecting which it will not allow the confidence to be violated." Is the rule in *Totten* limited to barring breach of contract suits, alleging a breach of an espionage agreement with the government? Is the Court's ruling more expansive, prohibiting litigation that would disclose any secret government activities or programs?

2. Does *Totten* involve a balancing test, requiring the district court to balance the government's need for secrecy and the plaintiff's right to pursue a judicial remedy? What is the justification for a total ban on lawsuits seeking to enforce an espionage agreement?

3. Would the Court reach a different result if the suit was filed under the Federal Tort Claims Act, 28 U.S.C. § 1346, alleging that the government was responsible for the plaintiff's death or injury?

4. The Court's ruling in *Totten* creates friction between national security and the plaintiff's right to seek a judicial remedy for breach of contract or other alleged injury. Does the government's interest in protecting national security always trump a plaintiff's right to seek a civil judicial remedy? Stated another way, when should an aggrieved plaintiff be denied his or her day in court because of national security concerns related to the subject matter of the litigation?

5. What is the legal standard for determining whether an aggrieved plaintiff should be deprived of a judicial remedy because of the secretive or confidential nature of the subject matter of the litigation? In order to justify dismissing the civil complaint, must the government prove that the litigation would cause "exceptionally grave damage" to national security? Should the civil suit be dismissed if the litigation could harm national security, or advantage any foreign nation?

EXECUTIVE PRIVILEGE

In *United States v. Nixon*, 418 U.S. 683 (1974), the Court recognized an executive privilege. The Court stated:

> The expectation of a President to the confidentiality of his conversation and correspondence . . . has all the values to which [the Court] accord[s] deference for the privacy of all citizens and, added to those values, is the necessity for protection of the public interest in candid, objective, and even blunt or harsh opinions in Presidential decisionmaking. A President and those who assist him must be free to explore alternatives in the process of shaping policies and making decisions and to do so in a way many would be unwilling to express except privately. These are the considerations justifying a presumptive privilege of Presidential communications.[3]

However, the Court qualified the privilege, stating: "But this presumptive privilege must be considered in light of our historic commitment to the rule of law. . . . [G]uilt shall not escape or innocence suffer. . . . [W]e must weigh the importance of the President's responsibilities against the inroads of such a privilege on the fair administration of criminal justice." *Id.* at 711-12. Further, as it pertains to criminal matters, the Court stated that executive privilege claimed only on the grounds of "the generalized interest in confidentiality . . . cannot prevail over the fundamental demands of due process of law in the fair administration of criminal justice." *Id.* at 713.

b. The State-Secrets Privilege

The state-secrets privilege (SSP) is a common law evidentiary privilege not explicitly set forth in any statute. The SSP permits the government to bar the disclosure of information if there is a "reasonable danger" that such disclosure would "expose military matters which in the interest of national security, should not be divulged." *United States v. Reynolds*, 345 U.S. 1, 10 (1953). The privilege is based on the premise that "in exceptional circumstances courts must act in the interest of the country's national security to prevent disclosure of state secrets, even to the point of dismissing a case entirely." *Mohamed v. Jeppesen Dataplan, Inc.*, 614 F.3d 1070, 1077 (9th Cir. 2010) (en banc). The scope and application of the SSP are examined in the following cases.

United States v. Reynolds
345 U.S. 1 (1953)

Mr. Chief Justice VINSON delivered the opinion of the Court.

These suits under the Tort Claims Act arise from the death of three civilians in the crash of a B-29 aircraft at Waycross, Georgia, on October 6, 1948.

---

3. *Id.* at 708-09.

Because an important question of the Government's privilege to resist discovery is involved, we granted certiorari.

The aircraft had taken flight for the purpose of testing secret electronic equipment, with four civilian observers aboard. While aloft, fire broke out in one of the bomber's engines. Six of the nine crew members, and three of the four civilian observes were killed in the crash.

The widows of the three deceased civilian observers brought consolidated suits against the United States. In the pretrial stages the plaintiffs moved, under Rule 34 of the Federal Rules of Civil Procedure, for production of the Air Force's official accident investigation report and the statements of the three surviving crew members, taken in connection with the official investigation. The Government moved to quash the motion, claiming that these matters were privileged against disclosure pursuant to Air Force regulations promulgated under R.S. § 161.4. . . . The claim of privilege under R.S. § 161 was rejected on the premise that the Tort Claims Act, in making the Government liable "in the same manner" as a private individual had waived any privilege based upon executive control over governmental documents.

[In response,] the Government further objected to production of the documents "for the reason that the aircraft in question, together with the personnel on board, were engaged in a highly secret mission of the Air Force." An affidavit . . . was also filed with the court, which asserted that the demanded material could not be furnished "without seriously hampering national security, flying safety and the development of highly technical and secret military equipment." The same affidavit offered to produce the three surviving crew members, without cost, for examination by the plaintiffs . . . , and authorized testimony as to all matters except those of a "classified nature."

The District Court . . . entered an order, under Rule 37(b)(2)(i), that the facts on the issue of negligence would be taken as established in plaintiffs' favor . . . [, and] final judgment was entered for the plaintiffs. The Court of Appeals affirmed, both as to the showing of good cause for production of the documents, and as to the ultimate disposition of the case as a consequence of the Government's refusal to produce the documents.

We have had broad propositions pressed upon us for decision. On behalf of the Government it has been urged that the executive department heads have power to withhold any documents in their custody from judicial view if they deem it to be in the public interest. Respondents have asserted that the executive's power to withhold documents was waived by the Tort Claims Act.

. . .

The Tort Claims Act expressly makes the Federal Rules of Civil Procedure applicable to suits against the United States. The judgment in this case imposed liability upon the Government by operation of Rule 37, for refusal to produce documents under Rule 34. Since Rule 34 compels production only of matters "not privileged," the essential question is whether there was a valid claim of privilege under the Rule. We hold that there was, and that, therefore, the judgment below subjected the United States to liability on terms to which Congress did not consent by the Tort Claims Act.

We think it should be clear that the term "not privileged" as used in Rule 34, refers to "privileges" as that term is understood in the law of evidence. When the Secretary of the Air Force lodged his formal "Claim of Privilege," he attempted therein to invoke the privilege against revealing military secrets, a privilege which is well established in the law of evidence. . . .

The principles which control the application of the privilege emerge quite clearly from the available precedents. The privilege belongs to the Government and must be asserted by it; it can neither be claimed nor waived by a private party. It is not to be lightly invoked. There must be formal claim of privilege, lodged by the head of the department which has control over the matter, after actual personal consideration by that officer. The court itself must determine whether the circumstances are appropriate for the claim of privilege, and yet do so without forcing a disclosure of the very thing the privilege is designed to protect.

. . .

Judicial control over the evidence in a case cannot be abdicated to the caprice of executive officers. Yet we will not go so far as to say that the court may automatically require a complete disclosure to the judge before the claim of privilege will be accepted in any case. It may be possible to satisfy the court, from all the circumstances of the case, that there is a reasonable danger that compulsion of the evidence will expose military matters which, in the interest of national security, should not be divulged. When this is the case, the occasion for the privilege is appropriate, and the court should not jeopardize the security which the privilege is meant to protect by insisting upon an examination of the evidence, even by the judge alone, in chambers.

. . .

In each case, the showing of necessity which is made will determine how far the court should probe in satisfying itself that the occasion for invoking the privilege is appropriate. Where there is a strong showing of necessity, the claim of privilege should not be lightly accepted, but even the most compelling necessity cannot overcome the claim of privilege if the court is ultimately satisfied that military secrets are at stake. *A fortiori*, where necessity is dubious, a formal claim of privilege, made under the circumstances of this case, will have to prevail. Here, necessity was greatly minimized by an available alternative, which might have given respondents the evidence to make out their case without forcing a showdown on the claim of privilege. By their failure to pursue that alternative, respondents have posed the privilege question for decision with the formal claim of privilege set against a dubious showing of necessity.

There is nothing to suggest that the electronic equipment, in this case, had any causal connection with the accident. Therefore, it should be possible for respondents to adduce the essential facts as to causation without resort to material touching upon military secrets. Respondents were given a reasonable opportunity to do just that, when petitioner formally offered to make the surviving crew members available for examination. We think that offer should have been accepted.

Respondents have cited us to those cases in the criminal field, where it has been held that the Government can invoke its evidentiary privileges only at the price of letting the defendant go free. The rationale of the criminal cases is that, since the Government which prosecutes an accused also has the duty to see that justice is done, it is unconscionable to allow it to undertake prosecution and then invoke its governmental privileges to deprive the accused of anything which might be material to his defense. Such rationale has no application in a civil forum where the Government is not the moving party, but is a defendant only on terms to which it has consented.

The decision of the Court of Appeals is reversed and the case will be remanded to the District Court for further proceedings consistent with the views expressed in this opinion.

NOTES AND QUESTIONS

1. In *Reynolds*, when may a court in a civil case deny evidence to plaintiffs? What is the legal standard for triggering the state-secrets privilege? What must the government allege? What must the court find before denying evidence to plaintiffs?
2. In *Reynolds*, the Court stated: "Judicial control over the evidence in a case cannot be abdicated to the caprice of executive officers." What is the role of the court in deciding whether the state-secrets privilege applies and the government is protected from disclosure and discovery of documents requested by plaintiffs?
3. May the court conduct an *in camera* hearing to determine whether the government's national security concerns are justified?
4. What is the difference between the *Totten* bar and the state-secrets privilege?
5. Does the state-secrets privilege apply in criminal cases? In the criminal setting, a conflict arises between the government's interest in protecting national security and a criminal defendant's right to present a meaningful defense. How should this conflict be resolved? Must the government's interest always give way when the information is helpful to the defense of the accused?

The following case raises the question of whether plaintiffs are barred under *Totten* or the state-secrets privilege from suing a U.S. corporation for assisting the government in operating the CIA's clandestine terrorist detention and interrogation program.

Mohamed v. Jeppesen Dataplan, Inc.
614 F.3d 1070 (9th Cir. 2010) (en banc)

This case requires us to address the difficult balance the state secrets doctrine strikes between fundamental principles of our liberty, including justice, transparency, accountability and national security. Although as judges we strive to honor *all* of these principles, there are times when exceptional circumstances create an irreconcilable conflict between them. On those rare occasions, we are bound to follow the Supreme Court's admonition that "even the most compelling necessity cannot overcome the claim of privilege if the court is ultimately satisfied that [state] secrets are at stake." *United States v. Reynolds*, 345 U.S. 1, 11 (1953). After much deliberation, we reluctantly conclude this is such a case, and the plaintiffs' action must be dismissed. Accordingly, we affirm the judgment of the district court.

. . .

A. Factual Background

1. The Extraordinary Rendition Program

Plaintiffs allege that the Central Intelligence Agency ("CIA"), working in concert with other government agencies and officials of foreign governments, operated an extraordinary rendition program to gather intelligence by apprehending foreign nationals suspected of involvement in terrorist activities and transferring them in secret to foreign countries for detention and interrogation by United States or foreign officials. According to plaintiffs, this program has allowed agents of the U.S. government "to employ interrogation methods that would [otherwise have been] prohibited under federal or international law.". . .

. . .

2. Jeppesen's Alleged Involvement in the Rendition Program

Plaintiffs contend that publicly available information establishes that defendant Jeppesen Dataplan, Inc., a U.S. corporation, provided flight planning and logistical support services to the aircraft and crew on all of the flights transporting each of the five plaintiffs among the various locations where they were detained and allegedly subjected to torture. . . .

B. Summary of the Claims

Plaintiffs brought suit against Jeppesen under the Alien Tort Statute, 28 U.S.C. § 1350, alleging seven theories of liability marshaled under two claims, one for "forced disappearance" and another for "torture and other cruel, inhuman or degrading treatment."

With respect to the forced disappearance claim, plaintiffs assert four theories of liability: (1) direct liability for active participation, (2) conspiracy with agents of the United States, (3) aiding and abetting agents of the United States and (4) direct liability "because [Jeppesen] demonstrated a reckless disregard as to whether Plaintiffs would be subjected to forced disappearance through its participation in the extraordinary rendition program and specifically its provision of flight and logistical support services to aircraft and crew that it knew or reasonably should have known would be used to transport them to secret detention and interrogation."

On the torture and degrading treatment claim, plaintiffs assert three theories of liability: (1) conspiracy with agents of the U.S. in plaintiffs' torture and degrading treatment, (2) aiding and abetting agents of the U.S. in subjecting plaintiffs to torture and degrading treatment and (3) direct liability "because [Jeppesen] demonstrated a reckless disregard as to whether Plaintiffs would be subjected to torture or other cruel, inhuman, or degrading treatment by providing flight and logistical support to aircraft and crew it knew or reasonably should have known would be used in the extraordinary rendition program to transport them to detention and interrogation.". . .

C. Procedural History

Before Jeppesen answered the complaint, the United States moved to intervene and to dismiss plaintiffs' complaint under the state secrets doctrine. The then-Director of the CIA, General Michael Hayden, filed two declarations in support of the motion to dismiss, one classified, the other redacted and unclassified. The public declaration states that "[d]isclosure of the information covered by this privilege assertion reasonably could be expected to cause serious—and in some instances, exceptionally grave—damage to the national security of the United States and, therefore, the information should be excluded from any use in this case.". . .

The district court granted the motions to intervene and dismiss and entered judgment in favor of Jeppesen, stating that "at the core of Plaintiffs' case against Defendant Jeppesen are 'allegations' of covert U.S. military or CIA operations in foreign countries against foreign nationals—clearly a subject matter which is a state secret." Plaintiffs appealed. A three-judge panel of this court reversed and remanded, holding that the government had failed to establish a basis for dismissal under the state secrets doctrine but permitting the government to reassert the doctrine at subsequent stages of the litigation. *Jeppesen I*, 579 F.3d at 953, 961-62. . . .

. . .

III. THE STATE SECRETS DOCTRINE

The Supreme Court has long recognized that in exceptional circumstances courts must act in the interest of the country's national security to prevent disclosure of state secrets, even to the point of dismissing a case entirely. *See Totten v. United States*, 92 U.S. 105, 107 (1876). The contemporary state secrets doctrine encompasses two applications of this principle. One completely bars adjudication of claims premised on state secrets (the "*Totten* bar"); the other is an evidentiary privilege ("the *Reynolds* privilege") that excludes privileged evidence from the case and *may* result in dismissal of the claims. *See United States v. Reynolds*, 345 U.S. 1 (1953). We first address the nature of these applications and then apply them to the facts of this case.

A. The *Totten* Bar

In 1876 the Supreme Court stated "as a *general principle* [ ] that public policy forbids the maintenance of any suit in a court of justice, the trial of which would inevitably lead to the disclosure of matters which the law itself regards as confidential." *Totten*, 92 U.S. at 107 (emphasis added). The Court again invoked the principle in 1953, citing *Totten* for the proposition that "where the very subject matter of the action" is "a matter of state secret," an action may be "dismissed on the pleadings without ever reaching the question of evidence" because it is "so obvious that the action should never prevail over the privilege." *Reynolds*, 345 U.S. at 11 n.26. This application of *Totten*'s general principle—which we refer to as the *Totten* bar—is "designed not merely to defeat the asserted claims, but to preclude judicial inquiry" entirely. *Tenet v. Doe*, 544 U.S. 1, 7 n.4 (2005).

Plaintiffs contend that the *Totten* bar applies *only* to a narrow category of cases they say are not implicated here, namely claims premised on a plaintiff's espionage relationship with the government. We disagree. We read the Court's discussion of *Totten* in *Reynolds* to mean that the *Totten* bar applies to cases in which "the very subject matter of the action" is "a matter of state secret." *Reynolds*, 345 U.S. at 11. "[A] contract to perform espionage" is only an example. This conclusion is confirmed by *Weinberger*, which relied on the *Totten* bar to hold that a case involving nuclear weapons secrets, and having nothing to do with espionage contracts, was "beyond judicial scrutiny." *See Weinberger*, 454 U.S. at 146-47; *see also Tenet*, 544 U.S. at 9 (characterizing *Weinberger* as a case applying the *Totten* bar). Thus, although the claims in both *Totten* and *Tenet* were premised on the existence of espionage agreements, and even though the plaintiffs in both *Totten* and *Tenet* were themselves parties to the espionage agreements, the *Totten* bar rests on a general principle that extends beyond that specific context. We therefore reject plaintiffs' unduly narrow view of the *Totten* bar and reaffirm our holding in *Al-Haramain* that the bar "has evolved into the principle that where the very subject matter of a lawsuit is a matter of state secret, the action must be dismissed without reaching the question of evidence." *Al-Haramain*, 507 F.3d at 1197. As we explain below, the *Totten* bar is a narrow rule, but it is not as narrow as plaintiffs contend.

We also disagree with plaintiffs' related contention that the *Totten* bar cannot apply unless the *plaintiff* is a party to a secret agreement with the government. The environmental groups and individuals who were the plaintiffs in *Weinberger* were not parties to agreements with the United States, secret or otherwise. The purpose of the bar, moreover, is to prevent the revelation of state secrets harmful to national security, a concern no less pressing when the plaintiffs are strangers to the espionage agreement that their litigation threatens to reveal. Thus, even if plaintiffs were correct that the *Totten* bar is limited to cases premised on espionage agreements with the government, we would reject their contention that the bar is necessarily limited to cases in which the plaintiffs are themselves parties to those agreements.

B. The *Reynolds* Privilege

In addition to the *Totten* bar, the state secrets doctrine encompasses a "privilege against revealing military [or state] secrets, a privilege which is well established in the law of evidence." *Reynolds*, 345 U.S. at 6-7. A successful assertion of privilege under *Reynolds* will remove the privileged evidence from the litigation. Unlike the *Totten* bar, [however,] a valid claim of privilege under *Reynolds* does not automatically require dismissal of the case. . . .

. . .

IV. APPLICATION

... The government contends that plaintiffs' lawsuit should be dismissed, whether under the *Totten* bar or the *Reynolds* privilege, because "state secrets are so central to this case that permitting further proceeding[s] would create an intolerable risk of disclosure that would jeopardize national security.". . . Plaintiffs argue that the *Totten* bar does not apply and that, even if the government is entitled to some protection under the *Reynolds* privilege, at least some claims survive. The district court appears to have dismissed the action under the *Totten* bar, making a "threshold determination" that "the very subject matter of the case is a state secret." Having dismissed on that basis, the district court did not address whether application of the *Reynolds* privilege would require dismissal.

We do not find it quite so clear that the very subject matter of this case is a state secret. Nonetheless, having conducted our own detailed analysis, we conclude that the district court reached the correct result because dismissal is warranted even under *Reynolds*. Recognizing the serious consequences to plaintiffs of dismissal, we explain our ruling so far as possible within the considerable constraints imposed on us by the state secrets doctrine itself.

A. The *Totten* Bar

... The Court has applied the *Totten* bar on just three occasions, involving two different kinds of state secrets: In *Tenet* and *Totten* the Court applied the *Totten* bar to "the distinct class of cases that depend upon clandestine spy relationships," *see Tenet*, 544 U.S. at 9-10; *Totten*, 92 U.S. at 107, and in *Weinberger* the Court applied the *Totten* bar to a case that depended on whether the Navy proposed to store nuclear weapons at a particular facility, *see Weinberger*, 454 U.S. at 146-47. Although the Court has not limited the *Totten* bar to cases premised on secret espionage agreements or the location of nuclear weapons, neither has it offered much guidance on when the *Totten* bar applies beyond these limited circumstances. Because the *Totten* bar is rarely applied and not clearly defined, because it is a judge-made doctrine with extremely harsh consequences and because conducting a more detailed analysis will tend to improve the accuracy, transparency and legitimacy of the proceedings, district courts presented with disputes about state secrets should ordinarily undertake a detailed *Reynolds* analysis before deciding whether dismissal on the pleadings is justified.

Here, some of plaintiffs' claims might well fall within the *Totten* bar. In particular, their allegations that Jeppesen conspired with agents of the United States in plaintiffs' forced disappearance, torture and degrading treatment are premised on the existence of an alleged covert relationship between Jeppesen and the government—a matter that the Fourth Circuit has concluded is "practically indistinguishable from that categorically barred by *Totten* and *Tenet*." *El-Masri*, 479 F.3d at 309. On the other hand, allegations based on plaintiffs' theory that Jeppesen should be liable simply for what it "should have known" about the alleged unlawful extraordinary rendition program while participating in it are not so obviously tied to proof of a secret agreement between Jeppesen and the government.

We do not resolve the difficult question of precisely which claims may be barred under *Totten* because application of the *Reynolds* privilege leads us to conclude that this litigation cannot proceed further. We rely on the *Reynolds* privilege rather than the *Totten* bar for several reasons. First, the government has asserted the *Reynolds* privilege along with the *Totten* bar, inviting the further inquiry *Reynolds* requires and presenting a record that compels dismissal even on this alternate ground. Second, we have discretion to affirm on any basis supported by the record. Third, resolving this case under *Reynolds* avoids difficult questions about the precise scope of the *Totten* bar and permits us to conduct a searching judicial review, fulfilling our obligation under *Reynolds* "to review the [government's claim] with a very careful, indeed a skeptical, eye, and not to accept at face value the government's claim or justification of privilege." *Al-Haramain*, 507 F.3d at 1203.

B. The *Reynolds* Privilege

There is no dispute that the government has complied with *Reynolds'* procedural requirements for invoking the state secrets privilege by filing General Hayden's formal claim of privilege in his public declaration. We therefore focus on the second and third steps in the *Reynolds* analysis: *First*, whether and to what extent the matters the government contends must be kept secret are in fact matters of state secret; and *second*, if they are, whether the action can be litigated without relying on evidence that would necessarily reveal those secrets or press so closely upon them as to create an unjustifiable risk that they would be revealed. In doing so, we explain our decision as much as we can without compromising the secrets we are required to protect.

1. Whether and to What Extent the Evidence Is Privileged

The government asserts the state secrets privilege over four categories of evidence. In particular, the government contends that neither it nor Jeppesen should be compelled, through a responsive pleading, discovery responses or otherwise, to disclose: "[1] information that would tend to confirm or deny whether Jeppesen or any other private entity assisted the CIA with clandestine intelligence activities; [2] information about whether any foreign government cooperated with the CIA in clandestine intelligence activities; [3] information about the scope or operation of the CIA terrorist detention and interrogation program; [or 4] any other information concerning CIA clandestine intelligence operations that would tend to reveal intelligence activities, sources, or methods." These indisputably are matters that the state secrets privilege may cover. *See, e.g., Tenet*, 544 U.S. at 11 (emphasizing the "absolute protection" the state secrets doctrine affords against revealing espionage relationships); *CIA v. Sims*, 471 U.S. 159, 175 (1985) ("Even a small chance that some court will order disclosure of a source's identity could well impair intelligence gathering and cause sources to 'close up like a clam.'"); *In re Sealed Case*, 494 F.3d at 152 (prohibiting "all discussion of intelligence sources, capabilities, and the like"); *Al-Haramain*, 507 F.3d at 1204 (applying the privilege to "the means, sources and methods of intelligence gathering"); *Ellsberg*, 709 F.2d at 57 (applying the privilege to the "disclosure of intelligence-gathering methods or capabilities").

We have thoroughly and critically reviewed the government's public and classified declarations and are convinced that at least some of the matters it seeks to protect from disclosure in this litigation are valid state secrets, "which, in the interest of national security, should not be divulged." *Reynolds*, 345 U.S. at 10. The government's classified disclosures to the court are persuasive that compelled or inadvertent disclosure of such information in the course of litigation would seriously harm legitimate national security interests. . . .

2. Effect on the Proceedings

Having determined that the privilege applies, we next determine whether the case must be dismissed under the *Reynolds* privilege. . . .

[W]e do not rely on the first two circumstances in which the *Reynolds* privilege requires dismissal. . . . Instead, we assume without deciding that plaintiffs' prima facie case and Jeppesen's defenses may not inevitably depend on privileged evidence. Proceeding on that assumption, we hold that dismissal is nonetheless required under *Reynolds* because there is no feasible way to litigate Jeppesen's alleged liability without creating an unjustifiable risk of divulging state secrets. . . .

We reach this conclusion because all seven of plaintiffs' claims, even if taken as true, describe Jeppesen as providing logistical support in a broad, complex process, certain aspects of which, the government has persuaded us, are absolutely protected by the state secrets privilege. Notwithstanding that some information about that process has become public, Jeppesen's alleged role and its attendant liability cannot be isolated from aspects that are secret and protected. Because the facts underlying plaintiffs' claims are so infused with these secrets, *any* plausible effort by Jeppesen to defend against them would create an unjustifiable risk of revealing state secrets, even if plaintiffs could make a prima facie case on one or more claims with nonprivileged evidence. . . .

Here, our detailed *Reynolds* analysis reveals that the claims and possible defenses are so infused with state secrets that the risk of disclosing them is both apparent and inevitable. Dismissal under these circumstances, like dismissal under the *Totten* bar, reflects the general principle that "public policy forbids the maintenance of any suit in a court of justice, the trial of which would inevitably lead to the disclosure of matters which the law itself regards as confidential, and respecting which it will not allow the confidence to be violated." *Totten*, 92 U.S. at 107.

. . .

VI. CONCLUSION

We, like the dissent, emphasize that it should be a rare case when the state secrets doctrine leads to dismissal at the outset of a case. Nonetheless, there are such cases—not just those subject to *Totten*'s per se rule, but those where the mandate for dismissal is apparent even under the more searching examination required by *Reynolds*. This is one of those rare cases.

For all the reasons the dissent articulates—including the impact on human rights, the importance of constitutional protections and the constraints of a judge-made doctrine—we do not reach our decision lightly or without close and skeptical scrutiny of the record and the government's case for secrecy and dismissal. We expect our decision today to inform district courts that *Totten* has its limits, that every effort should be made to parse claims to salvage a case like this using the *Reynolds* approach, that the standards for peremptory dismissal are very high and it is the district court's role to use its fact-finding and other tools to full advantage before it concludes that the rare step of dismissal is justified. We also acknowledge that this case presents a painful conflict between human rights and national security. As judges, we have tried our best to evaluate the competing claims of plaintiffs and the government and resolve that conflict according to the principles governing the state secrets doctrine set forth by the United States Supreme Court.

For the reasons stated, we hold that the government's valid assertion of the state secrets privilege warrants dismissal of the litigation, and affirm the judgment of the district court. . . .

NOTES AND QUESTIONS

1. The court in *Jeppesen Dataplan* resolved the cause of action under the *Reynolds* privilege rather than the *Totten* bar. What are the advantages of resolving the matter under the state-secrets privilege versus the *Totten* bar?
2. What categories of evidence does the government claim constitute state secrets?
3. Why did the court dismiss plaintiffs' suit under the state-secrets doctrine?
4. The court states that "this case presents a painful conflict between human rights and national security." What violations of international human rights were committed under the government's secret detention and interrogation program?
5. What are the implications of the court's ruling? Are U.S. corporations that assist the government in executing programs that violate international human rights immune from civil liability? Moreover, if the government refuses to criminally prosecute the persons responsible for the government's unlawful detention and interrogation program, does impunity result? In the end, is no one held accountable? As a result, are certain government officials and contractors above the law?

B. Preventing Disclosure in Criminal Litigation

Classified Information Procedures Act

The Classified Information Procedures Act (CIPA), 18 U.S.C. App. 3 §§ 1-16, enacted in 1980, "provides a framework for determining how to proceed with discovery and admissibility of classified information in criminal cases." *United*

States v. Sterling, 724 F.3d 482, 515 (4th Cir. 2013). CIPA was designed to balance the defendant's interest in a fair trial and the government's interest in protecting national security information. The purpose is "to harmonize a [criminal] defendant's right to obtain and present exculpatory material with the government's need to withhold information from discovery when disclosure would be inimical to national security." *In re Terrorist Bombings of U.S. Embassies in East Africa*, 552 F.3d 93, 115-16 (2d Cir. 2008). While CIPA does not outright grant the government a privilege to refrain from disclosing classified information, it presupposes such a privilege. "The privilege it presupposes has its origins in the common-law privilege against disclosure of state secrets, which allows the government to withhold from discovery or prohibit disclosure at trial information that would threaten national security." *United States v. Abu-Jihad*, 630 F.3d 102, 140 (2d Cir. 2010). However, the protection or restriction of classified information must not impair the defendant's right to a fair trial. *United States v. Aref*, 533 F.3d 72, 78 (2d Cir. 2008).

Sections 4, 5, and 6 are essential to understanding how CIPA protects the disclosure of classified information. Section 4 of CIPA governs the pretrial discovery of classified information by defendants in criminal cases. After a defense request for discovery under the Federal Rules of Criminal Procedure, the government may submit a written statement to be inspected by the district court *in camera*, seeking a protective order to "(1) delete specified items of classified information, (2) substitute a summary of the information for such classified documents, or (3) substitute a statement admitting relevant facts that the classified information would tend to prove." *Id.* § 4. Section 5 provides that if a defendant reasonably expects to disclose classified information during the criminal trial or pretrial proceedings, he must give notice to the government attorney. *Id.* § 5(a).

Finally, § 6 sets out procedures to safeguard classified information, both before and during trial. Under § 6, the government may request the court to conduct a hearing "to make all determinations concerning the use, relevance, or admissibility of classified information" during trial or pretrial proceeding. Any such hearing shall be held *in camera* if the Attorney General certifies that a public proceeding may result in the disclosure of classified information. *Id.* § 6(a). Before the district court holds such a hearing, the government must give the defendant notice of the classified information at issue. *Id.* § 6(b)(1). Further, if a district court authorizes "the disclosure of specific classified information," the government may move to substitute "for such classified information . . . a statement admitting relevant facts that the specific classified information would tend to prove . . . or a summary of the specific classified information." *Id.* § 6(c)(1). A district court must grant the government's motion for a protective order "if it finds that the statement or summary will provide the defendant with substantially the same ability to make his defense as would disclosure of the specific classified information." *Id.* Ultimately, the disclosure of classified information under CIPA requires the district court "to determine whether the criminal defendant's interest in the information at issue outweighs the government's interest in withholding it." *In re Terrorist Bombings of U.S. Embassies in East Africa*, 552 F.3d 93, 124 (2d Cir. 2008).

United States v. Aref
553 F.3d 72 (2d Cir. 2008)

Both defendants were convicted on charges arising out of a sting operation. The jury found that they conspired to conceal the source of what a cooperator represented to be proceeds from the sale of a surface-to-air missile. According to the cooperator, the missile was to be used by terrorists against a target in New York City. Before trial, the Government sought, pursuant to the Classified Information Procedures Act ("CIPA"), 18 U.S.C. app. 3, two protective orders restricting discovery of certain classified information that, arguably, would have been otherwise discoverable. The district court granted the motions in part and denied the rest.

. . .

BACKGROUND

In a thirty-count indictment, both defendants were charged with conspiracy and attempt to commit money laundering and to provide material support to a designated terrorist organization. Aref was also charged with making false statements to federal officers.

The Government alleged that the defendants agreed to work with a cooperator in a scheme to conceal the source of $50,000. The cooperator told the defendants that the money came from the sale of a surface-to-air missile to a designated terrorist group called Jaish-e-Mohammed. The missile was to be fired at a target in New York City. A jury found Hossain guilty on all twenty-seven counts against him. Aref was convicted on ten counts and acquitted on the others. We address the defendants' challenges to the evidence against them in the accompanying summary order, and we recount only those facts relevant to the district court's handling of classified information.

. . .

DISCUSSION

The defendants argue that the district court improperly denied them access to classified information during discovery. . . .We reject these arguments.

I. CIPA

CIPA establishes procedures for handling classified information in criminal cases. The statute was meant to "protect[ ] and restrict[ ] the discovery of classified information in a way that does not impair the defendant's right to a fair trial." *United States v. O'Hara*, 301 F.3d 563, 568 (7th Cir. 2002).

CIPA section 4 sets out procedures for "[d]iscovery of classified information by defendants":

> The [district] court, upon a sufficient showing, may authorize the United States to delete specified items of classified information from documents to be made available to the defendant through discovery under the Federal Rules of Criminal Procedure, to substitute a summary of the information for such

classified documents, or to substitute a statement admitting relevant facts that the classified information would tend to prove. The court may permit the United States to make a request for such authorization in the form of a written statement to be inspected by the court alone.

18 U.S.C. app. 3 § 4.

This provision clarifies district courts' power under Federal Rule of Criminal Procedure 16(d)(1) to issue protective orders denying or restricting discovery for good cause. S. Rep. No. 96-823, at 6 (1980), *as reprinted in* 1980 U.S.C.C.A.N. 4294, 4299-4300. The Advisory Committee notes to Rule 16 make clear that "good cause" includes "the protection of information vital to the national security." Fed. R. Crim. P. 16 advisory committee's note to 1966 amendment.

It is important to understand that CIPA section 4 *presupposes* a governmental privilege against disclosing classified information. It does not itself *create* a privilege. *United States v. Mejia*, 448 F.3d 436, 455 & n.15 (D.C. Cir. 2006); *see also* H.R. Rep. No. 96-831, pt. 1, at 27 (1980) (noting that CIPA "is not intended to affect the discovery rights of a defendant"). Although Rule 16(d)(1) authorizes district courts to restrict discovery of evidence in the interest of national security, it leaves the relevant privilege undefined.

The most likely source for the protection of classified information lies in the common-law privilege against disclosure of state secrets. *See Zuckerbraun v. Gen. Dynamics Corp.*, 935 F.2d 544, 546 (2d Cir. 1991). That venerable evidentiary privilege "allows the government to withhold information from discovery when disclosure would be inimical to national security." *Id.* It would appear that classified information at issue in CIPA cases fits comfortably within the state-secrets privilege. *Compare id. with* Classified National Security Information, Exec. Order No. 13,292, § 1.2, 68 Fed. Reg. 15315, 15315-16 (Mar. 25, 2003) (recognizing three levels of classified national security information, all of which require the classifying officer to determine that disclosure reasonably could be expected to damage national security).

We are not unaware that the House of Representatives Select Committee on Intelligence stated categorically in its report on CIPA that "the common law state secrets privilege is not applicable in the criminal arena." H.R. Rep. 96-831, pt. 1, at 15 n.12. That statement simply sweeps too broadly.

The Committee relied on three cases for this remarkable proposition: *United States v. Reynolds*, 345 U.S. 1 (1953), *United States v. Coplon*, 185 F.2d 629 (2d Cir. 1950), and *United States v. Andolschek*, 142 F.2d 503 (2d Cir. 1944). *See* H.R. Rep. 96-831, pt. 1, at 15 n.12. A close reading of these cases does not support the Committee's conclusion.

In *Reynolds*, the Supreme Court held that a court in a civil case may deny evidence to plaintiffs if "there is a reasonable danger that compulsion of the evidence will expose military matters which, in the interest of national security, should not be divulged." 345 U.S. at 10. In contrast, the Court explained that in criminal cases such as *Andolschek*, the Government was not permitted to "undertake prosecution and then invoke its governmental privileges to deprive the accused of anything which might be material to his defense."

Id. at 12 & n.27. Similarly, we acknowledged in *Coplon* that the Government possesses a privilege against disclosing "state secrets," but held that the privilege could not prevent the defendant from receiving evidence to which he has a constitutional right. *See* 185 F.2d at 638. These cases, therefore, do not hold that the Government cannot claim the state-secrets privilege in criminal cases. Instead, they recognize the privilege, but conclude that it must give way under some circumstances to a criminal defendant's right to present a meaningful defense.

Accordingly, we hold that the applicable privilege here is the state-secrets privilege. *See United States v. Klimavicius-Viloria*, 144 F.3d 1249, 1261 (9th Cir. 1998) (holding that state-secrets privilege applies in CIPA cases). That said, *Reynolds, Andolschek*, and *Coplon* make clear that the privilege can be overcome when the evidence at issue is material to the defense. *See Reynolds*, 345 U.S. at 12 & n.27. This standard is consistent with *Roviaro v. United States*, 353 U.S. 53 (1957), where the Supreme Court held in a criminal case that the Government's privilege to withhold the identity of a confidential informant "must give way" when the information "is relevant and helpful to the defense of an accused, or is essential to a fair determination of a cause." *Id.* at 60-61. Indeed, we have interpreted "relevant and helpful" under *Roviaro* to mean "material to the defense." *United States v. Saa*, 859 F.2d 1067, 1073 (2d Cir. 1988). We have also noted that the government-informant privilege at issue in *Roviaro* and the state-secrets privilege are part of "the same doctrine." *Coplon*, 185 F.2d at 638.

We therefore adopt the *Roviaro* standard for determining when the Government's privilege must give way in a CIPA case. Other circuits agree. *See Klimavicius-Viloria*, 144 F.3d at 1261; United States v. Varca, 896 F.2d 900, 905 (5th Cir. 1990); *United States v. Yunis*, 867 F.2d 617, 623 (D.C. Cir. 1989); *United States v. Smith*, 780 F.2d 1102, 1107-10 (4th Cir. 1985) (en banc); *United States v. Pringle*, 751 F.2d 419, 427-28 (1st Cir. 1984).

Applying this standard, the district court must first decide whether the classified information the Government possesses is discoverable. If it is, the district court must then determine whether the state-secrets privilege applies because: (1) there is "a reasonable danger that compulsion of the evidence will expose . . . matters which, in the interest of national security, should not be divulged," and (2) the privilege is "lodged by the head of the department which has control over the matter, after actual personal consideration by that officer." *Reynolds*, 345 U.S. at 8, 10 (footnote omitted).

If the evidence is discoverable but the information is privileged, the court must next decide whether the information is helpful or material to the defense, i.e., useful "to counter the government's case or to bolster a defense." *United States v. Stevens*, 985 F.2d 1175, 1180 (2d Cir. 1993) (interpreting materiality standard under Federal Rule of Criminal Procedure 16(a)(1)). To be helpful or material to the defense, evidence need not rise to the level that would trigger the Government's obligation under *Brady v. Maryland*, 373 U.S. 83 (1963), to disclose exculpatory information. *See id.* at 87. "[I]nformation can be helpful without being 'favorable' in the *Brady* sense." *Mejia*, 448 F.3d at 457.

The district court's decision to issue a protective order under CIPA section 4 and Federal Rule of Criminal Procedure 16(d)(1) is reviewed for abuse of discretion. *See United States v. Delia*, 944 F.2d 1010, 1018 (2d Cir. 1991). Whether evidence is "helpful" or "material to the defense" is also within the district court's discretion. *See DiBlasio v. Keane*, 932 F.2d 1038, 1042 (2d Cir. 1991).

We find no abuse of discretion here. For purposes of this opinion, we assume without deciding that the classified information the Government presented to the district court was discoverable. We have carefully reviewed the classified information and the Government's sealed submissions and agree with the district court that the Government has established a reasonable danger that disclosure would jeopardize national security. *See Reynolds*, 345 U.S. at 10.

The Government failed, however, to invoke the privilege through the "head of the department which has control over the matter, after actual personal consideration by that officer." *Id.* at 8. This is not necessarily fatal. We have previously excused the Government's failure to comply with this formality where involvement of the department head would have been "of little or no benefit" because disclosure of classified information was prohibited by law. *See Clift v. United States*, 597 F.2d 826, 828-29 (2d Cir. 1979) (Friendly, J.) (internal quotation marks omitted). We similarly excuse the failure to involve the department head here. It would "be of little or no benefit" for us to remand for the purpose of having the department head agree that disclosure of the classified information would pose a risk to national security here. Based on our holding today, however, we trust that this issue will not arise in future CIPA cases.

Finally, we agree that the district court did not deny the defendants any helpful evidence. Indeed, we commend the district court for its thorough scrutiny of the classified information.

We also reject Aref's contention that the district court improperly held *ex parte* hearings with the Government when evaluating the classified material. Both CIPA section 4 and Rule 16(d)(1) authorize *ex parte* submissions. *See* 18 U.S.C. app. 3 § 4; Fed. R. Crim. P. 16(d)(1). "In a case involving classified documents, . . . *ex parte, in camera* hearings in which government counsel participates to the exclusion of defense counsel are part of the process that the district court may use in order to decide the relevancy of the information." *Klimavicius-Viloria*, 144 F.3d at 1261. When the "government is seeking to withhold classified information from the defendant, an adversary hearing with defense knowledge would defeat the very purpose of the discovery rules." H.R. Rep. 96-831, pt. 1, at 27 n.22.

. . .

CONCLUSION

For the foregoing reasons, and for those stated in the accompanying summary order, we . . . AFFIRM Aref's and Hossain's convictions. . . .

NOTES AND QUESTIONS

1. In *Reynolds*, the Supreme Court held that a court in a civil case may deny evidence to plaintiffs if "there is a reasonable danger that compulsion of the evidence will expose military matters which in the interest of national security, should not be divulged." 345 U.S. at 10. Should the state-secrets privilege be applied with the same effect in criminal cases?
2. Is the government's privilege under the state-secrets doctrine absolute? In a criminal case, when must the government's privilege give way to the defendant's right to present a defense? Conversely, when does the government's interest in protecting national security trump the defendant's interest in disclosing classified information in criminal proceedings?
3. What is the multi-step process for determining whether classified information should be disclosed in a criminal case? Who must assert the state-secrets privilege? Is non-compliance with this formality fatal?
4. The *Aref* court states that to be helpful or material to the defense, evidence need not rise to the level that would trigger the government's obligation under *Brady v. Maryland*, 373 U.S. 83 (1963). In *Brady*, the Supreme Court established an affirmative duty on the part of the prosecution to disclose upon request by the defendant evidence that is "material either to guilt or punishment." *Id.* at 87. Further, in *United States v. Agurs*, 427 U.S. 97 (1976), the Court extended the prosecution's affirmative duty imposed under *Brady* to require disclosure of favorable evidence even in the absence of a specific request by the defendant. *Id.* at 107. In *Aref*, the court stated that information can be helpful or material under CIPA without being favorable in the *Brady* sense. It therefore appears that the term "material" has one meaning under *Brady*, and a broader application in the CIPA context. Can you think of a situation where the government would not have an affirmative duty to disclose classified information under *Brady*, but such evidence would be subject to disclosure under CIPA?
5. In *Aref*, the court held that the district court's decision to issue a protective order under CIPA § 4 was not an abuse of discretion. Why not? What was the reasoning of the court?
6. Does excluding the defendant from hearings at which classified information is discussed violate the defendant's right to be present at a crucial stage in the proceedings guaranteed by the Fifth and Sixth Amendments? Always? Sometimes? *See In re Terrorist Bombings of U.S. Embassies in East Africa*, 552 F.3d 93, 130 (2d Cir. 2008) (holding that exclusion from hearings at which classified information was discussed did not violate defendant's due process right to be present at a crucial stage in his trial).

United States v. Sedaghaty
728 F.3d 885 (9th Cir. 2013)

Th[is] appeal illustrates the fine line between the government's use of relevant evidence to document motive for a cover up and its use of inflammatory, unrelated evidence . . . that prejudices the jury. This tension was evident both before and during trial and dominates much of the briefing on appeal.

. . .

II. CIPA CLAIMS

Although this is a tax fraud case, the prosecution discovered that the government possessed some relevant classified information, which was handled under CIPA procedures. Those procedures endeavor to harmonize a defendant's right to a fair trial with the government's right to protect classified information. While the government must safeguard classified information in the interest of national security, "courts must not be remiss in protecting a defendant's right to a full and meaningful presentation of his claim to innocence." *United States v. Fernandez*, 913 F.2d 148, 154 (4th Cir. 1990).

The government filed six motions seeking protection for classified materials, all of which were granted by the district court. [Pirouz Sedaghaty (known as Pete Seda)] . . . challenges the court's handling of these classified matters, including its approval of an unclassified summary. . . .

A. CIPA Provisions

Congress enacted CIPA in 1980 "to help ensure that the intelligence agencies are subject to the rule of law and to help strengthen the enforcement of laws designed to protect both national security and civil liberties." S. Rep. No. 96-823, at 3 (1980), reprinted in 1980 U.S.C.C.A.N. 4294, 4296. CIPA does not expand or restrict established principles of discovery and does not have a substantive impact on the admissibility of probative evidence. *United States v. Johnson*, 139 F.3d 1359, 1365 (11th Cir. 1998); S. Rep. No. 96-823 at 8, reprinted in 1980 U.S.C.C.A.N. at 4301-03. Instead, CIPA "establishes procedures for handling classified information in criminal cases," *United States v. Aref*, 533 F.3d 72, 78 (2d Cir. 2008), so that district courts may rule "on questions of admissibility involving classified information before introduction of the evidence in open court," *United States v. Sarkissian*, 841 F.2d 959, 965 (9th Cir. 1988) (citation omitted). Two sections of CIPA are relevant here: § 4 governs the pretrial discovery of classified information by defendants, and § 6 sets out procedures to safeguard classified information, both before and during trial.

CIPA § 4 was intended "to clarify the court's powers under Fed. R. Crim. P. 16(d)(1) to deny or restrict discovery in order to protect national security." *Sarkissian*, 841 F.2d at 965; S. Rep. No. 96-823 at 6, reprinted in 1980 U.S.C.C.A.N. at 4299. Section 4 provides that:

> [t]he court, upon a sufficient showing, may authorize the United States to delete specified items of classified information from documents to be made

available to the defendant through discovery under the Federal Rules of Criminal Procedure, to substitute a summary of the information for such classified documents, or to substitute a statement admitting relevant facts that the classified information would tend to prove.

18 U.S.C. app. 3 § 4.

When considering a motion to withhold classified information from discovery, a district court must first determine whether, pursuant to the Federal Rules of Criminal Procedure, statute, or the common law, the information at issue is discoverable at all. *United States v. Rewald*, 889 F.2d 836, 847-48 (9th Cir. 1989). If the material at issue is discoverable, the court must next determine whether the government has made a formal claim of the state secrets privilege, "'lodged by the head of the department which has actual control over the matter, after actual personal consideration by that officer.'" *United States v. Klimavicius-Viloria*, 144 F.3d 1249, 1261 (9th Cir. 1998) (quoting *United States v. Reynolds*, 345 U.S. 1, 7-8 (1953)). Once a court concludes that the material is discoverable and that the state secrets privilege applies, then the court must determine whether the evidence is "relevant and helpful to the defense of an accused." *Roviaro v. United States*, 353 U.S. 53, 60-61 (1957); *United States v. Gurolla*, 333 F.3d 944, 951 (9th Cir. 2003). If the information meets the "relevant and helpful" test, CIPA § 4 empowers the court to determine the terms of discovery, if any. 18 U.S.C. app. 3 § 4.

CIPA § 6, which applies to both pre-trial and trial proceedings, guides the procedures for making "determinations concerning the use, relevance, or admissibility of classified information. . . ." 18 U.S.C. app. 3 § 6(a). Specifically, CIPA § 6(c)(1) deals with substitutions and provides that a court may authorize a substitution for classified material in the form of a statement or summary "if it finds that the statement or summary will provide the defendant with substantially the same ability to make his defense as would disclosure of the specific classified information." 18 U.S.C. app. 3 § 6(c)(1). This requirement arises out of the Constitution's guarantee that all criminal defendants must have "'a meaningful opportunity to present a complete defense.'" *Holmes v. South Carolina*, 547 U.S. 319, 324 (2006) (quoting *Crane v. Kentucky*, 476 U.S. 683, 690 (1986)). Indeed, the "need to develop all relevant facts in the adversary system is both fundamental and comprehensive." *United States v. Nixon*, 418 U.S. 683, 709 (1974).

The substitution need not be of "precise, concrete equivalence," and the "fact that insignificant tactical advantages could accrue to the defendant by the use of the specified classified information should not preclude the court from ordering alternative disclosure." H.R. Rep. No. 96-1436, at 12-13 (1980) (Conf. Rep.), reprinted in 1980 U.S.C.C.A.N. at 4310-11. Nevertheless, the fundamental purpose of a substitution under CIPA is "to place the defendant, as nearly as possible, in the position he would be in if the classified information . . . were available to him." *United States v. Moussaoui*, 382 F.3d 453, 477 (4th Cir. 2004). . . .

B. THE SUBSTITUTION

The government acknowledged in advance of trial that it had classified information that was helpful to Seda's defense. The government proposed, and the court authorized, the following unclassified summary of classified material responsive to Seda's discovery requests:

The U.S. Government obtained information that Sami 'Abd Al 'Aziz Al-Sanad worked during 2000 and 2001 for the Al-Haramain organization and was responsible for providing currency supplied by Al-Haramain, including the currency obtained by codefendant Soliman Al-Buthe from Al-Haramain USA, to a representative of Muhammad Al-Sayf, aka Abu Umar, to be smuggled into Chechnya. Al-Sanad has claimed that the monies he provided to Al-Sayf's representative were destined for needy Chechen families.

Seda objected to the substitution and asked either for "an uneditorialized summary" or for the production of the underlying material. After careful review of the materials at issue, we conclude that the substitution's language unfairly colored presentation of the information and, even more problematic, that the substitution omitted facts helpful to Seda's defense. Further detail and analysis of the substitution is contained in the classified opinion with respect to the substitution. The substitution is statutorily inadequate because it does not provide Seda with "substantially the same ability to make his defense as would disclosure of the specific classified information." 18 U.S.C. app. 3 § 6(c)(1).

The brief summary contains both inculpatory and exculpatory information. On the one hand, it supports the government's theory that the El-Fiki donation went to fund the mujahideen in Chechnya because it indicates that Al-Sanad gave the money to a representative of Al-Sayf, who the government established at trial was a religious leader associated with the Chechen mujahideen at the time. On the other hand, it supports Seda's claim that, as far as he knew, the donation was to be used to fund humanitarian relief.

The wording of the summary bolsters the inculpatory section while discrediting the exculpatory section. For example, the first sentence presents Al-Sanad's transfer of the El-Fiki donation to Al-Sayf's representative as a fact about which the government has "obtained information." The second sentence, by contrast, embeds skepticism into Al-Sanad's exculpatory statement about the destination and use of the funds, dismissing it as something Al-Sanad "has claimed." This is but one example of the neutrality deficiencies in the statement. It is no surprise that Seda ultimately chose not to use the substitution at trial.

Because the underlying documents are classified, we are constrained in our comments about the summary. But it is a fundamental principle underlying CIPA that the summary should be evenhanded, worded in a neutral fashion and not tilted or shaded to the government's advantage. See S. Rep. No. 96-823 at 9 (1980), reprinted in 1980 U.S.C.C.A.N. at 4302-03 (stating that the "judge should ensure that a substitution . . . is crafted so that the Government obtains no unfair advantage in the trial").

In isolation, the characterization of the evidence may not be a sufficient basis to reject the substitution. More troubling, however, is the exclusion from the summary of further information that is helpful to Seda's defense. The classified nature of the material highlights the awkward nature of our review: Seda is forced to argue for the relevance of the material without actually knowing what the classified record contains, while we know what it contains but are unable to describe it on the public record. . . . We can say, however, that the summary excludes exculpatory information and fails to provide crucial context for certain information that it does convey.

Although there is no indication of bad faith, the government appears to have looked with tunnel vision at limited issues that it believed were relevant. Even granting the district court wide latitude in its evidentiary decisionmaking, as we must, we conclude that the summary is inadequate not only because of its slanted wording but more fundamentally because it is incomplete. *United States v. Clegg* ("*Clegg I*"), 740 F.2d 16, 18 (9th Cir. 1984) (upholding rejection of a substitution where the classified documents "are relevant to the development of a possible defense" and the "government's proposed summaries of the materials are inadequate"). It would be illogical to conclude that a substitution that excludes non-cumulative exculpatory information could "provide the defendant with substantially the same ability to make his defense as would disclosure of the specific classified information" as required by CIPA § 6. 18 U.S.C. app. 3 § 6(c)(1); see also *Moussaoui*, 382 F.3d at 478-79 (rejecting proposed substitutions that failed to include exculpatory information); *Fernandez*, 913 F.2d at 158 (upholding rejection of proposed substitutions because the "substitutions would have required the jury to judge [the defendant's] role . . . , and thus the truth of his statements about it, in a contextual vacuum").

. . . Not surprisingly, in the face of a slanted and unhelpful summary, Seda's counsel ultimately withdrew the substitution as a stipulated exhibit just before trial. But defense counsel ought not be put in a Catch-22 situation whereby it has to accept the government's deficient summary or none at all.

. . . Seda filed objections to the summary substitution and moved for "an uneditorialized summary." Without being able to access any of the underlying documents, Seda objected that the summary omitted relevant and helpful information about the individual to whom Al-Sanad transferred the funds. He also objected to the fact that the summary included language that questioned Al-Sanad's veracity and argued that the defense should be entitled to offer the exculpatory statements actually provided by Al-Sanad. Alternatively, Seda moved for access to more complete unclassified versions of the underlying materials on which the summary was presumably based. Seda never withdrew or waived this objection.

At a hearing the week before trial, the defense reiterated its objections to the summary substitution. The government replied that it would stipulate to the admission of the summary, but would not revise or alter it, saying, "we think it's either all or nothing." In response, the court said only, "Okay," and moved on to another topic. Later in that same hearing, as the judge was making final rulings on the exhibits, the government reiterated its position with regard to the summary and stated that the only decision was whether the defense wanted to accept the summary in its current form or not. The defense responded, "At this time, Your Honor, we would not be offering it. *We've pointed out what we believe needs to be done.*" (emphasis added). The defense withdrew the exhibit in that form, at that time, but explicitly referenced and reiterated its objection. Seda did not withdraw or waive his objection to the court's approval of the government's summary substitution. Nor could Seda's counsel have been expected to offer an intelligent substitution or alternative language, since he did not have access to the underlying classified documents. Having been unsuccessful at challenging the substitution before trial, Seda's recourse is in this appeal.

We are fully cognizant of the delicate task entrusted to the district court in matters involving classified information. To that end, CIPA lays out a defined process for substitutions such that, when classified information is relevant and helpful to his defense, the defendant should be placed, "as nearly as possible, in the position he would be in if the classified information were available to him." *Moussaoui*, 382 F.3d at 477; see also, 18 U.S.C. app. 3 § 6(c)(1). In the end, the inadequate substitution interfered with Seda's ability to present a complete defense. Although the government argues that substitution was sufficient, it does not make any argument that the facts omitted are harmless.

* * *

Affirmed in Part, Reversed in Part, and Remanded for a New Trial.

NOTES AND QUESTIONS

1. What is the purpose of CIPA § 4? What does CIPA § 6 provide? What types of substitutions are permitted under §§ 4 and 6?

2. Under CIPA § 6(c)(1), a court may authorize a substitution for classified material in the form of a statement or summary "if it finds that the statement or summary will provide the defendant with *substantially the same ability to make his defense* as would disclosure of the specific classified information." *Id.* § 6(c)(1) (emphasis added). The court states that the substitution need not be of "precise, concrete equivalence." Further, the "fact that insignificant tactical advantages could accrue to the defendant by the use of specified classified information" should not preclude alternative disclosure. What is the fundamental purpose of a substitution under CIPA? What factors are probative of whether the government's substitute statement or summary satisfies the statutory standard?

3. What was the problem with the government's unclassified summary of the classified material? The court states that a CIPA summary should be "evenhanded, worded in a neutral fashion and not tilted or shaded to the government's advantage." Did the summary provide the defendant with "substantially the same ability to make his defense" as would disclosure of the specific classified information? If not, why not?

4. If the information requested during discovery is classified, how does the defendant know whether the summary provides him with "substantially the same

ability to make his defense"? Is the defendant wholly reliant on the district court to make that determination? If so, is the court adequately positioned to make that decision?

United States v. Sterling
724 F.3d 482 (4th Cir. 2013)

TRAXLER, Chief Judge:

Jeffrey Sterling is a former CIA agent who has been indicted for, *inter alia*, the unauthorized retention and disclosure of national defense information, in violation of the Espionage Act, 18 U.S.C. § 793(d) & (e). The indictment followed the grand jury's probable cause determination that Sterling illegally disclosed classified information about a covert CIA operation pertaining to the Iranian nuclear weapons operation to James Risen, for publication in a book written by Risen, and that he may have done so in retaliation for the CIA's decision to terminate his employment and to interfere with his efforts to publish such classified information in his personal memoirs. Prior to trial, the district court made three evidentiary rulings that are the subject of this appeal. We affirm in part, reverse in part, and remand for further proceedings.

. . .

VII. CIPA RULING

Prior to trial the Government moved for a protective order, pursuant to the Classified Information Procedures Act ("CIPA"), 18 U.S.C. app. 3 § 6, prohibiting the disclosure of classified and sensitive information. The list of protected information included:

> [ ] The true name of any current or former covert CIA employee, or other information (such as a physical description) that reasonably could be expected to identify any current or former covert CIA employee, with the exception of those current or former covert CIA employees who testify using their full, true names.
>   [ ] The true name of any CIA employee, covert or overt, who testifies using his or her last initial only.

. . . The Government sought to protect the identities of some of its witnesses — as relevant here, current or former CIA operatives — through use of a screen or light disguises (wigs, false beards, half glasses), use of a non-public entrance to the courtroom, and, of critical importance to this appeal, by allowing the witnesses to use last initials rather than their full names (for example, "Mr. D." instead of John Doe).

Sterling . . . contended that the security measures proposed by the Government would infringe upon Sterling's right to a public trial and to confront the witnesses against him. He contended that the use of screens or disguises was unduly suggestive of the existence of national defense information, problematic because one of his planned defenses was that the information in Risen's book was not, in fact, national defense information. . . .

... The court agreed to permit a screen between the trial participants and the public seating section of the courtroom. And although the witnesses could use pseudonyms while testifying, the Government was ordered to provide to defense counsel, Sterling, and the jury a key with the witnesses' true names. The Government appealed the portion of the order requiring it to provide a key with the witnesses' true names to Sterling and the jury.

Sterling contends we do not have jurisdiction to review the order requiring disclosure of the witnesses' true identities to Sterling and the jury. The Government raises two bases for its argument that the disclosure order is immediately appealable: 18 U.S.C. § 3731, and CIPA section 7, 18 U.S.C. app. 3, § 7. Section 3731 ... does not confer jurisdiction for an immediate appeal as to this issue because the order is not one suppressing or excluding evidence. Thus, we turn to CIPA.

A.

CIPA provides a framework for determining how to proceed with discovery and admissibility of classified information in criminal cases. *See United States v. Moussaoui*, 591 F.3d 263, 281-82 (4th Cir. 2010). It was designed to balance the defendant's interest in a fair trial and the government's interest in protecting national security information. *United States v. Passaro*, 577 F.3d 207, 219 (4th Cir. 2009). When classified information may come into play at trial, the government may move for a hearing in the district court "to make all determinations concerning the use, relevance, or admissibility of classified information that would otherwise be made during the trial or pretrial proceedings." 18 U.S.C. app. 3, § 6(a). The district court's order was, we conclude, an order concerning the use of classified information encompassed by CIPA section 6.

It is true, as Sterling contends, that this is not a run-of-the-mill CIPA appeal. CIPA generally comes into play when the defendant seeks to obtain, or plans to disclose, national security information, and the government opposes disclosure. *United States v. Moussaoui*, 333 F.3d 509, 514 (4th Cir. 2003). In *Moussaoui*, we held that an order permitting a deposition of an enemy combatant witness was not immediately appealable under CIPA. We reasoned that CIPA was concerned with disclosure of classified information at trial, rather than the defendant's pretrial discovery of classified information. Thus, we concluded, CIPA was only applicable by analogy, and in that instance CIPA § 7 did not authorize an interlocutory appeal.

Following *Moussaoui*, we considered a case in which the government introduced classified information at trial, and relied upon CIPA in protecting that information from disclosure. *United States v. Abu Ali*, 528 F.3d 210, 255 (4th Cir. 2008). There, the government used classified information to which neither Abu Ali nor his counsel was privy. We held that:

> If classified information is to be relied upon as evidence of guilt, the district court may consider steps to protect some or all of the information from unnecessary public disclosure in the interest of national security and in accordance with CIPA, which specifically contemplates such methods as redactions and

substitutions so long as these alternatives do not deprive the defendant of a fair trial.

Id. The procedural posture of this case is, of course, different from *Abu Ali*; *Abu Ali* was an appeal following conviction, not an interlocutory appeal. Nevertheless, it is illustrative; evidence sought to be admitted at trial by the government, like that proffered by the defense, is subject to the protections afforded by CIPA.

The order at issue authorizes disclosure of classified information at trial, unlike the order in *Moussaoui*, which involved the defendant's pretrial discovery request. *Cf. United States v. Moussaoui*, 336 F.3d 279, 280 (4th Cir. 2003) (Wilkins, C.J., concurring in the denial of en banc rehearing) (noting that CIPA § 6 applies to the use of classified information at trial or in pretrial proceedings, and not to pretrial discovery of classified information). Given our recognition in *Abu Ali* that CIPA applies to evidence proffered by the government for use at trial, we have jurisdiction over this interlocutory appeal pursuant to Section 7 of CIPA, which provides:

> An interlocutory appeal by the United States taken before or after the defendant has been placed in jeopardy shall lie to a court of appeals from a decision or order of a district court in a criminal case authorizing disclosure of classified information, imposing sanctions for nondisclosure of classified information, or refusing a protective order sought by the United States to prevent the disclosure of classified information.

18 U.S.C. app. 3, § 7(a). Having determined that we have jurisdiction to review the district court's order, we turn to the merits, reviewing for abuse of discretion. *Abu Ali*, 528 F.3d at 253-54 (applying abuse of discretion standard, but striking a balance between the defendant's Confrontation Clause rights and the government's need to protect classified information).

B.

There can be no doubt that the identity of CIA operatives is sensitive information. The identity of CIA operatives is, and always has been, subject to rigorous protection. *See, e.g., In re Grand Jury Subpoena, Judith Miller*, 438 F.3d 1141 (D.C. Cir. 2006). To disclose the identities of CIA operatives, even if not to every spectator in the courtroom, subjects the operatives to targeting by hostile foreign intelligence services and terrorist organizations, and creates a grave danger to the operatives, their families, and the operations in which they are engaged. *Cf. United States v. Ramos-Cruz*, 667 F.3d 487, 500 (4th Cir. 2012) (recognizing that defendant's rights under the Confrontation Clause to identifying information about witnesses is not absolute; if the government shows an actual threat, the district court has discretion to determine whether effective cross-examination is possible if the witness's identity is concealed).

We find no abuse of discretion in the district court's decision to make available to Sterling and his counsel a key to the witnesses' true names. Sterling knows, or may know, some of the witnesses at issue, and depriving him of the ability to build his defense in this regard could impinge on his Confrontation

Clause rights. *See generally Maryland v. Craig*, 497 U.S. 836, 848-49 (1990). Moreover, and unlike the usual cases where witnesses have been permitted to use pseudonyms, the Government in this case has made no showing that Sterling or his counsel pose an actual threat to the safety of these witnesses. Thus, we discern no potential for harm from disclosure of their identities to Sterling and his counsel. We cannot, however, take the same approach when it comes to the jury.

Sterling contends that the security measures proposed by the Government will serve to impermissibly heighten the jury's sensitivity to the classified nature of the information Sterling is accused of disclosing, increasing the odds of his conviction. The district court understandably sought to limit to the extent possible the elements of secrecy in this case, and we, too, are mindful of the risk of tainting the jury if unduly suggestive security measures are used at trial. If a security measure is inherently prejudicial, it may be employed "only where justified by an essential state interest specific to each trial." *Holbrook v. Flynn*, 475 U.S. 560, 568-69 (1986). However, we can discern no real benefit that would inure from providing the jury with the full, true names of the CIA operatives at issue. The court sought to limit the risk of disclosure by proposing to instruct the jurors not to write down the witnesses' true names, but nothing will prevent a juror from remembering the names — and, for that matter, the other classified information presented at trial. Unlike the information Sterling is charged with disclosing to Risen, though, the true names of the CIA operatives at issue will do nothing to enhance the jury's understanding of the facts and legal issues presented at trial. And although we are mindful that the jurors are unlikely to disseminate the names in contravention of the district court's instructions, it simply is not worth the risk to the lives of these operatives (and their families and associates) to disclose the operatives' true names to anyone who does not have a genuine need to know their identities.

Although Sterling may dispute at trial that the information at issue was classified, or that he was the person who passed to Risen the information in [his book] there is no escaping the fact that Sterling has been charged with disclosing classified information, and the jury will be well aware of that fact from the very outset of the proceedings. The district court has made clear that it will instruct the jury that Sterling's guilt cannot be inferred from the use of security measures in the courtroom. Balancing Sterling's concerns with the very real danger to the CIA operatives if their identities are disclosed, we conclude that a proper jury instruction will alleviate any potential prejudice, and that the district court abused its discretion in taking the more perilous approach of ordering that the jury be given a key with the operatives' true names. Thus, we reverse this portion of the district court's order. We affirm, however, the portion of the order permitting Sterling and his counsel to receive the key with the operatives' true names.

C.

For the foregoing reasons, we reverse the court's exclusion of two Government witnesses, and affirm in part and reverse in part the court's ruling pursuant to CIPA. We remand for further proceedings consistent with this opinion.

NOTES AND QUESTIONS

1. CIPA is not concerned solely with the use of classified information by defendants, but also protects against the disclosure of classified information by the government in criminal cases. In *Sterling*, the court stated that "evidence sought to be admitted at trial by the government, like that proffered by the defense, is subject to the protections afforded by CIPA." However, the sanitized version of the classified information offered by the government would not have to satisfy the statutory standard of providing defendant with "substantially the same ability to make his defense" as would disclosure of the specific classified information.

2. Does CIPA § 7 authorize a party to challenge any adverse ruling on the discovery or protection of classified information on interlocutory appeal? When may the government file an interlocutory appeal? Does CIPA § 7 authorize an interlocutory appeal for the decision denying the defendant pretrial discovery of classified information?

3. The Fourth Circuit in *Sterling* found no abuse of discretion in the district court's decision to make available to the defendant and his counsel a key to the witnesses' true names. However, the court held that the district court abused its discretion in making available to the jury a key to the witnesses' true names. What is the reasoning of the court?

4. Are the defendant's rights under the Confrontation Clause to identify information about witnesses absolute? When may the district court conceal the witness's identity? Would the court in *Sterling* have reached the same result if the government had sought to prevent Sterling and his counsel (not merely the jury) from knowing the identity of the government's witnesses, claiming that disclosure of such information could pose an actual threat to the safety of these witnesses?

5. In addition to violating the Espionage Act, 18 U.S.C. §§ 793(d) and (e), the disclosure of the identity of a covert agent violates the Intelligence Identities Protection Act of 1982, 50 U.S.C. § 3121. Section 3121 prohibits the disclosure of the identity of a covert agent by persons who learn of the identity as a result of having access to classified information. The statute punishes

   > [w]hoever, having . . . authorized access to classified information that identifies a covert agent, intentionally discloses any information identifying such covert agent to any individual not authorized to receive classified information, knowing that the information disclosed so identifies such covert agent and the United States is taking affirmative measures to conceal such covert intelligence relationship to the United States.

   In *United States v. Kirakou*, 2012 WL 3263854 (E.D. Va. 2012), the court stressed the serious nature of the conduct proscribed under the statute, stating that "[t]he identity of a covert agent is information that goes to the heart of the nation's intelligence activities, and its disclosure could very well threaten the personal safety of the agent whose identity is revealed as well as undermine confidence in the Government's ability to protect its covert officers." *Id.* at *8.

ASSESSMENT QUESTIONS

1. Multiple Choice: Which statement most accurately states the concerns regarding over-classification of government information?

    The over-classification of government information runs a reasonable risk of
    (a) undermining government transparency;
    (b) covering up government misconduct;
    (c) covering up illegal government programs;
    (d) protecting government agency turf;
    (e) b and c only;
    (f) a, b, c, and d.

2. True or False: It is a defense to criminal charges under 18 U.S.C. §§ 793(d) and (e) that the defendant disclosed classified information to a representative of the media to reveal government waste, fraud, and abuse.

3. True or False: The *Totten* bar applies only to a narrow category of cases involving a plaintiff's claims based on a contract to perform espionage for the government.

4. True or False: Under the *Reynolds* privilege, the court may dismiss the plaintiff's civil action if there is no feasible way to litigate the claim without creating a risk of divulging state secrets.

5. Multiple Choice: Which of the following statements are correct?

    Under CIPA § 6(c)(1), a court may authorize the government to submit a substitution for classified information in the form of a statement or summary so long as the summary
    (a) is of "precise, concrete equivalence" to the classified statement;
    (b) is "worded in neutral fashion and not tilted or shaded to the government's advantage";
    (c) provides the defendant with the "same ability to make his defense";
    (d) provides the defendant with "substantially the same ability to make his defense";
    (e) does not deprive defendant of tactical advantages that would accrue by the use of specified classified information.

ASSESSMENT ANSWERS

1. The correct answer is f. The over-classification of government documents certainly undermines government transparency, and runs the risk of concealing government misconduct and illegal government programs. Over-classification is also a way to protect information from being shared with other government agencies.

2. The statement is false. In *United States v Morison*, 844 F.3d 1057 (4th Cir. 1988), the court rejected the defendant's First Amendment defense, holding: "Section 793(d) and (e) unquestionably criminalize such conduct by a delinquent government employee and, when applied to the defendant in the position of the defendant here, there is no First Amendment right implicated." *Id.* at 1069-70.

3. The statement is false. In *Mohamed v. Jeppesen Dataplan, Inc.*, 613 F.3d 1070 (9th Cir. 2010) (en banc), the court stated that the *Totten* bar is not limited to espionage relationships between plaintiff and the government, but applies to cases in which "the very subject matter of the action" is "a matter of state secret."

4. The statement is true. In *Mohamed v. Jeppesen Dataplan, Inc.*, the court dismissed plaintiffs' cause of action, finding that "plaintiffs' claims are so infused with these secrets, any plausible effort by Jeppesen to defend against them would create an unjustifiable risk of revealing state secrets, even if plaintiffs could make a prima facie case on one or more claims with non-privileged evidence. . . ."

5. The correct answers are b and d. In *United States v. Sedaghaty*, 728 F.3d 885 (9th Cir. 2013), the court stated that CIPA § 6(c)(1) requires that the substitute summary provide the defendant with "substantially the same ability to make his defense," as if the specified classified information were made available to him. To that end, the summary should be worded in a neutral fashion and not shaded in the government's favor. However, the summary need not be the precise, concrete equivalent of the classified statement, nor provide the defendant with the same ability to make his defense. Further, "the fact that insignificant tactical advantages could accrue to the defendant by the use of specified classified information" does not preclude alternative disclosure.

CHAPTER 14

National Security and the Press

The press . . . a conspiracy of the intellect, with the courage of numbers.
—Justice Potter Stewart

The First Amendment states that "Congress shall make no law . . . abridging the freedom of speech, or of the press. . . ." What have those words meant to the relationship between the state and the "Fourth Estate" over the course of our nation's history, particularly in times of war? Thomas Carlyle attributed that phrase to Edmund Burke:

> Burke said there were Three Estates in Parliament; but, in the Reporters' Gallery yonder, there sat a Fourth Estate more important far than they all. It is not a figure of speech, or a witty saying; it is a literal fact,—very momentous to us in these times. Literature is our Parliament too. Printing, which comes necessarily out of Writing, I say often, is equivalent to Democracy: invent Writing, Democracy is inevitable. Writing brings Printing; brings universal every-day extempore Printing, as we see at present. Whoever can speak, speaking now to the whole nation, becomes a power, a branch of government, with inalienable weight in law-making, in all acts of authority. It matters not what rank he has, what revenues or garnitures: the requisite thing is, that he have a tongue which others will listen to; this and nothing more is requisite.[1]

Carlyle wrote these words in 1840. But they resonate even more powerfully in the twenty-first century. In the age of the internet, who or what exactly is "the press"? In the age of globalization, and global terrorism, should its restraint *vel non* for reasons of national security be governed by the principles that persuaded the Framers?

The metaphor of the press as an institutional layer in the social order (like clergy or aristocrats) was embraced by Justice Potter Stewart, who believed the

---

1. Thomas Carlyle, *Lecture V: The Hero as a Man of Letters*, in Sartor Resartus, and On Heroes, Hero-Worship, and the Heroic in History 392-93 (Everyman's Library 2007).

Supreme Court's jurisprudence rightly accepted the role of the Free Press Clause as "a structural provision of the Constitution." In contrast to most other liberties protected by the Bill of Rights, which protect individuals, Stewart noted that this one "extends protection to an institution. The publishing business is, in short, the only organized private business that is given explicit constitutional protection." Potter Stewart, *Or of the Press*, 50 HASTINGS L.J. 705, 707 (1999) (republished from original at 26 HASTINGS L.J. 631 (1975)). Noting Burke's famous phrase, Stewart argued that the American approach was a lesson learned from English history:

> For centuries before our Revolution, the press in England had been licensed, censored, and bedeviled by prosecutions for seditious libel. The British Crown knew that a free press was not just a neutral vehicle for the balanced discussion of diverse ideas. Instead, the free press meant organized, expert scrutiny of government. The press was a conspiracy of the intellect, with the courage of numbers. This formidable check on official power was what the British Crown had feared—and what the American Founders decided to risk.[2]

It is for that reason, "to create a fourth institution outside the Government as an additional check on the three official branches," that John Adams drafted the Free Press Clause in the Massachusetts Constitution: "The liberty of the press is essential to the security of the state." *Id.*

These lofty thoughts were not always matched by deeds. The first part of this chapter describes some of the country's reactions to contrarian views in times of war. The second part of this chapter then examines three topics of particular relevance to the role of the press in reporting on government action during national security crises: prior restraints, access to courts, and access to information. Finally, the chapter concludes with a question: Who is "the press" in an age of blogs, social media, paperless periodicals, and a growing cadre of journalists whose credential is a large online following rather than a newspaper-as-employer or a press card?

I. A BRIEF AMERICAN HISTORY OF PRIOR RESTRAINTS AND SEDITIOUS LIBEL

The most egregious form of control of a private press is state censorship. A close second, perhaps, is the crime of seditious libel. Under the infamous Sedition Act of 1798, the crime was committed

> if any person shall write, print, utter or publish, or shall cause or procure to be written, printed, uttered or published, or shall knowingly and willingly assist or aid in writing, printing, uttering or publishing any false, scandalous and malicious writing or writings against the government of the United States, or either house of the Congress of the United States, or the President of the United States, with intent to defame the said government, or either house of the said Congress, or the said President, or to bring them, or either of them, into contempt or disrepute; or to excite against them, or either or any of them, the hatred of the good people of the

_____

2. *Id.* at 708.

United States, or to stir up sedition within the United States, or to excite any unlawful combinations therein, for opposing or resisting any law of the United States, or any act of the President of the United States, done in pursuance of any such law, or of the powers in him vested by the constitution of the United States, or to resist, oppose, or defeat any such law or act, or to aid, encourage or abet any hostile designs of any foreign nation against the United States, their people or government[.]

Punishment was by fine and imprisonment up to two years. Act of July 14, 1798, Ch. 74, § 2, 1 Stat. 596. It is hard to untangle the complex webs of reasons for the statute, but the context in which these formed was impending war and claimed fears for national security. The French Revolution had descended into a reign of terror and guillotine-enforced repression, sparking war in Europe. Despite efforts to preserve American neutrality, a "Quasi War" kindled between the United States and France (leading, in fact, to the rebuilding of a U.S. Navy essentially decommissioned after the Revolutionary War). The emerging political party system fueled acrimony and suspicion in debates over national security (and just about everything else). Whatever the stated grounds for passing the statute—and it was passed along party lines—its implementation was partisan and vindictive.

Over the course of the next two and a half years, "the Federalists arrested approximately twenty-five well-known Republicans under the act. Fifteen of these arrests led to indictments. Ten cases went to trial, all resulting in convictions." GEOFFREY R. STONE, PERILOUS TIMES: FREE SPEECH IN WARTIME 63 (2004). A Federalist-dominated judiciary kept First Amendment challenges at bay and the Act expired on the last full day in office for Federalist President John Adams. His successor, Thomas Jefferson, almost immediately pardoned those convicted under the Act. By 1840, all fines collected under the Act had been repaid; ironically, the last refund was paid, with interest, to the heirs of the first person convicted under the Sedition Act, Congressman Matthew Lyon. Act of July 4, 1840, Ch. 45, 6 Stat. 802. As Justice Brennan concluded in his opinion for the Court in *New York Times v. Sullivan*, "[a]lthough the Sedition Act was never tested in this Court, the attack upon its validity has carried the day in the court of history." 376 U.S. 254, 276 (1964) (footnote omitted).

Nevertheless, the Supreme Court did not demonstrate particular vigor in protecting freedom of speech and the press during the Civil War and Reconstruction period. In spring 1863, former Ohio congressman Clement Vallandigham (who, like Lambdin Milligan, introduced in Chapter 1, was a prominent Copperhead as well as a lawyer) was seized in the night from his home in Dayton, Ohio, and transported in military custody to Cincinnati. There he was convicted by military commission and imprisoned for having violated a military order issued by Union General Ambrose Burnside; in particular, he was sentenced "for having uttered, in a political speech at a public meeting, disloyal sentiments and opinions, with the object and purpose of weakening the power of the Government in its efforts for the suppression of an unlawful rebellion." *Ex parte Vallandigham*, 68 U.S. 243, 244 (1863).[3]

---

3. General Order No. 38 decreed, among other things, that "[t]he Commanding General publishes, for the information of all concerned, that hereafter all persons found within our lines who commit acts for the benefit of the enemies of our country will be tried as spies or traitors, and, if

Vallandigham challenged the constitutionality of this charge and the jurisdiction of a military commission to try him, a civilian, for it. Habeas corpus had not been suspended in Ohio, but Vallandigham's petition was nonetheless denied by the district court. The Supreme Court held that "[w]hatever may be the force of Vallandigham's protest, that he was not triable by a court of military commission," the Court lacked jurisdiction to issue a writ of certiorari to a military commission. *Id.* at 251. President Lincoln, who seems to have been taken by surprise by these actions, commuted the sentence from imprisonment until the end of the war to exile, declaring Vallandigham banished to the Confederacy. In a famous letter in which he admitted that trial by military commission had been a mistake, Lincoln nevertheless defended the substance of the charge: "Must I shoot a simple-minded soldier boy who deserts while I must not touch a hair of a wily agitator who induces him to desert? . . . I think that in such a case, to silence the agitator, and save the boy, is not only constitutional, but, withal, a great mercy." Letter to Erastus Corning and Others, June 12, 1863.

If Vallandigham's case suggested the disinterest of the judiciary to protect his freedom of expression in wartime, *Ex parte McCardle* demonstrated that the legislative branch could be just as unsympathetic to sentiments that seemed to endanger post-war Reconstruction. William McCardle, editor of the *Vicksburg Times*, was no friend to Union efforts to rebuild after the war. In an editorial published a few days before his arrest, McCardle used his newspaper to insult the local military commander by name, among other Union officers, describing them as "infamous, cowardly, and abandoned villains who, instead of wearing shoulder straps and ruling millions of people, should have their heads shaved, their ears cropped, their foreheads branded, and their persons lodged in a penitentiary." William W. Van Alstyne, *A Critical Guide to Ex parte McCardle*, 15 ARIZ. L. REV. 229, 236, n.42 (1973). For these printed remarks and others, he was convicted by a military commission for disturbing the peace, inciting to insurrection and disorder, libel, and impeding reconstruction.

McCardle, like Vallandigham, petitioned for a writ of habeas corpus, which was denied. After oral argument in the Supreme Court (but before the Court could release an opinion), Congress repealed the Court's jurisdiction to hear the appeal. A unanimous Court upheld the repeal and dismissed the case for want of jurisdiction.[4]

The Sedition Act of 1798 was not the only such act passed by Congress in U.S. history. And the unwillingness of Civil War–era courts to protect free expression in

---

convicted, will suffer death. . . . The habit of declaring sympathies for the enemy will not be allowed in this Department. Persons committing such offenses will be at once arrested, with a view to being tried as above stated, or sent beyond our lines into the lines of their friends. It must be distinctly understood that treason, expressed or implied, will not be tolerated in this Department. All officers and soldiers are strictly charged with the execution of this order."

4. Van Alstyne's detailed history of the case suggests a number of institutional reasons why the Court was not unwilling to forgo jurisdiction in the case, which could very well have held a key piece of federal Reconstruction legislation unconstitutional. In a letter written three weeks after the unanimous opinion, Chief Justice Chase told a friend: "I may say to you that had the merits of the *McCardle* case been decided the Court would doubtless have held that this imprisonment for trial before a military commission was illegal." Van Alstyne, *supra*, at 238, n.46.

wartime conditions was not the last instance of underwhelming enforcement of the First Amendment. Recall the discussion of the Espionage Act of 1917 and the Sedition Act of 1918 from Chapter 2, as well as the cases of *Schenck v. United States*, 249 U.S. 47, 51 (1919), and *Abrams v. United States*, 250 U.S. 616 (1919), that sustained these statutes against First Amendment challenges.

In debates over the Espionage Act, President Wilson aggressively sought the power to censor the press. In a letter to Congressman Edwin Y. Webb, Chairman of the House Judiciary Committee, he urged retention of the controversial power in the conference version of the bill: "[A]uthority to exercise censorship over the press . . . is absolutely necessary to the public safety. . . . I have every confidence that the great majority of the newspapers of the country will observe a patriotic reticence about everything whose publication could be of injury, but in every country there are some persons in a position to do mischief in this field who cannot be relied upon and whose interests or desires will lead to actions on their part highly dangerous to the nation in the midst of war." *Wilson Demands Press Censorship*, N.Y. TIMES, May 23, 1917, at 1.

In debates over the Sedition Act, some members of Congress supported an amendment to protect the freedom "to publish or speak what is true, with good motives, and for justifiable ends." 56 CONG. REC. 4826 (Apr. 9, 1918). Attorney General Gregory objected to the amendment: "[S]ome of the most dangerous types of propaganda were either made from good motives, or else their traitorous motives were not provable." PAUL L. MURPHY, WORLD WAR I AND THE ORIGIN OF CIVIL LIBERTIES IN THE UNITED STATES 83 (1979) (quoting Official Bulletin of the Committee on Public Information). The amendment failed to pass and elicited sharp criticism, including an accusation from one senator that "every Senator who votes against this conference report can have the satisfaction of knowing that he has voted for an amendment that will throw a cloak of protection around every spy in this country and every traitor and every Bolshevik and every I.W.W. that is denied to a loyal American citizen." 56 CONG. REC. 6050 (May 4, 1918).

NOTES AND QUESTIONS

1. How united should a country be in time of war? How supportive should the press be of calls for national unity and a common front against the enemy?
2. Twenty-five arrests were made under the Sedition Act between 1798 and 1801. Is this a big number or a small one? It is an old technique to arrest a few to deter the many. How could a social scientist measure the effect of the law on the role of the press? What should be made of the temporal proximity of the Sedition Act to the adoption of the First Amendment?
3. On July 4, 1917, under the headline "Jails Are Waiting for Them," the *New York Times* editorial board (an institution with a reputation today for valuing the First Amendment) had this to say about an organization formed to provide legal support to conscientious objectors:

> "Freedom of speech" is a fine thing, well worth fighting for, and even dying for, in case of need, but sensible people of good will do not make the mistake

of believing that speech can be literally and completely free in any civilized country. Inevitably there must be restrictions on speech, as on the "exercise of religion," even in lands with constitutions guaranteeing both, for between liberty and license there is a distinction, and though opinions may differ honestly as to the exact point where the one turns into the other and becomes intolerable, every Government must and does draw the line somewhere. Just where it shall be drawn is and must be determined, in countries properly called free, by public sentiment as formally expressed by majorities through their voluntarily chosen representatives, and in others according to the special interests of an autocratic ruler or a self-constituted ruling class. That is the distinction between the two sorts of countries — not that in the one anybody may, and in the other may not, say whatever he chooses, no matter how offensive to his neighbors.

These simple principles are entirely ignored by the little group of malcontents who for present purposes have chosen to call themselves "The National Civil Liberties Bureau." On other days of the week they are "The People's Council of America," or "The American Union Against Militarism," but always the same names appear on their proclamations and always they are engaged in the same task — that of antagonizing the settled policies of our Government, of resisting the execution of its deliberately formed plans, and of gaining for themselves immunity from the application of laws to which good citizens willingly submit as essential to the national existence and welfare.

The freedom of speech wanted by these troublesome folk is that of talking sedition and of lending aid and comfort to our enemies. They declare that they have found lawyers willing to aid them in the attainment of these preposterous ends, and they assert — very unconvincingly — their readiness to accept martyrdom of some unnamed and indeterminate kind rather than forego what they deem their right to oppose the national will. But they are an unimportant and minute minority — noisy out of all proportion to their numbers, and gaining attention just as crimes and accidents do, merely because they are abnormal and therefore "news."

II. LITIGATING PRESS FREEDOMS IN NATIONAL SECURITY CASES

A. Prior Restraint

Daniel Ellsberg, an analyst with the Rand Corporation, obtained access to a 7,000-page, classified Defense Department study of the war in Vietnam. After excluding those portions he personally felt could threaten national security if publicly revealed, he gave the remainder of the so-called Pentagon Papers to a journalist for the *New York Times*. After intense debate within the newspaper about how to proceed, the *Times* began to publish a ten-part series revealing and analyzing the leaked material. A few days later, the Justice Department asked the paper to stop its series and return the material. The *Times* refused and the Justice Department filed suit for an injunction. (Ellsberg also gave parts to the *Washington Post* with a similar result at that paper and at the Justice Department.)

New York Times Co. v. United States
403 U.S. 713 (1971)

PER CURIAM.

[T]he United States seeks to enjoin the *New York Times* and the *Washington Post* from publishing the contents of a classified study entitled "History of U.S. Decision-Making Process on Viet Nam Policy."

Any system of prior restraints of expression comes to this Court bearing a heavy presumption against its constitutional validity. The Government thus carries a heavy burden of showing justification for the imposition of such a restraint. The District Court for the Southern District of New York in the New York Times case, and the District Court for the District of Columbia and the Court of Appeals for the District of Columbia Circuit, in the Washington Post case held that the Government had not met that burden. We agree. The stays entered June 25, 1971, by the Court are vacated.

Mr. Justice BLACK, with whom Mr. Justice DOUGLAS joins, concurring.

I believe that every moment's continuance of the injunctions against these newspapers amounts to a flagrant, indefensible, and continuing violation of the First Amendment. In my view it is unfortunate that some of my Brethren are apparently willing to hold that the publication of news may sometimes be enjoined. Such a holding would make a shambles of the First Amendment.

The Bill of Rights changed the original Constitution into a new charter under which no branch of government could abridge the people's freedoms of press, speech, religion, and assembly. Yet the Solicitor General argues and some members of the Court appear to agree that the general powers of the Government adopted in the original Constitution should be interpreted to limit and restrict the specific and emphatic guarantees of the Bill of Rights adopted later. I can imagine no greater perversion of history. Madison and the other Framers of the First Amendment, able men that they were, wrote in language they earnestly believed could never be misunderstood: "Congress shall make no law . . . abridging the freedom . . . of the press. . . ."

In the First Amendment the Founding Fathers gave the free press the protection it must have to fulfill its essential role in our democracy. The press was to serve the governed, not the governors. The Government's power to censor the press was abolished so that the press would remain forever free to censure the Government. The press was protected so that it could bare the secrets of government and inform the people. Only a free and unrestrained press can effectively expose deception in government. And paramount among the responsibilities of a free press is the duty to prevent any part of the government from deceiving the people and sending them off to distant lands to die of foreign fevers and foreign shot and shell.

To find that the President has "inherent power" to halt the publication of news by resort to the courts would wipe out the First Amendment and destroy the fundamental liberty and security of the very people the Government hopes to make "secure." No one can read the history of the adoption of the First

Amendment without being convinced beyond any doubt that it was injunctions like those sought here that Madison and his collaborators intended to outlaw in this Nation for all time.

The word "security" is a broad, vague generality whose contours should not be invoked to abrogate the fundamental law embodied in the First Amendment. The guarding of military and diplomatic secrets at the expense of informed representative government provides no real security for our Republic.

Mr. Justice DOUGLAS, with whom Mr. Justice BLACK joins, concurring.

There is [] no statute barring the publication by the press of the material which the Times and the Post seek to use. Title 18 U.S.C. § 793(e) provides that "(w)hoever having unauthorized possession of, access to, or control over any document, writing . . . or information relating to the national defense which information the possessor has reason to believe could be used to the injury of the United States or to the advantage of any foreign nation, willfully communicates . . . the same to any person not entitled to receive it . . . (s)hall be fined not more than $10,000 or imprisoned not more than ten years, or both."

The Government suggests that the word "communicates" is broad enough to encompass publication.

There are eight sections in the chapter on espionage and censorship, §§ 792-799. In three of those eight "publish" is specifically mentioned: § 7 94(b) applies to "Whoever, in time of war, with intent that the same shall be communicated to the enemy, collects, records, publishes, or communicates . . . (the disposition of armed forces)."

Section 797 applies to whoever "reproduces, publishes, sells, or gives away" photographs of defense installations.

Section 798 relating to cryptography applies to whoever: "communicates, furnishes, transmits, or otherwise makes available . . . or publishes" the described materials.

Thus it is apparent that Congress was capable of and did distinguish between publishing and communication in the various sections of the Espionage Act.

The other evidence that § 793 does not apply to the press is a rejected version of § 793. That version read: "During any national emergency resulting from a war to which the United States is a party, or from threat of such a war, the President may, by proclamation, declare the existence of such emergency and, by proclamation, prohibit the publishing or communicating of, or the attempting to publish or communicate any information relating to the national defense which, in his judgment, is of such character that it is or might be useful to the enemy." 55 Cong. Rec. 1763. During the debates in the Senate the First Amendment was specifically cited and that provision was defeated. 55 Cong. Rec. 2167.

So any power that the Government possesses must come from its "inherent power."

The power to wage war is "the power to wage war successfully." *See Hirabayashi v. United States* (1943). But the war power stems from a declaration of war. The Constitution by Art. I, § 8, gives Congress, not the President, power "(t)o declare War." Nowhere are presidential wars authorized. We need not decide therefore what leveling effect the war power of Congress might have.

These disclosures[3] may have a serious impact. But that is no basis for sanctioning a previous restraint on the press.

The Government says that it has inherent powers to go into court and obtain an injunction to protect the national interest, which in this case is alleged to be national security.

The dominant purpose of the First Amendment was to prohibit the widespread practice of governmental suppression of embarrassing information. It is common knowledge that the First Amendment was adopted against the widespread use of the common law of seditious libel to punish the dissemination of material that is embarrassing to the powers-that-be. See T. Emerson, The System of Freedom of Expression, c. V (1970); Z. Chafee, Free Speech in the United States, c. XIII (1941). The present cases will, I think, go down in history as the most dramatic illustration of that principle. A debate of large proportions goes on in the Nation over our posture in Vietnam. That debate antedated the disclosure of the contents of the present documents. The latter are highly relevant to the debate in progress.

Secrecy in government is fundamentally anti-democratic, perpetuating bureaucratic errors. Open debate and discussion of public issues are vital to our national health. On public questions there should be "uninhibited, robust, and wide-open" debate. *New York Times Co. v. Sullivan* (1964).

Mr. Justice BRENNAN, concurring.

The error that has pervaded these cases from the outset was the granting of any injunctive relief whatsoever, interim or otherwise. The entire thrust of the Government's claim throughout these cases has been that publication of the material sought to be enjoined "could," or "might," or "may" prejudice the national interest in various ways. But the First Amendment tolerates absolutely no prior judicial restraints of the press predicated upon surmise or conjecture that untoward consequences may result. Our cases, it is true, have indicated that there is a single, extremely narrow class of cases in which the First Amendment's ban on prior judicial restraint may be overridden. Our cases have thus far indicated that such cases may arise only when the Nation "is at war," *Schenck v. United States* (1919), during which times "(n)o one would question but that a government might prevent actual obstruction to its recruiting service or the publication of the sailing dates of transports or the number and location of troops." *Near v. Minnesota ex rel. Olson* (1931). Even if the present world situation were assumed to be tantamount to a time of war, or if the power of presently available armaments would justify even in peacetime the

---

3. There are numerous sets of this material in existence and they apparently are not under any controlled custody. Moreover, the President has sent a set to the Congress. We start then with a case where there already is rather wide distribution of the material that is destined for publicity, not secrecy. I have gone over the material listed in the in camera brief of the United States. It is all history, not future events. None of it is more recent than 1968.

suppression of information that would set in motion a nuclear holocaust, in neither of these actions has the Government presented or even alleged that publication of items from or based upon the material at issue would cause the happening of an event of that nature. Thus, only governmental allegation and proof that publication must inevitably, directly, and immediately cause the occurrence of an event kindred to imperiling the safety of a transport already at sea can support even the issuance of an interim restraining order. In no event may mere conclusions be sufficient: for if the Executive Branch seeks judicial aid in preventing publication, it must inevitably submit the basis upon which that aid is sought to scrutiny by the judiciary.

Mr. Justice STEWART, with whom Mr. Justice WHITE joins, concurring.

In the governmental structure created by our Constitution, the Executive is endowed with enormous power in the two related areas of national defense and international relations. This power, largely unchecked by the Legislative and Judicial branches, has been pressed to the very hilt since the advent of the nuclear missile age. For better or for worse, the simple fact is that a President of the United States possesses vastly greater constitutional independence in these two vital areas of power than does, say, a prime minister of a country with a parliamentary form of government.

In the absence of the governmental checks and balances present in other areas of our national life, the only effective restraint upon executive policy and power in the areas of national defense and international affairs may lie in an enlightened citizenry—in an informed and critical public opinion which alone can here protect the values of democratic government. For this reason, it is perhaps here that a press that is alert, aware, and free most vitally serves the basic purpose of the First Amendment. For without an informed and free press there cannot be an enlightened people.

Yet it is elementary that the successful conduct of international diplomacy and the maintenance of an effective national defense require both confidentiality and secrecy. Other nations can hardly deal with this Nation in an atmosphere of mutual trust unless they can be assured that their confidences will be kept. And within our own executive departments, the development of considered and intelligent international policies would be impossible if those charged with their formulation could not communicate with each other freely, frankly, and in confidence. In the area of basic national defense the frequent need for absolute secrecy is, of course, self-evident.

I think there can be but one answer to this dilemma, if dilemma it be. The responsibility must be where the power is. If the Constitution gives the Executive a large degree of unshared power in the conduct of foreign affairs and the maintenance of our national defense, then under the Constitution the Executive must have the largely unshared duty to determine and preserve the degree of internal security necessary to exercise that power successfully. It is an awesome responsibility, requiring judgment and wisdom of a high order. I should suppose that moral, political, and practical considerations would dictate that a very first principle of that wisdom would be an insistence upon avoiding secrecy for its own sake. For when everything is classified, then nothing is classified, and the system becomes one to be disregarded by the cynical or the careless, and to be manipulated by those intent on self-protection or self-promotion. I should suppose, in short, that the hallmark of a truly effective internal security system would be the maximum possible disclosure, recognizing that secrecy can best be preserved only when credibility is truly maintained. But be that as it may, it is clear to me that it is the constitutional duty of the Executive — as a matter of sovereign prerogative and not as a matter of law as the courts know law — through the promulgation and enforcement of executive regulations, to protect the confidentiality necessary to carry out its responsibilities in the fields of international relations and national defense.

This is not to say that Congress and the courts have no role to play. Undoubtedly Congress has the power to enact specific and appropriate criminal laws to protect government property and preserve government secrets. Congress has passed such laws, and several of them are of very colorable relevance to the apparent circumstances of these cases. And if a criminal prosecution is instituted, it will be the responsibility of the courts to decide the applicability of the criminal law under which the charge is brought. Moreover, if Congress should pass a specific law authorizing civil proceedings in this field, the courts would likewise have the duty to decide the constitutionality of such a law as well as its applicability to the facts proved.

But in the cases before us we are asked neither to construe specific regulations nor to apply specific laws. We are asked, instead, to perform a function that the Constitution gave to the Executive, not the Judiciary. We are asked, quite simply, to prevent the publication by two newspapers of material that the Executive Branch insists should not, in the national interest, be published. I am convinced that the Executive is correct with respect to some of the documents involved. But I cannot say that disclosure of any of them will surely result in direct, immediate, and irreparable damage to our Nation or its people. That being so, there can under the First Amendment be but one judicial resolution of the issues before us. I join the judgments of the Court.

Mr. Justice WHITE, with whom Mr. Justice STEWART joins, concurring.

I concur in today's judgments, but only because of the concededly extraordinary protection against prior restraints enjoyed by the press under our constitutional system. I do not say that in no circumstances would the First Amendment permit an injunction against publishing information about government plans or operations. Nor, after examining the materials the Government characterizes as the most sensitive and destructive, can I deny that revelation of these documents will do substantial damage to public interests. Indeed, I am confident that their disclosure will have that result. But I nevertheless agree that the United States has not satisfied the very heavy burden that it must meet to warrant an injunction against publication in these cases, at least in the absence of express and appropriately limited congressional authorization for prior restraints in circumstances such as these.

The Government's position is simply stated: The responsibility of the Executive for the conduct of the foreign affairs and for the security of the Nation is so basic that the President is entitled to an injunction against publication of a newspaper story whenever he can convince a court that the information to be revealed threatens "grave and irreparable" injury to the public interest; and the injunction should issue whether or not the material to be published is classified, whether or not publication would be lawful under relevant criminal statutes enacted by Congress, and regardless of the circumstances by which the newspaper came into possession of the information.

At least in the absence of legislation by Congress, based on its own investigations and findings, I am quite unable to agree that the inherent powers of the Executive and the courts reach so far as to authorize remedies having such sweeping potential for inhibiting publications by the press. Much of the difficulty inheres in the "grave and irreparable danger" standard suggested by the United States. If the United States were to have judgment under such a standard in these cases, our decision would be of little guidance to other courts in other cases, for the material at issue here would not be available from the Court's opinion or from public records, nor would it be published by the press. Indeed, even today where we hold that the United States has not met its burden, the material remains sealed in court records and it is properly not discussed in today's opinions. Moreover, because the material poses substantial dangers to national interests and because of the hazards of criminal sanctions, a responsible press may choose never to publish the more sensitive materials. To sustain the Government in these cases would start the courts down a long and hazardous road that I am not willing to travel, at least without congressional guidance and direction.

The Criminal Code contains numerous provisions potentially relevant to these cases. Section 797 makes it a crime to publish certain photographs or drawings of military installations. Section 798, also in precise language, proscribes knowing and willful publication of any classified information concerning the cryptographic systems or communication intelligence activities of the United States as well as any information obtained from communication intelligence operations. If any of the material here at issue is of this nature, the newspapers are presumably now on full notice of the position of the United States and must face the consequences if they publish. I would have no difficulty in sustaining convictions under these sections on facts that would not justify the intervention of equity and the imposition of a prior restraint.

The same would be true under those sections of the Criminal Code casting a wider net to protect the national defense. Section 793(e) makes it a criminal act for any unauthorized possessor of a document "relating to the national defense" either (1) willfully to communicate or cause to be communicated that document to any person not entitled to receive it or (2) willfully to retain the document and fail to deliver it to an officer of the United States entitled to receive it.

It is thus clear that Congress has addressed itself to the problems of protecting the security of the country and the national defense from unauthorized disclosure of potentially damaging information. It has not, however, authorized the injunctive remedy against threatened publication. It has apparently been satisfied to rely on criminal sanctions and their deterrent effect on the responsible as well as the irresponsible press. I am not, of course, saying that either of these newspapers has yet committed a crime or that either would commit a crime if it published all the material now in its possession. That matter must await resolution in the context of a criminal proceeding if one is instituted by the United States. In that event, the issue of guilt or innocence would be determined by procedures and standards quite different from those that have purported to govern these injunctive proceedings.

Mr. Justice MARSHALL, concurring.

The Government contends that the only issue in these cases is whether in a suit by the United States, "the First Amendment bars a court from prohibiting a newspaper from publishing material whose disclosure would pose a 'grave and immediate danger to the security of the United States.'" With all due respect, I believe the ultimate issue in this case is even more basic than the one posed by the Solicitor General. The issue is whether this Court or the Congress has the power to make law.

In these cases there is no problem concerning the President's power to classify information as "secret" or "top secret." Congress has specifically recognized Presidential authority, which has been formally exercised in Exec. Order 10501 (1953), to classify documents and information. See, e.g., 18 U.S.C. § 798; 50 U.S.C. § 783. Nor is there any issue here regarding the President's power as Chief Executive and Commander in Chief to protect national security by disciplining employees who disclose information and by taking precautions to prevent leaks.

The problem here is whether in these particular cases the Executive Branch has authority to invoke the equity jurisdiction of the courts to protect what it believes to be the national interest. The Government argues that in addition to the inherent power of any government to protect itself, the President's power to conduct foreign affairs and his position as Commander in Chief give him authority to impose censorship on the press to protect his ability to deal effectively with foreign nations and to conduct the military affairs of the country. Of course, it is beyond cavil that the President has broad powers by virtue of his primary responsibility for the conduct of our foreign affairs and his position as Commander in Chief. And in some situations it may be that under whatever inherent powers the Government may have, as well as the implicit authority derived from the President's mandate to conduct foreign affairs and to act as Commander in Chief, there is a basis for the invocation of the equity jurisdiction of this Court as an aid to prevent the publication of material damaging to "national security," however that term may be defined.

It would, however, be utterly inconsistent with the concept of separation of powers for this Court to use its power of contempt to prevent behavior that Congress has specifically declined to prohibit. There would be a similar damage to the basic concept of these co-equal branches of Government if when the Executive Branch has adequate authority granted by Congress to protect "national security" it can choose instead to invoke the contempt power of a court to enjoin the threatened conduct. The Constitution provides that Congress shall make laws, the President execute laws, and courts interpret laws. It did not provide for government by injunction in which the courts and the Executive Branch can "make law" without regard to the action of Congress. It may be more convenient for the Executive Branch if it need only convince a judge to prohibit conduct rather than ask the Congress to pass a law, and it may be more convenient to enforce a contempt order than to seek a criminal conviction in a jury trial. Moreover, it may be considered politically wise to get a court to share the responsibility for arresting those who the Executive Branch has probable cause to believe are violating the law. But convenience and political considerations of the moment do not justify a basic departure from the principles of our system of government.

Mr. Chief Justice BURGER, dissenting.

We do not know the facts of the cases. No District Judge knew all the facts. No Court of Appeals Judge knew all the facts. No member of this Court knows all the facts.

Why are we in this posture, in which only those judges to whom the First Amendment is absolute and permits of no restraint in any circumstances or for any reason, are really in a position to act?

I suggest we are in this posture because these cases have been conducted in unseemly haste. Mr. Justice Harlan covers the chronology of events demonstrating the hectic pressures under which these cases have been processed and I need not restate them. The prompt settling of these cases reflects our universal abhorrence of prior restraint. But prompt judicial action does not mean unjudicial haste.

Here, moreover, the frenetic haste is due in large part to the manner in which the Times proceeded from the date it obtained the purloined documents.

The newspapers make a derivative claim under the First Amendment; they denominate this right as the public "right to know"; by implication, the Times asserts a sole trustee-ship of that right by virtue of its journalistic "scoop." The right is asserted as an absolute. Of course, the First Amendment right itself is not an absolute, as Justice Holmes so long ago pointed out in his aphorism concerning the right to shout "fire" in a crowded theater if there was no fire. There are no doubt other exceptions no one has had occasion to describe or discuss. Conceivably such exceptions may be lurking in these cases and would have been flushed had they been properly considered in the trial courts, free from unwarranted deadlines and frenetic pressures. An issue of this importance should be tried and heard in a judicial atmosphere conducive to thoughtful, reflective deliberation, especially when haste, in terms of hours, is unwarranted in light of the long period the Times, by its own choice, deferred publication.[1]

Would it have been unreasonable, since the newspaper could anticipate the Government's objections to release of secret material, to give the Government an opportunity to review the entire collection and determine whether agreement could be reached on publication? Stolen or not, if security was not in fact jeopardized, much of the material could no doubt have been declassified, since it spans a period ending in 1968. With such an approach — one that great newspapers have in the past practiced and stated editorially to be the duty of an honorable press — the newspapers and Government might well have narrowed the area of disagreement as to what was and was not publishable, leaving the remainder to be resolved in orderly litigation, if necessary. To me it is hardly believable that a newspaper long regarded as a great institution in American life would fail to perform one of the basic and simple duties of every citizen with respect to the discovery or possession of stolen property or secret government documents. That duty, I had thought — perhaps naively — was to report forthwith, to responsible public officers. This duty rests on taxi drivers, Justices, and the New York Times. The course followed by the Times, whether so calculated or not, removed any possibility of orderly litigation of the issues. If the action of the judges up to now has been correct, that result is sheer happenstance.[2]

The consequence of all this melancholy series of events is that we literally do not know what we are acting on. As I see it, we have been forced to deal with litigation concerning rights of great magnitude without an adequate record, and surely without time for adequate treatment either in the prior proceedings or in this Court. I agree generally with Mr. Justice Harlan and Mr. Justice Blackmun but I am not prepared to reach the merits.[3]

We all crave speedier judicial processes but when judges are pressured as in these cases the result is a parody of the judicial function.

---

1. As noted elsewhere the Times conducted its analysis of the 47 volumes of Government documents over a period of several months and did so with a degree of security that a government might envy. Such security was essential, of course, to protect the enterprise from others. Meanwhile the Times has copyrighted its material and there were strong intimations in the oral argument that the Times contemplated enjoining its use by any other publisher in violation of its copyright. Paradoxically this would afford it a protection, analogous to prior restraint, against all others — a protection the Times denies the Government of the United States.

2. Interestingly the Times explained its refusal to allow the Government to examine its own purloined documents by saying in substance this might compromise its sources and informants! The Times thus asserts a right to guard the secrecy of its sources while denying that the Government of the United States has that power.

3. With respect to the question of inherent power of the Executive to classify papers, records, and documents as secret, or otherwise unavailable for public exposure, and to secure aid of the courts for enforcement, there may be an analogy with respect to this Court. No statute gives this Court express power to establish and enforce the utmost security measures for the secrecy of our deliberations and records. Yet I have little doubt as to the inherent power of the Court to protect the confidentiality of its internal operations by whatever judicial measures may be required.

Mr. Justice HARLAN, with whom THE CHIEF JUSTICE and Mr. Justice BLACKMUN join, dissenting.

With all respect, I consider that the Court has been almost irresponsibly feverish in dealing with these cases.

Both the Court of Appeals for the Second Circuit and the Court of Appeals for the District of Columbia Circuit rendered judgment on June 23. The New York Times' petition for certiorari, its motion for accelerated consideration thereof, and its application for interim relief were filed in this Court on June 24 at about 11 A.M. The application of the United States for interim relief in the Post case was also filed here on June 24 at about 7:15 P.M. This Court's order setting a hearing before us on June 26 at 11 A.M., a course which I joined only to avoid the possibility of even more peremptory action by the Court, was issued less than 24 hours before. The record in the Post case was filed with the Clerk shortly before 1 P.M. on June 25; the record in the Times case did not arrive until 7 or 8 o'clock that same night. The briefs of the parties were received less than two hours before argument on June 26.

This frenzied train of events took place in the name of the presumption against prior restraints created by the First Amendment. Due regard for the extraordinarily important and difficult questions involved in these litigations should have led the Court to shun such a precipitate timetable.

Forced as I am to reach the merits of these cases, I dissent from the opinion and judgments of the Court. Within the severe limitations imposed by the time constraints under which I have been required to operate, I can only state my reasons in telescoped form, even though in different circumstances I would have felt constrained to deal with the cases in the fuller sweep indicated above.

It is plain to me that the scope of the judicial function in passing upon the activities of the Executive Branch of the Government in the field of foreign affairs is very narrowly restricted. This view is, I think, dictated by the concept of separation of powers upon which our constitutional system rests.

I agree that, in performance of its duty to protect the values of the First Amendment against political pressures, the judiciary must review the initial Executive determination to the point of satisfying itself that the subject matter of the dispute does lie within the proper compass of the President's foreign relations power. Constitutional considerations forbid a complete abandonment of judicial control. Moreover the judiciary may properly insist that the determination that disclosure of the subject matter would irreparably impair the national security be made by the head of the Executive Department concerned—here the Secretary of State or the Secretary of Defense—after actual personal consideration by that officer. This safeguard is required in the analogous area of executive claims of privilege for secrets of state.

But in my judgment the judiciary may not properly go beyond these two inquiries and redetermine for itself the probable impact of disclosure on the national security.

"(T)he very nature of executive decisions as to foreign policy is political, not judicial. Such decisions are wholly confided by our Constitution to the political departments of the government, Executive and Legislative. They are delicate, complex, and involve large elements of prophecy. They are and should be undertaken only by those directly responsible to the people whose welfare they advance or imperil. They are decisions of a kind for which the Judiciary has neither aptitude, facilities nor responsibility and have long been held to belong in the domain of political power not subject to judicial intrusion or inquiry." *Chicago & Southern Air Lines, Inc. v. Waterman Steamship Corp.* (1948) (Jackson J.).

Even if there is some room for the judiciary to override the executive determination, it is plain that the scope of review must be exceedingly narrow.

Accordingly, I would vacate the judgment of the Court of Appeals for the District of Columbia Circuit on this ground and remand the case for further proceedings in the District Court. Before the commencement of such further proceedings, due opportunity should be afforded the Government for procuring from the Secretary of State or the Secretary of Defense or both an expression of their views on the issue of national security. The ensuing review by the District Court should be in accordance with the views expressed in this opinion. And for the reasons stated above I would affirm the judgment of the Court of Appeals for the Second Circuit.

Pending further hearings in each case conducted under the appropriate ground rules, I would continue the restraints on publication. I cannot believe that the doctrine prohibiting prior restraints reaches to the point of preventing courts from maintaining the status quo long enough to act responsibly in matters of such national importance as those involved here.

Mr. Justice BLACKMUN, dissenting.

The New York Times clandestinely devoted a period of three months to examining the 47 volumes that came into its unauthorized possession. Once it had begun publication of material from those volumes, the New York case now before us emerged. It immediately assumed, and ever since has maintained, a frenetic pace and character. Seemingly once publication started, the material could not be made public fast enough. Seemingly, from then on, every deferral or delay, by restraint or otherwise, was abhorrent and was to be deemed violative of the First Amendment and of the public's "right immediately to know." Yet that newspaper stood before us at oral argument and professed criticism of the Government for not lodging its protest earlier than by a Monday telegram following the initial Sunday publication.

The country would be none the worse off were the cases tried quickly, to be sure, but in the customary and properly deliberative manner. The most recent of the material, it is said, dates no later than 1968, already about three years ago, and the Times itself took three months to formulate its plan of procedure and, thus, deprived its public for that period.

The First Amendment, after all, is only one part of an entire Constitution. Article II of the great document vests in the Executive Branch primary power over the conduct of foreign affairs and places in that branch the responsibility for the Nation's safety. Each provision of the Constitution is important, and I cannot subscribe to a doctrine of unlimited absolutism for the First Amendment at the cost of downgrading other provisions. First Amendment absolutism has never commanded a majority of this Court. What is needed here is a weighing, upon properly developed standards, of the broad right of the press to print and of the very narrow right of the Government to prevent. Such standards are not yet developed. The parties here are in disagreement as to what those standards should be. But even the newspapers concede that there are situations where restraint is in order and is constitutional.

It may well be that if these cases were allowed to develop as they should be developed, and to be tried as lawyers should try them and as courts should hear them, free of pressure and panic and sensationalism, other light would be shed on the situation and contrary considerations, for me, might prevail. But that is not the present posture of the litigation.

The Court, however, decides the cases today the other way. I therefore add one final comment.

I strongly urge, and sincerely hope, that these two newspapers will be fully aware of their ultimate responsibilities to the United States of America. Judge Wilkey, dissenting in the District of Columbia case, after a review of only the affidavits before his court (the basic papers had not then been made available by either party), concluded that there were a number of examples of documents that, if in the possession of the Post, and if published, "could clearly result in great harm to the nation," and he defined "harm" to mean "the death of soldiers, the destruction of alliances, the greatly increased difficulty of negotiation with our enemies, the inability of our diplomats to negotiate. . . ." I, for one, have now been able to give at least some cursory study not only to the affidavits, but to the material itself. I regret to say that from this examination I fear that Judge Wilkey's statements have possible foundation. I therefore share his concern. I hope that damage has not already been done. If, however, damage has been done, and if, with the Court's action today, these newspapers proceed to publish the critical documents and there results therefrom "the death of soldiers, the destruction of alliances, the greatly increased difficulty of negotiation with our enemies, the inability of our diplomats to negotiate," to which list I might add the factors of prolongation of the war and of further delay in the freeing of United States prisoners, then the Nation's people will know where the responsibility for these sad consequences rests.

NOTES AND QUESTIONS

1. The "black letter law" on prior restraints makes clear that "the protection even as to previous restraint is not absolutely unlimited. But the limitation has been recognized only in exceptional cases. When a nation is at war many things that might be said in time of peace are such a hindrance to its effort that their utterance will not be endured so long as men fight and that no Court could regard them as protected by any constitutional right. No one would question but that

a government might prevent actual obstruction to its recruiting service or the publication of the sailing dates of transports or the number and location of troops." *Near v. State of Minnesota ex rel. Olson*, 283 U.S. 697, 716 (1931) (quotation marks and internal citation omitted). What else, by analogy, should be subject to prior restraint from publication?

2. At least three Justices (Douglas, White, Blackmun) admit to personally reviewing the material sought to be enjoined from publication. Was that their role? What expertise would they employ? Should they be conducting a balancing test of harms? On the other hand, without looking at the materials, what point would there be to judicial review?

B. Access to Courts

Recall the discussion in Chapter 2 (p. 61) of the order by Chief Immigration Judge Michael Creppy to close "special interest" immigration hearings to the press and public shortly after the attacks of September 11, 2001. A circuit split developed between the Sixth and Third Circuit Courts of Appeals in cases pursued by news media and others.

Detroit Free Press v. Ashcroft
303 F.3d 681 (6th Cir. 2002)

KEITH, Circuit Judge.

The primary issue on appeal in this case is whether the First Amendment to the United States Constitution confers a public right of access to deportation hearings. If it does, then the Government must make a showing to overcome that right.

No one will ever forget the egregious, deplorable, and despicable terrorist attacks of September 11, 2001. These were cowardly acts. In response, our government launched an extensive investigation into the attacks, future threats, conspiracies, and attempts to come. As part of this effort, immigration laws are prosecuted with increased vigor. The issue before us today involves these efforts.

The political branches of our government enjoy near-unrestrained ability to control our borders. These are policy questions entrusted exclusively to the political branches of our government. While the Bill of Rights jealously protects citizens from such laws, it has never protected non-citizens facing deportation in the same way. In our democracy, based on checks and balances, neither the Bill of Rights nor the judiciary can second-guess government's choices. The only safeguard on this extraordinary governmental power is the public, deputizing the press as the guardians of their liberty. An informed public is the most potent of all restraints upon misgovernment.

Today, the Executive Branch seeks to take this safeguard away from the public by placing its actions beyond public scrutiny. Against non-citizens, it seeks the power to secretly deport a class if it unilaterally calls them "special interest" cases. The Executive Branch seeks to uproot people's lives, outside the public eye, and behind a closed door. Democracies die behind closed doors. The First Amendment, through a free press, protects the people's right to know that their government acts fairly, lawfully, and accurately in deportation proceedings. When government begins closing doors, it selectively controls information rightfully belonging to the people. Selective information is misinformation. The Framers of the First Amendment did not trust any government to separate the true from the false for us. They protected the people against secret government.

On September 21, 2001, Chief Immigration Judge Michael Creppy issued a directive (the "Creppy directive") to all United States Immigration Judges requiring closure of special interest cases. The Creppy directive requires that all proceedings in such cases be closed to the press and public, including family members and friends. The Record of the Proceeding is not to be disclosed to anyone except a deportee's attorney or representative, "assuming the file does not contain classified information." "This restriction on information includes confirming or denying whether such a case is on the docket or scheduled for a hearing."

On December 19, 2002, Immigration Judge Elizabeth Hacker conducted a bond hearing for Rabih Haddad ("Haddad"), one such special interest case. Haddad was subject to deportation, having overstayed his tourist visa. The Government further suspects that the Islamic charity Haddad operates supplies funds to terrorist organizations. Haddad's family, members of the public, including Congressman John Conyers, and several newspapers sought to attend his deportation hearing. Without prior notice to the public, Haddad, or his attorney, courtroom security officers announced that the hearing was closed to the public and the press. Haddad was denied bail, detained, and has since been in the government's custody. Subsequent hearings, conducted on January 2 and 10, 2002, were also closed to the public and the press.

Haddad, several newspapers (the "Newspaper Plaintiffs"), and Congressman Conyers filed complaints for injunctive and declaratory relief. Among the claims asserted, the Newspapers Plaintiffs (separately from Haddad) sought a declaratory judgment that the Creppy directive, facially and as applied, violated their First Amendment right of access to Haddad's deportation proceedings. They further sought to enjoin subsequent closures of proceedings in Haddad's case and a release of all transcripts and documents from previous proceedings.

The district court granted the Newspaper Plaintiffs' motion. [The court found] that the Newspaper Plaintiffs had a First Amendment right of access to the proceedings. The Government timely filed its notice of appeal. In the interim, on April 10, 2002, the Government obtained a temporary stay of the district court's order from this Court. On April 18, 2002, we dissolved the temporary stay and denied the Government's motion for stay pending this appeal.

We review the grant of a preliminary injunction for an abuse of discretion, but questions of law are reviewed de novo. To determine whether to grant a motion for a preliminary injunction, a court must analyze the following four factors:

> "(1) whether the movant has a strong likelihood of success on the merits; (2) whether the movant would suffer irreparable injury without the injunction; (3) whether issuance of the injunction would cause substantial harm to others; and (4) whether the public interest would be served by issuance of the injunction."

The Government argues that the district court erred in ruling that the government's plenary power over immigration did not warrant deferential review. The Government argues that it has plenary authority over not only substantive immigration laws and decisions, but also non-substantive ones, like the Creppy directive. Therefore, whether or not there is a First Amendment right of access to deportation proceedings, the Government argues, it can implement any non-substantive policy infringing upon that right if it is facially legitimate and bona fide.

It would be ironic, indeed, to allow the Government's assertion of plenary power to transform the First Amendment from the great instrument of open democracy to a safe harbor from public scrutiny. In the words of Justice Murphy, "[such a] conclusion would make our constitutional safeguards transitory and discriminatory in nature. . . . [We] cannot agree that the framers of the Constitution meant to make such an empty mockery of human freedom." *Bridges v. Wixon* (1945) (Murphy, J., concurring). As a result, the Government's stated position finds no authority in the Constitution and is untenable.

As old as the first immigration laws of this country is the recognition that non-citizens, even if illegally present in the United States, are "persons" entitled to the Fifth Amendment right of due process in deportation proceedings. Therefore, the Fifth Amendment limits non-substantive immigration laws.

As firmly established as the due process rights of deportees is the rule that non-citizens seeking initial entry have no right to due process. Non-citizens seeking initial entry have no ties to the United States, and are, therefore, not "persons" within the meaning of the Fifth Amendment. Whatever process the government affords them, no matter how minimal, illusory, or secret, is due process of law, beyond the scope of judicial review.

Therefore, in stark contrast to a deportation hearing, the Government may exclude a non-citizen seeking initial entry without a hearing or disclosure of the evidence and reasons relied upon. The difference between these two situations demonstrates not only that the Bill of Rights limits the government's power over non-substantive immigration laws, but also that the limitation is meaningful. The Government is not entitled to special deference in this area.

Non-deferential review does not begin and end with the Fifth Amendment. As long ago as 1896, the Supreme Court recognized that the Fifth and Sixth Amendments limited Congress from enforcing its powers over immigration. In *Wong Wing v. United States* (1896), Congress had passed a statute requiring that "any . . . Chinese person, or person of Chinese decent, convicted and adjudged to be not lawfully entitled to be or remain in the United States" be "imprisoned at hard labor for a period not exceeding one year, and thereafter removed from the United States." The government argued that this law was enacted under its plenary power over immigration. As such, trials of aliens under this section could be conducted by an administrative, summary hearing.

While noting the broad powers enjoyed by the political branches to expel and exclude aliens, the Court held that such powers were limited by the Fifth and Sixth Amendments: "But to declare unlawful residence within the country to be an infamous crime, punishable by deprivation of liberty and property, would be to pass out of the sphere of constitutional legislation, unless provision were made that the fact of guilt should first be established by a judicial trial."

Although the question had never been addressed specifically, there is ample foundation to conclude that the Supreme Court would also recognize that non-citizens enjoy unrestrained First Amendment rights in deportation proceedings. For example, in *Bridges v. Wixon* (1945), a non-citizen was deported because of his allegiance to the Communist Party. The Court invalidated the deportation on statutory grounds. A concurrence by Justice Murphy, however, noted that deportees had unqualified First Amendment rights in deportation hearings:

> [O]nce an alien lawfully enters and resides in this country he becomes invested with the rights guaranteed by the Constitution to all people within our borders. Such rights include those protected by the First and Fifth Amendments and by the due process clause of the Fourteenth Amendment. None of these provisions acknowledges any distinction between citizens and resident aliens. They extend their inalienable privileges to all "persons" and guard against any encroachment on those rights by federal or state authority.

Id. (Murphy, J., concurring).

Similarly, the Court seemed to acknowledge a First Amendment right in deportation hearings in *Harisiades v. Shaughnessy* (1952). Like *Bridges v. Wixon*, the deportees in *Harisiades* were deported for their allegiance to the Communist Party, which Congress had found advocated government overthrow by force or violence. While upholding the statutes and the deportations against a First Amendment challenge, the Court held that threat of violence and force was not protected by the First Amendment. Even while not finding a protected First Amendment right, the Court seemed to acknowledge that the First Amendment operated in deportation proceedings.

More support for independent, non-deferential review of non-substantive immigration laws can be found in *INS v. Chadha* (1983). *Chadha* involved a statute allowing a congressional veto over any decision by the Attorney General that allowed a deportable alien to remain in the United States. The Court held that the law violated the Presentment Clause. The government, in part, argued that they were entitled to deference due to their plenary power over immigration. The Court, however, stated:

> The plenary authority of Congress over aliens under Art. I § 8, cl. 4, is not open to question, but what is challenged here is whether Congress has chosen a constitutionally permissible means of implementing that power. As we made

clear in *Buckley v. Valeo* (1976): "Congress has plenary authority in all cases in which it has substantive legislative jurisdiction . . . so long as the exercise of that authority does not offend some other constitutional restriction."

More recently, the Supreme Court has again applied non-deferential review to non-substantive immigration law. In *Zadvydas v. Davis* (2001), two non-citizens were being held indefinitely beyond the normal statutory-removal period of ninety days, because no country would accept them. A post-removal-period statute authorized such detention. The issue, however, was whether the post-removal statute authorized a detention indefinitely, or for a period reasonably necessary to secure removal. The language of the statute set no such limit. The Court read an implicit reasonableness limit into the statute to avoid "serious constitutional problems." Significantly, the Court dismissed the government's argument that Congress's plenary power to create immigration law required deference to the political branches' decision-making. The Court repeated the mantra that the plenary power was "subject to important constitutional limitations."

The Government correctly notes that the Court in *Zadvydas* twice indicated that it might be deferential in situations involving terrorism. However, nothing in *Zadvydas* indicates that given such a situation, the Court would defer to the political branches' determination of who belongs in that "small segment of particularly dangerous individuals" without judicial review of the individual circumstances of each case,[9] something that the Creppy directive strikingly lacks. The Court repeated the importance of strong procedural protections when constitutional rights were involved: "[T]he Constitution may well preclude granting 'an administrative body the unreviewable authority to make determinations implicating fundamental rights.'"

Importantly, the Creppy directive does not apply to "a small segment of particularly dangerous" information, but a broad, indiscriminate range of information, including information likely to be entirely innocuous. Similarly, no definable standards used to determine whether a case is of "special interest" have been articulated. Nothing in the Creppy directive counsels that it is limited to "a small segment of particularly dangerous individuals." In fact, the Government so much as argues that certain non-citizens known to have no links to terrorism will be designated "special interest" cases. Supposedly, closing a more targeted class would allow terrorists to draw inferences from which hearings are open and which are closed.

While we sympathize and share the Government's fear that dangerous information might be disclosed in some of these hearings, we feel that the ordinary process of determining whether closure is warranted on a case-by-case basis sufficiently addresses their concerns. Using this stricter standard does not mean that information helpful to terrorists will be disclosed, only

---

9. It should also be noted that this language concerning terrorism was strictly dicta. In *New York Times v. United States*, the Court applied no deferential review to the Government's actions when faced with a national security threat.

that the Government must be more targeted and precise in its approach. Given the importance of the constitutional rights involved, such safeguards must be vigorously guarded, lest the First Amendment turn into another balancing test.

We next consider whether the First Amendment affords the press and public a right of access to deportation hearings. The Newspaper Plaintiffs argue that the right of access should be governed by the standards set forth in *Richmond Newspapers, Inc. v. Virginia* (1980) and its progeny. The Government, on the other hand, contends that *Richmond Newspapers* and its progeny are limited to judicial proceedings, and therefore, the standards articulated in these cases do not apply to deportation hearings, which are administrative proceedings. According to the Government, review of claims of access to administrative proceedings are governed by the more deferential standard articulated in *Houchins v. KQED, Inc.* (1978). The Government also argues that even if the standard articulated in *Richmond Newspapers* and its progeny is the appropriate test, the Newspaper Plaintiffs cannot demonstrate a right of access to deportation hearings by the standards articulated therein.

First, *Houchins* is not the applicable standard to resolve the First Amendment claim of access now before us. The issue before the Court in *Houchins*, decided two years before *Richmond Newspapers*, was "whether the news media have a constitutional right of access to a county jail, *over and above that of other persons*, to interview inmates and make sound recordings, films and photographs for publication and broadcasting by newspapers, radio and television." (emphasis added). Here, the Newspaper Plaintiffs do not claim a "special privilege of access" to the deportations hearings. Rather, the Newspaper Plaintiffs simply request that they be able to attend the hearings on equal footing with the public.

Next, *Houchins* rested its holding on the Court's interpretation of the press clause, a First Amendment clause distinct from the speech clause, which is here at issue.

The *Richmond Newspapers* two-part test has also been applied to particular proceedings outside the criminal judicial context, including administrative proceedings. Thus, we reject the Government's assertion that a line has been drawn between judicial and administrative proceedings, with the First Amendment guaranteeing access to the former but not the latter. The First Amendment question cannot be resolved solely on the label we give the event, i.e., "trial" or otherwise.

Finally, to the extent that the standard in *Houchins* remains good law, we do not find *Houchins* applicable to the facts of the present case. Here, the Newspaper Plaintiffs seek access to a demonstrably quasi-judicial government administrative proceeding normally open to the public, as opposed to *Houchins*, where the plaintiffs sought access to a government facility normally restricted to the public.

Deportation hearings, as quasi-judicial proceedings, are fundamentally different than a prison facility. Drawing sharp lines between administrative and judicial proceedings would allow the legislature to artfully craft information out of the public eye.

Under the two-part "experience and logic" test from *Richmond Newspapers*, we conclude that there is a First Amendment right of access to deportation proceedings. Deportation hearings, and similar proceedings, have traditionally been open to the public, and openness undoubtedly plays a significant positive role in this process.

As stated earlier, to paraphrase the Supreme Court, deportation hearings "walk, talk, and squawk" very much like a judicial proceeding. Substantively, we look to other proceedings that have the same effect as deportation. Here, the only other federal court that can enter an order of removal is a United States District Court during sentencing in a criminal trial. At common law, beginning with the Transportation Act of 1718, the English criminal courts could enter an order of transportation or banishment as a sentence in a criminal trial. As *Richmond Newspapers* discussed in great length, these types of criminal proceedings have historically been open.

Next, we turn to the "logic" prong, which asks "whether public access plays a significant positive role in the functioning of the particular process in question." Public access undoubtedly enhances the quality of deportation proceedings. Much of the reasoning from *Richmond Newspapers* is also applicable to this context.

First, public access acts as a check on the actions of the Executive by assuring us that proceedings are conducted fairly and properly. In an area such as immigration, where the government has nearly unlimited authority, the press and the public serve as perhaps the only check on abusive government practices.

Second, openness ensures that government does its job properly; that it does not make mistakes. Congressional oversight hearings can prevent future mistakes, but they can do little to correct past ones. In contrast, openness at the hearings can allow mistakes to be cured at once. Moreover, the natural tendency of government officials is to hold their meetings in secret. They can thereby avoid criticism and proceed informally and less carefully. They do not have to worry before they proceed with the task that a careless remark may be splashed across the next day's headlines.

These first two concerns are magnified by the fact that deportees have no right to an attorney at the government's expense. Effectively, the press and the public may be their only guardian.

Third, after the devastation of September 11 and the massive investigation that followed, the cathartic effect of open deportations cannot be overstated. They serve a "therapeutic" purpose as outlets for "community concern, hostility, and emotions." As the district court stated:

> It is important for the public, particularly individuals who feel that they are being targeted by the Government as a result of the terrorist attacks of September 11, to know that even during these sensitive times the Government is adhering to immigration procedures and respecting individuals' rights. . . . And if in fact the Government determines that Haddad is connected to terrorist activity or organizations, a decision made openly concerning his deportation may assure the public that justice has been done.

Detroit Free Press, 195 F. Supp. 2d at 944.

Fourth, openness enhances the perception of integrity and fairness. The most stringent safeguards for a deportee would be of limited worth if the public is not persuaded that the standards are being fairly enforced. Legitimacy rests in large part on public understanding.

Fifth, public access helps ensure that the individual citizen can effectively participate in and contribute to our republican system of self-government. Public access to deportation proceedings helps inform the public of the affairs of the government. Direct knowledge of how their government is operating enhances the public's ability to affirm or protest government's efforts. When government selectively chooses what information it allows the public to see, it can become a powerful tool for deception.

Additionally, the Government has not identified one persuasive reason why openness would play a negative role in the process. Nothing like the excessive financial burdens noted by the Supreme Court in *Houchins* would be applicable here.

Having found a First Amendment right of access to deportation hearings, we now determine whether the Government has made a sufficient showing to overcome that right.

Under the standard articulated in *Globe Newspaper*, government action that curtails a First Amendment right of access "in order to inhibit the disclosure of sensitive information" must be supported by a showing "that denial is necessitated by a compelling governmental interest, and is narrowly tailored to serve that interest." Moreover, "[t]he interest is to be articulated along with findings specific enough that a reviewing court can determine whether the closure order was properly entered." The Government's ongoing anti-terrorism investigation certainly implicates a compelling interest. However, the Creppy directive is neither narrowly tailored, nor does it require particularized findings. Therefore, it impermissibly infringes on the Newspaper Plaintiffs' First Amendment right of access.

[Interim rules regarding special interest cases] indefinitely restrain a deportee's ability to divulge all information, including information obtained independently from the deportation proceedings. The Government certainly has a compelling interest in preventing terrorism. According to the additional affidavits, public access to removal proceedings would disclose the following information that would impede the Government's investigation:

> "Bits and pieces of information that may appear innocuous in isolation," but used by terrorist groups to help form a "bigger picture" of the Government's terrorism investigation, would be disclosed. The Government describes this type of intelligence gathering as "akin to the construction of a mosaic," where an individual piece of information is not of obvious importance until pieced together with other pieces of information.
>
> The identifications of the detainees, witnesses, and investigative sources would be disclosed. Terrorist groups could subject these individuals or their families to intimidation or harm and discourage them from cooperating with the Government.

Methods of entry to the country, communicating, or funding could be revealed. This information could allow terrorist organizations to alter their patterns of activity to find the most effective means of evading detection. "Information that is *not* presented at the hearings also might provide important clues to terrorist[s], because it could reveal what the investigation has not yet discovered." The Government provides this example: "If the government discloses the evidence it has about a particular member of a terrorist organization, but fails to mention that the detainee is involved in an impending attack, the other members of the organization may be able to infer that the government is not yet aware of the attack."

See Gov't Brief at 47-49.

Inasmuch as these agents' declarations establish that certain information revealed during removal proceedings could impede the ongoing anti-terrorism investigation, we defer to their judgment. These agents are certainly in a better position to understand the contours of the investigation and the intelligence capabilities of terrorist organizations.

[However,] the blanket closure rule mandated by the Creppy directive is not narrowly tailored. The Government offers no persuasive argument as to why the Government's concerns cannot be addressed on a case-by-case basis. The Newspaper Plaintiffs argue, and the district court agreed, that the Creppy directive is ineffective in achieving its purported goals because the detainees and their lawyers are allowed to publicize the proceedings. According to the Newspaper Plaintiffs, to the extent that Haddad had discussed his proceedings (and disclosed documents) with family, friends and the media, the information that the Government seeks to protect is disclosed to the public anyway. We are not persuaded by the Government's argument in response that few detainees will disclose any information and that their disclosure will be less than complete public access. This contention is, at best, speculative and belies the Government's assertion that *any* information disclosed, even bits and pieces that seem innocuous, will be detrimental to the anti-terrorism investigation.

It is clear that certain types of information that the Government seeks to keep confidential could be kept from the public on a case-by-case basis through protective orders or in camera review—for example, the identification of investigative sources and witnesses. The Government, however, argues that it is impossible to keep some sensitive information confidential if any portion of a hearing is open or if the immigration court conducts a hearing to determine if closure is proper. Stated differently, the Government argues that there is sensitive information that would be disclosed if closure occurred on a case-by-case basis. First, the Government contends that the identities of the detainees would be revealed if closure occurred on a case-by-case basis, and such information would impede the anti-terrorism investigation. This information, however, is already being disclosed to the public through the detainees themselves or their counsel. Even if, as a result of the interim rule, a detainee remains silent, a terrorist group capable of sophisticated intelligence-gathering would certainly be made aware that one of its operatives, or someone connected to a particular terrorist plot, has disappeared into the Government's custody. Moreover, if a deportee does have links to terrorist organizations, there is nothing to stop that deportee from divulging the information learned from these proceedings once deported.

Next, the Government argues that open hearings would reveal the amount of intelligence that the Government does not possess. The Government argues that evidence concerning a particular detainee could be incomplete, and an incomplete presentation of evidence would permit terrorist groups to gauge how much the Government knows and does not know about their operations. The issue in a removal hearing is, however, narrowly focused, and the Government has enormous control over what evidence it introduces.

Here, the Government has detained Haddad and instituted removal proceedings based on his overstay of a tourist visa. Thus, the Government need only establish that Haddad obtained a visa, the visa has expired, and that he is still in the country. Very little information is required. The fact that the Government may have to contest the non-citizen's application for discretionary relief is similarly unavailing. At oral argument, it was brought to our attention that Haddad intends to apply for asylum, a form of discretionary relief available to non-citizens in deportation proceedings. We see no reason why, in making its case against the applicant's request for discretionary relief, the Government could not seek to keep confidential, pertinent information, as the need arises.

Finally, the Government seeks to protect from disclosure the bits and pieces of information that seem innocuous in isolation, but when pieced together with other bits and pieces aid in creating a bigger picture of the Government's anti-terrorism investigation, i.e., the "mosaic intelligence." Mindful of the Government's concerns, we must nevertheless conclude that the Creppy directive is over-inclusive. While the risk of "mosaic intelligence" may exist, we do not believe speculation should form the basis for such a drastic restriction of the public's First Amendment rights.

Furthermore, there seems to be no limit to the Government's argument. The Government could use its "mosaic intelligence" argument as a justification to close any public hearing completely and categorically, including criminal proceedings. The Government could operate in virtual secrecy in all matters dealing, even remotely, with "national security," resulting in a wholesale suspension of First Amendment rights. By the simple assertion of "national security," the Government seeks a process where it may, without review, designate certain classes of cases as "special interest cases" and, behind closed doors, adjudicate the merits of these cases to deprive non-citizens of their fundamental liberty interests.

This, we simply may not countenance. A government operating in the shadow of secrecy stands in complete opposition to the society envisioned by the Framers of our Constitution.

The Government states that special interest cases represent "a small, carefully chosen subset of the universe of aliens facing removal proceedings." Yet, to date, the Government has failed to disclose the actual number of special interest cases it has designated.

In sum, we find that the Government's attempt to establish a narrowly tailored restriction has failed.

When a party seeks a preliminary injunction on the basis of the potential violation of the First Amendment, the likelihood of success on the merits often will be the determinative factor. Nonetheless, the other three factors also favor granting an injunction. The Newspaper Plaintiffs will undoubtedly suffer irreparable injury if they are denied access to Haddad's upcoming hearings. The Supreme Court has held that even a minimal infringement upon First Amendment rights constitutes irreparable injury sufficient to justify injunctive relief. As the district court noted, no subsequent measures can cure this loss, because the information contained in the appeal or transcripts will be stale, and there is no assurance that they will completely detail the proceedings. Moreover, the injunction will not cause substantial harm to others because the Government can seek closure in individual cases at appropriate times.

Lastly, the public's interests are best served by open proceedings. A true democracy is one that operates on faith — faith that government officials are forthcoming and honest, and faith that informed citizens will arrive at logical conclusions. This is a vital reciprocity that America should not discard in these troubling times.

For the foregoing reasons, we AFFIRM.

* * *

The Court of Appeals for the Third Circuit reached the opposite conclusion from Judge Keith in the Sixth Circuit. In *North Jersey Media Group v. Ashcroft*, 308 F.3d 198 (3d Cir. 2002), Chief Judge Becker wrote the opinion for a 2-1 judgment reversing a district court's order enjoining the Attorney General from denying access to "special interest" deportation hearings under the Creppy Memo in a similar case brought by a consortium of media groups.

As to the appropriate test to adopt, Judge Becker observed that "[w]hile we believe that the notion that *Richmond Newspapers* applies is open to debate as a theoretical matter, we must yield to the prior precedent of this Court, and hence will apply it to the facts." However, he criticized the application of this two-part "experience and logic" test by the district court below (which, like Judge Keith in the Sixth Circuit, found for the media plaintiffs):

> With respect to the experience inquiry, the District Court relied especially on a line of Third Circuit cases which has applied *Richmond Newspapers* to find access to a number of auxiliary criminal proceedings, as well as to civil cases. The Court also relied on two cases in which we applied *Richmond Newspapers* to determine whether access should be granted to administrative proceedings, although we concluded in each instance that there was no access. . . . Turning to the logic prong, the District Court held that policy considerations strongly favored media access. Significantly, however, in evaluating the logic prong, the Court did not consider the policies militating against media access, including those identified in a declaration filed by Dale Watson, Counterterrorism Chief of the Federal Bureau of Investigation, which explained the danger of security breaches entailed in opening the hearings. In brief, the Watson Declaration represents that insight gleaned from

open proceedings might alert vigilant terrorists to the United States' investigative tactics and could easily betray what knowledge the government does—or does not—possess. Watson submits that even details that seem innocuous in isolation, such as the names of those detained, might be pieced together by knowledgeable persons within the terrorist network, who could in turn shift activities to a yet-undiscovered terrorist cell. Because immigration judges cannot be expected accurately to assess the harm that might result from disclosing seemingly trivial facts, Watson explains, seeking closure on a case-by-case basis would ineffectively protect the nation's interests.

Although existing caselaw on the logic prong has discussed only the policies favoring openness, we are satisfied that the logic prong must consider the flip side of the coin. Indeed, the Supreme Court seems to have contemplated this, for in formulating the *Richmond Newspapers* test it asked "whether public access plays a significant *positive* role in the functioning of the particular process in question." (emphasis added). Any inquiry into whether a role is positive must perforce consider whether it is potentially harmful. The District Court, however, failed to consider the Watson Declaration under its logic inquiry, examining it only in conjunction with the Newspapers' argument that the Creppy Directive failed strict scrutiny, a position that it endorsed.

Judge Becker also took issue with the approach taken by the Sixth Circuit:

The only Circuit to deal with these issues has resolved them in favor of the media. *See Detroit Free Press v. Ashcroft* (6th Cir. 2002). However, we find ourselves in disagreement with the Sixth Circuit. In our view the tradition of openness of deportation proceedings does not meet the standard required by *Richmond Newspapers*, or even its Third Circuit progeny. Deportation procedures have been codified for approximately 100 years but, despite their constant reenactment during that time, Congress has never explicitly guaranteed public access. Indeed, deportation cases involving abused alien children are mandatorily closed by statute, and hearings are often conducted in places generally inaccessible to the public. While INS regulations promulgated in 1964 create a *rebuttable* presumption of openness for most deportation cases, we conclude that a recently-created regulatory presumption of openness with significant statutory exceptions does not present the type of "unbroken, uncontradicted history" that *Richmond Newspapers* and its progeny require to establish a First Amendment right of access.

We also disagree with the Sixth Circuit as to the import of the *Richmond Newspapers* logic prong. We note preliminarily that, in the jurisprudence developed thus far, the logic prong does not appear to do much work in the *Richmond Newspapers* approach, for we have not found a case in which a proceeding passed the experience test through its history of openness yet failed the logic test by not serving community values. Under the reported cases, the second prong of the *Richmond Newspapers* test has been applied to inquire whether openness plays a positive policy role in a given proceeding. But, as we have explained, that calculus perforce must take account of the flip side—the extent to which openness impairs the public good.

This case arises in the wake of September 11, 2001, a day on which American life changed drastically and dramatically. The era that dawned on September 11th, and the war against terrorism that has pervaded the sinews of our national life since that day, are reflected in thousands of ways in legislative and national policy, the habits of daily living, and our collective psyches. Since the primary national policy must be self-preservation, it seems elementary that, to the extent open deportation hearings might impair national security, that security is implicated in the logic test. When it is factored in, given due consideration to the attorney general's statements of the threat, we do not believe that the *Richmond Newspapers* logic prong test favors the media either.

As we will now explain in detail, we find that the application of the *Richmond Newspapers* experience and logic tests does not compel us to declare the Creppy Directive unconstitutional. We will therefore reverse the Order of the District Court.

While the Framers clearly expected criminal and civil trials to be open to the public, Judge Becker argued, the "history of access to political branch proceedings is quite different." A review of that history (quoting Patrick Henry and Thomas Jefferson and referencing both the workings of Congress and the secret deliberations of the Constitutional Convention itself) convinced the court that there was no "unqualified right of access to the political branches" because some government functions require varying degrees of open access for their success. The court also pointed to more recent examples:

Even today, the Senate operates under a resolution limiting public access to "routine Senate records" for 20 years after their creation and to "sensitive records, such as investigative files" for 50 years after their creation, and each Senate committee retains the right to extend that access period for its own records.

This tradition of closing sensitive proceedings extends to many hearings before administrative agencies. For example, although hearings on Social Security disability claims profoundly affect hundreds of thousands of people annually, and have great impact on expenditure of government funds, they are open only to "the parties and to other persons the administrative law judge considers necessary and proper." 20 C.F.R. § 404.944. Likewise, administrative disbarment hearings are often presumptively closed. *See, e.g.*, 12 C.F.R. § 19.199 (Office of Comptroller of Currency); 12 C.F.R. § 263.97 (Federal Reserve Board of Governors). The Government lists more than a dozen other examples of mandatorily or presumptively closed administrative proceedings. For instance, hearings on charges of wrongdoing may often be closed at the administrator's discretion for "good cause," to protect the "public interest," or under similar standards. Hearings on adverse passport decisions by the Department of State "shall be private." 22 C.F.R. § 51.87. *See also* 5 C.F.R. § 2638.505(e)(2) (hearings on ethics charges against government employees may be closed "in the best interests of national security, the respondent employee, a witness, the public or other affected persons").

Faced with this litany of administrative hearings that are closed to the public, the Newspapers cannot claim a general First Amendment right of access to government proceedings without urging a judicially-imposed revolution in the administrative state. They wisely avoid that tactic, at least directly. Instead they submit that, despite frequent closures throughout the administrative realm, deportation proceedings in particular boast a history of openness sufficient to meet the *Richmond Newspapers* requirement. We now assess that claim, and find that we disagree.

The court then turned to the logic prong of the *Richmond Newspapers* test:

[W]e are troubled by our sense that the logic inquiry, as currently conducted, does not do much work in the *Richmond Newspapers* test. We have not found a case in which a proceeding passed the experience test through its history of openness yet failed the logic test by not serving community values. Under the reported cases, whenever a court has found that openness serves community values, it has concluded that openness plays a "significant positive role" in that proceeding. But that cannot be the story's end, for to gauge accurately whether a role is positive, the calculus must perforce take account of the flip side — the extent to which openness impairs the public good. We note in this respect that, were the logic prong only to determine whether openness serves some good, it is difficult to conceive of a government proceeding to which the public would not have a First Amendment right of access. For example, public access to *any* government affair, even internal CIA deliberations, would "promote informed discussion" among the citizenry. It is unlikely the Supreme Court intended this result.

In this case the Government presented substantial evidence that open deportation hearings would threaten national security. Although the District Court discussed these concerns as part of its strict scrutiny analysis, they are equally applicable to the question whether openness, on balance, serves a positive role in removal hearings. We find that upon factoring them into the logic equation, it is doubtful that openness promotes the public good in this context.

The court found the government's national security concerns to be persuasive, including those raising the "mosaic theory" dismissed by the Sixth Circuit. While finding some degree of speculation in the FBI's Watson Declaration, the court concluded:

We are quite hesitant to conduct a judicial inquiry into the credibility of these security concerns, as national security is an area where courts have traditionally extended great deference to Executive expertise. The assessments before us have been made by senior government officials responsible for investigating the events of September 11th and for preventing future attacks. These officials believe that closure of special interest hearings is necessary to advance these goals, and their concerns, as expressed in the Watson Declaration, have gone unrebutted. To the extent that the Attorney General's national security concerns seem credible, we will not lightly second-guess them.

We are keenly aware of the dangers presented by deference to the executive branch when constitutional liberties are at stake, especially in times of national crisis, when those liberties are likely in greatest jeopardy. On balance, however, we are unable to conclude that openness plays a positive role in special interest deportation hearings at a time when our nation is faced with threats of such profound and unknown dimension.

The importance of this case has not escaped us. As we approached it, we were acutely aware that the countervailing positions of the parties go to the heart of our institutions, our national values, and the republic itself.

Because we find that open deportation hearings do not pass the two-part *Richmond Newspapers* test, we hold that the press and public possess no First Amendment right of access. In the absence of such a right, we need not reach the subsequent questions whether the Creppy Directive's closures would pass a strict scrutiny analysis and whether the District Court's "national in scope" injunction was too broad.

The judgment of the District Court will be reversed.

Judge Scirica filed a dissenting opinion, arguing that the issue was "not whether some or all deportation hearings of special interest aliens should be closed, but who makes that determination." Applying *Richmond Newspapers*, he concluded that its two-part test was satisfied. However, his remedial approach would have been a more limited one:

> I would find a qualified right of access to deportation hearings. Because I believe that Immigration Judges can make these determinations with substantial deference to national security, I would affirm the District Court's judgment.
>
> I would hold that the District Court abused its discretion by issuing a nationwide injunction that bars enforcement of the Creppy Directive in any special interest proceeding and against any member of the general public or press. A narrower remedy will provide full relief to plaintiffs and allow other courts to explore this difficult constitutional question.
>
> In this case, the only plaintiffs are North Jersey Media Group and New Jersey Law Journal. An injunction protecting these plaintiffs alone would remedy any violation of plaintiffs' First Amendment rights. Enjoining enforcement of the Creppy Directive against other parties goes beyond providing relief to plaintiffs, and it deprives the Supreme Court of the opportunity to review the decisions of several courts of appeals. For these reasons, I would reverse the District Court's nationwide injunction.

NOTES AND QUESTIONS

1. In *Detroit Free Press*, Judge Keith distinguished the *Houchins* case from *Richmond Newspapers*, observing: "*Houchins* rested its holding on the Court's interpretation of the press clause, a First Amendment clause distinct from the speech clause, which is here at issue." In *Richmond Newspapers*, as in *Detroit Free Press*, both individuals and media representatives sought access to a murder trial in its fourth iteration (after a reversal and two mistrials). The *Richmond* Court spoke in general terms about the First Amendment, noting that the Speech, Press, Association, and Petition Clauses "share a common core purpose of assuring freedom of communication on matters relating to the functioning of government," 448 U.S. 555 at 575, even going so far as to refer to "the amalgam of the First Amendment guarantees of speech and press," *id.* at 577. Mixing the Speech and Press Clauses together, the Court held: "In guaranteeing freedoms such as those of speech and press, the First Amendment can be read as protecting the right of everyone to attend trials so as to give meaning to those explicit guarantees. The First Amendment goes beyond protection of the press and the self-expression of individuals to prohibit government from limiting the stock of information from which members of the public may draw. Free speech carries with it some freedom to listen." *Id.* at 575-76 (quotation marks and citation omitted). In a footnote, the Court finally distinguished individuals from journalists, but for purposes of the Court's holding this appeared to be a distinction without a difference: "That the right to attend may be exercised by people less frequently today when information as to trials generally reaches them by way of print and electronic media in no way alters the basic right. Instead of relying

on personal observation or reports from neighbors as in the past, most people receive information concerning trials through the media whose representatives are entitled to the same rights to attend trials as the general public." *Id.* at 577, n.12 (quotation marks and citation omitted).

2. Where do the Sixth Circuit and the Third Circuit part ways? Is this a dispute about the interpretation of the First Amendment or a disagreement about the outcome of a balancing of incommensurable interests? If the latter, are courts better placed to weigh those interests, on the argument that the executive branch will naturally prioritize security interests over all others and that the population subject to these immigration hearings, being non-voting and often unlawfully present aliens, is unlikely to attract the interest of the legislative branch? How do you explain the interest of Congressman John Conyers (D-MI) in the *Detroit Free Press* case?

3. Assess the concerns expressed in the government affidavits in these cases. How can these theories and anxieties be tested? Are they based on an expertise uniquely possessed by these officials? How would you challenge them in litigation? Some of their arguments (e.g., the "mosaic theory") have appeared in other contexts (e.g., to justify exceptions to the release of documents under the Freedom of Information Act). What limits can or should be placed on such arguments to prevent the exceptions from swallowing the rule—if it is a rule—of public access to the workings of government?

4. In *Detroit Free Press*, Judge Keith distinguished the government's preferred case (*Houchins*), *inter alia*, because that case concerned access to a county jail, a government facility normally restricted to the public. Suppose that the government restricted access to immigration proceedings not through the vehicle of something like the Creppy Memo, but simply by transferring proceedings from courthouses to immigration detention centers. If the government justified the move by citing security concerns, efficiency in dealing with a backlog, or to prevent the dissemination of particularly dangerous information, how should a court decide a case raising a similar First Amendment challenge?

5. Carol Rosenberg is a reporter for the *Miami Herald*. She is the only reporter in the United States (and, for that matter, the world) to have made Guantanamo Bay her beat. In May 2014, she delivered the Pringle Lecture at the Columbia School of Journalism, in which she remarked on the tradecraft of journalism in that context and the difficulties of sheer access to this story. She expressed her view that one reason Guantanamo was chosen was because of its remoteness: Being hard to reach would make it harder to report on and think about.

Access to the military commission proceedings at Camp Justice on the naval station at Guantanamo Bay requires military permission to enter the naval station itself. Once there, journalists and other observers may watch proceedings from behind a triple glass enclosed gallery into which audio is subject to a forty-second delay and the possibility of censorship to protect possibly classified information. Transcripts may similarly be redacted even if audio was not silenced during the proceeding. *See* Carol Rosenberg, *Guantánamo Prosecutor Defends Retroactive Censorship of Public Hearing in 9/11 Case*, Miami Herald, Feb. 4, 2016.

C. Access to Information

The Freedom of Information Act provides that "each agency, upon any request for records which (i) reasonably describes such records and (ii) is made in accordance with published rules stating the time, place, fees (if any), and procedures to be followed, shall make the records promptly available to any person." 5 U.S.C. § 552(a)(3)(A). However, this broad policy of open access—"freedom of information"—is constrained by a number of factors. Some are found in the statute itself. Most obvious are nine "exemptions" from this broad policy. § 552(b).[5] This section requires that portions of a record "reasonably segregable" from exempt information must be disclosed; in most cases, deletions must be indicated on the record. Despite statutorily mandated time periods for compliance, FOIA offices established by agencies obliged to respond to requests are notoriously backlogged.

---

5. This section does not apply to matters that are—

(1)(A) specifically authorized under criteria established by an Executive order to be kept secret in the interest of national defense or foreign policy and (B) are in fact properly classified pursuant to such Executive order;

(2) related solely to the internal personnel rules and practices of an agency;

(3) specifically exempted from disclosure by statute (other than section 552b of this title), if that statute—

(A)(i) requires that the matters be withheld from the public in such a manner as to leave no discretion on the issue; or

(ii) establishes particular criteria for withholding or refers to particular types of matters to be withheld; and

(B) if enacted after the date of enactment of the OPEN FOIA Act of 2009, specifically cites to this paragraph.

(4) trade secrets and commercial or financial information obtained from a person and privileged or confidential;

(5) inter-agency or intra-agency memorandums or letters which would not be available by law to a party other than an agency in litigation with the agency;

(6) personnel and medical files and similar files the disclosure of which would constitute a clearly unwarranted invasion of personal privacy;

(7) records or information compiled for law enforcement purposes, but only to the extent that the production of such law enforcement records or information (A) could reasonably be expected to interfere with enforcement proceedings, (B) would deprive a person of a right to a fair trial or an impartial adjudication, (C) could reasonably be expected to constitute an unwarranted invasion of personal privacy, (D) could reasonably be expected to disclose the identity of a confidential source, including a State, local, or foreign agency or authority or any private institution which furnished information on a confidential basis, and, in the case of a record or information compiled by criminal law enforcement authority in the course of a criminal investigation or by an agency conducting a lawful national security intelligence investigation, information furnished by a confidential source, (E) would disclose techniques and procedures for law enforcement investigations or prosecutions, or would disclose guidelines for law enforcement investigations or prosecutions if such disclosure could reasonably be expected to risk circumvention of the law, or (F) could reasonably be expected to endanger the life or physical safety of any individual;

(8) contained in or related to examination, operating, or condition reports prepared by, on behalf of, or for the use of an agency responsible for the regulation or supervision of financial institutions; or

(9) geological and geophysical information and data, including maps, concerning wells.

In fiscal year 2015, the federal agencies subject to FOIA received 713,168 requests; over 39 percent of these requests were directed to the Department of Homeland Security, with the Department of Justice (9.5 percent) and Department of Defense (8 percent) in second and third place, respectively. *See* Department of Justice, Summary of Annual FOIA Reports for Fiscal Year 2015, at 2 (*available at* https://www.justice.gov/oip/reports/fy_2015_annual_foia_report_summary/download). Litigation is often the "squeaky wheel" mechanism that compels actual compliance.

American Civil Liberties Union v. Department of Justice
681 F.3d 61 (2d Cir. 2012)

Wesley, Circuit Judge:

The Central Intelligence Agency ("CIA"), the Department of Justice ("DOJ"), and its component Office of Legal Counsel ("OLC") (collectively the "Government") appeal from a portion of an October 1, 2010 judgment of the United States District Court for the Southern District of New York (Hellerstein, J.), requiring the Government to disclose, pursuant to the Freedom of Information Act ("FOIA"), information redacted from two memoranda prepared by the OLC. The Government contends that the redactions are justified under FOIA because the information pertains to a highly classified, active intelligence method. We conclude that the Government may withhold this information under FOIA Exemption 1. We thus reverse the district court's judgment insofar as it required disclosure.

The American Civil Liberties Union ("ACLU"), Center for Constitutional Rights, Incorporated, Physicians for Human Rights, Veterans for Common Sense, and Veterans for Peace (collectively "Plaintiffs") appeal from the same judgment insofar as it upheld the Government's withholding of records relating to the CIA's use of the Enhanced Interrogation Technique ("EIT") of waterboarding and a photograph of high-value detainee Abu Zubaydah, taken while he was in CIA custody abroad. Plaintiffs contend that the records and photograph may not be withheld under either FOIA Exemption 1 or 3 because the President has declared the practice of waterboarding illegal and the Government has failed to justify adequately its withholding of the photograph. We disagree and hold that the President's declaration and prohibition of the future use of waterboarding do not affect the Government's otherwise valid authority to withhold the records under Exemption 3. We agree with the district court that both the records and photograph are exempt from disclosure under FOIA Exemption 3 and thus affirm that part of the judgment.

BACKGROUND

On October 7, 2003, Plaintiffs submitted a FOIA request to the CIA, DOJ, and other federal agencies, seeking the disclosure of records concerning (1) the treatment of detainees; (2) the deaths of detainees while in United States custody; and (3) the rendition, since September 11, 2001, of detainees and other individuals to countries known to employ torture or illegal interrogation methods. On January 31, 2005, Plaintiffs served a FOIA request on the OLC, incorporating by reference their October 7, 2003 request and enumerating a non-exhaustive list of documents falling within the scope of Plaintiffs' request.

Within a year of each request, Plaintiffs filed separate complaints seeking to compel the Government to release any responsive documents it had withheld from disclosure. With respect to the first action, the district court ordered the Government to produce or identify all records responsive to Plaintiffs' request. *ACLU v. Dep't of Def.*, 339 F. Supp. 2d 501, 505 (S.D.N.Y. 2004). Since that time, the Government has disclosed thousands of documents in response to Plaintiffs' FOIA requests.

I. FACTS AND PROCEDURAL HISTORY RELEVANT TO THE GOVERNMENT'S APPEAL

Among the documents disclosed by the Government are four memoranda authored by the OLC between August 1, 2002 and May 30, 2005, analyzing legal questions with respect to the application of EITs to detainees held in CIA custody abroad. The Government initially withheld these memoranda in full, but subsequently, on April 16, 2009, released unclassified versions of the memoranda with limited redactions. The classified information at issue in the Government's appeal is discussed in two of these memoranda, dated May 10, 2005 and May 30, 2005, respectively. The Government redacted references to the classified information—along with other information not relevant to this appeal—pursuant to FOIA Exemptions 1 and 3 on the basis that records related to "intelligence methods," "intelligence activities," and CIA "functions" are exempt from disclosure.[1] The parties filed cross-motions for summary judgment with regard to these redactions from the OLC memoranda.

The district court reviewed the unredacted OLC memoranda in a series of *ex parte, in camera* sessions. It also reviewed several declarations from high-level executive branch officials supporting the Government's withholding of the redacted information. At the first session, the district court issued a preliminary ruling that all but one of the references to the classified information must be disclosed, without explaining why it treated that sole reference differently. With respect to the other references, the district court held that publicly disclosing that information would reveal not an intelligence method but only a source of the CIA's authority. The district court also found that the references are so general in nature that their disclosure would not compromise national security. The district court nevertheless permitted the Government to submit additional declarations justifying its position that the information was exempt from disclosure.

---

1. Exemption 1 provides for the nondisclosure of matters that are "(A) specifically authorized under criteria established by an Executive order to be kept secret in the interest of national defense or foreign policy and (B) are in fact properly classified pursuant to such Executive order." 5 U.S.C. § 552(b)(1). Exemption 3 provides for the nondisclosure of matters that are "specifically exempted from disclosure by statute," provided that the statute "requires that the matters be withheld from the public in such a manner as to leave no discretion on the issue" or "establishes particular criteria for withholding or refers to particular types of matters to be withheld." *Id.* § 552(b)(3).

During a subsequent *in camera* session, the district court reaffirmed its preliminary ruling and explained that it viewed the classified information as a "source of authority" for interrogation rather than a "method of interrogation." As a compromise, however, the district court offered to allow the Government to replace references to the classified information with alternative language meant to preserve the meaning of the text. The district court acknowledged the national security concerns potentially raised by the disclosure of some of the classified information, but nevertheless ordered that the Government either disclose the information or comply with the court's proposed compromise. The district court also ordered that references to the classified information in the transcript of the first *ex parte, in camera* proceeding be disclosed or otherwise released in accordance with the compromise. The district court memorialized its oral ruling in a December 29, 2009 order. The Government now appeals from that order.

II. Facts and Procedural History Relevant to Plaintiffs' Cross-Appeal

Many of the documents released by the Government in response to Plaintiffs' FOIA requests relate to the use of EITs. During the course of this litigation, the President prohibited the future use of certain EITs, including waterboarding, formerly authorized for use on high-value detainees.[2] On May 7, 2009, the district court ordered the Government to compile a list of documents related to the contents of 92 destroyed videotapes of detainee interrogations that occurred between April and December 2002 and which would otherwise have been responsive to Plaintiffs' FOIA requests. Pursuant to that order, the CIA identified 580 documents and selected a sample of 65 documents for the district court to review for potential release. Specifically, the sample records comprise:

- 53 cables (operational communications) between CIA headquarters and an interrogation facility;
- 3 emails postdating the videotapes' destruction;
- 2 logbooks detailing observations of interrogation sessions;
- 1 set of handwritten notes from a meeting between a CIA employee and a CIA attorney;
- 2 memoranda containing descriptions of the contents of the videotapes;
- 1 set of handwritten notes taken during a review of the videotapes;

---

2. On January 22, 2009, the President issued an executive order terminating the CIA's detention and interrogation program and mandating that individuals in United States custody "not be subjected to any interrogation technique or approach, or any treatment related to interrogation, that is not authorized by and listed in Army Field Manual 2-22.3." Exec. Order No. 13,491, 74 Fed. Reg. 4,893, 4,894 (Jan. 22, 2009). Moreover, in an April 29, 2009 news conference, the President explained the basis for his ban on the use of waterboarding: "[W]aterboarding violates our ideals and our values. I do believe that is torture. I don't think that's just my opinion; that's the opinion of many who've examined the topic. And that's why I put an end to the practices." President Barack Obama, News Conference by the President (Apr. 29, 2009).

▓ 2 records summarizing details of waterboard exposures from the destroyed videotapes; and

▓ 1 photograph of Abu Zubaydah dated October 11, 2002.

The Government withheld these records pursuant to FOIA Exemptions 1 and 3, and the parties filed cross-motions for summary judgment with regard to whether the records were exempt from disclosure.

The Government defended its withholding of the records with three declarations of then-CIA Director Leon Panetta. The declarations explained that the records consist primarily of communications to CIA headquarters from a covert CIA facility where interrogations were being conducted, and include "sensitive intelligence and operational information concerning interrogations of Abu Zubaydah." With respect to Exemption 3, the declarations explained that, if disclosed, the records would "reveal intelligence sources and methods" employed by the CIA, as well as "the organization and functions of the CIA, including the conduct of clandestine intelligence activities to collect intelligence from human sources using interrogation methods." With respect to Exemption 1, the declarations asserted that the records were properly classified pursuant to Executive Order No. 12,958 and that their disclosure could reasonably be expected to result in harm to national security.

In response, Plaintiffs argued that the EITs were not "intelligence methods" within the meaning of the CIA's withholding authorities because they had been repudiated, and, in the case of waterboarding, declared unlawful by the President. Plaintiffs also argued that the CIA had failed to provide any explanation for withholding the photograph of Abu Zubaydah under either Exemption 1 or 3.

On September 30, 2009, the district court reviewed the photograph and a portion of the sample records in an ex *parte, in camera* session. With respect to the photograph of Abu Zubaydah, the Government asserted that it was "actually a CIA photo of a person in custody," and the court accepted the Government's position that a photograph of a detainee reveals "a lot more information" than the detainee's identity. During the public hearing, the district court rejected Plaintiffs' argument that the President's declaration was a sufficient basis for rejecting the Government's position. The district court explained that it would "decline to rule on the question of legality or illegality in the context of a FOIA request." Rebuffing Plaintiffs' argument that the photo should be produced because the Government offered no justification for its withholding, the district court sustained the withholding and explained that "the image of a person in a photograph is another aspect of information that is important in intelligence gathering."

In sustaining the withholding of the records under FOIA Exemption 3, the district court concluded that the CIA had satisfied its burden of showing that the release of the records could reasonably be expected to lead to unauthorized disclosure of intelligence sources and methods. The district court also rejected Plaintiffs' argument that records relating to illegal activities are beyond the scope of Exemption 3.

Plaintiffs limit their cross-appeal to those records reflecting the CIA's use of waterboard[ing and to the photograph of Abu Zubaydah.

DISCUSSION

The Freedom of Information Act calls for broad disclosure of Government records. But public disclosure of certain government records may not always be in the public interest. Thus, Congress provided that some records may be withheld from disclosure under any of nine exemptions.

An agency withholding documents responsive to a FOIA request bears the burden of proving the applicability of claimed exemptions. Affidavits or declarations giving reasonably detailed explanations why any withheld documents fall within an exemption are sufficient to sustain the agency's burden. We review the adequacy of the agency's justifications *de novo*. In the national security context, however, we must accord *substantial weight* to an agency's affidavit concerning the details of the classified status of the disputed record. Summary judgment is appropriate where the agency affidavits describe the justifications for nondisclosure with reasonably specific detail, demonstrate that the information withheld logically falls within the claimed exemption, and are not controverted by either contrary evidence in the record nor by evidence of agency bad faith. Ultimately, an agency may invoke a FOIA exemption if its justification appears logical or plausible.

I. The Government's Appeal — The OLC Memoranda

The Government contends that the information redacted from the OLC memoranda may be withheld from disclosure under either FOIA Exemption 1 or 3. In our view, Exemption 1 resolves the matter easily.[4] Exemption 1 permits the Government to withhold information "specifically authorized under criteria established by an Executive order to be kept secret in the interest of national defense or foreign policy" if that information has been "properly classified pursuant to such Executive order." 5 U.S.C. § 552(b)(1). The Government contends that the redacted information was properly classified under Executive Order No. 12,958, as amended, which authorized the classification of information concerning "intelligence activities (including special activities), intelligence sources or methods, or cryptology." Exec. Order No. 12,958 § 1.5(c) also required as a condition to classification that an original classification authority "determine[ ] that the unauthorized disclosure of the information reasonably could be expected to result in damage to the national security" and "is able to identify or describe the damage." Id. § 1.1(a)(4).

The district court held that the exemption was inapplicable because, in its view, the information pertains to a "source of authority" rather than a "method of interrogation." On appeal, as it did in the district court, the Government contends that the information pertains to an intelligence method and an intelligence

---

4. Because the FOIA Exemptions are independent of each other, we need only discuss why we conclude that the Government may invoke FOIA Exemption 1 to justify withholding the redacted information in the OLC memoranda.

activity, and that each category provides a basis for classification under Executive Order No. 12,958. In support of this contention, the Government has submitted declarations from General James L. Jones, then-Assistant to the President for National Security and National Security Advisor; General Michael V. Hayden, then-Director of the CIA; Leon Panetta, then-Director of the CIA; and Wendy M. Hilton, Information Review Officer for Detainee-Related Matters for the CIA.

Based on our *ex parte* and *in camera* review of the unredacted OLC memoranda and the Government's classified declarations, we agree with the Government that the redacted information was properly classified because it pertains to an intelligence activity. Plaintiffs concede that, even if we were to characterize the information as a "source of authority," "withholding [a] source of authority itself is . . . proper if disclosing it would reveal . . . intelligence sources, methods, or activities." Pls.' Br. 40-41. We give substantial weight to the Government's declarations, which establish that disclosing the redacted portions of the OLC memoranda would reveal the existence and scope of a highly classified, active intelligence activity.

We reject any notion that to sustain the Government's assertion that the withheld information concerns a protected "intelligence activity" under Executive Order No. 12,958 is effectively to exempt the CIA from FOIA's mandate. In response to Plaintiffs' FOIA requests and related court orders, the Government has already produced substantial information about its use of EITs, including almost all of the contents of the OLC memoranda. With regard to the limited material it has withheld from disclosure, the Government has sustained its burden by "giving reasonably detailed explanations" of how the information pertains to a classified intelligence activity.

On appeal, Plaintiffs do not dispute that the Government has established that public disclosure of the redacted information "reasonably could be expected to result in damage to the national security." Nor do we. We have consistently deferred to executive affidavits predicting harm to the national security, and have found it unwise to undertake searching judicial review. Recognizing the relative competencies of the executive and judiciary, we believe that it is bad law and bad policy to second-guess the predictive judgments made by the government's intelligence agencies regarding whether disclosure of the information redacted from the OLC memoranda would pose a threat to national security.

The Government's declarations describe in persuasive detail how revealing the redacted information would cause exceptionally grave harm to national security by (1) "damaging on-going activities and relationships with foreign intelligence liaison partners, which are of utmost importance to the CIA's overseas intelligence operations,"; (2) "alerting our adversaries of the existence of [the] intelligence method, which would give them the opportunity to alter their conduct to adapt to this new information and make future intelligence operations more dangerous and less effective,"; and (3) "increasing the risks for all individuals involved in those operations, including CIA officers and assets." According substantial weight and deference to the CIA's declarations, we conclude that it is both logical and plausible that the disclosure of the information pertaining to a CIA intelligence activity would harm national security.

Furthermore, we reject the district court's suggestion that certain portions of the redacted information are so general in relation to previously disclosed activities of the CIA that their disclosure would not compromise national security. It is true that the Government has disclosed significant aspects of the CIA's discontinued detention and interrogation program, but its declarations explain in great detail how the withheld information pertains to intelligence activities unrelated to the discontinued program. And even if the redacted information seems innocuous in the context of what is already known by the public, minor details of intelligence information may reveal more information than their apparent insignificance suggests because, much like a piece of jigsaw puzzle, each detail may aid in piecing together other bits of information even when the individual piece is not of obvious importance in itself. Again, it is both logical and plausible that disclosure of the redacted information would jeopardize the CIA's ability to conduct its intelligence operations and work with foreign intelligence liaison partners.

Both parties contend that the district court's compromise, whereby the Government could avoid public disclosure of the redacted information by substituting a purportedly neutral phrase composed by the court, exceeded the court's authority under FOIA. We agree. FOIA does not permit courts to compel an agency to produce anything other than responsive, non-exempt records. If the Government altered or modified the OLC memoranda in accordance with the compromise, the Government would effectively be "creating" documents—something FOIA does not obligate agencies to do. Moreover, given the "relative competencies of the executive and judiciary," the district court erred in "second-guess[ing]" the executive's judgment of the harm to national security that would likely result from disclosure, by crafting substitute text that—in its own view—would avoid the harms that could result from disclosure of the information in full.

The district court's apparent reliance on the Classified Information Procedures Act ("CIPA"), 18 U.S.C. app. 3, §§ 1-16, as a basis for the compromise was erroneous. Contrary to the district court's assertion, CIPA applies exclusively to criminal cases. Indeed, CIPA is codified as the third appendix to Title 18 of the U.S. Code, which concerns *crimes and criminal procedure*, and we have found no case law supporting the district court's adoption of CIPA in a FOIA context such as this.[9]

[The] Government has sustained its burden of proving that the information redacted from the OLC memoranda is exempt from disclosure under FOIA

---

9. The procedures of CIPA contrast sharply with those of FOIA. For example, under CIPA, when the court authorizes a defendant to disclose classified information during trial, the Government may move for the substitution of a summary of such classified information in lieu of the information itself, 18 U.S.C. app. 3, § 6(c), "to harmonize a defendant's right to obtain and present exculpatory material upon his trial and the government's right to protect classified material in the national interest," *United States v. Pappas*, 94 F.3d 795, 799 (2d Cir. 1996) (internal quotation marks omitted). Significantly, the Government retains ultimate control and may prevent a criminal defendant from disclosing classified information, with the consequence of the court either dismissing the indictment or taking another action adverse to the prosecution. *See* 18 U.S.C. app. 3, § 6(e). By contrast, the Government cannot walk away from a FOIA case in order to avoid disclosure of classified information.

Exemption 1. We therefore reverse the district court's judgment insofar as it required disclosure of the information—either in full or in accordance with the district court's compromise—in the OLC memoranda and the transcript of the district court's *ex parte, in camera* proceeding.

II. Materials at Issue in Plaintiffs' Cross-Appeal

The district court agreed with the Government that the records related to the contents of destroyed videotapes of detainee interrogations and a photograph of high-value detainee Abu Zubaydah in CIA custody may be withheld from disclosure under FOIA Exemption 3. Plaintiffs challenge the withholding of only those records relating to the CIA's use of waterboarding and the photograph.

Exemption 3 permits the Government to withhold information from public disclosure provided that: (1) the information is "specifically exempted from disclosure by statute"; and (2) the exemption statute "requires that the matters be withheld from the public in such a manner as to leave no discretion on the issue" or "establishes particular criteria for withholding or refers to particular types of matters to be withheld." 5 U.S.C. § 552(b)(3). Here, the Government contends that the records and photograph pertain to an "intelligence method" under section 102A(i)(1) of the National Security Act of 1947 ("NSA") and CIA "functions" under section 6 of the Central Intelligence Act of 1949, which include the collection of intelligence through human sources, see 50 U.S.C. § 403-4a(d).[10] Plaintiffs do not dispute that these statutes qualify as exemption statutes under Exemption 3. Thus, our only remaining inquiry is whether the withheld material relates to an intelligence method or functions of the CIA.

A. The Interrogation Records

Plaintiffs contend that the records regarding the use of waterboarding in particular instances do not relate to an "intelligence method" because the President has declared the practice of waterboarding illegal. Relying on the Supreme Court's decision in *CIA v. Sims*, Plaintiffs argue that the CIA may decline to disclose only records relating to those intelligence methods that fall within the CIA's charter. Plaintiffs argue that because an illegal activity cannot be said to "fall within the Agency's mandate to conduct foreign intelligence," waterboarding cannot be an "intelligence method" within the meaning of the CIA's withholding authorities.[12]

---

10. Section 102A(i)(1) of the National Security Act of 1947, as amended, 50 U.S.C. § 401 *et seq.*, requires the Director of National Intelligence to "protect intelligence sources and methods from unauthorized disclosure." 50 U.S.C. § 403-1(i)(1). Section 6 of the Central Intelligence Act of 1949, as amended, 50 U.S.C. § 403 *et seq.*, provides that the CIA shall be exempted from "the provisions of any other law which require the publication or disclosure" of the "functions" of the Agency. 50 U.S.C. § 403g.

12. Plaintiffs concede that an illegal act may produce information that may be properly withheld under FOIA Exemptions 1 and 3. Plaintiffs do not seek disclosure of information that may otherwise be classified for reasons apart from the fact that it would disclose details of the use of waterboarding. To the extent the records discuss such information, such as questions asked during an interrogation or intelligence gathered from an interrogation session, Plaintiffs agree that the information should be segregated and may remain classified.

We do not agree. *Sims* offers no support for Plaintiffs' proposed limitation upon the CIA's ability to protect information relating to intelligence methods. On the contrary, the *Sims* Court emphasized that the NSA "vested in the Director of Central Intelligence very broad authority to protect all sources of intelligence information from disclosure," and that judicial "narrowing of this authority not only contravenes the express intention of Congress, but also overlooks the practical necessities of modern intelligence gathering — the very reason Congress entrusted this Agency with sweeping power to protect its 'intelligence sources and methods.'" According to the Court, the "plain meaning" of "intelligence sources and methods" in this context, "may not be squared with any limiting definition that goes beyond the requirement that the information fall within the Agency's mandate to conduct foreign intelligence."

Here, Plaintiffs argue that the provision of the NSA requiring the Director of National Intelligence to "ensure compliance with the Constitution and laws of the United States," *see* 50 U.S.C. § 403-1(f)(4), delimits the Director's obligation under section 102A(i)(1) to "protect intelligence sources and methods from unauthorized disclosure," *see* 50 U.S.C. § 403-1(i)(1), and the concomitant rights under FOIA to decline to disclose. The statutory language does not, however, draw any such limitation, and to do so by judicial device would flout *Sims*'s clear directive against constricting the CIA's broad authority in this domain. Again, *Sims* expressly rejected any limitation on the CIA's duty to protect information "beyond the requirement that the information fall within the Agency's mandate to conduct foreign intelligence." Plaintiffs' argument lacks support in either the statute's text or in the case law interpreting that text.

Moreover, we are wary of the practical difficulties that would likely arise were the category of protectable intelligence methods circumscribed as Plaintiffs propose. In FOIA actions in which the government seeks to withhold information related to an intelligence method, an information officer and then the court would potentially be forced to engage in a complex inquiry to determine whether the government has sufficiently demonstrated the legality of the method to justify withholding. In this respect, we question how the court and the agency would handle varying assessments of legality. What becomes of information concerning a method that the President, on advice of counsel, considers legal, but which is later declared unlawful by a federal court or by a subsequent administration? Relatedly, is the legality of a method to be determined as of the time of the method's use or may a forward-looking proscription also apply retroactively to prevent reliance on an exemption? The matter currently before us helps illustrate the point. Even if we assumed that a President can render an intelligence method "illegal" through the mere issuance of public statements, or, more formally, through adoption of an executive order, and if we further assumed that President Obama's Executive Order coupled with his statements describing waterboarding as "torture" were sufficient in this regard, we would be left with the difficult task of determining what retroactive effect, if any, to assign that designation. In our view, such an "illegality" inquiry is clearly beyond the scope and purpose of FOIA.

Finally, we also note that prior courts faced with similar questions have declined to address the legality of an intelligence method as part of a FOIA analysis. In *ACLU v. U.S. Department of Defense*, the District of Columbia Circuit rejected the very argument raised by Plaintiffs here: that an interrogation technique formerly authorized for use on high-value detainees is no longer a protectable "intelligence method" for FOIA purposes if the President bans its future use. After noting that *Sims* "says nothing suggesting that the change in the specific techniques of intelligence gathering by the CIA renders unprotected sources and methods previously used," the court held that "the President's prohibition of the future use of certain interrogation techniques . . . does not diminish the government's otherwise valid authority to . . . withhold [information] from disclosure under exemptions 1 and 3."

In *Wilner v. NSA*, our Court considered whether the government could refuse to confirm or deny the existence of records obtained under the since-discontinued Terrorist Surveillance Program ("TSP"). The plaintiffs in *Wilner* claimed that the government had illegally obtained information about them through the TSP. They argued that the NSA improperly refused to disclose this information because any such records would have been obtained in violation of the U.S. Constitution. In concluding that the government properly withheld the information at issue under FOIA Exemption 3, we declined to reach "the legality of the underlying Terrorist Surveillance Program," reasoning that this question was "beyond the scope" of the plaintiffs' FOIA action.

We recognize that the plaintiffs in *Wilner* did not make the precise argument advanced here: that the statutory meaning of "intelligence methods" precludes the government from employing that label for a technique that the President has declared to be unlawful and thus outside the CIA's charter. But in our view, *Wilner*'s principle is equally applicable here—a judicial determination of the legality of waterboarding is beyond the scope of this FOIA action. For the foregoing reasons, we reject Plaintiffs' argument that the Government could not withhold information relating to waterboarding on the grounds that waterboarding is now "illegal" and therefore beyond the CIA's mandate.

According substantial weight to the CIA's declarations, we have no difficulty in concluding that the records in question, which we have reviewed *in camera*, relate to an intelligence method within the meaning of the NSA, and, accordingly, may be withheld. The parties agree that waterboarding was an interrogation method used by the CIA in connection with its foreign intelligence-gathering activities. Because the CIA's declarations are not contradicted by the record or undermined by any allegations of bad faith,[14] the Government has sustained its burden of proving that the records relating to the CIA's use of waterboarding are exempt from disclosure under FOIA Exemption 3.

---

14. In addition, Director Panetta confirmed that the records were withheld not to suppress evidence of any unlawful conduct but rather to protect intelligence sources and methods. We accord a "presumption of good faith" to this declaration.

B. The Photograph of Abu Zubaydah

Plaintiffs contend that the CIA failed to provide any justification for withholding a photograph of Abu Zubaydah taken while he was in CIA custody abroad and that the post hoc explanations offered by the Government's counsel do not suffice to justify the withholding. We disagree. In a June 8, 2009 unclassified declaration, Director Panetta explained that all of the records he reviewed in connection with his invocation of FOIA Exemptions 1 and 3, including the photograph, are "related to the contents of 92 destroyed videotapes of detainee interrogations that occurred between April and December 2002." Director Panetta further declared that "miscellaneous documents" in the sample records, including the photograph, "contain[ ] TOP SECRET operational information concerning the interrogations" of Abu Zubaydah. On appeal, the Government has expanded upon Director Panetta's justification for withholding by explaining that the photograph necessarily "relates to" an "intelligence source or method" because it records Abu Zubaydah's condition in the period during which he was interrogated.

We have reviewed the photograph *in camera*. Our examination has been informed by our contemporaneous review of other sample records. Like the district court, we observe that a photograph depicting a person in CIA custody discloses far more information than the person's identity. We agree with the district court that the image at issue here conveys an "aspect of information that is important to intelligence gathering," and that this information necessarily "relates to" an "intelligence source or method." The Government's justification for withholding the photograph is thus both "logical and plausible." Moreover, Director Panetta's declaration is entitled to substantial weight, and this Court must adopt a "deferential posture in FOIA cases regarding the uniquely executive purview of national security." Accordingly, we affirm the district court's conclusion that the Government has adequately justified its withholding of the photograph under FOIA Exemption 3.

NOTES AND QUESTIONS

1. The court references "the contents of 92 destroyed videotapes of detainee interrogations that . . . would otherwise have been responsive to Plaintiffs' FOIA requests." These videotapes, recording the waterboarding of Abu Zubaydah, Abd al Rahim al Nashiri, and Khalid Sheikh Mohammed, were deliberately destroyed on November 9, 2005, by order of Jose Rodriguez Jr., head of the CIA's clandestine service. Rodriguez, who was reprimanded by the CIA but not prosecuted, explained his reasoning to a journalist: "You really doubt that those tapes would not be out in the open now, that they would not be on YouTube? They would be out there, they would have been leaked, or somebody would have ordered their release." Tabassum Zakaria, *Ex-CIA Official Says Tapes Destroyed to Prevent al Qaeda Reprisals*, REUTERS, Apr. 30, 2012. In his memoirs, Rodriguez explained that he was tired of the "seemingly endless debate" and string of

"[j]ust another lawyer saying: 'I'd rather you not. . . .'" Jose A. Rodriguez, Jr., Hard Measures: How Aggressive CIA Actions After 9/11 Saved American Lives 191-92 (2013). Rodriguez explains:

> To make sure we got the right question, so that we could give the right answer, . . . our own lawyers who were separate from the larger contingent in the General Counsel's Office . . . drafted a cable that could be sent to the field with instructions that they cut and paste the appropriate language from the cable and put it into their own cable back to us. The instructions basically were: "Ask us in this way and we will say yes." The draft language was sent to the Office of the General Counsel for coordination at the same time it was sent to the field.
>
> The next day, a Saturday, the field dutifully sent a cable to headquarters asking for permission to destroy the tapes. The language was just right, of course, since our lawyers had drafted it. I asked my chief of staff to prepare a cable granting permission. On most matters I would just instruct my staff on what action to take and let them handle the administrative details. But this had been such an ordeal that I wanted to personally handle [it.] My chief of staff drafted a cable approving the action that we had been trying to accomplish for so long. The cable left nothing to chance. It even told them *how* to get rid of the tapes. They were to use an industrial-strength shredder to do the deed. On Tuesday, . . . after scrutinizing the cable on my computer for a while, I thought about the decision. I was not depriving anyone of information about what was done or what was said, I was just getting rid of some ugly visuals that could put the lives of my people at risk. I took a deep breath of weary satisfaction and hit Send.[6]

Assume that Rodriguez did not commit a crime in ordering the destruction of the tapes and that he was fully within the authority of his office to make such a decision. Does his action nevertheless call into question the "presumption of good faith" that the court was willing to give to CIA declarations? What would or should be sufficient to overcome such a presumption in this context?

2. Consider the two now iconic photographs, on the next page, from the Abu Ghraib prison outside Baghdad. These were leaked to the press. But imagine the following hypothetical. You represented a government agency in possession of these photographs, which have *not* been leaked or otherwise publicly disclosed. A FOIA request is made seeking the disclosure of records concerning "conditions of confinement of detainees in U.S. custody in Iraq." How should you respond? Consider that Exemptions 6 and 7 are among the most commonly invoked grounds to withhold agency records, amounting to 84.7 percent of exemptions cited by federal agencies in FY 2015. *See* Department of Justice, Summary of Annual FOIA Reports for Fiscal Year 2015, at 7. Now put yourself into the shoes of the FOIA requester. Did your request "reasonably describe" these pictures (which you have not seen and few would have imagined possible before they were revealed)?

---

6. *Id.* at 192-93.

3. David McCraw is the lead lawyer at the *New York Times* for its FOIA litigation. He is not sanguine about the value of the Freedom of Information Act to uncover information for timely reporting on national security issues: "[M]eaningful victories in national security FOIA cases remain legal unicorns." In a post on the website "Just Security," a blog devoted to national security legal issues, he noted some of his sharpest concerns:

> The case for disclosure is often compelling as a matter of democracy and self-governance, but in FOIA lawsuits a cluster of small-bore but powerful rules shape the narrative and too often defeat transparency. Anyone looking to [sic] for places to reform FOIA might start with these:
>
> **A presumption of good faith attaches to the Government's affidavits.** Virtually every FOIA case gets decided on competing motions for summary judgment. The Government makes its case through affidavits from agency officials, who inevitably proclaim in generic language, literally repeated from case to case, how important secrecy is. . . . The agencies then get the powerful advantage of having a "presumption of good faith" attach to their declarations, making them largely unchallengeable.
>
> **Discovery is almost never allowed in FOIA cases.** The defining feature of American civil litigation is discovery, where the parties get to depose witnesses. Then there is FOIA, largely a discovery-free zone, even when the facts used to justify withholding are critical and dubious.
>
> The rationale for barring discovery is murky. Some argue it makes no sense in a case involving secrecy to ask witnesses to testify about what they cannot reveal—even though the same is true in trade secret cases where discovery rages on unabated.
>
> **The Government doubles down on secrecy with the National Security and CIA Acts.** FOIA's Exemption 1 allows agencies to withhold material that is properly classified under Executive Order 13526. As wide-ranging as the Executive Order is, the Government is still required to show that disclosure "reasonably could be expected to cause identifiable or describable damage to national security." Not so with the National Security and CIA Acts. They allow secrecy with no showing that any harm might result from disclosure.
>
> **The waiver doctrine remains an absurdity.** When *The New York Times* and the ACLU won the release of two Justice Department memos providing the legal justification for the killing of Anwar al-Awlaki in Yemen, we did so on the basis of waiver. Simply put, officials had disclosed so much about the topic publicly, they had lost the right to keep the memos secret.
>
> Yet to get to that result, the Second Circuit had to put aside what most FOIA waiver cases have held: Any waiver extends only to information that is a "match" of what is publicly disclosed. As the Second Circuit said, if the waiver doctrine were taken literally, it would allow FOIA requesters to obtain only what they already know—which is precisely the opposite of what FOIA is supposed to be about.
>
> **The Government gets too much credit from the courts for faux releases.** After a dozen national security FOIA cases, I have become accustomed to the "faux release." We sue, and the agency then tells the court that it will review the documents and release what it can. Several months later, we begin receiving documents. Were redaction an art form, we could open a gallery. . . . The Government

then comes back to the court to talk about the hundreds or thousands of pages that were dutifully reprocessed and released. Few courts are interested in doing a deep dive into the documents to see what has actually been disclosed.[7]

III. WHO IS THE PRESS? THE STORY OF WIKILEAKS . . . AND BEYOND

As the citation to Mr. McCraw's "Just Security" blog post suggests, the internet is a brave new world to explore in search of the meaning of "the Press."[8] "Just Security," like "Lawfare," and other internet-only resources, are very serious enterprises for cutting edge news and analysis about national security issues. But are the people who post content on those platforms "journalists"? Are the platforms themselves the equivalent of newspapers, magazines, or other traditional news sources entitled to the full protection of the First Amendment? The website-as-newspaper presents the Court the same dilemmas that it confronted with other emerging technologies in the past. *Cf. Red Lion Broadcasting Co. v. FCC*, 395 U.S. 367 (1969) (unanimously upholding "fairness doctrine" regulation of broadcast media, requiring equal time and opportunity-to-reply on public issues) *with Miami Herald v. Tornillo*, 418 U.S. 241 (1974) (unanimously striking down similar fairness doctrine regulation of print newspapers), *and Turner Broadcasting System Inc. v. FCC*, 512 U.S. 622 (1994) (holding that lower *Red Lion* standard of review did not apply to cable television) *with Reno v. ACLU*, 521 U.S. 844 (1997) (holding that internet-based content is entitled to full First Amendment protection, distinguishing cases upholding regulation of broadcast media as inapplicable to cyberspace). As Justice Stevens observed, distinguishing the internet from media subject to greater regulation (and lower levels of judicial scrutiny): "Through the use of chat rooms, any person with a phone line

---

7. David McCraw, *FOIA Litigation Has Its Own Rules, But We Deserve Better*, Just Security, Mar. 15, 2016.

8. The Freedom of Information Act—which, as Mr. McCraw's post suggests, is not considered the most felicitous of vehicles for journalistic discovery—contains a surprisingly progressive definition of "a representative of the news media," who is considered (for purposes of assessing processing fees) to be

> any person or entity that gathers information of potential interest to a segment of the public, uses its editorial skills to turn the raw materials into a distinct work, and distributes that work to an audience. In this clause, the term "news" means information that is about current events or that would be of current interest to the public. Examples of news-media entities are television or radio stations broadcasting to the public at large and publishers of periodicals (but only if such entities qualify as disseminators of "news") who make their products available for purchase by or subscription by or free distribution to the general public. These examples are not all-inclusive. Moreover, as methods of news delivery evolve (for example, the adoption of the electronic dissemination of newspapers through telecommunications services), such alternative media shall be considered to be news-media entities. A freelance journalist shall be regarded as working for a news-media entity if the journalist can demonstrate a solid basis for expecting publication through that entity, whether or not the journalist is actually employed by the entity.

5 U.S.C. § 552(a)(4)(A)(ii).

can become a town crier with a voice that resonates farther than it could from any soapbox. Through the use of Web pages, mail exploders, and newsgroups, the same individual can become a pamphleteer." *Id.* at 870.[9]

What about the people who post material to "WikiLeaks"? Are they journalists and is that forum the digital equivalent of a newspaper or periodical? Is it entitled to the same protections as the institutional press? WikiLeaks provides a good source for such questions, but few answers about the relationship between the rule of law, a free press, the internet, and national security. Recall Justice Potter Stewart's description of the power of a free press as "a conspiracy of the intellect, with the courage of numbers." That doesn't quite seem to capture the idea of WikiLeaks, which its founder Julian Assange described as an "uncensorable system for untraceable mass document leaking."[10] WikiLeaks is a repository of leaked, often highly classified, government documents made public through the internet.

In *Bartnicki v. Vopper*, 532 U.S. 514 (2001), a cell phone conversation between union officials about a public collective-bargaining negotiation was unlawfully intercepted by an unknown person, who supplied a tape for broadcast on radio and publication in newspapers. The Court held that "a stranger's illegal conduct does not suffice to remove the First Amendment shield from speech about a matter of public concern." *Id.* at 535. The case, decided less than four months before 9/11, has been taken to protect news media who find themselves in possession of government documents supplied by would-be whistleblowers or less altruistic leaks of information. Of course, the "Pentagon Papers" case, *New York Times v. United States*, itself concerned stolen documents, although the focus in that case was on the validity of a prior restraint in the form of a court injunction, not criminal liability for its publication.

The availability of First Amendment protections for a WikiLeaks-type enterprise is, at best, undecided. The same cannot be said about the legality of the actions of some who have provided WikiLeaks its most widely known documents. Private First Class Bradley Manning (now known as Chelsea Manning) was convicted at a court-martial and sentenced to thirty-five years in prison for, *inter alia*, violating the Espionage Act of 1917 for giving WikiLeaks hundreds of thousands of classified government documents including diplomatic cables, video, and other materials concerning military action in Iraq, Afghanistan, and Guantanamo Bay.[11] Over the course

---

9. On the other side of the spectrum from those who might consider themselves to be journalists are individuals who would use the new "public square" that social media presents for speech that most would regard as in the highest degree odious, if not dangerous. What are the national security implications for uses of social media that glorify violence or share propaganda about terrorists and terrorist groups? Such speech is unprotected by the First Amendment only when it can be said to be intended, and likely, to cause imminent, illegal conduct. *See, e.g.*, Rachel VanLandingham, *Words We Fear: Burning Tweets and the Politics of Incitement*, 85 Brook. L. Rev. 37 (2019) (discussing the limits of government pressure on social media companies to remove content protected by the First Amendment).

10. Stephen Moss, *Julian Assange: The Whistleblower*, The Guardian, July 13, 2010.

11. An attempt to obtain greater public access to the court-martial, citing the Sixth Circuit's *Detroit Free Press* opinion, was unsuccessful. *See Center for Constitutional Rights v. Lind*, 954 F. Supp. 2d 389 (D. Md. 2013).

of 2010, WikiLeaks made much of this material publicly accessible with the help of traditional print media such as the *New York Times* and *The Guardian* (UK).[12]

After the involvement of WikiLeaks in these publications became clear, the U.S. Department of Justice began a criminal investigation of the organization and its founder, Julian Assange, including for possible violation of the Espionage Act (including as conspirators with Manning). In June 2012, Assange sought political asylum from Ecuador, avoiding arrest by sheltering in its embassy in London. A complaint was filed and arrest warrant issued in a sealed case in the U.S. District Court for the Eastern District of Virginia in late December 2017. The case was unsealed following Assange's arrest on April 11, 2019, after the Ecuadorian government withdrew asylum and permitted British police to forcibly remove Assange from its embassy. A superseding indictment filed in May 2019 charged Assange with multiple counts of violating the Espionage Act as well as with conspiracy to commit computer intrusion under 18 U.S.C. 371 and 1030. *See* Superseding Indictment, United States v. Julian Paul Assange, 1:18-cr-00111-CMH (E.D. Va. May 23, 2019).

The multiple Espionage Act counts were added in the 37-page superseding indictment; the original, six-page indictment alleged in only a single count that Assange had conspired with Manning to access a government computer without authorization. Assange, imprisoned in the United Kingdom, opposes his extradition to the United States on the grounds that (in violation of the extradition treaty between the US and the UK) he is being prosecuted for "political offenses". At the time of this writing, his extradition hearing has been postponed due to the coronavirus pandemic.

Is Julian Assange a journalist? Are his actions through WikiLeaks distinguishable (as a matter of fact or law or both) from the work of a national security investigative reporter for the *New York Times*?

---

12. In 2013, Edward Snowden, then a contractor at the National Security Agency, provided an extraordinary volume of information about classified NSA surveillance programs to journalists Glenn Greenwald and Laura Poitras, who then used the material to disclose the programs in *The Guardian* and other newspapers. Snowden was also charged under the Espionage Act but fled to Moscow where the Russian government granted him asylum.

ASSESSMENT QUESTIONS

1. Assume that you are a popular blogger on a website devoted to national security questions. A highly sensitive document that is unclassified but marked "For Official Use Only" comes into your possession. It is the manual used by the intelligence community to create, manage, and use terrorist watchlists (such as the "No-Fly List"). The editors of the website are concerned about the effect of publishing the material. What cases and legal principles should you consider as you decide what to do with the material?

2. Although the Third Circuit Court of Appeals and the Sixth Circuit Court of Appeals came to different conclusions about the right of access to deportation proceedings, they agreed on the applicable legal test. What is the test and how did the courts differ in its application?

3. Evaluate the legal and practical impediments to journalistic reliance on the Freedom of Information Act as a news-gathering source for national security issues.

ASSESSMENT ANSWERS

1. What is the nature of the document itself? Is the document more analogous to the "Pentagon Papers" (*New York Times v. United States*) or "the sailing dates of transports or the number and location of troops" (*Near v. State of Minnesota ex rel. Olson*)? Exploring answers to these questions will aid you and your colleagues in deciding whether the government would succeed in enjoining publication (if you either decide to notify the government in advance or serialize the release of the document and articles about it). What is the relationship between you and the person who supplied the document? If the document fell into your lap without any interaction with the source, *Bartnicki v. Vopper* might protect you ("a stranger's illegal conduct does not suffice to remove the First Amendment shield from speech about a matter of public concern"). Close interaction with the source could lead to potential criminal exposure, as the ongoing case of WikiLeaks and Julian Assange suggests.

2. The test is the two-part "experience and logic" test in *Richmond Newspapers, Inc. v. Virginia*, 448 U.S. 555 (1980). The Sixth Circuit (*Detroit Free Press v. Ashcroft*) found that the Creppy Directive closing the hearings violated both prongs of the test. First, such hearings have traditionally been open to the public. Second, the Sixth Circuit found that public access played "a significant positive role in the functioning of the particular process in question." The Third Circuit (*North Jersey Media Group v. Ashcroft*) adopted the same test but concluded that the experience prong should be applied to the broader category of "political branch proceedings" (which presented no such overarching tradition of open, public

access). Even if the narrower category of deportation hearings was examined in isolation, these did not present a "tradition of openness sufficient to satisfy *Richmond Newspapers.*" Next, turning to the logic prong, the court concluded that "the extent to which openness impairs the public good" had to be examined alongside any "significant positive role" to open public access. Seen in this dual light, the court was "unable to conclude that openness plays a positive role in special interest deportation hearings at a time when our nation is faced with threats of such profound and unknown dimension."

3. As a legal matter, the general policy toward disclosure found in the FOIA is most restricted in the national security context. Exemptions 1, 3, 7, and arguably others provide the legal basis to withhold documents from disclosure. In addition, courts tend to defer to agency judgments in this area. As a practical matter, the FOIA process is slowed by large backlogs and delays that make it unwieldy in a fast-paced reporting environment.

PART V

ECONOMIC SANCTIONS AND OTHER NATIONAL SECURITY TOPICS

CHAPTER 15

Economic Powers and National Security

I. INTRODUCTION

Historically, the United States has used economic sanctions to influence the conduct of foreign governments that threaten vital national security interests.[1] For example, for decades economic sanctions have been imposed against Iran for sponsoring acts of terrorism and to prevent Iran from developing nuclear weapons of mass destruction. The Iranian economic sanctions have their genesis in the Iranian revolution and American embassy hostage crisis of 1979, and continue to the present. Economic sanctions have been imposed against other nations such as Afghanistan, North Korea, Sudan, and Syria for threatening United States national security.

Economic sanctions have been imposed against non-state entities such as al Qaeda, the Islamic State of Iraq and Syria (ISIS), and affiliated terrorist organizations, as well as suspected terrorists and their financial sponsors. Generally, economic sanctions prohibit U.S. persons from conducting financial transactions with sanctioned countries and designated entities and individuals, and require that their assets located in the United States or otherwise subject to the jurisdiction of the United States be blocked or frozen. However, economic sanctions advance several other important goals. These sanctions deny terrorists access to the United States financial system and commercial markets. Investigating terrorist financial networks may "expose terrorist financing 'money trails' that may generate leads to previously unknown terrorist cells and financiers."[2] Moreover, blocking the assets

---

1. For a comprehensive discussion of economic sanctions to protect national security, see Geoffrey S. Corn et al., National Security Law — Principles and Policy 372-425 (2015) (hereinafter "National Security Law").

2. U.S. Dep't of Treasury, National Money Laundering Strategy 7 (2003), *available at* http://www.treasury.gov/offices/enforcement/publications/ml2003.pdf. *See also* National Commission on Terrorist Attacks, The 9/11 Commission Report: Final Report of the National Commission on Terrorist Attacks upon the United States 382 (2004) ("The government has recognized that information about terrorist money helps us to understand their networks, search them out, and disrupt their operations.").

of terrorist front companies, shutting down corrupt charities, and arresting terrorist donors may deter others from providing financial support to terrorist organizations. Further, "disrupting the channels of funding may force terrorists to use riskier and less efficient and reliable means to move money globally to finance terrorist activities."[3]

Both Congress and the President play an important role in implementing economic sanctions. For example, Congress passed the Comprehensive Iran Sanctions, Accountability, and Divestment Act of 2010 (CISADA), Pub. L. No. 111-195, 124 Stat. 1312 (2010) (codified in part at 50 U.S.C § 1701 (note)). CISADA expanded the Iran Sanctions Act by targeting Iran's ability to make or import gasoline and placing new restrictions on financial institutions.[4] At the same time, presidential executive orders targeting suspected terrorists, foreign terrorist organizations, and their financial sponsors have been a powerful counter-terrorism tool.[5] Ultimately, the use of economic sanctions is an essential component of any effective national security strategy.

The International Emergency Economic Powers Act (IEEPA), 50 U.S.C. §§ 1701 et seq., the legal authority for imposing U.S. economic sanctions, will be examined at length in this chapter. More specifically, the chapter will explore the scope of application of the IEEPA, and constitutional challenges to the statute, including claims that the IEEPA violates separation of powers and the nondelegation doctrine and whether economic sanctions imposed under the IEEPA fail to provide adequate notice to the targets of blocking actions in violation of the void-for-vagueness and overbreadth doctrines. The chapter will also consider whether blocking actions under the IEEPA constitute an unreasonable seizure under the Fourth Amendment.

II. INTERNATIONAL EMERGENCY ECONOMIC POWERS ACT (IEEPA)

A. General Overview

The legal authority to block the assets of state sponsors of terrorism, suspected terrorists, and foreign terrorist organizations derives from the International Emergency Economic Powers Act (IEEPA), 50 U.S.C. §§ 1701 et seq. The IEEPA was enacted in 1977 to amend the Trading with the Enemy Act of 1917 (TWEA), 50 U.S.C. App. §§ 1-44. The TWEA grants the President the authority to regulate financial transactions involving enemy nations, including their nationals and allies, during a "time of war." 50 U.S.C. App. § 5(b)(1). However, TWEA has not always been limited to time of war, and has been used to regulate international trade during a "national emergency." *United States v. Amirnazmi*, 645 F.3d 564, 572 (3d

---

3. JIMMY GURULÉ & GEOFFREY S. CORN, PRINCIPLES OF COUNTER-TERRORISM LAW 295-96 (2011).

4. For a discussion of legislation enacted by Congress to curtail Iran's ability to develop a nuclear weapon and support acts of international terrorism, see NATIONAL SECURITY LAW 385-90.

5. For a discussion of Executive Order 13224, which is intended to block the assets of members of al Qaeda and associated groups and individuals, see NATIONAL SECURITY LAW 402-20.

Cir. 2011). In 1977, Congress amended TWEA, restricting the President's authority to times of declared war—as provided in the original Act. Contemporaneously, Congress enacted IEEPA, which authorizes the President to impose economic sanctions during national emergency situations.

The IEEPA grants the President broad authority to impose economic sanctions to deal with peacetime emergencies originating abroad. To trigger these powers, the President must declare a national emergency with respect to "any unusual and extraordinary threat, which has its source in whole or in substantial part outside of the United States, to the national security, foreign policy or economy of the United States." 50 U.S.C. § 1701(b). Once a national emergency has been declared, the IEEPA affords the President sweeping powers to impose controls over economic transactions and property in which a foreign nation or foreign person has any interest. *Id.* § 1701(a)(1). Under IEEPA, for example, the President may block (1) any foreign exchange transaction; (2) any transfer of credit or payments involving any interest of a foreign state or national thereof; and (3) the import or export of currency or securities, subject to the jurisdiction of the United States. *Id.*

The exercise of powers authorized under IEEPA involves a three-step process. First, the President issues an executive order declaring a national emergency that threatens the national security, foreign policy, or economy of the United States. The order describes the nature of the national emergency and the foreign country, persons, and entities that are covered by the order. The executive order usually includes a list of individuals and entities subject to economic sanctions under IEEPA. Second, the government cabinet member delegated the responsibility of implementing the order may designate additional foreign individuals and entities meeting the President's sanctions criteria and covered by the executive order. Third, the Treasury Department's Office of Foreign Assets Control (OFAC)—the federal agency charged with enforcement of economic sanctions—orders the blocking of all property of, and prohibits transactions involving, the designated individuals and entities.

Under 50 U.S.C. § 1705(a), it is "unlawful for a person to violate, attempt to violate, conspire to violate, or cause a violation of any license, order, regulation or prohibition" issued pursuant to IEEPA. *Id.* § 1705(a). The IEEPA provides a civil penalty of up to $250,000 or twice the amount of the culpable transaction for each IEEPA violation. *Id.* § 1705(b). However, a person who "willfully" violates, attempts, conspires to commit, or aids and abets a violation of any license, order, regulation, or prohibition issued under the IEEPA may be fined up to $1 million or imprisoned for not more than twenty years, or both. *Id.* § 1705(c).

B. Iranian Economic Sanctions

The United States has used economic sanctions against Iran since the Iranian revolution and the hostage crisis of 1979, making it the longest standing and most comprehensive sanctions regime that the United States has imposed against a nation-state.[6] For decades, U.S. presidents have issued executive orders in response

---

6. The general discussion of Iranian economic sanctions is taken in large part from Jimmy Gurulé & Geoffrey S. Corn, National Security Law: Principles and Policy 393-410 (2d ed. 2019).

to Iran-sponsored acts of terrorism.[7] In January 1984, the State Department declared Iran a state sponsor of terrorism (SST) after Iran's support of Hizballah, the foreign terrorist organization that claimed responsibility for the 1983 suicide bombings of the American embassy and U.S. Marine Corps barracks in Beirut, Lebanon. Iran's designation as an SST resulted in the imposition of a wide range of economic sanctions including a ban on arms sales and direct U.S. financial assistance to Iran. Even so, the United States continued to buy petroleum from Iran and by 1987, the regime had become the second largest supplier of oil to the United States. On March 6, 1995, President Clinton issued Executive Order (E.O.) 12957, prohibiting U.S. investment in Iran's energy sector, and E.O. 12959 two months later, banning all trade with Iran, including trade by the foreign subsidiaries of American corporations. By broadly prohibiting all imports from and exports to Iran, E.O. 12959 formed the foundation of the United States' sanctions regime against Iran. However, E.O. 12959 still did not prevent Iran from selling its oil to other foreign countries. In response, Congress enacted the Iran and Libya Sanctions Act of 1996 (ISA), which imposed sanctions against foreign firms that satisfied requisite threshold levels of involvement in Iran's energy sector. This was the first time the United States imposed "secondary sanctions," forcing foreign firms to choose between participating in the U.S. commercial market and doing business with Iran. The ISA was widely unpopular and criticized by the international community because of the restrictions it imposed on U.S. trading partners.

Since the mid-2000s, U.S. sanctions have focused on preventing Iran from developing weapons of mass destruction, or at least ensuring that its nuclear program be used only for civilian purposes. In 2005, President George W. Bush issued Executive Order 13382, imposing economic sanctions against Iran to prevent the development of nuclear, biological, and chemical weapons.[8] President Obama continued to expand the sanctions regime against Iran by issuing multiple executive orders that prohibited various foreign entities from doing business with Iran.[9]

On July 14, 2015, President Obama signed the Joint Comprehensive Plan of Action (JCPOA), an agreement between the United States, Russia, China, France, Great Britain, and Germany (P5+1), the European Union, and Iran.[10] The purpose of JCPOA is to prevent Iran from obtaining a nuclear weapon and ensure that Iran uses its nuclear program exclusively for peaceful purposes. On May 8, 2018,

---

7. President Carter: Exec. Order No. 12170, 44 Fed. Reg. 65729 (Nov. 14, 1979); Exec. Order No. 12205, 45 Fed. Reg. 24099 (Apr. 7, 1980); Exec. Order No. 12211, 45 Fed. Reg. 26685 (Apr. 17, 1980). President Reagan: Exec. Order No. 12282, 46 Fed. Reg. 7925 (Jan. 19, 1981); Exec. Order No. 12613, 52 Fed. Reg. 41940 (Oct. 28, 1987). President Clinton: Exec. Order No. 12957, 60 Fed. Reg. 14615 (Mar. 15, 1995); Exec. Order No. 12959, 60 Fed. Reg. 24757 (May 6, 1995); Exec. Order No. 13059, 62 Fed. Reg. 44531 (Aug. 21, 1997).

8. President George W. Bush: Exec. Order No. 13382, 70 Fed. Reg. 38567 (June 28, 2005).

9. President Obama: Exec. Order No. 13590, 76 Fed. Reg. 72609 (Nov. 20, 2011); Exec. Order No. 13599, 77 Fed. Reg. 6659 (Feb. 5, 2012); Exec. Order No. 13608, 77 Fed. Reg. 26409 (May 1, 2012); Exec. Order No. 13622, 77 Fed. Reg. 45897 (July 30, 2012); Exec. Order No. 13645, 78 Fed. Reg. 33945 (June 3, 2013).

10. Joint Comprehensive Plan of Action, July 14, 2015, https://2009-2017.state.gov/documents/organization/245317.pdf.

President Trump announced that the United States would terminate its participation in the JCPOA.[11] As a result, nuclear-related sanctions that the United States lifted pursuant to the JCPOA were re-imposed. President Trump maintained that Iran entered into the agreement in bad faith and that the agreement had undermined any leverage the United States had gained from previous sanctions. The reinstatement of U.S. sanctions has damaged the Iranian economy by prohibiting U.S. and foreign companies from purchasing oil from Iran. As such, U.S. sanctions against Iran continue to play a strategic role in U.S. foreign policy and national security, while the courts continue to assess the scope of their application.

C. Legal Challenges

Economic sanctions imposed under IEEPA have been challenged on constitutional grounds, including claims that IEEPA regulations are the product of an unconstitutional delegation of legislative authority to the executive branch, that IEEPA violates the separation of powers, that IEEPA is unconstitutionally vague in violation of the Fifth Amendment Due Process Clause, and that blocking actions violate the Fourth Amendment ban on unreasonable search and seizure. Furthermore, in the case of a criminal prosecution for a willful violation of IEEPA, defendants often maintain that the government failed to establish the requisite mens rea to sustain a conviction. The following cases examine the constitutional challenges to IEEPA.

United States v. Amirnazmi
645 F.3d 564 (3d Cir. 2011)

Scirica, Circuit Judge.

In pursuit of his stated goal of transforming the Islamic Republic of Iran into a global chemical powerhouse, Ali Amirnazmi, a chemical engineer, marketed a dynamic software program to Iranian actors and entered into agreements with various Iranian entities in which he pledged to provide technology to facilitate the construction of multiple chemical plants. Following a jury trial, Amirnazmi was convicted on ten charges—four counts stemming from violations of the International Emergency Economic Powers Act (IEEPA), three counts of making false statements, and three counts of bank fraud. Amirnazmi moved both for a judgment of acquittal and for a new trial. The District Court denied both motions and sentenced him to a four-year prison term. We will affirm.

I.

Amirnazmi, a dual citizen of the United States and Iran, founded a company called TranTech Consultants, Inc., in 1981. Billed as a business geared

---

11. Remarks by President Trump on the Joint Comprehensive Plan of Action, May 8, 2018, https://www.whitehouse.gov/briefings-statements/remarks-president-trump-joint-comprehensive-plan-action/.

toward providing "an innovative approach to strategic decision making for the Chemical Process Industries," TranTech marketed its primary product — a computer software program called ChemPlan — as an "exclusive, fully integrated, worldwide database" designed to allow chemical companies to assess product viability and cost based on a number of variables. ChemPlan had two principal functions. As a database that illuminated how chemical reactions could be disaggregated into their component parts, it included both public information and proprietary data derived from Amirnazmi's expert analysis of the various processes. And as a dynamic planning tool, ChemPlan enabled end users to determine individualized production costs and the feasibility of embarking on prospective projects by allowing them to change the input variables in order to generate "what if" scenarios accounting for market fluctuations. These features made ChemPlan attractive to major manufacturers such as the Dow Chemical Company, LyondellBasell Industries, and Rohm and Haas Company.

Aiming to facilitate Iran's transformation into "an independent chemical powerhouse," and seeking to spur "a flow of Iranian [ ] [scientists] back to Iran" where he would ultimately join them to impart his expertise, Amirnazmi began, in the mid-1990s, to explore business partnerships with Iranian entities. First, he initiated efforts to sell ChemPlan to the state-owned National Petrochemical Company of Iran (NPC). In August 1997, TranTech and NPC executed a Software/Data License Agreement whereby NPC agreed to purchase a subscription to ChemPlan for $64,000. Amirnazmi directed NPC to wire payment to a European bank account, and he traveled to Iran to demonstrate the product's functionality to NPC officials. In 1998, NPC purchased a software update for $18,000. In 2000, NPC enlisted Amirnazmi's assistance in its quest to obtain an off-the-shelf software package called BoxScore, a suite of programs manufactured in the United States and consequently unavailable to Iranian entities affected by U.S. trade sanctions. Amirnazmi procured the software, sent it to an intermediary in Germany, and charged NPC $667.85 for his efforts. . . .

After indicating he was willing to conduct business with Iran, Amirnazmi was granted a private audience with Iranian President Mahmoud Ahmadinejad at an event in New York City in September 2006. At this meeting and in subsequent correspondence, Amirnazmi expressed his desire to transfer ChemPlan's technical and economic knowledge to Iran and sought President Ahmadinejad's assistance in helping him return to Iran so that he might serve the country in his "field of expertise." In a January 2007 letter, Amirnazmi beseeched President Ahmadinejad to arrange an in-person meeting in Tehran so that he might unveil his "plan" to help Iran, and he decried the United States' "cruel and tyran[nical]" treatment of the Iranian people.

Having brought himself to President Ahmadinejad's attention, Amirnazmi's efforts to improve Iran's chemical capacities began to show results. In December 2007, Amirnazmi (on behalf of TranTech) signed a Memorandum of Understanding with the Institute for Business Analysis and Consultancy (IBACO), an Iranian company, regarding the provision of technology for a proposed polyvinyl butyral chemical plant to be constructed in Iran. In May 2008,

Amirnazmi entered into a separate confidentiality agreement with IBACO in which he agreed to have TranTech provide software licensing, equipment and chemicals in connection with the construction of a glacial acrylic acid and super absorbent polymer plant in Iran. . . .

Amirnazmi drew the attention of U.S. Customs and Border Protection by traveling to Iran in 2007 and twice more in 2008. Customs agents interviewed Amirnazmi upon his return to the United States in both April and June of 2008. Upon questioning, he claimed both trips were to visit his elderly mother and that the latter trip also permitted him to attend a petroleum conference. Although Amirnazmi repeatedly disavowed any commercial purpose for his travels, the presence of ostensibly business-related possessions cast doubt on the credibility of his responses. In April he claimed the sundry business cards and documents found in his briefcase were personal effects he had not made use of on his trip. In June 2008, confronted by Customs officials with computer files and hard copy documents detailing plans to build chemical plants in Iran, he declined to offer an explanation.

On June 4, 2008, the day after his second encounter with Customs officials, Amirnazmi contacted the OFAC compliance hotline to inquire in general about U.S. restrictions on commercial activity with Iran. Without either delving into the specifics of how ChemPlan operated or mentioning his prior business dealings with Iranian companies, he asked whether making public documents available on a website would fall within the informational-materials exemption to IEEPA and whether exporting an unidentified "good" would theoretically require dispensation in the form of a license issued by OFAC.

Two days after this telephone conversation, Amirnazmi was questioned by agents from the Internal Revenue Service and the Federal Bureau of Investigation. He acknowledged meeting President Ahmadinejad but denied having conducted business on either of his 2008 trips to Iran, and he claimed his only two financial transactions with Iran had been the disallowed wire transfers much earlier in the decade. The agents subsequently obtained a search warrant for Amirnazmi's business. Despite Amirnazmi's protestations that none of the documents named in the warrant were located on the premises, the authorities seized numerous physical documents and the hard drive from his computer, which also contained pertinent documents. Upon further interrogation, Amirnazmi conceded he had business relations with NPC both in 1997 and in the more recent past, and he acknowledged having met with Iranian state officials during his trips abroad.

II.

. . .

The jury convicted Amirnazmi on all but one of the IEEPA counts and on all of the false statement and bank fraud counts. . . . Amirnazmi moved for a judgment of acquittal under Fed. R. Crim. P. 29 on the IEEPA counts, the false statement counts and one of the bank fraud counts. He reiterated his argument that IEEPA unconstitutionally delegates to the Executive authority to criminalize commercial conduct, and he added an argument that the accompanying OFAC regulations under which he was convicted are unconstitutionally vague. . . . The court denied Amirnazmi's motion in its entirety. It rested on its previous ruling concerning the nondelegation doctrine, concluded that the IEEPA regulations are not unconstitutionally vague, and determined the government had produced sufficient evidence to sustain each conviction. . . . Amirnazmi timely appealed.

III.

On appeal, Amirnazmi principally challenges the constitutionality of IEEPA and the accompanying OFAC regulations. We will first address the constitutionality of the statute itself, which Amirnazmi challenges on two fronts. First, he argues that Congress—when delegating the authority to create criminal offenses—must articulate the standards by which executive conduct will be governed with greater precision than is required in the context of delegations of civil authority. IEEPA, Amirnazmi contends, lacks the requisite specificity. Second, he claims Congress's failure to comply with its statutory responsibility to oversee the implementation of the Iranian sanctions regime left the Executive's discretion wholly unchecked. Because IEEPA reserves for Congress the final word in determining trade policy during peacetime emergencies, Amirnazmi alleges, Congress's abdication of its oversight role rendered the delegation unconstitutional.

A.

As the source of statutory authority for the Executive's exercise of emergency economic powers in response to peacetime crises, IEEPA traces its provenance to § 5(b) of the Trading with the Enemy Act of 1917, Pub. L. No. 65-91, § 5, 40 Stat. 411, 415 (1917), as amended, 12 U.S.C. § 95a (TWEA). *Dames & Moore v. Regan*, 453 U.S. 654, 671 (1981). TWEA endowed the President with sweeping powers to regulate international trade in times of war or "national emergency," but it lacked a countervailing mechanism to divest the President of such authority once the emergency had ebbed. Because Presidents had displayed a tendency to allow "emergency" declarations to linger "even after the circumstances or tensions that had led to the declaration could no longer be said to pose a threat of emergency proportion to the Nation," some expressed concern that TWEA effectively served as a "one-way ratchet to enhance greatly the President's discretionary authority over foreign policy." *Regan v. Wald*, 468 U.S. 222, 245 (1984) (Blackmun, J., dissenting).

In an effort to address TWEA's evolution into a "flexible instrument of foreign policy in nonemergency situations," *id.* at 246, Congress amended § 5(b) in 1977, restricting the Executive's ability to act under that statute strictly to times of war. . . . Contemporaneously, Congress enacted the International Emergency Economic Powers Act to serve as the locus of executive economic authority during national-emergency situations. *See id.* at Tit. II, 91 Stat. at 1626 (codified at 50 U.S.C. § 1701 *et seq.*). Although the powers conferred in

IEEPA closely mirror those granted in its progenitor, IEEPA removed certain tools from the President's peacetime kit. And, significantly for our purposes, IEEPA subjected the President's authority to a host of procedural limitations designed to ensure Congress would retain its essential legislative superiority in the formulation of sanctions regimes erected under the Act's delegation of emergency power.

The predicate for an exercise of executive authority under IEEPA is the declaration of a national emergency under the National Emergencies Act (NEA). *See* 50 U.S.C. §§ 1621, 1701(b). Under IEEPA, the emergency must stem from an "unusual and extraordinary threat, which has its source in whole or substantial part outside the United States, to the national security, foreign policy, or economy of the United States." *Id.* § 1701(a). After declaring such an emergency, the President may, through "regulations . . . instructions, licenses, or otherwise,"

> (A) investigate, regulate, or prohibit—
>> (i) any transactions in foreign exchange,
>> (ii) transfers of credit or payments between, by, through, or to any banking institution, to the extent that such transfers or payments involve any interest of any foreign country or a national thereof,
>> (iii) the importing or exporting of currency or securities,
> by any person, or with respect to any property, subject to the jurisdiction of the United States;
> (B) investigate, block during the pendency of an investigation, regulate, direct and compel, nullify, void, prevent or prohibit, any acquisition, holding, withholding, use, transfer, withdrawal, transportation, importation or exportation of, or dealing in, or exercising any right, power, or privilege with respect to, or transactions involving, any property in which any foreign country or a national thereof has any interest by any person, or with respect to any property, subject to the jurisdiction of the United States. . . .

Id. § 1702(a)(1).

In tandem, IEEPA and NEA subject the President's exercise of emergency economic powers to an assortment of procedural requirements. The President must consult with Congress before exercising any of his powers under IEEPA "in every possible instance," and he "shall consult regularly with the Congress so long as such authorities are exercised." *Id.* § 1703(a); *see also id.* § 1703(c) (stipulating that the President must report to Congress "[a]t least once during each succeeding six-month period after" the initial exercise of any authority granted by the IEEPA). Whenever the President acts pursuant to IEEPA, he must provide Congress with a report detailing:

> (1) the circumstances which necessitate such exercise of authority;
> (2) why the President believes those circumstances constitute an unusual and extraordinary threat, which has its source in whole or substantial part outside the United States, to the national security, foreign policy, or economy of the United States;

(3) the authorities to be exercised and the actions to be taken in the exercise of those authorities to deal with those circumstances;

(4) why the President believes such actions are necessary to deal with those circumstances; and

(5) any foreign countries with respect to which such actions are to be taken and why such actions are to be taken with respect to those countries.

Id. § 1703(b). After each six-month interval, Congress "shall meet to consider a vote on a joint resolution to determine whether that emergency shall be terminated." *Id.* § 1622(b); *id.* § 1706(b) (providing for the cessation of presidential authority under IEEPA upon congressional termination of an emergency declared under NEA).

Substantively, the regulations contain several exemptions and constraints. That is, regulations promulgated under IEEPA may not impinge upon transactions incident to travel or curtail the free exchange of personal communications, humanitarian aid, or "information or informational materials." *Id.* § 1702(b). Moreover, criminal penalties under IEEPA are reserved exclusively for those who "willfully commit[ ], willfully attempt[ ] to commit, or willfully conspire[ ] to commit" a violation of any license, order or regulation issued pursuant to IEEPA. *Id.* § 1705(c). And the Act exempts those who act in "good faith" reliance on IEEPA, or on "any regulation, instruction, or direction" issued under IEEPA, from both civil and criminal liability. *Id.* § 1702(a)(3).

On March 15, 1995, President Bill Clinton issued Executive Order 12957, which declared a national emergency to deal with the "unusual and extraordinary threat" posed to the national security, foreign policy and economy of the United States by "the actions and policies of the Government of Iran," and which prohibited United States involvement with petroleum development in Iran. 60 Fed. Reg. 14615 (Mar. 17, 1995). On May 6, 1995, President Clinton signed Executive Order 12959, which fortified the sanctions regime by banning U.S. firms from exporting to Iran, importing from Iran, or investing in Iran, subject to the exemptions provided in IEEPA. *See* 60 Fed. Reg. 24757 (May 9, 1995); *see also* Exec. Order No. 13059, 62 Fed. Reg. 44531 (Aug. 21, 1997) (clarifying the preceding Orders). The Executive Orders authorized the Secretary of the Treasury, in consultation with the Secretary of State, "to take such actions, including the promulgation of rules and regulations . . . as may be necessary to carry out the purposes" of the Orders. *See, e.g.*, 60 Fed. Reg. 14615 at § 3. The Treasury Department subsequently issued the Iranian Transactions Regulations (ITR). *See generally* 31 C.F.R. Part 560.

Subject to limited exemptions and to licenses issued by OFAC, the ITR prohibits, in part, the "exportation, reexportation, sale, or supply, directly or indirectly, from the United States, or by a United States person, wherever located, of any goods, technology, or services to Iran or the Government of Iran," 31 C.F.R. § 560.204, and "any new investment by a United States person in Iran or in property (including entities) owned or controlled by the Government of Iran," *id.* § 560.207; *see also id.* § 560.206(a) (generally prohibiting "any transaction or dealing in or related to . . . [g]oods, technology, or services for exportation, reexportation, sale or supply, directly or indirectly, to Iran or the Government of Iran"). . . .

B.

The maxim that Congress may not delegate legislative power to the President is "universally recognized as vital to the integrity and maintenance of the system of government ordained by the Constitution." *Marshall Field & Co. v. Clark*, 143 U.S. 649, 692 (1892). Nevertheless, the Supreme Court has invoked the unconstitutional delegation doctrine—which derives its constitutional underpinning from Article I's vesting of "all legislative powers" with Congress—to strike down a law only twice in its history. *See Panama Ref. Co. v. Ryan*, 293 U.S. 388 (1935) (invalidating delegation under section 9(c) of the National Industrial Recovery Act permitting the President to prohibit the interstate transportation of petroleum goods); *A.L.A. Schechter Poultry Corp. v. United States*, 295 U.S. 495 (1935) (striking down section 3 of the same Act, which authorized trade and industrial associations to propose "codes of fair competition" that would become legally binding if approved by the President). The Court's jurisprudence has been animated by a "practical understanding that in our increasingly complex society, replete with ever changing and more technical problems, Congress simply cannot do its job absent an ability to delegate power under broad general directives." *Mistretta v. United States*, 488 U.S. 361, 372 (1989). Accordingly, in assessing a permissible delegation, the Court has decreed it will be " 'constitutionally sufficient if Congress clearly delineates the general policy, the public agency which is to apply it, and the boundaries of this delegated authority.' " *Id.* at 372-73.

Congress's ability to endow a coordinate branch of government with a measure of discretion is circumscribed by the requirement that it must "lay down by legislative act an intelligible principle to which the person or body authorized to [exercise the delegated authority] is directed to conform." *J.W. Hampton, Jr. & Co. v. United States*, 276 U.S. 394 (1928). Whereas Congress must itself elucidate "the standards of legal obligation" in order to fulfill its "essential legislative function," it may devolve to "selected instrumentalities [responsibility for] the making of subordinate rules within prescribed limits and the determination of facts to which the policy as declared by the legislature is to apply." *Schechter Poultry*, 295 U.S. at 530. . . .

The Supreme Court has upheld Congress's delegation to the President of civil authority to nullify certain attachments and transfers of assets under IEEPA. *Dames & Moore*, 453 U.S. at 675. But Amirnazmi contends IEEPA's delegation of authority to define criminal conduct is inherently more suspect and that, consequently, only a lesser degree of executive discretion is constitutionally permissible in this context. The Court has expressly refrained from deciding whether Congress must provide stricter guidance than a mere "intelligible principle" when authorizing the Executive "to promulgate regulations that contemplate criminal sanctions." *Touby v. United States*, 500 U.S. 160, 165-66 (1991). After concluding the contested delegation would pass constitutional muster even under a heightened standard, the Court refrained from resolving the petitioner's argument that criminal regulations promulgated under congressional delegations of authority should be subject to more searching scrutiny on account of the "heightened risk to individual liberty" they pose. *Id.* at 166.

C.

1.

. . .

We [ ] conclude that IEEPA "meaningfully constrains" the President's discretion. *See Touby*, 500 U.S. at 166. Under the Controlled Substance Act provision examined in *Touby*, the Attorney General could not temporarily schedule a drug without first finding that doing so would be "necessary to avoid an imminent hazard to the public safety." *Id.* Similarly, to activate IEEPA, the President must find that an "unusual and extraordinary threat . . . to the national security, foreign policy, or economy of the United States" originating on foreign soil has reached "national emergency" proportions. *See* 50 U.S.C. § 1701. In *Touby*, the Court found the Attorney General was constrained by the requirement that he abide by several of the more rigorous features of the permanent scheduling process designating illegal drugs. 500 U.S. at 166-67. Likewise, IEEPA prohibits the President from regulating certain exempt transactions, 50 U.S.C. § 1702(b), from prosecuting unwitting violators or holding liable those who act in good faith reliance on the statute and regulations, *id.* §§ 1705(c), 1702(a)(3), and from obviating Congress's role as ultimate arbiter of emergency trade policy, *see id.* §§ 1622(b), 1703, 1706.

In effecting the shift of peacetime authority from TWEA to IEEPA, Congress "placed several procedural restrictions on the President's exercise of the national-emergency powers, including congressional consultation, review, and termination." *Regan*, 468 U.S. at 249 (Blackmun, J., dissenting). In so doing, Congress reaffirmed its "essential legislative function," and struck a careful balance between affording the President a degree of authority to address the exigencies of national emergencies and restraining his ability to perpetuate emergency situations indefinitely by creating more opportunities for congressional input. Therefore, IEEPA meets the same standard of constraint outlined in *Touby*; that is, IEEPA meaningfully constrains the Executive's discretion. Accordingly, it is unnecessary for us to address the unsettled question of whether something more demanding than an "intelligible principle" is necessitated within the context of delegating authority to define criminal conduct.

2.

Second, Amirnazmi claims Congress has violated fundamental separation-of-powers precepts by neglecting its statutory responsibility to monitor the implementation of the Iranian sanctions regime established under IEEPA. In so doing, Amirnazmi claims, the legislature has allowed the President to arrogate "virtually unlimited power over foreign trade," thereby fomenting a "serious threat to public liberty [that] necessitates judicial intervention." This allegation implicates interrelated issues of foreign policy, congressional authorization, and statutorily mandated oversight. Because these considerations are intertwined, we consider them in concert.

The linchpin of Amirnazmi's claim is 50 U.S.C. § 1622(b), which reads: "Not later than six months after a national emergency is declared, and not later than the end of each six-month period thereafter that such emergency continues, each House of Congress shall meet to consider a vote on a joint resolution to determine whether that emergency shall be terminated." In *Dhafir*, the Second Circuit noted in passing that Congress's failure to fulfill its oversight responsibilities might conceivably raise "complicated and sensitive issues concerning separation of powers" but declined to expound in light of an inadequate factual record. 461 F.3d at 217 n.3. Given the conventional wisdom that the shift in authority from TWEA to IEEPA was inspired in part by a prevailing sentiment that Congress's role in devising emergency trade policy warranted strengthening, its failure to police executive conduct would appear counterintuitive.

As a threshold matter, we must determine whether a national emergency properly declared under NEA terminates automatically when Congress fails to meet in conformance with the language of § 1622(b). In *Beacon Products Corp. v. Reagan*, 814 F.2d 1, 4 (1st Cir. 1987), the First Circuit answered that question in the negative. The court reasoned that the disparity between § 1622(d), which explicitly provides for the automatic termination of a national emergency should the President fail to extend it, and § 1622(b), which is devoid of a parallel congressional provision, suggests Congress deliberately withheld automatic termination as a remedy for violation of the "periodic meeting" clause. *Id.* at 4. Next, the court noted Congress eliminated a sunset provision from an earlier draft of NEA, reserving for itself "the burden of acting affirmatively" by substituting in that provision's place the requirement that it pass a resolution to end an emergency. *Id.* (referencing 50 U.S.C. § 1622(a)). The court then concluded Congress likely intended "to give those who want to end the emergency the chance to force a vote on the issue, rather than to *require* those who do *not* want to end the emergency to force congressional action to prevent automatic termination." *Id.* at 5. We agree that Congress did not effectively terminate the emergency against Iran simply by virtue of its failure to hold the periodic meetings addressed in § 1622(b)....

The constitutionality of IEEPA's delegation of criminal authority does not rest on Congress affirmatively renewing its approval of each ongoing emergency at regular six-month intervals. Equating inaction with a withdrawal of authorization would be particularly improper with a statute that concerns foreign affairs, "a sphere in which delegation is afforded even broader deference." *Dhafir*, 461 F.3d at 215. "Congress—in giving the Executive authority over matters of foreign affairs—must of necessity paint with a brush broader than that it customarily wields in domestic areas." *Zemel v. Rusk*, 381 U.S. 1, 17 (1965).... Mindful of the heightened deference accorded the Executive in this field, we decline to interpret the legislative grant of authority parsimoniously. Congress may act to terminate the national emergency; NEA does not necessarily compel Congress to take affirmative steps to prolong the President's charted course.

Congress's failure to satisfy the periodic meeting requirements of § 1622(b) does not ineluctably lead to a conclusion that the President's continued prosecution of trade sanctions under IEEPA has ceased to be "pursuant to an express or implied authorization." *See Youngstown Sheet & Tube Co. v. Sawyer*, 343 U.S. 579, 635 (1952) (Jackson, J., concurring) (setting forth the familiar tripartite framework for evaluating executive action and explaining the President's power is "at its maximum" when he acts according to congressional directive). In *Haig v. Agee*, 453 U.S. 280, 300-01 (1981), the Court inferred congressional approval of a "longstanding and officially promulgated" executive policy from both inaction and statutory developments that "'left completely untouched the broad rule-making authority granted in the earlier Act.'" *Id.* Under *Agee*, we must generally defer to a consistent administrative construction of a statute. *Id.* at 291. "This is especially so in the areas of foreign policy and national security, where congressional silence is not to be equated with congressional disapproval." *Id.* The Court's analysis in *Agee* was buttressed by its determination that Congress had "endorsed not only the underlying premise of Executive authority in the areas of foreign policy and national security, but also its specific application" to the subject matter at issue. *Id.* at 294.

Similarly, this regulatory embargo against Iran has been in place since 1995. Far from sitting by as successive Presidents maintained a sweeping sanctions regime, Congress has expanded, deepened and formalized the sanctions in a comprehensive legislative effort to target Iran through economic measures. In 1996, Congress passed the Iran Sanctions Act, Pub. L. No. 104-172, 110 Stat. 1541 (1996) (codified in part at 50 U.S.C. § 1701 (note)), which mandated the imposition of specified sanctions against foreign firms that reached threshold levels of involvement with Iran's energy sector. Subsequently, in 2006, Congress passed the Iran Freedom Support Act. Pub. L. No. 109-293, 120 Stat. 1344 (2006) (codified in part at 50 U.S.C. § 1701 (note)). In addition to appropriating funds earmarked for the support of persons and organizations "working for the purpose of supporting and promoting democracy for Iran," *id.* § 302, the Act placed Congress's imprimatur on executive sanctions against Iran. . . .

And in 2010, Congress passed the Comprehensive Iran Sanctions, Accountability, and Divestment Act of 2010. Pub. L. No. 111-195, 124 Stat. 1312 (2010) (codified in part at 50 U.S.C § 1701 (note)). CISADA expanded the Iran Sanctions Act by targeting Iran's ability to make or import gasoline and placing new restrictions on financial institutions. Most significantly for our purposes, however, is § 103(b)(2), in which Congress codified the prohibitions on the exportation of goods, services and technology of United States origin to Iran that were then in effect under executive orders promulgated pursuant to IEEPA. Therefore, when Amirnazmi was tried and convicted, Congress had already ratified the OFAC regulations under which he was charged. And, in the aftermath of his conviction, Congress once more manifested its approval of executive conduct by again codifying the extant prohibitions on exports issued pursuant to IEEPA. These measures demonstrate Congress's approval of the emergency measures undertaken against Iran notwithstanding its failure to adhere to the meeting requirements of § 1622(b).

Far from being unaware or indifferent, in the case of Iran, Congress has clearly and consistently demonstrated its support of the Executive's agenda. This is not a scenario in which we are compelled to divine the significance — if any — of congressional silence. Nevertheless, given the number of countries against which trade sanctions have been leveled pursuant to IEEPA, it is not difficult to envisage a situation in which Congress's position is less robustly documented. Although Congress's failure to periodically meet neither automatically terminates an emergency nor bespeaks its dissatisfaction with the President's policies, § 1622(b) provides a regularized mechanism for disquieted representatives to initiate a dialogue about or even contest the wisdom of continuing on with the President's strategy. Once the President has invoked his power to criminalize certain conduct under IEEPA, Congress retains an ongoing part in ensuring the Executive's actions remain "meaningfully constrained" so as to satisfy the requirements of *Touby*.

The Supreme Court has held that "[m]atters intimately related to foreign policy and national security are rarely proper subjects for judicial intervention," *Agee*, 453 U.S. at 292, and federal courts have historically declined to review "the essentially political questions surrounding the declaration or continuance of a national emergency," *United States v. Spawr Optical Research, Inc.*, 685 F.2d 1076, 1080 (9th Cir. 1982) (internal quotation marks omitted). Although such considerations do not preclude enforcing compliance with statutory dictates, NEA places the onus on Congress to ensure emergency situations remain anomalous and do not quietly evolve into default norms.

. . .

B.

Next, Amirnazmi contends OFAC's regulations are imprecisely drafted and consequently void for vagueness. His core argument is that the carve-outs to the informational-materials exemption fail to provide "clear principles." According to him, it is impossible to determine whether a work is "fully created and in existence" without necessarily invoking "an untethered subjective judgment." Again, we find Amirnazmi's argument unconvincing.

"A statute is void on vagueness grounds if it: (1) 'fails to provide people of ordinary intelligence a reasonable opportunity to understand what conduct it prohibits'; or (2) 'authorizes or even encourages arbitrary and discriminatory enforcement.'" *United States v. Stevens*, 533 F.3d 218, 249 (3d Cir. 2008) (quoting *Hill v. Colorado*, 530 U.S. 703, 732 (2000)). In the criminal context, "since vagueness attacks are based on lack of notice, 'they may be overcome in any specific case where reasonable persons would know their conduct puts [them] at risk' of punishment under the statute." *San Filippo v. Bongiovanni*, 961 F.2d 1125, 1138 (3d Cir. 1992) (quoting *Maynard v. Cartwright*, 486 U.S. 356, 361 (1988)). Criminal statutes need only give "fair warning that certain conduct is prohibited" to survive constitutional challenges. *Id.* (internal quotation marks omitted).

Furthermore, the Supreme Court has stated that:

> [E]conomic regulation is subject to a less strict vagueness test because its subject matter is often more narrow, and because businesses, which face economic demands to plan behavior carefully, can be expected to consult relevant legislation in advance of action [and may] clarify the meaning of the regulation by [their] own inquiry, or by resort to an administrative process.

Village of Hoffman Estates v. Flipside, Hoffman Estates, Inc., 455 U.S. 489, 498 (1982). And, significantly, "the Court has recognized that a scienter requirement may mitigate a law's vagueness, especially with respect to the adequacy of notice to the complainant that his conduct is proscribed." *Id.* at 499.

The District Court rested its conclusion that the regulation is not unconstitutionally vague on two grounds. First, it reasoned that the sophisticated nature of those required to consult the IEEPA regulations coupled with the availability of guidance from OFAC officials on electronic and telephone hotlines negated any notice concerns. And second, it noted that IEEPA's scienter requirement counseled against a vagueness finding.

As to the latter point, the government had to prove beyond a reasonable doubt that Amirnazmi willfully violated the trade restrictions. *See* 50 U.S.C. § 1705(c) (restricting IEEPA convictions to those who "willfully commit[ ], willfully attempt[ ] to commit, or willfully conspire[ ] to commit" a violation of any license, order or regulation issued pursuant to IEEPA). As the District Court noted, "this is a case where ignorance of the law *is* a defense; the inability to appreciate the meaning of the law negatives the *mens rea* required for conviction, and Defendant was free to, and did, argue this to the jury." The jury unanimously concluded Amirnazmi knew his conduct was unlawful.

And, as to the former point, the record reveals Amirnazmi only halfheartedly availed himself of the opportunity to receive definitive guidance from OFAC. Amirnazmi first contacted OFAC upon his return from Iran on June 3, 2008. He indicated he was curious as to whether consolidating publicly available documents in a single location to increase the ease of access for individuals in Iran would fall within the informational-materials exemption, and he alluded to the possibility of exporting a good to Iran. He did not mention the computations that could be done with the data, nor did he ask if confidential trade secrets were exempt. . . . On June 11, he sent a letter to OFAC confirming his unsupported understanding that ChemPlan fell within the exemption but again failed to disclose how ChemPlan functioned as a dynamic planning tool. Amirnazmi once more contacted OFAC on June 17 and was told to submit a "detailed explanation of the transactions he wanted to carry out" if he wanted authoritative guidance. One month later, he was indicted. The District Court concluded Amirnazmi did not contact OFAC "in good faith or with the intention of actually procuring guidance in complying with the OFAC regulations." Amirnazmi's refusal to provide OFAC with the detailed information that might have allowed the agency to offer reasoned guidance supports the District Court's conclusion. . . .

In sum, we agree with the District Court's conclusion that, in light of the "narrow subject matter and reach of the IEEPA regulations, as well as the sophisticated nature of the persons they affect and the ability of such persons to obtain guidance from OFAC itself, the IEEPA regulations are not unconstitutionally vague." Because OFAC's regulations are neither *ultra vires* nor unconstitutionally vague, we will deny Amirnazmi's request to vacate his IEEPA convictions on these grounds. . . . For the foregoing reasons, we will affirm the jury's verdict and the District Court's imposition of a four-year prison sentence.

NOTES AND QUESTIONS

1. Why did the court reject the defendant's argument that IEEPA violates the non-delegation doctrine? Does IEEPA "meaningfully constrain" the President's discretion? If so, how?
2. Did Congress violate fundamental separation-of-powers principles by neglecting its statutory responsibility to monitor the implementation of the Iranian sanctions regime established under IEEPA? What role has Congress played with respect to economic sanctions against Iran? Do these actions demonstrate support of the Executive's Iranian sanctions regime?
3. Why did the court conclude that IEEPA is not unconstitutionally vague? Are economic regulations subject to a less strict vagueness test? If so, why?
4. In order to sustain a criminal violation of IEEPA, the government must prove beyond a reasonable doubt that Amirnazmi willfully violated the Iranian trade restrictions. Does the IEEPA scienter requirement mitigate against a vagueness finding? If so, why?
5. IEEPA does not prohibit all transactions with a sanctioned country or entity. IEEPA recognizes a humanitarian exception. The authority granted to the President does not extend to regulating or prohibiting donations of food, clothing, or medicine intended to be used to relieve human suffering, unless the President determines that such donations "would seriously impair his ability to deal with any national emergency." 50 U.S.C. § 1702(b)(2).
6. What is the "good faith" defense under IEEPA?
7. Pursuant to regulations issued by OFAC, a party may seek a license to engage in transactions otherwise prohibited by an executive order issued under IEEPA. These regulations authorize OFAC to issue both "general" and "specific" licenses. For example, OFAC has issued several general licenses authorizing United States persons to engage in certain transactions with the Palestinian Authority. The purpose of issuing a license is to ameliorate the harsh effects of OFAC blocking actions under IEEPA. OFAC regulations permit a party to seek a specific license to engage in a particular transaction. In *Global Relief Foundation, Inc. v. O'Neill*, 207 F. Supp. 2d 779, 788, 805 (N.D. Ill. 2002), OFAC exercised its discretion to grant a U.S.-based charity, whose assets had been designated for blocking under IEEPA, licenses to pay legal fees, establish a legal defense fund, pay employees' salaries, payroll taxes, health insurance, rent, utilities, and other recurring expenses.

Epsilon Electronics, Inc. v. United States Dep't of Treasury
857 F.3d 913 (D.C. Cir. 2017)

GRIFFITH, Circuit Judge:

In 1995, President Clinton imposed trade sanctions against Iran that are enforced by the Office of Foreign Assets Control within the Department of the Treasury. OFAC is authorized to impose civil penalties against any person who exports goods to a third party who it has reason to know intends to send them to Iran. The principal question raised by this appeal is whether OFAC must also show that the goods actually ended up in Iran. We agree with the agency that the government need not make that showing and affirm the district court on that ground. But we also conclude that OFAC did not adequately explain parts of its determination that the exporter here had reason to know that its shipments would be sent on to Iran.

I

When the President identifies an "unusual and extraordinary threat" to the American economy, national security, or foreign policy that originates from abroad, *see* 50 U.S.C. § 1701, the International Emergency Economic Powers Act authorizes him to declare a national emergency and address the threat by regulating foreign commerce, *see id.* § 1702. In 1995, President Clinton determined that Iran's "support for international terrorism, its efforts to undermine the Middle East peace process, and its efforts to acquire weapons of mass destruction" represented a national emergency, *see* Iranian Transactions Regulations and, invoking his authority under the Act, imposed comprehensive trade sanctions on Iran by executive order, *see* Exec. Order No. 12,959, 60 Fed. Reg. 24,757, § 1 (May 6, 1995).

OFAC implemented the President's executive order in September 1995 by promulgating the Iranian Transactions and Sanctions Regulations, which are now codified, as amended, at 31 C.F.R. pt. 560. Among other prohibitions, the regulations forbid "the exportation, reexportation, sale, or supply, directly or indirectly . . . of any goods, technology, or services to Iran" by United States individuals and businesses, including exportation to a third country with "knowledge or reason to know" that the goods are "intended specifically" for reexportation to Iran. *See* 31 C.F.R. § 560.204.

The agency has invoked that prohibition against appellant Epsilon Electronics, a California-based wholesaler of sound systems, video players, and other accessories for cars. The company's wares can be found across the globe, from Latin America to Africa and the Middle East. Asra International Corporation, a distributor based in Dubai, has been one of Epsilon's trading partners. Between 2008 and 2012, Epsilon sent thirty-nine shipments of consumer goods to Asra, valued at about $3.4 million.

OFAC began investigating Epsilon in 2011, when the agency learned about a 2008 shipment from Epsilon's California headquarters to an address in Tehran, Iran. In response to an administrative subpoena, Epsilon's president denied knowledge of the shipment and suggested that a lower-level employee had sent the package without the company's knowledge.

Later in 2011, OFAC also learned that Epsilon had received multiple wire transfers from a Dubai bank, made on behalf of Asra International. The agency examined Asra's website, which touted the company's success in the Iranian market, contained a directory of dealers who were all located in Iran, and displayed photos from trade shows in various Iranian cities. Some of these photos also appeared on Epsilon's website. OFAC suspected that the company's shipments to Asra were "destined for Iran," and opened a second investigation on Epsilon in December 2011. The agency issued an administrative subpoena to Epsilon's bank, seeking information about the company's transactions with Asra.

In the meantime, OFAC decided to close its investigation of the 2008 shipment. In January 2012, the agency sent Epsilon a letter explaining that the shipment appeared to have violated OFAC regulations, and warning that those regulations "prohibit virtually all" American trade with Iran. OFAC explained that it would not penalize Epsilon for the shipment but that the agency could take this apparent violation into account in any future case.

But OFAC did not close its parallel investigation of Epsilon's dealings with Asra. In May 2012, the agency sent Epsilon another administrative subpoena, requesting further details on the company's transactions with Asra and with Iran. Epsilon responded that it had no dealings with Iran and that none of its shipments to Asra were intended for Iran. The company submitted invoices chronicling thirty-four shipments to Asra.

Between February and May 2012, while OFAC's investigation continued, Epsilon sent Asra five more shipments. During this period, Epsilon managers corresponded by email with an Asra manager, Shahriar Hashemi, who described plans to launch a Dubai retail store under "Asra's flag." The emails record Hashemi and Epsilon negotiating several orders, and show Hashemi mentioning plans for his showroom, complaining about another Dubai shop selling Epsilon products, worrying about whether Epsilon products could endure Dubai's heat, and anticipating sales to African and Central Asian customers. An Epsilon manager promised Hashemi that the Dubai retail market was "all yours."

In May 2014, OFAC tentatively concluded that all thirty-nine of Epsilon's shipments to Asra violated 31 C.F.R. § 560.204 because each was made with knowledge, or reason to know, that Asra intended to reexport the goods to Iran. The agency sent Epsilon a Prepenalty Notice, declaring its intent to impose a civil monetary penalty of $4,073,000, subject to Epsilon's response. OFAC arrived at that dollar amount by applying its penalty guidelines, which required the agency to determine whether any of the violations were voluntarily disclosed and whether any were "egregious." OFAC found that none of Epsilon's violations was voluntarily disclosed, and that the last five shipments, made after Epsilon received OFAC's January 2012 cautionary letter, were egregious. Though the agency has authority to depart upward or downward from the guideline penalty, it decided not to do so after balancing the aggravating and mitigating factors.

In July 2014, OFAC issued a final Penalty Notice, formally imposing a $4,073,000 civil penalty. The agency had not been persuaded by Epsilon's response to the Prepenalty Notice, which again denied any knowledge or reason to know that Asra distributed Epsilon's products in Iran. The Penalty Notice explained that "multiple facts tend to show that the goods exported to Asra were sent to Iran and that Epsilon knew or had reason to know that the goods were intended specifically for supply, transshipment, or reexportation, directly or indirectly, to Iran." Although the Notice recited much of the evidence against Epsilon, it never mentioned the emails between Epsilon management and Hashemi.

The issuance of the Penalty Notice was final agency action. In December 2014, Epsilon sued OFAC in district court. Epsilon's complaint sought declaratory and injunctive relief against enforcement of the civil penalty. On March 7, 2016, the district court granted summary judgment in favor of the government.

Epsilon timely appealed. We have jurisdiction under 28 U.S.C. § 1291, and review de novo the district court's entry of summary judgment in favor of the government. *Islamic Am. Relief Agency v. Gonzales (IARA)*, 477 F.3d 728, 732 (D.C. Cir. 2007). As the Administrative Procedure Act requires, our review is "highly deferential" to the agency, meaning we may set aside OFAC's action "only if it is arbitrary, capricious, an abuse of discretion, or otherwise not in accordance with law." *IARA*, 477 F.3d at 732 (quoting 5 U.S.C. § 706(2)(A)). Under that standard, we will uphold agency findings that are supported by substantial evidence, even if we might have reached a different conclusion in the first instance. That deference has a caveat: although the APA does not permit us to substitute our judgment for the agency's, we must ensure that the agency has "articulate[d] a satisfactory explanation for its action including a 'rational connection between the facts found and the choice made.'" *Motor Vehicle Mfrs. Ass'n of the U.S. v. State Farm Mut. Auto. Ins. Co.*, 463 U.S. 29, 43 (1983) (quoting *Burlington Truck Lines, Inc. v. United States*, 371 U.S. 156, 168 (1962)).

Epsilon asks us to set aside these fundamental doctrines of administrative law by reviewing OFAC's decision de novo instead of under the APA's arbitrary-and-capricious standard. We have described de novo review in an APA case as "extraordinary and rare," so rare, in fact, that we have never done so. *Zevallos v. Obama*, 793 F.3d 106, 112 (D.C. Cir. 2015). . . . Accordingly, we will adhere to the "arbitrary [and] capricious" standard set out in 5 U.S.C. § 706(2)(A).

II

Epsilon offers three challenges to the civil penalty that OFAC imposed. First, the company contends that none of its thirty-nine shipments to Asra were in violation of the Iranian Transactions and Sanctions Regulations. Second, Epsilon claims that the amount of the penalty assessed is not only arbitrary and capricious, but also an "excessive fine" forbidden by the Eighth Amendment. Third, the company argues that its due process rights were violated because it had insufficient notice of the evidence that OFAC intended to rely on.

A

We first consider whether OFAC properly found Epsilon liable for thirty-nine violations of section 560.204 of the Iranian Transactions and Sanctions Regulations. In addressing that issue, we face a threshold question of regulatory interpretation. To hold a party liable for a breach of section 560.204, must OFAC prove that goods shipped by that party actually arrived in Iranian territory? Or can liability rest solely on a showing that the party shipped goods to a third party, with reason to know that the recipient specifically intended to reexport them to Iran?

Epsilon advances the former position, and contends there is no substantial evidence that the thirty-nine shipments at issue ever entered Iran. OFAC responds that the regulation's plain text does not require such a showing. . . . The agency also urges us to defer to its interpretation if we find the regulation ambiguous. However, the reading of section 560.204 that OFAC has adopted is the same reading that we would have adopted in the absence of any agency interpretation.

i

We begin with the regulation's text. Section 560.204 provides:

> Except as otherwise authorized pursuant to this part . . . the exportation, reexportation, sale, or supply, directly or indirectly, from the United States, or by a United States person, wherever located, of any goods, technology, or services to Iran or the Government of Iran is prohibited, including the exportation, reexportation, sale, or supply of any goods, technology, or services to a person in a third country undertaken with knowledge or reason to know that:
>
> (a) Such goods, technology, or services are intended specifically for supply, transshipment, or reexportation, directly or indirectly, to Iran or the Government of Iran. . . .

The analysis at first glance appears straightforward. The regulation prohibits "the exportation [ ] of any goods [ ] to a person in a third country undertaken with knowledge or reason to know that [s]uch goods [ ] are intended specifically for [ ] reexportation [ ] to Iran." *See id.* That prohibition, on its face, has only two elements: (1) the exportation of goods to "a person in a third country" and (2) "knowledge or reason to know" that the third-country recipient plans to send the goods on to Iran. *Id.* The goods' actual arrival in Iran is not mentioned, meaning that proof of this event is not required for a liability finding under the prohibition on third-country exports.

Epsilon, in response, points to the word "including." The rule just discussed is "includ[ed]" within a broader prohibition on "exportation . . . to Iran." *See id.* The company argues that the "word 'including' makes clear there is no separate prohibition on exports to third countries independent from reexportation to Iran." This argument relies on an unstated premise: that goods have not been exported "to Iran" until they actually reach Iranian territory. OFAC, by contrast, assumes that the phrase "to Iran" refers to the sender's intent, not the ultimate arrival of the goods. In other words, on OFAC's interpretation, goods have been "export[ed] . . . to Iran" when the exporter puts them in transit, with Iran as the intended final destination.

We think OFAC's reading more closely aligns with ordinary English usage. Suppose you put a birthday card in the mail, addressed to your brother. While the card is still en route, your mother asks you, "Did you send a card to your brother?" In line with OFAC's usage, you would respond, "I sent a card to him, but it hasn't arrived yet," because you put the card in transit, intending it to reach him. Following Epsilon's usage, though, you would have to say, "I didn't send a card to him," because the card has not yet arrived. (Stranger still, if you were uncertain whether the card had reached his mailbox, you might answer, "I don't know if I sent a card to him or not.") The first statement is more consistent with the way ordinary English speakers talk.

The agency's argument draws further support from the definition of the word "exportation" in export rules that are closely related to OFAC's. The regulations in question are the Department of Commerce's Export Administration Regulations (EAR) which control the export of items that have both civilian and military uses. *See* 15 C.F.R. § 730.3. The Iranian transaction regulations do not expressly incorporate this EAR definition, but they often refer to the EAR. . . . The EAR defines "export" as "an actual shipment or transmission of items out of the United States." 15 C.F.R. § 772.1 (2014). In other words, the occurrence of an "export" is not contingent on the goods' arrival at their final destination. What's more, "the export or reexport of items subject to the EAR that will transit through [Country A] or be transshipped in [Country A] to [Country B] or are intended for reexport to [Country B], are deemed to be exports *to* [Country B]." *Id.* § 734.2(b)(6) (2014) (emphasis added). Note the use of forward-looking language: the export of items "that *will transit*" or "*are intended* for reexport." If an exporter can say, "I have exported items to Country B that will transit through Country A," then exportation to B occurs before "transit through" A, and thus before the goods reach A, let alone B. The EAR definition of "export" indicates that OFAC's reading of section 560.204 reflects the meaning of that word as it is used in trade regulations.

The EAR, like OFAC's interpretation of section 560.204, embodies the understanding, drawn from broader legal usage, that exportation is an "act," specifically, "[t]he act of sending or carrying goods and merchandise from one country to another." *Exportation*, BLACK'S LAW DICTIONARY (10th ed. 2014). An "act," in turn, is an actor's voluntary conduct: for example, placing goods on a ship bound for Iran. *See Act*, BLACK'S LAW DICTIONARY (10th ed. 2014) ("The word 'act' . . . denote[s] an external manifestation of the actor's will and does not include any of its results, even the most direct, immediate, and intended." (quoting RESTATEMENT (SECOND) OF TORTS § 2 (1965))). If an exporter has taken all the steps he must personally take to put goods in transit to Iran, and the goods are out of his control, no further "voluntary conduct" or "external manifestation of [ ] will" by the exporter is necessary for the goods to arrive in Iran. . . . The arrival of the goods is a "result" of his "voluntary conduct," not part of the conduct itself, and thus is not a component of the "act" of exportation.

Epsilon's gloss on section 560.204 would also subvert the ordinary meaning of the word "including." That word typically introduces one or more illustrative examples. Whatever follows the word "including" is a subset of whatever comes before; any conduct that comes within the "including" clause comes, by definition, within the preceding clause as well. For example, imagine a regulation that reads: "All disruptive activity is prohibited in the park, including the playing of loud music." The word "including" indicates that "playing of loud music" is part of the broader category of "disruptive activity." And if a court (or an agency) adopted a definition of "disruptive activity" that *excluded* "playing of loud music" in many circumstances, that court (or agency) would distort the plain meaning of the regulation.

That principle guides us here, and further illustrates why Epsilon's interpretation of the phrase "to Iran" cannot be correct. Section 560.204 is divided into two clauses. First is the prohibitory clause, which contains the general ban on "exportation . . . to Iran." Second is the "including" clause, which contains the specific prohibition on third-country shipments that is at issue in this case. If we adopted the company's reading of the words "exportation . . . to Iran" in the prohibitory clause, certain conduct would be covered by the including clause, but *not* by the prohibitory clause. Consider a case where an exporter ships goods to a distributor in a third country, knowing that the distributor intends to send those goods on to Iran. In this hypothetical, there is no dispute that the goods entered the third country, but no showing that they actually made it to Iran. On Epsilon's reading, such a case would satisfy the text of the including clause (because the goods arrived in the third country, and the exporter had the necessary mental state), but not the text of the prohibitory clause (because the goods did not arrive in Iran). That interpretation turns the word "including" on its head. . . .

ii

Epsilon contends, in the face of the text, that OFAC has recognized a safe harbor in section 560.204: the "inventory exception." This exception, according to the company, is "well understood in the industry as a negative reading of § 560.204, creating a safe harbor for re-exports to Iran of non-sensitive . . . products so long as the U.S. exporter does not know, or have reason to know, such products are specifically intended for Iran." Appellant Br. 14. Thus, Epsilon explains, if it ships goods to a Dubai company that are taken up into the Dubai company's "general inventory," Epsilon cannot be held liable if the Dubai company later ships those same goods to Iran.

Nobody argues that section 560.204 is a strict-liability rule. After all, liability for shipment of goods to a third country explicitly depends on the shipper's knowledge or "reason to know" that the third-country recipient specifically intends to reexport those goods to Iran. *See* 31 C.F.R. § 560.204. Conversely, when an exporter *does* have reason to know that its third-country trading partner specifically intends to reexport the exporter's goods to Iran, the exporter cannot avoid liability by asserting that the exports passed through the middleman's "general inventory." The regulation does not provide support for

Epsilon's proposed freestanding exception. . . . Epsilon thus was properly found liable for violating section 560.204 if it had reason to know that its shipments to Asra were specifically intended for reexport to Iran, regardless of whether Asra treated those shipments as "general inventory."

. . .

B

We have explained that an exporter may be found liable under section 560.204 if it ships goods from the United States to a third country, with reason to know that those goods are specifically intended for reexport to Iran, even if the goods never arrive in Iran. OFAC found that Epsilon made thirty-nine such shipments, in each case with the requisite reason to know. We now consider whether the agency's determinations were arbitrary and capricious. This case turns on OFAC's factual determination that Epsilon's conduct contravened section 560.204, and so the central question in the arbitrary-and-capricious analysis is whether substantial evidence supported that determination.

The APA's substantial evidence standard "requires more than a scintilla, but can be satisfied by something less than a preponderance of the evidence." *Town of Barnstable v. FAA*, 740 F.3d 681, 687 (D.C. Cir. 2014) (quoting *Fla. Gas Transmission Co. v. FERC*, 604 F.3d 636, 645 (D.C. Cir. 2010)). If that threshold is met, we must uphold the agency's judgment regarding the relevant facts, even if we think the "evidence tends to weigh against the agency's finding." *See United Steel Workers*, 707 F.3d at 325. However, we cannot examine the agency's proffered evidence in isolation; we must also consider "whatever in the record fairly detracts from its weight." *Town of Barnstable*, 740 F.3d at 687 (quoting *Universal Camera Corp. v. NLRB*, 340 U.S. 474, 488 (1951)).

We begin our exploration of the facts on the parties' common ground: Epsilon sent thirty-nine shipments of car accessories from the United States to Asra International, and those accessories arrived in Dubai. The only disputed question, in light of our textual analysis above, is whether Epsilon knew, or had reason to know, that Asra International specifically intended to reexport those shipments to Iran. OFAC's guidance explains that "reason to know" can be established "through a variety of circumstantial evidence," including "course of dealing, general knowledge of the industry or customer preferences, working relationships between the parties, or other criteria far too numerous to enumerate." Transshipments Guidance at 2. We consider the thirty-nine shipments in two groups: the thirty-four shipments sent between 2008 and 2011, and the five shipments sent in 2012. We conclude that OFAC's findings regarding the first group (the 2008-2011 shipments) were adequately justified, but the agency's findings regarding the latter group (the 2012 shipments) were not.

i

Record evidence tends to show that Asra International distributed exclusively in Iran as late as December 2011. Specifically, Asra International's English-language website presented Asra International ("Dubai Asra") as an affiliate of the Asra Electronic Trading Company of Tehran ("Tehran Asra"). The website's "Contact Us" page, under the heading "Asra International Corporation L.L.C.," listed only two addresses: one for Asra International Corporation in Dubai, United Arab Emirates, and one for Asra Electronic Trading Company in Tehran, Iran. The same website's "About Us" page, again under the "Asra International Corporation" heading, announced that "Asra Trading Company revels in its 10 long years of experience on Iran's car audio & video market," having established "the broadest car audio & video systems distribution and sales network in Iran, supported by 150 of Iran's most reputable sales agents in different cities." A.A. 85. The marketing copy made several references to Asra's success in "the country," implying that the company served only a single country, Iran; indeed, no other countries were mentioned on this page. Finally, the website's "Dealers" tab displayed a long list of sales agents, all located in Iran. OFAC could reasonably infer from this website that Dubai Asra distributed only in Iran, by reexporting goods to Tehran Asra, which then transported those goods to dealers throughout the country.

Epsilon had reason to know these facts, which were available on Asra's public, English-language website. There is also direct evidence that Epsilon had actual knowledge of Asra's website and its contents. Specifically, Epsilon copied images found there to its own website, displaying them in a photo gallery labeled "Iran" as recently as 2012. Thus, in addition to demonstrating Epsilon's awareness of Asra's website, these photos suggest that Epsilon actually knew of Dubai Asra's distribution in Iran. Further evidence that Epsilon knew of Dubai Asra and Tehran Asra's connection came in the form of a 2008 freight manifest, recording a shipment from Epsilon's address directly to Tehran Asra's address. . . .

The information available to Epsilon indicated that everything Dubai Asra purchased before 2012 was sent to Iran. On the record before us, OFAC surely had much "more than a scintilla" of evidence . . . to support its finding that Epsilon's first thirty-four shipments to Dubai Asra violated section 560.204.

ii

We cannot say the same, however, for the final five shipments. Although a court applying the APA's arbitrary-and-capricious standard "is not to substitute its judgment for that of the agency," *State Farm*, 463 U.S. at 43, the agency must "articulate a satisfactory explanation for its action including a rational connection between the facts found and the choice made." *IARA*, 477 F.3d at 732 (quoting *State Farm*, 463 U.S. at 43). Certain evidence in the record indicated that Epsilon did not have reason to know its last five shipments were intended for reexport to Iran. OFAC failed to explain adequately why it discounted that evidence. We do not hold that OFAC *could not have* imposed liability for the last five shipments. That is, we do not opine on whether the record contained substantial evidence supporting a determination of liability for these shipments. We hold instead that the agency did not explain why its conclusion about the first thirty-four shipments held for the last five as well, in light of the countervailing evidence presented. In other words, the agency failed to "exercise[ ] its judgment in a reasoned way." *U.S. Sugar Corp. v. EPA*, 830 F.3d 579, 652 (D.C. Cir. 2016) (per curiam).

The countervailing evidence in question consists of several email conversations between Epsilon's sales team and Dubai Asra manager Shahriar Hashemi. These emails covered the period between September 2011 and July 2012, the time frame when the last five shipments were sent. Epsilon explained that these emails "contemplate[d] [Epsilon] products being sold out of the Asra store in Dubai." A.A. 132. The emails' content seems to bear out Epsilon's characterization. The emails tend to show that Hashemi planned to open a store in Dubai, styled "Actel Trading" but operating under "Asra's flag." A.A. 118. In one conversation, Hashemi expressed concern about a competing retailer selling Epsilon products in Dubai. An Epsilon co-owner reassured him, "We are not selling to anyone in Dubai. It is all yours." A.A. 119. In other emails, Hashemi referred to his "showroom," A.A. 122, and fretted that he would have "nothing to display" to prospective customers from Central Asia, Africa, and Jordan, A.A. 109. The emails appear to connect the final five shipments to this retail store: each shipment has a contemporaneous email chain that implies the shipment was meant for Hashemi's own business. Several refer explicitly to market conditions in Dubai. Epsilon, reading Hashemi's correspondence, might well have believed these five shipments were intended for a Dubai retail store, which suggests that it did not have reason to know those shipments were specifically intended for reexport to Iran.

Government counsel explained at oral argument that OFAC did not consider the emails credible evidence. We can infer as much from the agency's liability finding. But we lack an explanation, from the record, of *why* they are not credible, and why they do not counsel against liability for the final five shipments. The Prepenalty Notice and Penalty Notice do not mention the emails at all, and instead treat the thirty-nine violations as a unit, as though the same set of evidence applied to each one. The agency did include a limited discussion of the emails in an internal OFAC memorandum, circulated a month before the Prepenalty Notice issued. But even this memo does not set forth a reasoned basis for rejecting the email evidence.

The memo occasionally approaches the necessary explanation, but in each case falls short. First, the memo notes that every email in the record was sent *after* Epsilon received OFAC's first administrative subpoena. At least two inferences could be drawn from that fact. Perhaps Epsilon and Asra concocted the emails to cover up Asra's continued exports to Iran (and Epsilon's knowledge thereof) in the face of OFAC scrutiny. Or perhaps Epsilon read and understood OFAC's January 2012 cautionary letter, and continued exporting to Asra only because it honestly believed its new shipments were meant for Dubai retail. Nowhere in the administrative record does OFAC state any reason for choosing one inference over the other.

Second, the memo mentions that Hashemi's Dubai retail store opened in April 2012, after all but two of the last five shipments had already been dispatched. The relevant question, though, is not whether the goods in the last five shipments were actually sold in the store, but whether Epsilon had reason to know that those last five shipments were intended for Iran. The store's opening date does not rebut evidence that Epsilon believed its goods were slated for eventual sale there. Third, the memo notes that the Dubai store was named Actel Trading but that the last five shipments, like the first thirty-four, were addressed to Asra, not Actel. From these facts, the memo suggests that the last five shipments could not have been intended for retail sale in Dubai. But the memo also observes that Actel appears to be "a subsidiary or affiliate acting on behalf of Asra." Thus, the fact that the shipments were addressed to Asra does not contradict the theory that they were intended for Actel. We also note the low value of the last five shipments, two of which were worth just over one hundred dollars apiece. At the time those shipments were sent, Epsilon knew its dealings with Asra were under OFAC investigation. OFAC did not explain why Epsilon would knowingly risk fines of up to $250,000 per shipment in return for such a small reward.

In cases like this one, our doctrine offers two principles that pull in opposing directions. We must "uphold a decision of less than ideal clarity if the agency's path may reasonably be discerned," *State Farm*, 463 U.S. at 43 (quoting *Bowman Transp.*, 419 U.S. at 286), but we "may not supply a reasoned basis for the agency's action that the agency itself has not given," *id.* (quoting *SEC v. Chenery Corp.*, 332 U.S. 194, 196 (1947)). Though the question is close, we hold that OFAC failed to offer a sufficient explanation for why it did not credit the email evidence. Because OFAC failed to justify its conclusion that Epsilon should be held liable for the last five shipments as well as the first thirty-four, the final five liability determinations were arbitrary and capricious.

*   *   *

III

The order of the district court granting the government defendants' motion for summary judgment is affirmed in part and reversed in part. The order is affirmed as to OFAC's determination that Epsilon's thirty-four shipments to Asra International between August 2008 and March 2011 violated section 560.204 of the Iranian Transactions and Sanctions Regulations. The order is reversed as to OFAC's determination that Epsilon's five shipments to Asra International in 2012 violated the same regulation. The case is remanded to the district court, with instructions to remand the matter to OFAC for further consideration of the five alleged 2012 violations, and of the total monetary penalty imposed for all liability findings, in a manner consistent with this opinion.

NOTES AND QUESTIONS

1. The first issue decided by the court was the meaning of the text of § 560.204, which prohibits the exportation of goods "to Iran." Epsilon argued that goods have not been exported "to Iran" until they actually reach Iranian territory. OFAC took the position that proof of the goods' actual arrival in Iran is not required to violate the statute. The court sided with OFAC, rejecting Epsilon's proposed reading of the statute. Why? What was the court's reasoning? Do you agree?

2. The court affirmed OFAC's determination that Epsilon's thirty-four shipments to Asra International between August 2008 and March 2011 violated § 560.204 of the Iranian Transactions and Sanctions regulation, but reversed OFAC's determination that Epsilon's five shipments to Asra International in 2012 violated the same regulation. Why did the court uphold OFAC's determination that Epsilon knew, or had reason to know, that Asra International intended to re-export the first thirty-four shipments to Iran? Why was liability for the last five shipments arbitrary and capricious?

3. OFAC found that all thirty-nine of Epsilon's shipments to Asra International violated 31 C.F.R. § 560.204 and imposed a civil monetary penalty of $4,073,000. Epsilon argued that the size of the penalty imposed by OFAC constituted an excessive fine in violation of the Eighth Amendment. However, the court found that the imposition of liability for the last five shipments was arbitrary and capricious. The court stated that the question remains "whether the penalty for the first thirty-four shipments is severable from the penalty for the last five" to address the lawfulness of the penalty. Ultimately, the court had "substantial doubt" that "OFAC would have imposed the same penalty for the first thirty-four shipments in the absence of its liability finding for the last five shipments" and remanded the matter to OFAC to determine what liability it would impose for the first thirty-four shipments. The important takeaway from the case is that the Eighth Amendment Excessive Fines Clause imposes a constitutional limitation on civil monetary penalties imposed by OFAC for violations of economic sanctions. What factors are probative on whether OFAC's civil monetary penalty of $4,073,000 is unconstitutionally excessive?

4. On June 11, 2020, President Trump issued an executive order under IEEPA threatening to impose sanctions on parties associated with the International Criminal Court (ICC). Specifically, Trump declared that the ICC's investigation of the Afghanistan situation and whether U.S. soldiers committed war crimes and crimes against humanity constitutes an "unusual and extraordinary threat to the national security and foreign policy of the United States." The imposition of sanctions would not only impact the work of the ICC, but also affect the livelihood of ICC prosecutors, judges, staff, and other persons associated with the ICC. Designation under the Executive Order would require blocking or freezing the assets of such individuals located in the United States. Furthermore, United States persons would be prohibited from engaging in any transactions with persons designated under the Executive Order. The Order was clearly intended to have a chilling effect on the work of the ICC and sets a dangerous precedent. Is this a lawful use of IEEPA? Does the use of IEEPA against the ICC reinforce calls for reforming the statute? If so, what reforms or amendments would you propose?

WHAT IS THE OFFICE OF FOREIGN ASSETS CONTROL (OFAC)?

"The primary mission of OFAC is to administer and enforce economic sanctions against targeted foreign countries and regimes, terrorists and terrorist organizations, weapons of mass destruction proliferators, narcotic traffickers, and others, in furtherance of U.S. national security, foreign policy, and economic objectives. OFAC acts under Presidential national emergency powers, as well as specific legislation to prohibit transactions and block (or 'freeze') assets subject to U.S. jurisdiction." Fed. Reg. Vol. 74, No. 215, Nov. 9, 2009.

United States v. Homa International Trading Corp.
387 F.3d 144 (2d Cir. 2004)

Defendant-appellant Mazyar Gavidel appeals from the district court's judgment of conviction, dated May 30, 2003, following a jury trial in which Gavidel and Homa International Trading Corp. ("Homa"), a Manhattan business owned and operated by Gavidel, were found guilty of the following crimes: conspiring to commit money laundering, in violation of 18 U.S.C. § 1956(h); laundering purported narcotics proceeds, in violation of 18 U.S.C. § 1956(a)(3)(B); and violating a trade embargo against Iran (the "Embargo") by transferring $277,045 from the United States to Iran, in violation of 50 U.S.C. §§ 1702, 1705(b), Executive Order 12959, and 31 C.F.R. §§ 560.203, 560.204, and 560.406(b). Gavidel was also convicted of structuring cash transactions (totaling $614,806) to avoid reporting requirements, in violation of 31 U.S.C. § 5324(a)(1) and (c)(2). Although he claimed entrapment, Gavidel did not call witnesses or submit evidence in his defense. At sentencing, Judge Griesa ordered Gavidel to forfeit $614,000 and sentenced him to seventy months' imprisonment, followed by three years' supervised release, and a mandatory $800 special assessment.

The Government launched its investigation of Gavidel and his company in the fall of 1999, after agents of the U.S. Customs Service received a tip that Gavidel was laundering drug money. The investigation included a sting operation, during which a confidential informant (the "C.I.") hired Gavidel to help him launder funds, purportedly from the sale of illegal narcotics, through Homa. At trial, the Government established that from November 1999 through August 2000, Gavidel laundered the C.I.'s money by wiring hundreds of thousands of dollars he believed were the C.I.'s narcotics proceeds to bank accounts in London.

Before wiring the money overseas, Gavidel made cash purchases of small-denomination money orders and then deposited those money orders in a Homa bank account. Testimony at trial established that postal officials must record purchases of money orders in excess of $3,000, and that it is illegal to purchase money orders in amounts less than $3,000 to evade reporting requirements. During an eighteen-month period, Gavidel deposited 882 postal money orders, each valued at less than $3,000, with a total value of $614,459 into a Homa bank account in the United States. Gavidel's girlfriend testified that she purchased numerous money orders several times per week at Gavidel's direction. On a number of occasions, Gavidel accompanied her and purchased money orders also.

In addition to these illicit activities, Gavidel violated the Embargo in the summer of 2000 by indirectly transferring money into bank accounts in Iran. The Government established its case in this regard by offering as evidence Gavidel's faxes. The faxes indicated correspondence between Gavidel, his brother in Iran, and third parties planning and implementing the transfer of funds from the United States to bank accounts in Iran via Dubai, U.A.E. They also depicted copies of deposit tickets and statements from Iranian banks. On two occasions, Gavidel's bank declined transfer requests involving Gavidel's account when the bank suspected that Gavidel was attempting to funnel money to Iran. On both occasions, the Treasury Department's Office of Foreign Assets Control ("OFAC") issued a letter to Gavidel inquiring of his business relations with Iran and referencing Treasury Department regulations relating to the Embargo.

DISCUSSION

The Embargo prohibits the "exportation . . . directly or indirectly, from the United States . . . of any goods, technology, or services to Iran." 31 C.F.R. § 560.204. In our view, the execution on behalf of others of money transfers from the United States to Iran is a "service" under the terms of the Embargo. The term "services" is unambiguous and refers to the performance of something useful for a fee. *See United States v. All Funds on Deposit in United Bank of Switzerland*, 2003 WL 56999, at *1 (S.D.N.Y. Jan. 7, 2003) ("*All Funds*") (Rakoff, J.).

This plain interpretation of the meaning of "services" is corroborated by the Iranian Transaction Regulations, which permit qualifying depository institutions to execute certain specified types of money transfers to Iran. Under those regulations, depository institutions may transfer funds to or from Iran if the transfer arises from a non-prohibited transaction, such as a family remittance unrelated to a family business, and does not involve debiting or crediting an Iranian account. *See* 31 C.F.R. § 560.516(a)(3). Certainly, if the provision of money transfers were not a service under the Embargo, as Gavidel argues, there would be no need for the exception.

The Embargo's prohibition on the exportation of services applies "where the benefit of such services is . . . received in Iran, if such services are performed . . . [i]n the United States." 31 C.F.R. § 560.410(a). Plainly, the individual or entity in Iran that received the transferred funds benefited from Gavidel's services.

> The obvious purpose of the order is to isolate Iran from trade with the United States. . . . This broad export ban reflected the President's appraisal of the nation's interest in sanctioning Iran's sponsorship of international terrorism, its frustration of the Middle East peace process, and its pursuit of weapons of mass destruction.

United States v. Ehsan, 163 F.3d 855, 859 (4th Cir. 1998). Gavidel's activities—transferring a customer's money to Iran for a fee—clearly fall within the sweep of the statute.

We also reject Gavidel's challenge to the district court's jury instruction on the willfulness requirement for criminal liability under the Embargo. "[T]o establish a 'willful' violation of a statute, the Government must prove that the defendant acted with knowledge that his conduct was unlawful." *Bryan v. United States*, 524 U.S. 184, 191-92 (1998) (internal quotation marks omitted). The district court properly instructed the jury that it could not convict Gavidel of violating the Embargo unless "the defendant knew that such transmission of funds was a violation of the Iranian embargo, and was, thus, illegal." The instruction clearly articulated that Gavidel had to violate knowingly the Embargo.

Furthermore, we reject Gavidel's challenge to the sufficiency of the evidence of his willfulness to violate the Embargo. On two occasions, Gavidel's bank refused to complete questionable transactions. Following each of these incidents, OFAC wrote letters to Gavidel inquiring of his business purposes and alerting him to the Embargo's regulations. Moreover, Gavidel conducted his business practices in stealth, using code words to reference money transfers. Sometimes he described his clandestine transactions in terms of the sale of newspapers; other times he surreptitiously referred to the sale of tea. This activity clearly confirms that Gavidel knew his activities ran afoul of the law.

Accordingly, we affirm the district court's judgment.

NOTES AND QUESTIONS

1. What conduct is prohibited under the Iranian sanctions? What is the scope of the prohibited conduct? The Iran embargo prohibits the "exportation . . . directly or indirectly, from the United States . . . of any goods, technology, or services to Iran." 31 C.F.R. § 560.240. Would the result have been different if Gavidel had not charged a fee for the money transfers?
2. Is the term "service" unconstitutionally vague? In *Holder v. Humanitarian Law Project*, 561 U.S. 1 (2010), the Court held that the term "service" for purposes of the material support statute, 18 U.S.C. § 2339A(b)(1), was not unconstitutionally vague as applied. Is the Court's ruling dispositive of the vagueness issue in the context of IEEPA?
3. Why did the court find that the defendant "willfully" violated the Iranian economic sanctions?

ECONOMIC SANCTIONS AGAINST NATION STATES

OFAC is currently enforcing economic sanctions against the Balkans, Burundi, Central African Republic, Cote d'Ivoire (Ivory Coast), Cuba, Democratic Republic of the Congo, Iran, Iraq, Lebanon, Libya, Mali, Nicaragua, North Korea, Somalia, Sudan, Syria, Russia, Venezuela, Yemen and Zimbabwe. *See* OFAC's website: http://www.Treasury.gov/resources-center/sanctions/Programs/Pages/Programs.aspx.

III. TERRORIST FINANCING — EXECUTIVE ORDER 13224

After the September 11, 2001 terrorist attacks, President George W. Bush issued Executive Order 13224, invoking his authority under the IEEPA, 50 U.S.C. §§ 1701 et seq. E.O. 13224 declared a national emergency with respect to "grave acts of terrorism and threats of terrorism committed by foreign terrorists, including the terrorist attacks . . . committed on September 11, 2001 . . . and the continuing and immediate threat of further attacks on United States nationals or the United States." Exec. Order No. 13224, Blocking Property and Prohibiting Transactions with Persons Who Commit, Threaten to Commit, or Support Terrorism, 66 Fed. Reg. 49079 (Sept. 23, 2001). Initially, the order designated twelve individuals and fifteen entities as "Specially Designated Global Terrorists" (SDGTs), and identified them in the Annex to E.O. 13224. *Id.* To date, the number of SDGTs has grown to over 1,400 individuals and entities.[12]

E.O. 13224 authorizes the Secretary of the Treasury, in consultation with the Secretary of State and the Attorney General, to designate and block the property of additional persons who (1) "act for or on behalf of" or are "owned or controlled by" designated terrorists, (2) "assist in, sponsor, or provide financial, material, or technological support for" SDGTs, or (3) are "otherwise associated with" SDGTs. *Id.* §§ 1(c)-(d). Further, E.O. 13224 authorizes the Secretary of State, in consultation with the Secretary of the Treasury and the Attorney General, to designate as SDGTs persons determined "to have committed, or to pose a significant risk of committing, acts of terrorism that threaten the security of United States nationals or the national security, foreign policy, or economy of the United States." *Id.* § 1(b).

Multiple constitutional challenges have been raised against blocking actions under E.O. 13224. Plaintiffs have advanced the following legal theories: (1) blocking actions under E.O. 13224 failed to provide them meaningful notice and opportunity to be heard; (2) use of classified information without disclosure to the designated party violates due process; (3) OFAC's authority under IEEPA and E.O. 13224 is unconstitutionally vague; (4) OFAC blocking actions constitute an unconstitutional taking under the Takings Clause of the Fifth Amendment; and (5) blocking actions constitute an unlawful seizure under the Fourth Amendment. Legal issues have also been raised with respect to the scope of E.O. 13224. These constitutional arguments are discussed in the following cases.

---

12. *See* OFAC, U.S. Treasury, Terrorists Asset report to the Congress, 27th annual, at 6 (2018), *available at* http://www.treasury.gov/resource-center/sanctions/OFAC-Enforcement/Pages/20150506 .aspx. As of December 31, 2018, a total of 1,411 individuals and entities had been designated SDGTs under E.O. 13224, which includes 67 Foreign Terrorist Organizations designated by the Secretary of State pursuant to the Antiterrorism and Effective Death Penalty Act of 1996.

DEFINITION OF TERRORISM

Executive Order 13224, issued by President Bush on September 23, 2001, defines terrorism to mean "an activity that involves a violent act or an act dangerous to human life, property or infrastructure; and appears to be intended to intimidate or coerce a civilian population; to influence the policy of a government by intimidation or coercion; or to affect the conduct of a government by mass destruction, assassination, kidnapping, or hostage-taking." Exec. Order No. 13224 § 3(d).

Global Relief Foundation, Inc. v. O'Neill
315 F.3d 748 (7th Cir. 2002)

EASTERBROOK, Circuit Judge.

Following the terrorist attack of September 11, 2001, the President issued an executive order declaring a national emergency and authorizing the Secretary of the Treasury to freeze the assets of groups that "assist in, sponsor, or provide financial, material, or technological support for, or financial or other services to or in support of, such acts of terrorism" to the extent that statutes permit freezes. Executive Order 13224 § 1(d)(i), 66 Fed. Reg. 49079 (Sept. 23, 2001). Authority for this order lies in the International Emergency Economic Powers Act (IEEPA), 50 U.S.C. §§ 1701-07, which after Executive Order 13224 was amended by the USA PATRIOT Act, Pub. L. 107-56, Title I, § 106, 115 Stat. 272 (Oct. 26, 2001). On December 14, 2001, the Secretary used the delegated authority to block all assets of Global Relief Foundation, Inc., an Illinois charitable corporation that conducts operations in approximately 25 foreign entities, including Afghanistan, Albania, Bosnia, Kosovo, Iraq, Lebanon, Pakistan, Palestine (West Bank and Gaza), Russia (Chechnya and Ingushetia), Somalia, and Syria. The provision underlying this action is § 1702(a)(1)(B), which provides that the President may

> investigate, block during the pendency of an investigation, regulate, direct and compel, nullify, void, prevent or prohibit, any acquisition, holding, withholding, use, transfer, withdrawal, transportation, importation or exportation of, or dealing in, or exercising any right, power, or privilege with respect to, or transactions involving, any property in which any foreign country or a national thereof has any interest by any person, or with respect to any property, subject to the jurisdiction of the United States[.]

Global Relief Foundation (which goes by the acronym GRF) denies that any "foreign . . . national" has an "interest" in its assets, and it asked the district court to enjoin the blocking order for this reason and several others said to be rooted in the Constitution. The district court denied this request, see 207 F. Supp. 2d 779 (N.D. Ill. 2002), and GRF has appealed.

When the district court acted, the blocking order was an interim step pending investigation. The freeze on December 14 was accompanied by a search of

GRF's headquarters, and the Treasury Department planned to use evidence obtained from the search, plus submissions it invited from GRF, to decide whether to extend the freeze. One element of relief that GRF requested was an injunction against the extension, which would be accomplished by naming GRF a "Specially Designated Global Terrorist" under Executive Order 13224. On October 18, 2002, shortly before oral argument, the Office of Foreign Assets Control listed GRF as a Specially Designated Global Terrorist. See <http://www .treas.gov/offices/enforcement/ofac/actions/20021018.html>. Designation does not change the status of GRF's assets and records, which remain in Treasury's control. But it does affect the scope of arguments available on appeal. Because the designation is a *fait accompli*, a court cannot enjoin its making—though a court might direct the Office of Foreign Assets Control to lift it. To the extent that GRF was attacking the factual support for the interim order, time has passed that issue by; the right question now is whether the designation of October 18 is supported by adequate information, and that question cannot be resolved until the district court has assembled a new record. What is more, some of GRF's principal legal theories drop out of the case. It contended, for example, that Executive Order 13224, which was issued before enactment of the USA PATRIOT Act, could not have delegated to the Secretary of the Treasury those powers added to the IEEPA by the new law. The change that potentially affected this case was the addition to § 1702(a)(1)(B) of language authorizing asset freezes pending investigation. Now that the investigative stage is over, however, the amendment to the IEEPA does not matter to the freeze, and it is correspondingly inappropriate for us to decide whether Executive Order 13224 delegates powers enacted after September 23, 2001.

. . .

Let us turn, then, to GRF's contention that the IEEPA does not apply to corporations that hold charters issued within the United States. The argument is straightforward: a U.S. corporation is a U.S. citizen; the corporation owns all of its property (including its bank accounts); this property therefore cannot be "property in which any foreign country or a national thereof has any interest" for the purpose of § 1702(a)(1)(B). The district court observed that two of the three members of GRF's board are foreign nationals, but this does not alter the fact that GRF is itself a citizen of the United States. Neither membership on the board nor ownership of stock affects the citizenship of the firm, which as a matter of corporate law has an existence separate from that of the directors and investors. Cases such as *Sumitomo Shoji America, Inc. v. Avagliano*, 457 U.S. 176 (1982), illustrate the application of this principle to federal statutes. Treaties that the United States has negotiated with many foreign nations allow citizens (including corporations) of those nations certain privileges within the United States. *Avagliano* holds that a U.S. subsidiary of a foreign corporation is a U.S. citizen, not a foreign citizen, for the purpose of these treaties, which meant that the subsidiary must comply fully with U.S. law even though 100% of its stock may be held by foreign nationals. Some statutes prescribe a different rule. The Foreign Sovereign Immunities Act, for example, treats a corporation as having the sovereign attributes of a government that owns the majority of its stock. 28 U.S.C. § 1603(b)(2). . . . But under the Foreign Sovereign Immunities Act a corporation chartered within the United States always is treated as a private U.S. citizen, even if a foreign nation owns all of its stock. 28 U.S.C. § 1603(b)(3). Given the holding of *Avagliano* and the norm reflected in § 1603(b)(3), does it not follow that the property of any corporation chartered within the United States is domestic U.S. property?

No, it does not follow, and for a simple reason. GRF reads the word "interest" in § 1702(a)(1)(B) as referring to a *legal* interest, in the way that a trustee is legal owner of the corpus even if someone else enjoys the beneficial interest. . . . The legal interest in GRF's property lies in the United States, but we need to know whether § 1702(a)(1)(B) refers to legal as opposed to beneficial interests. The function of the IEEPA strongly suggests that beneficial rather than legal interests matter. The statute is designed to give the President means to control assets that could be used by enemy aliens. When an enemy holds the *beneficial* interest in property, that is a real risk even if a U.S. citizen is the legal owner. Consider for a moment what would happen if Osama bin Laden put all of his assets into a trust, under Illinois law, administered by a national bank. If the trust instrument directed the trustee to make the funds available for purchases of weapons to be used by al Qaeda, then foreign enemies of the United States would have an "interest" in these funds even though legal ownership would be vested in the bank. The situation is the same if al Qaeda incorporated a subsidiary in Delaware and transferred all of its funds to that corporation — something it could do without any al Qaeda operative setting foot in the United States. What sense could it make to treat al Qaeda's funds as open to seizure if administered by a German bank but not if administered by a Delaware corporation under terrorist control? Nothing in the text of the IEEPA suggests that the United States' ability to respond to an external threat can be defeated so easily. Thus the focus must be on how assets could be controlled and used, not on bare legal ownership. GRF conducts its operations outside the United States; the funds are applied for the benefit of non-citizens and thus are covered by § 1702(a)(1)(B).

This understanding is consistent with the portion of *Dames & Moore v. Regan*, 453 U.S. 654, 675 (1981), on which GRF relies. The Court observed that "claims of American citizens against Iran are not in themselves transactions involving Iranian property or efforts to exercise any rights with respect to such property." GRF reads this as excluding any claims or other property owned by citizens of the United States. We read it, to the contrary, as focusing on the nature of the property rather than the identity of its owner. Claims *against* Iran not only were owned by U.S. citizens but also were designed to generate funds that would be used beneficially within the United States. Claims owned nominally by U.S. citizens but effectively controlled by Iran, or designed to raise funds for the operation of the Iranian government, would have been treated differently, we are confident. See also *Centrifugal Casting Machine Co. v. American Bank & Trust Co.*, 966 F.2d 1348, 1353-54 (10th Cir. 1992) (looking to the nature of the interest, rather than the citizenship of its legal owner, to determine whether it is within scope of IEEPA). So the fact that GRF as a U.S. corporation owns all of its assets does not mean that the assets are free of any foreign national's interest.

A foreign beneficial interest does not automatically make the funds subject to freeze. We have nothing to say here about whether GRF supports terrorism (as Treasury has concluded) or instead provides humanitarian relief (as it describes itself). That question is open to review in the district court, on the record compiled by the agency before it named GRF as a Specially Designated Global Terrorist. What we hold is that the phrase "property in which any foreign country or a national thereof has any interest" in § 1702(a)(1)(B) does not offer GRF a silver bullet that will terminate the freeze without regard to the nature of its activities.

None of GRF's constitutional arguments has that effect either. There is no separation-of-powers problem, as *Dames & Moore* shows. The Steel Seizure Case, *Youngstown Sheet & Tube Co. v. Sawyer*, 343 U.S. 579 (1952), dealt with a seizure of private assets under a President's inherent powers, which the Court deemed insufficient; Executive Order 13224, by contrast, delegates to the Secretary only those powers provided by statute.

Administration of the IEEPA is not rendered unconstitutional because that statute authorizes the use of classified evidence that may be considered *ex parte* by the district court. 50 U.S.C. § 1702(c). *Ex parte* consideration is common in criminal cases where, say, the identity of informants otherwise might be revealed, see *Roviaro v. United States*, 353 U.S. 53 (1957), and in litigation under the Freedom of Information Act—where public disclosure would divulge the very information that the case is about and thus make it impossible for the government to maintain confidentiality even when the FOIA does not create a right of public access. . . . A part of the Antiterrorism and Effective Death Penalty Act of 1996 parallel to § 1702(c) has been sustained against constitutional challenge in two decisions with which we agree. See *Iran Council of Resistance v. Department of State*, 251 F.3d 192, 196 (D.C. Cir. 2001); *People's Mojahedin Organization v. Department of State*, 182 F.3d 17, 19 (D.C. Cir. 1999). See also, e.g., *United States v. Ott*, 827 F.2d 473, 476 (9th Cir. 1987), and *United States v. Belfield*, 692 F.2d 141, 147 (D.C. Cir. 1982), which hold that use and *ex parte* judicial review of classified information under the Foreign Intelligence Surveillance Act are constitutionally proper. The Constitution would indeed be a suicide pact, *Kennedy v. Mendoza-Martinez*, 372 U.S. 144, 160 (1963), if the only way to curtail enemies' access to assets were to reveal information that might cost lives.

Nor does the Constitution entitle GRF to notice and a pre-seizure hearing, an opportunity that would allow any enemy to spirit assets out of the United States. Although pre-seizure hearing is the constitutional norm, postponement is acceptable in emergencies. See, e.g., *Gilbert v. Homar*, 520 U.S. 924, 930 (1997); *FDIC v. Mallen*, 486 U.S. 230, 240 (1988). Risks of error rise when hearings are deferred, but these risks must be balanced against the potential for loss of life if assets should be put to violent use. Opportunity to obtain recompense under the Tucker Act, 28 U.S.C. § 1491(a), if the blocking turns out to be invalid, provides the private party with the very remedy that the Constitution names: just compensation. If the freeze is sustained on the merits, however, GRF does not have any grievance, any more than a cocaine ring has a right to recover the value of the illegal drugs or a thief a right to be paid the value of confiscated burglar's tools. See *Paradissiotis v. United States*, 304 F.3d 1271 (Fed. Cir. 2002). GRF's takings claim not only is premature—it must await decision on the validity of the Global Terrorist designation—but also is in the wrong court. It belongs to the Court of Federal Claims under the Tucker Act.

Other constitutional theories—such as GRF's contention that application of the IEEPA is an ex post facto law—are defective for too many reasons to count. For example, only criminal statutes are deemed ex post facto laws, and the IEEPA does not define a crime. Moreover, the IEEPA predates GRF's activities, and at all events aid to the enemies of the United States has been unlawful since the Nation's founding. Application of the IEEPA is not a bill of attainder; implementation of the statute is in the hands of the Executive and Judicial Branches, while a bill of attainder is a decision of guilt made by the Legislative Branch. See *United States v. Lovett*, 328 U.S. 303, 315 (1946). It is unnecessary to recite and reject the rest of this lot individually.

Because we have dealt exclusively with legal contentions, our resolution of them is conclusive and not subject to reexamination in the district court when deciding whether GRF is entitled to a permanent injunction. But we have avoided any inquiry into the facts and do not attempt to anticipate the ultimate resolution of GRF's claim. The central question now becomes whether the evidence supports the agency's belief that GRF uses its assets to support terrorism. That question should be addressed and resolved expeditiously in the district court. The judgment denying GRF's request for an injunction that would compel the release of its assets while that issue remains open is affirmed.

NOTES AND QUESTIONS

1. Section 1702(a)(1)(B) of IEEPA authorizes the President to block any property in which any "foreign country or a national thereof" has any interest, subject to the jurisdiction of the United States. IEEPA doesn't authorize blocking orders against U.S. persons, only foreign countries and their nationals. The Treasury Department issued a blocking order against the Global Relief Foundation (GRF), a corporation that holds a charter issued in the United States. Isn't GRF a U.S. person? If so, doesn't it follow that the property of a corporation chartered within the United States is domestic U.S. property? Why then did the court uphold the blocking action against GRF? What's the reasoning of the court?

2. The court held that classified information may be considered by the court *ex parte* in determining the legality of a blocking action under IEEPA. Doesn't the use of secret evidence deprive the property owner of due process? Without

access to the secret evidence, how can the property owner mount an effective legal defense to the blocking action?

3. In support of the court's ruling on the use of classified information, the court cited *Roviaro v. United States*, 353 U.S. 53 (1957). However, the Supreme Court in *Roviaro* did not hold that the identity of a confidential informant may always be withheld from the defendant. Instead, the government's interest in protecting the safety of the confidential informant by withholding his identity must give way when the evidence would be relevant and material to the defense. Should a similar rule apply with respect to blocking a person's property?

4. Is the government required to provide notice and a hearing to the property owner before her assets are frozen under E.O. 13224? Is the property owner entitled to a pre-seizure hearing? If not, why not?

BLOCKING ACTIONS

Blocking terrorist-related assets is an administrative, rather than a criminal action. Designation as a Specially Designated Global Terrorist (SDGT) therefore does not require that the party be criminally prosecuted and convicted, or even charged with committing acts of terrorism. Because designations and blocking orders are administrative in nature, the government is not required to satisfy the standard of proof beyond a reasonable doubt. Instead, a lower standard of proof is applied. An individual may be designated and his assets frozen if there is "reason to believe" that he may have engaged in activities prohibited by E.O. 13224.

Humanitarian Relief Project v. United States Dep't of Treasury
484 F. Supp. 2d 1099 (C.D. Cal. 2007)

FACTUAL AND PROCEDURAL BACKGROUND

On November 21, 2006, the Court issued an Order ("Order") granting in part and denying in part Plaintiffs' Motion for Summary Judgment and Defendants' Motion to Dismiss and Cross-Motion for Summary Judgment. *See Humanitarian Law Project v. U.S. Dept. of Treasury*, 463 F. Supp. 2d 1049 (C.D. Cal. 2006). On January 18, 2007, the Court issued a Judgment (entered on January 24, 2007) and a minute order informing the parties of its view that the November 21, 2006 Order resolved all issues in the case, and that the judgment should be made final. However, the Court also allowed any party that disagreed with this view to submit, by January 30, 2007, a brief setting forth any such objection, and identifying any outstanding issues prior to the Court's closing the case.

On January 30, 2007, Defendants filed the instant Motion, seeking reconsideration of two aspects of the Court's Order. First, Defendants contend that the Court should reconsider its decision that the "otherwise associated with" provision of Executive Order 13224 ("EO"), section 1(d)(ii), is unconstitutionally vague on its face and overbroad. Defendants state that on January 26, 2007, in response to the Order, the Office of Foreign Assets Control ("OFAC") issued a new regulation (31 C.F.R. § 594.316) defining "otherwise associated with." Defendants contend that this new regulation cures the unconstitutionality of EO § 1(d)(ii). Thus, Defendants ask the Court to assess the new regulation, find EO § 1(d)(ii) constitutional, and vacate its Order and injunction against enforcing EO § 1(d)(ii) against Plaintiffs.

Second, Defendants seek reconsideration of the Court's decision that the President's designation of twenty-seven individuals and groups as SDGTs in the Annex to the EO was unconstitutional. Defendants contend that the Court did not consider governing law, and thus arrived at an incorrect decision. Plaintiffs oppose each of Defendants' arguments.

DISCUSSION

. . .

A. The "Otherwise Associated With" Provision

Defendants seek reconsideration of the Court's finding that the "otherwise associated with" provision is unconstitutional on the ground that a change of law occurred after the Order was issued, and that this change of law remedied the constitutional infirmities identified in the Order. Before disputing Defendants' arguments on their merits, Plaintiffs urge the Court to decline to consider the new regulation on a number of grounds, including that the motion is untimely, that Defendants have not demonstrated how their request meets the requirements for reconsideration, and that Defendants' motion amounts to a request to find the Order moot on the unsound ground that Defendants voluntarily changed their illegal conduct.

. . .

2. Whether 31 C.F.R. § 594.316 Remedies the Vagueness and Overbreadth of EO 13224, § 1(d)(ii)

As stated, Defendants contend that the new regulation remedies the constitutional infirmities identified in the Order. Specifically, the Order found the "otherwise associated with" provision of the EO unconstitutionally vague because the term is not itself susceptible of clear meaning, was not defined by OFAC's implementing regulations, its application was not subject to any identifiable criteria, and its enforcement was therefore subject only to the Government's unfettered discretion. The Order also found the provision unconstitutionally overbroad because it imposed penalties for mere association with SDGTs, and that this overbreadth was substantial in relation to the potentially constitutional scope of the provision. *See Humanitarian Law Project*, 463 F. Supp. 2d at 1070-1071.

Defendants now contend that, in direct response to the Order, OFAC revised its regulations implementing and interpreting the EO by adding a new section, 31 C.F.R. § 594.316, to define "otherwise associated with" as it is used in the regulation that corresponds to EO 13224, § 1(d)(ii). Section 594.316 states:

> The term "to be otherwise associated with," as used in [31 C.F.R.] § 594.201(a)(4)(ii), means:
>
>   (a) To own or control; or
>
>   (b) To attempt, or to conspire with one or more persons, to act for or on behalf of or to provide financial, material, or technological support, or financial or other services, to.

Defendants contend that this newly-issued definition sets forth criteria governing the Secretary of the Treasury's (hereafter, "Secretary") discretion to designate SDGTs that are sufficient to avoid violating the First and Fifth Amendments to the United States Constitution. Plaintiffs disagree, contending that the new regulation is null and void because it exceeds the Secretary's designation authority under section 1(c) of the EO. Plaintiffs further argue that even if the new regulation is not null and void, it does not cure the constitutional infirmities of the "otherwise associated with" provision. The Court agrees with Defendants.

First, the new regulation does not exceed the scope of the Secretary's designation authority. Plaintiffs contend that the regulation expands the Secretary's designation authority under section 1(c) of the EO. Specifically, Plaintiffs claim that while section 1(c) authorizes the designation of persons who are "owned or controlled by" already-designated SDGTs, the new regulation reaches to those who themselves "own or control" SDGTs. This argument is not well-taken.

The new regulation relates to the Secretary's designation authority under EO § 1(d)(ii), the "otherwise associated with" provision, not to section 1(c). As such, the new provision simply defines the operative term of the designation authority delegated to the Secretary in section 1(d)(ii). In addition to this express delegation of authority to designate SDGTs, the Secretary is authorized, under EO § 7, "to take such actions, including promulgation of rules and regulations, and to employ all powers granted to the President by IEEPA and UNPA as may be necessary to carry out the purposes of this order." Thus, the EO also expressly authorizes the Secretary to issue regulations to interpret the designation authority granted therein. As such, OFAC's regulations do not exceed the scope of the Secretary's authority "unless they contradict express statutory language or prove unreasonable." *Consarc Corp. v. Iraqi Ministry*, 27 F.3d 695, 701 (D.C. Cir. 1994). Here, in stating that to be "otherwise associated with" an SDGT means that a person "own[s] or control[s]" an SDGT, or "attempts" or "conspires" to provide "financial, material or technological support" to an SDGT, the regulation does not contradict express statutory language. Indeed, it is clear that such conduct is consistent with being "otherwise associated with." Accordingly, the Secretary has the authority to construe the term "otherwise associated with" as used in EO § 1(d)(ii), and the definition established by 31 C.F.R. § 594.316 is a reasonable construction of that term.

The new provision also remedies the constitutional defects of the "otherwise associated with" provision. The full language of the new provision states that to be "otherwise associated with" means "[t]o own or control" an SDGT, or "[t]o attempt, or to conspire with one or more persons, to act for or on behalf of or to provide financial, material, or technological support, or financial or other services, to" an SDGT. 31 C.F.R. § 594.316. In the Order, the Court analyzed nearly identical language in the EO, and found that it satisfied the Constitution. Specifically, the Court held that the Secretary's authority to designate a person who is "owned or controlled by, or . . . act[s] for or on behalf of" other SDGTs (EO § 1(c)), or someone who has provided "financial, material, or technological support for, or financial or other services to or in support of" acts of terrorism or other SDGTs (EO § 1(d)(i)), was not vague and did not violate Fifth Amendment due process requirements. *See Humanitarian Law Project v. U.S. Dept. of Treasury*, 463 F. Supp. 2d 1049, 1065-1066 (C.D. Cal. 2006). The Court sees no reason to depart from its earlier reasoning, and it applies equally to the same language in the new provision.

The new provision's language varies from that previously analyzed only in that it identifies "to own or control" and "[t]o attempt, or to conspire" as additional bases for designation. Plaintiffs do not challenge the constitutionality of the "to own or control" element of the provision. However, Plaintiffs do claim that the phrase "to attempt, or to conspire" to do anything "on behalf of" can reach "any" associational activity, such as filling out a membership card or communicating with an SDGT about its interests, and that this language is therefore unconstitutional.

Plaintiffs' conclusory argument does not specify whether they believe that the provision is vague, overbroad, or both. In any case, Plaintiffs' argument is not persuasive. The Court already found that the phrase "on behalf of" was not vague. *See Humanitarian Law Project v. U.S. Dept. of Treasury*, 463 F. Supp. 2d at 1065-1066. In addition, unlike the term "otherwise associated with," the phrase "to attempt, or to conspire" does not on its face reach mere association and is not vague on its face. Indeed, to attempt, or to conspire to engage in, an unlawful activity is routinely considered criminal in innumerable contexts. Nor is the provision vague even as to the hypothetical conduct Plaintiffs posit. Filling out a membership card or communicating for informational purposes cannot be construed as "to attempt, or to conspire" to do something illegal on the organization's behalf. Ultimately, the meaning of the phrase "to attempt, or to conspire" is "sufficiently clear so as not to cause persons 'of common intelligence . . . necessarily [to] guess at its meaning and [to] differ as to its application.'" *United States v. Wunsch*, 84 F.3d 1110, 1119 (9th Cir. 1996) (quoting *Connally v. General Constr. Co.*, 269 U.S. 385, 391 (1926)). Thus, "to attempt or to conspire" is not unconstitutionally vague.

Nor is the phrase "to attempt, or to conspire" unconstitutionally overbroad. A law is overbroad if it punishes a substantial amount of protected conduct judged in relation to the statute's legitimate sweep, until and unless the law is narrowed to remove the threat. *See Virginia v. Hicks*, 539 U.S. 113, 118 (2003). Here, "to attempt, or to conspire" does not on its face reach mere association, nor do Plaintiffs provide any credible scenarios wherein the provision could be employed beyond its legitimate scope, nor can the Court formulate one. Accordingly, the definition of "otherwise associated with" supplied by 31 C.F.R. § 594.316 is sufficiently precise to satisfy the Constitution. Thus, the injunction issued against enforcement of EO 13224, § 1(d)(ii), the "otherwise associated with" provision, is no longer warranted and the injunction is hereby lifted.

NOTES AND QUESTIONS

1. The court held that the OFAC regulation defining the "otherwise associated with" in E.O. 13224 was not unconstitutionally vague on its face. How does the new OFAC regulation remedy the constitutional defects of "otherwise associated with" provision?
2. Under the new provision, who may be designated under E.O. 13224 and subjected to a blocking order?
3. Plaintiffs argued that the phrase "to attempt, or to conspire" to do anything "on behalf of" a Specially Designated Global Terrorist (SDGT) reaches associational activity, such as filling out a membership card or communicating with an SDGT, and this language is therefore unconstitutionally vague. Why did the court reject this argument?
4. The new provision prohibits "to attempt, or to conspire with one or more persons" to provide "financial or other services" to an SDGT. Is the term "other services" unconstitutionally vague?

Al Haramain Islamic Foundation, Inc. v. United States Dep't of Treasury
686 F.3d 965 (9th Cir. 2011)

Plaintiff Al Haramain Islamic Foundation, Oregon ("AHIF-Oregon"), is a nonprofit organization, incorporated in Oregon, whose stated purpose is to promote greater understanding of Islam. The United States government suspected AHIF-Oregon of supporting terrorism. In 2004, the Office of Foreign Assets Control ("OFAC"), a part of the United States Department of the Treasury, froze AHIF-Oregon's assets and designated AHIF-Oregon as a "specially designated global terrorist" pursuant to Executive Order ("EO") No. 13,224. President George W. Bush had issued EO 13,224 pursuant to the International Emergency Economic Powers Act ("IEEPA"), 50 U.S.C. §§ 1701-1707, in the wake of the events of September 11, 2001.

AHIF-Oregon eventually filed this action, asserting that OFAC has violated a variety of its statutory and constitutional rights. Plaintiff Multicultural Association of Southern Oregon, which the government has not accused of supporting terrorism, challenges certain laws that bar it from providing services to designated entities such as AHIF-Oregon. With the exception of one claim not at issue on appeal, the district court granted summary judgment to OFAC.

. . . We affirm the district court's ruling that substantial evidence supports OFAC's redesignation of AHIF-Oregon as a specially designated global terrorist, and we affirm the district court's rejection of AHIF-Oregon's due process claims. We reverse the district court's rejection of AHIF-Oregon's Fourth Amendment claim and remand for the district court to determine what judicial relief, if any, is available. Finally, we reverse the district court's dismissal of Plaintiffs' First Amendment claim.

FACTUAL AND PROCEDURAL HISTORY

. . .

Shortly after the events of September 11, 2001, President Bush exercised his authority under the IEEPA by issuing EO 13,224. 66 Fed. Reg. 49,079 (Sept. 23, 2001). Under the IEEPA, the President may, in specified ways, "deal with any unusual and extraordinary threat, which has its source in whole or substantial part outside the United States, to the national security, foreign policy, or economy of the United States, if the President declares a national emergency with respect to such threat." 50 U.S.C. § 1701(a). Relevant here, the President may

> (B) investigate, block during the pendency of an investigation, regulate, direct and compel, nullify, void, prevent or prohibit, any acquisition, holding, withholding, use, transfer, withdrawal, transportation, importation or exportation of, or dealing in, or exercising any right, power, or privilege with respect to, or transactions involving, any property in which any foreign country or a national thereof has any interest by any person, or with respect to any property, subject to the jurisdiction of the United States[.]

Id. § 1702(a)(1)(B). A person who violates the IEEPA is subject to civil penalties and, for willful violations, criminal penalties, including a fine up to $1 million and imprisonment for up to 20 years. *Id.* § 1705.

In the Executive Order, the President declared that the "September 11, 2001, acts . . . constitute an unusual and extraordinary threat to the national security, foreign policy, and economy of the United States." EO 13,224 pmbl. The Order "blocked" "all property and interests in property" of 27 persons designated by the Order, and it delegated to the specified agency head the authority to designate other persons with substantial connections to terrorist activities and organizations. *Id.* § 1. Specifically, Section 1 of the Order states that

> all property and interests in property of the following persons that are in the United States or that hereafter come within the United States, or that hereafter come within the possession or control of United States persons are blocked:
> (a) foreign persons listed in the Annex to this order;
> (b) foreign persons determined by the Secretary of State, in consultation with the Secretary of the Treasury and the Attorney General, to have committed, or to pose a significant risk of committing, acts of terrorism that threaten the security of U.S. nationals or the national security, foreign policy, or economy of the United States;

(c) persons determined by the Secretary of the Treasury, in consultation with the Secretary of State and the Attorney General, to be owned or controlled by, or to act for or on behalf of those persons listed in the Annex to this order or those persons determined to be subject to subsection 1(b), 1(c), or 1(d)(i) of this order;

(d) except as provided in section 5 of this order and after such consultation, if any, with foreign authorities as the Secretary of State, in consultation with the Secretary of the Treasury and the Attorney General, deems appropriate in the exercise of [her] discretion, persons determined by the Secretary of the Treasury, in consultation with the Secretary of State and the Attorney General;

(i) to assist in, sponsor, or provide financial, material, or technological support for, or financial or other services to or in support of, such acts of terrorism or those persons listed in the Annex to this order or determined to be subject to this order; or

(ii) to be otherwise associated with those persons listed in the Annex to this order or those persons determined to be subject to subsection 1(b), 1(c), or 1(d)(i) of this order.

. . . In the years following the issuance of EO 13,224, OFAC periodically designated new persons and entities. Relevant here, by February 1, 2004, OFAC had designated AHIF organizations in six countries: Somalia, Bosnia, Indonesia, Kenya, Tanzania, and Pakistan. But OFAC had not designated AHIF-Oregon, AHIF-Saudi Arabia, or any AHIF organization other than those six in the countries just listed.

. . .

DISCUSSION

. . .

B. Procedural Due Process Challenges

AHIF-Oregon argues that OFAC violated its procedural due process rights by using classified information without any disclosure of its content and by failing to provide adequate notice and a meaningful opportunity to respond. We apply the balancing test set forth in *Mathews v. Eldridge*, 424 U.S. 319 (1976). . . . Under the *Mathews* balancing test, we "must weigh (1) [the person's or entity's] private property interest, (2) the risk of an erroneous deprivation of such interest through the procedures used, as well as the value of additional safeguards, and (3) the Government's interest in maintaining its procedures, including the burdens of additional procedural requirements." *Foss v. Nat'l Marine Fisheries Serv.*, 161 F.3d 584, 589 (9th Cir. 1998) (citing *Mathews*, 424 U.S. at 334-35).

There are strong interests on both sides of the scale, generally encapsulated in the first and third *Mathews* factors. The private party's property interest is significant. By design, a designation by OFAC completely shutters all domestic operations of an entity. All assets are frozen. No person or organization may conduct any business whatsoever with the entity, other than a very narrow category of actions such as legal defense. Civil penalties attach even for unwitting violations. 50 U.S.C. § 1705(b). Criminal penalties, including up to 20 years' imprisonment, attach for willful violations. *Id.* § 1705(c). For domestic organizations such as AHIF-Oregon, a designation means that it conducts no business at all. . . . In sum, designation is not a mere inconvenience or burden on certain property interests; designation indefinitely renders a domestic organization financially defunct.

On the other side of the scale, the government's interest in national security cannot be understated. We owe unique deference to the executive branch's determination that we face "an unusual and extraordinary threat to the national security" of the United States. EO 13,224 pmbl. It is beyond dispute that "the Government's interest in combating terrorism is an urgent objective of the highest order." *Holder v. Humanitarian Law Project*, 130 S. Ct. 2705, 2724 (2010).

Striking a balance between those two strong competing interests cannot be done in the abstract. As the *Mathews* balancing test makes clear, we must carefully assess the precise "procedures used" by the government, "the value of additional safeguards," and "the burdens of additional procedural requirements." *Foss*, 161 F.3d at 589 (citing *Mathews*, 424 U.S. at 334-35). As explained in more detail below, the Constitution certainly does not require that the government take actions that would endanger national security; nor does it require the government to undertake every possible effort to mitigate the risk of erroneous deprivation and the potential harm to the private party. But the Constitution does require that the government take reasonable measures to ensure basic fairness to the private party and that the government follow procedures reasonably designed to protect against erroneous deprivation of the private party's interests.

1. OFAC's Use of Classified Information

AHIF-Oregon argues that OFAC's use of classified information violates its procedural due process rights. The first two *Mathews* factors support AHIF-Oregon's position. As noted above, its private interests are significant. And, as we have held previously with respect to the use of classified information without disclosure: "One would be hard pressed to design a procedure more likely to result in erroneous deprivations." *ADC*, 70 F.3d at 1069. "[T]he very foundation of the adversary process assumes that use of undisclosed information will violate due process because of the risk of error." *Id.* But the third *Mathews* factor—the government's interest in maintaining national security— supports OFAC's position.

Given the extreme importance of maintaining national security, we cannot accept AHIF-Oregon's most sweeping argument—that OFAC is not entitled to use classified information in making its designation determination. *See generally Gen. Dynamics Corp. v. United States*, ___ U.S. ___, 131 S. Ct. 1900, 1905 (2011) ("[P]rotecting our national security sometimes requires keeping information about our military, intelligence, and diplomatic efforts secret.").

In AHIF-Oregon's view, if classified information concerning national security demonstrates that an entity is supporting terrorism, OFAC either must decline to designate the entity or must reveal the classified information to the entity that OFAC believes supports terrorist activities. Common sense dictates that AHIF-Oregon is overreaching. Not surprisingly, all federal courts to have considered this argument have rejected it. *Holy Land*, 333 F.3d at 164; *Global Relief Found., Inc. v. O'Neill*, 315 F.3d 748, 754 (7th Cir. 2002); *KindHearts for Charitable Humanitarian Dev., Inc. v. Geithner* (*KindHearts II*), 710 F. Supp. 2d 637, 660 (N.D. Ohio 2010); *Al-Aqeel v. Paulson*, 568 F. Supp. 2d 64, 72 (D.D.C. 2008). . . .

The only case that could be read to yield the contrary conclusion is our decision in *ADC*, 70 F.3d 1045. There, the government used classified information in summary proceedings to exclude certain long-time resident aliens. *Id.* at 1052-54. The aliens brought suit, alleging that the use of classified information violated their due process rights. *Id.* at 1054. The district court, after viewing the classified information ex parte and in camera, agreed. *Id.*

Applying the *Mathews* balancing test, we affirmed. *ADC*, 70 F.3d at 1068-70. We found that the first two factors strongly favored the plaintiffs. And, under the facts of that case, we held that the government's claims of national security were "insufficient to tip the *Mathews* scale towards the Government." *Id.* at 1070. We reached that conclusion because of *the content of the classified information.* Specifically, the government had argued that the aliens threatened national security, but the classified information contained nothing about the aliens themselves; the classified information demonstrated only that the aliens were nominal members of a foreign organization that had engaged in terrorist activities. *Id.* at 1069-70. Notably, we stated that "[t]hese aliens have been free since the beginning of this litigation almost eight years ago, without criminal charges being brought against them for their activities. . . . [The classified evidence] does not indicate that either alien has personally advocated those [impermissible] doctrines or has participated in terrorist activities." *Id.* at 1070. We concluded that the use of classified information "should be presumptively unconstitutional. Only the most extraordinary circumstances could support one-sided process." *Id.* Because extraordinary circumstances did not exist in that case, the use of the classified information was impermissible. *Id.*

AHIF-Oregon argues that *ADC* is directly on point and "controls here." AHIF-Oregon is mistaken. We did not hold that classified information can never be used. Instead, we held that such use is "presumptively unconstitutional" subject to the government's overcoming the presumption in "the most extraordinary circumstances." *Id.* Even assuming that the standard enunciated in *ADC* remains good law, the use of classified information in the fight against terrorism, during a presidentially declared "national emergency," qualifies as sufficiently "extraordinary" to overcome the presumption. . . . In sum, we join all other courts to have addressed the issue in holding that, subject to the limitations discussed below, the government may use classified information, without disclosure, when making designation determinations.

AHIF-Oregon's more nuanced argument, however, presents a different question. AHIF-Oregon argues that, even if OFAC may use classified information, it must undertake some reasonable measure to mitigate the potential unfairness to AHIF-Oregon. AHIF-Oregon proffers that OFAC could, for example, provide an unclassified summary of the classified information or permit AHIF-Oregon's lawyer to view the documents after receiving a security clearance and pursuant to a protective order. In essence, AHIF-Oregon argues that, to the extent possible, OFAC must take reasonable measures that do not implicate national security and impose only a small burden on the agency.

Under the *Mathews* test, we must consider "the value of additional safeguards" against the risk of error and "the burdens of additional procedural requirements." *Foss*, 161 F.3d at 589. The value of AHIF-Oregon's suggested methods seems clear. Without disclosure of classified information, the designated entity cannot possibly know how to respond to OFAC's concerns. Without knowledge of a charge, even simple factual errors may go uncorrected despite potentially easy, ready, and persuasive explanations. To the extent that an unclassified summary could provide helpful information, such as the subject matter of the agency's concerns, and to the extent that it is feasible to permit a lawyer with security clearance to view the classified information, the value of those methods seems undeniable. . . .

We find significant that there may be means of providing information to the potential designee that do not implicate national security. For example, an unclassified summary, by definition, does not implicate national security because it is unclassified. Similarly, a lawyer for the designated entity who has the appropriate security clearance also does not implicate national security when viewing the classified material because, by definition, he or she has the appropriate security clearance.

We recognize that disclosure may not always be possible. For example, an unclassified summary may not be possible because, in some cases, the subject matter itself may be classified and cannot be revealed without implicating national security. Depending on the circumstances, OFAC might have a legitimate interest in shielding the materials even from someone with the appropriate security clearance. . . . In many cases, though, some information could be summarized or presented to a lawyer with a security clearance without implicating national security.

Indeed, OFAC has not defended its failure to provide an unclassified summary or access by a lawyer with the proper security clearance on the ground that any such measure would have implicated national security. Instead, OFAC asserts that any mechanism would be unduly burdensome. OFAC points to the large number of designated persons and argues that any of the proposed measures could overwhelm the agency, diminishing its ability to carry out its important mission of protecting national security.

We acknowledge the agency's abstract concerns but find that they have little practical reality. Here, for instance, OFAC eventually presented a list of unclassified reasons to AHIF-Oregon, which could have been augmented by a short unclassified summary of classified evidence. The small expenditure in time and resources would not outweigh the entity's interest in knowing the charges and evidence against it. . . .

. . . We agree that a case-by-case approach is proper. As we have alluded to earlier, the proper measures in any given case will depend on a number of factors. We expect the agency (and, if necessary, the district court) to consider, at a minimum, the nature and extent of the classified information, the nature and extent of the threat to national security, and the possible avenues available to allow the designated person to respond more effectively to the charges.

2. Adequate Notice and Meaningful Opportunity to Respond

AHIF-Oregon argues that OFAC violated its due process rights by failing to provide adequate notice and a meaningful opportunity to respond to OFAC's designation and redesignation determinations. Specifically, AHIF-Oregon asserts that OFAC refused to disclose its reasons for investigating and designating AHIF-Oregon, leaving AHIF-Oregon unable to respond adequately to the agency's unknown suspicions.

"Due process requires notice 'reasonably calculated, under all the circumstances, to apprise interested parties of the pendency of the action and afford them an opportunity to present their objections.'" *United Student Aid Funds, Inc. v. Espinosa*, 559 U.S. 260 (2010) (quoting *Mullane v. Cent. Hanover Bank & Trust Co.*, 339 U.S. 306, 314 (1950)). "'Due process is flexible and calls for such procedural protections as the particular situation demands.'" *Gilbert v. Homar*, 520 U.S. 924, 930 (1997). . . . Once again, the *Mathews* balancing test applies. . . .

We hold that all three *Mathews* factors support the conclusion that OFAC violated AHIF-Oregon's due process rights. First, OFAC's blocking notice deprived AHIF-Oregon of its ability to use any funds whatsoever, for any purpose. Second, because AHIF-Oregon could only *guess* (partly incorrectly) as to the reasons for the investigation, the risk of erroneous deprivation was high. Finally, and perhaps most importantly, although national security might justify keeping AHIF-Oregon in the dark, OFAC makes no effort to demonstrate that its failure to provide AHIF-Oregon with reasons for its investigation promoted national security. OFAC presents three different arguments to justify its failure to provide a statement of reasons.

First, OFAC argues that its September 2004 press release constituted sufficient notice. We agree with OFAC that the press release states with some clarity that AHIF-Oregon supported Chechen terrorists (the third reason given in the 2008 redesignation notice). OFAC also claims that there was sufficient information in the press release to apprise AHIF-Oregon of OFAC's concern about control by Al-Aqil and Al-Buthe (the first and second reasons given in the 2008 redesignation notice). But, as the district court correctly pointed out, the press release stated nothing about ownership or control of AHIF-Oregon. OFAC provided notice concerning only one of three reasons for its investigation and designation, and that notice occurred seven months after it froze AHIF-Oregon's assets. Such a significantly untimely and incomplete notice does not meet the requirements of due process.

Second, OFAC argues that it was impractical to provide reasons to AHIF-Oregon during the four-year investigation. We are unpersuaded for many of the same reasons, just discussed, concerning OFAC's failure to provide mitigation measures regarding the classified information. It is clear that OFAC *had* its reasons for investigating AHIF-Oregon (otherwise its investigation would be unjustified), so the summary of those reasons would not present a practical burden. . . .

We can envision situations in which OFAC acts so quickly between the original deprivation and its decision to designate that it may be impractical to provide a statement of reasons. But the seven-month period of the original investigation, and certainly the four-year period of the entire redesignation determination, gave OFAC ample time to provide AHIF-Oregon with, at a minimum, a terse and complete statement of reasons for the investigation. There is no reason why OFAC could not have given notice in this particular case. If a notice requirement is unduly burdensome in some future case, OFAC may present that argument to the appropriate court.

Finally, OFAC argues that the circumstances of its investigation and the documentation that it submitted to AHIF-Oregon provided that entity with sufficient information from which AHIF-Oregon could *guess* OFAC's reasons. In any event, OFAC asserts, AHIF-Oregon's guesses proved partly correct. We have rejected that argument in an analogous situation; the opportunity to guess at the factual and legal bases for a government action does not substitute for actual notice of the government's intentions. . . .

OFAC leans heavily on two decisions by the District of Columbia Circuit. In *NCORI*, 251 F.3d at 208-09, the court addressed what process is due in the closely similar context of designation of a foreign terrorist organization under AEDPA. In that case, the government had provided no notice at all and no opportunity for the entity to be heard. *Id.* at 208. The court held that due process requires notice of pending designation, a copy of the unclassified administrative record, and an opportunity to respond. *Id.* at 208-09. That court did not address the issue at hand here: whether the notice must contain some statement of reasons for the investigation. Thus the court did not state that the government must supply its reasons for investigating.

Similarly, in *Holy Land*, 333 F.3d at 164, the District of Columbia Circuit addressed a challenge to OFAC's designation under EO 13,224, including the argument that OFAC provided insufficient process. Applying *NCORI*, the court rejected the due process argument:

> Treasury notified both Holy Land ["HLF"] and the district court that it was reopening the administrative record and considering whether to redesignate HLF as an SDGT [specially designated global terrorist], on the basis of additional evidence linking HLF and Hamas. Holy Land was then given thirty-one days to respond to the redesignation and the new evidence. Holy Land did respond and the Treasury considered its response as well as the new evidence before deciding to redesignate HLF in May 2002. Therefore, Treasury provided HLF with the requisite notice and opportunity for response necessary to satisfy due process requirements.

Id.

Both decisions by the District of Columbia Circuit may suggest that a statement of reasons is not required by due process, because neither decision mentions that issue. But it appears that the plaintiffs in those cases never raised that specific issue and that the notice given in *Holy Land* sufficiently stated the reasons for the investigation. We do not read those decisions as holding definitively that due process does not require a statement of reasons. . . . We hold that OFAC violated AHIF-Oregon's due process rights by failing to provide an adequate statement of reasons for its investigation.

. . .

C. Fourth Amendment

AHIF-Oregon argues that OFAC's failure to obtain a warrant supported by probable cause violated its Fourth Amendment right to be free of unreasonable seizures. "In the ordinary case, the [Supreme] Court has viewed a seizure of personal property as *per se* unreasonable within the meaning of the Fourth Amendment unless it is accomplished pursuant to a judicial warrant issued upon probable cause and particularly describing the items to be seized." *United States v. Place*, 462 U.S. 696, 701 (1983). In most circumstances, searches and seizures conducted without a warrant are "*per se* unreasonable under the Fourth Amendment—subject only to a few specifically established and well-delineated exceptions." *Katz v. United States*, 389 U.S. 347, 357 (1967). Here, OFAC argues that its seizure falls within one of those well-delineated exceptions to the warrant requirement: the "special needs" exception.

1. "Special Needs" Exception

"The 'special needs' exception is 'an exception to the general rule that a search [or seizure] must be based on individualized suspicion of wrongdoing.'" *Friedman v. Boucher*, 580 F.3d 847, 853 (9th Cir. 2009) (quoting *City of Indianapolis v. Edmond*, 531 U.S. 32, 54 (2000)). "Under this exception, suspicionless searches [and seizures] may be upheld if they are conducted for important non-law enforcement purposes in contexts where adherence to the warrant-and-probable cause requirement would be impracticable." *Id.* (internal quotation marks and emphasis omitted). . . . AHIF-Oregon concedes that OFAC blocking orders are "conducted for important non-law enforcement purposes," specifically, to prevent the funding of terrorist organizations. But the parties dispute whether the application of the warrant requirement would be impracticable.

The Supreme Court has held that the "special needs" exception applies in several different contexts. The exception requires a weighing of the nature and extent of the privacy interest at hand against the nature and immediacy of the government's concerns and the efficacy of the procedures employed in meeting those concerns. *Bd. of Educ. v. Earls*, 536 U.S. 822, 830-34 (2002). Because those interests vary with the factual context, a brief survey of the major cases is helpful.

In *Camara v. Municipal Court*, 387 U.S. 523 (1967), the Court held that periodic, routine building inspections for health code reasons fell within the exception. The Court explained that (1) "such programs have a long history of judicial and public acceptance"; (2) "the public interest demands that all dangerous conditions be prevented or abated, yet it is doubtful that any other canvassing technique would achieve acceptable results"; and (3) the searches "involve a relatively limited invasion of the urban citizen's privacy." *Id.* at 537.

In *O'Connor v. Ortega*, 480 U.S. 709 (1987), the Court held that a government employer may search the files and drawers of its employees for work-related reasons. The Court held that "requiring an employer to obtain a warrant whenever the employer wished to enter an employee's office, desk, or file cabinets for a work-related purpose would seriously disrupt the routine conduct of business and would be unduly burdensome." *Id.* at 722 (plurality). . . . Additionally, "the privacy interests of government employees in their place of work . . . , while not insubstantial, are far less than those found at home or in some other contexts." *Id.* at 725 (plurality). . . .

In *Earls*, 536 U.S. at 825, the Court held that a public school's policy of requiring drug testing of all students participating in extracurricular activities fell within the "special needs" exception. "A student's privacy interest is limited in a public school environment. . . ." *Id.* at 830. Because the school conducted the test with many procedural safeguards and used the results only in connection with permitting the student to participate in extracurricular activities, the Court held that, "[g]iven the minimally intrusive nature of the sample collection and the limited uses to which the test results are put, we conclude that the invasion of students' privacy is not significant." *Id.* at 834. Finally, the Court considered the school's strong interest in "preventing drug use by schoolchildren," especially because of "specific evidence of drug use" at the school in question. *Id.*

In *Griffin*, 483 U.S. at 875-80, the Court held that a probation officer's search of a probationer's home on a tip by a police officer that the probationer illegally possessed a gun fell within the exception. . . . "A warrant requirement would interfere to an appreciable degree with the probation system," particularly because "the delay inherent in obtaining a warrant would make it more difficult for probation officials to respond quickly to evidence of misconduct." *Id.* at 876. . . . Overall, the Court concluded that "the probation regime would . . . be unduly disrupted" by requiring probable cause and a warrant. *Id.* at 878. . . .

In *Michigan Department of State Police v. Sitz*, 496 U.S. 444 (1990), and *United States v. Martinez-Fuerte*, 428 U.S. 543 (1976), the Court held that traffic checkpoints where officers screened vehicles for intoxicated drivers or illegal aliens survived Fourth Amendment scrutiny. In both cases, the Court's decision resulted largely from the "minor interference" involved in responding to a traffic checkpoint. *Martinez-Fuerte*, 428 U.S. at 565; *see Sitz*, 496 U.S. at 451 (holding that the intrusion on motorists is "slight"). . . .

Here, the domestic entity's interest in being free from blocking orders is great. A blocking order effectively shuts down the private entity. Indeed, blocking orders do so *by design.* Unlike in the Court's other cases, such as a one-time drug test, a search of files at a person's office, a search of a home while on probation, or a brief traffic stop, there is no limited scope or scale to the effect of the blocking order. The only limit is temporal, and that limitation is quite small. Once OFAC concludes its investigation (which took more than half a year here), then the party has a right to very limited judicial review and a right to request administrative reconsideration. Both of those actions take considerable time, as the facts of this case . . . demonstrate. In the meantime, the entity's doors are closed.

Additionally, OFAC's potential reach is extensive. Unlike the Court's cases, which concerned well-defined classes of persons such as probationers, public school students, public employees at work, drivers on the road, and so on, OFAC can issue a blocking order against *any person* within the United States or elsewhere. And, of course, OFAC does so without warning. There certainly is no "long history of judicial and public acceptance." *Camara*, 387 U.S. at 537. Relatedly, unlike in the school and probation cases, in which those persons who conduct the search or seizure also are entrusted with protecting the targeted person's interests, OFAC is not at all tasked with protecting the interests of the blocked entities.

On the other side of the scale, the government's interest in preventing terrorism and the funding of terrorism is extremely high. But the sensitive subject matter is no excuse for the dispensing altogether with domestic persons' constitutional rights. . . . Rather, the dispositive question here is whether it is impracticable for OFAC to achieve its undeniably important aims without securing a warrant.

On this point, OFAC asserts that it does not and cannot know the location of the assets it seeks to block and must rely on property holders other than the blocked entity to identify such assets. OFAC also asserts that it would be impractical to update its warrants whenever it discovered additional assets owned by the entity. Finally, OFAC asserts that the timing of its blocking orders is coordinated with other governments, which makes it impractical to obtain a warrant.

We are not persuaded. As an initial matter, we reiterate that the number of designated persons located within the United States appears to be very small. The warrant requirement therefore will be relevant in only a few cases.

We acknowledge that the issue of "asset flight" is a legitimate concern; that coordination may be required with different agencies of this government or even with foreign governments; and that additional assets may be discovered in the future. To the extent that those concerns are present in any given situation, OFAC can protect its interest in stopping the funding of terrorism by seizing the assets *initially* pursuant to an emergency exception to the warrant requirement. . . . After OFAC has blocked the assets so that asset flight is foreclosed, OFAC then can obtain a warrant specifying the particular assets.

In any event, OFAC has not given us any reason why it could not have obtained a warrant *here.* We hold that the "special needs" exception does not apply to the seizure of AHIF-Oregon's assets by OFAC under EO 13,224. . . .

2. "General Reasonableness" Test

OFAC also argues that, apart from any well-delineated exception to the warrant requirement, its blocking orders "are not susceptible to Fourth Amendment challenges" because they are per se reasonable under the "general reasonableness" test. "'[R]easonableness in all the circumstances of the particular governmental invasion of a citizen's personal security'" is the "touchstone" of Fourth Amendment analysis. *Pennsylvania v. Mimms*, 434 U.S. 106, 108-09 (1977) (quoting *Terry v. Ohio*, 392 U.S. 1, 19 (1968))....

Under this approach, "we examine the totality of the circumstances to determine whether a [seizure] is reasonable within the meaning of the Fourth Amendment." *Samson*, 547 U.S. at 848. "Whether a search is reasonable is determined by assessing, on the one hand, the degree to which it intrudes upon an individual's privacy and, on the other, the degree to which it is needed for the promotion of legitimate governmental interests." *Id.* (internal quotation marks omitted).

Most of our reasoning above, concerning the special needs exception, applies equally here. The cases in which the Court has found warrantless searches to be reasonable all involve very special circumstances and greatly diminished privacy interests—a point repeatedly emphasized by the Court. For instance, in *Flores-Montano*, 541 U.S. at 154, the Court held that a person's privacy interest in the interior of an automobile's gas tank is not sufficient to overcome the government's interest in preventing drug smuggling at the border. Similarly, in *Samson* and *Knights*, the Court explained at length that probationers and parolees, who are subject to a clearly disclosed search condition of parole or probation, have greatly diminished expectations of privacy such that warrantless searches survived Fourth Amendment scrutiny. *Samson*, 547 U.S. at 850-52; *Knights*, 534 U.S. at 119-21. Here, however, as we have explained, the reach of OFAC's authority extends to *all persons and entities*, without limitation. Nothing diminishes the privacy expectation of persons and entities potentially subject to seizure by OFAC because that class includes everyone.

We reiterate that OFAC's interest in preventing terrorism is extremely high. But we cannot accept OFAC's contention that its blocking orders are per se reasonable in all circumstances, solely by virtue of that vital mission. As we noted above, an exception to the warrant requirement would permit OFAC to seize assets without obtaining a warrant in some situations. But, because there is no diminished expectation of privacy and because nothing prevents OFAC from obtaining a warrant in the normal course, we reject OFAC's argument that its blocking orders are per se reasonable under the "general reasonableness" approach.

In summary, no exception applies to OFAC's warrantless seizure of AHIF-Oregon's assets and the seizure is not justified under a "general reasonableness" test. We therefore hold that OFAC violated AHIF-Oregon's Fourth Amendment right to be free of unreasonable seizures. Because the district court did not reach the issue of remedy and because the parties did not brief that issue before us, we remand to the district court to determine, in the first instance, what remedy, if any, is available.

NOTES AND QUESTIONS

1. The court applied the *Mathews* balancing test in determining whether the use of classified information in designating AHIF-Oregon a Specially Designated Global Terrorist violated the entity's due process rights. What factors must the court consider under the *Mathews* balancing test? Do the *Mathews* factors weigh in favor of AHIF-Oregon or the government?

2. What is the court's view on the use of classified information to make designation determinations under E.O. 13224? What is the legal standard? When is the use of classified information permissible? Why did the court find that the use of classified information violated AHIF-Oregon's due process rights?

3. The court held that the government may use classified information, without disclosure, when making designation determinations, subject to certain limitations. What limitations did the court impose on the government's use of classified information in making a designation determination?

4. Why did the court find that the notice OFAC provided failed to provide adequate notice and a meaningful opportunity for AHIF-Oregon to respond to OFAC's designation determination? Why was the notice provided by OFAC deficient?

5. The court held that OFAC's failure to obtain a warrant supported by probable cause prior to blocking AHIF-Oregon's assets violated the Fourth Amendment. More specifically, the court held that the "special needs" exception did not apply. When may suspicionless searches and seizures be upheld under the special-needs exception?

6. What factors did the court consider in finding that the special needs exception did not apply? Did the court apply the *Mathews* balancing test, focusing on the domestic entity's interest in being free from blocking orders and the government's interest in preventing the financing of terrorism? Did the court apply the wrong standard?

7. Why did the court find that blocking AHIF-Oregon's assets was not per se reasonable under the "general reasonableness" test? What factors did the court consider?

Islamic American Relief Agency v. Gonzales
477 F.3d 728 (D.C. Cir. 2007)

SENTELLE, Circuit Judge.

The Islamic American Relief Agency ("IARA-USA"), based in Columbia, Missouri, challenges the district court's decision upholding the blocking of its assets. The government concluded that the organization was a branch office of a Specially Designated Global Terrorist and invoked its authority under antiterrorism laws to block IARA-USA assets. In this appeal, IARA-USA contends that the district court erroneously held that the record supports the government's conclusion, and that it erroneously dismissed and entered summary judgment for defendants on IARA-USA's claims under the Administrative Procedure Act and the Constitution. IARA-USA also argues that it should have been permitted to amend its complaint to request access to its blocked funds for payment of attorneys' fees. Because we conclude that the designation was supported by the record and was not contrary to law, we affirm the district court's disposition of the case, but on the question of attorneys' fees we remand for further proceedings.

I

In 1985, a Sudanese immigrant founded IARA-USA as the Islamic African Relief Agency. Since then, the entity has engaged in humanitarian activities around the world, often in partnership with similar organizations. In 2000, IARA-USA changed its name from the "Islamic *African* Relief Agency" to the "Islamic *American* Relief Agency" (emphasis added). Meanwhile, the entity in Sudan calling itself the Islamic African Relief Agency ("IARA") continued to exist under that name.

On October 13, 2004, the Office of Foreign Assets Control in the Department of the Treasury ("OFAC") designated IARA as a Specially Designated Global Terrorist ("SDGT"). The designation was based on OFAC's conclusion that IARA "provides financial support or other services to persons who commit, threaten to commit or support terrorism" in violation of anti-terrorism laws. Although IARA-USA was not independently designated, OFAC considered it to be the United States branch of IARA and included it in the blocking notice. This meant that none of IARA-USA's financial assets or property could be "transferred, withdrawn, exported, paid, or otherwise dealt in without prior authorization from OFAC." IARA-USA could not receive "any contribution of funds, goods, or services," nor could it continue to use its offices or remove any items of corporate property. Any violation of the blocking notice could subject IARA-USA to criminal and civil penalties.

IARA-USA immediately contested the blocking, maintaining that it is a separate entity from IARA. It requested that OFAC review the designation and permit IARA-USA to access its blocked funds for the limited purpose of paying attorneys' fees. In late December 2004, having failed to persuade OFAC to unblock its assets, IARA-USA filed a complaint in district court, naming as defendants the Attorney General, the Secretary of the Treasury, and other unidentified FBI agents and Treasury personnel. Relevant to this appeal, it claimed that (1) the blocking is unsupported by the record and thus violates the APA and the International Emergency Economic Powers Act, 50 U.S.C. §§ 1701-1707; (2) the blocking violates IARA-USA's constitutional rights of equal protection, free exercise of religion, and free association; and (3) IARA-USA should be permitted to pay attorneys' fees from the blocked funds. In a memorandum opinion and order issued on September 15, 2005, the district court dismissed or entered summary judgment in favor of defendant on all claims. *Islamic Am. Relief Agency v. Unidentified FBI Agents*, 394 F. Supp. 2d 34 (D.D.C. 2005) ("*IARA-USA*"). The district court held that the record supported OFAC's conclusion that IARA-USA was a branch of IARA, and that the blocking was proper under applicable laws and the Constitution. It also denied the motion to access blocked funds for attorneys' fees.

In this appeal, IARA-USA argues that the district court erred in rejecting the three arguments described above, and that it erred in failing to ensure that the Government complied with an internal regulation requiring it to declassify record evidence and in denying discovery before entering summary judgment. IARA-USA does not challenge the district court's ruling on its other claims.

II

We note at the outset that the designated entity, IARA, is not a party to this case, and IARA-USA does not challenge the evidentiary basis for the designation of its alleged parent. Rather, the question here is whether the record supports OFAC's conclusion that IARA-USA is a branch of IARA. If so, as IARA-USA conceded at oral argument, OFAC's blocking of its assets was a proper consequence of the designation.

. . .

Our review of an SDGT designation falls under the APA, and thus its highly deferential standard of review applies. *See Holy Land Found. for Relief & Dev. v. Ashcroft*, 333 F.3d 156, 162 (D.C. Cir. 2003). Under that standard, we will set aside OFAC's action only if it is "arbitrary, capricious, an abuse of discretion, or otherwise not in accordance with law." 5 U.S.C. § 706(2)(A). We may not substitute our judgment for OFAC's, but we will require it to "examine the relevant data and articulate a satisfactory explanation for its action including a rational connection between the facts found and the choice made." *Motor Vehicle Mfrs. Ass'n of the U.S., Inc. v. State Farm Mut. Auto. Ins. Co.*, 463 U.S. 29, 43 (1983). Thus, with respect to the APA claims, if OFAC's actions were not arbitrary and capricious and were based on substantial evidence, we must affirm the district court's decision. 5 U.S.C. § 706(2)(A).

A

This case is the first in this Court challenging an SDGT designation based on a branch relationship with an entity that supports terrorists. Our prior cases involved entities that directly supported terrorists. IARA-USA suggests that because of this factual difference, we should review the blocking as we would review an alias designation in a Foreign Terrorist Organization ("FTO") case. In those cases, we require evidence that the designated entity "so dominates and controls" the alleged alias entity that they can be considered one and the same. *Nat'l Council of Resistance of Iran v. Dep't of State*, 373 F.3d 152, 157 (D.C. Cir. 2004) ("*NCRI*"). On IARA-USA's theory, then, blocking its assets based on the designation of IARA was proper only if IARA "dominates and controls" IARA-USA. The Government disagrees, arguing that the alias test is not applicable here because this blocking was not based on an alias theory. It urges instead that the blocking may stand if there is sufficient evidence that IARA-USA and IARA are the same organization, even in the absence of evidence that one controls the other.

We conclude that the Government has the better argument. To determine whether the evidence is sufficient, we must employ a test that reflects the theory on which the assets were blocked. The "dominates and controls" test is appropriate for reviewing the existence of a principal-agent relationship because, where there is sufficient evidence to find an agency relationship, substantial evidence of the principal's unlawful activity is sufficient to justify the designation or blocking of the agent. *See NCRI*, 373 F.3d at 157 (concluding that the "dominates and controls" test is an appropriate basis for upholding an alias designation, because of the "ordinary principle[ ] of agency law" that "where a corporate entity is so extensively controlled by its owner that a relationship of principal and agent is created . . . one may be held liable for the actions of the other") (internal quotation marks and citation omitted). In this case, however, OFAC's theory was that IARA-USA and IARA, along with other branch offices, comprised a single global organization. The Government argues that their relationship, therefore, is more accurately described as one between different offices of the same entity. It follows that, if the record contains substantial evidence that IARA-USA is a branch of IARA, then it was proper for OFAC to subject IARA-USA to the blocking as a result of IARA's designation. . . .

With this framework in mind, we turn to the unclassified record. While the record contains a great number of documents, we discuss here only a sampling of the most pertinent. IARA-USA was founded by an immigrant from Sudan, the site of IARA's offices, and was incorporated with a name identical to IARA's from its founding until 2000, when IARA-USA made the minor change of replacing "African" in its name with "American." IARA-USA's Articles of Incorporation describe it as "Islamic African Relief Agency United States Affiliate" and include the purpose of "effect[ing] the Objectives and Means of the Islamic African Relief Agency as set forth in its Constitution." In the event of IARA-USA's dissolution, the Articles of Incorporation provided that IARA, among other entities, should receive its assets.

Since its founding, IARA-USA has continued to engage in conduct that evinces a branch relationship with IARA. In 1998, for example, IARA-USA applied to the Treasury Department for a license to transfer funds to "Islamic African Relief Agency, Sudan," in which it described itself as "The Islamic African Relief Agency, United States Affiliate." It described "the Islamic African Relief Agency, Sudan" as its "partner in Sudan." In a letter to the *Washington Times* on October 10, 1995, IARA-USA's Executive Director identified himself as speaking on behalf of "IARA and its partners," implicitly accepted the newspaper's characterization of IARA as the "Khartoum-based 'Islamic Relief Agency,'" and acknowledged IARA's "branch offices in the United States" and other countries. Solicitation materials used by IARA-USA stated that its "international headquarters are in Khartoum, Sudan." Additionally, IARA-USA maintained financial connections with at least one other IARA branch and its address was listed on IARA websites as a United States branch office.

    . . .

We acknowledge that the unclassified record evidence is not overwhelming, but we reiterate that our review—in an area at the intersection of national security, foreign policy, and administrative law—is extremely deferential. *Cf. Holy Land*, 333 F.3d at 166 (noting the unique nature of reviewing an SDGT designation as "involving sensitive issues of national security and foreign policy"); *Humanitarian Law Project v. Reno*, 205 F.3d 1130, 1137 (9th Cir. 2000) (noting that, where a "regulation involves the conduct of foreign affairs, we owe the executive branch even more latitude than in the domestic context" and stating that the high degree of judicial deference to the decision to designate an entity as an FTO "is a necessary concomitant of the foreign affairs power"). Under that standard, the record—containing various types of evidence from several different sources, and covering an extended period of time—provides substantial evidence for the conclusion that IARA-USA is part of IARA. Furthermore, although we deem it unnecessary to sustain OFAC's actions, the classified record contains extensive evidence that IARA-USA is a branch of IARA.

OFAC's conduct was also lawful under the relevant statute and Executive Orders. In the wake of the attacks of September 11, 2001, the President invoked the authority of the International Emergency Economic Powers Act, 50 U.S.C. §§ 1701-1707 ("IEEPA") by declaring a national emergency with respect to the "unusual and extraordinary threat to national security" posed by terrorists. *Blocking Property and Prohibiting Transactions With Persons Who Commit, Threaten to Commit, or Support Terrorism*, Exec. Order No. 13,224, 66 Fed. Reg. 49,079 (Sept. 23, 2001), as amended by Exec. Orders No. 13,268, 67 Fed. Reg. 44,751 (July 2, 2002) and No. 13,372, 70 Fed. Reg. 8499 (Feb. 16, 2005). In that Order, the President described the types of conduct that could subject an entity to blocking of its assets, such as providing financial support to terrorists. He named a number of entities whose assets would be blocked immediately, and authorized the Treasury Department to designate additional entities that it determines are within the purview of the Order.

IARA-USA argues that OFAC cannot block an entity's assets unless it determines that the entity itself poses an "unusual and extraordinary threat to national security." The district court rejected this argument, holding that the threat need not be found with regard to each individual entity. *IARA-USA*, 394 F. Supp. 2d at 46. We agree with the district court. The President may exercise his authority under the IEEPA "to deal with any unusual and extraordinary threat, which has its source in whole or substantial part outside the United States, to the national security, foreign policy, or economy of the United States, if the President declares a national emergency with respect to such threat." 50 U.S.C. § 1701(a). Thus, once the President has declared a national emergency, the IEEPA authorizes the blocking of property to protect against that threat. *Id.* § 1702(a)(1)(B). It is that authority OFAC invoked when it blocked IARA-USA's assets. We hold that the district court correctly dismissed this claim because IARA-USA could prove no set of facts that would entitle it to relief.

B

We turn next to IARA-USA's claims that the blocking violated its rights under the Constitution. . . . As we have noted previously, "there is no First Amendment right nor any other constitutional right to support terrorists." *Holy Land*, 333 F.3d at 166; *see also Humanitarian Law Project*, 205 F.3d at 1133 ("[T]here is no constitutional right to facilitate terrorism" with materials or funding.).

Our analysis of IARA-USA's constitutional arguments is informed by our recent decision in *Holy Land*, 333 F.3d at 164-67. In that case, Holy Land Foundation ("HLF") challenged its designation as an SDGT under the First, Fourth, and Fifth Amendments. *Id.* The district court rejected HLF's First and Fifth Amendment claims, and we affirmed, on the basis that "the law is established that there is no constitutional right to fund terrorism." *Id.* at 165. Thus, where an organization is found to have supported terrorism, government actions to suspend that support are not unconstitutional. *Id.* (noting that HLF could not have "produced evidence upon which a reasonable trier of fact could have found that the designation and the blocking of assets violated its First or Fifth Amendment rights" because "there is no constitutional right to fund terrorism" and the record evidence established that HLF did fund a terrorist organization).

IARA-USA contends that OFAC violated its right to equal protection under the Fifth Amendment by singling it out as a Muslim organization. As evidence that OFAC treated it differently than similar organizations, IARA-USA notes that UNICEF's funds were not blocked even though it also provided financial support to IARA. The district court entered summary judgment after concluding that IARA-USA had not shown that it was similarly situated to UNICEF. *IARA*, 394 F. Supp. 2d at 50-51. As the district court noted, to survive summary judgment IARA-USA must show that it was treated differently than a similar organization with similar ties to an SDGT. . . . IARA-USA asserts that UNICEF entered into a contract in which it agreed to provide financial support to IARA. But a single contact of this nature does not begin to approximate the extensive relationship between IARA-USA and IARA. As the district court held, IARA-USA and UNICEF are not similarly situated, and as a result their disparate treatment by OFAC cannot itself support a claim that IARA-USA has been denied equal protection of the law. IARA-USA's equal protection claim thus was properly rejected by the district court.

IARA-USA also argues that OFAC violated its rights of association and free exercise of religion under the First Amendment. Its freedom of association claim is that the blocking inhibits its ability to engage in the associational activity of making financial contributions and that its association, even with an unpopular entity, cannot form the basis of the decision to block its assets. Following *Holy Land*, the district court dismissed the claim, concluding that the blocking did not implicate IARA-USA's association rights because it did not prevent or punish the associational activity of IARA-USA, but rather was directed at its funding of terrorists, as a branch of IARA. *IARA-USA*, 394

F. Supp. 2d at 54. We agree with the district court. Our decision in *Holy Land* relied on the Ninth Circuit's recent decision in *Humanitarian Law Project. Holy Land*, 333 F.3d at 166 (holding, with regard to HLF's freedom of association claim, "that there is no First Amendment right nor any other constitutional right to support terrorists" with funding) (citing *Humanitarian Law Project*, 205 F.3d at 1133). In *Humanitarian Law Project*, entities designated as FTOs argued that preventing them from making donations in support of humanitarian and political activities violated their First Amendment right of association, at least where it was not shown that they intended their donations to support unlawful activities. 205 F.3d at 1133. The Ninth Circuit noted that freedom of association is implicated where people are punished merely for "membership in a group or for espousing its views, whereas the statute in question only prohibited the act of giving material support." *Id.* (citing *NAACP v. Claiborne Hardware Co.*, 458 U.S. 886, 920 (1982)). Similarly, it held that the requirement to show intent to aid unlawful acts was not applicable in the context of donations to terrorist groups, because the money could be used for unlawful activities regardless of donor intent. *Id.* at 1133-34.

Here, as in *Holy Land*, we adopt the Ninth Circuit's reasoning. The blocking was not based on, nor does it prohibit, associational activity other than financial support. The blocking of IARA-USA's assets does not punish advocacy of IARA's or any other entity's goals. *See Humanitarian Law Project*, 205 F.3d at 1133-34 (distinguishing financial support from advocacy and noting that, just as "there is no constitutional right to facilitate terrorism by giving terrorists the weapons and explosives with which to carry out their grisly missions," neither is there any "right to provide resources with which terrorists can buy weapons and explosives"). We hold that OFAC's blocking of IARA-USA's assets does not implicate IARA-USA's First Amendment right of association.

Nor is the Government required to show that IARA-USA funded terrorist organizations with an intent to aid their unlawful activities. Although the Supreme Court has previously imposed such an intent requirement, it is limited to cases in which liability was imposed by reason of association alone. *See Healy v. James*, 408 U.S. 169, 186 (1972) (noting that where First Amendment rights are denied based on "guilt by association alone, without (establishing) that an individual's association poses the threat feared by the Government . . . [t]he government has the burden of establishing a knowing affiliation with an organization possessing unlawful aims and goals, and a specific intent to further those illegal aims"). In this case, however, OFAC's decision to block IARA-USA's assets was not based on association. Rather, as we have explained above, the decision was based on OFAC's finding that IARA-USA is a branch of an SDGT. Thus we do not require a showing that IARA-USA intended its funding to support terrorist activities. . . .

As to IARA-USA's free exercise of religion claim, we conclude that the district court properly entered summary judgment for defendants. IARA-USA argues that the blocking "substantially burdens" the religious exercise of its members because they intended their donations to fulfill their religious obligation to engage in humanitarian charitable giving. Blocking those funds before they could be distributed, IARA-USA contends, interfered with that religious expression. As we explained in *Holy Land*, "[a]cting against the funding of terrorism does not violate the free exercise rights protected by ... the First Amendment. There is no free exercise right to fund terrorists." 333 F.3d at 167. We have already concluded that there was sufficient evidence in the administrative record that IARA-USA did, through its relationship with IARA, support terrorism. We thus affirm the district court's dismissal of IARA-USA's free exercise claim.

. . .

III

As the district court held, the blocking of IARA-USA's assets was not unlawful. OFAC's determination that IARA-USA functions as a branch of IARA was supported by substantial evidence in the unclassified record, and was proper under the relevant anti-terrorism laws, the APA and the Constitution. Accordingly, IARA-USA's claims are without merit and were properly dismissed or disposed of on summary judgment by the district court. The judgment of the district court is affirmed in all respects except that portion relating to IARA-USA's motion for leave to amend its complaint. On that issue, the case is remanded to the district court for further proceedings.

NOTES AND QUESTIONS

1. A person designated as an SDGT bears a heavy burden to overturn the designation on the grounds of insufficient evidence. Under the Administrative Procedure Act, the court may reverse an agency action only if the action was "arbitrary, capricious, an abuse of discretion, or otherwise not in accordance with the law." 5 U.S.C. § 706(2)(A); *see also Marsh v. Oregon Natural Resources Council*, 480 U.S. 360, 377 (1989). Judicial review under this standard is highly deferential and the court may not substitute its judgment for OFAC's. Based on this standard of review how often do you think OFAC designations are overturned by the court?

2. IARA-USA argued that OFAC violated its right to equal protection under the Fifth Amendment by singling it out as a Muslim organization. Why did the court reject this argument?

3. IARA-USA argued that OFAC violated its First Amendment right of association by inhibiting its ability to provide funding to unpopular groups. The court rejected this argument. Why? Does the blocking action punish or prohibit IARA-USA from public advocacy of IARA's or any other entity's goals?

4. The court held that the government is not required to show that IARA-USA funded foreign terrorist organizations with the intent to aid their unlawful

activities. What's the reasoning of the court? Do you agree? Some foreign organizations engage in humanitarian as well as terrorist-related activities. Should a person be permitted to provide funding to support the legitimate, humanitarian activities of the foreign organization or should all donations be prohibited?

5. The court denied IARA-USA's First Amendment free exercise of religion claim. Does the OFAC blocking action "substantially burden" the religious exercise of its members because they intended their donations to fulfill their religious obligations to engage in humanitarian charitable giving? Did blocking funds before they could be distributed interfere with the members of IARA-USA's religious expression?

6. Should funds needed to pay attorneys' fees be exempt from OFAC blocking actions?

ASSESSMENT QUESTIONS

1. Multiple Choice: Which of the following statements are correct?
    (a) In order to exercise the President's authority to impose economic sanctions under IEEPA, the President must declare a national emergency that has its source outside of the United States.
    (b) Under IEEPA, the requisite national emergency must pose an "unusual and extraordinary threat" to the national security, foreign policy, or economy of the United States.
    (c) Once the President declares the requisite national emergency, the President may block the assets of any person, including a U.S. person, wherever the property is located.
    (d) The government doesn't need a court order to block assets under IEEPA because the seizure falls within the "special needs" exception to the warrant requirement.

2. True or False: Under E.O. 13224, the government may only block the property in which a designated party has a legal interest, not merely a beneficial interest.

3. True or False: The Fifth Amendment Due Process Clause affords a designated party the right to notice and a hearing before his assets may be seized under E.O. 13224.

4. True or False: Under E.O. 13224, OFAC must decline to designate the entity or must reveal the classified information to the entity that OFAC believes supports terrorist activities.

5. True or False: A person designated a Specially Designated Global Terrorist under E.O. 13224 bears a heavy burden to overturn the designation on the grounds of insufficient evidence.

ASSESSMENT ANSWERS

1. Statement b is the only correct statement. IEEPA, 50 U.S.C. § 1701(a), authorizes the President to declare a national emergency "to deal with any unusual and extraordinary threat, which has its source in whole or in substantial part outside the United States, to the national security, foreign policy, or economy of the United States." Statement a is incorrect because the threat must have its source in whole or "substantial part" outside of the United States. The source of the threat need not emanate entirely outside of the United States. Statement b is correct because the national emergency must pose an "unusual and extraordinary" threat to the "national security, foreign policy or economy" of the United States.

   When such a national emergency is declared, the President may block the transfer of any property in which "any foreign country or national thereof has any interest. . . ." *Id.* § 1702(a)(1)(B). IEEPA does not authorize blocking the property of U.S. persons. Therefore, statement c is wrong. Further, the statute does not apply extraterritorially. The property subject to blocking must be located in the United States or subject to the jurisdiction of the United States. Finally, in *Al Haramain Islamic Foundation, Inc. v. United States Dep't of Treasury*, 686 F.3d 965 (9th Cir. 2011), the court held that the "special needs" exception did not apply to the seizure of AHIF-Oregon's assets by OFAC under E.O. 13224. Therefore, statement d is incorrect.

2. The statement is false. In *Global Relief Foundation, Inc. v. O'Neill*, 315 F.3d 748 (7th Cir. 2002), the court held that the word "interest" in 50 U.S.C. § 1702(a)(1)(B) is not limited to "legal" interest in property. The court stated: "The statute is designed to give the President means to control assets that could be used by enemy aliens. When an enemy holds the *beneficial* interest in property that is a real risk even if a U.S. citizen is the legal owner."

3. The statement is false. The courts have consistently held that while the Due Process Clause requires that a designated party be afforded notice and a hearing to challenge the blocking action, pre-seizure notice is not required. In *Global Relief Foundation*, the court posited: "Nor does the Constitution entitle GRF to notice and a pre-seizure hearing, an opportunity that would allow any enemy to spirit assets out of the United States."

4. The statement is false. In *Al Haramain Islamic Foundation*, the court rejected AHIF-Oregon's argument that OFAC must either decline to designate the entity or reveal the classified information relied on by OFAC to support the designation. However, the court stated that OFAC should provide the designated party an unclassified summary whenever possible.

5. The statement is true. Appellate review of SDGT designations falls under the Administrative Procedure Act, which requires that an administrative action, including an OFAC designation, be set aside only if it is "arbitrary and capricious, an abuse of discretion, or otherwise not in accordance with law." 5 U.S.C. § 706(2)(A). This is a highly deferential standard of review. *See Islamic American Relief Agency v. Gonzales*, 477 F.3d 728 (D.C. Cir. 2007).

CHAPTER 16

Responding to Domestic Emergencies

I. INTRODUCTION

Threat to the security of the nation are not limited to the external realm. As a result, the federal government may be called upon to respond to threats to the homeland. These threats can take a variety of forms, ranging from violent action by state or non-state actors, to internal dissident activities, to natural disasters. As a result, planning to protect the nation from such threats is an unfortunately increasing aspect of national security practice. However, unlike projecting power externally, domestic security actions will often involve legal issues of a very different nature, not the least of which is the allocation of authority between state and federal authorities. With the exception of protecting the homeland from an armed attack, this federalism-based legal foundation almost always places the federal government in a secondary or supporting role to the states. But there are important exceptions.

Indeed, the complexity and significance of this area of emergency response authority gained national attention during the protests and civil disturbances in response to the killing of Mr. George Floyd in the Summer of 2020. Such domestic use may at times be considered necessary or perhaps most efficient, but it also implicates concerns over military intrusion on civil liberties that are deeply embedded in the U.S. constitutional tradition. As a result, the domestic use of military assets will be the primary focus of the chapter. Understanding the limits on such use, and the federal government's domestic emergency response authority more generally, begins with an introduction to the allocation of the general police power in our federal system of government.

II. THE GENERAL POLICE POWER

A government response to a domestic emergency will almost always require an exercise of what is known as the general police power. This power allows the government to take necessary measures to protect the public from such emergencies. Because the federal government is one of limited powers, states retained this power and the accordant primacy in the response equation. The basis for this principle is the Tenth Amendment to the Constitution, in which the states reserved to themselves all powers that had not been delegated to the federal government. Recall from Chapter 4 that in *United States v. Curtiss-Wright Export Corp.*, 299 U.S. 304 (1936), Justice Sutherland noted:

> It will contribute to the elucidation of the question if we first consider the differences between the powers of the federal government in respect of foreign or external affairs and those in respect of domestic or internal affairs. That there are differences between them, and that these differences are fundamental, may not be doubted.
>
> The two classes of powers are different both in respect of their origin and their nature. The broad statement that the federal government can exercise no powers except those specifically enumerated in the Constitution, and such implied powers as are necessary and proper to carry into effect the enumerated powers, is categorically true only in respect of our internal affairs. In that field, the primary purpose of the Constitution was to carve from the general mass of legislative powers then possessed by the states such portions as it was thought desirable to vest in the federal government, leaving those not included in the enumeration still in the states.[1]

In contrast to the federal government, the powers of a state government to respond to internal threats and emergencies is limited only by state laws bounded by the requirement to comply with the Fourteenth Amendment to the Constitution. This is the basis for understanding why unlike the federal government, each state is vested with an inherent police power—a power to exercise government authority for the general well-being of the state population. It is therefore logical that the states would be the presumptive initial response authority to an emergency, disaster, or other crisis within its borders. It is equally logical, however, that states will look to the federal government to augment or support their emergency response efforts. But it is also important to understand that many of the powers vested in the federal government by the Constitution create an overlap with state authority, and that in some instances the federal government may be authorized to take a primary or lead role in responding to a domestic emergency, even though it lacks "general" police powers.

A Congressional Research Service Report entitled "Federalism, State Sovereignty, and the Constitution: Basis and Limits of Congressional Power" (RL30315, Sept. 23, 2015) explains the contrast in powers as follows:

Powers of the States
States may generally legislate on all matters within their territorial jurisdiction. This "police power" does not arise from the Constitution, but is an inherent attribute of the States' territorial sovereignty. The Constitution does, however, provide certain specific limitations on that power. For instance, a state is relatively limited in its authority regarding the regulation of foreign imports and exports or the conduct of foreign affairs. Further, states must respect the decisions of courts of other states, and are limited in their ability to vary their territory without congressional

---

1. *Id.* at 315.

permission. In addition, the Supreme Court has found that states are limited in their ability to burden interstate commerce.

Powers of the Federal Government

The powers of the federal government, while limited to those enumerated in the Constitution, have been interpreted broadly, so as to create a large potential overlap with state authority. For instance, Article I, § 8, cl. 18 provides that "[t]he Congress will have power . . . To make all laws which will be necessary and proper for carrying into Execution the foregoing Powers and all other Powers vested by this Constitution in the Government of the United States, or in any Department or Officer thereof." Early in the history of the Constitution, the Supreme Court found that this clause enlarges rather than narrows the powers of Congress.

But the general police power is not unlimited. Instead, the state must ensure that the exercise of that power — even in an emergency — does not result in a deprivation of rights protected by the Fourteenth Amendment. As you read the next case, consider how the test the Court utilizes to assess the validity of the state action would apply to modern day threats to the general public.

Jacobson v. Massachusetts
197 U.S. 11 (1905)

Mr. Justice HARLAN delivered the opinion of the court:

This case involves the validity, under the Constitution of the United States, of certain provisions in the statutes of Massachusetts relating to vaccination.

The Revised Laws of that commonwealth, chap. 75, § 137, provide that "the board of health of a city or town, if, in its opinion, it is necessary for the public health or safety, shall require and enforce the vaccination and revaccination of all the inhabitants thereof, and shall provide them with the means of free vaccination. Whoever, being over twenty-one years of age and not under guardianship, refuses or neglects to comply with such requirement shall forfeit $5."

An exception is made in favor of "children who present a certificate, signed by a registered physician, that they are unfit subjects for vaccination." § 139.

Proceeding under the above statutes, the board of health of the city of Cambridge, Massachusetts, on the 27th day of February, 1902, adopted the following regulation: "Whereas, smallpox has been prevalent to some extent in the city of Cambridge, and still continues to increase; and whereas, it is necessary for the speedy extermination of the disease that all persons not protected by vaccination should be vaccinated; and whereas, in the opinion of the board, the public health and safety require the vaccination or revaccination of all the inhabitants of Cambridge; be it ordered, that all the inhabitants habitants of the city who have not been successfully vaccinated since March 1st, 1897, be vaccinated or revaccinated.". . .

The above regulations being in force, the plaintiff in error, Jacobson, was proceeded against by a criminal complaint in one of the inferior courts of Massachusetts. The complaint charged that on the 17th day of July, 1902, the board of health of Cambridge, being of the opinion that it was necessary for the public health and safety, required the vaccination and revaccination of all the inhabitants thereof who had not been successfully vaccinated since the 1st day of March, 1897, and provided them with the means of free vaccination; and that the defendant, being over twenty-one years of age and not under guardianship, refused and neglected to comply with such requirement.

The defendant, having been arraigned, pleaded not guilty. . . .

The defendant . . . asked numerous instructions to the jury, among which were the following:

> That § 137 of chapter 75 of the Revised Laws of Massachusetts was in derogation of the rights secured to the defendant by the preamble to the Constitution of the United States, and tended to subvert and defeat the purposes of the Constitution as declared in its preamble; That the section referred to was in derogation of the rights secured to the defendant by the 14th Amendment of the Constitution of the United States, and especially of the clauses of that amendment providing that no state shall make or enforce any law abridging the privileges or immunities of citizens of the United States, nor deprive any person of life, liberty, or property without due process of law, nor deny to any person within its jurisdiction the equal protection of the laws. . . .

Each of defendant's prayers for instructions was rejected, and he duly excepted. The defendant requested the court, but the court refused, to instruct the jury to return a verdict of not guilty. . . . And the court ordered that he stand committed until the fine was paid.

We come, then, to inquire whether any right given or secured by the Constitution is invaded by the statute as interpreted by the state court. The defendant insists that his liberty is invaded when the state subjects him to fine or imprisonment for neglecting or refusing to submit to vaccination; that a compulsory vaccination law is unreasonable, arbitrary, and oppressive, and, therefore, hostile to the inherent right of every freeman to care for his own body and health in such way as to him seems best; and that the execution of such a law against one who objects to vaccination, no matter for what reason, is nothing short of an assault upon his person. But the liberty secured by the Constitution of the United States to every person within its jurisdiction does not import an absolute right in each person to be, at all times and in all circumstances, wholly freed from restraint. There are manifold restraints to which every person is necessarily subject for the common good. . . . This court has more than once recognized it as a fundamental principle that "persons and property are subjected to all kinds of restraints and burdens in order to secure the general comfort, health, and prosperity of the state. . . ."

Applying these principles to the present case, it is to be observed that the legislature of Massachusetts required the inhabitants of a city or town to be vaccinated only when, in the opinion of the board of health, that was necessary for the public health or the public safety. The authority to determine for all what ought to be done in such an emergency must have been lodged somewhere or in some body; and surely it was appropriate for the legislature to refer that question, in the first instance, to a board of health composed of persons residing in the locality affected, and appointed, presumably, because of their fitness to determine such questions. To invest such a body with authority over such matters was not an unusual, nor an unreasonable or arbitrary, requirement. Upon the principle of self-defense, of paramount necessity, a community has the right to protect itself against an epidemic of disease, which threatens the safety of its members. It is to be observed that when the regulation in question was adopted smallpox, according to the recitals in the regulation adopted by the board of health, was prevalent to some extent in the city of Cambridge, and the disease was increasing. If such was the situation, — and nothing is asserted or appears in the record to the contrary, — if we are to attach, any value whatever to the knowledge which, it is safe to affirm, in common to all civilized peoples touching smallpox and the methods most usually employed to eradicate that disease, it cannot be adjudged that the present regulation of the board of health was not necessary in order to protect the public health and secure the public safety. Smallpox being prevalent and increasing at Cambridge, the court would usurp the functions of another branch of government if it adjudged, as matter of law, that the mode adopted under the sanction of the state, to protect the people at large was arbitrary, and not justified by the necessities of the case. . . .

Whatever may be thought of the expediency of this statute, it cannot be affirmed to be, beyond question, in palpable conflict with the Constitution. Nor, in view of the methods employed to stamp out the disease of smallpox, can anyone confidently assert that the means prescribed by the state to that end has no real or substantial relation to the protection of the public health and the public safety. Such an assertion would not be consistent with the experience of this and other countries whose authorities have dealt with the disease of smallpox. And the principle of vaccination as a means to prevent the spread of smallpox has been enforced in many states by statutes making the vaccination of children a condition of their right to enter or remain in public schools. *Blue v. Beach*, 155 Ind. 121, 50 L.R.A. 64, 80 Am. St. Rep. 195, 56 N.E. 89; *Morris v. Columbus*, 102 Ga. 792, 42 L.R.A. 175, 66 Am. St. Rep. 243, 30 S.E. 850; *State v. Hay*, 126 N.C. 999, 49 L.R.A. 588, 78 Am. St. Rep. 691, 35 S.E. 459; *Abeel v. Clark*, 84 Cal. 226, 24 Pac. 383; *Bissell v. Davison*, 65 Conn. 183, 29 L.R.A. 251, 32 Atl. 348; *Hazen v. Strong*, 2 Vt. 427; *Duffield v. Williamsport School District*, 162 Pa. 476, 25 L.R.A. 152, 29 Atl. 742. . . .

The defendant offered to prove that vaccination "quite often" caused serious and permanent injury to the health of the person vaccinated; that the operation "occasionally" resulted in death; that it was "impossible" to tell "in any particular case" what the results of vaccination would be, or whether it would injure the health or result in death. . . .

. . . But the defendant did not offer to prove that, by reason of his then condition, he was in fact not a fit subject of vaccination at the time he was informed of the requirement of the regulation adopted by the board of health. . . . The matured opinions of medical men everywhere, and the experience of mankind, as all must know, negative the suggestion that it is not possible in any case to determine whether vaccination is safe. Was defendant exempted from the operation of the statute simply because of his dread of the same evil results experienced by him when a child, and which he had observed in the cases of his son and other children? Could he reasonably claim such an exemption because "quite often," or "occasionally," injury had resulted from vaccination, or because it was impossible, in the opinion of some, by any practical test, to determine with absolute certainty whether a particular person could be safely vaccinated?

It seems to the court that an affirmative answer to these questions would practically strip the legislative department of its function to care for the public health and the public safety when endangered by epidemics of disease. . . .

. . . Until otherwise informed by the highest court of Massachusetts, we are not inclined to hold that the statute establishes the absolute rule that an adult must be vaccinated if it be apparent or can be shown with reasonable certainty that he is not at the time a fit subject of vaccination, or that vaccination, by reason of his then condition, would seriously impair his health, or probably cause his death. No such case is here presented. . . .

We now decide only that the statute covers the present case, and that nothing clearly appears that would justify this court in holding it to be unconstitutional and inoperative in its application to the plaintiff in error.

The judgment of the court below must be affirmed.

NOTES AND QUESTIONS

1. Why is this somewhat dated opinion considered to provide an important foundation for state emergency response authority?
2. What limit, if any, does *Jacobson* establish for a state exercise of emergency police powers?
3. Why was the assumption the statute included an implicit exemption based on an actual finding that the vaccine would seriously endanger the health of the patient so important to the decision? What principle of the general concept of necessity does this assumption reflect?

Jacobson dealt with vaccinations, but obviously the holding extends to other measures implemented by government authorities to protect the public from serious dangers, for example, limiting intra- and inter-state movement by imposing a quarantine or other restrictions on individual liberty. As all Americans learned during the Coronavirus pandemic of 2020, states possess broad authority to invoke their general police powers to implement intra-state control measures such as lockdowns, quarantines, travel restrictions, and social distancing. But it is the federal government that will act when the danger implicates inter-state movement or entry into the nation itself. The following excerpt from the Center for Disease Control website summarizes the nature and sources of federal authority to respond to a widespread public health threat.

Legal Authorities for Isolation and Quarantine

Federal isolation and quarantine are authorized for these communicable diseases

- Cholera
- Diphtheria
- Infectious tuberculosis
- Plague
- Smallpox
- Yellow fever
- Viral hemorrhagic fevers
- Severe acute respiratory syndromes
- Flu that can cause a pandemic

Federal isolation and quarantine are authorized by Executive Order of the President. The President can revise this list by Executive Order.

Isolation and Quarantine

Isolation and quarantine help protect the public by preventing exposure to people who have or may have a contagious disease.

- **Isolation** separates sick people with a quarantinable communicable disease from people who are not sick.
- **Quarantine** separates and restricts the movement of people who were exposed to a contagious disease to see if they become sick.

In addition to serving as medical functions, isolation and quarantine also are "police power" functions, derived from the right of the state to take action affecting individuals for the benefit of society.

Federal Law

The federal government derives its authority for isolation and quarantine from the Commerce Clause of the U.S. Constitution.

Under section 361 of the Public Health Service Act (42 U.S. Code § 264), the U.S. Secretary of Health and Human Services is authorized to take measures to prevent the entry and spread of communicable diseases from foreign countries into the United States and between states.

The authority for carrying out these functions on a daily basis has been delegated to the Centers for Disease Control and Prevention (CDC).

CDC's Role

Under 42 Code of Federal Regulations parts 70 and 71, CDC is authorized to detain, medically examine, and release persons arriving into the United States and traveling between states who are suspected of carrying these communicable diseases.

As part of its federal authority, CDC routinely monitors persons arriving at U.S. land border crossings and passengers and crew arriving at U.S. ports of entry for signs or symptoms of communicable diseases.

When alerted about an ill passenger or crew member by the pilot of a plane or captain of a ship, CDC may detain passengers and crew as necessary to investigate whether the cause of the illness on board is a communicable disease.

State, Local, and Tribal Law

States have police power functions to protect the health, safety, and welfare of persons within their borders. To control the spread of disease within their borders, states have laws to enforce the use of isolation and quarantine.

These laws can vary from state to state and can be specific or broad. In some states, local health authorities implement state law. In most states, breaking a quarantine order is a criminal misdemeanor.

Tribes also have police power authority to take actions that promote the health, safety, and welfare of their own tribal members. Tribal health authorities may enforce their own isolation and quarantine laws within tribal lands, if such laws exist.

Who Is in Charge

The Federal Government

- Acts to prevent the entry of communicable diseases into the United States. Quarantine and isolation may be used at U.S. ports of entry.
- Is authorized to take measures to prevent the spread of communicable diseases between states.
- May accept state and local assistance in enforcing federal quarantine.
- May assist state and local authorities in preventing the spread of communicable diseases.

State, Local, and Tribal Authorities

- Enforce isolation and quarantine within their borders.

It is possible for federal, state, local, and tribal health authorities to have and use all at the same time separate but coexisting legal quarantine power in certain events. In the event of a conflict, federal law is supreme.

Enforcement

If a quarantinable disease is suspected or identified, CDC may issue a federal isolation or quarantine order.

Public health authorities at the federal, state, local, and tribal levels may sometimes seek help from police or other law enforcement officers to enforce a public health order.

U.S. Customs and Border Protection and U.S. Coast Guard officers are authorized to help enforce federal quarantine orders.

Breaking a federal quarantine order is punishable by fines and imprisonment.

Federal law allows the conditional release of persons from quarantine if they comply with medical monitoring and surveillance.

In the rare event that a federal order is issued by CDC, those individuals meeting standards for federal quarantine will be provided with an Order for Quarantine or Isolation. . . . This document outlines the rationale of the federal order as well as information on where the individual will be located, quarantine requirements including the length of the order, CDC's legal authority, and information outlining what the individual can expect while under federal order.

The following is an example of a CDC issued quarantine order:

U.S. Department Of Health And Human Services Centers For Disease Control And Prevention (CDC)
Order For Quarantine Under Section 361 of the Public Health Service Act 42 Code of Federal Regulations Part 70 (Interstate) and Part 71 (Foreign)

Section A: Subject Person

[NAME OF SUBJECT PERSON], WHO WAS DETERMINED TO HAVE BEEN IN HUBEI PROVINCE, PEOPLE'S REPUBLIC OF CHINA, (CHINA) IN THE LAST 14 DAYS, WHO WAS ONBOARD [AIRLINE] FLIGHT #[X] ARRIVING AT [NAME OF AIRPORT].

Section B: Findings

Based on the attached medical declaration, I find:

1. Based on the scientific evidence collected concerning COVID-19, the disease meets the definition of "severe acute respiratory syndromes" as specified under Executive Order 13295, as amended by Executive Orders 13375 and 13674.

2. The Director General of the World Health Organization has declared that the 2019-nCoV/COVID-19 constitutes a Public Health Emergency of International Concern. The Secretary of the U.S. Department of Health and Human Services has declared that 2019-nCoV/COVID-19[1] constitutes a public health emergency.

3. CDC reasonably believes that the subject person arriving into the United States is infected with or has been exposed to COVID-19. 1 42 C.F.R. §§ 71.32(a), 71.33.

---

1. For the reasons set forth in this Declaration, the individual listed in this order additionally meets the standards for quarantine under 42 C.F.R. § 70.6 because the subject person is reasonably believed to be in a qualifying stage of the disease and if released from the place of quarantine would be moving or are about to move from one State into another or constitute a probable source of infection to others who may be moving from one State into another. Qualifying stage is defined under 42 U.S.C. § 264(d)(2) and 42 C.F.R. § 70.1 to mean: (1) The communicable stage of the of a quarantinable communicable disease; or (2) The precommunicable stage of the quarantinable communicable disease, but only if the quarantinable communicable disease would be likely to cause a public health emergency if transmitted to other individuals.

4. COVID-19 is a quarantinable communicable disease in the United States, meaning that CDC may quarantine and restrict the movement of individuals who are arriving into the United States and have been infected with or exposed to the disease.

5. Quarantine[2] is authorized by section 361 of the Public Health Service Act (42 U.S.C. § 264) and federal regulations at 42 CFR §§ 70.6, 71.32(a) and 71.33. The facts listed in the attached medical declaration support the conclusion that quarantine is appropriate. This order meets the requirements of 42 CFR §§ 70.14, 71.37.

6. Based on these reasonable beliefs, I find that the subject person meets the standard for federal quarantine under 42 U.S.C. § 264 and 42 CFR §§ 70.14, 71.37.

7. CDC may legally detain you until it finds that you are no longer at risk of becoming ill and spreading the disease to others. This is commonly referred to as the incubation period for the disease. The incubation period for COVID-19 is currently believed to be up to 14 days. You will be reassessed while you are detained. CDC will count the beginning of the incubation period from when you left Hubei Province, China.

8. This order will take effect immediately.

Section C: Place of Quarantine

You will be housed at [Location, City, State].

Section D: Requirements

1. While under quarantine, you must take precautions, as directed by healthcare staff and CDC personnel, to prevent the possible spread of the quarantinable communicable disease to others.

2. You must cooperate with the efforts of federal and state or local health authorities to contact other exposed people to prevent the possible spread of the quarantinable communicable disease. This includes providing information regarding people you had contact with, places you visited or traveled to, and your medical history.

3. This order prohibits you from traveling in any manner onboard any type of transportation without a written travel permit issued by the CDC Director under 42 C.F.R. § 70.5. Contact information for questions about travel permits is provided under "How to Obtain More Information about This Order" below.

[The order then provides the individual with notice of legal rights, including a right to request medical review and notice of penalties for non-compliance.]

---

2. Quarantine means separation of an individual or group reasonably believed to have been exposed to a quarantinable communicable disease, but who is/are not yet ill, from others who have not been so exposed, to prevent the possible spread of the quarantinable communicable disease.

NOTES AND QUESTIONS

1. Note how the CDC information indicates federal government authority is limited to controlling international and inter-state movement, while states may invoke their general police power at the intra-state level.
2. Enforcement of a large-scale quarantine would obviously present many challenges. The CDC summary indicates that Customs and Border Protection and the U.S. Coast Guard may be called upon to assist in enforcement. Keep this in mind as you read the rest of the chapter and consider what legal barriers must be overcome before the President orders federal armed forces to participate in enforcement.
3. The CDC summary includes a paragraph with a heading titled "Who Is in Charge." For the federal government, the answer is in some ways simple and in others complicated. Overall authority is vested in the President, but the answer becomes less obvious below that level. This is because many federal agencies, to include the Department of Defense, could play a role in a pandemic response. 42 U.S.C § 264 vests the Surgeon General, with approval of the Secretary of Homeland Security, with authority to order and enforce regulations to control communicable diseases:

> *(a) Promulgation and enforcement by Surgeon General*
>
> The Surgeon General, with the approval of the Secretary, is authorized to make and enforce such regulations as in his judgment are necessary to prevent the introduction, transmission, or spread of communicable diseases from foreign countries into the States or possessions, or from one State or possession into any other State or possession. For purposes of carrying out and enforcing such regulations, the Surgeon General may provide for such inspection, fumigation, disinfection, sanitation, pest extermination, destruction of animals or articles found to be so infected or contaminated as to be sources of dangerous infection to human beings, and other measures, as in his judgment may be necessary.

The limited powers of the federal government, coupled with the inherent police power possessed by the individual states, explains in large measure why state governments will be the "first responders" to domestic emergency situations. When such an emergency is the result of a national security threat, especially if that threat emanates from outside the country—such as a terrorist attack—the necessity to call for federal assistance will increase. In some situations, this assistance will be civilian in nature.

A. Humanitarian Assistance and Damage Mitigation

In order to mitigate the suffering caused by a domestic emergency, federal assistance may take the form of what is best understood as "humanitarian" aid—assisting in recovery efforts by providing everything from food, to temporary housing, to debris removal. FEMA—the Federal Emergency Management Agency—is the principal federal agency that will coordinate such assistance, usually relying on contributions from other federal agencies (like the Department of Defense or the Department of Transportation), and managing the contracting process to procure support resources. The principal statutory authority for this federal humanitarian type of support is the Stafford Act. Pursuant to the Act, a governor may request the President to declare the existence of either a major disaster or major emergency, either of which will trigger federal response authority. According to the Act:

Sec. 401. Procedure for Declaration (42 U.S.C. 5170)

(a) In General—All requests for a declaration by the President that a major disaster exists shall be made by the Governor of the affected State. Such a request shall be based on a finding that the disaster is of such severity and magnitude that effective response is beyond the capabilities of the State and the affected local governments and that Federal assistance is necessary. As part of such request, and as a prerequisite to major disaster assistance under this Act, the Governor shall take appropriate response action under State law and direct execution of the State's emergency plan....

Sec. 501. Procedure for Declaration (42 U.S.C. 5191)

(a) Request for Declaration—All requests for a declaration by the President that an emergency exists shall be made by the Governor of the affected State. Such a request shall be based on a finding that the situation is of such severity and magnitude that effective response is beyond the capabilities of the State and the affected local governments and that Federal assistance is necessary. As a part of such request, and as a prerequisite to emergency assistance under this Act, the Governor shall take appropriate action under State law and direct execution of the State's emergency plan.

The Stafford Act also allows the President to invoke the Act by declaring the existence of a major emergency without request from a governor, but only if it is an emergency that the President concludes implicates a "primary" federal responsibility:

Certain Emergencies Involving Federal Primary Responsibility—The President may exercise any authority vested in him by section 5192 of this title or section 5193 of this title [Sections 502 or 503] with respect to an emergency when he determines that an emergency exists for which the primary responsibility for response rests with the United States because the emergency involves a subject area for which, under the Constitution or laws of the United States, the United States exercises exclusive or preeminent responsibility and authority. In determining whether or not such an emergency exists, the President shall consult the Governor of any affected State, if practicable. The President's determination may be made without regard to subsection (a) of this section.

Once triggered by such a declaration, the Stafford Act provides both the authority for federal assistance to the states and, of equal importance, substantial federal funding for such assistance.

B. Military Support to Civil Authorities[2]

A domestic emergency may necessitate the involvement of military forces to assist in both humanitarian assistance and the maintenance of law and order. What mission

---

2. For a comprehensive treatment of the role of the U.S. military in response to domestic challenges, see WILLIAM C. BANKS & STEPHEN DYCUS, SOLDIERS ON THE HOME FRONT: THE DOMESTIC ROLE OF THE AMERICAN MILITARY (2016).

is assigned to such forces, and whether they fall under state or federal authority, is essential for assessing the legal authority for their actions. This importance flows from statutory and constitutional limitations on the use of federal military forces to enforce law. However, these limitations are not absolute, and therefore *if* federal military forces are employed to execute missions that fall within the scope of law enforcement, it is necessary to assess the legal authorities for such missions. But this also means that use of either state or federal military forces in a non-law enforcement role—for example, to assist with humanitarian relief efforts conducted pursuant to the Stafford Act—will not implicate these limitations and restrictions.

Certain domestic emergencies and/or threats may necessitate the use of military forces to augment civilian law enforcement capabilities. Not all military forces are, however, the same for assessing the legal authority for such missions. Each state, the District of Columbia, and Puerto Rico maintain National Guard units. These forces normally fall under the command and control of the state governor. When operating in a state status (commonly referred to as Title 32 Status, referring to the chapter of the United States Code that provides for federal recognition of state National Guard units), these military forces are not restricted by federal law limiting the function of the armed forces, although like any other state officials they do fall within the scope of the Due Process Clause of the Fourteenth Amendment. This means that each governor may order the use of National Guard units to assist in law enforcement in the states. Further, National Guard units may be deployed to other states and placed under the operational control of that state's governor and military commanders without being placed in a federal status.

National Guard forces are also subject to being "federalized"—called into the service of the nation pursuant to laws and regulations promulgated to implement the Militia Clause of the Constitution. When this occurs, these National Guard units fall under national command and control, and are, for purposes of legal authority, no different than federal active duty and reserve forces.

All Army and Air Force forces under federal authority must comply with the Posse Comitatus Act, 18 U.S.C. § 1385, which provides:

> Whoever, except in cases and under circumstances expressly authorized by the Constitution or Act of Congress, willfully uses any part of the Army or the Air Force as a posse comitatus or otherwise to execute the laws shall be fined under this title or imprisoned not more than two years, or both.

This law was enacted following the Reconstruction era to limit the interference of federal military forces in state and local affairs. A posse comitatus refers to the practice of a local law enforcement official calling all able-bodied men in the jurisdiction into service to enforce the law. This law essentially prohibited federal military forces from participating in such a posse, although in practice it prohibits any use of federal military forces in a law enforcement role (the restriction is extended to the Navy and Marine Corps by Department of Defense regulation). While the prohibition is not absolute, allowing for such use when authorized by "the Constitution or an Act of Congress," it is presumptive. But what qualifies as "law enforcement" for purposes of the PCA? The following two opinions provide the framework for answering this question.

Laird v. Tatum
408 U.S. 1 (1972)

Mr. Chief Justice BURGER delivered the opinion of the Court.

Respondents brought this class action in the District Court seeking declaratory and injunctive relief on their claim that their rights were being invaded by the Department of the Army's alleged "surveillance of lawful and peaceful civilian political activity." The petitioners in response describe the activity as "gathering by lawful means . . . (and) maintaining and using in their intelligence activities . . . information relating to potential or actual civil disturbances (or) street demonstrations." . . .

On appeal, a divided Court of Appeals reversed and ordered the case remanded for further proceedings. We granted certiorari to consider whether, as the Court of Appeals held, respondents presented a justiciable controversy in complaining of a "chilling" effect on the exercise of their First Amendment rights where such effect is allegedly caused, not by any "specific action of the Army against them, (but) only (by) the existence and operation of the intelligence gathering and distributing system, which is confined to the Army and related civilian investigative agencies." 144 U.S. App. D.C. 72, 78, 444 F.2d 947, 953. We reverse.

The President is authorized by 10 U.S.C. § 331 to make use of the armed forces to quell insurrection and other domestic violence if and when the conditions described in that section obtain within one of the States. Pursuant to those provisions, President Johnson ordered federal troops to assist local authorities at the time of the civil disorders in Detroit, Michigan, in the summer of 1967 and during the disturbances that followed the assassination of Dr. Martin Luther King. Prior to the Detroit disorders, the Army had a general contingency plan for providing such assistance to local authorities, but the 1967 experience led Army authorities to believe that more attention should be given to such preparatory planning. The data-gathering system here involved is said to have been established in connection with the development of more detailed and specific contingency planning designed to permit the Army, when called upon to assist local authorities, to be able to respond effectively with a minimum of force. As the Court of Appeals observed,

> "In performing this type function the Army is essentially a police force or the back-up of a local police force. To quell disturbances or to prevent further disturbances the Army needs the same tools and, most importantly, the same information to which local police forces have access. Since the Army is sent into territory almost invariably unfamiliar to most soldiers and their commanders, their need for information is likely to be greater than that of the hometown policeman.
>
> "No logical argument can be made for compelling the military to use blind force. When force is employed it should be intelligently directed, and this depends upon having reliable information—in time. As Chief Justice John Marshall said of Washington, 'A general must be governed by his intelligence and must regulate his measures by his information. It is his duty to obtain

correct information. . . .' So we take it as undeniable that the military, i.e., the Army, need a certain amount of information in order to perform their constitutional and statutory missions." 144 U.S. App. D.C., at 77-78, 444 F.2d, at 952-953 (footnotes omitted).

The system put into operation as a result of the Army's 1967 experience consisted essentially of the collection of information about public activities that were thought to have at least some potential for civil disorder, the reporting of that information to Army Intelligence headquarters at Fort Holabird, Maryland, the dissemination of these reports from headquarters to major Army posts around the country, and the storage of the reported information in a computer data bank located at Fort Holabird. The information itself was collected by a variety of means, but it is significant that the principal sources of information were the news media and publications in general circulation. Some of the information came from Army Intelligence agents. . . . And still other information was provided to the Army by civilian law enforcement agencies.

Our examination of the record satisfies us that the Court of Appeals properly identified the issue presented, namely, whether the jurisdiction of a federal court may be invoked by a complainant who alleges that the exercise of his First Amendment rights is being chilled by the mere existence, without more, of a governmental investigative and data-gathering activity that is alleged to be broader in scope than is reasonably necessary for the accomplishment of a valid governmental purpose. We conclude, however, that, having properly identified the issue, the Court of Appeals decided that issue incorrectly.

In recent years this Court has found in a number of cases that constitutional violations may arise from the deterrent, or "chilling," effect of governmental regulations that fall short of a direct prohibition against the exercise of First Amendment rights. E.g., *Baird v. State Bar of Arizona*, 401 U.S. 1, 91 S. Ct. 702, 27 L. Ed. 2d 639 (1971); *Keyishian v. Board of Regents*, 385 U.S. 589, 87 S. Ct. 675, 17 L. Ed. 2d 629 (1967); *Lamont v. Postmaster General*, 381 U.S. 301, 85 S. Ct. 1493, 14 L. Ed. 2d 398 (1965); *Baggett v. Bullitt*, 377 U.S. 360, 84 S. Ct. 1316, 12 L. Ed. 2d 377 (1964). In none of these cases, however, did the chilling effect arise merely from the individual's knowledge that a governmental agency was engaged in certain activities or from the individual's concomitant fear that, armed with the fruits of those activities, the agency might in the future take some other and additional action detrimental to that individual. Rather, in each of these cases, the challenged exercise of governmental power was regulatory, proscriptive, or compulsory in nature, and the complainant was either presently or prospectively subject to the regulations, proscriptions, or compulsions that he was challenging. . . .

The decisions in these cases fully recognize that governmental action may be subject to constitutional challenge even though it has only an indirect effect on the exercise of First Amendment rights. At the same time, however, these decisions have in no way eroded the "established principle that to entitle a private individual to invoke the judicial power to determine the validity of executive or legislative action he must show that he has sustained, or is immediately in danger of sustaining, a direct injury as the result of that action. . . ." *Ex parte Levitt*, 302 U.S. 633, 634, 58 S. Ct. 1, 82 L. Ed. 493 (1937).

The respondents do not meet this test; their claim, simply stated, is that they disagree with the judgments made by the Executive Branch with respect to the type and amount of information the Army needs and that the very existence of the Army's data-gathering system produces a constitutionally impermissible chilling effect upon the exercise of their First Amendment rights. That alleged "chilling" effect may perhaps be seen as arising from respondents' very perception of the system as inappropriate to the Army's role under our form of government, or as arising from respondents' beliefs that it is inherently dangerous for the military to be concerned with activities in the civilian sector, or as arising from respondents' less generalized yet speculative apprehensiveness that the Army may at some future date misuse the information in some way that would cause direct harm to respondents. Allegations of a subjective "chill" are not an adequate substitute for a claim of specific present objective harm or a threat of specific future harm; "the federal courts established pursuant to Article III of the Constitution do not render advisory opinions." *United Public Workers of America (C.I.O.) v. Mitchell*, 330 U.S. 75, 89, 67 S. Ct. 556, 564, 91 L. Ed. 754 (1947). . . .

The concerns of the Executive and Legislative Branches in response to disclosure of the Army surveillance activities—and indeed the claims alleged in the complaint—reflect a traditional and strong resistance of Americans to any military intrusion into civilian affairs. That tradition has deep roots in our history and found early expression, for example, in the Third Amendment's explicit prohibition against quartering soldiers in private homes without consent and in the constitutional provisions for civilian control of the military. Those prohibitions are not directly presented by this case, but their philosophical underpinnings explain our traditional insistence on limitations on military operations in peacetime. Indeed, when presented with claims of judicially cognizable injury resulting from military intrusion into the civilian sector, federal courts are fully empowered to consider claims of those asserting such injury; there is nothing in our Nation's history or in this Court's decided cases, including our holding today, that can properly be seen as giving any indication that actual or threatened injury by reason of unlawful activities of the military would go unnoticed or unremedied.

Reversed.

Mr. Justice DOUGLAS, with whom Mr. Justice MARSHALL concurs, dissenting.

I

If Congress had passed a law authorizing the armed services to establish surveillance over the civilian population, a most serious constitutional problem would be presented. There is, however, no law authorizing surveillance over civilians, which in this case the Pentagon concededly had undertaken.

The question is whether such authority may be implied. One can search the Constitution in vain for any such authority. . . .

The start of the problem is the constitutional distinction between the "militia" and the Armed Forces. By Art. I, § 8, of the Constitution the militia is specifically confined to precise duties: "to execute the Laws of the Union, suppress Insurrections and repel Invasions."

This obviously means that the "militia" cannot be sent overseas to fight wars. It is purely a domestic arm of the governors of the several States, save as it may be called under Art. I, § 8, of the Constitution into the federal service. Whether the "militia" could be given powers comparable to those granted the FBI is a question not now raised, for we deal here not with the "militia" but with "armies." The Army, Navy, and Air Force are comprehended in the constitutional term "armies." Article I, § 8, provides that Congress may "raise and support Armies," and "provide and maintain a Navy," and make "Rules for the Government and Regulation of the land and naval Forces." And the Fifth Amendment excepts from the requirement of a presentment or indictment of a grand jury "cases arising in the land or naval forces, or in the Militia, when in actual service in time of War or public danger."

Acting under that authority, Congress has provided a code governing the Armed Services. That code sets the procedural standards for the Government and regulation of the land and naval forces. It is difficult to imagine how those powers can be extended to military surveillance over civilian affairs.

The most pointed and relevant decisions of the Court on the limitation of military authority concern the attempt of the military to try civilians. The first leading case was *Ex parte Milligan*, 4 Wall. 2, 124, 18 L. Ed. 281, where the Court noted that the conflict between "civil liberty" and "martial law" is "irreconcilable." The Court which made that announcement would have been horrified at the prospect of the military—absent a regime of martial law—establishing a regime of surveillance over civilians. The power of the military to establish such a system is obviously less than the power of Congress to authorize such surveillance. For the authority of Congress is restricted by its power to "raise" armies, Art. I, § 8; and, to repeat, its authority over the Armed Forces is stated in these terms, "To make Rules for the Government and Regulation of the land and naval Forces."

The Constitution contains many provisions guaranteeing rights to persons. Those include the right to indictment by a grand jury and the right to trial by a jury of one's peers. They include the procedural safeguards of the Sixth Amendment in criminal prosecutions; the protection against double jeopardy, cruel and unusual punishments—and, of course, the First Amendment. The alarm was sounded in the Constitutional Convention about the dangers of the armed services. Luther Martin of Maryland said, "when a government wishes to deprive its citizens of freedom, and reduce them to slavery, it generally makes use of a standing army." That danger, we have held, exists not only in bold acts of usurpation of power, but also in gradual encroachments. . . .

Thus, we have until today consistently adhered to the belief that "(i)t is an unbending rule of law, that the exercise of military power, where the rights of the citizen are concerned, shall never be pushed beyond what the exigency requires." *Raymond v. Thomas*, 91 U.S. 712, 716, 23 L. Ed. 434.

It was in that tradition that *Youngstown Sheet & Tube Co. v. Sawyer*, 343 U.S. 579, 72 S. Ct. 863, 96 L. Ed. 1153, was decided, in which President Truman's seizure of the steel mills in the so-called Korean War was held unconstitutional. As stated by Justice Black:

"The order cannot properly be sustained as an exercise of the President's military power as Commander in Chief of the Armed Forces. The Government attempts to do so by citing a number of cases upholding broad powers in military commanders engaged in day-to-day fighting in a theater of war. Such cases need not concern us here. Even though 'theater of war' be an expanding concept, we cannot with faithfulness to our constitutional system hold that the Commander in Chief of the Armed Forces has the ultimate power as such to take possession of private property in order to keep labor disputes from stopping production. This is a job for the Nation's lawmakers, not for its military authorities." Id., at 587, 72 S. Ct., at 867. . . .

II

The claim that respondents have no standing to challenge the Army's surveillance of them and the other members of the class they seek to represent is too transparent for serious argument. The surveillance of the Army over the civilian sector — a part of society hitherto immune from its control — is a serious charge. It is alleged that the Army maintains files on the membership, ideology, programs, and practices of virtually every activist political group in the country, including groups such as the Southern Christian Leadership Conference, Clergy and Laymen United Against the War in Vietnam, the American Civil Liberties Union, Women's Strike for Peace, and the National Association for the Advancement of Colored People. The Army uses undercover agents to infiltrate these civilian groups and to reach into confidential files of students and other groups. The Army moves as a secret group among civilian audiences, using cameras and electronic ears for surveillance. The data it collects are distributed to civilian officials in state, federal, and local governments and to each military intelligence unit and troop command under the Army's jurisdiction (both here and abroad); and these data are stored in one or more data banks.

Those are the allegations; and the charge is that the purpose and effect of the system of surveillance is to harass and intimidate the respondents and to deter them from exercising their rights of political expression, protest, and dissent "by invading their privacy, damaging their reputations, adversely affecting their employment and their opportunities for employment, and in other ways." Their fear is that "permanent reports of their activities will be maintained in the Army's data bank, and their 'profiles' will appear in the so-called 'Blaklist' and that all of this information will be released to numerous federal and state agencies upon request."

Judge Wilkey, speaking for the Court of Appeals, properly inferred that this Army surveillance "exercises a present inhibiting effect on their full expression and utilization of their First Amendment rights." 144 U.S. App. D.C. 72, 79, 444 F.2d 947, 954. That is the test. The "deterrent effect" on First Amendment rights by government oversight marks an unconstitutional intrusion, *Lamont v. Postmaster General*, 381 U.S. 301, 307, 85 S. Ct. 1493, 1496, 14 L. Ed. 2d 398. Or, as stated by Mr. Justice Brennan, "inhibition as well as prohibition against the exercise of precious First Amendment rights is a power denied to government." Id., at 309, 85 S. Ct., at 1497. . . .

The present controversy is not a remote, imaginary conflict. Respondents were targets of the Army's surveillance. First, the surveillance was not casual but massive and comprehensive. Second, the intelligence reports were regularly and widely circulated and were exchanged with reports of the FBI, state and municipal police departments, and the CIA. Third, the Army's surveillance was not collecting material in public records but staking out teams of agents, infiltrating undercover agents, creating command posts inside meetings, posing as press photographers and newsmen, posing as TV newsmen, posing as students, and shadowing public figures.

Finally, we know from the hearings conducted by Senator Ervin that the Army has misused or abused its reporting functions. Thus, Senator Ervin concluded that reports of the Army have been "taken from the Intelligence Command's highly inaccurate civil disturbance teletype and filed in Army dossiers on persons who have held, or were being considered for, security clearances, thus contaminating what are supposed to be investigative reports with unverified gossip and rumor. This practice directly jeopardized the employment and employment opportunities of persons seeking sensitive positions with the federal government or defense industry."

Surveillance of civilians is none of the Army's constitutional business and Congress has not undertaken to entrust it with any such function. . . .

[Dissenting opinion of Mr. Justice Brennan, with whom Mr. Justice Stewart and Mr. Justice Marshall join, omitted.]

NOTES AND QUESTIONS

1. The Court held that the Army's intelligence collection activities did not violate the constitutional rights of any citizens. Why not?
2. What conduct on the part of Army intelligence operatives would have led to a different outcome here?

While *Laird v. Tatum* held that the Army's "passive" collection of intelligence related to U.S. citizens did not violate the Constitution, this does not mean that such activity is necessarily appropriate. In fact, subsequent to this decision, and in large measure in response to post-Vietnam criticisms of these and other intelligence activities, domestic intelligence surveillance by the military was subjected to significant statutory and regulatory restrictions. These laws and regulations require findings of a genuine relationship between the collection and the military mission or interest (for example, allowing military counter-intelligence agents to conduct surveillance to protect the military command or installation from a foreign intelligence threat).

In the next case, the Eighth Circuit Court of Appeals, drawing on *Laird v. Tatum*, considered the legality of using federal military assets to assist in a federal law enforcement mission. Note how the court links the Posse Comitatus Act to a much deeper constitutional aversion to the use of military forces in the domestic realm and the Fourth Amendment protection against unreasonable search or seizure.

Bissonette v. Haig

776 F.2d 1384 (8th Cir. 1985), *aff'd*, 800 F.2d 812 (8th Cir. 1986) (en banc),
aff'd, 485 U.S. 264 (1988)

ARNOLD, Circuit Judge.

This is an action for damages caused by defendants' alleged violations of the Constitution of the United States. The complaint alleges, among other things, that the defendants seized and confined plaintiffs within an "armed perimeter" by the unlawful use of military force, and that this conduct violated not only a federal statute but also the Fourth Amendment. The use of federal military force, plaintiffs argue, without lawful authority and in violation of the Posse Comitatus Act, 18 U.S.C. § 1385, was an "unreasonable" seizure of their persons within the meaning of the Fourth Amendment. We hold that the complaint states a claim upon which relief may be granted. The judgment of the District Court, dismissing the complaint with prejudice for failure to state a claim, will therefore be reversed, and the cause remanded for further proceedings consistent with this opinion.

I.

This case arises out of the occupation of the village of Wounded Knee, South Dakota, on the Pine Ridge Reservation by an armed group of Indians on February 27, 1973. On the evening when the occupation began, members of the Federal Bureau of Investigation, the United States Marshals Service, and the Bureau of Indian Affairs Police sealed off the village by establishing roadblocks at all major entry and exit roads. The standoff between the Indians and the law-enforcement authorities ended about ten weeks later with the surrender of the Indians occupying the village. . . .

In their amended complaint, plaintiffs allege three sets of substantive claims. First, they claim that they were unreasonably seized and confined in the village of Wounded Knee contrary to the Fourth Amendment and their rights to free movement and travel. Second, they claim that they were unreasonably searched by ground and aerial surveillance. In both cases, plaintiffs assert that the seizures and searches were unreasonable because "Defendants accomplished or caused to be accomplished those actions by means of the unconstitutional and felonious use of parts of the United States Army or Air Force. . . ." Third, plaintiffs claim they were assaulted, deprived of life in one instance, and deprived of property contrary to their rights under the Fifth and Eighth Amendments. Again, plaintiffs allege that these actions were unconstitutional "for the reason that the arms used in the force or threat of force were parts of the United States Army or Air Force. . . ." This case comes to us on appeal from a dismissal for failure to state a claim, and we therefore accept for present purposes the factual allegations of the complaint.

These allegations must be viewed against the background of the Posse Comitatus Act of 1878, 18 U.S.C. § 1385, which plaintiffs claim was violated here. The statute provides:

> § 1385. Use of Army and Air Force as posse comitatus
> Whoever, except in cases and under circumstances expressly authorized by the Constitution or Act of Congress, willfully uses any part of the Army or the Air Force as a posse comitatus or otherwise to execute the laws shall be fined not more than $10,000 or imprisoned not more than two years, or both.

The first two sets of claims raise the question whether a search or seizure, otherwise permissible, can be rendered unreasonable under the Fourth Amendment because military personnel or equipment were used to accomplish those actions. We believe that the Constitution, certain acts of Congress, and the decisions of the Supreme Court embody certain limitations on the use of military personnel in enforcing the civil law, and that searches and seizures in circumstances which exceed those limits are unreasonable under the Fourth Amendment.

The Supreme Court has recently indicated that a seizure can be unreasonable even if it is supported by probable cause. *Tennessee v. Garner*, 471 U.S. 1, 105 S. Ct. 1694, 1699, 85 L. Ed. 2d 1 (1985) (seizure with deadly force of fleeing burglar who was apparently unarmed is unreasonable under the Fourth Amendment, whether or not probable cause exists to believe the fugitive has committed a crime). Reasonableness is determined by balancing the interests for and against the seizure. 105 S. Ct. at 1699-1700. Usually, the interests arrayed against a seizure are those of the individual in privacy, freedom of movement, or, in the case of a seizure by deadly force, life. Here, however, the opposing interests are more societal and governmental than strictly individual in character. They concern the special threats to constitutional government inherent in military enforcement of civilian law. That these governmental interests should weigh in the Fourth Amendment balance is neither novel nor surprising. In the typical Fourth Amendment case, the interests of the individual are balanced against those of the government. See, *e.g.*, *Tennessee v. Garner*, 105 S. Ct. at 1700. That some of those governmental interests are on the other side of the Fourth Amendment balance does not make them any less relevant or important.

Civilian rule is basic to our system of government. The use of military forces to seize civilians can expose civilian government to the threat of military rule and the suspension of constitutional liberties. On a lesser scale, military enforcement of the civil law leaves the protection of vital Fourth and Fifth Amendment rights in the hands of persons who are not trained to uphold these rights. It may also chill the exercise of fundamental rights, such as the rights to speak freely and to vote, and create the atmosphere of fear and hostility which exists in territories occupied by enemy forces.

The interest in limiting military involvement in civilian affairs has a long tradition beginning with the Declaration of Independence and continued in the Constitution, certain acts of Congress, and decisions of the Supreme Court. The Declaration of Independence states among the grounds for severing ties with Great Britain that the King "has kept among us, in times of peace, Standing Armies without Consent of our Legislature . . . [and] has affected to render the Military independent of and superior to the Civil power." These concerns were later raised at the Constitutional Convention. Luther Martin of Maryland said, "when a government wishes to deprive its citizens of freedom, and reduce them to slavery, it generally makes use of a standing army."

The Constitution itself limits the role of the military in civilian affairs: it makes the President, the highest civilian official in the Executive Branch, Commander in Chief of the armed services (Art. II, § 2); it limits the appropriations for armed forces to two years and grants to the Congress the power to make rules to govern the armed forces (Art. I, § 8, cl. 14); and it forbids the involuntary quartering of soldiers in any house in time of peace (Third Amendment).

Congress has passed several statutes limiting the use of the military in enforcing the civil law. As already noted, 18 U.S.C. § 1385 makes it a crime for anyone, "except in cases and circumstances expressly authorized by the Constitution or Act of Congress . . . [to use] any part of the Army or Air Force as a posse comitatus or otherwise to execute the laws." Title 10 U.S.C. §§ 331-335 delimit the circumstances under which the President may call upon the national guard or military to suppress insurrection or domestic violence. See also 32 C.F.R. § 215 (1984).

The Supreme Court has also recognized the constitutional limitations placed on military involvement in civilian affairs. A leading case is *Ex parte Milligan*, 4 Wall. 2, 124, 71 U.S. 2, 124, 18 L. Ed. 281 (1866), a Civil War case where the Court held that military commissions had no authority to try civilians in States not engaged in rebellion, in which the civil courts were open. More recently, in *Laird v. Tatum*, 408 U.S. 1, 15-16, 92 S. Ct. 2318, 2326-27, 33 L. Ed. 2d 154 (1972), statements the Court made in dicta reaffirm these limitations:

> The concerns of the Executive and Legislative Branches . . . reflect a traditional and strong resistance of Americans to any military intrusion into civilian affairs. That tradition has deep roots in our history and found early expression, for example, in the Third Amendment's explicit prohibition against quartering soldiers in private homes without consent and in the constitutional provisions for civilian control of the military. Those prohibitions are not directly presented by this case, but their philosophical underpinnings explain our traditional insistence on limitations on military operations in peacetime. Indeed, when presented with claims of judicially cognizable injury resulting from military intrusion into the civilian sector, federal courts are fully empowered to consider claims of those asserting such injury; there is nothing in our Nation's history or in this Court's decided cases, including our holding today, that can properly be seen as giving any indication that actual or threatened injury by reason of unlawful activities of the military would go unnoticed or unremedied.

The governmental interests favoring military assistance to civilian law enforcement are primarily twofold: first, to maintain order in times of domestic violence or rebellion; and second, to improve the efficiency of civilian law enforcement by giving it the benefit of military technologies, equipment, information, and training personnel. These interests can and have been accommodated by acts of Congress to the overriding interest of preserving civilian government and law enforcement. At the time of the Wounded Knee occupation, Congress had prohibited the use of the military to execute the civilian laws, except when expressly authorized. 18 U.S.C. § 1385. And it had placed specific limits on the President's power to use the national guard and military in emergency situations. 10 U.S.C. §§ 331-335. For example, under 10 U.S.C. § 332, the President may call upon the military only after having determined that domestic unrest makes it "impracticable to enforce the laws of the United States by the ordinary course of judicial proceedings," and under 10 U.S.C. § 334, he may do so only after having issued a proclamation ordering the insurgents to disperse. Those steps were not taken here.

We believe that the limits established by Congress on the use of the military for civilian law enforcement provide a reliable guidepost by which to evaluate the reasonableness for Fourth Amendment purposes of the seizures and searches in question here. Congress has acted to establish reasonable limits on the President's use of military forces in emergency situations, and in doing so has circumscribed whatever, if any, inherent power the President may have had absent such legislation. This is the teaching of *Youngstown Sheet & Tube Co. v. Sawyer*, 343 U.S. 579, 72 S. Ct. 863, 96 L. Ed. 1153 (1952). . . .

The District Court took the view that there is no "separate private cause of action for damages for the involvement of military personnel simply because they *were* military personnel. . . ." *Lamont v. Haig, supra*, 539 F. Supp. at 560 (emphasis in original). In large part, we agree. As will be seen shortly when we come to discuss plaintiff's allegations under the Due Process Clause of the Fifth Amendment, the essence of due process is that no governmental power, civilian or military, may be used to restrain the liberty of the citizen or seize his property otherwise than in accordance with the forms of law, including, in most instances, judicial proceedings. In the context of the Fourth Amendment, however, we believe plaintiffs' theory that the use of military force is in a class by itself has merit. The legal traditions which we have briefly summarized establish that the use of military force for domestic law-enforcement purposes is in a special category, and that both the courts and Congress have been alert to keep it there. In short, if the use of military personnel is both unauthorized by any statute, and contrary to a specific criminal prohibition, and if citizens are seized or searched by military means in such a case, we have no hesitation in declaring that such searches and seizures are constitutionally "unreasonable." We do not mean to say that every search or seizure that violates a statute of any kind is necessarily a violation of the Fourth Amendment. But the statute prohibiting (if the allegations in the complaint can be proved) the conduct engaged in by defendants here is, as we have attempted to explain, not just any act of Congress. It is the embodiment of a long tradition of suspicion and hostility towards the use of military force for domestic purposes.

Plaintiffs' Fourth Amendment case, therefore, must stand or fall on the proposition that military activity in connection with the occupation of Wounded Knee violated the Posse Comitatus Act.

In *United States v. Casper*, 541 F.2d 1275 (8th Cir. 1976) (per curiam), *cert. denied*, 430 U.S. 970, 97 S. Ct. 1654, 52 L. Ed. 2d 362 (1977), we specifically held that military assistance given to civilian authorities at Wounded Knee did not violate this statute. (Surprisingly, neither side cites or discusses *Casper* in its brief on this appeal.) In *Casper*, several defendants who were convicted of attempting to interfere with United States Marshals and FBI agents during the Wounded Knee disorder appealed their convictions on the ground that the District Court had erred in rejecting their defense that the federal officials allegedly interfered with had been acting in violation of the Posse Comitatus Act. Specifically, the District Court had found on a stipulated record that the following activities did not violate the Act: the use of Air Force personnel, planes, and cameras to fly surveillance; the advice of military officers in dealing with the disorder; and the furnishing of equipment and supplies. *United States v. McArthur*, 419 F. Supp. 186, 194-95 (D.N.D. 1976). We affirmed "on the basis of the trial court's thorough and well-reasoned opinion." 541 F.2d at 1276.

Casper does, however, stand as a binding precedent in this Circuit on the interpretation of the Act. Therefore, unless plaintiffs now allege that the defendants took actions that went beyond those alleged in the *Casper* case, the actions alleged in the complaint now before us cannot violate the Act.

In *Casper*, quoting from Judge VanSickle's opinion for the District Court, 419 F. Supp. at 194, we approved the following standard for determining whether a violation of the Posse Comitatus Act had occurred:

> Were Army or Air Force personnel used by the civilian law enforcement officers at Wounded Knee in such a manner that the military personnel subjected the citizens to the exercise of military power which was regulatory, proscriptive, or compulsory in nature, either presently or prospectively? 541 F.2d at 1278. This formulation, see 419 F. Supp. at 194 n.4, is based on language found in the Supreme Court's opinion in *Laird v. Tatum*, 408 U.S. 1, 11, 92 S. Ct. 2318, 2324, 33 L. Ed. 2d 154 (1972). *Laird* involved a claim that First Amendment rights were chilled by the existence of a data-gathering system maintained by Army Intelligence, a system described by plaintiffs in that case as involving the surveillance of lawful civilian political activity. The Court rejected this claim on the ground that no justiciable controversy existed. It held that the mere existence of this challenged data-gathering system infringed no rights of plaintiffs, since there had been no showing of objective harm or threat of specific future harm.

When this concept is transplanted into the present legal context, we take it to mean that military involvement, even when not expressly authorized by the Constitution or a statute, does not violate the Posse Comitatus Act unless it actually regulates, forbids, or compels some conduct on the part of those claiming relief. A mere threat of some future injury would be insufficient. . . .

. . . We of course have no way of knowing what plaintiffs would be able to prove if this case goes to trial, but the complaint, considered simply as a pleading, goes well beyond an allegation that defendants simply furnished supplies, aerial surveillance, and advice. It specifically charges that "the several Defendants maintained or caused to be maintained roadblocks and armed patrols constituting an armed perimeter around the village of Wounded Knee. . . ." Defendants' actions, it is charged, "seized, confined, and made prisoners [of plaintiffs] against their will. . . ." These allegations amount to a claim that defendants' activities, allegedly in violation of the Posse Comitatus Act, were "regulatory, proscriptive, or compulsory," in the sense that these activities directly restrained plaintiffs' freedom of movement. No more is required to survive a motion to dismiss. We hold, therefore, that plaintiffs' first set of claims, alleging an unreasonable seizure in violation of the Fourth Amendment because of defendants' confinement of plaintiffs within an armed perimeter, does state a cause of action.

As to the second set of claims . . . plaintiffs charge that they were searched and subjected to surveillance against their will by aerial photographic and visual search and surveillance. As we have already noted, *Casper* holds that this sort of activity does not violate the Posse Comitatus Act. It is therefore not "unreasonable" for Fourth Amendment purposes. . . .

The third set of claims invokes the Due Process Clause of the Fifth Amendment. Plaintiffs argue that they were deprived of liberty, property, and, in the case of the son of one of the plaintiffs, life without due process of law. In the ordinary case, a claimed lack of due process relates to the absence of a notice and hearing or certain other procedural deficiencies. Plaintiffs' theory here is quite different. They claim a due-process violation by reason of the mere fact that the confinement and other deprivations inflicted upon them derived from military action instead of civilian. Plaintiffs cite a number of 19th-century cases which they say supports this view. *E.g., Ex parte Merryman*, 17 Fed. Cas. 144 (No. 9487) (Taney, C.J., in chambers) (1861). We have carefully examined each of these authorities and find in them no clear support for the novel theory advocated by plaintiffs. In *Merryman*, for example, the Chief Justice did mention the Due Process Clause of the Fifth Amendment, and the petitioner in that habeas corpus proceeding was in military custody, but the result in the case would have been exactly the same had the custody been civilian, because Merryman was seized and imprisoned without any judicial process. It was the absence of that process, rather than the military character of Merryman's custodian, that caused the Chief Justice to take the view that the petitioner was unconstitutionally confined. . . .

Our decision to reject plaintiffs' due-process theory is reinforced by the knowledge that all of the proof relevant under such a theory will still come in if and when the Fourth Amendment search-and-seizure theory goes to trial. In other words, plaintiffs do not really need the due-process theory in order to secure relief here, the Court having already held that an unauthorized action by a military officer can be "unreasonable" under the Fourth Amendment even though the same thing, if done by a civilian official, would not. . . .

NOTES AND QUESTIONS

1. Note that the court cites several statutes that actually authorize military support to civilian law enforcement, both at the state and local level. In fact, Congress has enacted a range of statutes that allow the military to provide various types of logistics, training, intelligence, and equipment support to law enforcement. As the court properly noted, activities conducted pursuant to such statutes are consistent with the PCA's "Act of Congress" exception.

2. What is the "test" the court adopts for determining when federal military activity qualifies as law enforcement and therefore falls within the scope of the PCA? Can you think of examples under each of the three prongs of this test?

3. How does the court link compliance or non-compliance with the PCA to the constitutional protections provided by the Fourth Amendment?

4. Does the court's due process analysis provide the government with important flexibility in the means it uses to respond to a domestic emergency? How is the court's Fourth Amendment analysis functionally aligned with its due process analysis?

5. The court offered an interesting discussion of the history of aversion to military involvement in civil affairs, and how this aversion should frame any assessment of the propriety of such involvement. How can the broad state authority to use the National Guard for law enforcement activities without implicating the PCA be reconciled with this discussion?

6. *Laird* and *Casper* are important for two reasons. First, a perceived necessity of action alone does not provide per se legal authority to employ federal military forces domestically. Second, when Congress provides statutory authorization for such use, it will be treated as presumptively constitutional and serve as a specific exception to the PCA. Congress has enacted a number of laws authorizing military support to law enforcement, ranging from loan of equipment, to training, to provision of intelligence and other expert advice. These types of activities would fall outside the scope of the PCA not only because they are authorized by statute, but also because they do not result in federal military forces engaging in regulatory, compulsory, or proscriptive action. The statutory authority described below goes much further.

C. Statutory Authority for Use of Federal Forces in a Law Enforcement Role

As noted in *Bissonette*, the PCA prohibits the use of federal military forces from engaging in conduct that is "regulatory, proscriptive, or compulsory" in nature. But the PCA also provides for an exception when such activities are authorized by an "Act of Congress."

Congress has, in fact, provided statutory authority for such use of federal military forces: The Insurrection Acts, enacted pursuant to Congress's Article I authority, "Provide for calling forth the Militia to execute the Laws of the union, suppress Insurrections, and repel Invasions." The current version of the Insurrection Act is the successor to a law that was originally enacted in 1792, the Militia Act.

The Insurrection Act, 10 U.S.C.A. §§ 251-255, authorizes the President to order use of federal military forces to conduct or augment law enforcement efforts (whether active duty, federal reserve forces called to active duty, or National Guard forces called into federal service) in several situations. While the title of the Insurrection Act may suggest that it should be used only in response to some type of uprising against a state or the federal government, this is misleading. Any domestic disturbance that overwhelms state and local response authorities or interferes with the enforcement of federal law or the protection of federal constitutional rights may trigger invocation of the Act. Examples include the Los Angeles riots of 1992, the race riots in various U.S. cities following the assassination of Dr. Martin Luther King, Jr., and the use of federal military forces to enforce desegregation of public schools in Little Rock, Arkansas and the University of Alabama. But the controversy generated when President Trump declared himself the "president of law and order" and vowed to mobilize every available federal force both "civilian and military" to put an immediate end to protests sparked by Mr. George Floyd's killing in the Summer of 2020—controversy which included a public statement by Secretary of Defense Mark Esper expressing his opposition to President Trump's threat to invoke the Insurrection Act to use federal military personnel and commentary from numerous former senior retired military leaders condemning the President's threat—the Act is historically perceived as a measure of last resort that should never be invoked absent a situation of genuine extremis.

Pursuant to § 251, the President may invoke the Act in response to a request for assistance from a state governor or legislature:

> Whenever there is an insurrections in any State against its government, the President may, upon the request of its legislature or of its governor if the legislature cannot be convened, call into Federal service such of the militia of the other States, in the number requested by that State, and use such of the armed forces, as he considers necessary to suppress the insurrection.

In contrast to § 251, other provisions of the Act do not require a request from the state for assistance as a condition to presidential invocation. Section 252 authorizes the President to invoke the Act on his own initiative in response to any obstruction that makes it impracticable to enforce federal law through normal judicial process:

> Whenever the President considers that unlawful obstructions, combinations, or assemblages, or rebellion against the authority of the United States, make it impracticable to enforce the laws of the United States in any State by the ordinary course of judicial proceedings, he may call into Federal service such of the militia of any State, and use such of the armed forces, as he considers necessary to enforce those laws or to suppress the rebellion.

As an example, President Eisenhower invoked this provision of the Act to utilize the U.S. Army 101st Airborne Division to assist in enforcing federal judicial decisions related to desegregation in Little Rock, Arkansas when the state refused to do so.

Under § 253:

> The President, by using the militia or the armed forces, or both, or by any other means, shall take such measures as he considers necessary to suppress, in a State, any insurrection, domestic violence, unlawful combination, or conspiracy, if it—
>
> (1) so hinders the execution of the laws of that State, and of the United States within the State, that any part or class of its people is deprived of a right, privilege, immunity, or protection named in the Constitution and secured by law, and the constituted

authorities of that State are unable, fail, or refuse to protect that right, privilege, or immunity, or to give that protection; or

(2) opposes or obstructs the execution of the laws of the United States or impedes the course of justice under those laws.

In any situation covered by clause (1), the State shall be considered to have denied the equal protection of the laws secured by the Constitution.

Section 254 of the Act requires the President to issue a proclamation to disperse or otherwise retreat as soon as he invokes the Act, although in practice such proclamations are *pro forma* in nature. For example, when President George H.W. Bush invoked the Insurrection Act to provide assistance to the state of California in response to the 1992 Los Angeles riots that broke out following the Rodney King verdict, he issued the following proclamation:

By the President of the United States of America

A Proclamation

WHEREAS, I have been informed by the Governor of California that conditions of domestic violence and disorder exist in and about the City and County of Los Angeles, and other districts of California, endangering life and property and obstructing execution of the laws, and that the available law enforcement resources, including the National Guard, are unable to suppress such acts of violence and to restore law and order;

WHEREAS, such domestic violence and disorder are also obstructing the execution of the laws of the United States, in the affected area; and

WHEREAS, the Governor of California has requested Federal assistance in suppressing the violence and restoring law and order in the affected area.

NOW, THEREFORE, I GEORGE BUSH, President of the United States of America, by virtue of the authority vested in me by the Constitution and the laws of the United States, including Chapter 15 of Title 10 of the United States Code, do command all persons engaged in such acts of violence and disorder to cease and desist therefrom and to disperse and retire peaceably forthwith.

IN WITNESS WHEREOF, I have hereunto set my hand this first day of May, in the year of our Lord nineteen hundred and ninety-two, and of the Independence of the United States of America the two hundred and sixteenth.

/s/ George Bush[3]

Any use of military forces to enforce law and/or establish law and order domestically is by its nature unusual and may create the perception of an overzealous assertion of federal authority. This may explain, at least to some extent, why the Insurrection Act has been invoked relatively infrequently. Another pragmatic explanation for the infrequent invocation of the Act is that the State National Guard — military units normally under the command of the State Governor (unless called into federal service by the President acting through the Secretary of Defense) may provide law enforcement support to state civilian officials without implicating either the PCA or the Insurrection Act. So long as National Guard forces operate pursuant to state authority they may engage in law enforcement operations no differently than police. Each state governor may therefore call on the state National

---

3. Pres. Proc. No. 6,427 (May 1, 1992), reprinted at 57 Fed. Reg. 19381.

Guard to augment law enforcement capabilities whenever such action is deemed necessary. Even when the state National Guard forces might be insufficient, interstate support agreements will allow the governor to call for National Guard augmentation from other states and in so doing avoid the need to call on the federal government for military augmentation.

This reliance on National Guard forces operating under state authority tends to be the normal response to disturbances or emergencies that overwhelm civilian police capabilities. However, the Insurrection Act provides an important source of authority for using the immense power of federal military forces to respond to many domestic emergencies that threaten the federal function and the constitutional rights of citizens, or results in a request for assistance from the state.

However, it is unclear how far this Insurrection Act authority extends, especially in the absence of a state request for support. May the President invoke the Act to order military forces to enforce a quarantine in response to a pandemic? Or to allow federal military forces to engage in border security operations to prevent an influx of migrants seeking asylum in the United States? The text of the Act suggests that some type of violent domestic disorder is a predicate to invocation, but the terms of the Act are certainly subject to executive interpretation. However, when assessing what qualifies as a triggering event pursuant to the Act, it is significant to consider that Congress substantially expanded the terms of the Act in 2006 and then quickly repealed that expansion. This expansion was incorporated into the 2007 Defense Authorization Act, which amended the Insurrection Act as follows:

(1) The President may employ the armed forces, including the National Guard in Federal service, to—

(A) restore public order and enforce the laws of the United States when, as a result of a natural disaster, epidemic, or other serious public health emergency, terrorist attack or incident, or other condition in any State or possession of the United States, the President determines that—

(i) domestic violence has occurred to such an extent that the constituted authorities of the State or possession are incapable of maintaining public order; and

(ii) such violence results in a condition described in paragraph (2); or

(B) suppress, in a State, any insurrection, domestic violence, unlawful combination, or conspiracy if such insurrection, violation, combination, or conspiracy results in a condition described in paragraph (2).

(2) A condition described in this paragraph is a condition that—

(A) so hinders the execution of the laws of a State or possession, as applicable, and of the United States within that State or possession, that any part or class of its people is deprived of a right, privilege, immunity, or protection named in the Constitution and secured by law, and the constituted authorities of that State or possession are unable, fail, or refuse to protect that right, privilege, or immunity, or to give that protection; or

(B) opposes or obstructs the execution of the laws of the United States or impedes the course of justice under those laws.

This amendment, motivated by both the September 11th attacks and Hurricane Katrina, triggered a backlash based on concerns it made it too easy for the President to order federal military forces to engage in domestic law enforcement. In response,

Congress repealed the amendment and reverted back to the prior version of the law (which is the current version) in the 2008 National Defense Authorization Act. This series of amendments to the Act certainly suggest a congressional intent to narrow the scope of what qualifies as a triggering insurrection.

Once invoked, a complex regulatory process—beyond the scope of this discussion—is triggered for executing the domestic mission. The central tenet of this operational execution process is ensuring civilian authority over the mission. Accordingly, the military forces committed to any domestic response will function under the authority of a civilian official from the Department of Justice: the Senior Civilian Representative of the Attorney General. This official will coordinate with the military commander detailed to command the military component of the response mission, but will have ultimate authority, reporting directly to the Attorney General and the President.

Federal Domestic Response Authority

Humanitarian Aid	Law and Order	Response to Armed Attack
Stafford Act	Insurrection Act	Prize Cases/AUMF
Scope of Power: Provide Resources to Facilitate Disaster Recovery	Scope of Power: Statutory Exception to PCA that Allows Use of Federal Military to Enforce Law	Scope of Power: • Meet the Challenge in the Manner It Presents Itself; or • Pursuant to All Necessary Means Authorization
Trigger: Presidential Declaration of National Emergency	Trigger: • Domestic Violence, Terrorist Attack, Epidemic, "Other Situation": • Threatens Federal Function • Beyond Capability of State	Trigger: • War Being "Thrust" upon the Nation • Action Directed Against a Defined Enemy Belligerent Operating Domestically
Role of the Military: Provide Support to Augment Civilian Response	Role of the Military: • NG Can Be Federalized • May Enforce Law	Execute Wartime Missions
Lead Agency: DHS/FEMA	Lead Agency: DOJ/SCRAG	Lead Agency: DOD/NORTHCOM

D. Martial Law

Martial law is a concept that raises a myriad of legal and policy questions, not the least of which is the very definition. A rarely invoked theory of government power, martial law is probably most easily understood as a domestic version of military occupation: Military authority assumes responsibility for governing functions normally performed by civilian authorities in response to some catastrophic event that disables normal government function. Thus, in a situation of martial law a military commander would replace the role of a local mayor or governor, exercising all aspects of government function, to include issuing orders that ostensibly have the force of law. In a situation necessitating imposition of martial law by the federal government, it is likely the President would invoke the Insurrection Act, authorizing military personnel to perform the full spectrum of law enforcement functions.

The text of the Constitution makes no reference to martial law. But this does not mean the concept is per se unconstitutional. Recall that in *Ex parte Milligan* (Chapter 1), the Supreme Court offered what is widely considered the test for assessing when the federal government may, pursuant to the Constitution, invoke martial law.

Lambdin P. Milligan, a resident of Ohio, was allegedly involved with a group known generally as "Copperheads" that supported the Confederacy during the Civil War. A federal grand jury considered evidence against him but did not return an indictment. Milligan was then arrested by the local military commander and tried and convicted by a military commission. The Supreme Court struck down his conviction, holding that subjecting him to military criminal jurisdiction violated his constitutional rights and represented an improper intrusion of military authority into civil affairs. The Court did suggest that such authority could be properly exercised during a period of martial law, although it concluded no such situation existed at the time of Milligan's trial. The Court summarized the government position as follows:

> It is claimed that martial law covers with its broad mantle the proceedings of this military commission. The proposition is this: that, in a time of war, the commander of an armed force (if, in his opinion, the exigencies of the country demand it, and of which he is to judge) has the power, within the lines of his military district, to suspend all civil rights and their remedies and subject citizens, as well as soldiers to the rule of *his will*, and, in the exercise of his lawful authority, cannot be restrained except by his superior officer or the President of the United States.

The Court rejected the contention that Milligan's sympathy for and efforts to support the Confederacy justified subjecting him to military authority. The invalidity of using a military tribunal as a substitute for an Article III court rested on two critical conclusions: First, Milligan was not a member of the Confederate armed forces, and therefore not subject to military detention or jurisdiction pursuant to the laws and customs of war; and second, the situation in Indiana did not justify invoking martial law. On this latter point, the Court explained:

> It will be borne in mind that this is not a question of the power to proclaim martial law when war exists in a community and the courts and civil authorities are overthrown. Nor is it a question what rule a military commander, at the head of his army, can impose on states in rebellion to cripple their resources and quell the insurrection. The jurisdiction claimed is much more extensive. The necessities of the service during the late Rebellion required that the loyal states should be placed within the limits of certain military districts and commanders appointed in them, and it is urged that this, in a military sense, constituted them the theater of military operations, and as, in this case, Indiana had been and was again threatened with invasion by the enemy, the occasion was furnished to establish martial law. The conclusion does not follow from the premises. If armies were collected in Indiana, they were to be employed in another locality, where the laws were obstructed and the national authority disputed. On her soil there was no hostile foot; if once invaded, that invasion was at an end, and, with it, all pretext for martial law. Martial law cannot arise from a *threatened* invasion. The necessity must be actual and present, the invasion real, such as effectually closes the courts and deposes the civil administration.

> It is difficult to see how the *safety* for the country required martial law in Indiana. If any of her citizens were plotting treason, the power of arrest could secure them until the government was prepared for their trial, when the courts were open and ready to try them. It was as easy to protect witnesses before a civil as a military tribunal, and as there could be no wish to convict except on sufficient legal evidence, surely an ordained and established court was better able to judge of this than a military tribunal composed of gentlemen not trained to the profession of the law.
>
> It follows from what has been said on this subject that there are occasions when martial rule can be properly applied. If, in foreign invasion or civil war, the courts are actually closed, and it is impossible to administer criminal justice according to law, *then*, on the theatre of active military operations, where war really prevails, there is a necessity to furnish a substitute for the civil authority, thus overthrown, to preserve the safety of the army and society, and as no power is left but the military, it is allowed to govern by martial rule until the laws can have their free course. As necessity creates the rule, so it limits its duration, for, if this government is continued *after* the courts are reinstated, it is a gross usurpation of power. Martial rule can never exist where the courts are open and in the proper and unobstructed exercise of their jurisdiction. It is also confined to the locality of actual war. . . .

Consider how these requirements for a valid assertion of martial law, or lack thereof, could impact a military response to a domestic emergency that is *not* the result of a foreign invasion.

In *Milligan*, the Court noted that "martial law cannot arise from a *threatened* invasion. The necessity must be actual and present, the invasion real, such as effectually closes the courts and deposes the civil administration." The following decision provides rare insight into how the Supreme Court assessed the existence of such a situation.

Duncan v. Kahanamoku
327 U.S. 304 (1946)

Mr. Justice BLACK delivered the opinion of the Court.

The petitioners in these cases were sentenced to prison by military tribunals in Hawaii. Both are civilians. The question before us is whether the military tribunals had power to do this. The United States District Court for Hawaii, in habeas corpus proceedings, held that the military tribunals had no such power, and ordered that they be set free. The Circuit Court of Appeals reversed, and ordered that the petitioners be returned to prison. 146 F.2d 576. Both cases thus involve the rights of individuals charged with crime and not connected with the armed forces to have their guilt or innocence determined in courts [of] law which provide established procedural safeguards, rather than by military tribunals which fail to afford many of these safeguards. Since these judicial safeguards are prized privileges of our system of government we granted certiorari. 324 U.S. 833.

The following events led to the military tribunals' exercise of jurisdiction over the petitioners. On December 7, 1941, immediately following the surprise air attack by the Japanese on Pearl Harbor, the Governor of Hawaii by proclamation undertook to suspend the privilege of the writ of habeas corpus and to place the Territory under "martial law." Section 67 of the Hawaiian Organic Act, 31 Stat. 141, 153 authorizes the Territorial Governor to take this action "in case of rebellion or invasion, or imminent danger thereof, when the public safety requires it." His action was to remain in effect only "until communication can be had with the President and his decision thereon made known." The President approved the Governor's action on December 9th. The Governor's proclamation also authorized and requested the Commanding General, "during . . . the emergency and until danger of invasion is removed, to exercise all the powers normally exercised" by the Governor and by "the judicial officers and employees of the Territory."

Pursuant to this authorization, the Commanding General immediately proclaimed himself Military Governor and undertook the defense of the Territory and the maintenance of order. On December 8th, both civil and criminal courts were forbidden to summon jurors and witnesses and to try cases. The Commanding General established military tribunals to take the place of the courts. These were to try civilians charged with violating the laws of the United States and of the Territory, and rules, regulations, orders or policies of the Military Government. Rules of evidence and procedure of courts of law were not to control the military trials. In imposing penalties the military tribunals were to be

> "guided by, but not limited to the penalties authorized by the court martial manual, the laws of the United States, the Territory of Hawaii, the District of Columbia, and the customs of war in like cases."

The rule announced was simply that punishment was "to be commensurate with the offense committed," and that the death penalty might be imposed "in appropriate cases." Thus, the military authorities took over the government of Hawaii. They could and did, by simply promulgating orders, govern the day-to-day activities of civilians who lived, worked, or were merely passing through there. The military tribunals interpreted the very orders promulgated by the military authorities, and proceeded to punish violators. The sentences imposed were not subject to direct appellate court review, since it had long been established that military tribunals are not part of our judicial system. *Ex parte Vallandingham*, 1 Wall. 243. The military undoubtedly assumed that its rule was not subject to any judicial control whatever, for, by orders issued on August 25, 1943, it prohibited even accepting of a petition for writ of habeas corpus by a judge or judicial employee or the filing of such a petition by a prisoner or his attorney. Military tribunals could punish violators of these orders by fine, imprisonment, or death.

White, the petitioner in No. 15, was a stockbroker in Honolulu. Neither he nor his business was connected with the armed forces. On August 20, 1942, more than eight months after the Pearl Harbor attack, the military police arrested him. The charge against him was embezzling stock belonging to another civilian in violation of Chapter 183 of the Revised Laws of Hawaii.

Though by the time of White's arrest the courts were permitted "as agents of the Military Governor" to dispose of some nonjury civil cases, they were still forbidden to summon jurors and to exercise criminal jurisdiction. On August 22nd, White was brought before a military tribunal designated as a "Provost Court." The "Court" orally informed him of the charge. He objected to the tribunal's jurisdiction but the objection was overruled. He demanded to be tried by a jury. This request was denied. His attorney asked for additional time to prepare the case. This was refused. On August 25th, he was tried and convicted. The tribunal sentenced him to five years' imprisonment. Later, the sentence was reduced to four years.

Duncan, the petitioner in No. 14, was a civilian shipfitter employed in the Navy Yard at Honolulu. On February 24th, 1944, more than two years and two months after the Pearl Harbor attack, he engaged in a brawl with two armed Marine sentries at the yard. He was arrested by the military authorities. By the time of his arrest, the military had to some extent eased the stringency of military rule. Schools, bars, and motion picture theaters had been reopened. Courts had been authorized to "exercise their normal functions." They were once more summoning jurors and witnesses and conducting criminal trials. There were important exceptions, however. One of these was that only military tribunals were to try "Criminal Prosecutions for violations of military orders." As the record shows, these military orders still covered a wide range of day-to-day civilian conduct. Duncan was charged with violating one of these orders, paragraph 8.01, Title 8, of General Order No. 2, which prohibited assault on military or naval personnel with intent to resist or hinder them in the discharge of their duty. He was therefore tried by a military tribunal, rather than the Territorial Court, although the general laws of Hawaii made assault a crime. Revised L.H. 1935, ch. 166. A conviction followed, and Duncan was sentenced to six months' imprisonment.

Both White and Duncan challenged the power of the military tribunals to try them by petitions for writs of habeas corpus filed in the District Court for Hawaii on March 14 and April 14, 1944, respectively. Their petitions urged both statutory and Constitutional grounds. The court issued orders to show cause. Returns to these orders contended that Hawaii had become part of an active theater of war constantly threatened by invasion from without; that the writ of habeas corpus had therefore properly been suspended and martial law had validly been established in accordance with the provisions of the Organic Act; that, consequently, the District Court did not have jurisdiction to issue the writ, and that the trials of petitioners by military tribunals pursuant to orders by the Military Governor issued because of military necessity were valid. Each petitioner filed a traverse to the returns, which traverse challenged, among other things, the suspension of habeas corpus, the establishment of martial law, and the validity of the Military Governor's orders, asserting that such action could not be taken except when required by military necessity due to actual or threatened invasion, which, even if it did exist on December 7, 1941, did not exist when the petitioners were tried, and that, whatever the necessity for martial law, there was no justification for trying them in military tribunals, rather than the regular courts of law. The District Court, after separate trials, found in each case, among other things, that the courts had always been able to function but for the military orders closing them, and that, consequently, there was no military necessity for the trial of petitioners by military tribunals, rather than regular courts. It accordingly held the trials void, and ordered the release of the petitioners.

The Circuit Court of Appeals, assuming without deciding that the District Court had jurisdiction to entertain the petitions, held the military trials valid and reversed the ruling of the District Court, 146 F.2d 576. It held that the military orders providing for military trials were fully authorized by Section 67 of the Organic Act and the Governor's actions taken under it. The Court relied on that part of the section which, as we have indicated, authorizes the Governor, with the approval of the President, to proclaim "martial law" whenever the public safety requires it. The Circuit Court thought that the term "martial law" as used in the Act denotes, among other things, the establishment of a "total military government" completely displacing or subordinating the regular courts, that the decision of the executive as to what the public safety requires must be sustained so long as that decision is based on reasonable grounds, and that such reasonable grounds did exist.

In presenting its argument before this Court, the government, for reasons set out in the margin, abandons its contention as to the suspension of the writ of habeas corpus and advances the argument employed by the Circuit Court for sustaining the trials and convictions of the petitioners by military tribunals. The petitioners contend that "martial law," as provided for by § 67, did not authorize the military to try and punish civilians such as petitioners, and urge further that, if such authority should be inferred from the Organic Act, it would be unconstitutional. We need decide the Constitutional question only if we agree with the government that Congress did authorize what was done here.

Did the Organic Act, during the period of martial law, give the armed forces power to supplant all civilian laws and to substitute military for judicial trials under the conditions that existed in Hawaii at the time these petitioners were tried? The relevant conditions, for our purposes, were the same when both petitioners were tried. The answer to the question depends on a correct interpretation of the Act. But we need not construe the Act insofar as the power of the military might be used to meet other and different conditions and situations. The boundaries of the situation with reference to which we do interpret the scope of the Act can be more sharply defined by stating at this point some different conditions which either would or might conceivably have affected to a greater or lesser extent the scope of the authorized military power. We note first that, at the time the alleged offenses were committed, the dangers apprehended by the military were not sufficiently imminent to cause them to require civilians to evacuate the area, or even to evacuate any of the buildings necessary to carry on the business of the courts. In fact, the buildings had long been open and actually in use for certain kinds of trials. Our question does not involve the well established power of the military to exercise jurisdiction over members of the armed forces, those directly connected with such forces [for example, civilian contractors accompanying the armed forces during operations], or enemy belligerents, prisoners of war, or others charged with violating the laws of war. We are not concerned with the recognized power of the military to try civilians in tribunals established as a part of a temporary military government over occupied enemy territory or territory regained from an enemy where civilian government cannot and does not function. For Hawaii, since annexation, has been held by and loyal to the United States. Nor need we here consider the power of the military simply to arrest and detain civilians interfering with a necessary military function at a time of turbulence and danger from insurrection or war. And finally, there was no specialized effort of the military, here, to enforce orders which related only to military functions, such as, for illustration, curfew rules or blackouts. For these petitioners were tried before tribunals set up under a military program which took over all government and superseded all civil laws and courts. If the Organic Act, properly interpreted, did not give the armed forces this awesome power, both petitioners are entitled to their freedom.

I

In interpreting the Act, we must first look to its language. Section 67 makes it plain that Congress did intend the Governor of Hawaii, with the approval of the President, to invoke military aid under certain circumstances. But Congress did not specifically state to what extent the army could be used, or what power it could exercise. It certainly did not explicitly declare that the Governor, in conjunction with the military, could for days, months, or years close all the courts and supplant them with military tribunals. *Cf. Coleman v. Tennessee*, 97 U.S. 509, 97 U.S. 514. If a power thus to obliterate the judicial system of Hawaii can be found at all in the Organic Act, it must be inferred from § 67's provision for placing the Territory under "martial law." But the term "martial law" carries no precise meaning. The Constitution does not refer to "martial law" at all, and no Act of Congress has defined the term. It has been employed in various ways by different people and at different times. By some, it has been identified as "military law" limited to members of, and those connected with, the armed forces. Others have said that the term does not imply a system of established rules, but denotes simply some kind of day-to-day expression of a General's will dictated by what he considers the imperious necessity of the moment. *See United States v. Diekelman*, 92 U.S. 520, 92 U.S. 526. In 1857, the confusion as to the meaning of the phrase was so great that the Attorney General, in an official opinion, had this to say about it: "The Common Law authorities and commentators afford no clue to what martial law, as understood in England, really is. . . . In this country, it is still worse." 8 Op. Atty. Gen. 365, 367. What was true in 1857 remains true today. The language of § 67 thus fails to define adequately the scope of the power given to the military and to show whether the Organic Act provides that courts of law be supplanted by military tribunals.

II

Since the Act's language does not provide a satisfactory answer, we look to the legislative history for possible further aid in interpreting the term "martial law" as used in the statute. The government contends that the legislative history shows that Congress intended to give the armed forces extraordinarily broad powers to try civilians before military tribunals. Its argument is as follows: that portion of the language of § 67 which prescribes the prerequisites to declaring martial law is identical with a part of the language of the original Constitution of Hawaii. Before Congress enacted the Organic Act, the Supreme Court of Hawaii had construed that language as giving the Hawaiian President power to authorize military tribunals to try civilians charged with crime whenever the public safety required it. *In re Kalanianaole,* 10 Hawaii, 29. When Congress passed the Organic Act, it simply enacted the applicable language of the Hawaiian Constitution, and, with it, the interpretation of that language by the Hawaiian Supreme Court.

In disposing of this argument, we wish to point out at the outset that, even had Congress intended the decision in the *Kalanianaole* case to become part of the Organic Act, that case did not go so far as to authorize military trials of the petitioners for these reasons. There, the defendants were insurrectionists taking part in the very uprising which the military were to suppress, while here, the petitioners had no connection with any organized resistance to the armed forces or the established government. If, on the other hand, we should take the *Kalanianaole* case to authorize the complete supplanting of courts by military tribunals, we are certain that Congress did not wish to make that case part of the Organic Act. For that case did not merely uphold military trials of civilians, but also held that courts were to interfere only when there was an obvious abuse of discretion which resulted in cruel and inhuman practices or the establishment of military rule for the personal gain of the President and the armed forces. But courts were not to review whether the President's action, no matter how unjustifiable, was necessary for the public safety. As we shall indicate later, military trials of civilians charged with crime, especially when not made subject to judicial review, are so obviously contrary to our political traditions and our institution of jury trials in courts of law that the tenuous circumstance offered by the government can hardly suffice to persuade us that Congress was willing to enact a Hawaiian Supreme Court decision permitting such a radical departure from our steadfast beliefs.

Partly in order to meet this objection, the government further contends that Congress, in enacting the *Kalanianaole* case, not only authorized military trials of civilians in Hawaii, but also could and intended to provide that "martial law" in Hawaii should not be limited by the United States Constitution or by established Constitutional practice. But, when the Organic Act is read as a whole and in the light of its legislative history, it becomes clear that Congress did not intend the Constitution to have a limited application to Hawaii. Along with § 67, Congress enacted § 5 of the Organic Act, which provides "that the Constitution . . . shall have the same force and effect within the said Territory as elsewhere in the United States."... Congress thus expressed a strong desire to apply the Constitution without qualification.

It follows that civilians in Hawaii are entitled to the Constitutional guarantee of a fair trial to the same extent as those who live in any other part of our country. We are aware that conditions peculiar to Hawaii might imperatively demand extraordinarily speedy and effective measures in the event of actual or threatened invasion. But this also holds true for other parts of the United States. Extraordinary measures in Hawaii, however necessary, are not supportable on the mistaken premise that Hawaiian inhabitants are less entitled to Constitutional protection than others. For here, Congress did not, in the Organic Act, exercise whatever power it might have had to limit the application of the Constitution. *Cf. Hawaii v. Mankichi*, 190 U.S. 197. The people of Hawaii are therefore entitled to Constitutional protection to the same extent as the inhabitants of the 48 States. . . . Whatever power the Organic Act gave the Hawaiian military authorities, such power must therefore be construed in the same way as a grant of power to troops stationed in any one of the states.

III

Since both the language of the Organic Act and its legislative history fail to indicate that the scope of "martial law" in Hawaii includes the supplanting of courts by military tribunals, we must look to other sources in order to interpret that term. We think the answer may be found in the birth, development, and growth of our governmental institutions up to the time Congress passed the Organic Act. Have the principles and practices developed during the birth and growth of our political institutions been such as to persuade us that Congress intended that loyal civilians in loyal territory should have their daily conduct governed by military orders substituted for criminal laws, and that such civilians should be tried and punished by military tribunals? Let us examine what those principles and practices have been with respect to the position of civilian government and the courts, and compare that with the standing of military tribunals throughout our history.

People of many ages and countries have feared and unflinchingly opposed the kind of subordination of executive, legislative, and judicial authorities to complete military rule which according to the government Congress has authorized here. In this country, that fear has become part of our cultural and political institutions. The story of that development is well known, and we see no need to retell it all. But we might mention a few pertinent incidents. As early as the 17th Century, our British ancestors took political action against aggressive military rule. When James I and Charles I authorized martial law for purposes of speedily punishing all types of crimes committed by civilians, the protest led to the historic Petition of Right, which, in uncompromising terms, objected to this arbitrary procedure and prayed that it be stopped and never repeated. When later the American colonies declared their independence, one of the grievances listed by Jefferson was that the King had endeavored to render the military superior to the civil power. The executive and military officials who later found it necessary to utilize the armed forces to keep order in a young and turbulent nation did not lose sight of the philosophy embodied in the Petition of Right and the Declaration of Independence that existing civilian government, and especially the courts, were not to be interfered with by the exercise of military power. In 1787, the year in which the Constitution was formulated, the Governor of Massachusetts colony used the militia to cope with Shay's rebellion. In his instructions to the Commander of the troops, the Governor listed the "great objects" of the mission. The troops were to "protect the judicial courts . . . ," "to assist the civil magistrates in executing the laws . . . ," and to "aid them in apprehending the disturbers of the public peace. . . ." The Commander was to consider himself "constantly as under the direction of the civil officer, saving where any armed force shall appear and oppose . . . [his] . . . marching to execute these orders." President Washington's instructions to the Commander of the troops sent into Pennsylvania to suppress the Whiskey Rebellion of 1794 were to the same effect. The troops were to see to it that the laws were enforced, and were to deliver the leaders of armed insurgents to the regular courts for trial. The President admonished the Commanding General "that the judge cannot be controlled in his functions." In the many instances of the use of troops to control the activities of civilians that followed, the troops were generally again employed merely to aid, and not to supplant, the civilian authorities. The last noteworthy incident before the enactment of the Organic Act was the rioting that occurred in the Summer of 1892 at the Coeur d'Alene mines of Shoshone County, Idaho. The President ordered the regular troops to report to the Governor for instructions and to support the civil authorities in preserving the peace. Later, the State Auditor, as agent of the Governor, and not the Commanding General, ordered the troops to detain citizens without trial and to aid the Auditor in doing all he thought necessary to stop the riot. Once more, the military authorities did not undertake to supplant the courts and to establish military tribunals to try and punish ordinary civilian offenders.

Courts and their procedural safeguards are indispensable to our system of government. They were set up by our founders to protect the liberties they valued. *Ex parte Quirin*, 317 U.S. 1, 317 U.S. 19. Our system of government clearly is the antithesis of total military rule, and the founders of this country are not likely to have contemplated complete military dominance within the limits of a Territory made part of this country and not recently taken from an enemy. They were opposed to governments that placed in the hands of one man the power to make, interpret, and enforce the laws. Their philosophy has been the people's throughout our history. For that reason, we have maintained legislatures chosen by citizens or their representatives and courts and juries to try those who violate legislative enactments. We have always been especially concerned about the potential evils of summary criminal trials, and have guarded against them by provisions embodied in the constitution itself. *See Ex parte Milligan*, 4 Wall. 2; *Chambers v. Florida*, 309 U.S. 227. Legislatures and courts are not merely cherished American institutions; they are indispensable to our government.

Military tribunals have no such standing. For as this Court has said before:

> "... the military should always be kept in subjection to the laws of the country to which it belongs, and that he is no friend to the Republic who advocates the contrary. The established principle of every free people is that the law shall alone govern, and to it the military must always yield."

Dow v. Johnson, 100 U.S. 158, 100 U.S. 169. Congress, prior to the time of the enactment of the Organic Act, had only once authorized the supplanting of the courts by military tribunals. Legislation to that effect was enacted immediately after the South's unsuccessful attempt to secede from the Union. Insofar as that legislation applied to the Southern States after the war was at an end, it was challenged by a series of Presidential vetoes as vigorous as any in the country's history. And, in order to prevent this Court from passing on the constitutionality of this legislation, Congress found it necessary to curtail our appellate jurisdiction. Indeed, prior to the Organic Act, the only time this Court had ever discussed the supplanting of courts by military tribunals in a situation other than that involving the establishment of a military government over recently occupied enemy territory, it had emphatically declared that "civil liberty and this kind of martial law cannot endure together; the antagonism is irreconcilable, and, in the conflict, one or the other must perish." *Ex parte Milligan*, 4 Wall. 2, 71 U.S. 124-125.

We believe that, when Congress passed the Hawaiian Organic Act and authorized the establishment of "martial law," it had in mind and did not wish to exceed the boundaries between military and civilian power in which our people have always believed, which responsible military and executive officers had heeded, and which had become part of our political philosophy and institutions prior to the time Congress passed the Organic Act. The phrase "martial law," as employed in that Act, therefore, while intended to authorize the military to act vigorously for the maintenance of an orderly civil government and for the defense of the island against actual or threatened rebellion or invasion, was not intended to authorize the supplanting of courts by military tribunals. Yet the government seeks to justify the punishment of both White and Duncan on the ground of such supposed Congressional authorization. We hold that both petitioners are now entitled to be released from custody.

Reversed.

NOTES AND QUESTIONS

1. How does the structure and function of the Insurrection Act support the Court's holding in *Duncan*?
2. Based on *Milligan* and *Duncan*, under what circumstances other than recovery of territory from an enemy, if any, would imposition of martial law be justified?
3. If you were advising a military commander tasked with imposing martial law in an area of the United States, when would you advise termination of this authority?

4. *Duncan* illustrates that Congress is capable of providing statutory authority for imposition of martial law. Would it be wise for Congress to enact such a statute for potential emergencies in the United States? What would be the constitutional authority for enacting such a statute? What would be the essential provisions you would expect would be included in such a statute?

5. In the absence of statutory authority similar to that invoked in *Duncan*, would a presidential invocation of martial law be constitutionally valid?

ASSESSMENT QUESTIONS

1. In response to an outbreak of smallpox in Houston, a combined state and federal response is implemented. All evidence indicates that the outbreak is limited to Houston and surrounding communities (all in Texas). The primary objectives of the response are to stop the spread of this highly contagious disease beyond the Houston metropolitan area; provide essential medical treatment to infected individuals; provide adequate supplies of food, water, and fuel to the community; and ensure the maintenance of public order. The mayor of Houston requests support from the governor and from the President to establish movement control, infection screening stations, and food and water supply and distribution, and to apprehend individuals who violate movement restrictions. What resources would you advise the mayor he is likely to receive in response to these requests?

2. In a recent incident, Abilene Airport was closed in response to a bomb threat. The local police responded, and immediately requested that the Commander of Dyess Air Force Base dispatch several teams of Air Force military security police with bomb-sniffing dogs to assist in sweeping the airport for concealed explosives. The Commander granted the request, and the Air Force personnel conducted the mission in cooperation with the local police. No bombs were found, the airport resumed operation, and the military personnel returned to their base. Prior to the bomb sweep, all non-law enforcement personnel had been evacuated from the airport at the direction of local police officials. A passenger at the airport that day is disturbed by the use of federal military forces, and seeks your advice on whether she can successfully sue the government alleging a civil rights violation. How would you respond?

3. Briefly explain the difference between military support to civil authorities under the Stafford Act and military support to civil authorities under the Insurrection Act.

ASSESSMENT ANSWERS

1. The mayor should expect the state to provide support for controlling the population and enforcing law, and the federal government to support the effort to provide food, water, and other resources. Unlike the federal government, the state is vested with "general police powers." This will allow the governor to impose emergency movement restrictions. The governor may also order the National Guard to assist in enforcing the law, to include movement restrictions, so long as the National Guard is operating under state control. The federal government may invoke the Stafford Act to provide resources and support to respond to the emergency, and federal military forces may contribute to that effort. However,

absent invocation of the Insurrection Act (or martial law), military forces under federal control may not participate in law enforcement or movement control activities, as such missions would violate the Posse Comitatus Act. It is therefore important that National Guard forces remain under state authority (Title 32), and are not called into federal service (Title 10).

2. The passenger will not be successful in suing the government for a civil rights violation. The use of federal military forces is restricted by the Posse Comitatus Act. However, that restriction only prohibits use of these forces as a posse comitatus. This has been interpreted by federal courts as prohibiting conduct that is regulatory, proscriptive, or compulsory in nature. Such activity, when it impacts a citizen, results in a violation of the Fourth Amendment because it is inherently unreasonable. However, use of federal military forces to provide support to local, state, or federal law enforcement agencies in a manner that does not involve such activities does not implicate the PCA. Here, nothing the Air Force personnel did crossed that line, and therefore it would not be treated as unreasonable within the meaning of the Fourth Amendment.

3. The Stafford Act establishes authority for the federal government to provide what is in essence "humanitarian aid" to state and local governments in response to a natural disaster or emergency. This support is coordinated through FEMA (the Federal Emergency Management Agency). FEMA will frequently request that the Department of Defense contribute to these humanitarian response efforts. So long as federal military forces are merely providing support, and not engaged in activities that implicate the restrictions of the Posse Comitatus Act, their involvement in such activities is lawful. In contrast, the Insurrection Act is a statutory exception to the Posse Comitatus Act. Accordingly, when properly invoked, the Act authorizes the use of federal military forces to enforce laws of the United States and the states. When invoked, federal military forces will operate under the authority of the Senior Civilian Representative of the Attorney General.

CHAPTER 17

National Security in the Digital Age

I. OVERVIEW

Advances in technology have always presented unique national security challenges and opportunities. Just consider the broad-ranging and profound impacts on national security ushered in by the nuclear age. On the one hand, nuclear technology and weapons enabled the United States to project power in support of national interests in unprecedented ways. On the other hand, as the technology proliferated and fell in the hands of adversaries, the threat landscape changed fundamentally. This shift necessitated new strategies, policies, and attendant legal frameworks to manage traditional inter-state relationships and activities and protect national security.

The rapid and accelerating shift from the analog to the digital age has been no less impactful, and perhaps more so. The transformative power of digital computing that began in the middle of the last century is by now obvious. And from the moment the first host-to-host digital message was sent across the ARPANET in 1969 — the first step toward rapidly establishing a ubiquitously interconnected digital world — the national security landscape changed forever. At the outset of this digital revolution, few if any could have predicted the degree to which the technology of the internet would create an entirely new realm, cyberspace, through which states could engage in traditional statecraft and conflict in novel and dynamic ways. The explosion of information technology over the last half-century has reshaped the world, transforming nearly every aspect of society, including international relations and security.

The unprecedented speed of development and diffusion of globally interconnected information technology has been staggering. Unfortunately, the tremendous benefits engendered by the digital revolution have also been matched and perhaps outpaced by accompanying threats to individual and national security. The significance and potential impact of cyber-threats have grown exponentially over the past few decades to the point where cyber-threats are now considered a major, if not the most significant strategic threat to the United States.

This threat manifests in myriad ways. Cyberspace and digital technology afford threat actors the means to degrade or disrupt the functionality of devices, networks, machines, and infrastructure vital to national health, welfare, and security. It also puts at risk the integrity, availability, and confidentiality of the information we all rely on to function effectively, individually and as a nation. And as we have learned over the last several election cycles, cyberspace and its component technology provides a fertile and effective environment for the spread of propaganda, misinformation, and disinformation as part of hostile influence campaigns.

While some of these cyber-threats can and have manifested as part of ongoing armed conflicts, the vast majority of malicious cyber operations have taken place in the so-called gray zone — the distinct and uncertain environment falling along the conflict continuum somewhere between peacetime geo-political interactions and overt warfare. Exploiting inherent legal, policy, and factual ambiguities prevalent in this "gray zone," state and non-state actors have been engaging in a range of progressively more aggressive actions designed to alter the status quo and achieve strategic objectives normally associated with war. However, these actions are deliberately calibrated to remain below the threshold of a use of force prohibited by the U.N. Charter to avoid the risk of conventional armed conflict. Although not confined to any single domain or modality, cyberspace is very conducive to gray-zone confrontation, as evidenced, for example, by Russia's well-documented efforts to sow dissention and interfere with elections in the United States and other Western democracies.

Extant national security law and the premises it was built on do not align well with the technological structure and global interconnectedness of the digital world. Cyberspace is predominantly owned, operated, and managed by the private sector; does not correspond to geography and national borders; is integrated with the operation of critical infrastructures; and forms the backbone of commerce, governance, and national security. As such, it is a unique medium through which state and non-state actors can affect a wide array of targets and interests with decreased risk of detection and free from the physical constraints of geography and territorial boundaries. And while their strategic goals may find historical analogs, like using cyber capabilities as a means of conducting traditional espionage, the scope, scale, depth, and speed of their tactical actions can place intense pressure on existing legal frameworks and raise difficult legal questions about how they apply to unanticipated fact patterns.

Consider, for example, the Supreme Court's handling of cell-site location data in *United States v. Carpenter*, 138 S. Ct. 2206 (2018). Prior to *Carpenter*, the prevailing view was that a person could claim no reasonable expectation of privacy in either "information he [or she] voluntarily turns over to third parties,"[1] nor in his or her movements from one place to another when "traveling in an automobile on public thoroughfares. . . ."[2] Yet in *Carpenter*, the Court came to the exact opposite

---

1. *United States v. Miller*, 425 U.S. 435, 443 (1976).
2. *United States v. Knotts*, 460 U.S. 276, 281-82 (1983).

conclusion when considering a Fourth Amendment challenge to the government's warrantless collection from a wireless carrier of cell-site location information. The Court declined to extend its prior precedents to what it described as a "seismic shift[] in technology that made possible the tracking of not only Carpenter's location but also everyone else's, not for a short period but for years and years. . . ." For the Court, the novel circumstances presented by the "exhaustive chronicle of location information" enabled by modern digital technology was too much for existing Fourth Amendment doctrine to bear.

Tracking the public movements of criminal suspects was not a novel method of law-enforcement surveillance, nor was doing so with the aid of technology. That was the exact situation in *Knotts*, where the government used a "beeper" to aid in the tracking of a vehicle, which the Court deemed not to constitute a search under the Fourth Amendment. Likewise, the government has long relied on the third-party doctrine established in *Smith v. Maryland*[3] and *United States v. Miller*[4] to obtain business records without triggering the Fourth Amendment. So why in *Carpenter* did the Court tack in such a different direction? Apparently, it was because of unease with the qualitatively and quantitatively different nature of surveillance and data collection and aggregation enabled by new technologies like cell phones, the use of which the Court viewed as practically a necessity of everyday life and an extension of the individual. For a majority of the Court, extant Fourth Amendment approaches are simply ill-suited to the digital age.

The specific implications of *Carpenter* to national security investigations are addressed in Chapter 9. For purposes of the present chapter, the case is offered to illustrate an important point when considering the national security law aspects of new technologies generally: They rarely serve as a catalyst for wholly unprecedented behavior, especially at the inter-state level, but rather offer new and unique means and methods for states and non-state actors to engage in traditional statecraft and conflict. This is an important starting point for analyzing whether and how the existing national security law frameworks set out in this book apply to the use of emerging technologies by state and non-state actors. With that in mind, this chapter will focus on the particular case of cyber technology.

According to the U.S. intelligence community's most recent assessment, "adversaries and strategic competitors will increasingly use cyber capabilities—including cyber espionage, attack, and influence—to seek political, economic, and military advantage over the United States and its allies and partners."[5] The cyber-threat posed by states like Russia, China, Iran, and North Korea have already materialized in the form of, *inter alia*, disruptive influence campaigns, substantial economic loss from intellectual property theft, the compromise of defense industrial base information, and attacks on the financial sector.

---

3. 442 U.S. 735 (1979).
4. 425 U.S. 435 (1976).
5. Daniel R. Coats, Statement for the Record, Worldwide Threat Assessment of the U.S. Intelligence Community 5 (2019).

Here is how the Commander of U.S. Cyber Command, General Paul M. Nakasone, characterized the evolving situation to the House Armed Services Committee in 2020:

> A decade ago, we trained and postured our cyber forces like any other military force: to prevail in future conflict. A central challenge today is that our adversaries compete below the threshold of armed conflict, without triggering the hostilities for which DoD has traditionally prepared. That short-of-war competition features cyber and information operations employed by nations in ways that bypass America's conventional military strengths.[6]

United States strategies have steadily realigned in response to this new reality, shifting from a narrow cyber security focus anchored in restraint to an emphasis on more proactive cyber operations as part of a return to great power competition.

Beyond countering cyber-threats, the United States may need to employ cyber capabilities in pursuit of broader national security objectives—for example, to collect intelligence, deter adversaries, control conflict escalation, or achieve lawful ends in war. Many of the activities or operations necessary to protect or advance U.S. national security in or through cyberspace will fall within the traditional lanes of federal departments or agencies, like the investigation and prosecution of cyber-related national security crimes. On the other hand, employing the military to defend against threats in cyberspace involves a far less traditional use of that element of national power. This chapter considers some of the legal complexities, both domestic and international, of employing cyber capabilities in defense of the United States and in furtherance of national security objectives, in particular, the conduct of military cyber operations in the complex and ambiguous security environment below the threshold of armed conflict.

II. A SHIFT IN STRATEGIC APPROACH

In 2016, the DoD acknowledged it had conducted sophisticated offensive operations against the Islamic State in Iraq and Syria (ISIS) as part of its campaign to defeat the terrorist organization. The Commander of U.S. Cyber Command subsequently noted that the lessons learned from these unprecedented operations informed later activities to defend the 2018 midterm elections from Russian interference. That effort, led by a U.S. Cyber Command-National Security Agency task force known as the Russia Small Group, involved a range of groundbreaking operations in support of wider U.S. government actions, including discrete offensive cyber operations to disrupt Russian capabilities and efforts to undermine the integrity of the 2018 elections.

A number of senior DoD and other U.S. government officials have cited the foregoing as reflective of a significant shift in the U.S. approach to addressing

---

6. *Before the H. Subcomm. on Intelligence and Emerging Threats and Capabilities*, 116th Cong. (2020) (statement of General Paul M. Nakasone, Commander, United States Cyberspace Command).

cyber-threats and using cyber operations as a tool of national power. According to U.S. Cyber Command's Executive Director, "[i]n the face of cyber threats, we've adjusted our strategic vision to one of persistent engagement with a persistent force. No longer reactive, but actually working in cyberspace in an area where there is no sanctuary or operational pause. It is the center of strategic rivalry in this era of renewed power competition. We are in constant contact with our adversaries. Success is determined on how we enable and act."[7]

The strategic shift alluded to traces to the *2017 National Security Strategy of the United States* with its emphasis on the return to great power competition and a commitment to deterring and disrupting malicious cyber actors before they are able to impact U.S. interests, all of which marked a shift from a policy of restraint to a more forward-leaning and active stance to countering cyber-threats. According to the *2018 DoD Cyber Strategy*:

> The Department must take action in cyberspace during day-to-day competition to preserve U.S. military advantages and to defend U.S. interests. Our focus will be on the States that can pose strategic threats to U.S. prosperity and security, particularly China and Russia. We will conduct cyberspace operations to collect intelligence and prepare military cyber capabilities to be used in the event of crisis or conflict. We will defend forward to disrupt or halt malicious cyber activity at its source, including activity that falls below the level of armed conflict. We will strengthen the security and resilience of networks and systems that contribute to current and future U.S. military advantages. We will collaborate with our interagency, industry, and international partners to advance our mutual interests.

Although multifaceted, a key component to this new strategic approach is the recognition that cyber national security requires persistent action to identify, track, and disrupt cyber-threats, including when appropriate the use of the United States' own cyber capabilities outside of DoD networks not just as a means and method of warfare, but to also "defend forward" in the gray zone.

Strategies are worth only the paper they are written on unless they are underwritten by resources and implementing direction and policies. In 2018, the President issued new cyber-operations policy in the form of National Security Presidential Memorandum 13, which although classified reportedly enabled the delegation of greater operational authority to departments and agencies and reduced bureaucratic hurdles to interagency coordination and approval.

And of course strategy and policy must be consonant with and underpinned by law. DoD leadership has consistently credited a slate of new legislation in the 2019 National Defense Authorization Act as key to implementing its new cyber strategy and successfully operating to disrupt Russia's election interference efforts. We will consider the impact of these and other domestic and international law provisions on the national security law landscape.

---

7. C. Todd Lopez, *Persistent Engagement, Partnerships, Top Cybercom's Priorities*, Defense.gov, May 14, 2019, https://www.defense.gov/Explore/News/Article/Article/1847823/persistent-engagement-partnerships-top-cybercoms-priorities/.

III. THE NATURE OF CYBER OPERATIONS

As with any use of the military, cyber operations are a means to an end. And like more traditional activities, the legal implications of a particular cyber operation are very fact and context specific, and require a deep understanding not only of the purpose for conducting the operation, but the technical details of the tool or capability that will be used and the anticipated effects it will generate. The following is a brief, general description of tactical cyber operations offered to better inform the legal issues set out in this chapter.

> The unique attributes of cyberspace compel one truism: no two cyber operations are (or better stated, can be) the same. A cyber operation's "attack" profile, including tool design and weaponeering, must be tailored particularly to account for variables such as the target configuration (i.e., its operating system, resident software, system vulnerabilities, and security software such as intrusion detection systems and anti-virus programs that may be running on the target system) and the type, scope, and scale of intended effect. [T]he cyber operational environment—including adversary security awareness and postures, intrusion detection systems and forensic capabilities of service providers, third-party cybersecurity vendors, and system owners along the path to target, as well as individual target characteristics—is constantly changing. The available vectors and opportunities to access a target system or device and successfully deliver effects can be extremely fleeting. Once an adversary is aware of its vulnerabilities it can mitigate or eliminate them, and it can adapt its security and defensive measures to render offensive tools ineffective. Operational security and the attendant concealment and secrecy it requires—achieve through a combination of clandestine operational [tactics, techniques, and procedures] and obfuscated infra-structure—are therefore vital in the cyber domain. . . .
>
> Each cyber operation will vary in accordance with the nature of the targeted system or device, its specific vulnerabilities, and the nature and combination of the tools employed against it. Notwithstanding these variables, several models have been developed to describe the basic steps commonly employed in a typical cyber operation. Although described differently, these models generally include the following phases: 1) reconnaissance (target discovery and enumeration); 2) exploitation (initial access); 3) privilege escalation and sustainment; 4) exfiltration or effect; and 5) assessment and concealment. Most operations, whether external or internal, start in the reconnaissance phase in order to identify and understand the target and the operational environment and proceed through the remaining four phases.
>
> [S]ituational awareness of the target in cyberspace can be achieved through both intelligence and non-intelligence enabling actions. Regardless of authorities employed, the reconnaissance phase involves the identification and selection of targets . . . as well as scanning and other techniques aimed at characterizing the target and identifying potential access and attack vectors, whether they be human or system vulnerabilities. Reconnaissance identifies basic information about potential targets needed to access or affect them, such as network information (e.g., IP addresses, domain names, and network topology), host information (e.g., user and group names, and operating system and version), human information (for both target identification and human exploitation), and security measures and posture (e.g., password complexity and

change frequency requirements, firewalls, intrusion detection systems). Target reconnaissance can be developed over a period of time and generally with relative stealth, and may involve both passive and active measures, such as IP address and port scans, and running network mappers. Initial reconnaissance may be sufficient to support a basic external effect operation, or may continue through follow-on phases to provide deepening insight into the targeted network or end-point device.

The means of achieving operational cyber effects generally can be divided into two broad categories: "those that attack from outside enemy systems [external], and those that attack from within [internal]." External effects operations, such as a denial of service (DoS) attack, focus on temporarily disrupting or degrading an adversary system's ability to communicate or access data. Internal operations involve gaining unauthorized access—hacking—into an adversary system to steal data, manipulate information, or degrade or disrupt the system's functionality. . . .

As noted, the objective of internal cyber operations—those that involve penetration of a target computer or network—is to gain sufficient access to an end-point device (such as a mobile phone or laptop) or a host within a network (a connected computer, router, or server) to either introduce a "payload" (the tool employed to carry out the cyber operations intended effects) or gain remote, root-level control of the device or host to achieve the operational objective of data exfiltration or system disruption, denial, degradation, or destruction. Leveraging information obtained during the reconnaissance phase to identify available access points, or vulnerabilities, the operation will move to the exploitation phase to gain initial, unauthorized access into the targeted system or node. . . . From this initial foothold, the operation may pivot to establish deeper access into the device, or establish access to other nodes within the network as a pathway to the ultimate target. Throughout its course, the operation will move into the privilege escalation phase as necessary to increase privileges within the host or the broader network to a level that will allow sustained access and remote control of the system. When the necessary conditions are set, the operation will move into the exfiltration or effect phase to achieve the ultimate operational objective.

Textbox drawn from Colonel Gary P. Corn, *Cyber National Security: Navigating Gray Zone Challenges in and Through Cyberspace*, in Complex Battlespaces: The Law of Armed Conflict and the Dynamics of Modern Warfare (2018) (internal citations omitted).

IV. THE NATIONAL SECURITY CONSTITUTION AND CYBER OPERATIONS

Recall from Section I that, even with respect to national security, the federal government is one of limited powers distributed across the three branches, and that any national security powers it may invoke must trace ultimately to an affirmative grant in the Constitution. When it comes to protecting important national interests, the Constitution confers broad, but not unfettered authority on the President. Ultimately, "[t]he President's authority to act, as with the exercise of any governmental power, 'must stem either from an act of Congress or from the Constitution itself.'"[8] That the Constitution confers on the President broad authority to direct the conduct

---

8. *Medellín v. Texas*, 552 U.S. 491, 524 (2008) (quoting *Youngstown Sheet & Tube Co. v. Sawyer*, 343 U.S. 579, 582 (1952)).

of military operations, including the use of cyber capabilities, to defend the nation against imminent or actual attack is fairly well settled. Similarly, the President would be on firm constitutional footing when directing cyber operations as part of ongoing, congressionally authorized hostilities. But what about military cyber operations, even ones that might involve some level of physical damage, conducted outside of and below the threshold of war, at least as that term is used in Article I, § 8 of the Constitution?

According to press reports, in June 2019, U.S. Cyber Command conducted an operation against a critical database used by Iran's Islamic Revolutionary Guard to plot attacks against oil tankers transiting the Strait of Hormuz. Earlier that month, Iran, according to the United States, was behind two limpet-mine attacks against tankers transiting the strait. The reported cyber operation, aimed at degrading Tehran's ability to target shipping traffic in the Persian Gulf, was conducted in response to Iran's downing of a U.S. drone.

On the same day the reported cyber operation against Iran took place, the President had approved, but then called off, airstrikes to respond to the drone shootdown. In the absence of a congressional authorization to use force, what basis would the President have relied on to conduct the airstrikes? Would the cyber operation be subsumed in the same analysis?

See Julian E. Barnes, *U.S. Cyberattack Hurt Iran's Ability to Target Oil Tankers, Officials Say*, N.Y. TIMES, Aug. 28, 2019.

Throughout the nation's history, presidents have invoked Article II as the basis for directing a wide range of military operations to protect and advance U.S. interests. Not all of these operations involved combat or armed force, but presidents have frequently asserted broad independent authority to use force for purposes beyond just repelling actual or imminent attacks on the homeland. Recall from Chapter 7 the Office of Legal Counsel's (OLC) *ex post facto* review of the 2018 airstrikes conducted against Syrian chemical-weapons sites.[9] It provides a window into the history and rationale behind presidents' approving combat operations in the absence of congressional authorization.

On April 13, 2018, the President directed the United States military to launch airstrikes against three Syrian chemical-weapons facilities. The President did so without seeking authority from Congress. The OLC determined prior to the strike that the President had reasonably determined that the use of force would be in the national interest and that the anticipated hostilities would not rise to the level of a war in the constitutional sense.

According to the OLC, the President's action was well grounded in historical practice. The precedent of "well over 100 instances of military deployments [over 230 years] without prior congressional authorization" established that "the

9. April 2018 Airstrikes Against Syrian Chemical-Weapons Facilities (Slip Opinion), DOJ OLC, May 31, 2018. https://www.justice.gov/olc/opinion/file/1067551/download.

President, as Commander in Chief and Chief Executive, has the constitutional authority to deploy the military to protect American persons and interests without seeking prior authorization from Congress." Congress's authority to "declare War," on the other hand, is limited to deciding "whether to commit the Nation to a sustained, full-scale conflict with another Nation."

For the OLC, the President's unilateral authority extends even to "commit[ing] American forces in such a way as to seriously risk hostilities, and also to actually commit them to such hostilities, without prior congressional approval." Thus, not every military operation or engagement rises to the level of a war in the constitutional sense.

According to the OLC, the scope of the President's authority to unilaterally commit the armed forces into hostilities distills down to two questions: whether the President can reasonably determine that the action serves important national interests, and whether the anticipated nature, scope, and duration of the conflict might rise to the level of a war under the Constitution.

The OLC memo pointed to several distinct interests that presidents have historically relied on to justify armed force, such as the protection of U.S. persons and property; assistance to allies; support for the United Nations; promoting regional stability; mitigating humanitarian disasters; and in the instance of the Syrian airstrikes, preventing the use and proliferation of chemical weapons. Given the absence of ground troops, the limited mission, and the finite time frame involved, as well as efforts the memo cited aimed at mitigating the risk of escalation, OLC considered the anticipated nature, scope, and duration of the airstrikes to fall "far short of the kinds of engagements approved by prior Presidents under Article II."

NOTES AND QUESTIONS

1. Does this robust view of Article II authority leave any meaningful space for Congress to exercise its constitutional role?
2. Does the OLC's analytical framing, derived from a long history of traditional, physical-world military deployments, map well to non-traditional cyber operations?
3. What important national interests might be served by defending forward in cyberspace?
4. Returning to the reported cyber operation against Iran cited above, how would the OLC analysis proceed?

Consider the remarks of the Department of Defense (DoD) General Counsel, the Honorable Paul C. Ney, Jr., at the U.S. Cyber Command Legal Conference in March of 2020. For the DoD, the legal analysis

> begin[s] with the foundational question of domestic legal authority to conduct a military cyber operation. The domestic legal authority for the DoD to conduct cyber operations is included in the broader authorities of the President and the Secretary of Defense to conduct military operations in defense of the nation. We assess whether a proposed cyber operation has been properly authorized using the

analysis we apply to all other operations, including those that constitute use of force. The President has authority under Article II of the U.S. Constitution to direct the use of the Armed Forces to serve important national interests, and it is the longstanding view of the Executive Branch that this authority may include the use of armed force when the anticipated nature, scope, and duration of the operations do not rise to the level of "war" under the Constitution, triggering Congress's power to declare war. Furthermore, the Supreme Court has long affirmed the President's power to use force in defense of the nation and federal persons, property, and instrumentalities. Accordingly, the President has constitutional authority to order military cyber operations even if they amount to use of force in defense of the United States. Of course, the vast majority of military operations in cyberspace do not rise to the level of a use of force; but we begin analysis of U.S. domestic law with the same starting point of identifying the legal authority.[10]

NOTES AND QUESTIONS

1. What national interests might be served by directing the military to conduct cyber operations outside of traditional combat operations?
2. What might the risks of those operations be, and how would those risks factor into OLC's analysis?
3. Of course, OLC's analysis presumes the employment of military forces will involve some level of armed hostilities, which as the memo points out is often not the case. For cyber operations not intended or likely to cause actual damage or destruction, is it enough for the President to simply determine that they would serve an important national interest? Would risk of escalation factor in the analysis, and if so, how?

In Chapter 5, we discussed Justice Jackson's concurring opinion in *Youngstown Sheet & Tube Co. v. Sawyer*, 343 U.S. 579 (1952), in which he set out his familiar tripartite framework for assessing presidential authority. When presidents act, they do so either in the absence of a congressional grant or denial of authority, with the express or implied authorization of Congress, or contrary to the expressed or implied will of Congress. Thus far we have considered whether the President has independent authority under Article II to direct "gray zone" cyber operations. But what if any role has Congress played in regard to these operations?

In his U.S. Cyber Command speech, Mr. Ney continued:

In the context of cyber operations, the President does not need to rely solely on his Article II powers because Congress has provided for ample authorization. As I noted earlier, Congress has specifically affirmed the President's authority to direct DoD to conduct military operations in cyberspace. Moreover, cyber operations against specific targets are logically encompassed within broad statutory authorizations to the President to use force, like the 2001 Authorization for the Use of

---

10. Hon. Paul C. Ney, Jr., *DOD General Counsel Remarks at U.S. Cyber Command Legal Conference*, Defense.Gov, Mar. 2, 2020, https://www.defense.gov/Newsroom/Speeches/Speech/Article/2099378/dod-general-counsel-remarks-at-us-cyber-command-legal-conference/.

Military Force, which authorizes the President to use "all necessary and appropriate force" against those he determines were involved in the 9/11 attacks or that harbored them. Congress has also expressed support for the conduct of military cyber operations to defend the nation against Russian, Chinese, North Korean, and Iranian "active, systematic, and ongoing campaigns of attacks" against U.S. interests, including attempts to influence U.S. elections.

Within the *Youngstown* framework, presidential power is understood to be at its zenith when exercised pursuant to an express or implied authorization of Congress, for in those instances the exercise "includes all that [the President] possesses in his own right plus all that Congress can delegate." Otherwise, in the absence of either a congressional grant or denial of authority, the President "can only rely upon his own independent powers," or upon powers resident in a constitutional "zone of twilight" in which the distribution between the President and Congress is either concurrent or uncertain. Mindful of the Supreme Court's later admonition in *Dames & Moore v. Regan,* 453 U.S. 654, 669 (1981), "that executive action in any particular instance falls not neatly in one of three pigeonholes, but rather at some point along a spectrum running from explicit congressional authorization to explicit congressional prohibition[,]" what, in Mr. Ney's view, is the "ample authority" Congress provided regarding cyber operations?

A. Congress and the Evolution of Cyber Authorities

1. Authorizations for the Use of Military Force

Since 2001, the United States has been engaged in near-continuous combat operations in some form or another. At the outset of this period, Congress passed two specific military force authorizations: the 2001 Authorization for Use of Military Force, and the 2002 Authorization to Use Military Force Against Iraq. The former authorized the President to use all necessary and appropriate force against all who "planned, authorized, committed, or aided the terrorist attacks that occurred on September 11, 2001, or harbored such organizations or persons," whereas the latter authorized the President to use the armed forces as "necessary and appropriate" to "defend U.S. national security against the continuing threat posed by Iraq" and to "enforce all relevant Security Council resolutions regarding Iraq." President's have relied on these congressional authorizations and Article II of the Constitution, both alternatively and in combination, to underpin the various combat operations conducted since 2001. The military has incorporated cyber capabilities into its operations as a new means of warfare.

In 2014, a U.S.-led coalition began substantial combat operations in Iraq and Syria under the banner of Operation Inherent Resolve to defeat the emergent Islamic State of Iraq and Syria, or ISIS. In 2016, the Department of Defense publicly acknowledged conducting cyber operations as part of its broader campaign to defeat ISIS. Putting aside senior DoD officials' hyperbole about dropping "cyber bombs," according to the

Secretary of Defense, U.S. Cyber Command had conducted offensive cyber operations to cause ISIS to "lose confidence in their networks, to overload their networks so that they can't function, and do all of these things that will interrupt their ability to command and control forces"[11]—all actions consistent with traditional warfighting. Based on declassified documents and public reports, U.S. Cyber Command formed a specialized joint task force—JTF Ares—to conduct the cyber campaign, part of which involved a highly sophisticated and coordinated operation, called Glowing Symphony, to degrade ISIS's digital media and propaganda production and dissemination infrastructure.[12]

NOTES AND QUESTIONS

1. What was the basis for the cyber operations targeting ISIS? Did they fall within the "broad statutory authorizations to the President to use force, like the 2001 Authorization for the Use of Military Force" that Mr. Ney referred to?
2. In December 2017, Senator Tim Kaine sent letters to both the Secretary of Defense and Secretary of State questioning the domestic legal basis for DoD's Counter-ISIS operations in Iraq and Syria. Both departments responded in January 2018, claiming authority under a combination of Article II, the 2001 AUMF, and the 2002 Iraq AUMF, not only for its operations against ISIS, but for limited strikes against the Syrian regime and regime-backed forces. Senator Kaine's questions reflect much broader skepticism about the applicability of the 2001 and 2002 AUMFs to operations against ISIS.
3. Could the President rely solely on her Article II authority to direct cyber operations not amounting to "constitutional war" against ISIS or other non-state threats?

B. Express or Implied Authorization?

Although successive administrations have given the 2001 and 2002 AUMFs an expansive reading, neither authorization addresses the vast majority of emerging and ongoing cyber-threats to the United States. Congress has taken notice of this distinct national security problem, passing a number of cyber-related provisions over the last several years relevant to assessing the President's authority to direct the military to conduct gray-zone cyber operations. These provisions have evolved from simple affirmations of the President's authority to what some have described as an actual, albeit narrow and specific, authorization to use military cyber force.

A review of the dense legislative record in this area reveals Congress's growing support, through appropriations and enabling legislation, for the development of substantial military cyber capability and capacity, including establishing and eventually elevating U.S. Cyber Command to full combatant-command status within

---

11. Sean Lyngaas, *The Business of Federal Technology*, FCW, Feb. 29, 2016, https://fcw.com/articles/2016/02/29/carter-isis-networks.aspx.

12. Dina Temple-Raston, *How the U.S. Hacked ISIS*, NPR, Sept. 26, 2019, https://www.npr.org/2019/09/26/763545811/how-the-u-s-hacked-isis.

DoD with a sizable cyber force under its command.[13] In addition, Congress has frequently waded into the realm of policy, expressing a consistent view that "in certain instances, the most effective way to deal with threats and protect U.S. and coalition forces is to undertake offensive military cyber activities . . . ."[14]

For example, in § 954 of the 2012 National Defense Authorization Act (NDAA), Congress seemed to affirm the President's authority to direct the military to conduct offensive cyber operations "to defend the United States, our allies and interests." Subsequently, in the wake of North Korea's cyber operation against Sony Pictures International, Congress again expressed its concern over "the growing number and severity of malicious cyber activities" against the United States and its view that "failing to impose meaningful consequences on those seeking to harm the United States through the cyber domain will embolden our adversaries and lead to more severe attacks in the future." In response, it passed § 1642 of the 2016 NDAA, directing the Secretary of Defense to develop and make ready the armed forces to conduct military cyber operations against foreign powers conducting cyber operations against the United States "when appropriately authorized to do so."

While it would be hard to describe these congressional pronouncements as "inertia, indifference, or quiescence," can they be described as explicit authorizations? When considering a subsequent amendment to § 1642 that would affirm the authority of the Secretary of Defense to conduct certain military activities and operations in cyberspace, the conferees were clear that the affirmation would "not itself authorize any specific military activities or operations and should not be treated as an authorization for use of military force."[15] Where do these congressional actions fall within the constitutional "zone of twilight" that Justice Jackson described?

In January 2017, the U.S. intelligence community published its assessment that Russia had engaged in a disruptive influence campaign, including extensive cyber operations and cyber-enabled information operations intended to interfere in the 2016 presidential election. Concerned with reports of increasing adversary cyber operations and that Russia planned a repeat performance in the run-up to the 2018 mid-term elections, Congress took up the mantle of cyber authorities yet again in the fall of 2018.

SEC. 1642. Active Defense Against The Russian Federation, People's Republic of China, Democratic People's Republic of Korea, and Islamic Republic of Iran Attacks in Cyberspace

(a) AUTHORITY TO DISRUPT, DEFEAT, AND DETER CYBER ATTACKS. —

(1) IN GENERAL. — In the event that the National Command Authority determines that the Russian Federation, People's Republic of China, Democratic

---

13. *See* National Defense Authorization Act for Fiscal Year 2017, Pub. L. No. 114-328, § 923, 130 Stat. 2000, 2357 (2016) (codified at 10 U.S.C. § 167b).

14. H.R. Rep. No. 112-329, at 686 (2011) (Conf. Rep.).

15. H.R. Rep. No. 115-874, at 1049 (2018).

People's Republic of Korea, or Islamic Republic of Iran is conducting an active, systematic, and ongoing campaign of attacks against the Government or people of the United States in cyberspace, including attempting to influence American elections and democratic political processes, the National Command Authority may authorize the Secretary of Defense, acting through the Commander of the United States Cyber Command, to take appropriate and proportional action in foreign cyberspace to disrupt, defeat, and deter such attacks under the authority and policy of the Secretary of Defense to conduct cyber operations and information operations as traditional military activities.

(2) NOTIFICATION AND REPORTING. —
(A) NOTIFICATION OF OPERATIONS. — In exercising the authority provided in paragraph (1), the Secretary shall provide notices to the congressional defense committees in accordance with section 395 of title 10, United States Code (as transferred and redesignated pursuant to section 1631).
(B) QUARTERLY REPORTS BY COMMANDER OF THE UNITED STATES CYBER COMMAND. —
(i) IN GENERAL. — In any fiscal year in which the Commander of the United States Cyber Command carries out an action under paragraph (1), the Secretary of Defense shall, not less frequently than quarterly, submit to the congressional defense committees a report on the actions of the Commander under such paragraph in such fiscal year.
(ii) MANNER OF REPORTING. — Reports submitted under clause (i) shall be submitted in a manner that is consistent with the recurring quarterly report required by section 484 of title 10, United States Code.
(d) RULE OF CONSTRUCTION. — Nothing in this section may be construed to —
(1) limit the authority of the Secretary to conduct military activities or operations in cyberspace, including clandestine activities or operations in cyberspace; or
(2) affect the War Powers Resolution (Public Law 93-148; 50 U.S.C. 1541 et seq.) or the Authorization for Use of Military Force (Public Law 107-40; 50 U.S.C. 1541 note).

National Defense Authorization Act for Fiscal Year 2019, Pub. L. No. 115-232, § 1642, 132 Stat. 2132-33 (2018).

NOTES AND QUESTIONS

1. In his Cyber Command speech, Mr. Ney referred to § 1642 as reflecting Congress's "support" for military cyber operations to defend against the specified threats. Is that a fair reading of the statute, or did Congress provide specific authorization to the President in this case?
2. On its face, the statute seems to delegate authority to the executive to conduct military cyber operations under the specified conditions. But given the executive branch's broad view of the President's inherent Article II authority to direct

military activity without seeking congressional approval, and the conditions and limitations contained in the statute, what new authority does it provide?

3. Why does § 1642 condition the defined cyber operations on a finding by the National Command Authority, which is understood to be the President and the Secretary of Defense, as opposed to the President alone?

4. Note the rule of construction included in § 1642. What "authority of the Secretary to conduct military activities or operations in cyberspace, including clandestine activities or operations in cyberspace . . ." is Congress referring to? Does Congress understand those operations to be different in kind than the "appropriate and proportional action in foreign cyberspace to disrupt, defeat, and deter" the specific cyberspace campaigns referenced in the main body of the statute?

5. Section 1642 also states that it is not to be construed to affect the War Powers Resolution or the AUMF. Similar language appears in 10 U.S.C. § 394. Does this imply the "appropriate and proportional" action in foreign cyberspace referenced in the statute must fall below a level that would constitute hostilities? Or is the better argument that § 1642 is sufficient congressional authorization on its own, satisfying without "affecting" the WPR?

C. A Note on the War Powers Resolution and Cyber Operations

The history and challenges of the War Powers Resolution (WPR) were addressed in Chapter 7. Leaving aside broader debates about the constitutionality of the WPR, whether and how its provisions might apply to specific cyber operations is a difficult question in its own right. The answer turns primarily on whether cyber operations constitute the *introduction* of U.S. armed forces into *hostilities*, as those terms are used in the WPR—a matter that is unclear at best.

When cyber operations are conducted as a component of larger military operations, the WPR reporting implications are subsumed in the broader analysis. Standing alone, it is unlikely that a military cyber operation would constitute either the introduction of armed forces into hostilities or a combat-equipped deployment as those terms are used in the WPR.

While only subsection (2) of § 1543(a) includes a geographic component, the executive branch has generally taken the position that subsection (1) is triggered only by the actual, physical "introduction" of members of the armed forces into a geographic area of operations under circumstances that place them at a certain level of risk, a requirement unlikely to be triggered by remote cyber operations where the forces conducting the operation remain in the United States or at least distant from the point of delivery of the cyber effect. Relatedly, the meaning generally accorded the term "hostilities" as used in the narrow context of the WPR seems to require a substantial level of armed force, again tied to actual risk to U.S. forces, which would not be met by most cyber operations standing alone, especially sub-use-of-force gray-zone cyber operations. Finally, an assessment under subsection (2) is unlikely to yield a different result based on the territorial component of the provision, and the executive branch's view that "equipped for combat" refers only to the deployment of forces armed with crew-served weapons. However, as the DoD has noted in response to inquiries from Congress, while cyber operations per se "might not include the introduction of armed forces personnel into the area of hostilities . . . the Department will continue to assess each of its actions in cyberspace to determine when the requirements of the War Powers Resolution may apply to those actions."

Even under circumstances triggering a WPR report, substantial uncertainty remains not only as to the enforceability of the WPR's termination provision generally, but also as to what constitutes the termination "of any use of U.S. Armed Forces" for purposes of the WPR and its applicability to cyber operations. First, leaving the larger constitutional questions aside, the WPR's termination provision has been understood to require the physical withdrawal of armed forces from areas of active or imminent hostilities, not necessarily the cessation of all operational activity. Under a narrow view of the purpose of the WPR—one linked to actual risk of harm to forces—this interpretation makes sense. Second, for many of the reasons cyber operations are unlikely to qualify as hostilities under that term's WPR meaning, they are unlikely to fall subject to the law's termination requirement. The executive branch has consistently emphasized "the distinction between full military encounters and more constrained operations, stating that 'intermittent military engagements' do not require withdrawal of forces under the resolution's 60-day rule." That is, cyber operations alone are likely to be viewed as the type of limited military means unregulated by the WPR, "not the kind of full military engagements with which the [WPR] is primarily concerned."

Textbox drawn from Colonel Gary P. Corn, *Cyber National Security: Navigating Gray Zone Challenges in and Through Cyberspace*, in COMPLEX BATTLESPACES: THE LAW OF ARMED CONFLICT AND THE DYNAMICS OF MODERN WARFARE (Oxford U. Press 2018) (internal citations omitted).

Concern over unintended consequences and escalation underlie criticisms of a more proactive use of offensive cyber operations as a tool of national power outside of situations of congressionally authorized hostilities. Perhaps these fears are overblown, but is a narrow, formalistic interpretation of the WPR consistent with the original intent of the statute? Should Congress have a role in managing the risk of escalation and involving the nation in broader armed conflict that cyber operations may present? Do the various cyber-operations reporting requirements in § 1642 and elsewhere in Title 10 assuage these concerns?

As cyber operations increase in scale and frequency, arguments for a more expansive reading of the WPR or for amendments designed to protect Congress's constitutionally assigned prerogatives may gain traction. For now, given the statute's incongruity with the nature of cyber operations, Congress's repeated admonishments to the President urging greater action, and the executive branch's narrow interpretation of the WPR, it is not likely to prove much of a constraint on the President's authority in this area.

D. Congressional Limitations on the President's Authority to Conduct Cyber Operations

We turn now to the final leg of Justice Jackson's *Youngstown* framework. As Mr. Ney noted in his Cyber Command speech, "[a]fter concluding that [an] operation has been properly authorized, DoD lawyers assess whether there are any statutes that may restrict DoD's ability to conduct the proposed cyber operation and whether the operation may be carried out consistent with the protections afforded to the privacy and civil liberties of U.S. persons." This is so because when "the President takes measures incompatible with the expressed or implied will of Congress his power is at its lowest ebb, for then he can rely only upon his own constitutional powers minus any constitutional powers of Congress over the matter."

1. Covert Action, Traditional Military Activities, and Clandestine Cyber Operations

In 2018, Congress passed a piece of legislation that a number of senior DoD officials have described as a sea change for military cyber operations and a foundational element supporting the DoD Cyber Strategy. Section 1632 of the 2019 NDAA amended § 130g of Title 10, redesignating it as § 394 and, more important, reducing a major obstacle to military cyber operations.

---

§394. Authorities concerning military cyber operations

(a) In General. — The Secretary of Defense shall develop, prepare, and coordinate; make ready all armed forces for purposes of; and, when appropriately authorized to do so, conduct, military cyber activities or operations in cyberspace, including clandestine military activities or operations in cyberspace, to defend the United States and its allies, including in response to malicious cyber activity carried out against the United States or a United States person by a foreign power.

(b) Affirmation of Authority. — Congress affirms that the activities or operations referred to in subsection (a), when appropriately authorized, include the conduct of military activities or operations in cyberspace short of hostilities (as such term is used in the War Powers Resolution . . . or in areas in which hostilities are not occurring, including for the purpose of preparation of the environment, information operations, force protection, and deterrence of hostilities, or counterterrorism operations involving the Armed Forces of the United States.

(c) Clandestine Activities or Operations. — A clandestine military activity or operation in cyberspace shall be considered a traditional military activity for the purposes of section 503(e)(2) of the National Security Act of 1947 (50 U.S.C. 3093(e)(2)).

(d) Congressional Oversight. — The Secretary shall brief the congressional defense committees about any military activities or operations in cyberspace, including clandestine military activities or operations in cyberspace, occurring during the previous quarter during the quarterly briefing required by section 484 of this title. . . .

(f) Definitions. — In this section:

(1) The term "clandestine military activity or operation in cyberspace" means a military activity or military operation carried out in cyberspace, or associated preparatory actions, authorized by the President or the Secretary that —

> (A) is marked by, held in, or conducted with secrecy, where the intent is that the activity or operation will not be apparent or acknowledged publicly; and
> (B) is to be carried out —
>> (i) as part of a military operation plan approved by the President or the Secretary in anticipation of hostilities or as directed by the President or the Secretary;
>> (ii) to deter, safeguard, or defend against attacks or malicious cyber activities against the United States or Department of Defense information, networks, systems, installations, facilities, or other assets; or
>> (iii) in support of information related capabilities.

The focus of § 1632 was to affirm not only that the Secretary of Defense can, when "appropriately authorized," conduct military activities or operations in cyberspace short of hostilities, but that those activities or operations could be clandestine. What problem was Congress addressing by passing § 1632? Consider this excerpt from the accompanying conference report:

> The conferees note that the Department of Defense faces difficulties within the interagency in obtaining mission approval. One of the challenges routinely confronted by the Department is the perceived ambiguity as to whether clandestine military activities and operations, even those short of cyber attacks, qualify as traditional military activities as distinct from covert actions requiring a Presidential Finding. As a result, with respect to actions that produce effects on information systems outside of areas of active hostilities, the Department of Defense has been limited to proposing actions that could be conducted overtly on attributable infrastructure without deniability — an operational space that is far too narrow to defend national interests. The conferees see no logical, legal, or practical reason for allowing extensive clandestine traditional military activities in all other operational domains (air, sea, ground, and space) but not in cyberspace. It is unfortunate that the executive branch has squandered years in interagency deliberations that failed to recognize this basic fact and that this legislative action has proven necessary.[16]

What is the distinction referenced between covert action and a traditional military activity, and why should that have proved such an obstacle to conducting military operations? The issue stems from the unique operational environment of cyberspace and the statutory oversight framework governing covert action — a specific class of sensitive executive branch activities.

Passed in 1991 to ensure congressional oversight over the executive branch's conduct of covert activities, the Covert Action Statute (CAS), 50 U.S.C. § 3093 (2012), requires specified presidential findings and congressional notifications prior to any department, agency, or entity of the U.S. government conducting any "activity or activities . . . to influence political, economic, or military conditions abroad, where it is intended that the role of the United States will not be apparent or acknowledged publicly." Prior to authorizing covert action, the President must

---

16. H.R. Rep. No. 115-874, at 1049 (2018).

first make a written finding noticed to Congress that the activity or activities is necessary to support identifiable foreign policy objectives of the United States, is important to the national security of the United States, and does not violate the Constitution or any statute of the United States.

On its face, the CAS only applies to activities deliberately constructed so as to allow plausible deniability for the U.S. government. Strictly speaking, the procedural requirements of the statute are not triggered simply because cover and concealment techniques are utilized to maintain security or achieve operational surprise. The CAS governs only where the intent of utilizing those measures is to conceal the sponsorship of the United States. However, the subtle distinction between hiding the fact of an operation versus its sponsorship can be very difficult to discern in practice. Owing to the unique nature of cyberspace where operational security is essential to success, operations are nearly always conducted in a concealed, unattributed, or undetectable manner. As such, compliance with § 3093 is directly implicated.

Nothing in the Covert Action Statute precludes the President from authorizing the DoD to conduct covert action. Yet prior to 2019, the statute proved to be a substantial impediment to DoD cyber operations. Since it was enacted, as a matter of standing executive policy the Central Intelligence Agency has been the only element within the executive branch authorized to conduct covert action, and the statute has often been framed in substantive terms as delimiting the boundaries of institutional roles and authorities. Unless an activity meeting the definition of covert action falls within one of the statute's enumerated exceptions, DoD is effectively barred from conducting it. For purposes of the present discussion, the most relevant among the exceptions are activities the primary purpose of which is to acquire intelligence, traditional counter-intelligence activities, and traditional military activities (TMA).

The intelligence-related exceptions are fairly straightforward. Unfortunately, the meaning of TMA is not and the statute does not define the term. As one can imagine, this ambiguity has generated friction both within the executive branch over which agencies may conduct certain activities, as well as between the executive branch and Congress over the jurisdiction of the relevant oversight committees. This was exactly what the conferees were referring to in the conference report passage reproduced above.

According to the Conference Report accompanying § 3093:

> It is the intent of the conferees that traditional military activities include activities by military personnel *under the direction and control of a United States military commander* (whether or not the U.S. sponsorship of such activities is apparent or later to be acknowledged) *preceding and related to hostilities which are either anticipated* (meaning approval has been given by the National Command Authorities for the activities and for operational planning for hostilities) to involve U.S. military forces, or *where such hostilities* involving United States military forces *are ongoing*, and, where the *fact of the U.S. role in the overall operation is apparent or to be acknowledged publicly.* In this regard, the conferees intend to draw a line between activities that are and are not under the direction and control of the military commander. Activities that are not under the direction and control of a military commander should not be considered as traditional military activities.[17]

---

17. H.R. Rep. No. 102-166, at 29-30 (1991) (emphasis added).

What does the Conference Report tell us about Congress's intent in including the TMA exception to the definition of covert action? Should the question turn on a straightforward, objective definition of TMA that looks only to whether the operation is commanded and executed by military personnel, and takes place in a context where overt hostilities are either underway or anticipated? Or did Congress intend a more historical approach to the analysis; one that looks to whether the activity in question is one the military *traditionally* conducted covertly prior to 1991, the year of the statute's passage?

Executive branch lawyers have generally followed the latter approach, looking to history as a guide in addition to distilling objective criteria from the statute's legislative history. For operations conducted as part of ongoing hostilities, especially when confined to active areas of hostilities, this approach generates little TMA debate. But cyber operations do not align neatly with geographic boundaries, and for operations taking place in the gray zone outside of armed conflict, the TMA hurdle proved nearly insurmountable. For these more difficult scenarios, Congress recognized that the TMA exception to covert action must account for the constantly evolving nature of military doctrine and operations as well as new technologies. Section 1642 reflects this recognition and brings greater definitional clarity to the Covert Action Statute's scope of applicability in the cyber context.

NOTES AND QUESTIONS

1. As a threshold question, would merely concealing the existence of an operation or activity bring it within the ambit of covert action? Does the specific intent for adopting measures of concealment matter to the analysis? Would all measures of concealment evince an intent "that the role of the United States will not be apparent or acknowledged publicly"?

2. DoD doctrine distinguishes between clandestine and covert operations. According to the DoD, a clandestine operation is one sponsored or conducted in such a way as to assure secrecy or concealment. A clandestine operation differs from a covert operation in that emphasis is placed on concealment of the operation rather than on concealment of the identity of the sponsor. Is this really a distinction? How would one discern the difference in practice? Does Congress's use of the term "clandestine" in § 1632 risk confusion?

3. The Conference Report accompanying § 1632 says that because of narrow interpretations of TMA, "with respect to actions that produce effects on information systems outside of areas of active hostilities, the Department of Defense has been limited to proposing actions that could be conducted overtly on attributable infrastructure without deniability." Is that an accurate reflection of how the Covert Action Statute was meant to apply?

4. How about the oversight concerns that the Covert Action Statute was meant to address? Section 1632 mandates briefings about any military activities or operations in cyberspace, including clandestine military activities, during the quarterly briefings required in § 484 of Title 10. Section 395 of Title 10 also requires the DoD to report any sensitive military cyber operations to the defense

committees within forty-eight hours of execution. Does this ensure sufficient congressional oversight over DoD cyber activities? Does it matter that these reporting requirements are to the defense, and not the intelligence committees?

2. Computer Hacking for National Security

Cyber operations frequently involve gaining unauthorized access to and possibly causing some level of harm to targeted computers and networks; in colloquial terms, computer hacking. The purpose of these operations might be to collect national security–relevant data or information from the hacked devices or it might be a means to intercept data and communications transiting the internet. Or the purpose might be to generate an intended effect, such as degrading the functionality of the targeted device or corrupting or manipulating the data resident thereon. In either instance, there is a rich body of laws that must be considered in determining whether the Constitution or statutes constrain the President's authority to direct these activities.

a. The Computer Fraud and Abuse Act

The Computer Fraud and Abuse Act (CFAA), 18 U.S.C. § 1030 (2012), is the primary federal statute proscribing computer hacking, providing for both criminal and civil penalties. The CFAA lists seven specific offenses, which fall into two broad areas: the sending of code or commands with the intent to damage or impair the operation of a protected computer without authorization; and the accessing of a protected computer without authority or by exceeding authorized access and thereby obtaining information or causing damage, impairment, or loss. The CFAA also criminalizes conspiracy to commit and attempts to commit the underlying offenses, and the statute has explicit extraterritorial scope.

As national security threats have moved online, the CFAA has figured prominently in the Department of Justice's toolkit for using domestic law to affirmatively counter this problem.

Department of Justice

Office of Public Affairs

FOR IMMEDIATE RELEASE
Monday, February 10, 2020

Chinese Military Personnel Charged with Computer Fraud, Economic Espionage and Wire Fraud for Hacking into Credit Reporting Agency Equifax

Indictment Alleges Four Members of China's People's Liberation Army Engaged in a Three-Month Long Campaign to Steal Sensitive Personal Information of Nearly 150 Million Americans

A federal grand jury in Atlanta returned an indictment last week charging four members of the Chinese People's Liberation Army (PLA) with hacking into the computer systems of the credit reporting agency Equifax and stealing Americans' personal data and Equifax's valuable trade secrets.

The nine-count indictment alleges that Wu Zhiyong (吴志勇), Wang Qian (王乾), Xu Ke (许可) and Liu Lei (刘磊) were members of the PLA's 54th Research Institute, a component of the Chinese military. They allegedly conspired with each other to hack into Equifax's computer networks, maintain unauthorized access to those computers, and steal sensitive, personally identifiable information of approximately 145 million American victims.

"This was a deliberate and sweeping intrusion into the private information of the American people," said Attorney General William P. Barr, who made the announcement. "Today, we hold PLA hackers accountable for their criminal actions, and we remind the Chinese government that we have the capability to remove the Internet's cloak of anonymity and find the hackers that nation repeatedly deploys against us. Unfortunately, the Equifax hack fits a disturbing and unacceptable pattern of state-sponsored computer intrusions and thefts by China and its citizens that have targeted personally identifiable information, trade secrets, and other confidential information."

According to the indictment, the defendants exploited a vulnerability in the Apache Struts Web Framework software used by Equifax's online dispute portal. They used this access to conduct reconnaissance of Equifax's online dispute portal and to obtain login credentials that could be used to further navigate Equifax's network. The defendants spent several weeks running queries to identify Equifax's database structure and searching for sensitive, personally identifiable information within Equifax's system. Once they accessed files of interest, the conspirators then stored the stolen information in temporary output files, compressed and divided the files, and ultimately were able to download and exfiltrate the data from Equifax's network to computers outside the United States. In total, the attackers ran approximately 9,000 queries on Equifax's system, obtaining names, birth dates and social security numbers for nearly half of all American citizens.

The indictment also charges the defendants with stealing trade secret information, namely Equifax's data compilations and database designs. "In short, this was an organized and remarkably brazen criminal heist of sensitive information of nearly half of all Americans, as well as the hard work and intellectual property of an American company, by a unit of the Chinese military," said Barr.

The defendants took steps to evade detection throughout the intrusion, as alleged in the indictment. They routed traffic through approximately 34 servers located in nearly 20 countries to obfuscate their true location, used encrypted communication channels within Equifax's network to blend in with normal network activity, and deleted compressed files and wiped log files on a daily basis in an effort to eliminate records of their activity.

"Today's announcement of these indictments further highlights our commitment to imposing consequences on cybercriminals no matter who they are, where they are, or what country's uniform they wear," said FBI Deputy Director David Bowdich. "The size and scope of this investigation—affecting nearly half of the U.S. population, demonstrates the importance of the FBI's mission and our enduring partnerships with the Justice Department and the U.S. Attorney's Office. This is not the end of our investigation; to all who seek to disrupt the safety, security and confidence of the global citizenry in this digitally connected world, this is a day of reckoning."

The defendants are charged with three counts of conspiracy to commit computer fraud, conspiracy to commit economic espionage, and conspiracy to commit wire fraud. The defendants are also charged with two counts of unauthorized access and intentional damage to a protected computer, one count of economic espionage, and three counts of wire fraud.

* * *

The details contained in the charging document are allegations. The defendants are presumed innocent until proven guilty beyond a reasonable doubt in a court of law.

https://www.justice.gov/opa/pr/chinese-military-personnel-charged-computer-fraud-economic-espionage-and-wire-fraud-hacking

The likelihood that the indicted PLA operatives will ever see the inside of a U.S. courtroom is low. So what is the purpose of the indictment? How valuable is this as means of protecting national security?

The CFAA is a complex statute. Since its passage in 1984, courts have struggled with the terms of the statute and the technology it was written for. It continues to raise difficult interpretive questions as digital technology and hacking tradecraft evolve. Federal courts are divided as to the meaning of key phrases in the statute, such as "authorized access," and the scope of the statute's overall applicability, and the Supreme Court has yet to weigh in to resolve these differences.

One of the more recent decisions out of the Ninth Circuit is illustrative. In *hiQ Labs, Inc. v. Linkedin Corp.*, 938 F.3d 985 (9th Cir. 2019), the court addressed the issue of whether a company may legally "scrape" data from another company's website. Data scraping comes in a variety of forms, but it generally involves the use of automated tools, or bots, to extract content and data from a website. As part of its business model, hiQ Labs was using a bot to scrape publicly facing data from LinkedIn profiles. LinkedIn sent hiQ Labs a cease and desist order, asserting violation of several provisions of law, including the CFAA, and implemented technical barriers to block the scraping. A week later, hiQ filed suit seeking injunctive relief and a declaratory judgment that LinkedIn could not lawfully invoke the CFAA under the circumstances because hiQ Labs had not accessed LinkedIn's servers "without authorization." The district court granted hiQ Lab's motion and LinkedIn appealed.

hiQ Labs, Inc. v. LinkedIn Corporation
(9th Cir. 2019)

May LinkedIn, the professional networking website, prevent a competitor, hiQ, from collecting and using information that LinkedIn users have shared on their public profiles, available for viewing by anyone with a web browser? HiQ, a data analytics company, obtained a preliminary injunction forbidding LinkedIn from denying hiQ access to publicly available LinkedIn member profiles. At this preliminary injunction stage, we do not resolve the companies' legal dispute definitively, nor do we address all the claims and defenses they have pleaded in the district court. Instead, we focus on whether hiQ has raised serious questions on the merits of the factual and legal issues presented to us, as well as on the other requisites for preliminary relief.

* * *

2. Computer Fraud and Abuse Act (CFAA)

The pivotal CFAA question here is whether once hiQ received LinkedIn's cease-and-desist letter, any further scraping and use of LinkedIn's data was "without authorization" within the meaning of the CFAA and thus a violation of the statute. 18 U.S.C. § 1030(a)(2). . . .

We have held in another context that the phrase "'without authorization' is a non-technical term that, given its plain and ordinary meaning, means accessing a protected computer without permission." *Nosal II*, 844 F.3d at 1028. *Nosal II* involved an employee accessing without permission an employer's private computer for which access permissions in the form of user accounts were required. *Id.* at 1028-29. *Nosal II* did not address whether access can be "without authorization" under the CFAA where, as here, prior authorization is not generally required, but a particular person—or bot—is refused access. HiQ's position is that *Nosal II* is consistent with the conclusion that where access is open to the general public, the CFAA "without authorization" concept is inapplicable. At the very least, we conclude, hiQ has raised a serious question as to this issue.

* * *

The CFAA was enacted to prevent intentional intrusion onto someone else's computer—specifically, computer hacking. *See United States v. Nosal (Nosal I)*, 676 F.3d 854, 858 (9th Cir. 2012) (citing S. Rep. No. 99-432, at 9 (1986) (Conf. Rep.)).

The 1984 House Report on the CFAA explicitly analogized the conduct prohibited by section 1030 to forced entry: "It is noteworthy that section 1030 deals with an 'unauthorized access' concept of computer fraud rather than the mere use of a computer. Thus, the conduct prohibited is analogous to that of 'breaking and entering'. . . ." H.R. Rep. No. 98-894, at 20 (1984). . . . Senator Jeremiah Denton similarly characterized the CFAA as a statute designed to prevent unlawful intrusion into otherwise inaccessible computers, observing that "[t]he bill makes it clear that unauthorized access to a Government computer is a trespass offense, as surely as if the offender had entered a restricted Government compound without proper authorization." 132 Cong. Rec. 27639 (1986) (emphasis added). . . .

In recognizing that the CFAA is best understood as an anti-intrusion statute and not as a "misappropriation statute," *Nosal I*, 676 F.3d at 857-58, we rejected the contract-based interpretation of the CFAA's "without authorization" provision adopted by some of our sister circuits. . . .

We therefore look to whether the conduct at issue is analogous to "breaking and entering." H.R. Rep. No. 98-894, at 20. Significantly, the version of the CFAA initially enacted in 1984 was limited to a narrow range of computers—namely, those containing national security information or financial data and those operated by or on behalf of the government. *See* Counterfeit Access Device and Computer Fraud and Abuse Act of 1984, Pub. L. No. 98-473, § 2102, 98 Stat. 2190, 2190-91. None of the computers to which the CFAA initially applied were accessible to the general public; affirmative authorization of some kind was presumptively required.

When section 1030(a)(2)(c) was added in 1996 to extend the prohibition on unauthorized access to any "protected computer," the Senate Judiciary Committee explained that the amendment was designed "to increase protection for the privacy and confidentiality of computer information." S. Rep. No. 104-357, at 7 (emphasis added). The legislative history of section 1030 thus makes clear that the prohibition on unauthorized access is properly understood to apply only to private information—information delineated as private through use of a permission requirement of some sort. As one prominent commentator has put it, "an authentication requirement, such as a password gate, is needed to create the necessary barrier that divides open spaces from closed spaces on the Web." Orin S. Kerr, *Norms of Computer Trespass,* 116 Colum. L. Rev. 1143, 1161 (2016). Moreover, elsewhere in the statute, password fraud is cited as a means by which a computer may be accessed without authorization, *see* 18 U.S.C. § 1030(a)(6), bolstering the idea that authorization is only required for password-protected sites or sites that otherwise prevent the general public from viewing the information.

We therefore conclude that hiQ has raised a serious question as to whether the reference to access "without authorization" limits the scope of the statutory coverage to computer information for which authorization or access permission, such as password authentication, is generally required. Put differently, the CFAA contemplates the existence of three kinds of computer information: (1) information for which access is open to the general public and permission is not required, (2) information for which authorization is required and has been given, and (3) information for which authorization is required but has not been given (or, in the case of the prohibition on exceeding authorized access, has not been given for the part of the system accessed). Public LinkedIn profiles, available to anyone with an Internet connection, fall into the first category. With regard to such information, the "breaking and entering" analogue invoked so frequently during congressional consideration has no application, and the concept of "without authorization" is inapt.

Neither of the cases LinkedIn principally relies upon is to the contrary. LinkedIn first cites *Nosal II,* 844 F.3d 1024 (9th Cir. 2016). As we have already stated, *Nosal II* held that a former employee who used current employees' login credentials to access company computers and collect confidential information had acted "'without authorization' in violation of the CFAA." *Nosal II,* 844 F.3d at 1038. The computer information the defendant accessed in *Nosal II* was thus plainly one which no one could access without authorization.

So too with regard to the system at issue in *Power Ventures,* 844 F.3d 1058 (9th Cir. 2016), the other precedent upon which LinkedIn relies. In that case, Facebook sued Power Ventures, a social networking website that aggregated social networking information from multiple platforms, for accessing Facebook users' data and using that data to send mass messages as part of a promotional campaign. *Id.* at 1062-63. After Facebook sent a cease-and-desist letter, Power Ventures continued to circumvent IP barriers and gain access to password-protected Facebook member profiles. *Id.* at 1063. We held that after receiving an individualized cease-and-desist letter, Power Ventures had accessed Facebook computers "without authorization" and was therefore liable under the CFAA. *Id.* at 1067-68. But we specifically recognized that "Facebook has tried to limit and control access to its website" as to the purposes for which Power Ventures sought to use it. *Id.* at 1063. Indeed, Facebook requires its users to register with a unique username and password, and Power Ventures required that Facebook users provide their Facebook username and password to access their Facebook data on Power Ventures' platform. *Facebook, Inc. v. Power Ventures, Inc.*, 844 F. Supp. 2d 1025, 1028 (N.D. Cal. 2012). While Power Ventures was gathering user data that was protected by Facebook's username and password authentication system, the data hiQ was scraping was available to anyone with a web browser.

In sum, *Nosal II* and *Power Ventures* control situations in which authorization generally is required and has either never been given or has been revoked. As *Power Ventures* indicated, the two cases do not control the situation present here, in which information is "presumptively open to all comers." *Power Ventures*, 844 F.3d at 1067 n.2.

* * *

Both the legislative history of section 1030 of the CFAA and the legislative history of section 2701 of the SCA, with its similar "without authorization" provision, then, support the district court's distinction between "private" computer networks and websites, protected by a password authentication system and "not visible to the public," and websites that are accessible to the general public.

Finally, the rule of lenity favors our narrow interpretation of the "without authorization" provision in the CFAA. . . . As we explained in *Nosal I*, we therefore favor a narrow interpretation of the CFAA's "without authorization" provision so as not to turn a criminal hacking statute into a "sweeping Internet-policing mandate." *Nosal I*, 676 F.3d at 858; *see also id.* at 863.

For all these reasons, it appears that the CFAA's prohibition on accessing a computer "without authorization" is violated when a person circumvents a computer's generally applicable rules regarding access permissions, such as username and password requirements, to gain access to a computer. It is likely that when a computer network generally permits public access to its data, a user's accessing that publicly available data will not constitute access without authorization under the CFAA. The data hiQ seeks to access is not owned by LinkedIn and has not been demarcated by LinkedIn as private using such an authorization system. HiQ has therefore raised serious questions about whether LinkedIn may invoke the CFAA to preempt hiQ's possibly meritorious tortious interference claim.

NOTES AND QUESTIONS

1. Where exactly does the court draw the line between what is and is not prohibited by the CFAA? Why didn't it matter to the court that LinkedIn issued the cease and desist order and set up technical measures to block hiQ Labs? How did it distinguish this case from its prior holding in *Power Ventures*? Does it matter that the case was on appeal from the grant of a preliminary injunction?

2. Should the fact that hiQ Labs was using an automated scraper make a difference?

3. Many argue that the CFAA is in need of reform, that its concepts of unauthorized access and exceeding authorized access are vague, and that the statute sweeps up a broad range of common internet usage. Several other circuits take a broader view of what is covered by the CFAA, holding that violating terms of service can constitute unauthorized access. What interests does the Ninth Circuit's "breaking and entering" approach serve?

4. What if a foreign government used the same technique to scrape LinkedIn data on members of the U.S. military or the intelligence community?

5. The CFAA criminalizes more than just gaining unauthorized access or exceeding authorized access. Several of the statute's provisions also cover intentionally causing damage to a protected computer by knowingly causing the transmission of a program, information, code, or command; recklessly causing damage to a protected computer as a result of gaining unauthorized access; or intentionally accessing a protected computer without authorization, and as a result of such conduct, causing damage and loss. Damage is defined in the statute as "any impairment to the integrity or availability of data, a program, a system, or information. . . ." Although these terms are not defined further, courts have generally treated them broadly as proscribing conduct that diminishes an owner's or a user's ability to use computer systems or the data resident thereon. This includes distributed denial-of-service (DDoS) operations that do not modify data or software on the targeted device, but temporarily degrade the system's functionality or availability. Disruption, denial, degradation, and even destruction of data and systems can all be intended effects of a military cyber operation.

Regardless of the uncertainty as to the CFAA's reach and the varied approaches courts take to the question of unauthorized access, the statute would seem to bring within its scope at least some of the activities conducted during the course of military cyber operations. Recalling the description of cyber operations at the beginning of the chapter, one can imagine how web scraping or similar techniques might serve an intelligence or reconnaissance purpose. And obviously, cyber operations might involve more intrusive and potentially harmful techniques. How does this square with Congress's encouragement, if not authorization, for the military to conduct more of these operations?

Returning again to the DoD General Counsel's Cyber Command speech, when addressing the impact of the CFAA on military operations Mr. Ney noted that the statute evinces no clear congressional intent to limit the President's authority to direct military cyber operations. According to Mr. Ney, "[c]ommon sense and long-accepted canons of statutory interpretation suggest . . . that the CFAA will not constrain appropriately authorized DoD cyber operations." What canons of construction was he referring to?

Nardone v. United States
302 U.S. 379 (1937)

Mr. Justice ROBERTS delivered the opinion of the Court.

The importance of the question involved—whether, in view of the provisions of § 605 of the Communications Act of 1934, evidence procured by a federal officer's tapping telephone wires and intercepting messages is admissible in a criminal trial in a United States District Court—moved us to grant the writ of certiorari.

The indictment under which the petitioners were tried, convicted, and sentenced, charged, in separate counts, the smuggling of alcohol, possession and concealment of the smuggled alcohol, and conspiracy to smuggle and conceal it. Over the petitioners' objection and exception, federal agents testified to the substance of petitioners' interstate communications overheard by the witnesses who had intercepted the messages by tapping telephone wires. The court below, though it found this evidence constituted such a vital part of the prosecution's proof that its admission, if erroneous, amounted to reversible error, held it was properly admitted, and affirmed the judgment of conviction.

Section 605 of the Federal Communications Act provides that no person who, as an employee, has to do with the sending or receiving of any interstate communication by wire, shall divulge or publish it or its substance to anyone other than the addressee or his authorized representative or to authorized fellow employees, save in response to a subpoena issued by a court of competent jurisdiction or on demand of other lawful authority, and "no person not being authorized by the sender shall intercept any communication and divulge or publish the existence, contents, substance, purport, effect, or meaning of such intercepted communication to any person."

Taken at face value, the phrase "no person" comprehends federal agents, and the ban on communication to "any person" bars testimony to the content of an intercepted message. Such an application of the section is supported by comparison of the clause concerning intercepted messages with that relating to those known to employees of the carrier. The former may not be divulged to any person, the latter may be divulged in answer to a lawful subpoena.

The government contends that Congress did not intend to prohibit tapping wires to procure evidence. It is said that this Court, in *Olmstead v. United States,* 277 U.S. 438, held such evidence admissible at common law despite the fact that a state statute made wiretapping a crime, and the argument proceeds that, since the *Olmstead* decision, departments of the federal government, with the knowledge of Congress, have, to a limited extent, permitted their agents to tap wires in aid of detection and conviction of criminals. It is shown that, in spite of its knowledge of the practice, Congress refrained from adopting legislation outlawing it, although bills so providing have been introduced. The Communications Act, so it is claimed, was passed only for the purpose of reenacting the provisions of the Radio Act of 1927 so as to make it applicable to wire messages and to transfer jurisdiction over radio and wire communications to the newly constituted Federal Communications Commission, and therefore the phraseology of the statute ought not to be construed as changing the practically identical provision on the subject which was a part of the Radio Act when the *Olmstead* case was decided.

We nevertheless face the fact that the plain words of § 605 forbid anyone, unless authorized by the sender, to intercept a telephone message, and direct in equally clear language that "no person" shall divulge or publish the message or its substance to "any person." To recite the contents of the message in testimony before a court is to divulge the message. The conclusion that the act forbids such testimony seems to us unshaken by the government's arguments.

True it is that, after this Court's decision in the *Olmstead* case, Congressional committees investigated the wiretapping activities of federal agents. Over a period of several years, bills were introduced to prohibit the practice, all of which failed to pass. An Act of 1933 included a clause forbidding this method of procuring evidence of violations of the National Prohibition Act. During 1932, 1933, and 1934, however, there was no discussion of the matter in Congress, and we are without contemporary legislative history relevant to the passage of the statute in question. It is also true that the committee reports in connection with the Federal Communications Act dwell upon the fact that the major purpose of the legislation was the transfer of jurisdiction over wire and radio communication to the newly constituted Federal Communications Commission. But these circumstances are, in our opinion, insufficient to overbear the plain mandate of the statute.

It is urged that a construction be given the section which would exclude federal agents, since it is improbable Congress intended to hamper and impede the activities of the government in the detection and punishment of crime. The answer is that the question is one of policy. Congress may have thought it less important that some offenders should go unwhipped of justice than that officers should resort to methods deemed inconsistent with ethical standards and destructive of personal liberty. The same considerations may well have moved the Congress to adopt § 605 as evoked the guaranty against practices and procedures violative of privacy embodied in the Fourth and Fifth Amendments of the Constitution.

The canon that the general words of a statute do not include the government or affect its rights unless the construction be clear and indisputable upon the text of the act does not aid the respondent. The cases in which it has been applied fall into two classes. The first is where an act, if not so limited, would deprive the sovereign of a recognized or established prerogative title or interest. A classical instance is the exemption of the state from the operation of general statutes of limitation. The rule of exclusion of the sovereign is less stringently applied where the operation of the law is upon the agents or servants of the government, rather than on the sovereign itself.

The second class—that where public officers are impliedly excluded from language embracing all persons—is where a reading which would include such officers would work obvious absurdity, as, for example, the application of a speed law to a policeman pursuing a criminal or the driver of a fire engine responding to an alarm.

For years, controversy has raged with respect to the morality of the practice of wiretapping by officers to obtain evidence. It has been the view of many that the practice involves a grave wrong. In the light of these circumstances, we think another well recognized principle leads to the application of the statute as it is written so as to include within its sweep federal officers, as well as others. That principle is that the sovereign is embraced by general words of a statute intended to prevent injury and wrong.

The judgment must be reversed, and the cause remanded to the District Court for further proceedings in conformity with this opinion.

Reversed.

NOTES AND QUESTIONS

1. *Nardone*, or at least its reference to a canon of excluding public officials from a statute's ambit when "a reading which would include such officers would work obvious absurdity," is often cited for the proposition that statutes should be read in light of the general public authority doctrine. That doctrine, usually applied as a justification in criminal law, holds that acts committed by a public official that otherwise would be criminal, such as taking or destroying property, taking hold of a person by force and against his will, placing him in confinement, or even taking his life, are not crimes if done with proper public authority. For example, the Department of Justice relied on the public authority exception and *Nardone* when it opined that the federal murder statutes did not apply to government officials involved in lethal strikes against members of al Qaeda, even when the target is a U.S. citizen.[18] According to the opinion, "it would not make sense to attribute to Congress the intent with respect to each of its criminal statutes to prohibit all covered activities undertaken by public officials in the legitimate exercise of their otherwise lawful authorities, even if Congress has clearly intended to make those same actions a crime when committed by persons who are not acting pursuant to such public authority."

2. In *Nardone*, the Court actually rejected the government's arguments to exclude its agents from the scope of the Federal Communications Act. Why should the outcome be different in the case of the CFAA?

3. The CFAA actually includes an express public authority exception for certain government activities. It "does not prohibit any lawfully authorized investigative, protective, or intelligence activity of a law enforcement agency of the United States, a State or political subdivision of a State, or of any intelligence agency of

---

18. Memorandum from the Dep't of Justice, Office of Legal Counsel for the Attorney General, Subject: Applicability of Federal Criminal Laws and the Constitution to Contemplated Lethal Operations Against Shaykh Anwar al-Aulaqi 16 (July 16, 2010), https://www.justice.gov/sites/default/files/olc/pages/attachments/2015/04/02/2010-07-16_-_olc_aaga_barron_-_al-aulaqi.pdf.

the United States." How does the absence of any reference to non-intelligence community military forces in § 1030(f) impact the public authority analysis?

4. Does applying the interpretive canon *expressio unius est exclusio alterius* (expressing one item of an associated group or series excludes another left unmentioned), undermine claims to a public authority exception? In light of Congress's purpose for passing the CFAA, which predates the development of military cyber operations, and the ample evidence of subsequent congressional action endorsing and enabling those operations, can it be said that "'circumstances support[ ] a sensible inference that the term left out must have been meant to be excluded.'" *See National Labor Relations Board v. SW General, Inc.*, 137 S. Ct. 929, 933 (2017) (citations omitted) (limiting applicability of the *expressio unius* canon).

E. The Law of Cyber Reconnaissance

No matter the domain of operations, operational success depends on national security decision makers and military commanders having sufficient information about the threats and adversaries they are tasked with influencing or defeating, as well as the complex and dynamic environments within which they have to operate. Generically referred to as intelligence, the information necessary to support effective decision making can be collected in myriad ways, not all of which constitute intelligence in the technical, and potentially legally relevant, sense of the term.[19]

Even before becoming the nation's first President, then General George Washington understood well the value of collecting information about an adversary. Under his direction, Major Benjamin Tallmadge organized a group of spies in the summer of 1778 known as the Culper Ring and ran an effective collection effort against the British then occupying New York at the height of the American Revolutionary War. Every President since Washington has followed suit, conducting espionage against foreign governments and to uncover threats in order to inform foreign relations, national defense, and national security decision making.

Throughout most of the nation's history, presidents exercised nearly unfettered authority under Article II to collect information against national security threats and foreign powers. However, beginning in the 1970s, Congress started taking a more active role in the regulation and oversight of information collection activities. It did so in response to the advent of new and more intrusive collection technologies, evolving understandings of the Fourth Amendment, and the discovery of a number of abuses of this power. This shift led to the development of complex statutory and regulatory frameworks governing the conduct of certain information collection activities — electronic surveillance and activities conducted by elements

---

19. Intelligence is "[t]he product resulting from the collection, processing, integration, evaluation, analysis, and interpretation of available information concerning foreign nations, hostile or potentially hostile forces or elements, or areas of actual or potential operations," as well as "[t]he activities that result in the product." U.S. Dep't of Def., DOD Dictionary of Military and Associated Terms 114 (Aug. 2017). Information alone does not constitute intelligence unless collected by an intelligence organization or under specific intelligence authorities.

of the intelligence community (IC) chief among them.[20] But not all information collection constitutes "intelligence" as that term is used in statutes, executive orders, and regulations.

> Elevated by statute in 2018 to become the DoD's combatant command responsible for directing, synchronizing, and coordinating cyberspace operations to defend and advance national interests, U.S. Cyber Command exercises command and control over the Cyber Mission Force (CMF)—over 6,000 military cyber operators organized into 133 teams. With very limited exceptions, Cyber Command is the only entity in the federal government tasked with conducting offensive cyber operations. And although the Commander is "dual-hatted" as the Director of the National Security Agency, Cyber Command is a military operational force, not an element of the IC. When members of the CMF conduct operations, they do so under "Title 10" military authorities, not "Title 50" intelligence authorities.

The information needed to plan and execute cyber operations comes from myriad sources. Some derive from standard intelligence processes like human and imagery intelligence conducted by elements of the IC with the appropriate mission and authorities. But a substantial amount is collected in and through cyberspace, including data both in transit and at rest ("stored" in the parlance of the Electronic Communications Privacy Act (ECPA)),[21] in order to identify, characterize, and pair effects tools against cyber targets. These collection activities are often the precursor to and may be indistinguishable from those intended to deliver a cyber effect. Some of this data may be collected under signals intelligence authorities, but frequently the military operational force executes all phases of the cyber operation, including reconnaissance as a "Title 10" operation. This implicates nuanced questions as to whether and how the complex set of existing legal and regulatory frameworks governing electronic surveillance and digital data collection apply in the emerging context of non-intelligence military personnel conducting cyber reconnaissance, especially the robust oversight processes and procedures developed for and often specifically applicable to intelligence activities.

---

20. The intelligence community is a defined set of federal departments and agencies and spe-. cific elements thereof. It includes, for example, the Office of the Director of National Intelligence, the Central Intelligence Agency, the National Security Agency, the Defense Intelligence Agency, the National Geospatial-Intelligence Agency, the National Reconnaissance Office, and the intelligence elements of the Army, the Navy, the Air Force, the Marine Corps, the Coast Guard, the Federal Bureau of Investigation, the Drug Enforcement Administration, and the Department of Energy. For a full listing of the departments and agencies comprising the intelligence community, see 50 U.S.C. § 3003(4) (2012).

21. Data at rest is data that is not actively moving from device to device or network to network, such as data stored on a hard drive, laptop, flash drive, or archived/stored in some other way. Data in transit is data actively moving from one location to another, such as across the internet or through a private network.

1. Cyber Collection and the Fourth Amendment

Since at least the late 1960s, Congress has sought to regulate the means, methods, and scope of the executive's use of new technologies to intercept communications and collect other digital data. In each instance, Congress has sought to strike a workable balance between individual rights and the legitimate investigatory and intelligence needs of the government. These statutory schemes are complex, interrelated, and generally context specific, reflecting the different balance of interests at play depending on which government actors are collecting information and for what purpose. For example, as we saw in Chapters 8 and 12, the rules governing law enforcement and intelligence collection can be very different.

Like Congress, the Supreme Court has also evolved its constitutional jurisprudence to account for advances in technology, most recently in *Jones* and *Carpenter*. Since its watershed decision in *Katz*, where, in the context of a non-trespassory wiretap, it established the reasonable expectation of privacy test as the touchstone for determining whether government action constitutes a search, the Fourth Amendment has become the start point for determining the legality of federal actors intercepting or collecting digital signals and data.

When applying the Fourth Amendment, the Court has also taken into account the specific context and purpose for which the government seeks to leverage new collection technologies. Consider, for example, its decision in *United States v. United States District Court*, 407 U.S. 297 (1972), commonly referred to as the *"Keith"* case. In *Keith*, although the Court unanimously rejected the government's claim to a national security exception to the warrant requirement in the context of domestic surveillance, it affirmatively declined to reach the Fourth Amendment's applicability to "the President's surveillance power with respect to the activities of foreign powers [or their agents], within or without this country." Further, because of the unique nature of non-criminal, domestic national security investigations, the Court held that the standards and procedures for conducting electronic surveillance for national security purposes can be different from those applicable to criminal investigations. The Court then implicitly invited Congress to enact legislation to govern such activities.

Rather than take up the Court's invitation directly, Congress instead passed the Foreign Intelligence Surveillance Act (FISA), discussed at length in Chapter 12. Whether the Court would still endorse a specialized regime like FISA in the case of domestic national security investigations is an open question—one that would likely be influenced by decades of subsequent practice applying traditional Fourth Amendment doctrine and the procedures in ECPA to data collection in the domestic context.

The Court's Fourth Amendment decisions also establish that the situs and target of collection are relevant factors. Recall that in *United States v. Verdugo-Urquidez*, 494 U.S. 259 (1990), the Court limited the scope of Fourth Amendment protection to only U.S. citizens and non-resident aliens that have "come within the territory of the United States and developed substantial connections with this country." Non-resident aliens abroad enjoy no protection under the Fourth Amendment. But

Verdugo leaves open a number of questions relevant to conducting cyber reconnaissance and collection against devices and data located overseas. The following Second Circuit opinion considers the role of the Fourth Amendment in the case of an extraterritorial search.

United States v. Odeh
(In re Terrorist Bombings of U.S. Embassies in East Afr.)
(Fourth Amendment Cases)
552 F.3d 157 (2d Cir. 2008)

Defendant-appellant Wadih El-Hage, a citizen of the United States, challenges his conviction in the United States District Court for the Southern District of New York . . . on numerous charges arising from his involvement in the August 7, 1998 bombings of the American Embassies in Nairobi, Kenya and Dar es Salaam, Tanzania (the "August 7 bombings"). In this opinion we consider El-Hage's challenge to the District Court's denial of his motion to suppress evidence obtained by the government from an August 1997 search of his residence in Nairobi, Kenya and electronic surveillance of telephone lines—land-based and cellular—conducted in Kenya between August 1996 and August 1997. . . .

American intelligence became aware of al Qaeda's presence in Kenya by mid-1996 and identified five telephone numbers used by suspected al Qaeda associates. From August 1996 through August 1997, American intelligence officials monitored these telephone lines, including two El-Hage used: a phone line in the building where El-Hage lived and his cell phone. The Attorney General of the United States then authorized intelligence operatives to target El-Hage in particular. . . . Working with Kenyan authorities, U.S. officials searched El-Hage's home in Nairobi on August 21, 1997, pursuant to a document shown to El-Hage's wife that was "identified as a Kenyan warrant authorizing a search for 'stolen property.'" At the completion of the search, one of the Kenyan officers gave El-Hage's wife an inventory listing the items seized during the search. El- Hage was not present during the search of his home. It is uncontested that the agents did not apply for or obtain a warrant from a U.S. court. . . .

EXTRATERRITORIAL APPLICATION
OF THE FOURTH AMENDMENT

[W]e must first determine whether and to what extent the Fourth Amendment's safeguards apply to overseas searches involving U.S. citizens. In *United States v. Toscanino*, a case involving a Fourth Amendment challenge to overseas wiretapping of a non-U.S. citizen, we observed that it was "well settled" that "the Bill of Rights has extraterritorial application to the conduct abroad of federal agents directed against United States citizens." 500 F.2d 267, 280-81 (2d Cir. 1974). . . . Nevertheless, we have not yet determined the specific question of the applicability of the Fourth Amendment's Warrant Clause to overseas searches. Faced with that question now, we hold that the Fourth Amendment's warrant requirement does not govern searches conducted abroad by U.S. agents; such searches of U.S. citizens need only satisfy the Fourth Amendment's requirement of reasonableness. . . .

The question of whether a warrant is required for overseas searches of U.S. citizens has not been decided by the Supreme Court, by our Court, or, as far as we are able to determine, by any of our sister circuits. While never addressing the question directly, the Supreme Court provided some guidance on the issue in *United States v. Verdugo-Urquidez*, where the Court examined whether an alien with "no voluntary attachment to the United States" could invoke the protections of the Fourth Amendment to suppress evidence obtained through a warrantless search conducted in Mexico. Relying on "the text of the Fourth Amendment, its history, and [the Court's] cases discussing the application of the Constitution to aliens and extraterritorially," the Supreme Court held that the Fourth Amendment affords no protection to aliens searched by U.S. officials outside of our borders. With respect to the applicability of the Warrant Clause abroad, the Court expressed doubt that the clause governed any overseas searches conducted by U.S. agents, explaining that warrants issued to conduct overseas searches "would be a dead letter outside the United States." Elaborating on this observation in a concurring opinion, Justice Kennedy concluded:

> The absence of local judges or magistrates available to issue warrants, the differing and perhaps unascertainable conceptions of reasonableness and privacy that prevail abroad, and the need to cooperate with foreign officials all indicate that the Fourth Amendment's warrant requirement should not apply in Mexico as it does in this country.

Both Justice Stevens, in a concurring opinion, and Justice Blackmun, in dissent, also took a dim view of applying the Warrant Clause to searches conducted abroad, noting that U.S. judicial officers have no power to issue such warrants. . . . Accordingly, in *Verdugo-Urquidez*, seven justices of the Supreme Court endorsed the view that U.S. courts are not empowered to issue warrants for foreign searches.

These observations and the following reasons weigh against imposing a warrant requirement on overseas searches.

First, there is nothing in our history or our precedents suggesting that U.S. officials must first obtain a warrant before conducting an overseas search. El-Hage has pointed to no authority — and we are aware of none — directly supporting the proposition that warrants are necessary for searches conducted abroad by U.S. law enforcement officers or local agents acting in collaboration with them; nor has El-Hage identified any instances in our history where a foreign search was conducted pursuant to an American search warrant. This dearth of authority is not surprising in light of the history of the Fourth Amendment and its Warrant Clause as well as the history of international affairs. As the *Verdugo-Urquidez* Court explained, "[w]hat we know of the history of the drafting of the Fourth Amendment ... suggests that its purpose was to restrict searches and seizures which might be conducted by the United States in domestic matters." In addition, the Warrant Clause appears to have been invested with a meaning at the time of the drafting that differs significantly from our modern view of the requirement. Justice White observed that "at the time of the Bill of Rights, the warrant functioned as a powerful tool of law enforcement rather than as a protection for the rights of criminal suspects," and "it was the abusive use of the warrant power, rather than any excessive zeal in the discharge of peace officers' inherent authority, that precipitated the Fourth Amendment." Accordingly, we agree with the Ninth Circuit's observation that "foreign searches have neither been historically subject to the warrant procedure, nor could they be as a practical matter." *United States v. Barona*, 56 F.3d 1087, 1092 n. 1 (9th Cir. 1995).

The interest served by the warrant requirement in having a "neutral and detached magistrate" evaluate the reasonableness of a search is, in part, based on separation of powers concerns—namely, the need to interpose a judicial officer between the zealous police officer ferreting out crime and the subject of the search. These interests are lessened in the circumstances presented here for two reasons. First, a domestic judicial officer's ability to determine the reasonableness of a search is diminished where the search occurs on foreign soil. Second, the acknowledged wide discretion afforded the executive branch in foreign affairs ought to be respected in these circumstances.

A warrant serves a further purpose in limiting the scope of the search to places described with particularity or "the persons or things to be seized" in the warrant. U.S. Const. amend. IV. In the instant case, we are satisfied that the scope of the searches at issue was not unreasonable.

Second, nothing in the history of the foreign relations of the United States would require that U.S. officials obtain warrants from foreign magistrates before conducting searches overseas or, indeed, to suppose that all other states have search and investigation rules akin to our own. As the Supreme Court explained in *Verdugo-Urquidez*:

> For better or for worse, we live in a world of nation-states in which our Government must be able to function effectively in the company of sovereign nations. Some who violate our laws may live outside our borders under a regime quite different from that which obtains in this country. Situations threatening to important American interests may arise halfway around the globe, situations which in the view of the political branches of our Government require an American response with armed force. If there are to be restrictions on searches and seizures which occur incident to such American action, they must be imposed by the political branches through diplomatic understanding, treaty, or legislation.

The American procedure of issuing search warrants on a showing of probable cause simply does not extend throughout the globe and, pursuant to the Supreme Court's instructions, the Constitution does not condition our government's investigative powers on the practices of foreign legal regimes "quite different from that which obtains in this country." . . .

Third, if U.S. judicial officers were to issue search warrants intended to have extraterritorial effect, such warrants would have dubious legal significance, if any, in a foreign nation. As a District Court in this Circuit recently observed, "it takes little to imagine the diplomatic and legal complications that would arise if American government officials traveled to another sovereign country and attempted to carry out a search of any kind, professing the authority to do so based on an American-issued search warrant." We agree with that observation. A warrant issued by a U.S. court would neither empower a U.S. agent to conduct a search nor would it necessarily compel the intended target to comply. It would be a nullity, or in the words of the Supreme Court, "a dead letter."

Fourth and finally, it is by no means clear that U.S. judicial officers could be authorized to issue warrants for overseas searches . . . although we need not resolve that issue here.

For these reasons, we hold that the Fourth Amendment's Warrant Clause has no extraterritorial application and that foreign searches of U.S. citizens conducted by U.S. agents are subject only to the Fourth Amendment's requirement of reasonableness.

NOTES AND QUESTIONS

1. The court went on to find the search of El-Hage's home and the year-long wiretapping of his phones to be reasonable. Applying a "totality of the circumstances" test, the court found that any intrusions on El-Hage's privacy were outweighed by the government's "manifest need to investigate possible threats to national security . . . ," at least in the case of "the extreme threat al Qaeda presented . . . to national security." What does *Odeh* tell us about military cyber operations involving overseas data collection?

2. What are the implications of *Verdugo*'s substantial connection requirement for resident aliens when they are outside of the United States or its territories? *See United States v. Barona*, 56 F.3d 1087, 1094 (9th Cir. 1995) (noting, but declining to answer, whether a resident alien has undertaken sufficient obligations of citizenship or developed a sufficient connection with the United States to be considered protected by the Fourth Amendment even when abroad).

3. In the age of the internet, can someone's online contacts establish a sufficient connection with the United States to qualify her for Fourth Amendment protection?

4. How does the Fourth Amendment apply when the government cannot determine with specificity where data is located?

5. The Ninth Circuit has held that when the U.S. government cooperates with foreign authorities to conduct a search or seizure, reasonableness requires compliance with the domestic law where the search occurs. *See United States v. Peterson*, 812 F.2d 486, 490 (9th Cir. 1987). How would such a standard apply to cross-border data collection?

Based on *Verdugo* and its progeny, "the Fourth Amendment does not apply to searches and seizures by the United States against a non-resident alien in a foreign country." *United States v. Zakharov*, 468 F.3d 1171, 1179 (9th Cir. 2006). It is exactly in this foreign space that the military operates, even in the cyber context notwithstanding the challenges presented by a borderless internet. The Posse Comitatus Act, 18 U.S.C. § 1385 (2012), regulations, and longstanding custom limit the military's authority to operate domestically. This holds true for cyber operations outside of DoD information networks, which are generally aimed at foreign powers and infrastructure located overseas. Because targeting the communications and data of non-U.S. citizens abroad for collection falls beyond the reach of the Fourth Amendment, these collection activities are subject only to restraints that the executive or Congress may, at their discretion, proscribe. Congress and the executive have done so only for a narrow set of circumstances through § 702 of the FISA Amendments Act of 2008 and Executive Order 12333, respectively. As we will see, neither of these frameworks apply neatly to non-intelligence military operations involving extraterritorial collection of information.

What about inadvertent or incidental collection[22] of a U.S. citizen's data or communications during the course of an extraterritorial cyber reconnaissance operation? Are there Fourth Amendment implications?

The Second Circuit recently addressed this issue in *United States v. Hasbajrami*, No. 15-2684 (2d Cir. 2019), a decision reviewing a challenge to the constitutionality of collecting, storing, and querying the electronic communications of a U.S. citizen—later used as evidence at his criminal trial—as part of the warrantless surveillance program authorized by § 702 of the FISA Amendments Act. The court ruled that the "incidental collection" of a U.S. citizen's communications under § 702 is permissible when the primary target of the surveillance is a foreign national located overseas. Relying on *Verdugo* and applying the "incidental overhear" doctrine of *United States v. Donovan*, 429 U.S. 413 (1977), the court found that the incidental collection was reasonable under the circumstances and that because the primary collection targeting a non-resident alien overseas was lawful, the government did not need to obtain a separate warrant for Hasbajrami's "overheard" communications with the target.

The court then went on to distinguish between initial collection and subsequent querying of data. Noting its concerns about § 702's sweeping technological capacity and broad scope, the court held that "querying [§ 702] stored data does have important Fourth Amendment implications, and those implications counsel in favor of considering querying a separate Fourth Amendment event that, in itself, must be reasonable." It based its conclusion, at least in part, on *Carpenter* and other Supreme Court cases in which the Court has "expressed increasing concern about the interaction between Fourth Amendment precedent and evolving government

---

22. Incidental and inadvertent collection are considered and treated differently. The former involves the collateral collection of communications or data of non-targeted individuals during the course of collecting against an authorized target. The latter involves targeting communications or data for collection based on the mistaken belief that the collection is authorized, such as in the case of targeting a U.S. citizen on the mistaken belief that the individual is a non-resident alien overseas.

technological capabilities." On this issue, the court remanded the case for further development of the record to assess the reasonableness of the government's queries. Finally, the court stated that inadvertent collection of communications or data also raised "complicated [constitutional] questions," but declined to address them, finding harmless error.

Compare the Second Circuit's approach to the query issue with that of the Foreign Intelligence Surveillance Court (FISC) in *Redacted*, 402 F. Supp. 3d 45 (FISA Ct. 2018). For the FISC, individual queries are not separate searches, but the standing procedures the government adopts to govern queries of incidentally collected U.S.-citizen data must be reasonable under the Fourth Amendment. Which is the better approach? What are the implications of each?

2. Beyond the Fourth Amendment

Like the courts, Congress has struggled to keep pace with the rapid evolution of digital technology. The result is a complex set of interrelated statutes that generally proscribe non-consensual wiretapping and digital data collection with public authority carve-outs "authorizing" the government to conduct these activities subject to elaborate approval and oversight procedures. The executive has also adopted extensive regulations governing these activities when conducted by elements of the intelligence community, all of which must be considered when military forces engage in cyber reconnaissance to collect data and information.

a. Electronic Communications Privacy Act (ECPA)

Congress passed ECPA in 1986 as an update to the Wire Tap Act and "to protect the privacy of an individual's electronic communications while also providing the government with a means for accessing these communications and related records." ECPA covers a broad range of data both in transit and at rest, including the content of e-mails, private instant messages, YouTube and similar videos, as well as some non-content metadata. With respect to stored data, ECPA's coverage extends only to electronic communications held by "electronic communication service" (ECS) providers and "remote computing service" (RCS) providers—in essence, internet service providers (ISP).

The Wire Tap Act is codified in Title I of the ECPA. It makes the interception of data in transit, i.e., electronic eavesdropping, a federal crime, but contains a public authority exception excluding from its scope both interceptions authorized pursuant to FISA and interceptions by federal agents of "foreign intelligence information from international or foreign communications, or foreign intelligence activities conducted in accordance with otherwise applicable Federal Law involving a foreign electronic communications system, utilizing a means other than" FISA electronic surveillance. The latter exception is subject to a set of procedural constraints, but those apply to the interception of *domestic* wiretapping for law enforcement purposes. Thus, ECPA's Title I procedures are the exclusive means by which the government can conduct *domestic* interceptions of electronic communications, other than FISA electronic surveillance. As such, they do not apply to non-law enforcement, extraterritorial collection of foreign intelligence or cyber reconnaissance information.

When it comes to collecting communications content stored with an ISP, the analysis is not as straightforward. Title II of ECPA, the Stored Communications Act (SCA), makes it a crime to intentionally obtain, alter, or prevent authorized access to stored electronic communications by means of accessing without authorization or in excess of authorization a facility through which an ECS or RCS is provided. Like the CFAA, the SCA potentially reaches a broad range of activity that might encompass some extraterritorial cyber data collection. At first glance, this would not seem to fall within the SCA's three enumerated exceptions.[23]

The better view is that military cyber reconnaissance operations to collect stored data outside the United States fall outside the scope of the SCA. First, the SCA's criminal provisions likely do not have extraterritorial reach. In *Microsoft Corp. v. United States (In re Warrant to Search a Certain E-Mail Account Controlled & Maintained by Microsoft Corp.)*, 829 F.3d 197, 209, 222 (2d Cir. 2016), the Second Circuit held that the SCA's warrant provisions do not apply overseas, as the statute has no "clear indication of extraterritorial application." There is nothing to indicate that the presumption against extraterritorial effect should not apply equally to the SCA as a whole. Second, § 2511(f) of ECPA specifically cross-references the SCA, thereby extending the same public authority exception applicable in the Title I context to the collection of foreign intelligence information.

b. FISA

Recall from Chapter 12 that traditional Title I FISA applies only to electronic surveillance—as defined in § 1801(f)—conducted in the United States. As originally enacted, Congress specifically intended to exclude extraterritorial collection of foreign intelligence from FISA's reach. When conducted by elements of the IC, that collection was governed by Executive Order (E.O.) 12333.

The provisions of the FISA Amendments Act operate slightly differently, addressing three distinct situations. Section 702 governs collection against foreign persons located abroad by means of electronic surveillance effected within the United States. Section 703 governs the targeting of a United States person reasonably believed to be outside the United States to acquire foreign intelligence information, "if the acquisition constitutes electronic surveillance or the acquisition of stored electronic communications or stored electronic data. . . ." Finally, § 704 prohibits any "element of the intelligence community" from targeting a U.S. person reasonably believed to be outside the United States to acquire foreign intelligence under circumstances where the targeted individual has a reasonable expectation of privacy and a warrant would be required if the acquisition were conducted in the United States.

FISA and the FAA are complicated statutes and the legal issues they raise are numerous. Whether FISA and the FAA apply to military forces conducting cyber reconnaissance and collection is critical for at least two reasons. First, FISA provides for the exclusive means to conduct electronic surveillance as defined by the statute. Engaging

---

23. Section 2701(c) provides three statutory exceptions to a violation of the SCA. Specifically, the SCA does not apply to conduct authorized "(1) by the person or entity providing a wire or electronic communications service; (2) by a user of that service with respect to a communication of or intended for that user; or (3) in section 2703, 2704 or 2518 of this title."

in electronic surveillance except as authorized by FISA implicates criminal and civil sanction. Second, FISA electronic surveillance aligns with the DoD definition of Signals Intelligence (SIGINT). Within the DoD, only the NSA may engage in SIGINT activities except pursuant to a delegation by the Secretary of Defense, after coordination with the DNI. The same holds true for electronic surveillance conducted under §§ 702 and 703 of the FAA. In contrast, § 704's scope is specifically limited to elements of the IC.

So, Title I FISA governs *any* collection of foreign intelligence within the United States by means of electronic surveillance. In the case of overseas collection, DoD elements of the IC must obtain authorization from the FISC to target U.S. persons abroad. In all other cases, intelligence activities targeting foreign persons abroad are governed by E.O. 12333 and DoD internal approval and oversight regulations that by their terms apply to defense intelligence components. Operational maneuver forces conducting cyber reconnaissance must adhere to the Reasonableness Clause of the Fourth Amendment when applicable. Otherwise, their operations are governed only by mission-specific constraints or restraints or other applicable policies or orders.

NOTES AND QUESTIONS

1. In the course of ongoing operations against ISIS elements in Syria, cyber operators propose an operation to access and exploit the data on the laptop of an ISIS fighter known to be a U.S. citizen. He is a key planner of ISIS's external attack operations. The operators believe they can effectively disrupt his planning by ultimately disrupting the functionality of his laptop, but they first need to collect information from it to develop the right tool to deliver the intended cyber effect. You are the assigned legal advisor. What would you advise your operators?
2. For cyber reconnaissance operations targeted against foreign personnel and infrastructure abroad, what measures should be emplaced to address the risks of incidental or inadvertent collection of U.S. citizen's data?

A NOTE ON END-TO-END ENCRYPTION

Even assuming the government complies with the requirements of the Fourth Amendment to access information, what happens when technology creates an impenetrable zone of privacy? Should the government be allowed to prohibit private companies from creating and marketing encrypted devices and end-to-end encrypted communications platforms, or to compel a private entity to produce an encryption key to enable access to data pursuant to a court order? What are the national security implications of bringing these products to market? The advantages encryption affords to terrorists and criminals are typically cited, but could end-to-end encryption facilitate cyber espionage and effects operations as well? Are there countervailing considerations to requiring companies to maintain some ability to allow the government to access this data?

Following the 2015 San Bernardino terrorist shootings, the FBI took Apple to court in an attempt to compel it under the All Writs Act of 1789 to assist the FBI with accessing a work-issued iPhone used by one of the shooters. The shooters managed to destroy their personal cell phones before both were killed in a shoot-out with law enforcement. The work phone was recovered intact but was locked with a four-digit password and was set to delete all data after ten failed login attempts—data that might have illuminated the shooters' connections to foreign terror organizations and broader plots. Apple did not maintain encryption keys for its iPhones and refused to assist the FBI by developing a technical solution to decrypting the phone's contents. The FBI abruptly dropped the court case, reportedly because it found a third-party supplier able to crack the device, but the event fueled the deeper "going dark" debate.

The encryption debate has only intensified with the increased number of end-to-end encrypted messaging platforms coming to market. End-to-end encryption is a system of communication where only the communicating users can read the messages. In principle, it prevents potential eavesdroppers—including telecom providers, internet providers, and even the provider of the communication service—from being able to access the cryptographic keys needed to decrypt the conversation. End-to-end encryption offers much greater communications security. Unbreakable end-to-end encryption also affords criminals, terrorists, and other national security threat actors a means to communicate without the possibility of their communications being intercepted.

The Department of Justice has consistently lobbied against device manufacturers and application developers producing and deploying encryption that can only be decrypted by the end user or customer, citing the risks to public safety and national security that "warrant proof" encryption creates.

These efforts have thus far fallen flat, however. For example, in December 2019 Facebook released an open letter refusing Department of Justice entreaties to stall applying end-to-end encryption to its Messenger platform, stating that any backdoor access into Facebook's products created for law enforcement would weaken security and let in bad actors who would exploit the access. Efforts in Congress to resolve this debate have similarly failed. At the same time, some countries, like Australia, have passed controversial encryption legislation.

For contrasting views on the encryption debate, see Geoffrey S. Corn & Dru Brenner-Beck, *"Going Dark": Encryption, Privacy, Liberty, and Security in the "Golden Age of Surveillance,"* in THE CAMBRIDGE HANDBOOK OF SURVEILLANCE LAW (David Gray & Stephen E. Henderson eds., 2017), and Jim Baker, *Rethinking Encryption*, LAWFARE, Oct. 22, 2019, https://www.lawfareblog.com/rethinking-encryption.

V. INTERNATIONAL LAW OF CYBER OPERATIONS AND THE *JUS* "CYBER" *BELLUM*

The emergence of cyberspace as a domain of interstate relations and conflict has engendered difficult questions and debates about international law's role in governing how states use cyber capabilities and operations to protect and advance their interests. As cyberspace and the attendant threats have evolved, the United States has been consistent in its commitment to the applicability of international law to states' interactions in cyberspace. As then State Department Legal Advisor

Brian Egan put it in a 2016 speech at Berkeley Law School, "[e]xisting principles of international law form a cornerstone of the United States' strategic framework of international cyber stability during peacetime and during armed conflict." The United States 2018 Cyber Strategy echoes this commitment, noting that "[i]nternational law . . . provide[s] stabilizing, security-enhancing standards that define acceptable behavior to all states and promote greater predictability and stability in cyberspace."

Early debates over this baseline question of whether international law even applies to states' use of cyber capabilities have effectively receded. For example, with the United States' participation and endorsement, the UNGGE[24] affirmed after years of debate that "[i]nternational law, and in particular the Charter of the United Nations, is applicable, and is essential in maintaining peace and stability and promoting an open, secure, peaceful and accessible ICT environment." A growing number of states have separately endorsed this view. On the more difficult question of how international law operates in the context of cyberspace, progress has been slow and uneven.

International legal obligations can derive from treaty or customary law, or both. But with the exception of the Convention on Cybercrime of the Council of Europe, otherwise known as the Budapest Convention, states have yet to consider, let alone adopt any international law conventions specific to cyber operations. Instead, states look to existing frameworks, engaging in what Professor and former State Department Legal Advisor Harold Koh describes as a "translation exercise" — looking to the "spirit" of existing law to adapt it to the "present-day situation."

This process of transposing extant international law principles and norms to new contexts is generally reactive, slow, and iterative. The novel, rapidly evolving nature of cyberspace hampers efforts to resolve the many open questions and ambiguities in the law, creating challenges to the existing framework of international peace and security and the international legal structure undergirding it. States set on challenging the international rules-based order routinely exploit these ambiguities in the gray zone between war and peace, engaging in increasingly frequent and threatening cyber operations. Reducing uncertainty and evolving international law's role in the cyber context must play a part in any strategic response to these growing threats.

Identifying the state practice and *opinio juris* necessary to establish customary international law and its applicability in the cyber domain is further complicated by the clandestine nature of cyber operations. The list of serious and harmful cyber operations continues to grow, such as the release of the Wannacry, Petya, and Not-Petya malware, the operation directed against Sony Pictures, and the hacking of the Democratic National Committee and related information operations directed at the 2016 U.S. presidential elections, to name a few. But the parties responsible for these operations went to great lengths to obscure their involvement, obviously offering no rationale to support them. And while the victims of these operations

---

24. United Nations Group of Governmental Experts on Developments in the Field of Information and Telecommunications in the Context of International Security.

have shown increasing capability and willingness to attribute them, clear statements about the international law implications of these events have been wanting.

A small but growing number of states have offered official statements setting out their views on how certain principles of international law apply to cyber operations—Australia, France, Estonia, the Netherlands, the United Kingdom, and the United States among them. These statements help to bring some clarity to the field, but they have also highlighted some core disagreements over certain fundamental questions. Returning to Mr. Ney's speech at the U.S. Cyber Command Legal Conference, discussed above, he laid out the DoD's views about key aspects of international law as applied to cyber operations, building on prior speeches by State Department Legal Advisors Harold Koh and Brian Egan in 2012 and 2016 respectively, and the 2014 U.S. submission to the UNGGE.

> We recognize that State practice in cyberspace is evolving. As lawyers operating in this area, we pay close attention to States' explanations of their own practice, how they are applying treaty rules and customary international law to State activities in cyberspace, and how States address matters where the law is unsettled. . . . Initiatives by non-governmental groups like those that led to the Tallinn Manual can be useful to consider, but they do not create new international law, which only states can make. My intent here is not to lay out a comprehensive set of positions on international law. Rather . . . I will tell you how DoD lawyers address some of the international law issues that today's military cyber operations present.
>
> . . . It continues to be the view of the United States that existing international law applies to State conduct in cyberspace. Particularly relevant for military operations are the Charter of the United Nations, the law of State responsibility, and the law of war. To determine whether a rule of customary international law has emerged with respect to certain State activities in cyberspace, we look for sufficient State practice over time, coupled with opinio juris—evidence or indications that the practice was undertaken out of a sense that it was legally compelled, not out of a sense of policy prudence or moral obligation.
>
> As I discussed a few minutes ago, our policy leaders assess that the threat environment demands action today—our clients need our advice today on how international legal rules apply when resorting to action to defend our national interests from malicious activity in cyberspace, notwithstanding any lack of agreement among States on how such rules apply. Consequently, in reviewing particular operations, DoD lawyers provide advice guided by how existing rules apply to activities in other domains, while considering the unique, and frequently changing, aspects of cyberspace.
>
> First, let's discuss the international law applicable to uses of force. Article 2(4) of the Charter of the United Nations provides that "All Members shall refrain in their international relations from the threat or use of force against the territorial integrity or political independence of any state, or in any other manner inconsistent with the Purposes of the United Nations." At the same time, international law recognizes that there are exceptions to this rule. For example, in the exercise of its inherent right of self-defense a State may use force that is necessary and proportionate to respond to an actual or imminent armed attack. This is true in the cyber context just as in any other context.

Depending on the circumstances, a military cyber operation may constitute a use of force within the meaning of Article 2(4) of the U.N. Charter and customary international law. In assessing whether a particular cyber operation—conducted by or against the United States—constitutes a use of force, DoD lawyers consider whether the operation causes physical injury or damage that would be considered a use of force if caused solely by traditional means like a missile or a mine. Even if a particular cyber operation does not constitute a use of force, it is important to keep in mind that the State or States targeted by the operation may disagree, or at least have a different perception of what the operation entailed.

Second, the international law prohibition on coercively intervening in the core functions of another State (such as the choice of political, economic, or cultural system) applies to State conduct in cyberspace. For example, "a cyber operation by a State that interferes with another country's ability to hold an election" or that tampers with "another country's election results would be a clear violation of the rule of non-intervention." Other States have indicated that they would view operations that disrupt the fundamental operation of a legislative body or that would destabilize their financial system as prohibited interventions.

There is no international consensus among States on the precise scope or reach of the non-intervention principle, even outside the context of cyber operations. Because States take different views on this question, DoD lawyers examining any proposed cyber operations must tread carefully, even if only a few States have taken the position publicly that the proposed activities would amount to a prohibited intervention.

Some situations compel us to take into consideration whether the States involved have consented to the proposed operation. Because the principle of non-intervention prohibits "actions designed to coerce a State ... in contravention of its rights," it does not prohibit actions to which a State voluntarily consents, provided the conduct remains within the limits of the consent given. . . .

For cyber operations that would not constitute a prohibited intervention or use-of-force, the Department believes there is not sufficiently widespread and consistent State practice resulting from a sense of legal obligation to conclude that customary international law generally prohibits such non-consensual cyber operations in another State's territory. This proposition is recognized in the Department's adoption of the "defend forward" strategy: "We will defend forward to disrupt or halt malicious cyber activity at its source, including activity that falls below the level of armed conflict." The Department's commitment to defend forward including to counter foreign cyber activity targeting the United States—comports with our obligations under international law and our commitment to the rules-based international order.

The DoD OGC view, which we have applied in legal reviews of military cyber operations to date, shares similarities with the view expressed by the U.K. Government in 2018. We recognize that there are differences of opinion among States, which suggests that State practice and *opinio juris* are presently not settled on this issue. Indeed, many States' public silence in the face of countless publicly known cyber intrusions into foreign networks precludes a conclusion that States have coalesced around a common view that there is an international prohibition against all such operations (regardless of whatever penalties may be imposed under domestic law).

NOTES AND QUESTIONS

1. Mr. Ney notes that "[i]nitiatives by non-governmental groups like those that led to the Tallinn Manual can be useful to consider, but they do not create new international law, which only states can make." The *Tallinn Manual 2.0 on the International Law Applicable to Cyber Operations*—the product of a group of nineteen academics—has been described as the most comprehensive guide on how existing international law applies to cyber operations. Why do you think Mr. Ney made specific reference to the *Tallinn Manual* in the way he did? How does his point align with Article 38 of the Statute of the International Court of Justice?

2. Mr. Ney addresses several international law principles the DoD considers most relevant to assessing cyber operations, starting with the *jus ad bellum*. Each is explored further below. He also acknowledged without elaboration that cyber operations are subject to a number of other legal and normative considerations. What might these rules be? Because cyber operations can cut across all operational domains, they can implicate multiple international law regimes, such as international human rights law, the law of the sea, and even space law.

THE DEVELOPMENT OF CYBER NORMS

In his U.S. Cyber Command speech, Mr. Ney also noted the DoD's commitment to "U.S. State Department-led initiatives to build and promote [a] framework for responsible State behavior in cyberspace," which "includes participation in the UN Group of Governmental Experts and an Open-Ended Working Group on information and communications technologies in the context of international peace and security."

Under the auspices of the United Nations, there have been five Groups of Governmental Experts that have convened since 2004. The Groups have examined existing and potential threats in the cyber-sphere and possible cooperative measures to address them. The 2010, 2013, and 2015 GGEs produced consensus reports that included non-binding peacetime norms of state behavior in cyberspace. In December 2018, the General Assembly established both a new GGE and an Open-Ended Working Group (OEWG) to continue these discussions for the period of 2019-2021 and 2019-2020, respectively.

For the DoD, "[t]hese diplomatic engagements are an important part of the United States' overall effort to protect U.S. national interests by promoting stability in cyberspace." How do these political commitments by states help to prevent miscalculation and conflict escalation? What relationship do they have to the development of international law?

A. The *Jus* ad *Bellum*

Consistent with the Department of Defense Law of War Manual's treatment of the subject, Mr. Ney conveys a fairly conventional view that the prohibition on the use of force is breached when there is some element of armed force involved, or at least actions resulting in physical injury or damage. The United Kingdom and Australia share this approach. But does this view sufficiently account for the nature of emerging cyber threats?

Commenting on Mr. Ney's remarks, Professor Michael Schmitt, the General Editor of the *Tallinn Manual* and *the Tallinn Manual 2.0 on the International Law Applicable to Cyber Operations*, expressed a slightly different perspective:

In 2019, the Netherlands addressed this question head on, stating that "at this time it cannot be ruled out that a cyber operation with a very serious financial or economic impact may qualify as the use of force." It explained:

> It is necessary, when assessing the scale and effects of a cyber operation, to examine both qualitative and quantitative factors. The Tallinn Manual 2.0 refers to a number of factors that could play a role in this regard, including how serious and far-reaching the cyber operation's consequences are, whether the operation is military in nature and whether it is carried out by a state. These are not binding legal criteria. They are factors that could provide an indication that a cyber operation may be deemed a use of force, and the government endorses this approach.

The same year, employing reasoning analogous to that of the Netherlands, France adopted the position that a use of force need not be destructive or injurious:

> France does not rule out the possibility that a cyberoperation without physical effects may also be characterized as a use of force. In the absence of physical damage, a cyberoperation may be deemed a use of force against the yardstick of several criteria, including the circumstances prevailing at the time of the operation, such as the origin of the operation and the nature of the instigator (military or not), the extent of intrusion, the actual or intended effects of the operation or the nature of the intended target. This is of course not an exhaustive list. For example, penetrating military systems in order to compromise French defence capabilities, or financing or even training individuals to carry out cyberattacks against France, could also be deemed uses of force.

In my estimation, it is very unlikely that a State facing calamitous cyber operations, such as a devastating attack on its economy or disruption of its national defense capabilities, would hesitate to treat such operations as a use of force because they were neither physically destructive nor injurious. On the contrary, even States that reject the U.S. view that there is no sunlight between the use of force and armed attack thresholds would characterize such operations as armed attacks entitling them to resort to kinetic or cyber force in self-defense.

Michael N. Schmitt, *The Defense Department's Measured Take on International Law in Cyberspace*, JUST SECURITY, Mar. 11, 2020, https://www.justsecurity.org/69119/the-defense-departments-measured-take-on-international-law-in-cyberspace/.

NOTES AND QUESTIONS

1. In *The Case Concerning Military and Paramilitary Activities in and Against Nicaragua*, the International Court of Justice described armed attacks as the gravest form of a use of force. Most states, including France and the Netherlands, adopt this view and consider there to be a so-called force gap between a use of force and an armed attack. The United States and a handful of other states take the opposite view, considering use of force and armed attack to be synonymous.

2. For the majority of states, whether a particular action constitutes a use of force does not turn on the means used, but rather on the effects produced. Where France and the Netherlands go further is in their apparent willingness to consider non-physical effects as potentially constituting a use of force. How much might this position be influenced by the view that not all uses of force amount to armed attacks under Article 51 of the U.N. Charter, which triggers the victim state's inherent right of self-defense? What are the risks of adopting the approach of the Netherlands and France?

3. In *Paramilitary Activities*, the ICJ looked to the scale and effects of a hostile action to determine whether it amounted to an armed attack. The *Tallinn Manual 2.0* adapted this standard to the use-of-force question and suggested a series of factors states should consider. The DoD *Law of War Manual* opts for a totality of the circumstances approach. Which approach is more practical?

4. Not only will France consider non-physical harm as potentially crossing the use-of-force threshold, apparently it also subscribes to the "accumulation theory" of use of force. In France's view, cyber operations that viewed separately would not reach the threshold of an armed attack may nevertheless be classified as such if their accumulated effects are either sufficiently grave or if they occur in a coordinated fashion with other actions that may be classified as an armed attack and emanate from the same entity or different entities acting in concert.

5. During the drafting of the U.N. Charter, and later during the proceedings leading to the U.N. General Assembly's Declaration on Friendly Relations, states rejected the notion that economic coercion or other forms of political pressure having the effect of threatening the territorial integrity or political independence of any state could constitute a use of force. How can one reconcile this rejection with the views of France and the Netherlands?

6. In 2016, the Department of Justice indicted seven Iranians alleged to have been behind sustained Iranian government DDoS operations against forty-six U.S. financial institutions. According to the U.S. Attorney for the Southern District of New York, the "onslaught of cyber-attacks on 46 of our largest financial institutions, many headquartered in New York City, resulted in hundreds of thousands of customers being unable to access their accounts and tens of millions of dollars being spent by the companies trying to stay online through these attacks." Although the United States attributed the DDoS operations to Iran, it did not assert that they amounted to a use of force. Does this represent the type of harmful effect France and the Netherlands have in mind? Or should the threshold of economic harm be more substantial?

B. Prohibited Intervention

To date, no state has condemned a malicious cyber operation as constituting a use of force, and those states employing cyber capabilities seem to be calibrating their actions to avoid causing the type of harmful effects that might cross the use-of-force boundary and risk a forceful response. Cyber operations are playing out below this threshold. However, this does not negate or diminish the harmful impact of these operations. Nor does it mean there is no law to apply.

Below the use-of-force threshold, states have evolved the customary international law principle of non-intervention as an additional protection against impairments of their sovereignty. Like the prohibition on the use of force, the non-intervention rule derives from the general principle of sovereignty and is intended to protect the same basic sovereign interests in states' territorial integrity and political independence. As the United Kingdom's attorney general noted in a 2018 speech on cyber and international law, "[t]he international law prohibition on intervention in the internal affairs of other states is of particular importance in modern times when technology has an increasing role to play in every facet of our lives, including political campaigns and the conduct of elections." As evidenced by the 2015 UNGGE report and subsequent official statements from a number of states, this prohibition applies to states' activities conducted in and through cyberspace.

According to the ICJ in its *Paramilitary Activities* judgment, the non-intervention rule comprises the "right of every sovereign State to conduct its [internal and external] affairs without outside interference. . . ." But like the use-of-force prohibition, the non-intervention rule is limited in scope. It has never been meant to cover all forms of interference. In essence, it prohibits states from using coercive measures to overcome the free will of a targeted state with respect to matters that fall within that state's core, independent sovereign prerogative.

To be internationally wrongful, an intervention must first bear on what is commonly referred to as the state's "domaine réservé"— those "matters in which each State is permitted, by the principle of State sovereignty, to decide freely" such as the right to choose a political, economic, social, and cultural system, and to formulate and execute foreign policy. Second, the measures employed must be forcible or dictatorial, or otherwise coercive, in effect depriving the state intervened against of control over the matter in question. That is, only actions that deprive or substantially impair a state's freedom of choice over a protected matter in a way that forces it to take or refrain from taking an action against its will are prohibited. Unfortunately, the concepts of coercion and domaine réservé are ill defined.

Commentators and now some state pronouncements point to intervening in electoral processes to manipulate the outcome as a paradigmatic example of a prohibited intervention. What of Russia's well-documented election interference efforts? In January 2017, the U.S. intelligence community published its unclassified findings on Russia's interference in the 2016 presidential election:

Russian efforts to influence the 2016 US presidential election represent the most recent expression of Moscow's longstanding desire to undermine the

US-led liberal democratic order, but these activities demonstrated a significant escalation in directness, level of activity, and scope of effort compared to previous operations.

We assess Russian President Vladimir Putin ordered an influence campaign in 2016 aimed at the US presidential election. Russia's goals were to undermine public faith in the US democratic process, denigrate Secretary Clinton, and harm her electability and potential presidency. We further assess Putin and the Russian Government developed a clear preference for President-elect Trump. We have high confidence in these judgments.

  ▪ We also assess Putin and the Russian Government aspired to help President-elect Trump's election chances when possible by discrediting Secretary Clinton and publicly contrasting her unfavorably to him. All three agencies agree with this judgment. CIA and FBI have high confidence in this judgment; NSA has moderate confidence.
  ▪ Moscow's approach evolved over the course of the campaign based on Russia's understanding of the electoral prospects of the two main candidates. When it appeared to Moscow that Secretary Clinton was likely to win the election, the Russian influence campaign began to focus more on undermining her future presidency.
  ▪ Further information has come to light since Election Day that, when combined with Russian behavior since early November 2016, increases our confidence in our assessments of Russian motivations and goals.

Moscow's influence campaign followed a Russian messaging strategy that blends covert intelligence operations—such as cyber activity—with overt efforts by Russian Government agencies, state-funded media, third-party intermediaries, and paid social media users or "trolls." Russia, like its Soviet predecessor, has a history of conducting covert influence campaigns focused on US presidential elections that have used intelligence officers and agents and press placements to disparage candidates perceived as hostile to the Kremlin.

  ▪ Russia's intelligence services conducted cyber operations against targets associated with the 2016 US presidential election, including targets associated with both major US political parties.
  ▪ We assess with high confidence that Russian military intelligence (General Staff Main Intelligence Directorate or GRU) used the Guccifer 2.0 persona and DCLeaks.com to release US victim data obtained in cyber operations publicly and in exclusives to media outlets and relayed material to WikiLeaks.
  ▪ Russian intelligence obtained and maintained access to elements of multiple US state or local electoral boards. DHS assesses that the types of systems Russian actors targeted or compromised were not involved in vote tallying.
  ▪ Russia's state-run propaganda machine contributed to the influence campaign by serving as a platform for Kremlin messaging to Russian and international audiences.

We assess Moscow will apply lessons learned from its Putin-ordered campaign aimed at the US presidential election to future influence efforts worldwide, including against US allies and their election processes.

Office of the Director of National Intelligence, *Intelligence Community Assessment: Assessing Russian Activities and Intentions in Recent US Elections* (Jan. 6, 2017), https://www.dni.gov/files/documents/ICA_2017_01.pdf.

NOTES AND QUESTIONS

1. Based on the IC's assessment, did Russia commit a prohibited intervention? What aspects of Russia's efforts might fall short? Some have argued forcefully that Russia did violate international law. *See* Steven J. Barela, *Zero Shades of Grey: Russian-Ops Violate International Law*, Just Security, Mar. 29, 2018, https://www.justsecurity.org/54340/shades-grey-russian-ops-violate-international-law/. For a more in-depth analysis of the implications of election interference, see Michael N. Schmitt, *"Virtual" Disenfranchisement: Cyber Election Meddling in the Grey Zones of International Law*, 19 Chi. J. Int'l L. 30 (2018).

2. Although the element of coercion is the touchstone of the non-intervention rule, there is little agreement among states as to the definition of the term or the types of action that might fall within the rule's scope. In an official letter the government of the Kingdom of the Netherlands transmitted to its Parliament in 2019 detailing its views on international law applicable to cyber, it stated that "[i]n essence [coercion] means compelling a state to take a course of action (whether an act or an omission) that it would not otherwise voluntarily pursue. The goal of the intervention must be to effect change in the behaviour of the target state." But they also noted that "the precise definition of coercion, and thus of unauthorized intervention, has not yet fully crystallized in international law."

3. Compare the Netherland's view that intervention requires a specific goal or intent with Australia's approach, articulated in its 2019 *Supplement to Australia's Position on the Application of International Law to State Conduct in Cyberspace*, that focuses on the impact and not the intent of an intervention: "A prohibited intervention is one that interferes by coercive means (in the sense that they effectively deprive another state of the ability to control, decide upon or govern matters of an inherently sovereign nature), either directly or indirectly, in matters that a state is permitted by the principle of state sovereignty to decide freely." What is the value of imposing a scienter requirement on this rule?

4. Both the United Kingdom and Australia have indicated they would consider intervention in the stability of a state's financial systems as internationally wrongful. Based on Mr. Ney's speech, does the DoD agree with this interpretation of the non-intervention rule?

THE CONVERGENCE OF CYBER OPERATIONS AND COVERT DISINFORMATION CAMPAIGNS

Russia's interference efforts have not been limited to cyber espionage and effects operations. As the IC's 2016 election assessment makes clear, Russia is engaged in a broader campaign to undermine Western democracies and the international rules-based order. Information operations, especially covert deception activities, figure prominently in this campaign and are facilitated by the global information and telecommunications infrastructure.

According to multiple news sources and official reporting, Russia has engaged in a far-reaching disinformation campaign regarding the novel coronavirus, which causes the respiratory disease COVID-19. According to multiple sources, including the

State Department's Global Engagement Center, Russia deployed its full information-operations toolkit of official state media, proxy news sites, and a vast infrastructure of false social media personas to disseminate multiple false narratives with the aim of aggravating the public health crisis in Western countries. The reports are consistent with Russia's broader and well-documented efforts to sow division in the West and undermine democratic institutions, with the added consequence of putting lives at risk.

But propaganda and influence operations are longstanding forms of statecraft not prohibited by international law. At what point might states consider disinformation campaigns to be coercive and cross the intervention threshold? Is there a legal distinction between overt propaganda and influence, on the one hand, and covert information campaigns aimed at intervening in and overcoming the free will of the targeted state on the other?

Prior to the pandemic, Russia's documented election interference had come the closest of any state action to violating the non-intervention rule. In fact, it arguably did. Election processes are a paradigmatic example of the type of sovereign prerogatives protected by the non-intervention rule, leading some legal experts to assert that Russia's election interference crossed the line. Yet beyond the general statements alluded to above, no state has publicly asserted that Russia's election interference violates international law — let alone taken action based on such a claim.

If Russia were to unleash a deadly biological weapon against another state, there is no doubt it would be condemned as a use of force. Yet, as much as death and illness are likely and foreseeable consequences of Russia's spreading of COVID-19 disinformation, it is unlikely that states will go so far as to condemn Russia's actions as crossing the use-of-force threshold out of concerns for escalation. But the rule of prohibited intervention can be, and should be, a different story.

To date, state responses to Russian disinformation operations have been grounded in domestic law, as with Special Counsel Robert Mueller's indictment related to Russia's interference in the 2016 elections and Australia's recently adopted foreign interference law. The focus on fraud and deceit as the *actus reus* of the offenses charged in the special counsel's indictment should serve as a guidepost for clarifying or evolving the coercion element of the prohibited intervention rule. It demonstrates that covert deception and disinformation can be just as harmful to sovereign prerogative as more overt coercive measures, if not more so.

Gary P. Corn, *Coronavirus Disinformation and the Need for States to Shore Up International Law*, Lawfare, Apr. 2, 2020, https://www.lawfareblog.com/coronavirus-disinformation-and-need-states-shore-international-law.

C. The Role of Sovereignty

When appropriately applied, and perhaps adjusted to account for the novel threats presented by emerging technologies, the rule of prohibited intervention can serve as a powerful tool for enforcing acceptable state behavior in cyberspace. However, the prohibition does not bring within its scope all sub-use-of-force cyber activities and must be distinguished from mere interferences in the internal affairs or against the sovereign interests of another state. This raises the important question of whether, and if so, how international law regulates cyber activities that fall below the threshold or outside the scope of a prohibited intervention.

Some point to the principle of sovereignty as the answer to this question. The importance of sovereignty as a basic constitutional doctrine of the law of nations cannot be overstated. Nevertheless, the exact meaning of the term is susceptible to many uses, and its exact contours have been described as frustratingly indeterminate. In broad terms, it refers to "the collection of rights held by a state, first in its capacity as the entity entitled to exercise control over its territory and second in its capacity to act on the international plane, representing that territory and its people."[25] The ICJ described sovereignty in the *Corfu Channel Case* as encompassing "the whole body of rights and attributes which a state possesses in its territory, to the exclusion of all other states, and also in its relation with other states."

But as much as sovereignty involves freedom from certain outside interference, it also means freedom of action on the international plane. And no issue has generated as much debate in the context of cyber operations as the question of sovereignty's normative status and application. There are many facets to this question, but debate has revolved principally around whether sovereignty exists as a primary rule of international law applicable to cyber operations, the violation of which would be an internationally wrongful act in and of itself, or as a foundational principle, which could only be violated by infringing on some other sovereignty-based primary rule such as the prohibition on the use of force.

THE LAW OF STATE RESPONSIBILITY AND THE LOTUS PRINCIPLE

The sovereignty question should be considered against the backdrop of the customary laws of state responsibility—reflected in the International Law Commission's *Draft Articles on Responsibility of States for Internationally Wrongful Acts*—and certain basic premises of international law. Most notable among these is the so-called *Lotus* principle.

The law of state responsibility establishes the baseline premise that states are legally responsible only for acts or omissions that are attributable to them and which constitute a breach of an international obligation. In other words, states are obligated to conform their activities to the terms of applicable primary rules of international law and can be held legally accountable for breaches of those obligations only when sufficient evidence exists to attribute violations to them.

The question of whether an act breaches an international obligation turns first on whether an obligation exists *vel non*. That is, not all state activities, whether conducted in and through cyberspace or otherwise, are regulated by international law and state responsibility is simply not implicated when states engage in acts that are unregulated by international law. This may include acts that are objectionable and even prejudicial to the targeted state, but unless they implicate a binding legal obligation, responses are confined to the realm of diplomacy and retorsions (actions that are considered "unfriendly," such as sanctions, but not unlawful).

The process of identifying and transposing existing international law to the cyber context to determine whether a particular cyber operation would constitute a breach

---

25. James Crawford, Brownlie's Principles of Public International Law 448 (8th ed. 2012).

of an international obligation must be done mindful of the unique aspects of the domain, the central, near exclusive role states play in the making of international law, and the generally permissive structure of international law itself, reflected in the *Lotus* principle.

The principle derives from the Permanent Court of International Justice's (PCIJ) 1927 judgment in *The SS Lotus* case. It stands for the proposition that states are free to act on the international plane except to the extent that their actions are proscribed by treaty or customary international law. The case arose out of an at-sea collision between a French steamship and a Turkish collier resulting in the death of eight Turkish nationals. In rejecting France's claim before the PCIJ that Turkey had violated international law by asserting criminal jurisdiction over the French officer in charge of the *S.S. Lotus*, the court noted that

> [i]nternational law governs relations between independent States. The rules of law binding upon States therefore emanate from their own free will as expressed in conventions or by usages generally accepted as expressing principles of law and established in order to regulate the relations between these co-existing independent communities or with a view to the achievement of common aims. *Restrictions upon the independence of States cannot therefore be presumed.*

The PCIJ's positivist approach continues to shape international law to this day.

The core issue at play in *Lotus* and at the heart of the international law principle drawn from the cited passage is the question of state sovereignty and the normative role it plays in international law. The gravamen of France's claim in the case was that Turkey had over-asserted its sovereignty to the detriment of France's competing sovereign prerogative to exercise exclusive proscriptive jurisdiction over its own nationals. Faced with this clash of external and internal sovereign interests, the court declined to restrict Turkey's exercise of jurisdiction absent clear evidence of an established rule of international law circumscribing its freedom to do so.

The sovereignty debate surfaced with the launch of the *Tallinn Manual 2.0* and its treatment of sovereignty in Rule 4 as a violable primary rule of international law. For a brief time, the debate was confined to unofficial circles. In 2018, however, the United Kingdom offered the first official state view on the issue, when the Attorney General stated the following in a speech:

> Some have sought to argue for the existence of a cyber specific rule of a "violation of territorial sovereignty" in relation to interference in the computer networks of another state without its consent.
>
> Sovereignty is of course fundamental to the international rules-based system. But I am not persuaded that we can currently extrapolate from that general principle a specific rule or additional prohibition for cyber activity beyond that of a prohibited intervention. The UK Government's position is therefore that there is no such rule as a matter of current international law.

The Right Honourable Jeremy Smith, QC MP, Attorney General, Cyber and International Law in the 21st Century, Address before Chatham House (May 23, 2018), https://www.gov.uk/government/speeches/cyber-and-international-law-in-the-21st-century.

In contrast to the U.K.'s position, the Netherlands subsequently endorsed the *Tallinn Manual 2.0* view, stating its belief that "respect for the sovereignty of other countries is an obligation in its own right, the violation of which may in turn constitute an internationally wrongful act." This view draws from the exclusivity of internal sovereignty and the general mandate that states respect the personality, territorial integrity, and political independence of other states.

Judging from Mr. Ney's speech, the DoD, and perhaps the United States, finds clear solidarity with the U.K.'s position. Most other states that have offered views on the international law applicable to cyber operations have been silent on the issue, notwithstanding the currency and importance of the debate. What do these varied state pronouncements tell us about the state of the issue as a matter of customary international law?

Even for proponents of the sovereignty rule, not all non-consensual cyber operations would constitute a violation of international law. The *Tallinn Manual 2.0* recognized that "[t]he precise legal character of remote cyber operations that manifest on a State's territory is somewhat unsettled in international law." The contributors could not agree on the types or levels of effect that a cyber operation would have to generate to violate the sovereignty rule.

NOTES AND QUESTIONS

1. How can the sovereignty-as-a-rule position be reconciled with the ubiquitous state practice of espionage, which frequently involves sending state agents into the territory of another state without consent? Some of the contributors to the *Tallinn Manual 2.0* argued that state practice has created an exception to a generally accepted premise that non-consensual activities attributable to a state while physically present on another's territory violate sovereignty. The majority rejected this view, adopting the position that espionage is not prohibited per se by international law. Here is what the DoD General Counsel had to say on the question of espionage:

   > Traditional espionage may also be a useful analogue to consider. Many of the techniques and even the objectives of intelligence and counterintelligence operations are similar to those used in cyber operations. Of course, most countries, including the United States, have *domestic* laws against espionage, but international law, in our view, does not prohibit espionage *per se* even when it involves some degree of physical or virtual intrusion into foreign territory. There is no anti-espionage treaty, and there are many concrete examples of States practicing it, indicating the absence of a customary international law norm against it.

   Some argue that espionage is not lawful but tolerated as a matter of state practice. How does such a position align with the *Lotus* principle?

2. Mr. Ney asserts that "States' public silence in the face of countless publicly known cyber intrusions into foreign networks precludes a conclusion that States have coalesced around a common view that there is an international prohibition against all such operations (regardless of whatever penalties may be imposed

under domestic law).” What relevance does states’ public silence have on determining the existence or lack thereof of customary international law?

3. In *The Application of International Law to Cyberspace: Sovereignty and Non-Intervention,* Chatham House endorses the sovereignty-as-a-rule approach. However, beyond stating that there is a de minimis rule in effect, the report could discern no standards in customary international law for assessing a breach of sovereignty. For a critique of the Chatham House Report, see Gary P. Corn, *Punching on the Edges of the Grey Zone: Iranian Cyber Threats and State Cyber Responses,* Just Security, Feb. 11, 2020, https://www.justsecurity.org/68622/punching-on-the-edges-of-the-grey-zone-iranian-cyber-threats-and-state-cyber-responses/.

4. In his Berkeley speech, then State Department Legal Advisor Egan stated: “As an initial matter, remote cyber operations involving computers or other networked devices located on another State’s territory do not constitute a per se violation of international law. In other words, there is no absolute prohibition on such operations as a matter of international law. This is perhaps most clear where such activities in another State’s territory have no effects or de minimis effects.” De minimis means too trivial or minor to merit consideration. Is that a realistic or workable standard?

5. What is the significance of the sovereignty debate to the United States’s defend-forward cyber strategy? Mr. Ney draws a direct linkage, stating that the DoD’s position is reflected in the Department’s adoption of the defend-forward strategy. Given the nature of the cyber domain and standard operating frameworks, adversary cyber infrastructure will often be globally dispersed, implicating infrastructure in the territory of multiple states. In that environment, how would the sovereignty-as-rule position impact the ability to conduct effective counter-cyber operations?

6. For a more in-depth discussion of sovereignty and cyber operations, see the American Journal of International Law’s *Symposium on Sovereignty, Cyberspace, and Tallinn Manual 2.0,* at https://www.cambridge.org/core/journals/american-journal-of-international-law/ajil-unbound-by-symposium/sovereignty-cyberspace-and-tallinn-manual-2-0.

COUNTERMEASURES

The right of states to employ countermeasures in response to breaches of international law committed against them by other states is well established in customary international law. Countermeasures are sub-use-of-force actions or omissions by an injured state directed against another state that would themselves violate international law but for the fact that they are proportionate self-help measures employed to respond to and remedy antecedent breaches of international law against the injured state. Like self-defense, countermeasures are the evolutionary progeny of the historical law of peacetime reprisals. Unlike self-defense, however, countermeasures are the descendant of the non-forcible branch of peacetime reprisals and are bound by a number of constraints unsuited to the emerging realities of cyber threats.

The first of these arguable constraints is a requirement, at least in the view of the International Law Commission, that countermeasures must be preceded by notice to the responsible state. The United Kingdom, France, the Netherlands, and based on the DoD General Counsel's speech, perhaps the United States reject an absolute requirement in this regard, at least in the context of cyberspace. Most states also regard countermeasures involving a use of force to be impermissible. Based on Judge Simma's separate opinion in the ICJ's *Oil Platforms Case* in which he endorses such measures, some commentators question this limitation.

Unlike the law of self-defense, the prevailing view is that countermeasures do not include a collective right. Finally, the prevailing view is that countermeasures are only available against states. Again, unlike current views of self-defense, countermeasures cannot be taken against non-state actors unless it can be determined that they are operating under the effective control of a state. This is a particularly significant limitation in light of the ubiquity of cyber activities that have been attributed to non-state actors and states' use of loosely affiliated proxies. The continuing difficulty of determining who is responsible for a particular cyber event, combined with the high standard under the rules of state responsibility for attributing the acts of a non-state actor to a state, make this limitation on the use of cyber countermeasures problematic.

For a discussion of the challenges to applying the law of countermeasures in the cyber context, *see* Gary P. Corn & Eric Talbot Jensen, *The Use of Force and Cyber Countermeasures*, 32 Temp. Int'l & Comp. L.J. 127 (2018).

NOTES AND QUESTIONS

1. In 2019, during a speech on international law and cyber operations, the President of Estonia articulated her country's view that states can engage in collective countermeasures. France and other states have officially rejected the notion of collective countermeasures. What is the logic behind limiting collective action only to self-defense and not countermeasures?
2. What is the interplay between the questions regarding sovereignty and the law of countermeasures?

A NOTE ON ATTRIBUTION

Attribution is frequently cited as a problem in relation to cyber security, deterrence, and operations. The basic operating construct of cyberspace lends itself to obfuscation and makes technical (i.e., factual) attribution difficult. From a policy perspective, this renders attribution claims particularly vulnerable to public criticism and second-guessing.

As a matter of international law, these factual and policy challenges should be distinguished from the customary international law requirement that a breach of an international obligation must be attributable to a state in order to hold that state legally responsible. States are responsible for the internationally wrongful cyber activities of their organs, such as the armed forces, intelligence services, and law enforcement agencies, as well as for the acts of persons or entities exercising elements of governmental authority. States can also be held accountable under international law for the conduct of non-state actors where the person or group of persons is in fact acting on the instructions of, or under the direction or control of, that State in carrying out the conduct. The ICJ has interpreted this standard as one of effective control.

International law does not set any particular burden of proof for establishing attribution. Rather, according to the State Department Legal Advisor, "international law generally requires [only] that States act reasonably under the circumstances when they gather information and draw conclusions based on that information." Cyberspace presents unique attribution challenges, but these are primarily in the nature of factual and policy questions and less so about the legal standards to be applied.

D. Cyber *in Bello*

The original purpose for developing military cyber capabilities was to integrate them as another tool in the DoD's warfighting toolkit. This remains a core DoD mission. In this regard, cyber capabilities are a means, and their operational employment are a method of warfare. In the view of the United States, the LOAC regulates how states conduct hostilities regardless of the technological novelty of the means and methods employed.

> The *DoD Law of War Manual* sets out the Department's position on the applicability of the law of war to cyber operations:
>
> Specific law of war rules may be applicable to cyber operations, even though these rules were developed long before cyber operations were possible.
>
> The law of war affirmatively anticipates technological innovation and contemplates that its existing rules will apply to such innovation, including cyber operations. . . . For example, the rules on conducting attacks do not depend on what type of weapon is used to conduct the attack. Thus, cyber operations may be subject to a variety of law of war rules depending on the rule and nature of the cyber operation. . . .
>
> Cyber operations may pose challenging legal questions because of the variety of effects they can produce. For example, cyber operations could be a non-forcible means or method of conducting hostilities (such as information gathering), and would be regulated as such under rules applicable to non-forcible means and methods of warfare. Other cyber operations could be used to create effects that amount to an attack and would be regulated under the rules on conducting attacks.
>
> . . . [A] cyber attack that would destroy enemy computer systems could not be directed against ostensibly civilian infrastructure, such as computer systems belonging to stock exchanges, banking systems, and universities, unless those computer systems met the test for being a military objective under the circumstances. A cyber operation that would not constitute an attack, but would nonetheless seize or destroy enemy property, would have to be imperatively demanded by the necessities of war.

NOTES AND QUESTIONS

1. The term "attack" is at the heart of many of the *jus in bello* rules regulating the conduct of hostilities, or armed conflict, such as the prohibitions on attacking civilians or civilian objects, the ban on indiscriminate attacks, and the rules of precaution and proportionality in the conduct of attacks. The generally accepted definition of attack is found in Additional Protocol I to the Geneva Conventions, where attacks are defined as "acts of violence against the adversary, whether in the offense or in the defence." Where a cyber operation generates an effect amounting to physical damage to objects or death or injury to individuals, AP I's definition of "attack" is triggered, assuming the operation is conducted as part of, or itself constitutes the initiation of, armed conflict. The *DoD Law of War Manual* reflects this approach. According to the *Tallinn Manual 2.0*, de minimis damage or destruction does not meet the threshold of harm to be considered an "attack" for purposes of the LOAC.

2. What about cyber operations that do not amount to acts of violence? The *DoD Law of War Manual* states that cyber operations that do not constitute attacks are not subject to the full array of LOAC targeting rules, and "[s]ince such operations generally would not be considered attacks under the law of war, they generally would not need to be directed at military objectives, and may be directed at civilians or civilian objects." The *Manual* suggests that factors to consider would include whether the operation causes only temporary or reversible effects. It lists as examples webpage defacement; minor, brief disruption of internet services; brief disruption or interference with communications; and disseminating propaganda. What limiting principles might still apply to the conduct of "non-attack" cyber operations?

3. Perhaps one of the more controversial positions set out in the *Tallinn Manual 2.0* is the view the contributors expressed that data are not a tangible object that can even be the subject of an attack. This would mean that a cyber operation that completely wipes data would not be constrained by the LOAC's targeting rules. How does this view comport with the realities of today's digitally dependent world?

4. What humanitarian benefits do the use of cyber capabilities as a means of warfare offer? For a discussion of this point, see Colonel Gary P. Corn, *The Potential Human Costs of Eschewing Cyber Operations*, ICRC Blog: Humanitarian Law & Policy, May 31, 2019, https://blogs.icrc.org/law-and-policy/2019/05/31/potential-human-costs-eschewing-cyber-operations/.

5. The principle of distinction is a "cardinal principle" that lies at the heart of the LOAC. As we have seen, secrecy and surprise are operational imperatives in cyberspace, which raises challenging distinction issues. Applying the LOAC to covered or concealed cyber operations, out of necessity executed across predominantly civilian infrastructure, raises difficult questions not only as to the affirmative obligation to discriminate between adversary forces and civilians in the conduct of operations amounting to attacks, but also with respect to the obligation of combatants to distinguish and, when feasible, separate themselves and their activities from the civilian population. In this regard, where the line

between permissible and impermissible deception, ruses, perfidy, and the passive obligation of distinction lies has never been entirely clear and has varied with state practice over time. Discerning where this line lies for operations using or simulating civilian cyberspace infrastructure can be even more elusive. For an in-depth analysis of these issues, see Colonel Gary P. Corn & Commander Peter Pascucci, *The Law of Armed Conflict Implications of Covered or Concealed Cyber Operations—Perfidy, Ruses, and the Principle of Passive Distinction,* in THE IMPACT OF EMERGING TECHNOLOGIES ON THE LAW OF ARMED CONFLICT (Michael N. Schmitt et al. eds., 2019).

ASSESSMENT QUESTIONS

1. You are the legal advisor for U.S. Cyber Command. The Secretary of Defense has directed the command to conduct cyber operations in support of U.S. Central Command's combat operations against ISIS in Iraq and Syria. Intelligence assessments have determined with a high degree of confidence that John Smith is a senior member of ISIS located in Syria. Smith's specific role within ISIS is to develop and oversee all of ISIS's online recruitment and propaganda operations, which include online incitement of external attacks against the United States. John Smith was born in Ohio but travelled to Syria to join ISIS sometime after converting to Islam. The cyber operations forces assigned to Cyber Command are tasked with conducting cyber operations to disrupt Smith's online operations. They come to you seeking legal advice on whether they can first conduct operations to access Smith's individual laptop, which they believe he uses to plan and direct ISIS's media operations in order to identify its operating system, characterize the programs and data, and collect information necessary to plan and conduct a follow-on cyber effects operation against Smith's laptop. Must the command seek authority for this cyber collection operation from the Foreign Intelligence Surveillance Court?

2. Based on an initial scan of Smith's laptop, the operators discover that it is running an outdated version of Windows with a known security vulnerability. They have developed a malware exploit of this vulnerability that they will use to gain full, clandestine access to the laptop with full administrative privileges in order to copy and exfiltrate the necessary data. Do they need to worry about violating the Computer Fraud and Abuse Act (CFAA)?

3. As a result of the collection operation, the operators learn that Smith actually maintains nearly all the data used to develop and disseminate ISIS's incitement propaganda on a contracted virtual private server (VPS) located in Burundi. They have obtained the login credentials to the VPS from Smith's laptop and propose an operation to use the credentials to seize control of the VPS and wipe all of the data. For operational security reasons, the operators want to conduct the operation so that it cannot be detected or attributed. First, is the proposed operation subject to the procedural requirements of the Covert Action Statute? Second, as a matter of international law, must the United States first obtain Burundi's consent before proceeding?

ASSESSMENT ANSWERS

1. This is not an intelligence operation. U.S. Cyber Command is not a DoD intelligence component or a member of the intelligence community. Neither are the operations forces proposing to conduct this cyber collection operation intelligence forces. Because the operation proposes the collection of data at rest from

a device located overseas, it does not meet the definition of electronic surveillance for purposes of FISA. Section 704 of the FISA Amendments Act requires FISC approval before targeting a U.S. person reasonably believed to be outside the United States to acquire foreign intelligence; however, this provision only applies when the collection is conducted by an "element of the intelligence community." However, because Smith is a U.S. citizen, the operation must still satisfy the reasonableness standard of the Fourth Amendment. Because he is located overseas, the search can be conducted as an exception to the Warrant Clause.

2. Generally, gaining unauthorized access in this manner would violate the criminal provisions of the CFAA. However, although the CFAA's public authority exception does not specifically extend to military cyber forces, under the *Nardone* canon of construction and the public authority doctrine, applying the statute to bar these operations would be an absurd result. The CFAA was passed before the advent of military cyber operations and Congress has subsequently evidenced its support for these types of operations through various official statements as well as multiple funding and authorizing statutes.

3. As to the first question, although the operation would seem to qualify as a covert action as defined in the Covert Action Statute, it would be carried out under the exception for traditional military activities as set out in § 1632 of the 2019 NDAA. As to the second question, obtaining consent would only be legally required if the cyber operation would otherwise constitute a breach of an international obligation owed to Burundi and there was no justification available to preclude the wrongfulness, such as acting in legitimate self-defense or taking a countermeasure. As described, the operation would not amount to a use of force as it does not implicate a sufficient level of physical damage to meet that threshold. Nor would it constitute a prohibited intervention in Burundi's internal affairs because it is neither coercive in nature nor directed at Burundi's domaine réservé. That leaves the question of whether sovereignty is a separate rule of international law, and if so, whether deletion of the data without more would constitute a breach of that rule. The evidence of customary international law is insufficient to answer the first question in the affirmative. As for the second, it is unlikely that adherents to the sovereignty rule would consider these effects as sufficient to amount to a breach of Burundi's territorial sovereignty.

Table of Cases

Principal cases are italicized.

Table of Statutes

Miscellaneous United States Code

Other Federal Statutes

Federal Regulations

Index